THE
GLADSTONE
DIARIES

Gladstone at Westminster, 1833.
Oil sketch by Hayter, now at Fasque.

THE
GLADSTONE
DIARIES

VOLUME II · 1833–1839

Edited by

M. R. D. FOOT

PROFESSOR OF MODERN HISTORY
IN THE
UNIVERSITY OF MANCHESTER

CLARENDON PRESS · OXFORD
1968

Oxford University Press, Ely House, London, W.1

GLASGOW NEW YORK TORONTO MELBOURNE WELLINGTON
CAPE TOWN SALISBURY IBADAN NAIROBI LUSAKA ADDIS ABABA
BOMBAY CALCUTTA MADRAS KARACHI LAHORE DACCA
KUALA LUMPUR SINGAPORE HONG KONG TOKYO

MADE AND PRINTED IN GREAT BRITAIN BY
WILLIAM CLOWES AND SONS, LIMITED, LONDON AND BECCLES

CONTENTS

VOLUME II

LIST OF ILLUSTRATIONS

A.D. 1833. Jan. 1. Tuesday[1]

The cholera is declared to have ceased: God crowns the opening year with blessings. I made but a bad beginning. Heard from Anstice, Gaskell, Mr Caparn, Mr Wilson:[2] wrote to Bruce, the Duke of N. and R.G.—At Warwick—read Barcley—& papers. Heming Tom's friend dined here.[3] At Lady Eastnorr's evening party. Made up the year's accounts &c.

2.

Wrote to Robn. Heard from Uncle Colin—newspapers—which occupy more time than I could wish. Barcley on Slavery, and Notes thereon—an Article for the Liverpool Standard[4]—Scott's Nap[oleon] & Analysis—Spade cultivation papers[5]—a game at commerce. Lecture from Mr G. on currency. Scrap book.

3.

Wrote to Mr Finlay—and a long letter to Gaskell. Barcley, and notes thereupon. Called on Mrs Hook, & Lady Eastnor. met Sir Coutts Trotter[6] there —& walked with him after my visit. Found him a most agreeable man. Scott's Nap. and parts of two Articles for the Lpool Standard. Backgammon —papers—heard from Bruce, Price, T.G. Heard from Phillimore.

4. Friday.

Wrote to R.G.—T.G.—Anstice—heard from Ward (of Wadham).[7] Wrote parts of two long articles for the Lpool Standard—& sent my packet for Tuesday's number. Out with J.N.G. Began a concern to be called "the human heart"[8] read Scott's Nap. & analysed a little. Dined at Ld Eastnorr's—introduced to Lady Farnham,[9] Mr Sanderson,[10] Mr Fox,[11] Mr Alexander,[12] Mr Crichton.[13]

[1] Lambeth MS 1420 ctd.
[2] John Wilson, secretary of Newark savings bank.
[3] Thomas Heming, 1804?–36; Christ Church graduate; barrister.
[4] Untraced.
[5] Untraced; cp. 23 Mar. 33.
[6] Sir Coutts Trotter, 1767–1837, partner in Coutts's bank; cr. bart 1821.
[7] E. L. Ward.
[8] Add MS 44722, ff. 94–95; see 9 Dec. 34.
[9] Juliana Lucy Annesley, 1772?–1833, d. of 1st earl of Mountnorris, m. 1789 John Maxwell-Barry, 1767–1838, 5th Lord Farnham 1823, Irish representative peer 1825.
[10] Probably Richard Sanderson, 1783?–1857, Quaker bill-broker; cons. M.P. Colchester 1831–47; m. 1833 Charlotte Matilda, da. of the speaker, *Manners-Sutton (see 29 Jan. 33).
[11] Probably William Sackville Lane-Fox, d. 1874, tory M.P. Helston 1831–5, son-in-law of 6th duke of Leeds.
[12] Perhaps William M. Alexander, a West Indian proprietor.
[13] Possibly James Crichton of Graymount, Alyth, Perthshire.

5. Sat.

Papers—heard from T.G. Wrote to R.G. A short Art. for the Lpool Standard.[1] Rode & walked with J.N.G. Aunts went to their house—Scott's Nap. & Analysis—Barclay on Slavery. Whist. Calld on Mrs Hook.

6. Sunday.

Mr Riddell (mg); & Mr Gayfor (aftn), very good. Read Hook's Lectures—Dean Hook's Sermon before Christ. Knowl. Soc. and that on Eph. 4.3.[2]—Bible—walked. read a sermon of Blunt's at night.

7. M.

Tom came. Scott's Nap. Wrote to Price—Ward—Mr Crampern[3]—& Luigi Lamonica (the last in Italian). Part of an art. in Qu. Rev "how it will work"[4]—and wrote part of an art. for the Lpool Standard—At Lady Farnham's party—played whist—Wrote some lines.

8. T.

Wrote for the Liverpool Standard[5]—and to Rn G. A supply of papers from Lpool—bores, & consumers of time. Scott's Nap. & Analysis. Finished Art. in Quart Rev. rode with J.N.G.—whist—began to analyse with a view to various points a list of the returns & account of the elections given in the last 'Weekly Dispatch'.[6]

9. W.

Scott's Nap. & Analysis. Hewitt came to see me—walked with him. called on Lady Farnham. walk with J.N.G. Heard from Mr Tallents & Mr Caparn. Wrote to R.G., Cole, Crampern, and Uncle Divie—also a little for the Standard. Whist.

10. Th.

Wrote to Mr Tallents & Mr Caparn[7]—and a long article for the [Liverpool] Standard.[8] Scott's Nap. & Analysis. Rode 7 or 8 miles with Hewitt on his way homewards. Read the Bible with H.J.G. in the Evening. Papers.

[1] Perhaps on ballot, 8 January 1833, 112.

[2] James *Hook, dean of Worcester, father of W.F.*; on 2 Chron. xvii. 8–9 (1819), and (1812).

[3] John Callis Crampern, corn dealer, of 92 Jermyn Street; cp. 24 Jan. 33.

[4] *Quarterly Review*, xlviii. 542 (December 1832), on church reform.

[5] 'Working of the Reform Bill', 11 January 1833, 120.

[6] 'An Analysis of the First Reformed Parliament' in *Weekly Dispatch*, 6 January 1833, and its supplement.

[7] Declining invitations to a ball on 17 January (Add MS 44353, ff. 47–53).

[8] 15 January 1833, 128; on church reform.

11. Fr.

Wrote to Tupper—& an Article for the Lpool Standard.[1] Papers. A long
ride with T.G. & J.N.G. Weather frosty & fine. At night *they* went to the
Warwick Dispensary Ball. Scott's Nap—three or four hours—& Analysis.

12. Sat.

Wrote to Robn, twice—to Mr Bacon[2]—to Aunt M. & to Mr McDowall.[3]
Walk with J.N.G. at Dr Jephson's in the evening to hear Phillips, an extraordinary player on the pianoforte. Scott's Napoleon—and Analysis.—Got
into Vol. 8.

13. Sunday.

Read Christian Year—Hook's Lectures—and Whitty's Memoir with some
of his letters.[4] Scrapbook. At night read aloud 'Man created & renewed in
the image of God'[5] Mr Downes mg & Mr Gayfor aft. at Church.

14. M.

Two articles for Lpool Standard[6]—wrote to C. MacGrigor.[7] Scott's Nap. &
Analysis. Walk & papers. At night, attended a ball at the Swinfen's. Got
letters from Newark pressing me to one there—to which I am exceedingly
averse to go.

15. T.

Conv. with Mrs G. abt Newark. It was at last agreed that I should not go—
my Father was kind as usual. Wrote an Art. for the Lpool Standard.[8] Rode
with T.G.—Scott's Nap. & Analysis. Drs Jephson & Geldart[9] dined here—
whist. Wrote to Mr Tallents, Mr Godfrey, R.G., & Cole.

16. W.

Wrote to R.G.—Jones at Lpool, Williams at Oxford[10]—walk. called on
Miss Swinfen, & Miss Legh. Two long articles for the Standard.[11] Papers.
Scott's Nap., & Analysis. Girdlestone's 1st letter on Church Reform[12]—

[1] Untraced.
[2] Possibly James Bacon of Lincoln's Inn.
[3] Possibly Charles MacDowall, 1790–1872, fashionable London watchmaker.
[4] Irwine Whitty, *A selection of Letters and Meditations* (2 ed. 1833).
[5] Untraced: presumably a tract.
[6] Perhaps 18 January 1833, 136; on new parliament, and against ballot.
[7] Charles Rhoderic, 1811–90, succ. Sir James *McGrigor as 2nd bart. 1858.
[8] Untraced.
[9] Perhaps John Geldart, later in practice in London.
[10] Adin Williams, tailor and robe-maker, High Street, Oxford; reply in Add MS 44353,
f. 61, about fancy waistcoats.
[11] One printed, on church establishments: 22 January 1833, 144.
[12] Charles *Girdlestone, 'A letter on Church Reform addressed to the Regius Professor
of Divinity in the University of Oxford' (1832).

heard from Pusey. Hunted long for Cicero de Amicitiâ—Hewitt got it me, & I consulted it about ballot.[1]

17. Th.

Wrote to Puller. Wrote three or four concerns for the Liverpool Standard.[2] Rode with T.G.—Papers. Scott's Nap. and Analysis.

18. Fr.

revising—wrote to R.G. to Mr Williams at Oxford. walked with J.N.G. Scott's Nap. & Analysis. Backgammon with Aunt E. Girdlestone's 2nd Letter on Church Reform.[3] Papers.

19.

Qu. Rev. on Sarrans. Breakfasted at Mr Grant's to meet the Bruces, & with them till past 11. Paper—news of collision between the French Chambers.[4] Scott's Nap. & Analysis. called on Mrs Galton[5]—Lady Eastnorr—Mrs Proby. Backgammon. Tea at Mrs Hook's—singing—met Ashby[6]—an old Etonian & contemporary.

At night I read the account in Scott of Napoleon's last days & death.[7] While going through the detail, I literally felt an internal weakness and my stomach turned, with such a feeling as is excited upon hearing of some sudden & terrible catastrophe—with such a feeling as I should behold the sun removed out of the face of the heaven. What is so awful, as the transition of such a Spirit!

20. Sunday.

Finished Hook's Lectures—a sound & solid book. Bible. read to H.J.G.— wrote on 'good' in black b.[8] read 'the Rose', & Mrs Sherwood.[9]—Two strangers officiated. Polit[ical] sermon (I hear) at the Baptist Chapel.

21. M.

Arranging papers. Scott's Nap. Analysis.—Read two of Dr. Hook's pam-

---

[1] xxv–vi. Cp. next entry.
[2] Two printed: on thanksgiving after cholera, 25 January 1833, 152, and on 'Rome and the Ballot', 29 January 1833, 160.
[3] (1833).
[4] The French chamber of deputies wished to abolish, and the chamber of peers to retain, 21 January as a day of national mourning for the execution of Louis XVI in 1793. The lower house won.
[5] Probably Frances Anne Violetta, eldest da. of Erasmus *Darwin; m. S. T. Galton 1807; mother of (Sir) Francis*; of Duddeston House, Birmingham.
[6] Edward Quenby Ashby, 1805?–71, Christ Church; rector of Dunton, Buckinghamshire, 1842.
[7] Sir W. *Scott, Life of Napoleon Buonaparte, ix. 254–302 (1827).
[8] In Add MS 44820, ff. 27–28.
[9] A short tract on the glories of creation; and some improving work by M. M. *Sherwood, prolific evangelical authoress.

phlets & began a third 'anguis in herbâ'.[1] Calls. Backgammon. papers. Wrote to Mr Oliver[2]—Mr Bailey[3]—Mr Cotton[4]—Mr Crampern.

22.

Finished Analysis of Vol. 7. of Scott's Nap. & Dean Hook's Anguis in Herbâ. papers. wrote to R.G. & to Mrs Conway. Packing—plenty to do. Called on Mrs Hook—a long convn, chiefly on religion & parties therein— also with Mr Grant his Lady[5] & Lady M. Bruce, on Irvingites, politics, and poetry—& at night with my dear Mother, on our own serious family matters.

23.

Breakfd & left Leam[ington] at 8½. Reached Oxford before two. Went to see Harrison—Wordsworth—Canning—Mayow—Bruce—J. Wishlade—W. Harris—Mrs Albutt—Mrs Charriere—old Wale[6]—Mr Rockall[7]—Dodd[8]— at Parker's picking pamphlets—at Williams's about my clothes—Wheeler's[9] to get a map & settle, &c.—Tea with Wordsworth. Harrison & Bruce there. Long conv. on Ch Reform.

24.

Called on Veysie—Williams—A. Short—J. Ley—Pusey (sat & talked long with him) Liddell,[10] Scott, Boyle, Brandreth &c. settled affairs with Rockall, gave directions about my things—came up to town by the Triumph: found everything at Mr Crampern's prepared & comfortable. Reading on Church Reform. Wrote to Mrs G.

25.

Breakf. in Bedf. Square.—wrote to T.G.—Mr G—Harrison—heard from H.J.G. & J.N.G. Read Lpool Standard, with my father's 1st letter on Currency[11]—arranged matters & entered at Lincoln's Inn, by favour of Heming and Puller: eat my first dinner: met young B. Montagu[12] in Hall— also Farr and others—chamberhunting with Uncle D.—saw & staid some

---

[1] A defence of church pluralities (1802).
[2] John Oliver, Newark draper.
[3] Neale Bailey, Newark excise officer.
[4] Perhaps John Cottam, Newark maltster.
[5] See 30 Nov. 32 n.
[6] An object of his charity.
[7] Probably a senior college servant at Christ Church.
[8] Joseph Dodd, 1810–91, of Queen's College; rector of Hampton Poyle near Oxford 1838–72.
[9] Stationer and publisher, High Street.
[10] Henry George *Liddell, 1811–98, lexicographer; double first 1833; published Greek lexicon, 1843; headmaster of Westminster, 1846; dean of Christ Church, 1855–91; f. of Alice in Wonderland.
[11] 'Mercator' of 23 January, in *Liverpool Standard*, 25 January 1833, 149, against paper currency.
[12] Son and namesake of Basil *Montagu.

time with Anstice & Puller—Tupper came to me in the evg & had tea. Arranged a few of my things *pro tempore*—wrote a little for Lpool Standard: to Mr G & B. Harrison.

26. Saturday.

Breakf in Bedf. Square—tea at Anstice's in Bulstrode Street—Mrs A.[1] pretty, clever, & agreeable—*he* works too hard I fear. Spent three hours there very pleasurably.—At Pusey's—Cole's—calld on Mr Tallents in Cov[ent] Garden, & recd a letter from him: wrote to R.G. & an art for the Lpool Standard.[2] Unpacked a box from Naples—dined again at Lincoln's Inn—read paper: read Winstanley Hull on Church Reform,[3] and most of Dr Burton's sequel.[4]

27.

Breakf. Bedf. Square—reading Articles—St Giles's mg[5]—St James's aftn. a good sermon on 1 Cor.VIII. & 'liberty'. Dined at Lincoln's Inn: went thence with Rogers to Mr Irving's evg service—a scene pregnant with melancholy instruction.[6]—Tea with F. Cole. Talked much about his brother —read Girdlestone—& wrote something about his book for the Liverpool Standard.[7]

28.

Cole breakfd with me. Dinner at Lincoln's Inn. 8–12 p.m. in T.G.'s rooms— reading Tasso's Aminta & Ld Lauderdale's Public Wealth.[8] Tea with him when he came. Wrote to Mr G. Miss G. and B.H.—Read on Church Reform. —B. Montagu—Liverpool Standard—Calamy.[9]

29. Tuesday.

Breakf. in Bedf. Square. with T.G. at his interview with Messrs Sharp & Alexander[10]—Gaskell came to us & we went down to the Ho. of C. where the members began to assemble before one. Called on Sir R. Inglis—introduced to Mr C. Grant—Mr Hyett[11]—Mr Serj. Merewether.[12] Debate on the Speaker-

[1] Joseph *Anstice m. in 1832 (Add MS 44353, f. 37).
[2] On church reform, 1 February 1833, 168.
[3] W. W. *Hull, 'Thoughts on Church Reform' (1832), lawyer's pamphlet.
[4] E. *Burton, 'Sequal to Remarks upon Church Reform with Observations Upon the Plan Proposed by Lord *Henley' (1832).
[5] St Giles in the Fields, Bloomsbury, of which *Tyler was rector.
[6] Edward *Irving, 1792–1834, Scottish religious enthusiast, held services this winter at the newly formed Holy Catholic Apostolic Church in Newman Street, north Soho.
[7] C. *Girdlestone, *Seven Sermons*, reviewed in *Liverpool Standard*, 5 February 1833, 176.
[8] James *Maitland, 8th earl of Lauderdale, *Inquiry into the Nature and Origin of Public Wealth* (2 ed. 1819).
[9] Perhaps the autobiography of the youngest Edmund *Calamy, nonconformist scholar (1829).
[10] Probably some Portarlington business.
[11] William Henry Hyett, b. 1795; changed name from Adams 1813; whig M.P. for Stroud 1832–5.
[12] Henry Alworth *Merewether, 1780–1864; serjeant-at-law 1827; town clerk of London 1842–59.

ship—we all in the majority.[1] Wrote a very hurried article on it for the Lpool S.[2]—dined with T.G. & saw him off. read Pusey, & wrote in scrap-b[ook] at night.—also wrote to R.G. & Mr Basil Montagu—Phillimore came in & sat long.

30.

Morng Church at St James's. Breakf at Uncle D's: dined, to complete my term, at Lincoln's Inn.—Wrote to Mr G. & R.G. Wrote divers matters for Lpool Standard.[3] & in Scrap Book. Finish'd Pusey's & Arnold's pamphlets. both remarkable—but how different! Call'd on Mr R. Hook[4]—Gaskell—Farr—Wood (A.C.) came to see me—& Phillimore.

31.

Walked to the Charterhouse to breakf with Saunders. James there—lionised partially. Called on Anstice—Mr Tallents—& the M.G.s. Wrote to Mr G.—Tupper—Mr Hughes. Made up monthly accts. At the House: went with the Speaker to the Lords: his part admirably acted, & Brougham's too[5]—wrote in Red Book[6]—& read Townsend.

February One. Friday.

Wrote to my Brother—B. Harrison—and Jones. read Miss Martineau—& Townsend. Heming—R. Hook—& Phillimore—here. Walkd: calld on Wood (C.A.) & Wood (S.F.) met Doyle, &c. read accts by the Jam[aic]a packet, &c. Dined at Unc D's; met Mr Tyler: much conv. with him. Wrote two articles for the Lpool Standard.[7]

Sat. 2.

Wrote an Art for Lpool Standard.[8] Wrote to R.G., J.N.G. and Brandreth at Ch. Ch.—met Hawtrey in Bond Street. finished Townsend's Plan, and Bird's "What will the Bishops do?"[9] Began Jeremie's pamphlet.[10] At night, at Mrs Phillimore's[11]—met Hallam, Gaskell, Saunders, Anstice, Puller,

[1] Charles *Manners-Sutton, 1780–1845; M.P. for Scarborough 1806–32, for Cambridge University 1833–5, speaker 1817–35; cr. Viscount Canterbury 1835; was elected unanimously after E. J. *Littleton had been rejected by 241–31. *H* xv. 35. (Edward John *Littleton, 1791–1863, changed name from Walhouse, 1812; M.P. Staffordshire 1812–35; Irish secretary 1833–4; cr. Lord Hatherton 1835.)
[2] 1 February 1833, 168.
[3] On slavery, *Ewart, and cholera: 5 February 1833, 176.
[4] Robert Hook of 18 King Street, St. James's.
[5] The speaker requested and obtained from the lord chancellor the customary assurances of the commons' freedom of debate: *H* xv. 83.
[6] Probably undated notes in Add MS 44819.
[7] One, on church reform, on 8 February 1833, 194.
[8] Untraced.
[9] Pamphlet on church economy by 'A Beneficed Clergyman' (1833).
[10] (Sir) J. *Jeremie, 'Four essays on colonial slavery' (1831).
[11] Elizabeth, née Bagot, d. 1859; m. Joseph *Phillimore 1807; mother of R.J.*

Pearson, & others.—very pleasant. finished Miss Martineau's Life in the Wilds.[1]

3. Sunday.

Walked to Sir R. Inglis's to breakfast. Heard Dr Dealtry morng & aftn[;] in mg on the sin against the Holy Ghost.[2] Finished Girdlestone's Seven Sermons—read Scougal's Serm. on "few to be saved"[3]—& the chap in 'Sat. Evg' on the Church and the World.[4]—Conv. with Sir R.

4. M.

breakfd at Mr Harrison's—and came to town with Mrs H.[5] read Lpool papers: wrote an art for L[iver]p[ool] St[andard],[6] wrote to Rn G. and to Brandreth. Looking at rooms in Albany[7]—unpacked my box of alab[aste]rs; very little damage: dined with Saunders at the Charterhouse: met Mr Hale,[8] H. Denison, J. Talbot,[9] &c. then went to Wood's for 1½ hours conv.—read Miss Martineau's Ireland.[10] Referring at S's to Cicero & Adam on Ballot.[11]

5. T.

Finished Miss Martineau's Ireland—reading West Indian Evidence.[12] Also wrote to Harrison—& read part of E. Evans's pamphlet on Ireland.[13] Early dinner with Gaskell—at Ho. at 12 to prayers—again to hear King's Speech—debate began ¼ before 5. till 12. O'Connell able: Stanley admirable.[14]

6. W.

Very busy reading Cicero's Third Book de Legg. & writing on Ballot for the

---

[1] H. *Martineau, *Illustrations of Political Economy* (1832–4), no. 1.

[2] Mark iii. 29.

[3] Henry *Scougal on Luke xiii. 23 (ca. 1675).

[4] [Isaac *Taylor] *Saturday Evening* (1832), 77–98.

[5] Mary, née Le Pelly, m. 1797 Benjamin *Harrison the elder.

[6] Untraced.

[7] See 2 Mar. 33.

[8] William Hale *Hale, 1795–1870, scholar and tory; chaplain to *Blomfield 1824; archdeacon of London and master of the Charterhouse 1842.

[9] John Chetwynd Talbot, 1806–52; Charterhouse and Christ Church; recorder of Monmouth 1834–9, and Windsor 1836–52; Q.C. 1843.

[10] H. *Martineau, *Illustrations of Political Economy*, no. 9 (1832).

[11] *De Legibus*, iii, and Alexander *Adam, *Roman Antiquities*, i. 71–93 (in 10 ed., 1825).

[12] *PP* (Lords) 1832 xi.

[13] Eyre Evans, 'Evils affecting Ireland'.

[14] Debate on address. *O'Connell denounced the proposed Irish coercion bill. *Stanley riposted. *H* xv. 87, 139; and see Sir G. *Hayter's painting (1848) in National Portrait Gallery. Edward Geoffrey Smith-*Stanley, 1799–1869, orator; M.P. 1822–44, Irish secretary 1830–3, colonial secretary 1833–4, 1841–5; styled Lord Stanley 1834, cr. Lord Stanley of Bickerstaffe 1844, succ. as 14th earl of Derby 1851; prime minister 1852, 1858–9, 1866–8; see Add MS 44140.

Lpool Paper.[1] Wrote to J.N.G. and R.G. Read W.I. evidence (analysed). Debate again—Macaulay,[2] C. Grant, Sheil,[3] & W. Harvey.[4]

7. Th.

Read W.I. Evidence—& 'Order in Council considered with ref. to Mag. Charta'.[5] Wrote to Goodenough—& pt of an Art. on Irving. Called on Pusey—& Hallam on me. House 6½—1 A.M. Peel made a really splendid speech.[6] Read Girdlestone's Serm. on Church & Dissenters.[7]

8.

Hallam breakfasted with me—Cole and Tupper each called. Calld on Mr Larkins—dined at Uncle D's. went to the House past nine. Shaw made a good speech.[8] Adjourned 2¾ A.M. Div. on

O'Connell's am.	Maj.	428.
	Min.	40.
on Tennyson's	Maj.	393.
	Min.	60.

Read W.I. Evidence—wrote to my Father—read B. Montagu's Thoughts[10] —& paper: also votes &c.

9. Sat.

Up late. wrote to R.G. & an art. for L.S.[11] Calld on Sir C. Trotter & Mr Handley—read B. Montagu, & began Keith's 'Signs of the Times'[12] & Pecchio's Osservazioni.[13] Dined at house. read paper.

10. Sunday.

Breakf. with Anstice—my Father came. dined with Uncle D. Marg. Chapel

[1] *Liverpool Standard*, 8 February 1833, 184.
[2] Debate on address continued: *H* xv. 238. Thomas Babington *Macaulay, 1800–59, whig historian and orator; M.P. 1830–47, 1852–6; member of Indian supreme council 1834–8; paymaster-general 1846–7; cr. Lord Macaulay 1857.
[3] Richard Lalor *Sheil, 1791–1851, dramatist and orator; K.C. 1830; Irish M.P. 1830–50; vice-president, board of trade, 1838–41; master of mint 1846–50.
[4] Daniel Whittle *Harvey, 1786–1863; radical M.P. Colchester 1818–20, 1826–34, Southwark 1835–40; then first commissioner of city of London police. Cp. 21 May 34, &c.
[5] Untraced pamphlet.
[6] *H* xv. 366; still on address.
[7] C. *Girdlestone, 'Affection between Churchmen and Dissenters', on Luke ix. 49–50 (1833).
[8] (Sir) Frederick *Shaw, 1799–1876; recorder of Dublin, 1828, and tory M.P. for it, 1830–31, and for Dublin University, 1832–48; succ. as 3rd bart. 1869; on the horrors of life in the ascendancy class in Ireland. *H* xv. 435.
[9] Both amdts—the latter, by Charles Tennyson (*D'Eyncourt), the milder—pleaded for better treatment for Ireland. *H* xv. 393; division lists, 458.
[10] Either Basil *Montagu's *Some Thoughts upon Liberty, and the Rights of Englishmen* (1819) or his *The Private Tutor* (1820).
[11] Perhaps 'Duty of Conservative Body' in *Liverpool Standard*, 12 February 1833, 192.
[12] Alexander *Keith, *The Signs of the Times, illustrated by the Fulfilment of Historical Predictions* (1832).
[13] G. Pecchio, *Osservazioni semi-serie, di un Esule sull'Inghilterra* (1831), gossip.

mg—Mr Dodsworth—good, & hard-headed, on the Fall.[1] Westmr Abbey in evg. Anth[em] B.137 & good serm. Read Sermm. & 'Signs of the Times' with astonishment.

11. M.

Keith's 'Signs' & Townsend's "Facts on Irish Clergy".[2] went with Mr G. & Tom about chambers. wrote to Seymer & Mr Tallents—Read Com.'s report on Petitions[3]—I look over these documents, to pick up information on the forms of the House. Down early—came away with T.G. in his cab near St Martin's Church—driver mercifully preserved: but the driver of the cab which ran us down, seemed very faulty. Dined however at Uncle D's—& retd to the House. Cobbett most disgusting—divided agst him 323 to 23.[4]

12. T.

Went to police office with T.G. Read Townsend's Facts—Pecchio—and Tennyson's Poems.[5] dined with M.G[askell]. Offer made by Mr G. for Chambers in Albany.[6] Called on H.H. J[oy]; Parr (ill) & Mrs Phillimore. House 5–10½. Irish Church Reform. Lord Althorp's speech more alarming, than the plan itself.[7] Peel spoke well; & Stanley.

13. W.

Breakf. at 22. B. Sq.—dinner at Sir J. Hall's.[8] Met Mr Tooke M.P.[9]—Singular discussion between my Father and him on Slavery. I could not help feeling some disgust at his manner of treating it. "We must have immediate abolition—the petitions are all prepared—at present we are keeping them back. We cannot hold Jamaica—but we have the right of the strongest—Reform Law". I saw no enthusiasm, religious or political, which would I trust have commanded my respect. I saw not anything save this, that Mr Tooke appeared to consider the question a good practical joke. No doubt at times he entertains it more seriously: but I say he ought not to permit himself to treat it as he did, on any occasion. It is a question, of

[1] William *Dodsworth, 1798–1861, anglican priest, res. orders on conversion to Rome 1851; on Genesis iii; in chapel in Margaret Street, Cavendish Square.
[2] T. S. Townsend, 'Facts and circumstances relating to the condition of the Irish Clergy of the Established Church, and to the present state of Ireland' (1832).
[3] PP 1833 xii. 153.
[4] William *Cobbett, 1762–1835, radical author, M.P. Oldham 1832, moved (on report) amendment to address calling for relief for poor and Irish: H xv. 477, 524.
[5] Alfred *Tennyson's new book of lyrics [1832].
[6] Cp. 2 Mar. 33.
[7] John Charles *Spencer (1782–1845; styled Viscount Althorp 1783; succ. as 3rd Earl Spencer 1834; master of Pytchley; M.P. Okehampton 1804, St. Albans 1806, Northamptonshire 1806–34; widowed 1818; chancellor of exchequer and leader of commons 1830–34; farmer, 1834–45) moved for leave to bring in a bill to halve the Irish protestant episcopate. H xv. 561.
[8] Sir John Hall, 1787–1860; b. at Edinburgh; F.R.S. 1820; 5th bart. 1832; Basil *Hall's b.
[9] William *Tooke, 1777–1863; solicitor and philanthropist; a founder of University College, London and of the S.D.U.K.; whig M.P. Truro 1832–7.

which he seems very ignorant: which he seemed to view only in one practical respect—that which embraces its relation to the hustings. Has he a right to habituate himself to extreme levity and merriment, on this solemn and awful question, of which it is the lightest part, that it involves the properties of many thousand Englishmen: for it also involves the heavy responsibilities of an entire nation, and the temporal and eternal interests of an extensive & an oppressed population.

Read Keith—Pecchio—wrote to Mr Tallents—Mr Pusey—Mr Rawson —Mr Barry[1]—R. Ward[2]—Rn G.—A. Pakenham. Wrote something for Lpool St[andard].[3] Called on Sir J. Hanmer & Mr Handley. Exam[ine]d some of the Irish comm[unio?]n translation.[4]

14. Th.

[Read] Keith—Townsend—L[iverpool] St[andar]d—Mercator's two first letters on free trade—analysed them.[5] Wrote to J.N.G. and B. Harrison— cop[ie]d a long document about slavery. heard my Father's evidence.[6] House—divn on Hume's motion for aboln of Mil. & Nav. sinecures.

Maj. 232.
Min. 138.[7]

15.

Breakf. & dinner at Gaskell's—Doyle & Pusey with me—read Keith— Pecchio—Tennyson—paper. House 4¼ to 11¾ P.M. Peel spoke admirably— Dr Lushington cleverly.[8]

16. Sat.

Mr Godfrey called on me. Called on Sir F. Doyle & Mr Oliverson.[9] At Police Office giving evidence agst cabdriver. the owner was fined £5, & costs.[10] Wrote an art. for L. St.[11] & wrote to J.N.G. & Jones. Keith—Pecchio— paper—dined at Uncle D's—red book & a *reverie* afterwards.

17. Sunday.

Two charity sermons at St James's. Twisleton[12] & Gaskell with me long—

---

[1] Probably Charles Upham Barry, a Bloomsbury neighbour of Divie Robertson's.
[2] Robert Ward, d. 1843, Norfolk gentleman, lived in Albany.   [3] Untraced.
[4] Possibly from French translation of Church of Ireland Liturgy (1704, 1715).
[5] By John *Gladstone in *Liverpool Standard*, 5 and 12 February 1833, 173 and 189.
[6] Perhaps on Liverpool's affairs.
[7] Joseph *Hume, 1777–1855, radical; Scottish born; served in India 1800–8; M.P. 1812, 1818–41, 1842–55; eminent financial reformer. *H* xv. 660. *Gladstone voted against him: Morley, i. 106.
[8] Stephen *Lushington, 1782–1873, judge and reformer; M.P. 1806–8, 1820–41; defended Queen *Caroline; admiralty judge 1838, dean of arches 1858, res. 1867. Discussion on trade with Netherlands: *H* xv. 770.
[9] Richard Oliverson, insurance broker, of Portland Place.
[10] See 11 Feb. 33.
[11] Untraced.
[12] Edward Boyd Turner *Twisleton, 1809–74; b. of 13th Lord Saye and Sele; chief commissioner of poor laws in Ireland 1845–9; on Oxford University commission, 1855.

dined at Uncle Divie's—read Blunt's Sermon on Jehu,[1] and a good deal of Keith. Prophecy affords matter for most interesting study: and important indeed, tho' dangerous. In the present uncertainty of calculation founded upon human affairs, it becomes more than ever desirable that we should know whereabouts we stand in the immovable dispensations of God.

18. M.

Wrote to R.G.—H.J.G.—D. of Newcastle—E. of Lincoln. Paper—Keith. Public documents. at Christie's. called on Mr Godfrey & Mr Tallents—& on the Gaskells. Ho. of C. 3¾–11¼. Powerful speech of O'Connell.[2]

19. T.

T.G. & Mr Tallents breakfasted with me. Keith—Pecchio—Townsend. House 4¾–8¾.[3]—At Christie's. Gaskell had tea with me. Wrote to Blakesley & Mrs G: also two short art.s for L. St.[4]—This day is memorable.[5] Portarl[ingto]n petition.[6]

20.

Mr Godfrey with me. Finished Vol. 1. of Keith. Dined at Mr Hallam's—met E. of Kerry,[7] Ld Mahon, Sotheby,[8] & Gally Knight.[9] At St James's—but only for half the service. public documents—mending alabasters[10]—drew up a statement about El[ection] petitions—ans[we]r from Ireland & matters almost arranged.

21.

Furniture shops & Christie's sale—wrote to R.G. Paper. Count Pecchio. Making some Abstracts—read Ld Grey's Sp. on Irish Coercion, and Lord Althorp's & Stanley's on Church Reform, in the Mirror[11]—House 4¾–8¼. T.G. spoke on Lpool petition—I only heard one or two sentences.[12]

22.

Furniture shops, & arranging with Luxmoore.[13] Also mending alabasters.

[1] Henry *Blunt, 'The Zeal of Jehu not Christian Zeal' (1833), on II Kings x. 16.
[2] On woes of Ireland: *H* xv. 873.   [3] Irish grand juries: *H* xv. 955.
[4] One perhaps printed, on 'Ministerial Tactics', 22 February 1833, 216.
[5] Cp. 19 Feb. 29.
[6] Thomas Gladstone's return for Portarlington was disputed: see 28, 30 Mar. 33.
[7] William Thomas Petty-Fitzmaurice, 1811–36, eldest son of 3rd marquis of *Lansdowne; styled Earl Wycombe, 1811; earl of Kerry 1818; whig M.P. Calne 1833–6.
[8] Probably William *Sotheby, 1757–1833, author, translator of Homer.
[9] Henry Gally *Knight, 1786–1846, traveller and writer on architecture; tory M.P. Aldborough 1824, Malton 1830, north Nottinghamshire 1835–46.
[10] See 4 Feb. 33.
[11] *Mirror*, i. 232, 274, 187 (1833); cp. *H* xv. 718, 561, 607.
[12] *H* xv. 1026. John Benett, 1773–1852, whig (later tory) M.P. for Wiltshire 1819–52, presented a petition on corruption of Liverpool local elections. Thomas Gladstone's speech in reply was wrongly attributed to his brother in *Mirror*, i. 351. Debates followed on corporation abuses and on public walks. *H* xv. 1030, 1049.
[13] W. T. Luxmoore, manager at the Albany.

Mayow breakfasted with me. Ho: of C. 5½–8½.[1] At night, read Count Pecchio, Appx to Townsend's Facts and 'Outlines of History',[2] with Abstract.

23.

Hallam Breakfasted with me—day occupied in[3] discussing bookcases & curtains carpets beds &c. inquiry for serv[an]ts—wrote to Mr G. & an art. for L. St.[4] calld on Mrs Hallam (whom I liked *much*)[5] Gaskell, Lincoln: introduced to Lady L: much struck with her manner as well as, or more than, face—dined at Uncle D's. Looking over Rept on enlargement of Ho. of C.[6] Business with Luxmoore.

24.

Breakf. in Bedf. Square. St Giles's—Mr Tyler; good. Kept at home rest of day on acct of cough. Read much of Keith: Cox's "Secession Considered"[7]: Barber's Serm. on "Party Spirit in the Church".[8] Wrote some notes on the Irish Extract Book.[9]

25.

Wrote to R.G.—to Sherriffs. Busy inspecting furniture & my rooms till near dinnertime—called on Lady Scott[10] to break my engagement for Wednesday: & broke an engagement with Gaskell for today—read papers —Coercion Bill—Count Pecchio—and Lardner's Outlines—with notes therefrom.

26.

Che folla degli affari![11] Furniture & servants with arrangements for divers articles of use. Called on Gaskell: & in Bedford Square. at Ho. of C. to attend the Petersfield Ballot[12]—wrote to Mr G—R.G. and Jones: also an Art. for Lpool Standard.[13] Home before eight. Read Pecchio: Rowe on the Ballot:[14] & finished Eyre Evans's certainly clever pamphlet on Ireland. Read too the Extracts from minutes of Evidence on B. & Ln. Railway.[15]

[1] On disturbances in Ireland, and members in office. *H* xv. 1110, 1107.
[2] By Dionysius *Lardner (1831).
[3] 'furnishing &' deleted.   [4] On Irish church reform, 26 February 1833, 224.
[5] Julia Maria Elton, 1783–1840, da. of 5th bart; m. 1807 Henry *Hallam, 1777–1859, historian; lived at 67 Wimpole Street.
[6] *PP* 1831 iv. 655 and 1833 xii. 465, 487.
[7] A pamphlet by Robert Cox in reply to one by J. L. Harris (1832?).
[8] In J. Barber, *Sermons* (1809).
[9] Untraced: cp. 13 Feb. 33.
[10] Anne, née Ommaney, d. 1849; m. 1796 (Sir) Samuel Scott, 1772–1849, banker, 2nd bart. of Lytchet Minster 1830.
[11] 'What press of business!'
[12] Thirty-three members' names drawn by lot to inquire into alleged corruption at the last Petersfield election.
[13] On Irish coercion, 1 March 1833, 232.
[14] Pamphlet by W. H. Rowe, political writer (1833).
[15] London and Birmingham railway bill under consideration.

27.

Wrote to Caparn—Welby[1]—Dry[2]—Mr G.—R.G.—Rockall—read Pecchio
—looked over all the names (abt 2800) to the Lpool petition—& copied a
good many—called on the Mayor,[3] & on Mr Moss & his party—Looking
after my rooms. House at 12. Again at 5 till half past one. Ld Althorp on
Irish Coercion very bad—Stanley splendid.[4] Wrote to Gaskell about poor
Wishlade.[5]

28.

Pecchio—seeing servants—and shopping: ordered my breakft service:
provided for fitting up my little bronzes. Wrote to H.J.G.—and J. Wishlade. House 4¾–11¾. Sheil's speech extremely able and ingenious: Macaulay's no answer.[6] Went out & read Burnet's Preface to his Ref. &c.—
making notes.[7] made up monthly accts. Answered in the negative the
application for aged & infirm actresses.[8] Elected a member of the Oxford
and Cambridge [club].

March 1. Friday.

Servants & furniture still on hand. breakf. in Bedfd Square—calld on
Mayor of Lpool & H.H. Joy to inquire for Parr who is much better. Wrote
to R.G. & to Mr Bartlett. House 5¼–1¾. Very clever speech from D.W.
Harvey, & a magnificent one from Peel—beyond any, I think, which I ever
heard.[9]

2.

Same work. Mr Shand[10] with me in mg. Wrote to Mrs Chisholm: & an art.
for Lpool Standard.[11] Got my things moved into the Albany.[12] How humiliating is the coil that attends the affairs of life, how many wants, how few
results: Dined at Sir F. Doyle's[13]—a very pleasant party.—arranging till
one.

Sunday March 3.

Breakfasted in my rooms with comfort enough. How largely am I supplied

---

[1] Probably Thomas Earle Welby, 1810–99, army officer 1826–37, bp. of St Helena
1861.
[2] Thomas Dry, clerk at Christ Church.
[3] Charles Horsfall, merchant, mayor of Liverpool 1832–3.
[4] *H* xv. 1210, 1250. Cp. *DNB* liii. 364.
[5] Cp. Add MS 44353, f. 92, for a warm letter of thanks from Wishlade.
[6] Again on Irish coercion. *H* xv. 1299, 1326.
[7] G. *Burnet, History of the Reformation of the Church of England*, i (1679).
[8] Add MS 44722, f. 167.
[9] Irish coercion bill: *H* xvi. 40, 77.
[10] Probably Charles Shand of Everton.   [11] Untraced.
[12] On 29 November 1832 the Albany trustees had consented to John *Gladstone's purchase of the chambers L2 (S. Birkenhead, *Peace in Piccadilly* (1958), 116; photograph of
their entrance at 195).
[13] At 10 Wimpole Street.

with the conveniences and treasures of this life! It is their very multitude which makes them a burden and a care, & gives them power to distract the mind: may God enable me to make them an occasion of thankfulness.—St James's mg & aft. Sacrament there. Met Seymer in aft. & walked with him. Dined at Uncle D's—read a good deal of Keith, & two Family Sermons.

4. Monday.

Engaged James Horsnell[1] at 12 s. a week board wages, 18 g[uinea]s, & his clothes.

Making inventory—unpacked a box—shopping—called on the Gaskells, & on Mrs Tupper.[2] Wrote to J. Wishlade—Jones—and J.N.G. Dined with the Mayor of Lpool & his companions—met Lord Sandon; & Sir H. Douglas to whom I was introduced—very gentlemanly & agreeable. Went to the H[ouse] with Lord Sandon $9\frac{3}{4}$–$1\frac{1}{4}$.[3] Read papers at the O. & C. Club to wh I paid my first visit.

5. T.

Busy about my rooms in morng. read papers—wrote divers notes, & to R.G., Mrs G., & Mr Welby.[4] Exam[ine]d the Lpool Dock petition, acc[ording] to request. House 4–2. Placed on Bedfd El[ectio]n Committee.[5] Very long speech from O'Connell; too long[6]—Read Burnet—made notes: & read Huskn's Sp. on giving franchise to 3 great towns.[7]

6. W.

Rose late: still at work about my rooms. Papers. El. Comm. 1–5. & House 5–11. Tea &c. &c. Had the intention of speaking: but the occasion was lost. L[iver]p[oo]l petition got a Committee—but with limited inquiry.[8]

7. Th.

El. Comm. 11–4. Then came home—went to see the Coles. Owen is in a sad state—spent my evening in quiet. Reading paper—Antislavery Abstract of Lords' Evidence[9]—and Macdonnell's Letter to Buxton.[10] T.G. came in, late.

---

[1] As valet.

[2] Ellen Devis, d. 1847; wife of Martin Tupper 1779–1845, physician, of New Burlington Street, m. of M. F. *Tupper.

[3] Coercion debate continued. *H* xvi. 120.

[4] Probably John Erle Welby, 1786–1867, rector of Harston, Leicestershire; father of T. E. and R. E. *Welby; connexion of *Glynnes.

[5] *Gladstone kept the minutes for this cttee. (Add MS 44722, ff. 168–93). It decided that the sitting member, the whig Samuel Crawley, had been duly elected; he sat till 1837. H. of C. *Journals* 1833, 165.

[6] Still on coercion. *H* xvi. 202, 228–72. *Gladstone voted for the first reading, carried 466–377.

[7] *Huskisson, favouring *Russell's bill to enfranchise Manchester, Leeds, and Birmingham, 23 February 1830, *NSH* xxii. 889.

[8] Liverpool's affairs debated; Thomas Gladstone spoke. *H* xvi. 293–5, 305.

[9] *H* xvi. 281.

[10] Pamphlet by A. *Macdonnell (1833).

Made an Estimate of my expences in Furnishing. Elected *without* my will (but not more than without it) a member of the Carlton Club.[1]

8. *Fr.*

Committee on Bedf. El. 11–3½. An important day. Continued my notes of the proceedings. Some business before & after. Wrote to H.J.G. & dined in Bedf. Sq. to meet my Father. Went to Ho. of C. at 9½. read a little Burnet in the Library—remained till 12¼.[2] Went to the Carlton & looked about me there—read H. of Lord's Evidence.

9.

Comm. El. at 11. Kept waiting for Mr Wood.[3] Sat till 4½. Scrutiny proceeding.[4] Wrote to R.G. Dined at O & C. Club. Getting things set to rights in my rooms. Finished Macdonnell's pamphlet—read J.G. on Free Trade—a little Machiavelli.

10. *Sunday.*

Mr Ward mg, on Sabbath.[5] Bp aft. on the *example* of the rich: most admirable. Invited to dine with Lord Mahon—wh I declined—Dined in Bedf. Sq. to meet my Father: he went by Mail. Bible—notes—finished Keith—a serm of Evans,[6] & one of Benson.[7]

11. *M.*

11–5. Committee. copied a letter—wrote to H.J.G. & Cousin Jane. Read papers & Burnet. House again 6½–1½: but staid out some time. Divided for time on Irish Ch Bill, 47 to 187, & 363 to 84 on the Coercion Bill.[8]

12. *T.*

11–4. Committee. Burnet—House 5–8¼.[9] Dined at Club—& went to Unc. D's to meet the Oliversons. Breakft at Mrs Cole's. O.C. drove me to the House. Read some of Baxter's Tract at nt.[10]

13. *Wed*

Cole came to breakfast with me—and I had a conversation with him curtailed indeed & most feeble on my part, but deeply interesting. May God

---

[1] Morley, i. 98; cp. Robbins, 159.   [2] Irish coercion: *H* xvi. 406.
[3] Probably (sir) Charles *Wood, 1800–85, whig M.P. 1826–66; m. *Grey's da. 1829, 3rd bart. 1846, chancellor of exchequer 1846–52, admiralty 1855–8, Indian secretary 1859–66, Cr. Viscount Halifax 1866.
[4] i.e., cttee. considered validity of individual suffrages.   [5] J. G. Ward.
[6] R. W. *Evans, *The Church of God in a Series of Sermons* (1832).
[7] C. *Benson.
[8] Irish church bill read 1°; 2° debate fixed for 14 March, against tory pleas for delay. Coercion bill read 2°. *H* xvi. 477, 489.
[9] Affairs of Liverpool: *H* xvi. 538.
[10] Robert Baxter, *Narrative of Facts* (1833), attack on *Irving by a former adherent.

enable me so to deport myself to him as neither to do harm, nor to omit receiving good. El Comm. 11–5. Wrote (in it) to Mr G. & Mr Dobson.[1] Began to read & analyse Irish Ch. Bill[2]—attended Ho. 5¼–9.[3] Afterwards reading Baxter's very remarkable & interesting work.

14. Th.

El. Comm. merely to wind up. A little business—& calld on the Gaskells, with whom I had an early dinner. Paper. Ho. of C. 4–9¾. Irish Church Bill agreed by Govt. to be put off.—& Counsel granted to Lpool Corpn.[4] At night finished Mr Baxter's (I think) *convincing* book. Wrote to R.G.—the Cashkeeper &c.

15. Fr.

Cole came to breakf. Conv. with him till past one. Wrote to H.J.G., Mr Rawson,[5] & Dry. Shopping. Read Palmer's reply to Arnold.[6] Dined at Sir S. Scott's—& went to a musical party at the Miss Christies.[7] House at midnight for one halfhour.[8]

16. Sat.

Much shopping and paying bills—ordered Court Dress.[9] Read Finlay's Letter to Ld Ashley, and Part 1 of Expos[ition] of B[ritish] For[eign] Policy towards Holland[10]—dined at Sir F. Doyle's—& came home with Wood who sat with me till 12½.

17.

St James's mg & aft. Dined at Unc. D's to meet Unc. C. Began Faber on Sacrifice[11] & Palmer's Origines.[12] Also read some of the Armenian Liturgy, & Instructions for the Mass. Wrote down a few thoughts.

18. M.

Breakf at Mr Gordon's.[13] Met Mr Finch[14]—Mr Pringle[15]—Mr Urquhart.[16]

---

[1] Possibly Thomas Dobson, city bullion dealer.   [2] *PP* 1833 i. 339.
[3] Coercion bill in cttee.: *H* xvi. 589.
[4] Irish church bill held up on a procedural difficulty: *H* xvi. 647. Agreed that Liverpool council should have legal representation at impending cttee.: ibid. 643.
[5] Replying to Rawson on Irish church, 12 March; Add MS 44353, ff. 100–2.
[6] William *Palmer, 'Remarks on . . . *Arnold's principles of Church Reform' (1833).
[7] Scott lived in Mansfield Street, Portland Place; and Langham Christie, 1789–1861, s. of a Bombay Engineer, Northamptonshire gentleman, lived half a mile west in Cumberland Street.
[8] Supply: *H* xvi. 698.   [9] See 20 Mar. 33.
[10] *PP* 1833 xlii. 1, the blue book on the Belgian question.
[11] G. S. *Faber, *Origin of Expiatory Sacrifice* (1827).
[12] W. *Palmer, *Origines Liturgicae*, 2v. (1832).
[13] Robert Gordon, 1787–1864, West India proprietor: whig M.P. Wareham 1812–18, Cricklade 1818–37, Windsor 1837–41.
[14] George Finch, d. 1870; Rutland magnate; tory M.P. for Stamford 1832–7.
[15] Robert Pringle, d. 1841, whig M.P. for Selkirkshire 1833–4.
[16] David *Urquhart, 1805–77, anti-Palmerstonian radical; fought in Greece 1827–8; secretary at Constantinople embassy 1837–8; M.P. for Stafford 1847–52.

Much conv.—Wrote to Mr Godfrey—Mr Rawson—Mr G—J.N.G.—Shopping—a *job* cleaning alabasters: House:[1] & delightful musical party at Sir F. Doyle's. Mrs Groom (*feu* Miss Wilkinson)[2] sang splendidly.

19.

Papers. Hallam came to breakft. Still shopping. Called on Mr Tallents. papers. Dined at O. & C. C[lub]. Boxes arrived from Oxford—a little unpacking at nt. House 4–1. But in Ho. of Peers to hear Bp of Exeter, &c.[3] Divided for the C[ourt] Martial Clause 270 to 130.[4]

20.

Went to the Levee. presented by Sir R. Inglis. Walk with Wood. Most of my day spent among my book boxes, in unpacking. Dined with Mr Williams in Grosv. Square.[5] Read papers. Going down to H. of C. late in evg, stopped, hearing there was nothing.

21.

Breakf. in Bedf. Square. Books, unpacking & arranging—a formidable affair. At the Queen's drawing room.[6] House 4–11¾. Div. on Attwood's motion 192 to 158[7]—Wrote to Mrs G. and R.G.

22.

Breakf. with Mr Gordon, to meet Bp of Exeter:[8] a person of great conversational power, & courtesy very finished but beyond my taste. Labouring again with my books, papers, & wine—& managed by 3 o'clock in the morng (after H. of C.) to get my things into something like order. Wrote to Scott. Papers. H. of C. 8–10½.[9]

23.

C. Larkins breakftd with me. Attended Meeting of Agricult[ural] Employment Institution[10]—& put down my name. Shopping—left cards or called for [*sc.* on] D. of N.,[11] Sir F. Doyle, Mrs Williams, Mrs Mundy, Lady Scott,

[1] Coercion bill, cttee. *H* xvi. 731.

[2] Wife of Richard Groom of Henrietta Street, Cavendish Square, and gd. of Abraham Wilkinson, M.D., of Whiteweb Park, Enfield.

[3] On Irish education. *H* xvi. 802.

[4] Clause 10 of the coercion bill enabled military courts martial to try political offenders in Ireland, in emergencies. *H* xvi. 827.

[5] Robert Williams, 1767–1847, banker and East India proprietor; Dorset magnate; tory M.P. for Dorchester 1812–35.

[6] Queen *Adelaide, 1792–1849, m. *William (IV) 1818.

[7] Thomas *Attwood, 1783–1856, democrat and currency reformer; founded Birmingham political union, 1830; M.P. Birmingham 1832–9. His motion for inquiry into distress among the industrious classes was beaten: *H* xvi. 918.

[8] Henry *Phillpotts, 1778–1869, fellow of Magdalen 1795–1804, rector of Stanhope 1820, dean of Chester 1828, bp. of Exeter 1830 and canon of Durham 1831.

[9] British Museum Add MSS catalogue and bribery at Stafford: *H* xvi. 990, 991.

[10] At the Freemasons' Tavern, Lincoln's Inn Fields; agreed to promote allotments for the deserving country poor.   [11] In Portman Square.

Mrs Labalmondiere, Mrs Denison.[1] Wrote to Mr Godfrey—R.G.—& Jeffries. Made a further approxn to tidiness, by arranging my pamphlets. Dined at Sir Jas MacGrigor's, Camden Hill.[2]

24. S.

Trin Chapel & St James's. Dottrina Cristiana[3]—Began Strype's Cranmer[4] —finished Evans's Church of God—read some of the Canons.

25.

Phillimore breakfd with me—Wrote to Mr G—R.G.—Childers—Mr Wakefield[5]—Warwick postm[aste]r. Called on Mr Tallents & Parr—Carlton meeting at 4—House at 5 and to near one. Navy estimates.[6] Read 'Plan for amending Taxn' & 'a Prop. Tax the only remedy' &c[7]—Mrs Wallis came.[8]

26.

A. Acland breakfd with me—& sat. Conv. on religion. which he has taken much to heart. Arranging still. Dinner at home—for the first time. Walked across the park with Bp Phillpotts. House 4–6½—and 10–1½. Prop. Tax. voted agst it: 221–155—& Peel's explanation.[9]

27.

Wordsworth & Palmer[10] breakfasted with me—read Memorial of residents in China[11]—paper—Pecchio—Burnet (at House)—and in Burke's Speeches. House at one P.M. & again 5½–9¼—divided for Shaw's amendment 44 to 123.[12]

28.

Read paper—part of Hale on Tithes[13]—Sir A. Agnew's Sabbath Bill[14]—&

[1] Charlotte, da. of Samuel Estwick, M.P.; m. 1797 as his 2nd wife John Denison (formerly Wilkinson), of Ossington; mother of J.E.*, E.*, G.A.*, &c; and stepmother-in-law to the speaker. She also lived in Portman Square.

[2] On the ridge between north and south Kensington.

[3] St. Robert Bellarmine's catechism, in shortened Italian version (1831).

[4] John *Strype, *Memorials of Thomas *Cranmer* (1694); notes in Add MS 44722, ff. 23–6.

[5] Begging letter from Edward Wakefield of Newark, subaltern in Sherwood Foresters, in Add MS 44353, ff. 104–5.

[6] *H* xvi. 1005.   [7] Untraced pamphlets.

[8] Housekeeper in Albany.

[9] George Richard Robinson (East India merchant, whig M.P. Worcester 1826–37, Poole 1847–52), proposed an inquiry into a property tax, as a means of simplifying taxation; Sir R. *Peel and Sir E. *Codrington (1770–1851, victor of Navarino) discussed slave trading in the Levant. *H* xvi. 1072, 1119.

[10] William *Palmer, 1811–79, theologian; elder b. of Roundell *Palmer; convert to Rome 1855.

[11] *PP* 1833 xxv. 471, dated Canton, 24 December 1830, requesting a permanent British envoy in China.

[12] *Shaw moved to reduce powers of lord lieutenant of Ireland: *H* xvi. 1149.

[13] W. H. *Hale, 'An Essay on the . . . division of tithes in England' (1832).

[14] *PP* 1833 iii. 561.

began Botta's Napoleon.[1] Read also Br[itish] Critic (Burton I am sure) on "Riland on the Liturgy".[2] House 4–7. Portarln Ballot. T.G., Gaskell, & I, were all called. They could not stand on the list—& I was struck.[3] Wrote to H.J.G. Mayow calld.

29. Friday.

Blakesley & Tupper called—each sat some time. Read C. Beamish's case[4]— & finished Hall's Essay on Tithes. Shopping—& called on D. of N., & the Gaskells—with whom I dined. D. of Buckm there.[5] Called on the Anstices. House 9–12¼. Third Reading of Disturbances Bill. 345 to 86.[6]

30. Sat.

Bad sore throat. Blakesley breakfasted with me. Tom's petition settled between one and three![7] Walked with A. Wood. Went to Mend[icant] Soc. about Fowler. Read their Report.[8] Wrote to Mr G—R.G.—Mr Godfrey— Mr Bartlett—Mr H. Hilton[9]—Speaker's levee in the evening—this being the last for the season. Read Botta—& Newland on Tithes.[10]

31. Sunday.

Lay in bed, in order to quell, if possible, my sore throat, till 4 P.M. Read &c. all the evg. Faber on the Prophecies[11]—Strype's Cranmer—Bible.

Looked through the services in my "Settimana Santa"[12]—& recalled this day twelvemonth with interest. I wish we made more use of times & seasons.

April 1.

Tupper breakfd with me. Mr Wilmot came, & sat two hours—talking chiefly about the Irish Church. Unwell this day. Went however to see

[1] C. G. G. Botta, *History of Italy during the Consulate and Empire of Napoleon Buonaparte*, 2v., tr. (1828).
[2] xiii. 42 (January 1833).
[3] Thirty-three M.P.s were chosen to consider the petition against Thomas Gladstone's return for Portarlington in cttee.; his brother, originally chosen by lot, being struck off the list. H. of C. *Journals* 1833, 229.
[4] Navy pay clerk since 1805, protesting in a pamphlet (1833) against superannuation.
[5] Richard Temple Nugent Brydges Chandos *Grenville, 1776–1839, magnate; styled Earl Temple 1784 to 1813 when he succ. as 2nd marquess of Buckingham; cr. duke of Buckingham and Chandos 1822; over-spent lavishly, chiefly at Stowe.
[6] Irish coercion. *H* xvi. 1236.
[7] Thomas Gladstone was confirmed in his seat for Portarlington. H. of C. *Journals* 1833, 244.
[8] Some Warwickshire trouble; see 12 Apr. 33.
[9] Henry Hilton, youngest brother of a Newark merchant family—another brother was on *Gladstone's election cttee.—sought merchanting work in Liverpool. Add MS 44353, ff. 108–12, 188.
[10] Pamphlet by H. Newland on tithes in Ireland (1832).
[11] G. S. *Faber, *Dissertation on the Prophecies*, 2v. (1807) or *Prophecies relative to the Conversion of Judah and Israel*, 2v. (1808).
[12] *Uffizia della Settimana Santa . . . con osservazioni dell'Ab. A. Mazzinelli* (1806), services for holy week.

Canning at Lady C's.[1] She very kindly brought me down in her carriage. House 5–12¾. Irish Church Resolutions.[2] T.G. had tea with me afterwards.

2.

Wood breakftd with me. papers. Wrote to Mrs G.—the Mayor of Warwick[3] —& Hallam. Still under the influence of medicine: but dined with T.G. & House 5–12. Church Resolutions—division avoided. Div. on Hume's motion against army flogging in England: voted 151 to 140.[4] I had occupied two hours of my morning in thinking over the Church question so far as regarded the taxation of the living incumbents, with a view to speaking —but I felt far more relieved than baffled, when Ministers averted the debate by making their concession.[5]

3. W.

Breakfast in Bedf Sq. Sat an hour with Parr—called on Duke of N.—Lady M'Kenzie—Mr Gordon—Mr Murchison[6]—Mr Freshfield.[7] paying bills & arranging household matters. House 6½–11¼: paired off with Herbert, for Wilson Patten's motion.[8] Prepns for departure.

4. Thursday.

Went down[9] with T.G. by Crown Prince. Travelled well. Arrived 6¼. T.G. not at all well. Found Mrs G. & Helen better—Jane & Miss Trench[10] here. In the evening read 'Sett[imana] Santa', Poor Law Reports,[11] and some of Seaward's narrative.[12]

5. Good Friday.

Church—sacrament morng: & very good serm. from Mr Gayfor aft. Walked about with Bruce who has been ill. Wrote to Jas Stewart—& Pusey. Read 'Sett[imana] Santa'—papers—and Poor Law Reports.

[1] 37 Chester Terrace, Regent's Park.

[2] *Althorp moved three resolutions on machinery for implementing the Church Temporalities (Ireland) bill; the first, giving the viceroy power to appoint ecclesiastical commissioners, was carried. *H* xvi. 1354.

[3] Thomas Collins, 1775?–1856, retired tradesman; mayor 1832–4.

[4] *Hume's motion was lost: *H* xvii. 68. Cp. Morley, i. 106.

[5] *Althorp's resolutions abolishing Irish first-fruits and vestry assessments agreed; *Althorp offered *Peel prospect of amdts. in cttee. *H* xviii. 36.

[6] (Sir) Roderick Impey *Murchison (1792–1871), of Kintail; geologist; fought at Corunna; president, geological society, 1831, 1841, and geographical society 1843–58; kt. 1836; cr. bart. 1866.

[7] James William Freshfield, 1775?–1864; solicitor to Bank of England; Surrey landowner; tory M.P. Penryn 1830–2, 1837–41, 1852–7, and Boston 1851–2.

[8] John *Wilson Patten (1802–92, Lancashire notable, tory M.P. Lancashire 1830–74, Irish secretary 1868, cr. Lord Winmarleigh 1874) sought a commission on factory labour: carried, 74–73. *H* xvii. 79, 113.

[9] To Leamington.

[10] Perhaps Eliza, d. unm. 1869, niece of Thomas Trench, 1761–1834, dean of Kildare 1809.

[11] *PP* 1831 viii. 321.

[12] Jane *Porter, *Narrative of Sir Edward Seaward's shipwreck*, 3v. (1831), historical novel.

6. Easter Eve.

Began Sismondi's It. Rep. making notes.[1] Continued 'Poor Laws'. Wrote to Aunt M—Williams at Oxford—& R.G.—Rode. A good deal of time occupied in sitting with my Mother—T.G.—Aunt E.—& Mr Grant at the Clarendon.

7. Easter Sunday.

Communion. A stranger preached in aftn. Tom still very unwell. It is providential that he came here. Read Bible—Sett. Santa—Faber on the Prophecies—& a Sermon of Arnold's aloud at night.

8. M.

Calld on Mrs Hook—likewise at Warwick, to see Sir J. Mordaunt and the Mayor. Heming dined with us. Wrote to F.B. Cole, and Gaskell—Read papers—Penny mag.[2]—Poor Law Reports—and Sismondi, which is delightful.

9. T.

Little improvement in Tom. Sismondi—Poor Law report—and paper— singing lesson from Meyrick, and singing in evg. John & Miss Joy[3] came. Called on Mrs Proby—Lady Farnham—Mrs C. Swinfen[4]—Mrs Lane.[5] Wrote to Phillimore—& some notes for T.G.

10. W.

Another day of unmitigated nausea for Tom—a severe trial. almost no food since Thursday! singing lesson—& practice at night. Rode with J.N.G. Wrote to Aunt D. for Tom. Read & analysed Sismondi—& read the Poor Law Report.

11. Th.

Sismondi and Poor Law Report—paper—saw Aunt E. as usual & called with Mr G. on Sir R. Vaughan.[6] Dined at Lord Eastnor's—& evg party there. Wrote at some length on hered[itary] aristocracy,[7] & to S. Denison on the same subject.[8] Wrote to Uncle D. papers.

---

[1] J. C. L. de Sismondi, *Histoire des républiques italiennes du moyen âge* (1807–18). Notes in Add MS 44723, ff. 11–13.

[2] Charles *Knight edited the *Penny Magazine* for the S.D.U.K. (1833–46).

[3] H. H. Joy's sister.

[4] Unidentified; perhaps of Swinfen Hall, Lichfield.

[5] Wife of C. N. Lane.

[6] Probably Sir (Charles) Richard *Vaughan, 1774–1849; Sir Henry *Halford's b.; minister to Washington 1825–35; cr. G.C.H. when on leave in England 1833.

[7] Add MS 44722, ff. 194–201.

[8] Denison had asked for an outline for a speech in the Oxford Union against the motion that 'Hereditary Aristocracy is an Evil' (Add MS 44373, ff. 118–19).

12. Fr.

Miss Joy and Jane went early. Sismondi & Poor Law Report. Mayor of Warwick & his legal adviser here about Fowler.[1] Rode. papers. wrote to Uncle Colin. Singing lesson with Meyrick.

13. Sat.

Sad account of Parr. May his bed of sickness be gilded by the rays of that hope which is fixed upon eternity. Read Sismondi: extremely interesting: & Poor Law Report—paper—singing lesson from Meyrick—called on Lady Eastnor—tea at Mrs Hook's—rode with J.N.G. Sat with Aunt E. [who was] still confined [to bed] & in pain—read to her.

14. Sunday.

The day of Thanksgiving.[2] Services admirably chosen. & good sermons from Mr Gayfor & Mr Downes. May God bless the appointment of this day. Read Bible—Christ[ian] Year—Faber—Prop. Gosp. Soc's Report.[3] With Aunt E.

15. Monday.

Cold & headach. Put off going. Wrote to Rogers—Sir R. Inglis—Robn. With Aunt E. & called on Mrs Jephson—copied two letters and read paper and Sismondi. Medicine at nt.

16. Tuesday.

Had intended going today: but gave it up yesterday. With Aunt E. Called on Mr Galton. Wilmot came. papers: finished Sismondi—excessively interesting—& read Poor Law Report.

17. Wednesday.

After going down all prepared, disapp[ointe]d of a place & did not go up!— papers—read Lord Byron's Doge of Venice with some of the Appendix.[4] The play contains a good deal of fine writing, but is I think defective as a drama. Hamilton & Hope came over from Rugby—& wished me to go back & see Arnold.[5] Walked about with Wilmot. With Aunt E.

18.

Breakfd with Wilmot—off by Crown Prince; arrived safely in town soon after 8—went to Ho of C.—no div. expected[6]—thence to Carlton—read the

---

[1] Unidentified; business untraced.   [2] For relief from cholera.
[3] 'On the Condition of the Negro Population on the Codrington Estate . . . in Barbados' (1831).
[4] 'Marino Faliero, Doge of Venice', blank verse tragedy (1821).
[5] Dr. Thomas *Arnold, 1795–1842, headmaster of Rugby 1828, originator of 'public' school system.
[6] Debates on tithes, sinecures, and Irish crime; one division on the last point, late at night. H xvii. 273, 292, 304.

Jews Debate[1]—tea at home—& read Whiteley's pamphlet on Jamaica[2]—rectifying matters.

19.

Breakf in Bedf Square—Busy hanging pictures & making arrangements in my rooms. Wordsworth & Mr Shand called—Dined at Lincoln's Inn—went to Parr's afterwards. Wrote to T.G. House of C. 6½–9. Budget.[3] Tea at O. & C. C[lub]—read Qu. Rev. on Poor Laws, & made notes. Making up furniture list.

20. Sat.

Shand—Doyle—Rogers—Egerton, here. Called on Bruce & Mr Finlay—rode with Gaskell—arranging papers (Parlty) Made Abstract of Lord Althorp's Speech.[4] read Poor Law Report.—wrote to J.N.G. Dined in Bedford Square—read paper.

21. S.

St James's morning & aft.—Went to see Parr, & sat with him some time; I found him better: but I turned the interview to no profit. Such is the return we make for the mercies of God! Had he been worse I should not have dared to do otherwise (I trust) than speak plainly. Went to A. Acland's, but did not see him. Read Bible—Strype's Cranmer (making notes)—some Catholic Ritual—Palmer's Origines; &c.

22. M.

Wrote to Mr & R.G. Mr Shand—Sutherland—& Mr Finlay here—occupied in looking over & making some notes upon a document drawn up by him. Rode—& dined at Lincoln's Inn—but I cannot tell how my day fled. House of C. 6¼–12¾. Debate on Attwood's motion.[5]

23. T.

Wrote to T.G. & E. Wishlade. Rode in the Park. Attended meeting of the Factory people in Bridge Street[6]—Read Jews & Patents Bills,[7] 'Exposition of the Factory question'[8] & began Mr Husk[isso]n on the Bullion Report.[9] House 6¼–2¼. Splendid speech from Peel.[10] Bruce breakfd with me.

---

[1] Of the previous day: H xvii. 205.

[2] Henry Whiteley, 'Three Months in Jamaica in 1832' (1833), against flogging of slaves.

[3] H xvii. 326.   [4] Budget speech of the previous day.

[5] Matthias Attwood (1779–1851, London banker, radical tory M.P. for Callington 1826–30, Boroughbridge 1830–2, Whitehaven 1832–47, b. of Thomas*) moved for inquiry into monetary system as cause of distress; debate adjourned. H xvii. 384.

[6] Probably a meeting of the supporters of *Sadler's and *Ashley's ten hours bill.

[7] PP 1833 ii. 569, iii. 169.

[8] 'Remarks on the propriety and necessity of making the Factory Bill of more general application' (1833).

[9] W. *Huskisson, The Question concerning the Depreciation of our Currency (1810).

[10] Currency debate continued, H xvii. 506; *Peel supported the gold standard.

24.

Mr Shand read his 'Letter to Mr Stanley'[1] to me—then came two gentn interested in steamboats, agst the St George Co's Bill[2]—then Irlam[3]—& Mayow. Calld on the D. of N[ewcastle] & Mrs M. Gaskell. rode with Milnes. Dined at Lincoln's Inn. paper—Huskisson's pamphlet—and "Letter to Ld A[shley] by a Lanc[ashire] Cotton Spinner"[4] with other papers on the Bill. House at 10½ but staid in the Library &c. till 12½—then till three—we had three divs. the minorities were 139–155–and 49 : the last agst 271.[5]

25.

Called on & saw D. of N., & Mrs Hagart. Read paper & Poor Law Report. Dined at Mr Farquhar's[6]—whist. Mr Shand with me a fearful time! looked over &c. his letter to Mr Stanley : I am a wretched critic : he admits remarks very good naturedly. Wrote to Mr G. House 4–5¼ : & 10–12½. Div. on Ballot 211 to 106.[7]

26. Friday.

Wilberforce breakfd with me. Mr Finlay here : I kept him long, and got an admirable lecture on currency and manufactures. Rode—and wrote to T.G. —Divers others with me. Read Huskn[8] and Poor Law Report—& paper. Dined at the Duke of Hamilton's[9]—Mr Finlay, Sir W. Clinton,[10] M. Attwood, &c. there. Came down too late for the division on the Malt Duties : at which I felt excessively disgusted, not on account of a failing to swell the majority, but because absent from my duty. Numbers 162 to 152.[11] Lincoln, Attwood & Maxwell,[12] shut out with me.—However I accepted the invitation believing there would be nothing of importance. And I trust this may not happen again.[13] Carlton afterwards.

[1] Untraced.

[2] The company traded between Liverpool and Cork. Bill for its better regulation lost 3°, 19 June 1833 (H. of C. *Journals*, 499).

[3] W. Irlam ; not otherwise identified.

[4] Anonymous pamphlet on factory bill by Henry *Ashworth (1833).

[5] Currency debate continued : *H* xvii. 540, 586, 590.

[6] James Farquhar of Johnstone Lodge, Laurencekirk ; his town house was in Duke Street, Westminster.

[7] George *Grote (1794–1871, historian of Greece; radical M.P., city of London, 1832–41)'s motion for ballot in future parliamentary elections lost. *H* xvii. 608, 667. Cp. H. *Grote's *Personal Life* of him, 83–4 (1873); and Morley, i. 106.

[8] J. *Wright, *Memoirs of *Huskisson* (1831).

[9] Alexander Hamilton *Douglas, 1767–1852, duke of Hamilton and Brandon 1819; whig M.P. Lancaster 1802 ; called up to house of lords as Lord Dutton 1806 ; magnifico, collector and freemason. By Susan Euphemia, 2nd da. of William *Beckford, whom he m. 1810, he had William A. A. *Douglas, 1811–63, 11th duke, styled marquess of Douglas and Clydesdale 1819–52, Etonian, at Christ Church 1829–32; and Lady Lincoln.

[10] Sir William Henry *Clinton, 1769–1846, general; seized Madeira, 1801 ; fought in Spain, 1812–14 ; M.P. for Boroughbridge, 1806–18, and for Newark, 1818–30.

[11] Reduction in malt duty carried against government, on motion of Sir William Aincoats Ingilby, 1783–1854, 2nd bart., M.P. for Lincolnshire 1823–35. *H* xvii. 689.

[12] (Sir) John Maxwell, 1791–1865, M.P. for Renfrewshire 1818–30, Lanarkshire 1832–7 ; 8th bart. of Pollock 1844.

[13] See Morley, i. 102.

3—II.

27. Sat.

T.G. came. Read Memoirs of Husk[isso]n. Mr Finlay with me. Philharm. rehearsal (by favour of T.G.) 12¼–3 P.M. Dined with the Hagarts at 7. Conv. with T.G. afterwards. Called on D. & Dss of Hamilton—A. Acland— Mrs Farquhar[1]—Lord Mahon—Colin Mackenzie—Mrs Christie[2]—Price— D. Milligan—Mr Foster (had left town)[3]—also shopping & household affairs. Mr Gordon with me.

28. Sunday.

Breakf. in Bedf. Sq.—St Giles's—& St James's. Read Bible—Strype—Rose on the Prevs Dispositions towards Christy.[4]—H[anna]h More—and a serm. to my servants at night. Walk &c.

29. M.

Divers visitors. papers. Wrote to Mr G. & J.N.G. House 5–7. Tea with Farr. Read Poor Law Report—and began 'Travels of an Irish Gentleman'[5] &c. which made me also look to Faber's 'Facts & Assertions'.[6]

30. T.

Poor Law Report. Petition from Newark—examined & presented it, saying a few words.[7] Lincoln with me at my (?) dinner. Setting papers &c. to rights : no end to this. House 4 P.M.–3 A.M. Divided in 355 to 157 for keeping the House & Window Taxes. Left purposely before the 2nd division.[8] papers. Read a very long petition from Bath on the W.I. Quest[ion].[9]

May 1. Wednesday.

Wm Larkins[10] breakfd with me. Paper. Poor Law Report. Looked over Carrickf[ergu]s Election Report[11] & divers other documents. Messrs Burge & Duncan brought me the Edinburgh petition.[12] Divers calls—and shopping. Read 'Travels of an Irish Gentn' &c. *Grey mare came.*

2. Th.

Read Appx to P[oor] L[aw] Report—& part of Ld Mahon's new pamphlet.[13] paper. Called on Lord M[ahon]—Mrs Hagart—Mr Duncan—Miss Joy. Saw

---

[1] Mrs James Farquhar.
[2] Margaret Elizabeth, née Gosling, d. 1866; m. Langham Christie 1829.
[3] John *Foster, 1787?–1846, architect to Liverpool corporation *ca.* 1816–32.
[4] Hugh James *Rose, *Brief Remarks on the Disposition towards Christianity generated by prevailing Opinions and Pursuits* (1830).
[5] [T. *Moore] *Travels of an Irish Gentleman in search of a religion* 2v. (1833).
[6] An anti-Roman S.P.C.K. tract by G. S. *Faber (1833).
[7] Morley, i. 102; against house and window taxes. H. of C. *Journals*, 329.
[8] Against the malt tax: *H* xvii. 833.   [9] Presented 14 May 1833.
[10] Presumably his young cousin Walter Larkins.
[11] *PP* 1830–31 iii. 179.
[12] See 21 May 33. Charles or William Burge, hatters; James Duncan. merchant, or William, W.S.; all of Edinburgh.
[13] 'Lord John *Russell and Mr. *Macaulay on the French Revolution'.

Mrs J.[1] Admired her looks most. House 4–6½.[2] Wrote to Mr G. & Mr Lee of Newark.[3] Dined in B. Square. House 10–2.[4]

3. Fr.

Wrote to H.J.G.—also a note to Lord Sandon, on the Lpool poll. Reading "Evidence" & making notes. Also read Newland—& paper—Rode: called at Parr's: he is better: dined at Lincoln's Inn. John came: had tea with me: also Tom. House 6¼–8.[5] Cousin Wm here.

4. Sat.

Newland on Tithes—Lpool Boro' Report—wrote to Mrs G—R.G.—& Mr Lee of Newark. paper: calls: rode in the Park—arranged letters for April: dined at Mr Mundy's[6]: heard of Aunt Murray's decease.[7]

5. S.

Dined at Uncle D's—Mrs Wallis ill: ∴ no reading aloud at nt. Communion. much thought on its nature: may God lead me. Read Bible—Palmer—Mosheim[8]—Strype's Cranmer & a Serm.

6.

Papers. wrote to Mr G—& Mr Huddlestone.[9] Rode. called on the Larkins: went to view Mr Niewenhuy's[10] pictures at Christie's. Liked much Raphael's Madonna & child—Garofalo's Holy Family—and Vandyck's portrait of Francis du Quesnoy. Read Newland, Blackstone, & Townsend, making notes on tithes &c. House 5¼–1½. Divided in 78 agst 317.[11]

7. T.

Out early, at Mr Escott's[12] Committee Room—then the National Gallery (first time) and then Mr Escott's nomination. A stormy scene. Got cut over on the nose with a piece of wood.[13] House 4–5¼, and 8¼–9.[14] J.N.G. breakfd

[1] Wife of H. H. Joy.
[2] Taxation: H xvii. 842.
[3] John Would Lee, attorney at Newark.
[4] Irish poor laws: H xvii. 846.
[5] Taxation: H xvii. 913.
[6] Charles Godfrey Mundy, d. 1838; f. of C.J.H.; town house in Park Crescent.
[7] Murray Gladstones' wife Susanna died on 1 May.
[8] J. L. von Mosheim, Institutionum historiae ecclesiasticae libri iv (1726).
[9] P. Huddlestone of Lincoln's Inn Fields.
[10] John Nieuwenhuys of Argyle Street.
[11] Against 2° Irish church reform bill: H xvii. 966.
[12] Bickham Sweet Escott, 1800–53; barrister; tory M.P. for Winchester 1841–7; contested seven other seats.
[13] At the by-election in Westminster, where Sir J. C. *Hobhouse sought his constituents' opinion on his conduct, Escott stood as a tory against him and another radical, (Sir) George de Lacy *Evans, 1787–1870, who fought in Spain and America, at Waterloo, and in the Crimea, and commanded British legion in Spain, 1835–7; M.P. 1833–41, 1846–65. On 11 May *Evans was declared elected; Escott a bad third.
[14] Irish vagrants; misc. business. H xvii. 1022; 1031.

& dined here. Read Moore's 'Travels' &c—finished Newland: & read
Reform Soc's Reports.[1]

8. W.

Breakf in B. Squ. Shopping—at W. India meeting—Rode—read Church
Petition & divers public papers, also finished Moores first vol. of Travels[2]:
House $5\frac{1}{4}$–$6\frac{1}{4}$[3]; made inquiries of Lord Althorp abt I[rish] Ch. informn &
Savings B.s Annuities Acts[4]—wrote to Mr Wilson of Newark—dined at Col.
Conolly's.[5]

9. Th.

Wrote to Mrs G—R.G.—Mr Macdowall—Jones—Dry. Rode with Tom.
Canvassed a little in the Strand for Escott. Reading Lpool Evidence—
Moore's 'Travels &c' and 'Account of Insurrn in St Domingo'.[6] also,
Outlines of History.

10. Fr.

Breakf. with Mr Gordon. Ref. Soc. $11\frac{1}{4}$–$2\frac{3}{4}$. then W.I. meeting till $4\frac{1}{2}$.[7]
Wrote to R.G.—Dined—rode—House 7–11.[8] Read Pope's Encycl. Letter[9]
& W.I. Evidence.

11. Sat.

Rode—dined at Lady Lucy Puseys[10]—wrote to E.L. Ward—attended W.I.
meeting: violent speech from Godson[11]: much excitement; Ld Harewood
poured oil on the waves.[12] Employed in reading Evidence—Jeremie—and
papers of conferences between Deputn & Govt.—also Petitions on Irish
Church Bill.—Calls.

12.

Sunday. Fr[ench] Chapel mg.[13] St James's aftn. Bp of London preached:

[1] Untraced.   [2] *Of an Irish gentleman.*
[3] Misc. business; general registry of deeds. *H* xvii. 1034, 1044.
[4] Cp. Add MS 44353, ff. 135–7.
[5] Edward Michael Pakenham, 1786–1849; cousin of 2nd Lord Longford; changed
name to Conolly, 1821, on inheriting estate; tory M.P. co. Donegal from 1831; militia
colonel.
[6] A pamphlet on the troubles of the 1790's.
[7] To hear details of government's slave compensation plan (*Times*, 11 and 13 May
1833, 5/1).
[8] Dutch embargo: *H* xvii. 1074.
[9] By Gregory XVI, August 1832.
[10] In Grosvenor Square. Lucy, née Sherard, 1769–1858, da. of 4th earl of Harborough,
m. 1791 Sir Thomas Cave, bart., who d. 1792, re-m. 1798 Philip Pusey, né Bouverie,
1748–1828; mother of Philip and E. B. *Pusey.
[11] Richard Godson, 1797–1849; wrangler 1818; lib.-cons. M.P. St. Albans 1831,
Kidderminster 1832–5, 1837–49; Q.C. 1841.
[12] Henry *Lascelles, 1767–1841, beau; M.P. 1796–1820; styled Viscount Lascelles
1814; succ. as 2nd earl of Harewood 1820; West India proprietor.
[13] Roman catholic chapel in Portman Square.

dined in Bedf Square; on acct of my Father's being there. Read some Fenelon there. Burnet & J. Taylor on Eucharist—Strype's Cranmer—& read a Serm. to servants.

13. M.

Wrote to Mr Wilson (Newark)—Macdowall—C. Larkins[1]—Girdlestone—all briefly. W.I. meeting 1–4. Godson again: as before. Dined with Bp of Exeter. Introd[uce]d to E. Roden[2]—Ld Bexley[3]—Bp of Rochester.[4] Read Times Art[icle] (strange!)[5]—Burnley's letter[6]—& two Speeches of Mr Canning's on the Slave Quest. House $10\frac{1}{2}$–$12\frac{1}{2}$.[7]

14. T.

Finished 'Minutes of Proceedings'—and read other papers connected with the W.I. House $3\frac{1}{2}$–$12\frac{3}{4}$. Stanley spoke 3 h: Ld Howick[8] 2, & very ably.[9] At the Brunswick[10] & consulting with my Father, who came under the Gallery. Howick attacked Vreedenhoop.[11]

15. Wed.

Anstice came to breakf. House 11–$12\frac{1}{4}$. ag[ai]n 5–$5\frac{3}{4}$—stopped on my way down the 3d time at nt, finding there was no house.[12] Called on Acland: conv. & discussions with him for $1\frac{1}{2}$ hour, with Twisleton in evg. for $2\frac{1}{2}$—all however *very* amicable. Robn came. We all dined together in Tom's rooms. Read Pecchio—Slavery Evidence, &c.

16. Th.

Acland breakfd with me. Copied a longish document on W.I.—paper—W.I. meeting 1–$3\frac{1}{4}$. House 4–$6\frac{3}{4}$, and $8\frac{1}{2}$–$2\frac{1}{2}$. Read part of a pamphlet of Cropper.[13] Peel & Cobbett. Divided in 73 to 79 for the Lord's Day Bill.[14]

---

[1] Presumably also a cousin.

[2] Robert *Jocelyn, 1788–1870, 3rd earl of Roden 1820; M.P. Dundalk 1810–20; strong protestant Orangeman.

[3] Nicholas *Vansittart, 1766–1851; M.P. 1796–1823, when cr. Lord Bexley; secretary for Ireland 1805, chancellor of exchequer 1812–22, of duchy of Lancaster 1822–7; ineffectual debater, ardent Christian.

[4] George *Murray, 1784–1860; gs. of 3rd duke of *Atholl; bp. of Sodor and Man 1814, of Rochester 1827, with deanery of Worcester 1828.

[5] Hedging first leader on slave emancipation.

[6] W. H. Burnley of Trinidad, 'Opinions on Slavery' (1833).

[7] Irish church bill in cttee.: *H* xvii. 1113.

[8] (Sir) Henry George *Grey, 1802–94; styled Viscount Howick, 1807; whig M.P. 1826–45; colonial under-secretary 1830–3; secretary of war 1835–9; 3rd Earl Grey 1845; colonial secretary 1846–52.

[9] Colonial slavery: *H* xvii. 1193, 1231.

[10] Brunswick Hotel, Jermyn Street.

[11] See 3 June 1833. Not in *Hansard, Mirror*, ii. 1772.

[12] Various petitions; house counted out. *H* xvii. 1262.

[13] James *Cropper, 'A Vindication of a Loan of £15,000,000 to the West India Planters' (1833).

[14] *Cobbett had a protracted quarrel with *Peel. A Lord's Day Observance bill was defeated 2°. *H* xvii. 1277, 1325.

17.

J.N.G., R.G., & Mr Gordon to breakft. Review in Hyde Park 11–1; with Wood. Such a sight affords[1] much excitement, strongly mingled with a disposition to tears. Wrote to Wishlade—& Mr Peart. H. of C. 1–3, Commees, & again 11–12½. Divided in 305 to 106 for the present Corn Laws[2]—dined with Mr Alexander—a W.I. party.

18. Sat.

Late rising. Accompts &c. Made fourteen calls. read W.I. Evidence—rode in the Park—Eton dinner[3]—not up to what it should [be]—paper—Hallam & others with me.

19. Sunday.

Breakf. with the Anstices. Marg. Chapel—Dodsworth: very able. Notes in Bible—Strype's Cranmer—Archdn Eliot's Three first Lectures[4]—read a serm. to servants. St James's in aftn.

20. M.

Read W.I. Parl. papers—& Notes on Hayti[5]—House (Commee &c) 11½–2½ —and 6¾–12½.[6] Wrote to Mr G—Mr Tallents—Duke of N—B. Harrison. Rode with John.

21. T.

House 12¾–2¾ and 4–6. Presented Ed[inburg]h petition: spoke 2 or 3 min.![7] Mr G. came. rode—read Sismondi & other history—Mackenzie—paper—and was occupied several hours in making a copy of my Father's 'plan'.

22. Wed.

Read W.I. Evidence—Mackenzie—Pecchio—called on the Hagarts & the Gaskells—House 4–12¾—of which ¾ of an hour riding—Divided in 52 to 189 on the Jew Bill.[8]

23. Th.

Breakf. & dinner in Bedf. Sq. Rode. Read Pecchio—Evidence—Cropper on

[1] 'me' here deleted.
[2] *H* xvii. 1349.
[3] At Willis's rooms, King Street, St. James's.
[4] E. Eliot, archdeacon of Barbadoes, *Christianity and Slavery: in a course of lectures preached at . . . St. Michael, Barbadoes* (1833).
[5] C. Mackenzie, *Notes on Hayti* 2v. (1830); notes in Add MS 44649. ff. 34–44; used in speech on 3 June 1833.
[6] Misc. business; Irish church bill in cttee. *H* xvii. 1381.
[7] Morley, i. 102. Petition against immediate abolition of slavery: *H* xviii. 2.
[8] Bill to remove Jewish civil disabilities read 2°: *H* xviii. 47.

the Loan—& took a lesson in German from a Pole of Posen, who came to me in distress.

24. Fr.

W.I. documents. & Hertford Evidence. 2nd German lesson. Dined with Mr G at Brunswick. Rode—called on D. of N. Potter's Concert 2–5.[1] House 7½–12½. Voted agst Bernal in 55 to 227—.[2] Pasta & Schröder[3] splendid. Arnold's Postscript.[4]

25. Sat.

Pecchio—Mackenzie—Germ. Grammar. My Pole did not appear—inquired for him in vain—Rode—dined with the Smith Wrights.[5] Shopping. Sat some time with Mrs Hagart—as did Puller with me. Wrote to R.G. and H.J.G.

26. Sunday.

York St Chapel mg. Sacrament.[6] St James's aftn. Dined at Lincoln's Inn. Wrote a note to Mr R. Douglas[7] in answer to a request that I would second a resolution tomorrow. Read Faber—Strype's Cranmer—Elliot (finished)—and one of Close's Sermons aloud.

27. M.

Pecchio—Mackenzie—& W.I. Evidence. W.I. meeting 1–4½.[8] Dined at Lincoln's Inn. Mrs Rolles musical party in Evg.[9] Wrote to Dr Jephson.

28. T.

Wrote to A.C. Wood—Sir Jas Macdonald[10]—Mr Caparn—Mrs G. paper—W.I. Ev[idence]—Mackenzie—Pecchio—Rode. Striving now to get my information into shape.

[1] Philip Cipriani Hambly *Potter, 1792–1871, pianist and composer; principal, Royal Academy of Music 1832–59; conducted public concerts there.
[2] Ralph *Bernal, d. 1854 (whig M.P. for Lincoln 1818–20, Rochester 1820–41 and 1847–52, Weymouth 1841–7; art collector; and West India proprietor), chairman of Hertford election cttee., carried motion deploring bribery there. *H* xviii. 68.
[3] Wilhelmine Schröder-Devrient, 1804–60, German soprano, called 'the Queen of Tears'; thrice m., twice divorced.
[4] T. *Arnold, 'Postscript to Principles of Church Reform' (1832).
[5] John Smith Wright, 1773–1851?, of Rempstone Hall, Nottinghamshire; m. 2ndly 1821 Sarah Caroline, née Stovin, d. 1860, widow of Sir Sitwell Sitwell, 1st bart. of Renishaw. His eldest da. Kythe Caroline, 1811?–34, m. 1829 a clansman of the diarist's, Sir Francis Alexander Mackenzie, 1798–1843, 5th bart. of Gairloch 1822; and d. in childbirth.
[6] York Street, now renamed Duke Street, on north side of St. James's Square.
[7] W. R. Keith Douglas, F.R.S.?
[8] Cp. Robbins, 171, and *Annual Register* for 1833, 196–7.
[9] Miss Rolle, of Hudscot, Devonshire; town house in Gloucester Place; a connexion of the Clintons.
[10] But Sir James Macdonald, b. 1784, whig M.P. from 1806, at India board 1830, had d. of cholera in 1832. Presume Sir John*, adjutant general 1830, who d. 1850.

29. W.

Finished Mackenzie. Read part of the Extracts from Lords' Evidence. Arranging matter & references to it: & arranging notes for a speech. Also reading Stanley's: & other documents. Rode in Park. Dined at Sir S. Scott's.

30. Th.

Read Pecchio—& W.I. papers—got my matter arranged: rode. House $11\frac{1}{2}$–$12\frac{1}{4}$, and 5–$12\frac{1}{4}$.[1] Attempted to speak after Buxton, but Bernal gave it in favour of Ward.[2] Wrote to Lincoln on Collerton Railway.

31. Friday.

Pecchio—and Sir H. Parnell's Financial Reform.[3] House $11\frac{3}{4}$–$12\frac{1}{2}$ and $5\frac{1}{2}$–12.[4] Saw no good opportunity for speaking. The emotions through which one passes, at least thro' which I pass, in anticipating such an effort as this, are painful and humiliating. The utter prostration and depression of spirit: the deep sincerity, the burdensome & overpowering reality of the feeling of mere feebleness and incapacity, felt in the inmost heart, yet not to find relief by expression because the expression of such things goes for affectation; these things I am unequal to describe, yet I have experienced them now.[5] And may they have their use towards me: and teach me to cast my regards towards the Almighty Father whose care is about the paths of us all. May I look up to him in hope tho' in shame, and find from him both fortitude & peace: thro' Jesus Christ our Lord.

June 1. Saturday.

Shand, & Caparn, & Rogers, with me. Copying for my father. Finished Pecchio. Meeting at Brunswick H. to deliberate on W.I. affairs—a set of Res[olution]s. arranged. Paper. Rode. dined with Colin Mackenzie. Calls. Miss Milnes Gaskell born 4 P.M.[6]

2. Sunday.

St James's morng & aftn. And the Sacrament: which now alone exercises power over my mind excited & kept in a state of tension by public affairs during the week. Dined at Uncle D's. Read Bible—Strype's Cranmer— Canons—& a Serm. of Close's aloud.

---

[1] Slavery debate continued: *H* xviii. 112.
[2] *Bernal was chairman of cttees. (Sir) Henry George *Ward, 1797–1860; travelled in Mexico; M.P. for St. Albans 1832–7, Sheffield 1837–49; administered Ionia 1849, Ceylon 1855, Madras 1860. Opposed immediate abolition of slavery.
[3] 4th ed. (1832).
[4] Slavery debate ctd: *H* xviii. 204.
[5] These two sentences in Morley, i. 103.
[6] Isabel Milnes Gaskell; m. 1855 Fitzgerald Thomas Wintour, 1829–98, rector of High Hoyland, Yorkshire, 1867.

3. M.

Began Le mie prigioni.[1] W.I. meeting of members at one, at Ld Sandons. Resolutions discussed & agreed upon. At Gaskell's—dined early—rearranged my notes for the debate—rode. House 5–1. Spoke. my first time—for 50 min. My leading desire was, to benefit the cause of those, who are now so sorely beset. The House heard me very kindly, and my *friends* were satisfied. Tea afterwards at the Carlton.[2]

4. T.

Read Le Mie Prigioni—Macbeth over once more—Lpool Evidence—Lord's Debate—& diff[eren]t reports of my unfortunate speech, all ludicrous enough, some incredibly. Rode—dined at Lincoln's Inn—House: counted out.[3] Nat[ional] Gallery. Wrote to H.J.G. & Aunt E. Heard from the latter with great delight. Indulged myself in a little classical inquiry.

5. W.

Le Mie Prigioni. T.G. & J.N.G. came to breakfast. paper—divers callers—Wrote to Canning—& to R.G. 12–6. Went to Harrow with Glynne, Egerton, & Mordaunt—heard the speeches. Sir R. Peel[4] came up to me most kindly & praised the affair of Monday night. No house—dined with the Hagarts. Miss Watts Russell[5] & Mr Callender[6] there: a work afterwards, till 2½, in preparing my speech for the Mirror.[7]

6. Th.

Ryder came to breakfast. Wrought at my speech. Wrote to H.J.G.—Took Aunt D[ivie] to the ventilator.[8] Rode. Read paper—& Silvio Pellico. Dined with the Wrights. In evg at the House— divided in 98 to 301 on Portugal.[9]

7. Fr.

Caparn & Branston with me on Newark matters, public houses &c. May I be kept straight in this matter. W.I. meeting 11¾–1. Calls—rode. finished writing out speech—wrote to Mrs G—read Pellico—rode. House 5½ P.M.–2½ A.M.[10] Conv there with Lord Howick about Vreeden Hoop & his motion.

---

[1] Silvio Pellico's celebrated account of ten years' imprisonment by the Austrians in northern Italy (1832).

[2] Slavery debate continued: *H* xviii. 308. *Gladstone's maiden speech defended his father's estate at Vreedenhoop, Demerara, from imputations by *Howick: ibid. 330. Notes for it in Add MS 44649, ff. 34–44. See Morley, i. 103.

[3] During discussion of trade with China: *H* xviii. 377.   [4] An old Harrovian.

[5] Isabel, 3rd da. of Jesse Watts-Russell, 1786–1875, of Ilam Hall, co. Stafford, M.P. Gatton 1820–6.

[6] James Henry Callender of Ardkinglass, Perthshire gentleman; whig M.P. for Argyllshire 1832–5.

[7] *Mirror*, ii. 2079.   [8] The ladies' gallery of the old house of commons.

[9] Against motion by Thomas Henry Hastings Davies, peninsular war veteran, whig M.P. for Worcester 1818–35, 1837–41, approving current British policy in Portugal. *H* xviii. 391.

[10] Colonial slavery: *H* xviii. 458.

8. Sat.

Up late. read Pellico—papers—W.I. Evidence. Conv. with Mr G. on Newark affairs—& Vreeden Hoop. Wrote at some length to the D. of N[ewcastle] on the former. Calls. Dined with Sir R. Inglis—rode out & home. How much kindness I have received on account of my speech: there is great room for gratitude to God and man: and may I "live in the Spirit of this creed".

9. Sunday.

Trinity—Mr Beamish.[1] St James's—Bp. but only heard half the service, as the D. of Newcastle came in upon me at 2¾ to speak about these Newark bills. St. Bride's[2] in evg—walked to Moorfields, but found Cath. Chapel shut.[3] Read a serm. aloud—Strype—& Armenian Liturgy.[4]

10. M.

Caparn breakfd with me—talk about Newark—Wrote at some length to Mr Tallents—read W.I. Evid. & papers—meeting at one—wrote to Mr G rode with J.N.G.—Dined with the Mayor of Lpool—house at 6½, and again 9–2. 3d Res. passed—voted in 324 to (I think) 35.[5] Waited for Lord Howick's motion on Vreeden Hoop—spoke a few minutes on it—withdrawn.[6] read Silvio Pellico.

11. Tuesday.

Hurricane. Read Pellico—Husk[isso]n on currency—& part of 'Wages or the Whip'.[7] Calls. J.N.G. dined with me. Rode. House 5¼–6 and 6¾–1¾. Voted in 277 agst 142 on Buxton's amendment, and in three other divisions.[8] Wrote to Mr G. and R.G.

12. Wed.

Wind abated. Read Pellico—finished 'Wages or the Whip'—went with Mrs Hagart to the microscope exhibn[9]—calls—rode—dined at Mr Oliversons—evening party at Mrs Hallam's.

---

[1] Henry Hamilton Beamish, 1795–ca. 1870, incumbent of Trinity Chapel, Conduit Street, 1832; later also rector of Kinsale, co. Cork.

[2] *Wren's church in Fleet Street.

[3] Fashionable Roman catholic chapel in Finsbury.

[4] P. G. Aredichian, *Liturgia Armena*, tr. into Italian (1832).

[5] Colonial slavery. The vote, of 324–42, opposed an amendment of *O'Connell's specifying that wages must be paid to freed slaves. *H* xviii, 515.

[6] *Howick withdrew demand for mortality statistics from Vreedenhoop on *Gladstone's protest that the estate was unfairly singled out. Not in *Hansard*. *Mirror*, iii. 2207; Morley, i. 105.

[7] J. *Conder, (1833); on the comparative cost and productivity of slave and free labour.

[8] Irish railways, briefly; main debate in committee on colonial slavery. *Buxton's motion, which was lost, sought to shorten apprenticeships. *Stanley's four resolutions were eventually passed by 286–77. *H* xviii. 566, 573.

[9] Untraced.

13. Th.

Read Pellico—paper—wrote to Mr G. Stirred up the Hagarts & went with them & Miss Watts Russell to St Paul's. We were late & consequently fared ill—but both sight & sound were glorious—and they possessed that remarkable criterion of the sublime, a grand result from a combination of simple elements.[1] Dined with Mr Murchison—at Lady Lansdowne's Ball.[2] House $5\frac{1}{2}$–$6\frac{1}{2}$. Grant speaking.[3]

14. Fr.

J.N.G. came to breakft. read Huskisson—Pellico—paper—Tupper, Caparn, &c here. Rode. dined with Sir R. Vyvyan.[4]—House $10\frac{3}{4}$–$1\frac{1}{4}$.[5] Arranging in rooms—& endeav[ourin]g to design a bookcase. Conv with C. Buller.[6]

15. Sat.

Wrote to Mrs G. Mr Tallents with me: Parr, Mordaunt, & others. Rode to Sir R. Inglis's infant school fete: a pretty & pleasing sight. Read Pellico—paper—finished Huskn on Currency: dined at Mayow's.

Sunday June 16.

St James's mg & aftn. Dined at home—walk afterwards. Read Bible—Arm[enian] Liturgy (finished)—J. Taylor—& Strype's Cranmer—also a serm. to servants. The Arm. Liturgy is curious enough: it involves (I think) transsubstantiation and prayers for the dead, but not for release from purgatory tho difference is wide. Wrote.

17.

Tupper & J.N.G. to breakft. Mr Tallents repeated his visit (by app[oin]t-m[en]t) & we consulted on the Newark bills—Wrote a long letter to Mr Godfrey in consequence—& copied it out[7]—wrote to Mr G. & Mr Blundell. Read Lpool Evidence—a pamphlet on the Factory system—& S. Pellico. rode—House 7–$12\frac{1}{4}$. Ir. Ch. Bill in Comm.[8]

18. Tuesday.

T.G., J.N.G., & D. Milligan, to breakft. Read Pellico—Sir H. Parnell—Lpool Evidence—& papers: also 500 L. of Æneid. Wrote divers—Rode—Calls—House $5\frac{3}{4}$–$12\frac{1}{4}$[9]: an hour absent to tea at Gaskell's.[10]

[1] No special serviced traced.
[2] Louisa Emma Fox-Strangways, 1785–1851; 5th da. of 2nd earl of Ilchester; m. 1808 Lord Henry *Petty-Fitzmaurice, 3rd marquis of Lansdowne 1809.
[3] C. *Grant on East India charter: H xviii. 698.
[4] Sir Richard Rawlinson *Vyvyan, 1800–79; 8th bart. 1820; tory M.P. Cornwall 1825–31, Okehampton 1831–2, Bristol 1832–7, Helston 1841–57.
[5] Irish tithes, and miscellaneous business. H xviii. 811.
[6] Charles *Buller, 1806–48; radical M.P. Looe 1830–1, Liskeard 1832–49; author of *Durham report (see 12 Feb. 39 n.).
[7] Godfrey fell out with the rest of *Gladstone's finance committee at Newark about propriety of payment of innkeepers' bills in 1832 election; cp. Add MS 44353, ff. 151–80.
[8] H xviii. 915. [9] Mainly the same: H xviii. 955.
[10] Mary Gaskell had a house in New Ormond Street, Bloomsbury.

19. Wed.

Wrote to Mr G. Godfrey (with draught) & Mr Caparn. Farewell call to the Hagarts. Finished Pellico—began Allemagne[1]—read Parnell—& Æneid—rode—dined with T.G.—House 5–5¾, and 10¾–1½.[2]

20. Th.

No house. a reading day—comparatively. Parnell—Allemagne—King Lear, for the nth time—Polybius on origin of society, ars imperatoria, & character of Hannibal[3]—calls—early dinner with the Gaskells—rode—conv. with young Acland.

21. Fr.

Breakf. in B. Square. Read Achille Murat[4]—Parnell—& L'Allemagne. Wrote to Mr Finlay—D. of N.—Mrs G.—Rode. House 12¼–1¼, and 6½–1 A.M. Divided in 59 to 85, and in 280 to 148, on I.C. Bill in Committee.[5]

22. Sat.

L'Allemagne—Parnell. Reports of Corp. & Beer Committees.[6] Conv. of about 1½ hour with D. of N. Wrote to Mr Godfrey—& Mr Tallents—draughts & copies—also to Mr G. J.N.G. dined with me—Mrs [Smith] Wright's, & also Mrs Warburton's,[7] in evg.

23. Sunday.

French Chapel, & St James's. Bible—& Notes. Strype—Two first parts of Homily against Idolatry—a sermon of Arnold's aloud—&c. Walk in evg. I feel painfully the want of some extrinsic influence on my mind during the Lord's day : which should *quell* the remaining excitement of the week, and effectually reduce it to peaceful exercises on matter of religion.

24. M.

T.G., J.N.G., & Phillimore, breakfd with me. Wrote to Mr G., Aunt E., Mr Godfrey, Mr Caparn, Sir Jas Macdonald—House, & Patents' Committee 12¼–3¼. Rode—dined at home—House 6–12¾. Ir. Church.[8]

---

[1] By Mme de Stael (suppressed in Paris, 1810; published in London, 1813).
[2] Shipping in Irish Sea; Irish church bill; misc. business. *H* xviii. 994.
[3] *Histories*, vi. 3–9, ix. 12–21, 22–26.
[4] Napoleon Achille Murat, Napoleon's nephew and Washington's great-nephew-in-law, *Exposition des principes du gouvernement républicain . . . en Amérique* (1833).
[5] Road and railway bills; in main debate on Irish church bill, an amendment (by William *Parsons, 1800–67, Lord Oxmantown 1807, whig M.P. for King's Co. 1821–34, astronomer, 3rd earl of Rosse 1841) favouring holders of bishops' leases was carried, 85–49; on government motions, an important clause on sale of perpetuities was deleted. *H* xviii. 1065. The house divided 280–149.
[6] *PP* 1833, xxxi. 323 on Sunday elections to municipal office, and perhaps xxxiii. 183.
[7] Perhaps wife of Major Warburton of Congleton, who lived off Manchester Square.
[8] Cttee. continued: *H* xviii. 1135. He was also on select cttee. for a Patents Bill: H. of C. *Journals*, 297.

25. T.

Tradesmen's business—& calls—rode—dined in Bedf. Square. Wrote to my
Mother: heard from Mr Tallents: but no answer required. Read L'Allemagne
—& began 'A view of the Banking Question'.[1] Ho. of Peers 10½–12¼—
Slavery Resolutions debate.[2]

26. W.

Wrote to H.J.G., & Mr Tallents. Read L'Allemagne—Banking Question—
Parnell—Rode—&c. Dined with Sir R. Peel: a large party, almost all
members: he did me the favour to ask me to take wine. House 10¾–1½.
Voted in two divisions on the Jew Bill.[3]—Read some speeches &c. in
'Choix de Rapports'.[4]

27. Th.

Wrote to Mr G.[5] & a few lines to Mr Nicholl[6] & Miss Bethune.[7] Rode.
House 5–8¼. Divided in 8 to 78! agst Political Unions.[8] Dined at home.
Obliged to speak about my sugar, wh disappears strangely. Read L'Alle-
magne—Achille Murat—Troilus & Cressida—& Banking System.

28. Fr.

Dear Helen's birthday.—Wrote to Mr Caparn—Mr Tallents—& Rn G.
House 12–1½, and 9¼–12¾.[9] Anstice breakfd & John dined with me. Childers
called & staid some time. Rode.

29. Sat.

Seymer & J.N.G. to breakft. Read paper—& L'Allemagne. Wrote to Mr
Hall Dare (for Luigi)[10] & Mr Caparn. Calls—at Camden Hill. & in Park.
Dined at Sir R. Inglis's—walked home with Mr Light . . .,[11] an agreeable
man.

30. Sunday.

St Anne's Soho in morng to hear Mr Melvill:[12] who appeared to me an extra-

[1] *Review of the banking system of Britain* (1821).
[2] *Ripon moved adoption of commons' resolutions on slavery. The lords agreed. *H*
xviii. 1163.
[3] Main debate on Royal Burghs (Scotland) Bill, which passed cttee.; so did Jewish
Civil Disabilities Bill, in spite of five divisions by a score of members headed by *Inglis.
H xviii. 1243, 1251.
[4] Untraced.   [5] Part in Bassett, 27–28.
[6] Thomas Nicholl, 1797?–1867?; priest 1830; lived in Duke Street, St. James's.
[7] Alice Margaret, da. of Gilbert Bethune of Balfour who was b. 1765.
[8] Finch moved that all political unions were subversive: *H* xviii. 1263.
[9] Irish communications; Bank of England charter. *H* xviii. 1291.
[10] Robert Westley Hall Dare of Cranbrook, d. 1836; tory M.P. for Essex 1832–6; s. of
a West India proprietor.   [11] Untraced: diarist's dots.
[12] Henry *Melvill, 1798–1871; wrangler 1821; priest at Camberwell 1829–43; principal
of Haileybury 1843–57; canon of St. Paul's 1856, and rector of Barnes, Surrey, 1863;
celebrated preacher.

ordinary man. His sentiments are manly in tone: he deals powerfully with all his subject: his language is glowing and unbounded, his imagery varied and intensely strong. Vigorous and lofty as are his conceptions, he is not I think less remarkable for the soundness and healthiness of mind with which he seems to have apprehended the grand and deep truths of revelation. St James's in aftn. Read Bible—Strype—a sermon of Close's aloud—analysed the first two parts of the Homily on Idolatry: & wrote.

July 1. Monday.

Read L'Allemagne—papers—finished 'a view of the Banking Question'— breakfd with T.G. Spent 1½ hour in seeing Mr O'Neill's pictures[1]—at Carlton. House 6–1½ A.M. Voted in 156 to 214 on legal tender.[2]

2. T.

L'Allemagne—Parnell. Wrote to Mr & R.G., to Mr Hagart & Darbyshire at Newark.[3] Went to Mrs Vansittart's.[4] thence to see the balloon ascend from Hungerfd Market[5]—much time spent. House 6–8½—and 11–2. Voted in 154 to 70 on the Q. of a new House.[6] Aft[er] din[ne]r at Uncle D's.

3. W.

Gillanders[7] & Ogilvy breakfasted, T.G. & J.N.G. dined with me. Read L'Allemagne—& Lpool Evidence: Also made some classical references. Convs with T. & J.N.G., each on matters somewhat nearly affecting them. House 9¾–11¾: voted in 88 to 176 for a Commee on the Bank Bargain[8]: read papers, & West. Rev. on Rad. Policy.[9]

4. Thursday.

Read L'Allemagne—Lpool Evidence—& "Refu[t]ation of Statement on the Evidence".[10] House 12–3—discussion on I.C. Bill. Rode: & House 6¼–2 A.M.—Spoke some 20 min. or more on Lpool Question: anything but satisfactorily to myself.[11] Voted in 84 to 166 agst pursuit of inquiry.[12]

---

[1] Charles O'Neil of Newman Street?
[2] Bank Charter acts considered in cttee.; government amendment carried, to make £5 Bank of England notes payable in gold. H xviii. 1361.
[3] William Darbyshire, coachmaker.
[4] Caroline Eden, 1782?–1851; da. of 1st Lord *Auckland; m. 1806 Arthur Vansittart, 1775–1829, and had 14 children.
[5] To celebrate the opening of the new Hungerford market in the Strand. It came down after an hour in North Ockenden, Essex. See Times, 3 and 5 July 1833.
[6] He voted against a motion of *Hume's that proposed a new house of commons; H xix. 59. Main debate on Irish tithes: H xix. 37.
[7] George Gillanders, 1805–46; of Highfield, co. Ross; Calcutta merchant; eventually partner in John *Gladstone's Liverpool merchanting house.
[8] M. Attwood moved for a cttee. to inquire into proper rates of payment to Bank of England for its public services: H xix. 32.
[9] Westminster Review, xviii. 493 (April 1833), on petitions.
[10] Refutation of a Statement, intitled 'Result of the Evidence given before the Select Cttee. appointed to enquire into the Petition on Liverpool Borough' (1833).
[11] Morley, i. 105. Irish church bill, report stage: H xix. 117. Select cttee. appointed to inquire into affairs of Liverpool borough. H xix. 129, 135 ('Mr Edward Gladstone').
[12] H xix. 142.

5. Friday.

Late up—Read L'Allemagne. House 2–3.[1] W.I. meeting 3–5½—rode—wrote to Aunt J., R.G., H.J.G., Mr G: House 8¼–1. Voted in 164 to 141 agst ref[errin]g Factory Bill to a Select Committee.[2] Striking conv. returning home.

6. Saturday.

Late rising. Foster & Nicholl with me: wrote to the former, declining to go down to Liverpool. Wrote also to R.G., and to Mr Finlay. Rode. Calls. Went to see the works of West,[3] Reynolds, & Lawrence. Dined with Lord Sandon. Liked Lady Frances extremely.[4] Read L'Allemagne, & part of 'a Letter on Country Banking'.[5]

7. Sunday.

St James's mg & aft. Sacrament. A very good antifashionable sermon from Mr Ward in aft. Walk. Read Sumner aloud—Strype—Pascal—& began Abbott's Young Christian.[6]—Tired with the week's work.

8. M.

L'Allemagne. Wrote to Mrs G. & Harrison. Thinking for speech: also wrote a little. Rode: dined at home: read 'Letter on Country Banking'. H. Joy with me. House 6¼–3¾. Spoke some 20 or 25 min. on Ir. Ch. Bill. Div[ide]d in 94 to 274?[7]

9. T.

W.I. meetings 11–1 and 2–4. House 10–1½. Div[ide]d in 177 to 95 agst Poland Address.[8] L'Allemagne—& finished Letter on Country Banking. Dined with T.G. Wrote home—& to D. of N. Rode.

10. Wed.

Breakfd & dined in B. Square. Papers. L'Allemagne. Correcting my Lpool speech for the Mirror.[9] W.I. meetings 12–1½ and 2¼–5.[10] Apptd on Commee to consider the Bill! Acceded very reluctantly. Wrote to Mr G. and R.G. Rode.

[1] Factories bill: *H* xix. 219.
[2] Morley, i. 106. I.e. bill to be kept on floor of house. *H* xix. 219, 254.
[3] Benjamin *West, 1738–1820, historical painter to *George III.
[4] Lady Frances, née Stuart, d. 1859, 4th da. of 1st marquis of Bute, m. 1823 Dudley *Ryder, Viscount Sandon, later 2nd earl of Harrowby.   [5] Untraced.
[6] Jacob Abbott, *The Young Christian* (1833), improving American work.
[7] Notes for speech in Add MS 44649, ff. 45–46. Closing stages: bill finally carried, 274–94. *H* xix. 257, 292, 301.
[8] Robert Cutlar *Fergusson, d. 1838 (East India Company director; whig M.P., Kirkcudbright, 1826–38) held the current state of Poland to violate the treaty of Vienna; his proposed protest rejected as untimely. *H* xix. 319.
[9] *Mirror*, iii. 2755.
[10] Planters' pressure group, meeting at Thatched House Tavern. Cp. 22 Jul. 33.

11.

J.N.G. breakfd with me, J.N.G. & Robert Gladstone dined. W.I. meeting 2–4.[1] Reading L'Allemagne & W.I. Bill. rode. calls. wrote to Lincoln. Mr Tallents here on Newark matters. House $8\frac{3}{4}$–$2\frac{1}{2}$.[2]

12.

Mr Tallents to breakft. Wrote to Young—& Mr G.—11–2 with Rose & Hyndman,[3] discussing W.I. Bill—also getting it up alone—papers. L'Allemagne (finished vol 1) and Burnley's pamphlet.[4] Rode. House $2\frac{3}{4}$–$3\frac{1}{2}$, and again at $10\frac{1}{2}$. but did not remain.[5]

13. Sat.

J.N.G. to breakft. L'Allemagne—finished Mr Burnley's pamphlet—and read W.I. Bill. 1–5. occupied with discussing the same in the W.I. Committee apptd on Wedy. Wrote to Mr G. Rode: bid goodbye to John, dear John. Dined at Sir R. Bromley's,—an agreeable party.

14.

St Philip's[6] (Bp) & St. James's (Mr Ward). Dined at Uncle D's. Read Charges of Bps of Lichfield[7] & Chester[8]—Mad. de S's chapters on Protestantism, Catholicism, & the Moravians,[9] & some parts of Father Clement.[10]

15.

Papers. L'Allemagne. Factory Report & Evidence. Wrote to Mr & Mrs G. W.I. Commee 3–6, and House $6\frac{1}{4}$–$7\frac{1}{4}$. Voted in 160 to 124 agst Sir J. Wrottesley's motion.[11] Read 'Taming of a Shrew'.

16.

Paper. L'Allemagne. Factory Rep. Wrote to Mr G.—R.G.—Reinhard Bassermann[12]—Dined with Mr Moss—Rode—calls—W.I. Committee 1–3.

---

[1] On British Guiana; his brother Thomas and John went with him. Compensation terms approved: cp. PRO CO 318/116.

[2] Mainly affairs of police of New South Wales: *H* xix. 592.

[3] John Beckles Hyndman, Barbados proprietor; father of H. M. *Hyndman, the socialist.

[4] W. H. Burnley, *Opinions on Slavery and Emancipation in 1823* (1833).

[5] East India Charter: *H* xix. 616.

[6] In Waterloo Place.

[7] H. *Ryder, *A Charge delivered to the Clergy of . . . Lichfield and Coventry* (1832).

[8] J. B. *Sumner, *A Charge delivered to the clergy of . . . Chester* (1832).

[9] *De l'Allemagne*, iii, chapters 2, 4, 3.

[10] Grace *Kennedy, *Father Clement* (1823).

[11] Sir John *Wrottesley (1771–1841; 9th bart. 1787; whig M.P. Lichfield 1799–1806, Staffordshire 1823–37; farmer; cr. Lord Wrottesley 1838) moved that the whole house be called to consider the fate of the Irish church bill in the lords: lost by 125 to 160. *H* xix. 650, 662.

[12] Possibly a brother of F. D. Bassermann, 1810–55, Mannheim bookseller and politician, prominent in 1848 revolution.

17.

Remonstrances from Committee at Newark—wrote and copied out my answer.[1] Also wrote to Mr Mcdowall and to J.N.G. R.G. came. Dined with him & the Mayor [of Liverpool]. Rode. Home business. paper. Read L'Allemagne—Factory Rep.—& Thoughts on the Present Threatening aspect &c.[2] House $11\frac{1}{4}$–$1\frac{1}{2}$.[3]

18.

L'Allemagne—paper—Fact. Report. West I. Commee & House $12\frac{1}{2}$–3.[4] Rode. Dined with T.G. at Madrigals—great treat—H. of Lords $9\frac{1}{2}$–$1\frac{1}{2}$.[5] Did not vote in Commons on Cl. 1. of Factory Bill.[6] Wrote to my Father.

19.

L'Allemagne. papers. Seymer came to breakfast. Wrote to my Father. W.I. meeting 1–2, and 3–4. Spoke. Went to dine at Greenwich. a pleasant party, curious conv. with Miss Shipley.[7] H. of Lords afterwards.[8]

20. Sat.

R.G. & T. Horsfall[9] to breakf. Paper. Parted with James.[10] Seemed to discover afterwards, that I thought too well of him. Some trouble & occupn. Dined in Bedf. Sq.—with R.G.—L'Allemagne. W.I. meeting in city 1–3. Rode.

Finis.

[The closing pages of this volume are filled with the notes below, which begin on the back page.]

Poetry does not coalesce with the *essence* of Prose—nor prose with the *form* of poetry—but vice versâ.

The mind often retains disjointed *fragments* of an idea: and after the lapse of a certain time loses the power of identifying them.

e.g. in reading some verses, the notion of sameness strikes me: I cannot however explain wherein it consists—but on looking back, find the same expression had occurred a few lines before.

---

[1] Trouble about bills for 1832 election: Add MS 44353, ff. 186–90.
[2] Untraced.
[3] East India bill: *H* xix. 797.
[4] Factories bill: *H* xix. 883.
[5] Irish church bill, 2°: *H* xix. 807.
[6] *Ashley's first attempt to get young people's working hours in factories limited to 10 was beaten, 238–93: *H* xix. 883, 898.
[7] Charlotte, d. 1871; cp. 24 June 35.
[8] Irish church bill, 2°: *H* xix. 918.
[9] Son of the mayor of Liverpool.
[10] Horsnell.

Some have never been led so far in mental analysis, as to consider the distinctness of the essences of words & ideas. They look upon both as we ordinarily contemplate the moving bodily form of a man, not considering that he is made up of the sensual & the spiritual. Not that the mind *denies* the latter: but it has never thought of it apart from its husk, as an individual thing: and this idea remains *involved* in the first.

Good is the interest of man. In essences, it is. In appearances, it is not universally. Hence to him it is not. For a man acts on appearances not on essences. Hence, infer as to doctrine of moral obligation.

General questions

What effort have I made this day to advance any of my fellow creatures in the knowledge of the truths of salvation?

What acts have I done this day, which would scandalise a brother and cause the ways of God to be evil spoken of?

What distinct struggle with any impulse or propensity have I gone through this day, and with what success?

What proof has my mind given this day of having an eye unceasingly fixed on God, and of its readily reverting with concentrated attention to him, escaped from out of the midst of the cares of this world?

Books read on the Continent.

Danl Wilson's Tour, 2 vols.
Forsyth's Italy, 2 vols.
Burton's Rome, 1 vol.
Shelley's Revolt of Islam.
Coleridge's Transl. of Wallenstein.
Selections from Wordsworth's Poetry.
Pitt's select Speeches.
Fox's select Speeches.
Volney's Ruins of Empires.
Pascal's Provincial Letters 2 vols.
Bossuet's Funeral Orations.
Hall's Balm of Gilead.
Lardner's Outlines of History.
Divers Pamphlets and Reviews.

In London, some Sermons, pamphlets, tracts, & Parl. Debates.

Register of Books read, beginning

Aug. 19, 1832, & containing

reference to some of the more remarkable

Passages

Memoir of Bp Sandford.—

> p.79. Method.
> p.97. Old writers & old Church services.
> 126. Jephtha's daughter.
> 136. Ideas among Esquimaux of future life.
> 137. St Paul's eloquence—of ratiocination.
> 307. Letter on the principle of honour. Steele's Christn Hero.
> 332, 3. Holy Communion.
> II.13. death of an infant.

Lord Henley's Plan of Church Reform—

> p.10. doing work by deputy.
> Makes very light of the spirit of *general insubordination* now existing and spreading: and is *wholly unsatisfactory* where he ought to show how the presence of the Bishops can be dispensed with: otherwise an excellent book. He seems strongly to support the national Church, but not to feel the evils of schism as such.

A Dissenting Ministers fourteen reasons.

> p.13. Baptism.
> 15, 16. Burial service. "take unto thyself".

Corinne, ou, l'Italie.

> I. p.8–10. Common errors concerning travelling.
> 31. Value of natural, readymade, attachments.
> (1794)   "France, ou la societè est tout—Londres, où les interêts politiques absorbent presque tous les autres".
> 32. Roman Campagna.
> 37. Italian taste: requisites of greatness.
> 45. Observation of human nature. In what countries prevalent.
> 62. Rome makes one "in love with death".
> 63. Melodies of English & Italian tongues.
> 88, 9. Charms of Italian tongue.
> 91, 2. Mood of a poet.
> 112. Effect of fellowship in the contemplatn of grandeur.
> 119. Eloquent passage on St Peters. & 120.

122. Mysteries in all *sizes*.
203. Letter of Oswald.
208. Answer of Corinne.
237. Independent character of genius.
309, 10. Religious subjects why preferable in painting.
322. Sentiment of ruins.
364. Internal mechanism of the mind, varied to infinity.
367. Roman preachers. entire Chapter.
384. Comparisn of the religious.

Protestantism Succumbing to Popery.

p.42. Sentiments of Mr Bradbury 1791.
56. "The Tax of the Apostolic Chancery".
59. Preface & Notes to Rhemh Translation.
63. Pius VII's Bull of 1816.

Quart. Rev. on "Stages of the Revolution".
          "Lord Nugent's Hampden".
"A Church Establt lawful" &c.
Blomfield's Duty of Prayer.
Bishop Sandford's Select Sermons—
(appended to his other remains).

p.129–33. Faith historical—philosophical—real.
185–90. Knowledge—belief—practical refutation of the
          Socinian arg. in every man's conduct.

Benj. Harrison's Essay on Languages.

p. 1. Twofold view.
26. Doctrine of general consent—& notes.
30. inference from particles of all kinds.
33. Horne Tooke on "truth" floored.
41. "right". But very equal & sustained throughout.

Orlando Furioso. Canto . . .

I. 77, 8. changes in love.
III. 30. Posterity of Bradamante evoked. Q. idea for Macbeth?

Trollope's domestic manners of the Americans.

I. 40. Miss Wright's experiment.
97. Character of Jefferson.
103. Description of a revival.
207. Mr Owen's discussion.
229. A Campmeeting.
398. Want of discipline for children.

II. 94. Observance of the Sabbath—chains in streets.
100. Exclusive concentration of Amn enthusiasm.
101. Influence of literary habits there.
116. Thunderstorm.
159. Jefferson's works.
171. American Reviews.
181. Good tone in mentioning a Negro preacher.
196. Girl's boarding school Establishment.
216. Reception & nature of Capt. Hall's work.
284. Tints of American scenery.
294. & seqq. General remarks on the Institutions.

Edinburgh Review on Mrs Trollope.
. . . . Political condition of Italian States.
. . . . Lord Henley's Church Reform.
. . . . Working & prospects of the Reform.
Blunt's Twelve Lectures on the History of Abraham.
Duke of Newcastle's Address to all Classes.
. . . . Pamphlet on Catholic Relief.
Pusey's Sermon on the Consecration of Grove Church.
Captain Basil Hall's Travels in America.

I. 32. Comparative abilities of black & white children.
36. N. York exhibn of pictures.
38. Mode of removing brick houses.
54. Prison at Sing Sing.
83. West Point Military Academy.
96, 7. Militia—population—
109. Disposition to praise America.
124. Principle of genuine admiration for scenery.
139. State of negroes—& (II.77)—population.
147. No local attachments—(So, in Greece).
215. Welland Canal—Navigation of the St Lawrence—defence of the frontier. to end of Ch.
249. Loyalty of the Canadas—their means of defence.
253. Effect of continuance of fine scenery—America.
257. Reclamation of the Mississagua Indians.
275. Camp Meeting.
282. Emigrants at Peterborough, sent in 1825.
307–46. Letters from settlers.
352–4. Effect of the falls of Niagara on the mind.

II. 29. Government of State of New York & Conditions of Federation—Debate: wordy. also pp.52, 3.
40. Ladies & Gentn sit apart at parties.
43. Difficulty of understanding & being understood.
59. Electioneering spirit—means rather than end.

85. Society *must* take its tone from the lower order, & why—
Report of Boston Temperance Society.
101. Tariff—for protection of N.E.
107. Free Trade in England &c.
112. Unitarianism—Dr Channing (?)
135. Lowell Factories.
146. Strict naval discipline.
154–61. Constant Electioneering—cheap Justice—destruction of
domestic habits—and station of women.
164. American education. Abundant quant. deficient qual.
184. Good temper of the people.
192. Hartford Retreat for the insane.
216. Chapters XI–XIV. American Constitution. Tendency towards
pure democracy. Substitution of political for domestic habits.
Lax morale of legislation.
359. Effect of solitary confinement. Philadelphia.
266. Libraries & literary institutions there.
381. Attention to females.
384. Account of Steam Engines.   ⎧Idea (London) 1737
394. Comparative local advv. of N.Y., ⎨Watt's Patents 1769–84
N.O., Philada, Balt[imor]e, Boston. ⎩Fulton's boat 1807.
405. Extracts from "The American Chesterfield".
409. Ch.XIX. American Judiciary.

III. p.45. A Slave Law.
79. Uneducated state of the Slaves.
90. Impressment, absence of.
93. Army flogging, absence of. Discontent: & want of discipline
in consequence.
117. Whites in the slave estates.
121. Highlanders in N. Carolina.
129. Families may be parted.
133. Columbia (S. Car.) College. Youths *will* not *remain.*
156. Opinion of an Amn on state of slavery.
179. 189–91—& to 200.—same question.
204–11. Difficulties of the case.
222–47. Slave question—quantities of labour &c.
254. Conjecture on the 'rolling country' of Georgia.
282–6. Embryo city of Columbus.
293–305. Indian ball-play game.
322. The arks of the Mississipi.
348. Price of firewood. 128 cubic feet 10s6d to 12s6d.
368. 1430 miles up stream in 9 days. He averaged $5\frac{1}{2}$ miles an hour.
400. Advv. of Established Church.

Quart. Rev. on Count Pecchio's Osservazioni.
.... Prince Polignac & the Three Days.

.... Flint's Ten Years in the Vale of the Mississipi.
.... Fashionable Novels.
.... Works of Robert Hall.
England and France: or, a Cure for the Ministerial Gallomania.
Lady Canning's amplified half-volume of Stapylton.
Rousseau et la religion de nos Pères.
Les Morts enterrant leur Mort.
Temoignage rendu a l'Evangile.   by Malan.
p.1. Règlement of May 1817.   *suspended*[1] *in 1823*
  35, 39. Desire to escape the name of
     Schismatic or Sectarian.
Foreign Quart. on Government of Louis Philippe.
.... Sorelli's Translation of Milton.
.... Works of Chateaubriand.
.... Gouverneur Morris. mem. to buy.
Sarrans' Memoirs of La Fayette I. II.
Proceedings at West India Meeting of 1832.
Le Bas's Life of Wiclif.
Meek's Reasons for Conformity to the Church of Engld.
Bourrienne's Memoirs of Napoleon (Engl. Ed) I. Vols. I.
Scott's Napoleon. I. II. III.
Miss Kemble's Francis the First.
Quart. Rev. on 'How will it work'.
           Sarrans's Memoirs.
Girdlestone's 1st & 2nd letter on Reform in Church.
Navigation of the Scheldt.
Hook's Last days of our Saviour's Ministry.
    p.200. 'Son of God' how understood.
     227. Departure of the sceptre.
Dean Hook's Sermon before Christ. Knowl. Society.
.... Letter to Mr Fox.
.... Opinion of an old Englishman.
.... Sermon on Eph.4.3.
.... Anguis in Herba.
    p.45. Pluralities before Ref.
     63–70. Henry 8's proceedings.
     £3,277,000. present Rev. 1,500,000.

Scott's Napoleon. IV.V.VI.VII.VIII. and of IX Chaps 1, 2, 3,& 8.
Pusey's Benefits of Cathedral Institutions.

    8. Better to renovate than substitute.
   12. General edn tends to correct narrowmindedness.
   14. Previous professl instruction nec. for Clergy.
   21. Use of theological study.

---

[1] Instead of 'agreed' [?].

23. Evils. 1. Excitement ⎫ with reciprocal
          2. Superficiality ⎬ action. —
26. New discoveries expected in religion : of a wrong kind.
29. The Rationalists.

Bird's "What will the Bishops do?"

12. Defence of commuttn in land.
29 & seq. Chapter property to defray Church Rates. Miss-
      managemt of Parl. Commes.
15, 16. Landed property really assailed. Tithes in the van of rent.
51, 2. Quasi contradictory statement of the doctrine of the
      Trinity.
79. & seq. Ch.VIII. On the resummoning of Convocn. practically
      defunct since 1664.

<table>
<tr><td>Prov. of Cant.</td><td>U. House.</td></tr>
<tr><td></td><td>twenty Bishops.</td></tr>
<tr><td></td><td>L. House.</td></tr>
<tr><td></td><td>22 Deans</td></tr>
<tr><td></td><td>53 Archdeacons</td></tr>
<tr><td></td><td>24 Chapter proctors.</td></tr>
<tr><td></td><td>44 Parochial proctors.</td></tr>
<tr><td>Prov. of York.</td><td>Only one House.</td></tr>
</table>

Girdlestone's Seven Sermons on Cholera.
Townsend's Plan of Church Reform.
Winstanley Hull's Thoughts on Church Reform.
Arnold's principles of Church Reform.
Burton's Sequel to his Thoughts on Church Reform.
Lord Henley's Union of Lord H's & Dr B's Plans.
Miss Martineau's Life in the Wilds.
————————————— Ireland.
Keith's Signs of the Times Vol.1.
Townsend's Facts & Circumstances in the condn of Ir. Ch.
Girdlestone's serm. on Conduct to Dissenters.
Cicero de Legg. B.III.
Cox's Letter on Secession.
Barter's Sermon on Party Spirit in the Church.
Extracts from Evidence on the Bm & Ln Railway.
Rowe's pamphlet on the Ballot.
E. Evans's pamphlet on the Evils affecting Ireland.

[The back flyleaf contains the following notes :]

Scholarship.

'piety'—Maseres 1.185.
'subdue'—America—B. Hall.

March 5. James Horsnell's
           service commenced.
           £1.15 a month.

       Right of sovns Opinion.
       Hollis Maseres 1.193.

Principle may dwell in a man like fire in a flint.

[At right angles to the rest:]

       Our conversation is in heaven.[1]
       Knowledge without Grace.[2]
       Holding the unity of the Spirit in the bond of peace.[3]

[1] Phil. iii. 20.
[2] Perhaps 1 Cor. viii. 2–3.
[3] Eph. iv. 3, misquoted.

[VOLUME VII[1]]

Jul. 21. 33–Mch. 1 34 (No 7)[2]
London Sunday July 21. 1833.

St James's morng & evg. Wrote some lines—and prose also. Finished Strype—read Abbott—& Sumner aloud. Thought for some hours on my own future destiny—& took a solitary walk to & about Kensington Gardens.[3]

22. Monday.

Newark matters—wrote to Mr Tallents—Mr Hagart—Mr Finlay—& my Father. W.I. meetings—1–4. Went to Col[onia]l Office, as one of a Deputn bearing a protest from Six Colonies.[4] Rode—at Carlton in evg—House &c. 5½–8.[5] Read paper—L'Allemagne—Fact. Report[6]—Bulwer's England.[7] Worrying disclosures about James.[8]

23. Tuesday.

Read L'Allemagne—paper—Rape of the Lock—& finished Factory Report. Wrote to Mr G.—Mr Richmond[9]—Mrs Bartlett—Mr Hayter[10]—D. of N— H. Wilberforce—Mr Grant—all briefly. House 5¼–6, and 9–12½. Voted agst Tennyson in 213:164.[11]

24. W.

L'Allemagne—paper—Sir H. Parnell—Mr Canning on Slave Quest.[12] Rode

---

[1] Lambeth MS 1421. 25ff.

[2] Morley jotted down, more correctly, on an outer leaf: 'No. 7. July 21 1833 to Mar. 24. 1834.

[3] Morley, i. 106.

[4] The cttee. apptd. on 10 July 1833, representing British Guiana, Grenada, Tobago, St. Vincent, Trinidad and Mauritius, saw *Stanley to urge fuller attention to planters' interests over emancipation (PRO CO 318/116).

[5] Slave emancipation, 2°; East India charter. H xix. 1056, 1069.

[6] Factories Inquiry Commission, first or second report: PP 1833 xx. or xxi.

[7] E. G. E. L. Bulwer(-*Lytton), England and the English, 2v. (1833), social chit-chat with a hard core of observation.

[8] Horsnell.

[9] Thomas *Richmond, 1771–1837, miniaturist; f. of George.*

[10] (Sir) George *Hayter, 1792–1871, portrait and historical painter, kt. 1842; then engaged in painting members of H. of C.

[11] Tennyson (*D'Eyncourt) moved the repeal of the septennial act: H xix. 1107.

[12] Probably speeches of 16 March 1824, on improving slaves' conditions; NSH x. 1091. Possibly speech of 1 March 1799, 27 May 1802, 15 May 1823, or 19 May 1826.

—wrote to Mr G—more matter from Newark—House $5\frac{3}{4}$–$1\frac{3}{4}$. Divided in 158 to 151 against Buxton's instruction.[1]

25. *Th.*

L'Allemagne. paper. Went to breakfast with old Mr Wilberforce[2]—heard him pray with his family. Blessing & honour are upon his head.[3] Different scenes succeeded! House $12\frac{1}{4}$–3, and $6\frac{1}{4}$–$12\frac{1}{2}$. Stanley announced, that he wd propose 7 years for 12: without any previous intimation. Spoke a few sentences on the subject, in much confusion: for I could not easily recover from the sensations caused by the sudden overthrow of an entire & undoubting reliance.[4] Wrote to Mr G.—rode. T.G's birthday.

26. *Fr.*

L'Allemagne. Parnell. paper. Wrote draught to Burnaby & copied out.[5] Wrote to Mr G.—Mrs Charriere—Lincoln. House $6\frac{1}{2}$–7 and $9\frac{1}{2}$–$11\frac{1}{2}$.[6] Rode to Beulah[7] to see Mrs M[ilnes] G[askell] with Tom. He dined with me.

27. *Sat.*

L'Allemagne—paper—Sir H. Parnell. Dined at Sir R. Inglis's—went on horseback. Wrote for bl[ack] b[ook][8] & wrote to Mr Tallents (& copy),[9] R.G., & H.J.G.

28. *Sunday.*

Breakf. in Bedford Square. Foundling[10] in mg. St James's aft.—Saw the Foundling children dine. Walk. Read Bible—Davies's Memoir[11]—Abbott[12] —Wrote in Bible, & a letter to Cole.

29. *M.*

L'Allemagne. Wrote to Mrs G—Dry—Mrs Wishlade.[13] Paper. rode. House $12\frac{1}{4}$–3, and 7–$12\frac{1}{2}$. W.I. Bill in Committee. Took some part.[14]

[1] (Sir) Thomas Fowell *Buxton, 1786–1845, philanthropist; M.P. for Weymouth 1818–37; headed anti-slavery group in commons from 1824; moved to reduce apprenticeships for freed slaves to minimum. *H* xix. 1184.

[2] William *Wilberforce, 1759–1833, evangelical philanthropist; friend of *Pitt; secured abolition of transatlantic slave trade, 1807.

[3] Version in Morley, i. 105–7.

[4] Version in Morley, i. 105. *Stanley intimated, as the cttee. stage of the bill to abolish slavery began, that the government would propose to reduce from 12 years to 7 the period of apprenticeship for freed slaves. *Gladstone protested that on so important a matter the sense of the house should have been taken. *H* xix. 1252.

[5] Thomas Fowke Andrew Burnaby, 1808–93, Newark lawyer and landowner; town clerk 1833–73. Draught in Add MS 44353, ff. 205–6.

[6] East India charter bill, 3°: *H* xx. 14.

[7] Then fashionable spa at Norwood, some 6 miles south of St. Paul's.

[8] On West Indian apprenticeship; dated on previous day in Add MS 44819, f. 3.

[9] In Add MS 44353, f. 207.

[10] Thomas *Coram's hospital for foundling children; in east Bloomsbury 1745–1935; then at Berkhampstead.

[11] T. *Davies, *Memoirs of the Life of David *Garrick*, 2v. (1780).   [12] *Scott.

[13] Mary Ann, w. of J.E., Wishlade.

[14] Short speech on cost to proprietors of money payments to freed slaves: *H* xx. 60.

30. T.

L'Allemagne. Bulwer's England. Parnell. Looked at my Plato. Rode.
House 1¼–3: and at 6¾ did not stay—again 10–11 in H. of Lords.[1] Dined
with T.G.—Mrs Wallis taken ill in the evening.

31. W.

T.G. & Hallam breakf[aste]d with me. Rode to & dined at Beaulah with
the Gaskells. House at 2¼, & again 7–11¾. Commee on W.I. Bill finished.
(Howick & P. Stewart.)[2] German lesson from Mr Tropponeger: L'Allemagne: paper: made up accounts: part of a letter to Mr Tallents. Report
on Stafford Borough.[3]

August 1. Thursday.

Draught & letter to Mr Tallents[4]—wrote to J.N.G.—Paper. Report on
public walks[5]—L'Allemagne—worked German Grammar. rode. dined at
Uncle D's—[read] Sir H. Parnell. House ½ hour bef. dinner[6]—Went to inquire for the Wilberforces.

2. Fr.

Worked German several hours. Read half of the Bride of Lammermoor.
paper—L'Allemagne. wrote to Mr Sylvester[7]—Freshfield—Aunt E. Rode
House 5–6½.[8] German lesson. I like Troppaneger, my master, much.[9]

3. Sat.

German lesson: & worked alone. Paper. L'Allemagne. Wrote to H.J.G.
Attended Mr Wilberforce's funeral.[10] it brought solemn thoughts, particularly about the slaves. That is a burdensome question. Rode to Beulah &
dined there: staid also to tea: & rode home alone.[11]

4. Sunday.

St James's m[orning] & aft.—Sacrament. Verses. Third part of Homily on
Images—Bible—wrote to Mrs G.—Christian Year—Abbott—Walk.

---

[1] Slave emancipation and education in commons; Irish church bill 3° in lords. *H* xx.
129, 139; 113.
[2] Stewart and *Howick fell out over the former's allegation that the latter had
changed his mind on resigning: *H* xx. 196. Patrick Maxwell Stewart, 1791?–1846,
banker; agent for Tobago; whig M.P. Lancaster 1831–7, and co. Renfrew 1841–6.
[3] Extracts in Morley, i. 107. *PP* 1833 xi. 1.
[4] About election expenses. Add MS 44353, ff. 218–19.
[5] *PP* 1833 xv. 337.
[6] Misc. business: *H* xx. 256.
[7] Charles or John Sylvester, civil engineers, Bloomsbury.
[8] Lords' amdts. to Irish church bill agreed to: *H* xx. 285.
[9] Extracts in Morley, i. 107.
[10] *Wilberforce had died on 29 July. He was buried in Westminster Abbey.
[11] Extracts in Morley, i. 107.

5. M.

German—and lesson therein. Rode. L'Allemagne—finished Sir H. Parnell. Wrote to Saunders—Lincoln—Mr G.—Mr Girdlestone—paper. House $5\frac{1}{4}$–$9\frac{1}{4}$.[1]

6. Tuesday.

German—and lesson. Calls—& rode. Attended Committee on Sir J. Key's affair, merely to fix the course of proceeding. $12\frac{1}{2}$–$1\frac{1}{4}$.[2] Read Bride of Lammermoor.—Tasso—Rousseau—D'Haussez on England[3]—paper—& finished L'Allemagne with regret.

7. W.

House $12\frac{1}{2}$–$3\frac{1}{2}$. $5\frac{1}{2}$–7 and $10\frac{3}{4}$–$2\frac{1}{2}$.[4] Wrote to Mr G. & R.G. German & German lesson. Read Tasso—finished Bride of Lammermoor. Wrote out part of speech on Irish Church Bill. Heard from Mr Tallents.

8. Th.

German; but no lesson. Breakf. in Bedf. Square. Wrote to John and Mr Tallents.[5] paper—Black Dwarf[6]—Ovid, Am[ores] and Remed[ia] Am[oris] —[Key] Committee $12\frac{1}{2}$–5. House 5–6. Moved for some Irish Educn papers.[7] Rode with Sir R. Bromley—Dined with T.G.

9. Fr.

German, and lesson. Wrote to Mrs G. & Mr Blundell. [Key] Committee 1– $3\frac{1}{2}$. House $9\frac{1}{4}$–2. Voted in 48 to 87 agst legal tender clause.[8] T.G. dined with me. Rode—calls—read Tasso.[9]

10. Sat.

German, and lesson—Tasso—Black Dwarf. [Key] Commee 1–$4\frac{1}{4}$. Dined at Sir R. Inglis's. Wrote to J.N.G.—paper.

11. Sunday.

St James's mg and aft. Read Bible—Abbott (finished)—and a serm. of

[1] Slavery abolition bill, in cttee.: *H* xx. 336.
[2] Sir John *Key, 1794–1858, stationer; alderman of London 1823; lived in Bedford Square; lord mayor 1830 and 1831; cr. bart. 1831; junior M.P. City of London 1832, resigned 1833 on outcry at appointment of his son (Kingsmill Grove Key, 1815–99) to a job in stationery office. *Gladstone was appointed on 4 August to the commons' cttee. of inquiry. His notes on it in Add MS 44722, ff. 202–16. See *PP* 1833 xvi. 69 ff.
[3] C. L. d'Haussez, *Great Britain in 1833* (2v., tr.), an under-informed account.
[4] Slavery abolition bill, 3°; customs; and miscellanea. *H* xx. 409; 428; 430.
[5] Election expenses again. Copy in Add MS 44353, f. 227.
[6] *Scott.
[7] Misc. business: *H* xx. 433. He asked for data on Dublin schools and their textbooks.
[8] Bank of England charter: *Gladstone opposed making the bank's notes legal tender. *H* xx. 453.
[9] Extracts in Morley, i. 107. Torquato Tasso *Gerusalemme liberata* (1581).

Blomfield's aloud. Wrote a paraphrase of part of Chap 8 of Romans. Dined at Uncle Divie's.[1]

12. M.

Interesting letter from Cole. Wrote to him at great length in reply. Wrote also to H.J.G.—& (draught & copy) to Mr Tallents. Went with Aunt D. to see Mrs Wadd. Germ. & lesson. Finished Black Dwarf. Rode. at House little.[2]

13. Tuesday.

German, and lesson. [Key] Committee 1–4½. In the midst, however, went out to call with Tom on the Spottiswoodes. Rode—dined with him—House in Evg 10–11¼[3]—conv. with Mr Peter[4]—Wrote to Aunt M—Sir C. Greville —J.N.G.—Mr G. Finished writing out my speech on the Irish Church.

14. W.

German and lesson—Gaskell & T.G. breakfd, Gaskell dined, with me. Rode to Clapham. [Key] Committee 1½–3¾, House 5¼–9.[5] Wrote to Mr G., R.G., Harrison, and Manning.

15. Th.

Committee 1–3¼. Wrote to Mr G. Cousin Divie breakfd with me—Gaskell dined. Rode. read papers—Plato—finished Tasso Canto 1—Antislavery Obss. on Bill—German vocabulary and exercise.[6]

16. Fr.

Committee 2¾–3½. Finished.[7] Wrote to Lincoln—Wilberforce—Mr Hagart —Mrs Hagart—Sir R. Inglis. Breakf. with Gaskell—dined at Uncle D's. Calls—rode—shopping. German and lesson. Finished Plato Rep. V. Pre-paring to pack.[6]

17. Sat.

Going undecided till one, when Tom had seen Stanley & we resolved to start: with Joy. Packed—T.G. & Patk Stewart dined with me—papers— wrote to Doyle—and to Mrs G. Paid bills &c—Left Albany 9¼ P.M.—

---

[1] Extracts in Morley, i. 107.
[2] Factories regulation bill, or Irish tithes. *H* xx. 527; 537.
[3] Factories bill: *H* xx. 576.
[4] William *Peter, 1785–1853; whig M.P. for Bodmin 1832–4; consul at Philadelphia from 1840; his son, John Thomas Henry, 1810?–83, fellow of Merton 1836–56, was at Christ Church with the diarist.
[5] Cambridge writ; miscellaneous estimates. *H* xx. 597; 610.
[6] Extracts in Morley, i. 107.
[7] The cttee. reported that day that there was no evidence to support a charge of a corrupt system at the stationery office, and laid all the evidence given to it before the house. *PP* 1833 xvi. 101.

started for Aberdeen on board Queen of Scotland at 12. Need not have been on board before 11½ at least.[1]

18. Sunday.

Rose to breakfast but unwisely: uncomfortable all day: sick in the evening. Attempted reading, & read most of 'Letter on Baxter's Narrative'[2]—not too unwell to reflect. Eat nought af[te]r a tiny breakft.[1]

19. Monday.

Remained in bed—much better in consequence—eat, not much, but without inconvenience at the three meals. Read Goethe and transl[ate]d a few lines. Also, Beauties of Shakespeare.[3] In Evg, it blew—very sick, tho in bed. Tom *nearly* sick in undressing. Could not help admiring the crests of the waves even as I stood at our cabin window.[1]

20. Tuesday.

Arrived 8½ A.M. The Queen is a slow boat. 56½ hours. Rigged at the Hotel —breakfd—met Wm Gladstone—Translating from Goethe—My Father came over in the Phaeton & took us back—dined at Stonehaven.[4] Arrived before nine: much pleased with what I saw of the interior of the house.[5]

21. Wednesday.

Employed chiefly in lionising, within and without: *much* pleased. Delightful to find my Mother & Helen as they are. Unpacked & arranged Read Quart. on Dom. & For. Pol., also began Gifford's Life of Pitt.[6]

22. Th.

Quart. on Fr. Rev. of 1830, & on 'The Port Admiral'. Gifford's Pitt & Analysis—German—began 'The Virgin Martyr'[7]—wrote to Uncle Divie.

23. Fr.

Bible (began Acts) & Alfieri Ag[amemnon] with H.J.G.—Quart. on Rush— finished Virgin Martyr—Pitt's Life—rode to Laurencekirk with T.G. & J.N.G. & to call on Sir J. Forbes.[8]

[1] Extracts in Morley, i. 107.

[2] 'A Letter to a Friend in the Country on reading Mr [Robert] Baxter's Narrative of Facts' (1833), a fragment of the Irvingite controversy.

[3] By W. *Dodd (1752, often reprinted). Cp. *DNB* xv. 157.

[4] Port 15 miles SSW. of Aberdeen.

[5] First visit to Fasque, 16 miles SW. of Stonehaven; see 15 Aug. 31n.

[6] J. *Gifford, *Political Life of William *Pitt the younger*, 6v. (1809); notes in Add MS 44722, ff. 217–32.

[7] Tragedy by *Massinger and *Dekker.

[8] Sir John Stuart Hepburn Forbes, 1804–66; 8th bart. of Pitsligo 1828; lived at Fettercairn House.

24. Sat.

Bible—& Alfieri—with H.J.G. Rode with her. Wrote to Bruce & Canning. Pitt's Life. German—Quarterly on Tennyson's Poems.[1]

25. Sunday.

Church in mg. read after prayers alone. In garden. Hooker E[cclesiastical] P[olity] B.V (+) began: began Memoirs of Oberlin[2]—Bible.

26. M.

Bible, & Alfieri with H.J.G.—paper—wrote to Mr Bartlett—& housekeeper —read Quart. on Novels, and on Ref[orme]d Parlt.—began "die deutschen kleinstädter"[3]—went with Mr G. to see Mr Hutton: found him with a friend at their toddy: liked him: went to the River, & walked up the beautiful banks of the Esk.[4]

27. T.

Af[te]r breakf. rode to the Mill of Kincairn[5] to see Mackay who was shot last night: he was suffering much at times & seemed near death. Read the + Scriptures to him (Pss. 51, 69, 71. Is. 55. Joh 14.Col 3. Then interrupted.), sent for Mr White.[6] His Mother & brothers there—pleased with them. I could not find anything decisively satisfactory concerning his state, but far from anything the reverse. Left my prayerbook.[7]

Read Quart on Martineau—Shirley.[8] Read paper—Kotzebue—Gifford's Pitt—wrote to Marshall, & P. Stewart.

Read part of the D[avid] G[ladstone] and T[homas] O[gilvy] correspondence.

28. W.

Went again to see Mackay: he was better & more hope was entertained. The mother seemed fully impressed with the sentiments belonging to her situation.—Finished the correspondence—read Quart. on Church & Landlords—& Kotzebue. began Foscolo's letters.[9]

29. Th.

Bible & Alfieri with H.J.G.—Kotzebue. Gifford's Pitt—Quart on Le Vasseur —Roscoe's Letter on Reform.[10] Morrison's to Moss[11]—papers—rode John's

---

[1] xlix. 81, April 1833.
[2] Thomas Sims, *Brief Memorials* of J. F. Oberlin, Alsatian pastor and teacher (1830).
[3] 'The little German towns', comedy by Kotzebue (1803).
[4] Hutton was the minister at Edzell, 6 miles SW. of Fasque.
[5] Kincardine?, 1½ miles east of Fasque.
[6] Alexander Whyte, the minister at Fettercairn.
[7] Extracts in Morley, i. 108, dated a week earlier.
[8] Presumably the Caroline dramatist*.
[9] Ugo Foscolo, *Letters of Jacopo Ortis* (1798).
[10] W. *Roscoe, 'Letter to Henry *Brougham on Reform Representation in Parliament' (1811).   [11] Untraced.

horse—after dinner went down to see Mackay, who is not so well today. He really seems in good hands.

30. Fr.

Bible & Alfieri (began Oreste—) with H.J.G.—Paper: rode to the top of the hills towards Drumtochtie[1]—very fine view. Pitt's Life—began Piccolomini, using Coleridge's Translation[2]—Quart. on Neff's Mem.[3]—singing.

31. Sat.

Bible and Alfieri with H.J.G. Paper. walked to see Mackay, who is again somewhat better. Mrs G. ill. Copied a long letter. Schiller. Gifford's Pitt. Quarterly on Halford's Essays.

Sunday September One.

Bible. Oberlin—Hooker—finished Letter on Baxter's Narrative. Church mg. conv. with Mrs & H.J.G.—Walked towards Mackay's abode, but met T.G. coming away so turned back.

2.

Bible & Alfieri with H.J.G.—Rush[4]—Piccolomini—Gifford's Pitt. paper—rode. Went to ask for Mackay: he is better. My cousins came. Wrote to R.G. & Mrs Wallis.

3.

Bible with H.J.G.—& Alfieri—arranged books of prints. Billiards with J. Macadam[5]—transln of Goethe—Piccolomini—Rush—singing—wrote to Mr Tallents, & draught.

4.

Bible & Alfieri—finished [his] Oreste. The play seems adapted to produce great effect on the stage, & the story is perhaps skilfully modernised: but on the whole I think it loses by comparison with the artless and yet awful grandeur of the fable as in Æschylus. And the death of Clytemnestra seems awkwardly contrived: as likewise her previous conduct incongruous.— Wrote to Doyle. Read paper—Rush—and Schiller. Rode. billiards with John Macadam. the Finlays came: walked with Mr F. & my father.

---

[1] Drumtochty forest stretches from 2 to 8 miles to the NE. of Fasque, on the edge of the Grampians.

[2] First part of S. T. *Coleridge's translation of Schiller's *Wallenstein* (1800); vocabulary in Add MS 44722, ff. 241–51.

[3] *Quarterly Review* xlix. 47, on S. W. *Gilly *Memoir of Felix Neff*, protestant preacher in the Dauphiné (April 1833).

[4] Richard Rush, *Memoranda of a Residence at the Court of London 1817–1825* (1833), when he was American minister.

[5] John McAdam Gladstone, 1808–35, 2nd son of Robert Gladstone; lost at sea. Cp. 7 Nov. 35.

5—II.

5. Thursday.

Paper. Rush. Gifford. Schiller: little, alas. Backgammon &c. with J. M[acadam]—wrote to Pakenham. Out deer-shooting: got half the credit of one killed, at which J.M. & I shot together; but I think I did not deserve so much.—Poor Mackay died yesterday afternoon.

6. Friday

Rode with Mr Finlay &c. Backg[ammo]n & billiards with J. Macadam—Bible & Alfieri with H.J.G.—paper—Rush—Gifford's Pitt, and Piccolomini little.

7. Sat.

Bible & Alfieri with H.J.G.—papers—Hamilton[1]—Rush—Gifford's Pitt—little German.

Attended young Mackay's funeral with my father. Perhaps sixty persons were assembled in a barn, swept for the occasion. Each sipped from a glass of whisky on entering—and wine with cake & bread were afterwards handed round, of which all partook, some repeatedly. The brothers of the deceased administered. This was preceded by a prayer from Mr White, the only religious service of the day: all standing: the body not present. Before they "lifted", the father & brothers came severally, & drank to the company present. The female connections & friends were assembled within the House. The father & brothers were much affected. When we arrived at the Churchyard the body was lowered at once & the grave filled. On the way one of the chief mourners walks at its head—the guests carried it, those at least who were pedestrians. The company melted away: & all is considered over when the sods are laid. No care had been taken to hide the bones which were about the grave in great numbers: & on which I heard one of the brothers remark. It would perhaps have been more delicate. The behaviour of those present was reverent, & there was, contrary to the custom in England, no attendance at the tomb except of mourners. The service however is sadly deficient. We are I trust allowed to hope, that the soul now taken sleeps in Jesus: and may our nearness this day to the house of mourning, & the receptacle of decay, not be without its fruit.

8. Sunday.

The Mackays all at Church. Calvinistic Sermon on " & if I be lifted up " &c.[2]—good. Read Hooker—Oberlin—Carpenter on Arnold[3]—and wrote some "Thoughts".[4]

---

[1] [Thomas *Hamilton], *Men and Manners in America*, 2v. (1833).
[2] John xii. 32.
[3] Pamphlet by Lant *Carpenter on Thomas *Arnold's *Principles of church reform* (1833).
[4] 'Thoughts on the State and Prospect of Religion in this Country', Add MS 44794, ff. 1–8.

9. M.

Wrote draught & copy to Mr Godfrey: wrote to E. Wishlade & S. Ashton[1]: read Rush and Gifford's Pitt, also Bible & Alfieri with H.J.G. Rode by Fordun to Drumtochtie, and back between the hills.[2] Singing—Backgn with Miss Finlay. Mr & Mrs Whyte & Mr Tyrrell[3] dined here.

10. T.

Bible & Alfieri with H.J.G. Wrote to Mrs Wallace. paper. singing: Gifford's Pitt—copied a letter—finished Rush. The spirit of the book very amicable. Occasional felicity of expression, but great general deficiency in style, & in what we term general education. His characters & passages on court ceremonies—the press—the colonies—& English country life—seem valuable.

Rode to Edzell Castle with Miss Finlay & Cous. John. Remarkable cornice of the principal tower, which is very perfect. Garden wall: square apertures for flowers: niches, for images?—the Virtues, on one side—sciences on another—and Pagan deities (we were told) on a third—all in rude bas relief: date on a scutcheon 1604, but were not these older?[4] Backgn.

11. W.

Rain—billiards, a rubber at.—Bible & Alfieri with H.J.G. paper—Gifford's Pitt, and Schiller: also Hamilton's "Men & Manners in America"—a very clever book apparently. wrote in Red Book.[5] Backgn with Miss F[inlay].

12. Th.

Mr Aspinall & Crombies of Thornton Castle dined here.[6]—Rode to the Burn,[7] & looked over the library. Bible and Alfieri with Helen. copied a letter—wrote to Gaskell—billiards, backgn—singing. Gifford's Pitt—and Hamilton. I think the description of the Mississippi[8] is one of the most poetical passages I ever read in a prose work—paper.

13. Fr.

The Finlays went. Mr F. is certainly gifted with a remarkable capacity to please in society, full of heart & humour. May the crowning gift not be wanting. Mr Aspinall went.—Called at Stracathro.[9] paper—singing. Hamilton—Schiller—Gifford's Pitt (finished Vol. 1.) & analysis.

[1] Possibly Samuel Ashton, Liverpool merchant.
[2] Fordoun lies 5½ miles ENE., and Drumtochty Castle 4 miles NE., of Fasque.
[3] Possibly John Tyrrell, victualler, of Peter's Lane, Liverpool.
[4] Edzell castle, in ruins, belonged to the earls of Crawford whose fortunes failed in the seventeenth century. (J. B. *Burke, *Vicissitudes of Families*, i. 197 (1869).)
[5] On 'pleasure and duty', Add MS 44803H, f. 30.
[6] Alexander Crombie of Thornton Castle, Laurencekirk, and his wife.
[7] House beyond the Esk, 4 miles WSW. of Fasque.   [8] ii. 191–200.
[9] Six and a half miles south of Fasque, a seat of Sir James Campbell, 1818–1903; 5th bart. of Aberuchill 1824; m. 1840 Caroline, da. of Sir R. H. Bromley. Margaret Lady Campbell, d. 1871, née Coldstream, m. the 4th bart. 1816.

14. S.

Bible & Alfieri with H.J.G.—copied a long letter. paper—also Demerara papers. Gifford's Pitt—a little Schiller—Hamilton. Rode with my Father & J.N.G.—singing.

15.

Church. Walked to Mackays. Read Oberlin—part of the Abbé Dubois, and Heber as bearing upon his work[1]—also wrote in red book and "Thoughts".[2]

16.

T.G. went.—Wrote to Freshfield—Wilmot—R.G.—Bible and Alfieri with Helen. Piccolomini—Gifford's Pitt—Tennyson's Poems—Hamilton's America—singing.

17. Tuesday.

Bible & Alfieri with H.J.G. Finished Filippo: much struck with it. I thought it would have been still better if Gomez had been made sincerely penitent: Filippo himself would have had more grandeur of position, if the springs of all the crimes had been concentrated in him, & if his will had been represented as compelling from all around him that hateful service. Besides Gomez is another Philip, differing in position only: and hereby the effect of the character of the King is committed. Also the acts which are alleged as Carlo's crimes should it seems have been more fully developed: it is too weighty a matter for the spectator to be able to realise it upon hearsay.

Gifford's Pitt—Schiller—wrote to Mrs Wallace—Hamilton—Butler's Catholics.[3] rode—sang.

18. W.

Bible & Alfieri with H.J.G.—began Antigone—Gifford's Pitt—Schiller—Hamilton. paper—singing—out shooting with John $1\frac{1}{2}$-$5\frac{3}{4}$—shooting? if a man can be said to have shot, who hit nothing. The Frasers came.

19. Th.

Bible & Alfieri with H.J.G. Gifford's Pitt—Schiller—Hamilton. & began "Recc. of a Chaperon"[4]—paper—singing rode with H.J.G. wrote to Aunt E. & Mr Allen.[5]

[1] J. A. Dubois, *Descriptions of the . . . People of India* (1805, tr. 1817), a lengthy discussion of Brahman caste, and R. *Heber, *Narrative of a journey . . . from Calcutta to Bombay, 1824–1825*, 2v. (1828).
[2] Add MS 44803 H, f. 32.
[3] Charles *Butler, *The Book of the Roman-Catholic Church* (1825), an attack on *Southey's *Book of the Church*: dedicated to Charles Blundell.
[4] [A. J. Sullivan] *Recollections of a Chaperone*, 3v. of novelettes, ed. by Lady *Dacre (1833).
[5] Joseph Allen, stable-keeper at Philpot Farm, Uxbridge, who had charge of *Gladstone's grey mare.

20. Fr.

Bible and Alfieri with H.J.G.—Copied a little. rode to Balmeno.[1] Schiller: I have now a new transln to compare, from the Montrose Library. Recc. of a Chap. The Arbuthnots & Miss Forbes[2] dined here. Found Miss F. a very nice person. sang, ill indeed.

21. Sat.

The Arbuthnots went. rode to Phesdo &c. paper—Hamilton—Piccolomini —Gifford's Pitt—singing—wrote to Cousin Divie & J.E. Wishlade.

22. Sunday.

"Thoughts".[3]　Bible—Hooker—finished　Oberlin—finished　Dubois—a strange book.

23. M.

Bible & Alfieri with H.J.G. Finished Antigone: began Virginia. Dislike the former. It seems to have the faults of both the ancient & modern dramas. Antigone & Argia are ill distinguished from each other: rather Amphipolish.[4] Artificial & wiredrawn discussions where one expects simple energetic sentiment & action consequent. Creon's affection is unamiable, while there is nothing grand in his tyranny: vice unrelieved by power of any description, while its unity is only spoiled by the remains of parental attachment. Hoemon's part required more decisive action. Want of incident. Why was not the capture of Argia and Antigone introduced otherwise than as a naked fact? The sentiment is exaggerated, caricatured, & diluted thereby in its results: while there is a grievous want of simplicity & strength, & of a sustained interest & tone of character.—Gifford's Pitt— Piccolomini—Recc. of a Chapn—finished Hamilton. The Aspinalls dined here, with Mrs Swinburne.[5] Sang—wrote to T.G.—& to Sec. King's Coll.— paper.

24. T.

Bible & Alfieri with H.J.G.—Gifford's Pitt—finished Piccolomini—began Plat[o] Rep[ublic] B.6—in boat—Aspinalls went—singing—read Recc. of a Chaperon.

25. W.

Bible & Alfieri—wrote to Mr G. & Freshfield—Gifford's Pitt—began death of Wallenstein[6]—a little Plato. Warenne. Rode with H.J.G.

[1] Balmano House, Marykirk, 6 miles SSE. of Fasque, belonged to James Calvert.
[2] Jane, elder da. of Sir William, 7th bart.; d. 1871.
[3] Perhaps in Add MS 44815 F.　　　　　　　　[4] Cp. 'amphibolic' = equivocal?
[5] Helen, eldest da. of James Aspinall; m. 1826 Major-General Thomas Swinburne of Marcus Lodge, Forfarshire; d. 1860.
[6] Second part of S. T. *Coleridge's translation of Schiller's *Wallenstein*. Vocabulary in Add MS 44722, ff. 233–40.

26. Th.

J.N.G. went. Bible & Alfieri—ride—boat—paper—singing—'An old Tale': imperfect tho' wellmeaning in the highest particular?[1] Death of Wallenstein—Plato—Gifford's Pitt—wrote to Lincoln.

27. Fr.

Bible. Alfieri—wrote to Mr G.—rode—music—Gifford's Pitt—Wallenstein —Plato—paper. Recc. of a Chaperon.

28. Sat.

Bible—finished Virginia: has merits & faults? most of the latter candidly pointed out by the author in his "parere".[2] Life of Pitt—Wallenstein—Plato —wrote to Robn—sang—finished Recc. of a Chaperon: Ellen Wareham is a tale of much power & feeling & extraordinary interest, and was not the mind of the writer good to God-ward? boat with H.J.G. & walk.—Exceedingly kind letter from Sir R. Inglis.

29. S.

A good serm. on Matt. 16.26. Long conv. with my Mother & Helen on the painful subject of our domestic condition in reference to religion—Read Scriptures aloud at night—Hooker—M'Crie's Ref. in Italy[3]—'thoughts'.[4]

30. M.

Bible—Alfieri (began Mirra)—Gifford—Wallenstein—Plato (progress very slow)—began Biographia Litteraria[5]—singing—was to meet Aunt M.— conversation (premature) with my Father about W.I. education.[6]

Tuesday, October one.

Bible—Alfieri—Canning's Speech on Sard[inian] treaty & on Address in 1795[7]—Gifford's Pitt—Death of Wallenstein—singing—rode with H.J.G.— Plato.

2.

Copied a letter—Bible—Alfieri—Pitt—began Vol. 3—Tennyson's Poems— Death of Wallenstein—Finished Plat. Rep. B.6—paper, Rode to Drumtochtie: *walked out with* gun for ½ hour.

---

[1] Perhaps a tract.
[2] 'advice' to the reader, in V. Alfieri, *Opere*, ix. lxxxvii (1807); but, cp. 10 Oct. 33, they may have been reading him in French.
[3] T. *McCrie, *History of the Progress and Suppression of the Reformation in Italy* (1827).
[4] Untraced.
[5] *S. T. Coleridge (1817).
[6] See 11 Oct. 33.
[7] 31 January, 30 December 1794; the first two speeches in *Therry's edition, 6v. (1828).

3.

Bible—Alfieri (finished Mirra)—Giff. Pitt—Biographia Litteraria—Wallenstein's Tod—Plato—paper—out with gun—Mirra is unassuming in diction,
and simplicity of plot is preserved, but the suspense is very long and the
denouement very rapid. We miss I think the calmness of the Greek tragic
dialogue in the modern imitations.—Wrote to J.N.G. Father Mo[ther] &
Helen go to Craigs.[1]

4. Fr.

Gifford's Pitt—Wallenstein—ride & walk—wrote some verses—Biogr.
Litt.—Plato—wrote to Girdlestone—paper. My Mother returned ill.

5. Sat.

Gifford's Pitt. Bible & Alfieri—began Merope—paper—wrote to Freshfield
—red book[2]—Wallenstein—Biogr. Litt.—My Mother somewhat better—
Long ride with Mr G., whose horse came down.

6. Sunday.

Post hour today brought me a melancholy announcement—the death of
Arthur Hallam.[3] This intelligence was deeply oppressive, even to my selfish
disposition. I mourn in him, for myself, my earliest near friend: for my
fellow creatures, one who would have adorned his age and country, a mind
full of beauty and of power, attaining almost to that ideal standard, of
which it is presumption to expect an example in natural life. When shall I
see his like? Yet this dispensation is not all pain: for there is a hope, and
not (in my mind) either a bare or a rash hope, that his soul rests with God
in Jesus Christ. I walked upon the hills to muse upon this very mournful
event, which cuts me to the heart. Alas for his family and his intended
bride!—Read Bible—Hooker—MacCrie—Wrote to Doyle—& Gaskell.[4]

7. M.

My usual occupations: but not without many thoughts, in spite of selfish-
ness, upon my departed friend. Bible, Alfieri, Wallenstein, Plato, Gifford's
Pitt, Biogr. Litt., paper—wrote to Sir R. Inglis. Rode with my Father &
Helen. All objects lay clad in the softness and solemnity of autumnal decay
—alas! my poor friend was cut off in the spring of his bright existence.[5]

8.

Bible—Merope—some Lat. verses—Wallenstein—Gifford's Pitt—paper—
Shelley—rode. Wrote to Doyle—& T.G. Sang: only the concluding part of
the Tempest: it is a dirge for Hallam.

[1] James Wylie's house at Mid-Calder, 12 miles WSW. of Edinburgh.
[2] Add MS 44803 H, ff. 35–36.
[3] Very suddenly, of heart failure, during an afternoon rest in his father's study at
Vienna, 15 September 1833.
[4] Extracts in Morley, i. 108–9.   [5] Version in Morley, i. 109.

9.

Bible—Merope—Cenci[1]—Wallenstein—Gifford's Pitt—boat—Plato—dined at Stracathro—a large party. I did not expect an exciting party: or shd not have wished to go.

10.

Bible. Finished Merope: & Alfieri for the present. A great stage effect must one wd think be produced by these plays: as regards human character & passions, the highest object of the drama. Philip seems by far the best of the eight in the Paris selection.

Paper—Wallenstein—Gifford's Pitt—part of 'the Cenci'. Not unlike Filippo. Rode.

11. Friday

Letter from Mr Tallents—wrote to him, & to the Duke—conv. with my Father, who was most kind. I feel much difficulty & embarassment: not from doubt as to principles, but from ignorance of facts.[2] But there is help, unworthy as I am to look for it.

Gifford's Pitt—Wallenstein—Plato—copied a paper for my Father—rode —finished the Cenci.

My Father said spontaneously, he wd write to Maclean,[3] strongly & fully, on W.I. Education.

12. Sat.

Bible with H.J.G. Wrote to Seymer—& Mrs Wallace—Rode—Gifford's Pitt—Wallenstein—read Shelley—paper—Christabel[4]—some points of similarity in part 1 with the Bride of Corinth—Plato—a little whist—drew out some questions to go to Maclean, about already existing education.

13. Sunday.

T.G. & J.N.G. returned.—Bible—Butler's Memm. of R.C.s—McCrie's Ref. in Italy—& Hooker's E[cclesiastical] P[olity].

14. M.

Bible with H.J.G.—Heard from & wrote to Doyle: still on the same deeply & painfully interesting subject [of Hallam's death]. Rode with T.G. paper— Biogr. Litt—Gifford's Pitt—death of Wallenstein: wrote over my education queries to go to Mr Maclean.

---

[1] *Shelley's tragedy (1819).
[2] Continued dispute about election expenses; see 30 Oct. 33.
[3] Unidentified: several Macleans, of the families of Westfield, co. Elgin, and Pennycross, co. Argyll, were in the West Indies at this time.
[4] *S. T. Coleridge (1816).

15. T.

Wrote to R.G. & B. Harrison. Bible with Helen. paper. Finished Mr Robertson's paper on Demerara population.[1] finished Wallenstein. Gifford's Pitt—Coleridge Biogr. Litt. Sang—rode—sailed. The Miss Arbuthnots came.[2]

16. W.

Bible—read up omitted passages in Wallenstein—from which I part with regret. Viewing it as a strictly historical drama, & therefore not of that class which gives the widest range to the imagination, it is very masterly: in variety & fidelity of character: in the structure & unfolding of the plot: & there are many very beautiful pieces of imagery. Pitt's Life—paper—red book[3]—Plato—rode—cards evg.

17. Th.

Began Mary Stuart:[4] progress somewhat slower, as I have no translation. Gifford's Pitt. Biogr. Litt. Singing. Copied two papers for my Father. Wrote the draught of a letter to Mr Hallam: with which I am very ill satisfied. Medicine.

18. Fr.

Mary Stuart—Gifford's Pitt—wrote to Mr Hallam. rode to Laurencekirk. Plato Canning's Speeches—Heard with deep regret of the death of my friend Francis Cole: now I trust "in pace".—The Cruickshanks[5] & Swinburnes dined here—singing. paper.

19.

paper. Gifford's Pitt—Mary Stuart—Plato finished B.VII. Biogr. Litt. Canning's Speeches. singing—rode with my Father—wrote to Tupper.

20. Sunday.

Church—& in aft. read the aftn Service of *our* Church—& a sermon of Arnold's. Fourteen persons present. I was greatly pleased: may God grant that even this little light be not put out. Wrote to Cole.—"Thoughts".[6] Hooker—Bible.—It. Refn.[7]

[1] Untraced MS.

[2] Perhaps Anne, only da. of Sir William Arbuthnot, who m. 1849 her cousin Hugh Inglis; and Jane, d. 1892, 2nd da. of his b. George, 1772–1843, Madras banker. Jane m. 1846 Sir George Stephens Gough, 1815–95, 2nd Viscount Gough, 1869.

[3] Add MS 44803 H, ff. 37–38.

[4] Schiller; vocabulary in Add MS 44722, ff. 252–7.

[5] Either James Cruickshank of Langley Park, Montrose, or Alexander Cruickshank of Brechin.

[6] Add MS 44803 H, f. 38, on guilt.

[7] *McCrie.

21. M.

The Frasers went.—Gifford's Pitt—Maria Stuart—Plato—Biogr. Litt.—paper—wrote to D. of N., Mr Tallents, & Freshfield. Rode with T.G. Heard of Susan Gladstone's death: which has long been deemed inevitable: but we have learned that she was prepared.[1] Bible & Racine (Les Freres Ennemis) with Helen.

22. T.

Finished Gifford's Life of Pitt. It seems honest & straightforward: but abounds in strong epithets. Allowance however must be made, on the score of the time at which it was written. Mary Stuart. Bible & Racine with Helen—Plato & Canning's Sp.—singing—walk & ride: wrote to Montrose (Shipping Co's agent)[2] for my Father—he being confined to bed by lumbago.

23. W.

Bible. Racine: finished Les Freres Ennemis. What butchery! Every character of note cut off—yet there is not that sense of desolation which oppresses the mind in reading Lammermoor or the Cenci. Creon's wickedness is not energetic enough to deserve or suit his catastrophe.—Maria Stuart—began Hallam's Middle Ages, with Analysis[3]—copied a letter: wrote to Gaskell. finished Biogr. Litt. Vol.1.—Mr Canning's 2nd Sp. on Ir. Union.[4] Rode in Glenesk. Plato.

24. Th.

Hallam—Maria Stuart—Plato—Froissart—wrote to R.G. & H.J.G., now at Ld Arbuthnott's.[5]

25. Fr.

Cousin Divie came—out with him. Uncle C. expected. Hallam—Mary Stuart—Plato—began Maffei's Merope[6]—whist—paper.

26. Sat.

Hallam. Plato finished B.8. Mary Stuart. Copied a paper for Mr G.—Merope—paper—whist—went to Arbuthnot to bring Helen home—there near 1½ hour, & 4 on the road.

[1] A child of Uncle Thomas Gladstones'.
[2] Fasque lies 12 miles north of the port of Montrose.
[3] In Add MS 44722, ff. 258–73.
[4] 22 April 1799, in *Cobbett, Parliamentary History, xxxiv. 958.
[5] John Arbuthnott, 1778–1860; 8th viscount 1800; lord lieut. of Kincardineshire 1805–47; lived at Arbuthnott House, 10 miles east of Fasque, between Fordoun and Inverbervie.
[6] Italian tragedy (1713).

27. Sunday

Church—& Evg. prayers in aftn with a Sermon. Walk. Newman's & Keble's papers on the Church[1]—Butler, & MacCrie—Bible—Wrote 'Thoughts'.[2]

28. M.

Hallam—Mary Stuart—Plato (B.9.)[3]—Merope—papers—wrote to B. Harrison. Mr G. & T.G. at Durris.[4]—Bible and Racine with Helen.

29. T.

A kind & straightforward letter from the D. of N.—and a very moving one from Mr Hallam.[5]—Wrote to Mr Hancock (Grantham)[6] & Sir Jas Macdonald. Also draught of a longish letter to Mr Tallents. Bible—Alexandre[7]—Plato—Hallam. Mary Stuart—Merope—whist—singing.

30.

Reconsidered, & wrote over my letter to Mr Tallents for tomorrow's post: sent him a short letter with the money £650: also one to Mr Caparn £150.[8] & wrote to Mr Franceys.[9]—Hallam—Bible—Racine—Mary Stuart—Plato—Merope—but all curtailed. Whist.

31. Th.

Bible with H.J.G. Hallam, & Chronological tables. $11\frac{3}{4}$–$2\frac{1}{2}$—out with my brothers & Divie after roes. paper. Finished Mary Stuart: & read Walter Scott's Scotch Hist Chh 34–6, to enable me better to appreciate the admirable judgment of Schiller both where he has adhered to history & where he has gone beyond it.[10] Made up accts.

Friday Nov 1.

Bible—Racine—(began Andromaque)—hurricane all day. Messrs Hutton & Whyte dined here.—Hallam and Chronol[ogica]l tables—Began Joan of Arc[11]—wrote to R.G.—papers—whist—arranged my letters for the period since leaving London.

---

[1] Probably *Keble's assize sermon on 'National Apostasy' of 14 July 1833 and the first three *Tracts for the Times*, all by *Newman: the beginnings of the Oxford movement. Cp. 10 Nov. 33.

[2] Add MS 44803 H, f. 39, on conscience.

[3] Notes in Add MS 44722, ff. 292–7.

[4] Anthony Mactier's house near Drumoak, on Deeside, 10 miles WSW. of Aberdeen.

[5] In Add MS 44353, ff. 269–70.

[6] Possibly Edward Hancock of Loughborough.

[7] Racine.

[8] Election expenses and agent's fee.

[9] Samuel Franceys published the *Liverpool Standard*, and sold books.

[10] These two lines in Morley, i. 108.

[11] Schiller.

2.

Bible—Racine. Hallam, with references to Sismondi—Joan of Arc—a little
Plato—rode with Divie to the Burn & lionised him about the Esk—whist—
and Ed. Rev. on Overton's poem—DHaussez's England—& 'Ref. Min. &
Ref. Parl'.[1]

3.

Church mg—Eng. service, & sermon, in aftn—14 persons present. Went to
see old Finlayson.[2] Bible—Finished M'Crie's Ref. in Italy—read Hooker.

4. M.

Hallam—began Vol 2—made a map of Spain, very small & very rude.
Bible with H.J.G.—Racine—Joan of Arc—rode with T.G.—whist—sang—
Quarterly on 'Bergami et la Reine d'Angleterre'[3]—Copied *two* [docu-
ments].

5. T.

Hallam. Bible (finished 2 Cor.)—Racine (finished Andromaque). Joan of
Arc. Divie went. At 3 went to Arbuthnott with my father & brothers—
dined & slept. singing.

6. W.

Read paper—'remarks on Engl. & Sc. Establishments':[4] vicious enough;
with some melancholy truth. wrote to Mrs Wallace. Hallam, & Chronol.
table—(analysis every day)—Joan of Arc. It seems a good plan to read
along with history historical plays of the same events, for mutual illustration, as well as aid to the memory.[5] finished Vol 1 of Canning's Sp.

7. Th.

Hallam—table—& map of Germ[any]. Bible (St Peter) & Racine—Joan of
Arc. wrote to Harrison. Mad. de Stäl's Chapters on Schiller.[6] Gillanders
dined here. Called on Mr White. Sang.

8. Fr.

Hallam—& map of France. Bible & Racine. Joan of Arc. Wrote to Bruce.
Packing for London & Edinburgh. paper. a little Plato—whist—Rode.

9.

Bible.—finished Les Plaideurs:[7] I never read a play in which there was so
much to be supplied by the mind of the reader: and after all to no great

---

[1] D. *Le Marchant, 'The Reform Ministry and the Reformed Parliament' (1833).
[2] A cottager.   [3] Cp. 6 July 32.
[4] Untraced pamphlet.   [5] Version in Morley, i. 108.
[6] *L'Allemagne*, part ii, chs. 17–20.   [7] A comedietta by Racine (1668).

purpose: tho on the stage I doubt not it might have good effect. Hallam—
& Chronol. Table.—wrote to Tupper—Joan of Arc.

10. Sunday

Church. read prayers & a serm. of Bradley's in aftn. 10 persons. Oxf. Tract
on the Church—ably drawn.[1] "Thoughts".[2] Nat. Hist. of Enthus.—three
of More's Moral Sketches—and part of Dean Stanhope's Meditations.[3]

11. Monday

Bible—Joan of Arc—Biogr. Litt (Vol.2.)—Hallam—wrote a long letter to
Pakenham—paper. Began with T.G. to call upon the Tenants. Near having
an accident—Lion broke loose when Tom was off, and rushed furiously
about the field where we were, kicking and rearing. The power of sympathy
kept him near John's horse which I was riding, with all his fury: but did
not prevent his bursting out and renewing his very energetic performances:
so his neighbourhood was not agreeable: but, singular enough, I was obliged
to remain perfectly still, as the least motion renewed his rage. a little corn
attracted him & he submitted.

12. T.

Hallam. Biogr. Litt.—paper—arranged divers matters about several poor
people—a three hours excursion calling on the tenants with Tom—they
really seem to be a people whose acquaintance is well worth cultivation. It
is delightful to see so much industry, cheerfulness, & content, and in such
close connection with the fear of God.—Whist. and wrote a paper on
Racine,[4] & note to Sherriffs.[5] Packed.

13. W.

8¾–3¾—to Perth—George Inn: good. wrote to Bruce—Robn & P. Stewart.
Walked. whist—Joan of Arc—part of Ref. Min. & Ref. Parl.—& Quarterly's
Art. thereupon.

14. Th.

7–12½—to Queensferry—breakfasting at Kinross.[6] Joan of Arc—& Esdaile
on Church Establishment: good.[7] Took chaise over to Broom Hall.[8] Walk
there mit den fraülein M., & L.G.[9]—Liked my hosts much—a day of much

---

[1] By *Newman: the first of the *Tracts for the Times*, dated 9 September 1833.
[2] Untraced.
[3] More probably George *Stanhope's *Pious Meditations* (1701) than his paraphrase of
Marcus Aurelius (1697).
[4] In Add MS 44722, ff. 274–5.
[5] William Sherriffs of Broomhill on Deeside, west of Aberdeen.
[6] Kinross, some 60 miles SW. of Fasque, lies 20 miles NW. of Edinburgh, 10 north of
Dunfermline, and 15 north of Queensferry.
[7] 'Civil and Religious Institutions . . . inseparably connected' (1833?), pamphlet by
James Esdaile of Perth, father and namesake of the mesmerist*.
[8] Lord *Elgin's seat SW. of Dunfermline.   [9] Untraced: governesses?

very interesting conversation, with Lady E.,[1] Lady M.B.[2] & Jas B. particularly.

15. Fr.

Wrote to H.J.G.—finished Joan of Arc—read Excursion & "Ref. Min. & Ref. Parl ".—walked a little—ride of four hours, to Dunfermline, rail road, hill for view (dire fog) and Sir Robert Preston's.[3] paper—scraps—Dear Robns birthday.

16. Sat.

Long conv. with Lady E. after breakfast—scarcely in time for the Steamer to Newhaven[4] at twelve. Home[5] between three and four. Found my Mother unwell. Unpacked—read papers—and Duchess of Berri in La Vendée.[6]

17. S.

St Johns. Mr Ramsay, & Dean of Carlisle[7]—walk—Read Hooker, and Faber's Sermm. on Atonement & Predestinarian Controversy.[8] Wrote a paper on the fall &c.[9] Wrote to R.G., Aunt E.

18. M.

Long work with the books—called on Mrs Fraser—at Blackwood's[10]—specially about tradesmen, filling up Mrs Oswald's[11] lists. papers—Duchess of Berri &c—Hallam.

19. T.

Shopping—and ride. Again with Blackwood.—Hallam, finished Vol.II. Schiller—began "die braut von Messina". Finished La Duchesse de B. dans la Vendée.

20. W.

Long work arranging books. Shopping—& ride. Quart. on D'Haussez & Dermoncourt. Hallam & Analysis. Bride of Messina—& papers.

[1] Elizabeth Oswald, m. 1810, d. 1860.
[2] Lady Matilda (Harriet) Bruce, 1802–57, *Elgin's second da. by his first wife (divorced, 1808); b. in Athens where her father collected the marbles from the Parthenon; m. 1839 Sir John Maxwell, bart.
[3] Sir Robert Preston, 7th bart. of Kirkforther, Fife, d. 1847.
[4] Fishing port west of Leith and north of Edinburgh.
[5] In Atholl Crescent.
[6] By E. A. Dumas and General Dermoncourt, who arrested her (1833).
[7] Robert Hodgson.
[8] G. S. *Faber, Sermons, i. 23, 405 (1816), on Romans iii. 23–6 and 1 Thessal. v. 21.
[9] Untraced.
[10] In Prince's Street, William *Blackwood, publisher.
[11] Wife of James Townshend Oswald of Dunnikeir, Fife, and Lady Elgin's mother.

21. Th.

Hallam—analysis & Chronol. table—shopping—Mr P. Robertson,[1] Mr Miller,[2] & Mr Blackwood here.—I saw them in my father's absence: they came again to him (R. & M.) at 4½.—Wrote to Mrs Wallace. Bride of Messina—and Shakespeare's Richard II.

22. Friday.

Hallam and Analysis. Braut von Messina—part of Henry IV—(P.I.)—papers—my Mother very ill—T. & J. returned. Called on & saw Lady Arbuthnot.—Mr Ramsay—& the Goalens.

23. S.

Hallam &c. Braut von Messina—finished P.1. of H[enry]4. Attended Zaba's first Lecture on Poland[3]—papers—wrote to B. Harrison—sang. Called on Moncreiff, & walked with him.

24. Sunday.

Mr Williams mg—Mr Tyrrit aft.[4] Wrote to Cole—and for Ethics X. Read Hooker and began 'Guide to an Irish Gentleman'.[5]

25. M.

Bible with H.J.G. renewed—& began 'La Clemenza di Tito'.[6] Hallam as usual. Began Henry IV p[art] 2.—read papers. Second Polish Lecture—wrote to Mr Tallents & Mr Whyte.

Polish Dates.	First dynasty	992.
	Second Jagellon.	1486.
	Consttl monarchy ab.	1360–1574.
	Elective monarchy—	1574.
	John Sobieski at Vienna.	1683.
	Augustus II.	
	Stanislaus expelled by foreign arms.	
	Elr of Saxony—Augustus III.	
	Stanislaus Poniatowski—	
	First partition	1772.
	Constitution	1789–91.
	Second partition..	1793.
	Third	1795. Sept.

[1] Patrick Robertson, advocate.

[2] Perhaps James Miller, advocate; or a partner in J. Miller and sons, Edinburgh merchants.

[3] N. F. Zaba, Polish exile.

[4] Charles Hughes *Terrot, 1790–1872; priest 1817, dean 1837, and bishop 1841, in Edinburgh.

[5] M. *O'Sullivan, A Guide to an Irish Gentleman in his search for a Religion (1833), protestant reply to Thomas *Moore's Travels.

[6] By Pietro Trapassi, known as Metastasio, Italian eighteenth-century poet and librettist.

26. T.

Hallam—Braut von Messina—Draught & Letter to Duke of N.—whist—singing—seeing pictures. Bible & Metastasio with H.J.G.—Maffei's Merope.

27. W.

Hallam. Braut von Messina—finished H[enry] 4., Part II. papers—sale of pictures, with my Father—whist—wrote to Crabb[1]—finished Maffei's Merope—Bible & Metastasio with Helen. Maffei does not make Polifonte aware of the existence of Creophontes, as Alfieri does, by arranging the eclaircissement in his presence.

28. Th.

Bible. & Metastasio. Finished La Clemenza di Tito—it is warm and interesting—but Vitellia resembles Racine's Hermione, and the rapid transfer of affections as also the numerous transitions from love to hatred, are repugnant I think to our English notions of the truth of human nature and the seriousness of the heart: particularly as the former seems degraded by being an expedient to complete the mere mechanism of the play.—Hallam—Bride of Messina—paper—rode—dined at Mr Pringle's[2]—at Mr Alison's[3] in evg heard Emiliani[4] again, with great delight.—Calls.

29. Fr.

Bible & Metastasio (Temistocle) with H.J.G.—Hallam—copied a paper—Bride of Messina—dined at Mr Craig's—several calls—conv. with my Mother in evg.

30. Sat.

Bible & Metastasio—Hallam—Bride of Messina—rode—dined at Mr Tytler's[5]—paper—read aloud to my Father. Walk also. Heard from Cole. Made up my letters &c.

N.B. Hallam names as memorials of Chivalry

Memoirs of St Palaye
La Tremouille
Bayard.
(3.511.N.)[6]

Hist. of philosophy—Tennemar—Tiedeman. Buhle: 531.N.[7]

[1] Possibly J. Crabbe, Edinburgh surgeon.
[2] Probably J. Pringle, deputy clerk of session.
[3] Archibald *Alison, 1757–1839, priest in Edinburgh 1800–30, f. of the historian*.
[4] Cesare Emiliani, Bolognese violinist.
[5] Patrick Fraser *Tytler, 1791–1849, historian of Scotland; or James Tytler, writer to the signet, a neighbour at 5 Atholl Crescent.
[6] H. *Hallam, State of Europe, iii. 511 n, refers to the Memoirs of Ancient Chivalry of J. B. La Curne de St. Palaye (tr., 1784), and to Le Panegyric du Chevallier sans Reproche, M. de La Tremoille and La tres joyeuse . . . histoire . . . du bon Chevalier sans Paour et sans Reprouche, le gentil Seigneur de Bayart, in M. Petitot, Collection complète des Mémoires, xiv., xv. (1826–7).
[7] *Hallam refers, ibid. iii. 531 n., to [J.G.] Buhle [Geschichte der neueren Philosophie, 6v. (1800–5)] as a valuable recent work on the history of philosophy; and names also [D.] Tiedemann and [W.G.] Tennemann as sound untranslated authors on same subject.

Sunday December 1.

Sacrament—perhaps eighty. Excellent sermon in aftn from Mr Ramsay. Wrote 'Thoughts'[1] & to Cole. Read Hooker and 'Guide to an Ir. Gent'.

2. M.

Bible and Metastasio. Finished Hallam & Analysis. The 'Middle Ages' I should suppose to be one of the most useful books of the age. It comprehends a wide extent of diversified information and research: you are carried through many details without ever being permitted to lose sight of the general objects had in view: more ornament is attached to the style than in such a subject matter might have seemed possible, yet without any sacrifice of solidity and clearness. There is no rigorous love of system, yet enough of classification to give the most connected views of the subjects. The spirit is *national,* and the graces and powers of intellect[2] are recorded and described with sympathetic animation. Whiggism is the creed of the writer: but it is neither extreme nor exclusive. To view the book in the most important of all relations—there is not I think any disposition to shut out from view the agency of God—yet I could have wished that distinctions had been more sedulously drawn, where the writer speaks of the *three* spirits moving on the face of the waters, and of a possible separation of virtue from belief. I have had an additional pleasure in reading this book at this time, because my studies in it connected themselves with the recollection of my departed friend.

My method has usually been 1. to read over regularly—2. to glance again over all I have read, and analyse.[3]
N.B. More dates might with advantage be added, in the last half of the work.

Bride of Messina—Began Henry V. Paper—& read it to my Father. Wrote to Mr Hagart. Whist. Long walk with Moncreiff: & conv. on Patronage, Episcopacy, &c.

3. T.

Finished Temistocle. Metastasio is too humane. History should not be violated without a reason. Nay the mind is not satisfied by a commonplace Consummation, after being studiously prepared by[4] emotion for great and adequate events. Not only is history overset in one point, namely, the deliverance of Themistocles to[5] death: but in another, in order to procure this, namely, the continued enmity of Xerxes. The latter caused the former. It is too much to change both cause and effect. History may be set aside, to fill up poetical verisimilitude. If history assigns a cause inadequate to its effect, or an effect inadequate to its cause, poetry may supply the deficiency for the sake of an impressive whole. But it is too much to *overset* a narration,

---

[1] Add MS 44815, f. 13v.
[3] Morley, i. 108; antedated.
[5] Instead of 'from'.

[2] 'fixed' here deleted.
[4] 'str' here deleted.

6—II.

and call it an historical play.[1]—We liked the play however, much—and the working up of the mind of Themistocles to the dreadful resolution seems admirably managed—and beautiful[ly] illustrates the position of the heathen, who might see himself placed between two conflicting duties, each apparently imperative, without possessing the Christian secret which solves the enigma, by teaching that duty is but *one*, and that we have only to ascertain among acts offering themselves to us, which is most agreeable to conscience and the law of God, as by the answer to that question, all the rest are set aside.

Bible—finished Bride of Messina. The early part seems cold and distant —the éclaircissement not happily arranged—the last scene, when Isabella relents, very beautiful, & the Chorus there dignified. This play might suggest a lengthened criticism. It is enought here to say, that if the reasonings of the Preface on a Chorus be admitted, it still remains difficult to understand his introducing two partisan choruses, which goes to destroy the Greek character of a Chorus; might he not have had one, attached to neither son, but rather to Isabella? Alas too for the religion.

Began Robertson's Charles V.[2] Wrote to Mr Sherriffs, & Mrs Wallace— whist—calls (Mrs Craig & Mr Sinclair[3]) & shopping—finished Henry V. Copied a letter.

4. Wednesday.

Disappointed in going at one—went at 4½—rough night. At Bantaskine[4] by eight, with kind friends. Sang a little.—copied two letters—wrote to Aunt J.—Robertson's Charles V—Bible—Metastasio (began Zenobia) & "die Deutschen Kleinstädter" resumed.

5. Th.

Deutsche kleinstädter—Robertson—billiards—singing—walk. The Vernies[5] came to dine—&c.

6. Fr.

reading as yesterday—billiards with Miss Hagart—long conv. with Mrs H. on her son's prospects (Js),[6] and general—Left at 3½ for Carnock[7]—drove

[1] Antedated version in Morley, i. 108.
[2] William *Robertson, *History of . . . Charles V*, 3v. (1769), with a sketch of the development of European society from the third to the sixteenth century, once an historical classic; notes in Add MS 44722, ff. 276–91.
[3] John *Sinclair, 1797–1875, priest 1820; worked in Edinburgh; vicar of Kensington 1843.
[4] The Hagarts' place at Camelon, on the west side of Falkirk; a journey of some 24 miles.
[5] Probably Sir Harry *Verney, 1801–94; s. of General Sir Harry *Calvert, 1st bart.; succ. 1826; changed name to *Verney 1827; whig M.P. Buckingham 1832–41, 1856–74, and 1880–5 and Bedford, 1847–52; and his b. Frederick, 1806–91, M.P. Aylesbury 1850–1; had a house on the Forth at Carriden, 10 miles east of Falkirk.
[6] James McCaul Hagart.
[7] Three miles west of Dunfermline.

Lion over—Met the Miss Forbeses, &c. Made to sing much, for want of a better performer, Tom being hoarse.—Curious house, and people *notorious* for being agreeable.

7. S.

Rode to join the Stirling Mail—in Edin[burgh] by 3—dined at Lord Moncreiff's—scraps—papers—wrote to R.G., and Cole.

8. Sunday

Two beautiful sermons from Mr Ramsay—Gen. 1.1. and Math. 7.16.—walk with John. Heard from Childers that he is to be married[1]—and wrote my hearty congratulations. Bible. Hooker—Guide to an I.G.—black book—&c. Mrs G. ill.

9.

My Mother still ill. Helen too. Attended Forbes's Lecture[2]—walk—Robertson—Deutsch. Kleinst—began Henry 6. P.1.—paper.

10.

Our invalids somewhat better. Mr Finlay, Mr Thomson,[3] Mr Learmunth,[4] Mr Robinson,[5] dined here. Robertson—and Deutsch Kl.—arranging papers &c. Ride—and strumming at piano : made out for the first time the chords to an air.

11.

Continued but not great improvement. My dear father's birthday—crowned with many mercies—may they be consummated in one. Robertson—Hen.6—paper—Deutsch. Kl. At Mrs Ogilvy's—dined at Lady Arbuthnot's. Mr Logan played. Sir W. Rae[6] of the party. Wrote to Mrs Hagart.

12.

Singing lesson. Robertson's Ch.V—finished Vol 1. The manner is very attractive : the Notes very useful. Deutsch. Kl—Shakespeare—paper—wrote to Childers. Mr Learmunth took me to Heriot's Hospital[7]—the Poor's House—400 in—the University. went with my father to call on Dr Chalmers.

[1] To Dulcibella, d. 1865; da. of Sir Robert Chester of Bush Hall, near Hatfield.
[2] James David *Forbes, 1809–68, professor of natural philosophy.
[3] James Gibson Thomson, wine and general merchant.
[4] John Learmonth, Edinburgh merchant.
[5] Perhaps a son of Captain James Robinson of Rankeillour Street.
[6] Sir William *Rae, 1769–1842; 3rd bart. of Inveresk 1815; M.P. 1819–32, incl. Portarlington 1831–2, and for Buteshire from 1833; lord advocate 1819–30, 1834–5, 1841–2.
[7] Founded 1624 in memory of George *Heriot, goldsmith and banker.

13.

Breakfast with Dr Chalmers. His modesty is so extreme, that it is oppressive to those who are in his company, especially if his juniors: since it is impossible for them to keep their behaviour in due *proportion* to his. He was on his own subject—the poor Laws—very eloquent earnest and impressive. Perhaps he may have been hasty in applying maxims drawn from Scotland to a more advanced stage of society in England.[1]

Robertson—Deutsch. Kl[einstädter]—Emiliani's concert—*he* was the only great attraction; Vaccajs voice inadequate to the room.[2] calls. papers. wrote to R.G. finished Henry VI P.II. My Mother & Helen better.

14.

Earned my breakfast by a walk to Mrs Ogilvy's—sat with her a little. Robertson—Deutsch. Kl—Singing Lesson—paper—began Chalmers's Tracts on Pauperism[3]—& Henry 6. Part 3. Much struck: by the scene between York & Margaret in particular.

15. S.

Mr Ramsay yet more acceptable.—two walks. wrote 'Thoughts'[4] & Notes on passages. Bible—Hooker—Guide to Irish Gentn.

16. M.

Robertson (at length) found time to resume my Plato & finished B.9.—finished Deutsch. Kleinst.—Chalmers on Pauperism—paper. Attended Royal Society in evg[5]—& Mr Russell's supper after it.[6] I fear I got little benefit from the meeting, it is impossible to drop into the middle of a science & find one's self at home there, even tho it be of the lower class.

17. T.

Robertson—Plato (began B.10)—began Kotzebue's Wirrwarr[7]—Chalmers —paper—singing lesson & practice—whist. Letter from Mr Tallents. I could have wished other accounts—but I still believe I am *there* at least in the path of duty.[8] Copied two letters.—Walked on the Glasgow road 1st mile stone to 4th & back in 70 min.—the returning *three* miles in about 33¾. Ground in some places rather muddy & slippery.[9]

[1] Version in Morley, i. 109.
[2] Nicola Vaccaj, 1790–1848, Italian composer, who also sang.
[3] T. *Chalmers, *Speeches and Tracts* (1823).
[4] Add MS 44815, f. 19v.
[5] Charles Murray *Cathcart, 1783–1859; styled Lord Greenock 1814; fought in Spain and at Waterloo; 2nd Earl Cathcart 1843; governed Canada 1846; general 1854; read a paper on geology of Edinburgh Castle Hill (*Trans. of Royal Society of Edinburgh*, xiii. 39 (1836)).
[6] James Russell of Abercromby Place, born in Barbadoes, M.D. Edinburgh 1822, was a vice-president.
[7] 'Confusion', a farce (1803). Notes on vocabulary in Add MS 44722, ff. 298–300.
[8] In Add MS 44353, f. 300: more about unpaid Newark publicans' bills.
[9] Extracts in Morley, i. 109.

18. W.

Robertson—finished Vol.2.—Plato—Wirrwarr—Chalmers—paper—whist calls—a little singing—Sinclair's Uniomachia[1]—seems to me to have a good deal of spirit. Long letter to Lincoln.

19. Th.

Robertson. began Vol 3—Plato—Chalmers—out—singing lesson 4th— Wirrwarr—singing (practice)—dined at Mr Ramsay's: liked my host much, & Mr Earl.[2] heard from Cole. paper.

20. Fr.

Robertson—Plato—finished Henry VI part III. wrote to T.G. & Mr Tallents—dined at Mr Horn's[3]—walk—singing—paper. Two morning callers (G. Sinclair[4] & Dr Russell) curtailed my work today.

21. S.

Robertson—Plato—paper—singing lesson.[5] Wirrwarr. Went with Mr Sinclair to Lady Carnegie's.[6] Dined at Sir J. Sinclair's.[7] Went to meet R.G., who came at $3\frac{1}{2}$.

22. Sunday.

Mr Ramsay—Mr Hughes in aftn.—Wet still. Bible—Hooker—Guide— Wrote for prayers &c.

23. M.

Robertson—Plato—Wirrwarr—part of MacCrie's pamphlet on patronage[8] —paper—whist—a good many calls. Found out Mr Glasgow Robertson jun.[9] medicine of last night ineffective—a stronger dose. Wrote to Pusey— & Dry.

24. Tuesday.

—The birthday of our ever beloved sister Anne. Robertson. Plato (finished the Republic)—finished Dr M'Crie on Patronage & Chalmers on Pauperism —Wirrwarr—singing—Wrote to Tupper.—Followed up my pills & kept the house.

---

[1] A macaronic Oxford squib by, among others, William *Sinclair (Cp. 28 Dec. 33).
[2] Edward Earl, gentleman, of Abercrombie Place.
[3] Perhaps Robert Horn(e), advocate, of Darnaway Street.
[4] George M. Sinclair, secretary to School of Arts library.
[5] 'fin[ishe]d' here deleted.
[6] Charlotte, née Lysons, d. 1848; m. at Naples 1825 Sir James Carnegie, 5th bart. 1805.
[7] Sir John *Sinclair, 1754–1835, cr. bart. of Ulbster 1786, creator and president of board of agriculture 1793–8 and 1806–13.
[8] T. *McCrie the elder 'On Church Establishments' (1833).
[9] Robert Robertson-Glasgow, 1811–60, advocate and Ayrshire J.P.

25. Christmas Day.

Perhaps 250 communicants. Six of ourselves—may God give his blessing. Wrote to Aunt E. & Mr Allen—Bp preached in aftn. Hooker—Le Bas's Serm. on the day—began Inglis on Church Establishments.[1] In the evening whist—questionable?—Pills.

26.

A feeble day! Three successive callers, & a conv. with my Father about young Hagart, occupied the morng.—Read a good allowance of Robertson: an historian who *leads his reader on* I think more pleasurably than any I know. A long letter to Mrs Hagart. Whist. The Goalens & Mrs O[gilvy] dined here. Pills.—Singing lesson.[2]

27. W.

Robertson—& Dem[osthenes] Olynth[iac] I (+). wrote to Gaskell. went with Mr Learmunth to Trinity College, the Leith Docks, &c. Singing in the evg. our teacher came to tea. Bruce here. Divie dined. Calomel.

28.

Robertson's Charles V—Demosth. Second Olynth—paper—wrote to Pakenham—a little singing. Not very well. Long conv. with W. Sinclair.[3] Out, not very long. The Frasers, Myddletons[4] &c. dined here—doses continued. The last day of my year! "I am borne darkly fearfully afar"[5]— some verses.

29. Sunday.

Twenty four years have I lived. And they seem a great void specked from point to point with some acts, and some changes—but where is the *continuous* work, which ought to fill up the life of a Christian without intermission?

Particularly[6] this last year has been one of *opportunities*: may the next be more fruitful in their use and results.

I have been growing, that is certain: in good or evil? Much fluctuation: often a supposed progress, terminating in finding myself at or[7] short of the point which I deemed I had left behind me. Business and political excitement a tremendous trial: not so much alluring as forcibly dragging down the soul from that temper, which is fit to inhale the air of heaven.

Yet unless I altogether delude myself I still continue to read in the habitual occurrences of my life the sure marks of Providential care and love: I see all things great and small fitted into a discipline: I therefore

---

[1] John *Inglis of Edinburgh, *A Vindication of Ecclesiastical Establishments* (1833).
[2] Version, with interpolation from 30 December 1833, in Morley, i. 109.
[3] William *Sinclair, 1804–78; capt., Madras cavalry, then ordained; priest at Leeds, 1837–57, canon of Chichester 1874.
[4] Possibly George Middleton, minister at Strathmiglo, Fife, and his wife.
[5] End of *Shelley's 'Adonais'.
[6] 'in' here deleted.   [7] 'be[yond?]' here deleted.

believe that God is still my Father, Christ still my Saviour, the Spirit still a Spirit warning, striving, pleading, within me: and not to me only, but to all those who are embraced within the body of the Church, by right if not in act.

The coincidence of Sunday and a birthday was painful, because Sunday is full alas! of stumbling blocks. May it not be so again.

Bible—Hooker—Guide—Church twice—walk with John—wrote a paper[1]—& a letter to Cole.

Rather sick.—Helen ill.[2]

30. M.

Robertson—finished Charles V. The style most attractive, but the mind of the writer does not set forth the loftiest principles.[3] Dem[osthenes] Third Olynthiac—paper—singing lesson. Whist—Wirrwarr. Helen better. Read Mr Blake's letters on Bengal Sugar works,[4] with interest.

31. T.

Began the fifth vol. of Raynal, where he commences with the West Indies.[5] Full of gross infidelity. Dem[osthenes] Phil[ippic] 1.—Wrote to Mr Bartlett —& the bookkeeper—sorted my letters & made up my accounts pretty fully. Walked, & rode with R.G. Singing, and whist.

And thus farewell to the year: God's mercies are no sooner departed with the old than they recommence with the new.

[1] On words and meaning, in Add MS 44722, ff. 301–9.
[2] Extracts in Morley, i. 109.
[3] Misdated ibid.
[4] Untraced.
[5] G. T. F. Raynal and others (including Diderot), *A Philosophical and Political History of the Settlements and Trade of the Europeans in the East and West Indies*, new tr., 6v. (1782). Notes in Add MS 44723, ff. 5–10.

1834. Jan. 1. Wednesday.

Raynal—Demosthenes—papers—shopping &c. Singing lesson—wrote to Mr Tallents. read W. Sinclair's papers on currency—& wrote notes thereupon.[1] Church at 11 A.M. Perhaps 120 there.—R.G. fixed to go to Jamaica —Arranged my own plans for moving S.

2. Th.

Raynal—Demosthenes—calls—Singing lesson, wh generally reached $1\frac{1}{2}$ hour. Walter Goalen came to dine. Wrote to Aunt E—at a musical party at Lord Medwins (Stuart Henry)[2]—a sad discussion at tea—Remade my plans.

3.

Raynal. paper. Wrote to Mrs Hagart. & Gaskell. a little singing. Walk with John. Divers calls. much pleased with Mrs Ramsay's[3] sentiments— seventeen to dinner—a very pleasant party. Hard abstract conv. with Mr Sinclair nearly all dinnertime—Church matters after it—and a conv. with Captain Wellesley[4] on religion, especially[5] Baptism: struck by his singular ingenuousness.—W. Forbes sang. Bad acct of Mr Hugh G.

4. Sat.

Raynal. finished Vol 5—wrote to Mr Macdowal[6]—Pusey—Girdlestone.[7] —Dined with Mr Learmunth. Walked with R.G. Singing and lesson in do.— Conv. with G. Sinclair[8] on the prayer society.

5. Sunday.

St John's, Sacrament. There seemed about 80. St Paul's in aft. also went into Mr Craig's & heard a stranger preaching well. Sad account of Aunt E. —Better of Mr Hugh G. Read Hooker (finished B.5)—finished "Guide to an I.G". Fenelon. wrote.

6. Jan. Monday.

Raynal—began Vol VI—paper. Chapel at eleven. Walked to the Goalens,

---

[1] William *Sinclair, father, Sir John* of Ulbster, published in 1829 a pamphlet favouring bimetallism and a paper currency. Notes untraced.

[2] Untraced.

[3] Isabella, née Cochrane; Canadian-born; m. Dean *Ramsay 1829; d. 1858.

[4] William Henry George Wellesley, 1806–75; b. of (dean) Gerald*; lieut. R.N. 1825, capt. 1829.

[5] 'discipl' here deleted.

[6] Perhaps John McDowall, Edinburgh advocate.

[7] Sending £10 for a new church (see Add MS 44354, f. 3).

[8] (Sir) George *Sinclair of Ulbster, 1790–1868; acquitted of espionage by Napoleon 1806; whig M.P. Caithness 1817–20, 1831–41; 2nd bart. 1835.

Mrs Watson's,[1] & Mrs Ogilvy's. Mrs W. is heavily afflicted: one daughter in health nurses a sick mother and a sick sister: a school perhaps in which she may be educated to happiness brighter than that which glares around many an one more wealthy but not more comely.

A party—the Moncreiffs, W. Sinclair, Glasgow Robertson, &c. Wrote to Pakenham. read Wirrwarr—sang.

7. T.

Raynal. Wirrwarr. Singing lesson. Moncreiff's review of Inglis.[2] Went with my father to see pictures. W. Forbes called on me.—Chalmers on Pauperism, gathering my notions.

8. W.

Breakfast with Dr Chalmers. Attended his lecture 2–3. Divers calls. Raynal. Wirrwarr. paper. singing—tea with Aunt M.—More than ever struck with superabundance of Dr C's gorgeous language—which leads him into repetitions, continued until the stores of our tongue be exhausted on each particular point. Yet the variety & magnificence of his expositions must fix them very strongly in the minds of his hearers. In ordinary works great attention wd be excited by the very infrequent occurrence of the brilliant expressions & illustrations, with which he clogs the palate. His gems lie like paving stones.[3] He does indeed seem to be an *admirable* man.[4]

9. Th.

Raynal finished Hist of the *West Indies*. Finished Wirrwarr. Singing lesson. Party to dinner—& accession in the evening. Singing. Many calls p.p.c.— Kind note from Mrs Ramsay. Comm[unicatio]ns with Aunt M. Packing & arranging till 2 A.M. of 10th.

10.

Little or no sleep—up & off at 6½—from Ed[inburgh] at 7 with R.G.

> I would be, and I would seem,
> Like the happy mountain stream
> That from its cradle to its grave,
> From its first infantine motion
> To its deep repose in ocean
> Bears no speck upon its wave
> Rendering up its life to heaven
> Bright and clear as it was given.
>
> But I am of a traitor seed
> Fair in word & false in deed . . .

---

[1] Possibly Mrs Watson of Moray Street.

[2] Untraced.

[3] 'But' here deleted.

[4] Version in Morley, i. 109–10.

11. Sat.

In Lpool at 8. Dressed &c. at R.G's house[1]—lionised it. At Seaforth 11¼—found Aunt E., in body as I had feared—in mind, as I had hoped. Presented my books—saw the Rawsons— in Lpool at 1½—called on Moss—Horsfall —Uncle R—Ld Sandon. Wrote to Mrs G., T.G. Bushnell,[2] Mrs Wallace, Allen, Williams, Pusey, Mr Bacon, &c—dined at Mr T. Tobin's;[3] met Ld Sandon: heard conv. on impressment. Read a little Lingard.[4]

12. Sunday.

Heard Mr Peck's farewell Sermon[5]—began Whyte on Prayer[6]—at Seaforth for aftn Church—enjoyed it. Dined and slept at the Parsonage—much conv. 1½ hour with my Aunts—read Beveridge, & some of the Prayers to them.— Even the wind howling upon my window at night was dear and familiar.[7]

13. M.

Breakfast with Aunt J.—at Mrs Conway's, in the garden &c—saw Aunt E. afterwards, & read some prayers. Wrote to my Father—and Uncle Divie, after return to town—called on Mrs D.G.—Mrs S.G.—Mrs Brandreth—Mrs Grant—Mr Jones—a party at Robns—whist—read some of Lingard's Henry VIII[8]—Long conv. with Rn at night.

14. T.

Lingard—wrote to Mr G. 12–3—went to Seaforth—saw my Aunts—on the subject of their departure—& (Aunt J. only) wills—called on Mrs Myers.— at the Parsonage—& on Mrs Staniforth & the Mayor—at the Town Hall about some Corp. matters, with Ld Sandon—dined at Mr Grant's with him & a large party. wrote out a sketch of will. at Mr Eden's.[9]

15. W.

Af[te]r breakfast in the Park—seven calls; saw am[on]g others, Mrs Thos G. & Helen—in deep mourning: very kind: how have they been afflicted![10] with Mr Moss on Moravian missionaries—wrote to Mr G.—Aunt M—Miss Benwell—copied out a sketch of will—at Eden's but did not see him—packed—dined, & off at 5¾ for Wolverhampton by Erin go Bragh—good coach.

---

[1] At 3 Abercromby Square.
[2] Perhaps John Hext Bushnell, b. 1814?, then an undergraduate at Worcester; priest 1839.
[3] Thomas Tobin, merchant, of Bold Street.
[4] J. *Lingard, History of England, 8v. (1819–30), from a Roman catholic view.
[5] Kenrick Peck, 1769?–1837, rector of Ightfield, Shropshire, 1820.
[6] Alexander Whyte, The Duty of Prayer (1834).
[7] Version in Morley, i. 111.
[8] In his vol. iv (1820).
[9] Probably John Eden, attorney, of Mount Pleasant.
[10] Cp. 21 Oct. 33.

16. Th.

At Wolv. 4¾ A.M. Left it 6¾ for Sedgley 4 miles off. Found Mr Girdlestone up[1]—after breakf. out with Pusey, then with him, seeing Churches, Schools, iron foundry, & nailing. Much & interesting conv.—read Christn Obs. on his Cholera Sermon—& on his Comprehension plans[2]—also Divers Tracts on Amer[ica]n Episcopacy &c.—Afternoon prayers & Lecture at 3. —Mr Lewis his curate[3] came to dine.

17. Fr.

Left Sedgley 8½—Birm[ingham]—10¾ for Oxford—arrived 6½. engaged lodgings at Green's[4]—unpacked—read Gibbon—& went upon a voyage of discovery for acquaintances and friends in Ch. Ch—with little success. Found Brandreth—began to count term.[5]

18. Saturday.

John's birthday—may God richly crown him with all blessings.—indifferent accounts of Aunt E. Many letters. Wrote T.G.—J.N.G.—R.G.—Aunt E.— Bushnell—Mrs Wallace. convv. with Williams, & Jeffreys—the latter had tea with me. Began Palgrave on Corpp.[6] sundry matters consequent on arrival—went out to Tetsworth,[7] met & brought in my grey mare.

19. Sunday.

Read the 1st lesson in morning Chapel. A most masterly sermon of Pusey's preached by Clarke. Lancaster in aftn on the Sacrament. good. Walk. Wrote to Aunt E. read Whyte—3 of Girdlestone's Sermm. on Sact[8]— Pickering on Adult Baptism (some clever & some[9] *singularly* insufficient reasoning)[10]—Am. Episc. Pastoral Letter for 1832[11]—Doane's Ordination Sermon 1833, admirable.[12] Wrote some 'Thoughts'.[13]

20. M.

Called on the Dean—the Clintons[14]—Short—Pusey—Churton—rode—read paper—Zenobia[15]—Sismondi's Italian Repp—wrote to H.J.G.—Dined at

---

[1] Charles *Girdlestone was vicar of Sedgley, 1826–37.
[2] *Christian Observer*, xxxiv. 1, 26 (January 1834).
[3] William Lewis, d. 1870; ordained 1824; vicar of Sedgley 1837.
[4] A lodging-house, probably in St. Ebbe's.
[5] University statutes required him to reside for three weeks to qualify for his master's degree.
[6] Sir F. *Palgrave, *Observations on . . . New Municipal Corporations* (1832).
[7] Nearly 12 miles east of Oxford on the main road to London.
[8] C. *Girdlestone, *Seven Sermons on the Lord's Supper* (1833).
[9] Instead of 'much'.
[10] Possibly J. Pickering, *Practical Sermons* (1821), i. 278, on John iii. 3.
[11] 'A Pastoral Letter to the . . . Protestant Episcopal Church . . . from the Bishops'.
[12] Probably the one reprinted in W. C. Doane, *Life and Writings of G. W. Doane*, bp. of New Jersey, ii. 541 (1860).
[13] Version in Morley, i. 111.   [14] Lord Thomas and Lord William.
[15] James Ward, *Zenobia, A Drama; with Other Poems* (1833).

Merton, and spent all the evening there, in interesting convn—I was Hamilton's guest. It is delightful, it *wrings* joy even from the most unfeeling heart, to see religion on the increase as it is here.—Chapel in mg, which I hope to continue. visits from old Wale & W. Harris—looked over some of the library pictures.[1]

21. T.

Breakf. & conv. with Harrison. Calls from E. Denison & Palmer—rode to Holton[2]—wine with Thornton. Wrote to Aunt J—Mr Allen—R.G.—read Carwithen & Short's first Chapters[3]—paper—Excursion—Zenobia— finished Palgrave.

22. Wed.

Walk with Harrison—mare a little lame from a stone—dined at Merton, as Tancred's guest. Wrote to Anstice—Mr G—T.G.—read Short & Carwithen —finished Zenobia—continued transln of Br[aut] von. Cor[inth].

23. Th.

Breakf. with Brandreth—dinner at sen. masters' table, & Com. Room after-wards—Sismondi & Analysis—& Carwithen—Wrote to Uncle D. upon hearing of Jane's marriage[4]—to Rob. Gladstone— & T.G.—calls &c. Much of today, it fell out, spent in conversations of an interesting kind—with Brandreth & Pearson, on eternal punishment—with Williams (High St.) on Baptism—with Churton, on *faith*, & rel[igio]n in Univ—with Harrison, on prophecy & the papacy[5]—read Doane's charge & Address to Convn.[6]

24. Fr.

Breakfast with Churton at B.N.C.—walk with Tancred & E. Denison— dined at Merton, as Guest of the latter. Began "Essay on Saving Faith"— & wrote thereon.[7] Carwithen, Short, & Analysis. Wrote to R.G. & Mr Allen.

25. Sat.

Surpl. prayers. breakf. with Clintons. wine with Jeffreys. At Ramble Society —Lushington had tea with me. Paper—wrote to Unc. D.—Mr G.—Mr Bartlett—Bushnell—Mrs Wallace—Short, Carwithen & Analysis—Essay on Saving Faith.

[1] Extracts in Morley, i. 111.
[2] Five and a half miles east of Oxford.
[3] J. B. S. Carwithen, *History of the Church of England*, 3v. (1829–33); T. V. *Short, *A Sketch of the History of the Church of England to . . 1688*, 2v. (1832).
[4] Divie Robertson's only da. Jane was engaged to their Bedford Square neighbour, J. E. *Tyler the rector of St. Giles'; see 3 Feb., 6 Mar. 34.
[5] Extracts in Morley, i. 111.
[6] G. W. Doane, primary charge to his clergy, 29 May 1933; and a sermon on Philip-pians i. 27, to the annual convention of the Protestant Episcopal Church (Boston, 1832).
[7] *Essay on the Extent of Human and Divine Agency in the Production of Saving Faith* (1827). This sentence in Morley, i. 111.

26. Sunday.

Symons preached on intercessory prayer. walk with Lushington. Tea at Churton's. read "Four Dialogues on Bapt".[1]—Began Jerram's conv. on Inf. Bapt.[2] read Bible, & Essay on Saving Faith—wrote a few notes.

27. Monday.

Carwithen & Analysis. paper—Essay on Faith—wrote to Mr Jackson (Newark) & draught[3]—& to Mrs Wallace. At Wise's[?]. Calls & shopping: mare still unserviceable—call from Price & conv. on pol. & social matters—dined at Jacobson's—a very pleasant party—Burton, Macbride, Head,[4] Hamilton, Harrison, G. Denison &c. &c.

28. T.

Breakf. & walk with Lushington. Dined with Churton. Finished the Essay on Saving Faith. Wrote to R.G. & Anstice. Carwithen and Analysis. Began Sinclair's pamphlet.[5]

29. W.

Visits from one or two old folks &c. Walked with Hamilton to Wolvercot,[6] & visited with him—delighted. Called on Sinclair & Mr Badcock.[7] Dined at Oriel: conv. with Newman chiefly on Church matters. Wrote to Aunt E.— also, on reason & understanding, &c—Carwithen & Analysis—Doane's Address on founding Princeton Church.[8] I excuse some idleness to myself by the fear of doing some real injury to my eyes. Tea with Brandreth.[9]

30. Th.

Charles I's service. Finished Sinclair's very able & well written pamphlet. Carwithen & Analysis—with Short for reference—Papers. Went with Ham[ilto]n to Water Eaton[10] rode a little—conv. with Mr Pusey, on Convocation: dined with Williams, & renewed the subj[ect] in common room. Ham[ilto]n & Harr[iso]n had tea with me. Much time now goes in conversations, yet I hope not unprofitably spent.

[1] Joshua *Toulmin, *Four Discourses on Baptism* (1811).

[2] Charles *Jerram, *Conversations on Infant Baptism and some popular objections against the Church of the United Kingdom* (1819).

[3] Francis Jackson, innkeeper of the King's Head, Newark, seeking payment for £32 election entertainment: see Add MS 44354, ff. 6, 10.

[4] (Sir) Edmund Walker *Head, 1805–68; 8th bart. 1838; fellow of Merton 1830–9; governor-general of Canada 1854–61.

[5] Probably a tract by John *Sinclair, 1797–1875.

[6] Now a northern suburb of Oxford.

[7] Probably William *Sinclair, then at St Mary Hall; and John Badcock of Watlington, Oxfordshire, whose s. Arthur William, b. 1814? was a scholar of Pembroke.

[8] G. W. Doane, at the laying of the cornerstone of a new church at Princeton, N.J., 4 July 1833.

[9] Extracts in Morley, i. 111.

[10] Three and a half miles north of Oxford.

31. Fr.

Breakf. with Rogers. Short, Carwithen, & Analysis. Read "Obss. on Tithes". wrote on them.[1] Wrote to T.G. & Mr Macdowal. Dined with G. Denison at Oriel. Made up accounts &c. papers.

Saturday February 1.

Short, Carwithen, & Analysis—ride & calls. Dined with Harrison—part of my packing—wrote to J.N.G. and Aunt E. A distrusting acct of her bodily health from Mr Rawson.

2. Sunday.

Clerk[2] in mg—Ogilvy aft. finished Jerram's Convv. on Baptism—dined with Hamilton—& in evg had a lecture from Harrison on the Revv—read no 24 of the Tracts.[3] Walk with Lushington & Pugh.[4] Wrote directions to servs—query to B. Square—.

3. M.

Paying bills & packing—breakf. with Brandreth—left at 1½—in London 8½ —went to B[edford] Square by appt; found all well Jane & Mr Tyler seemed very happy.—At night unpacking &c. till late.

4. T.

Further unpacking & arranging—called on Walter Farquhar[5]—read Registration report[6]—& paper. House 2¼–6¾. Speech savoured little of re- form—& dealt rudely, at least, with the Reformers.[7] Wrote to Mr Ramsay —Col. Coles, to inquire about Wallace[8]—T.G.—R.G.—J.N.G.—Aunt J.— dined at Uncle D's to meet Mrs Wadd & Andrew & Divie—house 10¼–11¾. —Debate wonderfully placid, & division little more than nominal.[9]

5. W.

More arranging, books & papers. Calls from Parr & W.H. Larkins—called on Lincoln, Anstice, Doyle, & Mr Hallam—who is about to print some of his son's remains, as I am glad to find. Wrote to R.G.—Mr Macdowal—Mr

---

[1] Perhaps D. Bain, 'Tithes, their origin, and their proper use' (1832).

[2] C. C. Clerke.

[3] 'The Scripture view of the Apostolic Commission'.

[4] John William Pugh, 1810?–52, of Balliol; vicar of Llandilo-Vawr, Glamorgan, 1838.

[5] Sir Walter Rockliff Farquhar, 1810–1900; Eton and Christ Church; 3rd bart. 1836. See Add MS 44155.

[6] PP 1833, xiv. 505.

[7] The king opened the new session; commons debated address in reply to his speech. H xxi. 33.

[8] Robert Bartlett Coles, later lieutenant-general; colonel, 65th. Wallace was the housekeeper's son.

[9] Amendment by *O'Connell, seeking not to deplore Irish repeal agitation, lost 23–189. H xxi. 83.

G.—papers. Read 'Letter to both houses on Dissn petitions &c'[1]—and Messrs Tyler & Hales's evidence on registration.[2] House 6½–8½—discussion on Sheil's business—exceedingly painful viewed with reference to God's law: and much unfairness shown towards Sheil.[3] Wrote out heads of Church Reform.[4]

6. Th.

Morning principally occupied in perusing such of Hallam's letters as I have here. Alas! it is a painful office, they are pleasurable as reviving old recollections—but most painful to me, inasmuch as I can now partially discern how utterly incapable I was of comprehending his mind or meriting any of its affection.—Doyle also with me, on these and his poetry much conv. of melancholy interest. Anstice & A. Acland here. Walk with Doyle. Called on D. of N. and Mrs Cole—at House early:[5] wrote to T.G. & dined at Uncle D's—Mr Tyler there as usual—paper—1st Chap. of the Politics: how full of matter![6]—read V.C's judgmt on the Hewley Case[7]—Dissenter's Memorial (of Glasgow)—& reply, evidently I should think Chalmers's.[8]

7. Fr.

Anstice, Doyle, A. Acland, to breakf. Doyle staid—more conv. of Hallam. Pakenham also here, and Farquhar—each on diff. subjj.—read Tennyson's book—shopping. Wrote to Gaskell—Mrs G—Mr Ramsay—W. Sinclair—Aunt E.[9]—Girdlestone—paper.

8. Sat.

Accts. Journey to Oxf. 9½–4. Shopping there—dined at Merton with Ham[ilto]n. Wrote to Mrs Wallace—wrote in Bl. Book[10]—and read a little Carwithen.

9. Sun.

Two Univ. Serm. & St Peter's (Walker).[11] Round the meadow with Williams

---

[1] A. P. *Perceval, 'A letter to the Members of Both Houses of Parliament on the Dissenters' Petitions' (1834).

[2] *PP* 1833, xiv. 600, 540.

[3] After a three-sided quarrel between *O'Connell, *Althorp, and *Sheil, in which *Sheil's veracity was impugned, he and *Althorp were arrested by the sergeant-at-arms lest they fight a duel. *H* xxi. 119.

[4] Untraced.

[5] Breach of privilege, arising from the quarrel of the previous day: *H* xxi. 150.

[6] Aristotle. And cp. 15 Aug. 34.

[7] Sir Lancelot *Shadwell, 1779–1850, last vice-chancellor of England 1827, gave judgement on 23 December 1833, in *Attorney-General v. Shore*, that unitarians could not benefit under Lady Sarah *Hewley's will (1707).

[8] Untraced.

[9] One sentence in Bassett, 28.

[10] Untraced.

[11] Richard Walker, 1791?–1870, fellow of Magdalen 1821–52, master of Magdalen College School 1828–44.

—dined with him : Common room. Tea & a pleasant conv. with Harr[isso]n. Black book.[1] began Chrysost de Sacerd[otio].[2] & Cecil's Friendly Visit.[3]

10. M.

Chapel—from wh I am sorry to part. Breakfast with Rogers. Bills to pay &c. &c.—packed a box of books—off at 11¼. Arrived at Gerard's Cross, 35 m. (from West's) at 5½. one bait, below Stokenchurch Hill.[4] A nice house— the Bull.[5] Saw my man dressed—read Ar[istotle] Pol[itics] & St Chrys. de Sacerdotio.

11. T.

8–10¾—to the Albany, above 20 m. Many letters accumulated—among others, news of Aunt E. which leads to the expectation that we shall hear of her no more as alive according to the flesh. Live then her Spirit. Wrote to T.G.—Helen—John—Gaskell—Ld Eastnor (about Warwick).[6] House 5¼– 6.[7] Calls given & recd—dined at D. of Hamilton's—a family party.

12. W.

Received the expected intelligence of Aunt E's departure—in the faith and fear of Christ, we trust. May we too die in the Lord—and to this end, live in the Lord.

Wrote to Gaskell—Mrs G.—Mr G.—T.G.—Ld Sandon. finished Cecil's Friendly Visit, a beautiful little book—finished Tennyson's Poems—wrote a paper on ἠθικὴ πίστις[8] in poetry—read paper, & recollections of Robert Hall. Mr Rose[9] here : also Uncle D.—Went to the King's Bench to inquire for Mr C. . . . . le[10]—whom I could not find to be there.[11]

13. Th.

Breakf. in B. Sq.—called on Mrs Cole,[12] OB C[ole], thank God, seems much better by a letter recd this day. With Doyle : long & solemn conversation on *the* doctrine of the Trinity. Papers—began Wardlaw's Chrn Ethics[13]— Wrote to Mr Ramsay—Mrs G.—J.N.G.—Left Cov[entry] St 10 m. bef[ore] 7 by Peveril—Peacock, soon afr 8.[14]

[1] Untraced.
[2] 'On Priesthood', late fourth-century treatise by St. John Chrysostom.
[3] Richard *Cecil, *A Friendly Visit to a House of Mourning* (1792). Extracts in Morley, i. 111.
[4] At the Lambert Arms, at the foot of the Chiltern hanger.
[5] At Gerrard's Cross.
[6] Eastnor urged *Gladstone to oppose a projected radical motion to deprive Lord Warwick (Henry Richard Greville, 1778–1816, 3rd earl 1816) of the lord lieutenancy of his county : see Add MS 44354, ff. 18–23.
[7] Misc. business : *H* xxi. 206.   [8] Sincerity, power to convince.
[9] Peter Rose of Demerara.
[10] Diarist's dots. Perhaps Charles or Thomas Kirk Constable, of Symond's Inn.
[11] Extracts in Morley, i. 111.
[12] Jane Eliza, née Owen, wife of Henry Cole of Adam Street, Adelphi, and mother of O. B. Cole.   [13] R. *Wardlaw, *Christian Ethics* (1834).
[14] Slow travelling : the Peacock was only 3 miles north, in Islington. Extracts in Morley, i. 111.

14.

Upset at 7.20 A.M. 1½ m. S. of Leicester. Thank God, no one hurt. How small was our thankfulness! We went down gradually. God commanded it so. Instead of blessing him for that commandment, we use the fact, its result, to justify our withholding praise from Him to whom it is due.—Delayed 1½ hour. In Manchester 7¼ P.M. Slept at the Star. Read the Ed[inburgh] Presbytery Statement[1]—Sedgwick's 2d Letter[2]—& Scripture at night with Mr Farlong a clergyman & fellow traveller.[3] Inn fair.

15.

7–9 Railway to Lpool. Divers delays in getting to Seaforth. Found the sombre train in waiting. Aunt J. much worn & depressed. She went to the Church. Aunt E. was laid by her holy niece and her aged mother: both we trust with God. "These all died in faith".[4] What more can be said? So may we live in faith, in *the* faith.

Dined at Rns & slept again under his hospitable roof. Wrote to Mrs G— Dr Chalmers—Cole—Lord Eastnor—T.B. Horsfall[5]—read papers, and Lingard. Had a *little* time of thought on our service of today.

I was murmuring at the loss of time on this journey! Very selfishly. And even already it has given me an opportunity of consulting my Father on the Warwick business, which I could not easily have dispensed with.[6]

16. Sunday.

Two Sermm. of Wolfe's[7]—St Andrew's morn & *ev.*: much pleased. At Seaforth with Aunt J. in the interval—dined with her. She will, I trust be sustained: as she has been. Saw the Rawsons—tea at Mr Grant's—left by Mail at 10.20m. P.M.

17. M.

Arrived in London soon after 9 P.M. good travelling: best from Stoney Stratford to town. Met Andrew in the *down* [coach]. Unpacking & arranging —T.G. here to tea.

18. T.

Breakf in B.S.—Shopping—rode—read McNeile's Serm. of 6 Feb. 1834[8]— wrote to Ld Eastnor—Gaskell—Williams—Harrison—Mr G.—House 5¼—

---

[1] Report of proceedings on house rent for ministers' stipends, 24 April 1833.

[2] One of four letters written to the *Leeds Mercury* between January and June 1834, by Adam *Sedgwick, 1785–1873, professor of geology at Cambridge, defending the university against charges of corruption.

[3] Charles Joseph Furlong, 1803?–74?; vicar of Warfield, Berkshire, 1834–60 and minister at Boulogne, 1847–68; author.

[4] Heb. xi. 13.

[5] Thomas Berry Horsfall, merchant, lived at Everton.

[6] Cp. 11 Feb. 34 n.

[7] In J. A. Russell, *Remains of Charles *Wolfe*, the elegist of Sir John *Moore, 2v. (1825).

[8] H. *McNeile on 'Discrimination in Doctrine', Jer. xv. 19.

7—II.

12¼. Voted in 190 to 182! on Pensions Committee.[1]—Arranging papers & pamphlets. Read over the remainder of Hallam's letters. I *hope* I have derived a lesson from this review. I had a friend: but knew not how to use him.

19. W.

Began Les Dix Ans de mon Exil.[2] Read Answer to the Auditors Reports[3]— & Burton on Separation of Church and State[4]—papers—Corinne—Wrote 'Moi' &c. verse & prose.[5] House 5½–6¾.[6] Wrote (there) to Mr G—Mrs G— Aunt J., Robn, Keate.[7] Went to see Mrs Hallam. not remembering at the time, how appropriate was the day.[8] It was a melancholy interview, yet pleasant to me.—Rode.

20. Th.

Read Les Dix Ans—papers—& old compositions of my own—wrote to John, and Mrs Charriere—House 5¼–6½—and 9½–10½—dined at Uncle D.s. —Divers callers. At the Vet[erinar]y College—sad account of my mare. Two divv.[9]

21. Fr.

Les Dix Ans—papers—wrote to Selwyn—Ward—J.N.G.—Girdlestone. Rode. Papers from Sir C. Greville. House 5–7. Then T.G. dined with me—& House 8¾–3 A.M. Voted in 202 to 206 with Lord Chandos—& 161 to 155 with Sir E. Knatchbull.[10] Saw Lord Eastnor & arranged with him. Calls.

22. Sat.

The Mayor & Mr Foster here abt Lpool.—Seymer & Anstice to breakfast— dined at Mrs Cole's, to meet Lady Trench.[11] Wrote to Ld Eastnor—Mr G.— Ch. Ch postman—waggon office—& T. Carson[12]—read pt of Merewether's Address on Warwick[13]—& part of Hallam's Volume of MS. Poems[14]—divers calls.

[1] Libel laws; pensions policy, *H* xxi. 468; 480.
[2] Mme de Staël, *Dix années de mon exil* (1821, written 1810–13), her autobiography.
[3] Untraced.
[4] Edward *Burton, *Thoughts on the Separation of Church and State* (1834).
[5] Untraced.
[6] The house discussed county coroners and rose at 6.15. *H* xxi. 557.
[7] *Keate was worried about railway development near Eton: Add MS 44354, f. 24.
[8] The anniversary of Anne's death.
[9] On amendments to resolution on Irish tithes; both defeated: *H* xxi. 572.
[10] *Chandos drew attention to agricultural distress, and *Knatchbull to an alleged Irish judicial irregularity. *H* xxi. 694, 752. Sir Edward *Knatchbull, 1781–1849; 9th bart. 1819; tory M.P. Kent 1819–30, 1832–45; paymaster-general (in cabinet) 1834–5, 1841–5.
[11] Letitia Susanna, née Dillon, d. 1865; m. 1805 Sir Robert Le Poer Trench, 1782–1824, army colonel, 5th s. of 1st earl of Clancarty.
[12] Thomas Carson, attorney at Seaforth.
[13] Untraced.
[14] See 18 June 34.

23. Sunday.

York St Chapel, & St James. Mr Tallents called. Dind at Uncle D's. Read Bible. Wardlaw—Wolfe—& Benson's Serm. on Maintenance :[1] wrote on the principle of Ethics & other points.[2] Read aloud Wolfe on Gen. I.27.

24. M.

Papers. found Conserv[atives] in Div.1 of Friday, 90—in div.2., 86, or including pairs, 97.—Dix Années—finished Hallam's MS. Poems : with much admiration on my mind. Sir F. Doyle here—also F.—dined at Sir R. Inglis's—Mrs Somervile[3] &c. there. Wrote to Aunt J., Mrs Charriere, & Anstice with books.

25. T.

Paper. Dix Années. Called on Mr Tallents—Mrs Hallam—the Doyles. Saw all. rode with Seymer. House 5½–6½.[4] Dined with T.G.—singing a little—he with me : concocting a scheme for a grand party next week—wrote to Mrs G—Mrs Charriere—Mr Strangford.[5]

26. W.

a busy day—yet of little palpable profit. Mr Rose here—the Mayor of Lpool &c—& Gaskell. Read two important Demerara papers. MS. Comm[itme]nt of Tithes plan, & went over Newark accts. Rode—at the Levee—wrote to Mrs Wishlade, & home to Mr G. House 5½–11. Wished to speak : but deterred by the extremely ill disposition of the House to hear. much sickened at their unfairness in the judicial character ; more still, at my own wretched feebleness & fears. God help me.—Div. 33 to 190.—Tea at Carlton afterwards.[6]

27. Th.

Papers. Dix Années. Rode—several calls—dined with the Lpool gentn. Wrote to Mr G. & J.N.G. House 5–8¾, and 11¾.[7]

28. Fr.

Paper. Arrangements about dinner—also for glass & dinner ware & other matters of furniture. Wrote to Mr G.—R.G.—Mr Tallents—Cole. House

[1] Christopher *Benson, *A Certain and Sufficient Maintenance, the Right of Christ's Ministers* (1834).
[2] Add MS 44820, f. 112.
[3] Mary *Somerville, 1780–1872 ; née Fairfax ; m. 1804 Samuel Grieg (d. 1807) ; re-m. 1812 Dr. William *Somerville (1771–1860) ; scientist, and 'the most remarkable woman of her generation' (*DNB* liii. 255) ; Somerville College named after her.
[4] Irish libel case : *H* xxi. 791.
[5] Charles Stuart Strangford, Trinity College Dublin, friend of the Coles and editor of *Dublin University Magazine*.
[6] Version in Morley, i. 112. The house carried 2° by 38 to 190 the Disfranchisement of Liverpool Freemen bill : *H* xxi. 846, 861.
[7] Repeal of the Malt Duty ; Scottish Church Patronage. *H* xxi. 876 ; 926.

$5\frac{3}{4}$–$12\frac{1}{4}$. Voted in 281 to 45 on Army Ests.[1] Dix Années—Monthly accts. Rn sailed.

Saturday March 1.

Paper—shopping—divers MS. on W.I. matters—wrote to Mr G., Mrs G., R.G.—$\frac{1}{2}$ doz. calls—rode—Finished Vol I of Dix Années—dined at Dr Phillimore's—made up my letters since Jan 1—they grow bulky upon me & henceforward I must adopt a new mode & discriminate.—Wrote herein.[2]

2. Sunday.

St James's. Mr Ward—& the Bp.—Tea with Acland—read Bible—Wolfe (him too aloud)—Wardlaw, & two or three Sermons in 'The Preacher'.[3]

3. M.

Cameron breakfasted with me. conv. with Sir R. I[nglis] on H. of C. Society.—also with Bennet[4] on Liverpool. Papers. Began Mad. de S[taël]'s Essais Dramatiques[5]—"Impressment of Seamen"[6]—dined at Uncle D's— arrangements for tomorrow's dinner—wrote to Mr G—rode—Ancient Music 1st rehearsal—liked much some Choruses and two madrigals.[7]

4. T.

Paper. Essais Dramat.—Interesting Christian Knowledge Meeting, tho' painful too, 1–$4\frac{3}{4}$. House $5\frac{3}{4}$–$6\frac{1}{4}$ to find a *pair* on Impressment.[8]—righting rooms &c. All the B. Sq. party (five), Mr Tyler, & Colin Mackenzie dined here![9] 10 more came in the evg, when we had tea, music, &c. in Tom's rooms! a fête for the marriage of Thursday.

5. W.

Paper. At $7\frac{3}{4}$ in Portman Square—read Rogers, Pl. of Mem[10]—breakf—& off with Lincoln to Eton—There 11–3—saw Keate, Knapp, Mrs Ward,[11] Okes, Chapman[12] &c., & two Selwyns—G. & T.—sorry to come away so

[1] For them: *H* xxi. 963.

[2] '(*Robn sailed*)' here deleted.

[3] *The Preacher, containing sermons by Eminent Living Divines* (1831–5); a weekly paper.   [4] Unidentified.

[5] (1821).

[6] Anonymous pamphlet (1834).

[7] The Concert of Ancient Music, established 1776, performed works more than 20 years old; usually, at this time, by *Handel and Mozart. Last performance 1848.

[8] Later in the evening, *Buckingham's motion against naval impressment was lost, 130–218: *H* xxi. 1063.

[9] Menu in Add MS 44723, f.. 18.

[10] Samuel *Rogers, *The Pleasures of Memory* (1792).

[11] Possibly Emily Elizabeth, da. of Sir J. E. Swinburne, 6th bart.; m. 1824 (Sir) H. G. *Ward; d. 1882.

[12] James Chapman, 1799–1879, assistant master 1822; rector of Dunton-Waylett, Essex, 1834; 1st bp. of Colombo 1845–61; fellow of Eton 1862.

soon. House 6–7$\frac{3}{4}$[1]—dined at D. of Hamilton's—House again 10–12$\frac{1}{2}$[1]—
Ess[ais] Dram[atiques]—wrote to Sir T. Acland.

6. Th.

To the marriage (in col[oure]d clothes) at 9$\frac{1}{4}$—Bp of London performed it.
It is beautiful & touching—Breakf. in B. Square afterwards—also dinner,
chiefly family.[2] Wrote to J.N.G. & Aunt J. Paper—Ess. Dram.—calls—
rode—House 5$\frac{1}{2}$–6$\frac{1}{2}$—and 11–12.[3]

God's blessing we may hope will be on the union formed today: and may
his power defend those who have so lately sailed from its gales.

7. Fr.

Ess. Dram—papers. T.G. & Kelso to breakf.—Anstice & Farquhar to
dinner.—Wrote to Mrs G—T. Finlay—Wm Gladstone—Mr Simpson—H.
Hilton[4]—Sumner—House early: & again 9$\frac{3}{4}$–1. Div[ide]d in 312 to 154 on
the Corn Laws.[5] At Vet[erinary] College again. Analysed Sir J. Graham's
Speech.

8. S.

Finished Essais Dramatiques. Read papers—Tennyson's Speech[6]—wrote
to Robn, Mr Posnett,[7] Mrs Hagart, Williams—rode with T.G. dined at Mr
Marryatt's[8]—Speaker's Levee, and tea at T.G's in evening.

9. S.

Trinity Chapel (Mr Daly)[9] & St. James's (Mr Ward). Walk. Bible—Wardlaw; a sound Christian book—Newman's Arians (began)[10]—Wolfe (one
aloud)—Chrys. de Sacerdotio. Notes on Bible.

10. M.

Breakf. in B. Sq: to hear & sign marriage Settlements. House 12$\frac{1}{2}$–2$\frac{3}{4}$, and
9$\frac{1}{4}$–11$\frac{1}{4}$. Voted in 92 agst 182, agst 2nd reading of the Reading Railway
Bill.[11] Began "Jane Gray".[12] Papers. wrote to Mr Richardson[13]—H.J.G.—
John—dined with T.G.—rode—Gaskell to tea.

[1] Carrickfergus and Stafford Disenfranchisement Bills; Warwick Election Bill. *H* xxi.
1155; 1172; 1177.
[2] J. E. *Tyler's marriage to Jane Robertson, at St. Giles.
[3] Repeal of Corn Laws: *H* xxi. 1195.
[4] Henry Hilton, b. 1811?; at Worcester; rector of Milstead, Kent, 1843–50; canon of
Canterbury 1874.
[5] Motion for lower duty defeated 312–155: *H* xxi. 1266.
[6] C. Tennyson (*D'Eyncourt) on reform, 19 May 1828: *NSH* xix. 780.
[7] Leonard Possnett was the Wesleyan Methodist preacher at Newark 1832–4.
[8] Joseph Marryatt, banker and West Indies proprietor; whig M.P. Sandwich 1826–34;
lived in Richmond Terrace.
[9] In Seymour Street, Portman Square. Robert *Daly, 1783–1872, evangelical preacher;
dean of St. Patrick's 1842, bp. of Cashel 1843.
[10] J. H. *Newman, *The Arians of the Fourth Century* (1833).
[11] Read 2°: *H* xxi. 1352.   [12] Early verse tragedy by Mme de Staël (anon., 1787).
[13] Possibly William Richardson, city solicitor.

11. T.

Dined with the Gaskells. House 6–12½. Voted in 137 to 182 on one of Sir A. Agnew's bills.[1] Rode—went with T.G. to see hotels. Finished Jane Gray—paper—wrote to Mrs Hagart, Scott, T. Finlay, Mrs G., Thomson.

12. W.

Paper. Hunting Mordaunt, for Sir R.I. & why. Took my mare to Mavor's. Rode. Read 'Sophie'—paper—wrote to B. Harrison. House 5½–12. Up several times in Lpool Commee. On the whole gained confidence. Divided in 14 to 116.[2]

13. Th.

Paper. Read 'Some Remarks on Eton'—& Reply. Began writing thereupon.[3] Wrote to Mr G.—Mr Ramsay—Mr Tyler—Read pt of 'Eloge de M. Guibert'[4]—dined at Uncle D.s.—calling &c. corrected Mirror's Reports of what I said last night.[5]

14. Fr.

House 12¼–1¼ and 8¼–12¾. Voted in 227 to 94 agst abolition of Military Flogging.[6] Finished Eloge de M. Guibert; contined the smaller pieces: pt of Bp Exeter's Charge[7]—wrote to Franceys—inv. from Sir R. Peel for Sunday (23d) to my regret.[8]

15. Sat.

Paper. Black book[9]—divers calls. Wrote to Aunt J.—Mr Bartlett—B. Harrison. Read Madame de Stael. & finished Bp of Exeter's very able charge. Dined at the Speaker's: about 36, Tories: but Cripps & Sir C. Burrell included.[10] Canvassed some for the Lpool 3d reading.

16.

Breakf. in B. Sq.—St Giles's—& St James's: Bp preached for Nat[ional] Schools. Acland to dinner & tea. Read Bible—Wolfe—Wardlaw—Slade on

[1] Bill to enable local authorities to alter the days of fairs and markets; lost 181 to 137. *H.* xxii. 61.
[2] *H* xxii. 104, 108, 115.
[3] *Some Remarks on the Present Studies and Management of Eton School*, by a parent (1834); and *A Few Words in Reply to 'Some Remarks'*, by 'Etoniensis' (1834).
[4] Mme de Staël [1790].
[5] *Mirror*, i. 681, 683, 685.
[6] *H* xxii. 193, 221.
[7] Henry *Phillpotts, *Charge Delivered to the Clergy of the Diocese of Exeter, by the Bishop of Exeter at his Primary Visitation*, (1833).
[8] Cp. Hammond and Foot, *Gladstone and Liberalism*, 15.
[9] Untraced.
[10] Joseph Cripps, d. 1843?, whig M.P. for Cirencester 1807–41; Sir Charles Merrick Burrell, 1774–1862, 3rd bart. 1796; east India proprietor; M.P. for Shoreham from 1806; paired in favour of reform bill.

the Psalms[1]—part of Pusey on Fasting (liked it extremely)[2]—wrote in Bl. BB.[3]

17.

Paper—Parl. papers—wrote to Mr G. & J.N.G.—Mad. de Stael—Ancient Music rehearsal. House $5\frac{1}{4}$–$2\frac{1}{4}$.[4]

18. T.

De Stael. finished Vol.III (save the Denouement of Delphine) began Memorie di Silvio Pellico[5]—Poor Law Report—paper—wrote to Mary Anne—Mrs Hagart—Mr G—J.N.G.—Williams. House $5\frac{1}{2}$–9. Shall we not have warm work on the Church after Easter?[6] Tea with the Gaskells.

19.

Paper. Maroncelli.[7] Wrote to Finlay—Mr Astley[8]—J.N.G.—House & Commee $12\frac{1}{2}$–3 and 6–$12\frac{1}{2}$. Spoke on Lpool Freeman's Bill—(& voted in 63 to 120 and 52 to 109) most unsatisfactorily.[9]

20.

Paper. Went to Trinity Chelsea—Mr Blunt[10] preached; both my Aunt & I liked the sermon extremely. Joh. VI.37.—House & Commees $1\frac{1}{2}$ $4\frac{1}{4}$.[11] An evening at home. Read A Dissrs Letter to the King[12]—Maroncelli—& Poor Law Rept.[13] Wrote to Kynaston—Mr G—Miss J. Mackenzie[14]—Sir H. Verney.

[1] J. *Slade, An Explanation of the Psalms as read in the Liturgy of the Church (S.P.C.K. 1832).
[2] E. B. *Pusey, 'Thoughts on the benefits of the system of fasting, enjoined by our Church', Tracts for the Times, no. 18.
[3] Untraced.
[4] Slavery Abolition Act; Malt Tax; Russian and Turkish Treaties. H xxii. 280, 284, 307.
[5] S. Pellico, Le mie prigioni (1832), celebrated account of a suspected carbonaro's captivity.
[6] Church rates: H. xxii. 381.
[7] P. Maroncelli, Addizioni alle mie prigioni (1833), further notes by Pellico's gaol companion.
[8] Probably Francis Bickley Astley, b. 1782, 3rd b. of 1st bart.; rector of Manningford Abbots, Wiltshire, 1810; had Warwickshire connexions.
[9] The bill passed: H xxii. 468, 474, 480. Notes for speech in Add MS 44649, ff. 47–51.
[10] Henry *Blunt, 1794–1843; vicar of Clare, Suffolk, 1819–32; of Trinity Church, Sloane Street, Chelsea, 1832–6; rector of Streatham, Surrey, 1835–43; writer and eminent preacher.
[11] Liverpool corn laws petition: H xxii. 482.
[12] Josiah *Conder, The Design of the Dissenters, a Letter to the King (1834).
[13] PP 1834 xxvii.1.
[14] Jane, da. of (Sir) Colin Mackenzie (cr. bart. 1836); m. 1853 James Wardlaw, of co. Ross, who d. 1867.

21.

Paper. House & Commee[1] 1–2¼ and 5¼–7.[2] Read Maroncelli—Poor Law Report—Parnell's Chap. on the W.I. Sugar Duties &c[3]—& 'Lay of the Last Minstrel' afresh. Wrote to H.J.G.—Lincoln here.

22.

Paper. Harr[isso]n & Lushington to br[eakfast]. Long conv. with the former on tithe &c. ride—calls—wrote to Mrs Hagart—Mr Bartlett—Mr G.— J.N.G.—dined at Glee Club[4]—musical party at the Doyle's in evg.—read a little Maroncelli & corrected part of Mirror Report. Began morning prayers.

23.

All Saints. (Dr. Chandler):[5] called on Mrs Cole. St James's—Mr Ward. Tupper to tea. Finished Wolfe: read most of Stanhope's Holy Week.[6] & Uffizio della Domenica delli Palmi.

24.

Finished Stanhope—Lunedi Santo—Maroncelli—paper—wrote to Mr G— House & Commee 12½–3½, & 5¼–7.[7] St Giles's—& tea in B. square. T.G. & Seymer to breakf. Hope & J. Ley to dinner. Finished correcting speech for Mirror.[8]

   2. Externality of criteria—
   3. Indisp[ensable] to sink into those relations wh God has preconstituted for us—e.g. church religion—family religion.

There is danger when we are led to fix our thoughts on possession, rather than use. Here one peril arising from money's becoming the basis of all relations: because it has no intrinsic value.   21.

It is true that we have hitherto seen but too often the principle of intellectual excellence & the spirit of religious zeal in collision rather than in harmony, but let us hope that it may be otherwise, even as the elements of fire and water, which of old never wrought together save in the fatal con-

---

[1] '1½' here deleted.
[2] Liverpool petition on free trade: *H* xxii. 522.
[3] Sir H. B. *Parnell *On Financial Reform* (4 ed., 1832), ch. xv.
[4] A society founded in 1787, which met at the Freemason's Tavern. Motets, glees and canons were sung after dinner.
[5] George Chandler, 1779–1859, rector of All Souls, St. Marylebone, 1825; dean of Chichester 1830.
[6] George *Stanhope, *A Paraphrase and Comment upon the Epistles and Gospels appointed to be used in the Church of England* (1705–8); from which was taken *The Holy Week*, 1828.
[7] Cambridge Petition on Dissenters' Grievances: *H* xxii. 569.
[8] The following passage was written from the other end of the page.

currency of inundation and volcano, now are blended to accelerate the passage of man over the wide ocean.   25.[1]

Strait between the
inward & the outward
thoughts & deeds.
bridged over March
25. 1834.
WEG.

δ.τ.Θ.[2]

---

[1] Next seven lines at right angles to the rest.
[2] δόξα τῷ Θεῷ, glory be to God. Cp. Morley, i. 189.

[VOLUME VIII][1]

March 25, 1834–Sept 30, 1835.

March 1834.

25.

Tuesday in Passion Week.

"Martedi Santo"—Maroncelli—papers—House & Commee $12\frac{1}{2}$–$4\frac{1}{4}$.[2] dinner in B[edford] Square. St Giles's Church. Wrote to Aunt J., Mr G., Wason,[3] J.N.G.

26.

"Mercoledi Santo", read—Maroncelli—paper—began Sewell on Admn of Dissrs[4]—House $12\frac{1}{4}$–$3\frac{1}{4}$.[5] Rode to Clapham. Dined at Nicholl's.[6] Wrote on the Lord's Supper.[7]

27.

Part only of "Giovedi Santo". Maroncelli—papers—Sewell—Quarty on Adam Clarke's life—dined with the Doyles. Rode to Charterhouse &c— Wrote to Mrs G. and J.N.G.—read to servv. before prayers some of what I had written. Hope came to breakfast.

28.

Sac[ramen]t 8 A.M.—St James's mg: Bp of London. St Giles's evg (dinner with Uncle D.)–part of 'Venerdi Santo'—wrote briefly home & to T.G.— read paper—W.I. letters. Raikes (began)[8]—Sewell (finished)—wrote in bl. book.

29.

paper—Maroncelli—rode—summoned two hackney coachmen[9]—began Doyle's Poems—part of 'Sabato Santo'. singing lesson from Cittadini[10]—

---

[1] Lambeth MS 1422. 53 ff.   [2] University tests: *H* xxii. 623.
[3] Peter Rigby Wason, 1799–1875, of Ayrshire; whig M.P. for Ipswich 1831–37, 1841; prominent in recent Liverpool debates.
[4] W. *Sewell, 'Letter on the Admission of Dissenters to the University of Oxford' (1830).
[5] University tests. *H* xxii. 674.
[6] At 28 Curzon Street, with Dr. John Nicholl, 1797–1853, s. of the judge*; Peelite M.P. Cardiff 1832–53; whip 1835; judge advocate general 1841–6.
[7] Untraced.
[8] H. *Raikes, 'Remarks on Clerical Education' (1831) or one of his sermons.
[9] See 4 Apr. 34.   [10] A singing-master.

he & Gaskell to tea—spoke to Wallace about Sac[ramen]t & found him anxious: thank God. Wrote to Aunt J.—J.N.G.—&c.

30.

Sacrament at 8. St Philip's mg. Mr Harvey.[1] St James's aft—Mr Gay.[2] dined with Uncle D.—wrote in Bible & Bl. b.—read Pearson on Resurrn &c[3]—Sumner (aloud)—3 Sermm. of Paley's, which seem to have great merits & serious defects: not (I thought) fit for the Chr. Kn. List as they are—"Domenica della Risurrezione"—finished Pusey on Fasting.

Mar 31.

lesson with Cittadini—papers—wrote to M'Dowal—J.N.G.—Mr S. Mackenzie—Raby—at Horse Guards for Withers[4]—began Prideaux on Tithes[5] —& Helen[6]—finished Maroncelli—Dined at Sir R. Inglis's—met Ld. Sidmouth,[7] Bp Philpotts, Sir R. Peel—Mr Hallam with Moberly[8] & others. A very interesting party, delightful listening after dinner.

Tuesday Ap. 1.

Paper—began Schlegel's Tempest—Prideaux. Helen, which I find very heavy—wrote to Sir J. Macdonald—dined at Sir R. Peel's. Herries,[9] Sir G. Murray,[10] Chantry,[11] &c. Sir R.P. very kind in his manner to us.[12] Went to see Luigi's prints &c.—Doyle's poems.[13]

2. W.

Moberley to Breakft—Cittadini (3)—Hallam's Const. Hist.—wrote to Caparn, Allen, Williams—dined in B[edford] Square—Read Helen—

---

[1] Chapel in Waterloo Place. Richard Harvey, 1798–1889; *Shelley's fag at Eton; rector of Hornsey 1829–80; canon of St. Paul's 1843, of Gloucester 1858.

[2] William Gay, 1801?–46, rector of Bidborough, Kent, 1830.

[3] Article v of John *Pearson's *Exposition of the Creed* (1659).

[4] No doubt pursuing some untraced money trouble.

[5] Humphrey *Prideaux, *Original and Right of Tithes* (1710).

[6] Maria *Edgeworth's last novel (1834).

[7] Henry *Addington, 1757–1844; speaker 1789; prime minister 1801; resigned 1804; cr. Viscount Sidmouth 1805; in cabinet 1812–24, notorious advocate of repression; tory elder statesman.

[8] George *Moberley, 1803–85; fellow of Balliol 1826–34; headmaster of Winchester 1835–66; bp. of Salisbury 1869; high churchman.

[9] John Charles *Herries, 1778–1855, tory administrator; held financial posts 1801–27; M.P. Harwich 1823–41, Stamford 1847–53; chancellor of exchequer 1827–8; president, board of control 1852.

[10] Sir George *Murray, 1772–1846, general; fought in Flanders, Egypt, and Denmark 1793–1807; senior staff officer under *Wellington; M.P. for Perthshire 1823–32 and 1834; colonial secretary 1828–30.

[11] (Sir) Francis Leggatt *Chantry, 1781–1842, sculptor; son of a Sheffield carpenter; carved most great Englishmen of his day; knighted 1835.

[12] Extract in Morley, i. 112.

[13] (Sir) F. H. *Doyle, *Miscellaneous Verses* (1834).

Sewell's 2nd letter[1]—Doyley's on Church Rate[2]—Taylor's on Lord's Day.[3]

3. Th.

Paper—Hallam Ch.IX—Schlegel's Tempest—Helen (finished Vol 2)—rode with Bruce—Cittadini in Eveng—arranged dinner for Saturday—calls—wrote to H.J.G.

4. Fr.

Paper—Diss[entin]g Min[iste]rs Letter to Lord Grey[4]—part of "Trades Unions"[5]—wrote in bl. b. on Church Rates—rode—wrote to Mr Macdowal —Cittadini—Blakesley here—dined with Walter Farquhar—at Police Office, settled my business quietly—remained (by advice) to hear a horrid charge—read Oxf. Mag. on Shelley.[6]

5. Sat.

Breakf. in B. Square—wrote to R.G.—Williams—and Mr G. Rode. Read Prideaux—paper—der Sturm[7]—had Saunders. G. Denison, F. Bruce,[8] Chr. Wordsworth, Doyle, & T.G., to dine.[9]

6. Sunday.

Trin. Chapel, Mr Beamish, mg. Sacrament—only about 35—and Margaret St, Mr Dodsworth, evening. Walk—Wood dined with me—wrote, in Bible, & on Sac[ramen]t. Read Blunt on the Lord's Supper[10] (also aloud)—Homily on Do. Rose's Div. Lecture[11] & Wilson's letter on Chr. Knowl. Society.[12]

7. M.

Ward, J. Moncreiff, T.G., to breakfast. Anc. Mus. Rehearsal—dined at Mr Hallam's—rode—paper. Prideaux—& Lorimer's 1st pamphlet on reln in America.[13] Wrote to Allen—J.N.G.—Mr Finlay.

[1] W. *Sewell 'A second letter to a Dissenter on the opposition of the University of Oxford to the Charter of the London College' (1834).
[2] George *D'Oyley, 'A letter to . . . Earl *Grey on . . . Church Rates' (1834).
[3] C. B. Tayler, 'The Lord's Day' (1830).
[4] 'A letter to Earl *Grey containing a vindication of the Established Church and remarks on the claims of the Dissenters', by a Dissenting Minister (1834).
[5] Trades' Unions and Strikes (1834).
[6] Oxford University Magazine, i. 3 (1834).
[7] Schlegel's translation of The Tempest.
[8] (Sir) Frederick William Adolphus *Bruce, 1814–67; 4th s. of 7th earl of *Elgin; minister in Washington 1865–7.
[9] Menu in Add MS 44723, f. 18.
[10] Henry *Blunt, Two Discourses upon the Sacrament of the Lord's Supper (1825).
[11] Hugh James *Rose, 'An Apology for the Study of Divinity' (1834).
[12] Possibly 'Clericus Kensingtonensis', 'A Letter to the . . . Bishop of London, on the Present state of the S.P.C.K.' (1834).
[13] J. G. Lorimer, 'The Past and Present Conditions of Religion and Morality in the United States of America: an Argument for Established Churches' (1834).

8. T.

Robt G., Murray G., & W. Irlam, to breakfast—paper—Prideaux—Lorimer Trade's Unions (finished)—wrote to Mr G—Chr. Knowl. Soc. 1–4¼.—rode. attempted to resume my "Braut von Korinth" transl.

9. W.

paper—Schlegel—Prideaux—Lorimer—rode—dined with Colin Mackenzie —calls—wrote to Lincoln & Mr G.—& in Bl. b. Perused Sir R. Inglis's Speech in MS.[1]

10. Th.

J.N.G. came—he & T.G. to breakfast—dined at Mr Williams's—Mr Dodsworth there—he expounded & prayed.—A long time in the Brit. Instittn —pleasure & the reverse.[2] Prideaux—finished Lorimer—paper—wrote to Mr G.—rode.

11. Fr.

dined at Mr Harrison's. paper. Schlegel's Hamlet—finished Prideaux— began Selden.[3] wrote to Rn G. and Parker.

12. Sat.

Breakf. with T.G.—paper—wrote to Aunt J. and Mrs G—rode—dined with Cumming Bruce[4]—read Selden on Tithes, & Schlegel's Hamlet.

13. Sun.

Trin. Chap. mg & aft. Mr Philips[5] & Mr Mosley.[6] Bible—Wardlaw—Newman's Arians—Blunt on Lord's Supper, aloud—Scougal's Life of God[7] abridged, through.—wrote.

14. M.

T.G. & J.N.G. to breakf. dined with T.G.—Glasgow Lottery Comm. 12¼– 3½[8]—and voted agst the St Pancras Bill[9]—at Peel's in evg. Did a very absurd thing in speaking to him: as usual. paper—Selden—Schlegel's Hamlet—Began Wolfe Vol 1.[10] Wrote to Mr G—and Mr Finlay.

---

[1] In favour of retaining university tests, 26 March 1834. *H* xxii. 674.
[2] Public gallery in Pall Mall.   [3] John *Selden, *History of Tithes* (1618).
[4] Charles Lennox Cumming-Bruce, 1790–1874, of Kinnaird, Perthshire; tory M.P. for Inverness 1818–26, 1833–7, and for Elginshire 1840–68; minor office 1852; his da. Elizabeth Mary, d. 1843, m. in 1841 James *Bruce, 8th earl of Elgin.
[5] Probably George *Phillips, 1804–92, orientalist; wrangler 1829; priest 1832; president of Queen's, Cambridge, 1857.
[6] Henry *Moseley, 1801–72, mathematician; wrangler 1826; priest 1828; professor, King's College London, 1831; inspector of schools 1844; canon of Bristol 1853.
[7] H. *Scougal, *Life of God in the soul of man* (1677).
[8] *PP* 1834 xviii. 87, 91; *Inglis in the Chair.
[9] St. Pancras paving bill rejected 2° by 35 to 29: *Mirror*, ii. 1013.
[10] Cp. 16 Feb. 34.

15. T.

paper—Letter on Hand Loom Weavers[1]—Selden—Wolfe. House 5.40–6.55[2]—dined at Mr Lyall's—rode—calls. wrote to H.J.G.—& on Ld Warwick's case some notes.[3]

16. Wed.

paper, & Tithe Debate &c. rode—wrote to Mr Bartlett—read, Wolfe—Rose on prevalent opns towards Christianity[4]—Schlegel's Hamlet—and Selden—Mordaunt dined with me meaning to go to the House: but there was none: he staid the evening.

17. Th.

T.G. & J.N.G. to breakf. Read Selden—Wordsworth's pamphlet[5]—wrote to T. Hagart—T. Finlay—Mr Crombie (Aberdeen)[6]—Commee 12–3,[7] and House 5¼–1¼—voted in miserable division on Univv.[8]

18. Fr.

A day of disturbance—placing, & filling, my new bookcase. Paper—Selden—Wolfe—dined at Lady M'Kenzie's—sang a little—went to Carlton—read Quart. on Fr. Drama—to the House at midnight; finding to my sorrow & surprise that the Irish Estt. had come on, & the Educn vote passed.[9] Wrote to Mr G.

19. Sat.

Paper—Selden—Wolfe (finished his Remains). Rode. several Nos of the Pioneer[10]—by favour of Mrs Mundy—rode—dined at Lincoln's Inn—read a Volume of 'Paris & London'; personal, licentious, & not very interesting.[11] J.N.G. to tea. Wrote to Mrs G.

20. Sund.

Trin. Mr Phillips.—& St James's—the Bp. Dined at Lincoln's Inn. read Bible—Wardlaw—Rose's Sermons—Massillon's 1st sur une profession religieuse—one of Girdlestone's aloud—some Bible notes.

---

[1] Untraced.
[2] Status of Berwick-on-Tweed: *Mirror*, ii. 1045.
[3] Cp. 11 Feb. 34 n.
[4] Probably Hugh James *Rose, *The Tendency of Prevalent Opinions about knowledge considered* (1826); but see 17 May 34 n.
[5] Christopher *Wordsworth, 'On the Admission of Dissenters to Graduate in the University of Cambridge. A letter to the Right Hon. Viscount *Althorp, M.P.' (1834).
[6] Lewis Crombie, Aberdeen advocate.
[7] Glasgow lotteries.
[8] Leave to bring in a bill to abolish university tests was given by 185 to 44: *H* xxii. 928.
[9] Cttee of supply, Irish estimates: *H* xxii. 965.
[10] *The Christian Pioneer* (Glasgow, 1826–45).
[11] J. T. Trueba y Cosió, *Paris and London*, 3v. (1831), a novel.

21. M.

Immense procession of Unionists—no accident, thank God![1] As also that events *in* the House of Commons were more propitious than we could hope. *He* is gracious. Glasgow Comm. 12–3—House 5.45–6.45 and 10–1. Voted in 5 divisions. 256 to 140 on Church Rates[2]—264 to 137 on the same—and 109 to 143 on Hertford—two others on the same.[3] J.N.G. & Mr Furlong to breakf—dined at Sir S. Scott's—read Selden & paper—wrote to Mr G.

22. T.

paper[4]—"the Pioneer" more Nos from Mrs Mundy—Wrote to Mr Simpson —and Aunt J.—The travellers arrived at 3—dined with them. Glasgow Lott. (Exam[inin]g Minutes & commee) $11\frac{1}{2}$–$3\frac{3}{4}$. House 5–6—and $8\frac{1}{2}$–$11\frac{3}{4}$.[5] The Wilsons & J.N.G. to breakfast.

23. W.

paper—Selden. Endeavouring to arrange for Wallace. Dined at Unc. D's. Anc[ient] Music afterwards—very delightful. Grisi sang.[6] Wrote to Mrs Wishlade. Rode. read Helen Vol.3—abler. Went out of mourning. Carlton, on Lpool business.

24. Th.

paper. Selden. Rose. Glasgow L. Comm. 12–4. House $10\frac{3}{4}$–$1\frac{1}{2}$. voted in 14 and 9 agst For. Enl. Act. repeal and Jews.[7] Dined at Uncle D's. Wrote to Hamilton. Pakenham Phillimore & J.N.G. to breakfast.

25. Fr.

Wrote to Lushington—& W. Duke, of Newark.[8] Papers—calls. dined at Linc. Inn—read a Chap. on the Spanish Church[9]—& 'Bubbles from Brunnens'.[10] Tea at Bailey's.[11] Rode. Arranged to take Best[12] from J.N.G.—Long conv. with Mrs G. House $9\frac{3}{4}$–3. Splendid speech from Peel.[13] Wilberforce here—he & G. Ryder are to be married.[14]

---

[1] Some 30,000 trade unionists processed through the west end to the home office, bearing a petition that deplored the transportation of six Dorsetshire labourers (the 'Tolpuddle martyrs') for administering illegal union oaths.   [2] 'and' here deleted.

[3] Resolved by 256 to 140 to abolish church rates, reaffirmed by 263 to 136; Hertford borough bill, extending borough boundaries, read 3°—*Peel's attempt to retain boundaries lost by 109 to 143, and *Evans's to establish ballot by 82 to 182. *H* xxii. 1060, 1076.

[4] 'Selden' here deleted.   [5] Union with Ireland: ibid. 1090.

[6] Giulia Grisi, 1811–69, Italian soprano prima donna.

[7] Foreign enlistment act repeal bill, 2°, 65–14; leave to discuss civil disabilities of Jews, 53–9. *H* xxii. 1371, 1373.

[8] Unidentified.   [9] A tract?

[10] [F. B. *Head] *Bubbles from the Brunnens of Nassau* (1834).

[11] i.e. at Hatchett's hotel in Piccadilly.   [12] A manservant.

[13] Favouring continued union with Ireland. *H* xxiii. 69.

[14] H. W. *Wilberforce and George Dudley Ryder, 1810–80, nephew of 2nd earl of *Harrowby, convert to Rome 1846, married sisters, Mary and Sophia Lucy, das. of John Sargent, rector of Lavington; their eldest sister Emily had m. S. *Wilberforce in 1828, and Caroline another sister m. H. E. *Manning in 1833. Cp. H. Sumner, *Life of C. R. *Sumner* (1876), 231.

26. Sat.

Best's service began. Bubbles—Bp. of Exeter's Speech[1]—paper—wrote to Pusey[2]—calls—dined at Mrs Denison—Justice J. Park's afterwards[3]—wrote to Mayor of Lpool—& a paper of conditions for Best. Some thought on the Univ. quest. which will require much if I am to speak[4] on it.

27. Sunday.

Trinity. Mr Beamish & Mr Murray. Dined at Lincoln's Inn—tea at Bailey's —Wardlaw—Newman—Rose's Sermons—Hall on the Holy Spirit[5]—read one of Girdlestone's on Sact aloud—wrote upon it—Bible.

28. M.

Paper. Selden. calls. ride. "bubbles from the brunnans". House (Gl. Lott.) 12–3½–& late in evg.[6] Dined with Gaskell. At Bailey's. Wrote to Mr Stewart—& Mr Ramsay.

29. T.

Paper. Selden. finished 'Bubbles'. Schlegel's Hamlet. Tea in B[edford] Square. Temperance (Assn) Report.[7] Calls on Lady Canning & others. House 10¾–1¾. Div[ide]d in 523:38 on Repeal [of Irish union]—and 100 to 15 for introducing a Beer Bill.[8] Rode. Arranged dinner for Thursday.

30. W.

Breakf. with T.G. paper. Selden. rode. House 5–11¾. Div[ide]d in 125:161 for 2d reading of Sir A. Agnew.[9] Schlegel's Hamlet. Accounts—& letters.

Thursday May One.

Papers. Selden. G.L. Commee 12¼–2¾.[10] Mr G., J.N.G., Mr Monteith,[11] Mr Tallents to dinner—others asked, but did not come.[12] Rode. In B. Square twice—wrote to B. Price. Read a little of "Eustace Conway".[13]

---

[1] *H* xxii. 997, 21 April 1834, on Cambridge petition against dissenters.
[2] Cp. *Liddon, *Pusey, i. 293–4.
[3] Sir James Alan *Park, 1763–1838, protégé of *Mansfield; K.C. 1799; common pleas judge 1816; lived at 32 Bedford Square. Altered from 'Parke': cp. 17 Jan. 35.
[4] 'Worth[ily]' here deleted.
[5] Robert *Hall, *On the Work of the Holy Spirit* (1809).
[6] Repeal of union debated: *H* xxiii. 127.
[7] Untraced.
[8] *H* xxiii. 286, 294.
[9] Sir Andrew *Agnew (1793–1849, 7th bart. 1809, M.P. Wigtonshire 1830–7) moved 2° Lord's day observance bill. *H* xxiii. 314.
[10] He took the chair (*PP* 1834 xviii. 189–92).
[11] Henry Monteith, d. 1848; of Carstairs near Lanark; M.P. Falkirk burghs 1820–6, 1830–1.
[12] Menu in Add MS 44723, f. 18v.
[13] A 3v. novel [by F. D. *Maurice, 1834].

2.

Paper—Began 'Essays on the Church'[1] & 'Becher's anti-pauper system'.[2] Interview with Mr Tallents 11½–Chr. Knowl. Soc. 12¾–3½—rode to Clapham —wrote to Mr S. Wilberforce & Mr Rawson—House 5½–6¼ & 10–2—voted in 241 to 74 on Irish Tithes[3]—tea at Thomas's. Providentially, matters were most amicably arranged at the Chr. Knowledge meeting.

3.

Seymer to breakf. Mrs G., H.J.G., T.G., J.N.G. to lunch. with D. of N. about Newark; he approves of my going. Dined with the Tuppers[4]—a little singing. Bailey's thrice. Read Essays on the Church & (finished) Becher's Anti-pauper system—paper. Rode with J.N.G.—& bade him a reluctant farewell. Wrote to Steuart G.

4.

Trin. mg & aft. At Uncle D.s—tea in Berkeley Square—finished writing on Sact. Read one of Girdlestone's aloud—Rose's Sermm—Newman—Mr Beamish preached zealously for the Church & public worship. But it seems to me as if it might have been shown more as a primary function of the Church of Christ, & necessary result & condition of membership. Sacrament.

5. M.

Mayow & Tupper to breakfast. 'Essays on the Church' & Moberley's pamphlet.[5] Paper. Wrote to Wilberforce—J.N.G.—Mr Monteith—Mr Stewart. House 12–2½, 5¾–7½, 10–1¼. Voted in 390 to 148, and 311 to 230.[6] Rode—tea in B. Square.

6. Tuesday.

Cardwell—Rob. G—Suth[erlan]d, to breakfast. B. Square twice. Selden, & Essays on the Church. House & Comm. 12–3.[7] Dined at D. of Newcastle's. Reports of Mr G's standing for Leith.[8] Wrote to Caparn—& Monteith—rode —calls.

7. W.

Selden (finished)—Essays on the Church—Schlegel's Hamlet. House 4¾–6½[9]

---

[1] Also anonymous (1833).

[2] J. T. *Becher, *The anti-pauper system* (1828) on poor relief in Nottinghamshire.

[3] To continue debate: *H* xxiii. 471.

[4] M. F. *Tupper's parents; he did not marry till 1835.

[5] George *Moberley, 'A Few Remarks on the Proposed Admission of Dissenters into the University of Oxford' (1834).

[6] Dissenters' petitions, *H* xxiii. 505; and against inquiry into royal pension list, *H* xxiii. 584.

[7] Petitions on Irish Church: *H* xxiii. 622. And Glasgow lotteries, preliminary report.
[8] Nothing in them.   [9] General register bill, rejected 2°: *H* xxiii. 696.

8--ii.

—rode—calls—paper—Ancient Music Concert with Mrs & H.J.G.—wrote to Wilberforce—Mr Ramsay—Harrison—Mr Burnaby—Mr Finlay—J.N.G.

8. Th.

paper. Essays on the Church, finished—Excursion, Bb. 4 and 5. analysis of Prideaux on Tithes—Schlegel's Hamlet—rode—singing—copied two letters —wrote to R.G. & to Hicklin. House 5½–6 only.[1] St James's with H.J.G. Mr Wigram[2] preached.

9. Fr.

Copied two letters. began Macneile on the Church.[3] rode. wrote to B. Harrison. House 8.40–12.15. voted in 319:20 for 2nd reading of Poor Law Bill.[4] At Festival of the Sons of the Clergy. 3h.¾–12. waiting. 1–5¾. The music very fair: but on the whole I was rather induced to suspect that the Bp of London's opinion was right.

10. Sat.

Williams & Pusey here about Univ. pettn.[5] Calls—rode—paper—Analysis of Prideaux—Shelley—began Crabbe's Life[6]—at riding school with H.J.G. —Dinner & evg. with them—thought & wrote on Univ. Adm[issio]n Bill.

11.

Trinity m. & aft. walk with H.J.G. Tea at Bailey's. Read Bible—Newman —Macneile—Hervey's Life[7]—a Girdlestone Serm. aloud.—Rose.

12. M.

House 12–3. (Two petitions) & 11¾–1.[8]—read Gibbon's Ch.XV—Rose on the spread of Christ[ianit]y[9]—paper—Br. Critic on "Internal State of the Church".[10] Wrote to J.N.G.—Dry—Sumner.

---

[1] Repeal of the union: *H* xxiii. 753.

[2] Joseph Cotton *Wigram, 1798–1867, wrangler 1820; assistant preacher at St. James's 1827; rector of East Tisted, Hampshire, 1839; of St. Mary's, Southampton, 1850; bp. of Rochester 1860.

[3] Hugh *McNeile, 'Letter to a Friend who Has Felt it his duty to Secede from the Church of England' (1834).

[4] *H* xxiii. 842.

[5] See n. 8 below.

[6] By his son and namesake George, in an edition of his poems (1834).

[7] John Brown, *Life of the Rev. James *Hervey* (1832).

[8] He presented petitions against the universities' admission bill from members of the universities of Oxford and Cambridge, and from the gentry of Newark. Late at night, Central Criminal Courts Bill: *H* xxiii. 860, 878.

[9] Henry John *Rose, tr. J. A. W. Neander *History of the Christian Religion and Church during the First Three Centuries*, 2v. (1831).

[10] xiii. 465 (April 1833), reviewing John *Sinclair, *Dissertations* cp. 5 Oct. 34.

13. T.

paper. Gibbon Ch.XVI—Rose—they contrast well. Schlegel's Hamlet—wrote to Aunt J. & H.J.G.—dined at Uncle D.s—singing in evg. Met Mr Richardson.

14. W.

Rose—Mr Barnes's 'Appeal'—Mr B.[1] & Mr Swan[2] with me 1½ hour or more on the subject. Rode & dined with Gaskell. Wrote to Dr Burton—Tallents—Burnaby—House 6–6¾, and 10–3. Divided in 37:60 against Commee on Rel. Ass. Bill at 1¾ A.M. a painful business.[3] paper—in B. Square.

15. Th.

Rob. & W.G., & Barnes, to breakft.—paper—Rose—Schlegel—walked with H.J.G.—dined in Bedf. Square—house before—& again 10½–11¾—voted in 235:185 on shortening parlts—abt 85 tories.[4] Wrote to Williams (Rev. J.)—Williams (A.)—Freshfield—Stanford[5]—J.N.G.—began to write a paper for D.U.M.[6]

16. Fr.

paper. proceedings of Manch[este]r Diss[ente]rs meeting[7]—Schlegel's Hamlet. House 7¼–9¼. voted in 157 to 27 for Beer Bill.[8] rode—continued my paper for D.U.M.—wrote to Sumner—in B. Square—Mrs Wilson Patten's musical party at night. A cram, in an oven.[9] Lady Lansdown's afterwards: home pretty early. Picture hanging.—Doyle's sister to be married.[10]

17. Sat.

paper. Schlegel's Hamlet. Rose. 'Prevg Opinions'.[11] calls: on the Doyles to congratulate. rode. wrote to Stanford—D.M. Peter[12]—A. Williams—Harri-

[1] Ralph Barnes, 1781–1869, attorney and author; secretary to bps. of Exeter, 1830; wrote 'An Appeal to the People of England on the Proposed Transfer of all Testamentary Business to London' (1834).

[2] Robert Swan, legal author.

[3] Poor law bill in cttee., *H* xxiii. 952. Religious assemblies bill committed, on a division ibid. 1006.

[4] Tennyson (*D'Eyncourt)'s bill to shorten parliaments rejected, ibid. 1087.

[5] John Frederick Stanford, 1815–80; Etonian; F.R.S. 1844; Peelite M.P. Reading 1849–52.

[6] Draft political article for *Dublin University Magazine*, unpublished, in Add MS 44681, ff. 12–28.

[7] On 5 March 1834, to adopt petition to commons (*Times*, 10 March, 3).

[8] Read 2°. *H* xxiii. 1135.

[9] Anna Maria Patten-Bold, m. 1828 her cousin, John *Wilson Patten; and d. 1846.

[10] See 17 June 34.

[11] Probably Hugh James *Rose 'Brief Remarks on the Disposition towards Christianity generated by prevailing opinions and Pursuits' (1830); but see 17 Apr. 34.

[12] William *Peter, 1788–1853, reforming M.P. Bodmin 1832–4; verse translator; consul at Philadelphia from 1840.

son—finished my paper : a sorry affair. Dined at the Mundy's. Mrs Wynn's afterwards : late.[1]

18. Sunday.

Trin. & St James's—Sacrament. Mr Stewart,[2] & the Bp—both excellent. walk. tea at Bailey's. Wrote. read a Serm. of Close's aloud—Bible—Bp Reynolds[2] on "Sinfulness of Sin"—& Rose a good deal.

Monday 19.

Rose's commencement Sermon.[3] packing &c. Anc. Mus. Rehearsal 12–1½. 2¼–8 to Oxford per Defiance. wrote to Mrs G.—J.N.G.—my Latin Epistles —tea with Short—read a little of Whittle Harvey's case.[4]

20.

Many calls—Epistles delivered[5]—breakf. with Harrison—Williams's & Parkers—wrote to Bp of Exeter & T.G.—dined in Hall & at Common Room—tea with Hamilton—read some Corinne. Surplice prayers.

21.

breakf. with Pusey. read the Hough[6] & Alban Francis pamphlets[7]—at Short's for the articles &c. Convocation 10¼–12[8]—off in a great hurry to town 12–6¼ (Regulator). House immediately—& again 11–1. Voted agst Jews (32 to 123) & for Fleetwood's Bill.[9] in Berk. Square—read Chr. Words-worth's 2nd Edn,[10] paper, & some Whittle Harvey.

22. Thursday.

Whittle Harvey's Report—Rose on St Simonianism[11]—paper—wrote to B.

[1] Mary, née Cunliffe, d. 1838; eldest da. of Sir Foster Cunliffe, bart.; m. 1806 Charles Watkin Williams *Wynn, 1775–1850, M.P. Old Sarum 1797–9, Montgomeryshire 1799–1850, who was president, board of control, 1822–8; secretary at war 1830–1; chancellor, duchy of Lancaster 1834–5; and a master of parliamentary forms.
[2] James Arrott Stewart, 1800?–1851?, rector of Vange, Essex, 1834–49.
[3] E. *Reynolds, bp. of Norwich 1660.
[4] Preached by Hugh James *Rose at Cambride in 1826 (1831).
[5] See Morley, i. 112 n. *Gladstone sat on the commons' cttee to investigate the refusal of the inns of court to allow *Harvey to become a barrister. See PP 1834 xviii. 331 and Add MS 44723, ff. 36–101.
[6] He went to Oxford to take his M.A. degree; epistles asked for the leave of the govern-ing body to do so; the university required adhesion to the 39 articles.
[7] 'Attempt of King *James II to force a Dissenter [John *Hough] upon Magdalen College, Oxford, April, 1687' (1834).
[8] 'Attempt of King *James II to force a Dissenter [Alban *Francis] upon the University of Cambridge, February, 1687' (1834).
[9] Jewish disabilities bill carried 2°; Lord's Day (no. 1) bill lost 2°; H xxiii. 1176, 1179. (Sir) Peter *Hesketh-Fleetwood, 1801–66, M.P. Preston 1832–47; cr. bart. 1838.
[10] Christopher *Wordsworth, On the Admission of Dissenters . . . to the University of Cambridge, 2 ed. (1834).
[11] Hugh James *Rose, The Gospel an Abiding System, with some Remarks on the 'New Christianity' of the St. Simonians (1832).

H[arrison]—J.N.G.—Parker—Williams—in Berk. Square—rode—dined at Mr Oliverson's—House 10¾–12¼.[1]

23.

Breakf. in Bedf. Square—House 1–2¼. Wrote to Mr Stanford.[2] Whittle Harvey's Report—& Art. in Law Magazine.[3] Dined at Lincoln's Inn—rode —Schlegel's Hamlet—papers—at Bailey's.

24.

Breakft at Sir H. Verney's. Ld Mandeville,[4] Mr Plumptre,[5] Mr C. Bruce, Mr Forster,[6] Mr Sinclair, & Mr Blunt, who prayed &c. A pleasing meeting. Busied with Tom about a private matter. Wrote to J.N.G. & Mr M'Dowal— read Harvey's Report & finished Rose's Chr. Advocate publications—in B. Square—at Eton dinner. Lincoln in the Chair. Keate's farewell.[7] D. of Newcastle & other great folk.

25.

Late. Trinity mg & aft.—dined at Lincoln's Inn—tea at Bailey's. Wrote in Bible &c. read MacNeile (finished) on the Church—Newman—one of Arnold's aloud. My plan[8] is to strengthen or qualify or omit expressions as I go along.

26.

T.G., Thomas,[9] & S. Denison to breakfast. rode. calls. paper. Harvey's "Report". Muster's Certificate—Schlegel's Hamlet—dined at H. Joy's— House 10¾–12½[10]—Duc de Berri's pictt. with Mr G.—

Lingelback	Two Teniers	Two Moeris.
Pynaka	Two Ostade	G. Dow.
N. Berghem		Schalken
	Van der Veld	Ruysdael
	Backhuysen	Hobbema

cf and contr[ast][11]

27.

paper. Began 6th Common Law Report—and read Schlegel—wrote to Rogers—& Williams. Committee 12¾–3½ House 6¼–7¾.—Debate ad-

---

[1] Reporting of debates: *H* xxiii. 1228.

[2] Perhaps Major Stanford of Ballina, co. Mayo; f. of J.F.

[3] xi. 94 (February 1834).

[4] George Montagu, 1799–1855; styled viscount Mandeville; M.P. Huntingdonshire 1826–37; succ. as 6th duke of Manchester, 1843.

[5] John Pemberton Plumptre, 1791–1864, protectionist M.P. for east Kent 1832–52.

[6] Charles Smith Forster, d. 1850; banker; tory M.P. Walsall 1832–7; f. of 1st bart.

[7] *Keate was about to retire.   [8] When reading at family prayers.

[9] Perhaps Morgan Thomas, 1803–67, changed name to Treherne 1857, cons. M.P. Coventry (at 7th attempt) 1863.   [10] Poor laws: *H* xxiii. 1320.

[11] Seventeenth-century painters, of the Dutch and Flemish schools.

journed & why[1]—tea in B. Square—dined at Lincoln's Inn—rode to Sir R. Inglis's.

28.

Finished Schlegel's Hamlet—read paper, & 6th Report, &c. on the Harvey case. At the Drawing room— $3\frac{3}{4}$ hours; $2\frac{1}{4}$–6, nearly[2]—rode—dined with the Tylers—sang—Carlton afterwards—wrote to Mr Pritt,[3] & Macdowall. A day of public festivities; amidst symptoms of an awful future.

29.

paper—6th Report—Commee $12\frac{3}{4}$–$2\frac{1}{4}$[4]—rode. dined with the Gaskells. wrote to Cole—Stanford—Ld Sandon (on Mr Ross's matter).[5] Mignet's introduction[6]—Turton on increased difficulty in reorganising the govt.[7]

30. Fr.

Messrs Wilson & Pritt[8] here, on Harvey's business 11–$12\frac{1}{2}$. paper—Pearson on Admn of Dissrs—finished 6th Report (on Harvey's case)—Mignet—rode —dined with the Doyles. Somerset House exhibn $12\frac{3}{4}$–3—with Mr Mrs & H.J.G.[9]

31. Sat.

Mignet, & analysis—paper—calls—rode—made up accts & letters. Mr Mrs & H.J.G., to dinner.[10]

Sunday June 1.

Trinity mg & evg—did not go to the Sacrament—Read Mr Wilberforce's holy prayers, & his son's good & able preface[11]—Reynolds on 'Sinfulness of Sin'—Newman's Arians—Bible—wrote—dinner at Lincoln's Inn. A serm. of Arnold's aloud.

2.

T.G., Farr, E. Hamilton[12] to breakfast. Gaskell to dinner. rode. went to see Hope's house—pictures delightful, & everything splendid.[13] Wrote to Mr

---

[1] Irish church: adjourned because *Althorp had news of the resignation of *Stanley and his friends ('the Derby dilly'). H xxiii. 1368, 1400; DNB liv. 56.

[2] Queen *Adelaide held a drawing-room at St. James's to celebrate *William IV's birthday; no doubt the first occasion when the diarist and the future queen, Alexandrina *Victoria, 1819–1901, succ. 1837, set eyes on each other.   [3] See 30 May 34.

[4] 'called' here deleted.   [5] Probably electoral: cp. 10 Dec. 34.

[6] F. A. M. Mignet, History of the French Revolution (1824, tr. 1826, 2v.). His work on the Spanish succession, to which Morley refers this passage (i. 112), was still unpublished.

[7] T. *Turton's 'Thoughts' on admitting dissenters to degrees (1834).

[8] Neither identified.

[9] Version in Morley, i. 112.   [10] Menu in Add MS 44723, f. 18v.

[11] R. *Wilberforce ed. his father's Family Prayers (1834).

[12] Edward William Terrick Hamilton, 1809–98; br. of W.K.*; Eton and Trinity, Cambridge; wrangler 1832, fellow 1834–42; in New South Wales, 1845–65; lib. M.P. Salisbury 1868–9.

[13] But *Hope(-Scott) was in Holland at the time (Ornsby i. 68–69).

Duke, & J.N.G. read Mr Ward's Speech (corrected),[1] Canning, & papers. House at prayers and 5–12¼. Voted in 396:120.[2]

3.

Mignet—paper—and Bencher's certificate of 1834.[3] Wrote to Harrison—calls—rode—dined with Baring Wall.[4] House 11–11½.

4.

Bruce to breakfast. Paper—Mignet—Burke—Harvey evidence, began—Anc. Mus. Concert—dined at Lincoln's Inn. House 11¾–12¾.[5] rode.[6]

5.

Mignet—Harvey-Evidence: Ho & Committee 12¼–4¼.[7]—at Nat. Gallery—rode—Bedford Square in evening—sang—& worked again at Harvey's case, upon Rigge's evidence[8]—wrote to Williams.

6.

Mignet—Harvey Evidence—Commee 12¼–4½—& H of C. & H. of Lords 8½–12.[9] wrote to Hamilton—Mr Grant—Mrs Hagart—rode.

7.

Mignet: & analysis—City, on Aunt E's property as executor and Albany (£2) deeds—walked with Helen—paper—wrote to Robn, Harrison, Williams —rode—dined in Bedford Square.

8. Sunday.

Trin. mg & aft—dined at Bailey's—walk—Bible—wrote—Newman—Hervey's Life—Par. Lost—began Leibnitz's Tentamina Theodiceæ.[10]

9. M.

papers—Mignet, began Vol 2—Harvey's case—Commee 12¼–4, and House 7–9.[11] Evidence on do [sc. Harvey]—rode—dined at home—wrote to T.G.— & a paper at some length on alienation &c. of Church property.[12]

[1] Of 27 May: H xxiii. 1368.
[2] Irish church; *Ward's motion defeated. H xxiv. 86.
[3] Part of *Harvey's case: PP 1834, xlviii. 95.
[4] Charles Baring Wall, d. 1853, tory M.P. Guildford 1819–26, 1830, 1832–47; for Wareham 1826–30; for Weymouth 1831–2; for Salisbury 1847–53.
[5] Prisoners' Counsel Bill: H xxiv. 158.
[6] Version in Morley, l. 112.
[7] Petitions, &c: H xxiv. 174.
[8] PP 1834 xviii. 343, xlviii. 27; Samuel Rigge had been *Harvey's managing clerk ca. 1810.
[9] Lords debated Irish church; commons, poor laws. H xxiv. 244; 309.
[10] Leibnitz, Essais de Theodicée sur la Bonté de Dieu, la Liberté de l'homme, et l'origine du mal (1710).
[11] Poor laws. H xxiv. 324. Antedated extract in Morley, i. 112.   [12] Untraced.

10. T.

Mignet—Harvey's case—calls—rode—wrote on Church property—dined at Sir T. Farquhar's—papers.

11. W.

Mignet. Harvey Comm. $12\frac{1}{4}$–$3\frac{3}{4}$—& House $5\frac{1}{2}$–2.

Voted in 33 : 88 agst Rel. Ass. Bill—
    in 14 : 50 agst Jews' Bill.[1]

read Pitt's Speeches on the Union in Jan 1799—& Grattan on Cath. Petn 1805[2]—Wrote to Mrs Hagart—and T.G.—rode.

12. Th.

Mignet—callers—House & Edn Comm. $1\frac{3}{4}$–$5\frac{1}{4}$[3]—dined at (J. E.) Denison's —Mignet, & Harvey Evidence. papers. Pitt's Sp. Ap. 21. 1799.[4]

13. Fr.

Mignet—paper—Harvey Evidence—wrote to Franceys—Lt Col. Bradley's case[5]—Commee $12\frac{1}{2}$–4 : & House 7–$8\frac{3}{4}$[6]—rode—tea at Bailey's.

14. Sat.

Mignet—paper—Buckingham Evidence—rode—calls—dined at Lady Mordaunt's, liked them well[7]—wrote to Cole, Mr Tallents, Mr Cotton, Rigg,[8] Hamilton.

15. Sunday.

Trin. mg & aft. Bp of Winchester in mg.[9] Bible—Newman (finished)— Arnold Vol II (begun), one aloud—Brown on Establishments (begun)[10]— Hervey—tea in B. Square—and read some passages in the latter part of Corinne, which always work strongly on me. wrote.

16. M.

Finished Mignet. paper—part of Anstice's Essay,[11] & of Quarterly on

---

[1] Both bills read 3°: *H* xxiv. 364, 383.
[2] Henry *Grattan's speech of 14 May 1805: *Cobbett's Parliamentary Debates*, iv. 969.
[3] First meeting of cttee. to inquire into popular education in England and Wales: *PP* 1834 ix. 5. In house, poor laws amdt. bill in cttee.: *H* xxiv. 385.
[4] On 31 January 1799, on union with Ireland; *Parliamentary History*, xxxiv. 254.
[5] Army discipline: cp. *Mirror*, iv. 2880–1.
[6] Poor laws again: *H* xxiv. 427.
[7] Marianne, née Holbeck, d. 1842, m. Sir Charles Mordaunt 1807; widowed, 1823.
[8] Perhaps Jonathan Rigg, b. 1808, London merchant; or John Rigg, 1811?–60, St. Edmund Hall; priest at Glossop, Derbyshire, 1848.   [9] C. R. *Sumner.
[10] C. J. Brown, *Church Establishments Defended, with special references to the Church of Scotland* (1833).
[11] J. *Anstice, 'The influence of the Roman Conquests upon Literature and the Arts in Rome', Oxford English prize essay (1834).

Macintosh. Rode. Committees 12½–5, & Ho. 10¼–12¼.[1] Arranged a small dinner for tomorrow.

17. Tuesday.

Began Guizot's Revolution of England[2]—attended Miss E. Doyle's marriage breakfast: she was much overcome. Are meetings just of this kind well timed?[3] paper—read Rns 11 sheet letter—very interesting matters in it. Hamilton, Sir H. Verney, Mordaunt, Harrison, to dinner[4]—out with Hamilton afterwards—rode. Twice on my way to the House, not there at all.

18.

Hamilton, Anstice, Blakesley, T.G., to breakfast. paper. rode. Comms & House 12¼–5¼, and 8¼–9½[5]—in B. Sq. twice. Guizot. Coming home to dine, found 'Remains of A.H.H.' Yesterday, a bridal at a friend's: today a sad memorial of Death! It is a sad subject, a very sad one, to me. I have not seen his like: and probably if I were *now* to meet one such, still the old affection might be imitated but could not be renewed. The memory of him reposes gently in my inmost heart, a fountain of tears which soften and fertilise it in the midst of pursuits whose tendency is to dry up the sources of emotion by the fever of excitement. I read his memoir. His father has done me much and undeserved kindness there. Would to God I *had* been able to appreciate his beloved & departed son; but my words are as far below my feelings, as my feelings are short of the truths of the case. I read some of the contents of the book.[6]

19. Th.

House 1–3 and 10½–11¼.[7] Dined at Madrigals Society. A treat.[8] rode—read Guizot—A.H.H.—thought on Univv.

20. Fr.

House 12¼–3½—and 5¼–2¼. read D.W. H[arvey] papers—most of my time went in thinking confusedly over the University question—very anxious to speak: tortured with nervous anticipations: could not get an opportunity —certainly my inward experience on these occasions *ought* to make me

---

[1] Poor laws again: *H* xxiv. 446.

[2] *Histoire de la Révolution de l'Angleterre depuis l'avènement de Charles Ier jusqu'à la restauration de Charles II*, 2v. (1826–7).

[3] Francis *Doyle's sister Emily Josephine Eliza, 1811–72, m. William Leveson-Gower, 1806–60, of Titsey Place, Surrey; a gt-gs. of 1st earl *Gower.

[4] Menu in Add MS 44723, f. 19.

[5] Poor laws continued: *H* xxiv. 520.

[6] Henry *Hallam circulated privately a memoir of, and some poems and essays by, his dead son (published 1863). Extracts in Morley, i. 112.

[7] Beer bill; legal business. *H* xxiv. 551, 592.

[8] The Madrigal Society, founded 1741, met fortnightly to sing, and monthly to dine, at the Freemason's Tavern, Lincoln's Inn Fields, 1827–82.

humble.—Herbert's maiden speech—very successful.[1]—I ought to be thankful for my *miss*: perhaps also because my mind was so much oppressed that I could not I fear have unfolded my inward convictions. What a work it is, and how does it require the Divine power and aid to clothe[2] in words the profound and mysterious thoughts which the mind entertains on these subjects most connected with the human soul, thoughts which the mind does not command as a mistress, but entertains reverentially as honoured guests: content with only a partial comprehension, hoping to render it a progressive one, but how difficult to define in words a conception many of whose parts are still in a nascent state with no fixed outline or palpable substance. 321:147.[3]

21. Sat.

Sewell's Chapel[4]—sermons—& began Charriere's book.[5] A sad letter from his mother. Wrote to him, Mrs C., Mr Tyler, Mr Rawson, Sir R. Inglis, Sir H. Verney, in consequence. Also draft for a note to Mr Hallam, that I may consider of it. House 2–3½—voted for Miles's Clauses in 114:33 (I think).[6] rode, partly with Helen: dined at Mrs Labalmondiere's—at Doyle's afterwards.

22. Sunday.

Trinity mg & aft—tea in Berk. Square—walk. Bible—Arnold's Sermm—one aloud—Essays on Interpn of Scriptures; very dangerous I fear[7]—Leibnitz—Par. Lost B.1—Hallam still much in my mind.

23. M.

Commee 12½–4—House before dinner—& again 10½–12½—voted in 360:99 on I.C.[8]—dined at Sir S. Scott's—rode—paper—A.H.H.—finished Charriere's first *part*—Guizot. Wrote to Mr J.E. Gordon[9]—Mr Hallam.

24. T.

A.H.H. on Rossetti's Dante[10]—Guizot—wrote on Church property—Edn Commee & House 3¼–6.[11] paper—evening at home; & in B. Square. rode.

[1] Universities Admission Bill 2°: *H* xxiv. 640.
[2] Instead of 'paint'.
[3] Version of extracts in Morley, i. 112–13.
[4] Perhaps York Street chapel, off St. James's Square; to hear Thomas Sewell, 1795–1865?, of Trinity Hall, or Henry Doyle Sewell, 1806?–86, vicar of Headcorn, Kent, 1850.
[5] Ernest Charrière, *St. Hélène* (1826), lyric poem.
[6] Poor laws: new clause, imposing charges on putative fathers of bastards, inserted by 114 to 39: *H* xxiv. 718. Proposed by (Sir) William Miles, 1797–1878, M.P. Chippenham 1818–29, Romney 1830–2, Somerset 1834–65; cr. bart. 1859.
[7] Perhaps T. *Turton 'Text of the English Bible . . . considered' (1833).
[8] In cttee. on Tithes (Ireland) Bill: *H* xxiv. 805.
[9] Secretary of the Protestant Association.
[10] A. H. *Hallam, 'Remarks on Professor Rossetti's "Disquisizioni sullo spirito anti-papale"', (1832) in *Remains* (1834).
[11] Police obstruction of access to house: *H* xxiv. 826.

25. W.

Wrote to Sir G. Grey[1]—Parker—Doyle. D.W.H. comm. $12\frac{1}{2}$–$4\frac{1}{4}$. rode—paper—Guizot—finished Anstice's Essay—& wrote on the same subject. Tea at Bailey's—Clarendon.

26.

Cousin[2]—Guizot—Quart Rev. on Revv. of 1688 & 1832—House $1\frac{1}{2}$–$3\frac{1}{4}$—and $10\frac{1}{2}$–12—voted for Lord's Day Bill in 4 divv—agst Game Bill in 2[3]—Dined at Mr Lyall's—rode—late lunch at T.G's—wrote to Girdlestone.

27.

Cousin—Guizot—papers—Commees & House $12\frac{1}{2}$–$5\frac{1}{4}$[4]—tea & conv. at Bailey's in evg—rode—wrote to Charriere—& Parker—Gaskell breakfasted with me.

28.

Helen's birthday—wrote a letter to her, with my second copy of A.H.H. —breakf. in B. Square—dinner at T.G's—whist in evg. paper—calls—rode —Guizot—Cousin—wrote sundries[5]—read Mr Allen's benevolent pamphlet.[6]

29. Sunday.

Trinity & St James's—Helen to dinner, & walk afterwards. Bible—Brown —Girdlestone's Sermons &c. very kindly sent me for the negroes[7]—read one aloud—Par. Lost—wrote—copied my 'Prepp. for Sacrament'.[8]

30. M.

Breakf at Bailey's to meet Mr Leigh. Commees 1–5. Dined at Uncle D.s— Guizot—Education Evidence papers—wrote to Parker—Girdlestone—Dry —Mordaunt on his marriage announced by him to me as in contempln., to Miss C. Murray[9]—rode—accts &c. for the month.

---

[1] Sir George *Grey, 1799–1882, 2nd bart. 1828; whig M.P. Devonport 1832–47, Northumberland 1847–52, Morpeth 1853–74; colonial under-secretary, 1834 and 1835–9; home secretary, 1846–52, 1855–8, 1861–6; gf. of foreign secretary. See Add MS 44162.

[2] Victor Cousin, tr. Sarah *Austin, *Report on the State of Public Instruction in Prussia* (1834).

[3] Lord's Day (no. 2) Bill passed through cttee.; Game Laws amdt. bill defeated 2°; *H* xxiv. 851, 854.

[4] Poor laws: *H* xxiv. 913.

[5] Including a paper on Irish church property, Add MS 44723, ff. 106–15.

[6] William *Allen, *A Plan for Diminishing the Poor Rates in Agricultural Districts* (1833).

[7] Charles *Girdlestone, *A course of Sermons For the Year*, 2v. (1834). Cp. 20 July 34.

[8] Add MSS 44813E or 44831.

[9] Sir John Mordaunt m. 7 August 1834 Caroline Sophia, 2nd da. of George *Murray, bp. of Rochester; she re-m. 1853 Gustavus Smith of Goldicote House, Stratford. Cp. also 15 June 39 n.

Tuesday July one.

The Messiah in Westr Abbey. "For unto us" & the Hallelujah Choruses— "Comfort ye" by Braham among the solos &c. delighted me most. House $4\frac{1}{4}$–5.[1] Rode—tea at Bailey's—Guizot—Cousin—Buckingham evidence[2]— wrote to Mr Tallents.

2. W.

Saw our party depart at about $10\frac{1}{2}$—Guizot—Cousin—Bossuet (Hist. Univ.)—wrote to[3] Caparn—Cole—Parker—Duke—Commee & House $12\frac{1}{2}$– 5—and $8\frac{1}{4}$–4—waiting to see Univ. Bill thro. Commee.[4] rode—Curious detail from O'Connell of his interview with Littleton &c.[5]

3.

Guizot—Cousin—paper—Doyle's poems—rode—Comm. & House $3\frac{1}{4}$–$6\frac{1}{4}$[6]— dined at Mordaunt's—Bp of Rochr & his family there: the intended looked charming. Wrote to Aunt J.—Mr Rawson—Mr G—Mr Macdowall—J.M.G.

4.

Guizot—Harvey's "Narrative" of 1810—wrote to H.J.G.—read Fitz- maurice on Ireland: an able pamphlet.[7] Commee & House $12\frac{1}{2}$–5 and $10\frac{3}{4}$– $12\frac{3}{4}$. voted in 354:71 and in 171:235 on Irish Tithes.[8] rode—dined at H.H. Joy's.

5.

Guizot—Cousin—wrote to Mr G—rode—calls—wrought a little at my Tr. from Göthe—papers—dined at Sir E. Kerrison's[9]—party of great folks— good music.

6.

St Margaret's; in H. of C. pew. Mr Melvill preached a magnificent sermon for the Westmr Hospital. Trin in aft. Walk—tea with A. Acland—Bible— Whyte on Prayer—Brown on Establishment. Conc[ilium] Trid[entinum] on a Church &c[10]—wrote.

[1] Poor laws, closing stages: *H* xxiv. 1027.
[2] James Silk *Buckingham, 1786–1855, radical M.P. Sheffield 1832–7 and journalist, was examined at length by a select cttee., on which *Gladstone sat, inquiring into sup- pression of *Buckingham's *Calcutta Journal* eleven years before: *PP* 1834 viii. 48.
[3] 'divers' here deleted.   [4] Universities Admission Bill, cttee. stage: *H* xxiv. 1088.
[5] Extracts in Morley, i. 113. For the interview, on 23 June, a celebrated misunder- standing, see *DNB* xxxiii. 370–1.
[6] Irish coercion: *H* xxiv. 1099. *O'Connell gave his version of the interview.
[7] Perhaps Sir W. *Petty, the Fitzmaurices' ancestor, *Political Anatomy of Ireland* (1691).
[8] Cttee. stage of Church Temporalities (Ireland) bill; financial details. Amdt. defeated, bill advanced: *H* xxiv. 1211.
[9] Sir Edward *Kerrison, 1774–1853, fought in Spain and Flanders; tory M.P. Shaftes- bury 1812–18, Northampton 1818–24, Eye 1824–52; cr. bart. 1821; general 1851.
[10] Council of Trent, session vii (1547), on the sacraments.

7. M.

Guizot—Cousin—papers—wrote to Mrs G—Hamilton—Lushington—Franceys. Commee 12½–4¾—House 9½–12. voted in 174:190 for Lord Chandos.[1] Rode—&c.

8. T.

Not quite well: some trifle in the stomach. How rarely have I to write even this! Guizot—Cousin—paper—wrote to Mrs G—made a paper of travelling hints for Martyn[2]—rode—House 7¼–8¾[3]—Lady Bromley's ball for an hour. A. Acland breakfd with me.

9. W.

Guizot—papers—Commees & H. of C. & L. 12–3¾, and 5¼–7. Rode—in evg at Unc. D's—wrote home to Mr G—to Mr Tallents—& Gaskell.. Explanations: very interesting, nay awful.[4] (Finished Guizot).

10. Th.

7¼ A.M.–7½ P.M. to Coggeshall & back with O'Connell & G. Sinclair (see Memoranda) to examine Skingley, which was done with little success.[5] Read Aeneid—papers—Cousin—Irish Report of 1832. No *news* worthy of the name.

11. Friday.

No news till the afn then heard on very good authority, that the Grey govt *is* definitively broken up & that attempts at reconstruction have failed—Cousin—Hanmer's Poems[6]—papers—D.W.H. Commee 12½ 3¾—rode—attended the Italian refugee performance—excellent music—the drama had much false sentiment—wrote to Cole & J.M.G.[7]

12. Sat.

Breakf. in B. Square—Hamilton with me—dined with Mr Finlay—rode; twice at Carlton—no news worth having—read papers—Cousin—Francesca da Rimini[8] (began)—Hanmer's poems (finished). Wrote to J.M.G.—Mr G—Doyle—Morng Post (for Gaskell)—Wm Robertson.

---

[1] *Chandos drew attention to distress on the land: *H* xxiv. 1284.
[2] Charles Cecil Martyn, 1809?–66; Christ Church and Lincoln's Inn; M.P. Southampton 1841–2.
[3] Misc. business: *H* xxiv. 1204.
[4] In commons, *Althorp explained *Grey's resignation: *H* xxiv. 1336. In lords, *Grey announced it; the cabinet having fallen out over Irish policy: ibid. 1305.
[5] Coggeshall, Essex, 42 miles NE. of Westminster. Henry Skingley's evidence in *PP* 1834 xviii. 636. Memoranda in Add MS 44819, ff. 3–4. Skingley, then an old man, had been the original purchaser in the deal that aroused suspicion of *Harvey.
[6] Sir J. *Hanmer, *Proteus* (1833).
[7] Version in Morley, i. 113.
[8] S. Pellico, *Francesca da Rimini* (1818), verse tragedy.

13. Sunday.

Breakf. with Farquhar. Hamilton dined with me—Capt. Wellesley here:
Trin. Chelsea[1] mg with H. & F.—Long Acre[2] evg with H. & Wilberforce.
Bible—Whyte—Mr Tayler's Sermon—& wrote on social intercourse.

14.

$7\frac{1}{2}$ started for Harrow—turned back at half-way, meeting Mr Cunningham.
Wrote to Aunt J[3]—Mrs G—Gaskell—Doyle—House & Commee $12\frac{1}{4}$–4 and
$5\frac{1}{4}$–$6\frac{1}{4}$[4]—Wood dined with me—read Fr. da Rimini—Cousin—papers—$\frac{1}{2}$
vol of Ivanhoe—and $\frac{1}{2}$ of Sir C. Wetherell's Sp. on London U[niversity]
Charter.[5]

15.

Seymer & Bruce to breakf.—paper—Sismondi's Introduction[6]—Cousin—
(finished) Fr. da Rimini—Dined at Sir E. Kerrison's: sang![7] Harvey's
Comm. $12\frac{3}{4}$–$5\frac{1}{4}$. Spoke to Mrs Wallace a little on her son's religious education.

16.

A black day as touching the House:[8] Read however Edn & Harvey papers
—Cousin—(began) Eufemia di Messina[9]—rode—dined again at Sir E.
Kerrison's—sang a little: wrote to H.J.G. papers.

17. Th.

Hayes & T.G. to breakf—paper—Ed. Comm. $2\frac{1}{4}$–5: H. of P[eers] & C. 5–7,
and 9–$1\frac{1}{2}$—several divv. on Beer Bill[10]—rode—read Cousin & (finished)
Eufemia di Messina, which has interest, though deficient I think in harmony both of the plot & the sentiment. Wrote to Aunt J.

18. Fr.

paper. Sismondi. Harvey Commee & House (except a call on Sir J. Sinclair)
$12\frac{1}{2}$–$11\frac{1}{2}$—voted for Coercion Bill.[11] Wrote to Mr G.

---

[1] Cp. 20 Mar. 34.
[2] Long Acre episcopal chapel, near St. Martin's Lane.
[3] In Bassett, 29.
[4] Miscellaneous: H xxv. 23.
[5] Sir Charles *Wetherell, 'On Incorporating the London University' (1834).
[6] J. C. L. de Sismondi, *Italian Republics*, tr. (1832).
[7] Anecdote in Add MS 44819, f. 5.
[8] Commons still adjourned; lords rejected religious assemblies bill and discussed Irish
coercion. H xxv. 25.
[9] Also Pellico's (1822).
[10] Irish disturbances in Lords. *Althorp announced *Melbourne's government; beer
bill in cttee. H xxv. 31, 58, 83.
[11] Leave to bring in bill, 140–26: H xxv. 192.

19.

Had last night a very curious dream of an appearance of our Saviour. Oh that he were ever present to the eye of my mind, as other visions often are.

Wrote to Mrs G—Mr Tallents—sat to Hayter[1]—papers—Junius— Cousin—Sismondi—Tutti Frutti, which I dislike much[2]—singing—copied (& enlarged a little) O'Connell's remarks.[3]

20.

Breakf. in B.S.—heard Short at Bloomsbury; a *very* thin congregation: & Mr Ward—walk—read Bible—several Chr. Knowl. Tracts; (completed my selection for the W.I.)—and Whyte on Prayer.

21.

Cousin—Sismondi—Educn Evidence—paper—wrote to Charriere—Mr Grant—Gaskell—Doyle—Mr G—rode. Commee & House, 1–4¼, 5½–6¼, and 7½–10.[4]

Today not for the first time felt a great want of courage to express feelings strongly awakened on hearing a speech of O'Connell. To have so strong an impulse & not obey it seems unnatural: it seems like an inflicted dumbness.[5]

22.

Expected Charriere to breakft he did not come. Cousin—Sismondi—Educn Commee Evidence—papers—wrote to Mr G. & Mr Tallents—rode—House, 5¼–6¼, and 7¼–8[6]—worked over the old Univ. Adm[issio]n subject, in great fear & trembling. At Chantrey's: saw the bust & cast of A.H.H.—could not like the former, but the latter is deeply interesting.[7]

23.

Sismondi—Cousin—part of Harvey's 'Speech & Reply'—wrote to Girdle-stone—& some verses. Papers. Harvey's & Gl. L. Comm. 12–4—House 6–11—voted in 34 to 114 for a Committee about Ellice.[8] Tea at House with P.A.P[ickering] & Spedding.

24.

Spedding breakfd with me—I shd be glad to see more of him. Papers— wrote to Mr G.—Mr Tallents—Capt. Wellesley. Ed. Comm. 2–4½—rode—

---

[1] (Sir) George *Hayter, 1792–1871, painter, knighted 1842. His portrait of *Gladstone, now at Fasque, is reproduced in Reid, *G*, 168.

[2] Prince Hermann Puckler-Muskau, *Tutti Frutti: From the Papers of the Departed*, 2v. (1834).

[3] Cp. 10 July 34 n.

[4] Irish coercion bill, 2°, 146–23: *H* xxv. 323; anecdote in Add MS 44819, f. 5.

[5] These two sentences in Morley, i. 113. Contrast Blake, 148–50.

[6] Miscellaneous business: *H* xxv. 334.   [7] Illustrated in Reid, *G*, 5.

[8] *O'Connell failed to get inquiry into alleged bribery in 1832 by Edward *Ellice, 1781–1863, fur trader ('the Bear'); m. *Grey's sister Hannah 1809; whig whip 1830–2; secretary at war 1832–4; founded Reform Club 1836; elder statesman. *H* xxv. 400.

dined at Uncle D.s—read Cousin—Sismondi—Introduction & began Philip Van Artevelde.[1]

25.

Sat to Hayter—Harvey Comm. 1–4½—rode—papers—Cousin—Harvey papers & making notes—Philip Van Artevelde (finished Part 1)—Tom's birthday: may all his days be days of blessing.

26.

Payment of bills &c—calls—rode—wrote to Robn & Mrs G—Cousin— paper—Philip Van Artevelde (began Part II)—dined in B. Square—beginning to rout out for departure—already!

27. Sunday.

Breakf. in B. Square. St. Giles. Excellent serm. from Mr Tyler on Eph.I.3,4. St James's aft.—walk—wrote a little—Whyte on Prayer (finished, except the forms)—Bible—Slade on the Ps[alm]s[2]—Brown on Establishments[3]— an Arnold aloud.

28. M.

Cousin—paper—Wrote to Aunt J—Mr G—Mr Mundy—Mr Stanford— Ed[i]n[burgh] housekeeper—rode—T.G. dined with me—Harvey Comm. 1–5¼—and House 7¼–1¾—spoke 30 to 35 min. on Univ. Bill, with more ease than I had hoped, having been more mindful or less unmindful of Divine aid. Divided in 75:164, & made a list afterwards.[4]

29.

Sat to Hayter. I fear he draws a bow. At Sir R.I's on Gl. Lott & Comm. 1–3¼. Wrote to Mr G—T.G.—Gaskell (who had a daughter on Sunday),[5] Mr Tallents, Manning. Pleasant House dinner at Carlton—Sir R.P. very kind[6] —House 10¾–12½.[7] Papers. finished Cousin—wrote "Political Memoranda".[8]

30. Wed.

Wrote to Mr Wynne—Mrs G—T.G.—Farquhar—Dry—Lawton—Mr Tallents—Mr Grant—read papers—Speech at Camb. agst political Unions[9]

---

[1] The play that made Henry *Taylor famous (1834).
[2] James *Slade, *An Explanation of the Psalms* (1832).
[3] Cp. 15 June, 34.
[4] University Admissions Bill, 3°: *H* xxv. 635, 653. Extracts in Morley, i. 113. Notes for speech in Add MS 44649, ff. 53–7.
[5] Died in infancy.
[6] Cp. Morley, i. 113–4, and Add MS 44819, ff. 5–7.
[7] Irish tithes: *H* xxv. 713.   [8] Untraced.
[9] Probably at trial at Cambridge assizes, 22–23 July, of E. J. Dixon and J. Phipps, acquitted of forming illegal unions.

—D.U.M. on Protestant emigration.[1] Harvey Comm. & House, &c. 1–6.—Difference of opinion on the Report declared.[2]

31. Th.

Wrote to J.N.G.—Mr G—Lawton—Mordaunt—Gl. Lottery $11\frac{1}{4}$–$3\frac{1}{2}$[3]—papers—finished Brown on Establishments—packing & arranging for departure—corrected my speech of Monday for the Mirror—very irksome work.[4] arranged accts & Letters &c. Wrote to the Chairman of Codrington's Committee.[5]

August one. Friday.

A momentous day in the W.I.—May God govern it aright.[6] further arrangements—paper—House 11–$4\frac{1}{4}$[7]—Harvey (divided 1:10 against impeaching the verdict in Collis's case)[8]—Educn Comm (Bp of London examd)[9]—went to Portman Square—dined, read State & Pr[ospects] of Toryism[10]—wrote notes for Lincoln—also wrote to Mr G., Mr Wynn[11]—started in L[incoln]'s carriage at $6\frac{3}{4}$.[12] began Paroles d'un croyant[13]—trav[elle]d all night.

2.

Newark at $10\frac{1}{2}$. Convv. with L[incoln], T.G. & Mr Tallents. Abt 35 calls—found most at home: received with civility in all cases, in many kindness & even warmth (Branston, Hardy,[14] Lang,[15] Harvey, Wilson, Boler,[16] Bishop,[17] &c)—more than expected. Find very much turning on Mr Godfrey. Lincoln long with him. Dined at Mr Tallents. Wrote to Mrs G—& Aunt J. Much political conv. with L. on my way.—Everything tended to point out Mr Godfrey at the centre of offence & necessary channel of reconciliation.

3. Sunday.

Ch. mg & aft. Mr Simpson & Mr Massey[18]—walk—Sacrament. read Bible—

[1] *Dublin University Magazine*, iv. 1 (July 1834).
[2] Cttee.'s last day of hearing evidence, *PP* 1834 xviii. 796; it reported, exonerating *Harvey, on 4 August (ibid. 337); intervening debates not recorded.
[3] Drawing up final report: *PP* 1834 xviii. 91.
[4] *Mirror*, iv. 3047, for 28 July 1834.
[5] *Bernal: a cttee. of the whole house was inquiring into *Codrington's claim for rewards for combatants at Navarino.
[6] From this day, slaves became free apprentices. These two sentences added later.
[7] Misc. business: *H* xxv. 888.
[8] A side-issue, dropped by the cttee., about the evidence of Christopher Annett Collis, Essex brewer and baker.
[9] *PP* 1834 ix. 191.
[10] Reprinted from *Fraser's Magazine*, ix. 1, 364 (1834).
[11] Charles W. W. *Wynn, *Gaskell's father-in-law.
[12] Fragment of conversation in Add MS 44819, f. 7.
[13] By H. F. R. de Lammenais (1834), marking his severance from the Roman church.
[14] Thomas Hardy, Newark maltster.   [15] William Lang, Newark glazier.
[16] William Boler, Newark merchant.   [17] Robert Bishop, Newark maltster.
[18] Thomas Massey, 1810?–88; curate at Newark 1833–6 and second master of grammar school; rector of Hatcliffe, Lincolnshire, 1840.

Wordsworth's Eccl. sonnets—Hallam's Theodicaea[1] (+)—Chrys[ostom] de Sacerdo[tio] (finished).

4. M.

Papers—dined with Mr Tallents—read Wordsw. & Quart. on Phil. van Artevelde—calls continued—meeting with Duke. much conv. with Mr Lee —He again mentioned the rumour of Caparn as aggrieved—did not know notices had been sent. Missed Mr. Godfrey again.

5. T.

Wrote to Lincoln—home—Gaskell—saw Hemstock.[2] some more calls— bulk of the day passed in long convv. with Mr Godfrey—Branston—Butler[3] —& at night longest of all, Mr Tallents.—I am really & sorely tried in this matter: may God help me, first by enabling me to confide, and then by answering the call.

6. W.

Wrote to Aunt J—Mr Grant—& in evg to Lincoln—Mr Finlay—Mr G. The latter letter detailed most of what had passed in the day, most of which was occupied in anxious reconsideration of the questions at issue with Mr Branston, Caparn, Tallents, Godfrey, one or more: drew a paper expressing briefly the terms: may I trust that God *has* helped me? Let me wait for the issue. But this morning I despaired: and a way was opened. I hope conscience has not been slighted.

Dined with Mr Tallents. Read Quarterly on Sir E. Brydges and Beckford. Arranged to go to Lpool tomorrow.

7. Th.

6½–4¼. Newark to Manchr 77 miles. and 5–6½ 31 to Lpool. Arranged for departure tomorrow—& walked out to Seaforth. Tea & slept at Aunt J's— much conversation—found her in a very perilous state, yet I fully believe with God's help she may soon again be both useful & happy: in her almost more than any other the two are united—Remarkable country in Derbyshire.

8. Fr.

Left my Aunt at 10½—at the Rawsons'—Felt the air delightfully exhilarating. Poor Seaforth; I never come here without a twinge: on this spot I feel, what is the power of a child's imagination: how the local associations of boyhood can neither be eradicated, nor replaced.—Left Lpool at one ½ by the Vulcan[4]—little sickness, & slept well.

[1] A. H. *Hallam, 'Theodicaea Novissima', in his *Remains* (1834).
[2] Richard Hemstock, Newark victualler.
[3] Henry Butler, Newark draper.
[4] Steam packet plying between Liverpool and Glasgow.

9. Sat.

Made a good breakfast on board! after starving yesterday. Greenock at 10¾ —head wind all the way.—Detained at Greenock till one—Toward at 3½— went up the hill: a splendid view: such alone give one an idea of the *earth*.[1]

10. Sunday.

Dunoon church*yard*—good serm on Rom.12.2[2]—rode home—read Bible— some of Newton's Life, & Letters,[3] & some of Miss Graham's life.[4]

11. M.

Wrote briefly to Mrs G. & Farquhar—read Ed. Rev. on Tory proceedings —Quart. on Guizot's Gibbon—Black Book, &c.—billiards. (rain)—lionised.

12. T.

9½–2½—Toward to Glasgow by Steam[er]. 4–8.20 Gl. to Ed[inburgh]— Went to take pl[ace] by Defiance—slept at A[tholl] Cr[escent]—tea & began Promessi Sposi.[5]

13. W.

5½–4½. Ed. to Fasque by L[aurence]kirk—105 miles. So here I am safe & sound thank God.—How easily is a journey of 660 miles accomplished— read papers—& For. Quart on Mad de Stael.[6] Sorry to find my dear Mother lame.

14. Th.

Arranging my books & meditating great doings, to work 2 h. (at least) before breakf—& go to bed at 11—being satisfied it is of importance for eyes & health.[7]

Paper—Prom. Sposi—& began Dobson's Petrarch[8]—wrote to Lady Kerrison[9]—Wishlade—Storr.[10]

15. Fr.

Manzoni—paper—Rns letters—Aristotle's Politics (began)[11]—rode—rowed Divie[12]—conv. with Mr G. about Newark—wrote to Caparn & Aunt J.—my dear Mother very ill.

[1] The Gladstones had a house for the summer on the west bank of the Firth of Clyde, near Toward, which lies 10 miles SW. of Greenock, and 7 south of Dunoon.
[2] Probably by Dr. Macintosh Mackay, minister at Dunoon.
[3] John *Newton of Olney's autobiography (1764) and *Omicron* (1774).
[4] *Life of Mrs Isabella Graham* (1832); a pious Scotswoman who kept a girls' school in New York.
[5] A. Manzoni's celebrated novel (3v. 1825–7) 'The Betrothed'. Notes in Add MS 44723, ff. 243–6.
[6] *Foreign Quarterly Review*, xiv. 1 (August 1834).   [7] '15. Wed.' here deleted.
[8] Susannah *Dobson, *Life of Petrarch*, 2v. (1775). Notes in Add MS 44723, ff. 232–3.
[9] Mary Martha, née Ellice, m. 1813 Sir E. *Kerrison; d. 1860.
[10] Richard Storr, Newark publican.   [11] Lengthy notes in Add MS 44723, ff. 120–95.
[12] The lake at Fasque is a third of a mile long.

16. Sat.

My Mother little better.—Manzoni—Ar. Pol.—paper—Petrarch—began Brougham's Col. Policy[1]—rode—wrote to Farquhar, Gaskell, Doyle.

17. Sunday.

My Mother better. Fettercairn—& read aftn service with a Serm. at home. Bible—began Pearsons Swartz,[2] & Milner's Church History: I cannot think all the sentiments of the Introdn appropriate[3]—read Life of Abp Leighton.[4]

18. M.

Brougham—Prom. Sposi—Petrarch's Life—papers—Notices of Whyte on Prayer & divers artt. in Scotch Reviews—Barrett's Sp. May 18, 1833[5]— wrote to Cole & Mr Stanford: rode—brought over Uncle D[ivie]—calls.[6]

19.

Brougham. Pr. Sposi—Burge's Speech[5]—Petrarch—Caulfield's Remarkable characters[7]—paper. rode—Party.

20.

Brougham. Pr. Sposi—Virgil with [Cousin] Divie—copied a letter: wrote to Mayor—on the hill: shot a brace: the Miss Forbeses here—Whist &c— "Remarkable characters"—Petrarch.

21.

Brougham. Pr. Sposi. "Crockford's".[8] Singing at night. at Sherriffs's &c. Arist. Pol.—wrote to Lushington—billiards.

22.

Brougham. Pr. Sposi—Virgil construing with Divie: a lecture about something at billiards yesterday. "Crockford's". Billiards.—A rubber in evg— Arist. Pol.

[1] Henry *Brougham, *An Inquiry Into the Colonial Policy of the European Powers*, 2v. (1803). Notes ibid. ff. 234–42.

[2] H. N. *Pearson, *Memoirs of the Life and Correspondence of C. *Swartz*, 2v. (1834).

[3] Joseph *Milner, *History of the Church of Christ*, ed. and ctd. by his b. Isaac*, 5v. (1810).

[4] Thomas *Murray, *The Life of R. *Leighton* (1828).

[5] 'The speeches of Mr. Barret and of Mr. Burge at a general meeting of Planters and others Interested in the West India Colonies' (1833).

[6] 'Gave Divie an hour with his Virgil' here deleted.

[7] James *Caulfield, *Portraits, Memoirs, and Characters, of Remarkable Persons*, 4v. (1819–20).

[8] Deale, *Crockford's; or, Life in the West*, 2v. (1828), a novel.

23. Sat.

Brougham—Pr. Sposi—Arist. Pol.—"Crockford's"—rode to make a round of calls.

24. Sunday.

Church, & aftn home service. A serm. of Bradley's. wrote on "God is love" —Leighton—Pearson's Swartz—Bible—Church of Scotland Mag.[1]

25.

Wrote to Lincoln—Doyle—Mr Tyler—Mrs Wallis—Hatchard—Farquhar —read Brougham—Manzoni—"Crockford's" (finished), inadequate to cure the evils it exposes—billiards—rode—Uncle David went: & Mr G.— papers.

This morning I had a painful and appalling dream. I stood with ——, looking out towards the S. and E.—Over the sea there arose a light strange in colour, between blue and green, indescribably clear[2]—it extended its arch upon the heaven: "look, look, look!" and as we looked, it brightened into a clear flame, a white consuming flame, masses appeared to [be] crackling and dissolving in it: its advance was steady and rapid over the intervening space, it gathered up and devoured all the rival elements on its way: the truth flashed upon me, it is the coming of the Son of Man! I turned and saw one drawn by a resistless power, in convulsive struggles down, down to the ground, and under the ground: my tongue said mechanically, Glory to thee, O God! but I felt within me the mass of sin, of flesh, of self, a death from which I could not escape and along with which I too must surely and how deservedly be destroyed—but here my vision ended, I awoke. It should be useful: may it be.

26. T.

Brougham—Pr. Sposi—Petrarch—Ar. Pol.—papers—billiards—boat— rode—wrote to Charriere & Caparn.

27. W.

Brougham—Pr. Sposi—wrote to J.N.G.—rode—singing—Ar. Pol. Billiards —to Edzell & called on Mr Hutton.

28. Th.

Brougham—(finished Vol 1.) Pr Sposi—Ar. Pol.—Petrarch. Out after the roes with Sir J. Forbes, Heming, & T.G.—Heming killed one—papers.

29. Fr.

Brougham's Col. Pol.—Pr. Sposi (finished Vol 1)—Petrarch (began Vol 2.) —paper—wrote to Mr Stanford—on the hill in the fog with Heming— billiards—Arist. Pol.

[1] (Glasgow 1834).   [2] Instead of 'bright'.

30. Sat.

Brougham (began Vol 2)—Pr. Sposi (began Vol 2.)—Arist. Pol.—took my Uncle to the Burn—Petrarch—& a game of whist.

31.

Sunday. Began Augustine's Confessions, & greatly delighted with them. Pearson's Swartz—Bible & Nn—Leighton—read prayers in aft. & an abridged serm. of Blomfield—Fettercairn in the morning.

Monday September one.

My Uncle & Aunt went with Divie, & Heming. We were sorry to part, & they.—Brougham. Eccentricity, paradox, fast & loose reasoning & (much more) sentiment, appear to have entered most deeply into the essence of this remarkable man when he wrote his Col. Pol., as now. With the rarest powers of *expressing* his thoughts, has he any fixed law to guide them?[1]

Pr. Sposi. I am sorry the liberation turns on "Iddio perdona tante cose" &c.[2]—Ar. Pol. & analysis as usual—Quarterly on Coleridge. paper. rode with Mr G. Wrote to Lady Kerrison & Mrs Wallace.—Accts & letters.

2.

T.G. went. Brougham—Pr Sp[osi]—Petrarch—rode with Helen—singing— Arist. Pol.—wrote to Aunt D.

3.

Doyle came: went to meet him. Brougham—Pr. Sposi—Petrarch—Arist. Pol.—Convn with Doyle on *"epics"*; appeared to be

    1. of action.
    2. action rehearsed.
    3. with unity of action.
    4. but extended & diversified, with a great range & some marked views of human character.
    5. To be of very general interest, not merely rational —yet
    6. To have that interest concentrated (invariably?) in individuals.

And Obs[erve] in connection with the *extent* of action—the *drama* is more like sculpture; it depends usually on a single idea, & sculpture admits rarely of grouping with success. Epic assimilates to the nature of painting in which composition may be much more complicated.

4.

Went on the hill with Doyle: several shots & as many misses. Brougham— Pr. Sp.—Arist Pol.—Quart Rev. on France—papers—sang—conv. on the

---

[1] Morley, i. 117.   [2] 'God pardons so many things': ch. 36.

Apollo Belv. & Venus dei Med. with Doyle: he doubted whether the artist had done right in choosing the human side of the alternative for the execution of the Venus.

5.

Brougham—Pr. Sposi—Began Novum Organon[1] with Doyle—paper—wrote to Beighton[2]—rode with Doyle—& walked him from the Gannochy up to the open glen[3]—conv. on female excellence; held their intellect less, their goodness greater than that of man: inferred from experience: as that universally we have not seen them in the first rank of excellence: nor is this well to be accounted for by the supposition that circumstances & the law of strength have been against them for 1. Do not believe in the supremacy of circumstance over mind; 2. There would at all events be evidence of a struggle in the female mind against the impediments of its condition but this we do not see. 3. I might have added, arguments from Revelation.

6. Sat.

Brougham. Pr. Sposi. paper. Arist. Pol.—rode over the Cairn[4] with Doyle —billiards & backgammon—also convv. with him about Göthe & our friend Hallam. Petrarch's Life. Conv. on distinctions of orders among undergradd. at the University.

7. Sunday.

Swartz. Aug. Conf.—Leighton. Church, & our prayers in aft. with a good sermon of Mr Medland's.[5] walk with Doyle—found "old William" reading at 76; we stood before him while he read two chapters (I think) without lifting his eyes so as to perceive us!—I went to see young Molison: his mother asked me to pray by him and I did so: O may the rains of heaven descend upon my own heart.

8. M.

Brougham—Pr. Sp[osi]—Bacon—with Doyle—finished Life of Petrarch—papers. rain all day. billiards & backgammon. Wrote to T.G. & Bruce (invitation).

9. Tuesday.

Finished Brougham's Col. Policy.—Quarty on Eton—paper—rain most of day; billiards & backgammon. resumed transln of Bride of Corinth—Bacon with Doyle—Promessi Sposi.

---

[1] *Bacon.   [2] William Beighton, Newark baker.
[3] That is, over the edge of the Grampian rampart up to Glen Dye, some 5 miles north of Fasque.
[4] Cairn o' Mount, a summit on the road to Deeside, 3 miles north of Fasque.
[5] Thomas Medland, 1803–82; fellow of Corpus, Oxford, 1830–41; vicar of Steyning, Sussex, 1840; domestic chaplain to dukes of *Sutherland.

10. W.

Ride to Drumtochtie with Doyle—billiards—backgammon—paper. Bacon's Org. and Analysis—Promessi Sposi—began Roscoe's Lorenzo[1]—a *few* lines to my transn.

11. Th.

Prom. Sposi—Bacon with Doyle—paper. Roscoe's Lorenzo—Draughts & letters to Mr Branston & W. Beighton—Bride of Corinth. Rode with Doyle: Helen's mare came down with me—thank God, no hurt: & her knees not broken, but I fear she must be unsafe.

12. Fr.

Prom. Sposi—Bacon with Doyle—shooting—killed 3 partr[idges], & 2 rabb[its] sitting—Roscoe's Lorenzo—began to write an Irish paper—wrote to T.G. and Mr Caparn—backgammon—paper.

13. S.

Pr. Sposi—Irish paper for D.U.M. (pr[ospective?])[2]—Roscoe's Lorenzo. papers—rode to Stracathro—Bacon with Doyle, began B. II.—backgn.

14. Sunday.

Church & Sac[ramen]t at Laurencekirk. Read the Sc. Episc. Communion service (not used then)—the diff[erence]s between it & ours are worthy of note. Above 100 present. Doyle remained with us: to my great delight. Went to Molison: prayer. walk over the hills. Leighton—& Swartz (finished Vol 1.).

15. M.

Wrote on Irish Church quest. paper. backgammon. Prom. Sposi, finished. It is inartificial, well principled, & interesting: much that is graphic or eloquent in it—rather loaded with digressions.—Wrote to Mr Stanford. Rode with Doyle to the Old Castle of Dunottar[3]—(except 11 miles in the gig)— much delighted, especially with the *natural* features of the place. $1\frac{1}{2}$–8. Lion came down with me on the way back. My *care* will be rather in disrepute I fear from two such accidents so near together.—Lorenzo—[anniversary of] Hallam's death: kept, but little.

16. T.

Finished & dispatched my paper on Irish Church Prospects.[4] Bacon with Doyle—billiards—boat—walk—whist—Roscoe's Lorenzo—began Dante's Commedia, read Canto 1. Wrote to T.G.—Mrs Watson's funeral.[5]

---

[1] William *Roscoe, *Life of Lorenzo di Medici* (1795). Notes in Add MS 44723, ff. 359–62.   [2] See 16 Sept. 34.

[3] Ruined castle 2 miles south of Stonehaven, where the Scottish regalia were kept during the commonwealth. Poem in Add MS 44723, f. 395. Cp. 19 May 28.

[4] Add MS 44681, f. 12: not traced in print.   [5] Cp. 6 Jan. 34.

17. W.

T.G. returned.—boat—and archery a little: whist in evg.—finished Bride of Corinth, so much of it at least as is at all fit to translate: & the effect of this may be questionable—the project too probably bad. Lorenzo (finished Vol. 1.)—Dante, Cantos II, III.—papers—Inglis's Tyrol.[1]

18. Th.

Lorenzo.—The Tyrol (Hist. of the War). paper. whist. Bacon with Doyle; B.II of Nov.Org. billiards, & scrambling walk by Cranstoun Burn.[2] Dante, Cantos IV, V.

19. Fr.

Lorenzo. Dante VI, VII. Mr Hutton & W. Goalen to dinner. rode: bow & arrow. Busy most of my reading time in making extracts from Brougham's Col. Pol. & writing a letter therewith, draught & fair copy.[3] Singing a little. —Doyle went.

20. Sat.

Lorenzo. Dante's Inf. Cantos VIII, IX, X. Bacon, notes. papers. whist. rode with T.G. to Arbuthnot. Wrote to Rn of whose arrival we hope soon to hear, & Mr James Lee, Newark. A few lines on Dunottar.

21. Sunday.

At Edzell Church: Mr Hutton feeble: but his mind has both sweetness & grace. Lunch with him afterwards. Prayers at 3 & Arnold XXX—read with P. Anderson[4] & Molison: prayer with the latter. Swartz (began Vol.2.) Aug. Conf. & Leighton.

22.

Lorenzo. Robns letters—papers—Dante XI & XII—Arist. Pol.—Bacon Nov. Org. I am now reading over again; making Analysis & Notes[5]—bow & arrows—rode—A sermon of W. Goalens.

23.

Lorenzo. Bacon Nov. Org.—Arist. Pol. & Analysis. Memoirs of Lord Chatham[6]—Inferno XIII, XIV. wrote to Doyle—rode with T.G.—whist.

[1] H. D. *Inglis, The Tyrol, with a Glance at Bavaria (1833).
[2] SE. of the house.
[3] See 27 Sept. 34.
[4] A villager.
[5] *Bacon, Novum Organum (1620). Notes in Add MS 44723, ff. 196–231.
[6] Authentic Memoirs of . . . the Late Earl of *Chatham (1778). Notes in Add MS 44723, ff. 250–4.

24.

Lorenzo—Bacon Nov. Org.—Arist. Pol.—analysis of both—paper—rode & archery with Helen—Dante XV, XVI. Whist—Lord Chatham.

25.

Lorenzo—Dante XVII, XVIII—wrote to Doyle & Gaskell—heard from Selwyn—dined & slept at Stracathro (five)—Machiavelli's Principe (began) —paper—Bad news from W.I.

26.

Lorenzo, finished—Principe—Dante XIX, XX—Lord Chatham—paper— whist—wrote to Aunt J.—returned from Stracathro soon after 12.

27.

Lord Chatham. Dante XXI, XXII. Lord Bacon's Nov. Org.—paper: sad accounts from Demerara—sculled Helen—Mr Wilson & Dr Gregory[1] here. Wrote to J.N.G. & Lincoln—my letter on Brougham appeared, in Wednesday's morning Post[2]—copied Mr Grant's letter.

28. Sunday.

—Church—prayers in aftn & Arnold—saw Molison. prayer—Leighton— Aug. Conf. —& Swartz.

29. M.

They all went to Aberdeen at 10—Goalen came over for the evening. Worked among the books—& walked out with a gun—Chatham—Dante, two Cantos—Bacon—wrote to R.G.—Mr Simpson—& a long letter to Dr Chalmers. Copied two letters from Mr Stuart, Demerara:[3] accounts perhaps better for *us*, than might have been expected: but God seems to manifest displeasure. papers.

30. T.

Solitary, after breakfast. Dante XXV, XXVI—Lord Chatham—began Mrs H. More's Life[4]—Bacon Nov. Org. worked among the books—wrote to Mrs G—strumming. papers.

Wednesday October one.

The delightful news of R[o]b[ertso]ns arrival at Falmouth on the 27th. Thank God. Wrote to him—to Mr G.—T.G.—Dante XXVII, XXVIII—

---

[1] Possibly Dr. William Gregory of Cheltenham.

[2] Just over a column, signed 'Guato', accusing *Brougham of 'wanton inconsistencies'. Draft in Add MS 44723, ff. 247–9.

[3] No doubt John Stewart, John *Gladstone's agent there; cp. 30 July 26 n.

[4] William *Roberts, *Memoirs of the Life and Correspondence of Mrs. Hannah *More*, 4v. (1834). A few notes in Add MS 44723, f. 282.

Bacon Nov. Org.—paper. Chatham—Mrs H. More—Bravo of Venice[1]—Books—shooting: killed 4 partridges & wounded another.

2. Th.

A long day at the books. rode. More—Bacon—Dante XXIX, XXX—wrote to Mr G.—Chatham—Cotton's Poems[2]—finished Bravo of Venice—papers.

3. Fr.

Finished the books—out shooting—dined at Stracathro—returned in evg. Dante XXXI, XXXII—Chatham—paper—Decamerone, enough to give an idea of the book: & show a strange state of manners, & how religion is disconnected from conduct there: but is it not so in every one of us? At least in one.[3]

4. Sat.

Finished the Inferno: read Hallam on Rossetti—Chatham—More—Bacon—ride—paper—wrote to R.G.—they returned from Aberdeen at 6½—conv. with Mrs G. there anent.

5. Sunday.

Ch. in mg—prayers & one of Swartz's Sermons in aftn—saw Molison, & prayer: a cottage conv. on the Garrol.[4] Aug. Confess—began Sinclair[5]—Pearson's Swartz.

6. M.

Sadly late. Chatham (began V.3). More (finished Vol 1)—Bacon—wrote to Mr Tallents—rode with Mr G.—papers—began Schiller's Don Carlos.

7. T.

Went to L[aurence]kirk to meet Uncle C.—who did not come. Il Principe—Bacon—Chatham—paper—walked the Robertsons out—Don Carlos—Mr Alexander[6] came.

8. W.

Chatham—Don Carlos—Bacon—billiards—boat—wrote to Mr Ramsay. Sir J. F[orbes] & Gen A[rbuthnott][7] to dinner—Blackwood on Coleridge—& on Aust. Govt in Italy.[8]

---

[1] J. F. Cooper, The Bravo. A Venetian Story, 3v. (1831).
[2] Charles *Cotton, Poems (1689).   [3] See Morley, i. 117, and 20, 27 Oct. 34.
[4] The Burn of Garrol runs southerly, ½ mile east of Fasque.
[5] J. Sinclair, Dissertations Vindicating the Church of England (1833).
[6] William L. Alexander, priest, of Edinburgh.
[7] Hugh Arbuthnott, 1780?–1868, 2nd s. of 7th viscount; fought in Baltic and Spain; tory M.P. Kincardineshire 1826–65.
[8] Blackwood's Edinburgh Magazine xxxvi. 542, 530 (October 1834).

9. Th.

To L[aurence]kirk in mg to meet Uncle C. rode to Thornton[1] in aft: Chatham, Mrs More (began V.2), Don Carlos, Bacon, papers.

10. Fr.

Don Carlos, Chatham, began Leo X,[2] wrote on the Church, wrote to Selwyn —paper—Bacon—rode to L[aurence]kirk to meet Robn & welcomed him home heartily and (it ought to be) thankfully—music in evg.

11. Sat.

Morng—out for roe. fired at & wounded a *fox*—saw a grouse by the house— in aft. rode to the Burn Keithock[3] & Stracathro with J.G., R.G., & Wm Alexander. Music in evg—Chatham—Don Carlos—Ph. von Artevelde resumed, it having just arrived—paper—wrote to Caparn & J.W. Lee.

12. Sun.

Church: aftn prayers at 3, & a Serm. of Bp Sandford's. saw Molison: prayer there: also (upon request) with old Mary Hay.[4] Swartz—Aug. Conf.—Sinclair—Bible—Molison's Father told me the labourers thought they were now well with meal at 10d or 1/ a peck, & the Reform: but if a bad harvest came, & meal rose to 1/6 or 1/8, they wd not endure it & wd call for more Reform. How thankful should be we for our weather. Wrote in black book.

13. M.

dined at Sir J. Forbes—Ld & Lady Morton[5] there. papers. Don Carlos— began die Räuber instead[6]—Philip Van A.—wrote to Cole—; Machiavelli —Chatham—Mr Alexander went—singing.

14. T.

Chatham, vol 3 (finished)—Bacon—paper—Die Räuber—distressing news of William Robn[7]—shooting with Uncle C.—finished Ph. van Artevelde: I think Mr Taylor in his preface applies the peculiarities of the drama too much to poetry universally—whist—began Bulwer's France.[8]

15. W.

Bulwer's France. Roscoe's Leo. Die Raüber: it is hard, or I very stupid, or both—billiards—singing—a rubber [of whist].

[1] The Crombies' place, Thornton Castle, 3 miles SE. of Fasque, midway between Fettercairn and Laurencekirk.
[2] W. *Roscoe, Life and Pontificate of Leo X, 4v. (Liverpool, 1805). Notes in Add MS 44723, ff. 270–81.
[3] A hamlet beyond Stracathro, 3 miles north of Brechin.
[4] Another cottager.
[5] George Sholto Douglas, 1789–1858, succ. his cousin as 19th earl of Morton 1827.
[6] Both Schiller's. Notes in Add MS 44723, ff. 264–9, 368–78.
[7] Presumably an errant cousin; cp. 8 July 35.
[8] Sir H. *Bulwer, France, social, literary, political, 2v. (1834).

16. Th.

France—Leo—Räuber—Bacon—boat—a rubber—With Rn to Sir J. Forbes's—paper.

17. Fr.

Went to Montrose. Thought the spire *absolutely* rather tawdry, & *relatively* not in keeping with the Church. Walked back 2h.47 min[1]—much pleased with the views of Fasque & the Grampians.—France—Leo—Räuber, & a rubber—some vss.

18. S.

Stewarts came—Jane went with little Flora.[2] Walk with R.G.—singing—Räuber—Leo—Bulwer—paper—Chesterfield: pfui![3] Wrote to Aunt J. & Pakenham.

19. Sunday.

Swartz—Augustine—Sinclair—read prayers & Arnold XI—conv. with P. S[tewart] about Convocation &c. on which he seemed to agree. Saw Mollison, & prayer.

20. M.

Bulwer's France—Bacon—Räuber—Boccaccio's Decameron: the "Convcncvolc cosa[4] &c" at the beginning of I is curious, compared with some of what follows—papers—billiards with P.M. S[tewart] a little whist & singing—papers—the sad news of the burning of both Houses.[5] wrote to Doyle.

21. T.

12–6. Out after roe. Singing in evg. France—Raüber—paper—Boccaccio. Forbeses dined here.

22. W.

Singing—whist—Räuber—still hard, at least to me—paper—'France'—Hume on Liberty & Causation & writing thereupon[6]—wrote to Lincoln's Inn—

---

[1] See Morley, i. 116.

[2] Jane Tyler, with *Tyler's da. by his first wife, Elizabeth Ann, née Griffin, who d. 1830.

[3] The 4th earl of *Chesterfield's notorious *Letters to his son*, 2v. (1774).

[4] 'Decent matter'.

[5] Both houses of parliament were burned down on the evening of 16 October, through careless burning of exchequer tallies in the furnaces of the lords.

[6] David *Hume, *Enquiry concerning human understanding* (1758), chs. viii and vii; a few notes in Add MS 44814, ff. 63–64.

23. Th.

Stormy day. singing—whist—Raüber—Boccaccio—Bulwer—'An Account of all the Lord Bacon's Works'[1]—papers—at night the wind became terrific.

24.

Sad sad devastation among the trees—out to examine—wrote to Goalen—Papers—King of Prussias[2] works—billiards—singing—the Inneses[3] & Mrs Farquhar to dinner—wrote to Harrison—Raüber—a rubber. Leo X.

25.

Wind much abated from last evening. Out after roe. Singing; a game at commerce; papers. Bulwer's France—die Raüber—wrote to Gaskell—a few verses—this has been an idle week, but with company one's work dwindles.

26. Sunday.

Swartz—Sinclair—St Augustin—psalm-singing at night. read prayers & Arnold XII—prayer with Molison & old Mary Hay. Saw at the village church a great object: an old woman staggered up the aisle with a violent convulsive affection; she fell as it were from pew door to pew door, her head from time to time cast up, her face pale, eyes glazed: in her pew she was most agitated when she stood, but even when sitting she was very far from repose both limbs and head twitched uncontroulably, and her painful state was strangely set off by the remarkable cleanliness of her clothing—Alas! if the frame of Adam told that he was born to be admired and obeyed, it is not so with a portion at least of its descendants. But surely that soul must be healthy, which heeds not the public gaze, under such painful conditions, in order to hear the word of God.—Stewart tells me that in his neighbourhood the children do not attend church, any more than here: but Sunday School—So at Edzell—& q. generally?

27. M.

Stewart went. Cruickshanks & Carnegys to dine. Singing. went to the Burn with Uncle C. Leo X (finished Vol 1.) papers. Bulwer: wrote something about last week's storm.[4] Boccaccio, finished Giornata I which with some others I have read is enough.

28. T.

Robn went. Good news to Uncle C. from London—Now the reign of (comparative) diligence should return—wrote to Lincoln's Inn—Bacon—Leo—Bulwer—Raüber—whist—papers. Began Adv. of Learning.

---

[1] Possibly J. B. de Vauzelles, *Histoire de la vie et des ouvrages de Francis *Bacon*, 2v. (1833), ii. 207 ff.

[2] Frederick the Great.

[3] William Innes of Raemoir, 17 miles to the north.   [4] Cp. 31 Oct. 34.

29. W.

rode—Räuber—finished my Analysis of the Novum Organon to II.20, &c. —Mrs More's Life resumed—whist—Roscoe's Leo—rode with H.J.G.

30. Th.

Late up. Räuber—Leo—Mrs More—Machiavelli's Principe—wrote to Dry —Mrs Wishlade—Gaskell. Whist—The Principe very well illustrates Leo X.

31. Fr.

Leo.—Räuber. Principe. Bacon. Hannah More—wrote to Harrison. paper. wrote out my "Congratulation to the Beeches of the Garrol".[1] Walk with gun.

Saturday November one.

Leo: finished Vol 2.—finished the Robbers, and so read the preface which gives a pleasing picture of Schiller's mind: give my adhesion to Coleridge's opinion.[2]—wrote a little on Causation—rode—Mrs More—papers—& a game of dummy.

2. Sunday.

Church—prayers in aft. & Swartz's 4th—saw Molison; prayer: at two old folks' cottages. I am delighted to find them so, at the offer of Prayerbooks. Augustin—Sinclair on Liturgies—Bible—Leighton on St Peter.[3] Wm G. here.

3. M.

The Mackenzies came. Uneasiness about Helen's attack in the evg. Leo: resumed Don Carlos: Adv. Learning (finished B.1.)—Mrs More—out shooting: wrote to Bell & Bradfute.[4] papers.

4. T.

Dr Guthrie & Mr Fettis[5] here. The complaint appeared to be probably measles—the M'Ks went. Leo: Don Carlos: Mrs More: Adv. Learning (B.II): papers: read Education evidence: drew a paper of references & wrote to Harrison therewith.

5. Wed.

Helen much better: decided measles.—Leo: Adv. Learning: Don Carlos: Mrs More finished Vol 2: Bulwer: out shooting.

---

[1] On surviving the storm of 23–24 October: Add MS 44723, ff. 255–8.

[2] *Coleridge, in *Biographia Literaria*, ii. 257 (1817), describes Schiller's play as 'the first fruits of his youth, and, as such, the pledge and promise of no ordinary genius'.

[3] Robert *Leighton, *A Practical Commentary upon the first two Chapters of the first Epistle of St. Peter* (1693).

[4] Edinburgh publishers and booksellers.   [5] Surgeon, of Laurencekirk.

6. Th.

Leo: Adv. Learning. Coleridge's Christabel (+) &c: Don Carlos: paper:
Mrs More: among the hill woods. Saw Helen.

7. Fr.

Wrote to Bell & Bradfute—& to Mrs Wishlade's father. A day of rain:
billiards with T.G.—started Best with his French Grammar; tried to explain
how such things should stand, there is *one* more important. Papers. Leo:
Don Carlos: Mrs More: Adv. Learning—Bulwer's France—backgammon
with my dear father.

8. S.

Saw Helen again, Leo: Don Carlos: finished Pearson's Swartz: Adv. Learning: Mrs More: billiards with T.G. (a day of rain) (began Vol IV in Leo.)

9. Sunday.

Helen now improving we hope regularly. Church: prayers & Arnold aloud
—recommended Milner: Leighton: Aug. Conf: Sinclair: Bible. prayer with
Mollison.—Saw 'Sandy' sick.

10. M.

Leo: Don Carlos: papers: Mrs More: Adv. Learning: wrote to J.N.G: & a
long letter to John. At Fettercairn.

11. T.

Leo: Don Carlos: Mrs More: paper: gun & walk: wrote to Doyle: finished
Adv. of Learning—August. Conf. had to kill a wounded partridge: & felt
after it, as if I had shot the albatross. It may be said—this should be either
less or more.[1]

12. W.

ride: down with Blackwood[2]: not thrown, nor any damage to him. Leo:
Don Carlos: working at French Statistics: August[ine] Confess.—Mrs More.
On Monday mg I began to give Best a little chamber lesson in French, &
continue it daily: being habitual I shall not mention it here.

13. Th.

finished Don Carlos: began Whewell's Bridgwater Treatise.[3] Leo: paper:

---

[1] Version in Morley, i. 116.
[2] His horse.
[3] W. *Whewell, *Astronomy and General Physics considered with reference to Natural
Theology* (1833), the first published of eight works 'On the Power, Wisdom, and Goodness of God, as manifested in the Creation', written on a bequest of the 8th earl of
*Bridgewater. Notes in Add MS 44723, ff. 363–7.

Mrs More (finished Vol 3) Aug. Conf.—at Mr Whytes: the Fettercairn school:[1] Macdonald's & Ross's[2]—wrote to Pakenham.

14. Fr.

Mrs More (began Vol 4)—Whewell—began "Die Verschwörung des Fiesko"[3] —finished Leo, highly interesting, agreeable in style: of its fidelity and research I am not competent to speak, but it has though in some degree subdued the leaven of Unitarianism lowering its tone in reference to the most important subjects.[4] paper—wrote to Goalen.

15. Sat.

papers—Verschwörung—Whewell—Mrs More—began Shepherd's Poggio Bracciolini.[5] Lower in regard to religion than Roscoe: it seems scornful and licentious. Hor[ace] Walpole.—Visits on Balfour with T.G.

16. Sunday.

At Laurencekirk mg—reading & prayer with Molison—pr[ayer] with M. Hay—aft. prayers & a *Swartz* sermon (his 3d).—Augustine—Sinclair— Milner.

17. M.

Poggio: Verschwörung: Whewell: Mrs More: paper: Mr Hutton & the Whytes to dine: a delightful hillwalk, perhaps 2 m. beyond Clattering Brig:[6] wrote a few lines: wrote to Harrison.

18.

T.G. went. Poggio: Verschwörung: Whewell: Mrs More: shooting in aft: Hutton & Goalen dined here; & General Arbuthnott brought us an account that the Ministers were out.[7]—Papers.

19.

Poggio: Verschwörung: Whewell: Aug. Conf.: Mrs More: papers: wrote to T.G.—Aunt J.—& General Arbuthnott. Rather disturbed in my work to-day by the confirmation of yesterday's most extraordinary intelligence: God bear us through.

[1] James Nicholson, master.
[2] David Ross, Fettercairn blacksmith.
[3] By Schiller. Notes ibid. ff. 283–8.
[4] See Morley, i. 117.
[5] W. *Shepherd, Liverpool radical, *Life of Poggio Bracciolini* (1802), renaissance scholar. Notes in Add MS 44723, ff. 290–3.
[6] Two miles NNE. of the house; where the road over Cairn o'Mount to Glen Dye and Deeside crosses the Black Burn of Arnbarrow.
[7] *William IV dismissed *Melbourne on 15 November. See Morley, i. 118.

10—II.

20.

Poggio: Verschw: Whewell: paper: Mrs More: Aug. Conf: wrote to Mr Tallents—Mrs Wallace—out on cottage & farm visits &c.—No great light today on yesterday's news. *Thoughts* for a paper thereon.

21.

Poggio: Verschwörung: paper: wrote to Mr Tallents & to Ld Arbuthnott: Aug. Confess. Helen now a good deal advanced. Most of my[1] *reading day* occupied in writing a sort of political tract, for possible use.[2]

22.

Aug. Confess: Whewell: Verschwörung: read Wordsworth to H.J.G.— papers—finished Poggio. This & many other books in a religious or even only a moral view, require to be read with much jealousy. wrote to Doyle— and T.G.—rode to Fordun, saw Dr Leslie.[3]

23. Sunday.

Church: prayers in aft & Arnold 24—reading & prayer with Molison. finished Sinclair: several Chapp. of More on St Paul. Aug. Confess: yet this day of rest was more than usually invaded by the exciting thoughts of the time.

24. M.

The papers—now bulky reading. Gunning.[4] Wrote to Gaskell & Mr Finlay. Verschwörung: finished Whewell's able & amiable book: & Mrs More: wh will I hope do much good.—Goalen here in evg.

25. T.

finished Verschwörung: papers: Aug. Conf: began Forbes on Church Lands & Tithes[5]—copied a paper for Mr G—wrote to T.G. and R.G.

26.

Finished Notes of Pearson's Swartz[6]—finished Augustin's Confessions: there is a good deal of prolix & fanciful though acute speculation, but the practical parts of the book have a wonderful force, inimitable sweetness & simplicity.[7]—Forbes on Tithes—packing. Saw Molison & offered a farewell prayer. I would not have ventured upon this solemn office at all, but his

[1] 'day' deleted.
[2] Morley reports this 'has disappeared down the gulf of time' (i. 118). It is in Add MS 44723, ff. 294–308, still incomplete.
[3] James Leslie, 1764–1858; D.D. Glasgow; minister at Fordoun 1788–1843.
[4] Elizabeth *Gunning, 1769–1823; novelist.
[5] W. Forbes, *Church Lands and Tithes* (1705). A few notes in Add MS 44723, f. 289.
[6] In Add MS 44723, ff. 396–8.
[7] Version in Morley, i. 117. Notes in Add MS 44723, ff. 380–6.

good minister lives seven miles off.—Saw all the tenants on Balfour, & wrote an account of the entire for Sheriff's keeping.

27.

Russell's modern Europe—which I am about to commence from soon after Charles V.[1] 9.50–4.20 56 m. to Perth. read the papers & wrote a few verses at night: but more of thought upon political matters, public & private.

28.

10.10–4—44 miles to Edinburgh—same subjects continued on my mind: in the evening a long conversation expressed my feelings about treating to my dear & kind father, T.G. present—carried their concurrence to the length of inquiring from my Committee how they propose to proceed: wrote (draughts and letters) to Mr Tallents and the Duke accordingly. This is a great relief to my mind: the way is I hope now open though I do not yet see its issue: θεῶν ἐν γούνασι κεῖται.[2]

29. Saturday.

Signed the Address[3]—shopping—called on the Frasers & Ramsays—wrote to Robn—papers—& read "Autobiogr. of a Dissg Minister".[4]

30. Sunday.

Woke with sore throat. Ch mg & aft: read a little Wilberforce & so made my head worse—went to bed early, physic &c.

December. 1 & 2.

In bed—fever kept *off* by perspiration and purging—saw Dr Hunter[5] Tuesday night—my Mother's incessant kindness spoiled me: & seemed as though it would knock her up.

3. Wed.

began to read a little of the paper: some doses of which my throat & head have saved me. wrote a letter to Hamilton. Up in the evening.

4. Th.

Up earlier in the aft—wrote (draught & letter) to Mr Godfrey—Mr Tallents —Mr M'Dowal—T. D. Acland—[6] a few verses.

[1] W. *Russell, *History of Modern Europe*, 5v. (1779–84). Notes in Add MS 44723, ff. 314–26.
[2] 'It lies in the lap of the gods'.
[3] For Newark? Cp. 15 Dec. 34.
[4] W. P. *Scargill, *The Autobiography of a Dissenting Minister* (1834).
[5] J. D. Hunter, F.R.C.P.
[6] 'paper a little' here deleted.

5. Fr.

Again improved: my interruption has been such as should remind me of dependence. read Quarty on Mrs More—a mixture of good & *bad* spirit—finished the Dissenting Minister: good humoured but somewhat apathetic —wrote to Dry & Mrs Wallace—read Quart. on Louis Philippe.

6. Sat.

Wrote 'The old moorcock's song'.[1] Dr Hunter—to pay his last visit. The Excursion. Out. T.G. went to town—wrote to Crawfurd (about Knapp)[2]— Seymer—& Acland—read Quart. on Paroles d'un Croyant. paper.

7. Sunday.

Ch mg & aft.—Sacrament. read Wilberforce—(began) Mrs More's Strictures[3]—Bible—&c.

8. M.

papers—calls—wrote to T.G.—Aunt Divie—Wilmot. a short walk. Heard of the birth of Jane Tyler's daughter[4]—read Cook on Patronage[5]—Strictures —whist—verses.

9. T.

Wrote to Uncle C. finished Cook on Patronage. read For. Quart. on Italy.[6] Finished & wrote out some stanzas of Dec. 1832 on !! the human heart!! but I am not impudent enough to call them by that name.[7]—letters from Newark: strove to deceive myself at first: but Truth forced in her way, & I saw that I in duty could not close with them. An evening of *painful* thought and conversation: but how should I be taught herein to cast my care on God, when myself utterly baffled and perplexed within, tempted without? Wrote two draughts to Mr Godfrey.

10. W.

Arranged even beyond hope with my father a letter to Mr Godfrey, from a draught the fourth I had drawn.[8] Draughts & letters to the Duke & Mr T. —wrote to T.G. & R.G.—rode—calls—papers—Quarty on Louis Philippe:

[1] Add MS 44723, f. 309.
[2] Knapp's debts had forced him to flee the country. R. Craufurd was bringing out an ed. of Knapp's poems; to which *Gladstone did not subscribe. Cp. 30 Jan. 36.
[3] Hannah *More, *Strictures on the Modern System of Female Education*, 2v. (1799).
[4] See 3 Feb. 35.
[5] G. Cook, 'A Few Plain Observations on the Enactment of the General Assembly, 1834, relating to Patronage and Calls'.
[6] Foreign Quarterly Review, xiv. 298 (December 1834), on 'Italy and Europe'.
[7] Add MS 44722, ff. 94–95.
[8] Add MS 44723, ff. 18–19.

began a Clergyman's answer to the Case of the Dissenters.[1] With Ross about the Forfarshire burghs.[2]

11. Th.

My Father's seventieth birthday. His strength & energy are wonderful & give promise of many more.[3] may they come! and may each more and more unfold a character such as shall live in the sight of God for ever.

Began Locke on U[4]—Russell's Mod. Eur. Vol. 3.—papers—Strictures—wrote to Mr Tyler—calls.

12. Fr.

Russell—Locke—Answer to Diss[ente]rs Case (finished)—wrote to Mrs Wallace—Hamilton—Mr Tallents—papers—calls—finished Strictures Vol 1.—no favourable news yet from Tom.

13. Sat.

Russell—Locke—Politics—& notes (as usual) from all. resumed Best's morning French. Mr Lindsay[5] dined here: overflowing with Eastern information. papers—calls. So Stanley is gone to town. Thank God.[6]

14. Sunday.

St John's m. & aft—Mr R[amsay] admirable on Matt 25.46.—Wilberforce—Bible—began More's Practical Piety.[7] Attempted to speak to Best about the Sacrament: found him fav[ourabl]y disposed. And went to Aunt M. on the restoration of intercourse: may it succeed.

The earlier part of the day prepared me for the latter. more letters from Newark. I owe Branston much: but how do I need the Divine Guidance: perhaps I ask & expect it too visibly & palpably. Wrote (briefly) to Mrs Gaskell—R.G.—Mr M'Dowal.

15. M.

Wrote accordingly to Tallents & Branston. Russell—Locke—papers—large arrivals from Newark &c: far better than I dared have hoped: thanks be to God who works all for good. Excellent letter (especially) from the Duke: my Father delighted with it. And Orkney looks well for Tom.[8] Oh

---

[1] 'An Answer to a Letter Addressed to the Lord Chancellor on the Case of the Dissenters, in a Letter to the Same, by a Clergyman' (1834).
[2] Horatio *Ross, 1801–86; Scottish sportsman; whig M.P. Aberdeen 1831, Montrose burghs 1832–4 (i.e. Montrose, Aberbrothock, Brechin, Forfar, and Inverbervie); contested Paisley 1835.
[3] Version in Morley, i. 118.
[4] John *Locke, *An Essay concerning Humane Understanding* (1690). See 9 Apr. 36 and Morley, iii. 476–7. Notes in Add MS 44723, ff. 327–58.
[5] James Lindsay, 1793–1855, of Balcarres, co. Fife; cousin of earl of Balcarres.
[6] *Peel reached London from Italy on 9 December, and at once sent for *Stanley.
[7] Hannah *More, *Practical Piety* (1811).
[8] But see 26 Dec. 34 and 9 Jan. 35: he fought Leicester instead.

may we rise through these to higher things.—Wrote draughts to the Duke and Mr Godfrey, *accepting*.[1] *Aunt M. here.*

16. Tuesday.

Wrote to the Duke—Lincoln—Godfrey—Tallents—T.G.—read Locke, Russell—at Mr Wood's:[2] saw him & had an interesting conversation. He is I suppose another Howard.[3] He gave Bell[4] priority: mentioned want of *life*, & technicality: Directors of Br. & For. school disingenuous: principle of comprehension carried far enough in the Natl Schools.—catechism shd not be given up.

Aunt M. & the Frasers dined here. At Ld Medwin's in evg.

17. Wednesday.

Locke & Russell in morng: went to meet the Post: found a letter from Peel, desiring to see me dated 13th. All haste: ready by 4—no place. reluctantly deferred till the morning. Wrote to Lincoln—Sir R. Peel[5]—Mr Godfrey—Gaskell—Mr Tallents—Seymer—papers: & a game at whist!

This is a serious call. I got my father's advice, to take anything with work and responsibility. May God guide me: much has he done for me: surely this is providentially ordered—the call upon me comes but two days after I had made a settlement at Newark.[6]

18.

Off at 7.40 by mail. I find it a privation to be unable to read in a coach: the mind is distracted thro' the senses, & rambles: nowhere is it to me so incapable of continuous thought. Scotch accent in Northumberland: different character of the inclosures. All night on & on—Newcastle at $9\frac{1}{4}$ P.M.[6]

19.

The same again. At York $6\frac{1}{4}$ A.M. to 7. Ran to peep at the Minister & bore away a faint twilight image of its grandeur. At Newark sent a message to Mr T[allents] by Gilstrap.[7]

20.

Arrived safe thank God & well $5\frac{3}{4}$—Albany soon—Charriere had evacuated my rooms: found a very thankful letter: to bed for $2\frac{1}{4}$ hours—conv. with

[1] Nomination for Newark: see 31 Dec. 34, &c.
[2] John Wood, teacher at Edinburgh sessional school (cp. 1 Jan. 35).
[3] John *Howard, 1753–99, self-taught mathematician, kept schools at Carlisle and Newcastle.
[4] Andrew *Bell, 1753–1832, originator of a pupil-teacher system.
[5] Add MS 40406, f. 25.
[6] Extracts in Morley, i. 119.
[7] Extracts ibid. Joseph Gilstrap, innkeeper, ran the coach office at the Kirkgate.

Tom ever warm in interest—went to Peel about eleven:[1] by his offer & recommendation settled at the Treasury board[2]—in Bedf. Square & Wimpole Street. T.G. dined in my rooms & off by Mail to Lpool: I hope & think his matters will go well. Wrote to Mr G—Duke of N.—Lincoln—Mr Godfrey, Mr Tallents, Mr Stirling (Glasgow),[3] T. Ogilvy, Harrison, Sir J. Mordaunt, Gaskell—dined at the Carlton House dinner: a good deal of conv. with Lord G. Somerset, Mr Shaw, and Mr C. Ross.[4]

21. S.

St James's Bp (ordination) mg, & Mr Ward aftn. Dined in B. Square. Wood with me. Letters. Endeavoured to explain the sacrament to my servv. at night. Began Evans.[5]

22. M.

Dined with Doyle. Long with Merewether about Corporations. Wrote an Address for Newark:[6] submitted it to Uncle D., Mr Lefroy,[7] & Sir T. Freemantle,[8] before venturing to send one so much in detail. Arranging pamphlets &c.—wrote to Mr Tallents—H.J.G.—R.G.—Lincoln—Mrs Gaskell—Sir Hugh Campbell—Mrs Charriere—Mr Hagart. Papers. The Treasury Board is I learn completed.

23. T.

Harrison with me—& Mr Oliverson. letters from Tom: occupied with his matters: saw Mr Balfour: little encouragement. Wrote to Lincoln—T.G.—Mr G—Acland[9]—dined at the Mansion House: much expence, little comfort.[10] Peel's speech however was my object & repaid me. papers.

24. W.

This is a sacred day at least of right.[11] Mr Oliverson here again—saw Mr Balfour again—& Lord Meadowbank.[12]—long letters on Tom's matters &

---

[1] Version ibid.

[2] *Gladstone was appointed a junior lord of the treasury. Conversation in Add MS 44819, ff. 7–8.

[3] Probably Gordon Stirling, West India merchant.

[4] Charles Ross, 1800?–60, tory M.P. Oxford 1822–6, St. Germans 1826–32, Northampton 1832–7; m. a da. of Lord Cornwallis 1825; junior lord of admiralty 1830, of treasury 1834–5.

[5] R. W. *Evans, *Scripture Biography* (1834), published as vol. vii of *The Theological Library*.

[6] Draft in Add MS 44723, ff. 310–11. Text in Reid, *G*, 195–6.

[7] Thomas Langlois *Lefroy, 1776–1869; K.C. 1806; M.P. Dublin University 1830–41; Irish judge 1841–66.

[8] Sir Thomas Francis *Freemantle, 1798–1890; cr. bt. 1821; tory M.P. Buckingham 1827–46; chief whip *ca.* 1841–3; chairman, board of customs, 1846–74; cr. Lord Cottesloe 1874.

[9] In A. H. D. *Acland, *Memoirs and Letters of ... Sir T. D. *Acland* (1902), 75–77.

[10] See Magnus, 21.

[11] His dead sister's birthday.

[12] Alexander *Maconochie, 1777–1861, Scottish judge; Lord Meadowbank 1819.

busy therewith: also other calls. wrote to T.G. Mr G. Mr Tallents, Lord Stuart de Rothsay[1]—Treasury Commission announced in Evg papers— dined in B. Square—read "Tories Whigs & Radicals"[2]—my indoor time expended in arranging my Parlty papers to this time, not very agreeably.

25.

St James's mg & aft. Sacrament. Mrs Wallace (I hope) went—read Bible— Evans's Scr. Biography—papers—wrote to Mrs G—R.G.—Uncle C.—Mr Ramsay—W. K. Hamilton—dined in B. Square.

26.

T.G. came: with him at Carlton—Balfour's—Merewether's—& with the Liverpool folks. He behaved admirably to B. & B. well to him.[3] Wrote to Mr G.—Mr Tallents—Lord Winchilsea—Lord Middleton—Mr Holden— Mr. T. Manners Sutton—papers—read Excursion B.5.—acct of Newark— dined in Bedf. Square.

27. Sat.

T.G. to breakf & dinner—read Wordsworth's Excursion—Gisborne's Letter,[4] Disraeli's speech[5]—wrote to J.M.G., Sir H. Campbell[6], Mr G. (copied two letters), Horatio Ross, Cole, Childers, T. Ogilvy, Sherriffs, Mr Tallents—heard a great secret, of what will be on Tuesday—papers: a rattle at me with the net in the Globe[7]—preparing to pack again, up late.

28. Sunday.

St Giles's & St James's. Breakf. in B. Squ. & tea with the Anstices. Sumner aloud. Sacred Biogr. & the two first 'Essays on the Church'.[8] Bible. A troubled day with the plans of tomorrow. Packed.

29.

Wrote to Saunders & T.G. Off by the Highflyer at 8—Stamford $8\frac{1}{2}$ P.M. Posted on to Newark: arrived soon after 12—dressed & went to the ball: to reach which (by Mr G & T[allents]'s desire) was my object. Found many county folks & kind welcome—$12\frac{1}{2}$-$2\frac{1}{2}$.

---

[1] Sir Charles *Stuart, 1779–1845, diplomat; envoy to Lisbon 1810–4, to Paris 1814, 1815–24, 1828–31; kt. 1812; cr. Lord Stuart de Rothsay 1828; his da. Charlotte m. C. J. *Canning 1835.

[2] Untraced.

[3] Thomas Balfour of Balfour, 1810–38, was tory M.P. for Orkney, 1835–7.

[4] The younger Thomas *Gisborne's address to his Derbyshire constituents (1834).

[5] B. *Disraeli, 'The Crisis Examined', an address to the electors of High Wycombe on 16 December 1834.

[6] Sir Hugh Purves-Hume-Campbell of Marchmont, 1812–94, 7th bart. 1833, tory M.P. co. Berwick 1834–47; m. 1834 Margaret Spottiswoode, who d. 1839.

[7] A leader reviewing the new Treasury board that day said he 'exhibits the most zealous adherence to the most antiquated and obnoxious principles of his party'.

[8] R. W. *Evans, The Church of God, in a series of Sermons (1832).

My birthday. Twenty five years have passed over my poor head: the body they say is now compact & firm: but my mind at least remains incoherent and disjointed: void of the power to realise its desires & thoughts, and of the courage to seize upon occasion in its flight: though I think its mechanical aptitude for labour may have grown. But it were hypocrisy to pretend that *here* lay its worst fault. No, it is in the deadly taint of sin, manifest in every nascent suggestion of the heart, insinuating itself into and throughout every mental process. O! if we knew by sad experience that all even the slightest of our acts are capable of imbibing sinfulness by generating vainglory and selflove, how necessarily is it also true that in all things we may by their expulsion glorify God, and do all things in the name of the Lord Jesus! I am still one of that Body to whom the promises are assured: to whom God is a Father, and Jesus Christ an elder brother:

> O joy! that in our embers
> Is something that doth live!

still it is granted me to see in the ordinances with which I am blessed without, and the guidance of Providences about my path, that God's lovingkindness endures. As long as in many things I am convinced I see his design and operation keeping evil out of my way, so long may I be convinced I am not given over, even I: and is it not wonderful? and shall I not praise him? Alas rather shall I? May he teach me.

My journey was quiet & allowed of thought.

30.

Wrote to T.G.—Sir T. Freemantle—Dr Chalmers—Mrs G: F.H. Doyle. Convv. with the Duke of N. &c. Met my committee: all hearty from Mr G[odfrey] downwards, calls. Dined at Mr Tallents's. Made up my year's accounts—& wrote up my journal.

31.

Lardner's 'Outlines'. wrote to J.N.G.—Mr Back (Greenwich Park)[1]—T.G.—R.G.—Miss G.—Lord G. Somerset[2]—Uncle D.—dined at Mr Godfrey's—many calls. Handley retired!

Though this brings in Wilde, worse disposed I fear than H. towards the Govt and country, I am not the less bound to be thankful for it as a great personal mercy, that I am hereby (I trust) relieved from any fear of the difficulties which would have arisen, had the Committee been unable to realise the promises held out by Mr Godfrey, still more, of the demoralisation usually connected with treating. The year thus closes upon me with a new assurance of the Providence and mercy of God! May it have its effect. —Recd the Serjeant's congratulations.

---

[1] Possibly James Buck, clerk at horse guards.

[2] Lord Granville Charles Henry *Somerset, 1792–1848, 2nd s. of 6th duke of Beaufort; tory M.P. Monmouthshire from 1828; commissioner of woods and forests 1834–5; chancellor, duchy of Lancaster, 1841–6; notable sportsman.

Newark Jan. One. 1835.

9½–4. Canvass: speech afterwards. Committee dinner. Tea at Mr Godfrey's. Papers. Wood's 'Sessional School'[1]—On our progress, all went *most* agreeably. Good accounts from Tom. Wrote to J.M.G.

2. Friday.

Canvass 9¼–5. Short speeches, after it & after the dinner wh was as yesterday. Papers & Wood's Sessional School. Tea at Mr Tallents's. Very excellent success.

3. Sat.

Canvass 9–3½: finished the town: speech. Dined at Gilstrap's—speaking &c —tea at Mr Tallents's—read Wood—wrote to Mrs G.—Hatchard—Mr Stewart—Mr Grant—Mr Macdowal.—Mr Norman.[2]

4. Sunday.

Ch. morng & evg. The Lord's Supper: wh Best attended, to my great satisfaction. Dinner & tea at Mr Tallents's. Read Evans—pt of Simpson's pamphlet[3]—Bible—Chr[istian] Year.

5. M.

Went with very little mental preparation to the hustings at 10. Elected by 10.25—Spoke perhaps 50 min. & the Serjeant an hour—to a very Blue audience.[4] I have no reason to complain of him, quite the reverse: but cannot speak well of his character as far as inferred from his speaking. Chaired at two—the *best* feeling prevailed. We passed with cheers. Our procession was *very* large, & most orderly & respectable. I should say 2–3,000, confidently. A short speech afterwards. Dinner at 5½. Speeches afterwards: & a little singing: plenty of both from others. Seventy dined. The most cordial feeling. Sat till 11½. Wrote home, &c.

6. T.

Menteith breakfd with me. Considering several applications. near 40 calls. dined at Mr Godfrey's. papers: settlings afterwards. wrote to Rn G—Wm G—Sir R. Bromley—Mrs Wallace.

---

[1] John Wood, *Account of the Edinburgh Sessional School* (1829).
[2] John Norman, Newark maltster; or perhaps Richard Norman of Melton Mowbray, who m. a da. of the 4th duke of Rutland.
[3] Robert Simpson, curate of Newark, 'Remarks on a Pamphlet . . . by Rev. J. Waterworth, a Romish Priest in Newark' (1835).
[4] *Wilde's colours were blue, *Gladstone's red. Both were returned unopposed.

7. W.

Off at 9½ by Tuxford[1] to Clumber. Went out with the sportsmen, D of N., D. of H[amilton], and Lord Wm [Clinton]—All were very kind. D. of H. seems conservative though not ministerial. Duchess[2] & Lady L[incoln] sang in the evening: a very high treat for my poor ears. Paper: wrote to H.J.G. —Off at 10½—Missed the Highflyer at Tuxford: broke down in my chaise on the way to Newark: No injury—thanks to God. Remained 2½ hours alone: overtaken by the Wellington at

(8. Th.)

3½ A.M. Arrived in London before 8 P.M. Good travelling.[3] Now I should be very thankful this week to have escaped colds & bad ones. Saw the chairing in Huntingdon.[4]

9. Fr.

After some abortive Canvass calls, voted for Cochrane[5] & went to the Treasury: had my first lesson there from Mr Stewart:[6] the business of course in the first instance mechanical.—Tom is *in* for Leicester: a great victory.[7] Wrote to him—Mr G—R.G.—Macdowal—Mr Jones—Dr Chalmers—E. of Lincoln.—Papers: Wood. In evg attended Cochrane's Committee: & (privately) endeavoured to urge the publication of the pollbooks as a foundation for future organisation. Arranging.

10. Sat.

Wrote to Sir F. Doyle—Charriere—Mr Tallents—Mr Simpson—R. Moth[8] —Mr Willmer[9]—Lincoln—F.G.[10]—occupied 12–5 at the Treasury in going over many minutes—dined at Uncle D.s—papers—household work.

The elections proceed: well enough at least to show what *might* have been done in a short time. But God be praised.[11]

11. Sunday.

St Giles's & St James's. Lunch in B. Square. Arnold 11.30 aloud. Bible—

[1] On the great north road, 15 miles NNW. of Newark.
[2] Of Hamilton: *Newcastle had been a widower since 1822.
[3] Morley, i. 121–2.
[4] *Peel's brother Jonathan*, 1799–1879, soldier and racehorse owner, M.P. Norwich 1826–31, Huntingdon 1831–69, war secretary 1858–9, 1866–7; and Sir Jonathan Frederick *Pollock, 1783–1870, judge; a saddler's son; senior wrangler 1806; M.P. Huntingdon 1831–44; attorney-general 1834–5, 1841–4; lord chief baron of exchequer, 1844–66; both returned unopposed.
[5] Sir Thomas John *Cochrane, 1789–1872; kt. 1825; M.P. Ipswich 1837–42; admiral 1865; was easily beaten at Westminster by *Burdett and De Lacy *Evans.
[6] James Stewart, senior treasury official.
[7] Edward *Goulburn, 1787–1860, judge, and Thomas *Gladstone carried Leicester town by large majorities over William Evans and Wynne *Ellis. And cp. 26 Dec. 34.
[8] Unidentified.
[9] Perhaps Henry Willmer of Baker Street; or David Wilmer, 1804–70, of Highgate.
[10] Presumably slip of pen for 'T.G.'   [11] See 23 Jan. 35.

Carwithen—Mosheim—Arnold's Serm. Vol II—Evans's Scripture Biography.

12. M.

Carwithen—Coleridge's Poems—Wood's Sess. School—began 'Frankenstein'[1]—papers—wrote to Ld Winchilsea—Uncle Robert—Caparn—H. Green[2]—Mr G—T.G.—R.G.—Mrs Wishlade—Mr Sullivan (about M. Dixon)[3]—arranged my letters.

13. T.

Carwithen. Wood's Sess. School—Frankenstein—papers—saw Mr Balfour. Wrote to Mr G.—Williams—Wm Gabbitus[4]—Mr Ross (Rossshire)—Mr C[umming] Bruce—Sir R. Inglis.—Hunting up the Mirror about Stewart M'Kenzie.[5]—Treasury (Board day)[6]—Lecture on Superannuations.

14. Wed.

Carwithen—Finished Wood. papers. Coleridge and Shelley. Dined in B. Square. Went to see the ruins at Westmr[7]—Lesson in superannuations at the Treasury. Wrote to Mrs G—R.G.—Ferrand—Willmer—Cole—Mr Ross.

15. Th.

Carwithen: began Moore's Life of Sheridan[8]—papers—wrote to T. Ogilvy—
—Pusey—R.G.—Mr M'Dowal—Mr Ross—Mr G.—Treasury: superannuations—at Aunt D.s evening party.

16. Fr.

Treasury: Board Day. Lpool journey off, my brothers having got me a *pair*. Carwithen (finished V.2)—Moore's Sheridan—Frankenstein (finished) —papers—wrote to T.G.—R.G.—Miss G—Dr Chalmers—& notes on the proposed Westmr Consttl Club.[9]

17. Sat.

Treasury. Calls. papers. Moore's Sheridan. Mosheim. Wrote to Mr G—Sir E. Kerrison—Williams (Oxf)—Mr Anders.[10] Dined at the Lord Chancellor's.[11]

[1] Early science fiction (1818) by Mary Wollstonecraft *Shelley, the poet's second wife.
[2] Perhaps Robert Green, Newark maltster.
[3] Possibly to John Sullivan, shopkeeper, about a child of George Dixon, maltster; all of Newark.
[4] William Gabitas, Newark gentleman.
[5] Stewart-Mackenzie had hardly spoken at all in 1834.
[6] The lords of the treasury met twice a week to hear letters and direct replies: minutes in PRO, T 29/361.
[7] Cp. 20 Oct. 34.
[8] Thomas *Moore, *Memoirs of the Life of the Right Hon. R. B. *Sheridan* (1825).
[9] Add MS 44724, f. 1.
[10] James Anders, Newark surgeon.   [11] *Lyndhurst's.

Lord Abbinger,[1] & Justices J. Parke[2] & Patteson,[3] were there: these four
I fancy the flower of the bench.[4]

18. Sunday.

St James's m. & aft. Dined in B. Square. Arnold's Sermm. & one aloud—
one of Burton's—Scripture Biography—& (began) Hone's Usher.[5] Bible.

19. M.

Moore's Sheridan—[6] arranging work for the kitchen—papers—Treasury—
with Sir R. Peel on business—with Mr Florance[7] about the proposed club
—wrote to Mr Hay, Ld Granville Somerset, Mr G., Mr Wing,[8] Mr Stevenson,[9] J. T. Thomson.[10] Walked to Clapham, to Harrison's—dined & slept—
Newman there. Read Knox on Ch. Eng's doctrine of Baptism.[11]

20. T.

Treasury at 11½. Board day. papers. Wrote to Mr Balfour, Mr T.S. Rice,[12]
Lincoln, Mr Tallents, Mr Caparn, Summers,[13] Walter Goalen, Mr Anders,
Mr Stevenson. Read in evg Mosheim & Moore's Sheridan.

21. Wed.

Moore's Sheridan—Church Patronage Report[14]—papers. Wrote to R.G.—
Mrs G—Mr Stevenson—& an Address for Sir J.T.T.[15]—calls—dined at
H.H. J[oy]'s. Wrote to Sir F. Doyle about Shaw.[16]

22. Th.

Farquhar to breakfast. Moore's Sheridan. Excursion B.7.—Patronage

---

[1] James *Scarlett, 1769–1844; born in Jamaica; K.C. 1816; tory M.P. 1819–34;
attorney general 1827–8, 1829–30; lord chief baron of exchequer 1834; cr. Baron Abinger
1835.
[2] Sir James *Parke, 1782–1868; wrangler 1803; judge and kt. 1828; cr. Lord Wensleydale 1856.
[3] Sir John *Patteson, 1790–1861; king's bench judge 1830–52.
[4] *Disraeli, who was also present, found his fellow guests 'rather dull, but we had a
swan very white and tender, and stuffed with truffles, the best company there' (Lord
Beaconsfield's correspondence with his sister (1886), 30). See also Morley, i. 122–3, Magnus,
21, and Bassett, 30.
[5] R. B. Hone, Lives of Eminent Christians . . . Archbishop *Usher (1833).
[6] 'sett[ling]' here deleted.
[7] James Florance, parliamentary agent, of Parliament Street.
[8] William Wing, Newark book-keeper.   [9] George Stevenson, Newark gentleman.
[10] John, chairmaker, or James Thompson, maltster; both of Newark.
[11] Alexander *Knox, On the Doctrine Respecting Baptism Held By The Church of
England (1820).
[12] Thomas *Spring-Rice, 1790–1866; whig M.P. Limerick 1820–32, Cambridge 1832–9;
war and colonial secretary 1834; exchequer 1835–9; cr. Baron Monteagle 1839.
[13] Joseph, painter, or John Summers, shoemaker; Newark voters.
[14] PP 1834 v. 1, on the Church of Scotland.
[15] Sir John Tyssen Tyrell, 1795–1877; 2nd bart. 1832; M.P. Essex 1830–1, 1832–57;
protectionist tory.
[16] William Shaw was a Newark bricklayer; cp. 24 Jan. 35.

Report—Br. Critic on Rd Watson.[1] At the treasury, superannuations &c. & with Sir R. Peel. papers. Wrote to Ld Ashley—Mr Hay—Caparn—Lt Magrath[2]—Mr G.

23. F.

Mr E Crafer[3] made up his book for *England*, yesterday—friends 239—foes 228—Doubtful 33.
Upon estimate, I add,
Ireland—friends 45—foes 60—
(after petition, we hope 50—and 55—)
Scotland—friends—16—foes 30—doubtful 7.
This would give as
totals ....300 ....318 ....40.[4]
But this is clipping the middle party on both sides. I would take off 20 from the friends—38 from the foes—& consider the two great parties 280 each, and the doubtfuls 98.

We have reason to be thankful, fearful, & hopeful.—In the city, Hyndman's & Natl Debt Office for Mr G. Treasury: board day. wrote to Mr G— Mrs Temple[5]—Mr A. Sinclair[6]—Seymer. papers. Moore's Sheridan. dined at Uncle D's.

24. Sat.

Phillimore to breakfast. Calls. papers. Treasury (superannuations). Wrote to Mr Dean—Mr W. Peel[7]—Lincoln—Sir J. Mordaunt—W. Shaw, Bulson,[8] Mr Stevenson, at Newark—Wordsworth—Hamilton—Rev. Mr Wilson. Dined at Sir R. Peel's. A small party. Moore's Sheridan. (—aet.14—)

25. Sunday.

Bible—Mosheim—Evans—finished Life of Usher—Arnold—Wigram on Sunday Schools.[9] Arnold aloud—St Philip's (no more) & St James's.

26. M.

Moore's Sheridan. Wrote to A. Robertson—T.G.—R.G.—Mr Godfrey— Lincoln—Mr S. Wilberforce—& my Father. Treasury (Superannuations.)— papers.

[1] xxxi. 1 (July 1834), reviewing Thomas *Jackson's *Memoirs* of Richard*Watson the methodist.
[2] Perhaps Nicholas Magrath, surgeon R.N. 1829.
[3] Edward T. Crafer, from a family of treasury officials; junior clerk.
[4] Diarist's dots.
[5] Wife of Christopher Temple of Lincoln's Inn, Denbigh magnate?
[6] Andrew Sinclair, Edinburgh surgeon?
[7] William Yates *Peel, 1789–1858, 2nd s. of 1st bart.; M.P. 1817–37, 1847–52; minor office 1826–30, 1834–5.
[8] David Bilson, Newark book-keeper.
[9] J. C. *Wigram, *Practical Hints on the Formation and Management of Sunday Schools* (1833).

About 4½, Sir R. Peel sent for me: & offered me the Colonial Under Secretaryship. I accepted this great responsibility: God be with me in its discharge. He said to me most emphatically when I left him, "May *God* bless you, wherever you are". I saw next Ld Aberdeen:[1] then Mr Hay[2] & Mr Stephen:[3] & so I am transplanted. Honestly & truly do I wish they had had Lord Sandon.[4]

Dined at H. Joy's—Mr Brackenbury[5] there. Afterwards to Sir H. Halford's lecture which I could not hear—saw many friends there.

27. Tuesday.

Breakf. in B.S.—Calls. Wrote to Mr G.—R.G.—Mr Wolseley[6]—Gaskell— Saw Sir F. Doyle—Mr Marryat—; Mr Tyler, & A. Robertson on business. Dined at Mr Wynn's. Col. Office 11½–5¾—& reading papers up at home, connected with business there.

28. Wed.

Moore's Sheridan (began V.2.)—Colonial Office: working at old papers, & general business—dined in B. Square. paper. At night worked late at Superannuation cases, wh I hope to clear off in one more sitting. Wrote to Mr G —Mr Bardsley[7]—Mr W. Peel.

29. Th.

Mr Brackenbury to breakft. Canning Doyle Saunders Anstice Phillimore to dinner. Superannuation cases afterwards. Paper. Colonial Office nearly all day. Wrote many letters there[8]—for which, see my journal there (not *yet* made).

30. Fr.

Price to breakfast: conv. with him. Also with Pakenham in evg. Col. Office nr all day.—*began journal &c. there*[9]—Moore's Sheridan. Finished Stephen & Hay's printed paper on Canada[10]—Superannuations.

[1] George Hamilton-*Gordon, 1784–1860; styled Lord Haddo 1791; 4th earl of Aberdeen 1801; at Leipzig 1813; foreign secretary 1828–30, 1841–6; colonial secretary 1834–5; prime minister 1852–5. See Add MSS 44088–9; and for this interview, Sir A. *Gordon *Aberdeen* (1893), 111.

[2] Permanent under-secretary in the colonial office.

[3] (Sir) James *Stephen, 1789–1859, administrator ('Mr Over-Secretary'); assistant 1834–6, and under-secretary 1836–47, in colonial office; K.C.B. 1847; regius professor of history, Cambridge, 1849. Cp. H. *Taylor, *Autobiography* (1885), i. 229.

[4] Morley, i. 123–4, gives fuller accounts of the interviews with Peel and Aberdeen. And see 7 Feb. 35.

[5] Perhaps Henry Brackenbury, 1790–1862; rector of Scremby, Lincolnshire, 1816.

[6] William Bertie Wolseley, 1797–1881, gs. of 6th bart. of Wolseley; civil servant in British Guiana.

[7] Joseph Bardsley, gentleman; of Newark.

[8] As political under-secretary, he signed most correspondence with other govt. departments.

[9] See 21 Feb. 35.

[10] In PRO, CO 7.

31. Sat.

Mr Brackenbury & Pakenham to breakfast. Moore's Sheridan. paper. Tea in B. Square. Wrote Address for Newark.[1] Wrote to J.N.G. called on Mrs Price.[2] Office 11½–6¾—accounts &c.

Sunday Feb. one.

St James's mg & aft. The Holy Sacrament. Mr Wigram & Mr Ward. Script. Biogr—Bible—Hammond's Life[3]—Mosheim—some Hammond aloud.

2.

Farquhar, Tancred, Tupper, to breakft. Col. Office, 11½–6½. papers at home, & part of Senior's pamphlet[4]—dined in B. Square—papers.

3.

J.E. Gordon & Anstice to breakft—finished Senior's pamphlet. Col. Office 11¾–6, Canning there, brought the gratifying news of Sir R. Peel's offer to him.[5] At the christening of Mr Tyler's child : I am godfather : may my duty be fulfilled, and her blessed privilege.[6]—dined with him—Canada papers at night.

4.

Canada papers. Colonial Office 11½–7. Br. Guiana papers[7]—read Denison's pamphlet[8]—at Mrs Vansittart's—paper.

5.

Finished Canada papers. Moore's Sheridan. Newsp.—Col. Office 11½–5¼. dined with Farquhar.[9]

6. Friday.

Honduras papers. Colonial Office 11½–6¾. dined at Sir F. Doyle's. newsp. Moore's Sheridan.

7. Sat.

Brackenbury to breakf.—Newsp. Moore's Sheridan. Dined at Mr Hallam's :

[1] Acceptance of under-secretaryship entailed re-election.
[2] Mrs. John Price, of Bryanston Square.
[3] R. B. Hone, *Lives of Eminent Christians . . . Life of Henry *Hammond* (1833).
[4] Naussau William *Senior, *On National Property and on the Prospects of the Present Administration* (1835).
[5] Of a lordship at the treasury ; his mother declined it for him (M. Maclagan, '*Clemency*' Canning (1962), 9).
[6] Mary Jane Tyler, b. 5 December 1834, christened in her father's church of St. Giles.
[7] Court of policy quarrelling with governor : PRO, CO 111/135.
[8] Edward *Denison, 'A Review of the State of the Question Respecting the Admission of the Dissenters to the Universities' (1835).
[9] The entry in Morley, i. 126, headed '*Feb. 4 or 5*' is not from the diary.

a place to me of solemn recollections[1]—wrote an acct of my interview with Sir R.P. Jan 26[2]—Col. Off. 11½–6½.

8. Sunday.

St Giles's (Mr Tyler) & St James's (Bp.) Talked the W.I. Educn quest. with Mr T. and Colvile. Tea in B. Squ.—Bible—Arnold (& aloud)—Scripture Biogr—Mosheim—& part of Bp Wilson's Life.

9. M.

Colonial Office 11¼–6½. Dined in B. Square. Newsp. Moore's Sheridan—& pt of Merewether's Introduction to his 'History of Boroughs & Municipal Corporations'.[3] *Mare up*

10. T.

Colonial Office 11½–6½. Dined at Sir F. Doyle's. Stephen on Grenada Laws.[4] Finished Merewether's Introduction. Moore's Sheridan. wrote to Mr Balfour.

11. W.

Col. Off. 11½–7½. breakf. in B. Square. Br. Museum's Elgin marbles, a treat tho' short. wrote in Pol. Mema[5]—finished Moore's Sheridan; a most melancholy book—St Kitt's Martial Law papers.[6] Quarterly on Peel's Address.

12. Th.

Quarty on Coleridge's Table Talk. Col. Off. 11¾–7. dined at Ld Aberdeen's. Quarterly on Church & Voluntary System.

13.

Divers papers—Col. Office 11½–6½. dined at Uncle D.s—went to Sir R. Inglis's in evg & saw the Aclands—Quarterly on Turkey question.

14.

Papers morng & evg—& Col. Office 11¾–6¾.—newsp—Quart. on Bennett's New S. Wales. wrote to Wm G.

15. Sunday.

Farquhar to breakf. Longacre (Mr Sandford, very good)[7] & Sact.—Walk

[1] Fragment of conversation with Sydney *Smith, 1771–1845, wit, in *Gleanings*, vii. 220.
[2] Add MS 44819, f. 9.   [3] H. A. *Merewether (1835).
[4] Early draft of dispatch no. 8 to Grenada, 28 February 1835, in PRO, CO 101/78.
[5] On *Peel's offer to *Canning, in Add MS 44819, f. 11.
[6] First papers in PRO, CO 239/39.
[7] John *Sandford, 1801–73; canon of Worcester 1844; archdeacon of Coventry 1851.

with Farquhar: I am unworthy to walk with him: St James's. Read Bible, finished Scr. Biography—finished Life of Wilson—read Ep[istl]e of St Barnabas,[1] & Arnold 'Man created & renewed' aloud.[2]

16. M.

Manning to breakf. Col. Off. 11¾–7. Dined at H. Joy's. Quarty on Populn and began Paine's 'Rights of Man'.[3]

17. T.

Pakenham to breakf.—Col. Off. &c. 11¾–6¾. dined at Mr Hays. Croker,[4] Ld Vesey.[5] &c. read Paine—and wrote in Polit. Mem.[6]

18. W.

Col. Office &c. 10¾–1½, & 3½–6½. Uncle D. & Mr Tallents to dinner. Read Appx to Bp Coleridge's Charges[7]—drew a table from them—Mr Stephen on Br. Guiana judicial procedure.[8]

19. Th.

Col. Office 11–2. Br. Guiana Jud[icia]l papers. H. of C. 2–6½. Stanley's Speech most effective. Divided in 306 : 316.[9] Of the state, of wh this div. is a symptom, I can form but one opinion: but God has not deserted us: and surely He will not. O may He be intreated! T.G., Farquhar, R. Williams,[10] and Gaskell, to dinner: long conv with T.G. to one in the morng.

20. Fr.

Acland to breakf. He is a delightful person. House:[11] Col. Office 12½–6½. dined at Uncle D.s. At Lady Peel's evening party.[12] read newsp. & Paine.

21. Sat.

Wm Gladstone to breakft.—Paine's Rights of Man finished—They do not startle me now. Col. Office & swearing in at H. of C. 11½–6½.[13] Saw D[ivie]

---

[1] Apocryphal gospel, composed *ca.* A.D. 75.   [2] Untraced.

[3] Thomas *Paine's classic (1790–92).

[4] John Wilson *Croker, 1780–1857, political manager and essayist; secretary to admiralty 1810–30; M.P. 1807–32; attacked *Keats, quarrelled with *Macaulay, derided by *Disraeli.

[5] Fitzgerald.   [6] On *Croker, in Add MS 44819, f. 13.

[7] W. H. *Coleridge, *Charges delivered to the Clergy of Barbados and the Leeward Islands* (1835).

[8] In PRO, CO 111/134.

[9] Speakership debated; Manners *Sutton defeated by Sir James *Abercromby 1776–1858; M.P. Midhurst 1807, Calne 1812–30, Edinburgh 1832–9; cr. Lord Dunfermline 1839. *H* xxvi. 59; and cp. Morley, i. 125.

[10] Robert Williams, 1811–90, s. of banker, cons. M.P. Dorchester 1835–41.

[11] The speaker and some members took the oaths: *H* xxvi. 63.

[12] *Peel m. 1820 Julia, da. of General Sir John Floyd, bart.; she d. 1859. Their town house was in Whitehall Gardens.

[13] *H* xxvi. 63.

R[obertson]—Forbes—Taylor[1]—wrote to Mr G—Dr Duncan[2]—finished a very bungling draft for Trinidad.[3] review, & divers papers—obliged to give up journalising at Col. Office—dined at Mr Colville's.[4]

22. Sunday.

Farquhar to breakft & walk. Long Acre—& St James's (Bp). Began Coleridge's Vol. of Charges &c—Mosheim. Bible. Ventured upon an expl. of Joh. 13.34 in evg: I fear perhaps rashly. Went into the Newman St Chapel.[5]

23. M.

read Halliday's long & interesting paper on Br. Guiana.[6] Col. Office 12–6$\frac{1}{2}$. Dinner at Sir R. Peel's. King's Speech read—it is good & will puzzle carpers.[7]—paper &c.

24. T.

Carwithen (V.3.)—newsp—papers—Col. Office 12–4$\frac{1}{4}$. rode. dined at Mr Tyler's—House 4$\frac{1}{2}$–7 & 9$\frac{1}{4}$–1$\frac{3}{4}$. Peel's splendid speech.[8] From convv. with Sinclair & the Stewarts I augur well of the middle party.[9]

25. W.

Carwithen. Col. Office 12$\frac{1}{4}$–5. House 5–1.[10] wrote to Mr G—Mrs G—Mr Godfrey—Good hopes.

26. Th.

West India Church paper. Carwithen. Col. Off. 12–4$\frac{1}{2}$. rode. House 8–2. Williams fm Oxford with me—div. in 302:309.[11]

27. Fr.

W.I. Church paper (very long) finished. Harrowing details.[12] Col. Office 12$\frac{3}{4}$–4$\frac{1}{2}$. saw Bp of Barbadoes[13] & Mr Campbell.[14] wrote to Mr Campbell—

---

[1] (Sir) Henry *Taylor, 1800–86, author, clerk in colonial office 1824–72. See Add MS 44355, &c; and his *Autobiography*, i. 228–9.

[2] Andrew Duncan, professor of medicine at Edinburgh, where he became M.D. 1794.

[3] Excusing colony from sending supplementary estimate: PRO, CO 295/109.

[4] Andrew Wedderburn Colvile, d. 1856, of Ochiltree, Fifeshire; f. of (Sir) J.W.*

[5] Irvingite.

[6] Sir Andrew *Halliday on medical condition of colony, in PRO, CO 111/132.

[7] *H* xxvi. 63.

[8] Debate on address; *Peel on how he had come to power, and what he proposed. Ibid. 151, 214.

[9] i.e. those M.P.s not firmly committed either to government or to opposition: cp. 23 Jan. 35.

[10] Debate on address: *H* xxvi. 243.

[11] Whig amdt. to address carried: ibid. 410.

[12] Probably one of the statements on education by various denominations in PRO, CO 318/122.

[13] William Hart *Coleridge, 1789–1849, nephew of S.T.*; bp. of Barbados 1824–41.

[14] Perhaps Lachlan T. Campbell, lawyer in Jamaica.

Ld Sandon—Mr Cunningham. House 5–8¾.[1] Answered two questions of Buxton's—very ill.[2] read Carwithen—& Æschylus.

28. Sat.

Carwithen's Hist.—wrote to Mrs G—newsp—dined at Lady Farquhar's—at Lady Salisbury's (perfunctory) afterwards[3]—rode—Col. Office 12–1¾[4]—then to Court with the Address—& 3½–4¾.

Sunday, March one.

St James's mg & aft. Mr Ward very good on Eph. 6.10 & seqq. Sacrament. —read Bible—Coleridge's Charges—began Evelyn's Life,[5] & Sandford's Lectures on Fellowship with God.[6]

2. M.

Col. Office 12–4½ & papers at home mg & evg. House 5.10–6.30[7]—rode. newsp. wrote to Mr G.—E.L. Ward—Mrs Ramsay—Mr Tallents—& Sir J. Sinclair. read Carwithen—began Ettore Fieramosca.[8] Made lists for Col. Mil. Exp[enditur]e & Educn Commees—A conv. with Col. Doyle from Jamaica.[9]

3. T.

Papers mg & aft. Breakf. with T.G.—rode with Farquhar. Col. Office 12–4. H. of C. 5–8¾.[10] read Carwithen. Wrote to Mrs Hagart.—An ominous conv. with Ld Aberdeen on W.I. Educn[11]—and also a startling one with H. J[oy] about Mr Hay.—Pamphlet on the Jews' case.[12]

4. W.

Papers mg. newsp. wrote to Mrs G—R.G.—E.L. Ward—St James's—Mr Ward preached. Col. Office 12¾–4; House 4–5 and 6–12½.[13] rode. read

[1] Mainly report on address: H xxvi. 425.
[2] On negro education, and independence of magistrates in Jamaica: ibid. 464, 465. (Sir Thomas) Fowell *Buxton, 1786–1845; M.P. Weymouth 1818–37; led anti-slavery group in commons; cr. bart. 1840.
[3] Frances Mary, née Gascoigne, d. 1839; m. 1821 James Brownlow William (Gascoigne-) Cecil, 1791–1868, succ. as 2nd marquess of Salisbury 1823; parents of prime minister.
[4] Minute on British Guiana finance and draft dispatch in PRO, CO 111/136.
[5] By R. B. Hone in his Lives of Eminent Christians (1833).
[6] John *Sandford, Eight Lectures on Fellowship with God (1835).
[7] Discussion on dissolution: H xxvi. 471.
[8] Life of Italian renaissance hero by Massimo d'Azeglio (1833).
[9] (Sir) Charles Hastings Doyle, 1804–83, soldier; served in east and west Indies and in Crimea; K.C.M.G. 1869.
[10] Misc. business: H xxvi. 490.
[11] *Gladstone was already contemplating the first of many resignations: see Morley, i. 125.
[12] An Appeal to the Public in Behalf of the Jews (1834).
[13] Misc. business: H xxvi. 526, incl. carrying motion for cttee. on colonial military expenditure.

"L[ower] Canada Petn & remon[stratio]n."[1] Saw Mr Surtees:[2] and Dr Madden.

5. Th.

Papers—newsp. Col. O. 11½–2—Drawing room (entrée)[3] and Col. O. 3¾–4¼. rode. A drive with Ld Mahon & a conv. on *Women*. dined at Ld Aberdeen's—dress for the birthday. Much conv. with Ld C. Hamilton.[4] Wrote to Col. L. Hay[5]—Mr R. Earle[6]—Mr G—Mrs Hagart. Conv. with Mr Pringle about Irish Educn—finished Carwithen's Hist. of the Church.

6. Fr.

Seymer to breakft. Pamphlet on the Timber Trade—Ettore Fieramosca—Canada papers. rode, Col, Office 11¾–4¼—House 5¼–10½.[7] Another ominous conv. with Ld Aberdeen. With Mr Baring.

7. Sat.

Began Cook's Scotch Church History[8]—Col. Office[9] & Malt Tax meeting 12–4¾. Wrote to Rn G—Williams. newsp. dined with E.I. Directors—a sumptuous feast. Walking & calls.

8. Sunday.

St James's. Mr Ward & Bp. Tea in B. Square. Farquhar to breakf.—Wrote on experience.[10] read B.—Sandford—Evelyn—Coleridge's Charges (& aloud).

9. M.

Canada papers. newsp. Cook's Hist. Ettore Fieramosca—Col. O. 12½–4½[11]—House 4½–9¾.[12] Saw Dr Bunting &c. on W.I. Education.[13]

10. T.

Cook's Hist. Ettore Fieramosca. Office 11¾–4¼.—Rode. House 5¼–7¾ and

---

[1] See *H* xxvi. 660, 9 March 1835.
[2] Perhaps Edward Surtees, who m. *ca.* 1810 Walker Ferrand's sister Anne Catherine; Durham magistrate.
[3] As a member of the government. *Adelaide, though b. 13 August, had her official birthday on 5 March.
[4] Lord Claud Hamilton, 1813–84, a b. of *Abercorn, M.P. co. Tyrone 1835–7, 1839–74.
[5] (Sir) Andrew Leith *Hay, 1785–1862, soldier, reforming M.P. Elgin burghs 1832–8, 1841–7; writer on architecture.
[6] Richard Earle, 1796–1848, b. of 1st bart.
[7] Orange societies: *H* xxvi. 504. And see *The Times*, leading article, 22 May 1835.
[8] George *Cook, *The History of the Church of Scotland*, 3v. (1815).
[9] Draft dispatch to British Guiana in PRO, CO 111/136.
[10] 'Considerations upon Christian Experience', in Add MS 44724, ff. 54–71; cp. 17 Apr. 35.
[11] Draft dispatch to British Guiana in PRO, CO 111/133.
[12] Canadian grievances: *H* xxvi. 660.
[13] Jabez *Bunting, 1779–1856, leading Wesleyan, and two companions brought Wesleyan Missionary Society's plan for W.I. education: PRO, CO 318/122.

$9\frac{3}{4}-1\frac{1}{2}$.[1] Wrote to Mr Arnold—Mr Harrison—Mr Bagshaw[2]—Mr Earle—Ld Stanley.

11. Wednesday.

Ettore Fieramosca. Wrote a painful letter to my father. Conv. with Tom about his petn. Wrote to Sir J. Byng[3]—Mr Dorington[4]—Col. O. $12\frac{3}{4}-4\frac{1}{4}$.[5] Rode. House—dined at H. Taylor's to meet the revered Wordsworth—& House 9–1.[6]. Walk home with L[incol]n & conv. on politics.

12. Th.

Cook's Church Hist.—household matters—newsp—wrote to A. Williams— Mr J. Wood. Col. Office $12-5\frac{1}{4}$: House to $6\frac{3}{4}$, and 8–12.[7]

13. Fr.

Breakf in B. Square. Col. Office $11\frac{3}{4}-2$. Col. Mil. Commee Office $2\frac{3}{4}-4$—ride & Office 5–6. House. dined with Sir J. Mordaunt & House $9\frac{1}{4}-1$.[8] read Cook's Church Hist. wrote to Dr Chalmers.

14. Sat.

Cook's Ch. Hist.—newsp. Col. Office $11\frac{3}{4}-4\frac{1}{2}$. and $5\frac{1}{2}-7$: saw Mr Colvile & Ld Mahon. Wrote long letters for Br. G.[9] & St Lucia.[10] rode. dined at Sir E. Kerrison's—& sung! at Lady Salisbury's—home & wrote to H.J.G.

15. S.

The Sacrament at 8. Ch mg & aft. Messrs Wigram & Ward. read Bible— Evelyn—Sandford (finished) & aloud—Knox[11]—wrote on last Sunday's subject.

16. M.

Cook's Hist (finished Vol 1)—finished Evelyn's Life. Newsp. Husk[isso]ns Speeches. Col. Off. $12-4\frac{1}{4}$. House $4\frac{1}{4}-5$—rode—wrote to Mr G—House 8– $11\frac{1}{2}$[12]—Lady Farquhar's party.

---

[1] Malt tax: *H* xxvi. 737.
[2] John Bagshaw, whig M.P. Sudbury 1835–7, Harwich 1847–51, 1853–7.
[3] Sir John *Byng, 1772–1860, soldier; fought in Flanders, Ireland, and Spain 1793– 1815; M.P. Poole 1831–5; cr. Lord Strafford 12 May 1835, earl of Strafford 1847, field- marshal 1855. He chaired the cttee. set up on 4 March, on which *Gladstone sat; cp. *PP* 1835 vi. 1.
[4] John Edward Dorington, b. 1786, clerk of the fees to the commons.
[5] Consultations with *Aberdeen on British Guiana marriage laws, PRO, CO 111/133.
[6] Election bribery: *H* xxvi. 873.
[7] Misc. business, mainly Irish: *H* xxvi. 888.
[8] Embassy to Russia; navy estimates. *H* xxvi. 938, 990.
[9] On finance, in PRO, CO 112/19, f. 50.
[10] On litigation, in PRO, CO 253/48.
[11] Alexander *Knox, *Remains* (1834–7), vols i and ii.
[12] Canada; navy estimates. *H* xxvi. 1013, 1031.

17. T.

Cook's Hist.—Newman's pamphlet on Suffragans[1]—newsp. Col. Office & ballot at H. of C. 12–5¼ and 8–12.[2] wrote to Acland—Mr Godfrey—Mr Caparn—Mr Stevenson.

18. W.

Cook's Hist. Breakfd at Taylors to meet Wordsworth. Office papers—newsp—Office 11¾–2. then went to the Borough Road School[3] with Taylor —Wordsworth—Josh. Watson.[4] Great vivacity & excitement. Wordsworth held a disc[ussio]n with Dunn[5] on the principles. Office again—ride—House 8–9[6]—Williams to tea & a convn. on the religious world & a Church—examining Best about matters between him & Mrs Taylor.[7]

19. Th.

Cook—Smith (on Edn)[8]—Tyler on Oaths[9]—Arfwedson's America[10]—wrote to Mr G—R.G—Bp of Barb[adoe]s—Farquhar—newsp. Col. Office 11½–1.[11] House of C. Commee 1–3. Office 3–4¼. House 5¼–10½. Introduced a new Passengers' Bill in a confused speech.[12]

20. Fr.

Cook. Breakfast at Mr Wynn's. Newsp. Col. Off. 12–4¼. ride. House 5–11¾. Div. in 213:198 on Tithe Resolutions.[13] Educn papers at home. wrote to Farquhar & Ld Ashley.

21. Sat.

Cook. Acland to breakf.[14] Newsp. wrote to Mr G[15]—R.G.—Mr Godfrey—Col. Off. 12¼–5. Talked over with Lincoln the W.I. Edn & my position therein. Dined at Mr Williams's, & had the pleasure of introducing Canning (by his request) to Sir R. Peel at his house—began to write on W.I. E[ducation].[16]

[1] J. H. *Newman, 'The Restoration of Suffragan Bishops Recommended' (1835).
[2] Dissenters' marriages; imprisonment *H* xxvi. 1073; 1120. He was put on select cttee. on education: *PP* 1835 vii. 763.
[3] In Southwark; headquarters and model school of the British and Foreign School Society.
[4] Joshua *Watson, 1771–1855, philanthropist, first treasurer of the National Society, 1811–42.
[5] Henry Dunn, secretary of the British and Foreign School Society.
[6] Imprisonment for debt: *H* xxvi. 1144.
[7] Presumably another servant.
[8] Sydney *Smith, 'On Mrs. *Trimmer on *Lancaster's Plan of Education', *Edinburgh Review*, ix. 177 (October 1806).
[9] J. E. *Tyler, *Oaths: their Origin, Nature and History* (1834).
[10] C. D. Arfwedson, *The United States and Canada in 1832–3–4* (1834).
[11] He forwarded *Bunting's paper (see 9 Mar. 35) to *Aberdeen: PRO, CO 318/122.
[12] Irish poor laws; and leave to introduce bill to improve emigrants' ships: *H* xxvi. 1206, 1235.
[13] For substitution of rent charge for tithe: *H* xxvii. 83.
[14] Cp. A.H.D. *Acland, *Sir T.D. *Acland*, 77–78.
[15] Proposing that *Canning should contest Liverpool; see Maclagan, *Canning*, 9, 365.
[16] In Add MS 44724, ff. 4–36.

22. Sunday.

Knox. Arnold aloud. Ladies Negro Ed. Rep.[1] wrote on exp[erience]. St James's—Mr Ward & Bp—dined with Saunders & went in evg to Christ's Hospital.

23. M.

Buchanan[2]—divers papers & letters—Col. O. 12–3¾—ride—House 5–8¼[3]—tea at Taylor's—Mr Wordsworth's conv. on Education—House 9¾–1¼.[4] newsp—letters: saw Mr Sterling on Edn.[5]

24. T.

Wrote to Mr Baring—Mr J. Wood—C.O. & Commee 12¼–4. Ballot[6]—ride—dined in B. Square—House 10–12¾[7]—finished Buchanan's "Facts & Obss."

25.

Cook. Edn—Church (Mr Cavendish)[8]—newsp—C.O. 12¾–4. ride. C.O. & House to 7¼—dined at Sir C. Burrells—House 10–1.[9] read "Effects of Sea Insurance"[10] & "Infn on Emigrn".[11]

26. Th.

Cook—wrote on Edn—Col. Office & Mil. Exp. Commee 12–3¼—ride—House 4—7¼—dined with Uncle D. & House 9½–1. divided in 101:146 on Leicester petn! & in 136:246!! on London Univ.[12]—wrote to Rogers & Lushington.

Evil rumours for next week thicken around us—but the Lord God Almighty reigns.

27. Fr.

Cook. Turner's Hist. Engl.[13]—wrote to Mr G—& others—consulting with

---

[1] Report (of 18 March) by 'The Ladies' Society for Promoting the Early Education & Improvement of the *Children of Negroes* & People of Colour in the *British West Indies*': copy in PRO, CO 318/122. The duchess of Beaufort was patron of the society, founded in 1825.

[2] James Buchanan, *Facts and Observations in Relation to the Extension of State Prisons in England* (New York 1834).

[3] Irish tithes: *H* xxvii. 102.　　　　　　　　　　　　[4] Orange lodges: ibid. 135.

[5] John *Sterling, 1806–44, author, s. of Edward *Sterling, 1773–1847, of *The Times*.

[6] He was appointed to the select cttee. to inquire into sinecures in the colonies: cp. 2 July 35 and *PP* 1835 xviii. 441.

[7] Chatham election; timber duties. *H* xxvii. 204, 213.

[8] Augustus, 1798?–1864, or Thomas (Union) Cavendish, 1801?–59; vicars successively of Doveridge, Derbyshire, 1823, 1839; ss. of 2nd Baron Waterpark.

[9] Misc. business: *H.* xxvii. 218.

[10] Untraced.

[11] *Practical Information to Emigrants* (1832).

[12] Muddle over formal error in Leicester petition (division was 101:147); crown asked to grant limited charter to university of London. *H* xxvii. 270, 301.

[13] Sharon *Turner, *History of England*, 9v. (1799–1823).

T.G., Mr Goulburn, & Mr Wynn, on reviving the Leicester case—agreed.[1]
C.O. 12¼–4½—House—ride—House 7–1. In four divv.–victorious, but this
is in no degree a symptom. We all appear to see whither (at first) we are
going.[2]

28. Sat.

Cook (finished Vol 2.)—wrote on Edn in W.I.—Col. O. 12½–4¼. rode—
dined at Bp of London's—a truly valuable acquaintance—looked up my
Irish Church papers & pamphlets & put some notes & figures together—At
Lady Salisbury's in evg. Vss in bed at nt.[3]

29. S.

Charity sermon. Bp of Exeter & Mr Ward. Tea with Anstice—& in B.
Square—wrote in Bl. book[4]—: Bible: Knox: Massillon: an Arnold aloud.

30. M.

Mr Canning on "Unlawful Societies".[5] Wrote to Ld Sandon—Farquhar—
Mr R.M. Martin, on an insult from me; this should be a lesson on the use of
the tongue.[6] C.O. 12½–2½—sinecure Commee & rode—House 4¾–1¼. Wished
to speak on Irish Church—no opp[ortunit]y—: wrote on it. A nobly high-
minded speech from Sir James Graham.[7]

31. Tuesday.

Breakf. with T.G. Canning on Cath. Quest.[8]—newsp.—rode. C.O. 12–1¼
commee to 3¼—C.O. & House to 12¾. Brought forward Jennings's Leicester
petition[9]—debate adjourned after Gisborne's Speech[10]—Spoke on the Irish
Church—under 40 m. I cannot help here recording that this matter of
speaking is really my strongest religious exercise. On all occasions & today
especially was forced upon me the humiliating sense of my inability to
exercise my reason in the face of the House of Commons, and of the

[1] See 1 Apr. 35.
[2] Army estimates carried, publication of poor laws board correspondence refused,
H xxvii. 355, 359; but government's days clearly numbered.
[3] Perhaps Add MS 44724, f. 53.
[4] Add MS 44821C, ff. 17–19.
[5] On suppression of unlawful associations in Ireland, 15 February 1825; NSH xii. 463
and *Therry, Speeches, v. 328.
[6] Add MS 44354, f. 193: quarrel with colonial historian, Robert Montgomery *Martin,
1830–68; at once patched up.
[7] Extracts in Morley, i. 126. Discussions on Irish church; *Graham explained why he
had resigned in 1834. H xxvii. 361, 419. Sir James (Robert George) *Graham, 1792–1861,
2nd bart. of Netherby 1824; whig M.P. 1818–21, 1826–37; tory M.P. from 1838; admiralty 1830–4, 1852–5; home secretary 1841–7; led Peelites after 1850. See Add MSS
44163–4.
[8] For 2° Roman Catholic Relief Bill, 21 April 1825; NSH xiii. 84 and *Therry, Speeches,
v. 386.
[9] Charles Jennings was the sitting members' agent.
[10] H xxvii. 462, 464. Thomas *Gisborne, 1794–1852; radical M.P. Stafford 1830–2,
Derbyshire 1832–7, Carlow 1839–41, and Nottingham 1843–7. See next entry.

necessity of my utterly failing unless God gave me strength and language. It was after all a poor performance—but would have been poorer had He never been in my thoughts as a present and powerful aid. But this is what I am as yet totally incompetent to effect—to realise in speaking any thing however small which at all satisfies my mind. Debating seems to me less difficult (tho' unattained): but to hold in serene contemplative action the mental faculties in the turbid excitement of debate, so as to see truth clearly and set it forth such as it is—this I cannot attain unto.[1]

Wednesday April one.

Cook (began Vol. 3.) newsp—Col. Office & Sinecure Commee[2] & B. of Trade 12–4¼. Wrote to J.N.G.—rode. House 5–7—voted in 216:200 on the Leicester business: petn discharged[3] to our great joy—dined at Lady M'Kenzie's[4]—House again 10–2.[5]

2. Th.

Breakf. at Mordaunt's—Cook—newsp—wrote to Mr G—R.G.—Dr Chalmers—Mr Bartlett—Mr Tallents. Office & Commee Room & B. of T. 11½–3¾—House 3¾–5¼—ride: delicious evening—dined at H. H. Joy's. House again 10½–3½—voted in 289:322 on I.C. question.[6] God be with us. Conv. with Ld Abn.

3. Fr.

Letters on Estabd Church[7]—newsp—wrote to Acland & Mrs G.—Another conv. with Ld Abn on political matters. C.O. 12¾–5 ride—House—dinner in B. Squ. House again 9½–11¾. voted in 140:178 on adjournment.[8]

4. Sat.

Finished "Letters" &c—Cook's Hist.—newsp. Wrote on I.C.—C. Office 1–5. wrote to Mr Tallents—Mr Bartlett—Sir G. Clark—S.F. Wood—saw Mr Greville[9]—dined at Sir J. M'Grigor's—rode.

5. S.

St James's—Mr Ward & Bp—Sacrament—Read Knox upon it: he tends much, (or should) to give fixedness and strength to the view of that high ordinance. Massillon—Arnold (& aloud)—a long letter to Manning, on the Church.[10]

[1] Morley, i. 126. Irish church discussion ctd. *Gladstone opposed *Russell's motion for inquiry. H xxvii. 507. Notes for speech in Add MS 44649, ff. 58–78.
[2] He gave evidence: PP 1835 xviii. 447.
[3] On formal grounds; leaving Thomas Gladstone M.P. for Leicester. H xxvii. 544–7.
[4] In Clarges Street.   [5] Irish church ctd.: H xxvii. 547.
[6] Against *Russell's motion to go into cttee.: H xxvii. 772.
[7] Letters on the Church. By an Episcopalian [R. *Whatley], 1826.
[8] Still on Irish church: H xxvii. 824.   [9] Cp. 26 June, 2 July 35.
[10] Lathbury, i. 23–28.

6. M.

Seymer to breakf—& dinner. read Kildare Soc's reports &c[1]—newsp. Col. Off. 1–4¾[2]—wrote on W.I. Edn—to Mr Tallents—Mrs Langbridge[3]—House —ride—House again 7–12½.[4]—Dark & ominous conv. with Ld Aberdeen on the fate of the govt. His (confidential) intimations corroborated by the feeling which had begun to be generally entertained in the evening. convv. with Mr Finch—T. Baring.

7. Tuesday.

Cook. Finished my long paper on W.I. Education.[5] Wrote to Mrs G—R.G. —C.O.[6] & Commee 1–4½. ride. House 6¾–1½. Divided in 258:285 after a noble speech from Peel.[7] No doubt had existed on my mind, from a previous conv. with my chief, that this vote would seal the fate of the ministry. God's will be done.

8. Wed.

Cook—Col. Office papers—C.O. 12–2. wrote to Mr Ewing—Mr Whyte—&c. At 5, heard the announcement of Peel's resignation—admirably given, of course. In so small a *book* I had better not speculate on consequences.[8] Rode. Dined at Ld Salisbury's. Introduced to the D. of Cumberland[9] (see Bl. B.).[10]

9. Th.

Cook. C.O. & Commee 12½–3. H. of C. at ballot[11]—wrote to Ld Mahon—Sir W. Follett[12]—Mr G.—J.N.G.—newsp. dined at Mr Lyall's—& went with his party to the Mansion house ball. Peel there, & in great spirits it was said.

10. Fr.

Finished Cook. wrote to Mr Burnaby—Mr Godfrey—Mr Cs Robertson[13]—

[1] Reports of the Society For Promoting the Education of the Poor in Ireland; of Kildare Place, Dublin (1813–33).

[2] Minute on British Guiana in PRO, CO 111/136.

[3] Perhaps wife of Henry Charles Langbridge, Birmingham bookseller.

[4] Irish church; naval estimates. *H* xxvii. 837, 864.

[5] Add MS 44724, ff. 4–37; fair copy in PRO, CO 318/122, f. 521. Cp. H. *Taylor, Autobiography*, i. 229.

[6] Draft dispatch to British Guiana in PRO, CO 111/136.

[7] Govt. beaten on Irish church: *H* xxvii. 878, 962.

[8] *H* xxvii. 980. See Magnus, 22–23; who, following Morley, i. 127, conflates the events of these two days.

[9] *Ernest Augustus, 1771–1851; served in Flanders, 1793–5, and Germany, 1806, 1813–4; cr. duke of Cumberland and Teviotdale, 1799; tory partisan; as king Ernest I of Hanover, 1837, suspended constitution; granted new one 1840; popular ruler.

[10] Add MS 44819, ff. 15–17.

[11] Cttee. on Cork city election set up: H.C. *Journ.* xc. 215.

[12] Sir William Webb *Follett, 1798–1845, advocate; solicitor-general 1834–5, 1841–4; attorney-general 1844–5; tory M.P. Exeter 1835; died of overwork.

[13] Possibly Charles Robertson, B.A. from St. John's, Cambridge, 1826, priest 1827.

Mr G—R.G.—Mr Halcomb[1]—C.O. & Commee 12–4¾—Took a Newark Address to Sir R. Peel—who was in excellent spirits—rode—dined at Sir E. Kerrison's—Lady Antrobus's splendid concert in evg.[2] newsp.

11. Sat.

Breakf. with Bp of Exeter: & conv.—newsp.—a beautiful letter from Manning. C.O. 11¾–4¼. rode. Began Lawson's Laud.[3] dined at the Carruthers's—at Sir F. Doyle's in evg—calls—wrote (rudely) La Fanatica: from last night.[4]

12. Sunday.

read "Domenica delle Palme"—3 of Milner's sermons (of Newark)[5]—Knox. Mr Tallents & Colvile here. Tea in B. Square—wrote—St James's—Mr Wigram (rather a low doctrine of the Sacrament) and Mr Ward—both very good.

13. M.

Rode to Richmond—breakf. with the Tylers—walk & conv. with him in the Park—on Sac[ramen]t &c.—Back at one. C.O. Commee, calls & House—wrote to R.G.—T. Sumner[6]—Mr Godfrey—dined at Peel's: his health drunk: an official party[7]—went to Ld Abns & with him to Lady Jersey's.[8] —Laud—'Lunedi Santo'—wrote to Mr Rose.

14. T.

"Martedi Santo"—Laud. Corrected my W.I. paper. calls. C.O. 1–4. dined with T.G.—Wrote to Mr Burnaby—Mr Baring—Mr Colquhoun—newsp.—rode.

15. W.

A final sitting to Hayter. St James's—Mr Wigram preached. C.O. 12¾–5¼. corrected my I.C. Speech for Mirror[9]—wrote Pol. Mema—Laud—Ettore Fieramosca—dined at Mr Mundy's—"Mercoledi Santo". Conv. with Ld Abn.[10]

[1] John *Halcomb, 1790–1852, candidate for Dover; carried it, as tory, 1833; beaten at Warwick as whig, 1835.

[2] Anne, née Lindsay, 1800–85, m. 1817 (Sir) Edmund Antrobus, 1792–1870, who succ. his uncle as 2nd bart. 1826; town house at 146 Piccadilly.

[3] J. P. *Lawson, Life and Times of William Laud, 2v. (1829).

[4] In Add MS 44724, ff. 42–45.

[5] J. T. Milner, Sermons on Important Subjects (1835).

[6] Probably s. of J. B. *Sumner.

[7] See Morley, i. 128, for *Peel's affectionate speech to his fallen colleagues; and *Gladstone's notes in Add MS 44819, ff. 17–18.

[8] Sarah Sophia, née Fane, 1785–1867; da. of 10th earl of Westmorland; m. 1804 George (Child-)*Villiers; 5th earl of Jersey 1805, racehorse owner; famous hostess.

[9] Mirror, ii. 647.

[10] Note in Add MS 44819, ff. 18–19.

16. Th.

newsp.—Laud—Ettore Fieramosca—St Giles's (Mr Tyler)—tea in B. Square—C.O.—conv. with Mr Wordsworth—wrote to Mr G—R.G.— J.N.G.—Simnitt,[1] Sumner, Mr Milner, Serj. Merewether, &c.—part of "Giovedi Santo". House.[2]

17. Fr.

St James's. Bp & Mr Ward. The Sacrament. How great Knox is on this high theme. Read him on Mysticism &c—Lawson's Laud—pt of Venerdi Santo—finished my paper on 'Experience'[3]—Bible to servv. as yesterday —newsp—tea in B. Squ—rode.

18. Sat.

Pt of Sabato Santo—newsp—Lawson's Laud—dined in B. Square—rode. The new ministry being formed, bad farewell to the Colonial Office: may my place be better filled.[4] Wrote divers Mema—& to Stormont[5]—Mr G— R.G.—T.G.—Mr Godfrey—Mr Finlay—read Lawson's Laud—Ettore Fieramosca.

19. Easter Sunday.

St James's—Mr Ward (exc[ellen]t) & Mr Gage.[6] The Sacrament.—read Knox—Domenica della Risurr.—Scripture aloud—Milner's Serm—Leibnitz on reunion.[7] revised &c. paper on 'Experience'—dined at Lincoln's Inn.

20. M.

Lawson's Laud—finished V.1.—newsp.—wrote to Mr M'Garel[8]—Mr Hay (two)[9]—Mr G.—R.G.—Mr Shand—arranging papers of the last 2 months— rode to Hillingdon to dinner[10]—at night began 'Confessions of an Opium Eater'.[11]

---

[1] Probably William Simnitt, Newark weaver.
[2] No useful business: *H* xxvii. 994.
[3] Cp. 8 Mar. 35 n.
[4] Sir G. *Grey filled it.
[5] William David Murray, 1806–98; Eton and Christ Church; styled Viscount Stormont till he succ. as 4th earl of Mansfield 1840; tory M.P. 1830–40; a lord of the treasury 1834–5.
[6] Probably Thomas Wentworth Gage, 1801?–37, gs. of 1st Viscount Gage, rector of Higham Ferrers, Northamptonshire, 1830,
[7] G. W. Leibnitz, *Systema theologicum* (1686, unpublished till 1819), sought common ground between catholics and protestants.
[8] Charles McGarel, d. 1876, of Magheramorne, co. Antrim, and of Wimpole Street.
[9] One recommends James McDonald of Berbice: PRO, CO 111/142.
[10] At Richard Heming's, father of T.J.; near Uxbridge, Middlesex, some 16 miles west of Westminster.
[11] *De Quincey (1821).

21. T.

finished Confessions—read Novelle Morali[1]—paper—left the Hemings, who are very kind, bef 3.—dined at Lincoln's Inn: papers: wrote to Mr G —Boler—Mr Pusey[2]—Pickering to tea & conv—Ettore Fieramosca. Laud (Vol 2).

22. Wed.

newsp. Laud. Conv. with T. Ogilvy, & Harrison, who called. wrote to Mr G. —Mr C. Robertson—Mr Lee (of Newark)—Mr Whyte—Rogers. dined at Lincoln's Inn—rode—read Homer's Hymn to Apollo. P. Tomkins & J. Jenkyns[3]—and divers of my old papers.

23. Th.

T. Ogilvy to breakf & long walk. Wood—S. Denison, &c. newsp.—read Laud—Homer—Fieramosca—dined at Mr Smith Wright's—Miss Dalbiac on the guitar.[4] rode—wrote to Mr G.

24. Fr.

Laud. Homer. Corpn Report (began)[5]—many calls—rode—dined with Sir R. Inglis: met Bp of Winchr & Mrs H. Goulburn jun.[6] wrote—read Quarty on Fisher Ames—newsp.—wrote to Mr G—Mr Ramsay—Mrs Hawkins.[7]

25. Sat.

Laud. Homer (began Merc.)[8] finished Corpn report—wrote papers—wrote to Mr G. & Raby—read Quarty on Beaumont—dined at Mr Goulburn's— newsp—rode—calls—read pt of B. Noel's letter to Bp of London.[9]

26. Sunday.

Breakf. in B. Square. Temple Church—Mr Benson:[10] a crowded & intensely

[1] Giovanni Soave (1788).
[2] In H. P. Liddon, *Life of* *Pusey, i. 306–7 (1893).
[3] Isaac Tomkins, *Thoughts upon the Aristocracy of England, with a Letter to Isaac Tomkins on the same subject by P. Jenkins* (2 ed., 1835). Isaac Tomkins and Peter Jenkins were pseudonyms of *Brougham.
[4] Susanna Stephania, 1814–95, m. 1836 the 6th duke of Roxburghe; lifelong friend of *Victoria's (cp. *LQV*, 3s. ii. 501); only child of Sir James Charles Dalbiac, 1776–1847, who fought in Spain; kt. 1831; tory M.P. Ripon 1835–7; lived in Albany; lieut.-gen. 1838.
[5] *PP* 1833 xiii.1.
[6] But Henry Goulburn, 1813–43, senior classic and 2nd wrangler 1835, eldest s. of the statesman, d. unmarried. His uncle Edward*, 1787–1868, sergeant-at-law, m. 3rdly 1831 his cousin Catherine Montagu, d. 1865, da. of 5th Lord Rokeby.
[7] Perhaps the wife of John Heywood Hawkins, nephew of 1st bart. of Trewithen; whig M.P. St. Michael 1830, Tavistock 1831, Newport (I.o.W.) 1832–41.
[8] One of the Homeric *Hymns* is to Hermes.
[9] Baptist W. *Noel, 'The State of the Metropolis Considered, in a Letter to the Bishop of London' (1835).
[10] Christopher *Benson, 1789–1868; first Hulsean lecturer 1820; canon of Worcester 1825–68; Master of the Temple 1826–45; noted preacher.

attentive audience. St James's in aft—Mr Ward. Dinner at L[incoln's] Inn. read Bible—Knox (began Vol 2)—B. Noel's letter (finished)—Leibniz Corresp. with Bossuet[1]—Arnold's Sermons (and one aloud).

27. M.

Cold & Headach. Wordsworth & Selwyn to breakfast. Lawson's Laud—Palgrave's protest[2]—papers—wrote to Bruce—rode. calls—dined with T.G.—Mr & Mrs G. came in evg: spent evg with them.[3] Eyes being painful could not read much. wrote to Mr Polson.[4]

28. T.

Cold & Headach still: however, breakf. in Conduit St—wrote to H.J.G.—Aunt M—Branston. Newsp. dined at Mrs Vansittart's—rode. finished Lawson's Laud, a most intemperate book; the foam swallows up all the facts—and part of "Candide".[5]

29. W.

Cold still: went to Court to present an Address.[6] Dined in B. Square—Mr Richards's Letter & sent him a note upon it[7]—newsp—finished Candide & wrote upon it[8]—read Wordsworth's "Postscript",[9] and began Ld J. Russell on the Consttn.[10]

30. Thursday.

Sore throat: endurable: but gave up dining with Harrison, as yesterday Rogers. dined in Conduit St.—accounts & letters—Ld J. Russell—(began) Hallam's Const. Hist.[11]—Ettore Fiera mosca—Virgil—wrote some verses, and letters to Lady Kerrison—Caparn—newsp. Mrs G. ill.

Friday May one.

Cold has almost fled. My dear Mother somewhat better. Calls. rode. newsp. wrote to J.N.G.—Caparn—Chairman of Court of Directors[12]—many notes.

---

[1] Correspondence between Bossuet, Leibnitz, and Molan on the unification of catholics and protestants (1815).

[2] Sir F. T. *Palgrave 'Remarks, submitted to . . . [Lord] *Melbourne' (1832), a row about records.

[3] They were staying at 38 Conduit Street, Mayfair.

[4] W. G. Polson of Lincoln's Inn?   [5] Voltaire.

[6] At a levée; from Kilmuir Easter, co. Cromarty, approving *Peel's government's policy.

[7] John Richards, whig M.P. Knaresborough 1832–7, Letter to Lord *Brougham (1835), in reply to 'Peter Jenkins'.

[8] Add MS 44724, f. 68.

[9] To Yarrow Revisited (1835).

[10] An Essay on the History of the English Government and Constitution (1821).

[11] H. *Hallam, Constitutional History of England, 2v. (1827).

[12] Of the East India company: Henry St. George *Tucker, 1771–1851, civil servant and merchant in India 1786–1815, director of company 1826–51, chairman 1834–5 and 1847–8.

dined at no 38 (Conduit St). read Hallam—Ettore—part of Qu. Rev. on poor Law[1]—wrote a supplement to W.I. Edn paper.[2]

2. S.

To Selwyn's (Richmond) to breakf—walk there with him—back at 1½— wrote to H.J.G. & Chisholm—newsp—finished Quart. on Poor Bill in E. Kent—read Hallam (Ch III)—Ettore—and Preface to Manzoni's Sulla Morale.[3] My dear Mother very little better. Dined at 38.

3. Sunday.

St James's. Sacrament. Mr Ward & the Bishop. My dear Mother still very unwell. Breakfast & dinner at 38. read Knox—Blunt on Artt[4]—Manzoni sulla Morale—& wrote.[5]

4. M.

Lyall to breakf.—Hallam Ch IV. household business. walk with W. Harrison.[6] paper. Wrote to A. Williams—Mrs Larkins. my mother very weak still & sick.—dined at Mr Colvile's—at Kensington Palace in evg.— What am I, to walk there?[7]

5. Tuesday.

Ross to breakf.—admirable news from Devonshire.[8] With Hamilton at the Church Miss[ionar]y meeting. 12¼–3. read J.N.G.'s letters—newsp—Statement of Scottish Dissrs & Counter Statement of Gen. Assrs case[9]—Dante's Ugolino.[10] wrote to Caparn & Ld Hill.[11] rode—calls—dined at Mr Tyler's. read Blunt's 3d Serm on Articles.

My dear mother continued to suffer but appeared in the evening easier: may God grant her a speedy return of strength.

6.

Mrs G. decidedly better: thank God. much in Conduit St. read Blunt—

---

[1] Instead of 'Laws'. [2] In Add MS 44724, ff. 38–39.

[3] A. Manzoni, *Osservazioni sulla morale cattolica* (1834), attack on Sismondi's view of moral influence of Roman church.

[4] Henry *Blunt, *Discourses on the Doctrinal Articles of the Church of England* (1835). [5] On Calvinism: Add MS 44821 C, ff. 21–26, and on God: Add MS 44820, f. 23.

[6] William Harrison, 1811–82; at Brasenose; court chaplain; canon of St. Albans 1877.

[7] Then the home of Victoria Mary Louisa, 1786–1861, of Saxe-Saalfeld-Coburg, m. 1803 prince Emich Charles of Leiningen, who d. 1814, and 2ndly 1818 Edward Augustus, 1767–1820, duke of *Kent; and of their da. *Victoria.

[8] Lord John *Russell, standing for re-election on becoming home secretary, was badly beaten at a by-election.

[9] 'Statement relating to Church Accommodation in Scotland' (1835) by the Scottish Central Board for vindicating the rights of Dissenters; and 'Exposure of the false principles contained' in it by the General Assembly of the Church of Scotland.

[10] *Inferno*, xxxii–xxxiii.

[11] Rowland *Hill, 1772–1842, general: fought at Toulon, in Egypt and Peninsula, and at Waterloo; tory M.P. Shrewsbury 1812; cr. baron 1814, and Viscount Hill 1842; commander-in-chief 1828–42.

newsp—Hallam—Ett. Fieramosca—& Eton Miscellany: I cannot keep my temper in perusing my own (with few exceptions) execrable productions. Dined at Mr Tuppers. rode. wrote.[1] wrote to Moncreiff[2]—H.J.G.—and J.N.G.

7.

Breakfd & spent some time in Conduit St. My dear mother as yet far from comfortable. read Blunt—"1835 compd with 1772"[3]—Hume (beginning Edw. VI)—Ld J. Russell—newsp—notes of Hallam. rode—dined at Col. Conolly's.

8.

Breakf. & morng again in Conduit St. Thank God a great improvement to day.—Read M'Donnell on R.C. Oath[4]—"a religious reason"[5]—paper— Hume—wrote a few verses—notes of Hallam: gathering quotns from papers &c. for H. of C. perhaps—rode—dined at Mr Smith Wrights: pleasant party. —read Bible to Mrs G.

9.

Breakf. & several hours in Conduit St.—paper—Ettore Fieramosca— Hallam & notes—wrote to Mrs Wadd—T.S. Godfrey & Mr Tallents, it being said that Wilde is to be Att[orne]y General.[6] rode—dined at Uncle D's—saw Mr Pinnock[7]—conv. with Ld Mahon, &c.

10. Sunday.

Mrs G. progressing. dinner at 38. St James's—Wigram & Ward. walk. wrote on Church of E.[8]—read Bible—Leibnitz—Knox—Blunt on Artt (finished)—Arnold (aloud).

11.

breakf. & forenoon at 38. With Mr G. at C[olonial] O[ffice]—rode—wrote to Mr Tallents—Bartlett—Ramsay—Harrison. read Hallam. Ettore. Wordsworth. At Peel's great dinner—his reception enthusiastic.[9] At Lady Antrobus's delightful concert afterwards.[10]

[1] Add MS 44821C, ff. 26–29.
[2] James *Moncreiff had just published a pamphlet in defence of the Church of Scotland on the accommodation question.
[3] *1835 and 1772: The Present Attack on Subscription compared with the Last* (1835).
[4] Eneas Macdonnell, 'The Roman Catholic Oath Considered' (1835).
[5] Possibly *Reasons for Christianity; and the Hope therein founded* (1833), or a review of it.
[6] *Wilde became solicitor-general in 1839, and attorney-general for a few weeks in 1841.
[7] William *Pinnock, 1782–1843, writer on education and speculator.   [8] Untraced.
[9] The London conservative merchants and bankers entertained *Peel in Merchant Taylors' Hall.
[10] Here no doubt began the diarist's attachment to Caroline (Eliza) Farquhar, d. 1890, Walter Farquhar's sister; see Magnus, 23–29. She m. 26 July 1836 Charles *Grey, 1804–70, 2nd s. of 2nd Earl *Grey; whig M.P. Wycombe 1831–7, private secretary to *Victoria 1862, and general 1865.

12.

breakf. & forenoon at 38. Saw Ld Abn. Wrote to R.G.—H.J.G.—Sir G. Grey—read Ettore—Hallam—Hume—newsp—Hilhouse's papers on B.G.[1] —dined at Col. Baillie's[2]—rode. H. of C. $4\frac{1}{2}$–$5\frac{3}{4}$[3]—Mrs G. better again.

13. Wed.

Breakf. & forenoon at 38—wrote draft to the Mint—Ettore Fieramosca— Hallam—Bradley's Sermon—a Sonnet—rode: conv. with Taylor—House— dined at Guy's as a Govr—Lady Sitwell's[4] in evg.—read papers in Mr Rose's case—newsp.—a sonnet!![5]

14. Th.

A check in my Mother's progress. Dinner & evg there. House 4–6.[6] wrote to Mr Wilson—Mr Rose—Gould—Pinnock—Caparn—Williams—Mrs Wishlade—Mr Pusey[7]—Messrs Hall[8] & M'Garel—Stephen—reperused my W.I.E. paper, with ref. to an inquiry of Taylors. Ettore—Hallam—newsp— Sinclair on Patronage—Pinnock's papers—copied a letter.

15. Fr.

Mrs G. still checked.—Mentieth & Garden to breakfast—Hume—Ettore— paper—walk with Farquhar—read Stirling's long & able paper on W.I.E.[9] —thought over the printing my own. dinner & evg at 38—House—wrote to Lushington—Wordsworth—Lincoln—Warden &c. of Winchester[10]— rode.

16. Saturday.

Tancred to breakf: LONG conv.—conv. with Farquhar on my W.I.E. paper: had I some object?[11]—wrote to Bp of London—dined at Lambeth, public day: splendid house & banquet: Abp's manners most pleasing. with Mrs G: learned from her I had been of use to Mollison. Alas!—Hallam—newsp —began J. Abbott's "teacher"[12]—calls—rode.

---

[1] William Hilhouse, *Indian Notices, Sketches of the Several Nations* [of British Guiana], (1825).

[2] Hugh Duncan Baillie, 1777–1866; of Tarradale, co. Ross; colonel, Surrey Rangers, 1810; lib.-cons. M.P. Rye 1830, Honiton 1835–47.

[3] Misc. business: *H* xxvii. 1024.

[4] Susan, née Tait, d. 1880 (sister of *abp.), m. 1818 Sir George Sitwell 1797–1853, 2nd bart. of Renishaw 1814.

[5] See Morley, i. 128.

[6] Misc. Irish business: *H* xxvii. 1071.

[7] In *Liddon, *Pusey*, i. 309.

[8] Perhaps (Sir) Benjamin *Hall, 1802–67, whig M.P. Monmouth 1831, 1832–7, Marylebone 1837–59; cr. bart. 1838, Baron Llanover 1859; commissioner of works, 1855–8.

[9] By John *Sterling; in PRO, CO 318/122, ff. 381–505. See *DNB* liv. 194, and T. *Carlyle, *Sterling* (1857), 261.

[10] Rupert Speckott Barter, 1790–1861, warden of Winchester College 1832.

[11] See 11 May 35 n.

[12] Jacob Abbott, *The Teacher: Moral Influences . . . in instructing The Young* (1833).

17. Sunday.

St James's. Mr Ward & the Bp: both exc[ellen]t: latter partic[ularl]y: dined in Conduit St. walk—read Bible to Mrs G.—Arnold aloud—wrote—read Leibniz—Morale Catholica—Knox—.

18. M.

Hallam—"the Teacher"—calls—Club—wrote to Mr Godfrey & Mr Caparn—House—dined & evg at 38—rode—read newsp—'the Foundn of the Faith assailed'[1]—Ettore Fier—Quarty on Mod. Germ. Litte—and Br. Cr. on religious parties[2]—also Bible to Mrs G.

19. T.

Hallam. "Teacher"—Morale Catholica—newsp—wrote to Mr Young—Mrs Ramsay—Caparn—Col. Hay—rode—dinner at Mr Williams's—Mr Stewart expounded Ps 96—Educn Commee—some convn & discussion on going to Oxford for tomorrow: decided in neg.—House 4–5¼.[3]

20. Wed.

My dear Mother still suffering very great pain: tho' in some respects better.
    wrote to Thos Godfrey—Caparn—read "Teacher"—Ettore—newsp.—wrote vss.[4]—rode—at examn of Nat. School Children—not satisfied—rode—dined at 38—conv. with Canning on Chichester.[5]

21. Th.

Breakf. & forenoon at 38—also dinner: my dear Mother thank God better. newsp—Ettore—Hume. Wrote to Sir G. Grey—Pinnock. At Aunt D.s—Lady Sitwell's—Lady Farquhar's—in evg: a strange dissipation; not without a purpose.

22. Friday.

Hume—Ettore Fieramosca—newsp—Ld Abns Canada despatches.[6] House 4–6½. rode. div. 185:171 on Lpool Police & Clergy Bill.[7] dined at 38. wrote to H.J.G.—at Christie's sale.

23. Sat.

Hume. Finished the Canada despatches. newsp. Finished Fieramosca—Isaac Comnenus.[8] calls. rode. dined at 38—Carlton. wrote to A. Williams—T.S. Godfrey—Mrs Bartlett.[9]—Mrs G. much the same.

---

[1] *The Foundation of the Faith Assailed in Oxford* (1835).
[2] *British Critic*, xvii. 390–425 (1835).
[3] Irish education: *H* xxvii. 1199.   [4] In Add MS 44724, f. 72.
[5] *Canning was still searching for a seat.
[6] *PP* 1837–8, xxxix. 863; no doubt seen in MS.
[7] Against a wrecking amdt. of *Ewart's; bill then read 2°. *H* xxviii. 30.
[8] Tragedy by Henry *Taylor (1828).
[9] Presumably wife of the vicar of Newark.

24. Sunday.

St James's—Mr Wigram & Mr Ward. Walk. Mrs G. better. dined &c. at
38. read Bible—Knox—Leibnitz—Morale Catholica—an Arnold [sermon]
aloud. Wrote on Knox.[1]

25. M.

Apsley House 10¼–11¾ seeing the pictures under G. Wellesley's tutelage—
much interested & gratified. then with Mr G. to Mr Norton's.[2] calls. rode.
read Hume & began "L'Esclavage"[3]—paper—House 4–5¼ and 10–12½.[4]
dined at 38. Mrs G. better.

26. T.

T.G., Wm G & Adam[5] to breakft—newsp—Hume—Sir P. Sidney—Educn
Commee—called on Sir R. Peel—rode—House 4–7.[6] evg at 38—read
"Marie ou L'Esclavage" & Ed. Rev. on "Recent Pol. Occurr[ence]s"
evid[entl]y Brougham? Wrote to Kynaston & Aunt J.

27. W.

Breakf at 38—Marie—Hume—newsp—Sir P. Sidney (Defence of Poesy)—
House 4–6¾[7]—dined at Ld Ashburton's:[8] fine pictures: saw Mr Brackenbury's—wrote to Sir R. Peel—Mr Pinnock—O.B. Cole—H.J.G.—calls.

28. Th.

Doyle & Acland to breakft: Farquhar came in to meet the latter. St
James's; the sacrament. Went (afternoon) to the Drawingroom.[9] rode.
dined at 38. Marie—newsp—Sir P. Sidney—Knox. Arranged for departure
tomorrow.

I went to the drawingroom really as an act of social duty. It may startle
one thus to bring its pomp into contact with the holy rite I had attended:
but believing both right I concluded at last to join them: and indeed in a
true view of the Sacrament, what is it but a supply of that substantial
nourishment upon which, if we be Christians, our souls are habitually to be
fed, of that which is to sustain even their momentary respiration, of that
which is [to] enable us to pass through all acts of relative duty, and the
varieties of social intercourse: therefore as upon occasion not selfsought I

[1] In Add MS 44724, f. 73.
[2] Perhaps (Sir) John David Norton, d. 1843; judge at Madras, kt. 1842; or George
Chapple Norton, 1800–75, M.P. Guildford 1828–32, Lambeth magistrate 1831–67,
husband of Caroline *Norton.
[3] Novel by Gustave de Beaumont about life in Maryland (1835).
[4] Church rates; agricultural distress. *H* xxviii. 51, 85.
[5] Adam Steuart Gladstone, 1814–63, 5th s. of diarist's uncle Robert; Liverpool
merchant.
[6] Misc. business: *H* xxviii. 150.
[7] Paving St. Pancras: *H* xxviii. 186.
[8] Alexander *Baring had been cr. Baron Ashburton 10 April 1835.
[9] At St. James's, to celebrate the king's birthday.

would go straight from a meal to bodily exercise, so today I thought it right to go at a short interval from the table of the Lord to the court of my earthly sovereign: how much ought we to feel there, and how much to learn!

29. Fr.

5–3.40. Posted to Leam[ingto]n. Breakf. at Brickhill 40 m.[1] read Marie & began Reynolds's Lectures[2]—wrote some lines, & notes—calls at Leamn—dined & slept at Dr Jephson's—whist. Glad to find H.J.G. well tho wanting care.

30. Sat.

8.5–6.30. Back to London. Another cause for thankfulness: found John at 38, rode. dined at the Watts Russells[3] read Reynolds.

31. Sunday.

St James's: Mr Ward & Bp—both admirable. breakf. & dinner at 38—read Bible—Arnold (& aloud)—Morale Catholica—Leibniz—Knox's Remains (finished).

Monday June one.

Breakf at 38—copied a letter—wrote to A. Williams—Mr Tallents—Mr T. Godfrey—attended O. & C. Committee meeting—calls—rode—house 5 6.[4] dined at Ld Abns. Hope's party: these places have a positive saddening effect on my mind.[5] read newsp—Marie—Reynolds.

2. T.

Farquhar—Acland—J.N.G.—to breakf. Mr Herbert[6] here. wrote to R.G. & Mr T. Godfrey. Edn Committee (Commn overthrown) and House 1–5. rode: dined at Mr Smith Wright's—voted in 317:144 agst ballot—Marie, Reynolds: house 10.40–1½.[7]

3. W.

Bruce & Geary[8] to breakf. wrote to T. Godfrey—newsp—M'Ghee's Sermon on North[9]—Isaac Comnenus (finished)—House 5–6½.[10] dined at Short's—

[1] i.e. 40 miles out of London, to the NW.
[2] H. W. *Beechey ed., Sir Joshua *Reynold's Literary Works, 2v. (1835).
[3] Jesse Watts Russell m. 1811 Mary, da. of David Pike Watts; and see 4 June 35.
[4] Church of Scotland: H xxviii. 209.
[5] Perhaps *Hope held his party at his father's; Sir Alexander *Hope, 1769–1837, general and M.P., who governed Chelsea hospital from 1826.
[6] Perhaps George Herbert, clerk of the bills in the treasury.
[7] *Grote again failed to carry ballot: H xxviii. 471.
[8] (Sir) Francis Geary, 1811–95; at Christ Church; 4th bart. 1877.
[9] R. J. MacGhee, 'A Sermon on the Death of J. H. North' (1831).
[10] Quarrel between *Hume and Edmund Lechmere Charlton, 1785?–1845, cons. M.P. Ludlow 1835–7: H xxviii. 486.

at Lady Bullers[1] & Bridgwater House[2] afterwards, with Mr G. at Christie's &c.

4. Th.

breakf at 38—at 10½ went to St George's: saw Watts Russell[3] married to Miss Mary (Smith) Wright: an interesting & touching ceremony admirably performed by the Bp of Lichfield.[4] May God's blessing be upon them. Went thence to St Paul's—the Anniversary:[5] the sight magnificent: the sound extraordinary, not perfectly agreeable: rather painful to my ears which are not strong. A crackling sound in the air as if it underwent broken & irregular propulsions, when the children sang out.—rode—calls—Reynolds (began Vol 2)—Maurice (began)[6]—wrote to Burnaby—dined at Sir J.Y. Buller's.[7]

5. Fr.

Mr Tallents here. with Lincoln—Lady L[incoln]—a long conv. with Lady Canning. wrote to Caparn & R.G.—House 5–7. Corpn Reform[8]—dined at Sir S. Scott's. read on Newark Corpn—Maurice—and Sir J. Reynolds.

6. Sat.

Reynolds—Maurice (finished) an admirable book—A.H.H.—rode to Hampstead (the Chief Justice's party)[9]—dined at Mordaunt's—at Mrs Wynn's—wrote to T. Godfrey—Dr Wordsworth—Rn G.—Chr. Wordsworth—Mrs Ramsay.

7. Sunday.

Breakf & dinner at 38—walk—Mr Ward & Bp: both excellent. The Holy Sacrament. read Bible—Arnold (Vol 3) & aloud—Morale Catholica—Leibniz.

8. M.

Left Piccadilly by Express 7.20 A.M. arrived at Newark 10.40 P.M. Went out to Beaconfield: found the Godfreys awaiting me: & as friendly as I could by possibility desire. Great heat.

---

[1] Elizabeth, née Wilson-Patten, d. 1857; m. 1823 (Sir) John Yarde-Buller (see next entry).
[2] Lord Francis *Egerton's palace in Cleveland Square. Lord Francis Leveson-Gower, 1800–57, grandee; M.P. 1822–46; changed name to *Egerton 1833, as heir of 8th earl of Bridgewater; poet and patron; cr. earl of Ellesmere 1846.
[3] (Jesse) David Watts Russell, 1812–79, s. of Jesse; at Christ Church; cons. M.P. Staffordshire 1841–7.
[4] Henry *Ryder, 1777–1836, 3rd s. of 1st Lord *Harrowby; bp. of Gloucester 1815, of Lichfield 1824.   [5] Charity children's service.
[6] F. D. *Maurice, Eustace Conway, a novel (1834).
[7] Sir John Yarde-Buller, 1799–1871; tory M.P. Devonshire 1835–58; succ. as 3rd bart. 1833; cr. Baron Churston 1858.   [8] H xxviii. 541.
[9] Sir Nicholas Conyngham *Tindal, 1776–1846; wrangler 1799; tory M.P. 1824–9; kt. 1826; chief justice of common pleas 1829; lived on Hampstead Heath.

9. T.

Heat continued. In Newark—seeing friends : conv. on Corpn business. The Tallentses &c. to dinner. conv. with Mr Caparn. wrote to Mrs G.—read in J. Reynolds. Robn came in evg.

10. W.

Heat still. Circuit with Robn made near 50 calls : almost every one (wisely) within doors. Sir J. Reynolds—paper— Party at Beaconfield : a little singing in evg : thought over points for tomorrow & notes.

11. Th.

In Newark early. Mr G. came, & gratified our friends much. Again at Beaconfield, & revolved my subject. Dinner—4–11. 180 dined, I am told. Spoke (in chief) near an hour : by no means to my satisfaction. Divers minor speeches. My Father expressed himself with beautiful and affectionate truth of feeling : and the party sympathised. I mean by truth of feeling not to imply an equal truth in fact. Robn [spoke] very well indeed. Tea at Clinton Arms.[1]

12. Fr.

1 A.M.–4½—to London outside the Highflyer with Rn G.—great heat still. rode—at L[incol]ns Inn—dined at 38—sang—papers—at Carlton.

13.

Began Talfourd's Ion :[2] wrote an answer to his very kind letter. rode. at Lns Inn. dined at Mr Herries's[3]—Speaker's levee—sat long with my Mother—& my Father. wrote notes for two dinners—& to Doyle—Mr Alexander—Hicklin[g]—Caparn—Dr Wordsworth—Girdlestone—saw Sir R. Peel.

14. Sunday.

Mr Wigram & Mr Ward. Sact—Bible—Chalmers's two pamphlets on Scotch Church questn[4]—Knox's Corresp[5]—Morale Catholica—an Arnold aloud : consid[erabl]e modifn is required. Lincs Inn.

15. M.

at meeting of members on Sc. Ch. quest—calls—Nat Gall—dined at Lns Inn—tea at 38—House 5¾–6½ & 10–12¼—heard Peel's Speech with sorrow,

---

[1] Dinner to diarist in town hall. See Morley, i. 129 ; and Cornelius Brown, *History of Newark*, ii. 252, and *Annals of Newark*, 285–6 ; and *Nottingham Journal*, 12 June 1835.
[2] (Sir) T. N. *Talfourd's tragedy of *Ion* was privately circulated for a year before its production in 1836.   [3] In Albemarle Street.
[4] Thomas *Chalmers, 'On the Evils which The Established Church in Edinburgh has ... suffered' and 'Specimens of the Ecclesiastical Destitution of Scotland' (both 1835).
[5] *Thirty Years' Correspondence Between John *Webb and A. *Knox*, 2v. (1834).

much sorrow[1]—read Ion and Marie—and Corpn Report on Newark—wrote to Mr Tallents.

16. T.

With Mr G. at Norton's—Edn Commee 12¼–2¼—calls—rode—finished Ion —read Sir J. Reynolds—wrote to Aunt M—evg at 38.

17. W.

read Marie—paper—arranged for two dinners tomorrow & Fr—House at 12—and 4.40–5.45, 7–8¼.[2] tea at 38—evg at Lady Sitwell's—a long work correcting & almost rewriting my speech at Newark for the Lpool St. very incompletely done after all.[3]

18.

read "Ch of Sc's India Mission"—very curious pamphlet on a subject of deep interest.[4] Wrote to Mrs Charriere & Wordsworth—read Marie—paper —rode—Ed. Comm. 12–3—saw Col. Fitzgibbon's house.[5] R.G., Taylor, J.M.G., Lyall, Pearson, Vansittart, Colvile, dined with me.

19. Friday.

Marie. paper. Cobbett is dead: alas! for the cloud that rests upon his memory: I have a painful recollection of something he said to me.

Corpn Bill meeting at Sir R. Peel's 11¼–2½. Chiefly on details. rode. House 5–11½—unable to join my poor? guests! (J.N.G., Mordaunt, Pringle, Chisholm, C. Hagart). Sir G. Grey's capital speech was however a great treat.[6]

20. Sat.

R.G. & Seymer to breakf.—Canning shd have come. Marie: Taylor's letter on public Offices.[7] Protestant meeting 11½–4¾. O'Sullivan[8] is indeed a noble speaker: far from a mere $\delta\eta\mu o\chi\alpha\rho\iota\sigma\tau\eta\varsigma$.[9] M'Ghee's too, very important.[10] rode. dined at Sir E. Kerrison's: delightful singing there.

[1] Municipal Corporations Bill 2°, with Peel's assent: *H* xxviii. 830.

[2] Misc. business: *H* xxviii. 843.

[3] *Liverpool Standard*, 19 June 1835.

[4] A. *Duff, 'The Church of Scotland India Mission' (1835); urging preaching of gospe in native tongues, by natives.

[5] 44 Belgrave Square. Richard Hobart Fitzgibbon, 1793–1865, fought at Talavera; M.P. co. Limerick 1818–37; succ. his b. as 3rd earl of Clare 1851; his only s. k. at Balaclava.

[6] Discussion on West Indian labour conditions: *H* xxviii. 918.

[7] Probably an early draft of *The Statesman*: cp. 7 Apr. 36.

[8] Mortimer *O'Sullivan, 1791?–1859, controversialist; convert from Rome; canon of St. Patrick's 1827–30; held various Irish rectories. He spoke on the woes of the Irish protestant clergy in Exeter Hall.

[9] 'Flatterer of the people'.

[10] Robert James MacGhee, 1799–1872, controversialist and protestant priest, opened the meeting.

21. Sunday.

St Margaret's Mr Hook. St James's Mr Cavendish. Charity sermons : both very good. Anstice dined with me : sadly hacked and torn by his cough : God I trust will spare his valuable and interesting life. Tea at 38. Read Bible—Knox—and Morale Catholica.

22. M.

Monteith & Garden to breakf. House at 12. Again $3\frac{3}{4}$–$5\frac{3}{4}$ (spoke for the Newark Corpn)[1]—(Rousseau Confns—I scarcely know whether to read on.)[2] rode—House $7\frac{1}{4}$–$12\frac{1}{4}$. div. in 192 : 279, and 321 : 97 on Corpns[3]—calls &c.

23. Tuesday.

Breakf. at Bp of Winchester's—Edn Commee $12\frac{1}{4}$–$2\frac{1}{4}$—wrote to J. Crane[4]—rode—dined at Serj. Merewether's—House 4–5, again $6\frac{1}{2}$. and $9\frac{1}{2}$–12—at Mrs Law's.[5] read Rousseau Conf. & two of Place's pamphlets[6]—divided in 232 to 279 on rights of freemen.[7]

24. W.

R.G. & Canning to breakf.—Marie—Rousseau Conf.—wrote to Mr Moss. at Lady H. Wynn's[8] in evg (to celebrate Miss Shipley's marriage)[9]—newsp. House $4\frac{3}{4}$–$9\frac{3}{4}$, and 11–1.[10]

25. Th.

The Wilberforces (S. and R.)[11] to breakf, also O'Brien.[12] conv. on W.I. quest. relative to Mr W's life. At Ld F. Egerton's,[13] Edn & Sinecure Comm!,[14] 12–$3\frac{1}{4}$. Rode—House—dined at Bp of Rochester's—House 1 –$11\frac{1}{2}$.[15] Carl-

[1] Presenting petition against Municipal Corporations Bill : *H* xxviii. 979. Debate on catholic members' oaths : ibid. 979.
[2] Jean-Jacques Rousseau's posthumous *Confessions* (1782), notorious for their frankness. Cp. Morley, i. 128.
[3] In cttee.: *H* xxviii. 1035, 1043.
[4] Joseph Crane, auctioneer in Southampton Row.
[5] In Portland Place. Elizabeth Sophia, née Nightingale, 1789?–1864, m. 1811 Charles Ewan *Law, 1792–1850, recorder of London 1833, tory M.P. Cambridge University from 1835.
[6] Francis *Place, 'Pamphlets for the People' (1835), on municipal reform.
[7] Corporations Bill, cttee.: *H* xxviii. 1112. The numbers were 278 : 232.
[8] Hester Frances, née Smith, d. 1854; da. of *Lord Carrington; m. 1813 (Sir) Henry Watkin Williams *Wynn, 1783–1856, minister in Copenhagen 1824–53, whose sister Charlotte m. 1806 lieut.-col. William Shipley.
[9] Charlotte, d. 1871, Col. Shipley's da., m. this day (col.) Richard Thomas Rowley, 1812–87, 2nd s. of 1st Lord Langford; cons. M.P. Harwich 1860–5.
[10] Corporations Bill, cttee.: *H* xxviii. 1181.
[11] Robert Isaac *Wilberforce, 1802–57, 2nd s. of William*; double first, 1823; fellow of Oriel, 1826–31; archdeacon of East Riding, 1841–54; *Manning's Anglican confessor, 1843–50; entered Roman church, 1854. S.* and R. I. *Wilberforce published a *Life* of their father, 5v. (1838).
[12] Cornelius O'Brien, whig M.P. co. Clare 1832–47, 1852–7.   [13] Cp. 3 June 35 n.
[14] Cp. *PP* 1834 vi. 339.   [15] Dorchester labourers : *H* xxviii. 1235.

ton. walk & strange conv.—Read Conf[essio]ns & M'Ghee's pamphlet.[1] Wrote to Mr Campbell. Tennyson.

26. Fr.

Breakf at 38. Rain. At Diorama.[2] read Reynolds. Wrote to Mr Greville— Mr Carson. House 5–6¾; dined with the Lushingtons—House 10–1¼[3]— papers. Greville's case.[4]

27. Sat.

Breakf with the Lushingtons—calls—O. & C. Commee accounts—rode— read 'Sunday in London',[5] Marie, paper—wrote to Tallents—Dry— Hicklin—dined with P.M. Stewart.

28. Sunday.

Helen's birthday—21; may she be blessed in them all. St James's mg & aft. dined at 38. Knox—Arnold—Morale Catholica—Arnold aloud.

29.

Breakf at 38. Reynolds—Oakeley's pamphlet (very good).[6] Mr Ross called. Calls. rode. paper. House 5¼–1¼[7] (rode 1¼ hour) finished "Sunday in London".

30. Tuesday.

Breakfast at 38. paper. Reynolds. Edn Comm.[8] & House 1–5: rode: dined 38: House 8½–12¾. voted in 204:262 on Corpn Bill—and in 176:220. (Clauses 20 & 22).[9] wrote to Caparn. Mrs Chisholm. Mr Moss. read a pamphlet of Place's.

Wednesday July one.

Saw Buck[ingha]m palace: much bad and paltry taste: the results poor compared with the means & time bestowed. Wrote on Oxf. questn—read

---

[1] R. J. MacGhee, 'A Letter to the Protestants of the United Kingdom', strongly anti-Roman, dated 12 June 1835.
[2] Perhaps at the Colosseum in Regent's Park.
[3] Ipswich election; leave to bring in Irish church bill. H xxviii. 1278.
[4] See 2 July 35 n.
[5] John Wight, *Sunday in London* (1833).
[6] Frederick *Oakley, 'A Letter to . . . the Duke of *Wellington . . . upon . . . a Bill . . . entitled "A Bill for abolishing Subscription to Articles of Religion in Certain Cases"' (1835).
[7] Governor-general of India: H xxix. 30.
[8] Some notes in Add MS 44724, ff. 93–101, on the evidence of Francis *Place, 1771–1854, the radical.
[9] For property qualifications for town councillors (204–267), and for less frequent local elections: H xxix. 120, 125.

Pusey's questt. ans[wer]s. & notes[1]—Marie—began Milnes.[2] House 6¾–10.[3] rode. at Lady Scott's concert: very delightful.

2. Th.

Milnes—began Dymond on Establts[4]—Committees &c. 1¼–5, and House 9–12. rode. wrote to Mayor of Newark,[5] Mr Greville,[6] Mr Stephen, Dr Wordsworth, Lincoln, Hankey.[7] voted in 166:211 on licensing[8]—saw panorama of Jerusm: disagreeable to the eye but, all say, very veracious.[9]

3. Friday.

Milnes—finished Dymond—dined at 38 to bid R.G. goodbye—House 5–5½ and 7¼[10]—at Lady Lansdowne's, at Hayter's with Mrs G—rode. Hamilton with me.

4. Sat.

[Millbank] Penitentiary rules—Ipswich Eln Evidence.[11] wrote to Tallents, Branston, & Mayor of Newark. Ipswich Commee 12–2 and Penitentiary 2–4. rode—dined at Mr Pusey's.[12] Finished Milnes. there is some great ability in him & vivid perceptions.

5. Sunday.

St James's mg & aft.—The Sacrament. Bible—Knox—Leibniz—Morale Catholica—papers on the Irish Islands &c.[13] tea at 38.

6. M.

8 A.M. went to see Mr Kelly.[14] heard him till near 9. came up by appt & found Dr Chalmers & Mr Simpson:[15] I am ashamed of my uselessness to them. 10–4 Ipswich El. Commee. rode. House. dined in B. square. House

---

[1] E. B. *Pusey, *Subscription to the 39 Articles* (1835); see Faber, *Oxford Apostles*, 343–4.

[2] R. M. *Milnes, *Memorials of a tour in . . . Greece* (1833).

[3] Church of Scotland: *H* xxix. 136.

[4] J. *Dymond *The Church and the clergy* (1834).

[5] William Thompson the younger.

[6] *Gladstone was helping Charles *Greville, 1794–1865, the diarist, to retain both the secretaryship of Jamaica, which *Greville never visited, and the clerkship of the privy council; each carried a substantial salary. See Greville, iii. 222–3, for 7 July 1835; and 17 July 35 below.

[7] Thompson Hankey, 1805–93; governor, bank of England, 1851–3; lib. M.P. Peterborough 1853–68, 1874–80.

[8] Against licensing powers for town councils: *H* xxix. 208.

[9] 'The Siege of Jerusalem' was showing at Astley's Royal Amphitheatre.

[10] Put on Ipswich election cttee.; corporations bill ctd. *H* xxix. 232.

[11] Diarist's record in Add MS 44724, ff. 103–25.

[12] Philip *Pusey, 1799–1855, b. of E.B.*; cons. M.P. Berkshire 1835–52; agriculturalist.

[13] Statement by the Ladies' Irish Islands Association (Dublin, January 1835) in Add MS 44563, ff. 13–14.

[14] Possibly John *Kelly, 1801–76, Liverpool independent preacher.

[15] Robert *Simpson, 1795–1867, presbyterian divine, not his namesake at Newark.

again 10–11½.[1] read M'Donnell's 2d pamphlet.[2] wrote to Miss Benwell—T. Ogilvy—Dr Wordsworth—Mr Baring.[3]

7. Tuesday.

10–4, Ipswich Committee. Wrote to Mr Baring—Mr Tallents—Mr Burnaby —M[blank]. at 5 rode to Roehampton with Farquhar & Williams—went over Sir T.F's place[4]—an agreeable evening there, & excessive enjoyment of the free night air from a bow window commanding London & the range of country which fronts Richmond hill. Began Jeremie.[5] wrote a letter to Canning.

8. W.

In London I cannot get up: here I could not but get up on awaking. continued Jeremie—& began Mrs Sullivan's Blanche.[6] After breakfast went reluctantly to town with my excellent friend: looking forward however to another visit next week by very kind invitn.[7] e veramente con piacere ho fatto questa visita, stamattina massimamente: ma perche? ne debbo dire ne posso, in quanto i sentimenti del cuore ne figura hanno dalla loro nascita, ne distinto e chiaro colore.[8] Heard of Wm Robertson's death: with gleams of unexpected mercy.

Commee 11–4. House. Dinner at 38. House in evg 10½–12¼. Paired off agt Stafford.[9] read Phipps on Eccl. impositions.[10] wrote,[11] & wrote to Mr Herbert. Mr Ward. May I see the hand of God.

9. Th.

Draft of a long letter & some lines before breakft. Awoke early & with an elasticity the residue of my country visit. Commee & House 11–4¼.[12] rode. dined with the elder Gaskells. wrote to Mr Christy[13]—Mr Neilson.[14] read (R.C.) "abridgm[en]t of Ch[istia]n doctrine"[15]—conv. at nt with my Mother abt R.G.

---

[1] Corporation Bill, and misc. business: H xxix. 262.

[2] Eneas Macdonnell, 'The Roman catholic oath illustrated by Roman Catholic Authorities' (1835).

[3] *Baring was chairman of the sinecures cttee.

[4] Magnus, 24–25, places the Farquhars near Dorking.

[5] (Sir) John *Jeremie, 'Recent events at Mauritius' (1835).

[6] Vol. iii of Lady *Dacre, Tales of the peerage and the peasantry (1835); and see Add MS 44724, f. 132.

[7] 'I have taken great pleasure in this visit, particularly especially' here heavily deleted.

[8] 'I have really delighted in this visit, this morning most especially: but why? Neither ought I to, nor can I say how much the inclinations of the heart may show their origin, in colours clear and distinct'.

[9] There was a long debate on Irish Poor-Laws Bill, 2°, but no division: H xxix. 308.

[10] J. *Phipps, Brief remarks on . . . Ecclesiastical Impositions . . . (1769).

[11] On the idea of beauty; Add MS 44724, f. 126.

[12] Corporation Bill, H xxix. 365.

[13] Presumably Langham Christie.

[14] A. Neilson, Liverpool merchant, an uncle.

[15] Catholic pamphlet, often reprinted.

10. Friday.

Commee 11–4. copied my long letter to T.G. it is in great measure tentative both of him & myself.[1] wrote to Miss Benwell—G. M'Kenzie.[2] House 4–4¾.[3] rode. dined at 38. read R.C. Catm—paper—Quarty on Corpns Bill—& cont[inue]d Blanche.

11. Sat.

Breakf at 38. my dear Mother unwell: afn worse. Somerset House with H.J.G. & Miss T.[4]—disapp[oin]t[e]d. Exeter Hall 11¼–2¼.[5] Saw Dr Chalmers. Milbank 3–4¾. to Norwood to dinner—walk &c. afr: read 'Abstract of Douay Catechism',[6] & finished 'Blanche'.

12. Sunday.

Breakf & dinner at 38. St James's—(Mr Cavendish & Mr Ward) with H.J.G.—Bible—Arnold (& aloud)—Morale Catholica—Leibniz—& pursued my review of the Penitentiary R.C. books. They have some good points; & some forcible ideas. "spiritual murder"—e.g.

13. M.

Mr Reddie with me at 9.[7] Breakf at 38. Commee & House 11–4½.[8] Dined at Dr Phillimore's.[9] Rode: wrote to T.G.—to Lady F[arquhar]—to Mayor of N[ewar]k—at Sir F. Doyle's musical party—read Mr Mills's Serm on Liberty,[10] Dr L. on Mauritius,[11] & part of Reddie.

14. T.

Having H.J.G's approval sent my letter to Canning & got a most kind answer:[12] as yesterday from T.G. How many causes to be thankful. Breakf at 38. Left them at 10¾, abt to start. Commee & House 11–4½ and 9½–2. wrote to T.G. Lord Morpeth—D. of N.[13]—O.B. Cole—read Reynolds & Countess of Nithsdale.[14] voted in 134:186 on Gt Yarmouth Commee.[15] finished Reddie's pamphlet.

[1] See Magnus, 29–30, on *Gladstone's objections to Thomas's marriage.
[2] George Alexander Mackenzie, d. 1874, 2nd s. of Thomas, of Applecross; Liverpool merchant; or possibly his sis. Geddes Elizabeth, who later m. John Cay, Edinburgh advocate; or George, ca. 1810–44, s. of Colin, in East India Service.
[3] Misc. business: H xxix. 400.　　　　　　　　　　　　　[4] Helen's governess.
[5] Another meeting of protest against Roman doctrines propagated in Ireland.
[6] Douay, 1718?.
[7] John Reddie, chief justice of St. Lucia from 1836, helped *Jeremie write his pamphlet on Mauritius, where he had also served (see 7 July 35, n. 1).
[8] Misc. business and supply: H xxix. 449.
[9] Joseph *Phillimore, 1775–1855, civilian; father of R.J.*
[10] Benjamin Mills 'On Christian Liberty' (1741); text from Gal. v. 13, 'Use not Liberty for an Occasion to the Flesh'.　　　　　　　　[11] Untraced.
[12] Answer in Add MS 44117, ff. 149–50; subject unclear.
[13] Proposing inscription on plate for Tallents, Add MS 44261, f. 60.
[14] The first half of Lady *Dacre's Tales of the peerage, &c.
[15] Against inquiry into bribery: H xxix. 593, gives 132 to 186.

15. W.

Marie—finished Reynolds's (most able & useful) works. What a valuable book to take into galleries—Countess of Nithsdale. Commee $11\frac{1}{4}$–$1\frac{1}{2}$. wrote to T.G. R.G. Caparn. 3–$4\frac{3}{4}$ Went over the Penitentiary[1]—with the Farquhars & Ld Douro.[2] rode. dined at Ld Eastnor's. Canning there.

16. Th.

J.N.G. & three Larkinses to breakft. Mr Willis before it—The post brought the deeply interesting news of Tom's engagement.[3] Oh may the blessings of the Most High bind it and sanctify if. Long conv. with John on the proceedings at Shotesham—and with Tom on his arrival at 8 P.M. J.N.G. dined with me. rode—in the City. House 5–6 and 9–$1\frac{1}{2}$. Div. in 234:262, 203:234, 165:234, & another, on freemen.[4] read Marie: finished & wrote out 'Roedeer'[5]—arranged papers—&c. wrote to Wm G.

17. Fr.

Canning to breakf. Marie—finished Winifred[6]—paper. Sinecures Comm. & House 1–$5\frac{1}{2}$. House again $9\frac{1}{2}$–$1\frac{1}{4}$.[7] rode. wrote to Ld Strafford—Mr Finlay— Rn G—Mr Charriere—Mr Fellowes (& draught)[8]—Mr Higgins.[9] In the course of some refl. on an interesting subject, I had this day some salutary truths brought home: let me remember that one thing is needful.[10]—div. 10:8 on Mr Greville's case.[11]

18. Sat.

Marie. Began Crawford's Penitentiary Report.[12] Framed res[olution]s. with Lord Strafford for Col. Mil. Exp. Commee.[13] at Penitentiary—wrote to Mr G. paper. Dinner & evg at Richmond with the Egerton party. On the water.

19. Sunday.

The Lord's Supper at 8. (How gratifying was Tom's occasion last Sunday). about 40. Knox—Arnold aloud—finished Morale Catholica—& read Miss

---

[1] At Millbank; he was about to become a visitor.

[2] Arthur Richard Wellesley, 1807–84, styled Marquess Douro 1814, succ. as 2nd duke of Wellington 1852, 6th earl of Mornington 1863; M.P. Aldeburgh 1830–1, Norwich 1837–52; lieutenant-general.

[3] To Louisa, d. 1901, 2nd da. of Robert Fellowes, d. 1869, of Shotesham Park, near Norwich; see 27 Aug. 35.

[4] 50:163; all on report stage of corporations bill. H xxix. 669, 677, 677, 678.

[5] Verses, in Add MS 44724, f. 129.　　　　　　　　　　[6] Untraced.

[7] Report stage concluded: H xxix. 697.

[8] Draft in Add MS 44354, ff. 205–6; answer ibid. ff. 207–8.

[9] Perhaps Charles Longuet *Higgins, 1806–85, philanthropist.

[10] See Add MS 44724, f. 131, on 'error of youthful anticipation'.

[11] Resolution in PP 1835 xviii. 444.

[12] W. *Crawford, Report . . . on the Penitentiaries of the United States, in PP 1834 xlvi. 349.

[13] After *Strafford's elevation to the lords, Robert Gordon took over the cttee. chairmanship: cp. 11 Mar. 35 n.

Graham's 'Test of Truth' & 'Freeness & Sovereignty': extremely interested partic[ularl]y in the first.[1] St James's & Long Acre—walk with Farquhar.

20. M.

J.N.G. & Mr Ross to breakf. read Appx to Marie—called in King St: sat $\frac{3}{4}$ hour.[2] rode. House $5\frac{1}{4}$–$8\frac{1}{2}$. tea in B. Square, House $9\frac{3}{4}$–1. spoke a few words on Corpns & Stafford.[3] wrote to Hamilton—Cousin Jane[4]—Rn G—Charriere.

21. T.

wrote to W. Goalen—Mr Cruickshank—Mr G.—Mrs Falkner[5]—Farquhar & Chisholm to breakf.—Ipswich Commee (Report) $12\frac{1}{4}$–4. Voted agt first Res., partly agreeing. House 4–4.15, ballot. rode—House 5.40–8.5, and 10–12.45.[6] read Marie & began Miss Graham's Life.[7]

22. W.

Breakf. with T.G. paper. wrote to Mr G. & Mr Tallents. read Miss Graham, and pt of 'The Hampshire Cottage'[8]—got up facts &c. on the I[rish] C[hurch] question.—rode—House $7\frac{1}{4}$–$12\frac{3}{4}$.[9]—Accosted by a young man who alleged distress & wished to get his poems published. Took part of them to read.[10]

23. Th.

T.G. to breakfast. I.C. papers again. Miss Graham—finished—Marie. Best ill. rode. wrote to Mr G. Saw H. Thompson who accosted me yesterday and (having perused his poems) referred him to Taylor with a note. House 5.25–3.15. voted in 232:319.[11] In hopes of speaking by arrangement with Ld Stanley: but was shut out by the length of the other speakers. so I had two useful lessons instead of one. For the sense of helplessness which always possesses me in prospect of a speech is a very useful lesson: and being disappointed after having attained some due state of excitement & anticipation is another.[12]

[1] By Mary Jane Graham (1831 and 1833).
[2] The Farquhar's town house was at 18 King Street, St. James's.
[3] Against corporations bill, which was read 3°; and distinguishing cases of Liverpoo and Stafford elections. *H* xxix. 755, 783.
[4] Tyler.
[5] Probably Louisa, née Grant, d. 1862; m. 1830 William Falconer, 1799–1846, 2nd s. of 7th earl of Kintore, capt. R.N.
[6] Church of Ireland Bill, cttee. *H* xxix. 790.
[7] C. *Bridges, *Memoir of Miss M. J. Graham* (1823).
[8] Another of Lady *Dacre's *Tales of the peerage, &c.*
[9] Irish church, ctd.: *H* xxix. 885.
[10] Henry Thompson, b. 1816?, s. of tax surveyor at Oakham, Rutland; cp. Add MS 44355, ff. 74–96.
[11] Irish church, ctd.: *H* xxix. 1067 gives 282:319.
[12] Morley, i. 128–9.

24. Fr.

T.G. off again. rode. dined in B. Square. Col. Commee 12¾–3¾. finished
Hampshire Cottage: much merit: read Br. & For. Rev. on Engl. literature:
insufficient.[1] Saw the Dr about Best. saw Taylor about H. Thompson: he
agreed with me: and I wrote two letters of inquiry to Oakham about him.
Wrote to Anstice. Perusing old scraps of verse.

25.

T.G's birthday: & not the least int[eres]t[in]g of them. Best better. Milbank
Commee & dined at Mr Harrison's. Paper. wrote out some old verses. wrote
to Stephen & Mr G. read pt of Stephen's on Corpns[2] and Miss Graham.
wrote Pol. Mem.[3]

26. Sunday.

St James's: Mr Cavendish & Mr Gage. Tea in B. Square. Best better.
wrote on Predestn; likewise finished & wrote out a kind of hymn from an
old MS book—read Knox—Miss Graham—Leibniz's correspondence on
reunion of Churches (finished).

27. M.

J.N.G. to breakf. H. Thompson's brother[4] here: an agreeable young man:
very grateful—for nothing. Aboriginees Commee[5]—House[6]—dined with Sir
F. Doyle: read Miss Graham, Crawford on Penity (finished) Procdgs of
Statl Socy.[7] wrote to Stephen—Mr Rose—read letter by Tomkins.[8]

28. T.

letter to Tomkins. Miss Graham. paper. House for ballot. J.N.G. & Murray
G. to breakft. wrote to T.G.—Uncle R—Mrs G—dined at Mr Wainewright's:[9] in evg at Lady Bromley's. went to Bedlam with the Farquhars.
saw Hatfield—Martin, full of excellent religious language: a poor woman
with dolls dressed as her children: but our party was too large & smart for
us to do justice to the institution.[10] wrote some lines. rode.

29. W.

read paper—Br. & For. Rev. on "Russia", & "Quadruple Treaty"—very

---

[1] British and Foreign Review, i. 190 (July 1835).
[2] A. J. Stephens, Treatise on the [Municipal] Corporation Act (1835).
[3] On dissolution of 1834; Add MS 44819, f. 20.
[4] Thompson had eight siblings.
[5] PP 1835 xxxix. 301 or 531; on South African natives.
[6] Colonial timber duties: H xxix. 1101.
[7] Statistical Society of London, Proceedings (1835).
[8] Jacob Tomkins [i.e. *Brougham], Epistle to Isaac Tomkins from his dutiful nephew Jacob, on the Free Grammar Schools of England (1835).
[9] Probably Reader Wainewright of Lincoln's Inn.
[10] Bethlehem hospital, founded 1274, the famous madhouse; then in Moorfields. James Hadfield missed *George III at Drury Lane, 1800; Francis Mardin, b. 1786?, in holy orders, entered Bedlam 1819.

able & important:[1] Holford's Preface:[2] Nat. Society's Report[3]—Miss Graham. Dined at Ld Mahon's: music. House—*told* for Clipperton's release:[4] wrote to T.G.[5] & Corden—calls—rode—wrote lines on a scene yesterday at Bedlam.[6] My thoughts are subject to a strong centrifugal force, but practice is I fear more likely to bewilder them than speculation, in which latter I seem to see my way.

30. Thursday.

Holford. Miss Graham. paper. in B. Square trying "Il Rival".[7] rode to Roehampton with Farquhar—evg there—music: at the House—paired. read La Martine Vol.1. in parts, specy the very singular account of his visit to Lady Esther Stanhope.[8] wrote to Acland & A. Williams.

31. Fr.

Lady Dacre's sonnets[9]—and Gonsalvo di Cordova.[10] At 11½, after a morning's conv. rode to see the Hallams at E. Moulsey:[11] returned at 6—found a party which broke up after 9—the Hallams kind and interesting as ever. The younger son is very promising: alas, now the only one.[12]—More conv. at night.

Sat. Aug. 1.

Read a little "Joseph" a French prose epic: it seemed very French.[13] Left Roehampton at 10½ after a conv. more than gossip & less than anything else.—Wrote to Mr G[14]—T.G.—S. Robinson[15]—D. of N.—Mr Baring (on Sinecures Report)—T. Nimmo[16]—read Holford—Miss Graham—Orange Report—paper—dined at Sir E. Kerrison's—music.

Sunday 2.

St James's bis. At the Sacrament: a humbling joy. Read Miss Graham—

---

[1] *British and Foreign Review*, i. 102 (July 1835).
[2] To G. Holford, 'Short Vindication of . . . Millbank', 3 parts (1825).
[3] National Society for Promoting the Education of the Poor in the Principles of the Established Church; founded 1811; afterwards National Society: Central Council of the Church for Religious Education.
[4] John Clipperton, Ipswich attorney, held in Newgate; release after reprimand by speaker next day ordered, 56–34. *H* xxix. 1195.
[5] Cp. Magnus, 23.   [6] In Add MS 44724, f. 136.
[7] Song from Bellini's *I Puritani di Scozia* (1835).
[8] Lamartine, *Souvenirs, Impressions, Pensées et Paysages pendant un Voyage en Orient*, 4v. (1835); especially i. 242–74.
[9] Lady Barbarina *Dacre, *Dramas, Translations and Occasional Poems*, 2v. (1829).
[10] Ibid., v. i; a play.
[11] East Molesey, on the Thames, 16 miles WSW. of Westminster.
[12] Henry Fitzmaurice *Hallam, 1824–50; Newcastle medallist, 1841; an 'Apostle'. See Morley, i. 230.
[13] A. Duval's opera (1807)??
[14] On marriage, in the abstract. See Magnus, 23.
[15] Unidentified; possibly a friend of C. R. Blundell.
[16] Thomas Nimmo, Glasgow pipe manufacturer, another uncle.
13—II.

Bible—Leibniz—Arnold (& aloud)—he requires modif. Social Duties—wrote—tea in B. Square.

3. M.

T.G. ret[urne]d: tea with the party: Miss F[ellowes] blooming as the earliest rose: may *the* blessing be with them.—finished Miss Graham: Oh for her spirit. 11¾–3; Sir R. Peel's—Edn, Sinecures, & Aborigines Commees. wrote to Mr G., H.J.G., Mr Johnson,[1] Wm G: 3–4½—singing lesson (Negri).[2] House 5½–6½, & again.[3] read Report of Ir. Ed. Commrs,[4] and Manning's capital Sermon.[5]

4. T.

debates—Holford—*spelling* my music—saw the F[ellowes]s—conv. with T.G. on divers matters, & important: dined in B. Square—wrote to Mr Tallents—Dry—Manning—Rn G—saw Canning—House 5½–6 and 10.20–1.[6]

5. W.

met the ladies to breakf. at T.G.s dinner & evg with them. rode. Wrote to Cole[7]—Tallents—Mrs G—J.N.G.—Signor Negri (2) and practice at home. read papers—Holford: wrote *Moi* & Pol. Mem. & Rel. points.[8]

6. Th.

T.G. and the ladies breakfd with me. Also [cousin] Divie. exam[ine]d him afterwards. saw Mr Reddie. Holford—paper—part of Hogg's protest[9]—spelling songs—House at 5[10]—rode to Roehampton. a very agr[eeable] evening—read Wetherell's Sp. on Corporation Bill.[11] Up late in my room.

7. Fr.

read Knight's Speech on Corpn Bill[12]—after breakft a long & *delectable* music lesson: rode to town. read Holford—Hogg—wrote to Mr G—Mr Simpson—Ld Abn—House 5¼–9¼. voted in 89:47 on Gen Darling.[13] wrote to Mr Jones—Mr Whyte. (Deus.)—tea at the Burlington.

[1] Possibly Charles Johnson, 1791–1880, professor of botany at Guy's 1830–73.
[2] Benedetto Negri, 1784–1854, taught pianoforte and singing, mainly at Milan.
[3] Slavery abolition; Irish church. *H* xxx. 13, 25.   [4] Probably *PP* 1834 xl. 65.
[5] H. *Manning, 'The English Church, its Succession and Witness for Christ' (1835).
[6] Command in Honduras; Orange lodges. *H* xxx. 49, 58.
[7] Cp. Magnus, 26.   [8] Add MS 44821C, ff. 29–32.
[9] T. J. *Hogg, one of the Municipal Corporations Commissioners, protested against their report: *PP* xl. 481.
[10] He cut a discussion on Yarmouth election: *H* xxx. 111.
[11] Sir Charles *Wetherall, at bar of Lords; see *Times* for 31 July and 1 August.
[12] Henry Gally *Knight, at bar of Lords; see *Times* for 3 August.
[13] (Sir) Ralph *Darling, 1775–1858, soldier; at Corunna and Walcheren; governed New South Wales 1825–1831, incurring much unpopularity; kt. 1835, but not re-employed. Diarist sat on cttee. which exonerated him (*PP* 1835 vi. 371). Vote forbade cttee. to review a relevant court-martial's proceedings: *H* xxx. 146.

8. Saty.

Saw the marriage party off at 9¾—Singing lesson (3d). Penitentiary—divers calls & business—wrote to, Mrs Chisholm—Uncle D. about Thompson—Mr G. Mrs G—Hay. dined with Brandreth[1] at the Guards: liked him. finished Holford—& read the Mauritius defence in MS.[2] wrote to Mr Irving[3] on the subject.

9. Sunday.

St James's—& St Martin's (Mr Duckinfield).[4] Walk. Acland came to me in evg. Read Bible—Arnold Sermm. & Appendices: not without pain. Serm. aloud. Knox. Wrote some vss.[5]

10. M.

Gaskell & Brandreth to breakf.—read Jeremie & finished Hogg. wrote to T.G.—Mr Rawson—Mr Cook—Mr Holford. paper. calls. saw Mr Richardson on Maur[itiu]s—dined with Sir H. Verney: sang: Commee & House 3–4¾ and 9¼–12½.[6]

11. T.

Adam's Case (Mauritius) & Consultn of Counsel.[7] Negri (4th) 11 to near 1. rode. House 8¼–2¼. voted in 43:123 on the last Orange Res.[8] wrote to Mr G—Mrs G—T.G.—J.N.G.—Mr Macewan[9]—Sir S. Scott—Mr Tennent[10]—Dr Gifford[11]—wrote some vss[12]—& a report for the Mirror.

12.

St James's to hear band. Darling's Commee at 12–1. rode. read Jeremie—Notes—Bp Wilson's First charge.[13] Wrote to Taylor—T.G.—House 5½–10½: anxious to speak on I.C. Bill, but the House was so perfectly dead that I did not.[14]—Singing. amazing[?].

---

[1] Frederick Brandreth, lieut. and capt., Scots Fusilier Guards, June 1835.

[2] Cp. 11 Aug. 35.

[3] John Irving, 1767?–1845, London merchant prince; cons. M.P. Bramber 1806–32, co. Antrim 1837–45; agent for Mauritius.

[4] (Sir) Henry Robert Dukinfield, 1791–1858, canon of Salisbury 1833, rector of St. Martin's-in-the-fields 1834–48; succ. as 7th bart. 1836.

[5] On St. James's; in Add MS 44724, f. 46.

[6] Stamp act; supply. *H* xxx. 202, 219.

[7] Mauritian slave owners were in course of securing compensation.

[8] Against specific reference to *Cumberland's part in setting up Orange lodges in army. *H* xxx. 310.

[9] Possibly James MacEwan, w.s., of Edinburgh.

[10] (Sir) James Emerson *Tennent, 1804–69; né Emerson, took wife's surname on marriage 1831; cons. M.P. Belfast 1832–7, 1838–41, 1842–5, Lisburn 1852; kt. 1845; cr. bart. 1867; secretary to India board, 1841–3, to govt. of Ceylon, 1845–50; author.

[11] Stanley L. Gifford, doctor in Clerkenwell.

[12] In Add MS 44724.

[13] On visiting Calcutta (1835).

[14] Bill read 3°; *H* xxx. 403.

13. Th.

Singing lesson (5) and practice at home. read Bp Wilson's 2d charge (exc[ellen]t)[1]—Jeremie—paper—Mrs Norton's 2d vol.[2]—rode—called on Sir T. Farquhar. House 5–6.[3] wrote to Mr G—Mr Cleghorn[?][4]—Raby.

14. Fr.

Taylor & J.M.G. to breakf. Thompson, Gen. Darling, & Ld Carrington[5] with me. paper. wrote to Burge—Mr G—J.N.G.—T.G.—Aborig. Commee. called at Roehampton—dined at Mr Harrison's—singing—read Jeremie, & Scotch Report on Schools 1835.[6] vss.[7]

15. Sat.

Finished Jeremie. Singing lesson (6th). Got a gig and left at $3\frac{1}{2}$ to drive 30 miles to Ld Carrington's, Wycombe Abbey.[8] Arrived $7\frac{1}{2}$. found Ld & Ly J. Eliot[9]—Ld & Lady Mahon[10]—Bp of Exeter—all very pleasant: & a sweet place in its kind. Singing.

16. Sunday.

Church mg only: 2nd service being in evg. Some Church prayers are read at 10. Walking & conv. with the bp. Ld M. & Ld E.; some good, but these Sundays out I do not like upon the whole. read Knox & wrote.

17. M.

$6\frac{3}{4}$–$11\frac{1}{4}$. to town—drove the Bp to Hillingdon[11]—& breakfasted there— Gen. Darling's Commee $12\frac{1}{4}$–$2\frac{1}{4}$. much incensed. Singing lesson. T.G. came. rode. began 'England & Russia'.[12] Wrote to Mr Rawson—Mr Cooke— Aunt J—singing.

18. T.

paper. arranging letters. wrote to Sir H. Hardinge[13]—Caparn—Rn G—

[1] Also on visiting Calcutta (1835).

[2] Caroline *Norton, Woman's Reward, a novel, 3v. (1835).

[3] Printed papers: H xxx. 466.

[4] Patrick Cleghorn, b. 1785?, at Lincoln's Inn; or Peter Cleghorn, d. 1863, lawyer at Madras.

[5] Robert *Smith, 1752–1838, banker; tory M.P. Nottingham 1779 till cr. Baron Carrington 1796; friend of *Pitt and *Cowper.

[6] Perhaps PP 1835 xl. 679.   [7] In Add MS 44724, f. 139.

[8] At High Wycombe, Buckinghamshire; WNW. of London; a girls' school since 1897.

[9] Edward Granville *Eliot, 1798–1877, diplomat, styled Lord Eliot 1823, envoy in Spain 1834–7, Irish secretary 1841–5, 3rd earl of St. Germans 1845, Irish viceroy 1852–5; and his w. Lady Jemima, née Cornwallis, 1803–56.

[10] *Mahon m. 1834 Emily Harriet, 1815–73, 2nd da. of Sir E. *Kerrison.

[11] Near Uxbridge.

[12] David *Urquhart, 'England, France, Russia, and Turkey' (1834), sensational anti-Palmerstonian pamphlet.

[13] Sir Henry *Hardinge, 1785–1856, soldier; fought in peninsula 1808–14 and at Ligny; M.P. Durham 1820–30, Newport (Cornwall) 1830–2, Launceston 1832–44; secretary at war 1828–30, 1841–4, for Ireland 1830, 1834–5; as viceroy of India 1844–8, served as 2nd-in-command in Sikh war 1845–6; commander-in-chief 1852–6; cr. Viscount Hardinge 1844, field-marshal 1855. Sat on *Darling cttee. 1835.

J.N.G.—Mr G. Discussions on Gen. Darling 12–3. saw Sir G. Grey. rode. paper. read Madden's W.I.[1] & 'Woman as she is & should be'—app-[arentl]y strange:[2] a gladdening note from Lady F. wrote vss.[3]—T.G. with me in evg. House. Singing.

19. W.

Sir W. Riddell, M. Wilson,[4] & T.G. to breakf. some business—rode with Hook—Commee $11\frac{3}{4}$–$2\frac{3}{4}$—T.G. & Gaskell to dinner—conv. with T.G.— wrote to Mr Simpson—Raby—Rn G—Mr Tennent. read Engl. & Russia. & Quarty on Macintosh's Life.

20. Th.

paper. two of Gen. Darling's pamphlets[5]—wrote notes on his case— Commee 12–$3\frac{1}{4}$: rode to Rochampton to tea, & music: back with R. Hook & to the House. wrote to Mr G., Rn G., Lady Scott, Dry.

21. Fr.

paper T.G. to breakf.—business—Darling Comm. 12–$2\frac{1}{2}$—read "England & Russia"—& Darling's 3d pamphlet[6]—wrote to Mrs G—Mr G—Mrs Chisholm—Mr Stirling—House 5–$8\frac{3}{4}$. Committed myself foolishly by a careless charge agt Rice.[7]

22. Sat.

paper. Paying bills & getting presents. Calls—Gen. Darling $12\frac{1}{2}$–$3\frac{1}{4}$. Peniten-tiary $3\frac{1}{2}$–$4\frac{3}{4}$. Much rumination at home in evg. wrote a paper on my posi-tion: and driven to prayer. Finished Engl. & Russia—wrote to Mr G— Caparn—T.G.—Lincoln—Dry—R.G.—M'Lauchlan.[8]

23. Sunday.

St James's, & St Luke's Chelsea on my way to Roehampton with R. Hook. From him I got useful religious statistics. Bible—Knox—& 3 Newman's Sermm[9]—very able. A large family party. made very scanty use of my opportunity: learned my blindness & stupidity by afterthought. ruminated long at night by my open window.

---

[1] R. R. *Madden, *A Twelvemonth's Residence in the West Indies during the transition from slavery to apprenticeship*, 2v. (1835).

[2] An anonymous novel, 2v. (1835).   [3] Add MS 44724, f. 149.

[4] (Sir) Mathew Wilson, 1802–91, s. of London solicitor; lib. M.P. Clitheroe 1841–2, 1847–53, Yorkshire 1874–85, Skipton 1885–6; cr. bart. 1874.

[5] (Sir) R. *Darling, 'A Few Plain Facts', and 'The Case of Lieut.-General Ralph *Darling' (1835), about a libel on him by Captain Robert Robison.

[6] Sir R. *Darling, 'Remarks on the Libel . . . by Mr R. Robison against Lieut-General R. *Darling' (1835).

[7] Supply: diarist joined in dispute between *Spring-Rice and *O'Connell about timing of appropriation clause, and was roughly handled. *H* xxx. 824.

[8] Perhaps Lachlan McLachlan, attorney, near Portland Place.

[9] In John Henry *Newman, *Parochial Sermons*, 6v. (1834–42).

24. M.

Mi destai ruminando mi medesimi pensieri. Non son andato che un pochino in avanti. Quella che mi piaceva mi piace: quella che mi mosse mi muove: sicuramente credo che il suo cuor sia a Dio: la mente bella siccome il volto. Ma mi bisognerebbe una gran forza del divino amore per sollevarmi sempre sempre dal pasto mondano alle cose celesti ed alla ricordazione del Redentore—Ebbene, l'aspetto: ma, che son io per nutrir una cotanta speme? Dopo aver fatto la colazione differi la partita fino al mezzogiorno. Spesa aggradevole di due ore nell udir ed imparar il canto. A Londra a piede.[1] Gen Darlings C. 2½–5. Wrote to Mr G—T.G.—Gaskell—Taylor—read Burke—& Bulwer's Student.[2] House 4–5¼.[3] dined at Lady Hope's[4]—sang.

25. Tuesday.

10.20. went to Sir M.F's marriage[5]—found it over: a merited disappt.—the most agreeable neighbourhood at the breakfast. calls—Darling's Committee 1½–4½. Walter Hamilton dined with me. Broke my secret to him. He most kindly gave up returning to Oxford by the Mail & remained with me in evg. His advice valuable: and his prayers will bless it. wrote in consequence a draft, & letter, to Sir T. F[arquhar].[6] I hope earnestly & believe that the hand of God points the way, especially since seeing this excellent friend.

26. W.

5¾ out. from Aldgate to Shotesham 7–7¼ P.M. late for dinner. found all ready for 27th—singing. Long convv. with T.G. and J.N.G. esp. on self, and Rn. Late up.

Thursday 27.

Marriage about 10½. All parties borne up admirably. Two hours after they went off: and may their union be holy in the sight of God, and their love be centered in him. Out with John & convv. read a letter from Hamilton on the way to church. It was all I could hope under my circumstances. Dinner at 6½. Off by Mail abt 7¾. outside—all night: no want of subjects for thought. Wrote to Hamilton—Aunt D[ivie]—Robn.

[1] 'Awoke ruminating the same thoughts. Have only advanced a very little. She who delighted me delights me: she who moved me, moves me: I surely believe that her heart is with God: her mind is as fair as her face. But I would need a great strength of divine love to raise myself always, always above worldly dross, towards heavenly things and the recollection of the Redeemer. Well, I hope for it; but, who am I to cherish so great a hope? After breakfast I put off leaving till the afternoon. At pleasing cost of two hours hearing and learning songs. Walked to London.'
[2] E. *Bulwer Lytton, The Student, satirical tales, 2v. (1835).
[3] Misc. business: H xxx. 936.
[4] Georgina Alicia, née Brown, m. 1805 (Sir) Alexander *Hope.
[5] Sir Walter Minto Townsend-Farquhar, 1809–1866; m. Erica, daughter of 7th Lord Reay; cons. M.P. for Hertford 1857–66.
[6] Part quoted in Magnus, 24–25.

28.

At the Albany soon afr 7. a letter from H[ele]n. Went to bed: slept (proh pudor) to 1 P.M. found an excellent letter svegliandomi dalla madre, la quale senza aggradir troppo al mio orgoglio spiega in un senso oltimo e la madre e la figliuola. Oh che debbo della grazie Addio qualunque sia l'esito della mia preghiera. Tutto mi incarisce l'oggetto che ho in mira.[1] Saw Sir G. Grey. Wrote to Lady F—Mr Dundas[2]—J.M.G. (twice)—Mrs G—R.G.— T.G.—Lady Kerrison—Raby—Claughton—Gaskell—Lincoln—House 3¼– 8.[3]—Vss in evg[4]—& Newman's Sermm.

29. Sat.

Milnes to breakf. Commee 11½–1¼. wrote to Mr G—Brooks—Raby— Hamilton—Farquhar—Uncle D—Cole. To Roeh[ampto]n at 2½ with Sir T.F. The ladies at home. Ella si mosse un pochino per un solo istante ve- dendo l'audace che avea i suoi pensieri fissi in lei. Con ambedui le donne passegiai buon pezzo: sempre sempre piu contento del contegno dell alma della beltà. Ma come andan in avanti? Questo non so io. Forse la strada s'aprira. C'è bonta c'è sapienza di Dio le quali guideranno le cose.[5] Family party, singing. began Croly[6]— read Dundas's papers.

30.

Putney,[7] uffizio della matina, anche dopo mezzo giorno. Passeggiata con compagni di jeri. Ma codardo di cuore e lasso del intelletto per oggi special- mente non soddisfaceva alla mia coscienza. Ella sempre sta volentieri per le cose di relligione. Venne a pranzo il zio. Th. Hook.[8] O che (siccome io credo) la bell' anima della donzella si farebbe contenta di consagrare tutta la vita una domenica.[9] Good serm. Bible. Knox. Newman.

---

[1] 'On awaking from the mother, which without being too flattering to my pride dis- plays mother and daughter alike in the best possible light. O how much I owe to the grace of God, whatever the result of my prayer may be. Everything makes dearer to me the aim I have in view.' Letter quoted in part in Magnus, 25.
[2] Thomas Dundas, 1795–1873, M.P. Richmond (Yorkshire) 1818–30, 1835–9, York 1830–2, 1833–5; succ. as 2nd earl of Zetland 1838; eminent freemason.
[3] Misc. business: *H* xxx. 1085.
[4] Add MS 44724, f. 141, on road to Genoa.
[5] 'For a single instant, she was a trifle moved, viewing my temerity in fixing my thoughts on her. Walked a good way with both ladies: more and more happy at the bearing of the fair one's soul. But how will it be in the future? That I do not know. Perhaps a road will open up. It is the goodness, the wisdom of God that will guide affairs.'
[6] D. O. Croly, 'An Essay Religious and Political on Ecclesiastical Finance, as Regards the Roman Catholic Church in Ireland' (1834).
[7] On the Thames a mile NE. of Roehampton.
[8] Theodore Edward *Hook, 1788–1841, comic novelist and defalcator; his brother James*, 1772?–1828, dean of Worcester 1825, m. 1796 Anne Farquhar, d. 1844, da. of the 1st bart.*
[9] 'Morning service, also afternoon. Walk with yesterday's companions. But, cowardly and slow-witted, I did not satisfy my conscience, today particularly. She delights always in things of religion. The uncle, Th[eodore] Hook, came to dinner. O that (as I believe) the maiden's fair soul may be happy to hallow all her life as a Sunday.'

31.

Dopo la colazione, tre ore di discorso colla madre. Parlammo liberamente di relligione; anche del stato presenta dei miei affari, e della maniera di proseguirli. Adesso abbiam capito l'un l'altro interamente come spero: e che io stia contento O Dio.[1] Walk & coach to town—business there—wrote to Mr Tallents—T.G.—J.N.G.—R.G.—Mr G—Ld Morpeth—With Mr Dundas at Comp[ensatio]n Office. House 4–7.40 and 10–12¼.[2] Trench's poems (delightful)[3]—Croly.

Tuesday Sept. 1.

Croly—Trench. Commee & H of C. 12¼–3½. rep[orte]d on Gen. Darling. House 5½–11¾. business. voted in 271:37 and 69:164.[4] wrote to Mrs G., J.N.G., H.J.G., T.G., Dr Gifford. much thought.

2. Wed.

House 5½–11½. div. in 155:67.[5] read Trench—Doyle to breakft—some classical retrospects with him—wrote vss[6]—accts—wrote to Raby—H.J.G. —Rn G—M'Lachlan—H.H. Joy—W.W. Farr. Heard from Farquhar. much thought.

3. Th.

Learned by post the deaths of Aunt Mary and Uncle Robert: the latter had an awful suddenness. A reverent hope remains to us. I believe he well knew the truths of redemption. Another letter from W.R.F. wrote a long one to Lady F. spiegandomi in matiera di credenza e di relligione, non senza preghiera, ma come debole! Ne so io, quai sentimenti muoverà, ne in qual misura mi esponga con chiarezza: ma questo l'ho voluto: è rimasto nelle mani di Dio. Domattina la risposta: che sia di Lui ispirata.[7] Gave up my engagement to Rn for today. Verses[8]—prepns to depart—Trench—and finished Burke on S. and B.[9] House 5–7½.[10] wrote to Mr G. and Mrs G. (stating my case)—Morley[11]—Caparn—Farquhar—Uncle D.

---

[1] 'After breakfast, three hours' talk with the mother. We spoke freely of religion; also of the present state of my affairs, and how they will develop. Now, as I trust, we entirely understand each other; and O God, may I be happy.'
[2] Lords' amdts. to corporations bill: *H* xxx. 1132.
[3] R. *Chenevix Trench, *The Story of Justin Martyr and Other Poems* (1835).
[4] Lords' amdts. to corporation bill; voting against widening local franchise, and for crown's unfettered right to name magistrates. *H* xxx. 1208, 1225.
[5] Same; voting in 155–56 for continuing property qualification of councillors in office. *H* xxx. 1279.
[6] Add MS 44724, ff. 47 and 151.
[7] 'Unfolding my views on matters of belief and religion; not without prayer, but how weak! I know neither by what feelings I will move her, nor to what extent I express myself clearly: but this I wanted: it remains in God's hands. Tomorrow morning the reply: may He inspire it.'
[8] Add MS 44724, f. 142.
[9] Jotting ibid. f. 143.
[10] Misc. business: *H* xxx. 1318.
[11] Perhaps Daniel Morley, Newark grocer.

4. Fr.

ricevetti alle dieci la risposta di Lady F. alla lettera di jeri : che finisce tutto. Anche scrissi un altra, sommettendomi. ma, malgrado mio. Fissi la partita per la sera, non trovando nulla di piu da quella parte : il giorno sunto nella preparativa : uscito prima delle nove, dritto al pachetto, che incominciava il viaggio da Londra a Aberdeen alle 11¼.—un piecol sonnetto[1]—scrissi a Mrs G.,[2] T.G., R.G., J.N.G., W.K.H., W.R.F., Mrs Tyler, Mr Butler.[3] Finished Knox Vol 1.

5. Sat.

The "City of Abn" made good way. Less squeamish than usual. Wrote to W.R.F. & a few vss.[4]

6. Sunday

Service on board. Chaplain gave thanks "that thou hast not visited us with any signal token of thy displeasure". Like yesterday a day of silence & thought. My Friday night on board was one of painful associations : dovevo dormire dalla famiglia F.—E poi quando giacevo mi credeban ammalato : ma lo fui solamente nella gravezza del cuore.[5]

7. M.

After arrival at midnight rem[aine]d asleep to 4½. Left Ab[erdee]n by Defiance at 6. Walked over from Laurencekirk : just in time for Uncle R.s funeral : his sons[6] sincerely affected. Found my dear Mother ill. Vss. on the contrast with the 27th.[7]—made up accts —unpacking.

8. T.

Up to see my cousins off. Wrote & wrote out Vss.[8] wrote to W.R.F. these things curiously mixed with Mr G's inquiries into W.I. comp[ensatio]n. Conv. with him on my own matters. singing in evg. My dear Mother still very unwell. Commenced reading the morning prayers.

---

[1] Add MS 44724, f. 144.

[2] 'Received at ten o'clock Lady F.'s reply to yesterday's letter : which puts an end to it all. Also wrote another, submitting. But, against my will. Fixed departure for the evening, finding no more from that quarter [Roehampton] : the day taken up in packing : left before nine, straight to the packet-boat, which began the voyage from London to Aberdeen at 11¼—a scrap of a sonnet—wrote to', &c. Magnus, 26–27, quotes parts of the letters from Lady Farquhar and to Mrs Gladstone : and has the diarist leave on the 7th.

[3] Pierce Butler, 1774–1846, 4th s. of 11th Viscount Mountgarret and b. of the mad earl of Kilkenny ; reforming M.P. for that co. from 1832.

[4] Add MS 44724, f. 144.

[5] 'I was to have slept at the F[arquhar]s'.—And then, when I lay down I thought I was ill ; but I was only sick at heart.'

[6] Thomas Steuart, William, Robert, Adam Steuart, Murray, and Montgomerie, 1817–80, Manchester merchants. And see 7 Nov. 35.

[7] 27 August 1835, the day of Thomas Gladstone's marriage ; in Add MS 44724, ff. 49–50.

[8] Add MS 44724, ff. 153, 155.

9. W.

Called at F[ettercair]n house &c. wrote to Stephen & T.G.—Mrs G. a little better. wrote vss. and began "Quindici giorni in Londra".[1] paper. singing.

10. Th.

Letters from W.R.F. & W.K.H.: very pleasing. wrote to W.K.G. and H.H. Joy. read paper—Spanish Grammar—Quindici giorni—singing—billiards with J.N.G.—my Mother but little better. Vss.—By dates, a fortnight since T.G's marriage: by my impressions, four times as long.

11. Fr.

Mrs G. much the same. T.G. & Louisa arrived. six hours on the hill: "can't afford it". finished "Quindici giorni". singing.

12. Sat.

My Mother worse in aft. wrote Vss[2]—& in Bl. Book.[3] Bible to her—began Ayesha[4] & Tocqueville's Democratie en Amerique.[5] Conv. with my mother.

13. Sunday.

To Ch. & Sact at Laurencekirk. prayers & Blunt to servv. in aftn. began Knox Vol 2, and Chillingworth.[6] my mother slightly better.

14. M.

Tocqueville. Ayesha. Finished Trench. Vss & arrangement of do. gun. Slight improvement in my Mother. Wrote to Storr—Mr Campbell—Parr—R.G.—Mrs Wallace—Murray.

15. T.

Tocqueville. Ayesha. Blackstone (resumed). Vss. Wrote to W.R.F. & Walter Goalen. rode. Mrs G. the same. Hallam's death: mistook it to be 19th.[7]

16. W.

Verses.[8] no change in my Mother. Tocqueville. Ayesha. rode to Johnstone.

---

[1] Untraced; probably autobiographical reflexions on 22 Aug.–4 Sept. 35.
[2] Add MS 44724, f. 154.
[3] On equality: Add MS 44821C, ff. 24–27.
[4] J. J. *Morier, *Ayesha, The Maid of Kars*, a novel, 3v. (1834).
[5] Tr. Henry *Reeve, 2v. (1835); notes in Add MS 44724, ff. 181–6, and on 3 Nov. 35.
[6] W. *Chillingworth, *The Religion of Protestants a Safe Way of Salvation* (1637).
[7] This sentence interlineated.
[8] 'To Violets in a Vaudois Valley', Add MS 44725, ff. 51–2; cp. 7 Mar. 32.

A long business for Mr G. calculating the comp[ensatio]n on all his Jamaica Estates. (comp £25 : val[ue] £53[,000].)[1]

17. Th.

Guthrie's[2] opinion more fav[ourable]—verses—rode to Stracathro—Tocqueville—Ayesha—Spanish Grammar. Saw my mother : a startling weakness in her.

18. Fr.

Dr Hunter came early and revealed a new cause of anxiety (com[parativel]y) in the exhaustion. After dinner we were much alarmed : tho' the erysipelas was subsiding. She was better from nine to twelve. At half past two worse : pulse weak & at 102. Dr H. then gave wine. It pleased God to bless its effects ; and at six in the morning (19) Helen wakened me to say our dear Mother was quiet with less fever & more strength. God be praised. This was indeed an evening for prayer to him. Even now how different is anxiety for her to what it would be for a soul far from God.—The Bp's prayer for the sick read.

In the day—read Tocqueville. Paul to his kinsfolk[3]—finished and wrote out my Epistle—wrote to Cole and to Mr Gibbon.[4] out shooting with J.N.G. in aftn.

19. Sat.

My dear Mother improved in the morning. At midday Dr Guthrie came : she was found worse & Dr Hunter agreed to stay all night, conceiving the danger increased. Last night he had said unless a fav[ourable] change took place by 12 today, there wd be little hope. In the morning we thought it had. All the aftn we were much depressed. After dinner the pulse abated & we went to rest less desponding.

read Tocqueville—'Paul's Letters'—wrote to Stephen and [blank]— and in the morning some hints upon my packet of Vss marked private.[5]

20. Sunday.

Awakened by Dr Hunter at 5 with the acct. of an unfav. change. pulse 130 —a hot flush : bowels much distended. We gathered at her bedside : and excited her by the unusual sight. My Father only absent then. She had no idea of *immediate* dissolution. At 8½ Dr H. said the declension had become

---

[1] In fact, according to the accounts of slave compensation claims (*PP* 1838 xlviii. 331), John *Gladstone appears only to have received about £14,000 for 806 former slaves in Jamaica, some of them owned jointly with Divie Robertson ; though three of his nephews were awarded a further £9,225 for 468 slaves, and he also received £58,000 for 1,094 in British Guiana (ibid. 345, 392, 632 ; 357 ; 454–5, 652).

[2] Thomas Guthrie, surgeon, of Bervie.

[3] Sir Walter *Scott, *Paul's Letters to His Kinsfolk* (1816).

[4] Perhaps David Gibbon of the Middle Temple.

[5] Notes on the diarist's verses, written in August and September 1835, to and about Caroline Farquhar ; Add MS 44724, f. 146.

much more rapid: he thought at 9½ when Dr Guthrie came that 3 or 4 hours wd terminate all. But wine was given, & spirits of turpentine with blessed effect: pulse came down to 110, and after Dr H's departure at 1¾ she continued rather to gain ground—At night and during it the pulse was 104–8. the turpentine given between 3 & 4 P.M. gave much relief. In the forenoon & up to post we wrote letters, all but hopeless. I wrote to Aunt J— Miss Benwell—Mrs Tyler—Miss Joy—Robn—Mrs Falconer[1]—Mrs Chisholm.[2]

Today outward exertion was very difficult—I read the mg & evg prayers & an aftn service; only.

21. M.

Sat by the beloved invalid except when sent out 2¼–5¼ A.M. The pulse wonderfully sustained—& no increase of debility. Dr Guthrie seemed equal to his arduous duties—and we have reason to magnify the mercy of God for the respite which has been afforded. He who has long said to her "thy sins be forgiven thee"—can also say "Arise take up thy bed and walk".[3]

Today we dispatched letters in a degree more hopeful to the same parties as yesterday. And I read Paul's letters, and Macintosh's life.[4]

The events of the illness I have detailed in a separate paper.[5]

22. Tuesday.

This was the day of pain: suspense was not removed though hope was extinguished. We again wrote our accounts—I added to my list Sir S. Scott and W. Goalen. Much impressed with Helen's nerve and fortitude. With perfect selfpossession as well as the deepest interest she watched the advances of Death upon the frame of her parent. A scene of emotion in the morning on my Father's reading prayers from my being alseep: as I had been in my Mother's room from eleven to five. We gathered finally in the evening to see her die.

23.

at a quarter past midnight her soul went to blessedness, her body to sleep. John & I waited for poor Robn who arrived at 4¼. We met for breakfast at ten. Much occupation afterwards in writing: I had near 20 letters and notes. My father wonderfully sustained. In turns we went into the Chamber of Death, and kissed the claycold face. In the evg & night wrote my recollections of her last days.[6] Bible. Long and interesting conv. with my Father.

[1] A connexion, m. of George Falconer Mackenzie.
[2] Perhaps Mrs. Roderick Chisholm, a distant connexion, whose s. James Sunderland succ. Duncan Macdonnell as The Chisholm in 1859 and d. 1885.
[3] Mark ii. 9.
[4] R. J. Mackintosh, *Memoirs of the Life of Sir James *Mackintosh*, 2v. (1835).
[5] See 23 Sept. 35.
[6] Add MS 44724, ff. 164–75.

24. Th.

Looked over my paper. Aunt J. arrived at 8½. Much occupied with her & with my Father about her. In the evening, God was pleased to open a way to peace. She suffered much, but by a pain orig[inall]y selfcaused. Another long list of communications: of which I had to write nearly as [many as] yesterday. Arrangements about mourning. At night, read a little of Macintosh.

25. Friday.

Wrote to Lewis[1]—Sir G. Grey—Mrs Wallace—and W.R.F. at much length in answer to a note from him apprising me from Lady F. che si rincrescessero di aver finito le cose cosi subito: e questo mi piace muovendo ringraziamente alla Sapienza di Dio senza troppo turbare il mio cuore fatto da mestizia piu stabile e piu chiaro.[2] Walk with John. My Father saw Aunt J.: treated her with the greatest kindness. finished Ayesha—read Macintosh & Reynolds. Most beautifully did my Father speak to me before dinner of the visitation, its wise and kind intent, & its softening effects: with the full recognition of the truth that such things are *necessary* for our peace. Conv. with my brothers in evg.

26. Sat.

walk with J.N.G. read paper—finished Paul's letters to his kinsfolk— began Mrs Butler's journal[3]—wrote to Mrs Williams[4]—Doyle—Gaskell— Bruce—Pulford.

27. S.

read Knox. Chillingworth. began Le Bas's Jewel[5]—read aloud two services (Blomfield & Arnold) & mg & evg family prayers. Wrote to Hamilton & Mrs Labalmondiere.

28. M.

Began Chalmers's Bridgwater.[6] Helen unwell. Wrote to Dr Hunter—Dr Jephson. read Mrs Butler. paper. walk with Mr G.

[1] Perhaps (Sir) G. C. *Lewis, 1806–53, whig M.P. Hertfordshire 1847–52, bart. and M.P. Radnor 1855; succ. diarist at exchequer, 1855–8; home secretary 1859, war secretary 1861. He was working on Irish education at the time.
[2] That she is sorry to have broken things off so abruptly; and this pleased me, impelling me to thank God's Wisdom without too much disturbing my heart, which has grown more stable and less turbid in the interval.'
[3] Fanny *Kemble, later Butler, *Journal*, 2v. (1835).
[4] Wife of Robert Williams the elder.
[5] Charles *Le Bas, *Life of Bishop *Jewel* (1835).
[6] Thomas *Chalmers, *On the Adaption of External Nature to the Moral and Intellectual Constitution of Man*, 2v. (1833); one of eight treatises by various authors, endowed by the Earl of *Bridgewater. And see 5 Oct. 35.

29. T.

Continued Chalmers (with notes).[1] wrote to Mr Jones—Mrs Chisholm—
Hamilton—Maclachlan. walk among the hills. My own matter more in my
mind than it ought. read Mrs Butler—(a strange mixture) and three
Cantos of the Faery Queen B I. Uncle Colin & Larkins came. Macintosh.

30. Wednesday.

The funeral. We laid a body in the grave: but, from whatever cause, I do
not feel separated from the spirit which possessed it: and which I rejoice to
think is now very near us, and associated again with that of her beloved
daughter, to whom almost if not quite her very last articulate words in the
flesh referred. "She was blessed". And now, they are both blessed. May the
fulness of the love of God make them glad for ever.

    rude interest of the people in the churchyard: but chiefly to look into the
vault: into wh they nearly thrust some of us. My dear Father bore up
wonderfully.—used some add[tiona]l prayer at night.

    Read Bible. Jewel's life. Spenser. Mrs Butler.

    Here closes my little book with a month of no ordinary interest and equal
to three or four of life.

[The last page of the book contains:]
from the overhanging penalty of sin? Primarily, but this is but an instrumental deliverance having an ulterior end. It is faith in a work whose
substantial object was to save us from the power of sin.

    What then is the logical position of him who says he has faith and that
holiness is unconnected with it. This: "I believe that Christ died to save
me from the power of sin:[2] therefore I will continue in the power of sin"—
But shall the purpose of God be made of none effect?

May 13. A nat[ural] though not nec[essary] connexion [be]tw[ee]n the doctrine of particular redemption & the hab[it] of viewing the church as a
portion selected out of the baptised world.

May 28. A spirit of doubt in religion keeps truth superseded in the region of
the understanding and precludes it from sinking deeper and acting upon the
affections: for which two things are required: time, and confidence.

    An acute intellect may lead a bad man to much religious truth: because
while his general selfwill biasses him *against* the humbling doctrine of the
Bible, that bias is redressed by his pride of understanding which piques
itself upon a strict adherence to the laws of reasoning, while the strength
of the faculty discerns the premisses aright.

[1] Add MS 44724, f. 176.
[2] Cp. Acts. xxvii. 18.

[VOLUME IX][1]

[The front fly leaf contains:]

Oct 35–Feb 38

PRIVATE   (NO 9)

In the waters are the six last cantos of the Faery Queen[2]

the great seal of England 1688[3]

St Stephen's Schools. Dr Muir.[4]

The siege of Londonderry.[5]

The Marquis of Hertford's undercle's[6]

June 1/ 36.[7]

Meditations of Pius—of Aurelius[8]—

Aug[ustine] de Util[itate] Credendi.[9]

B.3. contra Faust[um Manichaeum].[10]

Annales de l'ass[ociatio]n pour la Prop[agatio]n de la Foi. Paris & Lyons.[11]

Rime del Buonarrotti[12]

Petrarchs Ethics.[13]

---

[1] Lambeth MS 1423, 89 ff.
[2] Which Edmund *Spenser never completed.
[3] Thrown into the Thames by *James II when he fled from London, 1688; recovered several months later by a fisherman.
[4] Dr. William Muir, d. 1869, Scottish divine and educationist, minister at St. Stephen's, Edinburgh, 1829; prominent opponent of disruption.
[5] J. Graham, *Deriana, . . . A History of The Siege of Londonderry and Defence of Enniskillen* (1823).
[6] Some adventure of Francis Charles *Seymour-Conway, 1777–1842, diplomat and debauchee; 6th marquess of Hertford 1822; original of *Thackeray's Lord Steyne and *Disraeli's Lord Monmouth.
[7] Pencil jotting.
[8] References to Antoninus Pius, Roman emperor 138–161, are frequent in the *Meditations* of his nephew and successor Marcus Aurelius.
[9] Anti-Manichean tract (391); Migne *PL* xlii. 63.
[10] On genealogy of Jesus (*ca.* 400); ibid. 207.
[11] Untraced.
[12] Poems by Michaelangelo, 1623.
[13] S. *Dobson tr., *Petrarch's View of Human Life* (1787).

Fasque. October one. 1835.

Thursday.

The last month one of much disorganisation: but much exercise and discipline.

Chalmers (finished Vol I). Mrs Butler. Spenser which I like very much. walk with Mr G. and alone. paper. wrote to Mrs Wallace—Dr Chalmers.

2. Friday.

Chalmers (Vol II). Spenser. Finished Mrs Butler.[1] walk with Mr G.—songs in evg—wrote to Mr Rawson, Mr Simpson, Dr Hunter.

How mercifully is the removal of a beloved person softened by its gradations. Illness removed her from our eyes. Danger announced shook the hold of the heart upon her. Death visibly & measurably near wrought perhaps the greatest part of the separation. The flight of the spirit was less felt because it came at the close of long and intense expectation. Then the remains were taken from the eye by inclosure in the coffin: and at internment, sense was wholly deprived of its evidences of her existence, faith wholly in possession of the field of its exercise.

3. Sat.

Uncle C. went. This is my scheme for the weekday.

1. Blackstone.
2. Tocqueville.....to be foll[owe]d by Dante, Purgatorio.
3. Spanish Grammar..................Goethe.
4. Fox's James II............Smollett & Frederic.
5. Aristot. Politics.

add, a book for the evening—Spenser at present.[2]
    Walk with Mr G. verses.[3] analysis of "Politics" (Aristot.)—Chalmers—Spenser. began Italian Lives in Lardner[4]—[5]Gillies's Intrr to Pol. 1. & 2.[6]

4. Sunday.

Ch. & aftn home service. Blomfield aloud. read Jewel—Knox—Chillingworth—wrote, prose[7] & a few vss.

5. M.

Rn went. Began Fox's James 2.[8] Finished Chalmers. He is not in this work most in his element. rode. wrote to Aunt D. Spenser—Lardner's Italian Lives.

---

[1] A few notes in Add MS 44725, f. 233.
[2] A few notes on *The Faery Queene*, ibid. ff. 231–2.   [3] Perhaps ibid. f. 228.
[4] By Sismondi, in Dionysius *Lardner *Cabinet Cyclopaedia*, 133 v. (1829–44).
[5] 'a note to' here deleted.
[6] J. *Gillies ed. Aristotle *Ethics* and *Politics* (1797).
[7] On Scriptures; in Add MS 44724, f. 187.
[8] C. J. *Fox, *History of the Early Part of the Reign of James II* (1808).

6. T.

Began Hume at the Commonwealth.[1] Analysis of Ar. Pol. Wrote to W. Mackenzie—Huddlestone—C. Brooks[2]—read It. Biogr.—songs: out in the woods.

7. W.

Hume. wrote out Vss.[3] Arist. Pol. out with gun. It. Biogr. & Boccaccio's Tale of Griselda.[4] wrote to Mr Harrison.

8. Th.

Hume. Arist. Pol. It Biogr.—Faery Queen—singing—wrote to Mr T. Godfrey. Aunt J & the Larkinses went.

9. Fr.

Hume. Arist. Pol.—It Biogr.—Spenser—Blackstone—Tocqueville. Hill walk.

10. Sat.

reading as yesterday—wrote to Mrs Wallace—read paper. wrote in Bl. B.

11. S.

Bible. Knox—Chillingworth—Jewel—began Aug[ustine] de Civ[itate] Dei[5] —Sumner at aft. prayers.

12. M.

Hume. Tocqueville. Ar. Pol. began B.4—Blackstone—Italian Biogr. (finished Vol 1)—Spenser. papers.

13. T.

Hume. Tocqueville. Blackstone.[6] Spenser. Compensation calculations. Gillies's Acct. of San Marino.[7] On the hill.

14. W.

Hume (finished). Fox's James II. Ar. Pol. Blackstone. Tocqueville. Wrote

---

[1] D. *Hume, *History of England*, ch. lx. Notes in Add MS. 44724, ff 211–15.
[2] Possibly Charles William Shirley *Brooks, 1816–74; parliamentary reporter and light author; edited *Punch* 1870.
[3] Of 4 October, in Add MS 44724, f. 201.
[4] The last tale in the *Decamerone*.
[5] Migne, *PL*, xli. 12 (*ca.* 413–26). A few notes in Add MS 44724, f. 210.
[6] 'Ar. Pol.' here deleted.
[7] Appended to book ii of Aristotle, *Politics* in J. *Gillies' ed.
14—II.

to Mr Rawson—& H. Thompson.[1] Spenser—finished B.2. of Faery Queen. ride with T.G. &c. Quart. Rev. aloud to Mr G.

15. Th.

Fox's James II. Wrote to Aunt J. & O. Cole. Singing. Tocqueville. Ar. Pol. Mrs Macdonald bro[ugh]t me a cheese "for the sake of her that's awa." ride. Quart. aloud to Mr G. Also [therein] Artt. on Willis and Coleridge's Worthies.[2] Blackstone.

16. Fr.

Mr G. determined to go to Ed[inburg]h on Helen's acct, a wise measure I trust. Fox's James II. I am disappointed in him, not seeing such an acuteness in extracting and exhibiting the principles which govern from beneath the actions of men and parties, nor such a grasp of generalisation, nor such a faculty of separating minute from material particulars, nor such an abstraction from a debater's modes of thought & forms of expression, as I shd have hoped. It is however an unfinished fragment, & this may be a presumptuous opinion.—Ar. Pol.—Blackstone—began Smollett: a sad change from Hume. Singing. out shooting with Tom and John. Draft & letter to Mr Simpson.

17. Sat.

It is proposed to go [on] Tuesday—set about winding up my books summarily. (Wrote to Mrs Wishlade.) Visited the tenants on Fasque, &c. finished Smollett's 3d Chapter, & mean to cut him. I may be wrong but he seems to me a bad narrator & he has not I believe countervailing merits. Barillon (Fox's Appx)[3] wrote to Lady K[erriso]n & Moyle.[4]

18. Sunday.

Church—prayers & Sumners S.2. aloud. Read Aug. de Civ. Dei (finished B.1.) Le Bas's Jewel (finished) Chillingworth. 'Notes'.[5]

19. M.

Barillon—curious & interesting. wrote to Selwyn. called on the Balfour tenants. paper—(finished Barillon).

---

[1] Thompson spent this winter as an assistant at Rawson's school (Add MS 44355, ff. 75–77).
[2] Cp. 21 Oct. 35.
[3] The appendix to *Fox's *James II* included transcripts, made for *Fox in Paris in 1802, of the dispatches Louis XIV received in 1685 from his ambassador in London, Paul Barillon d'Amoncourt.
[4] George Moyle, 1816?–61, priest; master of Chudleigh grammar school 1850.
[5] Scrap in Add MS 44725, f. 230.

20. T.

7½–6½. miles 12 (at least), 13, 18, 13, 17, 16, 2, 10.[1] Shd have been ¾ hour earlier but for accid[enta]l delays. Dr Hunter called in evg to inquire.— read Macintosh.

21. W.

Arist. Pol.—wrote to T.G. commenced the satisf[actor]y acct wh Dr Hunter, thank God, has given of Helen. read Hartley Coleridge[2]—Macintosh—Tocqueville—paper—sat with the Ramsays.

22. Th.

Helen again improved. Wrote to R.G.—Aunt J.—and Mr G—walked with Mr Horne—read Ar. Pol.—Novelle Scelte[3]—Macintosh—paper—Russell's modern Europe (resumed)—Tocqueville.

23. Fr.

wrote to Mr Bonham.[4] Walk. read Macintosh—Russell—Tocqueville—Ar. Pol.—Coleridge (H.)—and Bacon's Essays. Helen proceeds.

24.

d[itt]o of H.—Mr G. came—wrote to J.N.G. & Merivale[?].[5] Vss. Macintosh, Tocqueville, Ar. Pol., Russell, and J.T. Reed's Narrative of Six Mo[nths] in a Convent.[6]

25. Sunday.

St John's mg & aft. with much pleasure. Mr G. went. Notes. Leighton— Pollok's Course of Time[7]—Hooker.

26. M.

Late last night waiting Dr Hunter—late this mg.—Russell—Ar. Pol.— paper—Tocqueville—wrote to Mr G and Mr Tyler—a sketch of a project touching "Peculiarities in Religion".[8]

27. T.

Russell. Ar. Pol. finished B.IV. & wrote a paper on CXII.[9] saw Mr Horne[10]—

[1] Post stages on journey to Edinburgh.
[2] *Lives of Illustrious Worthies of Yorkshire and Lancashire* (1835), by the poet's son*.
[3] Boccaccio's *Decamerone*, abbreviated for family reading (1812).
[4] Francis Robert Bonham, 1785–1863; conservative party manager 1831–46; M.P. Rye 1830–1, Harwich 1835–7 (see N. Gash, *Politics in the age of Peel* (1953), 412–18, 464).
[5] Perhaps Herman *Merivale, 1806–74; permanent under-secretary, colonial office 1848, India office 1859.
[6] By Rebecca T. Reed (1835); and see Add MS 44724, f. 201.
[7] R. *Pollock, *The Course of Time*, a poem, 2v. (1827). Cp. 29 Nov. 35.
[8] Add MS 44724, f. 203.
[9] On what sorts of constitution fit what sorts of people. Add MS 44724, f. 207.
[10] Donald Horne, w.s., of 10 Atholl Crescent.

Mr Grant—Mrs Ogilvy. Bacon's Essays. Tocqueville—wrote to Mr G. and Luigi Lamonica. A sketch of some writing on our Colonial system.

28.

Russell. Hist. Notes.[1] Ar. Pol.—Bacon's Essays—Tocqueville—singing—walk round Arthur's seat[2]—wrote to Lincoln—T. Godfrey—T.G.—and Mrs Chisholm.

29.

Russell (began Vol 5) Bacon's Essays (finished) Ar. Pol—Tocqueville—began King Lear aloud—singing—wrote to Mr Simpson.

30.

Mr G. came. wrote to Harrison. Paper &c. aloud to Mr G.—Russell—Ar. Pol.—Tocqueville—Hartley Coleridge.

31.

Russell. Ar. Pol.—Letters, papers, & Macintosh aloud to Mr G.—wrote to P.M. Stewart. walked up Arthur's seat. Tocqueville. finished Hartley Coleridge.

Sunday Nov. 1.

Sact. Perhaps 120. wrote Notes—read Pollok (pt aloud to Mr G) Knox, & began Russell's Church History.[3]

2. M.

Wrote to Lady Kerrison. dined at Mr Ramsay's to meet the Bp of N. Carolina.[4] Much conv. with him. Bp of Ed.[5] also there. A very pleasing evg. read Russell—Ar. Pol.—Tocqueville.

3. T.

Russell. Ar. Pol.—Tocqueville finished. a most able book—and beautifully arranged. Paper (O'Connell & Raphael!!)[6] to Mr G—J.N.G. came—wrote to Milnes—Lincoln—Mr Simpson.[7]

[1] Add MS 44724, f. 205.

[2] The hill, rising steeply south of Holyrood, on the eastern side of Edinburgh.

[3] M. *Russell, *History of the Church in Scotland*, 2v. (1834).

[4] Levi Silliman Ives, 1797–1867; bp. of North Carolina 1831; converted to Rome 1852.

[5] James *Walker, 1770?–1841; ordained 1793; as sub-editor, studied and wrote on Kant in *Encyclopaedia Britannica*; bp. of Edinburgh 1830; primus 1837.

[6] *O'Connell was imbrangled in controversy with Alexander Raphael, M.P. for Carlow at by-election in June 1835, unseated on petition, who charged *O'Connell with malversation of election funds. See 22 Apr. 36.

[7] And wrote fragment on substitute materials: Add MS 44725, f. 1.

4. W.

Russell (began Vol VI.)—Ar. Pol.—Macintosh to Mr G.—wrote to T.G.—L.G.—and Doyle—walk with J.N.G. Began Chateaubriand's Génie du Christianisme.[1]

5. Th.

Russell. Ar. Pol.—Gillies's Intrr. to BB. V & VI—breakfd with Mrs Ogilvy —some sore throat. Chateaubriand—wrote to Mrs Fyfe[2]—long conv. with Mr G. on the R.G. family matter.[3]

6. Fr.

Russell. Ar. Pol.—wrote to Rn—paper—Macintosh aloud to Mr G. Purgatorio I, II. Chateaubriand. Whist.

7. Sat.

It is now cons[idere]d nearly certain that John Macadam [Gladstone] is lost. This is indeed a painful death: how mercifully have we been dealt with. How arc we at once spared & warned. And yet this which is without assurance is not without hope.

Up Arthur's seat with John. [Read] Macintosh to Mr G. paper. Ar. Pol. Russell. wrote on Education.[4] wrote to Col. Coles. Chateaubriand.

8. S.

St John's mg & aft. Knox. Pollok. Russell Ch. Scotland. Chateaubriand. Wrote.[5]

9. M.

Russell. Ar. Pol.—Wrote on Edn—wrote to Bonham—Lincoln here. Bruce walked with me. singing. Chateaubriand.[6] Vss.

10. T.

Russell. Ar. Pol. (began B.VII). calls. wrote on Politics.[7] Purgatorio III, IV. Fudge Family[8] to Mr G.

[1] (1802); and see Add MS 44725, f. 41.
[2] Possibly wife of John Fyfe of Gordonloisk Cottage, near Dunoon.
[3] Robertson Gladstone proposed to marry Mary Ellen, d. 1865, da. of Hugh Jones, 1777–1842, unitarian banker, of Larkhill, Liverpool. See Magnus, 29–30; and below, 14–21 Nov. 35, 28 Jan. 36.
[4] Notes written from this date to 10 December 1835, Add MS 44725, ff. 44–102.
[5] On metaphysics; Add MS 44725, f. 2.
[6] 'Slave'[?] here deleted.
[7] Add MS 44725, f. 31.
[8] 'T. Brown the Younger' [i.e. Tom *Moore] *The Fudge Family in Paris* (1818), light verse.

11. W.

T.G. came. Russell. Ar. Pol. walk with J.N.G. read Picton's Memoirs[1] to Mr G.—Bruce here. Dante V, VI. Chateaubriand. Helen much troubled with earache.

12. Th.

Helen & Miss T. ill—Russell (finished Vol 6)—Ar. Pol.—Wrote on Educn &c—Picton to Mr G—Chateaubriand—wrote to Larkins. Rev. J. Sinclair here.[2]

13. Fr.

Helen still in much pain. Walk with J.N.G. read Russell. Ar. Pol.—Wrote Notes[3]—to Rn—copied a letter—Purgatorio VII, VIII with J.N.G. Picton to Mr G.—Alison's Introduction.[4]

14. Sat.

Helen better. Ar. Pol.[5]—Russell. Dante with J.N.G.—walked with him 10 m. on Queensferry Road[6] in 1 h. 53½ min.—both came in fresh. wrote to Col. Coles—& Rn G. in evg, on hearing of his contemplated marriage, which may God bless. wrote on Aristotle &c.—Milton's death in the paper. How are we warned. Hallam went down into the grave, his bridal in view, his lofty fame in an embryo it was not to burst: T. Selwyn in the fulness of academical distinction: & now Milton has left his blooming wife,[7] his high duties, his princely inheritance, to enter the dark valley, yet not I trust to remain in its darkness. All my contemporaries, all younger than myself: they are there, I here: but here or there our hope, our life, our God are the same.

15. Sunday.

St John's mg & aft. Wrote to Maurice. read Knox—Russell's Ch. Hist—and Pollok.—our evening clouded by a report at least ambiguous from Rn on *the* most important subject.

16. M.

Russell—Ar. Pol.—Dante [Purgatorio] XI—Génie du Christ. wrote to Wm

---

[1] H. B. Robinson, *Memoirs of . . . Sir Thomas *Picton*, 2v. (1835).

[2] John Sinclair, 1797–1875, b. of 2nd bart. of Ulbster; B.A. from Pembroke, Oxford, and ordained, 1819; vicar of Kensington 1842, and archdeacon of Middlesex 1843, and canon of St. Paul's 1844; built St. Mary Abbott's church.

[3] Add MS 44725, f. 35.

[4] A. *Alison, *History of Europe during the French Revolution* (1833–52); and see Add MS 44725, ff. 103–8.

[5] Cp. Add MS 44725, ff. 36–39.   [6] i.e. westwards.

[7] Lord Milton, who d. 8 November, had m. 1833 Lady Selina Charlotte Jenkinson 1812–83, 2nd da. of 3rd earl of *Liverpool; she re-m., as his 2nd w., 1845, George Savile Foljambe, 1800–69; earldom revived 1905 for their s.

Caparn.[1] Comm[unicate]d with Mr Ramsay about Ld Ramsay.[2]—Much conv. in evg on Rns matters. Another letter from him confirmed the worst interpretation of yesterday's. He is indeed in a fiery trial: may he who sent it, sanctify it. Mr G. resolved to go to Lpool.

17. T.

Russell. Ar. Pol.—Finished B.VII. Picton to Mr G. Dante Purg c[anto] XII with J.N.G.—wrote on Colonies. Walk with G. M'Kenzie to get his inf[ormatio]n touching N.S.W.—In evg a fresh & most sanguine letter from Rn: hopes & emotions soon alas to be dashed down. Callers.

18. Wed.

Russell. Ar. Pol.—Callers. went to see the Castle with T. and L. Purg XIII, XIV. Wrote to Mr Wilson.

La lettera quest'oggi da R. ricevuta spiega la credenza di MEJ. nelle lei parole. A mio padre ed ai fratelli, questi soddisfecero: a mi nondimeno non pajono di esprimer le prime verità del Vangelo, cioè le verità della prima necessità. I sentimenti di mia sorella sono d'accordo coi miei.[3] Questa e una gran ragione di doglia: ci troviamo divisi in materia di somma importanza l'un dell'altro; e dui fra noi da tutti e specialmente da quello a cui primieramente tocca. Che sia fatta la voglia di Dio: ma questo mi rincresce, per[4] ora non veggio che stia per esser fatta da noi. Come possiamo unirci, intanto che la credenza che dovesse riempire il cuore e regger la vita, formare la piu parte dell "Io", esistendo dall'una[5] parte, non si trova dell'altra? O questo non e conjugio—o quella non è credenza. Guardi O Dio in misericordia mio fratello e la casa nostra: ci leghi nel amore di Cristo, ci conduca per la via della croce al monte della tua gloria.[6]

19. Th.

Russell. Ar. Pol. and wrote out at length a paper with my views, at least in part, su quella materia con tanto c'interessa. Anche con mia sorella parlai

[1] Brother of Thomas Caparn?
[2] James Andrew Broun *Ramsay, 1812–60, Harrow and Christ Church; styled Lord Ramsay 1832; M.P. Haddingtonshire 1837–8; succ. as 10th earl of Dalhousie 1838, cr. marquess 1849; viceroy of India 1848–56. He m. 21 January 1836 Lady Susan (Georgiana) Hay, d. 1853, da. of 8th marquess of *Tweeddale.
[3] This phrase instead of 'i medesimi'.
[4] Instead of 'sta'.   [5] Instead of 'nell'uno'.
[6] 'The letters received from R[obertson] today unfolds the beliefs of ME J[ones] in her own words. These will satisfy my father and my brothers; nevertheless, to me they do not seem to express the first truths of the Gospel, that is, the most necessary truths of all. My sister's feelings accord with my own. [instead of 'are the same']. This is a great reason for sorrow: we find ourselves sundered one from another on a point of supreme import; and two of us are sundered from all the rest, especially from him who is most concerned. May God's will be done; but it pains me, that for the moment I cannot see what should be done by us to bring that about. How can we be united, while the creed that should fill the heart and rule the life, should fashion the greater part of the 'I', is there on one side, but not on the other? Either this is not marriage—or that is not belief. O God, guard in thy mercy my brother and our family; bind us in the love of Christ, lead us by the way of the cross to the mountain of thy glory'.

buon pezzo. Adesso non mi pare remedio: ma lo dovere s'unisce col disio del cuore, in sognandoci sperare.[1]

20. Fr.

Up to see Mr G. off. finished Russell. The design better than the execution. Finished Ar. Pol.: a book of immense value for all governors and public men. read Picton, & "Random Recollections of H. of C."[2]—princ[ipall]y trash, with some good & shrewd remarks, so far as I saw. Wrote on Colonies. met Aunt J. Diverted in spite of my more collected self by the last named book ad un'allegria che pessimamente s'accorda col spirito di dentro.[3]

Wrote to Mr G—M'Lachlan—Stevenson—Mrs Wallace—Wilde—Bain.[4]

21. Sat.

Notes on Russell. read Aristotle's Economics. Finished Picton Vol 1—and Génie du Christ Vol 1. began Madden's W.I.—sang: wrote on Edn. scrissi al fratello R.G. con sommo cordoglio:[5] kept draft.

22. Sunday.

Leighton on St Peter[6]—Pollok—Russell's Ch. Hist. St. John's mg & aft. Wrote to Mr G (W.W.)

23. M.

Bolingbroke's 5 first letters on History—wrote[7]—Dante Purg 15, 16— Random Recollections—paper—wrote to Mr Ramsay & to Bonham— Blackstone—my head swam in evg: so poor a creature every way. pensieri sulle mie cose; fa d'uopo disimbrogliarle: e più e più mi sento come sarei dono infelice per un sposo. E fra i voleri e le pratiche, c'e tanta differenza: e delle due parti di mia natura, quale si mariterebbe?[8]

24. T.

Finished Vol 1. of Bolingbroke. Resumé of the Politics—Blackstone— Purg. XVII, XVIII—Génie—singing—wrote on Edn.

---

[1] 'On this matter that concerns us so nearly. Also spoke of it with my sister a good deal. Up to now I can see no remedy: but duty unites with earnest heart's desire in fancying hope for us.'
[2] By James *Grant (1835).
[3] 'into a merriment which matched as badly as could be my inward feelings'.
[4] N. Bain, secretary and librarian, Royal Physical Society, Edinburgh.
[5] 'wrote to my brother R.G. with the keenest pain'.
[6] R. Leighton, A Practical Commentary upon the First Epistle of St. Peter (1819).
[7] Henry *St. John, Letters on the Study and Use of History, 2v. (1752), and see Add MS 44725, f. 40.
[8] 'Thought over my affairs; it is necessary to get out of the tangle: and more and more I feel what a wretched gift I would be as a husband. And there is such a difference between intention and practice; and of the two halves of my nature, which would mate?'

25. W.

Bolingbroke Vol. II. finished Synopsis of the Politics. Blackstone. Purg. XIX, XX. Génie. wrote to Mr G—Mr M'Lauchlan—Mrs Wallace. Singing.

26. Th.

Bolingbroke. Wrote on Mor[als][1]—Bruce here. rode with Louisa. Blackstone. Purg. XXI, XXII. Singing. wrote to Mr Allen. and Notes for a letter meant to be dispatched next week.

27. Fr.

Finished Bolingbroke. Wrote on Ed[ucation]—Purg. XXIII, IV. singing. Génie. Blackstone. Alison's French Rev. Ch. I.

28. Sat.

Alison. Wrote on Pol[itics].[2] Blackstone. Purg. XXV, VI. Génie. Madden's W.I.—wrote to Bonham—Lincoln—Acland.

29. Sunday.

St John's mg & aft. Finished Russell Vol. 1—Knox—Bible—Finished the Course of Time. Pollok seems to me to have had much talent, little culture, insufficient power to digest & construct his subject or his versification. His politics seem radical : his religious sentiments generally sound tho' perhaps hard. It was an interesting fate.[3] wrote draft of letter to Mr G. Helen at Church.

30. M.

Reconsidered, showed, & wrote letter to Mr G.[4] wrote to Hay & Mrs Wallace —singing—read Alison—Blackstone—Purg. XXVII,—paper—Madden— wrote on Pol. (concession).[5]

Decr. 35. (Edinbro.)
One. Tuesday.

Alison. Blackstone. Dante Purg. XXVIII, XXIX. Herschel on Nat. Phil.[6] paper. singing.—
     Heard of poor Lady Salisbury's awful death.[7]

---

[1] Untraced.   [2] Add MS 44724, f. 140.
[3] Robert *Pollok, a farmer's seventh son, qualified as a preacher in spite of poor health, and d. in 1827 before he was thirty.
[4] Part in Lathbury, ii. 231–3.
[5] Add MS 44725, ff. 184–9.
[6] W. *Herschel, *A Preliminary Discourse on the Study of Natural Philosophy*, in *Lardner's *Cabinet Cyclopaedia* (1831).
[7] Mary Amelia, née Hill, widow of 1st marquess, was burned alive in a fire at Hatfield (see Cecil, i. 2–4).

2. W.

Alison. Wrote on Hist. Blackstone. Purg. XXX, XXXI. paper. wrote to Mr G. Génie. singing.

3. Th.

Up at 6 to see T. & L. off. Alison. wrote on Mor. Locke (reviewing, to resume)—Blackstone. Grant Thorburn's Men & Manners[1]—singing—wrote to T.G. about Rn.—Childe Harold.

4. Fr.

Alison. wrote on Mor.—Locke—Blackstone. Dante's Purgatorio finished. The commentators writhe in the 32nd Canto.[2] wrote to Mr Finlay—and my long meditated letter to W.R. F[arquhar][3]—singing.

5. Sat.

Alison (entered Vol 2)—Blackstone—Locke—a conv. with H.J.G. on temper[4]—singing—wrote to Bonham—Mr G—Mrs Wallace—Bain. paper. Walked with Sir J. Riddell.[5] he told me a little of Peel. Childe Harold (finished C.I.)

6. Sunday

The Sacrament. Mr Ramsay in aft. wrote on Mor[als] (Rel[igion])[6]—read Par[adise] Lost I. Russell—Knox—sang.

7. M.

Alison. wrote on Mor (Rel)—Locke. Blackstone: Spanish (Cervantes, Novelas)[7]—Génie. singing—wrote to T.G. &c. Ross.

8. T.

Alison. wrote on Pol.[8]—Locke. Blackstone. Childe Harold. singing. Ma la sera fu principalmente occupata nel considerare e scrivere la risposta ad una lettera di T.G.[9]—also wrote a 2d to him.

[1] Grant *Thorburn, *Men and Manners in Britain* (1834).
[2] The poet's meeting with Beatrice; and some highly complicated symbolism about relations between Church and state. Cp. Add MS 44725, f. 109.
[3] Add MS 44155 includes letters on public subjects only; the private correspondence with the Farquhars is at St. Deiniol's library, Hawarden.
[4] Notes in Add MS 44725, f. 109.
[5] Sir James Milles Riddell, 1787–1861; succ. gf. as 2nd bart. 1797; at Christ Church; lieut.-col., Argyle militia, soon after going down.
[6] Add MS 44725, ff. 19–30; written on this day and next.
[7] *Novelas Ejemplares* (1613).
[8] Perhaps starting paper on social obligation, completed over next ten days; Add MS 44725, ff. 150–83.
[9] 'But the evening was principally taken up with considering, and writing an answer to, a letter from T.G.'

9. W.

Alison. Locke. Blackstone. La Gitanilla.[1] Childe Harold. singing. wrote to Mr G.

10. Th.

Alison. Wrote on Pol. Locke. Blackstone. letter from W.R.F. acc[oun]ting for delay. Childe Harold. singing. wrote to Uncle C—J.D. Acland—Bonham —W.R.F.—Hatchard—Mrs Wallace. Gitanilla. Finished Sumners St Mark at pr.

11. Fr.

Alison. Childe Harold (Began C.4). singing. Locke. Blackstone. wrote to T.G. heard from Lpool but not definitively. Gitanilla. wrote on Pol.[2] Began Sumner's St Luke.[3]

12. Sat.

Alison. Wrote on Pol. Locke. Blackstone. Pencillings by the way.[4] Gitanilla & Spanish Gram. Wrote to Caparn. Heard of our dear Father's sad fall on Thursday evg. Though we have no warrant for apprehension, we must look very anxiously for tomorrow's letters.

13. Sunday.

An ordination at St John's today. Rose at six to see John off. Gladdened in the afternoon by a most gratifying account of my Father for which we cannot be thankful enough. Russell—Leighton—Knox—wrote on Predest[inatio]n[5]—wrote to T.G.

14. M.

Alison. Blackstone. Locke. singing. paper. wrote to J.N.G. Finished Vol III of Pencillings by the Way.

15. T.

read Alison (finished Vol II), Locke, Blackstone. Wrote on Pol. read Quarty on Robespierre. rode. sang. paper. wrote to T.G. & Larkins.

16. W.

Rode with Helen (she af[te]r[wards] unwell from it) & alone to the Goalens. Wrote to Mr G. finished Notes on Alison—began Robertson's Scotland[6]—

[1] Cervantes, from *Novelas Ejemplares* (1613).
[2] Add MS 44725, ff. 140–9.
[3] J. B. *Sumner, *A Practical Exposition of the Gospel of St. Luke* (1832).
[4] By N. P. Willis, 3v. (1835).
[5] In Add MS 44725, ff. 115–32.
[6] William *Robertson, *The History of Scotland*, 2v. (1759).

Blackstone—Locke—Quarterly on Heyne's Allemagne—paper—wrote on Pol.[1]

17. Th.

Robertson—Locke—Blackstone—wrote on Pol.[2] rode—walked with Dr Chalmers for conv. on the Professorial salaries : a sad & app[aren]tly shameful case.[3] Childe Harold & Notes—paper—wrote to Mr G—Chateaubriand.

18. Fr.

Robertson. Locke. Blackstone. wrote on Pol. Chateaubriand. wrote to T.G. & J.N.G.—long conv. with Mr Menzies[4] on the Professorial salaries; I do not now see the *blame* imputable which appeared at first—but the case is *very* hard. paper—wrote on Absence of descriptive Poetry am[on]g anc[ien]ts.[5]

19. Sat.

Robertson. Locke. Wrote on Pol.[6] paper. wr to W. Sinclair & Mr G. reading Ed[inburgh] Univ. Commn Report[7]—a laborious and long evening divided between that, & the Lpool quest. with Helen.

20. Sunday.

Ch as usual. Russell. Leighton. Knox. Par. Lost B.II. wrote to J.N.G.—letter from W.R.F. & thought.[8]

21. M.

Robertson's Scotland—Finished Vol I. Locke. Blackstone—wrote to Mrs Hagart—J.N.G.—calls. nella mattina scrissi la risposta alla lettera ricevuta jeri.[9] Another long evg. upon the Univ. Report papers & notes.

22. T.

General Univ. Report; saw Mr Menzies again, walked with Dr Chalmers—& as the result of all wrote a letter with the facts to Ld Aberdeen.[10]

　　　Wrote to Mr G. Aunt J. Mr Tyler. Mr Caparn. Mrs Wallace. Crabb.[11] read Robertson—Locke—Blackstone—Chateaubriand.

[1] On prevalent theories of govt.; Add MS 44725, ff. 140–9, 190–206.
[2] On will in govt.; ibid. ff. 207–16.
[3] Notes ibid. ff. 217–25. Cp. 22 Dec. 35.
[4] Allan Menzies, Edinburgh lawyer; see next entry.
[5] Add MS 44725, f. 254.
[6] Ibid. f. 226.
[7] *PP* 1831 xii. 205, sent him that day by Menzies (Add MS 44563, f. 43).
[8] See Magnus, 27.
[9] 'In the morning, answered the letter received yesterday.'
[10] Reply in Add MS 44088, ff. 5–6; *Aberdeen under-informed.
[11] Possibly John Crabbe, Edinburgh surgeon.

23. Wed.

Reports, and drew a paper from them. Came in at the end of the Protestant Meeting. In evg went to hear Mr Simpson lecture the working classes in Cowgate Chapel: he told them that the applications of the particular dogmata of phrenology were as certain as that in chemistry from a gas & an alkali results an effervescence. Mr Menzies took me. Wrote to Mr G. Read Robertson—Locke—paper.

24. Th.

Robertson. Locke. Blackstone. wrote to Lincoln. Ld Aberdeen. J.N.G.— paper: dined with Mr G. Forbes.[1] walked with Dr Chalmers to the Water of Leith &c. Chateaubriand—& Chalmers's Sp. to Ass[embl]y Commissn.[2]

25. Friday. Christmas day.

A full communion: over 300 I think. My Father's letter to H.J.G. touching. Ch mg & aft.—Russell. Leighton (admirable)—Chateaubriand (finished Vol II)—wrote to Mr G—Mrs Wishlade. paper. wrote a little on M[orals].[3]

26.

Robertson (Diss[ertatio]n & Appx)—Locke—Blackstone—Account of Dick's bequest[4]—calls—dined at Sir Jas Riddell's—wrote to Mr G. oh come malgrado mio.[5]

27. Sunday.

Church as usual. Russel—reviewing the Confession &c. of 1643[6]—Leighton: still most admirable: Par. Lost B.III—Knox.

28. M.

Robertson, Appx: finished notes.[7] wrote on E[ducation]. papers. Locke. dined at Mr Ramsays. Wrote to T.G.—J.N.G.—Mr G—W.R.F. and Lady F. in answer to theirs which were important.[8]—to Lady Kerrison.

29. Tuesday

My birthday. Here closes an important year. Its first section brought to my life an enhancement of public interest: and its second has been not lightly charged with domestic cares. But *the* question for these anniversaries—

[1] George Forbes, of West Coates House, a few yards NW. of Atholl Crescent.
[2] T. *Chalmers, 'Speech on the Proceedings of the Church Deputation in London during their Recent Visit There' (1835).
[3] Perhaps Add MS 44725, ff. 276–8.
[4] Allan Menzies, 'Report to Trustees of the Bequest of the late James Dick Esq., for the Benefit of the County Parochial Schoolmasters in the Counties of Aberdeen, Banff and Moray' (1835).
[5] 'Oh how reluctantly.' Magnus, 30, quotes part of the letter, from Lathbury, ii. 233.
[6] The Solemn League and Covenant, sworn at Westminster on 15 September 1643.
[7] In Add MS 44724, f. 315.
[8] Presumably the 'paper' dated four days later by Magnus, 27–28.

special to them, but fit for every day—is, has the soul gained any growth into the Father's image? Is the mind which was in Christ more seen and known and transferred? I can only answer thus much: the heart condemns, but God is greater than the heart, and the evidences of His love in warnings and monitions and Providential combinations, remain abundant to sustain the soul. Onward then upon another year.

Vss[1]—Robertson (finished Appx)—Notes on Russell[2]—Locke—Blackstone—Finished Report of Dick's Trustees—paper—walk—wrote to Mr G —R.G. (in answer to a most kind letter on the day)—& Bonham.

30. W.

Began Robertson's America[3]—Notes on Russell. Locke. calls. walk with Moncreiff: conv. on necessity: floundered. wrote to Doyle—Mr G. & draught & letter to R.G. augurando mediante questa lettera di star meglio con lui in matiera delle nozze.[4] Blackstone. papers.

31. Thursday.

Robertson's America. Notes on Russell. Locke. Blackstone. Arranging letters & accounts. wrote to J.N.G.—T.G.—Robertson of Kindeace[5]—Miss J. Mackenzie. papers. Genie (began Vol III.)

And so died the old year: may the new be *better*: its happiness will then take care of itself.

---

[1] Add MS 44725, ff. 310–12.

[2] Ibid., ff. 313–14.

[3] William *Robertson, *The History of America*, 2v. (1777). Notes in Add MS 44726, f. 16.

[4] 'wishing by means of this letter to stand better with him on the marriage question'.

[5] William Robertson, 1765–1844, of Kindeace House, Ross-shire, on the northernmost shore of Cromarty firth; cousin of diarist's mother; cp. 7 Apr. 37.

Edinbro. Jan. One. 1836.

Church. Génie. papers. Robertson's Am. (finished Vol. 1.)—wrote to Mr G. —Blackstone—Locke—looked over my Analysis of [Bacon] Nov[um] Org[anum] & made an Abstract of it.[1] Notes on Russell.

2. Sat.

Génie. wrote on Classics. Locke. Blackstone. Notes on Russell. papers. Edwards's West Indies, began.[2] wrote to J.N.G. (heard from R.G. & W.R.F., *well*).

3. S.

Sacrament. Abt 130—an excellent sermon from W. Sinclair in aftn. God bless him.—Wrote to G. M'Kenzie on his loss.[3] To T.G. & J.N.G.—read Leighton, Knox, Russell (finished & finished Notes)—and the Confession of 1567.[4] wrote &c.s.[5]

4. M.

Chateaubriand. Notes on Robertson. Locke. Blackstone. Edwards & Notes. Don Quijote (with Transln). papers. wrote to Caparn—Uncle D.—Mr G.

5. T.

Chateaubriand. Locke. Blackstone. Don Quijote. Grammar. paper—rode to Penicuik to see Sir G. Clerk.[6] Edwards's W.I.

6. W.

Church in mg. calls. read Chateaubriand (finished Vol 3)—Locke—Blackstone—Don Quijote—Edwards. singing. wrote to Bonham—& Mr G.

7. Th.

Chateaubriand—Locke—Blackstone—Drove to Belmont. Newhaven, &c[7] —wrote on Pol.—wrote to T.G.—& Sir M. Stewart.[8] Edwards. Don Quijote.

---

[1] Cp. 29 Oct. 34.

[2] Bryan *Edwards, *The History, Civil and Commercial, of the British Colonies in the West Indies*, 3v. (1793–1801). Notes in Add MS 44726, ff. 3–7.

[3] Untraced.

[4] *A General Confession of Christian Churches*, drawn up by protestants in France (1561).

[5] He continued paper begun on 13 Dec. 35.

[6] Sir George *Clerk, 1787–1867; 6th bart. 1798; cons. M.P. Midlothian 1811–32, 1835–7, Stamford 1838–47, Dover 1847–52; secretary to treasury 1834–5, 1841–5; vice-president, board of trade, 1845–6. Lived at Penicuik House, 9 miles south of Edinburgh.

[7] i.e. westward and northward.

[8] Sir Michael Shaw-Stewart, 1788–1836, 6th bart. 1825, whig M.P. co. Lanark 1827–30, co. Renfrew 1830–6.

8. Fr.

Chateaubriand. Edwards. Locke. wrote to Chisholm & W. Forbes—paper—
Quarty on Lieber—at four, drove out to Sir G. Clerk's, Penicuik, for the
night.
(Capt. Wauchope's letter represents the Lib[erated] Afr[ica]ns as very
industrious—& advises that payment should be taken for att[endan]ce at
the schools.)[1]

9. Sat.

Left at 11.—Calls. Edwards W.I.—Chateaubriand—(mg)—wrote to Uncle
C—R.G.—T.G.—Sir R. Peel, from whom I have a very kind invitn.[2] Mr G.
arrived at 3: thin of course but we have much reason indeed to thank God
on his behalf. entretien long et penible a l'egard des noces, parce que je ne
peux pas vouloir d'y assister au moins qu'avec plus de lumières que je n'ai
a present. Bien que je suis frère indigne, il me semble que[3] en faisant mon
devoir je suis pas autant indigne que je serois en trahissant mes croyances.[4]

10. S.

Church as usual. Bible. Knox & Jebb (finished)[5]—Chateaubriand. Par. Lost
B.IV.—Much interrupted in these my closing days. Mais que la lettre qui
partoit d'ici la soir passée soit bénie de Dieu Toutpuissant.[6]

11. M.

Chateaubriand. Locke. Blackstone. Conv. with Helen on her letters. calls.
paper to Mr G. wrote to Pulford & Mrs Wallace. Edwards.

12. T.

Chateaubriand (finished). Trappist letters in Appx are curious & int[erest-
in]g. Calls & prepp. for leaving. Edwards. Wrote to R.G—W.R.F.—Caparn
—whist—singing.

W. 13.

Edwards (finished) Locke—(finished B III). He annihilates half creation.
Packed: sent off Best. wrote to Sir M.S. Stewart—Pulford—T.G.—Mr
Bradshaw[7]—Notes of Par. Lost & Ch[ilde] Harold.[8]

---

[1] Robert Wauchope, d. 1862; captain, R.N., 1814; in Thalia, 46, at Cape of Good Hope
1834–8; admiral 1861. Presumably in correspondence with *Clerk.
[2] See 18–25 Jan. 36.   [3] 'à présent' deleted.
[4] 'Long and painful conversation on the marriage, because I do not wish to be present,
unless I can have more light than has so far been accorded me. Unworthy brother though
I am, it seems to me that I am not as unworthy in doing my duty as I would be in betray-
ing my beliefs.'
[5] C. Forster, ed. Thirty Year's Correspondence between John *Jebb . . . and Alexander
*Knox, 2v. (1834).
[6] 'But may God Almighty bless the letter that left here last evening.'
[7] Joseph Hoare Bradshaw, d. 1845, London banker.
[8] Fragment on latter in Add MS 44726, f. 17.

Th. 14.

Off by Mail at 7 to Lpool. A terrible day: cd only get inside at Langholm.

15.

Lpool 7¾ A.M. breakf. with dear Rn.—calls—espec[iall]y on the [Hugh] J[ones]s—Mr Staniforth—Mr Moss—Mrs Grant—wrote to Mr G—and read Innes's letter on the W.I., an useful & sensible production, I think.[1] Dined with the [Hugh] J[ones]s[2]—music in evg: e questa prima prova fu piacevole. ed anche nelle cose della Fede trovai di contento.[3]

16. Sat.

Rode to Seaforth and to Ince—calls—dined at Otterspool—began Hull on Eccl. property.[4] wrote to H.J.G.—Pulford—Sir R. Peel.

17. Sunday.

Heard Mr Macneile[5] mg & evg: & on the whole much delighted, specy in mg. Services together 5½ hours. Breakf. with Steuart. Wrote to J.N.G. wrote on Church &c.

18. M.

8¼–6¾. Pier to Fazeley[6] by Woodside Mail. Found only Ld Harrowby at Drayton:[7] we dined *five*. wrote some notes of Conv. heard[8]—and read Hayward's Preff. to the Faust.[9]

19. T.

Party increased by arrivals of Ld G. Somerset, Mr Goulburn, Mr Herries, Sir H. Hardinge. began Lingard's England.[10] wrote to W.K. Hamilton—Doyle (criticm)—and Rn G. Sir R. [Peel] rather contracts in freedom of convn as the party expands.

20. W.

radunanza nella sala del maestro[11] per provar i sentimenti della compagnia con rispetto al 4to del mese prossimo: in quali generalmente caddero nel

---

[1] J. Innes, 'Letter to the Lord *Glenelg . . . on the Working of the New System in the British West India Colonies' (1835).

[2] In Rodney Street.

[3] 'and this first trial was agreeable. And I also found some satisfaction in matters of Faith.' Last three words instead of 'si trovò di aver gioja', 'pleasure was found'.

[4] Edward Hull, *The Institution and Abuse of Ecclesiastical Property* (1831).

[5] Hugh *McNeile, 1795–1879, evangelical; priest at Liverpool 1834–60; canon of Chester 1845–68; dean of Ripon 1868–75.

[6] Just south of Tamworth, on the Staffordshire–Warwickshire boundary.

[7] *Peel's place by Tamworth.

[8] In Add MS 44777, ff. 23–8; part in Morley, i. 132–3.

[9] A. *Hayward, *Faust . . . translated into English prose* (1833).

[10] John *Lingard, *A History of England*, 8v. (1819–30).

[11] Instead of 'oste' ('host').

15—II.

senso medesimo, rifiutando[1] la parte di quei che attaccano; stanno per aspettar.[2] D. of Wellington,[3] Ld Jersey, Ld Villiers,[4] Ld & Ly Lincoln, arrived afterwards. (L'intrattenimento fu lungo e libero: io mi tacqui.)[5]— wrote to J.N.G.—Blackwood. read Lingard—R.C. morality[6]—& Ld Hollands Parlty Talk.[7]

21. Th.

Wrote to Sir G. Clerk: Mr Grant: walk with Lincoln & Mr Goulburn. read Petronius, &c—began Bossuet's Variations[8]—paper—Sugden's letter to Ld Melbourne[9]—wrote notes.

22. Fr.

Wrote to Selwyn—Mr G[10]—Rn G—Mrs Wallace. read Petronius. Appuleius. Bossuet. Marmion. paper.

23.

Dante Paradiso I.II.—Appuleius. wrote to Glynne. Caparn. Mr Grant. walk with Lincoln & an int[erestin]g conv. on church matters. Messrs Perceval[11] & Sitwell[12] dined here: may we be like them in truth & singleness of heart. Bossuet. papers. Bossuet. Conv. on Univv. after dinner.

24.

mg Drayton Church with the family: aft Tamworth Church alone. At lunch, conv. on amusements: which was intercepted by time, or wd have been very interesting. Neither L[incoln], Lady L., nor Lady P[eel], showed any of that uncharitable spirit which often appears in attacks upon uncharitableness. read Bible. Perceval's paper[13]—& Bossuet, some of whose

---

[1] Instead of 'scegliendo' ('choosing').

[2] 'Meeting in the Chief's room to sound out the feelings of the company about the 4th of next month [when parliament was to reassemble]: on which they were generally agreed, holding back from the aggressive party; they fixed on waiting.'

[3] See Morley, i. 133–4.

[4] George Augustus Frederick Villiers, 1808–59, styled Viscount Villiers till he succ. as 6th earl of Jersey 1859; Eton and Christ Church; tory M.P. Rochester 1830, Minehead 1831, Honiton 1832–5, Weymouth 1837–42, Cirencester 1844–52; m. 1841 *Peel's da. Julia 1821–93, who re-m. 1865 Charles Brandling; who d. 1894.

[5] 'The conversation was long and free; I kept silent.'

[6] Pamphlet on doctrines taught at Maynooth (1836).

[7] 'Parliamentary Talk: or, The Objections to the Late Irish Church Bill, considered in a letter to a friend Abroad. By a disciple of *Selden.' (1836).

[8] *Histoire des Variations des Églises Protestantes*, 2v. (1688).

[9] E. B. *Sugden, 'A Letter to Viscount *Melbourne on the Present State of The Appellate Jurisdiction of the Court of Chancery and House of Lords' (1835).

[10] Bassett, 30–31.

[11] Arthur Philip *Perceval, 1799–1853, 5th s. of 2nd Lord Arden; royal chaplain from 1826, tractarian author.

[12] Perhaps William Hurt Sitwell, 1803–65, of Barmoor Castle, Northumberland, b.-in-law to Lady Smith Wright.

[13] Among *Perceval's large output, probably his *Letter* to *Peel (1835) on the state of the church.

theology seems to me very good. Bid goodbye at night with regret: the blessing of God be upon this house.

25.

Bossuet. Breakft; Mail to Lpool: Rn G.s[1] 9 P.M. read letters & papers: wrote to Mr G.[2] Read Hull's Eccl. property.

26.

Wrote to Hamilton. Williams. Mr Blundell. calls. read Lingard. paper. dined at Mr Bright's.[3] music.

27. W.

J.N.G. & T.G. came. dined at Mr [Hugh] Jones's. singing.—I am sure poor M.E. [Jones] must have been bored. calls. read Mr Jones's Sermon:[4] & Lingard. wrote on Rn. C. & Ch. Eng.m[5] wrote to Sir R.P.[6]

28. Th.

We saw the marriage take place soon af[te]r 9. At 10¼ they left Lpool. Would to God che potessi[7] pel loro benessere[8] alzar le sante mani e pregare da cuore affetuoso verso Iddio: ma la mia, sia talquale, e uscita almeno dalla bocca.[9] Dinner at Mr. J[ones]s conv. with P. Serjeantson[10] on their religious feelings & position. read Lingard. Wrote to Mr G: notices to the newspapers: called on Mr Jones (Rev) long conv. with his son.[11]

29. Fr.

T.G. & J.N.G. went. Wrote to Mr Blundell—Caparn—Thorpe—Glynne—Bradshaw. read Lingard—calls. wrote to Manson.[12] Mrs Wallace.

30. Sat.

Packed. finished Lingard Vol 1. Wrote to R.G.—H.J.G.—&—4 to Hawar-

---

[1] In Abercromby Square.
[2] Bassett, 31–32.
[3] Samuel Bright, merchant, lived in Rodney Street.
[4] Perhaps archdeacon *Jones on Rom. xiv. 17, 'The Characteristics of True Religion' (1834).
[5] Untraced.
[6] Describing how *O'Connell was shouted down that day at the Liverpool merchants' news room; in Parker, ii. 326–7.
[7] 'offrire' (offer) here deleted.
[8] 'la preghiera di' (the prayer of) here deleted.
[9] 'that I had been able to lift up my hands to bless them, and to pray for them with an affectionate heart; but my [blessing], such as it was, at least got out of my mouth.'
[10] Peter, partner with T. S. Gladstone in Gladstone & Serjeantson, Liverpool brokers.
[11] Perhaps (among seven sons) John Herbert Jones, 1823–1908, of Jesus, Cambridge; curate of St. Andrew's 1847–65, and vicar of St. John's Waterloo, Liverpool, 1865–1901.
[12] Alexander Manson, Birkenhead merchant.

den Castle.[1] read Southey's Pr. & Pr. of Socy.[2]—read thro' Knapp's Poems, wh leave a mournful impression.[3] made up monthly accounts.

31. Sunday.

Ch mg & aft. H.G.[4] preached well. Music in evg. read through Ellison's book "R.C. truths & Prot. Errors"[5]—a delicate subject, to the execution of wh he seems unequal. Wrote to Uncle D.—Read &c.

Monday February One.

Wrote to Mr G. Came to Chester 5 m[inutes] after the Mail had gone: got on by Albion. outside—all night: frost.[6]

2.

Rain. Arrived at Albany 11¾.[6] dined in B. Square. Horrid confusion of papers: what a science it requires to keep them in manageable order! my eyes being somewhat inflamed did not attempt reading: at Carlton: many friends: wrote to Hay (ejected!)[7]—to Mr G.—A. Williams—Mrs Hagart— Mr Penfold[8]—T.G.

3.

finished Short's good pamphlet on Natl Education.[9] read Barnes on H. of L—Abercrombies Inaugural Address[10] at Ab[erdee]n—& "Appeal" to the Heads of the Church[11]—wrote to Mr Gordon—Mr G—J.N.G.—W.K. Hamilton—Aunt J.—Pusey (Rev EB)[12]—H. Thompson—Charriere—dined in B. Square: but much of my day went in doing battle agt my letters & papers over wh by midnight I began to gain some slight advantage.

4. Thursday.

At Sir R. Peel's—House 1–2¾, and 4¾–10¾. Voted in 243:284.[13] A good opportunity of speaking offered; but in my weakness I did not use it. How

---

[1] Version in Morley, i. 134. Hawarden was the Glynnes' seat, 6 miles west of Chester; eventually the diarist's own.

[2] *Southey, Sir Thomas *Moore: or, Colloquies on the Progress and Prospects of Society (1829).

[3] R. Crawfurd ed. H. H. Knapp, Tempora Subseciva (1835). Cp. 6 Dec. 34.

[4] Henry Glynne, 1810–72, Sir Stephen*'s b.; whig M.P. Flint 1831–2; rector of Hawarden 1834, canon of St. Asaph 1855.

[5] N. T. Ellison, Protestant Errors and Roman Catholic Truths (1829); a tale, advocating peaceful coexistence with Rome.

[6] Version in Morley, i. 134.   [7] Cp. 30 May 36.

[8] Perhaps John Sandys Penfold; lived near Holborn; of Lincoln's Inn, 1819.

[9] T. V. *Short, 'National Education, and the Means of Improving It' (1835).

[10] J. *Abercrombie, 'Address delivered in . . . Marischal College, Aberdeen, on . . . his Installation as Lord Rector of the University' (1835).

[11] 'An Address to . . . the Archbishops and Bishops of the Church of England . . . by a Low Churchman' (1835), on church discipline.

[12] Cp. H. P. *Lidden, *Pusey, i. 369; on successor to *Burton, who had just d.

[13] *William IV opened new session; deb. on address; amdt. of *Peel's on Irish municipalities defeated. H xxxi. 22; 104.

entire[1] even for physical nerve is the dependence upon one above: how well that is should be so: & that the default & humiliation should be keenly felt, when the posture of the mind has not been true towards him. read Polish Appeal[2]—papers—state of Irish poor. wrote to Mr G—Mr Blundell— Mr Denby.[3]

5. Fr.

Breakf in B.S.—conv. with [T.V.] Short—arranging papers: some dawn of method. wrote to Anstice—Mr Finlay—Grant—T.G.—Miss Joy—House $4\frac{3}{4}$–$8\frac{1}{4}$.[4] read 1st Poor Law Commn Report—& Lond. Rev. on D'Israeli & Aristocracy.[5]

6. Sat.

Convv. with Bp Exeter (Ir[ish] Ed[ucation]) & Lady Canning. read "Catholicism in Austria",[6] & Stapylton's Canning.[7] wrote to T.G.—J.N.G. —B. Harrison—R.G.

7. Sunday.

Sacrament. St James's mg & aft.—read Tyndale on the Sacts[8]—began Sumner's St John (aloud)[9] & J. Taylor's Holy Living.[10] Went into the Newman St Chapel. Heard a discourse of wh part was excellent. Wrote.

8. M.

Home arrangements. Calls. Doyle with me. convv. with Perceval. Young. Sir L. Cole.[11] dined in B. Square. read "Cath[olicis]m in Austria" & began Sir J. Walsh[12]—wrote to Mr G—T.G.—Lawton—Grant. Dies nigerrimus.[13]— House.[14]

9. T.

at meeting of Conserve Socy.[15] Calls. read Cathm in Austria—Pt of Lewis's

[1] Instead of 'entirely'.
[2] Possibly 'Lays of Poland', a sympathetic verse pamphlet (1836).
[3] Perhaps Thomas Denby, attorney in Old Jewry. Version of extracts in Morley, i. 134.
[4] Deb. on address ctd.: H xxxi. 116.
[5] London Review, ii. 533 = Westminster Review, xxxi. 533 (January 1836) strongly hostile to B. *Disraeli, Vindication of the English Constitution (1835).
[6] F. dal Pozzo, Catholicism in Austria, . . . with a dissertation upon the rights and duties of the English Government with respect to the Catholics of Ireland (1827).
[7] A. G. *Stapleton, The Political Life of George *Canning (1831).
[8] William *Tyndale, A Brief Declaration of the Sacraments (1550?).
[9] J. B. *Sumner, A Practical exposition of the Gospel According to Saint John (1835).
[10] (1650).
[11] Sir Galbraith Lowry *Cole, 1772–1842, soldier; commanded 27th Inniskillings at Maida 1806, and 4th division at Albuera, Salamanca, Roncesvalles; G.C.B.; M.P. Fermanagh 1803–23; governed Mauritius 1823–8, and Cape 1828–33; general 1830.
[12] Sir J. B. *Walsh, Chapters of Contemporary History (1836).
[13] 'A very black day.'
[14] Agriculture; lighthouses. H xxxi. 147.
[15] Cp. 13 Apr. 36.

Report on Irish Immigrant poor,[1] & Tetley's[2] ir[r]it[a]t[in]g serm. on the atonement. wrote to Mr G—Mr Henderson[3]—Mr Denby—Sir H. Willock[4]—Mrs Bartlett—Mr Fox.[5] House 4–9½. div. in 93:171.[6]

10. Wed.

Mr Tallents here most of mg on Newark matters. In city abt Mrs Hagart's deed, &c. Mordaunt, Phillimore, J.M.G., F.H. D[oyle], to dinner: wrote to R.G., Mr G.—Mr Fox—Finished Sir J. Walsh's very able book, & read Oastler's letter to Abp York.[7]

11. Th.

T.G. & Mayow to breakf. T.G. to cold dinner. finished Lewis's Report—read Labouchere's Report.[8] Newark Statement on the Union[9]—finished Pozzo's Cathm in Austria: very curious if faithful. Wrote to Mr G—Mr Menzies—Mayor of Newark—Vicar of Nk[10]—Maurice—Mr Harrison—Serj. Wilde—House 4—9.[11] wrote vss "to grey mare".[12]

12. Fr.

T.G., Ross, & W.R.F., to breakfast. read Stapylton Ch. I & part of Stockenstrom's Evidence.[13] wrote to Dr Duncan—Ewing—Mr G—Aunt J—dined in B. Square—House bef. din[ner]. & 10–11¼.[14] Thankful it is not proposed to make marriage a civil contract—read Quarty on Bonnelier.—Saw divers persons.

13. Sat.

T.G. & WRF to breakft, Essendo partito il primo, ci intratenemmo della già tanto ventilata questione. Adesso è finita, è spenta. Sia fatta la gran

---

[1] Report by G. C. *Lewis published as appendix to the first report of the Irish Poor Inquiry Commission, *PP* 1836 xxxiv. 427.

[2] A slip of the pen. J. Ketley, 'Scriptural Views concerning the . . . Atonement' (1836), a sermon on Gen. ix. 17.

[3] Perhaps John Henderson, 1796–1858, collector; lived off Russell Square.

[4] Sir Henry Willock, 1788?–1858; chargé d'affaires in Persia 1814–27; kt. 1827; director, East India Co., 1838, chairman in 1844.

[5] John Fox, Newark attorney.

[6] Against providing M.P.s with free parliamentary papers: *H* xxxi. 224.

[7] Richard *Oastler, 'A Letter to the Archbishop of York' (1836); on creating a 'true Church of the People'.

[8] Probably *PP* 1835 xix, on timber duties. Henry *Labouchere, 1798–1869, whig M.P. St. Michael's 1826–30, Taunton 1830–59, was vice-president 1835–9, and president 1839–41, 1847–52, of board of trade, and Irish secretary 1846–7; cr. Lord Taunton 1859.

[9] Untraced; probably poor law business.

[10] John Garrett Bussell, 1804?–74; of Trinity College, Oxford; vicar of Newark 1835, and canon of Lincoln 1859.

[11] Carlow election; misc. business. *H* xxxi. 272.

[12] Add MS 44726, f. 1.

[13] *PP* 1836 vii. 49 ff. (Sir) Andries Stockenstrom, 1792–1864; lieut.-governor at Cape 1836–9; cr. bart. 1840.

[14] Orange societies; registration of births and marriages. *H* xxxi. 332; 367.

volontà.[1]—read paper—Stapylton—made indexes to music—at Milbank Commee—dined at Lady Canning's. Liked Mrs. C.[2] Glad to see Lincoln there. Wrote to Mr Ward: wishing to have *one* work of private charity on my hands.[3]

14. Sunday.

Gravi pensieri tratti dal affari di jeri.[4] wrote on Hypocrisy. on worship:[5] attempted to explain this to the servants at night. read Newman Serm— and J. Taylor. also Trench's Poems.[6]

15. M.

W.R.F. twice here. Inaspettata vicenda. e dubbj rinnovati. Cosa dirò? μέγας ἔν τουτοις θεός.[7] read Hampden & Mr G's pamphlet. Calls. wrote to Mr G. Draft & letter to WRF. House 6½ 11¾. Div.[8]

16. T.

T.G. to breakf. got good advice from him. Saw WRF.—wrote to Mr G— Mr Menzies. read Report of Ed. Trustees[9]—& finished Hampden's pamphlets.[10] Also Ed. Rev. on Cape. paper. Commee & House 2¾–9½.[11]

17. W.

Breakf. with W.R.F. in rebus jam notis[12] partim versabamus.[13] Church: Mr Ward preached very well, R. & M.E.G. came. read Stockenstrom's Evidence—& Stapylton. wrote to J.N.G. Caparn—Mr Bussell. Dined with the Lush[ington]s. House before & after[14] —singing.

18. Th.

read Stapylton—Newman on Hampden[15]—& pt of Ion (2d Ed.)—Col. Wade

[1] 'The first having left, we spoke of the question that has been so much aired already. Now it is finished—it is extinct. May the great Will be done.' But see 15, 18, 24 Feb. 36.
[2] *Canning had m., five months before, Charlotte Stuart, d. 1861, da. of Sir Charles, Lord *Stuart de Rothesay; with her sister, subject of Augustus *Hare, *Two Noble Lives* (1893).
[3] Cp. i. xxx above.
[4] 'Serious thoughts, drawn from the business of yesterday.'
[5] In Add MS 44726, f. 19.
[6] Extracts in Morley, i. 134. R. C. *Trench, *Story of Justin Martyr* (1835).
[7] 'An unexpected change, and doubts renewed. What can I say? God is in these things great.'
[8] *Roebuck failed to carry motion for inquiry into Mauritius courts: *H* xxxi. 429. John Arthur *Roebuck, 1801–79, radical M.P. Bath 1832–7, 1841–7, Sheffield 1849–68, 1874–9; felled *Aberdeen's govt. 1855; Q.C. 1843, P.C. 1878.
[9] Cp. 19 Dec. 35, 9 Apr. 36.
[10] Renn Dickson *Hampden, 'Observations on Religious Dissent' (1834); 'A Postscript to Observations on Religious Dissent' (1835).
[11] Placed on cttee, on aborigines in colonies; house discussed Carlow election. *H* xxxi. 445.
[12] Instead of 'usitatis' (customary).
[13] 'we were occupied partly with the matters already noted.'
[14] New house; Shannon navigation. *H* xxxi. 501; 508.
[15] J. H. *Newman, *Elucidations of Dr. *Hampden's Theological Statements* (1836).

with me > 2 hours.[1] wrote to Mr G—B. H[arrison]—House 5½–6½. & 10½–12. T.G., R.G., M.E.G., dined with me. singing.—With WRF again: no progress.

19.

A day of solemn but precious recollection.[2]—Stapylton. pt of Introdn to Cape Narrative.[3] Calls. dined in B. Square. Singing. Col Wade with me. & Cape [aborigines] Commee 1–3.20. wrote to Charriere. Larkins.

20. Sat.

Stapylton—Introdn to Cape Narrative—Hay here—trying to analyse Hampden a little—& write on him: but I fear in vain. Wrote to Mr G., Harrison, Jane Robn.[4] Accounts of Uncle C. still most indifft. dined at Mr B. Baring's.[5]

21. Sunday.

The Sacrament at 8.—Mr Wigram & Mr Ward. wrote. read Jer[emy] Taylor. Bossuet's Variations—"Fundamental Reform"[6]—Sumner's St John aloud. Tea at T.G.s.

22. M.

finished Stapylton Vol 1. Read Gurney's[7] 'New Poor Law the Poor man's friend'. Commee 12–1½. then Sir R. Peel's on Orange Lodges—then Carlton meeting. Wrote to Mr Gurney—Caparn—Mayor Nk—Mr G—Jacobson—conv. on Church extension with Sandon, Ashley, Pusey, Plumptre,[8] Finch. House 8½–12.[9]

23. T.

Ld Sandon & Pusey to breakft, & Ashley also to conv. on Church Extension. Wrote to Mr G., Mr Finlay. read Stapylton. House 4½–6½ and 10–1¾.[10]

24. W.

read Stapylton: Ion Ed. 2 (with deepened and riper pleasure (finished)) and Coleridge's Letters, mischievously Edited.[11] dined at Lady Hope's. Calls—

[1] Thomas F. Wade, lieut.-col. 1815; on half pay.
[2] Of his sister's death in 1829.
[3] *Introductory Remarks to a Narrative of the Irruption of the Kafir hordes* . . . (1835), by the editor of the *Grahamstown Journal* [Robert Godlonton].
[4] Miss J. C. Robertson.
[5] Henry Bingham Baring, 1804–69, tory and lib.-cons. M.P. Callington 1831, Marlborough 1832–68.
[6] 'Fundamental Reform of the Church Establishment' (1836), anonymous pamphlet.
[7] Probably slip of pen for J. Godley (1836?).
[8] John Pemberton Plumptre, 1791–1864, Canterbury banker, whig M.P. Kent 1832–52.
[9] Tithes commutation bill, 2°: *H* xxxi. 691.
[10] Carlow election, and Orange lodges. *H* xxxi. 762; 779.
[11] Thomas *Allsopp ed. *Letters, Conversations and Recollections of S. T. *Coleridge*, 2v. (1836). But see five notes later.

wrote. Wrote to Mr G—Conv. with W.R.F. συμπεραντικώτακτον.[1] Mare came up.

25. Th.

read Stapylton—Locke [on] U[nderstanding] (began B.IV)—Dante Paradiso I, II (+)—wrote to Larkins—Hamilton—dined in B. Square. House 5¼–6¼ & afr dinner.[2]

26. Fr.

Heard of Uncle Colin's death on Monday.[3] His will had bowed so often to the Lord, that I trust he is in peace. May that work proceed in us, merciful and blessed Father.

Wrote to S. MKenzie (Rosehaugh)—Mr G.—Aunt J—Pusey. read Stapylton. saw Mr Ward. Aborigines Commee 1–4.[4] House 4¾–6½ and 10–12.[5]

(25 Th. read some of Coleridge's Remains—very mischievously edited?)[6]

27. Sat.

Breakf. at C.G.[7]—read Stapylton—and Paradiso III, IV—veramente deliziosi.[8] At Hatchard's. 1–3 Church meeting. 3–5 Penitentiary. Wrote to Mr G.—Dr Chalmers—T.G.—W.R.F.—Hay—dined at Ld Salisbury's.

28. S.

Mr Ward & Bp. read Holy Living—Hist des Var[iations][9]—Newman's Serm—Sumner aloud—wrote—put some lines of Paradiso IV into blank verse[10]—tea at 6 C.G.

29. M.

—breakf at C.G.—saw them off at 9. Final conv. with W.R.F.—tête a tête dinner with Sir R. Inglis.—This is the day of my Uncle's funeral. Commee & House 1–6¼ and 9.40–12.[11] wrote to Mr G—T.G. Huddlestone— Cole—R.G.—read Locke—Stapylton. monthly accts.

Tuesday March One.

Finished Stapylton Vol 2—Introdn to Kafir narrative—read Paradiso V, VI.—wrote to Mr G—R.G.—dined in B. Square—saw Col. Wade. Aborigines Comm. 1–3¾.[12] wrote on Public Speaking.

[1] 'It is wholly concluded.' But see 29 Feb., 5, 9, 29 Mar. 36.
[2] Flogging; election business. H xxxi. 884; 896. [3] Colin Robertson.
[4] Interrogating Stockenstrom: PP 1836 vii. 225.
[5] Affairs of Spain: H xxxi. 952.
[6] This late entry heavily scored through. H. N. *Coleridge ed. S. T. *Coleridge, Literary Remains, 2v. (1836; 2 more v. 1838).
[7] John *Gladstone by now lived, with Thomas, at 6 Carlton Gardens.
[8] 'Truly delicious'. [9] Bossuet.
[10] In Add MS 44726, f. 24. [11] Irish municipalities, 2°: H xxxi, 1019.
[12] Again interrogating Stockenstrom: PP 1836 vii. 236.

2. Wed.

Heard to my deep sorrow of Anstice's death on Monday. His friends—his young widow—the world can spare him ill: so says at least the flesh.

Stapylton. Paradiso VII, VIII. calls. rode. wrote to Mr G—dined at Ld Ashburton's. House before, & 10.50–12½.[1] Stat[istica]l Socy's proceedings. wrote to [blank.][2]

3. Th.

Saw young Farrer[3] & P. Wood[4] on yesterday's sad subject. Mrs A's letters are wonderful. Such is Divine power. Commee on Compn 1.15–3.50. dined—by mistake! at Mr Hallam's (for 10th). wrote to Mr G.—read Stapylton—Locke—saw Taylor. Vss on A's death.[5]

4. Fr.

Commee 1–3¾.[6] read Stapylton. Paradiso IX & pt of X.—saw Phillimore (on A.s death) & Canning on Hull.[7] dined at Mr Colvile's—wrote—wrote to Mr Crampern—Serj. Wilde—Manning—Mr G.

5. Sat.

Read Stapylton—Paradiso pt of X & XI—Dodsworth No 1.[8]—meeting at Sir R.P's at 12. At my own rooms (1–3½) on Mr Gordon's Appeal.[9] Lds Chichester,[10] Galloway,[11] Lorton,[12] Sir O. Mosley,[13] Sir H. Verney, Mr Plumptre, Mr Hardy, Mr Coates,[14] Mr Wilks,[15] Mr [blank]. dined at Mr B. Baring's. Wrote to Mr G. and Hamilton. Saw WRF: pressed my point.

6. Sunday.

The Sacrament. Mr Wigram & Mr Ward preached.—Milnes here.—Tea in B. Square. Wrote.[16] read Jer. Taylor. Dodsworth Nos II, III. Sumner aloud.

---

[1] Misc. business: *H* xxxi. 1132.   [2] Version of extracts in Morley, i. 134.

[3] Perhaps Thomas Henry *Farrer, 1818–99, permanent secretary, board of trade, 1865–86, cr. bart. 1883, baron 1893; then still at Eton.

[4] Peter Almeric Leheup Wood, 1816–97, canon of Middleham 1844.

[5] Version of extracts, dated 2 March, in Morley, i. 134; verses in Add MS 44726, ff. 25–7.

[6] Again interrogating Stockenstrom: *PP* 1836 vii. 250.

[7] Another possible seat.

[8] W. *Dodsworth, *Discourses on the Lord's Supper* (1835).

[9] Presumably some Protestant Association business.

[10] Henry Thomas *Pelham, 1804–86, 3rd earl of Chichester 1826; cavalryman and patron of good works.

[11] Randolph Stewart, 1800–73, tory M.P. Cockermouth 1826–31, 9th earl of Galloway 1834.

[12] Robert Edward King, 1773–1854, soldier; Irish M.P. 1796–1800; acquitted of murder 1798; cr. Lord Erris 1800, Viscount Lorton 1806; general 1830.

[13] Sir Oswald Mosley, 1785–1871, 2nd bart. 1798; M.P. Staffordshire 1832–7; great-great-gf. of fascist.

[14] Perhaps Thomas Coates, of Coates & Sherwood, Lincoln's Inn Fields.

[15] John *Wilks, 1765?–1854, radical M.P. Boston 1830–7; or possibly his son and namesake,* d. 1846, swindler.

[16] On Christian truth: Add MS 44726, ff. 30–9.

7. M.

House at one ½—again 5¼–7¾ and 9.20–12¾.[1] at pt of Anc. Music rehearsal.
Wrote to H.J.G.—Mr Pusey—Harrison—finished Stapylton—read Colquhoun No 2.[2]

8. T.

recd letter from Lady F. Wrote to her[3]—Fox (Newark)—Dr Pusey.—read
Bickersteth's "Progress of Popery"[4]—Paradiso XII, XIII.—dined with
Sir R. Inglis to talk over the Oxford matter.[5] House at 1—and 7¾–3¾.
Stanley made a noble speech. Voted in 243:307! for abol[itio]n of Ir[ish]
Corpp.[6]—Pendulums & nothingarians all against us.[7]—Went to visit the
Natl Schools with Lady F. Egerton[8] & the Rector.

9. Wed.

Locke. Paradiso XIV, XV. dined at Uncle D.s. Anc. Mus. Concert—& Mrs
Ede's[9]—rode—wrote to Ld Sandon[10]—Mr Auld[11]—Harrison—Rn G.—Dry
—Williams— Aunt J—Commee 1¼–3¼. Saw Bp of Exr on R.D.Pp[12]—Saw
W.R.F.—finalmente.[13]

10. Th.

read Colquhoun's 2nd & able treatise—wrote a long letter to Mr G. on the
F[arquhar] matter.[14] wrote to Mr Kempe[15]—dined at Mr Hallam's. read
Paradiso XVI—hard. rode. House 5½–6¾.[16]

11. Fr.

Brownrigg's Evidence.[17] "Ministers of 98 & 36"[18]—Paradiso XVII & pt of

[1] Irish municipal reform: H xxxi. 1301.
[2] P. *Colquhoun, A Treatise on the Wealth, Power, and Resources, of the British Empire, 2 ed. (1815).
[3] 'and' here deleted.
[4] E. *Bickersteth, Testimony of the Reformers, with Introductory Remarks on the Progress of Popery (1836).
[5] R. D. *Hampden's appointment to the regius chair of divinity was making a stir.
[6] H xxxii. 119.
[7] These three sentences, dated a month early, are in Morley, i. 134.
[8] Harriet Catherine, née Greville, 1800–66, gd. of 3rd duke of *Portland; m. Lord Francis *Egerton 1822.
[9] Mrs. John Ede of Upper Harley Street?
[10] On the *Hampden affair: Add MS 44355, ff. 31–2.
[11] Robert Auld, secretary, Millbank penitentiary.
[12] On ecclesiastical revenues and duties; cp. PP 1836 xxxvi. 61.
[13] 'finally'. Cp. 4 Aug. 36.
[14] Part in Magnus, 28.
[15] Perhaps Edward Kempe, 1778–1858, priest and benefactor.
[16] Timber duties: H xxxii. 138.
[17] John Studholme Brownrigg, 1786–1853, cons. M.P. Boston 1835–47; evidence untraced.
[18] Untraced pamphlet.

XVIII—delightful. Commee & House 1–4½.[1] dined at Taylors. Lady Salisbury's in evg. Wrote to Hume—J.N.G.—and Mr Adams (Leic[este]r).[2]

12. Sat.

Paradiso pt of **XVIII, XIX**. "Orange Lodges"[3]—Bossuet. Wrote to Pusey—Miss Fellowes[4]—Selwyn. dined at Sir E. Kerrison's. Speaker's levee. Lady Stanhope's party.[5] rode. Meeting at 11 in my rooms: to suspend proceedings. Saw Ld Sandon & Ld Mansfield on R.D.Pp.[6]

13. Sunday.

St Jas & St Giles evg. tea in B.S.—wrote[7]—read Jer. Taylor—Variations— Pusey on Bapt[8]—& Bp Sumner aloud.

14. M.

Talbot to breakfast. read Statl Soc. Proceedings—Paradiso XX, XXI— paper—Locke on U[nderstanding]—Commees 1–4¼. House after dinner.[9] rode. wrote to T.G.—J.N.G.—tea with the Gaskells.

15. T.

Selwyn, Milnes, A. Acland, here. Calls. rode. dined in B. Square—House early and 10½–12½—voted in 125:195 on Soap Tax[10]—read Carlow Evidence.[11]

16. W.

Carlow Evidence. Commee 1¼–3½. rode. read Locke. wrote to J.N.G.—Dr Pusey—Dr Chalmers—dined with T.G.—no house. paper. Henningsen.[12] wrote out Vss. Lindsay's letter to Ld Palmerston.[13]

17. Th.

2nd Church Report. Began Sir R. Steel's transl[ate]d Vol on state of RCm.[14]

---

[1] Misc. business: *H* xxxii. 201.

[2] John Adams, publican, secretary of Leicester Conservative society (see A. Temple Patterson, *Radical Leicester* (1954), 196–7).

[3] *PP* 1835 xvii.

[4] Miss M. A. Fellowes, Louisa's aunt.

[5] Catharine Lucy, d. 1843, née Smith, da. of 1st Lord *Carrington, m. 1803 Philip Henry Stanhope, 1781–1855, 4th Earl Stanhope 1816.

[6] See 9 Mar. 36.   [7] On serving God: Add MS 44726, f. 41.

[8] E. B. *Pusey, 'Scriptural Views of Holy Baptism', in *Tracts for the Times*, 67–69 (1835, reissued 1836).

[9] Irish corporations: *H* xxxii. 254.

[10] Voting for its repeal: ibid. 382.

[11] Aftermath of *O'Connell-Raphael affair. Cp. H. of C. *Journals* 1836, 37; and 3 Nov. 35.

[12] C. F. Henningsen, probably *Scenes from the Belgian Revolution* (1832).

[13] H. H. Lindsay, 'Letter to Viscount *Palmerston on British Relations with China' (1836).

[14] Richard *Steele, *The Romish Ecclesiastical History of late Years* (1714).

Commees 12¾–4. paper. wrote to Mr G—Mr J. Mackenzie.[1] rode. Dante Par XXII, XXIII. Malvagna[2]—Locke.

18. Fr.

Pamphlet on Hampden.[3] paper (with his Lecture)[4]—Paradiso XXIV, XXV—State of RCm.—Commee & House 2–5½. In two divv.[5] dined in B. Square. Wrote to Pusey—Miss Bartlett[6]—Mr G—Kirwan[7]—R.G.—M'Lach[lan].

19. Sat.

finished State of R.Cm—Paradiso XXVI, VII. paper. wrote to Mr G—Finlay—Pusey. City meeting (priv.) abt a Conserve Society 12½–2¼. Milbank Penity—rode—Duchess of Kent's party; home at 11¾, am[on]g the first.

20. Sunday.

Mr Wigram & Mr Ward. The Sacrament at 8 P.M. wrote. read Pusey's pamphlet on Hampden: (finished) Holy Living: Bossuet: Sumner aloud.—Tea in B. Square.

21. M.

Paradiso XXVIII. Locke.—Obss. on the working of the Emancipn Act[8]—& other W.I. papers. Commees 1–3¼. saw Sir G. Grey—wrote to him (& copy)—to Pusey—R.G.—much conv. about going to Oxford: prevented by Buxton's impending Motion.[9]

22.

Several here. Paradiso XXIX. wrote to Mr G—Mr Finlay. at Col. Office, & reading, & making notes and references on W.I. quest.—House 5¼–9¾—spoke 50 min: kindly heard, & I should thank God for being made able to speak even thus indiff[eren]tly.[10] paper—tea with T.G. & Ed. Fellowes.[11] At nt Paradiso XXX.

[1] Perhaps John Mackenzie of Torridon, d. 1852.
[2] 'Riva malvagia'; *Inferno*, iii. 107.
[3] [E. B. *Pusey], 'Dr. *Hampden's Theological Statements Compared' (1836). Cp. *Liddon, *Pusey, i. ch. xvi.
[4] Inaugural, delivered on previous day. Cp. 8 Mar. 36.
[5] Misc. business; a Lambeth suspension bridge bill, 2°, and a Macclesfield small debts bill, 3°. *Mirror*, i. 676 (1836) and *H* xxxii. 400.
[6] Presumably sis. or da. of former vicar of Newark.
[7] Perhaps Anthony Latouche Kirwan, 1803–68, dean of Limerick 1849.
[8] A British and Foreign Anti-Slavery Society pamphlet.   [9] See next entry.
[10] See Morley, i. 134 and note, and 145–6; this speech marked *Gladstone's advance into prominence in politics. He gave qualified support to *Buxton's proposal for cttee. to inquire into West Indian apprentices, to which both were appointed that day. *H* xxxii. 486. Cttee. report comprises *PP* 1836 xv.
[11] Edward Fellowes, d. 1879, Louisa's younger brother; 78th regiment, later 11th Hussars; major-general 1877.

23. Wed.

Late: having been awake last night till twn 4 & 5, as usual after speaking: how useful to make me feel the habitual unremembered blessing of sound sleep.[1]

read Paradiso XXXI, pt of XXXII. Locke. Bossuet.—Wrote to Mr G.— Mr Ramsay—Gl. Prot. Ass[2]—dined at Mayow's—Ancient Music—Hh [*sc.* Houses) of P[arliamen]t designs Exhibn.

24. Th.

Jacobson, Milnes, OBrien, to breakfast. finished the dear Paradiso. read Bossuet.

wrote to Mr G., H.J.G., Dr Chalmers, Harrison, Allen.
Commees 12–2½.—dined at Egerton's. rode.
Wrote twice to Burge (bis)[3]—heard from him satisfactorily.

25.

Wrote to Mr G and [blank].
read Bossuet—& W.I. papers on Jam[aic]a Assy.
rode to Richmond to the Selwyns & Tylers.
House 6–10[4]—Lady F. Egerton's (music) afterwards.

26. Sat.

Bruce & Capt. Beresford to breakf—Bp Exeter, Milnes, T.G., here—called on Ld Abn abt Colonial matters—dined at S. M'Kenzie's (Richmond)— fire in the Arcade at night.[5] calls. wrote to Mr G and Sherriffs—read Hampden's past & pr. statements[6] & Bossuet.

27. Sunday.

Mr Ward & Bp. wrote.[7] tea in B. Square. [H.] Taylor here. read Bossuet (began Vol 2.)—Pusey Bapt—Newman's Sermm.—attempted speakg to servv. on Eph. 2.13.

28. M.

W.I. meeting 3–5. Poor Law Office. House 5½–6¾ and 9–2. Voted in 199 : 260 agst Irish Corp. Bill.[8] wrote to Mr Thompson. Began Gerusalemme Liberata anew.[9] & read pt of Matheson on China Trade.[10] Church at 11.

---

[1] Version in Morley, i. 134–5.   [2] Untraced.
[3] William Burge, K.C., agent for Jamaica, who shortly gave evidence to W.I. cttee.
[4] Tithes commutation: *H* xxxii. 592.
[5] The Burlington Arcade. Cp. Add MS 44720, f. 42.
[6] E. B. *P[usey], 'Dr. *Hampden's Past and Present Statements Compared' (1836).
[7] Add MS 44726, f. 42, on sin and thankfulness.
[8] 3°: *H* xxxii. 747.
[9] Tasso.
[10] J. Matheson, *The Present Position and Prospects of the British Trade with China* (1836).

29. T.

Finished Matheson. Gerusalemme. Church at 11. dined in B.S.—rode.
House 5–6.[1] wrote a hurried paper on Church Extension. wrote to Sir G.
Grey—Burge—Mr G—Rn G.

30. Wed.

Hale on Regn & Marr. Bills.[2] Church at 11. Cons[ervativ]e meetg at 2½.
Gerusalemme. Wrote to Mr Tyler, Mr G, T.G.—dined at Sir R. Peel's.
began [blank] on Church Reform.[3] House 5–7.20.[4]

31. Thursday.

Church at 11.—dined at Lincoln's. rode. wrote to Mr G—Mr Godfrey. read
Ger. Lib. C.IV—(began) Le Bas's Life of Laud[5]—Locke on Understanding.
Bossuet.

April One. Good Friday.

The Communion at 8. Church at 11 (Mr Ward pr.)—St Giles's at 7 P.M (Mr
Tyler pr.). tea in B. Square.—Venerdi Santo—Bossuet—Pusey on Baptm—
Life of Laud—Gerus. C.V.

2. S.

Church at 11. Went with Miss Fenwick's[6] party to the Midd[lese]x Lunatic
Asylum.[7] rode. dined at B. Wall's.[8] read Le Bas' Laud—Gerus. C.VI.—
W.I. Agr[icultural] Comp[en]s[ation][9]—Sabb. Santo. wrote to H.J.G.—
Aunt J.—T.G.—Allen.

3. Sunday.

St James's mg & aft. The blessed Communion.—In evg attempted to
expl[ain] the Epistle. Might one drop of the heavenly dew descend. Best at
C[ommunio]n—tea in B. Square. Wrote.[10] read Dom[enica] Santa. Pusey—
Bossuet. J. Taylor (began Holy Dying)[11]—Laud—& Vaudois Catechisms.

4. M.

Cold.—read Gerus. C.VII—Laud's Life—Tacitus (began Annales)—Locke

---

[1] Appointment of magistrates: *H* xxxii. 762.
[2] W. *Hale, *Remarks on the Two Bills . . . entitled, A Bill for Registering Births, Deaths
and Marriages in England, . . . and a Bill for Marriages in England* (1836).
[3] 'A clergyman', *Fundamental Reform of the Church Establishment* (1835).
[4] Misc. business, incl. fitness for command of James Thomas *Brudenell, 1797–1868,
7th Earl *Cardigan 1837, who led light brigade at Balaclava. *H* xxxii. 846.
[5] C. W. *Le Bas, *Life of Archbishop *Laud* (1832).
[6] Isabella Fenwick, cousin of Henry *Taylor and friend of the William *Words-
worths.
[7] At Hanwell, 10 miles west of Charing Cross.
[8] In Berkeley Square.   [9] Cp. *PP* 1836 xv. 302–5.
[10] On Col. iii. 1–7, briefly, in Add MS 44726, f. 40.   [11] (1651).

—Bulwer's Rienzi[1]—Corinne—papers—" Protestant Confederate "[2]—**wrote** to Mr G, T.G, H.J.G.—rode. Several here.

5. T.

Gerus. C.VIII & pt of IX.—Tacitus, finished B.I.—Bossuet. Laud's Life. Locke. Corinne. Harrison here. dined in B[edford] S[quare].

6. W.

Gerus. pt of IX and X. Tacitus began B.II.—Locke—wrote to Mr G—Mr Tallents. Dined with the Harrisons. began Von Raumer's England.[3]

7. Th.

Gerus. C.XI.—finished Laud's Life. It is somewhat too Laudish, I think, tho right au fond. Dr Pusey here from 12 to 3 about Church Building. rode. dined in B. Square. Wrote to H. Thompson. T.G. & Louisa came. At night (11–12) perusing Taylor's proofs on Statesmanship, & writing notes, presumptuous enough.[4]

8. Fr.

Gerusalemme XII.—a wretched pamphlet on the 20 millions[5]—reperused Taylor's sheets. A batch of calls. wrote to Taylor—Masterman[6]—Ld Rosslyn,[7] Ld F.E[gerton], Ld Sandon, Sir R. I[nglis]—read Bossuet. dined at Taylor's. a keen intellectual exercise: and thus a place of danger, especially as it is exercise *seen*.[4]

9. Sat.

Spedding to breakfast. Gerus. XIII. wrote to J.N.G.—dined with T.G—singing—rode—read Bossuet—finished Locke on Underst[an]d[in]g—it appears to me on the whole a much overrated tho in *some* respects a very useful book—read King of Oude's letter in MS.[8] Milbank—saw Sir R. P[eel] ab[out] Dr. Ch[almers].[9]

---

[1] E. G. E. L. Bulwer(-*Lytton)'s historical novel (1835).

[2] *The Protestant Confederate, and Mirror of Truth*, a short-lived Dublin periodical (1836).

[3] F. L. G. von Raumer, *England im Jahre 1835* (Leipzig 1836).

[4] Version of extracts in Morley, i. 135, all under date of 7 April.

[5] 'The Question of Compensation to the Owners of Slaves calmly considered'.

[6] John Masterman, East India director.

[7] Sir James St. Clair *Erskine, 1762–1837, 6th bart. 1765; whig M.P. 1781–1805; fought at Toulon 1793, and Walcheren 1809; succ. as 2nd earl of Rosslyn 1805; recommended peninsula campaign 1806; long tory whip in lords; privy seal 1824–30, lord president 1834.

[8] Nasīr-ud-dīn Haidar, king of Oudh 1827–37, had written to *George IV to propose a college of English studies in Oudh.

[9] Presumably on Edinburgh professors' salaries: cp. 18 Dec. 35, &c. Version of extracts in Morley, i. 135.

10. S.

St James mg & aft. tea in B.S.—wrote on the F[arquhar]s. read Bossuet—Bible—Jer. Taylor—Pusey on Baptism—Sumner aloud with ampl[ificatio]n.

11. M.

Taylor to breakft—Gerusalemme XIV. wrote to Gaskell. Mr Godfrey—Mr Masterman. My father came, looking wonderfully well. rode. House 5–7¼.[1] long conv. with J. E. Gordon on Protestantism &c.—evg at 7 C.G.[2]—Von Raumer. wrote a paper.[3]

12. T.

Gerusalemme XV & began XVI.—Saw Ld Aberdeen. rode—wrote for Mr G. to R.G.—J.N.G.—G. G[illanders?]—for self to Jos. Simpson. rode. read Bossuet—Terrot's Serm. for G. Epl Socy,[4] wh seems able & good. House 5¼–7: various business.[5] quest. to Sir R.P.—dined at Serj. Merewether's[6]—singing—till past 12.

13. W.

Gerus. finished XVI—pt of XVII.—wrote to G.G. & J.N.G. for my father. read Bossuet. rode: calls. City Cons. Dinner at C.G. Theatre—a magnif. sight.[7] House 10½–12½—voted in 212:95 on Mil. Flogging.[8]

14. Th.

Gerusalemme—finished XVII, pt of XVIII. Bossuet—Jacobson's excellent Ordinn Sermon[9]—read to Mr G—arranging for dinner—wrote out vss.—wrote to Pusey—Blakesley— Mr G., Sir R. Inglis, Chr. Wordsworth, Uncle D., Mr Tyler, Mr Tallents, Villiers, to dinner.

15. Fr.

Gerusalemme: finished XVIII, pt of XIX.—Bossuet—Burge's letters &c. to Ld Glenelg.[10]—Taylor's 2nd lot of proofs. Three Committees 12¼–4. House 5–7 and 8½–9½. spoke briefly on Jama Bill.[11] rode. wrote to Burge—W.K. H[amilton]—Miss G—Mrs Hagart.

---

[1] Supply: *H* xxxii. 869.   [2] *Abercromby's.
[3] On ideas, writing and speaking: Add MS 44726, ff. 43–44.
[4] Untraced sermon by C. H. *Terrot.
[5] *H* xxxii. 893.
[6] In Whitehall Place.
[7] Over a thousand people attended the City of London Conservative Association's anniversary dinner in Covent Garden theatre.
[8] For its retention: *H* xxxii. 1009.
[9] W. *Jacobson, 'Clerical Duties' (1835).
[10] Untraced; no doubt on Jamaica.
[11] On difference of opinion between Jamaican legislature and governor. Slavery Abolition [Jamaica] bill, 3°: *H* xxxii. 1106.

16. Sat.

Gerusalemme finished XIX. Bossuet. D. of W's Evidence on Flogging[1]—
began Alford's poems[2]—a few vss[3]—rode—dined at Mr Smith Wright's—
wrote to Taylor—J.N.G.—& one for Mr G—Wrote on Taylor's proofs.

17. Sunday.

Rector & Bp.—tea in C.G.—Bible, Bossuet (finished)—the last Book seems
to me show well the R.C. cause & where it fails—Newman—Pusey on Bapt.
Sumner aloud amplified.

18. M.

Mr G's operation at 1. with exc[ellen]t success, thank God, thus far. Ethical
conv with Taylor in evg—read St Pancras' brief. Finished the Gerusalemme;
beautiful in its kind but how can its author be placed in the same category
of genius with Dante? Commees & House 12–3½ and 7–10.[4] Lady Antrobus's
concert—rode.

19. T.

Taylor to *breakf.* & *ethics*—Bp of Exeter, Mr Innes, Mr Boler, here—wrote
to Sir J. Macdonald. Commees 12–3½[5]—House 5–6½ and 10½–12.[6]—notes
abt Chalmers.[7] rode. read Mil. Flogging Report—& began Ld E. Fitzgerald[8]
aloud to my Father—who progresses as well as possible. Vss.[9]

20. Wed.

Mr G. still very well. Wrote to Blundell, Marjoribanks,[10] & Sherriffs for him,
& read to him from Moore's Ld E.F.—Hamilton here (abt F.s)—& Mr
Burnley[11] on W.I. matters. Commee 2–3¾. wrote to R.G.—H.J.G.—B.H.—
Mr Maclauchlan—Lady Sitwell—reading the Carlow Evidence, went as
Visitor to Milbank. Wrote Vss.

21. Th.

breakf at Charterhouse. Hamilton here again. reading the Carlow Evidence
—correcting proofs for the Mirror[12]—House 5–1½.[13]

[1] *PP* 1836 xxii. 346.
[2] H. *Alford, *Poems and poetical fragments* (1833).
[3] Add MS 44726, f. 48.
[4] Registration of voters: *H* xxxii. 1168.
[5] The W.I. apprenticeship cttee. held its first meeting; *Labouchere took the chair.
[6] Pension list: ibid. 1198.
[7] In Add MS 44563, f. 52; cp. 9 Apr. 36.
[8] Thomas *Moore, *The Life and Death of Lord Edward *Fitzgerald*, 2v. (1831).
[9] Perhaps sonnet at Add MS 44726, f. 47.
[10] Probably Campbell, d. 1840, an East India director; or his br. Edward Marjoribanks,
1776–1868, partner in Coutts's Bank.
[11] William Hardin Burnley, Trinidad proprietor.
[12] *Mirror* i. 991.
[13] Carlow election: *H* xxxiii. 22.

22. Fr.

Crotty's letter[1]—Doyle to breakf.—Mr Hale here on the Registrn Bill—wrote to Caparn—Commees $12\frac{1}{2}$–$3\frac{3}{4}$, dined at Lincoln's Inn, rode, House $6\frac{1}{4}$–3.—Anxious to speak on the subject, deterred by its proximity to a personal one, & the insufficiency of my position for the purpose.[2]

23. Sat.

some vss. Rd Cavendish here—Hale's pamphlet of 1834.[3] Reading letters to Mr G. & copied a long one for him. Commee & Milbank $1\frac{1}{4}$–4—rode—dined at the Westr Conserve dinner[4]—left at 11 to go to C[arlton] Gardens—I write this after midnight—thank God that his day of peace has come, after a weary & exhausting week.

24. S.

Mr Ward excellent mg—Bp Bristol[5]—not so—at the Abbey in aft.—dined at Linc. Inn. wrote Vss—read Alford—Dealtry & pt of Appx[6]—Newman aloud—twice with Mr G as usual.

25. M.

Alford. Prussian Church papers.[7] Bp Warburton. Ld E. Fitzgerald (to Mr G)—pt of Jones on Tithe Commutn[8]—wrote half a doz. notes & letters for Mr G—Commees & House 12–$3\frac{3}{4}$, and 5–$8\frac{1}{2}$.[9]

26. T.

Alford. wrote. finished Jones's able pamphlet. Commees 1–$3\frac{3}{4}$, House 6–$7\frac{1}{2}$[10]—rode—dined at Linc. Inn—read Ld E. Fitzgerald to Mr G—wrote to Hamilton, Caparn, Mr Burge, Mr M'Lauchlan, Aunt J.

27. W.

Alford. Saw Mr Finlay & others—Dealtry's Appx. Wrote two letters for Mr G—Ld Ed. Fitzgerald—Commee, Abbey & House $1\frac{3}{4}$–6, dined at Sir E. Kerrisons, music, House $10\frac{1}{2}$–12.[11]

[1] Michael Crotty, *Letter Addressed to the Rev. Dr. Murray, Titular Archbishop of Dublin* (1836).
[2] Carlow election: *O'Connell absolved. *H* xxxiii. 122.
[3] W. *Hale, 'Some remarks on the probable consequences of establishing a General Registry of Births and Legalising the Registration of Dissenters' Baptism' (1834).
[4] With the Westminster Conservative Association, in Willis's rooms, King Street; a party rally of some 400 gentlemen.
[5] Joseph Allen, 1770–1845; *Althorp's tutor 1830; bp. of Bristol 1834, of Ely, June 1836.
[6] W. *Dealtry, 'The National Church a National Blessing', 2 ed. (1835).
[7] *PP* 1836 xl. 315.
[8] Richard *Jones, *A Few Remarks on the Proposed Commutation of Tithes* (1833).
[9] Irish tithes; registration of voters. *H* xxxiii. 204; 230.
[10] Misc. business: *H* xxxiii. 309.
[11] Agricultural distress: ibid. 333.

28. Th.

Finished Alford. No Commee! Calls. Began Machiavel's Discorsi.[1] House
4–6. rode. read Ld Ed. Fitzgerald to Mr G—Tea at T.G.s—songs—paper—
wrote to Mr Reddie—Mr Coates.

29. Fr.

Discorsi[2]—began Canadian papers[3]—wrote for Mr G—read pt of Sandar's
Evidence[4] to him—dined at Sir S. Scott's—writing out verses—rode—
W.I. Commee 1–4.

30. Sat.

Discorsi. Finished the Pty Canada papers. Wrote for Mr G. to Mr Grant—
for self to Caparn, J.N.G. & Aunt J.—dined with Mr Nicholls[5]—monthly
accts—rode—Ld E. Fitzgerald—began another lot of H. T[aylor]'s proofs.

Sunday May One.

St James's. Communion. Rector & Mr Wigram preached. Breakfast & tea
with Mr G. read some of Matheson[6] to him. dined at Ln's Inn. Vss—
Finished Pusey. Two of Dodsworth's Sermm.—Sumner aloud (ampl.).

2. M.

Breakf. with Mr G. & reading to him. finished Taylor's "Statesman" &
notes upon it. Wrote to Caparn—Lefevre.[7] Commee 2–3¾—House 6–9¼.[8]
rode. dined at Lns Inn. Mrs Russell Ellice's Concert.[9] read Mr Nihill's
pamphlet on convocation.[10]

3. T.

Taylor to breakf. conv. on social ethics. wrote letters for Mr G.—Wrote to
A. Larkins,[11] thanks for his kind present—Commee 1–3¾, rode, House 5¼–7¾,
dined at Lady Hope's, House 10½–12½[12]—Lady Y. Buller's party—Miss
Doyle[13] told me a ballroom always brought to her the thought of death, & I
said it seemed to me the two thoughts ought to be deliberately placed
together & compared.—finished Mr Nihill's pamphlet.

[1] (1531).   [2] A note in Add MS 44726, f. 46.
[3] 'Correspondence relating to grievances in the Canadas, PP 1836 xxxix. 1.
[4] A. O. Saunders employed coolie labour in Mauritius (PP 1837–8 lii. 95).
[5] H. J. or James Nicholls, of Lincoln's Inn.
[6] J. Matheson and A. Reed, Visit to the American Churches, 2v. (1835).
[7] (Sir) John George *Shaw-Lefevre, 1797–1879, official; wrangler, 1818; on slave compensation, poor law, and South Australia commissions; clerk of the parliaments, 1855–75.
[8] Tithe commutation: H xxxiii. 501.
[9] Harriet, née Chaplin (an aunt of Henry *Chaplin's) m. Russell Ellice, b. 1799, br. of Edward*; lived in Portman Square.
[10] D. Nihill, 'Suggestions on the Revival of Ecclesiastical Assemblies in the Church of England' (1834).
[11] Son of M. A. Larkins?
[12] Lord *Brudenell's fitness again (cp. 30 Mar. 36): H xxxiii. 533.
[13] Diana Emily Flora Doyle, 1805–79, da. of 1st bart.

4. W.

read Von Raumer—Machiavel's Discorsi—Pusey's Earnest Remonstrance[1]
—paper by Mr Nicholls to Mr G. aloud, &c—rode—wrote to Mr Baxter,[2]
dined at Mr Sm[ith] Wrights—Lady Parke's[3] in evg.

5. Th.

Whewell's Preface to Macintosh.[4] Machiavelli. Verses.[5] wrote 4 or 5 letters,
& read Von Raumer &c. to Mr G.—dined at Bp of Exeter's—Lady Lansdowne's afterwards.

6. Fr.

Read Pusey's Appx. Dublin (R.C.) review[6]—Machiavelli. O. Cole here.
Commee 1–4. House $4\frac{1}{2}$–$5\frac{1}{2}$.[7] rode. dined at Uncle D's. House again—Ld
Carrington's—wrote to Taylor, Hicklin, S. Bartlett,[8] & two letters for Mr G.

7. Sat.

read Matheson & Reed—Machiavelli—Tacitus. wrote to [blank]. Milbank
1–$3\frac{3}{4}$. rode. dined at Ld Mayor's.[9] Lady Salisbury's afterwards, Introduced
to the Duchess of Gloucester.[10]

8. Sunday.

St James's. Mr Ward twice. Sumner aloud. Bossuet sur les Promesses de
l'Eglise.[11] Dodsworth (finished). Dealtry[12] (finished). Pamphlet on King's
College[13]—Nova Scotia.[14]

[1] E. B. *Pusey, 'An Earnest Remonstrance to the Author of the "Pope's Pastoral
Letter to Certain Members of the University of Oxford"' (1836).
[2] Probably Edward, 1791–1870, or his younger br. (Sir) David *Baxter, 1793–1872, cr.
bart. 1863; Dundee merchant princes.
[3] Cecilia Arabella Frances, née Barlow, m. 1817 (Sir) James *Parke, lord Wensleydale;
lived in Park Street, Grosvenor Square.
[4] Sir J. *Mackintosh, *Dissertation on the Progress of Ethical Philosophy . . . with a
preface by W. *Whewell* (1836).
[5] Add MS 44726, f. 49: 'Zur Gräfinn M[ontgelas]'—i.e. to Ernestine née von Arco,
d. 1838, wife of Max Josef, count von Montgelas, 1759–1838, Bavarian statesman.
[6] The quarterly *Dublin Review* had just begun publication in London, edited by
M. J. *Quinn.
[7] Budget: *H* xxxiii. 635.
[8] Unidentified.
[9] William Taylor *Copeland, 1797–1868, eminent potter; sheriff, 1828, alderman, 1829
and lord mayor, 1835; cons. M.P. Coleraine 1833–7, Stoke 1837–52, 1857–65.
[10] *Mary, 1776–1857, 4th da. and last surviving child of *George III; m. 1816 her
cousin *William Frederick, 1776–1834, soldier, who succ. 1805 to dukedoms of Gloucester
and Edinburgh.
[11] *Instruction Pastorale sur les Promesses de l'Eglise* (1710).
[12] W. *Dealtry, 'Religious Establishments tried by the Word of God', sermon preached
in 1833, put out as S.P.C.K. tract (1836).
[13] *King's College, London. Report presented by the Council to the General Court* (1836).
[14] Papers on training of clergy, forwarded by its bp.; in Add MS 44355, ff. 33–43.

9. M.

Machiavelli—Bossuet sur les Pr[omesses]—Pusey on New Churches[1]—wrote to Mrs Ramsay, Mrs Charriere, Mrs Wishlade—for Mr G. to Grant, Sherriffs, Macewan[2]—Ch Past[oral] Aid Socy—Commees 1–3. Rode. House $6\frac{1}{4}$–$1\frac{3}{4}$.[3]

10. Tuesday.

Machiavelli. Bossuet sur les Pr.—Von Raumer—writing for Mr G.—wrote to Burge. W.I. Commee & House 1–$5\frac{1}{4}$. $9\frac{1}{4}$–$10\frac{1}{2}$[4]—Lady Ashburton's.[5] rode.

11. W.

Machiav.—Bossuet—Von Raumer—Hodgkin's paper[6]—newsp.—wrote to Pusey—M.A. L[arkins]—rode—dined at Ld Fr. Egerton's—A. Acland here —wrote for Mr G—Prot. Associatn meeting, as an auditor.[7]

12. Th.

Machiavelli—Bossuet. Tacitus (began B.3.) wrote to Ld Mansfield—rode— dined at Bp of Exeter's—many calls. Ly Trevelyans[8] 10 min—House— conv. with Mrs Williams.[9]

13. Fr.

Machiavelli. Bossuet (finished). Croly's Sermon on Marriage.[10] Childers to breakfast, & conv. with him. W.I. Commee 1–4.—Went as Visitor to Milbank. rode. Wrote to Bp of London—& for Mr G. to to T. Fraser [?].[11] at Mrs Hallams & C.G. in evg.

14. Sat.

Machiavelli—Tacitus. Reed & Matheson. paper. rode. dined at Uncle D.s— wrote to J.N.G.—looked over Vss. Wrote 3 letters for Mr G.—spoke to Ld Abn—wrote a little on Church.

[1] E. B. *Pusey, 'Churches in London', reprinted from *British Magazine*, viii. 581 (November 1835).
[2] Possibly Walter MacEwen, w.s. in Edinburgh.
[3] Factories Regulations bill: *H* xxxiii. 738.
[4] Misc. business; tithes commutation bill. *H* xxxiii. 803, 818.
[5] Anne Louisa, da. of Senator William Bingham of Philadelphia; m. 1798 Alexander *Baring, Lord Ashburton; d. 1848.
[6] Thomas *Hodgkin of Guy's, 'On the Importance of Studying and Preserving the Languages Spoken by Uncivilized Nations, with the View of Elucidating the Physical History of Man' (1835).
[7] The Protestant Association's first anniversary meeting, in Exeter Hall, 'very respectably, though not very numerously, attended' (*Times* the next day).
[8] Maria, née Wilson, m. 1791 Sir John Trevelyan, 5th bart., and d. 1852.
[9] Mrs. Robert Williams.
[10] G. *Croly, 'The Divine Origin, Appointment, and Obligation of Marriage' (1836).
[11] Perhaps Thomas Alexander Fraser of Lovat, of Strichen House, near Aberdour.

15. Sunday.

St James's.—The Eclipse: walk to Kens[ingto]n[1]—The Communion at 8 A.M.—Sumner aloud & ampl.—two of Poole's Sermons[2]—& a good deal of Reed & Matheson at diff. parts.—Tea &c. at C.G.—wrote.

16. M.

Mr Wordsworth, H. Taylor, & Doyle, to breakft.—Sat till 12¾. Conv. on Shelley—Trench—Tennyson—travelling—copyright—&c.[3]—Commee & House 1–4¼. House 5½–10½ (Canada). Sir G. Grey's speech injudicious.[4]— wrote to Ld Aberdeen.—Dr Pusey—Caparn. read Machiavelli, & Reed & Math[eson]—rode.

17. T.

wrote to Lush[ingto]n & a letter for Mr G.—Lionised at Lambeth Palace by Sir G. Beaumont,[5] very kindly. read Machiavelli & Ld E. Fitzgerald. rode. dined at T.G.s—saw the Coles. wrote a paper. Commee & House 1½–4, 6–6½, 9–10, and 11–12.[6]

18. Wed.

Mr Finlay with me on the Factory Bill. read Machiavelli—wrote for Mr G. Wrote to J.N.G.—Mrs Wadd—Commees & walk with Ld Mahon 12½–3¼— House 5¾–6¾. paired for Sir Andrew.[7]—dined at Mr R. Ellice's.—Lady F. Egerton's in evg. Vss.

19. Th.

Machiavelli. Bp of Exeter's Irish Educn Speech.[8] Many calls: on Bp Exr, Lady Bromley, the Lab[almondier]e[s?], the Mosses, & others, including that most singular of human beings Lady Cork.[9] wrote for Mr G several [letters]—wrote to Pusey & H. Thompson.—Vss.—House—dined with Mr Tallents. rode.

20. Fr.

Machiavelli. Reed & Matheson. Mr G. went. Commee & House 1–5¼.[10] T.G. to dinner. Rode. At Lady Cork's in evg. T.G., Cole, & Lush[ingto]n to breakft.

---

[1] An annular eclipse of the sun, in early afternoon.
[2] G. A. *Poole, 'The Divinity of Christ Asserted; and the Doctrine of the Atonement Vindicated, in Two Sermons' (1835). [3] Morley, i. 135.
[4] Opposing *Roebuck's request for detailed debate: *H* xxxiii. 930.
[5] Sir George Howland Willoughby Beaumont, 1799–1845, m. 1825 *Howley's da. Mary Anne; succ. his cousin the connoisseur* as 8th bart. 1827.
[6] Evictions in Co. Carlow: *H* xxxiii. 994.
[7] Sir Andrew *Agnew's Sabbath Observance bill beaten 2º, 43–75; diarist's pair not recorded. Ibid. 1078–9. [8] Of 15 March 1835: *H* xxxii. 274.
[9] Mary, née *Monckton, 1748–1840, youngest da. of 1st viscount Galway, widow 1798 of 7th earl of Cork, noted eccentric; lived in New Burlington Street, near Albany.
[10] Dublin election: *H* xxxiii. 1119.

21. Sat.

Machiavelli. Tacitus. Part of Fielden's pamphlet.[1] rode. wrote to T.G.—
Mr G—H.J.G.—Mrs Chisholm. Dined at Lady Cork's.

22. Sunday.

St J. mg & aft.—Communion—Poole. J. Taylor.—Sumner (alt[ere]d) aloud
—Reed & Mathn. Vss.[2] Eyes feeble. Tea in B.S.

23. M.

Breakf. with Taylor to meet Wordsworth. Staid till 12. then Anc. Mus.
Rehearsal. rode. wrote to Mr G—Wilde—Dr Gifford—dined in B.S.—
Philharmonic Concert. read Machiavelli—Unitn Letter[3]—& Carus Wilson's
to W. Patten.[4]

24. T.

Machiavelli (finished the Discorsi). Finished Fielden's pamphlet.—Wordsworth—Nat. Gall—rode—wrote to Mr G—R.G.—T.G.—Vss.[5] Tea at
Cole's, & music. Lady F.[6] is kindly & well principled. Lady E[7]—her sister,
rassomiglia alquanto a quella che un tempo mi fece il piacere e la speme:
ma questo sogno è andato via, ne ho più da farne, che impegnermi cosa sia
lo stare "dentro alla divina voglia".[8]
    Church 11 A.M.

25. W.

Began Toluck[9]—& Mably sur les Romains[10]—read Edmonstone on Ir. Ch.[11]
—wrote to Moscheles (& draft).[12] Mr Ward—Mr G—dined at Sir S. Canning's[; heard] tail[end] of Anc. Music [concert]. rode. calls. Blakesley here.

26. Th.

Mably—Fileen papers[13]—die lehre der Sünde—wrote to T.G.—Mr Ramsay.

---

[1] J. *Fielden, *The Curse of the Factory System* (1836).
[2] Add MS 44726, f. 52; 'Counterpart' to verses of 12 September 1835, ibid. f. 51.
[3] Untraced.   [4] Untraced.
[5] Add MS 44726, ff. 53–54, a preface to other verse of recent years.
[6] Frances Isabella, née Monck, b. 1809, 2nd da. of 1st earl of Rathdowne, m. O. B. Cole
1834.
[7] Lady Elizabeth Louise Mary Monck, 1814–92, 4th da. of 1st earl of Rathdowne,
m. 1844 her cousin Charles Stanley *Monck, 4th Viscount Monck 1849.
[8] 'is rather like her who once brought me pleasure and hope; but that dream is gone
away, I have no more to do with her, what will pledge me thus is her standing "within
the divine will".'
[9] F. A. G. Tholuck, *Die Lehre der Sünde und vom Versöhner* (1823), on sin.
[10] G. B. de Mably, *Observations sur les Romains* (1751).
[11] A. *Edmonstone, *Remarks on the State of the Established Church in Ireland* (1836).
[12] Ignaz Moscheles, 1794–1870, Bohemian pianist and composer; friend of Mendelssohn;
lived in London 1826–46, and conducted concerts there; at Leipzig conservatory 1846–66.
[13] On the claim of Judith Susannah Fileen to the Demerara estate of Jonas Fileen.
Cp. 30 Aug., 5 Oct. 36.

Calls—rode to Richmond, & on to Oatlands[1] to visit Ld F. Egerton—Macintosh.

27. Fr.

Walk with Ld Fr.—in aft. with the party: much talk in the place. Lady F. seems a valuable person. read Raumer—Macintosh—Carmichael[2]—&c. &c. as in a drawingroom one is wont.—Surprised by a paragraph in the Mg Herald.[3]

28. Sat.

Up early wrote a paper—Raumer. At 11, rode to town. Birthday drawing-room. wrote to Mr G—T.G.—Mr Fellowes. dined at Ln's Inn.—searching the papers with ref. to yesterday's—tea with Cole.

29. Sunday.

Communion. Very few.—Expected Rn. dined at Lincoln's Inn. Glad to meet Vaughan. read Newman. Poole. Lehre der Sünde. Jer. Taylor. Arnold aloud.

30.

Wordsworth, Milnes, Blakesley, Taylor, Cole, to breakf.—Church meeting at Abp of Armagh's[4]—Anc. Mus. rehearsal. House 6–8¼, and 9¼–12, on Estimates. Said something of Hay's case.[5] read Trench and Wordsworth—I needed them: it was a heavy day, my mind was unsetteld & needs time with grace.[6]

31.

read Trench. W.I. Commee 1–3¾. At Ln's Inn. House twice.[7] dined at B. Square—Mr Hallam's, & J.M.G.s in evg.—wrote Vss: alas, under Doyle's just censure for I "sing to give my spirit rest". Wrote to Mr G.

Wednesday June One.

read Wordsworth. R.G. to breakfast. wrote to Mr G.—Pusey—reading, & writing notes, on the Irish Church[8]—rode. House 5–12—spoke ab. 45 min.

[1] Oatlands Park, Weybridge, 8 miles SW. of Richmond; formerly seat of duke of *York.

[2] Mrs. A. C. Carmichael, *Domestic Manners and Social Condition of the White, Coloured and Negro Population of the West Indies*, 2v. (1833).

[3] Nothing in *Morning Herald*; but para. in that day's *Morning Chronicle* (of similar format), p. 2 col. 1, of gossip about *Mahon and Friedrich Ludwig Georg von Raumer, 1781–1872, historian.

[4] Lord John George de la Poer *Beresford, 1773–1862, 2nd s. of 1st marquess of Waterford; bp. of Cork 1805, Raphoe 1807, Clogher 1819; abp. of Dublin 1820, of Armagh and primate of all Ireland 1822.

[5] Protesting at R. W. Hay's dismissal from colonial office: H xxxiii. 1163.

[6] Extracts in Morley, i. 135: *Wordsworth's presence at breakfast is omitted.

[7] French affairs; service promotions. H xxxiii. 1191, 1210.

[8] Untraced.

I had this pleasure in my speech, that I never rose more intent upon telling what I believe to be *royal* truth: though I did it very ill, & farther than ever below the ἰδέα which I wd nevertheless hold before my mind.—wrote some notes for the Mirror.[1]

On Monday mg Wordsworth came in to breakft before I had had prayers & on my mentioning them asked particularly to join them.[2]

2. Th.

read Wordsworth. Saw Mr Sidebotham on a Vice Suppression Bill.[3] Singing at Cole's. Wrote to Mr G—H. Thompson—Aunt J—Mr Goal[en]—Mr Gordon: rode. House before dinner & 11½–1⁴—dined at Ld Mansfield's—commenced writing out a Report of my speech. 20 dined at Ld M's—19 of them had titles: povero me![5]

3. Fr.

W.I. Commee 1–4.—finished writing out my speech & sent it to (D.E. Mail) Mr Sheehan.[6] wrote to Mr G. rode. dined with T.G.—read Ld F. Egertons Trn "the Pariah".[7] Wordsworth—& pt of Quarterly on Ireland. House 10–3. div. in 261:300,[8] Robn went.[9]

4. Sat.

Wordsworth. Reed & Matheson. Domestic matters. wrote to J.N.G.—Mr Goulburn—Dr Chalmers. Saw Sir R. Peel. Milbank 2½–4¼. dined at Serj. Talfourd's to meet Wordsworth. rode. wrote.[10]

5. Sunday.

St James's. Commn. dined at Lns Inn. St Sepulchre's Church (Mr Dale)[11]—tea in B.S.—wrote.[12]—Jer. Taylor—Newman—began Nicole's Préjugés.[13] Arnold aloud.[14]

[1] Irish tithes: 2°, adjourned. *H* xxxiii. 1310; *Mirror*, ii. 1644.
[2] Version of extracts in Morley, i. 135; and see i. 136.
[3] E. V. Sidebottom of New Boswell Court; member of Suppression of Vice Society (founded 1802). Cp. 20 Mar. 37.
[4] Irish tithes: *H* xxxiii. 1337.
[5] 'Poor me!'
[6] Remy Sheehan, Irish journalist, opponent of *O'Connell; on Dublin *Evening Mail*.
[7] *Egerton tr. a play by Michael Beer (1829).
[8] Against Irish tithe bill, 2°: *H* xxxiv. 117.
[9] Extracts in Morley, i. 135.
[10] On morals, Add MS 44726, ff. 62–63. Extracts from entry in Morley, i. 135, dated 3 June.
[11] Thomas *Dale, 1797–1870, high church evangelical author; professor of English, U.C.L. 1828–30, K.C.L. 1836–9; vicar of St. Bride's 1835–46, St. Pancras 1846–61; dean of Rochester 1870. Evening lecturer at St. Sepulchre's, Snow Hill, 1828.
[12] On 'The New Life', Add MS 44726, ff. 64–67.
[13] P. Nicole, *Préjugez légitimes contre les Calvinistes* (1671).
[14] Extracts in Morley, i. 135.

6. M.

Mr Finlay to breakf.—Vss & writing out[1]—wrote to Rn G—Freeman[2]—House 7–10¾.[3] rode. read Reed & Matheson. Wordsworth—arrangements for party.

7. T.

breakf. in B.S.—Sir R. Peel's at 11 when the C[ape?] Land deputation came. Commee 1–4. rode. Wrote to Mr G—Learmonth—Innes—read Reed, Nicole.—Lincoln, Mahon, Wordsworth, Talfourd, Milnes, Cole, T. Godfrey, to dinner.

8. W.

Letter to a Lady[4]—Cape pamphlets—Bridgw[ater] House meeting—P. excellent—Commee,[5] Penity, & House 1–3¼.[6] Wrote to Mr G—"Mad d'Harcourt"[7]—dined at B. Baring's. Shiel there. wrote in "Memoranda".[8]

9. Th.

Peter Bell—& the new vol.[9]—Reed & Math.—Anster's Faust[10]—rode. House 5–6½, and 9.50–12.[11] dined at Sir W. Horne's.[12] wrote to J.N.G.—G. Grant—at Natl Gallery—ch[ic]fly to examine the question of the blue & the green, on wh I think I am on the whole right.[13]

10. Fr.

Moss to breakf.—Finished W[ordsworth]'s new vol. wh seems to me to have merit both great & popular. W.I. Commee[14] & House 1½–4¼—Ho 5–6½—& 10½–3.[15] dined at Ld Ashburton's. prepared to speak, but had not an opp[ortunit]y. Saw Mr T. Godfrey on N[ewar]k matters.

---

[1] 'The green and the blue', on the Rhone's junction with the Saône, and similar junctions in nature: Add MS 44726, f. 72.
[2] Perhaps William Peere Williams Freeman, 1811–73, of Fawley Court; Eton and Christ Church; high sheriff of Oxfordshire 1838.
[3] Registration of births: *H* xxxiv. 132.
[4] Untraced.
[5] He was placed this day on cttee. to inquire into modes of disposal of colonial lands: cp. *P.P.* 1836 xi. 499.
[6] Election bribery bill, cttee.: *H* xxxiv. 207.
[7] Perhaps *Maria Harcourt*, a society novel (1788).
[8] Morley's long extract for this day (i. 135–7) is not from the diary.
[9] W. *Wordsworth, *Peter Bell* (1819) and *Yarrow Revisited* (1835).
[10] Goethe's *Faust*, tr. J. *Anster (1835).
[11] Lords' amdts to Irish municipalities: *H* xxxiv. 217.
[12] Sir William *Horne, 1774–1860, K.C. and bencher of Lincoln's Inn 1818; M.P. 1812–18, 1831–4; solicitor-general 1830–4; master in chancery 1839–53; opposed death penalty.
[13] Cp. 6 June 36 n.
[14] First meeting since 6 May.
[15] Irish municipalities, lords' amdts: *H* xxxiv. 308.

11. Sat.

Moss to breakf. Commee 12–1½—wrote to Mr G. & Dr Newland.[1] read Browning's Paracelsus.[2] went to Richmond to dine with the Gaskells—a two hours walk home at nt.—called at the O. Palace.[3]

12. Sunday.

Bp of Winchr[4] & Mr Browne[5] preached—both very good.—tea in B.S.—twice at C.G. to see the F[ellowe]s—wrote Vss—read Holy Dying (finished)—Newman—Arnold aloud—Nicole.

13. M.

Moss to breakf.—wrote to Mr G—G.G—Parker[6]—calls—at the Zoological with Aunt D[ivie][7]—House 6½–8¾[8]—at Cole's (singing) & Mrs Praed's concert.[9] read Paracelsus.

14. T.

read Reed—Paracelsus (finished)—Church in Malta[10]—Commee 1–2½—House bef. dinner:[11] dined at Lady L. Pusey's—Mrs R. Ellice's afterwards—wrote to H.J.G. & Mr Fellowes—Vss. rode.

15. W.

read Reed—& Mably. Commees 12–4: dined at Mr Tallent's—at Lady F. Egerton's party—wrote to Mr G—R.G.—Uncle T.[12]—Mr Grant. rode.

16. Th.

Reed. Mably. Commee, West. Abbey, & House 1½–5¼.[13] dined at Mr Sm[ith] Wright's. Mrs Brownrigg's[14] & Lady Salisbury's afterwards—at nt, wrote two Sonnets.[15]—wrote to Poppins[16]—Mr G—Mr Ryder—Mr Finlay.[17]

---

[1] Henry Garrett *Newland, 1804–60, high churchman; sinecure rector of Westbourne, Sussex, 1829.

[2] By Robert *Browning (1835).

[3] Extracts in Morley, i. 137. The Old Palace of the bishops of London is at Fulham.

[4] C. R. *Sumner.

[5] Perhaps Henry Montague Browne, 1799–1884, dean of Lismore 1850.

[6] Probably John Henry *Parker, 1806–84, Oxford bookseller, publisher of *Keble and *Pusey, and writer on architecture.

[7] She was a fellow of the Zoological Society, which had a newly opened museum in Leicester Square and, then as now, a menagerie at the north side of the Regent's Park.

[8] Registration of marriages: H xxxiv. 490.

[9] Helen, da. of George Bogle, m. W. M. *Praed 1835, d. 1836.

[10] Untraced.

[11] Irish municipalities: H xxxiv. 511.

[12] Thomas Gladstones.

[13] Registration of voters: H xxxiv. 563.

[14] Elizabeth Rebecca, née Casamayor, m. J. S. Brownrigg 1812, and d. 1865.

[15] To a young lady: Add MS 44726, ff. 73–4.

[16] Unidentified.

[17] Fragment in Morley, i. 137.

17. Fr.

Reed. Wordsworth's Sonnets. Vss. finished & wrote out Braut von Korinth. Shall I ever dare or be able to make out a counterpart? wrote to Mr G.— J.N.G. came—some time with him—dined at Lady Canning's.[1]

18. Sat.

read Mably—Lehre der Sünde—finished Reed—began Torrens on Colonisation[2]—went with Lady K[erriso]n to the Duke [of Wellington]'s &c.[3]— rode—dined at Sir R. Bromley's[4]—singing—wrote to Mr G—Mr Ryder— papers.

19. Sunday.

Communion at 8 P.M.—Mr Wigram & Mr Ward preached—Tea at C.G.— Sumner aloud—read Nicole—Newman—Toluck—Wordsworth's Sermon.

20. M.

wrote to Mr Linning[5]—H.J.G.—Tomlinson[6]—Sidebottom—Fellowes—Mrs Chisholm. read Toluck—Mably—(began) Wordsworth's Attica[7]—Commee $1\frac{1}{4}$–$3\frac{1}{4}$—rode—dined with C. M'Kenzie—House 10–12.[8]

21. T.

Breakf at Mr Hallam's to meet Mr Wordsworth & Mr Rogers.[9]—W. spoke much & justly, about copyright. Conv. with Talfourd in evg, partly about that subject.—read Toluck. Nicole. Commee 1–$3\frac{3}{4}$—House 9–$12\frac{3}{4}$—two divv.[10]—Vss—wrote to Mr G—R.G—Mr Finlay.[11]

22. W.

Col. Torrens. Toluck. Vss. wrote to Mr Tyler—Mr Backhouse—Mr G.— Commee 12–$3\frac{3}{4}$—House 5–7.[12] Dined with the Milneses. Mrs Alexander's concert.

---

[1] Version of extract, misdated, in Morley, i. 137.
[2] R. *Torrens, *Colonization of South Australia* (1835).
[3] Sir E. *Kerrison, who had fought at Waterloo, attended the anniversary dinner at Apsley House.
[4] In Grosvenor Street.
[5] John Linning, general accountant for Scotland in excise office.
[6] George Tomlinson, 1801?–63; chaplain to *Blomfield and tutor to *Peel's family; sec., S.P.C.K., 1831–42; bp. of Gibraltar 1842.
[7] The younger Christopher *Wordsworth's *Athens and Attica* (1836).
[8] Stamp and excise duties: *H* xxxiv. 612.
[9] Samuel *Rogers, 1763–1855, poet, wit, and patron; refused laureateship 1850.
[10] Registration of voters, in cttee.: *H* xxxiv. 696.
[11] Version of extract in Morley, i. 137.
[12] Sugar duties: *H* xxxiv. 720.

23. Th.

Toluck—Torrens—Report of S. Aust. Co[1]—Col. Lands Commee 12–3.[2] paper. wrote to Mr G—R.G—: Pringle, Gaskell, J.N.G. to dinner. rode. House after dinner.[3] Mrs Denison's and Hope's—another look at the dear pictures.

24. Fr.

Breakf. with Mr Rogers: Mr Wordsworth only there. Very agreeable. W. read us aloud an American poem.[4]—Toluck (finished Abschnitt!)—Nicole— Vss. Commee & House 1¼–6.[5] rode. White Doe of Rylstone.[6]—wrote to Miss G—Tait.[7]

25. Sat.

J.N.G. & Cole to breakf—long conv. with him on Vss—wrote to Pusey— R. Cav[endish]—H.J.G.—rode—dined at Ld Harrowby's: read Wordsworth's Attica—finished White Doe—began Vaughan.[8]

26. Sunday.

Began Martin Boos.[9] Newman—& aloud. Nicole finished V.1.—Wrote[10]— & Vss. Tentamina Theodiceae, recommenced.[11]

27. M.

D. Robn to breakf.—wrote to Mr G—Parker—Commee 12¼–3¼—House 5.20–6.20, and 11–1. Two divv.[12] read Wordsworth—Boos—Buxton's Speech—& "Tales of Fashion & reality"[13]—sad!—saw Mr Miller on Edn.

28. T.

J.N.G. & D.R. to breakf.—Commee, Penit[entiar]y & House, 1.25–3.[14]

---

[1] The South Australia Company, a private firm recently founded, organized the first settlement there this autumn; first report of its directors issued in May 1836.
[2] Hearing, as on 22, 27, 29 June, Edward Gibbon *Wakefield, 1796–1862, radical imperialist, active in founding South Australia and New Zealand.
[3] Ballot: voted in 139:88 against it. H xxxiv. 137.
[4] Account in Add MS 44777, f. 29. *Wordsworth read 'The death of Bozzaris'.
[5] Tithe commutation bill in cttee.: H xxxiv. 856.
[6] *Wordsworth (1815).
[7] Extracts in Morley, i. 137, with additions from Add MS 44777, f. 29. Archibald Campbell *Tait, 1811–82; Edinburgh, Glasgow, and Balliol (fellow 1834); headmaster of Rugby 1842; dean of Carlisle 1850; bp. of London 1856; abp. of Canterbury 1869. Cp. Add MS 44330–1.
[8] R. *Vaughan, The Christian Warfare, 8v. (1832).
[9] J. Gossner (tr. C. Bridges) Life and Persecutions of Martin Boos (1836), German catholic divine who d. 1825.
[10] Continuing 'The New Life', Add MS 44726, ff. 68–71.
[11] Leibniz. Cp. 8 June 34.
[12] Tithes commutation, 3°. Just before the house rose, *Gladstone was snubbed by *Russell on a point of procedure. H xxxiv. 979; 983.
[13] By C. F. and H. M. Beauclerk (1836).
[14] Misc. business: H xxxiv. 1001.

dined at Ld Newark's[1]—rode! House 11–2. read Wordsworth. In three divv. on marriage bill.[2] H.J.G's birthday.

29. W.

Wordsworth—Torrens. wrote to Mr G—R.G.—Commee 12¼–4. Tea & singing at Cole's. rode. Vss. Jam[aic]a papers on Oldrey's case.[3] wrote on Egotism.[4]

30. Th.

Wordsworth's Attica. Torrens. Commee 12¼–3¾.—Nat. Gall.—House 5½–6¼.[5] rode. dined at Cole's—singing—Vss. wrote to Caparn—Mr Godfrey. Boos's Life.

Friday July one.

Arranging letters & accounts. Boos—Torrens—Wordsworth's Attica— Commee 1¼–4. wrote to Mr G.—Aunt J—Mrs Charriere—Rode—Archer's Lodge[6]—dined at Sir Ed. Kerr[iso]ns—singing.

2. Sat.

Heat again great.—reading vss.—calls (incl Lady Cork)—Lady Peel's breakf—dined at Sir E. Kerrison's—read Boos—Wordsw.—rode. wrote to Hemstock.

3. Sunday.

St James & Margaret Chapel.—Wood dined with me.—Saw Mr Ponsonby at the Chapel: an interesting object.[7] The Communion.—read Newland[8]— Boos—Nicole Prej.—Sumner aloud.

4. M.

Cole, Taylor, J.N.G., to breakf. read Boos—Wordsworth's Attica—Tupper's Sacra Poesis, through.[9] wrote to Mr G—Williams—Dry—Sir J. Mac-

[1] Charles Evelyn Pierrepont, 1805–50, s. of 2nd Earl Manvers, styled Viscount Newark; m. 1832 Emily Walhouse, who d. 1851, 2nd da. of 1st Lord *Hatherton.
[2] Three amdts. to registration bill of Anglican tendency defeated; bill passed. *H* xxxiv. 1021.
[3] William Oldrey, commander R.N. 1828, Jamaica magistrate who complained of persecution, was cross-questioned by diarist and others at W.I. Cttee. on 28 June and 1 July 1836.
[4] Add MS 44726, ff. 75–76.
[5] Irish municipalities: *H* xxxiv. 1067.
[6] Richmond Park?
[7] John George Brabazon Ponsonby, 1809–80, whig M.P. Bletchingley 1831, Higham Ferrers 1831–2, Derby 1835–47; 5th earl of Bessborough 1847; court office 1848–52, 1852–8, 1859–66, 1868–74. His first wife, Lady Frances Charlotte Lambton, b. 1812, da. of 1st earl of *Durham, d. in December 1835 three months after the wedding.
[8] H. G. *Newland, *An Examination of the Scripture Lessons, as Translated and Published by His Majesty's Commissioners of Education in Ireland* (1836).
[9] By M. F. *Tupper (1832).

donald—H. Thompson. Commee & House 12½–6.20 and 9½–1. An exc[ellen]t divn 266:290. thank God, I say solemnly.[1]

5. T.

Doyle, Cole, J.N.G., to breakf.—Boos—Wordsworth's Attica (finished)— Hoare's Letter to Buxton.[2] Commee & House 1.25–5.[3] rode. tea & singing at Cole's. wrote to cousin Divie—Mr G—Chr. Wordsworth—Harrison— F.C. Fraser.[4] Vss.

6. Wed.

Torrens. Mably. Boos. calls. Meeting at London House 2–4¼.[5] tea at Cole's & music. wrote to Mrs Charriere. Vss: wrote a sonnet (Div[ina] Comm[edia]) & finished another.

7. Th.

Torrens. Boos. Commee 1½–4. dined at H. Joy's—Bridgwater House Theatricals. rode. Phillimore to breakf. Germanised a little with him.— Scrope's Preface![6] wrote to Mr G—Mr Tyler. Ph. van Art[evelde].

8. Fr.

Comm. 1.25–3.35. House 10–12½. two divv.[7] dined at T.Gs—rode. wrote to Mr G—May.[8] finished Torrens—read Boos—Mably—Wakefield on Death[9] —Trench—Petrarch.

9. Sat.

J.N.G. & Phill[imor]e to breakf.—Penitentiary—singing—rode—dined at Sir R. Inglis's—wrote to Huddleston—G. M'Kenzie—Canning—R.G.— Vss. read Boos—Mably—recommenced Hymn to Mercury[10] with Shelley's Transln.

10. Sunday.

St James's bis.—Tea in B.S.—wrote Vss. Nicole (finished Préjugés). New-

---

[1] On inalienability of Irish church property: 264–290. *H* xxxiv. 1259.
[2] E. N. Hoare, *A Letter to Thomas Fowell *Buxton, Esq., M.P., in Reply to his Speech on the Irish Tithe Bill* (1836).
[3] Misc. business: *H* xxxiv. 1265.
[4] Perhaps Francis Garden Fraser, d. 1885, of Findrack, Aberdeenshire.
[5] At *Blomfield's, at 22 St. James's Square.
[6] G. J. Poulett *Scrope, M.P., *Principles of Political Economy* (1833).
[7] *Russell's Established Church bill, early stages: *H* xxxv. 53; 55.
[8] (Sir) Thomas Erskine *May, 1815–86, assistant librarian 1831, taxing master 1847, clerk assistant 1856, and clerk 1871, to house of commons, whose *Proceedings and Usage* he codified (1844, enlarged ed. still in use); K.C.B. 1866; cr. Lord Farnborough on retirement 1886. Corr. with diarist in Add MS 44154 (from 1861).
[9] E. G. *Wakefield, *Facts Relating to the Punishment of Death in the Metropolis* (1831).
[10] Homer.

man. Leibnitz—Objns to Ch. Discipline Bill[1]—Ch. Pastoral Aid Report[2]—
Life of Boos.

11. M.

Mably. Nicole (Additions aux Préjugés)—Vss—wrote to Mr G—T.G. twice
—Huddleston. Commee 12.20–3. House before & after dinner[3]—dined at
Sir F. Doyle's—rode——
    This morning Louisa was confined: the child born at 9 died at 3. Baptised
in the forenoon. L. is well. God be with them.

12. T.

Good accts of L.—read Mably—Wiseman's 1st Lecture.[4] Commee (W.I.),
Penit[entiar]y, & House, 1–6: House 10½–1.[5] rode. dined in B. Square
wrote to T.G. a few Vss.[6]

13. W.

Good accts.—finished Mably. Wiseman 2 & 3. House & ride 4.45–7.40.[7]
dined at Sir J. Buller's—music—Lady Cork's—wrote to H.J.G.—T.G—a
few Vss. saw H. Thompson on his matters—Cole (p.p.c.)—Mayow.

14. Th.

Accts still as good as we cd hope.—read Nicole—Anster's Preface[8] Wiseman Lect. 4—paper—rode. dined at Mr Tyler's—Commee 1.45 4: Penitentiary—wrote to Mr G—T.G.—Huddlestone—Corby.[9]

15. Fr.

Wiseman 5 & pt of 6 —Hymn to Mercury with Shelley's transl—Nicole,
finished Additions—T.G. & J.N.G. to dinner—House—Lady Cork's—
Somerset House Exhn (alas)[10] & Commee.

16. Sat.

Nicole "Les P.R. convaincus de Schisme"[11]—& finished Wiseman 6.—
dined with R. Williams—much Church Convn—[G.] Wellesley here: d[itt]o

---

    [1] Probably a petition, presented three days later to the lords, by clergymen objecting
to provision of clerical juries in bill: lords' *Journals*, 659.
    [2] Church Pastoral-Aid Society, report to first annual meeting on 9 May 1836.
    [3] Emigration; stamp duties. *H* xxxv. 96; 110.
    [4] N. P. S. *Wiseman, *Lectures on the Principal Doctrines and Practices of the Catholic
Church* (1836). And see 28 July 36.
    [5] Established Church bill: *H* xxxv. 150.
    [6] On the dead child: published long after, in *Good Words*, 365–8 (1871), without the
family context.
    [7] Hackney carriages (metropolis) bill: *H* xxxv. 169.
    [8] To his translation of *Faust* (1835).
    [9] Perhaps Thomas Corbyn of New Palace Yard.
    [10] Untraced.
    [11] P. Nicole, *Les prétendus réformés convaincus de schisme* (ca. 1670).
    17—II.

with him. Penitentiary at one—wrote to Sir S. Glynne & Mr G.—rode, twice.—J.N.G. to breakf—City & Somerset House Exhibn with him: little enough to like.

17. S.

St James's & Westr Abbey: Bp of Hereford, very impressive.[1] Tea in B.S.— read Nicole—Wiseman 7—Sumner aloud—began "Mammon"[2]—Church Miss. Reports.

18. M.

J.N.G., Capt. Wellesley, Tupper, to breakf. Pall Mall Exhn[3] with J.N.G.— paying bills. House $4\frac{1}{4}$–$5\frac{1}{2}$ and $9\frac{1}{2}$–$1\frac{1}{2}$. four divv.[4] read "Mammon"—paper —Art of Pluck,[5] & "papers" on d[itt]o—wrote to Mr G—R.G—Mrs Charriere—Jacobson—Wordsworth:—T.G. to dinner.

19. T.

Cousin Divie to breakf.—Commee, Penit[entiar]y & House $12\frac{1}{4}$–$6\frac{1}{4}$: House $8\frac{1}{2}$–$1\frac{1}{2}$—div in 88 : 133[6]—finished Mammon. read Wiseman. wrote to Mr G— Miss J. McK[enzie].[7]

20. W.

Hymn to Merc. & Shelley's Trans—(finished). finished Wiseman: remarkably able. Col. Lands Comm. $1\frac{1}{4}$–4.[8] Church Fund Commee—rode—dined at T.G's—paper—Anstice's Hymns.[9] Wrote to Mr G—Hamilton—Allen— Mahon—Mr Rawson. paper.

21.

Nicole—Vss—began Matheson's Ireland[10]—1.20–$2\frac{1}{4}$ Sir R. Peels. 6–$6\frac{3}{4}$ House.[11] rode. dined at Sir E. Kerrison's—music—wrote to Glynne—Hope —Sir A. Agnew—Mr G—Hanmer—up to see M.A. Fellowes off.

22.

Matheson—who is indeed excellent. Letters of Clericus Anglicanus.[12] wrote

[1] Edward Grey, 1782–1837, 5th s. of 1st Earl *Grey; had 16 children; bp. of Hereford 1832.
[2] By J. *Harris (1836).   [3] National gallery.
[4] Newspaper stamp duties, in cttee.: *H* xxxv. 270.
[5] *Fraser's Magazine*, xiii. 707 (June 1835).
[6] Against report on Charitable Trustees bill; Established Church bill, 3°, adjourned. *H* xxxv. 341.   [7] '& others' here deleted.
[8] Several divisions on report: *PP* 1836 xi. 504.
[9] *Hymns by the late Joseph *Anstice* (1836).
[10] Untraced; possibly slip of pen for (Sir) James Matheson 'Present position and prospects of the British trade with China' (1836).
[11] Plans for new houses of parliament: *H* xxxv. 398.
[12] 'Clericus Anglicanus', *Ecclesiastical Legislation . . . Three Letters on Church Property, Episcopacy, Cathedrals, and the Clergy* (1836); and *Letters Respecting the Suffering Irish Clergy* (1836).

to Mr G—Mr Grant. rode. Commee 12–4. J.N.G. to dinner—tea in B.S.—
at Coliseum—what an exemplifn of the 19th Century.[1]

23. Sat.

J.N.G., Jas Hope, & Mr Ramsay, to breakf.—Commee, Penity, & House,
$12\frac{1}{2}$–$4\frac{1}{4}$.[2] rode. J.N.G. went—dined in B. Square. read Matheson—& "Court
& Camp of D. Carlos"[3]—wrote to Mr G—Ld Mahon—W.K. H[amilton]—
Robn—T.G.

24. Sunday.

B.—Matheson—Nicole—(finished) Anstice's Hymns—Sumner aloud—
Newman—Duff's Statement on E.I. Mission[4]—Vss.—wrote—St James's
twice—tea in B.S.

25.

T.G's birthday.—Hope & Mr Ramsay to breakf—finished Matheson—
read Newland, & Missionary Correspondence & reports—saw Lady C[an-
nin]g—wrote to R.G.—H.J.G.—Canning—T.G.—House $4\frac{1}{2}$–$5\frac{3}{4}$ and 9–$1\frac{3}{4}$.[5]
E. Fellowes dined here.

26. T.

finished Newland. read Nicole. Commee $12\frac{1}{2}$–4. House 9–$1\frac{1}{2}$. many divv.[6]
wrote to Mr G—Allen. Began Simpson.[7] A Marriage.[8]

27. W.

Commee $1\frac{1}{4}$–4. dined in B.S. rode. wrote to R.G—Mahon—H. Thompson—
saw Mr Miller—Bp Exeter. D. Robn to breakf. read Nicole—'Court &
Camp of Don Carlos'—Vss. Finished Simpson. intemperate.

28. Th.

Breakfd with Milnes—to meet Wiseman. A longish *sederunt*.—Calls. saw
Lady Cg. wrote to Robn—Caparn—Mr G—Dr Chalmers—Innes—read
Nicole—began Brougham[9]—& a paper on rule of faith.

29. Fr.

Vss. Commee $12\frac{1}{2}$–4. House to $6\frac{1}{4}$ & again at 9[10]—tea with Sir R.I.—rode:

---

[1] Magic lantern shows were given at the Colosseum from its opening in 1824 to its
demolition in 1875 (*DNB* x. 247).
[2] Misc. business: *H* xxxv. 445.   [3] By M. B. Honan (1836).
[4] See 18 June 35.
[5] Established Church and Stamp Duties (Newspapers) bills passed: *H* xxxv. 523; 560.
[6] Charitable trustees, county elections, and beer. *H* xxxv. 585, 588, 590.
[7] R. Simpson, *Sermons, Doctrinal, Experimental, and Practical* (1836).
[8] See 4 Aug. 36. These two words, shakily underlined in pencil, a late entry.
[9] *Brougham, *A Discourse on Natural Theology* (1835).
[10] County Elections bill passed: *H* xxxv. 674.

farewell to thee pretty grey for $\frac{1}{2}$ year. read Brougham—Nicole—began Bakewell.[1] wrote to Glynne—Hanmer—T.G.—Robn—Mr G—Aunt J—& others.

30. Sat.

Commee & Penity 12$\frac{1}{4}$–5. dined in B.S.—singing—read Bakewell—raking up Irish Church matter. Wrote to Mr G—Hanmer—papers—read Buxton's proposed report.[2]—Accts.

31. Sunday.

St James's bis—tea in B.S.—read Nicole—Brougham—Newman (finished) —Sumner aloud.

August one. Monday.

Went to Ewell[3] to breakf. & spend the day. found Louisa going on very well. rode on the downs. read Nicole.

2. T.

Returned at 11. Commee 12$\frac{3}{4}$–4. House 5$\frac{1}{4}$–1$\frac{1}{4}$. Nicole. wrote to Caparn— Lady C[annin]g—H.J.G.—R.G—Acland. Govt disapp[oin]t[e]d with their 29.—Wished to speak.[4]

3. W.

Nicole. Went to Lady Cg again. Commee & House 3–6$\frac{3}{4}$—House 11–1.[5] wrote to Ld Carrington—Canning—R.G—Mr G—dined in B.S.

4. Th.

Saw Mr Ramsay who told me some facts about the 26th ult.[6]—I had not known of it before: it is as it was to me, in respect of pain: but in respect of good, I see distinct reasons for glorifying God: I therefore hope that even the pain will in his good time turn to good.

Jusqu'a present quand j'y ai reflechi, mes pensées ont toujours roulé sur ma perte: dorenavant je prie Dieu qu'il me fasse préalablement detourner mon esprit de ce côté là, e vivement sentir que c'est a cause de mes pêchés et de son amour qu'il m'a oté ce cher espoir afin que j'en faise profit. Que le regret[7] donc de ces pêchés étouffe celui du besoin et de la perte.[8]

---

[1] F. C. Bakewell, *Natural Evidence of a Future Life* (1835).
[2] This became *PP* 1836 vii. 3, on aborigines' cttee.
[3] Then a Surrey village, 12 miles SSW. of Westminster.
[4] Church of Ireland bill dropped, 260–231: *H* xxxv. 855.
[5] Railways and Jewish Disabilities bill. *H* xxxv. 860; 865.
[6] On 26 July 1836 Caroline Farquhar married Charles *Grey; see Magnus, 29.
[7] Instead of 'sentiment'.
[8] 'Up to now my reflexions on this have all turned on what I have lost; henceforward I pray to God that he may begin by deflecting my mind from this aspect, making me rather feel that he has taken this cherished hope from me for my own good, because of my sins and of his love. So may sorrow for these sins stifle regret for need and loss.'

read Dublin Rev. on Connelly, & recent poetry[1]—Bakewell—& Brougham. wrote Vss. O. & C. Club Commee at 4.—House $6\frac{1}{4}$–$9\frac{3}{4}$.[2] wrote to Acland—W.R. F[arquhar]—H. Thompson—Mr G—Mrs Chisholm—T.G.

5. Fr.

Bakewell—& 3d Irish Edn Report. Commee 12.40–5.[3] House 7–8.50, and $10\frac{1}{4}$–1.—No divn on one Report.[4] Wrote to Mr G. Aunt J. came.

6. Sat.

Bakewell—Brougham—Arranging papers &c. for departure. Garden here. Dined in B. Square. Wrote to J.N.G.—Simpson—Sir G. Grey—Dry—Jos. Geary[5]—T.G.—paying bills &c.

7. Sunday.

St Martin's (Commn) & Margt Chapel in Evg. Tea in B.S.—read Bible— Wardlaw—finished Nicole P.R.—Brougham—pt of Appx. Sumner aloud.

8. M.

finished Bakewell—& Brougham. packed. House 4–$5\frac{1}{4}$ & $7\frac{1}{2}$–9.[6] Off by Duke of Wellington[7]—on b. at 10—sailed at 11—wrote to Mr G—Mr Simpson—Sir R. Peel—W.R.F.—Bp of London—T.G.—Lady Canning—& others.

9. T.

On deck: some wind & motion: could not eat or read.

10. W.

in bed most of the day, & little motion. read (Sp[anish] N.T. & Guido Sorelli)[8] and fed. Afternoon & evg lovely. Fog at night—we overshot Aberdeen.

11. Th.

Owing to the fog, too late for Defiance—went by steam[er] to Stonehaven & posted home: found all well—hay making, cherries & gooseberries ripening.

wrote to G. M'Kenzie. read Miss Sinclair[9]—& pt of Quart. on Raumer. singing.

---

[1] i. 400 (July 1836).
[2] Warwickshire election; registration of voters bill in cttee. *H* xxxv. 904, 907.
[3] Final meeting of W.I. apprenticeship cttee.
[4] War in Spain, and supply; no divisions at all. *H* xxxv. 946, 967.
[5] Joseph Geary, Newark whitesmith.
[6] Supply; Irish education. *H* xxxv. 996, 1013.
[7] From Miller's wharf, just downstream from the Tower.
[8] *My Confessions to Silvio Pellico* (1836), autobiography of a Florentine exile settled in London.
[9] Catherine *Sinclair, *Modern Accomplishments or The March of Intellect* (1836).

12. Fr.

Went to the hill: but unfortunately with a sprained ancle: & obliged to give up early.[1] Quart. on Raumer & Fermoy—Sorelli—music.

13. Sat.

no walking today. finished Quart. on Fermoy. read Sorelli—Miss Sinclair —Backgammon—calls. wrote to T.G.—Col. Wade—Mr Hastings[2]—Dr Bigsby[3]—Mr G.—& copied three letters for him.

14. Sunday.

Began Nicole sur l'unité[4]—Milner's Church History[5]—Keith on Prophecies[6]—read aftn prayers & Sermon (Venn)[7] aloud. Music.

15.

Milner. Orator (began).[8] Miss Sinclair—Music. calls. wrote (long) to Dr Chalmers—and to Adjutant General.[9]

16.

Copied a letter. Milner—Orator—Sorelli—paper. Wrote to Mr Finlay— R.G. & M.E. came—the former looking very unwell.—made some envelopes.

17. Wed.

Milner. recommenced Whewell's Macintosh. Orator. wrote to Mrs Chisholm —Aberdeen[10]—Mr Mayor. Sorelli—Music.

18. Th.

Milner. Orator. Whewell. Miss Sinclair. several to dinner. billiards. boat. music. wrote part of a Butler Essay—& preface—.[11]

19. Fr.

wrote to Geo. Mackenzie—Abn—Mrs Chisholm. Milner—Sorelli—music— rode—finished Miss Sinclair—Journey to Dingwall given up—wrote Vss.

[1] Version in Morley, i. 137.
[2] Possibly Henry James Hastings, 1798–1875, rector of Arely Kings, 1831, of Martley, 1856, both in Worcestershire.
[3] John Bigsby, FRCP, of East Retford; MD Edinburgh 1814.
[4] P. Nicole, Essais de morale: De l'Unité de l'Eglise (1687).
[5] Joseph *Milner, The History of the Church of Christ (1794–7).
[6] A. *Keith, Sketch of the Evidence . . . From Prophecy (1823).
[7] Probably from Henry *Venn, A Volume of Sermons (1759).
[8] Cicero.
[9] Sir John *Macdonald. Extracts in Morley, i. 137.
[10] Perhaps to book a passage to Ross-shire: cp. 19 Aug. 36.
[11] Add MS 44725, ff. 236–45.

20. Sat.

Milner. Whewell. Orator. Sorelli. Began "Private Life"[1]—wrote to Mr Edmonston[2]—Wight[3]—.

21. S.

Church—& service at home. wrote on Rule of Faith.[4] read[5] Nicole—Aug[ustine] de Civitate Dei (recommenced)—& Sumner aloud.

22. M.

Milner—Orator—Macintosh—Sorelli—Private Life—rode with M.E., Miss G. & J.N.G.—Archery. papers.

23. T.

At the hill $10\frac{1}{2}$–$5\frac{1}{2}$. Milner—Sorelli—Private Life—wrote to J. Geary. papers. Canning's Eln.[6]

24. W.

At the hill 11–$5\frac{1}{4}$. read Milner—Sorelli—Macintosh. paper. wrote to T.G.—made envelopes. R.G. gains no ground app[aren]tly.

25. Th.

Rn improving. rode with M.E.G., J.N.G., Miss G. finished Orator—Milner—Macintosh. Wrote to Cole, Miss Aug. M'Kenzie—Mrs Chisholm. read paper—Sorelli.

26. Fr.

rode to Arbuthnot. Milner. Macintosh. Sorelli. Private Life (began Vol 2)—papers—music.

27. Sat.

on the hill—did all but nothing. read Macintosh. Milner. Sorelli. Private Life. T.G. came: Louisa looking pretty well.

28. S.

Communion at Laurencekirk. prayers in aftn—a good serm from W.M. G[oalen]—read Nicole, Milner, Augustin: but my eyes failed me.

---

[1] A tale by M. J. M'Kenzie (1829).
[2] Neil Benjamin Edmonstone, 1765–1841, East India Company director.
[3] Possibly Thomas Wight, Bloomsbury solicitor.
[4] Cp. 23 Sep. 36.
[5] 'Milner' here deleted.
[6] As M.P. for Warwick borough; by 464–434 against Henry William Hobhouse, 1791–1868, 3rd br. of J.C.*

29. M.

Milner. Macintosh. Augustin. Sorelli. wrote to Lady Canning. rode with
M.E.G. to the Cairno' Mont. dined at Sir J. Forbes's.

30. T.

Most of the day occupied with reading papers in the Fileen property question,[1] & writing the draft of a long letter for Mr G. to Sir G. G[rey]—Made
up accts. Milner. Private Life. Sorelli.

31. Wed.

Wrote to Jas Hope—Claypole[2]—dined at Stracathro. read Milner. Macintosh. (finished) Private Life, excellent. Again occupied in writing & copying
for Mr G. on the Fileen business.

Thursday Septr one.

read Milner (finished Vol 1). Macintosh—began Wraxall's Memoirs[3]—
wrote on Phil[osophy] &c. rode to Edzell. the Kerrs[4] dined here. Music.

2. Fr.

Milner. Macintosh. Wraxall. wrote on Eth. &c. Singing. making envelopes:
cont[emplatin]g Braemar tour.[5]

3. Sat.

Milner (began Vol 2) Wraxall. Macintosh. on the hill. music—envelopes.
θακοῦσιν ἱστουργοῦντες![6]

4. Sunday.

Fett[ercair]n & prayers in aftn. Sumner S.4—conv. with H.J.G.—read
Nicole & Milner.

5. M.

Milner. Macintosh. Aug. de Civ. Dei—Sorelli (finished)—Wraxall—paper—
wrote on Eth. &c.—wrote to Canning—C. Parker—Mavor.

6. T.

6.30–8.50—rode 17 m over the Cairn to Banchory with J.N.G.—breakft:
Inn avoidable: $11\frac{1}{4}$–$2\frac{1}{4}$ coach to Ballater:[7] inn very good. 4–$6\frac{1}{2}$ coach to

---

[1] See Sir G. *Grey to diarist, 27 Aug. 36, in Add MS 44162, fo. 145.
[2] James Claypole, Newark bank clerk.
[3] Sir N. W. *Wraxall, *Posthumous Memoirs*, 3v. (1836).
[4] Herbert J. N. Kerr of St. Ann's, Bankhouse, or William Kerr of Eskmount, both
near Brechin.   [5] See 6–10 Sep. 36.
[6] 'The men sit weaving at the loom!' (Sophocles, *Oedipus at Colonus*, 340).
[7] Twenty miles west of Banchory up Deeside.

Braemar: Invercauld Arms.[1] very comfortable. Our scenery has been splendid: though seen thro copious & almost incessant rain. wrote to Mr G. read "Sig. Gaudentio di Lucca"[2] and "Ildegonda" of Grossi.[3]

7. W.

Rain! impossible to attempt the mountain: walked in the aftn 7 miles to the Linn of Dee:[4] very fine: the river almost a flood: saw also the Linn of Cormutzie[5] wh is beautiful—& the whole glen much more than repays the trip. Pines of 12 f. at the Linn of Dee. read Gaud.—Ildegonda (finished) & Dee Guide[6]—wrote to T.G.

8. Th.

$8\frac{1}{2}$–4.25. Up Lochnagar.[7] fog at the top. The precipices are awful enough. The Forest thoroughly satisfies.[8] An old pine of 14 f. Went up in 3h.11m. of wh 30 m. rest, for distance under 11 m: the guide said more. Back about 13 m.—saw the Linn of Garrawalt.[9] Reddeer, roe, blackgame, grouse, ptarmigan. finished the Deeside Guide—most original—& read Gaudentio— The trip of today might be done in 6 hours—$6\frac{1}{2}$ with casc. Very cold on the top.

9. Fr.

9–$7\frac{1}{2}$. Up Ben Muickdhui: king of the Br. mountains.[10] Fine: & a noble view from the top to the N. Strathspey, Moray Firth & Rossshire: stepped into Invernessshire.[11] This is 10 hours good work. Mr Donald[12] went with us.

Places.	time going.	returning.	prob. distance
Cormutzie —	45 min.	46	$3\frac{1}{2}$ m.
Mar Lodge —	. . . .	22 m.	$1\frac{1}{2}$
Forester's hut —	1 h. 35 m.	1 h. 20 m.	5
Foot of the main ascent.	1 h.	1 h.	$3\frac{1}{2}$
Top.	2 h.	1 h. 5 m.	$4\frac{1}{2}$
	5 h. 20 m.	4 h. 31 m.	18 m.

[1] George Clark's, at Braemar, 13 miles west of Ballater.
[2] [S. Berington] *Memoirs of Signor Gaudentio di Lucca: Taken Down from His Confession and Examination before the Fathers at the Inquisition at Bologna in Italy* (1737, often re-issued), traveller's tales.
[3] T. Grossi (1820).
[4] Spectacular waterfall and rock rapids, west of Braemar.
[5] Corriemutzie, in the same glen, 4 miles west of Braemar.
[6] James Brown, [pseudonym of Joseph *Robertson,] *The Guide to Deeside* (1831).
[7] 3,796 ft.; 7 miles SE. of Braemar.
[8] Remains of the ancient Grampian forest of Marr.
[9] In Ballochbuie Forest, midway to summit.
[10] 4,796 ft.; 11 miles NW. of Braemar.
[11] Two miles NW. of summit of Ben Macdhui.
[12] Perhaps James Donald of Dorlarthers, near Turriff, Aberdeenshire.

and near 39 m. on the top.—A snowstorm descending. We got praise from the guide for good travelling—he rode. Our stoppages altogether were 1½ hours: of wh 1 h. was rest. We were not much tired. Finished Sig. Gaudentio di Lucca.

10. Sat.

Coach to Ballater. Then after delay started across the hills without a guide & laden with brushes &c. to Lochlee Manse: 4h. 15 miles. Crossed Month-keen.[1] Home 20 more m. in phaeton at 7½. . found Helen ill from toothach—read Wraxall.

11. Sunday.

Nicole de l'Unité finished Vol 1—Milner. Sumner aloud. Stowell's Sermon[2] —I have now resumed mg & evg daily prayers from H.J.G.—Aftn prayers.

12. M.

Milner. Wraxall. Willis's Gipsy of Sardis.[3] wrote to Mr Wills[4]—Mr Sandoz[5] —Rev Mr Campbell[6]—Claypole.

13. T.

Milner. wrote on "Signs".[7] wrote to B. Harrison. Began Cicero's Academica.[8] Wraxall. Headach in evg. Whist. took M.E.G. up the hill.

14. W.

Milner. Vss. Wraxall. Not quite well. Rode to Drumtochtie &c. with J.N.G. & M.E.G.—boat.

15. Th.

Milner. Wraxall. "The First part of Sir John Oldcastle".[9] billiards. whist: medicine in evg.

16. Fr.

Blackwood. Whist. Envelopes. My Father apprised me yesterday that he

[1] Mount Keen, 3,077 ft., 6 miles SSE. of Ballater; hamlet at eastern end of Loch Lee, on North Esk, 4½ miles beyond it.
[2] H. *Stowell, in First Annual Report of the Church Pastoral Aid Society (1836).
[3] N. P. Willis, Inklings of Adventure (1836).
[4] Possibly John Wills, ecclesiastical lawyer; or William Robert Wills(-Sandford), ca. 1770–1859, Irish gentleman.
[5] Frederic Sandoz, 1801?–63; of Swiss origin; a founder of Church Pastoral-Aid Society; auditor for East India Company.
[6] James William Campbell, 1810?–79?, Yorkshireman; Trinity, Cambridge; vicar of Eye 1838–64; rector of Palgrave, Suffolk 1864–79; both *Kerrison's livings.
[7] Extracts in Morley, i. 137.
[8] On philosophy; less than half has survived.
[9] By Michael *Drayton and others (1600).

meant me to have—God grant at a very distant day—the lands in Ross-shire: & with them the disposal of the almshouses at D[ingwa]ll.[1]

17. Sat.

Milner. Vss. & writing out. Wrote to Aunt J. Rode to Keithock[2] & Stra-cathro. Wraxall. Whist.

18. Sunday.

Fettn ch.—aftn prayers. read Augustin—Milner—Nicole (began Vol II)—[3] Sumner aloud.

19. M.

Milner. Macintosh (finished). wrote on Rule of F[aith].[4] Wraxall. Irish Legends.[5] rode with M.E.G. Wrote to Doyle—Childers—Mr Rawson.

20. T.

Milner. Finished Vol II—Cic. Acad.—Wraxall (finished Series 1)—Began Göthe's Iphigenia—wrote.[6] paper.—wrote to T. Ogilvy—Rev. Mr Wilson—Mrs Gaskell.

21. W.

Milner Vol III. Wraxall Series II. Cic. Acad B.II—wrote to Uncle David—Mr Tyler. Whist. took M.E.G. to the Burn. The Goalens came.

22. Th.

Milner. Cic. Acad. B.II—Iphigenia—wrote to Mr Brooks—Mr Jones—Claypole: read Wraxall. Whist.
  [7]Midnight brought solemn recollections!

23

—more cherished on this day, the sad anniversary of my dear Mother's departure to a distant land: I can call it no more: yet in this view it is still sad to us. With it I join an event of the same month in 1833, still very mournful.[8]
  read Milner—Cic. Acad. II—Iphig—Wraxall. Wrote on Rule of Faith.[9]

[1] Nothing came of this.
[2] Hamlet 8 miles S. by W. of Fasque.
[3] 'wrote' here deleted; but see Lathbury, ii. 429–30, on good use of money.
[4] Cp. 23 Sep. 36.
[5] Samuel *Lover, *Legends and Stories of Ireland* (1834).
[6] Extracts in Morley, i. 137.
[7] 'This' here deleted.
[8] *Hallam's death.
[9] Add MS 44726, ff. 155–174, dated this day.

24. Sat.

wrote to Lincoln. Mr Tallents.—read Milner—Aug. de Civ. Dei—Cic. Acad.
—Iphigenia. Wraxall.

25. Sunday.

Church at Laurencekirk. Prayers in aftn. Sumner Serm 7.—Aug. de Civ.
Dei.—Milner. Nicole. Wilson's "Work of an Evangelist".[1]

26. M.

Wrote to A. Acland—R. Williams. read Milner—Cic. Acad. (finished), very
useful for information—Augustin—Wraxall. rain ∴ billiards—whist.

27. T.

Milner. Cic de Finibus, began. Iphigenia. Wraxall. Whist. sculled H.J.G. &
M.E.G.

28. W.

Milner. Cic. de Fin. (began B.II). wrote to H. Thompson—Wraxall—whist.
Iphigenia—Mss. gun.

29. Th.

Wrote to Mr G. on Lpool invitation.[2] Milner. Mss. Cic. de Fin. Wraxall.
Iphigenia. whist. gun.

30. Fr.

Wrote to Jacobson. Milner. Cic de Fin. Aug. de Civ. Dei (began V) Wraxall.

Saturday Octr One.

a commencement of sore throat—Milner, Aug. de Civ. Dei, Cic. de Fin.
(began B.III), Wraxall (began Vol III), billiards (rain)—whist: Miss Doyle
came. Conv. long with H.J.G. on future plans.

2. Sunday.

Mustard plaister & dose (with calomel) acc[or]d[in]g[l]y to bed early. Not
at Fettn, but read aftn pr[ayers]. Milner—& Aug. de Civ. Dei.

3.

In bed. Eyes irritated: cd only read a few pages of Milner—came down late
in evg. A good conv with Robn G.

---

[1] Possibly a 40-page pamphlet by Daniel *Wilson in defence of the Church Missionary
Society (1818, often reprinted).
[2] See 4 and 18 Oct. 36.

4.

Turned out earlier. Milner. Wraxall. wrote to Aunt J.—Mrs Charriere—Mr Wilkinson:[1] accepting, as my Father wishes, the Lpool Conservative Socy's invitation—singing & whist.

5.

Tolerably convalescent, thank God.—Milner: Wraxall: whist & singing: my chief employment, in mg, a Petition from Judith Fileen to Mr G. in verse: wh having answered, late at night I manufactured a reply.[2]

6.

Robn & M.E.G. left us, to our sorrow. John kindly goes with them to Edinbro. wrote out again my Epistles.—Milner—rode to the Burn—Wraxall. Singing.

7. Friday.

Milner. Wraxall. a dinner party—wrote out a Sketch of an Essay on Justification.[3] Singing: whist: shooting. Copied a paper for Mr G.[4]

8. Sat.

Afr much doubt arranged to return N. afr Lpool, please God.—Milner. wrote to Mrs Wallace—Mr M'Cann[5]—Ld Aberdeen—Doyle—Cole. Finished Iphigenia, & Wraxall. Vss.

9. S.

Milner & Nicole. Fettn & read aftn prayers: Sumner aloud. Working up notes of Milner.

10. M.

Milner. Vss.[6] whist. singing. walked out lionising Miss Doyle. Read Quarty on Last Session. papers.

11. T.

Milner. Wrote on the Will.[7] wrote to Mrs Nimmo.[8] Shooting. music. whist.

---

[1] Edmund Wilkinson, Liverpool attorney. Cp. 18 Oct. 36.
[2] Add MS 44726, ff. 195–200. Cp. 26 May 36n.
[3] Ibid. ff. 201–3.
[4] Version in Morley, i. 137.
[5] Perhaps Nicholas McCann, 1802–67, London surgeon.
[6] Add MS 44726, f. 206.
[7] Add MS 44726, f. 208.
[8] Mrs T. Nimmo was his father's sister.

12. W.

a day on the hill for roe: 14 guns.[1] wrote to Rn G. Mr Tallents—Queensferry—Milner. finished Vol **IV**—whist—prepn to be off.

13. Th.

left Fasque at 8½ for NWater Bridge.[2] 9¾–8¼, 94 m. by Defiance to Edinbro.
Left Miss Doyle at Queensferry.—rain in part. paper—began Marco
Visconti.[3] The Waterloo fair *as a* coach Inn.[4]

14. Fr.

Left at 7 A.M. by Mail to Lpool—attempted to read, in vain—even in
England, much corn still out.

15. Sat.

7¾ A.M. arrived at P.O. Lpool thank God safe—found Rn, thank Him
again & more, much better. read Marco Visconti—wrote to Aunt D—Mr
Blundell—Mr G—saw Mr Holme[5] & T.B. Horsfall on the toasts—differed
about Shaw—went with M.E.G. to the Exhibn—it seemed to do credit—at
Mr Jones's in evg. music.

16. Sunday

St Jude's—& St Luke's[6]—with M.E.; Charles Lawrence preached, very
well.—read Keith. One of MacNeil's sermons aloud in evening. Mr Backhouse called.

17.

Canning came to breakfast. calls. wrote to Mr G—d[ined] in Rodney Street.[7]
Marco Visconti. music.

18. T.

wrote to Mg Herald—Acland—Miss G.—Calls—a short time for thought.
Dinner at 5 at the Amphitheatre. Most kindly heard.[8] Canning's debut
everything that could be desired—I thought I spoke 35 min: but afterwards found it was 55—read Marco Visconti.

19. W.

wrote to T.G.—Lord Aberdeen—Mr Masterman—Lady Canning—C. Canning, a note—calls. dined at Steuart's. singing. read Marco Visconti. Three

---

[1] Morley, i. 137.
[2] North Water Bridge, where the main road crosses the Esk, 6 miles south of Fasque.
[3] Romance by T. Grossi (1834; tr. C. Ward, 2v. 1836).
[4] James Scott's coaching inn, Waterloo Place.
[5] Samuel Holme, master builder.
[6] In London Road and Berry Street respectively.
[7] His uncle Thomas Gladstones lived at no 2.
[8] This sentence and next in Morley, i. 137. Summary of speech in Robbins, 239.

hours tough work in writing out my speech from the Report of the Courier:
I think it is now tolerably correct.[1]

20. Th.

Marco Visconti. Calls. wrote to Lincoln. Dined at Aspinall's. Party chiefly
of master tradesmen. Wrote out a *second* [part] for a te o cara.[2]

21. Fr.

Marco Visconti. Calls (uncles, park). wrote to Mr G. & Aunt J.—Operative
dinner at Amphitheatre—spoke perhaps 16 or 18 min.[3]—Away before
nine—music at Mr Jones's.

22. Sat.

finished Vol 1. of Marco Visconti. read 2d Letter to Councillor Blackburn.[4]
Mr Brooks here. Also Uncle T. on the bakers' affair. dined at Dr Brandreth's.
wrote to J.N.G.—Best.

23. Sunday.

A striking & bold sermon from M'Neile on perhaps too narrow a basis—
Subject, idolatry. St Luke's in aftn—Callers x—Keith—& 'Memorials of a
departed friend'—insufficient?[5]

24. M.

M. Visconti. papers. calls. packing. wrote to Mr G—Lady Canning—dined
with the Joneses—sailed 10 P.M. with C[annin]g by Vulcan.

25. T.

Bitten: ∴ not a very agreeable passage. M. Visconti—Greenock 8 P.M.—
Tea there. Gl[asgow] 12¼.

26. W.

breakf. with the Cannings. paper. Marco Visconti—Mail at 1. to Perth 8½.
On to Abn.

27. Th.

Abn 6¼. On to O. Meldrum & Haddo.[6] Terrible morning. Sleet froze as it

---

[1] *Liverpool Courier.* 19 October 1836.   [2] Love song from Bellini's *I Puritani.*
[3] This sentence in Morley, i. 137. Summary of speech in Robbins, 240.
[4] 'A Second Letter to Mr. Councillor Blackburn containing a Scriptural Refutation of
his "Defence of the system adopted in the Corporation Schools in Liverpool"' (1836).
Thomas Blackburn's pamphlet also appeared in 1836.
[5] C. *D[yson] ed. (1836), prayers and other writings by his wife.
[6] Old Meldrum, 16 miles NNW. of Aberdeen; Lord *Aberdeen's place, Haddo House,
6 miles NE. of Old Meldrum.

fell a cake ½ inch thick on the side of my hat, tho it was soaked. Wrote to Miss Doyle—Jas Bruce—Mr G—: journal: accounts: read papers: memoir of Mrs Hemans:[1]

28. Fr.

Wrote to T.G.—Rn G.—finished Marco Visconti—a long bout—but I could not let it go. papers. Buckland's opening Chapters[2]—on *the whole*, satisfactory. billiards. walk with Ld A.—political conv.—wrote Mema.[3]

29. Sat.

wrote to T.S. Godfrey—and H.J.G.—Mema—papers. began Mahon[4]—Mrs Hemans. Billiards & walk with Mr Forbes. In evg, conv. chiefly on the Deeside scenery.—wrote to Canning.

30. S.

Methlick kirk[5]—Evg. prayers. read Keith—& two strange Chapters of Tucker's.[6] A note to T.G. & long letter to R. Williams. Ld A. read prayers in evg with simple & earnest pathos.[7]

31. M.

7½–11. Coach to Abn.—11.55–3.10 walk to Stonehaven. 3.10–7.45 to Fasque: pr[etty] near 18 m: slow from the very bad state of the road after the snow. read papers—little of Mahon & the Lady of the Lake.

Tuesday November One.

Accounts. Copied a letter. paper. wrote to Sir R. Peel (declining an invitation), Serj. Wilde, Burnaby, T.S. Godfrey—read Mahon—Quarty on Brewster & Keith—dined [and slept] at Arbuthnott—singing.

2. W.

Back at 1.—Mahon—& Adventures in search of a horse[8]—whist—paper.

3. Th.

Wrote to Jacobson—H. Thompson—Mr Larkins—Walker. paper. copied a letter. Mahon: Adventures; whist. Up the cairn.

---

[1] H. F. *Chorley, *Memorials of Mrs. *Hemans* (1836).
[2] W. *Buckland, *Geology and Mineralogy Considered with reference to Natural Theology* (1836); No. 6 of the Bridgewater Treatises.
[3] Extracts in Morley, i. 137; memoranda in Add MS 44777, ff. 31–35, where Lord Arbuthnott's arrival on 28 Oct. is mentioned also.
[4] *History of England*, 7v. (1836–54).
[5] Six miles north of Old Meldrum and 2 west of Haddo.
[6] Perhaps from William Tucker, *Predestination calmly considered* (1821).
[7] Extracts in Morley, i. 137.
[8] Sir G. *Stephen, *The Adventures of a Gentleman in Search of a Horse* (1835).

4. Fr.

Mahon—finished—Milner: finished Vol IV. wrote to Tallents. Lincoln. H. Taylor. Downie,[1] & copied a letter—whist—paper.

5. Sat.

T.G. went with L., 6½. finished notes from Mahon.[2] Milner. Began Wilhelm Meister.[3] Shooting with J.N.G.—"Adventures"—began Monk Lewis's Journal.[4]—wrote to Canning.

6. Sunday.

wrote on Ser.—Keith—Aug. de Civ. Dei—Nicole—Milner.—Fettn—prayers in aftn—Sumner S.X aloud.

7. M.

Milner. Arranging papers in my new box wh I hope will conduce to order. Vss. Wilhelm Meister: Adventures: Lewis's Journal. L[ewis] seems to have humanity, but levity & flippancy amounting to profaneness—paper.

8. T.

Milner. Wrote to R.G.—Sir W.R.F.—T.D A[cland]—Mrs W. Wilhelm Meister. Walk & calls with J.N.G. resumed Cic. de Fin. B.III—Lewis—The Cannings came. music. paper.

9. W.

Rain, ∴ billiards & umbrella walk—Milner—Cic. de Fin.—Lewis—Wilhelmmeister—wrote to Mr T. Godfrey—music.

10. Th.

Milner. Cic de Fin. Wilhelm Meister: finished B.1. and there I mean to leave it, unless I hear a *better* report of the succeeding ones than I cd make of the first.[5] rode to the Burn[6]—music—whist—Lewis.

11. Fr.

Milner. Cic de Fin. wrote to T.G; Mr Goalen. Recommenced with great anticipations of delight the Divina Commedia.[5] Shooting with C[anning] & J.N.G.—Ld & Miss Arbuthnott to dinner. Whist. singing. papers.

---

[1] Possibly (Sir) Alexander Mackenzie Downie, 1811–52; s. of a Ross-shire minister; court physician; kt. 1840.
[2] Add MS 44726, f. 220.
[3] Goethe.
[4] M. G. *Lewis, Journal of a West Indian Proprietor* (1834).
[5] Versions in Morley, i. 137.
[6] Then William McInroy's.

18—II.

12. Sat.

Wrote to R.G.—Milner. Cic. de Fin. Inferno IV–VI. Rode to Edzell to attend the ladies. Lewis. paper. billiards with C[harles] C[anning]. music.

13. S.

Fettn., & aftn prayers. Sumner S.XI aloud. Finished Milner: good in spirit, a fair man in intent as well as a pious one. Fairness is a result of piety but not always worked out in the same degree. But defective in many historical points, even when a finished work? finished Nicole de l'Unité. I agree much with him on the *ministry*. Aug. de Civ. Dei.[1]

14. M.

Chronol[y] from Milner. Aug. de Civ. Dante VI–IX. (Inferno). Lewis. papers. wrote to B.H.—Mrs Chisholm. The Cannings went at 8, promising a return next year. whist. shooting. Cic. Fin.

15.

Aug de Civ.—Dante X–XII.—Cic de Fin. began B.V.—Lewis: finished. he seems a humane man in himself: sadly light & even profane. Began Rossetti sullo spirito Antipapale.[2] wrote to Mr Sandoz.

16.

Aug. de Civ.—Cic de Fin—wrote to Canning—Mr Tyler. Rossetti's Dante.[3] Dante XIII–XV. out shooting with J.N.G. whist—paper.

17.

Aug. de Civ. wrote to Caparn—Lincoln.—read Cic. de Fin—Dante XVI– XVIII. Joint Stock Bank C's Report[4]—Rossetti—whist. shooting with J.N.G. paper.

18.

Aug. de Civ. D.—Cic de Fin. finished.—Shooting exp[edition] to Balfour[5] 11–4½.—Dante XIX–XXI. whist. paper. Rossetti. saw 55 hares.

19.

Aug. de Civ. d[ei]. Began Cic's Tusculan Questions. wrote to H. Taylor (& notes on H. Thompson's case)—O.B. Cole—Mrs Wallis. Dante XXII–IV. whist. Rossetti. Shooting.[6]

---

[1] Extracts in Morley, i. 137.
[2] Gabriele Rossetti, *Sullo Spirito Antipapale che produsse la Riforma* (1832), literary and political disquisitions.
[3] *La Divina Commedia*, with an analytical commentary by G. Rossetti (1826).
[4] *PP* 1836 ix. 411, report of secret cttee. of commons.
[5] The Wood of Balfour lies along the edge of the Grampians, from 2 to 4 miles west of Fasque.   [6] Extracts in Morley, i. 138.

20. Sunday.

Fettn—& aftn Prayers—Sumner's S.—read Keith & (most of the day at Augustine. Trench.

21. M.

Aug.—Cic Tusc—[1]Inferno XXV–VII. Whist. Billiards. Wrote to Acland: reading papers about the C[hurch] P[astoral-]A[id] Society.

22. T.

Aug—Cic. Tusc—[2]Rossetti—Inferno XXVIII–XXX. whist. paper. wrote to R. Williams, & Mr Sandoz on the Qq. 5 and 8.

23. W.

Aug de Civ. Dei (I am now in B.XII)—Cic. Tusc. (finished B.I). wrote to Rn G—Mr Luxmoore—Mrs Wallis—Inferno XXXI–XXXIII—Rossetti. Dryden's Fables.[3]

24. Th.

Aug. de Civ. D.—Cic. Tusc II—wrote to Jas Bruce—T.G.—Dante Inf 34 & Purg 1.2.—Rossetti. a dose of whist. walk with J.N.G.—still snow & rain —perusing Vss &c.

25. Fr.

Aug de Civ. Dei. began B.XIV.—Cic. Tusc. finished B.II. wrote to Sir G. Clerk. Mrs Wallis. Rossetti. Purgatorio 3–5. paper. whist.[5]

26. Sat.

Rain & snow still continue. Wrote to T. Godfrey—Lincoln—Caparn: arranging or rather deranging—for the delay of my visit to Nk on acct of the Scotch dinners.[4]—Also to Mrs Wallis—Mrs Wishlade.

Aug.—Cic.—billiards—Purg. 6.8. whist. Began Dryden's Fables. My eyes are not in their best plight & I am obliged to consider type a little— Read however some Rossetti wh is tolerable in this.[5]

27. Sunday.

Fettn—Aftn prayers—a Sermon on Advent. S. Aug.—Keith—Par Lost Bb.1, 2.—

[1] 'Rosetti' here deleted.
[2] '(finished)' here deleted.
[3] *Fables Ancient and Modern* (1700).
[4] Cp. 13 Jan. 37.
[5] Versions of extracts in Morley, i. 138; with confusion between the days.

28. M.

Wrote to Sir J. Forbes. read S. Aug.—Cic. Tusc.—Purg. 9–11. went to the Burn—Dryden's Fables—papers—whist. translating from Inferno 33.

29. T.

S. Aug.—Cic. Tusc (finished 3)—Purg 12–14. Dryden's Fables. He professes to write a chaste book. Did he believe himself?—paper—whist—on the hill. transl a little.

30. W.

S. Aug. 10½–4 on an exp[edition] to the Burn sale, print-hunting. Not very successful.—Read Purg. 15–17 there. Cic. Tusc—Finished Dryden's Fables. Whist: the last.

Thursday December One.

J.N.G. went.—S. Aug.—Cic Tusc—accts—paper—Purg. 18–20. Wrote a long letter to Mr Sandoz on the C.P.A. matters—& read Ward's pamphlet.[1]

2. Fr.

Wrote to Chisholm—T.G.—Geo M'Kenzie—read S. Aug.—Cic. Tusc.—Dante transl.—paper—whist revived in dummy—Rossetti.

3.

S. Aug—Cic. Tusc.—Purg. 21–3.—paper—dummy—on the hill. wrote to H. Thompson—Rossetti.

4. Sunday.

Wrote to Mrs Wallis (money)—Fettn & aftn prayers. Sumner.—read S. Aug.—Keith—Par Lost 3 & 4.

5. M.

Wrote to Mrs Wallis—Gardiners (Bl.B.)[2]—read S. Aug (now in B.18)—Cic. Tusc—Purg. 24–6—called on some tenants—wrote to Williams & Harrison—whist—Rossetti—paper.

6. T.

Aug. C.D.—Cic. Tusc. (finished). Purg. 27—9. Rossetti. shooting—whist. wrote to J.N.G.—Goskirk.[3]

---

[1] Possibly Zion [i.e. John] *Ward, *The Fall of Lucifer* (1836).
[2] Gardiner & Son, stationers, of Prince's Street, Cavendish Square.
[3] Unidentified.

7. W.

Aug C.D.—Cic. de Nat. Deorum—Purg 30–32. Rossetti—at Fettn—calls—whist.

8. Th.

Aug C.D.—Cic. Nat. D.—wrote to Mayow—W.M. Goalen—Glasgow Commee—finished Purgatorio, & drew an abstract of the cycles of punishment in that & the Inferno.[1] paper.

9. Fr.

wrote to Taylor.—(at nt) Caparn—Mrs Hagart. St Aug C.D.—Cic. N.D. finished B 1—Rossetti—paper—Joint Stock Banks Report—rode to Lkirk &c.

10. Sat.

Gave Best notice. It went much agt the grain with both of us: but it is unavoidable.—Wrote to Mg Post—Mrs Wallis—Luxmoore—T.G.—arranging to advertise &c.—Mr Halliwell (organ).[2] read Aug. C.D.—Cic. N.D. (B.II)—Joint Stock Report—Rossetti. wrote to Froom[3]—Boyles.[4]   . . . .

11. Sunday.

A long & very able letter from Acland: wrote a reply = only in length. St Aug—Keith (finished) my eyes don't do their work well. Fettn—attn prayers & Sumners (excellent) 14th Serm. Visited old Mary Hay. Our dearest Father's birthday.

12. M.

Aug. Civ. D.—Cic. N.D.—wrote to Ld Haddington[5]—Lady Kerrison—& a controversial letter—faugh!—draft & copy, to Mr Kinnear.[6] Dummy. Rossetti. Joint Stock Banks—arranging books. Boccaccio.

13. T.

Wrote to J.N.G.—read Aug. Civ. D.—Cic. N.D.—Rossetti—J.S.B. Report —began Crabb's Tales[7]—dummy—visited old E. Taylor.[8]

---

[1] Add MS 44726, f. 275.
[2] Possibly John Hallewell, 1795–1871, E.I.C. chaplain at Madras 1823–39.
[3] Unidentified.
[4] Possibly the lord justice clerk (see 4 Jan. 37) and his 2nd wife, Camilla Catherine, née Smythe, d. 1880, da. of David, Lord *Methven.
[5] Thomas *Hamilton, 1780–1858; close friend of *Canning; tory M.P. 1802–27; cr. Lord Melros 1827; 9th earl of Haddington 1828; viceroy of Ireland 1834–5, refusing India 1841; first lord of admiralty 1841–6; lord privy seal 1846. See 4–7 Jan. 37.
[6] Patrick Kinnear, d. 1848, of Longforgan, near Dundee.
[7] *Crabbe, Tales (1812).
[8] A cottager.

14. W.

Began to write "directions for Best"—Aug. C.D. (B.21)—Cic. N.D. (B.3.)—J.S.B. Report—Crabb—dummy.

15. Th.

Aug. C.D.—Cic. N.D. B.3—Crabb—Rossetti—the Whytes & Mr Hutton to dinner—singing.

16. Fr.

Aug. C.D.—Finished Cic. N.D.—wrote to Mr Kinnear—J.S.B. Report. Rossetti. Crabb. Dummy.

17. Sat.

Aug. C.D.—Began Cic. Off. I.—wrote to R. Williams & Sir J. Forbes.[1] Crabb—Rossetti. Whist. Presb. Review on Dodsworth.[2]

18. Sunday.

Aug. C.D.—M'Crie's Knox.[3] Par L. B.5.—Fettn, & prayers in aft. Sumner S.15.

19. M.

Business about prints & rooms. Aug. C.D.—wrote to Mrs Wallis—Luxmoore—Mr Ogilvy—Rn G.—Munns.[4]

20. T.

Finished S. Aug. de Civ. D.—a noble work—Cic. Off.—Crabb—J.S.B. Report. Rossetti. Wrote to Luxmoore—Mrs Wallis—paper.

21. W.

Rossetti. Cic. Off. wrote to Gaskell—Mr Kelly—shooting, as for several days past. J.S.B. Report. Crabb. Whist. 'Oriental Trinn'.[5]

22. Th.

Rossetti. J.S.B. Report. paper.—Or. Trinn—Cic. Off.—whist. wrote to Goskirk. Kinnear. Lawton.[6] H. Thompson.

---

[1] 'J[oint] S[tock] B[anks] Report' here deleted.
[2] *Presbyterian Review* (November 1836), ix. 46, on W. *Dodsworth, *The Church of England a Protestor against Romanism and Dissent* (1836).
[3] T. *McCrie, *Life of John *Knox* (1812).
[4] Possibly R. Munns, Oxford Street upholsterers.
[5] T. *Maurice, *A Dissertation on the Oriental Trinities* (1800).
[6] Perhaps George Lawton, 1808–53, librarian of Manchester Mechanics' Institution 1832–45, director 1850.

23. Fr.

Heard of Sir M. Stewart's death. Wrote to his Mother.[1]—Rossetti. Cic. Off. —Oriental Trinities—Crabb (finished "Tales")—paper—J.S.B. Report— arranging letters. wrote to Harrison.

24. Sat.

Dearest Anne! but why remember her earthly birthday? the 19th Feby is her better birthday.
Cic. Off.—Rossetti (finished)—Oriental Trinities—papers—J.S.B. Report— wrote to Selwyn—Lady Kerrison—Pakenham—Rn G.—papers—whist.

25. Christmas day. Sunday.

Breakfd early to go to Lkirk; but the snow recommenced & I was obliged to give it up.
Mg prayers. Evg. prayers with Sermon.—Debarred on this great day from the Communion may we learn to value more its general accessibility.
M'Crie—Par L. B.VI—Acct of Jerusalem.[2] Or[iental] Trinn.

26. M.

J.S.B. Report.—Cic. Off.—wrote to Luxmoore—Mrs Wallis—Uncle D. (bis)—Mayow—Aunt J.—& in evg. two editions of a draft to Sir G. Grey on an annoying letter from Sir J.C. Smyth.[3] Wrote & gave full directions to Best. At Fettn—snow obstinate. paper. Crabb's Sir Eust, Grey & Justice Hall: both powerful.[4]

27. T.

Finished J.S.B. Report. read to Mr G. & copied out (with some verbal enlargements) my letter to Sir G. Grey—also wrote a long letter to Willmot on Irish Education.[5] Sent off Best to Montrose for Dundee. Wrote to Matthew[6] & Nicoll. read M'Crie. Quarterly on Mahon—& on Campbell.— whist. no post in.

28. W.

The last day of my 27th year; one wd lay hold on it, & stop it: but it cannot be.

[1] Catherine, youngest da. of Sir William Maxwell, bart., of Springkell, m. 1787 Sir Michael Shaw-Stewart, 5th bart., of Ardgowan, who d. 1825. His son and namesake d. 19 December 1836.
[2] *An Account of the Siege and Destruction of Jerusalem, with some Observations on the Present State of the Jews* (1822).
[3] Sir James Carmichael-*Smyth, 1780–1838, military engineer; served at Corunna and Waterloo; cr. bart. 1821; major-general 1825; governor of Bahamas, 1829, of British Guiana, 1833; accused diarist of partiality. Draft to Sir G. *Grey, much altered, in Add MS 44355, ff. 145–6.
[4] *Poems* (1807).   [5] His reply in Add MS 44355, f. 159: 4 Jan. 37.
[6] Possibly David Matthew, city merchant.

Wrote my 44 invitations for Newark: tough & tedious enough.[1] those to[2] Ln, Mr E.S. G[odfrey], Mr T.S. G[odfrey], Caparn & Mr Tallents, were letters.

Cic. Off.—Oriental Trinities. M'Crie's Knox.

29. Th.

Another birthday, with its monitory recollections. Every year the mercies of God seem to, and do accumulate: but the mixture of baseness and nothingness within is brought out more clearly & convincingly as their sad counterpart: have mercy, O God, have mercy.

At Fett[ercair]n exam[inin]g ground for almshouses. Visited two of the old women on the Garrol. wrote to T.G.—& W. Tancred.[3] the last whist: no S. mail: read M'Crie—Cic. Off. (finished B.3)—Oriental Trinities. a few Vss.

30. Fr.

Finished Oriental Trinities, & notes. M'Crie Vol 1 & notes. wrote to Mr Ramsay—Best—Shooting. Mr G. & Helen went off at 7½ A.M.—packed, & arranged divers matters.

31. Sat.

Read Hallam's Rossetti. 9¼–10½ to Edinbro by Defiance. A frost. The snow near Kinross where deep nearly as high as the coach. paper. Wrote to Ld Hadd[ingto]n—made up accts for the month.

[1] See 19 Jan. 37.
[2] Instead of 'of'.
[3] William Tancred, 1818–64, 3rd s. of 6th bart.; once archdeacon of Launceston, Tasmania.

Edinbro.

Sunday January One.

God pardon the past year & bless the coming.
St John's & Commn—wrote to Rev. C. Lawrence & B. Harrison: read
Cowper's Vss from de la Motte Guion.[1] tea at Mrs Frasers. St Andrews in
evg. & why.

2.

Calls. dined at Lady Arbuthnots—reading *up* the newsp. of 4 or 5 posts.

3. Tues.

Dined at Mr Ramsay's. breakfast with Dr Chalmers. began F. O'Connor.[2]
papers. wrote to Best—Mr Roberts. Basil Hall with us.[3]

4. W.

6–9½ journey to Tynninghame by Linton[4]—Found Ld & Lady Belhaven,[5]
Justice Clerk,[6] Ld Gillies,[7] &c. Sea walk there. read F. O'Connor: wrote to
Mayow. J.N.G.

5. Th.

wrote to Lincoln—Pakenham—Dr Chalmers—Mr G.—read 'La Royne
d'Ecosse'[8]—Charles I's prayer book—Walk.

6. Fr.

walk. read H. Walpole to Sir H. Mann[9]—convv. with Ld Haddington on
politics—as on Wed. abt Church & religion.

[1] W. *Cowper, *Poems Translated from the French of Madame de la Motte Guion* (1801).
[2] F. *O'Connor, *A Series of Letters . . . to Daniel *O'Connell . . . containing a review of Mr. *O'Connell's conduct during the agitation of the question of Catholic Emancipation* (1836).
[3] Extract, with addenda, in Morley, i. 138. Basil *Hall, 1788–1844, sailor and author; F.R.S. 1816; captain R.N. 1817; half-pay 1823; mad 1842.
[4] Tynninghame House, Lord *Haddington's place on the coast, 3 miles west of Dunbar and 2 miles NE. of East Linton, a village 22 miles east of Edinburgh.
[5] Robert Montgomery Hamilton, 1793–1868; 8th Lord Belhaven and Stenton 1814; whig Scottish representative peer, 1819–32; cr. Lord Hamilton (U.K. barony) 1831; m. 1815 Hamilton Campbell, 1790?–1873.
[6] David *Boyle, 1772–1853; M.P. Ayrshire 1807–11; lord justice clerk 1811 (Lord Boyle); lord president of court of session 1841–52.
[7] Adam *Gillies, 1760–1842; Scottish judge, 1811; lord of justiciary (Lord Gillies, 1812; judge in court of exchequer, 1837; 'strong, learned, and impartial' (*DNB*).
[8] 'Meditation faite par *Marie Royne d'Escoce et Dovariere de France' in 1572, in *Bannatyne Miscellany*, i. 339 (1837).
[9] H. *Walpole, *Letters to Sir H. *Mann. . . . British Envoy at the Court of Tuscany*, 3v. (1833).

7. Sat.

Sir H. Walpole to Sir H. Mann—could not finish Vol 1—1½–5½ cold ride to Edinbro: dined at Mr Ramsay's—headache.

8. Sunday.

Ch mg & aftn, then laid myself up & went to bed. My letters unread.

9. M.

Up in time to go by the carriage (how kind is my Father in matters small as well as great)[1] to Bantaskine, where we arrived at 4½—leaving at 1. A little music.

10. T.

Mr G. & H.J.G. went on. Unable to read or write with comfort: wrote however a note of necessity to Mr Jas Finlay—& an answer to the Notts Inv[itation]—by the hand of C. H[agart]—billiards—conv. with Mrs H. on the Ap[ostolica]l succession.

11. W.

No eyes usable yet. Wrote by proxy, to J.N.G.—Gaskell—Best. Billiards with C.H.—Music—whist: walked out to see the curling at Callander.[2]

12. Th.

paper, a little. read W.I. letters &c. wrote, by my proxy, a long draft (proposed) for Mr G. to send to Sir G. Grey[3]—wrote to Mr G—& by deputy to Blackwood—Lawton—& Sec. Agric. Empl. Inst.—Music. whist—billiards with Mr H. & J.H.

13. Fr.

9–12 to Glasgow. Called on Mrs Nimmo &c. To the dinner at 4½.—The pavilion astonishing: & the whole effect very grand. Near 3500. Sir R.P. spoke 1 h. 55 m.—explicit & bold: it was a great effort.—I kept within 15 min—quite long enough.[4]

14. Sat.

7½–5½ Mail to Carlisle. On all night.[5]

---

[1] Thus far, misdated, in Morley, i. 138.

[2] Callendar, the neighbouring estate 1½ miles to the east, belonged to William Forbes, d. 1855, tory M.P. for Stirlingshire, 1835–7 and from 1841.

[3] Add MS 44355, ff. 161–5. Cp. 26 Dec. 36, n.

[4] Version in Morley, i. 138. *Peel's address at his installation as rector of Glasgow university was published; see Parker, ii. 327–35. *Gladstone's speech summarised in Robbins, 242–4.　　　　　　　　　　[5] In Morley, i. 138.

15. Sunday.

Wetherby[1] at 7½. Leeds 10¼. Church there. walked over to Wakefield. Church there. Evg at Thornes.[2]

16. M.

Overpersuaded into remaining here today. billiards with J.M.G.—singing—walk—wrote to Mr G—Best—Caparn.

17. T.

10½–4¾. Wakefield–Newark. In time to hear Lincoln—& to speak ¾ hour. A very good meeting.[3] Ln spoke very well. wrote to Sir A. Grant[4]—Gaskell —Mrs Hagart—J.[N.]G.—Mr Cumming.[5]

18. W.

Calls & convv.—dined with G. Hutton[6]—Lincoln & his brothers to tea—music between—I have no eyes for reading yet. wrote to J.N.G.—T.G.—Beckett—Dr Bigsby (not sent).[7]

19. Th.

Calls on the Vicar,[8] Mr Simpson & others: the Church matter is painful & looks very impracticable. Also saw Dr Bigsby with Ln on the Mech. Institution. Went over the Workhouse. My dinner at 5—about 40—I was in the chair: had plenty of speaking & some singing. wrote to Mrs Wallace—Caparn (two notes of reference) Mr Fellowes—Mr G—Geo. Hutton, on a conv. of yesterday.

20. Fr.

Conv. with Lawton on railroads &c. Mail to Ollerton: Clumber before 12. Walk. wrote to Lady Kerrison—Mr G—Rev. B. Harrison—paper a little—singing in evg. Lady Lincoln has much of her usual buoyancy: but suffers much I believe—bravely & in secret.[9]

21. Sat.

Shooting, in Birk Holt & Long Cover[10]—abt 120 head killed, after 1 P.M.—an excellent specimen: galloped home. (wrote to Mr R. Thompson.)[11] Singing

---

[1] On the great north road, 11 miles NE. of Leeds.
[2] In Morley, i. 138.
[3] See Morley, i. 138–9, and summary in Robbins, 244–7.
[4] Sir Alexander Cray *Grant, 1782–1854, 6th bart. 1825; W.I. planter; M.P. 1812–32, 1840–3; on Indian board of control 1834–5; public accounts commissioner, 1843.
[5] Probably Alexander Cumming, minister at Bridge of Earn, by Perth.
[6] George Hutton, mayor of Newark 1846.
[7] A point of punctilio about Newark mechanics' institution; in Add MS 44355, f. 166.
[8] J. G. Bussell.   [9] Cp. 4 Feb. 37.
[10] Some 4 miles south, and 2 miles SW. of the house.
[11] Robert Thompson of Oakham, Henry's father.

again. left, with regret before 11 for Tuxford—Highflyer to Newark before 2 A.M. of

22. Sunday.

Ch. mg & aftn—the Vicar preached what I am sure none cd deny to be the principles of the gospel. Tea with Mr Tallents. Convv. with Mr Thorpe on the Church—Mr Caparn & T. Godfrey on that & a certain rule of the Conserve newsroom—Butler, on methodism & his illness.

23. M.

6–8¾ to Norwich, by Lynn 118 m.[1]—excellent dinner at the Globe—at Shotesham[2] by 10. Found Louisa advancing in health. Wrote to Lincoln. Sir R. Bromley. Mavor. M'Lachlan. Ridgway.[3]

24. T.

to Norwich with T.G.—saw Cathedral &c. I have no eyes yet for general work. looked over Vss at night. wrote to Mr G—H.J.G.—Tertius Thomson[4] —Sir R. Bromley—Doyle—Mr A. Cumming—Lady Kerrison—Hicklin.

25. W.

wrote to Mrs Falconer—Williams (Oxf) and Bonham. read State Trials, D. of Buckm, &c.[5] & papers—but not for any time being still unable. The J. Felloweses dined here.[6] singing.

26. Th.

7½–9¾. 19 m. to Oakley.[7] Shooting with Sir E.K. in the Park. sang. Still little or no reading. Finished & wrote out my transln of Ugolino.[8]

27. Fr.

Shooting at Broome.[9] Wrote draft of a long letter to Vicar of Nk—the most I have yet attempted.[10] Music at nt. Rev. Mr Campbell of Eye a good man app[aren]tly as well as musician. Ld Porchester's [copy of] Persius[11]— Chateaubriand's Engl Lit.[12]

[1] Lynn Regis, now King's Lynn, Norfolk, at southern corner of the Wash; 55 miles ESE. of Newark and 40 WNW. of Norwich.　　　　[2] Six miles south of Norwich.

[3] James Leech Ridgway, 1801–62, publisher; a proprietor of *Globe*.

[4] Unidentified.

[5] Perhaps Sir Henry *Wotton's life of George *Villiers, 1st duke of Buckingham (1812).

[6] John Fellowes, 1785–1838, Robert's younger b.; Jesus, Cambridge; vicar of Shottesham 1810–27; rector of Bramerton from 1827; m. 1811 Susan, née Lyon, gd. of 8th earl of Strathmore.

[7] *Kerrison's place at Hoxne, 20 miles south of Norwich and 3 NE. of Eye, Suffolk.

[8] Cp. 16 June 37.

[9] Brome Park, 1¼ miles west of Oakley Park; Sir Miles *Nightingall's.

[10] In Add MS 44355, ff. 174–7.

[11] Henry Howard Molyneux *Herbert, 1831–90, styled Lord Porchester 1833, 4th earl of Carnarvon 1849; colonial secretary 1866–7, 1874–8; Irish viceroy 1885–6.

[12] *Essai sur la littérature anglaise et considérations sur le génie des hommes, des temps et des révolutions*, 2v. (1836).

28. Sat.

Wrote to Pulford—Mrs Chisholm—Mr G—R.G—W. Selwyn[1]—Caparn—: also to J.N.G. & wrote over my long letter to the Vicar.—Shooting. Music at night.

29. S.

Hoxne ch. mg & evg.[2]—readg S.P.G. report & Appx—long conv. with Mr Heathcote[3] on Church matters & on E.K.s[4]—day I hope not all squandered.

30. M.

Chateaubriand. Saw Sir E.K. & Lady M. Off at 7. Left at 8. 9 A.M.–8¾ P.M. Phenomena to town. T.G. in it. Coachman for leaving off Sunday travelling.

31. T.

House at 2—& again 5–8¼—What surprise at the King's Speech.[5]—Wrote to Lincoln. Harrison. Mr G. M'Lachlan. Mr Blundell. In Hill St with T.G.— & a long hard day at unpacking & arranging Books &c.[6] Saw Townshend.[7]

Wednesday Feb. One.

Another day chiefly employed on my books & papers. Dined in B. Square. wrote to Sir G. Grey—J.N.G.—G. Grant. Saw Townshend again. Made up accts

The last month added no single volume to my poor list of books read. Now how *thankful* ought I to be that the slight weakness which made it prudent to abstain, occurred at a time when my occupations & movements bodily were such as to fill my time. Literally there is no end of God's goodness because we may continually follow & trace it further into minute things.

2. Th.

Arranging books & papers. A little daylight in my chaos. What useful advice might a man who has been buon pezzo[8] in Parlt give to one young

[1] On ecclesiastical legislation; *Selwyn had sent him on the 25th a printed memorial by the dean and chapter of Ely (Add MS 44355, f. 170).
[2] The vicar till 1843 was Dr. James Cox of Wadham, b. 1769?
[3] The Kerrisons' tutor.
[4] Edward Clarence Kerrison, 1821–86, the son of the house; succ. as 2nd bart. 1853; cons. M.P. Eye 1852–66, Suffolk 1866–7; m. 1844 Lady Caroline Margaret Fox-Strangways, d. 1895, 2nd da. of 3rd earl of Ilchester; celebrated coach-driver.
[5] Even more insipid than usual: H xxxvi. 2. Debate on address ibid. 21.
[6] Thomas Gladstone then lived at 2 Hill Street, Mayfair; the diarist had moved into his father's house at 6 Carlton Gardens.
[7] Perhaps Edward Venables Townshend, 1774–1845, Cheshire gentleman (cp. 27 Feb. 37), or one of his three sons, Lee Porcher, 1804–71, Edward Du Pré, b. 1806, or Henry, 1813–96.
[8] 'a good bit'.

in it on this mechanical portion of his business so forgotten.[1]—Dined in
B. Square. read A Jamaica Planter[2]—curious—& Bp of Exeter's charge.[3]
With Tom in Berk. Square.

3. Fr.

Working still at papers. Calls & shopping. Wrote to Mr G. & Caparn.
Consultn on a letter from Dr Giffard.[4] Dined at Mrs Vansittart's. Conv.
with Wm Blackwell afr 15 years separation.[5]

4. Sat.

Doyle—Acland—Bonham—here. long convv. with the two last. B[onham]
about Midd[lese]x—wh will not do.[6] Began Cabhunting.[7] Wrote to Mr G.
and to the Duke of N. in answer to an unfavourable acct of Lady L. Dined
at Mr B. Baring's—Ld Ashbn, Rice, Rogers, &c.—read Sydney Smith's
letter.[8]

5. Sunday.

St Giles's mg & evg. The Communion. Newman's three first of Vol II[9]—&
Blakesley's Discourse.[10] Alack my eyes.

6. M.

Again with B[onha]m & the Mx affair app[aren]tly closed. Wrote to Mr G.—
Rich. Dawson[11]—Blakesley—Caparn (bis)—Lady Peel. House 5–7 and
10–1.[12] hunting the Mirror on Church Rates. Calls.

7. T.

Three hours with Acland on P[arliamen]t in general & Som[er]s[ets]h[ir]e
in particular[13]—House 5–12¼.[14] Convv. with Mr B. Baring—Joplin[15] on
Joint Stock Banks. Calls &c.

[1] Misdated version in Morley, i. 139.
[2] Perhaps 'A Statement of Facts' (1837) on effect of abolition in Jamaica.
[3] H. *Phillpotts, 'Charge Delivered to the Clergy of the Diocese of Exeter' (1836).
[4] Stanley L. Gifford, Clerkenwell doctor, urged him to stand for Middlesex at next
election: Add MS 44355, f. 186.
[5] William Whitehead Blackwell, 1805?–66; Trinity, Cambridge; ordained 1830; curate
of Mells, Somerset, ca. 1845–60.
[6] Because it would cost his father a second £1,000 at least: Add MS 44355, ff. 188–9.
[7] See 8, 10, 11, 20 Feb. 37.
[8] A Letter to Archdeacon *Singleton, on the Ecclesiastical Commission (1837).
[9] In J. H. *Newman, Parochial Sermons, 6v. (1834–42).
[10] J. W. *Blakesley, 'Thoughts on the Recommendations of the Ecclesiastical Commission' (1837).
[11] Richard Dawson, 1783–1850, Liverpool merchant.
[12] Privilege; and joint stock banks. H xxxvi. 138, 155.
[13] T. D. *Acland was M.P. for west Somerset, 1837 and (unopposed) 1841.
[14] Irish municipalities: H xxxvi. 206.
[15] Thomas *Joplin, 1790?–1845, author; founder of National Provincial Bank, 1833.

8. W.

St Martin's—horse & cabhunting—our party arrived in aftn. House 8¾–2.[1] —Thank God they are well—to speak in general terms. May this Lent be blessed.

9. Th.

City—C[hurch] P[astoral-] A[id] Meeting 1–4¾. A good spirit but a blank in the place where church principle shd be, on many hands. But who am I? Dined with Serj. Merewether.[2] Music. arranging papers.

10. Fr.

Cab & horse hunting again with R.G. & alone. dined at Mr Lyon's.[3] Saw Alexander[4] who assures me my eyes are quite sound & the ailment in the lid easily remediable. Began Mr Watson. House 4¾–6½.[5] Wrote to Glynne. Selwyn. Harrison. Mr Tallents. Moved for Australian papers.[6]

11. Sat.

Hanging prints. Visit from Alexander: who restricts me for the present. Again after cabs: bought one: much ado about nothing! Dined at Ld Ashburton's. paper.

12. Sunday.

St Mathew's Chapel mg & aft.—Began mg prayers: went to see Aunt J.— pt of a Serm. of Newman's—otherwise still otiose as to reading.

13. M.

Exam[inin]g servants. hanging prints—calls—Ho. 5–8½ & 10–12. div. in 152 : 151 on Stafford Writ.[7] Wrote to P. Pusey—Harrison—J.N.G.—Conv. with J. Baring.[8] A 3d visit from Alexander.

14. T.

Servant & horse hunting. Wrote to J.N.G.—& G.N. Vansittart.[9] House 4½–6.[10] Dinner & whist with my Father.

[1] Irish municipalities, 1°: *H* xxxvi. 295.
[2] In Whitehall Place.
[3] Probably David Lyon, 1794–1872; s. of a Jamaica planter; of Goring Castle near Worthing and later of Balentore Castle near Forfar; tory M.P. Beeralston 1831–2.
[4] An oculist; possibly Henry Alexander of Cork Street, F.R.C.S. 1844.
[5] Misc. business: *H* xxxvi. 406.
[6] Ibid.
[7] Against delaying by-election: *H* xxxvi. 445; Irish poor law: ibid. 453.
[8] John Baring, 1801–88, 3rd s. of 2nd bart.
[9] George Nicholas Vansittart, 1814–89; Etonian; served in guards.
[10] Members' property qualification: *H* xxxvi. 524.

15. Wed.

My researches still continued. House 5–8.[1] Tea with R.G.—Lady Henniker's,[2] & music, in evg. Calls. wrote to Ld Abn—Mr Leathes[3]—Mr Ward—Vicar. Mr Thorpe—O.B. C[ole]—Selwyn.

16. Th.

C[hurch] P[astoral-] A[id] Society 12–5½. Spoke for Mr Dale's Amt: lost by 25:38. Mr Cunningham's carried by 38:33 agt. Mr Sandoz's—then lost agt the origl rule by 38:39.—House 6¼–9½—Voted in 197:92 agt expulsion of Bps[4]—pt of Mr Nicholl's Report.[5]

17. Fr.

a round of calls. papers. Mr Nicholls. Alexander—who reports well of my eyelids. House before & after dinner.[6] Long conv. with Mr West[7] on Irish matters—they are disheartening—wrote to Geo. M'Kenzie—Mrs Gaskell.

18. Sat.

Engaged a servant—Church Rate meeting 12–2½—Penitentiary—Coachmaker's—paper—wrote to Mr Alexander—Maurice—Mr Blundell—dined at Sir R. Peel's: Ld Stanley & his friends there.[8]

19. S.

Wild day. St Mathew's mg & evg. read 3 Newmans only.

20. M.

Turned out my cab.[9] Calls. Wrote to Manning—Blakesley—Robertson—Mr Russell (Glasgow)[10]—House 5–8¾ and 9¾–12½. Irish Mun. Bill.—wd have spoken but dared not.[11]

21. T.

read Crombie on the Ballot[12]—& pt of Wiseman's Evidence before the Edn

---

[1] English municipalities, cttee.: ibid. 568.
[2] Anna, née Kerrison, 1812–89, 1st da. of Sir E.*; m. 5 Jan. 37 John Henniker-Major, 1801–70, who succ. as 4th Lord Henniker 1832, and was conservative M.P. for Suffolk 1832–46 and from 1856 till cr. Lord Hartismere, 1866.
[3] Who had taken over his rooms in Albany: Add MS 44810 C, f. 1.
[4] *Lushington moved that bishops should leave parliament: H xxxvi. 609.
[5] 'wrote to Geo. McKenzie—Mrs Gaskell' here deleted.
[6] Irish municipalities, 2⁰; and misc. business. Ibid. 633.
[7] John Beatty West, 1793–1841, Irish Q.C. and landowner; conservative M.P. Dublin 1835–7 and 1841; constant and even-tempered opponent of *O'Connell.
[8] See Morley, i. 139.
[9] i.e. rigged it out, not discarded it.
[10] Michael *Russell, 1781–1848, dean of Edinburgh 1831, bp. of Glasgow 1837; or John Robert Russell of Glasgow Academy.
[11] Irish municipalities, in cttee.: H xxxvi. 657.
[12] A. *Crombie, A Letter to Henry William Tancred, Esq., M.P., on the Ballot (1837).

Committee.—wrote to Mr Simpson—dined at Ld Mahon's—House 4¾–6 and 9½–12.[1]

22. W.

Joplin on J.S. Banks[2]—pt of Barnes on Church Rates.[3] House 4½–6½ & 8½–3½. divided in 242:322 on Irish Corpns.[4] Attended meeting of Church Committee—wrote to Mr Walker—Walker Ord[5]—R. Palmer—Hope.[6]

23. Th.

Wrote to Mayor of Newark[7]—Vicar of do.—Mr Hallam—read Joplin. railroad business—conv. with Acland—meeting at Ashley's on C.P.A. Society. Calls. dined at Sir R. Peel's. GEO. HALL'S SERVICE BEGINS.

24. Fr.

finished Joplin. Arranging with Geo. Hall. Calls & business. Dined with the Larkinses. Aborigs Committee. MARE CAME FROM MAVOR'S TO COLLEY[8]. House 3¾–6¼ & 10–12.[9] Wrote to Mayor of Nk—A. Acland.

25. Sat.

House deranged in the morning by John's very severe attack of pain & [sc. both] face & head. Out for advice. read Fraser on Ch. Rates[10]—finished Barnes—at Milbank. wrote to R.G.—B. H[arrison]—Mayor of Nk—Browne —Reddie—Bartlett Vicar[??]—Wilmot and Col. Pocklington.

Last night in the Park I was stopped by two women both of whom as they said & I believed them had taken to their miserable calling from losing their livelihood by the death of their husbands. One had two children.

26. S.

St. Marg's—& St Matt's.—John's severe pains still continue. Shepherd's 'Autumn Dream'.[11]

27. M.

Present when Mr G. saw V. Townshend. Aborigs Commee House 4½–8 and 9½–11½. Poor Laws.[12] Finished Nicholl's Report. Began the Canadian Report.[13]

[1] Irish municipalities, ctd.: H xxxvi. 773.
[2] T. *Joplin, 'An Examination of the Report of the Joint Stock Bank Committee' (1836).   [3] R. Barnes, A Letter on Church Rates (1837).
[4] Irish municipalities: power to abolish refused. H xxxvi. 863. And an Irish scene: cp. Greville, iii. 355.
[5] John Walker *Ord, 1811–53; editor, Metropolitan Literary Journal (later Britannia).
[6] Cp. Ornsby, i. 112–1.6
[7] T. S. Godfrey.   [8] J. Colley, of Cockspur Street, saddler.
[9] Poor laws: H xxxvi. 986.   [10] Fraser's Magazine xv. 146 (February 1837).
[11] J. *Sheppard, An Autumn Dream: Thoughts in Verse on the intermediate state of the happy spirits (1837).
[12] Irish municipal reform, 3°; poor laws. H xxxvi. 1058, 1065. 'Had not courage to speak' here deleted.
[13] PP 1837 xxiv. 1, on grievances in Lower Canada.

19—II.

28. T.

Finished Records Report[1]—reading Canadn Report & Quarty on Cathedrals. wrote to Mr Ramsay—Robn—Mr Dawson—Mr Burnaby. dinner at home & whist. Calls. House 5–6¼.[2]—John relieved by losing his tooth.

Wednesday March One.

letters—accounts—wrote to Hicklin—Mr Lee—remounted my grey—dined at Mayow's—met Mrs Butler[3] there in evg: at Lady Antrobus's Concert. House 4½–6¼.[4] Canada Report—Bp Ward's Memorial.[5]

Thursday March 2.

Began La Fuggitiva[6]: ref. to Dem[erar]a Acts for Mr. G.—C.P.A. Comm^ee Meeting—writing out verses.[7] dined at 24 B.Sq.[8]—Mrs. Ede's—House 4¾–5¼ and after dinner.[9] God help me thro' these idle days.

3. Friday

Canada Reports. rode. House 5–9¾.[10] Discussion not desired by our leaders today. Wrote to Cubley (Nk).[11] Consulting Polybius on Roman religion.[12] Lady Stanhope's in evng.

4. Sat.

With Sir R.P. on Canada.[13] Wrote to Ld Ab^n—Party summoned. Dined at W.R.F's—rather sore—Canada Reports—Speaker's levee—rode. Milbank Committee.

5. S.

read Keble on Tradition[14] & Maurice's First Number: (rather a strain). It is admirable.[15] St. James's mg & aftn.—Communion.

[1] *Report from the Select Committee Appointed to enquire into the Management and Affairs of the Record Commission, and the Present State of Records in the United Kingdom.* PP 1836 xvi. 1.
[2] Misc. business: *H* xxxvi. 1161.
[3] Frances Anne *Kemble, 1809–93; actress; daughter of Charles *Kemble; m. 1834 Pierce Butler; author of poetical, dramatic and autobiographical works.
[4] Imprisonment for debt: *H* xxxvi. 1177.
[5] W. Ward, 'A Statement in reference to the proposed suppression of the Bishopric of Sodor and Man; contained in two memorials addressed to his Majesty's Commissioners appointed to consider the state of the Established Church with reference to Ecclesiastical duties and revenues' (1837).
[6] Romantic verse novel by T. Grossi (1816).
[7] In Add MS 44727, ff. 1–9.   [8] At the *Tylers'.
[9] Misc. business: *H* xxxvi. 1186.   [10] Church rates: ibid. 1207.
[11] Thomas Cobley, Newark sawyer.
[12] *Histories* vi. 56; one sentence formed the motto of the diarist's impending book (cp. ii. 351 below, n. 2). And cp. Add MS 44819, ff. 26–29.
[13] Account of talk in Morley, i. 139; conflated with that of 6 March.
[14] J. *Keble, *Primitive Tradition recognized in Holy Scripture* (1836).
[15] F. D. *Maurice, 'Letters to a Quaker', in ten parts, republished as *The Kingdom of Christ* (1837).

6. M.

Canada Reports (finished). Fuggitiva. Sir R.P's at 12. he read to Ld A. & me Ld S[tanley]'s letter.[1] Aborig^s Comm^{ee}—House $5\frac{1}{4}$-$12\frac{1}{4}$[2]—at home to tea—rode.

7. T.

read Horsley Palmer,[3] & Jones Loyd,[4] on the Bank & Money Market.— 2h conv. with Acland. rode. House 5-$6\frac{1}{4}$ and 9-$1\frac{1}{4}$. Voted agt Ballot in $265:153$.[5]

8. W.

read 'Letters on Canada'[6] Calls. House 5-$2\frac{1}{2}$. home to tea. Spoke about $\frac{3}{4}$ hour on Canada: unable to keep my engagement with Ld Cholmondeley.[7] Spoke with insuff[icien]t possession of the subject. 6 divisions—1st. $318:56$ —last $144:16$.[8]

9. Th.

read Ward on Emigration[9]—and Ricardo on the Bank.[10] Sat with Ld Cholmondeley. Dined at Sir E. Kerrisons. Hoarseness came on. Conv. with Mr Beaucham[11]—declined to attend Wesl. Miss. Soc^y & why. House 5-$6\frac{3}{4}$.[12] Wrote to Caparn, Falkner,[13] OBrien. O. & C. Club Comm^{ee}—Saw Dr Macleod.[14]

10 Fr.

Voice lost. read Kendall on the position of the Wesleyans.[15] Wrote on Ap[ostolica]l Succ[essio]n Factory Deputation. read Hook's Family Prayers. House 5-$6\frac{3}{4}$.[16] Dined at T.G's. began the Duke of N's book.[17]

[1] Cp. Add MS 44819, f. 26.
[2] Canada: *H* xxxvi. 1287. He was also put on select cttee. on Irish education.
[3] J. H. *Palmer, 'The Causes and Consequences of the Pressure upon the Money-Market' (1837).
[4] S. J. *Loyd, 'Reflections suggested by a perusal of Mr. J. Horsley *Palmer's pamphlet on the Causes and Consequences of the pressure on the Money-Market' (1837).
[5] *Grote's motion beaten: *H* xxxvi. 67.
[6] Catherine P. Strickland, *The Backwoods of Canada* (1836).
[7] George Horatio Cholmondeley, tory M.P. 1817–21, cr. Baron Newburgh 1822. 1792–1870, 2nd marquess 1827, m. 1830 a da. of duke of Beaufort.
[8] Extracts in Morley, i. 140. *Hume and *Roebuck failed to loosen the imperial connexion with Canada, for which *Gladstone spoke (*H* xxxvii. 95—105). Cp. E. Ryerson ed. J. G. Hodgins, *Story of My Life* (1884), 168.
[9] (Sir) H. G. *Ward, 'The first step to a Poor Law for Ireland' (1837).
[10] D. *Ricardo, 'Plan for the establishment of a national bank' (1824).
[11] John Beecham, secretary to Wesleyan missionary society.
[12] Shipping: *H* xxxvii. 164.
[13] Richard Philip Falkner, Newark attorney; mayor 1833.
[14] Roderick *Macleod, d. 1852; M.D. Edinburgh 1816; F.R.C.P. 1836; physician to St. George's hospital 1833–45; edited *London Medical and Physical Journal* from 1822.
[15] J. Kendall, *Miscellaneous and Free Strictures on the Practical Position of the Wesleyan Connexion Towards the Church of England* (1836).
[16] Supply, naval estimates: *H* xxxvii. 219.
[17] *Newcastle's *Thoughts in Times Past Tested by Subsequent Events* (1837).

11. Sat.

Finished the Duke of N.—& read 'Thoughts' Blakesley's letter to W.E.G.[1]
—Penitentiary—wrote to Mr Archer—Mr Smith Wright. paper: to the
detriment of my eyes. dined at Farquhar's. 1 h. out. House. $4\frac{3}{4}$–6.[2]

12. S.

read Maurices 2d number. Mr Ward & Bp preached Charity Sermons.—
rewrote some of my (supposed) Introduction, enlarging withal.[3]

13. M.

read Stephen on increase of crime[4]—La Pia[5]—Ed. Rev. on Evangelical
Preaching, very bad.[6]—Bp of Exeter's at 12. Peel's at 1.—Irish Comm^ee at
3. House till $7\frac{1}{4}$ and 11—12.[7] dined at Lady Salisbury's. Had not voice to
speak.

14. T.[8]

Interview with Bp of Exeter. Began Mr Hallam's new work.[9] House 5–$7\frac{1}{4}$:
came up to C.G. to dinner. House again $8\frac{3}{4}$–12[10]—and read pt of Quart on
Cathedrals. Also began La Pia.

15. Wed.

read Wilkins's letter[11]—mad!—Mr Hallam—shocked by Lady Canning's
death.[12] Went to Guy's Hospital at two to elect a Governor.[13] Looking up
Church Rate Question. Wrote to Caparn. House 5–$6\frac{3}{4}$ and $7\frac{3}{4}$–3.5. Spoke
for an hour or more: with more success than the matter or manner de-
served. Excellent division, 250:273—thank God! Broke my dinner engagement.[14]—

[1] J. W. *Blakesley, 'Thoughts on the . . . Ecclesiastical Commission', a pamphlet
on dons' low pay, addressed to *Gladstone.
[2] Questions by *Hume on army and navy: H xxxvii. 286.
[3] Progress with his book.
[4] Sir G. *Stephen, 'A Letter to . . . Lord John *Russell, on the probable increase of
Rural Crime in consequence of the introduction of the new Poor Law and Railroad
systems' (1836).
[5] B. Sestini, La Pia de' Tolomei (1822), verse drama based on Dante, Purgatorio, v.
130–6.
[6] lxiv. 428 (January 1837).
[7] Church rates: H xxxvii. 296.
[8] This entry originally written below the next one.
[9] H. *Hallam, Introduction to the Literature of Europe in the fifteenth, sixteenth, and
seventeenth centuries 4v. (1837–9).
[10] Church rates: H xxxvii. 384.
[11] G. *Wilkins, 'A Letter to Lord J. *Russell, on the subject of the Church Rates'
(1837).
[12] These five words instead of 'the touching legend of Nelda'.
[13] Mr Justice *Patteson. 'Interview alone' here deleted.
[14] Extracts in Morley, i. 139–40. Leave given to bring in bill to abolish church rates:
H xxxvii. 549. *Gladstone's speech, ibid. 489–502. Notes in Add MS 44649, ff. 119–33.
'Shocked' here deleted.

16. Th.

read Trench (2d Ed^n)[1] & Letter to Sir J. Campbell.[2] Wrote to Robertson—Mrs Phillips—D. of Newcastle—Blakesley—Mrs Chisholm. Dinner at No 6 —at Miss Fenwick's to see Wordsworth afterwards. House $5\frac{1}{2}$–$6\frac{1}{2}$ and 10–12. Div. in 223:89 on Corn Laws.[3] Went to Cannings. other calls.—conv. with Ashley.[4] Began my rondinella.[5]

17. Friday

Wrote in Pol.Memoranda.[6] Finished Quarty on Cathedrals: dined at Ld Lansdownes—Lady Antrobus's afterwards. calls. House 4–6.45.[7]—finished my rondinella. Wrote to Sir S. Canning asking to attend the funeral.[8]

18. Sat.

At Miss Fenwick's, to breakfast with Wordsworth. Library Committee at 12. Sir F. Palgrave[9] at 1—seeing the Records. Milbank. House. paper—Sismondi's Introduction.[10] Began Scotch Ch. Report.[11]

19. Sunday.

Communion at 8. St James's m. St Matt's[12] aft. saw Aunt J.—wrote on Ap^l Succession—Began Strype's Parker[13]—read two [sermons] of Newman.

20. M.

Saw Mr Sidebotham on his proposed Bill—finished Sc. Church Report. Cons[ultatio]n about Liverpool & wrote to Rob^n thereon. Calls. read Strype—Hallam. House $10\frac{1}{2}$–12.[14] wrote to Mr Boyd[15]—Mr Gye.[16]

21. T.

read Strype (Parker, & Annals.[17])—& Ward's Atticus.[18] St James's, aft^n—

[1] Melesina *Trench, *Thoughts of a Parent on Education*, new ed. (1837).
[2] R. Barnes, 'A Letter to Sir John *Campbell on the Law of Church Rates' (1837).
[3] Favouring variable duty, not fixed: *H* xxxvii. 615.
[4] Notes in Lathbury, ii. 344–7, from Add MS 44819, ff. 26–29.
[5] A nonce-word for 'little roundelay'.
[6] Add MS 44819, ff. 30–31.
[7] Blockade of Circassia: *H* xxxvii. 621.
[8] See 23 Mar. 37 and Add MS 44355, ff. 205–8.
[9] Francis Cohen, 1788–1861, historian; published translation of some Homer, 1797; took name of *Palgrave on marriage, 1823; edited Rolls Series; kt. 1832; deputy keeper of records, 1838.
[10] Either to his *History of the Fall of the Roman Empire*, tr., 2v. (1834); or to his *Etudes sur l'Economie Politique* (1837).
[11] First *Report* of the Commissioners of religious instruction in Scotland: *PP* 1837 xxi. 9.
[12] St Matthew's, Camberwell.
[13] (1711).   [14] Irish municipalities: *H* xxxvii. 672.
[15] Cp. 24 Oct. 37.
[16] Richard Gye, Newark victualler; or Frederick Gye, 1781–1869, tory M.P. Chippenham 1826–30; wine and tea merchant, ran Vauxhall Gardens 1821–40.
[17] Cp. Add MS 44727, f. 10.   [18] Untraced: slip of pen for 'Words[worth]'s *Attica*'?

wrote to Glynne & A. Williams. House 4–6. Dined at Mr Alexander's. Conv. with Mr Finch on the Fathers.—rode. Spoke on Pancras bill.[1]

22 Wed.

Calls. Dined with the Farquhars. read Strype's Parker. Warren's Address.[2] Wrote to Ouseley[3]—Mrs Gaskell—Geo. M'Kenzie. House 4–6.[4] Wrote on Apolst[l] Succession.

23. Th.

Breakfast with Gaskell, & thence to Lady Canning's funeral. We were but eleven in attendance. Her coffin was laid on that of her illustrious husband. C. showed a deep but manly sorrow. May we live as by the side of a grave and looking in. Prayers at the Abbey in aftn.[5]: Busy about my servant who has had an accident, a horse falling with him.

Saw Bp of Exeter. Mr Tallents—wrote to Boler—to Stewart M'Kenzie—House.[6]

Read Strype—& Dublin Review on Hampden.[7] recommenced the Paradiso.

24. Good Friday

Communion. St James's mg & aft.—wrote to Robn—read Strype & pt of Maurice's No 3.

25. Sat.

read Strype. Conv. with Mr Mills (Kildare Pl.Soc.)[8]—walk with Bp of Exeter. Aftn Church at St James's. Went to the Selwyns at Richmond. Paradiso in Evg.

26.

Communion, mg & evg Church. Kew Gardens with G.A.S[elwyn]—much conv.—finished Maurice No 3—and read Warter's Sermon[9] & Hooker (ma)[10] on Jerome.[11] This is a good Church family.

---

[1] Misc. business: H xxxvii. 678. St. Pancras paving bill defeated 2° by 51 to 33. *Gladstone's speech not in Bassett, Speeches, or Mirror or H; probably he presented a petition against it from proprietors on the Bedford estate. He told for the noes.

[2] T. A. Warren, 'An Address from a Country Minister', on vaccination (1803).

[3] Perhaps (Sir) William Gore *Ouseley, 1797–1866, diplomat; kt. 1852.

[4] Misc. business: H xxxvii. 700.

[5] Version of extracts in Morley, i. 139–40.

[6] Death penalty: proposed reductions. H xxxvii. 709.

[7] i. 250–65 (May 1836).

[8] L. Mills, inspector of schools for the Society for Promoting the Education of the Poor of Ireland, Kildare Place, Dublin.

[9] J. W. *Warter, 'Holy Matrimony: a sermon', on Matt. xix. 6 (1837).

[10] 'but': cp. Thomas Jones, 'Marginal Notes by Mr. *Gladstone', in National Library of Wales Journal, iv. 52 (1949).

[11] In Ecclesiastical Politie, book vii, on apostolic succession of episcopate.

27. Monday.

In town by 11. read Kildare Soc's 16th & last Report & Mr Killen's pamphlet.[1] Wrote to Blakesley & Doyle. Church in aft[n]. dined with the Doyles. At Lady Mackenzies afterwards on Rossshire matters & wrote a letter to her in her presence.[2]

28. T.

saw Mr Mills—Lady M'K.—Wm Forbes—Wrote to Mahon—Mr Stewart M'K.—copied letter to Lady M'K—out with Helen to the Pantechnicon.[3] $2\frac{3}{4}$–$6\frac{1}{4}$ drove to Betchworth, 25 m. by Croydon, to Mr Goulburn's.[4] read part of Wordsworth on Ch.Comm[n],[5] and of Evans's Biogr. of Early Church.

29. Wed.

Long conv. with H. Goulburn[6] on Church & religious matters. wrote to Mr G. —Warter—& Manning (part)—read Sullivan on Mon[etar]y System,[7] & finished Dr Wordsworth.—Several men to dinner.

30. Th.

read Horsely Palmer's reply:[8] paper: wrote to Mrs Wynn, Aunt D., J.N.G., Harrison, Lady M'Kenzie; finished Manning;[9] walk: $2\frac{1}{2}$–$5\frac{1}{2}$, 21 m. to Chevening thro' Reigate & Westerham: found the family alone.[10] Music. began Buxton's Draft Report.[11] A lesson in a little German Game.

31. Fr.

Walking the place wh is beautiful. reading Buxton's draft Report. polit[l] conv[n] & domestic with M[ahon]. billiards: backg[n]· & singing. wrote to R.G.—G.A. Selwyn.

Saturday Ap. 1.

Buxton. walk and violet gathering as yesterday. La Pia. Off at $2\frac{1}{2}$. Town at 5. Wrote to Mahon & Lady MKenzie. began 'Failure of Ref[n] in Ireland'.[12] made up accts & letters.

[1] W. D. *Killen, 'The Bible *versus* the Board' (1835): see his *Reminiscences* (1901), 73–80.

[2] Copy in Add MS 44527, f. 27.

[3] In Motcomb Street, Belgravia; then a bazaar; later a furniture warehouse.

[4] Three miles east of Dorking in Surrey. Henry *Goulburn, 1784–1856, tory M.P. from 1808, Irish secretary 1821–7, chancellor of exchequer 1828–30, home secretary 1834–5.

[5] Christopher *Wordsworth senior, *The Ecclesiastical Commission and the Universities* (1837). [6] The younger.

[7] Untraced. Possibly a paper by John Sullivan of the Indian board of control.

[8] J. H. *Palmer, *Reply to the Reflections of Mr. S. Jones* Loyd on the pamphlet Entitled "Causes and Consequences of the pressure on the Money Market"* (1837).

[9] Lathbury, ii. 234–7.

[10] Chevening, the *Stanhopes' seat NW. of Sevenoaks, lies some 17 miles ENE. of Betchworth: so this was fast walking. A later hand pencilled a red '!' in margin.

[11] First draft of *PP* 1837 vii. 1–87. Cp. Sir T. F. *Buxton, *Memoirs* (1848), 415–7.

[12] By W. *Harty (see 5, 6 Apr. 37).

2. *Sunday.*

wrote to Manning (long)[1] & Geo. Mackenzie. St James mg & aft—Mr Ward excellent & heavenly. Communion. Newman: Strype.

3. *M.*

Saw Bruce, Col. MacInnes,[2] Wordsworth (Chr.) Sadly disturbed hunting over town for a pair. rode. read a little Dante for quiet. Finished Buxton's draft Report & began A. Fonblanque.[3] wrote to Mr G.—Stewart M'K—Cadboll[4]—Capt Gordon,[5] Lincoln, Capt Fergusson,[6] Ld F. Egerton.

4. *T.*

Bruce & Wordsworth to breakfast. Again abt the Rossshire Election. wrote to A. Williams—Mr. G.—Mackenzie of Applecross—a long letter to Buxton[7]—Mr Nicholls—City of London School Sec^y—Robertson of Kindeace—H. Taylor—H. Thompson—read a little Dante & failure of Ref^n—House $4\frac{1}{2}$–6 and 10.50–$11\frac{3}{4}$.[8]—dined in B. Square.

5. *W.*

Music. copied my long letter to Buxton. wrote to Mrs. Charriere and H[orati]o Ross. read Sismondi—Hallam—[9] Br. Critic on Burgess's Lectures[10]—finished Harty's valuable Pamphlet. dined with the (young) Scotts.[11] House $4\frac{3}{4}$–$6\frac{1}{2}$ & in evg.[12]

6. *Th.*

read Hallam—Sadlier's Letter to Thorp[13]—Carlile's answer to Killen.[14] rode. dined at the Pusey's. wrote to Harty[15]—& A Simson.[16] Indexed all my Vols of Pamphlets.

[1] Lathbury, ii. 29–33.

[2] John MacInnis, 1779–1859; colonel, Bengal Native infantry, 1829; general 1856.

[3] A. Fonblanque the elder, *England under Seven Administrations*, 3v. (1837).

[4] Unidentified.

[5] William Hamilton-Gordon, 1785–1858; *Aberdeen's b.; captain, R.N., 1810, vice-admiral 1854; tory M.P. co. Aberdeen 1820–54.

[6] George Ferguson, 1786–1867, capt. R.N. 1814, admiral 1861, cons. M.P. co. Banff 1832–7.

[7] Copy in Add MS 44527, ff. 27–29; commenting adversely on *Buxton's draft report.

[8] Misc. business, mainly financial: *H* xxxvii. 734.

[9] 'began' here deleted.

[10] 1837, xxi. 427–42; on R. *Burgess, *Lectures on the Insufficiency of Unrevealed Religion and on the succeeding Influences of Christianity* (1832).

[11] (Sir) Claude Edward Scott, 1804–74, banker, 3rd bart. 1849, m. 1838 Mary, née Buckworth, who d. 1844; and his b. Samuel, 1807–69.

[12] Army estimates: *H* xxxvii. 778.

[13] F. *Sadleir, 'National Schools of Ireland defended in a letter to ... Dr Thorpe' (1837).

[14] Leaflet by James *Carlile the Irish education commissioner, summarised in W. D. *Killen, *Reminiscences*, 78.

[15] William *Harty, 1781–54, protestant physician in Dublin.

[16] Edinburgh notary, interested in education.

7. Fr.

read Carlile & other pamphlets on Ir. Ed[n] & pt of the Australian papers. wrote to Mr G & R.G. House $4\frac{1}{4}$–5 and $9\frac{1}{4}$–$11\frac{1}{4}$. Voted 167:72 on Mil. Flogging.[1] In the City seeing Mr Logan,[2] & went to see Mrs Wm Robertson.[3] Corrected pt of sp. on Canada.

8. Sat.

Australian & Ir.Ed[n] papers. Corrected remainder of speech on Canada. Rode. Dined at Mr Lyon's. Wrote Q[ns] for Ir.Ed. Comm[ee]. wrote to Mr G— R.G.—Boler—Pusey—Selwyn—Taylor.

9. S.

St Matt—& St James. Bp preached. walk. read Newman (on Annunc[n], alas.)[4] Strype, & finished Watson.[5] Wrote heads on Conscience in Governmts.[6]

10. Monday.

wrote to Mr. G.—R.G.—Mr Ramsay—Sir R. Peel—Makin[7]—Commees $1\frac{1}{4}$–$3\frac{1}{4}$. reading Irish Education papers and Evidence. House 10–1.[8]

11. Tuesday.

Irish Education Evidence & pamphlets. This subject & those it involves, haunt me day & night. Another batch of poem from H.T[hompson].—A letter from Manning. wrote to Mr. G—Rn G—Pusey. Saw Mr Mills. House 4–$5\frac{1}{2}$: and $9\frac{1}{2}$–1. Excellent division on Irish Corp. 247:302.[9]

12. Wed.

Reading on Irish Ed[n].—I have gone thro'
Lords' Evidence No.s 1.2.[10]
Carlile's Defence.[11]
Sadlier's Defence.[11]
Killens Two Pamphlets.[12]
Memorials to Abp of Dublin & Replies.[13]

---

[1] In favour of it: II xxxvii. 905.
[2] Robert Logan, banker?
[3] Mary, da. of Alexander Chisholm, of Chisholm, whose b. was killed in *Charles Edward's army at Culloden; m. 1789 William Robertson of Kindeace.
[4] J. H. *Newman, 'The Reverence Due to the Virgin Mary', in Parochial and Plain Sermons, ii. 142.
[5] Untraced.   [6] Add MSS 44727, ff. 28–29, and 44681, ff. 178–80.
[7] Perhaps Charles Makin, Liverpool gentleman.
[8] Irish municipalities, 3°, adjourned: H xxxvii. 929.
[9] Bill read 3°: ibid. 1110.
[10] Reprinted in PP 1837 viii. 2v.
[11] See 6 Apr. 37.
[12] 'The Board Unmeshed' (1836); and cp. 27 Mar. 37.
[13] 'Scriptural Education in Ireland' (1832).

Published documents of the Commissioners.[1]
Watson's Pamphlet.[2]
Address of the Derry Clergy.[3]
Brown St Schools Correspondence.[4]
Matheson's Introduction.[5]
Committee 1–4$\frac{1}{4}$. House till 6: ride. read "La Pia". House 9$\frac{1}{2}$–1. Voted in 177:84 on County Rates.[6] read Mr Hallam.

13. Th.

'Sederunt' with Mr Mills. began Gaskell's book[7]—dined at Lord F. Egerton's. House before dinner—& at 10$\frac{1}{4}$–1.[8] read paper—part of Blake's Evidence[9]—wrote to Mr G—Bp of London—A. Simson. began a paper on Irish Education—as my thoughts on it grow into shape[10]—rode.

14. Fr.

saw Mr Boler. Comm^{ees} 12$\frac{1}{4}$–4$\frac{1}{4}$ & House 8$\frac{3}{4}$–12$\frac{3}{4}$. Div. in 269:45 on Canada Resolutions.[11] read part of Swan's pamphlet[12]—Blake's Evidence. rode. wrote to Mrs Brigstock.[13]

15. Saturday.

Milbank. Calls. wrote to G. Denison. Wrote on Irish Edn. read Lords' Evidence No 4.—rode. dined with H.J.G. at the Kerrisons. music. Finished the Australian papers. Wrote to Sir G. Grey.[14]

16. Sunday.

Comm^n at 8. St Matth's & St James's. Mr Ward good & strong on covetousness. read Sheppard—Newman—Strype's Parker. music evg.

17. M.

Comm^{ees} 12$\frac{1}{4}$–4$\frac{1}{4}$. finished Blake's Ev. of 1835—& Lords' Ev. No 3.—rode. saw Mr Mills. read Gaskell. House 9$\frac{1}{2}$–12$\frac{1}{2}$.[15]

[1] *PP* 1837 ix. 585, 607 ff.
[2] By Alexander Watson, priest, on bible reading in Liverpool schools for poor children (1836).
[3] Cp. *PP* 1837 ix. 138.   [4] Ibid. 597.
[5] J. Matheson, 'Voluntary Churches the true Churches of Christ . . . introductory discourse' (1829).   [6] Against them, 2°: *H* xxxvii. 1150.
[7] Perhaps P. Gaskell, *Artisans and Machinery* (1836), on the moral defects of the factory system. J. M. Gaskell never published.
[8] Newspaper stamps; Scottish prisons. *H* xxxvii. 1162; 1201.
[9] Anthony Richard Blake, Dublin lawyer, an Irish education commissioner; testified in August 1835 before another select cttee. *PP* 1836 xiii. 303, 353.
[10] Add MS 44727, ff. 12–24.
[11] Against abolishing Canadian parliament: *H* xxxviii. 1200. The numbers were 269:46.
[12] R. Swan, *The Principle of Church Rates* (1837).
[13] Perhaps w. of William Papwell Brigstock, b. 1788?; of Christ Church and Lincoln's Inn.
[14] Copy in Add MS 44527, f. 29; on Australian religious education.
[15] Affairs of Spain: *H* xxxvii. 1329.

18. *T.*

Comm^{ee} 12½–4. Voted for Nk[1]—rode. read Mr Gaskell's book. wrote to Mr Pritchard.[2] Letters from Manning & Harrison. wrote on Irish Edⁿ—House 9½–12½.[3]

19. *Wed.*

read Gaskell—& part of Macnamara's Evidence.[4] wrote on Irish Edⁿ— went to Ir.Comm^{ee}, but could not get a quorum. rode. dined at Bp of London's. wrote to Caparn & A. Simson.—Long conv. with Colquhoun on Ir. Edⁿ—House 10½–3¾. voted in 242:278 on Sir H.H[ardinge].[5]

20. *Th.*

Wrote Vss: chiefly patching & piecing. No House. read Gaskell. & R.P.'s "Constitution as it is".[6] Went with Helen to the National Gallery.

21. *Fr.*

Comm 12¾–4. House 5½–6¾ & 8¾–1. on Canada chiefly.[7] read Kelly's Evidence No 10 before the Lords,[8] & some Ev^{ce} on Aborigines. calls.

22. *Sat.*

Wrote to Mr Estcourt.[9]—H. Thompson—B. Harrison & W.K. Hamilton (introd^y)—Caparn—H.A. Jeffreys—rode—accts—read Gaskell. wrote to R. Phillimore.

23. *S.*

St James mg & evg.—read Sheppard—Newman—Strype. wrote a long letter to Manning.[10]

24. *M.*

Commees & House 12–7 and 9½–10½—Canada Res[olution]s. finished[11]— read Sir C. Grey on the Proceedings—& Gaskell.

---

[1] Probably informal cttee. on Newark Estate Bill, introduced by E. J. *Stanley and *Baring on 21 April; cp. *PP* 1837 iii. 421.

[2] Probably John Pritchard, b. 1797, then at Lincoln's Inn; Shropshire gentleman; cons. M.P. Bridgnorth 1853–68.

[3] Spain again: *H* xxxvii. 1394.

[4] Dean Macnamara of Limerick's testimony to the previous inquiry on Irish education: *PP* 1836 xiii. 376.

[5] For his lost amdt., which deplored British help to Spanish legitimists: *H* xxxviii. 120.

[6] [R. J. *Phillimore] *The Constitution As it is, or Democracy?* (1837).

[7] *H* xxxviii. 198.

[8] Thomas F. Kelly, Irish education commissioner, in *PP* 1837 viii, *passim*.

[9] Thomas Grimston Bucknall Estcourt, 1775–1853; Gloucestershire gentleman; M.P. Devizes 1805–26, Oxford University 1827–47; tory backbencher.

[10] Lathbury, i. 33–9.

[11] *H* xxxviii. 230.

25. T.

Long interview with Dr Elrington[1] on Ir.Ed[n].—I gave him my paper: with scruples, for I feel the presumption of proposing anything upon it.—read Gaskell—began Greg on the Factory Question:[2] & 'Victims of Society'.[3] House 4–5, locked out.[4] rode. wrote to M.E.—Best—A. Williams.

26. W.

2d conv. with Dr Elrington: who thought favourably of the Sketch. read Mr Tyler's Sermon[5]—[6]Greg—& Victims of Society. Wrote to Col. Wade (bis) & Sir R. Peel. Comm[ees] & House 12–5¾.[7] rode.

27. Th.

Wrote to Mr Pritchard—Party at home—read Greg—Gaskell—and Strype. Rode. At Lns Inn.

28. Fr.

Sent books to Newark. Wrote to Caparn—& Selwyn. At Lns Inn. Comm[ee] 1–4, & House.[8] rode. dined at Ld Harrowby's. Finished Greg. read Gaskell.

29. Sat.

Viewing our new horses. Saw Mr Mills on Ir.Ed[n].—read Davies's Lecture on the state of Flatmen[9]—& Gaskell. rode. dined at Wilson Patten's. At Milbank. Elected Mr Nihill gov[r].

30. S.

St James (Bp of Ripon)[10] & St Matt.—Strype—Newman—Sheppard. Wrote on Hist. of Private Judgment. Walk.[11]

May 1. Monday.

Monthly letters & accts—Copied a letter for Mr G—read 'Victims' & pt of Carlile on Mixed Institutions.[12] Comm[ees] 12½–4¼. House 5–6½ & 10¼–11½.[13]

---

[1] Charles Richard *Elrington, 1787–1850; regius professor of divinity, Dublin, 1829; a founder of Church Education Society for Ireland.

[2] R. H. Greg, '*The Factory Question, considered in relation to its effects on the health and morals of those employed in Factories* (1837). Notes in Add MS 44727, f. 295.

[3] Novel by Lady *Blessington, 3v. (1837).

[4] Misc. business; house counted out. *H* xxxviii. 277.

[5] On Ephes. iv. 15, preached ten days earlier at Lambeth at *Denison's consecration as bp. of Salisbury.

[6] 'began' here deleted.

[7] Misc. business: *H* xxxviii. 278.

[8] Irish poor relief: ibid. 360.

[9] Untraced. Flatmen = bargees.

[10] Charles Thomas *Longley, 1794–1868; headmaster of Harrow 1829; bp. of Ripon 1836, of Durham 1856; abp. of York 1860, of Canterbury 1862.

[11] This became ch. vii of his book.

[12] James *Carlile, *System of Irish Education explained* (1832); *Gladstone was about to cross-examine him in cttee—*PP* 1837 ix. 112.

[13] Irish tithe and poor relief: *H* xxxviii. 408; 421.

wrote (suppl) on Ir.Ed[n].[1]—Saw Dr E[lrington] who reports well of the Primate[of Ireland]'s opinion on the paper.

2. T.

Finished Carlile on Mixed Institutions. read the Storm &c. in the Antiquary: & 'Victims of Society'—eyes weary.—Comm[ee] at 12—then Xn Knowl. Soc[y] where Dodsworth happily withdrew his Proposition—& calls passim—rode. House $5\frac{1}{2}$–$6\frac{1}{2}$.[2] Gaskell. wrote Mrs Wishlade.

3. W.

Finished Gaskell's book: and 'Victims of Society'. arranging bedroom—rode. Comm[ees] $12\frac{3}{4}$–$4\frac{1}{4}$. House before and after dinner.[3] dined at Mr Stanley's. wrote to Mr Gaskell—Dr Elrington—Began Sewell's Lecture.[4]

4. Th.

Church & Communion. read Hallam—Scotch Dissenters' Remarks[5]—Murray agt Nat. Edn Board.[6] Wrote to Rn G.—Secy of Cov. Garden Fund. party at home. Calls. House 4—$6\frac{1}{4}$ & aft[er] dinner.[7]

5. Fr.

read La Pia. Saw Rev. Messrs Bettridge & Cronyn from U. Canada[8]—Commees $12\frac{1}{4}$–$4\frac{1}{4}$. Rode. House $5\frac{1}{2}$–7. dined at Sir J. Mordaunts. House $10\frac{1}{4}$–$1\frac{1}{4}$: voted In 176 : 217 on Scotch Church Grant.[9]

6. Sat.

revising Vss and adding. read La Pia—& began Martin's Colonial Policy.[10] Dined at Mr Blackburne's.[11] Rode. wrote to Col. MacInnes. Calls.

7. Sunday.

St James & the Penitentiary in aft. The service there is impressive. Com-

[1] In Add MS 44727, ff. 26–27.
[2] Convocation: H xxxviii. 458.
[3] Grain imports; Libel bill, defeated 2°. Ibid. 465, 477.
[4] Perhaps W. *Sewell's inaugural as *White's professor of moral philosophy (1836).
[5] Untraced.
[6] Richard Murray, dean of Ardagh since 1801, in PP 1837 viii (2). 91, 108.
[7] Window tax; state of universities. H xxxviii. 503; 509.
[8] William Craddock Bettridge, 1791–1879; town major of Brussels 1815; in Neapolitan army 1822; ordained 1824; priest at Southampton 1828–34; rector of Woodstock, Ontario, 1834–74; canon; refused bishopric of Huron 1857. It was accepted by Benjamin Cronyn, 1802–71, s. of mayor of Kilkenny; at Trinity, Dublin; rector of London, Ontario, 1832–57.
[9] *Rae's motions for remedying state of Scotch episcopalians lost: H xxxviii. 652.
[10] Probably introduction to vol. iv of R. M. *Martin's British Colonial History, 10v. (1836).
[11] John Ireland Blackburne, 1783–1874, Lancashire gentleman; Peelite M.P. Newton (Lancashire) 1807–18, Warrington 1835–47.

munion. wrote on continuation of last S[unday]—read Strype—Shepherd (finished) and Newman's S[ermons] & began his Romanism.[1]

8. M.

Copied a letter. Finished Martin's Colonial Policy. Commees 12¾–4¼. rode. Dined with the Williamses. Mr Robins there.[2] House afterwards.[3] read Mr Nangel's & other Evidence.[4] Began to cons[ide]r of more Essays & read pt of Edn paper.

9. T.

Wrote on Ch & St.[5]—read La Pia (finished)—Sewell—(began) Lockhart.[6] House 5¼–8½: tea at H. Joy's—and House 10¼–11½. Voted in 129:81 on proxies.[7]

10. W.

Manning to breakf.—conv. on Church matters till near 1—Commee 1½–4¼. rode. dined at Ld Camden's: conv. with Capt. Fitzroy on Colonial matters. House in evg[8]—read Whately's Speech,[9] began Oakeley[10]—& a Voice from Ireland[11]—Wrote to Caparn. Mrs Law's.

11. Th.

Breakf. with Mr Rogers—there till past 12—wrote to R.G.—Geo M'Kenzie. House 5½–7.[12] Dined at Col. Baillie's. read Voice from Ireland—Lockhart— Hallam. Burdett's victory.[13]

12. Fr.

Judge Willis[14] to breakf. Very intelligent. Commee 1–4. Burdett took his seat; an interesting scene. rode. dined at Mr Tallents's. Ld Ch[o]lm[onde]-ley's afterwards. House before & after. 11–12½. Voted for settlement in Ireland. 68:120.[15] wrote to Mr S. Wilberforce. read Ir. N.B's Sacred Poetry[16]—& Hallam. & Oakley.

[1] J. H. *Newman, *Lectures on the Prophetical Office of the Church, viewed relatively to Romanism and Popular Protestantism* (1837).

[2] Perhaps Sanderson *Robins, 1801–62, priest and educationalist.

[3] Irish poor relief: *H* xxxviii. 690.

[4] Edward Nangle, priest, in *PP* 1837 viii. (1) 384.

[5] Preparing his book.

[6] J. G. *Lockhart, *Memoirs of the Life of Sir Walter *Scott, 7v. (1837–8).

[7] Against *Duncombe's motion, that they were 'incompatible with every principle of justice and reason': *H* xxxviii. 772. Thomas Slingsby *Duncombe, 1796–1861, radical M.P. Hertford 1826–32, Finsbury from 1834.

[8] Misc. business: *H* xxxviii. 775.

[9] On Irish education, in the lords, 19 Mar. 1833: *Mirror*, i. 835.

[10] F. *Oakeley, *Remarks upon Aristotelian and Platonic Ethics, as a Branch of the Studies Pursued in the University of Oxford* (1837).

[11] Untraced: pamphlet?   [12] Irish poor relief: *H* xxxviii. 806.

[13] Against *Leader, the govt. candidate, in Westminster by-election.

[14] John Walpole *Willis, 1793–1877; judge in Canada 1827; shortly amoved; in Demerara 1835–7; then in New South Wales, amoved 1842.

[15] For redistribution of Irish poor rate: *H* xxxviii. 850.   [16] Untraced.

13. Sat.

wrote on Ch & St.—at U. Canada meeting. Dined at Ld Skelmersdale's.[1] rode. Explanation with Leader. B. Noel on Unity.[2]—Hallam.

14. Sunday.

Newman on Romanism—Sermons—Strype's Appx—wrote on texts.[3] St James mg & evg. Communion. Hailstorm.

15. M.

Church—Hallam. Began Mahon Vol 2.—Wrote on Ch. & St.—dined at Mr Tallents's. Calls. rode.

16. T.

Hallam—Mahon. Party at home. Bp of Exeter's afterwards. rode. Attended meeting to form a Lay Union.[4] wrote on Ch. & St.

17. W.

Hallam—Mahon. Attended the Levee.[5] rode. calls. House & a div.[6]—rode. Anc. Music Concert. Wrote to T. Acland. Wrote on Ch & St.[7]

18. Th.

Copied two letters. Wrote (little) on Ch & St —at the drawingroom,[8] dinner party at home. rode. papers. read Hallam—Mahon—wrote to Acland.

19. Fr.

Hallam—Mahon. wrote to H. Ross—Mr Bowman[9]—Commees $1\frac{1}{4}$–$4\frac{1}{4}$. House $6\frac{3}{4}$–$9\frac{1}{4}$ and 10–$12\frac{1}{4}$. Voted in 73:72 agt Ewart's Instrn[10]—wrote on Ch. & St.—read Talfourd's Speech.[11]

20. Sat.

Hallam. Report of Excise Committee.[12] Mahon. rode. copied two letters.

---

[1] Edward Bootle-Wilbraham, 1771–1853, tory M.P. 1795 till cr. Baron Skelmersdale 1828.
[2] B. W. *Noel, 'The Unity of the Church' (1836).
[3] Add MS 44727, ff. 49–51.
[4] No trace.
[5] Held by the king in St. James's palace.
[6] Sunday travel on Glasgow, Paisley, and Ayr railway forbidden, by 51 to 47: H xxxviii. 858 (decision reversed two days later: ibid. 905).
[7] Add MS 44727, f. 52.
[8] Held by the king and his sister, Princess *Augusta, 1768–1840, at St. James's.
[9] Perhaps William Bowman, Newark bookkeeper.
[10] And in favour of death penalty for other crimes than murder: H xxxviii. 922.
[11] On copyright, 18 May: ibid. 866.
[12] PP 1837 xxx. 397.

Dined at Ld Ashburtons. wrote on Ch. & State—What an atmosphere! we have again relapsed into the middle of winter. God send other weather.

21. Sunday.

St James's mg & aft.—Communion. Strype—Newman Sermm—& Romanism—began Whyte's new book.[1] wrote on Ch. & St.

22. M.

Mahon. Hallam. U. Canada Clergy Commee 12–1. Irish Edn 1–4. rode. House 6½–7¾, again at 9½—Mrs W. Patten's—& House 10½–12¼.[2] wrote to Acland—Sandoz (retiring)—Ashley—C. Wood—read Cape papers[3] &c.

23. T.

Vss.—Hallam—Mahon—Miss Martineau's America[4]—wrote to Mr Ramsay—House 5–5¾: dined at Ld Stanley's—met H. Powys there—House 10¾–2¾. voted in 282:287 on Church Rates.[5] rode. calls.

24. W.

2 hours conv. with Acland. read Hallam.[6] Conv. with Hume & Baring, *vice* Commee.—dined at Mr Hogg's[7]—Anc. Music. Tea at Acland's. Rode.

25. Th.

Mahon. Miss Martineau. dined with the Heywoods.[8] Rode. calls. wrote on the Unities.[9] Wrote to Mr G—M. Welsh[10]—and [blank.]

Friday May 26.

Mahon. finished Vol 2.—& Lords' Evce. wrote to Mr G—Mr Sandoz—Mrs Phillips—Rode. Irish Commee 1¼–4. Lay Union Commee 4–4¾. Lincoln's Inn. rode. House 9.40–11.40.[11]—wrote out Vss.

Sat. 27.

Mahon Appx. Eckermann.[12] Ir. Edn Statistics. wrote to H. Hall[13]—A. Wil-

---

[1] A. Whyte, *The Heritage of God's People* (1837).
[2] Church rates: *H* xxxviii. 929.
[3] Dispatches on the Caffre war, not published till 12 July (*PP* 1837 xliii. 319); or newspapers.
[4] H. *Martineau, Society in America*, 3v. (1837).
[5] Against their eventual abolition: *H* xxxviii. 1073.
[6] A note in Add MS 44727, f. 53.
[7] (Sir) James Weir *Hogg, 1790–1876, barrister; at Calcutta 1814–35; Peelite M.P. Beverley 1835–47, Honiton 1847–57; East India director 1839–72; cr. bart. 1846.
[8] Probably (Sir) Benjamin *Heywood, 1793–1805, Manchester banker; M.P. Lancashire 1831; cr. bart. 1838; m. 1816 Sophia Ann, née Robinson, who d. 1852.
[9] The dramatic unities; in Add MS 44727, ff. 54–55.
[10] Perhaps Michael Henry H. Walsh, b. 1820? in Paris, s. of a Dublin barrister; graduate of Trinity College Dublin 1842.   [11] Irish poor relief: *H* xxxviii. 1095.
[12] J. P. Eckermann, *Conversations with Goethe*, undated American tr.
[13] Henry Hall, Newark draper.

liams—Mr G—O.B. Cole—Long conv. with G. Mackenzie on religious matters, Sacraments & Ap[ostolica]l Succ[essio]n especially. rode. dined at Mr Nicholls's. Lady Parke's aft[er]. Music. papers.

28. S.

Mr Ward & Bp. Dined at A. Lefroy's to see Dean Murray.[1] Long conv. with the L[efroy]s on Oxford doctrine &c. read Newman Serm—Romanism—& acct of School for sons of Irish Clergy.[2] Wrote.[3]

29. M.

Sir R. Peel's at 11½ on Church Rates. Canada Clergy Committee at 1.—Lincoln's Inn. rode—dined at Ld Cholmondeley's. Lady Domviles.[4] wrote to T.G.—read Miss Martineau—Moultrie[5]—finished Mahon's Appx.

30. T.

read Oakley—Moultrie—Lockhart. O. & C. Club Meeting at 1—Library Commee (Carlton) at 4—Lincoln's Inn—rode—House 6–9 and 11½–1¼. voted in 36:120 agt privilege resolution.[6]

31. W.

At work on Ir. Edn & Reln Statistics; too much for my eyes. Commees 1–4. Wrote to T.G.—read Moultrie—Oakley (finished). Dined at Col. Grant's.[7] Music. Lincoln's Inn. Rode.

Thursday June one.

Letters & accts.—Wrote to R.G.—dined at Sir O. Mosley's—sang. rode. First Fruits Commee 12–4[8]—except a call on Mrs Grant.[9] read Moultrie—Goethe—Old Statutes—Miss Martineau—House 4–5.[10]

2. Fr.

wrote to T.G.—Commee 1–4. dined at Ld Salisbury's. Lady Cork's afr. read Moultrie—Hallam (finished)—& James Williams's pamphlet.[11] rode. read Eckermann.

---

[1] Cp. 4 May 37 n.; and *PP* 1837 ix. 257, his testimony to education cttee. on 26 May.
[2] Untraced.   [3] On infallibility of the Church; Add MS 44727, f. 56.
[4] Maria, *née* Solly, d. 1863; she m. 1807 (Sir) William Domville, 1774–1860, 2nd bart. 1833. Their elder s. (Sir) James Graham Domville, 1812–87, 3rd bart., was at Christ Church and Lincoln's Inn.   [5] J. *Moultrie, Poems* (1837).
[6] With *Inglis, against *Peel and ministers; who claimed commons' privilege over courts of law. *H* xxxviii. 1134. The numbers were 126:36.
[7] Francis William Grant, 1778–1853, colonel, 1809; tory M.P. Elginshire from 1807 till he succ. his b. as 6th earl of Seafield 1840.
[8] Select cttee. to inquire into the constitution of the boards for receipt of first fruits and tenths: *PP* 1837 vi. 3.
[9] Mary Anne, *née* Dunn; m. F. W. Grant 1811; d. 1840.
[10] Flogging: *H* xxxviii. 1150.
[11] *A Narrative of events since the first of August, 1834* (1837); an account of his treatment as a negro apprentice in Jamaica.
20—II.

3. Sat.

Writing out Vss & piecing[1]—read Moultrie—Eckermann—Stanley (Bp) on Irish Education &c[2]—rode. dined at W. Alexander's.[3] Calls.

4. S.

St James's mg & aft.—Communion.—Newman Serm. & on Romanism.—Vss.[4]—Strype.

5. M.

Moultrie. Sturges W.I. Evidence.[5] First Fruits Commee $12\frac{1}{4}$–$3\frac{3}{4}$ and House 7–11. Voted agt Chaplains Clause in Ir. Poor Bill.[6] Lady E. Hardinge's ball.[7] I thought there of Lady Lincoln, in contrast.—Wrote to Messrs Ebden &c at the Cape—keeping draft[8]—to Buxton—Jas Doyle.[9] rode.

6. T.

Moultrie. Senior's letter on Irish Poor Law.[10] saw Jas Doyle, & Blakesley. Commee 1–4. Eckermann. Began Lang.[11] Dined at Sir S. Scott's. music. rode. Wrote to E. Bartlett[12]—T.G.—Sir G. Grey.

7. W.

Lang. At the Exhibition. Much better in sculpture than in painting?[13] Commee & C.O. to examine Australian papers about religion 2–$4\frac{1}{2}$. House 6–$10\frac{1}{2}$. Voted in 110:66 for Sir A. Agnew.[14] At Mrs Denison's.

8. Th.

Lang. perusing & correcting Vss. Eckermann: very interesting. Commee 1–$4\frac{1}{2}$. Rode. House $6\frac{1}{2}$–$7\frac{1}{4}$.[15] dined at Mr B. Baring's—House & Lady Y. Buller's afterwards. Moultrie.

---

[1] Some 600 lines of blank verse on 'Readings of Human Life'; in Add MS 44727, ff. 69–90.
[2] E. *Stanley, A Few Observations on Religion and Education in Ireland (1835).
[3] W. M. Alexander's.
[4] Add MS. 44727, ff. 69–90.
[5] Cp. 21 June 37.
[6] Cl. 43, empowering Irish workhouse commissioners to pay chaplains, carried 122–36: H xxxviii. 1210.
[7] Lady Emily Jane, née Stewart, 1789–1865, *Castlereagh's half-sister; m. Sir H. *Hardinge 1821.
[8] To a body of freeholders at the Cape of Good Hope, who had sent him a petition about aborigines; copy of hedging reply in Add MS 44527, f. 30.
[9] Possibly James Doyle, Liverpool customs officer.
[10] N. W. *Senior, 'A Letter to Lord *Howick on a Legal Provision for the Irish Poor; Commutation of Tithes, and a Provision for the Irish Roman Catholic Clergy' (1831).
[11] J. D. *Lang, An historical and statistical account of New South Wales, 2 ed., 2v. (1837).
[12] Cp. 18 Mar. 36.
[13] National Gallery.
[14] Lord's Day Bill, 2°: H xxxviii. 1242.   [15] Privilege: ibid. 1249.

9. *Fr.*

Lang. Moultrie. Saw Jeffries (Poor Law).[1] Dundee gentlemen.[2] Commee 1–4. Sad accounts of the King.[3] Calls. read Miss Martineau. trying to spell songs.

10. *Sat.*

Lang (finished)—Moultrie—Commee 1–4. wrote to T.G.—rode. dined at Mr Finch's. again at songs.

11. *S.*

St James' mg & evg. Read Newman's Romanism—Sermons—Strype. Walk.

12. *M.*

Moultrie (finished). His last not his best? Commee 1–3½. Song-spelling. papers. wrote to Mr Nicholls—Jones.[4] House 6–2, ½ hour at home for tea. Voted in 489:58, in 236:319, and in 265:291 in Church Rate motions.[5]

13. *T.*

Commee on Edn 1–4. read Atty General on Ch. Rates[6]—& pt of Nicholl. Wrote to Lincoln, & Mahon: sent the latter my Bride of Corinth—altered & transcribed it. Dined at Murchison's. Lady Mosley's[7] & Mr Herries's in evg. Conv. with Judge Willis on his evidence.

14. *W.*

Songs. Nicholl (finished). Bp Coleridge's charge in B. Guiana.[8] Commee 1–4¼. rode. wrote to Dean Murray—Lady F. Egerton's concert. Library Commee at Carlton. 4½–5½. House in evg.[9]

15. *Th.*

In Hill St, Louisa having been ill: is better[10]—began Maurice no 4—Strype—wrote on Priv. Judg. & on Doctrine. Commee 1–4. House 5¼–6¼.[11] dined at Mrs Labalmondière's. Lady A. Beresford's.[12]

---

[1] Possibly John Jeffreys, 1771?–1840, rector of Barnes, Surrey, 1795–1839; or his s. H.A. (see 8 Sept. 31).　　[2] Cp. 1, 8 July 37, &c.
[3] Cp. Add MS 44563, ff. 53–4, official prayer.　　[4] 'Report on' here deleted.
[5] Against abolition of church rate; against inquiry into it; and for wider means of religious education. *H* xxxviii. 1434.
[6] Sir J. *Campbell, in a 'Letter to . . . Lord *Stanley' (1837).
[7] Sophia Anne, d. 1859; 2nd da. of Sir Edward Every; m. 1804 Sir Oswald Mosley; of 25 Portland Place.
[8] W. H. *Coleridge, 'A Charge Delivered to the Church of England in British Guiana' (1837).
[9] Misc. business: *H* xxxviii. 1452.
[10] The Thomas Gladstones were living at 2 Hill Street, Mayfair.
[11] Hanwell lunatic asylum: *H* xxxviii. 1486.
[12] Lady Anne Beresford, d. 1841; 3rd da. of 2nd earl of Tyrone; lived in Charles Street, St. James's Square, with her siblings.

16. Fr.

reviewing Vss. read Deacon on Church Rates.[1] and Strype—Commee (Ir. Ed) 1–4¼. House in evg.[2] Dined at M[ary] Gaskell's[3] to meet the [Robertson] Glasgow's. Wrotc out my Ugolino transln, with the original.[4] rode.

Heard alas! of Miss Hallam's death.[5]

17. Sat.

Commee 12–3½. Penitentiary. St James's. Bad accounts of the King. Began Hale on Church Rates.[6] Rode. Dined with the Lyalls.

18. S.

The accounts of the King grow worse & worse. His light is waning fast. Here is another exercise of faith.

Communion.—Mr Ward & Bp preached. Read Chaplaincy Testimonials —Newman's Romm—Strype's Parker (II)—Maurice's No IV & Introduction. Walk.

19.

Apprenticeship Commee 1–4. Copied out Ugolino trans. & original. Finished Hall on Church Rates. Mrs R. Ellice's beautiful concert.—some to dine at home—rode.

20. T.

Between 2 & 3 A.M. the King died. He leaves a perilous legacy to his young successor![7]

At the House early. Sworn in.[8] read Warburton's Alliance.[9] Barnes on Church Rates. Wrote to Lincoln—dined at Baron Parke's.

21. W.

House at 1—attempted a W.I. Commee but in vain.[10] Conv. with Buxton & Sturge.[11] Ride with Mahon: conv. on my "Braut" &c—read Dublin Review

---

[1] E. A. Deacon, 'Another letter to . . . Lord *Stanley . . . on the Law of Church Rates' (1837).
[2] Poor laws: H xxxviii. 1507.
[3] In New Ormond Street, Bloomsbury.
[4] Draft and fair copy of translation of Dante, Inferno xxxiii. 1–78 in Add MS 44869, ff. 208–14.
[5] Henry *Hallam's da. Eleanor.
[6] W. H. *Hale, 'The Antiquity of the Church Rates Considered' (1837).
[7] Version in Morley, i. 140.
[8] H xxxviii. 1545.
[9] W. *Warburton, The Alliance between Church and State (1736).
[10] Members still swearing allegiance to *Victoria. Leave to cttees. to sit next day. H xxxviii. 1546.
[11] Joseph *Sturge, 1793–1859; quaker anti-slavery philanthropist; alderman of Birmingham 1835; visited West Indies early 1837; a founder of anti-corn law league; pacifist.

on Ch. E.[1]—& No Popery Cry[2]—Elia (popular fallacies)[3]—and Privilege Report.[4] wrote to T.G.—& copied Southey's letter to Miss Bronte.[5]

22. Th.

Commee 1–4. House 5–6¼.[6] rode. read pt of die Glocke & of Sotheby's trans[7]—Ch. of E. Rev. on Amn Episcl Church[8]—& pt of Lewis's remarks on Ir. Poor C's Report[9]—wrote draft & letter to D. of N—wrote to T.G.

23. Fr.

finished "die glocke" & transln—rode. dined at Lady Hope's—wrote pt of (a long) Address to Nk El[ecto]rs[10]—Commee & House 1–6¼—an even division[11]—Warburton's Alliance—note to Sir R. Peel. Finished Lewis's Report. Wrote to R.G.

24. Sat.

Concluded & wrote over my Address—Commee 12¼–3. read Strype. rode. spelling songs. dined at Abp of York's.[12] Eyes very poor. papers.

25. S.

2 Charity Sermm—Bp of Bangor[13] & Rector: both very good. read Strype—Newman—Maurice—Helen much better.

26. M.

read Maurice (finished No 4)—Pope—Edn Socy's publn[14]—Commee & House 1–5½, and 11¼–12½. voted in 12:52 agt Maynooth Grant.[15] wrote to T.G.—Caparn—Milnes[16]—N.W.R. Colborne[17]—Welsh—.

[1] 'The Present State and Prospects of the Anglican Church,' *Dublin Review* ii. 493 (April 1837).
[2] 'No-Popery Current, Liberal and Conservative,' ibid. 329.
[3] *Lamb, *Last Essays of Elia* (1833).
[4] *PP* 1837 xiii. 203.
[5] Add MS 44355, ff. 236–7; extract in Morley, ii. 538.
[6] Formalities of condolence: *H* xxxviii. 1554.
[7] Schiller, 'Das Lied von der Glocke' tr. in W. *Sotheby, *Italy and Other Poems* (1828), 225.
[8] *The Church of England Quarterly Review* i. 426 (April 1837).
[9] G. C. *Lewis, *Remarks on the third report of the Irish Poor Enquiry Commissioners* (1837).
[10] Several drafts in Add MS 44727, ff. 60–68.
[11] A tie, 41–41, on Caoutchouc Company bill, 3°; carried by speaker's vote. Impending dissolution made necessary by demise of crown, *H* xxxviii. 1583. H. of C. *Journals* 1837, 496.
[12] At 40 Grosvenor Square. Edward (Venables Vernon) *Harcourt, 1757–1847; canon of Christ Church 1783, and bp. of Carlisle 1791; abp. of York 1808; inherited Harcourt estates 1831; had 16 c.; gf. of Sir W. V.*.
[13] *Bethell.   [14] Untraced.
[15] Supply: only a grant of £8,928 to the R.C. seminary at Maynooth, co. Dublin, was challenged. *H* xxxviii. 1629.
[16] In T. W. *Reid, *Life of Lord *Houghton*, i. 199 (1890).
[17] Nicholas William Ridley, 1779–1854; added -Colborne to surname 1803; whig M.P. 1805–12, 1818–26, 1827–32, 1834–7; cr. Lord Colborne 1839; collected pictures.

Tuesday June 27.

Irish Commee 1–4. wrote to Taylor. Finished B. Noel's Evidence & read
Pope.[1] Saw Mr Scott—& Mr Macarthur: long conv. on NSW[2]—dined at Sir
S. Scott's & music 10–1—rewrote (by abbreviating) my address.

28.

Helen's birthday: blessing be with it. Taylor to breakfast. 2 hours of very
interesting conversation with him on the most solemn subject. wrote to
T.G. & Caparn: again rewrote address in some measure. dined with the
Fellowses.[3] rode. read Pope—papers—: at Library Committee.

29. Th.

Educn 1½–4. O. & C. Commee on *pew*-room for servants, an hour—Saw Mr
Scott—Macarthur—Acland. read Pope—Strype—dined at Mr Wainwright's. Election papers & convv. now sadly kill time—at York St Chapel[4]
surveying—rode—wrote to Jeffreys—Welsh.

30. Fr.

Conv. with Hamilton. Commee 1–4. Month's letters & accts—Pope—rode—
dined with the Joys—singing. At Lady Salisbury's. Beautiful sight of (alas)
a fire over the Park Gardens. read pt of Wyse's Speech.[5]

July one. Saturday.

Library Commee at 11. Calls. Penitentiary at 3 to choose a Chaplain.[6] rode.
dined at Abp of Armagh's. Lady Parke's afterwards—read Pope[7]—Strype
—Electioneering matters (Dundee Falmouth &c)[8] now kill a good deal of
time. Wrote to Ld Middleton & Ld Winchilsea.

2. S.

Church & Commn. Mr Wigram & Mr Ward. wrote a few Vss. 1½ hour with
Taylor on the same subject. Read nothing.

[1] A. *Pope tr. *The First Book of Statius His Thebais* (1712).
[2] Probably (Sir) Edward *Macarthur, 1789–1872; general; son of John*, 1767–1834,
founder of New South Wales colony; fought in peninsula; then secretary to lord chamber-
lain; commanded troops in Australia 1855–60; kt. 1862.
[3] Robert Fellowes had no town house.
[4] Off St. James's Square; ? under reconstruction.
[5] Of 19 May 1835, on Irish education: *H* xxvii. 1199.
[6] Daniel Nihill, 1791–1867, chaplain 1826–44, acted also as governor of the penitentiary, 1837–8.
[7] *Pope tr. *The First Book of Statius His Thebais*.
[8] His father was standing for Dundee. Penryn and Falmouth, a seat where govt.
influence was strong, was carried in August by Sir Robert Mounsey *Rolfe, 1790–1868,
whig M.P. there 1832–9, judge 1839, cr. Baron Cranworth 1850, lord chancellor 1852–8,
and by J. W. Freshfield; against (Sir) James Hanway *Plumridge, 1787–1863, who was
at Trafalgar; capt. R.N. 1822, whig M.P. there 1841–7, K.C.B. 1855, vice-admiral 1857.

3. M.

House 1–2, 5–6, 8½–12. Several Divv.[1] Library Commee at Carlton. Wrote to Caparn & T.G.—again rewrote Address; at last within reasonable limits.[2] rode. read Pope's 1st B. of Statius. eyes yet weak.—wrote to Wilde— Burnaby.

4. T.

read & epitomised the Rosshire petition: very trying to the eye. Wrote to Applex[3]—Mr Scott—Allen. Commee 12¼–3¼. House again 4½–5¼[4] and read Pope &c.[5]

5. W.

Commee at 1¼—Church Fund Commee at 2¼—House 3¼–6, Presented Cape petn with a statement.[6] Saw Applex on the Ross petn—Mr Dill[7] on a Presbn mission in Ireland—wrote out my statement for paper. Wrote to Caparn— Robert G.—Mr Leathes—John went to Leicester. Musical party at the Doyles'. Saw E. Hamilton on political matters. Acland on his Address.

6. Th.

saw Col. Wade—Applex—Ld Stanley—read Hook's Inaugural Discourse— excellent.[8] Pope. House 3–4. rode. dined at Mr Farrer's[9]—int[eres]ting conv. with Mr Gregson.[10] Wrote to J.N.G.—Mr Leathes. Presented Ross Eln petition[11]—wrote to Ld Advocate.[12]

7. Friday.

Eln letters &c.—wrote to J.N.G.—the Lord Advocate—Robert G.—dined with Farquhar & Hamn—inttg evg on Church matters till 12—Commee 1¼–4. Rode. music spelling. Vss—

8. Sat.

morning occupied with Dundee & other electioneering matters, & reading the Rossshire precognitions.[13] A few Vss. Eyes very poor. Helen fallen back. rode. dined at Mr Russell Ellice's. wrote to J.N.G.—Burnaby—Music.

I wd have given much to be at the King's funeral.[14]

[1] Mainly on supply, in a thin house: H xxxviii. 1763.
[2] Printed copy, dated this day, in Add MS 44727, f. 92; *Wilde's, dated 29 June, ibid. f. 59.   [3] Presumably Ross-shire election agent.
[4] Hand-loom weavers: H xxxviii. 1790.   [5] A note in Add MS 44727, ff. 93–94.
[6] On relations of colonists with aboriginals: H xxxviii. 1799.
[7] Samuel Mark Dill, priest, of Hillsborough, co. Dublin.
[8] W. F. *Hook, 'An Inaugural Discourse preached in the Parish Church of Leeds' (1837).
[9] Perhaps James William Farrer, 1785–1863; barrister; master in chancery from 1824.
[10] Perhaps John Gregson, 1806–79; barrister.
[11] On abduction of a drunken voter: H xxxviii. 1822.
[12] (Sir) John Archibald *Murray, 1779–1859; M.P. Leith 1832–9, lord advocate 1835–9, lord of session (as Lord Murray) from 1839.
[13] Scots law term for preliminary examinations of witnesses.
[14] At Windsor; M.P.s who were not privy councillors were not invited.

9. Sunday.

Ch. twice. walk to Aunt J.s &c.—wrote[1]—read a little of Newman's Romanism: as much as I dared—Helen better. Taylor again.

10. M.

read only the Poor Law Report, & papers. Election matters again: Walsall opened: saw Forster.[2]—House 3–5¼. Spoke on Rossshire petition, &c.[3] wrote to Allen—Caparn—J.N.G.—Graham's Town Committee—rode— dined in B. Square. Wrote to R. Dawson.

11. T.

Paying tradesmen's bills. Bookbuying, for Mr G., R.G., & Carlton Club.— read Newman, a little. Dined at Sir H. Dukinfield's. wrote to Wilde— Caparn—H. Thompson—& Ld J. Russell—out late.

12. Wed.

Saw Serj. Wilde on Nk matters. House 3–4¾. Apprp Commee Reported.[4] dined at Mr Taylor's—Carlton & (shd have been) meeting afterwards.— Election matters—bookbuying. Wrote to [blank]. read Poor Law Report.

13. Th.

Wrote to Caparn—T. Acland—House. read Pope (finished Vol I.)—Tal- fourd's Sp.[5]—R.C. Poll Catm—wrote a sketch on Poor Law—dined at Mr Mildmay's.[6] Lady Murray's concert.[7] O. & C. Club Commee—Eln matters— Out late. Vss.

14. Fr.

Wrote to Luxmoore—Burge—A & H.[8]—Robn G—Mahon. House 4–6.[9] saw Mr Brackenbury & settled a matter for him with Ld Sandon—went up with the Oxford Address: an interesting occasion.[10] rode. Evg at home & club.

---

[1] A note in Add MS 44727, f. 97.
[2] C. S. Forster decided in the end to stand again for Walsall; and was defeated by Francis Finch, who sat till February 1841, when J. N. Gladstone replaced him.
[3] Case of the Ross-shire voter made drunk re-stated; motion for inquiry withdrawn, on opposition from (Sir) J. A. *Murray. H xxxviii. 1856.
[4] Misc. business; mainly on colonial accounts cttee. H xxxviii. 1893.
[5] Of 1 April 1835, on Church of Ireland: H xxvii. 547.
[6] Probably Humphrey St. John Mildmay, 1794–1853, 6th son of 3rd bart.; lived in Berkeley Square.
[7] Sarah Maria Hay-Drummond, da. of 9th earl of Kinnoull, d. 1874; m. 1811 George *Murray, bp. of Rochester.
[8] *Acland and *Hamilton?
[9] West India compensation, on which he said a few words (not in H; Mirror, iii. 2224); church appointments (H xxxviii. 1908).
[10] Morley supposes this to have been the first meeting between *Gladstone and *Vic- toria (i. 140).

15. Sat.

J.N.G. retd. A busy day of packing & putting away: besides Eln matters. House 4–5¼.[1] rode. wrote to Caparn & Lawton. dined at Mr Estcourt's to meet the Oxford party. saw one afterwards.[2] Up late. Bill paying.

Sunday Jul. 16.

Commn at 8 A.M. Mr Ward twice. In Hill St, where Louisa attacked, but better. Finished Newman's Romanism. wrote to Hamilton—Stuart (Dem[erar]a)—Mr Cavendish—Mr G. Packing a little unavoidably.

17. M.

Wrote to Mr Bigg[3]— J.N.G.—8 a.m.–11 P.M. to Newark by Express coach. Found my friends awaiting me—Filicaja.[4]

18. T.

Canvass 9–5. Speech, & dinner, afterwards. read Filicaja: paper.

19. W.

Canvass 9–5½: speech afr—heard Serj. Wilde & Hichins[5] from Mr Tallents's —Saw the Manchester deputation:[6] recommdd them to Mr Granville Ryder.[7] paper. Filicaja—wrote to H.J.G.

20. Th.

Canvass 9–4. wrote to Lincoln—Mr [sc. Ld] Aberdeen— and J.N.G.—read paper—Filicaja. made reff. to Poor Law Act &c.[8]

21. Fr.

Canvass 9½–12—Lunch—& procession, afterwards. Dinner at C[linton] A[rms]—Speech of 40 m. at 7 P.M. to a large & quiet audience on the Poor Law Act.[9] wrote to Mr G—who stands for Dundee: T.G.—H.J.G.—Sir J. Macdonald. Wrote out two poems in Albums.

22. Sat.

Manchester rumour—considered—made a statement to my Commee— wrote handbill to contradict it.[10] Note to Mr Handley. calls. requested Mr Godfrey to propose me. Saw Sir R. Bromley—Hemstock & Watson[11] publi-

[1] Corporations bill: lords' amdts. accepted. *H* xxxviii. 1916. And see Morley, i. 140.
[2] i.e. was accosted, and remonstrated: cp. i. xxix–xxx above.
[3] Perhaps William Robert Bigg, b. 1804?, barrister of Lincoln's Inn.
[4] V. da Filicaja, *Poesie Toscane* (1827).   [5] Wilde's escort.
[6] See Morley, i. 141, for *Gladstone's unintended candidacy for Manchester.
[7] Granville Dudley Ryder, 1799–1879, of Westbrook Hay, Hemel Hempstead; lieut. R.N. 1819; 2nd son of 1st earl of *Harrowby; m. a da. of 6th duke of Beaufort.
[8] Note on ethics in Add MS 44727, f. 98.
[9] Not in Bassett, *Speeches.*
[10] In Cornelius Brown, *History of Newark* ii. 252 and Add MS 44727, f. 99; repudiating Manchester connexion.   [11] James Watson, Newark publican and pawnbroker.

cans on their bills—Mrs Wolfitt & her blind daughter[1]—sat to young Wilson[2]—attended the Odd Fellows in Evg, & spoke to them[3]—read paper—Filicaja.

23. Sunday.

Ch mg & evg. Mr Handley (Winthorpe)[4] & the Vicar. walk. Letters from Dundee—J.N.G.—Manchester—& others: material.—read Newman's Serm (Vol 3)—Filicaja—Chr. Kn. Tracts on Episcopacy—Edn of Childn—Ch. Establts (Dealtry).[5]

24. M.

Wrote to Mr G—draft & copy to Mr Crossley[6]—to H.J.G.—R.M. Milnes—Mr Godfrey—draft of Address of Thanks[7]—

Hustings at 10—Spoke near an hour: afr return, wh was before $10\frac{1}{2}$[8]—Chaired at $2\frac{1}{4}$ & speech—2 hours or more: dinner at 5 & speeches. Filicaja.

25. T.

Saw Wilde on town matters. Wrote to T.G.—Off by (the last place on) the Glasgow Mail to Carlisle. read Filicaja. T.G's birthday— & his lost election at Leicester, wh we much lament.[9]

26. W.

God be praised for the good accounts I received on my way. Is it not (implicitly) his cause? I believe so: but here a right frame of prayer is the security.

In Edinbro at 3. Saw Thomson[10] & L'Amy.[11] Got a little French & Italian on my way. In Dundee before 11. 340 miles in 37 hours.

27. Th.

Delighted to find my dear Father so supported in his truly patriotic labour. With him on his Canvass. With the Committee. One or two to dinner. Wrote to Rn G. and an Address[12] in answer to a bill agt me. At two meetings also with Mr G. Papers. Filicaja.

---

[1] Perhaps the wife and daughter of Joseph Woolfit, Newark fishmonger.

[2] Unidentified.

[3] Lodge 963, the Good Samaritan, founded 1835, of the Independent Order of Oddfellows.

[4] William Handley, 1811–73; rector of Winthorpe, Notts.

[5] S.P.C.K. tracts: T. Wilson, 'The True Christian Method of Educating Children' (1833), and W. *Dealtry, 'Religious Establishments Tried by the Word of God' (1835).

[6] James Crossley, Manchester lawyer; cp. 4 Aug. 37.   [7] Untraced.

[8] *Gladstone and *Wilde were again returned unopposed.

[9] Edward Goulbourn and Thomas Gladstone maintained their vote of 1835, but lost by some 350 each to Samuel Duckworth, made a master in chancery 1839, and (Sir) John *Easthope, 1784–1865, speculator, who was whig M.P. for St. Albans 1826–30, Banbury 1831, and Leicester 1837–47; cr. bart. 1841; owned *Morning Chronicle* 1834–47.

[10] Perhaps an Edinburgh advocate.   [11] James L'Amy, advocate.

[12] In Add MS 44796, f. 10: repudiating attack in *Manchester Guardian*.

28. Fr.

Quarty on Moxon. Filicaja, papers. dined at Mr Balfour's. Wrote to Sherriffs—T.G.—Mr Leathes. Nomination $11\frac{3}{4}$–$2\frac{1}{4}$. Mr G. not heard. Canvassing him.

29. Sat.

Canvassing. papers. Filicaja.

30. S.

Epl Church mg & aft. Newman. Dined at Mr Anderson's[1]—walked up the Law.

31. M.

Canvassing. Pelted with mud & stones. Complained to the police—wrote to R.G.—out again in evg. Our friends confident.

Tuesday August one.

My Father beaten after all; our promised voters in many cases holding back or going agt us.

Letters & accts made up—wrote to Mr Crossley—R.G.—determined on going South—200 promises broken—poll closed at

Parnell[2]	000.
Gladstone	381.[3]

It is not in human approbation that the reward of right action is to be sought.

Left at $4\frac{1}{2}$ amid the hisses of the crowd. Perth at $7\frac{1}{4}$. Went up Moncreiff hill for the view. Saw Stormont & his friends. Left at 1 (mg) for Glasgow.[4]

2.

Glasgow $8\frac{1}{2}$—Steamer at 11. Called on Mr Finlay. A breeze: miserably sick: deck all night.[4]

3.

Arrived [at Liverpool] at $11\frac{1}{2}$: refitted: very sore. papers—wrote to H.J.G. —Mr Symons—Mr Walther[5]—Caparn—Aunt J—Standard. music in evg. Calls.[4]

---

[1] Patrick Anderson, 1784?–1839, banker; four times provost ca. 1820.
[2] Sir Henry Brooke *Parnell, 1776–1842; writer on political economy; M.P. for Queen's county 1802 and 1806–32; for Dundee 1833–41; conspicuous supporter of Catholic emancipation; secretary at war 1831–2; paymaster general 1836–42; succ. as 4th bart. 1801; cr. Baron Congleton 1841; a suicide.
[3] Cp. *Roll of Eminent Burgesses of Dundee* (1887), 275–6.
[4] Extracts in Morley, i. 141.
[5] Perhaps David Walther, theological writer.

4.

Out at 8¼ to vote for S. Lanc^e—acted as representative in the booth ½ the day—Result of eln excellent.[1] Wrote to Mahon—Mr G—read A. Finlay[2]— Calls. papers. whist. music. Conv. with Mr Crossley.[3]

5. Sat.

Again in the booths. A great victory here.—Conv. with & about the Manchr people. Arranged to dine there on Wedy please God. read Finlay— papers. dined at Mr [Hugh] Jones's—music. wrote to Robert G.—& Walther. arranged the book bills: wh took so indifft an accountant some time.[3]

6. S.

St Andrew's: Communion: St Katherine's—wrote to T.G.—& Manning on the death of his wife.[4] Tom's daughter born.[5]—read Newman.[6]

7. M.

paper. Stanley's Prize Poem: capital.[7] A. Finlay's letters.[8]—wrote to Mr G. —revolving, for Wednesday—visited Seaforth—music—went to Larkhill: saw Wm Derbyshire.[9]

8. T.

Calls. paper. finished Finlay. dined at Otterspool. conv. with Rainy[10] on B. Guiana. again considering of matter for speech.

9. W.

Train at 11 to Manchr—papers—went to see & R. & Wm.s wives— pleased. Then to Mr Denison's at Rusholme.[11] Public dinner at 6. Lasted till near 12. Music excellent. Spoke 1½ hour—I am told. Proh pudor. wrote to Mr G.[12]

[1] Lord F. *Egerton and Richard Bootle Wilbraham, 1801–44, eldest son of 1st Lord Skelmersdale, M.P.s for south Lancashire from 1835, were returned by comfortable majorities over Edward Stanley, b. 1790, cons. M.P. for Cumberland 1832–52, and Charles Towneley.
[2] A. S. Finlay, *Letters on a Journey to Bombay, through Syria and Arabia in 1834–35* (1837).
[3] Extracts in Morley, i. 141.
[4] Caroline Manning d. of consumption on 24 July 1837.
[5] Louisa, d. unm. 1885.
[6] Extracts in Morley, i. 141. Note on *Newman in Add MS 44727, f. 101.
[7] A. P. *Stanley, 'The Gypsies'; *Newdigate prize, 1837.
[8] A. S. Finlay, *Letters on a Journey to Bombay, Through Syria and Arabia* (1837).
[9] A gardener, of Lark Hill, West Derby, 4 miles ENE. of central Liverpool.
[10] George Rainy, Demerara proprietor; a fifth cousin. (See P. C. Simpson, *Life of Principal *Rainy*, i. 5, 13 (1909).)
[11] Suburb 2 miles SSE. of city centre.
[12] Extracts in Morley, i. 141–2 and n.

10. Th.

retd to Lpool by train at 11. Read Elia—Filicaja. wrote to Mr G—Sherriffs. dined in A. Square.[1] walk afr & music. Saw Doyle.

11. Fr.

Headache. Doyle to breakft. walk with him. paper. wrote to Mr G—White—Luxmoore—Leathes—Caparn—Gaskell—Milnes—Mr Ramsay—Mrs Ogilvy—Bickers[teth]—Viant.[2]—Music with M.E. left Lpool at 6 by Steam. (Vulcan).

12. Sat.

A quiet passage. read Filicaja. Nay, dined in the Cabin. Greenock at $2\frac{1}{2}$ P.M.—Glasgow $5\frac{1}{2}$—Edinh 11—papers.

13. S.

St John's mg & aft. Most of the day with the Ramsays. Mr Sinclair too dined there. Interesting Church conv. as usual. read Newman.

14. M.

7–5 (by Defiance) to Fasque.[3] "The Captain" drove us from Perth. He has much infn on men & things of these parts. And here I have brought my uselessness again.—At the garden, stables, hayfield. Began Crabb "The Borough".

15.

On the hill. A healthful walk: shot as ill as possible. $2\frac{1}{2}$ br[ace], & a blue hare. wrote to Mr G., R.G., Acland,[4] Lady Mackenzie—Dined at Sir J. Forbes's. Music.

16. W.

Wrote to Mr G.[5]—Conning with Sherriffs. Hill again: & perhaps worse. 3 brace. Crabb. Poor Robert's wife very ill.—saw Preshaw:[6] read some of 'De Grimm & Diderot'.[7]

17. Th.

wrote to Mr G.—read Mrs Behn's Feigned Courtesans[8]—& Rabelais. paper. dined at Sir J. Forbes's—music. Saw Guthrie—Visited P. Anderson—Widow Fraser—Lawrence's school.

[1] Robert Gladstone lived at 17 Abercromby Square, Robertson at 3.
[2] A tax collector; cp. 18 Sep. 37.
[3] Morley, i. 142, places his arrival a day earlier.
[4] In A. H. D. *Acland, *T. D.* *Acland*, 84.
[5] And some notes on politics: Add MS 44727, ff. 102–4.
[6] William Preshaw, surgeon, of Fettercairn.
[7] *Correspondance littéraire, philosophique et critique . . . par le baron de Grimm et par Diderot* (1813).   [8] A. *Behn, *The Feigned Curtizans* (1679).

18. Fr.

Wrote to F. Baring—Mr G—T.G.—Ed. Abn Obsr[1]—Ed. Inv. Herald[2]—
Mr Russell Ellice.—read Rabelais—paper—Eloisa[3]—Hall Stevenson[4]—
Filicaja. wrote to H.J.G.

19. Sat.

paper. wrote to Mr Denison—J.G.—T.G.—Blakeslay—read Filicaja—King
James's Works—on the Hill—dined at Fettn H.—music.

20. S.

recommenced prayers—mg & evg: & reading service in aftn—with Sumner's
Serm 16[5]—very apposite. read Newman—& Coleridge on Ch—Par Lost
B.VII.—Fettn Ch. in mg.

21. M.

papers. analysing new H. of C.[6] wrote to Mr G.—Mordaunt—Bruce—read
Filicaja—Sir M. Shee's letter to Ld J. Russell[7]—Hist. of Buccaneers[8]—R.
Ascham on Edn.[9]

22. T.

Wrote to Mr G—on the hill—dined at Fettn H.—music—read papers—
Filicaja—Buccaneers.

23. W.

wrote to Mr G—Ingram—on the hill—read paper—Filicaja—unpacking &
arranging books—Sir W. Raleigh's poems.[10]

24. Th.

Mr G. came. Calls, riding. Don Juan Canto I. with notes. Filicaja. Eloisa.
wrote to Bonham.

25. Fr.

rain. Don Juan Canto II. Buccaneers. Quarterly on New Reign—& on

[1] Untraced; the *Aberdeen Observer* shortly expired.
[2] So did the *Inverness Herald*; also untraced.
[3] *Pope, 'Eloisa to Abelard' (1717).
[4] Probably *Crazy Tales* (1762), most famous work of John Hall–*Stevenson, 1718–85,
poetaster and pamphleteer.
[5] J. B. *Sumner, *A Series of Sermons on the Christian Faith and Character* (1821); in
9th ed of 1837, Sermon XVI p. 268 is on purity of heart, Matthew v. 8.
[6] Govt. retained a small working majority, under 40.
[7] Sir M. A. *Shee, 'A Letter to Lord John *Russell . . . on the alleged claim of the
public to be admitted gratis to the exhibition of the Royal Academy' (1837).
[8] A. O. Exquemelin, *History of the Bucaniers of America* (1678, tr. 1684; many eds.).
[9] *The Schoolmaster* (1570).
[10] First collected in 1813.

Hare's Sermons. wrote to Farquhar (on his marriage)[1]—T.G.—Mr Smith (Montrose).[2] arranging books. Read Stuart.[3] Demarara papers.

26. Sat.

Don Juan Canto III & remarks on the Blackwood critm[4]—Buccaneers. Pamphlet on the Rice Procln[5]—arranging books. Wrote to J.N.G.—& draft to Ld Glenelg.

27. Sunday.

Fettn Ch.—Evg prayers—went to Mackay's. read Newman—Leighton (resumed)—Coleridge on Church.[6]

28. M.

on the hill. Robert killed 3: I, 2—very wild—& packing. Wrote to Canning. read Filicaja & Don Juan Canto IV.

29. T.

wrote to T.G.—Monthly accounts & letters. began the Timaeus, with Abstract.[7] Spanish Grammar, resumed. Don Juan V—read Vss. Wrote to Buxton—Mahon.

30. W.

Filicaja. Timaeus. Juan VI. Wrote to Doyle. Wrote Adversa on Eth. &c.[8] —at Stracathro.

31. Th.

Filicaja. Timaeus, waxing thick. Juan VII & pt of VIII. Spanish Gr. & a page of Don Quijote. Wrote to Williams (Oxf.)—Mr Welby—Mr Dolier. (London).[9] Dined at Fettn H.—Music.

Friday September One.

Filicaja. Timaeus. Spanish, Don Quijote. Don Juan, VIII, IX. Drove to Mr G. to Johnstone & Balmakewan.[10]

[1] Sir W. R. Farquhar m., 28 November 1837, Lady Mary Octavia Somerset, 1814–1906, 8th da. of 6th duke of Beaufort.
[2] Perhaps Robert Smith, D.D., minister of the Old Church.
[3] Untraced.
[4] *Byron, 'Some Observations Upon an Article in Blackwood's Edinburgh Magazine' (1820, first printed in H. L. Bulwer ed., *Byron, Works 1835). It replied to 'Remarks on Don Juan' in Blackwood's Edinburgh Magazine v. 512 (August 1819).
[5] Untraced.
[6] Note on sin in Add MS 44727, f. 106; sonnet ibid. f. 108.
[7] Plato; abstract in Add MS 44727, ff. 111–16.
[8] In Add MS 44727, f. 119.   [9] William Dolier, Liverpool teacher.
[10] Alexander Gibbons lived at Johnstone, just south of Lawrencekirk; and Colonel William Fraser at Balmakewan, on the North Esk 4½ miles SW. of it.

2.

Wrote to Mordaunt—Ld Aberdeen—J.N.G.—R.G.—M'Lauchlan—Jno Ashley.

read Timacus—Hist. of Buccaneers—Don Juan X, XI—Spanish, Don Quijote.

3. *Sunday.*

Fettn mg—Prayers (& Sumner 18) aftn—one visit—read Leighton—Newman—Filicaja & Vss.[1]

4. *M.*

Wrote to M. Gaskell—J.N.G.
read Timaeus—Buccaneers—D. Juan C.XII—Don Quijote. At Fettn &c.

5. *T.*

Wrote to T.G.—Mrs Falconer.
read Timaeus—Filicaja—Hist. of Buccaneers—Don Juan XIII.—Drove Mr G. to Arbuthnott & Lkirk.

6. *W.*

wrote to Ld Aberdeen. Branston.
read Timaeus (tough)—Filicaja[2]—D.J. XIV & pt of XV. finished Hist. of Buccaneers. Began S. Aug. de peccatorum meritis & remissione B.1.[3]—Shooting. little to be found yet.

7. *Th.*

Wrote to Branston—Crabbe.
A day of rain. Billiards—twn my two hands. read Timaeus—(began) Leland's Hist. of Ireland[4]—S. Aug. de Pecc.—(finished) Don Juan (wh cannot be dismissed in a single remark)[5]—Don Quijote.

8. *Fr.*

wrote to Mr Peacock (Sleaford).[6]
In the bog for snipes with Sir J. & M'Kenzie—read Timaeus—Leland—(began) Byron's Life—my eyes refused any further progress. Vss.[7]

---

[1] In Add MS 44727, f. 121.
[2] A note ibid. f. 122, on God.
[3] Augustine on the deserts and forgiveness of sinners, and on infant baptism (412; in Migne, *PL*, xliv. 108). Abstract in Add MS 44727, ff. 124–5.
[4] T. *Leland, *The History of Ireland, from the Invasion of *Henry II*, 3 v. (1773). Abstract in Add MS 44727, ff. 126–32 and 237.
[5] Some notes ibid. f. 211.
[6] Anthony Taylor Peacock, Lincolnshire gentleman.
[7] Extracts in Morley, i. 142. Note on Timaeus in Add MS 44727, f. 156.

9. Sat.

Leland. Timaeus. Byron's Life. wrote to Mordaunt.—Again stopped.

10. S.

Fettn in mg. prayers in aft. Sumner XIX. Two visits. Wrote.[1] read Knox & pt of Pref. to Vol III of Remains[2]—Newman—Aug. de Pecc.

11. M.

Wrote to Aunt D.—Cousin Jane—M. Welsh—Rev. Mr Inglis[3]—G. Tallents.
read Timaeus[4]—Moore's Byron—Filicaja—Leland—S. Aug. de Pecc.—rode my mare.

12. T.

The Mordaunts do not come. Wrote to M: regretting the cause & its consequence. Copied a letter.
On Balmaine; I don't improve.[5]
S. Aug. de Pecc. Timaeus. Leland. M[oore's] B[yron]. finished Vol. I.

13. W.

wrote to T.C. read Timaeus. Leland. W.I. paper. S. Aug. M.B. The Fettn party dined here—music.

14. Th.

Finished Timaeus—wrote on do.[6]
read Leland—M.B.—(finished) Filicaja.
Sir J.F[orbes] & Ld A[rbuthnott] here about the M. Standard.[7]

15. Fr.

Wrote Caparn—D. of Newcastle—Mr Whyte. Snipe-shooting with F. in the bog.
read Critias[8] (began), 'Hours of Idleness',[9] Leland—considering some Vss of Doyle's.[10]

---

[1] On Filicaja and on the Virgin Mary; ibid., ff. 157–61. And see Lathbury, ii. 430–3.
[2] *Remains of Alexander *Knox*, 4v. (1834–7).
[3] John Inglis, 1778?–1850; s. of Charles*, first bp. of Nova Scotia; 3d. bp. of Nova Scotia 1825.
[4] More notes in Add MS 44727, ff. 162–3.
[5] Shooting at seat of Ramsay Alexander, half a mile south of Fettercairn.
[6] In Add MS 44727, ff. 164–6.
[7] John *Gladstone was a part owner of the Montrose Standard.
[8] Plato; abstract in Add MS 44727, f. 133.
[9] *Byron (1807); notes in Add MS 44727, ff. 168–9.
[10] Extracts in Morley, i. 142.

21—II.

16. Sat.

Wrote to Ld Abn, T.G.—Our journies brewed. rode.
read Critias—Leland—S. Aug. Byron. (finished H. of Idleness)[1]—Notes of
Mr G's earlier days—from a convn at dinner.[2]

17. S.

Fettn—Prayers in aft. Sumner XX—last: I regret to lose him. Read Knox
& Newman—wrote much.

18. M.

Mr G. went. Made arrangements for moving. wrote to T.G.—J.N.G.—Mr
Welsh—Viant (Assessed Tax)—read[3] Leland—S. Aug—Byron (finished
Vol VII of XVII)[4]—finished Critias & began νόμοι.[5]

19. T.

read Leland—& after breakf. & post left for Haddo. 17 m to Banchory
(two horses up hill) 8.55–11.20. Banchory to Inverury 19 m (went 20 by
error)[6] 11.30–2.5. Inverury to Haddo 12 m. 4–5½.
found a large party.
Read Sibilla Odaleta (began)[7]—paper.
wrote to Mr G.—Forbes—Wilmot—White.

20. W.

Overslept. wrote to Lady Kerrison.
read Νόμοι—Sibilla—Laird & Oldfield's Expn[8]—walkd to Tolquhoun[9] &
abt the place.

21. Th.

Wrote to Doyle—Hamilton.
read Νόμοι—Sibilla—Laird & Oldfield—drove to Formartine[10] & walked
afterwards with Ld Aberdeen.

22. Fr.

Wrote to Mr G—Austine.[11]
read Νόμοι (finished I.) Sibilla—Laird.
Otter hunting—senz'esito.[12] Hunting too in the library.[13]

---

[1] Extracts in Morley, i. 142.
[2] In Add MS 44727, ff. 176–7; and a note on Atlas and Columbus, ibid. f. 167.
[3] 'Critias' here deleted.
[4] Note ibid. f. 170.   [5] Plato, *Laws*; abstract in Add MS 44727, ff. 134–5.
[6] As the crow flies, 17; ENE. Inverurie lies 4 miles WSW. of Old Meldrum.
[7] C. Varese, *Sibilla Odaleta* (1828), an historical romance.
[8] M. *Laird and R. A. K. Oldfield, *Narrative of an Expedition into the interior of Africa
by the River Niger* (1837).   [9] Ruined castle 4 miles south of Haddo House.
[10] The east central plain of Aberdeenshire; its viscountcy was among Aberdeen's titles.
[11] Perhaps John *Austin, 1790–1859, the jurist.
[12] 'Without result'.   [13] Version of extracts in Morley, i. 142.

23. Sat.

Wrote to T.G.—White.

read Νόμοι—Laird (finished)—Alfieri on Tyranny[1]—Coleridge's Table Talk
—& his nephew's inttg preface.[2] walk with Lds A. & M.[3] & ride to see the
Tent.

24. S.

9¾–2¼ to Church at Old Meldrum. read Whyte and Smith's First Discourse.[4]
wrote Vss.[5] & on Justifn by Faith.[6]

25. M.

Vss. wrote to Mr G—Mr Ramsay—Mr Frascr (Gourock).
Left Haddo at 10.40—To Kintore[7] 17 m. 1 h. 40 m. (really not much over
15). To Banchory 15 m, 2h. 6m. (really 16). To Brig of Dye[8] 1 h.—pr[ob-
ably] 8 m. to Fasque 1 h. 20 m.—pr. 9 m. arrived at 6.50.
read Sibilla Odaleta—hunted Encycll., Phil, Trans. &c. about Echoes—also
Pennant & other Tours.[9]
wrote to H. Taylor, H. Thompson, Mr Trail—R.G.—J.N.G.—Housekeeper
C[arlton] G[ardens].

26.

wrote to Ld Aberdeen—Mr G.—T.G.—Vss. read paper—Leland—Sibilla.
much time in reverie.
wrote to Buxton. rode. walk.

27. Wed.

wrote to Mr G.—Mr Edmonston—Mr Macarthur—Mr Walther—D. of
Newcastle—read Sibilla—Leland[10]—& ditto—wrote to Manning—Shooting.

28. Th.

Read Manning's proof & wrote to him thereon.[11] rode to Laurencekirk—
walk. transl[ate]d (ma) "Lady Mary" into German[12]—read Leland—
Sibilla.

---

[1] Della Tirannide, 2v. (1801).
[2] H. N. *Coleridge ed. Specimens of the Table Talk of the late Samuel Taylor *Coleridge,
2v. (1835). [3] *Mahon?
[4] William Smith of Philadelphia, Discourses on Public Occasions During the War in
America (1759), explaining the protestant cause in British colonies.
[5] In Add MS 44727, f. 171. [6] Ibid., ff. 178–92.
[7] 4 miles south of Inverurie; also on the Don.
[8] Roadside hamlet midway between Banchory and Fasque.
[9] T. *Pennant, A Tour in Scotland (1769).
[10] Note in Add MS 44727, f. 172.
[11] On H. E. *Manning, 'The Principle of the Ecclesiastical Commission Examined in a
Letter to the Bishop of Chichester' (1838). In Lathbury, i. 40–42.
[12] 'Thou wert fair, Lady Mary' in [H. *Alford] 'Poems and Poetical Fragments'
(1833); translation in Add MS 44728, ff. 13–19; 22–29.

29. Fr.

wrote to Forbes—Brancker—read Leland—νόμοι[1]—Sibilla—Childe Harold
I. & N[otes]. shooting—monthly accts & letters made up.

30. S.

Vss (Dante &c) read Fr. da Rimini to consider of Mahon's advice—Wrote
to Mahon. Leland—Sibilla—νόμοι—Ch Harold II. Walk to the Cairn &
back, 2 h. From Cl[attering] Brig up,[2] 29½ m. down 25½ m. 2¼ miles.
Cl. Brig home, by drove rode 2 m. 3 f.—by the common road, 2 m. ¾.

Sunday Octr One.

Newman's Serm (finished Vol 3.)—Leighton—Knox.
wrote to Ld Abn—Finished Essay on Justification.[3]
walked to Lkirk to Ch. From Fasque by Phesdo 6¼ m. 1 h. 19 m. To
F[asque] by Fettn, 6¼ m., 1 h. 18 m.
Prayers at 3 & a sermon of Bp Blomfield.

2. M.

Wrote to Mr Ramsay. Miss Pittis.[4]
read Νόμοι (finished B.II) Sibilla Odaleta (finished) Leland (finished Vol 2.).
Shooting. W. Goalen & his wife came to dinner.[5]

3. T.

Wrote to T.G.—R.G.—J.N.G.—Doyle.
read Leland—Macarthur's N.S.W. (began)[6]—Childe Harold C.III.
Wrote (private) to Farquhar.

4. W.

wrote to W. Goalen.
read Leland—Macarthur—S. Aug. de Pecc. dined at Phesdo.[7] Conv. on
S. Australia—& Breeding. Shooting.

5. Th.

Wrote to Ld Arbuthnott. Crabb—Rn G.—Mr Ramsay—Mordaunt—read
Leland—S. Aug. de Pecc. (began B.III)—Ch. Har. pt of C.IV.—Macarthur's NSW—Sp. Grammar. our party still delayed.

[1] Note in Add MS 44727, ff. 173–4.
[2] Bridge 2 miles NE. of Fasque, on road to Cairn O'Mount and Deeside.
[3] Add MS 44727, ff. 178–92.
[4] Unidentified.
[5] Misc. notes ibid., ff. 193–7, and daily till 10 October, ff. 198–210.
[6] J. *Macarthur, *New South Wales, Its Present State and Future Prospects* (1837).
[7] At Mrs. Crombie's.

Fr. 6.

Wrote to T.G.—Stephen.
read Leland—S. Aug. de Pecc. (finished)—Macarthur. My Plato stopped
for want of next vol. shooting.
dined at Thornton.[1]

Sat. 7.

wrote to Jane Cath[erine Robertson]—Mrs Chisholm—Mr G.—read
Leland—S. Aug. de Nuptiis (began)[2]—Macarthur.
Out devising a hill road—dined at Balmakewan.

8. Sunday.

Wrote to Mr Edmondstone—H. Taylor (long). Fettn in mg—Prayers &
Blomfield S XI aft. Visited Widow Fraser—read Leighton (finished Vol.I.)
—Knox—S. Aug. de Nupt.

9. M.

wrote to H.J.G.—Crabb—saw Sherriffs &c. as usual. read Leland—S. Aug.
de Nupt. M'Arthur—Ch. Har. rode to Thornton to buy poney: to Phesdo,
to borrow a Plato from the Dr[3]—he had none here.

10. T.

wrote to Mr G.—shooting on Balfour. read S. Aug de Nupt (finished)—
Leland—Macarthur—Ch. Harold IV (finished)[4] (+).

11. W.

read Leland[5]—S. Aug ad Quodvultdeum (began)[6]—Macarthur: shooting—
Arbuthnott to dinner.

12. Th.

read Leland (finished)—S. Aug ad Q. (finished)—wrote to Buxton—Mr
Ramsay—Ld Aberdeen—rode to Fordoun—lionised by Dr Leslie: a
delightful specimen of his class. dined at Johnstone.

13. Fr.

read Macarthur (finished)—S. Aug. de V. Haeres.[7] (began)—and Moore's
Byron. Shooting on Balfour. Wrote to Doyle—T.G.—& on Ch. & St.

---

[1] At Alexander Crombie's.
[2] Augustine, *De Nuptiis et Concupiscentia* (419), on marriage and desire (Migne, *PL*,
xliv. 412); abstract in Add MS 44727, ff. 136–7.
[3] William Preshaw, or John Reith; both surgeons.
[4] Notes in Add MS 44727, ff. 212–4.   [5] Notes ibid. ff. 215–6.
[6] Augustine, *De Haeresibus ad Quodvultdeum* (ca. 428), list of heretics; Migne, *PL* xlii.
21. Notes in Add MS 44727, f. 149.
[7] *Tractatus Contra Quinque Haereses*; Migne, *PL* xlii. 1101. Notes in Add MS 44727,
f. 140.

14. Sat.

Wrote to Uncle D.—Mordaunt.—Read S. Aug. de V Haeres. (finished)—
Lingard—abstracting Vol 1 wh I have read before[1]—Moore's Byron—
Shooting on Balmain.[2]

15. Sunday.

Lkirk Ch. mg.—conv. with George.[3]—A Serm. of Bp Denison's with
prayers in aftn.
Read S. Aug. de Unit. Eccl. (began)[4]—Whyte—Knox.
Wrote on Apostl Succession.
Visited Mrs Martin—Our travellers again delayed.

16. M.

Wrote to Mr G.—Mr Horsman[5]—Hope—Ld Arbuthnott.
read Moore's Byron—Lingard—S. Aug. de Un. Eccl. dined at Stracathro.
Up the Cairn with a map, wh I enjoyed.

17.

Wrote to Mrs Wishlade—Mr Brown (Manchr)[6]—Mr Manley (Exeter)—[7]
Ld Morton.[8]
read Moore's B.[9]—Lingard—S. Aug. de Un. Eccl.[10]—Pastor Fido (began).[11]
Shooting on Fasque. wrote to J.N.G.

18.

My eyes in my way.—wrote to R.G.—Vss.[12] & on signs.
read Pastor Fido—S. Aug. de Un. Eccl.—Lingard[13]—Ubaldini's Descr. di
Scozia (began).[14]
Shooting. Then had a farming lecture from Bogindollo,[15] who is an intelligent man.—I then went to visit Mrs Martin—who sinks daily.

[1] Abstract in Add MS 44727, ff. 141–8.
[2] Note on Plato and women, ibid. f. 217.
[3] Possibly George McPherson, shopkeeper.
[4] Augustine, *Ad Catholicos Epistola Contra Donatistas* (*De Unitate Ecclesiae*) (*ca.* 402),
Migne, *PL* xliii. 391; abstract in Add MS 44727, ff. 150–1.
[5] Edward *Horsman, 1807–1876; liberal M.P. for Cockermouth 1835–52; Stroud
1853–68; Liskeard 1869–76; chief secretary for Ireland 1855–7.
[6] John Brown, boroughreeve of Manchester 1837–8.
[7] Orlando Manley, b. 1790, d. before 1860; priest at Dartmouth,1818; at Plymstock,
Devon 1834.
[8] See 20 Oct., 7 Nov. 37.
[9] Note in Add MS 44727, f. 219.
[10] Note ibid. f. 220.
[11] Pastoral tragicomedy by J. B. Guarini (1585).
[12] In Add MS 44727, f. 222.
[13] Note ibid. f. 221, on publicity.
[14] Petruccio Ubaldini, *Descrizzione del Regno di Scotia* (1588, reprinted 1829).
[15] John *Gladstone's factor.

19.

read Pastor Fido—S. Aug. de bono conjugali (began)[1]—Ubaldini—Lingard
—Moore's Byron.
In the hill woods. Visited Robert's wife again.

20.

ans. from Ld Morton. wrote to Farquhar—Lady Kerr[iso]n—read Pastor
Fido—S. Aug. de bono (finished) Moore's Byron—Ubaldini (finished).
Lingard.
Shooting in the bog.

21. Sat.

wrote to Bickers[teth]—Collier (Brechin)[2]—Bonham.—arranged my
F[arquhar] correspondence—read S. Aug. de Virg. (began)[3]—Lingard—
Pastor Fido—part of Romeo & Juliet (+). Moore's Byron. on the hill.

22. Sunday.

wrote to Mr G.—on 'latent tendency'.—walked to Church at Lkirk—
Prayers & pt of Bp Blomfield's Serm 12 in aftn—Visited Mrs Martin.
read S. Aug. de Virg.—Knox—& Whyte.

23. M.

wrote to Lady M'Kenzie—J.N.G.—read S. Aug. de Virg (finished)—Pastor
Fido—Romeo & Juliet. Our party arrived—& caused me a welcome
interruption. Helen's appearance quite up to my hopes.—Shooting.

24. T.

Wrote to Messrs Boyd (Cole's Stockbrokers)[4]—read S. Aug. de Epic. &
Sto.[5]—& began de Ut. Cred.[6]—Lingard—Blackstone (on benefit of Clergy)[7]
—Pastor Fido. Shooting.

25. W.

Wrote to J.N.G.—Collier—G. Tallents. read S. Aug. de Utilitate Credendi—
Pastor Fido—a little Lingard—and a good spell at 'Geraldine'[8]—shooting. whist.

[1] Migne, *PL* xl. 373 (*ca.* 390); abstract in Add MS 44727, f. 138.
[2] Lord F. *Egerton's librarian.
[3] *De sancta virginitate* (*ca.* 401), tract in praise of virginity; Migne, *PL* xl. 395; notes
in Add MS 44727, f. 139. Note on the Church, ibid. f. 224.
[4] Benjamin and Mark Boyd of Lothbury, City. Name much altered in MS.
[5] His sermon cl., on Acts xvii. 18–34, Migne, *PL* xxxviii. 809. Notes in Add MS
44727, f. 153.
[6] *De utilitate credendi* (*ca.* 391), Migne, *PL* xlii. 64. Notes in Add MS 44727, ff. 152,
228. Other misc. notes ibid. ff. 225–7.
[7] W. *Blackstone, *Commentaries on the Laws of England*, 4v. (1765–9), iv. 358.
[8] Martin *Tupper (1838).

26. Th.

Wrote to Capt. Gordon. Dean Murray. read hard at Geraldine (began Vol 2). Finished S. Aug. de Util. Credendi: beautiful & useful.[1] Convv. with H. on Geraldine.
Whist.

27. Fr.

Wrote to Bonham—M'Lachlan—monthly letters. read Geraldine—Lingard —Lady E.S. Wortley.[2]
my eyes are sadly peccant: but there is much of inward reading urgently required & not dependent on them but on an eye whose vigour ought to grow daily.
Wrote to Manning—Ld Morton—Mr Edmonstone—Defiance Bookk[eepe]r —Queensferry Landlord—W. Goalen.[3] Whist.

28. Sat.

Finished Geraldine—wh is highly interesting & contains much that is excellent. Also finished Lady E.S.W's 'Fragments & Fancies' & made a note of my impressions.[4]—Shooting on Pitgarvie[5]—Called on two tenants— whist.
Wrote to Doyle—Crabb.

29. S.

read Knox—Whyte (finished)—Denison's Sermons[6]—Coleridge.
Fettn & prayers with Denison 3d S. abbreviated—Visited Mrs Martin. I hardly like this praying: at least I have the fear that it does not tend much to create a praying frame of mind in the party principally conferred. Yet in extreme illness it seems better than to refuse them, & it enables one to recommend as preferable our own beautiful services. May God give light to my dark and weak thoughts.
wrote a long letter to Mr G—to be in retentis.[7] for a little.

30. M.

Wrote to T.G.—Hamilton. Mr Blundell is alarmingly ill.[8] Completed my circuit of calls on the Tenants: &c. Read Pastor Fido[9]—Coleridge's Ch. & St.—preparing for my move.

---

[1] Morley, i. 142.
[2] Lady E. C. E. *Stuart-Wortley, *Fragments and Fancies* (1837).
[3] And misc. notes, Add MS 44727, ff. 230–1.
[4] Ibid. ff. 233–3.
[5] Beyond Fettercairn, 4 miles SSE. of Fasque.
[6] E. *Denison, *Sermons preached before the University of Oxford* (1836).
[7] 'held back'. On the proposed chapel at Fasque: Lathbury, ii. 237–41.
[8] He had in fact d. on 27 October.
[9] Philological note in Add MS 44727, f. 235.

31.

Finished Coleridge's Idea—r[ea]d Pastor Fido. Monthly acct. Mr G—went to Lpool—Mr Hutton here to dinner. Shooting—wrote to J.N.G.—Conv. with Helen on R.Cm.

Nov. One. Wed.

finished Pastor Fido.
8¾–8¾, 100 miles to Dalmahoy:[1] found a very kind welcome.—Music. read Quart. on Cooper's England.

2. Th.

read Quart. on Etiquette—on Ld J.R. at Stroud[2]—Wesley's letters to Knox.[3]
Wrote to Mr Scott. Morning conv.
Shooting—music in evg. Jas Moncreiff dined here—& the Ramsays came.

3. Fr.

wrote to H.J.G.—Mr G.
read Knox—pt of Qu. on Univv.—Mr R[amsay]'s Sermon. Walk—& several hours conv. with that dear man. morning conv.—Music.

4. Sat.

wrote to R.G. (who is not Nov 7.[4] again a Councillor)—T.G.—Mrs Bartlett —Queensferry.[5]
read Knox—Quarty on Univv. finished—music. Shooting with Lord Aberdour.[6]—& convv.

5. S.

In Ed[inburgh] with the family to the Services & Communion. Called at Mrs Ogilvy's. Walked out—a little way Mr R[amsay] acc[ompanie]d me. read Knox. Wrote to H.J.G.

6. M.

read Quart. on Pickwick.[7] Byron's Dream (wh is very beautiful)[8]—& Hook's Story of Pascal & Bruno.[9] Wrote to R.G. walk to Knewton & Dalmahoy hill.[10] Convv & thoughts.

---

[1] The Mortons' great house 8 miles WSW. of Edinburgh.
[2] Sp. on 28 July 1837.   [3] In A. *Knox, *Remains*, 4v. (1834–7), iv. 1.
[4] These three words interlined.
[5] And religious notes, Add MS 44727, ff. 238–9.
[6] Sholto John Douglas, 1818–84; styled Lord Aberdour from 1827; succ. his f. as 19th earl of Morton 1858; representative peer from 1859.
[7] lix. 484 (October 1837).   [8] In 'The Prisoner of Chillon' (1816).
[9] Perhaps a preview of W. F. *Hook, *An Ecclesiastical Biography . . . of Ancient Fathers and Modern Divines*, 8v. (1841–51), on Pascal viii. 564, Bruno iii. 185.
[10] Kirknewton, 2 miles WSW., and the hill 1 mile south of the house.

7.

Obliged to propose my departure. Allowed tho' in great kindness to take it. Packed. Went in with the Moncreiffs. Saw the Mortons at Mr Ramsays again. Capt Wm Ramsay[1] (liked) went abt $10\frac{1}{2}$—Mrs Ramsay at 12. Much conv. before that time—then made a clean breast till three next mg.[2]

8. W.

$7-4\frac{3}{4}$. Defiance to N.W. Bridge—mixed dream & reminiscence. Walked to Fasque. Found Dear John in bed—but thank God going on well. Wrote "Saggi"[3] & a scrap from Forfar to Mr R.—read pt of Comedy of Errors (+).

9. Th.

Long with John. wrote to Mr G—Mr Ramsay. finished Comedy of Errors. Wrote.[4] walk.

10. Fr.

Wrote to G. Hall—Ingram[5]—T.G.—Mr G.—Bonham—Uncle D.—W. Goalen. Shooting. Afterwards, went to visit Martin's wife whose case is deemed hopeless. For the first time some of the children were present—I had suggested it. Had I a series of these duties to perform, they might draw off my mind from its restless cravings towards the quarter I have left. read pamphlet on Hist. of Convocations[6]—& pt of Macbeth (+).

11. Sat.

John improving fast. Wrote to R.G.—Manning—Lady Farquhar—Matthew & Nicoll[7]—Mr Ramsay (evg). rode to the Burn to lionise Jane. read Lingard—Macbeth. Visited Mrs Martin.

12. S.

Lkirk mg prayers in aft.—Saw Mrs M.—read Knox—began Hodge.[8]

13. M.

Wordsworth—Winters Tale. wrote to Mr G—Geo. Hall. Shooting. But what between enfeebled eyes & excited mind I can do little.

---

[1] William Maule Ramsay, 1809–59, 3rd s. of 1st Lord Panmure.
[2] The diarist wished to marry Morton's eldest da., Lady Frances (Harriet) Douglas, 1819–95; Lady Milton 1838, Countess Fitzwilliam 1857. She and her family held back. See Magnus, 30–32; and 14 Nov. 37.

[3] 'essays'.   [4] On free will; Add MS 44727, ff. 241–4.
[5] Unidentified.   [6] Untraced.
[7] Unidentified.
[8] C. Hodge, 'A Commentary on the Epistle to the Romans' (1835).

14. T.

A crushing letter from Mr Ramsay—I replied. The purposes of God are wise and good. Where we say thy will be done, we mean, our will be thine. May the prayer be fulfilled on me—whether I know its meaning or not—through Christ our Lord.

Wrote to G. Hall—Ingram—Matthews & Nicoll.

At night, another long letter to Mr R.—packed. Out visiting. saw Mrs M[artin] & four of the old: prayed with all. I do not know if but for my own matters I shd have done so: thus are my works contaminated even when plausibly Christian in appearance. Little rest—or rather sleep.

15.

Dear Rns birthday.

9½–3½ to Dundee. Left imm[ediatel]y by the 'London'. A day of oppression & pain.

16. Th.

A day of abject prostration. Probably more gloomy from severe seasickness—let the truth be told.

17.

I felt as if the bitterness were past: & what it is: & that it is good for me. Arrived in London (C. Gns) at 2¼ P.M. Saw many friends. Wrote to Mr G— J.N.G.—dined at Lincoln's Inn—read B. Noel. Tea with Milnes G[askell] & Cavendish.

18. Sat.

Wrote to Mr R—Mr G—T.G.—Uncle D—Harrison—D. of Wellington. read 'Vicar of Wrexhill'[1]—'Cons. Peers & Ref. Min'.[2]—at H. of C. to be sworn[3]—Milbank, Commee—Lincoln's Inn. to dine & keep exercise. Met Ld Ramsay in evg. *Horse up.*

19. S.

Commn at 8. How unfit: but how necessitous.—Ch mg & aft. read Pusey's Sermon & Pref.[4]—Acland's Tract[5]—began Keble's post-script.[6]

---

[1] F. *Trollope, *The Vicar of Wrexhill*, 3v. (1837). Cp. 27 Nov. 37.

[2] 'The Conservative Peers and the Reform Ministry' (1837).

[3] The new house, first meeting on the 15th, had re-elected *Abercromby speaker: *H* xxxix. 3. Members were sworn in on 16, 17, and 18th: ibid. 12.

[4] E. B. *Pusey, *Patience and Confidence. The Strength of the Church*, 2 pts (1836 and 1837).

[5] Perhaps H. D. Acland, 'A Brief Sketch of the History and Present Situation of the Valdenses in Piedmont' (1825).

[6] J. *Keble, 'A Postscript to the Third Edition of the Sermon entitled "Primitive Tradition Recognized in Holy Scripture" [1836], to which is subjoined "Catena Patrum" No. iii, being No. lxxviii of "Tracts for the Times"' (1837).

Conv. with Pringle on Ch. matters—unity. Wrote to Mr Ramsay.—A few lines from Dante's Pater Noster.[1] Hard, as usual.

20. M.

wrote to Miss G.—T.G.—R.G.—Sir G. Clerk—part of a long letter to Mr Ramsay in answer to Mrs R. Wrote to Mr Sheppard.[2]
Began to translate Nelda.[3] read 'the Vicar'.
House at 2[4]–5–9¾—dined with Mr Tyler & conv. on Synod & Convocation &c.

21. T.

Continued translating: & wrote the rest of my letter to Mr R. wrote to T.G.[5]
dined at Lincoln's Inn. read the Vicar. Penitentiary 3–4½. House 6–10.[6]

22. W.

Continued translating.
Hope & Manning with me—each on his subject.[7] Dined at Sir W. Young's.[8] Music.
read 'the Vicar'—Calls.
wrote to Mr G—D. Murray.[9]

23. W. [sc. Th.]

Out early—calls and shopping. saw Dr Locock[10] for H.J.G.—At two went to see Dr Farre[11] in Charterhouse Square. He orders me not to read or write more than ¼ hour without rest: but gives me a good account.—wrote to Mr Sheppard—Mrs Hagart—Mr G.—Mr Gould[12]—Dr Elrington—T.G.
Attended O & C. C. Commee—dined at Ln's Inn. read 'the Vicar'.

24. Fr.

read a *little* of 'New Zealand'.[13] finished & wrote out Nelda.

---

[1] In Dante's *Professione de Fede*, which reduced to terza rima the creed, the decalogue, the Lord's Prayer, the Ave, and the deadly sins.
[2] Thomas Sheppard, 1763?–1839, of St. Edmund Hall; rector of St. James's, Clerkenwell Green 1814.
[3] From Grossi; Add MS 44727, ff. 262–70.   [4] Debate on address: *H* xxxix. 31.
[5] And note on blessedness, Add MS 44727, f. 287.
[6] Address; and misc. business. Ibid. 91.
[7] *Hope on children's emigration to Cape; cp. Ornsby, i. 118 ff.
[8] Sir William Lawrence Young, 1806–42, 3rd bart. 1815, conservative M.P. Buckinghamshire 1837–42.
[9] David Murray, Fettercairn bootmaker. Cp. 6 Nov. 38.
[10] (Sir) Charles *Locock, 1799–1875, accoucheur, attended births of all *Victoria's children; cr. bart. 1857.
[11] John Richard *Farre, 1775–1862; M.D. Aberdeen 1806; a founder of Moorfield ophthalmic hospital; distinguished anatomist.
[12] Henry Gould, 1764?–1839, canon of Wells.
[13] E. G. *Wakefield, *The British Colonization of New Zealand: an Account of the Objects of the New Zealand Association* (1837).

Calls—opportune—from Mr Dawson—Mahon—Milnes with M'Arthy R.C.[1]
—Doyle with Lyall—Manning with Rogers.
dined at Mr Tylers. Billiards.
wrote to J.N.G.—Welsh—A. Williams—Caparn—Ch. Exchr—House 5–6½.[2]
Saw Twisleton on Club Pew.[3]

25. Sat.

Labouring to reduce my papers into order. wrote a paper thereon.[4]
Perused Nelda, with slight alterations. read New Zealand. Milbank Com-
mee 2½–4¼. dined at Ln's Inn. billiards—saw Grey at C.O. wrote to H.J.G.
—Mr G.

26. S.

St J. mg & aft.—translated Ld's Prayer from Dante. Read Bible, Knox,
Parker: little. wrote divers.[5]

27. M.

Saw Dr Spalding[6]—young M'Kenzie on his reading—Mr Campbell.
calls. wrote to Mr G—D of Wn[7]—Mr Edmonstone—G. Mackenzie—
Caparn—T.G.—R.G.—read 'the Vicar'—Scandalous indeed. House 4¾–10.
div. in 160:214.[8]

28. T.

read N. Zealand. 'the Vicar' (finished)—pt of Ld Nugent on the ballot.[9]
voted in 53:159 for Sodor & Man bishopric.[10] wrote to Mr G—H.J.G.—Mr
Gould—T.G.—saw D. of Wn on the Cape:[11] Mr Goulburn & Sir R. Peel on
Canada: D. of Newcastle on Nk matters—Ld Duncannon[12] (with Wilde) on
the Castle—calls. wrote Mema—Manning with me on Cathls.

29. W.

D of Wn at 12—Penitentiary at 2—Library Commee at 4. Long conv. with

[1] (Sir) Charles Justin MacCarthy, 1811–64, lifelong friend of *Milnes; secretary, 1851,
and governor, 1860, of Ceylon; kt. 1857.
[2] Conduct of business: *H* xxxix. 193.　　　　　　　[3] See 14 Dec. 37.
[4] 'Of Keeping Books and Papers'; Add MS 44727, ff. 256–7.
[5] Note on the Fall, ibid. f. 245.　　　　　　[6] James Spalding, surgeon.
[7] See *Wellington to *Gladstone, this day, offering appt., in Add MS 44355, f. 266;
and next entry.
[8] Against Controverted Elections Bill, 2°; poor laws followed. *H* xxxix. 284, 321.
[9] G. N. T. *Grenville, Baron Nugent, *The Ballot discussed in a letter to the Earl o
Durham (1837).
[10] Sir Harry Calvert failed to get leave to bring in a bill to keep this diocese separate
from that of Carlisle: *H* xxxix. 358.
[11] See Morley, i. 143.
[12] John William *Ponsonby, 1781–1847; s. of 3rd earl of Bessborough, styled Lord
Duncannon 1793; *Melbourne's b.-in-law; whig M.P. 1805–6, 1810–34, then cr. Lord
Duncannon; minor office 1831–4, 1839–41; home secretary Jul.–Nov. 1834; lord privy
seal, 1835–9; viceroy of Ireland 1846–7.

Farr on Church matters—& on Canada &c. with Spedding & Milnes. House.[1] Wrote to Mr G.[2]—wrote to (& heard from) Mr Ramsay—Jas Hope Sir G. Grey—Caparn—read Wilde's Poor Law Memorial.[3]

30. Th.

It was very pleasant to have so genial a convn with so old a schoolfellow as Farr.
At the Opera Buffa[4]—an exp[erimen]t—I doubt whether it will answer (eyesight). read 'Der Graf von Hapsburg'.[5] Wrote to Mr J.C. Chase[6]— J.E. Lyall—Mr G.
read B. Noel—New Zealand. With Sir R. Peel on Pr. Ass. &c.[7] O. & C.C. Commee (on Church Pew)[8] 4–5½. House.[9] Monthly letters & accts. Also made acct with H. Th[ompson].

London. Dec. 1. 37.
Fr.

read Bp Montreal's letter[10]—New Zealand. Reflected (as aliàs[11] of late) on the Cath[edra]l question. Calls. House 3¾–6.[12] dined in B. Square. Billiards. wrote to Mr G—J.N.G.—T.G.—R.G.—.[13]

2. Sat.

read Southey's Prefaces[14] & Joan of Arc 1[15]—New Zealand. Wrote to Mr G (bis)—Jacobson—W. Farquhar—MSS.[16] Made list of Comms for Monday with Ld G. S[omerset]. Milbank 2–4. dined at Mr Hoare's[17]—Lady Salisbury's afwds.

3. S.

St James's—Communion—St Giles in evg. Dined in B.S. 2–4½—with Taylor: I hope it has pleased God to give him progress. read Knox—& pt of S.P.G. report.

[1] Misc. business: *H* xxxix. 373.
[2] Bassett, 32–33.
[3] Presumably Newark business.
[4] Rossini, *L'Italiana in Algieri*, at the Lyceum.
[5] Prince E. M. Lichnowski, *Geschichte des Hauses Habsburgs*, 6v. (1836–42), i. *Stammbaum*. Cp. L. B. Namier, *Conflicts* (1942), 109 n.
[6] James Compigné Chase, 1811–90; Mill Hill and Queen's Cambridge; chaplain of Maidstone workhouse 1844; d. at Reading.
[7] Untraced.
[8] For Club servants.
[9] Irish constabulary: *H* xxxix. 396.
[10] G. J. *Mountain.
[11] 'at other times'.
[12] Bridgwater election (he asked a question) and Irish poor relief: *H* xxxix. 468, 477.
[13] And note on religious history, Add MS 44727, f. 246.
[14] *Specimens of the Later English Poets, with Preliminary Notices* (1807).
[15] (1796).
[16] Add MS 44727, ff. 247–8.
[17] Probably Samuel Hoare, 1783–1847, banker.

4. M.

New Zealand—Joan of Arc—(R. Palmer's) Miss[ionar]y Instructions[1]—B. Noel.
O. & C.C. Commee 1½–3½.
Wrote to Mr G—T.G.—R.G.—
Doyle, Acland, Mr L. Macdonald,[2] here. House 4–7. voted in 172:156 agt Grote's Instruction.[3] Dined at Ld Salisbury's.

5. T.

Wrote to Mr G—Caparn—Vss.
New Zealand—B. Noel.
House 5–6½ and 9½–1½.[4] Dined in B.S.

6. W.

Wrote to R.G.—M'Lauchlan—T.G. (with Vss)—O.B. Cole—J.N.G.—Dr Elrington.[5]
At Peel's 12—P.M. very int[eres]ting. Vid[e] Mema.[6] read New Zealand. House 4½–7: & at 10. Div 203:234.[7] Dined at Baron Parke's—music.

7. Th.[8]

New Zealand. Vss. Calls. H. Joy two hours here—on 5 min. business. O. & C. Commee at 4—& House 5–3. Div. in 389:91 and 331:121.[9] Wrote to H.J.G.—Mr G.—Mr Ramsay.

8. Fr.

New Zealand. Vss—began to translate Rodolph[10] at Mahon's recommn.
Wrote to Caparn—T.G.—Mr G.—Mr Waddilove[11]—Mr Nairne.[12] Mr Miller, Presbn clergyman[13] here two hours: an interesting convn on Educn went off

[1] Untraced.
[2] Lawrence *Macdonald, 1799–1878, sculptor; settled in Rome from 1832. His bust of John *Gladstone was in the Royal Scottish Exhibition in Edinburgh 1832.
[3] *Grote tried to extend dissenters' relief in Municipal Officers' Declaration Bill, in cttee.: *H* xxxix. 518.
[4] Irish municipalities; and the state of co. Armagh in 1795. Ibid. 602, 633.
[5] And note on faith in Add MS 44727, f. 249.
[6] See Morley, i. 144, and memoranda in Add MS 44777, ff. 36–39.
[7] Limerick election: William Smith *O'Brien failed to get his petition officially printed, but it was read during the debate: *H* xxxix. 707. *O'Brien, 1803–64, 2nd s. of 4th bart.; Harrow and Trinity, Cambridge; M.P. Ennis 1828–31, Co. Limerick 1835–49; failed to raise insurrection in SW. Ireland, 1848; sentenced to death; reprieved and exiled; pardoned 1856.
[8] 7, 8, and 9 Dec. 37 were originally dated 8, 9, and 10 in ink, and redated correctly in pencil.
[9] Limerick election again, *Gladstone now voting against *O'Brien: ibid. 837, 841.
[10] Novel by G. Touchard-Lafosse (1837).
[11] William James Darley Waddilove, 1783–1859; s. of R.D.*; b.-in-law of Sir J. *Graham; canon of Ripon, 1811.
[12] Perhaps James Mellis Nairne, d. 1848, of Dunsinane, Perthshire; or Charles, d. 1867, M.A. from Trinity, Cambridge 1829, canon of Lincoln 1845.
[13] Perhaps Samuel Miller, 1810–81, minister at Monifieth, near Dundee, 1835–43.

into the yet more int[eres]ting subject of Ap[ostolica]l Succn, wh we discussed at great length. Mr Macarthur also here.

9. Sat.

Joan of Arc. Vss.—Hope here an hour—Penitentiary 3–4½.
wrote to Mr G—Caparn—Sir G. Grey—Mr [blank] (Cape)—V. Townshend
—Sir F. Doyle.
Dined at Sir R. Peel's: most inttg—wrote Mema[1]—At Lady Parke's afwds.
music. conv. with Milnes on *Duty*.

10. Sunday.

St James—St Giles evg—dined at 22 B.S.—conv 2 h. with Acland on
Cathedrals &c—1 hour with Sir G. Clerk, chiefly on Scotch Church—Read
Knox—S.P.G. Report.

11. M.

Joan of Arc. Vss. Civil List Report. Wm Sinclair here 1½ hour. How thankful I should be for the many opportune & delightful visits & conversations I have had here in my need. He is going to be married to Miss Ellice.[2]
Wrote to Buxton—Bagshaw—Mr Ebden (Cape)[3]—Sir L. Cole—Sir F.
Doyle—Mr G's birthday: what a debt it brings. House 5½–6¾[4]—dined at
Sir S. Canning's: very pleasant party.—billiards with J.M.G.

12. T.

Finished Rodolph. Rewrote, from memory & draughts, 'the Grey Mare'
& 'Nelda'—Mahon having lost them at wh he is much more annoyed than
the cause requires.[5]
Sat to Miss Combe[6] 1½ hour for Aunt D.
Read W. Sinclair's Sermon.[7]
Wrote to Mr G—Sir F. Doyle—Caparn.
House 5–6.20 and 10–12¼.[8] dined at 22 B.S. Conv. with Maidstone[9] on
Pol. Ec.

13. W.

Vss.[10] read Knox on Cowper[11]—and Dub. Rev. on Vaudois.[12]

[1] In Add MS 44777, ff. 40–51, and in A. H. D. *Acland, *T. D. *Acland*, 106.
[2] William Sinclair, m. 28 December Helen, 4th da. of William and niece of Edward *Ellice; she d. 1842.   [3] John Bardwell Ebden, merchant, of Cape Town.
[4] Bradford poor law riots: *H* xxxix. 948.
[5] Perhaps to a pickpocket: Add MS 44317, f. 25.
[6] E. Combe, miniaturist, fl. 1834–40; perhaps da. of Henry Combe who lived by Bedford Square.
[7] Untraced; presumably MS.   [8] Misc. business: *H* xxxix. 978.
[9] George James Finch-Hatton, 1815–87; styled Viscount Maidstone, 1826; M.P. Northamptonshire 1837–41; 10th earl of Winchilsea 1858.
[10] Sonnet in Add MS 44727, f. 250, 'Imitated from Filicaja.
[11] A. *Knox, *Remains* iii. 331: on *Cowper's poetry.
[12] *Dublin Review* iii, 325 (October 1837).

1¼ hour at Mahon's—reading his orig[ina]l character of Walpole, & Peel's critique: with conv. thereon.[1]
dined at Mr Tyler's.
wrote to Elliot—Mr G—R.G.—B. Harrison.
billiards at the Carlton till 1 a.m. of

14. Th.

Read Knox on Cowper.
Recommenced writing on Rationalism.
wrote to Mr Sheppard—Mr G—Mr Holme.
12–2. Sat to Miss Combe. dined at B.S.—House[2]—Mr Rogers's—sat with him alone 1½ hour.[3]
4–5½ O. & C.C. Commee about Church att[endan]ce of servv.

15. Fr.

12 to 1¼ sat to Miss Combe—S.P.G. Meeting till 3½. House 4¼–7 and 10–2¼. Voted in two divv. on Civil List.[4] dined at Ld Abns. Conv. with both Aclands. Wrote Memoranda—read on New Zealand, & Joan of Arc. Wrote to Mr G—H. Thompson. Hamilton.

16. Sat.

Saw Mr M'Geachy[5] & H. Taylor.
read New Zealand
Wrote on private judgment—& to R.G.
House at 1¼[6]—Milbank 2–4¾.
dined at Sir R. Inglis's. Billiards with Perceval.

17. S.

St James's—ordination there—St Giles's evg—dined in B.S.—wrote on Rationalism[7]—read Knox.

18. M.

House 4¼–2¼.[8]
Wrote to Mr G—Hamilton—Pref. to Vss[9]—and on Rationalism.
Read New Zealand.

---

[1] *Mahon amended his *History of England*, i. 296 ff. (1836), to suit *Peel's criticisms.
[2] Navy: *H* xxxix, 1093. *Gladstone also raised a procedural point on an impending Municipal Boundaries Bill: ibid.
[3] See note in Add MS 44777, ff. 52—53.
[4] Civil List Bill read 2°, 184–52; two attempts to reduce part of it failed, by 199–19 and 173–41. *H* xxxix. 1181, 1182.
[5] Foster Alleyne McGeachey, 1809–87; at Balliol; conservative M.P. Honiton 1841–7.
[6] Slave compensation, cttee.: *H* xxxix. 1183.
[7] And note on morals in Add MS 44727, f. 251.
[8] Elections; pensions. *H* xxxix. 1220; 1226. 'Saw' here deleted.
[9] Add MS 44793, ff. 131–2.
22—II.

19. T.

Manning here at 11 on Cathls.
Sat to Miss Combe 12–2.
House 3–6 and 9–2½. In seven divisions.[1]
dined in B. Square. read a little Pusey.
wrote to Col Wade—R.G.—T.G.—W.B. Pusey.

20. W.

Read New Zealand & Mr Coates's Pamphlet[2]—Joan of Arc.
Saw Kynaston.[3]
Selecting Vss. of which I have about 150 pages in some sense producible.[4]
Shopping. dined in B. Square.
Wrote to Mr G—& on Rationalism.

21. Th.

Sat for likeness 12–2. Church at 3. House 5–6½.[5] dined at Bp of London's
(Fulham)—music. Wrote to J.N.G.—Huddlestone—Hemstock—Sir F.
Doyle—Kynaston—testimonials for do[6]—read Joan of Arc—Wrote on
Rat[ionalis]m.
Saw Mr W. Heseltine on his affair.[7]

22. Fr.

Finished New Zealand. Wrote on Ratm. wrote to Mr G.—Lincoln—
Lushington—calls.
Sat to Miss C[ombe] 12¼–1¾. Calls. Saw Mr Evans's pictures.[8] House 5–9.
Spoke (in a way) on Canadian matters.[9] At Mr Rogers's afwds—& conv.
with him when his party had dispersed till 12½.

23. Sat.

Saw Doyle—T.M. Gladstone—Walter Larkins on his studies & profession.
Went to Mr Rogers for Am[erica]n history with a view to Canada.
wrote to Lord Mahon—Dr D'Oyly[10]—Mr G—T.G.—Mr Paskin[11]—Mr

---

[1] Civil list; election business. *H* xxxix. 1320, 1324, 1326; 1335.
[2] D. Coates, 'Principles Objects and Plans of the New Zealand Association' (1837).
[3] '&' here deleted.
[4] Morley, i. 143, suggests these were all written during the previous summer.
[5] Duchess of *Kent's annuity: *H* xxxix. 1420.
[6] *Kynaston shortly became high master of St. Paul's school.
[7] William Heseltine, stockbroker and antiquary, was quarrelling with the chapter of
Canterbury about rent of a house in Lambeth.
[8] Perhaps George (Hampden) Evans, 1772?–1842; m. 1805 Sophia Parnell, *Congleton's s.; M.P. co. Dublin 1832 41; lived in Eaton Square.
[9] In a preliminary discussion: *H* xxxix. 1452. Notes in Add MS 44649, ff. 136–45.
[10] George *D'Oyly, 1778–1846, theologian; 2nd wrangler 1800; fellow of Corpus,
Cambridge 1801–13; joint ed. of bible with *Mant; succ. his f. as rector of Buxted,
Sussex 1815; rector of Lambeth, and of Sundridge, Kent, from 1820; a founder of King's
College, London.
[11] Charles Paskin, clerk in charge of the vote office of the commons.

Ramsay. dined in B. Square—read Joan of Arc—& papers: my eyes the worse for these latter. House 12–2: voted in 55:7 agt Ld G.B. for adjournment to the 28th [December].[1]
Milbank to 4½.

24. S.

St James's—Gray's Inn Lane[2] in evg. Finished Essay on Ch. E.—and put together most of that on Sacraments.
Saw Mr Larkins about his son. Tea in B.S. Sent Mr Edmonstone Mr Campbell's letter—with a few lines.
read only a little Bible & Knox. (A.M.G['s birthday].)

25. Xmas day.

Communion at 8. Service mg & aft.—wrote on Rule of Faith—& on Sacrts—read Knox—dined in B.S.
Wrote to Mr G—Gould—North—R.G.—Made up letters. Packed.

26. T.

6–6¼. 100 m. to Oakley by Phenomena. A kind welcome.
Began Franklin.[3]

27. W.

Franklin. paper. Shooting. A party here. Drafts & backgn—Conv. with Lady K[errison] about E.K.[4] wrote to Mr G—G.A. Selwyn—Sir R. Peel.

28. Th.

I tremble on the verge of another year! Yet I live for ever—but how?
read Franklin—& began Perceval's 'Roman Schism'[5]—papers.
Walked to Mr Campbell's at Eye. Drafts—backgammon: tried a piano Lesson, but my eyes I fear cannot afford it.
Wrote to Mr G—T.G.[6]

29. Fr.

Construing Virgil with E.K. & Mr Heathcote.
Shooting. Plenty of music: (Mr Campbell) Read Franklin.

[1] Misc. business: *H* xxxix. 1509. Motion (lost by 7 to 44: ibid. 1516) by Lord (William) George (Frederic Cavendish) *Bentinck, 1802–48, 5th child of 4th duke of Portland; his uncle *Canning's secretary 1822–5; M.P. Lynn from 1826; racehorse owner; *Disraeli's patron; led protectionists from 1846.
[2] Anglican chapel in Gray's Inn Square; evening reader from 1824, Edward Chaplin, 1772?–1858, Westminster and Trinity, Cambridge.
[3] Benjamin Franklin's autobiography, 3v. (1818). Notes in Add MS 44727, ff. 252, 259–61. [4] Her son E. C. Kerrison.
[5] A. P. *Perceval, *The Roman Schism illustrated from the records of the Catholic Church* (1836).
[6] And notes on prayer, Add MS 44727, ff. 253–4.

Wrote to H. Thompson—Mr G.—T.G.

Wrote a paper by way of "will".

In the retrospect of the past year I find accumulated cause for gratitude: but no progress made I am afraid against my besetting sins—unless it be in respect of envy.—Therefore I see my years pass away with dread: because their work is unfulfilled. O for a sense of the Divine will, an earnest and continual design to read accept and follow it and be incorporated and identified with it. O that the blessings of the Redeemer's covenant may with their power purge me to Himself and establish me in His love and service for ever.

30. Sat.

Aen[eid] 6 with E.K. & Mr H.—& Franklin—Shooting—music—drafts—backgammon—wrote to T.[1]G.—R.G.—J.N.G.—G.A. Selwyn—Sir R. Peel.

Sunday Dec. 31.

Brome Church & Communion. Eye Church aftn. Mr Campbell preached—excellently. Conv. & walk with him.

Wrote some supplemental sections. Read Perceval and Knox.

Wrote to Mrs Martindale.[2]

And thus died the year—*fuit* annus.[3]

---

[1] Instead of 'Mr'.

[2] A Bloomsbury neighbour of the *Tylers'.

[3] 'the year is done'.

January One 1838

read Franklin (& wrote therefrom)[1] & Perceval. Shooting with Cadogan[2] & E.K.

Drafts, backgn, cards.—The Mahons returned. Construing Aend with Mr H[eathcote] & E.K.—& conv. with the former about his interesting pupil. Monthly accts.

2. Tuesday.

Franklin—finished Vol.1—began 2. Wrote to T.G.—Dr Spry[3]—Doyle. Birthday rejoicings.[4]

Shooting with Mahon—drafts & backg[ammo]n.

3. W.

Construing Virgil (Cadogan joined us)—read Franklin—Russell's Hist. on the Amn war[5]—wrote to T.G.—Mr G.—R.G.—Music—backgammon. Conv. with Mr H. further about E.K. & with E.K.

4. Th.

Virgil—Mahon joined us. Began B.7. Read Washington's Letters[6]— Shooting in the Park. Pessimè.[7]

At the close, went over to Shotesham & got in to tea.

Wrote to Mr W. Heseltine—Mr Paskin.

5. Fr.

read papers—on Canada. Franklin's Mem.[8] Chatham's Life[9]—& Franklin's Correspondence.[10] wrote divers notes on Canada.

walk to High Shotesham.[11]

wrote to Mr Gould—Mr G—Mr Ramsay.

---

[1] In Add MS 44727, f. 259.

[2] Frederick William Cadogan, 1821–1904, liberal M.P. for Cricklade 1868–74, 4th s. of 3rd earl Cadogan of Oakley.

[3] John Hume Spry, 1777?–1854, Eton and Oriel; Bampton lecturer 1815; D.D. 1824; rector of St. Marylebone 1825, and canon of Canterbury 1828; involved in *affaire* Heseltine (see 21 Dec. 37).

[4] E. C. Kerrison was seventeen.

[5] *History of America*, ii. 409.

[6] J. Sparks, ed., *The Writings of George Washington . . . Correspondence, Addresses . . . and Other Papers*, 3v. (1833–37).

[7] 'As badly as possible'.

[8] *A Collection of the Familiar Letters and Papers of Benjamin Franklin* (Boston, 1833).

[9] F. *Thackeray, *A History of . . . William *Pitt, Earl of Chatham*, 2v. (1827).

[10] Included in 3rd ed. of his autobiography, 6v. (1818–19).

[11] Shottesham St. Mary, a mile east of the house.

6. Sat.

Franklin's Mem.—Pellew's Letter to Peel[1]—Washington's Life in Fam. Lib.[2]
Shooting in 'the little wood'[3] a little better. Belsham's Geo. 3.[4]—Music. Notes on Canada.

7. S.

Rode in to Norwich Cathl service: much delighted. High Shotesham in aftn. read Knox—& began "An Estimate of the Religion of the Fashionable world" 1791.[5]
Mr F[ellowes]'s sufferings are very great. I returned to the library for a book after leaving it at night & found him with his Bible. May his be purifying pains and prepare him for glory.

8. M.

Up early & answered another extinguishing letter from Mr R.[6]—at 8½ walked into Norwich to the Cathl service. I had been asked to choose an anthem but cd not make myself intelligible ∴ Mr Buck[7] the organist gave one. It was Ps.128—beautiful. Di quando in quando non mi potei[8] sapere se la musica venisse dal cielo o fosse della terra, e volentieri avrei restato fisso al luogo. Udiva la dicendomi "la sposa ti sarà come una vigna in sulle pareti della tua casa. Tuoi figli come i rami dell'uliva, dintorno alla tua tavola. . . . E vedrai gli figli de' tuo' figli e la pace in sull'Israele." Questa non mi fu veramente una Providenza? Ed affatto senza che io vi avessi parte. Ed anche un promesso: di nozze no, ma, siccome fissamente io credo, di quell'eterno amore che finora mi ha salvato.[9]

Called at the Bps.[10] Home before 2—Music. 'Estimate'. Preceded Wilberforce, I fancy: & (in the same line) partakes accordingly of a lower spirit.[11] Finished it.
Wrote to Paskin—R.G.—G.A. Selwyn—Mrs Martindale.
Long conv. with Mr Hudson Gurney.[12]

---

[1] G. *Pellew, 'A Letter to . . . Sir Robert *Peel . . . on the means of rendering Cathedral Churches most conducive to the efficiency of the Established Church' (1837).
[2] C. R. Edmonds, *The Life and Times of George Washington*, 2v. (1835–36).
[3] About 2 miles ESE. of the house.
[4] W. *Belsham, *Memoirs of the Reign of George III*, 4v. (1795).
[5] Hannah *More.   [6] See Magnus, 31.
[7] Zacchariah *Buck, 1798–1879; organist and composer; organist and choir-master of Norwich Cathedral 1819–77.   [8] Conjectured: much altered in MS.
[9] 'Sometimes I could not tell whether the music was made on heaven or on earth, and I willingly stayed rooted to the spot. I heard it saying to me, "Thy wife shall be as a vine, upon the walls of thine house. Thy children like the olive branches, round about thy table.—And thou shalt see thy children's children, and peace upon Israel.["] Was not this really a Providence for me? And entirely without my playing any part. And a promise as well: not of marriage, but—as I firmly believe—of that eternal love which hitherto has preserved me.'   [10] Edward *Stanley.
[11] W. *Wilberforce, *A Practical View of the Prevailing Religious System of Professed Christians* (1797).
[12] Hudson *Gurney, 1775–1864, M.P. Shaftesbury 1812, Newtown, Isle of Wight, 1816–32; friend of *Aberdeen's.

9. Tuesday.

Shooting in the snow. Dinner party here. Singing.
Read Franklin—& finished Pellew's letter. Also read Junius.[1]

10. W.

wrote to Sir E. Kerrison—Mr G.—Aunt J—again shooting in the snow.
Read Franklin—& Sidney's Life of Hill.[2] Singing.

11. Th.

Singing—a good *practise* with Louisa. Paper. Franklin and Thackeray's
Chatham. Wrote to Bishop—R.G.
Shooting in the snow again: fine bracing exercise.

12. Fr.

Up at 6. By Phenomena to Oakley for breakfast. Construing Horace Ep.
ad Pis. with E.K. & Mr H.—And began the Canadian papers.—Shooting
in Waterloo Wood.[3]—Music in evg. My account since the 6th is, shots 90:
killed 46.
Wrote to T.G.—Sir S. Scott—Backgn.

13. Sat.

Walk with Mahon to Brome. Music in evg. Backgn & drafts.
Construed a good piece of Il[iad] 4. with Ld M., Mr H. & E.K. finished
Franklin—Canadian papers—& read 'the Hanoverian Constitution'.[4]
Wrote to Mr G—N. Gould—W.F. McKenzie[5]—Mrs Rushton.[6] Metaphysical
& theoll conv. with Mr H.

14. Sunday.

Hoxne Ch. twice. Walk & much conv. with Mr Heathcote. Ref. to Paley:
astonished him. Also conv. with Mahon on some points of theology.
Our kind host quite laid up with gout. read Hook—Mr H. on Confirmation[7]
—&c. wrote.

15. M.

read Hook. 8½–9 P.M. Phenomena to town. wrote to Gould. reading
Franklin's Tracts—Burke.

[1] Notoriously malignant anonymous letters on politics (1769–72), usually attributed
to Sir Philip *Francis.
[2] E. Sidney, *The Life of the Rev. Rowland *Hill* (1834).
[3] Nearly a mile NE. of Eye.
[4] In *Foreign Quarterly Review*, xx. 378–402 (January 1838).
[5] William Forbes *Mackenzie, 1807–62, of Portmore; tory M.P. co. Peebles 1837–52;
elected for Liverpool 1852, unseated next year.
[6] Unidentified.
[7] Presumably Heathcote's MS.

16. T.

finished Burke on Amn Taxn[1]—read 'a plain statement'[2]—Words on
C[onfirmation]—Jefferson[3]—refd to Acts &c.
At Sir R. Peels $11\frac{3}{4}$–1[4]—there with Ld Aberdeen—House $4\frac{3}{4}$–$8\frac{1}{4}$ and
$9\frac{3}{4}$–$12\frac{3}{4}$.—div. in 188:28.[5] wrote to R.G.—Mr Viant. Mr MacLauchlan.

17. W.

Wrote to Mr Ramsay. La sapienza di Dio mi strugge in questa parte dove
anche piu dalle altre son stato peccatore.[6]
2 hours with Tancred on the Church. read Hints on Canada[7] & Elliot's
pamphlet.[8] wrote to Sir G. Grey—Jas Hope—Sir A. Willock—Barber
(Nottm)[9]—Mr Rogers. House $4\frac{3}{4}$–$9\frac{3}{4}$ and $10\frac{1}{2}$–$1\frac{1}{2}$. Two divv.[10]

18. Th.

read Lyall's pamphlet on Election Law[11]—& Mr Powell's on Tithe Commutation.[12]
wrote Vss. wrote to H. Thompson—Mr G—J.N.G.—R. Caparn—A.
Williams.
dined at Ln's Inn. H of Lords 9–11.[13] J.N.G.s b[irth]day.

19. Friday.

S.P.G. meeting 1–3. dined in B. Square. Conv. with Mr Kock[14] on Göthe
& Schiller &c.$1\frac{1}{2}$ hours with Sir G. Clerk in evg on the Apostolical Succession. Verses.[15]
read Gould's letter—began Colquhoun on Nat. Edn.[16] wrote to Pakenham—
Mr G—H.J.G.—Miss Joy—Gould.

[1] Urging repeal of tea duty (1774).
[2] H. W. Plumptre, 'A Plain Statement of Facts Relative to the Proposed New Church
in Nottingham' (1838).
[3] Probably president Thomas Jefferson, *Memoirs, Correspondence &c.*, 4 v. (1829).
[4] Presumably one of the three meetings referred to in Morley, i. 642; for the others,
see 20 and 22 Jan. 38.
[5] Against adjourning debate on Canada: *H* xl. 93.
[6] 'God in his wisdom afflicts me in this quarter where even more than in others I have
been a sinner.'
[7] 'Hints on the case of Canada, for the consideration of Members of Parliament'
(1838).
[8] E. Elliott, 'Pastoral Address on the Institution of a Prayer Meeting, in Connection
with the Established Church' (1834).
[9] Possibly Thomas Barber, b. 1805, of Greasley, Nottingham; Eton, Trinity, Cambridge, and Middle Temple.
[10] *Russell secured leave to bring in bill for temporary government of Lower Canada
(198–7); *Hume failed (13–61) to secure more papers. *H* xl. 157.
[11] Untraced.
[12] H. T. Powell, 'Tithe Commutation in 1969, or the Working of the Tithe Act illustrated by an Example of Commutation in 1705' (1837).
[13] Canada: *H* xl. 162.
[14] Of Frankfurt-am-Main: cp. 31 Jan., 10, 11 Sept., 38.
[15] Add MS 44728, ff. 13–15?
[16] J. C. *Colquhoun, *The System of National Education in Ireland, its principle and
practice* (1838).

20. Sat.

Wrote to Clark (Perth)[1]—Groom (at Fasque)—Mr G—Nicholl—Plumptre —R. Williams—Sir J. Buller—Acland.
Sir R. Peels 12¼ on Canada.[2] Penitentiary to 4¼, read Colquhoun—& Craigs despatch of 1810 with the answer.[3] Vss[4]—Mema.[5]
dined at Sir R. Inglis's.—At Milnes's afwds.

21. Sunday.

St James's 8 (Commn) 11, 3. Tea at 22 B.S. read Hook—Knox—Keble's Appx.
wrote to Ch. & St.

22. M.

Frost broke. At Milbank on Sat. the thermom. stood at 4°: at Hayes, in the night, at −½°: I hear of another place (from Mahon) where it was at −7°.
finished writing out 'a Tale'.[6]
Sir R. Peel's on Canada 12¼–2½.[7] and House 4¼–12. Spoke shortly on Roebuck's agency.[8]
Read part of Spedding (Ed. Rev.) on W.I. Apprn[9]—wrote to Mr Rodler.[10]
Referring to Constitl Act. &c. &c.[11] for the House.

23. Tuesday.

Wrote to Manning—Sir E. Kerrison—Mr G—T.G.
read Case of Sp. Emigrants[12]—Southey's Joan of Arc—Chalmers on Endowment.[13]
House 5–7¼ and 8.40–2 on Canada. Spoke. 1 h. 10 min up.—kindly recd & aided in a most defective execution of my idea. Div. in 262:16.[14]

24. Wed.

wrote to Mr G—T.G.—Mrs Tallents—Mr Sanderson (Nottm).

[1] George B. and David Clark, Perth lawyers.
[2] Account in Morley, i. 641–2.
[3] Sir James Henry *Craig, 1748–1812, governed Canada 1807–11; papers in PRO., CO 7/31, 32.
[4] Add MS 44728, ff. 5–12.
[5] On the meetings at *Peel's of this day and the previous Tuesday, both on Canada; see Add MS 44819, f. 32.
[6] 'The Pastor: A Tale'; long poem in Add MS 44728, ff. 5–12.
[7] See Morley, i. 641–2.
[8] Against recognition by house of *Roebuck as agent for house of assembly of Lower Canada. H xl. 257. Note in Add MS 44649, f. 146.
[9] 'The Negro Apprenticeship System'; Edinburgh Review, lxvi. 477–522 (January 1838).
[10] Unidentified.
[11] The Canadian constitution of 1791.
[12] Papers in PP 1838 xl. 29, annual report from agent for emigration in Canada.
[13] T. *Chalmers, On the Use and Abuse of Literary and Ecclesiastical Endowments (1827).
[14] For forwarding Lower Canada Government Bill (H xl. 419, 469); but he made a strong party speech against the administration. Notes for it in Add MS 44649, ff. 148–59.

read 'Defects in Eln Comm[ees]'[1]—Chalmers on Endowments—finished Spedding's Article. No House. Dined in B. Square.

25. Th.

read Chalmers.
dined at Lns Inn. Church 11 A.M.
Meeting at Peel's—12–2½ on Canada Bill.
O. & C.C. Commee at 4.
House 5–5½ and 10–12.[2]
Wrote to Buller—Kerrison—Mr G—Mr Taylor (Newark).[3] Saw Mr Zincke.[4]

26. Fr.

finished Chalmers—began Butlers Memoirs of (R.) Catholics.[5]
Wrote to Buller—Kerrison—Christian (Stonehaven)[6]—J.N.G.—Mema.[7]
Calls.
House 4¾–10¼. Govt yielded everything on the Canada Bill.[8]

27. Sat.

Wrote on 'Public Speaking'.[9]
wrote to Jelf—Zincke—W. Fretwell (Nk)[10]—Mr Russell (Caxton)[11]—T.G.—Burnaby.
read Butler—Colquhoun.
At Milbank Commee—saw Mr Heseltin's Library—curious advt to Par. Lost.[12]—at Clapham—Opera Buffa (Nozze di Figaro).[13]

28. S.

St James mg & aft.
Thinking, reading, & writing, on Cathls—also read 'Formularies of H.VIII'[14]—& Keble—dined at Ln's Inn—Tea in B.S.

[1] An Elector, 'Defects in Election Committees and in the Courts of Revising Barristers, with a Plan for Improving Them' (1838).
[2] Canadian bill: *H* xl. 476.
[3] William Taylor, victualler.
[4] Frederick Burt Zincke of Jamaica, f. of Foster Barham *Zincke, priest and antiquary.
[5] C. *Butler, *Historical Memoirs Respecting the English, Irish and Scottish Catholics from the Reformation to the Present Time*, 4v. (1819–21).
[6] Peter Christian, w.s., clerk of the peace.
[7] On previous day's Canada meeting at *Peel's; in Add MS 44819, f. 32v.
[8] Cp. ibid. f. 33v. Bill advanced in cttee.: *H* xl. 543.
[9] Add MS 44681, ff. 33v–36.
[10] William Fretwell, labourer.
[11] Arthur Tozer *Russell, 1806–74; author; vicar of Caxton, Cambridgeshire, 1830–52; held four successive livings 1852–74.
[12] In the fifth issue of the first edition of 'Paradise Lost' (1668), Simmons, the printer, inserted a preliminary notice explaining the addition of a synopsis before the text, and an apologia for blank verse.
[13] Mozart, at the Lycaeum Theatre; Frederick *Lablache, 1815–87, s. of Luigi*, played the Count.
[14] *A Necessary Doctrine and Erudition for any Cristen Man, sette furthe by the Kynges Majestie of England* (1543); probably C. *Lloyd's edition of 1825.

29. M.

Arranging papers.
read 4th Irish Edn Report[1]—Butler—Heseltine's pamph.[2]—wrote to Ld
Abn—Mr G—Mr Heseltine.
calls. House 4¾–6.[3] Convv with Lady Hope, & at her house in evg, on Apl
Succession & the Church.
Before this I have since coming to town in Novr held convv. (besides many
others with friends of the doctrine) with Lord Mahon—Sir G. Clerk—Rev.
Mr Miller—T. Tancred—Pringle—Ld Haddington.
A. Kinnaird[4] is very prepossessing from an evident earnestness and
sincerity of mind, at once frank and gentle, and set singly upon the truth.

30.

Church at 11.
read Butler—Joan of Arc—paper—wrote to E. Kerrison—Mr G—Mrs
Wishlade—billiards.

31.

W. Acland & Archdn Hoare[5] here 1½ hour on Cathls. Addl Curates Fund
Commee meeting 1–3: then at O. & C. Club & thro' the whole with Aunt D.
& Mrs R. Kock.
read Butler—Canada papers—& began the Nk Poor Law papers.
heard conclusively from Mr Ramsay—& wrote to Mr G. & to him there-
upon.[6]
Wrote to Mr Zincke. dined at Bridgwater House.
Monthly letters & accts.

Thursday Feb. one.

Wrote to Selwyn—Sec. Prot. Assn—Wells (Nk)[7]—read the Nk Poor Law
Papers—very bulky—& agt my eyes.—arranging & sifting Pty papers. read
Butler. calls. Acland here in evg. Newspapers (Canada accts).[8]

---

[1] Fourth Report of Commissioners of National Education in Ireland: *PP* 1838
xxvii. 49.
[2] [W. Heseltine] 'A Tenant's Statement of the Conduct Recently Pursued Towards
Him by the Dean and Chapter of Canterbury on the Occasion of Renewing His Lease'
(1838).
[3] Canada Bill, 3°: *H* xl. 616.
[4] Arthur Fitzgerald *Kinnaird, 1814–87, banker and philanthropist; 3rd s. of 8th
Lord *Kinnaird; liberal M.P. Perth 1837–9, 1852–78; succ. as 10th lord 1878; accompanied diarist abroad, see 6 Sept. 38 ff. And see Add MS 44230.
[5] Charles James *Hoare, 1781–1865; St. John's, Cambridge; double first, 1803; vicar
of Blandford, Dorset, 1807–21, of Godstone, Surrey, from 1821; archdeacon of Winchester, 1829–47, of Surrey, 1847–60; a leading evangelical.
[6] Cp. Magnus, 31–32.
[7] Probably Joseph Wells, gentleman.
[8] Of insurrections round Toronto; based on *Head's and *Colborne's dispatches of
19 and 22 December 1837, in *PP* 1838 xxxix. 461.

2. Fr.

read Joan of Arc (finished)—Colquhoun on N. Edn—Manzoni's Ode on
Napn[1]—Wr Rev.[2] on Canada.—Mr Miller—Taylor—Milnes—here.
Wrotc to Mr G[3] T.G.—H.K. Seymer.
dined at Dss (Dr) of Beaufort's.[4] Oxf. convn—much pleased with her.
Church at 3—House $4\frac{1}{4}$–$6\frac{3}{4}$.[5]

3. Sat.

Wrote to Mr Ramsay—Mr G—Col. Rolleston.[6]
dined at J. Stephens—Lady Parke's afr.
$12\frac{1}{4}$–$2\frac{1}{4}$. Addl Curates Sub Commee meeting—to determine forms of application. Then Milbank Peny to $4\frac{3}{4}$.
read Butler—began Channing's letter to Clay[7]—& pt of Morice's MS[8] on
State religion.

4. Sunday.

read Manzoni's Inni Sacri[9]—Hook, Serm. IV and V.
St James's & Communion. St Giles's in evg. Dinner in B. Square. Wrote on
the Church.[10]

5. M.

read Manzoni's Pref. to Carmagnola[11]—Quart. Rev. on Canada—and 3d
Scotch Eccl. Report.[12]
Wrote to T.G.—R. Caparn—Mr Nicholls—Mr Francken:[13] House 5–11.10—
three divv.—very bad.[14]
calls.
Wrote on the Church.

6. T.

Read Manzoni's Notizie Storiche[15] & began Carmagnola—finished Channing's Letter to Clay, a powerful & beautiful production—& read Canada
Correspondence (No 100).[16]
wrote to Mr G.

---

[1] 1821; see 9 Feb. 38.   [2] *Westminster Review*, xxviii. 502 (January 1838).
[3] Fragment in Magnus, 32.
[4] Charlotte Sophia, née Leveson-Gower, 1771–1854; da. of 1st marquess of *Stafford;
m. 1791 Henry Charles Somerset, 1766–1835, 6th Duke of Beaufort 1803.
[5] Misc. business; he asked a question on Canada. *H* xl. 715.
[6] Launcelot Rolleston, commanding the Royal Sherwood Foresters, then a militia
regiment with headquarters at Newark.
[7] W. E. Channing, *A Letter to the Hon. Henry Clay, on the Annexation of Texas to the
United States* (1837).   [8] Presumably F. D. *Maurice's.
[9] A few hymns (1824).   [10] Add MS 44821D, ff. 5 0, 15.
[11] Tragic drama (1820).
[12] Report on opportunities for public religious worship, religious instruction etc.:
PP 1838 xxxiii. 1.
[13] K. Francken, legal officer in Berbice?
[14] Electors Bill, in cttee.: *H* xl. 792, 806, 810.
[15] Historical notes, following preface to Carmagnola.   [16] *PP* 1838 xxxix. 477.

House 4–5.[1] Xn Knowl. Society at 1—Conv. with Ld Cholmondeley on Church matters.
Dined with the Selwyns at Richmond.

7. W.

1 hour Sub commee Addl Curates Society.
1¼ hour with Mr Nicholls on Newark Union—read Carmagnola—and Chr. Observer's Art. on New Zealand[2]—House 5–6¾.[3]
wrote to Caparn—Ly Kerrison—Mr Campbell—Sir R. Inglis.
Dined at Mr Colvill's.
wrote on Church.

8. Th.

read Carmagnola—began Beecham on New Zealand Colonisation.[4]
Mr Gillson[5] here 1½ h. on Nk Union.
Wrote to Lincoln.
House 3¾–7¼.[6] Mr G. & H.J.G. came.
At Mrs J. Morier's.[7]
Wrote on Church.

9. Fr.

Finished Beecham on New Zealand.
1½ hour with Capt. Fitzroy thereon.
Hope here 1 hour on Fellowship qualifications[8]—dined at Lady Hope's.
House before (5¼–6½), & after—to 12¼.[9]
learnt off Manzoni's Ode on Napoleon's death[10]—by way of sparing my eyes. Italian poetry does not take me near half the time of any other to learn by heart, I think.

10. Sat.

read Carmagnola (finished). S. Denison on the Ballot.[11]
Manning here 1 hour on Church.
Mr Rolleston[12] on Nk Union. Milbank 3–5 on the Estimates.
Wrote to R.G.—Mr Burnaby—Mr Gould—Mr Beecham. Dined at Mr Stirling's.

---

[1] Banks; Scottish schools. *H* xl. 816; 820.   [2] xxxviii. 131 (February 1838).
[3] Misc. business: *H* xl. 832.
[4] J. *Beecham, *Colonization, being remarks on colonization . . . with an examination of the proposals of the Association . . . for colonizing New Zealand* (1838).
[5] Thomas Gillson, Newark iron merchant.
[6] Misc. business: *H* xl. 889.
[7] Harriet, née Greville; died before her husband, James (Justinian) *Morier, 1780?–1849, diplomat and traveller, author of *Hajji Baba of Ispahan* (1824).
[8] See Ornsby, i. 134 ff.
[9] Mainly, Irish poor relief: *H* xl. 947.   [10] See 4 Jan., 8 Mar. 61.
[11] S. C. Denison, *Is the Ballot a Mistake?* (1838).
[12] Presumably the militia colonel (see 3 Feb. 38).

11. Sunday.

St James mg & aft.
Finished Essay on Church—that set is now, in a way, complete.[1]
Read Keble on Tradn[2]—& Provl Philosophy.[3]

12. M.

reading Buller's Bill[4]—& Denison on Ballot. wrote to Nicholls—and Lincoln.
Conv. with Colquhoun 1 h. on Newfoundland. Sir Jas Kempt[5] on Canada: T.G. 2 h. on my own recent matters.
Sir R. Peel's $12\frac{1}{2}$–2 on Buller's Bill.
House 5–$6\frac{1}{2}$ and $10\frac{1}{2}$–12.[6] Dined at C. M'Kenzie's.

13. Tuesday.

$1\frac{1}{2}$ h. with Mr G. on the matter of yesterday's with T.G.
read Göthes Critique on Carmagnola[7]—began Adelchi[8]—finished Denison on the Ballot—Educational Tracts No 2.
wrote to Aunt J—Mr Wells (Nk)—R. Scott.
House $3\frac{3}{4}$–6 and 10–12.[9]

14. W.

Mr Nicholls here on the Nk Union. H.H. J[oy] on Buller's Bill.
read Adelchi—Newfoundland papers—Hacket's Speech, Fuller &c. on that subject.[10]
Calls.—dined at Mr Mildmay's—met Lord Brougham.

15. Th.

Adelchi. Finished Newfoundland papers. Conv. with Colquhoun on them.—
"Justice to the Ch. of Eng".[11]—New Zealand papers.
House $3\frac{3}{4}$–6 and 9–$1\frac{1}{4}$. Voted in 315:198 on Ballot.[12]

---

[1] Preparing his book.
[2] J. *Keble, 'Primitive Tradition recognized in Holy Scripture', sermon on II Tim. i. 14 (1836).
[3] By Martin *Tupper (1838); cp DNB lvii. 318–9.
[4] Untraced.
[5] Sir James *Kempt, 1764–1854, general; commanded brigade at Maida, led assault at Badajoz, took over *Picton's division at Waterloo; governor-general of Canada 1828–30; master-general of ordnance 1834–8.
[6] Irish poor relief: H xl. 1007.
[7] In Theilnahme Goethes an Manzoni (1827), prefixed to Jena edition of Manzoni's works; strongly favourable. Italian tr. (also 1827).
[8] Another verse tragedy of Manzoni's (1823).
[9] Glasgow cotton spinners: H xl. 1059.
[10] Untraced.
[11] Anonymous (1838).
[12] Against *Grote's annual motion for it: H xl. 1221.

16. Fr.

Adelchi. La Trobe's Report on W.I. Edn.[1] Sir Jas. Graham's Cumberland Speech.[2]
Sir R. Peel's on Sc. Church at 12—S.P.G. Board $1\frac{1}{4}$–$3\frac{1}{2}$—Conv. with Bonham on Molesworth's motion[3]—with Bp of L[ondo]n & others on Education. with Capt. Alexander on Cape Affairs. with Kinnaird, wrote to Gould—R.G.

17. Sat.

Mr Innes here on B. G[uiana] Bank.
read Adelchi—part of Manning's letter.[4]
with Bp of Exeter $3\frac{1}{2}$–5 on Irish Education.
wrote on Church.[5]
dined at Colquhoun's (Putney). Lady Salisbury's afr. Wrote to Mr Wilson (Nk).

18. Sunday.

Commn 8 A.M. St James's mg & aft.
wrote to Manning, Finished his letter. read Close on Fasting[6]—Cave (Prim. Xty).[7] Helen kindly read me some of Philip's Whitfield &c.[8]

19. M.

wrote to Nicholls—R. Martin—J.N.G.—House 5–$6\frac{3}{4}$ and $9\frac{1}{2}$–12. Voted in 172:198[9] on P[arliamen]t[ar]y Electors Bill. In 134:75 on Shaw's Amendment (Ir. Poor Law).[10]
read part of Spry[11]—and finished Adelchi. In *parts* better than Carmagnola, as a whole inferior? read Archdn Hoare's Charge.[12]
Edn Commee $12\frac{1}{4}$–2.

20. T.

wrote to Nicholls.

[1] Report from C. J. *La Trobe on Negro Education in Jamaica: *PP* 1838, xlviii. 61. C. J. *La Trobe, 1801–75; governor of Australia, commissioned 1837 to report on working of money granted for West Indies negro education.
[2] Sir J. R. G. *Graham, 'Speech . . . at a dinner given to him in Carlisle, by the conservatives of East Cumberland' (1838).
[3] Cp. 6 Mar. 38. Note in Add MS 44819, f. 34, dated next day.
[4] H. E. *Manning, 'The Principle of the Ecclesiastical Commission Examined in a Letter to the Bishop of Chichester' (1838).
[5] And on colonial policy: Add MS 44819, f. 34.
[6] Probably F. *Close, *Nine Sermons*, 97 (4 ed., 1829), on Titus iii. 8.
[7] W. *Cave, *Primitive Christianity*, 2 v. (1672).
[8] R. *Philip, *The Life and Times of the Reverend George *Whitfield* (1837).
[9] The figures were 172:189.
[10] Electors Bill, 3°; *Shaw failed to secure further provision for destitute. *H* xl. 1261, 1282.
[11] J. H. Spry, 'Some Observations on a Measure for the Future Regulation of Cathedral and Collegiate Bodies' (1838).
[12] C. J. *Hoare, *A Charge Delivered to the Clergy of the Archdeaconry of Winchester* (1837).

read 'Discorso' (afr Adelchi)[1]—finished Spry.
Hope brought Mr Rassam (Chaldean)[2] here—long conv. on his Church & country.
Ch. Justice Boulton[3] & Capt. Spearman[4] here 2 h. on Newfoundland.
Mr [blank] on Nk Union.
House 4–6¼: and 11–1. Three divv.[5]—at Dss of Beaufort's in evg.

21. W.

read papers on Religious Instruction in Australia:[6] began Leslie's Regale.[7]
Edn meeting at Mr Beresford's 2¼–4. (St Andrew's) Mr Innes here on B.G. Bank—Manning on Church matters—Tancred on Mr Gualtier[8]—dined at Ld Cholmondeley's.
wrote to Lincoln—Mr Townsend (Antislav. petn).

22. Th.

Mr Langslow here on Baron de Bode.[9] R. Wilberforce on Colonial Church matters.—Conv. with Ch. Exchr[10] on W.I. Currency.
wrote to Mr Wilson (Nk)—Mr Huddlestone—Caparn.
House 3¾–5½ and 10–12½.[11]
read Manzoni's 'Discorsi'—the Regale.

23. Fr.

Mr Innes here on B.G. Bank. Mr Millar[12] on Education.
read Dean of Pet[erborough]'s Statement[13]—Hinds on N. Zealand[14]—Stat. Soc.s Westmr Edn Inquiry.[15]
Dined at Egertons. House 5–6½ and 10–12.[16] wrote to Lincoln—Edn Commee 12½–2.

24. Sat.

Matheson & Acland here on Edn. Meeting at Mr Burgess's on do (1½–3).—

---

[1] Manzoni's 'Adelchi' was followed by a discourse on Lombard history.
[2] Unidentified.
[3] Henry John Boulton, 1790–1870; b. in Kensington; solicitor-general, Upper Canada, 1818; attorney-general there 1829; dismissed 1833; chief justice of Newfoundland 1835; dismissed 1838.
[4] Unidentified.
[5] Right of petition; poor laws, leave to repeal act of 1834 refused. H xl. 1362; 1413.
[6] PP 1837 xliii. 21.
[7] C. *Leslie, The Case of the Regale and of the Pontificat Stated (1700).
[8] Untraced business.
[9] Robert Langslow, d. 1853; attorney-general in Malta 1832–8; judge in Ceylon 1840–4; complained at dismissal.
[10] *Spring-Rice.
[11] De Bode; intimidation of electors. H xli. 15; 40.
[12] James Millar, retired assistant secretary of the British and Foreign Schools Society.
[13] Untraced; by (bp.) T. *Turton.
[14] S. *Hinds, 'The Latest Official Documents relating to New Zealand, with Introductory Observations' (1838).
[15] Untraced.   [16] Irish poor relief: H xli. 61.

With F. Baring on N. Zealand—& conv. with Ld Ashburton on do.—
Penitentiary 3–4½.
dined at Ld Ashburton's.
read pt of Dunn's 'Natl Education'[1]—and Coate's Letter to Plumptre.[2]

25. *Sunday.*

St James mg. & aft.—walked to Wimpole St.—Wrote on Ch.[3]—read
Jewell.—& Catena Patrum.[4]

26. *M.*

finished Dunn.
wrote to Mr Brown (Boroughreeve Manchr)—Thos Wilson—Lincoln—
T.G.—Lushington—Hicklin.
Educn Comm. 12¼–3½.
House 4¾–12½. Voted on Maidstone's motion in
   263:254
   293: 85
   246:159.[5]

27. *T.*

A long conv. with Mr Bekker[6] on Church matters here, in Sweden, in
Denmark: &c. wrote to Mr Branston—read Dr Kaye on Training School.[7]
Milbank Penity 2½–3¾. House to 9¼ and again 10¼–12¼. Voted in
   249:225
   226:197
and in 87:100 on the marines.[8]
Busy about horses &c.

28. *Wed.*

Mr Bekker to breakfast—took him to the Clubs.
read Currie's W.I. infn[9]—Lester[10]—Pty Hist. on motions of censure in
Amn war.[11]
Sir R. Peel's 1¼–3¾. See Pol. Mema.[12]

[1] H. Dunn, *National Education, the Question of Questions* (1838).
[2] D. Coates, 'The Present State of the New Zealand Question Considered' (1838).
[3] Add MS 44821B, ff. 17–35.
[4] J. A. *Cramer, *Catena in Acta SS. Apostolorum* (1838).
[5] An Irish row; Maidstone's censure of *O'Connell carried. *H* xli. 162, 172, 184.
[6] Perhaps (A.) Immanuel Bekker, 1785–1871, German classicist, said by Schopenhauer
to be 'silent in seven languages'; more probably Bertel Petersen Bekker, 1797–1870,
Danish teacher.
[7] Untraced.
[8] Previous day's row ctd.: same result. Lennox's motion favouring faster marine
promotion carried. *H* xli. 218, 233, 261. Lord (John) George Lennox, 1793–1873, 2nd s.
of 4th duke of *Richmond, was M.P. for Chichester 1819–31, and for Sussex 1832–41.
[9] Presumably in a letter to John *Gladstone.
[10] Possibly Elizabeth B. Lester, *The Quakers*, a tale (1817).
[11] *Parliamentary History* xx. 174, 331, on 3, 22 March 1779; *Fox's motions.
[12] Add MS 44819, ff. 34v–37; on *Molesworth's motion.

23—II.

wrote to Lincoln. Wrote Pol. Mema.

dined at Gaskell's.

House 4¼–6.50.[1]

Prevented from attending Church.[2]

with
March one begins
another book.

1835, Before the Recess.[3]

Moore's Life of Sheridan. I, II.

Carwithen's Church History II, III.

Hope's Christian Biography. I, II.

Stephens's Canadian Papers.

Senior's pamphlet. Merewether's Introdn Corpn Report.

Palgrave's Protest. Hogg's Protest.

Paines Rights of Man.

Bp Coleridge's Charges.

Leibniz's Corresp. with Bossuet on Union between the Churches.

Miss Graham's Life.

Miss Graham's Test of Truth.

Miss Graham's Freeness of Salvation.

Cook's Hist of Scotch Ref. I, II, III.

Lawson's Life of Laud I, II.

Beaumont's Marie I, II.

Hallam's Const. Hist. I.

Holford on Milbank Penitentiary.

Crawfurd on Penitentiaries.

Ettore Fieramosca.

Knox's Remains. I, II.

Knox & Jebb's Correspe. I.

Evans's Scripture Biography I.

Frankenstein.

MSS, Reviews, Pamphlets not enumerated: Speeches do.

Sandford's Lectures on Fellowship with God. ⎫

Confessions of an Opium Eater.   ⎪

Voltaire's Candide.   ⎬ 1835 before

Ld J. Russell on the Constitution.   ⎪ recess

Blunt on the Articles.   ⎭

Read in the Recess of 1835

Le Bas' Life of Jewel.

Spenser's Faery Queen B.I, II.

---

[1] *O'Connell reproved by Speaker; tithes. *H* xli. 263; 273.

[2] It was Ash Wednesday.

[3] The following lists close the volume, beginning on the back flyleaf.

Chalmers's Bridgwater Treatise. I, II.
Hume Commonwealth—James II (Smollett 3 Chh.)
Russell's Modern Europe Vv. III, IV, V, VI, VII.
Ar. Pol. Libb. III, IV, V, VI, VII, VIII. & Econom.
Tocqueville's Democratie I. II.
Trench's Poems.
Mrs Butler's America.
Fox's James II and Appendix.
Ayesha.
Italian Lit. & Scient. Biography I.
Quindici Giorni in Londra.
J.T. Rudd's Six Months in a Convent.
Croly on Ecclesiastical Finance.
Paul's Letters to his Kinsfolk.
Bacon's Essays.
Harltey Coleridge's Poems I.
Life of M[ackintosh]
Purgatorio I–XXXIII.
Genie du Christme I. II. III. IV.
Herschel's [Natural Philosophy]

Manzoni sulla Morale Catholica.
England France Russia & Turkey.
Jeremy's Hist of Events at Mauritius.   }   1835 Before
Tales of the Peerage and the Peasantry.   recess.
Abbot's Teacher.
Isaac Comnenus.

Russell's Hist of the Church I. II.
Knox & Jebb's Correspondence I, II.
Memoirs of General Picton I.
Pollok's Course of Time. X.
Gillies's Introdns to Arist. Pol.
Bolingbroke's Letters &c. I. II.
Alison's History of Fr. Rev. I. II.
Robertson's History of Scotland I. II.
Child Harold I. II. III.   X.
Paradise Lost   X.
Blackstone's Commentaries I.
Pencillings by the way III.
Leighton on I. Peter Ch I. II.
Bp Sumner on St Mark.
Locke on the Understdg. I. II. III.
Robertson's America I.
Edwards's West Indies I. II.
Account of Dick's Educationall Bequest.

Reynolds's Works. I, II, III.
Talfourd's Ion.
Sunday in London.
Milnes's Sketches in Greece.
Burke on the Sublime & Beautiful.

Feb. 4.[1] Amt to Address 243:284.
9. Officers fees. 93:171
15. Mauritius Inquiry. 227:69.
23. Buckms Compensation. 125:81.
Mch 2. Poole Inquiry 70:188.
Mch 8. Irish Corpns. 243:307.
Mch 15. Soap Duty. 125:195.
28. Irish Corpns 199:260.
Ap. 13. Mil. Flogging. 212:95.
Ap. 19. Pensions Committee 268:146.
Ap. 22. ⎰Hardy's Ress............169:243
        ⎱Stanley's Ress (agt prev. quest) 166:238.
Ap. 27. Agricultural Relief............172:208.
    28. Edinbro Poor Rate Bill   .... 77:108.
May 3. Commee on Ld Hill (agt) 322:42.
    9. 2nd readg Factory Bill (agt) 176:178.   7?
June 3. Irish Church Bill. 261:300.
June 10. Ir. Mm. Bill. Ld's Amts 238:324.
June 20. Soap & newsp. stamps. 208:241.
June 23. Ballot. 139:83.
June 24. Lpool Docks. 173:197.
July 4. Approprn clause 266:290.
July 19. Charitable Trustees: 88:133.
July 25. Established Church 175:44.
Aug 2. Irish Tithe. 231:260.

Books read (1836 to recess—from Jan. 13)

Dante Paradiso.
Jeremy Taylor's Holy Living.
Newman's Ser
Bossuet's Histoire des Variations I. II (vol)
Sumner's
Stapylton's Canning I. II. III.
Talfourd's Ion (+) 2d Ed.
Sir J. Walsh's Chapters of Cont. Hist.
Knapp's Poems.
Protestant Errors & R.C. truths.
Locke on the Understanding B.IV.
Lingard's England Vol I.

[1] Notes follow of how he voted in 1836.

Pozzo's Catholicism in Austria.
Gerusalemme Liberata.
Pusey on Baptism.
Taciti Annales I.II.
J. Taylor's Holy Dying.
Taylor on Statesmanship.
The Hampden pamphlets generally.

Hayward's Preff. to Faust. R.C. Morality. Parliamentary Talk.
Sugden's L. to Ld M.—Perceval's Address. Jones's Sermon on Popery.
Tetlcy's on Atonement. Hampden's Obss.—do's Postscript—Newman's
Elucidations—Short on Nat. Edn.—

Baines to H. of Lords. Abercrombie's Inaugural Address—1st Poor Law
Commee Report—Polish Appeal. State of Irish Poor. Lond Rev. on
D'Israeli, & Aristocracy—Oastlee to Abp York—Lewis on Irish Immi-
grants. Quart. on Bonnellier. Labouchere's Report. Trustees Report.
Mr G's Examination of L –Ed Rev on Cape—Fundamental Reform.
Gurney on the New Poor Law (to Feb 22)
                    (No record of pamphlets &c. further.)

Bossuet sur les Promesscs de l'Eglise.
Dodsworth's Church of England a Protester.
Moore's Life of Ld Ed. Fitzgerald—I. II.
Von Raumer's—
Machiavelli's Discorsi.
Recd & Matheson's Visit to America I. II.
Wordsworth's Attica.
Browning's Paracelsus.
Torrens on Colonisation.
Wordsworth's Yarrow revis. &c.
Nicole's Préjugés Legitimes contre les Calvinistes.
Nicole's Additions to do.

Hom. Hymni ad Apoll. Del. Merc. (Shelley's Tr).
Mammon (88. 90. 93. 152. 195. 216. 272. 278. 300)
Mably on the Romans I. II.
Wiseman's Lecturers on the Church.
Anstice's Hymns.
Matheson's Tour in Ireland.
Newland's Exam. of Scripture Lessons.
Newman's Sermons. Vol 1.
Nicole's Pretendus R. convaincus de Schisme.
Brougham's Natural Theology.
Bakewell's Evidence of a Future Life.

From Aug. 9. Recess to Jan I.

Nicole de l'Unité I. II. (finished)
Miss Sinclair's Modcrn Accomplishments.
Sorelli's Confessions—(It.)
S. Aug. de Civ. Dei I–X. XI–XXII.
Milner's Church History I. II. III. IV. V.
[M. J. McKenzie] Private Life I. II.
Macintosh's Dissertn on the Hist of Ethics.
Ciceronis Orator—Academica—De Finibus.
Wraxall's Memoirs of his own Time. I. II.
Grossi's Ildegonda.
Signor Gaudentio di Lucca (Bp Berkeley.)

Wraxall's Posthumous Memoirs I. II. III.
Göthe's Iphigenie.
Göthe's Wilhelm Meister B.I.
Marco Visconti. I. II.
Ld Mahon's George the First. I.
Keith on the Prophecies.
Cic. Tusc. Quaest. I. II. III. IV.
The Inferno (+) Purgatorio (+)
The
Rossetti's Spirito Antipapale.
(Monk) Lewis's West Indian Journal.
Adventures in search of [a horse][1]
Evidence taken before Committee on Joint Stock Banks.
Dryden's Fables.
Par. Lost (+) 1–5.
Cicero de Naturâ Deorum.
Crabb's Tales.
Cicero de Officiis.
Dissertation on Oriental Trinities.
M'Crie's Knox Vol I.

[1] Cp. 2 Nov. 36.

[VOLUME X][1]
(*No 10.*)

Private Journal.

WEG. L[ondo]n Mch 1.
38.

The duties of the State towards the Church.[2]

Re consider persecution
   unity of Establ[t].
   corporate humanity
   activity of pr[ivate] judgment.[3]

Tour
for mending showerbath[4]
Simons[4]
Frost and Norton.[4]
Hart—[4]

Under pledge of £10 to Ir. Ch. Education[4] pd.
£1 to a schoolmaster (p. T. Tancred) for tour.[4]
£50. to College at Chichester cond[itionall]y.[5]
£20. to Educn at Liverpool pd.[4]
£50. to Educn at Newark condy.
£10. to Church at Paris, if Bp of L[ondon] approves.
£ . to Church at Athens.
£ to National Society[4]
£2.2. to Ld Arbuthnott's Subscription. (T.G.)[4]
£20 to Scotch Clergy Society & 2.2. annual.[4]
Miss Combe's Pictures.[4]
£50 to Bethnal Green.

---

[1] Lambeth MS 1424; 113 ff.
[2] This line pencilled faintly; draft title for his first book, *The State in its Relations with the Church*. Cp. 8 Dec. 38.
[3] Jottings for same book.
[4] These lines lightly erased.
[5] Cp. Purcell, i. 151n, and 2 May 38.

Ln. Mch. 38.

1. Thursday.

Wrote to G.A. Selwyn—Mr Moss—R. Blackwell.[1]
read Selwyn's admirable pamphlet on Cathedrals[2]—Glasgow Normal
School Report[3]—& Manzoni's Discorso
Educn Commee 12¼–3¼. Bp of London's Edn meetg. House 4–5.[4] Matheson
here 2 h. on Edn in Evg.
Party at Sir W. Wynn's.[5]

2 Fr.

Monthly letters & accts.—Wrote to Sir P. Laurie[6] and Mr R. Barnes.—Vss.
Calls—distributing Selwyn.
read Mr Lauries pamphlet on Prisons:[7] also on Music
House 4¾–6.[8] dined at Dr. Dss Beauforts. Lady Antrobus's afr.—

3 Sat.

Wrote to T.G.—Lincoln—Sir P. Laurie (rewrote) read Senior's pamphlet
on Factory Act[9]—Manchr Stat[istica]l Report on Labouring Poor.[10]—
Manual of V[ocal] Music[11]
Millbank 2½–4.
R. Wilberforce here on Church matters.
dined at Ph. Pusey's. Lady Parke's & Lady F. E[gerton]'s afr

4. Sunday.

St James mg & aft.—wrote to B. Baring—Lady F.E—Lady K.—with Edn
papers.
Read Maurice (Vol 2)—Leslie
I spoke to Mr G. after dinner on the point I opened to Mahon at B[ridge-
water] H[ouse][12]—viz. a definite principle on religious matters in the event
of any C[onservative] Govt being formed: & he said to me, spontaneously
'tu hai ragione, e quelle cose dovrebbero nettamente spiegarsi prima che
tu vi prenda qualch impiego'.[13]

---

[1] Robert Edward Blackwell, 1804–78, priest at Amberley, Gloucestershire, from 1836.
[2] G. A. *Selwyn, 'Are Cathedral Institutions Useless? . . . addressed to W. E. *Gladstone' (1838).
[3] Untraced.   [4] Slave trade: H xli. 321.
[5] Sir Watkin Williams Wynn, 1772–1840, 5th bart. 1789; m. 1817 Lady Henrietta
Antonia Clive, da. of 1st earl of *Powis; M.P. Beaumaris 1794–6, co. Denbigh from 1796.
[6] Sir Peter *Laurie, 1779?–1861; of Roxburghshire; contractor for Indian army; cr.
kt. 1824; lord mayor of London 1832–3; chairman of Union bank from 1839.
[7] P. *Laurie, Prison Discipline and Secondary Punishments (1837).
[8] Misc. business: H xli. 363.
[9] N. W. *Senior, Letters on the Factory Act, as it Affects the Cotton Manufacturer (1837).
[10] Untraced; cp. 6 Mar. 38.
[11] J. Turner, Manual of Introduction in Vocal Music, Chiefly With a View to Psalmody
(1833).
[12] See n. 3 below.
[13] 'you are right, and these things must be explained tidily before you take any office'.

5. M.

read Leslie—my eyes failed.
wrote to T.G.—Caparn—& to Ld Haddington, Sir J. Graham, Sir S. Canning, Pusey, Finch, R. Williams, Lady F. Egerton, on Selwyn's pamphlet & Matheson's plan—arranging distribution of both. rode.
Edn Commee 12¼–1¾. Peel's meeting 2–3½: wrote Pol. Mema¹—House before & aft dinner.²

6. T.

saw Matheson on his Edn plan—Lady F.E. on do—Tancred on Church. calls & distributing Selwyn.
House 3¾–6¼ and 8½–12½.³ I was anxious to think over the subject and speak—but totally incapable of effort. Peel however in the middle of the debate requested me to do so. It thus becomes my duty & I must hope to do it.
wrote to Manchr operatives—Mr Williamson—Mr Chase (Cape).⁴
read 'Killing no Murder'.⁵ rode.

7. W.

read Leslie—Sir C. Grey on Canadian Proceedings.⁶ forced myself to the Canadian subject against a strange depression.
arranged an exchange of horses—rode—calls.
House at 4— and 6–3. Spoke on Sandon's amt. Voted in 287:316.—I felt lighter, after my act of duty.⁷

8. Th.

Lushington here to breakf. Conv. till 12 on Church matters.
Edn commee 12½–2¾. Edn meeting at bp of London's. House again at four⁸—rode.
My beloved Father overrun—a most providential escape. dined and spent the evg with him alone.
Wrote to T.G.—Sir R. Heron⁹—Lord Aberdeen—G.A. Selwyn. read Manzoni.

9. Fr.

Wrote to Aunt J.—Mr Barnes—

---

¹ Add MS 44819, ff. 37v–38, on Bridgewater House two days before.
² Naval business: *H* xli. 404.
³ *Molesworth moved vote of lack of confidence in *Glenelg: *H* xli. 476.
⁴ Unidentified.
⁵ A pamphlet by E. *Sexby and S. *Titus (1657) calling for the assassination of Oliver *Cromwell; at once fatal to the first-named author.
⁶ Probably in MS: cp. *DNB* xxiii. 180.
⁷ See Morley, i. 145. *Molesworth ceded to *Sandon's lost amdt: *H* xli. 684. *Gladstone answered Sir G. *Grey: ibid. 626.   ⁸ Misc. business: *H* xli. 701.
⁹ Sir Robert *Heron, 1765–1854, 2nd bart. 1805; whig M.P. Grimsby 1812–18, Peterborough 1819–47.

read Burnet's Own Times[1]—Manzoni—Manual of Music.
Sir R. Peel's on Sp[anish] affairs 12¼–2: and conv. with Sir J. Graham and Stanley on the Education.
House 4–5¼ and 10–12½.[2]
Wrote a paper on a religious institution.[3]

10. Sat.

W.I. Edn papers from Dema.
Mr Macarthur here—conv on Church, do with Praed.
House 12¼–1½:[4] Penity 2½–3¾. rode. dined at Speaker's. Lady Salisbury's afr.—
Wrote to Miss Aug. Mackenzie.
No eyes for work.

11 Sunday.

St James' mg & aft.
read M.F. Tupper—Maurice Vol 2—Bp of London's Education Sermon & Preface[5]—
Wrote to Lincoln (on Cathls)—Bp of Salisbury.

12 M.

Wrote to Dr Hook[6]—Selwyn.
Edn Commee 12¼–3¾. rode. O. & C. Club Commee (Neate's case) 4½–5¼.[7]
House.[8] Miss Ede's (music) in evg. Taylor here to breakf.
Read Manual of Music—Leslie.

13. T.

Wrote to Hay—Ld Ripon—Mr Godfrey—Manning. read Krasinski[9]—
W.I. blue books to the best of my ability & beyond safety
rode—House 3¾–9¼[10] Dss of Beauforts & Mrs Colvile's. What a paltry course this seems: yet I do not see a better: & it is not here I think my dangers lie.
Grieved to hear of Matheson's illness.

[1] Gilbert *Burnet History of his own Time, 2v. (1723, 1734), on late seventeenth century.
[2] Misc.; and Irish poor relief in cttee.: H xli. 729; 732.
[3] Lathbury, ii. 433–7; on a new religious order to be devoted to almsgiving.
[4] The house did not sit.
[5] C. J. *Blomfield, 'Nation Education . . . A Sermon . . . On Behalf of the National Society' (1838).
[6] Extract in Morley, i. 148. W. F. *Hook had become an Oxford D.D. in 1837.
[7] Untraced.
[8] Supply: H xli. 786.
[9] W. S. Krasinski, Historical Sketch of . . . the Reformation in Poland, 2 v. (i, 1838; ii, 1840).
[10] Spain: H xli. 823.

14. W.

Wrote to Selwyn—Burnaby—Nicholls.
Edn Commee 12¼–2½. Bp of London's Comm. 2¾–4½.
read W.I. Blue Books.

15. Th.

Wrote to Manning[1]—Selwyn.
Breakf. with Acland & forenoon conv. on Educational matters. H. Powys
& Tancred made the carré.
House 3¾–6½ & 10–11¾ Voted in 300:95 for Corn Laws.[2] A long Church
conv. with Kinnaird.
Read obss. on Ld Glenelg[3]—began Froude.[4]

16. Fr.

Wrote to R.G.—Mr Hill (Salford)[5]—Mr Ramsay—read Froude—W.I.
Blue books.
House 5¼–7¾.[6] dinner party at home
S.P.G. meeting 1½–3½. conv. with Mr Dodsworth
rode—

17. Sat.

Wrote to Capt. Alexander—C. Lawrence. read Froude—Manzoni—& Helen
kindly read me 'a Letter to Ch. Commrs on their oaths'[7]
11¼–4. Educn (Metr) meetg—Addl Curates do—& Penity. rode—dined
at Mr Russell Ellices.

18. Sunday.

Communion 8 A.M. Ch. mg. & aft.
Wrote a little—singing in evg—walk with Mahon—read Leslie and Froude:
this latter very singular.

19 M.

Read Froude & blue book. H.J.G. read from R.C. Directory. wrote to Dr
Hook—Mr Paul (Leeds)[8]—Messrs D.R[obertson], Masterman,[9] & Lyall, on
the Calcutta order—Rn. G. & Aunt J.

---

[1] Part in Lathbury, i. 43.
[2] Against Charles *Villiers, 1802–98, younger b. of 4th Lord *Clarendon; radical M.P.
Wolverhampton from 1835, which he last visited 1875; eminent free trader. H xli. 946.
[3] Untraced.
[4] Editors J. H. *Newman and J. *Keble, Remains of the Late Rev. R.H.F., 4 v.
(1838–9).
[5] Perhaps Richard Hill, priest at Barton-on-Irwell—which like Salford lies just west
of Manchester—from 1843.
[6] Irish electoral register: H xli. 954.
[7] Untraced.
[8] William Paul, solicitor.
[9] John Masterman, director of the East India company.

House $5\frac{1}{4}$–$8\frac{1}{2}$.[1] Mrs Phillips's. rode.
Church conv. with W. Hamilton.

20 T.

Addl Curates comm. $12\frac{1}{4}$, Metrop. Edn 2, Ballot 4–5, House 6–$9\frac{1}{4}$ and $10\frac{1}{2}$–$12\frac{1}{2}$.[2]
Wrote to T.G.—Manchr Operatives—Selwyn.
read Froude—Close on Education[3]
rode—singing.
saw Farquhar about Matheson.

21 W.

Wrote to Burnaby.
read Froude—Lucretius—
at 1 went to see Chantrey's Sir Thos. Monro.[4]
at 3 Lay Union. House 4–7. voted in 139:68 for Lord's Day Bill.[5]
Convv & arrangements on Educn.
Dined at Ld Cholmondeley's.

22 Th.

Dined at Sir R. Peel's to meet Scotch Ch. Deputn. Mr Sidebottom here on the Hippodrome,[6] Mr V. Nolte on Medallions.[7] Mr Macarthur to breakfast. read Froude—Capt Alexander's Cape MSS[8]—& J.N.G. read me the Bp of Winchester's charge.[9]
rode. Ballot at 4.

23. F.

wrote to Dss Dr of Beaufort—Mr Francken—Selwyn—Manning—Dr Hook —Lincoln—Lawrence—Macarthur—Ld Cholmondeley. Made Register. read Froude.
Church at 11. O & C. with H.J.G.—S.P.G. $1\frac{1}{4}$–$2\frac{3}{4}$. Acland's (Edn) 4–$5\frac{1}{4}$.[10]
House 5.50–$8\frac{1}{2}$ and $10\frac{1}{4}$–$12\frac{3}{4}$.[11] Tea at Lady Hope's.

24. Sat.

wrote to Mr Godfrey—Caparn.
Selecting and arranging books for binding.

[1] Irish poor relief: *H* xli. 989.
[2] Misc. business: ibid. 1073.
[3] In F. *Close, *Sermons for the Times* (1837).
[4] Sir Thomas *Munro, 1761–1827, bart., administrator of India; carved on horseback by *Chantry; see *DNB* xxxix. 312.
[5] Plumptre moved it: *H* xli. 1119.   [6] At Notting Hill: cp. 2 Apr. 38.
[7] Untraced business: possibly with Charles or Peter van Notten, city merchants.
[8] Of J. E. *Alexander's *An Expedition into the Interior of Africa* (1838).
[9] C. R. *Sumner, *A charge delivered to the clergy . . . of Winchester* (1837).
[10] Cp. A. H. D. *Acland, *T. D. *Acland*, 89; and 14 Apr. 38.
[11] Irish poor relief, cttee. ctd.: *H* xli. 1179.

Conv. with Doyle on Ch—Mr G. on W.I.—called on Sir F. [Doyle]. Penity $2\frac{1}{4}$–4.

read Froude—with repeated regrets.

sent about more circulars.

rode—dined at Mr Lyon's—Lady Salisbury's afr.

25. Sunday.

St James mg & aft. Mr Ward & Bp. both excellent. walk & Church & conv. with Doyle.—music.

read Leslie (finished)—Froude—wrote—.[1]

26. M.

Wrote to Mr Wordsworth[2]—Mr Mills—R. Cavendish—Mr Smith Wright— Lushington—Jacobson—Mr Wood—Dr Wordsworth[3] –Rector Brooks.

read Scotch Prisons Report[4]—and Ld Brougham's Sp. on Slave Trade.[5]

Addl Curates comm at $12\frac{1}{2}$—rode—House $4\frac{3}{4}$–$6\frac{1}{2}$—dined at Ld Abns— House afr.—paired on Boldero[6]—Mrs Ede's (music) $10\frac{1}{2}$–$1\frac{1}{4}$.

Breakfd at Miss Fenwick's to meet Southey. His app[earan]ce is benignant, melancholy, & intellectual.[7]

27. T.

reading W.I. debates, Evidence, & papers, & endeavouring to reduce into order a great mass of matter.

arranging for the bindings of a lot of 214 vols—House 4–5. dined at Bp of London's. House $10\frac{3}{4}$–$12\frac{1}{2}$[8]

28. W.

read Froude. Lock Chapel at 11—Mr Blunt working up the W.I. question very much.

Millbank (Neale's inquiry) $2\frac{1}{4}$–5. House. Dined at Abp York's;[9] Anc. Music—excellent—& Lady Lansdowne's. 1–3 in the morng working W.I. accompts—absurd div. of 70 : 52—I was away, paired.[10]

29 Th.

wrote to Dr Hook—Dr Wordsworth—Mr Parkinson.[11] read Innes's[12] & Sharp's letters.[13]

[1] Add MS 44728, ff. 35–37.   [2] On copyright: see Add MS 44356, ff. 24–26.
[3] Cp. Robbins, 372.   [4] PP 1838 xxxi. 299.
[5] Of February 20, for immediate emancipation of Negro apprentices: H xl. 1284.
[6] Boldero's attempt to secure inquiry into flogging lost, 76–169: H xli. 1249. Henry George Boldero, 1797–ca. 1875, Royal Engineers; M.P. Chippenham, 1831, 1837–59; conservative; settled in Berkshire.
[7] Robert *Southey, 1774–1843; Poet Laureate 1813.
[8] Spain: H xli. 1320.   [9] Note in Add MS 44819, f. 39v.
[10] A muddle about Spain: H xli. 1384.
[11] Richard *Parkinson, 1797–1858, canon of Manchester 1830 and principal of St. Bee's 1846.   [12] J. Innes, Letter to Lord *Glenelg . . . on Negro Apprenticeship (1838).
[13] H. E. Sharpe, 'On the Abolition of Negro Apprenticeship, in a Letter to Lord *Brougham' (1838).

House at 3¾–5½–12. Unable to get in with my speech.[1] Tea at Carlton afr. rode.

30. Fr.

wrote to Mr Simpson—D. of Wellington—E.P. Vaughan.[2]
Finished Froude Vol 1—began Molesworth's Digest of the Transportation Evidence.[3]
rode, with H.J.G.—looked up a few remaining points. House at 4. and 6¼–1½. Spoke from 11 to 1—received with the greatest & most affecting kindness from all parties, both during & after. Through the debate I felt a most painful depression. Except Mr Plumtre & Ld John Russell, all who spoke damaged the question to the utmost possible degree. Prayer earnest for the moment was wrung from me in my necessity: I hope it was not a blasphemous prayer, for support in pleading the cause of injustice.
Isolated from love, and my greedy heart unappeased by a thousand consolations, I am half insensible even in the moment of delight to such pleasures as this kind of occasion affords: I feel as if the side of me, which lies towards the world, were ice, and all I see in it a dream: I long for that which is within, above: but this is a dangerous and a carnal state: indifference to the world is not love of God: May I have that love within me, as the central principle governing all others, cleansing me by discipline from my intolerable sinfulness, and filling me with an earnest affection to all my fellowmen heirs of less corruption in themselves, and of the same blessings in the covenant of grace.
God was merciful to me now as ever.[4]

31.

In the morning my Father was greatly overcome, & I could hardly speak to him.—Now is the time to turn this attack into measures of benefit for the negroes.[5]
I find the division of last night stands thus:

	Conservative		Ministerialist		Total.
Majority.	139	. . . .	130	. . . .	269
Minority	69	. . . .	136 or 146.		205
Total voted	208	. . . .	266	. . . .	474

 [1] Negro apprenticeship: *H* xlii. 40.
 [2] Edward Protero Vaughan; graduated from Balliol 1832; curate of Wraxall, Somerset 1835–57; rector there 1857.
 [3] (Sir) W. *Molesworth, *Report from the Select Committee . . . on Transportation . . . with notes* (1838).
 [4] Morley says that 'At the end of March Mr. Gladstone produced the strongest impression that he had yet made in parliament, and he now definitely took his place in the front rank', and quoted extracts from this entry: i. 145–6. Negro apprenticeship abolition, 2° by 269 to 215: *H* xlii. 257. Speech ibid. 224; notes for it in Add MS 44649, ff. 160–255, and see 2 Apr. 38. See also W. L. Burn, *Emancipation and Apprenticeship in the British West Indies* (1937), 153, 353–4.   [5] Morley, i. 147.

And, by subtraction,

Majority of ministerialists agt ministers 6
...... of Conservatives for them 70
...... of the House for them .... 64.

Monthly accts—letters—journal.
read Molesworth's Digest—Lucretius. Saw Mr Blair[1]—Mr Colvile & a deputn—at Penity—dined at Sir Ed. Kerrison's: music.
Wrote to Sir G. Grey—T.G.—Branston—Ld Morpeth—C. Lawrence—

Sunday April One.

St James mg & aft. & Communion. Read Froude & Dodsworth on Weekly Communion.[2]
Wrote to Ld Lansdowne—Capt. Saurin.[3]
Went to see Cavendish.—conv with Mr G. on W.I.

M. 2.

Saw McGarel[4] & Rainy—Sir G. Grey—& Labouchere—all on W.I. matters.
read Molesworth's Digest—a strange pamphlet on Extempore Prayer[5]
Curates Fund Comm.—U.C.C. Comm—House 4–6 (voted in 123:162 agt Notting Hill [Footway] Bill) and $8\frac{1}{2}$–$10\frac{1}{4}$.[6]
wrote a paper on B.G. provisions—& to Chanc. Exchr & Pease.[7]
at Lady Jersey's party.
Wrote a Preface & part of Appx to my speech.[8] On Saturday Mr Pitman[9] told me not to become vain for which I liked him. He little knows, by what disappointments I am (or should be) ballasted.

3. F.

wrote to Serj. Wilde—S.C. Denison—Mr Blair, (Chairman of Delegates,) with draft.
read Molesworth's Transportation papers. At Sir R. Peels on them 11.40–12.40: then with the D of Wn on Cape matters.
Commenced writing out my speech from the Reports in Times, M. Chron., & Post—all brief: aid me little.

[1] Perhaps Thomas Richard Arthur Blair, 1802–67; ordained in Calcutta, 1839, priest in Tasmania, 1843; vicar of Milbourne St. Andrew, Dorset, 1854. See 3 Apr. 38.
[2] W. *Dodsworth, *Discourses on the Lord's Supper* (1835).
[3] Edward, d. 1878, eldest s. of William *Saurin, who d. 1839; captain, R.N., 1814, admiral (retired) 1862; m. 1828 Lady Mary Ryder, 1801–1900, 2nd da. of 1st Lord *Harrowby.
[4] Perhaps Charles McGarel, d. 1876; of Magheramorne, co. Antrim, 1842.
[5] 'Extempore Prayer' (1837).
[6] Bill passed, blocking way through Hippodrome; later deb. on elections. H xlii. 274; 277.
[7] Joseph *Pease, 1799–1872, of Darlington; quaker mineowner and philanthropist; M.P. co. Durham, 1832–41. Cp. 9 Apr., 22 May 38.
[8] *Hatchard published his speech of 30 March.
[9] John Rogers *Pitman, 1782–1861, priest and author; preached in Kensington, 1833–48; then chaplain to duchess of *Kent.

House 4–5. rode. Dined at Ld Bandons. House 11–2½. Voted in 158:160 on Ld Durham's expences.[1] Lady de Salis's:[2] & a batch of speech till 4½.

4. W.

John began reading Ld Sligo's pamphlet[3] to me, working hard at speech. Dry and laborious.
At Millbank Commee.
House 3¾ and at 5¾[4] rode. dined at Ld Falmouth's. At Lady Williams's[5] afr.

5 Th.

Worked hard at my speech & appx, & finished the MS. at 3½. in the morning.
calls. House 3¾–7½.[6] Discussed the W.I. Bill with Sir G. Grey & prepared amendments.
Manning here to breakf. & conv. for the forenoon.
Mr Saintsbury[7] on the publishing. Arranged with Hatchard.
Wrote to Burnaby. Warden of Manchester.[8]
Dinner party at home. Music.

6. Friday.

Correcting speech, MS. with John's valuable aid, most kindly given: and arranging all my papers.—Memm on W.I. Bill.
Wrote to Mr Lyall—Mr Trew.[9]
rode. House 5–10½. Voted in 115–61. on Jama[ica] Appr[enticeshi]p.—conversational discussion in Committee.[10]
Lady Lansdowne's party afr.
Conv. with Dr Spalding on Jama.
read Dem[erar]a food reports—& Milnes's Poems.[11]
Bp of London's Educn meeting.

---

[1] Canada: *H* xlii. 422.
[2] Henrietta, née Foster, d. 1856; niece of 1st Lord *Oriel; m. *ca.* 1809 Jerome (Fane) de Salis, count de Salis 1807; he lived in Albany and she at Carlton Gardens.
[3] [P. B. Howe] 'Jamaica Under the Apprenticeship System' (1838).
[4] Misc. business: *H* xlii. 425.
[5] Mary, née Fortescue, d. 1874; 4th da. of 1st Earl Fortescue; m. 1823 (Sir) James Hamlyn Williams, 1790–1866, of Clovelly, who succ. as 3rd bart. 1829 and was whig M.P., Carmarthenshire, 1831 and 1835–7.
[6] Misc. business: *H* xlii. 432.
[7] John Sainsbury, bookseller and publisher of Red Lion Square, Holborn; father of W.N.*
[8] Thomas *Calvert, 1775–1840, changed name from Jackson, *ca.* 1820; divinity professor at Cambridge, 1814–24; warden of Manchester 1823.
[9] Henry Trew, secretary to the governor of Dominica in the Leeward Islands.
[10] He voted against ending it on 1 August 1838: *H* xlii. 474.
[11] R. M. *Milnes, *Poems of Many Years*, and *Memorials of a Residence on the Continent* (both 1838).

7. Saturday.

Wrote to Sir R. Heron[1]—H. Goulburn—Mr Huddlestone—Mr Landon.[2]
House at 12 for W.I. Bill.[3]
Conv. with Serg. Wilde on Newark Poor Law matters.
Educn meeting at Aclands $4\frac{1}{2}$–$5\frac{1}{2}$.
Milnes's poems. John read Ld Sligo to me.
dined at Ld Henniker's. music.

8. Sunday.

St James mg & aft.—Sat with Cavendish. read Mr Plumptre's Memoir of
his Sister[4] & part of 'The Faithful Friend'[5]—Dodsworth (finished) and
Trench's Poems.

9. M.

Ld Sligo (by J.N.G.)—Milnes. Thompson's 'Anti-slavery Crisis,'[6] Lunedi
Santo.
Wrote to Mr Colvile—Shand—Plumptre—Pease[7]—Ramsay—Huddlestone.
Canada Church Depn at 1—Mr Trew here on W.I. at $\frac{1}{2}$—Church at 3—
rode—House 5–$9\frac{3}{4}$. Voted in 124:120 and 117:121.[8] T. & L.G. came.

10. T.

Wrote to Saintsbury—Grey—Dr Spry— Sir E. Sugden.[9] Sir R. Heron—
Mr Brockden (Lincoln)[10]—Capt. Alexander.
read Milnes—Ld Sligo—Saintsbury's Extracts[11]—Cathl petition.
Church at 3.
corrected my proof sheets and made the remaining arrangements.
at Dss of Beaufort's in evg. conv. on amusements.

11. Wed.

Wrote to E.C. Kerrison.

[1] Sir Robert *Heron, 1765–1854, 2nd bart. 1805; whig M.P. Grimsby 1812–18,
Peterborough 1819–47.
[2] Perhaps Whittington Henry Landon, 1805?–83, b. of L.E.L.* the poetess; priest at
Slibeck, Pembrokeshire, 1851–77.
[3] He made two short speeches on report stage: *H* xlii. 474, 475. Notes in Add MS
44649, ff. 256–63.
[4] Presumably in MS. Frances Matilda Plumptre m. 1816 Robert Ramsden of Carlton
Hall, Notts., and d. April 1837.
[5] *The Faithful Friend . . . Conversations on Worldly Intercourse* (1834).
[6] *Eclectic Review*, iii. 458 (April 1838).
[7] Cp. Add MS 44356, ff. 34–35: *Pease excuses himself for not forwarding evidence
controverted by *Gladstone.
[8] Procedural divisions, ending debate on Shaftesbury election and adjourning slavery
debate: *H* xlii. 518, 525.
[9] Sir Edward Burtenshaw *Sugden, 1781–1875, tory lawyer; K.C. 1822; M.P. 1828–32
and 1837–52; solicitor-general (and kt.) 1829; lord chancellor of Ireland, 1834–5 and
1841–6, of England 1852; cr. Lord St. Leonards 1852.
[10] Possibly James Brogden, 1804?–64, then of Grosvenor Street; vicar of Deddington,
Oxfordshire, from 1848.
[11] *Dictionary of Musicians* (1825), compiled from various works and published by
Sainsbury.
24—II.

read Milnes—Acland & Wood's Edn MS.—S. Denison's P.S.[1]—Ld Ashburton's speech on Canada.[2]
Church at 11—Saw E.C. K[errison] on his studies. Acland on Edn—House.[3] rode.
dined at Sir A. Grant's.[4] Sir E. Kerrison's (private conv.) & Mrs Cunliffe's[5] afr.—Merc. Sant.

12. Th.

wrote to Lincoln—A. Williams—Robertson of Kindeace—Bonham.
Preparing copies of speech for distribution
Sir R. Fremantle's in evg—then Milnes's. conv. on copyright.
read Milnes—Burgess's Educational Statistics[6]—& John began Barrett's speech of 1833 to me.[7]
Church at 11. Edn meeting at 3. Giov[edi] Sant[o].

13. Good Friday.

Commn at 8. Church 11 & 3.
read Ld A. Hervey on Baptm—& on Popish Error: both excellent. It is delightful thus to revive acquaintance with an old friend.[8] Read Hook on Ath[anasia]n creed.[9]
music.
Wrote on amusements &c.[10] walk.
No fatto qualche digiuno in questa settimana: ma la notte passata mi risvegliava un poco ammalato, a cagione d'aver bevuto troppo del te e del caffè, prima di coricarmi: oggi ho fatto digiuno fino al pranzo: ma questo mi pare nuocermi un poco al viso specialmente. Poveraccio! 'Non hai potuto una sol'ora vegliare con me'?[11]

14. Easter Eve.

Finished Milnes. read part of Wordsworth's Inscriptions.[12] Ma, la mancanza di cibo benchè leggiera fa gli occhi, mi pare, più deboli.[13]
Church at 3.

[1] S. C. Denison, 'Is the Ballot a Mistake?' (1838).
[2] Of 8 February 1838, on 3° Canada Government bill: H xl. 847.
[3] Misc. business: H xlii. 545.
[4] Brief note in Add MS 44819, f. 38. Sir Alexander Cray *Grant, 1782–1854, 6th bart. 1825; West India planter; M.P. 1812–32, 1840–3; chairman of commons committees 1826–32; public accounts commissioner, 1843.
[5] Either Emma, née Crewe, d. 1850, who m. 1809 Cunliffe(-Offley), and was widowed 1832; or her niece-in-law Charlotte, née Howel, d. 1856, who m. ca. 1838 Robert Ellis Cunliffe, 1805–55, s. of 4th and f. of 5th bart., in EICS.
[6] R. *Burgess, Educational Statistics, a letter addressed to J. C. Colquhoun (1838).
[7] Cp. 18 Aug. 34.
[8] A. C. *Hervey, A Few Hints on Infant Baptism (1838); 'A Sermon Against the Errors of Popery' (1838).
[9] W. F. *Hook, A Letter to his Parishioners on the Use of the Athanasian Creed (1838).
[10] Add MS 44728, ff. 42 49; in Lathbury, ii. 437–43.
[11] 'I have done some fasting this week; but last night I woke up, rather poorly, because I had drunk too much tea and coffee before going to bed: today I fasted till dinner: but this seemed to harm me a little, my eyes particularly. Poor creature! "Could ye not watch one hour with me?"' (Matt. xxvi. 40.)
[12] Christopher *Wordsworth, Inscriptiones Pompeianae (1837).
[13] 'But the lack of food, though slight, seems to me to make the eyes weaker.'

At Lambeth 11–1: the Archbp most full & most gratifying on Education. Farquhar, Wood, & Acland, all alike pleased.
Sat to Miss Combe. Rode.
Wrote to Dr Hook—Mr Godfrey—Mr Wilkinson (Lpool)—Mr Saintsbury—Mr Jephson.
dined at Dss Dr of Beauforts—long conv. on worldly amusements &c. She is a noble lady indeed.

15. Easter Day.

Commn 8.—Ch 11.—Ch. 3.—read
Brown's Sermon on Daily Service. Trench's Poems. Began Newman on Justifn—I tremble.[1]—Domen. della Risurr.
wrote to Dr Spry—G.A. Selwyn.

16. M.

Church at 11.
wrote to Mr Jennings—Rev. J. Scott[2]—Mr Saunders—and H. Thompson.
Saw B. H[arrison] (to go to Dealtry) & S.F. Wood on the Edn plan.
calls.
at 4 to Sundridge.[3]—Music in evg.
Finished Trench. Read (Sewell) on the Eccl. Commn.[4]
took H[ugh] Jones to the National Gallery.

17. T.

Wrote to Lincoln. Farquhar. Mr G.—G. Hall—Finished Sewell on Eccl. Commn—read Fellowes's acct of La Trappe[5]—Luisa Strozzi (began)[6]—Leeke's 'Suggestion'.[7]
rode—music in evg.

18. W.

Wrote to Dr Spry—Serj. Wilde—Childers—P. Rose[8] read Luisa Strozzi—Glover's Ecclesia & Synodus (began)[9] rode—music in evening, plenty, (walk also with J.N.G.) I here draw a list of such speeches made by me as I should in any sense remember.

1. At Oxford on the Reform Bill. (Apl or) [17] May 1831. written out afr—but the MS. by some one mislaid.

[1] J. H. *Newman, *Lectures on Justification* (1838).
[2] Possibly Alexander John *Scott, 1805–66; friend of *Campbell of Row and of E. *Irving; first principal of Owen's College, Manchester, 1851.
[3] Sundridge Park, Bromley, the *Scotts' seat 9 miles SE. of London.   [4] Untraced.
[5] W. D. Fellowes, *A Visit to the Monastery of La Trappe* (1818).
[6] A novel by G. Rosini, 4 v. (1832–3), on sixteenth-century Florence.
[7] W. Leeke, *A Few Suggestions for Increasing the Incomes of Many of the Smaller Livings* (1838).
[8] Peter Rose wrote to him on 6 March about a new governor of Demerara (Add MS 44356, ff. 18–21).
[9] F. R. A. Glover, *Ecclesia et Synodus: or, the church's claim for self-deliberation* (1837).

2. H. of C. [3] June 1833. Slavery Abolition Act.
3. H. of C. June or [4] July 1833. on Liverpool Freemen.
4. H. of C. [8] July 1833. on Irish Church.
((2) and (3) are corrected in the Mirror. I have a corrected MS. of (4).)
5. H. of C. June or [28] July 1834. on the Universities' Bill. Corrected I
think for the Mirror.
6. H. of C. [31] March 1835. Irish Church. Corrected for the Mirror.
7. Newark. [11] June 1835. Public dinner. Reports in Nottm Journal.
Corrected for L'pool Standard.
8. H. of C. [22] March 1836. W.I. Apprenticeship. Ill report & very partially corrected in the Mirror.
9. H. of C. [1] June (?) 1836. Irish Church. Corrected for the Dublin
Evening Mail: copied thence I believe into the Mirror.
10. Liverpool. [18] Oct. 1836. Tradesmen's dinner. Corrected for the
Liverpool Mail.
11. Newark. [19] Jan. 1837. County dinner. Reported in Nottm Journal. Not
corrected.
12. H. of C. [8] Mch. 1837. Canada. Not corrected.
13. H. of C. [15] Mch 1837. Church Rates. Not corrected. These are however I think reported at considerable length in the papers.
14. [21] July. 1837. Newark. On the Poor Law. Not reported.
15. [9] Aug. 1837. Manchester. Public dinner. Not corrected. Several newspaper reports.
16. [22] Dec. 1837. H. of C. Canada. (only noted because the subject came
suddenly.)
17. [23] Jan. 1838. H. of C. Canada. Reported I believe pretty much at
length in the Times.
18. [7] Mch 1838. H. of C. Canada—the Ministry. In answer to Sir G. Grey.
19. Mch 30. 1838. H. of C. W.I. Apprenticeship. Corrected and published.

19. Th.

at 10, rode to town. Church at 3.
wrote to W. Selwyn[1]—Saunders (Sheffield)—F. Oakley—Mr Jennings
Jas Stephen—Mr Simpson—R.G.
read de Bry's voyages—very curious account of the object of Columbus.[2]—
M. Angelo, Rime—'Pluralism & Nonres[idence] indefensible'.[3]
rode. Dined with the Williams's. Music.
conv. with Mr G. Offered to go to W.I.—he disapproves.[4]

20. Fr.

Wrote to Sir G. Grey.
S.P.G. 1–2½.

---

[1] On cathedral establishments: see Add MS 44356, f. 55.
[2] T. de Bry, *Grands Voyages* (many eds.), part iv. (25 parts, 1590–1634).
[3] A clergyman, *Pluralism and Nonresidence Unnecessary, Injurious, and Indefensible*
(1838).
[4] See Morley, i. 148.

read Glover—Faber's Dedn & Preface[1]—John read me Barrett.
rode. dined in B. Square. Dss of Beaufort's afr & conv. Eyes very weak.

21 Sat.

Wrote to Mr Robertson (Zell)[2]—Chr. Wordsworth (with Testamt) G.A.
S[elwyn] here. Conv. on Cathls.
J.N.G. read Mr Burge's Speech of 1833.[3]—read Chalmers's Few words on
Politics[4]—Chase's correspondence.
Wrote to Dr Spry—Sir W.R.F.—A. Williams.
rode—dined at Mr Hallam's

22. Sunday.

Wrote on Thh.[5]
St James's mg & aft.
read Selwyn (p. J.N.G.)—Faithful Friend (finished) and Faber on Justifn.
Walk of 1½ hour & very interesting conv. with Sir Jas Graham on Church
matters.[6]

23. M.

Wrote to Sir R. Peel[7]—Ld Abn.
Newspapers (Apprn)—Wordsworth's Pompeii (finished)—Glovers Ecclesia
(finished)—Howick's speech.[8]
calls. in evg at Dss of Beaufort's.
Music by favour of L.G.

24. T.

Wrote to Saunders (Sheffield)[9].
read pt of Smith's False Witness:[10] & began Wilberforce's Life, wh I was
much gratified to receive.[11]
Saw G. Alexander. rode. dined at Col. Conolly's.—Music again.

25. W.

Wrote to Vanlerberghe[12]—Uncle D.—Watson (Nk).

[1] To G. S. *Faber's *The Primitive Doctrine of Justification* (1837).
[2] Zell-am-Hamersbach, a watering-place in Baden, 21 miles SE. of Strasburg.
[3] Cp. 18 Aug. 34n.
[4] T. *Chalmers, 'Reply to the Attempt to connect the Cause of Church Accommodation with Party Politics', four-page pamphlet reprinted from *Edinburgh Advertiser*
(1835).
[5] Add MS 44728, ff. 51–57.
[6] Note in Add MS 44819, f. 38.
[7] Forwarding *Selwyn on cathedrals: in Add MS 40425, ff. 53–54.
[8] Of 30 March 1838, against Negro apprenticeship: *H* xlii. 190.
[9] Unidentified. George Lemon Saunders was a Sheffield music teacher.
[10] Charles Smith, 'The Truths Hidden by the False Witness of Convocation' (1834).
[11] R. I. and S. *Wilberforce's *Life* of their father*, 5 v. (1838); cp. Add MS 44343, ff.
3–19.
[12] Unidentified.

at 11, Miss Milne's (Lady Galway's) marriage breakft.[1] 1½ hour with Mr Rogers afr.[2]
at 3 Church. U.C.C. conference at 4.[3] Acland on Edn. read Wilberforce.
began a long letter to S. Wilberforce.
House at 3.50 and again 5¼–10½.[4]

26. Th.

finished to Wilberforce. Wrote to Ld Jermyn[5]—Mr Mills. *Mr Collins*. Saw Miller on Sc. & Eng Ch.
Monday Evg I introduced the subject of a visit to the W.I.—my Father appears decided *agt*.[6]
House 3¼–8½.[7] Lady Hope's—Sir W. Wynn's. read Wilberforce's Life, wrote P. Mem[a8] rode.

27. Fr.

Wrote to Saunders (Sheffield)—Bonner (Belfast)[9]—Wainwright—Sir R. Peel—Bp of London—Mr Ramsay—Professor Forbes.
read Wilberforce & pt of Brougham on the Press.[10] 12–1¾ Conff. on Edn— Acland, Ld S[ando]n, Wood.
2–3¾. Dr Chalmers's 2d Lecture.[11]
rode. House. Mrs Russell Ellice's Concert. Cards on D. & Ly M.

28. Sat.

Wrote to Piercy.[12]
read Wilberforce—finished Vol 1 (with J.s aid)—& Buxton's Letter.
Saw Mr Farrer on the Milbank discovery[13]—Mr Leishman[14] & Mr Gordon on the Scotch Church: disclosed my objection to contributing: they received it very kindly, and I made no reserve.
Th. nt I had a conv. at Sir W.W.s on London amusements with Miss Seymer,[15] who spoke sensibly of them.
1–2¼ Nat. Soc. Sub Comm. on Educn—then to Kings College annual meeting. Chosen on the Council.[16]
rode, calls, evg at home.

[1] Henrietta Milnes m. her cousin George Edward Arundell Monckton-Arundell, 1805–76; 6th Viscount Galway 1834; conservative M.P. East Retford from 1847.
[2] Notes in Add MS 44819, ff. 38v–39v.
[3] Canadian clerical discussion.   [4] Copyright bill, 2°: *H* xlii. 555.
[5] Frederick William Hervey, 1800–64; styled Earl Jermyn, and Peelite M.P. Bury St. Edmund's, 1826–59; minor office 1841–6; 2nd marquess of Bristol 1859.
[6] Cp. 19 Apr. 38.   [7] Misc. business: *H* xlii. 597.
[8] Add MS 44819, f. 38.   [9] Unidentified.
[10] *Edinburgh Review*, lxvii. 1 (April 1838), on abuses of the press.
[11] Note in Add MS 44728, f. 60. *Chalmers was lecturing on the value of established churches: cp. *DNB* ix. 452 and M. C. Bowe, *Rio*, 156 n.
[12] Probably John Morpott William Piercy, 1816?–1902, then at Clare, Cambridge; vicar of Slawston, Leicestershire, from 1847.
[13] Untraced.
[14] Matthew Leishman, minister and author, moderator of the general assembly 1858.
[15] S. of H.K.   [16] At *Blomfield's invitation: Add MS 44356, f. 61.

Quei pochi che mi guardano, parebbero facilmente ingannarsi circa i miei perigli, i quali vengono, mi pare, da dentro massimamente. Tutto il di fuori è in qualche maniera disarmato per ora, mediante la freddezza, come di gelo, del cuore. Io se fossi stato maritato, credo che briacó avrei affatto smenticato mio Dio, e la santa di lui opra. Adesso cammino fra le pompe del mondo come morto, fra negozi come necribondo, portando il petto di pietra. adesso

'i floridi
Sentice della speranza'

per me porgon tutti e senza intervallo, a varcar nell' invisibile. Questo viene da pochissime agrissime cose che mi sono andate a contrappelo. Può cambiarsi. E mentre dura, bisogna aver cura: e non intendere il rammarico delle perdute come se fosse la voce dell'alma stanca del peccato ed invaghita del Redentore. O vivere o morire: o gioire o aver pena: riuscire o forte o debole, o sprezzato o ben stimato: che sia sempre pronto, stando da giorno in giorno nella Divina voglia; basi di speranza, castello di scampo e di salute.[1]

29. Sunday.

Wrote.—St. James mg & aft.
read Faber—Maurice's Sermon to Students[2]—and Froude (per J.N.G.)—

30. M.

Wrote to Ashley—Labouchere (& draft) R. Wilberforce. read Wilberforce's Memoirs.
Peel's at 11 on Church Rates. Addl Curates Fund at 1. Penitentiary at 3: concocted a letter for our need. House at $4\frac{1}{2}$. rode. House $8\frac{1}{2}$–$9\frac{3}{4}$.[3] Lady Clanricarde's (beautiful) concert.

Tuesday May one.

Breakfast with Acland to meet Dr Pusey: conv. on Ch. Govt & Cathl question—wh is now fermenting in my mind.
Church at 11.
Mr Berridge[4] here on Canadian Church.

---

[1] 'The few people who keep an eye on me might seem to deceive themselves easily about my dangers, which come, I think, to a very great degree from within. The world outside me seems somehow dismantled now, because of the icy coldness of my heart. Had I been married, I believe I would have been insensate enough to deny my God, and the holiness of his works. Now I walk among the splendours of the world like a dead man, and in business like one bound to death, with a heart of stone. Now all "the bright paths of hope", without a gap between, bring me to a pass into the invisible. This results from a very few very bitter things which have gone the wrong way for me. It may change. Meanwhile it is hard, and I must take care: and not hearken to regret for my loss as if it were the voice of a soul weary of sin and made fond of the Redeemer. Dying or living; rejoicing or suffering; turning out strong or weak, despised or well thought of; may I always be ready, waiting day by day in the will of God, the foundation of hope, the citadel of safety and salvation.'
[2] J. F. D. *Maurice, *The Responsibilities of Medical Students* (1838).
[3] Irish poor relief, 3°: *H* xlii. 675.   [4] W. C. Bettridge.

read Warburton's Alliance[1]—began 'Athenian Captive'.[2]
dined at Mr. Mildmay's.
Chalmers's Lecture at 2. House 4–7$\frac{3}{4}$.[3]

2.

Made up letters for the month past.
Manning here on Chichester Theologl College: &c.
finished "Athenian captive"—a fall from Ion?
At the Levee. Dr Spry here on Cathls.—Bp of Exeter on W.I. Apprp.—
Sat to Mr Bradley.[4] rode. dined at Mrs Wilson Pattens. Mrs Ede's afr.
Music. Sat to Bradley.

3. Th.

Wrote to Mr Ramsay—Selwyn—R.G.—Caparn Party at Home. rode.
Chalmers's Fourth Lecture 2–3$\frac{1}{2}$.[5]
Mr Macarthur here on N.S.W.
read Wilberforce.[6]
House 3$\frac{3}{4}$–4$\frac{3}{4}$ and 10$\frac{1}{2}$–1. Voted in 241:277 and 254:265 on Church leases
Commee[7]—Long conv. with Sir W. Heathcote.[8]
conv. with Mrs Watts Russell on the Church & Ministry.

4. Fr.

Wrote to Bp of London.
Railway Commee 12$\frac{3}{4}$–2$\frac{1}{2}$. Over Milbank with a party. rode. House 7$\frac{3}{4}$–12$\frac{1}{4}$.[9]
Acland on Edn.
read Wilberforce.

5. Sat.

Wrote to R.G.—(who became a father on Thursday)[10]—Mayor of Newark—
Mr Meymott.[11]
read Wilberforce.
[At] Acland's on Edn at 11—N.S. Subcommittee Conference 12$\frac{1}{4}$–2$\frac{1}{2}$.
Penitentiary Commee—sat to Bradley 4–5$\frac{1}{2}$. rode. Dined at Mr Greenes.[12]
Drew a paper for the Subcommee (if approved by my coadjutors.)[13]

---

[1] W. *Warburton, *The Alliance Between Church and State* (1736).
[2] By *Talfourd (1838).   [3] Misc. business: *H* xlii. 740.
[4] William *Bradley, 1801–57, portrait painter.
[5] Note in Add MS 44728, f. 64.   [6] 'Conv. wi' here deleted.
[7] Against setting up select cttee. to look into management of church property: *H* xlii.
892.
[8] Sir William Heathcote, 1801–81; 5th bart. 1825; tory M.P. Hampshire 1826–32,
1837–49, and Oxford university 1854–68.
[9] Church pluralities: *H* xlii. 906.
[10] Robertson Gladstone's eldest child John, d. 13 October 1852.
[11] Perhaps John Meymott, city solicitor.
[12] Thomas Greene, 1794–1872, tory M.P. Lancaster 1824–57; m. 1820 Henrietta, née
Russell, 4th da. of 1st bart.*, and gd. of Charles, Earl *Whitworth.
[13] Several of these papers on education are in Add MS 44728, *ca.* ff. 70–103.

6. *Sunday.*

Communion. Ch mg & aft.—Conv with George[1]—wrote over Edn paper. 2¼ hours with Acland on it.
read Faber.—and Burgess's 'What may this Edn be?'.[2]

7. *M.*

Wrote to Mr G.—W. Selwyn—Warden of Manchester.[3] A Kinnaird—Kinnear—Pease—Hansard[4]—Wilde.
Edn paper again discussed—with Acland—& with the Bp of Ln who made verbal alterations.
A conv. with Treasury Stanley[5] at nt on the Church and Cathedrals!
Railway Comm. 12¼–3¾. House again 5¾–6½: & 11–12¼.[6] Dined at Ld Galloway's. Church conv. with Mr Cummings.
read Wilberforce—Scobell's Speech.[7]
Tom read Mr G.s letter: accumulating our allowances almost beyond endurance. But what princeliness: what affection.[8]

8. *T.*

Wrote to Mr G.—Aunt J.
read Wilberforce.
Chalmers's 5th 2–4. Very good: the territorial question: sat to Mr Bradley & saw his profiles 4–5½.—rode conv. with Cavendish on his profession. Dined at Dss of Beaufort's—read them French. House Committee 12–1¼.

9. *W.*

Wrote to W. Selwyn—Dr Hook—Mrs [W.E.] Tallents—read Wilberforce—Pusey's Art.[9] (began).
Commee 12¼–2½ rode. House 6–8¼ and 9½–12¼. Voted in 220:150 on Bonded Corn Grinding 116:54 on Copyright.[10] Glynne & Gaskell to tea.—Calls

10. *Th.*

Wrote to Mr Cross (Glasgow)[11] Mr Gray (Glasgow):[12] Mr G., Bp of London,[13] Dr Chalmers.

---

[1] Hall.　　[2] R. *Burgess, *What may This System of National Education Be?* (1838).
[3] On education, see Add MS 44356, ff. 68–69.
[4] Luke Graves *Hansard, 1783–1841, printer to the H. of C.
[5] Edward John ('Ben') *Stanley, 1802–69; Eton and Christ Church; whig M.P. Hindon 1831, Cheshire 1832–41 and 1847–8; cr. Lord Eddisbury 1848; succ. as 2nd Lord Stanley of Alderly 1850; among other offices, whig chief whip 1835–41, board of trade 1855–8, postmaster-general 1860–6; refused office in diarist's first cabinet.
[6] Pluralities ctd.: *H* xlii. 952.
[7] J. Scoble, 'The Working of the Negro Apprenticeship System' (1838); his speech at Exeter Hall, 4 April 1838.　　[8] Cp. Magnus, 26.
[9] *Quarterly Review*, lxii. 390 (April 1838), on J. E. *Tyler's *Oaths* (1834).
[10] Bonded corn bill defeated, 2°; copyright bill into cttee. by 116 to 64. *H* xlii. 1042; 1073.　　[11] Perhaps Alexander Cross, merchant.
[12] Perhaps John Hamilton Gray, 1800–67, Glasgow born; traveller; vicar of Bolsover, co. Derby, 1833–66.　　[13] Cp. Add MS 44536, ff. 74–76.

read Wilberforce—& Pusey's Art.

Commees 12¼–3 & ¾ House to 4½ & again 5¾–7.[1] Dined at Ld Francis Egerton's. Queen's Ball afterwards[2] 'dry hearted as a stone'.

Conv. with Bp of London on Cathedrals—

11. Fr.

read 'Free thoughts on the Ministry'[3]—Bp of Lincoln on Eccl. Commn.—[4] Wilberforce.

Commee 2½–4: House 6–8½.[5] Lady Antrobus's Concert.

Wrote to Mr Tredgold.[6]

12. Sat.

Wrote to B. Harrison.

Eyes bad—cd not read.

Saw Mr Hodgson on N[ational] Society—Bp of Ex[ete]r on Ir. Edn— Chalmers's Lecture 2–4. rode. Dinner at Merchant Tailors. Left at 11.20. P. spoke 1 h. 20 m. He is not best after dinner.[7]

13. Sunday.

Ch. mg & aft: Bp of Winchr & Mr Dodsworth sermm. for new Ch.—each excellent.

read Faber on Just[ificatio]n.—Book of the Church[8]—The Prebendary[9] (p. J.N.G.).

2d conv. with George preparatory to his Confirmation. Mr G. talks of a Church at L'pool. Thank God.[10]

14. M.

Wrote to Manning[11]—Saunders. Dr Dss of Beaufort. and Oakley.

read Wilberforce—Pusey's Art, Dublin Rev. on Abp of Cologne.[12]

Commee 2–4. House 4¾–5½ and 9½–12.[13]

Acland on Edn.—

---

[1] Controverted elections: H xlii. 1080.

[2] *Victoria's first state ball.

[3] 'Free Thoughts on the Ministry in a letter to Lord *Lyndhurst' (1838).

[4] J. *Kaye, A Letter . . . to the Archbishop of Canterbury on the recommendations of the Ecclesiastical Commission (1838).

[5] Pluralities: H xlii. 1161.

[6] Perhaps Clarkson Sturge Tredgold, of Cape Town.

[7] 300 conservative M.P.s entertained *Peel in the merchant tailors' hall; he, *Stanley, and *Graham spoke at length.

[8] R. *Southey, The Book of the Church, 2 v. (1824).

[9] 'The Prebendary or Cathedral Establishments, Ancient and Modern; Being the Substance of Letters to the Morning Herald in 1836 and 1837', 2 pts. (1838).

[10] Eventually his youngest son inherited the advowson of the church of St. Thomas-in-the-Fields, Toxteth Park, built 1840.

[11] About *Chalmers: cp. Magnus, 36.

[12] ii. 168 (December 1836).

[13] Irish tithes: H xlii. 1173.

15. T.

Wrote to V. Nolte.
Wrote Resolutions for Suggestion to our Edn Commee & a paper on the training & licensing of school-masters.[1]
Read Wilberforce—(p. J.N.G.) Prebendary, finished I.
party at home. rode.
Commee 1½–4, House 4–5 looking up Ir. Ch. debates—& House 10–1¾.
Voted in 298:317 for rescinding Resolution of 1835.[2]

16. W.

Wrote to A. Wood (marriage)[3]—Saunders (Sheffield) read Wilberforce's Memoirs, & Miss Mitford's Tragedy,[4] 'Welcome & Farewell'[5] {46 sin. 52 marriage. 63 country 66. Scene with Villeroi & Margaret.
              'Yet who could see & know & love thee not?'
84.86, tree. 94 love. 100 scene.}
Bp of Exeters at 2. he out: read on Mann[ing?][6] Bradley 3–4½. rode: calls.
Lady Ashburton's & Lady Cross's[7] in evg.

17. Th.

Wrote to Burge. Manning.
Acland here on Education
Read the Jam[aic]a Committee's Report.[8] John read me the Prebendary No 2.—
Vss.[9] rode. party here. Lady Lansdowne's afr.—

18. Fr.

Wrote to Mr Campbell on S.P.G. matters. B. Harrison, Acland here on Edn.
—Mr Berridge on his petition & the Canadian Church. Commee at 2
Read Smith's Convocation[10] ([short blank])—J.N.G. finished the Prebendary to me.
Mr Hickson's Lecture on Music in Education at 3, & childrens singing.[11]
Very interesting. House afr, & Burge at 5½ on moving Jam[aic]a Report.

[1] Add MS 44728, paper ff. 72–74, resolutions f. 80.
[2] Irish tithes: *H* xlii. 1353.
[3] See 25 June 38.
[4] M. R. *Mitford, *Rienzi* (1828).
[5] Tragedy by William *Harness (1837).
[6] Untraced.
[7] Margaret, née Hyde, of Ardwick, Lancashire; m. 1802 Sir John *Cross, 1766–1842, kt. and bankruptcy judge 1831.
[8] On negro education, by C. J. *Latrobe: *PP* 1838 xlviii. 61 or 159.
[9] Probably the sonnets of which fair copies, dated 23 May, are in Add MS 44728, ff. 67–68.
[10] Cp. 24 Apr. 38.
[11] William Edward *Hickson, 1803–70, educational philanthropist; ed. *Westminster Review* 1840–52. The lecture was published.

Dined at Mr Longs.[1] Mrs Offley's,[2] Mrs Lucas's,[3] House $11\frac{3}{4}$–1, on Scotch prisons.[4]

19. Sat.

Wrote to Burge—Caparn.
read Wilberforce, Dunn.[5]
Sir R. Peel's 11–1 on Irish matters (Vid. Mem[a])[6]—N. School comm. & Penity.—2–$4\frac{1}{2}$. rode. Dined at Mr Gally Knight's.

20. S.

Communion 8 A.M.—Ch. mg & aft.
Walk with Cavendish. a third conv. with G. Hall for his confirmn.
read Hodgson's Apostolical Catechism[7]—& finished Faber on Justification.
Read Cosins.[8]

21. M.

Wrote to Dr Pusey, Hamilton, Jacobson (for R.C.)—[R.] B. Wilbraham, Fleetwood (for Mr Stanistreet)[9]—R.G. & Caparn.
Commee & House 2–$4\frac{1}{2}$.[10]
Read Dunn & the whole Scobell papers in V. No II.[11]
dined at Baring Wall's.
A[nti] S[lavery] Delegates here $1\frac{1}{4}$ hour.[11]—Mr Stanistreet—G. Mackenzie (looks as if not long for this poor world)—rode

22. T.

Wrote to Boler—read Dunn.
Scobell[12] & Pease here $1\frac{1}{2}$ hour.
Sub Commee B. meeting $2\frac{1}{2}$–4.[13] House 4–5. West Indian references and quotations. House $5\frac{3}{4}$–$10\frac{1}{2}$. Voted in 93 : 96 on Sir W. Wilmot.[14]—To prolong the debate I wd have spoken, not feeling satisfied of the state of the House: but had just been requested not to do it. After the div. I urged as strongly as I could the necessity of immediately rescinding—on Ellice, Rice, Goulburn, Ld Stanley.—Universal astonishment at the numbers.

---

[1] Walter Long, 1793–1871, cons. M.P. Wiltshire 1835–65.
[2] Probably a connexion of Sir Offley Penbury Wakeman, 1799–1868, s. of Sir Henry Wakeman, cr. bart. 1828, d. 1831, by his 2nd w. Sarah Offley of Hinton.
[3] Née Beesly; widow of James Lucas, Liverpool West India merchant; she d. 1849, when her 2nd s. James*, 1813–74, became 'the Hertfordshire hermit'.
[4] *H* xlii. 1421.
[5] H. Dunn, 'National Education, the Question of Questions; Being an Apology for the Bible in the Schools of the Nation', 2nd ed. (1838).
[6] Add MS 44819, ff. 39v–40.   [7] Presumably in MS.
[8] M. V. Cousins, *Rapport sur L'état de l'Instruction Publique en Prusse* (1833).
[9] Possibly to Charles Fleetwood, stockbroker, for Thomas Stanistreet of Clonmel, co. Tipperary.
[10] Registration of electors: *H* xliii. 75.
[11] Cp. next note.
[12] John Scoble of Newark, prominent opponent of slavery; cp. 7 May 38.
[13] National Society for the Education of the Poor. Cp. Robbins, 346–68.
[14] Against immediate end to negro apprenticeship: *H* xliii. 123.

23. W.

Wrote to Mrs Tallents. To Sir G. Grey mg, very strongly, for rescinding: and at night yet more strongly.

Peel's, meeting at 2–3$\frac{1}{2}$. Library Commee at 4. House 5–6.[1] rode. dined at Ld Salisbury's. Evg. party there. While in a discussion of the utmost anxiety about the vote of last night (many such today) my vision of joy crossed me, of human joy: O my God I recognise thy good hand in retribution, and yet I hope to feel that it has herein a sanctifying power, the daily sadness that is upon me in the midst of this painted life of inward trouble.

Geo. Mackenzie here: we advised him to move.

Busy reading Educational books to fulfil my Saturday engagement.— Theological conv. at Lady S.s with Teasdale[2] & Ld Exmouth.[3]—

24. Th. Ascension Day

Sent my letter to Sir G.G. after review with a strong P.S.—saw him at 3.— again in the House.—also Clerk,[4] Peel, Stanley, Irving,[5] & Ellice. Vide Mem. written this day.[6]

Church and Communion at 11.

read on Prussian Normal Schools.

House 5–6 and 8$\frac{1}{4}$–12$\frac{1}{4}$.[7]

25. Fr.

Wrote to Caparn—Mr Montagu—G. Mackenzie Nova Scotia Committee at 12: & S.P.G. Committee on until 3.—Thank God for the movement there, very cheering.

House 4$\frac{1}{2}$–5$\frac{3}{4}$ and 10–1. Voted in 250:272 on *Hawick*.[8]

finished Wilberforce Vol 2.—wrote on Schoolmasters.

Govt made their decl. about W.I.—too weak still.[9] Dined at Mr Sandersons.

26. Sat.

Wrote to Saunders (Sheffield) Read The Raphael Tapestries[10]—& (p. J.N.G) Hill on Education.[11] finished my long paper on Schoolmasters.[12]

[1] Lord's Day bill in cttee.: *H* xliii. 133.

[2] Thomas Walmsley Teasdale, b. 1801?; s. of priest at Coventry; at Lincoln College, Oxford; curate of Lackington, Wiltshire, *ca.* 1860.

[3] Edward Pellew, 1811–76; at Eton; Bengal civil service, 1829–39; 3rd Viscount Exmouth 1833.

[4] Sir George*.

[5] John Irving, d. 1853; cons. M.P. Bramber 1806–32, Antrim 1837–47; London merchant.

[6] Add MS 44777, ff. 54–9.

[7] Negro apprenticeship—he spoke briefly—and Hawick election. *H* xliii. 150; 175.

[8] He voted for disfranchising Hawick: *H* xliii. 345.

[9] Against doing anything to implement resolution hostile to apprenticeship carried on previous Tuesday: cp. H. of C. *Journals* 1837–8, 560–1.

[10] W. *Gunn, *The Raphael Tapestries in the Vatican* (1831).

[11] M. D. *Hill, *Public Education Plans for the Government and Liberal Instruction of Boys in Large Numbers* (1825).

[12] Add MS 44728, ff. 85–92.

Bp of London's Commee 2¾–4. Calls. rode.
read Von Waagen[1] & Cumming's 'Apology for the Church of Scotland'.[2]

27. Sunday.

Wrote to Dr Hook—Mr Wood.
read Newman on Just[ificatio]n.—Clericus Surriensis (p. J.N.G.).[3]
St James mg & aft.
At Carlton by summons resp[ectin]g tomorrows division.
Wrote a short paper for George [Hall].

28. M.

Wrote to Capt. Boldero.
Morning—Hill on Education & writing Notes for Sub Committees.
Getting up papers & House 4½–1¾. Waiting to speak after O'Connell:
Stanley came in then & it was too late. I only regret it on acct of the
personal matters, or rather *paternal*. Voted in 250:178 on Appr^p.[4]

29. T.

Wrote to Harrison—Lushington.
Hill on Educn—Notes for Sub Comms—B. & F. Manual.[5]
12–1¼ Sir T. Cochrane[6] & others here on Newfoundland.[7]
2–4½ Sub Committee B on boards.
House in evg.[8]

30. Wed.

Wrote to Hobhouse—G. Joy—Selwyn—Mr Cook.
read Areopagitica Secunda[9]—Sidney Smith's 2d letter[10]—& Hill on
Education.
dined at Sir H. Hardinge's. Ancient Music afr.
Library Commee 4–5¼. Rd. Cavendish here on his plans.

---

[1] H. E. Lloyd tr. G. F. Waagen, *Works of Art and Artists in England*, 3v. (1838).
[2] J. *Cumming, 'An Apology for the Church of Scotland; Or, an Explanation of its Character' (1837).
[3] Clericus Surriensis, i.e. J. Courtney, *An Earnest Protest against the Further Circulation of . . . Principles contained in the Pamphlet of . . . B. W. *Noel entitled 'The Unity of the Church'* (1837).
[4] Against immediate abolition of negro apprenticeship: *H* xliii. 430.
[5] *Manual of the System of Primary Instruction pursued in the Model Schools of the British and Foreign School Society* (1831).
[6] Sir Thomas John *Cochrane, 1789–1872, capt. R.N. (by nepotism) 1806, kt. 1812, admiral of the fleet 1865.
[7] Untraced business.
[8] Irish municipalities: *H* xliii. 434.
[9] 'Areopagitica Secunda: or Speech of the shade of John *Milton on Mr. Serjeant *Talfourd's Copyright Extension Bill' (1838).
[10] S. *Smith, 'Second Letter to Archdeacon *Singleton, being the Third of the Cathedral Letters' (1838).

31.¼Th.

Wrote to Thornton—Dr Hook—Farquhar.[1]
read Hill on Educⁿ (p. J.N.G.)—Byron's Parisina[2]—Benson's letter to the
Bp of Lincoln.[3]—Mr Pott here.[4]
House 3½–6½.[5] Dined at Sir T. Cochrane's. conv. with Sir J. Hobhouse.

Friday June One.

Read Hill on Education—Milnes Vol.2. B. Noel's Answer.[6]
Mr Miller here (Edn).
Vss. House 4–5¾.[7] Dined at Bp of Rochester's—Music after till 12.—

2. *Sat.*

Wrote to H. Thompson. Sir R. Inglis, Ld Stanley. Dr Hook. W. Selwyn.
read Milnes Vol 2—Hill on Education. Vss.
12½—4¼. N. Scotia Commee[8] Penitentiary & letters. rode. Dined at Abp
of Armagh's—music.
Monthly accts & letters.
Conv. with Bp of Winchʳ on the Dispensing power.

3. *Sunday.*

St James mg. aft.—Communion.
Walk & conv with Taylor 4¼–5¾. conv. on Edn & (most) on religion.
Read Newman—Chr. Wordsworth's Spital sermon[9] and Southey's book
of the Church.

4. *M.*

Eliza Robertson's funeral at ¼ to 12. The Cemetery: beautiful and soothing.
I am tempted to desire to follow, I ought to be happy here, having the
means to be useful: yet I live almost perpetually restless & depressed.
Active duty brings peace: what I have then to pray for is to be kept always
in it, and to be content, strictly, with my daily bread. Da oggi a noi la
cotidiana manna.[11] From the funeral to U.C.C. meeting. rode. Music in

---

[1] And on subjugating the will: Add MS 44728, f. 69.
[2] First published with *The Siege of Corinth* (1816).
[3] C. *Benson, 'On the Proceedings of the Ecclesiastical Commissioners. A Letter to
the Bishop of Lincoln' (1837).
[4] Joseph Holden *Pott, 1759–1847, vicar of St. Martin's 1812–24, and of Kensington
1824–42; archdeacon of St. Alban's 1789–1813, and of London 1813–42; canon of St.
Paul's 1822, and of Exeter 1826; also an author.
[5] Chaplains to the house: *H* xliii. 501.
[6] B. W. *Noel, 'A Defence of A Tract Entitled "The Unity of the Church": Being a
Letter to Clericus Surriensis in Answer to His Earnest Protest' (1837).
[7] Irish municipalities, cttee.: *H* xliii. 514.
[8] '&' here deleted. Cp. *PP* 1838 xxxix. 456.
[9] C. *Wordsworth, 'Heathen and Christian Philanthropy; Their Practical Results
Compared' (1838).
[10] Religious notes in Add MS 44728, ff. 104–5.
[11] 'Give us this day our daily bread.'

evg. at Mrs Greenes. Lady Jersey's afr—crossed the M[orton]s—& home frozen.[1]
read Milnes—Hill on Edn.—& began Beecham's 2d pamphlet on N. Zealand.[2]—Theol. conv. with Farquhar—copied a note for Mr G.

5.

Copied a note.—Vss.[3]—Church at 11—Hill on Edn (per J.N.G. & myself). Milnes. Beecham, rode, dined at Ld Kenyon's.[4] Mrs Wright's, Lady M. Wood's,[5] afr.
Wrote out a new Visiting Book.[6]

6.

Wrote to Tancred.
read Hill (p. J.N.G.)—Milnes—finished Vol 2—much beauty—Wakefield to Ld Glenelg[7]—finished Beecham.
dined at Mr B. Baring's—Lady Lansdowne's Concert.
conv with Stirling on Ch. &c.
House 5–7¼.[8] Comml. School meeting 3½–5.

7. Th.

Tancred here on Edn—2½–4 Subcommittee B.
read Sir T. Lawrence's Life.[9] W. Selwyn on Plurality Bill[10]—& the eloquent pamphlet on the Custody of Infants—evidently a woman's—probably Miss Norton's?[11]
Lady Galloway's[12] & Miss Mildmay's[13] in evg.
revising Vss.—House to the Ballot &c.[14]

8. Fr.

Wrote to P. Pusey—G. McKenzie.
read appx to Custody of Infants—Sir T. Lawrence—Milton—Edn Letters & papers.

[1] Cp. 23 May, 19 June 38.
[2] J. *Beecham, *Remarks Upon the Latest Official Documents Relating to New Zealand* (1838).
[3] In Add MS 44728, ff. 107–9; reflexion ibid. f. 106.
[4] George Kenyon, 1776–1855; 2nd Lord Kenyon 1802; m. 1803 Margaret Emma, d. 1815, who was *Hanmer's aunt.
[5] Lady Mary, née Grey, d. 1884, 5th da. of 2nd Earl *Grey; m. 1829 Charles *Wood, 1800–85, 3d bart. 1846, whig M.P. 1826–66, cr. Viscount Halifax 1866, privy seal 1870–4.
[6] Add MS 44810 B, 15 ff. And wrote on depression: Lathbury, ii. 433.
[7] E. G. *Wakefield, 'Mr. Coates and the New Zealand Association; in a Letter to Lord *Glenelg' (1837).   [8] Riot at Canterbury: *H* xliii. 543.
[9] D. E. Williams, *The Life and Correspondence of Sir T. *Lawrence* (1831).
[10] W. *Selwyn, *The Substance of an Argument . . . against those clauses of the Benefices Plurality Bill which confer additional powers on the Ecclesiastical Commissioners* (1838).
[11] C. E. S. *Norton, *The Separation of Mother and Child by the Law of 'Custody of Infants' Considered* (1838).
[12] Lady Harriet Blanche Somerset, 1811–85, 7th da. of 6th duke of Beaufort, m. 1833.
[13] Laetitia, 1803–44, da. of 3rd bart.; friend of Sydney *Smith.
[14] Misc. business: *H* xliii. 567.

Edn meeting 3½–5. House 5–9. Voted in 53:57 for limiting pluralities to contiguous parishes. Took some part on the Commn Clauses.[1]
Mrs Brownrigg's—Lady de Grey's.[2] Exquisitely furnished house.[3] Bp of N. Scotia here long on Church matters.

9. *Sat.*

Wrote to Selwyn—E. of Abn.—M. Rio.[4]
read Lawrence—Gauthey on Swiss Edn.[5]
Mr Rogers's 11–1. Edn Commee of Inquiry 2–4¼. Dined at Ld de Grey's.

10. *Sunday.*

St James mg & aft. Communion. Walk. Wrote on exemptions in N. Schools from Church & Catechisms. Read Newman—& Pusey's Article.

11. *M.*

Wrote to Caparn—Huddlestone[6]—Mr Wood (Ed.)—M. Rio here: interesting conv on Church &c. Then Mr Beecham—R.C. & Wesleyan in succession. After a conv. on N. Zealand, went to reunion. Spoke of unity & the perpetuity of the Church. He agreed: reordination the difficulty. Even this I said wd not prevent a prospective arrangement. I think he agreed.
Sutherland here on B.N.A. Church.
read Lawrence—Hill, finished (p. J.N.G.).
House 5 12¼. Lady Manvers's[7] Concert afr.
Voted in 288:285 for the £10 franchise.[8]
conv. with Acland on yesterdays MS.

12. *T.*

Wrote to W. Pusey.
Sir R. Peel on Scottish Church 12–1¾. Very curious.[9]
Subcomm. B. 2–3¾.
read the φβκ Oration[10]—Lawrence.
House.[11] rode. Dinner at home. Finished my N.S. paper on Exemptions.

[1] Benefices Plurality bill, report: *H* xliii. 597. Diarist not reported in *H* or *Mirror*.
[2] Lady Henrietta Frances Cole, 1784–1848, 5th da. of 1st earl of Enniskillen, m. 1805 Thomas Philip Weddell, 1781–1859; 3rd Lord Grantham 1786; changed surname from Robinson 1803, and to de *Grey 1833; 2nd Earl de Grey 1833; first lord of admiralty 1834–5; viceroy of Ireland 1841–4; K.G. 1844.   [3] At 4 St. James's Square.
[4] (Alexis) François Rio, 1797–1874, French catholic art historian, friend of Montalembert. Cp. M.C. Bowe, *François Rio* (1939), 151.
[5] L. F. F. Gauthey; perhaps an early draft of his *De l'école normale au canton de Vaud* (1839).
[6] Perhaps William Hudleston, 1826–94, in Madras civil service 1845–82.
[7] Mary Letitia Eyre, 1784–1860, m. 1804 Charles Herbert Pierrepont, 1778–1860, who served under *Nelson, 1798; whig M.P. Nottinghamshire 1801–16; styled Viscount Newark 1806; 2nd Earl Manvers 1816.
[8] Irish municipalities, cttee.: *H* xliii. 561, gives division figures as 286:266.
[9] Notes in Add MS 44819, f. 40.
[10] Phi Beta Kappa, the oldest American college fraternity; founded 1776, reorganized 1826. Oration in 1837 by R. W. Emerson on 'The American Scholar': cp. *Correspondence of *Carlyle and Emerson* (1883), i. 217–18.
[11] Breach of privilege: *H* xliii. 670.

13. W.

Wrote to Mr Nihill. Col Rowan[1]—Ld Duncannon—Selwyn—A. Cross (Glasgow).
Revised paper on Exemptions. Wrote Pol. Mema.[2]
read Lawrence—Guizot's interesting tract on L'Université Catholique.[3]
Rio here again: long conv. & read Dante.
Mr Dalton on Cath[edra]l petition.[4]
dined at Mr Dugdale's[5] Mrs Smith's Concert aft.—

14. Th.

Rio here. A Deputy in France said "il faut que la loi soit athée!" (It was Odillon Barrot, in a pleading) Lawrence. Report of Legisl. Council of U.C. (p. J.N.G.)[6]—M. Angelo—hard but beautiful.[7]
Comml School meeting $2\frac{1}{2}$–$3\frac{3}{4}$. House $5\frac{1}{2}$–$11\frac{3}{4}$ waiting for the 5th Edition of Apprenticeship. Voted in 74–70 agt Edn Commission.[8]

15. Fr.

Wrote to W. Selwyn—Geo. Mackenzie. Mr Rogers—Finished U. Canada Report—read Lawrence—papers on Patronage.
Dined at Lord Galloway's. House before dinner & 10 $\frac{3}{4}$–2—speaking on Sugar Duties[9]—S.P.G. meeting 1–$2\frac{1}{2}$—Sir R. Peel on Irish Corpp. at 11.

16. Sat.

Read Lawrence.
Mm. Rio & Carnet[10] here $10\frac{1}{2}$–$12\frac{1}{2}$. Conv. on rel. pol. & rel.
Edn Inquiry Comm. & Penity 2–$4\frac{1}{2}$. At Wr Abbey. Wrote P.S. on Catm question.[11] Dined at Mr [sc. Ld] Mansfield's.

17. Sunday.

Commn. 8. Ch. 11 & 3. Mr Ward & Bp. read James's Unitn Sermon.[12] (Bridgwater)

---

[1] (Sir) William *Rowan, 1789–1879; fought in Peninsula and at Waterloo; colonel 1837; civil and military secretary in Canada 1823–9; commanded forces there 1849–55; G.C.B. 1856; general 1862; field-marshal 1877.
[2] Add MS 44819, f. 40v.
[3] *Revue française*, v. 5 (1838), unsigned editorial.
[4] Untraced: Charles Browne Dalton, priest?
[5] William Stratford Dugdale, 1801–71; cons. M.P. Shaftesbury 1830, Bramber 1831, Warwickshire 1832–47; m. 1827 Harriet Ella, née Portman, 3d sister of 1st viscount*. Note on *Peel's conversation after dinner in Add MS 44819, ff. 40v–41.
[6] Perhaps *PP* 1837 xlii. 5.
[7] M. A. Buonarrotti, *Rime* (many eds).
[8] *H* xliii. 738.
[9] A short intervention; not in *H. Mirror*, vi. 4825.
[10] Louis Joseph Marie de Carné, 1804–76; comte de Carné Marcein; Breton diplomat, deputy, and liberal catholic journalist; retired from politics 1848.
[11] Untraced.
[12] W. James, 'The Leading Doctrines of Unitarian Christianity' (Bridgewater, 1837).

p. 8. 'It was after much reading & I hope diligent inquiry, *with prayer for divine assistance*, that I saw reason to change my views':[1] p. 32 acct of Unitarian deathbeds.[2]
read N[ational] S[ociety] draft report—Newman—Maurice. wrote.[3]

18. M.

Wrote to Nicholls (Surveyor)[4] Lecky[5]—Mrs Smith—Spedding. Rio here. 2 h. with Dr Hook & Acland on Edn. read Lawrence—(began) Rio's 'L'Art Chretien'[6]—House[7]—calls.[8]

19. T.

wrote to Lushington—Caparn. Edn Comm. 1½–3.[9] read Rio—finished Pusey on the Commissions.
Rio dined here. Dss of Buccleuch's[10] aftn—Ld Morton shook hands cordially—le nozze stan fisse: sian felici.[11] Col. Wood's[12]—Mrs G. Knight's[13] concert.

20 W.

Conv. with Rio again.
read Rio—Lawrence—Warburton.
House 5–10. Spoke agt New Zealand Bill. Voted in 92 : 32; & by concert, suggested postponement of Copyright Bill.[14]
Lady Cork's & Duchess of Buccleuch's concert,

21 Th.

Wrote to Ld Morton.[15]

[1] Ibid. 8: diarist's italics.   [2] Ibid. 32.
[3] On Christ, and morals: Add MS 44728, ff. 110–11.
[4] Thomas Nicholls of Holborn.
[5] John Hartpole Lecky, 1805?–52, Dublin gentleman; m. 1837 Mary Anne, d. 1839, da. of W. E. Tallents; their s., William Edward Hartpole*, 1838–1903, the historian, was b. 26 March.
[6] (1836; 2nd vol. 1841.)   [7] Misc. business: *H* xliii. 785.
[8] And note on 1688, Add MS 44728, f. 112.
[9] Draft in Add MS 44356, ff. 84–87, of protest to secretary, Robert Wilfred Skeffington Lutwidge, 1802–73, barrister, secretary to lunacy commission 1845.
[10] Charlotte Anne, née Thynne, 3rd da. of 2nd marquess of Bath, m. 1829 Walter Francis Montagu-Douglas-*Scott, 1806–84, 5th duke of Buccleuch 1819, lord privy seal 1842–6, lord president 1846. She was converted to Rome, 1860.
[11] 'The marriage is arranged: may they be happy'—i.e. Lady F. Douglas and Lord Milton. William Thomas Spencer Wentworth-Fitzwilliam, 1815–1902, Eton and Trinity Cambridge; styled viscount Milton 1835; m. 10 Sept. 38; lib. M.P. Malton, 1837–41, 1846–7, co. Wicklow 1847–57; succ. as earl Fitzwilliam 1857; lib. unionist.
[12] C. A. Wood's f. Thomas, 1777–1860, cons. M.P. Breconshire 1806–47, east India proprietor; lived in Richmond Terrace, Whitehall. Cp. 25 June 38.
[13] Henrietta, née Eyre, m. H. Gally *Knight 1828; lived in Grosvenor Street.
[14] N.Z. bill defeated 2°: *H* xliii. 873; division 882.
[15] To congratulate; see Magnus, 32. And note on self-distrust, Add MS 44728, f. 113; and to *Wordsworth, Add MS 44356, f. 88, copy.

read Quarterly on Art (Ld F.E's)—& part of Allies's Essay.[1]
dined with T.G.—Music at Mrs Greene's, practising—Bp of N.S. here—
U.C.C. meeting at 1—Edn (N.S.) at 2.
House before dinner & 10¾–1. Voted in 200:184 on Vixen.[2]

22. Fr.

Wrote to Mr Backhouse.
read Quarterly on Wilberforce—Buchanan's speech (p. J.N.G.).[3]
Sir R. Peel's on Corpns at 12[4]—S.P.G. meeting 1½–3. House 5½–6¼.[5]
dined at Dss of B's to meet Dr Hook. Lady Buller's afr & conv. with
F. Rogers on Church.

23 Sat.

Wrote to Freshfield's—Ld Duncannon—F. Fraser—Mr Heming—Lady
Coutts Trotter.[6]
Schools meeting at 12.—House at 1—Spelling "Bella immago" alone.[7]
A kind note from Ld Morton. So ends this to me saddening episode. It is
of the good counsel of God.
finished Allies—read Rogers—& the Prussian exposé.[8]
dined at abp. of York's.

24 Sunday.

St James mg & aft.
Wrote on Private Judgment.[9]
read Coronation Service—noble. Abercrombie's Harmony[10]—the Exposé—
& (p. J.N.G.) Hope on S.P.G.

25 M.

A. Wood's marriage[11] at 11 & breakf. afr.
Hope here on S.P.G.—Sir T. Cochrane on Newfoundland.
read Lawrence—Exposé—Spelling "bella immago". Warburton's Alliance.
rode. dined at Ld Manvers's. House 4¼–5½ & 10½–12½.[12]

26 T.

wrote to Wilmot.

---

[1] T. W. *Allies, On the Influence of Practical Piety on the Temporal and Eternal Interests of Mankind (1838).
[2] Against inquiry into seizure of this ship in Black Sea in 1836: H xliii. 959.
[3] He also wrote, but did not send, a letter to Buchanan: Add MS 44356, ff. 89–92.
[4] Note in Add MS 44819, f. 41.
[5] *Ashley's Factories Regulation bill: H xliii. 968.
[6] Cp. 3 Jan. 33.			[7] Untraced.
[8] Cp. 20 May 38.			[9] Add MS 44728, f. 114.
[10] J. *Abercrombie, The Harmony of Christian Faith and Christian Character (1835).
[11] To Sophia, d. 1906, da. of J. S. Brownrigg.
[12] Irish municipalities, 3° and passed: H xliii. 1044.

read Lawrence—Warburton—Smith on National Rel.[1] p. J.N.G.
rode. dined at Uncle D.s—Ld Abingers. House $3\frac{3}{4}$–$5\frac{1}{4}$, and 10–11.20.[2]
much anxiety & conv. about H.J.G.[3]

27. W.

Wrote to Selwyn.
My Father put off his purpose.[4]—Visited the Lincolns at Kew. House at $5\frac{1}{4}$.[5]
read Lawrence—Wilkins's Letter to Plumptre[6]—Exposé—Warburton.

28 Th.

Helen's birthday: and a gloomy one.
At 9 to the House & Abbey.[7] Left it after all had ended at $4\frac{1}{2}$: to Carlton
to see the procession. In evg to Bath House (to see fireworks) & the Duke's.
Home at $1\frac{1}{2}$.
The service is noble. The sight magnificent. Chanting greatly wanted.
Details should be either many or none.
read Lawrence.

29 Fr.

Conv. on H.J.G. again.—Church at 11.
read Lawrence—Hope's letter as printed.
SubComm B 2–$3\frac{1}{2}$. Mrs Greene's (singing) to $5\frac{3}{4}$. Dined at the Kerrisons.
Abp York's (music) & Lady Lansdowne's afr. Home at 1.

30. Sat.

Wrote to Grove Price[8]—Rev. R. Simpson—Macarthur. finished Lawrence.
Reading Coolie Bill.[9] Rogers.
12–$6\frac{1}{4}$ House[10]—N. School Commce—& O. & C.C. Commee. dined at Lady
Lucy Pusey's. With H.J.G. rode. One half the year has fled: more swift,
more shadowy, & yet more laden with pain, than its predecessors. But
Pain is not the great parent of regret.

Sunday July 1.

St James's mg & aft –Communion.
read Jewel[11]—& Abercrombie's Harmony (finished)—eyes indifferent.
Wrote.[12]

[1] J. P. *Smith, 'The Necessity of Religion to the Wellbeing of a Nation' (1834).
[2] Row about cttee. on Canterbury riot: *H* xliii. 1089.
[3] And note on Roman church, Add MS 44728, f. 115.
[4] Of being stern to Helen: cp. 21 July, 5 Aug. 38.
[5] Row appeased: *H* xliii. 1145.
[6] G. *Wilkins, 'A Letter Addressed to the Rev. H. W. Plumptre . . . on . . . his
Projected Church at Nottingham' (1838).
[7] For *Victoria's coronation. Cp. D. Hudson, *Martin *Tupper*, (1949), 25.
[8] Unidentified.
[9] Cp. *PP* 1838 lii. 1.   [10] Vestries: *H* xliii. 1154.
[11] J. *Jewel, *Apologia pro Ecclesia Anglicana* (1562). Cp. 7 Oct. 38.
[12] On religion: Add MS 44728, ff. 116–18.

2 M.

Wrote to Dry—Hamilton—Robn (bis)—Robt G.—Sir T. Cochrane.
read Warburton—Rogers—Hume on Drawback.[1]
Church Buildg Soc. 12–2¾. House 4½–8¼ & 9½–2. Voted in 188:167 agt 30 p.c.—& for 25, wh is shabby, I fear.[2]

3 T.

Wrote to Mr Ryder—Board of Excise—on Ch. & St.—Mr Sheppard.
read Rogers—Smith.
N[ational] S[ociety] Inq. Comm. 2–4¼. Lady Salisbury's in evg.

4 W.

Wrote on Ch. & St.[3]
read Chalmers's Lectures—Warburton—Smith—De Foe's Plague.[4]
House 4–5¾.[5] rode. dined at Sir W. Farquhar's. Sir W.W. Wynn's afr.

5. Th.

Wrote on Ch. & State.[6]
read Slaney's Educn Report.[7]
Saw Mr Atherstone[8] on Cape—De Foe.
Edn Comm. & conv. & O. & C. Club Comm. 2–5¾.
Dinner at home.

6 Fr.

Wrote on Ch. & St. My thoughts are all stray and ungovernable.
read Warburton—De Foe.
King's Coll. Council at 2½—Dss of Buccleuch's breakfast—House before dinner, & 3½–9½.[9]

7. Sat.

Wrote to Huddlestone—Mr Ramsay—Ld Duncannon—Mr Rawlins (Cape).[10]
Wrote on Ch. & State.
read Smith—De Foe (p. J.N.G.)—Warburton[11]—&c.
House & Edn Comm. 2¼–4¾.[12] Lady Parke's in evg.

[1] J. D. Hume, *Laws of the Customs* (1825).
[2] Irish tithes: size of rent charge. *H* xliii. 1177.
[3] And note in Add MS 44728, f. 119.
[4] Daniel *Defoe, *Journal of the Plague Year* (1722).
[5] Lord's Day bill in trouble in cttee.: *H* xliii. 1243.
[6] Note on bps., Add MS 44728, f. 119.
[7] Report on Education of the Poorer Classes in England and Wales: *PP* 1838 vii. 157.
[8] William Guyton Atherstone of Albany, Cape Province; surgeon; cp. *PP* 1837 vii. 114–16.
[9] Supply: *H* xliii. 1306.   [10] Unidentified.
[11] *Alliance*: notes in Add MS 44728, ff. 120–7.
[12] Scottish prisons: *H* xliii. 1315.

8. Sunday.

St James mg & aft.
Wrote hard on Church & State. My materials very unruly.
read Hooker B.VIII—& Smith.

9. M.

Wrote to Nagle.[1]
Again a long morng at Church & State—with ref.s to Hume, Hallam, &c.
read Smith: and finished Warburton's Postscript.[2]
rode. House $4\frac{1}{4}$–$5\frac{1}{2}$ and 9–$1\frac{1}{4}$.[3]

10 T.

Getting up the Cape case. Edn Commee $12\frac{1}{2}$–4. Duchess of Buccleuch's
$4\frac{1}{2}$–$5\frac{3}{4}$ and 7–7.50. House, speech on Cape, & Divn, in the interim.[4]
read Cape papers & Smith.
Lady Willoughby's[5] in evg.
Church and State.

11 W.

Wrote to Nihill—Col. Rowan—Lady C. Wood—Manning—Caparn.
Church and State.
read Hooker—Smith—Rogers's Poems. N.S. Comm. & House $2\frac{1}{4}$–6. &
House at 9.[6]—Music practice at Mrs Greene's.

12 Th.

Wrote to Talfourd[7]—Mrs Wishlade—Lady C. Wood—read Smith—De
Foe's Plague (p. JNG).
dined at Mr[8] Greene's—music. Lady F. Egerton's—Church conv. with
Lady Shelley.[9]
wrote on Church and State.
Educn Commee $1\frac{1}{2}$–4. & House.[10]

13 Fr.

Wrote to Sir F. Doyle—F. Doyle—Sir G. Grey. Church and State—read

---

[1] Perhaps William Cumming Nagle, 1810?–98; at Caius, Cambridge, 1834–9; chaplain in Madras 1842–63.
[2] Notes in Add MS 44728, ff. 120–7.
[3] Supply: *H* xliv. 42.
[4] His motion of an inquiry into relations with natives in South Africa was beaten, 32–41; *H* xliv. 114, 117.
[5] Margaret, née Williams, 1800?–80; 3rd da. of 1st bart.; m. 1829 Henry Peyto Verney, 1773–1852, 16th Lord Willoughby de Broke 1820, a strong tory.
[6] Misc. business: *H* xliv. 134.
[7] Cp. Add MS 44356, f. 97.
[8] Instead of 'Mrs'.
[9] Frances, née Winckley, m. Sir John Shelley, 6th bart., distant cousin of poet, 1806, and d. 1873.
[10] Coal: *H* xliv. 170.

Hooker and finished Smith's letters. House 1–4½.[1] Rode. dined at Dr Dss of Beaufort's. John's deeply interesting disclosure, on coming home: & conv. thereupon.[2] May God prosper it.

14. Sat.

Wrote to D. Morley (Nk)[3]—[a] Little on Ch. & St. Conv. on last night's news.
read Hooker—De Foe (p. J.N.G.).
H. of C—N.S. Comm—& Lady Shelley's music. Dined at Cannings.

15. Sunday.

Communion 8. 11 & 3.
Wrote & refd on Ch. & State—read Hooker.

16. M.

Wrote on Ch. & St. conv. with J. Hope thereon—he agrees to read the MS.
read Hooker (finished B.VIII)—Paley's 10th Chapter—Tupper's Ode[4]—Hook's Sermon—Rio.
House 5–6 and 9–10.[5] Mrs Gurney's in evg.

17. T.

Wrote to R.G.—Mr Ryder[6]—Sir R. Peel,[7] Sir T. Cochrane, Mr Nisbet.[8]
Revising parts of Ch & St.—Harrison here. Wrote on Ch & St.
read Rio. Rogers. rode.
House 3¾–6 and 10–11¾.[9]

18. W.

Wrote to Bp of Salisbury—Jas. Hope.[10]
Revising Ch & St. & writing—my eyes are tried.
Further conv in J.N.G's matter. Saw Mr Codner.[11]
read Rogers—Rio.
House 4¼–6 and 8¾–9½.[12] Singing at Mrs Greene's afr.

[1] Prisons bill in cttee.; he made one remark. *H* xliv. 191.
[2] His engagement to Elizabeth Honoria Bateson, d. 1862, 2nd da. of 1st bart.; they m. 7 Feb. 39.
[3] Daniel Morley, Newark grocer.
[4] M. F. *Tupper, *Coronation Ode* (1838).
[5] Irish tithes; prisons: *H* xliv. 229. Cp. 11 Sept. 38.
[6] Clergyman at Rathcormac, co. Cork; on Irish tithe.
[7] Also on Irish tithes: in Add MS 40425, ff. 230–2. Cp. Add MS 44819, f. 41v.
[8] James Nisbet, 1785–1854, bookseller, publisher, and educationist.
[9] Registration of electors: *H* xliv. 288.
[10] In Ornsby, i. 148.
[11] Unidentified.
[12] Parochial assessments: *H* xliv. 302. Conversation with speaker on importance of excluding popular influence noted in Add MS 44819, f. 42.

19. Th.

read De Foe—and "Consensus Omnium".[1] 11½–2. Private meeting at the Primate's on the Tithe.
House 4¼–7½ (ride between) & 9–11½.[2]
Copied my verses on T.G.s infant.[3]

20 Fr.

Wrote on Ch & St. & 1½ hour at Colonial Office consulting the Blue books on do. Also conv. with Bp of N. Scotia.
12–2 Private meeting at Sir R. Peel's on the Tithe.
House at 5. Paired to the Wimbledon breakfast, very beautiful[4]—House 9.40–12¼. Voted in 106:121 with Ashley.[5]
Conv. with J.N.G.—He is cruelly placed.

21. Sat.

Wrote to Lady F. Egerton—M'Kenzie—J.R. Hope.[6] Mr G. returned— c'est merveilleux comme il tranche les choses.[7]
Read De Foe (finished)—Thurlow's Sermons on 1 Tim. III 15.[8]
At C.O. Writing on Ch. & St.—reviewing &c. House 2½–4¼.[9] Lady Shelley's music. Conv with Lynch[10] on the Church.

22. S.

St James mg & aft.
read Leslie (Short method with Rom)[11] Newman, & D'Aubigne[12] p. J.N.G.

23. M.

Wrote to Abp Canterbury (& draft)[13] Bp of Exeter—Rn. G. Doran.[14] At C.O.—finished my Church & State.
Breakf with Mr Rogers 10–12¾. Lady Brabn[15] & the Miss Glynnes[16] our Ladies.

[1] [A Member of Oxford Convocation], 'Concensus Omnium; or the Test of Orthodoxy' (1838). [2] Irish tithes: H xliv. 324.
[3] Cp. 12 July 36. [4] Perhaps at *Lyndhurst's.
[5] *Ashley sought to improve laws on child labour in factories: H xliv. 443.
[6] Forwarding MS; see Ornsby, i. 149. [7] 'He is splendidly decisive'.
[8] C. A. Thurlow, 'The Church Established as the Guardian and Witness of the Truth' (1837). [9] Railway mails; prisons. H xliv. 447.
[10] Andrew Henry Lynch, barrister; lib. M.P. Galway 1832–41; master in chancery 1838.
[11] C. *Leslie, A Short Method with the Romanists (1835); in substance a reprint of The Case Stated between the Church of Rome and the Church of England (1713).
[12] Perhaps J. H. M. d'Aubigné, Histoire de la Réformation, 5 v. (1835–53).
[13] About non-Anglican prison chaplains: Add MS 44356, f. 102.
[14] Probably John *Doran, 1807–78, author; ed. Church and State Gazette 1841–52.
[15] Harriot, 2nd da. of Sir Richard Brooke, 6th bart.; 1811–98; m. 1837 William Brabazon, 1803–87, styled Lord Brabazon 1826, whig M.P. co. Dublin 1830–32, 1837–41, 11th earl of Meath 1851.
[16] Her cousins-in-law, Catherine, 1812–1900, and Mary, 1813–57, das. of Sir Stephen *Glynne, 8th bart. Cp. 25 July 39 for their double wedding, to the diarist and to George William *Lyttelton, 1817–76, scholar, 4th Lord Lyttelton 1837.

House $4\frac{1}{2}$–$6\frac{1}{2}$ and 8–11. Opposed Langdale's (R.C. Gaol Chaplains) Clause in 31: 131. How few care for a *naked* principle.[1]

Conv with Pusey. I told him for himself only—I thought my own Church & State principles within one stage of becoming hopeless as regards success in this generation.[2]

24. T.

Wrote to Jas. Jephson[3]—Caparn—Lewis—Mr Ryder. read Rio. Hallam & Lingard reff. Pt of Pusey's Plato—breakf. at Mr Roger's 10–1. Mrs Greene's, Music, at 3. Mr Atherstone's pictures $4\frac{3}{4}$–$5\frac{1}{2}$—House to $6\frac{1}{4}$ and 9–$12\frac{1}{2}$.[4]

25. W.

Wrote to T.G. (on his birthday)—Abp York—Pierre Bert[5]—read L. Da Vinci[6] & Mr Strahan's pamphlet[7].

Tithe meeting, the Primates $1\frac{1}{4}$–$3\frac{3}{4}$. Wrote mema.[8]

House $5\frac{1}{2}$–$6\frac{1}{2}$.[9] Dined at Lambeth Palace.

Copied Mr G.s letter on his property &c.

Saw Farquhar on E.I. idolatry—Bp Exeter on Prisons.—

26 Th.

Wrote to Bp of London—Hope.[10]

read Rio—Lingard. Howick's MS.

House $3\frac{3}{4}$–$6\frac{1}{4}$.[11] At home in evg on H.J.G.s case—seeing Locock & wrote Mema. for Mr G.

Interpolations for my Ch & St.

27. Fr

Wrote to Abp of York, Mr Saintsbury,[12] S. Wilberforce A formidable day of corrections & transpositions on my No II returned from Hope. Too deep in it to stop. Hope with me on it. He is of very great service.

Saw M. Jolivet[13] on W.I. question. Another conv with Lord Howick.

Dined in B. Square. House $9\frac{3}{4}$–$12\frac{1}{2}$.[14]

---

[1] In cttee. stage of Prisons Bill, which passed: *H* xliv. 493. Charles Stourton, 1787–1868, 3rd s. of 16th Lord Stourton; changed name to *Langdale, 1815; whig M.P. Beverley, 1832–5, and Knaresborough, 1837–41.

[2] Version of last sentence in Morley, i. 179.

[3] (Sir) James Saumarez Jephson, 1802–84, sec. to Carlton Club; 3rd bart. 1870.

[4] Post Office &c: *H* xliv. 582.

[5] No doubt to thank for Bert's edition, with dialect translation, of the gospels of Luke and John (1838); cp. 6–7 Mar. 32.

[6] L. da Vinci, *Trattata della Pittura* (many ed.).

[7] Untraced.   [8] Add MS 44819, f. 42.

[9] Naval officers supply: *H* xliv. 591.

[10] In Ornsby, i. 151.

[11] Indian idolatry; Irish tithes. *H* xliv. 646; 648.

[12] George Saintsbury of Trafalgar Square.

[13] Thomas-Marie Adolphe Jollivet, 1799–1848, Breton lawyer and deputy, strong opponent of negro emancipation.

[14] Supply: *H* xliv. 727.

28. Sat.

Wrote to Rio[1]—Mr Miles, Hatchard,[2] saw Mr Strahan. Working at Church & State. read Palmer Part V.
House 2–3¾.[3] Penitentiary, rode, dined at Ld Sandon's.

29. S.

St James mg & aft. called on Lady Shelley, about "Consensus Omnium". read Palmer. Wrought at Ch & S. (Private judgment) No V. read a little of Babbage.[4]

30. M.

Wrote to Hope.[5] Bp of London. Sir R. Peel. Rio. Mr Ryder—O.B. Cole[6]— Murray (Alb[emarle] St.).[7]
Breakf. (at 11½) at Lady Cork's. Paying bills. Saw Hatchard. read Palmer, & part of Gourier.[8]
House 4¼–6¼ and 8–10½—speaking on "Oxford Popery" &c.[9]

31. T.

Wrote to Pusey—Hope—Colquhoun. A. Williams. Hope (Ed). Monthly accts.
read Palmer—Burn's Eccl. Law (for Ch. & St.).[10]
N.S. Inq. Commee 2½–4½. House 4½–6¼.[11] Dined at Sir R. Inglis's. 10¼ P.M.– 1¾ revising No V.

Wednesday August One.

Putting away & preparing for journey. Saw (Young) Murray[12] about my book. Dined at Mr Roger's—Lady Cork's afr.—shopping.
wrote to Glynne—Mr Bradley.
read Rogers—Ph. Pusey's Article (finished)—Maurice on Ch. & St.

2. Th.

Wrote to Murray & sent him I. II. and V.
read Maurice.

[1] In Bowe, *Rio*, 155 n.; answering his of 26 July, Add MS 44356, ff. 103–4.
[2] John Hatchard, 1769–1849, Piccadilly bookseller and publisher, ed. *Christian Observer* 1802–45.
[3] China courts: *H* xliv. 744.
[4] No doubt one of the many works of Charles *Babbage, 1792–1871; mathematician and scientific mechanician.
[5] Extracts in Ornsby, i. 155.
[6] About *Tupper's *Coronation Ode*; extract in Hudson, *Tupper*, 25.
[7] John *Murray, 1778–1843, head of the publishing house.
[8] F. B. Gourrier, 'Letter to the Lord Bishop of London on the State of Religion in France' (1836).
[9] Irish education estimates: *H* xliv. 817, 818.
[10] R. *Burn, *Ecclesiastical Law*, 2v. (1763, 1765).
[11] Misc. business: *H* xliv. 843.
[12] John*, 1808–92; eldest s. of John *Murray; succ. as head of publishing house. Cp. Add MSS 44259–60.

conv. with Hope, Pusey, Acland, on my book.[1] With Macarthy on the Church. 2–3¾ sat to Miss Combe. House 5½–6½. and 9–12½.[2] Conv. with Kinnaird on our plans.[3]

3 Fr.

Wrote to H. Taylor—A. Williams—Ld Sandon—&c.
read Maurice—London & Wr on Milnes.[4]—House before & afr dinner[5]
Scotch Edn Commee 12½–1½.[6]
Again hard & late at work upon my MS.

4. Sat.

Wrote to A. Pakenham—Glynne—Pusey.
Rewrote one half of No. III. (Ch & St).
Edn Commee at 3—read Maurice—Reformatio Legum.[7]
dined at Ld Calthorpe's.[8] Correcting &c. again afr.

5. Sunday.

At 9¾ went with dear Helen to Whitehall Stairs, then with the carriage to the Batavier & assisted her.[9] Back just in time to find one door open—the last—at St James's for the Communion. I was the more anxious not to fail of that divine aliment, because I was now to have less frequent access to it for a time.—Ch in afternoon. read Maurice (No.X.) & two of Hare's Sermons.[10] Revising No III. &c. Saw Pusey.

6. M.

Wrote to T.G.—S P C K (for Mr G.) Mr Boulton—Ld Abn.
Correcting Ch & St. Nos VI, & VIII.
House 5–7½ on Pluralities Bill.[11]
Saw Mr Boulton (of Newfoundland) twice.
read Rio—Seeley's Essays[12]—Lanzi on Painting[13]—

[1] Discussing its publishability: cp. letter from P. Pusey in Add MS 44356, ff. 112–13. He also wrote a note on oaths, Add MS 44728, f. 128.
[2] Irish municipalities: *H* xliv. 871.
[3] Cp. 6 Sep. 38.
[4] *London and Westminster Review*, xxix. 308 (August 1838).
[5] Irish municipalities and pensions. *H* xliv. 986, 997.
[6] Cp. *PP* 1838 vii. 437.
[7] *Reformatio Legum Ecclesiasticarum* (1572), edited by *Fox; a code of ecclesiastical law drawn up in 1552 by commissioners headed by *Cranmer; never ratified by parliament.
[8] George Gough-Calthorpe, 1787–1851, 3rd Lord Calthorpe 1807; owned much of Edgbaston and of Clerkenwell; bachelor, lived in Grosvenor Square.
[9] She was going to Ems; cp. 16 Aug.–9 Sept. 38.
[10] A. W. *Hare, *Sermons to A Country Congregation*, 2 v. (1836).
[11] *H* xliv. 1015.
[12] R. B. *Seeley, *Essays on the Church* (1834).
[13] L. A. Lanzi, *History of Painting in Italy*, 6 v. (tr., 1828).

7. T.

Wrote to R. Williams—A. Williams (Oxf.)—M. Rio.[1]—Ld Skelmersdale.[2] Bp Barbadoes—J. Wilson—J. Stuart[3]—W.H. Burnley,[4] J. Reddie. Murray (with rem[ainin]g MSS.)—arranging books &c—bills—Commees 1–3½. read Rogers (finished)—Seeley. Kinnaird, Seymer, Hope, dined here.

8. W.

Wrote to Messrs Brooks, Campbell, Lawrence, Jones, Horsfall, Rn. G., Wood (Ed.), on Natl Educn. To Mr Ramsay, Manning, Glynne, Mahon. read Brydone,[5] Maurice (finished). calls. packing. Mr Severn dined here. Mr Rogers's in evg. Conv. with Doyle & Ph. Pusey.

9. Th.

Wrote to W. Selwyn. G. Selwyn—Simpson—Bussell. Warden of Manchr— Parkinson—Campbell (Eye)—on Edn.—And to Caparn—Huddlestone— Mad. Rio[6]—Hamilton—A. Williams—Luxmoore—Sheppard—Lutwidge– J.C. Colquhoun—Mr Kinnear. read Brydone Vol I & began 2. also read India Despatch of Feb. 33. Dined in B.S.

10. Fr.

Wrote to Bp of Barbadoes[8]—Mr Reddie—Lutwidge. Manning—T.G.— Murray—A. Robertson—Mr Rogers—V. Nolte. Finished Brydone. House 4¼–6.[9] Alarm of detention on Canada business at night. Settled in the Lords.[10] Got my release.[11] Packing & putting away. Read Seeley.

[1] In reply to his of 3 August, in Add MS 44356, ff. 114–15.
[2] Edward Boothe-Wilbraham, 1771–1853, Eton and Christ Church; Lancashire magnate; tory M.P. 1795–1828; cr. Lord Skelmersdale 1828; f. of R. B.-W.
[3] Demerara attorney.
[4] William F. Burnley was a Glasgow merchant.
[5] P. *Brydone, *A Tour Through Sicily and Malta*, 2v. (1773).
[6] Apollonia, née Jones, of Llanarth, Welsh catholic heiress; m. 1834.
[7] Cp. *Annual Register* 1833, 21–24.
[8] Cp. 24 Oct. 39.
[9] Trade with French Africa: *H* xliv. 1152.
[10] Ibid. 1146.
[11] I.e. a pair. The house rose on 16 August (ibid. 1321).

Saturday. Aug. 11.

Left Carlton Gardens at 6; the Tower, in the Giraffe,[2] at 7¼. 24½ hours passage to Rotterdam. Swell and much rolling in the channel. Most persons sick: I am usually in the van on these occasions.

The trade of London does not present by any means so imposing an aspect as that of Liverpool: but everyone must be struck by the manner in which space is economised even to inches on both sides of the river. The width of the Thames from Greenwich downwards, for a mere island river, is certainly respectable.

Read Jolivet's pamphlets on the French Emancipation[3]—'The permanent laws of the Emancipated Colonies'[4]—and Head's Letters to Brougham.[5]

12. Sunday.

Rotterdam. Pays Bas. Good.

English Church at 11 and 6. The clergyman[6] is a man of ability; scarcely well seconded by his manner.

Met Mackenzie (Portmore)[7] & Mr. Forbes.

At the Cathedral. The organ is fine. The pavement almost a puddle of saliva. The people,[8] or many of them, wear their hats during the sermon. The mass of voice very powerful.

The statue of Erasmus also appears a fine work. It is near the Cathedral.

The intermixture of houses, canals, ships, bridges, and trees, at almost every turn, has a singular and picturesque effect. The people are remarkably clean and well-dressed, and one looks in vain for signs of destitution.

Read Rio's Savonarola.[9] Saw Sir A. Ferrier.[10] Note to Murray.[11]

13 Monday.

Read Rio. Schreiber.[12]

[1] Entries from Add MS 44818 B till 12 Oct. 38, unless otherwise noted.

[2] Of the General Steam Navigation company; vessels ran from the Tower every Wednesday and Saturday.

[3] Pamphlets untraced; cp. 27 July 38.

[4] (1838.)

[5] F. B. *Head, 'Three Letters to Lord *Brougham on the Execution . . . Of Lount and Matthews' (1838).

[6] Joseph *Bosworth, 1789–1876, priest 1815; at St. Mary's, Rotterdam, 1832–40; professor of Anglo-Saxon at Oxford, 1858.

[7] William Forbes *Mackenzie, Tory M.P. Peebleshire 1837–52; elected for Liverpool 1852, unseated next year.

[8] 'even' deleted.

[9] Ch. VIII in F. Rio, De la Poésie chrétienne (1836).

[10] Sir Alexander Ferrier, K.H. 1834, kt. 1835, consul at Rotterdam.

[11] John *Murray was publishing *Gladstone's The State in its Relations with the Church (December 1838).

[12] A. Schreiber, Traveller's Guide to the Rhine (1836).

Out at 6. Again to Erasmus. Off at 7 by steamer. At Nimwegen[1] (why corruptly written by us Nimeguen?) 6 P.M. The river is monotonous: yet there are signs of life and industry all the way. The prospect from the Tower Belvedere here is beautiful: especially a bright sunset, down the river: which is commanded both ways. Behind the town, which slants down an elevation to the river is a singular raised table land with the dead flat on each side along the river. This ground seems to have been carved a hundred times by all sorts of military operations. It extends far back.

A garden near the tower seems to be abundantly frequented and by children, yet the flowers were unpicked, the grass untrodden and luxuriant. English children would be less manageable.

Pays Bas. Good, & reasonable. Porters rascally, as is too usual.

14. Tuesday.

6 A.M. Steamer to Cologne:[2] where we arrived at 7½ next morning. We averaged on the whole under five miles an hour. The river more tame and tedious—always excepting the stream downwards—than yesterday. 1½ hours at Emmerick,[3] hammering at the merchandise, which might have been made in the time. No search of the luggage.

Employed myself in correcting my proofsheets: and read Rio. Wished much to halt at Düsseldorf: but I did not venture it, being quite uncertain about my party. Those artists may be worth a journey of themselves.[4]

15 Wed.

Last night we slept twelve in a cabin which besides our boxes was 9 f. by 6, or less. However this encourages early rising. It is wonderful to see dinners of forty or fifty dishes served in these little boats, and the accounts of each passenger accurately kept. At Cöln went ashore to the Cathedral. Two schools came in at eight to hear mass in a side chapel with an organ of its own. The girls were there & the boys I learned were to follow. The teachers looked grave and kind. The chanting of the children was delightful: and strangely mixed with what I must call the grimaces of the priest. What divine art shall separate those opposite elements of mummery and devotion which are so subtly joined as to appear blended in the Roman Catholic system—like, however, and no more than like, the antagonist principles of flesh and spirit in a man. Cf. Usher, as cited in Palmer I 280.[5]

The archbishop[6] is in the shop windows on pocket handkerchiefs and especially on pipes. The agitation still continues and I see by the papers that the clergy have protested.

[1] Nijmwegen, Dutch frontier fortress town, 59 miles east of Rotterdam.

[2] On the Rhine, 100 miles SE. of Nijmwegen.

[3] 30 miles ESE. of Nijmwegen, just inside the Prussian frontier.

[4] At Dusseldorf, 24 miles north of Cologne, F. W. Schadow directed (1826–59) the academy of painting, then a notable centre of Christian art.

[5] W. *Palmer, A Treatise on the Church of Christ, 2 v. (1838).

[6] Clemens August Droste von Vischering, 1773–1845, vicar-general of Munich 1807–13, 1815–20; upheld Church's rights against Napoleon and Prussia; abp. of Cologne, 1835; arrested 1837; accepted coadjutor 1842, but remained under house arrest.

The picture of the Adoration is curious.

Had this Cathedral been completed, it could not have equalled Saint Peter's?[1]

Zeitungen. Schreiber.

$9\frac{1}{4}$–$8\frac{3}{4}$ to Coblenz,[2] $19\frac{1}{4}$ leagues. Looked well at the Rhine to get over my former disappointment, and in part succeeded. The Drachenfels, Rheineck, Hammerstein,[3] are very fine. Yet these hills are hardly mountains, and the great width of the river diminishes to the eye the height which they really have.

Plenty of English is spoken on the Rhine, but it appears to be written with gross inaccuracy. "My address carr is to have of the conductor," says a Johann Marie Farina on a very smart affiche in our cabin.

The weather showery, and the harvest less advanced than about London. These vine-yards are a sad delusion. They *sound* everything that is beautiful, and are the most insipid of all possible ingredients in a landscape.

16. Th.

Coblenz. Belle Vue. Good, and moderate. 6 A.M. Eilwagen[4] to Ems.[5] Three leagues: a good deal of hill: $2\frac{1}{4}$ hours. His Majesty's horses are not well adapted for draught. Found my party at the Vier Jahreszeiten. H. thank God doing well: J.N.G. out of sorts from suppressed seasickness. Wrote up Journal and accounts. Resumed private Journal. I had heard this place so accurately described, & seen so many views of it, that the actual sight just corresponded to the *type* in my mind ready to receive it: a valley hardly wider than to be a channel for the Lahn, with the walk, high road, and generally single row of houses beside it: the hills steep and wooded, rising to four or six hundred feet, here and there sharpened with rock: and luxuriant abundance of walks and rides: everything to apply a beneficial stimulus to a nervous invalid, besides the intrinsic qualities (ὅτι πότ᾽ ἐστιν)[6] of the waters.

16. Th.[7]

In aftⁿ settled myself in the Russie, whither all moved.—Up the Stations Hill[8]—read Palmer on the Church & worked German words a little. Wrote up journal. Sacksspringen &c.[9] Table d'hote very wearisome.

---

[1] Begun *ca.* 1300; left incomplete *ca.* 1520; finished 1842–80, in Gothic style; mined 1945, later rebuilt. The comparison was put forward in John *Murray's *Hand-book for Travellers . . . Along the Rhine* (1836), 207.

[2] 45 miles SE. of Cologne.

[3] The Drachenfels (1056 ft.) is one of the Siebengebirge, 10 miles upstream from Bonn on the opposite bank; the Hammerstein, also on the right bank, 12 miles NW. of Koblenz, is just upstream from Burg Rheineck, on the left.

[4] Diligence.

[5] Watering-place in Nassau, 6 miles ESE. of Koblenz.

[6] 'such as they are'.

[7] Next three entries from Lambeth MS 1423.

[8] On the south bank of the Lahn. 'which we' here deleted.

[9] See 18 Aug. 38, second entry.

17. Fr.

Wrote on Th.—& to Mr G.
read Palmer[1]—Wilberforce. paper. worked German & *proofs*.[2]
up the Mutterskopf (opposite)[3]

18. Sat.

Wrote Journal. & an account of the Sackspringen U[nd] Milchessen to go
to Selwyn as a proposal for Eton verses.
read Palmer. Worked German. Proofsheets. Walk to Tausenau.[4]

18 Sat.

On Thursday at dinner was announced by a printed notice, ein sackspringen,
und ein milchessen mit verbundenem augen,[5] at $5\frac{1}{2}$ in the evening, on the
Duke's ground. Repairing thither at the appointed time, we saw seventeen
donkey boys tied up in sacks,[6] by an inspector of police, under the eye of
the superintendent, and six started over the turf at once: three only reached
the flags, or pole-handkerchiefs which served the turn, one much before the
others. Then came the pinch: they had to race backwards to the point from
which they first started: they were off—one tumbled—the leader in the
first heat took the lead again—within two yards of success he fell—his sole
remaining competitor was working up, slow and sure: but the stranded
hero was not to be overcome and endeavoured to roll in—after one or two
turns he sprung vigorously up, and came in before his rival had quite
reached the prize. There were several other races: one when all the seventeen bags started together in a row: seven, generally of the most eager, were
immediately overset and betook themselves to tripping up others, amidst
general roars. Then came the milchessen. Two blindfolded boys, across a
narrow table, with a bowl between them, and a spoon apiece, were to put
milk into each other's mouths—or otherwise as it might be. Some was
discharged fairly over the shoulder, some descended on the head, but upon
the breast the streams were most abundant and rivalled those which sprang
to the touch of the thyrsus. But all this was so simple, so goodhumoured, so
nationally characteristic, and so amusing, that I formed a design of sending it to Eton to be proposed to Dr. Hawtrey for a subject for verses. This
I am accordingly about to do. We afterwards went up the hill of the Stations, which repays a short labour by a very beautiful view of the Amphitheatre of Ems.—Tonight, in honour of the little Princess's birthday,[7]
fireworks, a Prussian band from Coblenz, bonfires, an illumination, a ball.
To which the river added, thus early in the year, some fog. The general

[1] Add MS 44728, ff. 129–32.
[2] Of *The State in its Relations with the Church.*
[3] Malberg or Milbertskopf, on the south bank of the Lahn.
[4] Dausenau, 2 miles east of Ems, on the right bank of the Lahn.
[5] 'a sack-race, and blindfold milk-taking'.
[6] 'and six' deleted.
[7] Princess Helena of Nassau, 12 August 1831–1888, m. 1853 George Victor, 1831–93,
prince of Waldeck 1845.

effect, however, was very pretty: the light filling tolerably the basin in which we lie. Admittance to the ball seemed very free: a single pair of moustaches at the door. No one seemed ready to begin, whereupon the Superintendent of Police was applied to and gallantly turned out. At nine they commenced. At ten I went back, and the dance was over, the people outside too had dispersed. Not order only but perfect quiet reigned everywhere. How ductile and docile,[1] while with great intelligence, how far from everything egoistic while abounding in nationality, is this people. And how easily amused, their national relish standing in the place or rather not requiring the aid of strong seasoning.

19. Sunday.[2]

Our service in the Lutheran Church. Heard also a part of the L[uthera]n Service. read Palmer & wrote.[3] Walk up the opposite hill. Headache in evg & could do nothing. Church conv. at dinner.

20. M.

Palmer[4]—Wilberforce—Wrote to Mahon—head better. The ach Effect of change of diet & hours, I think. Walk to Fursthaus.[5] Learnt that R.C.s & Lutherans here sometimes attend one another's worship—& the children go to school together, & with the Jews.

21. T.

Church conv. &c. at breakf.
Proofs to p. 144 arrived—corrected them.
read Palmer & Wilberforce. Worked German.
Walk to top of the Kammenau hill.[6] Panoramic view, nearly.

22. W.

Wrote to Mr G.—G. Hall.—Kinnaird—Stephen—Mr Ramsay—Glynne—Selwyn.
reperused & corrected my proofsheets.
read Palmer. Hill walk.

23. Th.

Walk to Ehrenbreitstein[7] to breakf—saw John off. In Coblenz for money—read Palmer, Handbooks for my route S, Wilberforce. Note to Lincoln.

---

[1] 'and' deleted.
[2] Next five entries from Lambeth MS 1423.
[3] Add MS 44728, ff. 134–7.
[4] Notes ibid. ff. 138–9.
[5] The Kurhaus, property of the dukes of Nassau, a large gloomy hotel over the principal springs.
[6] Kemmenau, 2 miles ENE. of Ems.
[7] 6 miles WNW. of Ems, on right bank of Rhine opposite Koblenz.

24. Fr.

Yesterday we walked over to Ehrenbreitstein before breakfast. Weisser Ross, excellent. The distance is I think a good six miles. The road forks several times but generally reunites. The view down the Rhine from the top is fine: superior to that from Kemmenau in opening the gorge below Andernach[1] admirably: otherwise inferior. The view of Coblenz and the confluence[2] delightful. Here I passed within very short distance, a chapel unroofed, with trees growing inside of which one I should think 60 years old—used as a place of ordure—a statue of the Virgin and Child scrawled over with pencil—and in a few minutes, further on, another regularly wired in, with the usual tawdry images, evidently an object of resort and respect. How strange is this. Surely the images in the former should be removed if they cannot be secured. And how strange is the inequality of regard—one of the signs of idolatrous tendency. The Tyrolese glovers are delightful. One of them was quite pleased that I had bought gloves already from the other—his rival, but also his countryman, and the article one of his country's make. Their dark features kindle with joy if one mentions Hofer,[3] or has been or is going to Innspruck.

24. Fr.[4]

The Lincolns very kindly came over to breakf. A wretched morning to lionise them: walked 2m. back with him.
read Palmer,—Wilberforce—Handbook—worked German. Wrote to Mr Kock.[5]
Helen out (2d time) to ride donkey.

25. Sat.

Read Palmer—Wilberforce—Scotch Patronage Digest.[6] walk with Sir A. Murray[7] & lovely views. H. out again.

26. S.

R.C. Church at 9¾. missed serm. heard catechising. Engl. service. Wilberforce—Palmer—Cosin.

27 M.

I was surprised to see that the Russian Prince Heritier[8] attended the Lutheran Church yesterday.[9]

---

[1] 9 miles downstream from Koblenz.   [2] The Moselle joins the Rhine at Koblenz.
[3] Cp. 29 June 32.
[4] Next three entries from Lambeth MS 1423.
[5] In Frankfurt; see 11 Sep. 38.
[6] George Cook, *Few Plain Observations on the Enactment of the General Assembly of 1834 relating to Patronage and Calls* (1834), appx. Notes in Add MS 44728, ff. 140–1.
[7] Probably Sir Albert Joseph Murray, 1774–1849; of Melgun, Aberdeenshire.
[8] Alexander Nicholaevitch Romanov, 1818–1881; tsar 1855; emancipated serfs 1861 assassinated.
[9] Note on Lutheran beliefs, Add MS 44728, f. 142.

In the evening the Grand Duke[1] and all his company came in on donkeys wearing oakleaves—an annual feast I believe. The shops open on Sunday afternoon and the gambling-table, (which pays (for all the baths) 50,000 florins a year, and 4000 extra for the new Cursaal[2]) is more crowded on that day than any other. B. saw 160 crowns won at once by Fattie.

The R.C. Chapel was very crowded—fifty or more standing in the open air.

Miss Scott[3] and I went to Nassau.[4] Crone, seems good.

Leave the road at the bottom of the hill on coming in sight of the town and take the footpath to the right by the riverside. The view just under a walnut tree is lovely.

Observe the relative positions of the Lord's and vassals castles, the Nassau and Stein. On the same hill—the first higher & overlooking—a considerable cleft however between. This *proximity*, and command, yet with certain defences, are emblematic of the feudal system which certainly bore a witness however rude and imperfect, for great truths of humanity.

All begging is forbidden in the town—and every handlungsgeselle[5] must on entering it repair to the magistrate. (Not like travellers at Coblenz, who are only bound in case they make more than a *"temporal* stay"). How stringent is government here, in the form not of principles but of positive regulations.

I suppose the Rhine steamboats must be found convenient & consequently much frequented by honeymooning couples: this I take for an explanation of the incessant kissings there which meet the eye, and ear.

27. M.[6]

6.40.–11.50. to Nassau: breakf. & saw the castles. First view from the footpath the best. Wrote to J.N.G.
read Wilberforce—Palmer—worked German.

28. T.

Accounts settling—[7]journal—proofs. at R.C. Chapel at 8. Such a place always presents as the appropriate subjects for prayer, the unity and the purity of the Church, and that we may labour in the Lord for both.
Read Palmer, Wilberforce.
worked German. Out with H. in boat.

29 W.

accounts, writing out Vss for Miss S[cott].
read Wilberforce—Cook's Digest of Patronage Evidence (finished—curious)

---

[1] Wilhelm VII of Nassau, 1792–1839, succ. 1816.
[2] Opened 1839.
[3] Caroline Scott, 2nd da. of Sir Samuel; m. 1851 Peter Cracroft, R.N., who d. 1865; she d. 1879.
[4] 5 miles ESE. of Ems, higher up the Lahn.		[5] Trader.
[6] Next five entries from Lambeth MS 1423.		[7] '&' deleted.

the Lady of Lyons[1]—much talent, I admit.—Gally Knight's Sicilian Sketch.[2] Chess. the first for 15 years? a little singing. German, etwas.[3]

30. Th.

German, Etwas. wrote,[4] read Leila[5]—Palmer—Wilberforce. Walked over the Winterberg & beyond Heinrich's Hof; a fine view of Marksburg &c.[6]— Chess.

31 Fr.

German (etwas).
Wrote to Mr G. Wrote.[7]
Leila (finished)—Palmer—Wilberforce—Chess.

Sept 1. S.

Wrote[8]—Journal. read Palmer. Wilberforce. Calderon. Worked German. Chess.

Sept. 1. Saturday.

Yesterday to Spurchenburg.[9] Castle very decrepit. Wildflowers abundant. Follow the walk higher than the castle itself, for an echo from the wall which repeats about three syllables with the utmost distinctness.

Passing through old Ems, observed a dog turning a smith's bellows wheel; he stood within the periphery and worked it by walking on the treadmill principle. The man has several and works them by relays. In the same manner a wheel near the springs is turned by asses to supply the Vier Thürmen,[10] say 4 or 500 yards off, with the waters.

As we returned we saw the princes and their company practising at a stag painted on a board: this was on wheels, drawn across by lads running at a signal given. I afterwards found the distance to be about 55 yards.

Today a different dog wrought at the smith's wheel, and the labourer of yesterday was basking in the sun. It is said they easily learn this curious practice.

Passing through the fields I found the wheat larger I think than in England. Karl tells us most of the lower order get meat now and then: some of them every day. His family once a week in summer: in winter they

---

[1] Play by Bulwer *Lytton (1838).

[2] H. Gally *Knight, *The Normans in Sicily* (1838).

[3] 'some'.

[4] Add MS 44728, ff. 143–4.

[5] Bulwer *Lytton, *Leila, or the Siege of Granada* (1838).

[6] One of the more strenuous walks on the left bank of the Lahn. For Marksburg see 4 Sep. 38.

[7] Add MS 44728, ff. 145–6.

[8] On *Bulwer, ibid. ff. 147–8.

[9] Sporkenburg, a medieval castle about a mile beyond the old silver mines, on the left bank of the Lahn.

[10] One of the bath-houses.

kill a pig. Pork is at 13 kr.[1] per pound—good hog weighs 230–40 pounds. Potatoes are very much eaten by the labouring class. The towns and villages generally are possessed of woods. The Duke receives the tithes: pays both R.C. and Lutheran ministers.

The Schweingeneral[2] is a rough dirty drunken looking personage with a bloated and bulbous face, a terrific whip to which the valleys ring again, and an attendant boy who emulates his leader in the incessant flogging of the pigs—who even bleed under it. They were coming home when we returned. It is curious to see them drop off like children at their several homes as they pass the doors and alleys—one woman took up hers in her arms. The payment is 12 kr. per quarter for each. I doubt at this rate if the General's pay be more than six pounds a year.

One must be pleased with the easy and kindly manner in which persons of the highest rank here appear to move among the people. Yesterday the Russian Prince—who will have 60 millions (?) at his beck—with those of Nassau & other youths were walking in a string, boyishly, of five or six along the Cur Haus Square, at the top of their speed.

Sunday Sept. 2. Ems.[3]

R.C. Church. & Lutheran to have English service—but non c'era.[4]
read Palmer (finished)—Wilberforce (finished)—Cosin. Prayers.—Wrote.[5]

3. M.

Wrote to J.N.G.—Journal. Chess.
Began Bettridge's Hist. of U.C. Church.[6] Gally Knight—Rio.
Out with H. in illumination, &c.

Sept 3. Monday

Yesterday at 9½ to the R.C. Church. The priest (Miler) preached on the ten lepers whereof one, a Samaritan, returned to give thanks.[7] I caught his words most imperfectly, but was favourably impressed by his sermon, which was delivered with great earnestness & animation, & unwritten. Pride and unthankfulness were the one the first, the other the common & crying sin of the world; notwithstanding the mercies of God in our redemption by the Incarnate Saviour. When sin had shut against us the doors of Heaven, and left us heirs of wrath. The precious blood of Christ was the key with which He opened to us those doors. And this key He gave to Peter in the well known text. But men remained cold and unthankful, and religion hardly appeared to exist among them. Their pious forefathers flocked daily to the House of God, and then sought union with the Re-

---

[1] 13 Kroner were worth just over 14 pence.
[2] Cp. [F. B. *Head] Bubbles from the Brunnens, 95 ff.
[3] Next two entries from Lambeth MS 1423.
[4] 'there was none'.　　　　　　　　　　　　　[5] On theology, Add MS 44728, ff. 149–50.
[6] W. Bettridge, History of the Church in Upper Canada (1838).
[7] Luke xvii. 11–19.

deemer in His ordinances: but now how few answered to the call of the daily bell! Their business should be no excuse: apostles and saints had been workmen. In all things, according to St. Paul's command, they were to live to God, to do all things to his glory, by a godfearing and virtuous walk: and he earnestly besought and intreated them regarding these things to be ready to come with this pious Samaritan and render thanks to their Father. So he spoke, but this does him great injustice. The church was crowded, the people very attentive, on the whole, I judge by the blue frocks, more rustic & poorer than the Lutherans. The Russian Prince came here today —but did not enter until after the Sermon, when I left: and saw the gaming table in open preparation during the hours of worship. And these are both public institutions. Is God then no longer a jealous God?
I saw shops open at half past eleven. In the evening, I hear, the ladies raffled at the Curhaus for 2000 florins worth of *bijouterie* presented by the Russian Prince.

The Lutheran prayers, Carl tells me, are written; but different ones are used on successive Sundays. In their church we still see the demands of the *sense*. Wreaths of green, with ribbands attached to them, are hung all round—though faded. And in one aisle a tablet, within a scroll, supported by two cherubs, and inscribed with Dankbarkeit to God, Hochachtung[1] to the Great Reformers Luther and Calvin, and (I think) rejoicing in the reunion after 300 years of two several branches of the Church of Christ.

Sept 4. Tuesday.

Walked to Braubach[2] to breakfast. Zur Philipsburg: good. Bread beautiful. Distance 8½ miles, including 1 m. up and down to the castle of Marksburg.[3] Saw the ancient rack: consisting of three chief parts—an axle—pulleys, and a sort of pair of stocks. The two first perhaps five feet from the ground —the latter placed on it. Into these a prisoner's legs were inserted, so that, I suppose, he sat on the ground—a wooden frame with a ring was fixed on his neck and shoulders, and a rope worked by the axle, over the pulley, attached to the ring, brought the torture to bear on his frame. On to Lahnstein, 3 miles.[4]
And home to Ems, 9½ or 10—by 1¼ P.M. The three parts of the expedition presented three different classes of scenery, all quite distinct, but all belonging to the region intermediate between the purely picturesque and the purely romantic.

4. T.[5]

6½–1¼: walk of 20 or 21 miles to Braubach & Lahnstein. Afr, 3h. out with H.J.G.
Read Rio, German.

[1] 'thanks' and 'reverence'.
[2] SW. of Ems, on the right bank of the Rhine.
[3] Medieval castle towering over Braubach.
[4] Downstream, at the Lahn's junction with the Rhine.
[5] Next six entries from Lambeth MS 1423.

5. W.

Wrote to Murray—worked at proofsheets—read Sir H. Taylor's Reply to Ed. Rev[1]—Chess—Rio
A. Robertson here, & went off for a few days.

6. Th.

Wrote to Montrose Standard[2]—A. Robertson. Kinnaird came in evg.
Hard work at proofsheets—got through them. Read Southey's B. of the Church. Chess. Walk with Sir A. Murray.

7. Fr.

Wrote to Mahon—Mr G.—Mr Simpson (Nk)—B. Harrison[3]—Jas Hope[4]—Ld Abderdeen—T.G.
again revised Proofs: & dismissed them, much enjoying the release. Chess. read Southey. Lord Londonderry[5]—Strange! Rel[igious] conv. with K.

8. Sat.

Wrote to Sir C. Scott & Co—Deinhard & Jordan[6]—Lincoln.
Read Ed. Rev. on Whitfield & Froude—on Talleyrand & Chateaubriand. Long Church & rel. conv. with Kinnaird—as yesterday. paying accts & arrangements for departure.

9. S.

Journal. read Shuttleworth on Tradition[7]—finished Rio.—Church prayers *oben*.[8] R.C. & Luth[eran] sermons.

Sept 9. Sunday.

R.C. Church at 9½. Yesterday was the festival of the Annunciation: but the Priest gave notice last Sunday, that it would be kept today: a reluctant condescension, I suppose, to circumstances. He read most of Matt 1.— showed the humble circumstances of Jesus, and his mother: contrasted the honour which cometh of men with that which cometh of God: recited Rome and Greece, Manlius, Camillus, Lentulus, Scipio—where are they and their works, what were they once in worldly fame? But then of St. Peter, St Paul, . . . what were *they* in worldly fame, and how vast and enduring are

---

[1] General Sir H. *Taylor's 'Remarks' in reply to *Edinburgh Review*, lxvii (April 1838) —*Brougham on [Lady Charlotte *Bury], *Diary*, 2 v. (1838).
[2] Untraced; perhaps a business letter (his f. had been one of the paper's founders).
[3] To congratulate on being made chaplain to *Howley.
[4] Extracts in Ornsby, i. 171; answering letter brought by *Kinnaird, ibid. i. 168–71.
[5] *H* xliii. 806, 19 June 1838, on Spain; republished as pamphlet.
[6] Possibly Johann Heinrich Deinhardt, 1805–67, scholar, and Sylvester Jordan, 1792–1861, constitutionalist; each had written on education.
[7] P. N. *Shuttleworth, *Not Tradition but Revelation* (1838).
[8] 'upstairs'.

the results of their labours? Seek then for the life of God, for the witness of the Spirit to bear witness with your own, in and through the holy blood of Christ.—Truth compels me to add he ended with prayer to the Virgin accordingly.

(N.B. over the chief and one side altar are *escutcheons* fixed: this savours I suppose of *German* Romanism. So in the Lutheran Church, we find the *Fürstliches Nassauisches* Gesängbuch!)[1]

I then went to the Lutheran Sermon—O when shall we be one, "as the Father and the Son are one, *that the world may know*"[2] the Son's mission? The manner was manly & forcible: Miss Scott caught much more than I did. but from what appeared to both, his Sermon was less specifically Christian than that of the priest.

During the reading of prayers the people seemed but cold and distracted. A deeper shade of solemnity however was perceptible when the Lord's Prayer began.

Monday Sept 10.

8–6¾. Ems to Frankfurt.[3]

Hotel d'Angleterre; good: dear.

Slow as was our course today Glynne writes to me that he was until near 11 on the way to Langen Schwalbach[4]—leaving Ems before 4: so there is nothing to be gained by posting in point of speed here. We were in a supernumerary caléche—the one good point in the arrangements is, that you are not liable to be disappointed of your place.

K. is evidently a good traveller.

The harvest is late and not heavy. Much is still out.—Geese (from Wiesbaden to F.) Driven out to the stubbles in flocks—Langen Schwalbach inferior to Ems in appearance—air lighter—a good deal of its *umgegend*[5] bare—shops in Wiesbaden very attractive. Amused by one of our postillions stopping the carriage deliberately to wash his boots in a ditch by the roadside.

An Irish lady with her daughter got in at L.S.—"Certainly" she cried emphatically "next summer"—to persons at a door as we drove by: she had lodged in the house: and proceeded to remark that an English person would have been quite indifferent to the requests of these persons at parting, whereas she soothed them by an assurance which she had not the slightest intention to realise. She afterwards spoke of the very sad neglect of religion & the disappointment wh as a Prot[t.] she had experienced in the land of Luther: evidently a conscientious woman, but her countrymen are generally inconsequent.

Saw Mr. Koch—Sarg[6]—Cassino.[7] Read *Catholische Kirche Zeitung*[8]—on

---

[1] '*Royal Nassau* Hymnbook'.   [2] John xiv. 31.
[3] 42 miles ESE. of Ems.   [4] Resort 20 miles SE. of Ems, and 8 NW. of Wiesbaden.
[5] 'environs'.   [6] Frankfurt carriage-maker: see next entry.
[7] At Frankfurt.
[8] The *Katholische Kirchenzeitung* of Aschaffenburg (where was Döllinger) interested itself in the ideas of Lamennais and of Montalembert, even after they were rejected by Rome. Cp. *Annalen des Historischen Vereins für den Niederrhein*, cxlviii. 80 ff. (1949).

our Prison Chaplain's Debate[1]—monstrous! on the coronation—Montalembert[2] most interesting—on Bp Philpotts[3] & the Apostolic Succession.
Journal & Accounts.

Sept 11. Tues.

Up at 6. What with carriage—servant—sights—money—shopping—dinner at our kind friend Mr Kock's—& writing (Miss Scott & Mr G.)—a busy day enough.

Tolerable secondhand carriages are from 20£ to 50£. We bought a Courier Caleche at £29, Vienna build. We might have had a handsome light green britschka (i.e. double seated) from Sarg for £45. Sarg offered a strong carriage at £20—& a carriage at £10. Decided finally against a Courier.

I have copied out marrow and extracts this evening (after Mr. Kock's) respecting the Gaol Chaplain's Debate. Eccoli[4]

Katholische Kirchen Zeitung[5] Frankfurt Aug. 5. 1838
Lond. 16 July.

> Die gerechtigkeit wird der Torys zum trotz den sieg davon tragen, welche mit recht die gänzliche freigebung der Katholiken, als den untergang der durch das gesetz eingeführten herrschenden Kirche betrachten. Auch haben sie unerbittlich der kleinsten bill, welche die freiheit der Kirche begünstigen könnte, den Krieg erklärt.
>
> Befindet sich unter den gefangenen ein Quaker, Meth[odist], Unit[arier], Anab[aptist], Swed[enborger], oder irgend ein anderer sectarer, so findent man es ganz einfach, einen geistlichen ihrens glaubens zu ihm zu schicken: aber hat ein K[atholik] das unglück, gefängnissstrafe zu erleiden, so mag er seiner Kirche nur lebewohl sagen, &c—must hear anglican preacher, and[6] weigert er sich dessen, so ist ein Gensdarme da, den auch das gesetz eingesezt hat, um ihn anzuhalten, mitanzuhören, das Rom die grosse Babylon u[nd] der

[1] Cp. *H* xliv. 191, 492, 13 and 23 July 1832.
[2] C. F. R. de Montalembert, *Histoire de Sainte Elizabeth de Hongrie* (1836).
[3] H. *Phillpotts, 'Address . . . to the Clergy of his Diocese on the conduct of the Rev. Henry E. Head', and Head's 'Letter . . . in answer to the Circular about Confirmation' (both 1838).
[4] 'Here they are'.
[5] This entry was copied by the diarist on two slips of paper, pasted opposite and on the back of the entries for 10 and 11 Sep. 38.
'Catholic Church Journal Frankfurt Aug. 5 1838. Lond. 16 July.
'Justice will triumph in spite of the Tories, and they will rightly regard the complete emancipation of Catholics as the downfall of the Church by law established. They have mercilessly declared war also on the smallest Bill that might be favourable to the freedom of the Catholic church.
'If there is any Quaker, Methodist, Unitarian, Anabaptist, Swedenborgian or member of any other sect among the prisoners, it is taken for granted that a clergyman of his own faith be sent to him, but if a Catholic has the misfortune to be doing penal servitude, he may as well bid goodbye to his Church etc.—must hear anglican preacher, and if he refuses there is a gendarme ready, also provided for by law, to compel him to listen to Rome being denounced as Babylon the Great and the Pope as Antichrist. O'Connell and others required that a Catholic priest should be permitted to visit any prison in which 40 Catholics were present. The Tories it is true assert that such a law is an insult to the established Church.—&c.'
[6] 'if he ev' deleted.

Papst der AntiChrist sey. O'Connell & others required dass einem k[atholischen] priester erlaubt seyn solle, ein gefängniss, in welchem sich 40 K[atholiken] befänden, zu besuchen. Die Tory's haben zwar behauptet ein solches gesetz sey beleidigend für die herrschende Kirche—&c.

Danneker's Ariadne.[1] Executed with power, more than womanliness. The face expresses however *pracht*[2] admirably? The upper arms seemed somewhat thick & heavy. The balance, or *seat*[3], admirable. Would not the Ariadne of Catullus have afforded a more interesting and susceptible subject?[4]

Iuppiter omnipotens! utinam ne tempore primo
Gnossia Cecropiae tetigissent littora Classes[5]
&c. &c.

Saw the picture Gallery. Even Catalogues here provided Gratis. Observed.
1 a 'manner of Perugino'—*old*—& (consequently, ma) the Virgin kneeling, with other Saints, to the Infant Saviour.
2 A Giovan Bellini—Virgin & Infant, St John—a dark full grown man, & Elizabeth.
3 A Cima da Conegliano,[6] Virgin & Child—both these are very *grave* in their types—but the former has the deeper tone?

Mrs Kock says the English have more selfcommand, & more tact in expressing their opinions when they differ from one another, than continental persons. They have had longer *practice*. She put us on our H. of C. horses.

A long Church conv. with one of Judge Foster's daughters.[7] Most hospitably received. The Kocks must spoil all travellers. They should end & not begin here.

Sept. 12. Wed.

$6\frac{1}{4}$*A.M.*–8 *P.M.* Frankfurt to Brucksal.[8]—$16\frac{3}{4}$ German miles say 77 English. About $10\frac{1}{2}$d. per English mile.
Breakf. at Darmstadt,[9] Darmstadter Hof middling, and dear. 1h. at Heidelberg[10] to see the Castle, equally imposing from a distance & within its precincts. It might engage half a day, for one with an imagination to revel in the past—which it suggests copiously, continually, & in every form.

---

[1] J. H. von Dannecker (1758–1841), German sculptor. 'Ariadne' was then in the Bethmann Museum, Frankfurt.
[2] 'splendour'.   [3] Reclining on a panther.
[4] She was dishevelled: *Carmina*, lxiv. 61.
[5] *Carmina*, lxiv. 171: 'Almighty Jove! O that the Athenian ships had never come to the Cretan shores.'
[6] *Ca.* 1459–*ca.* 1517.
[7] John Leslie *Foster, d. 1842; tory M.P. 1807–12, 1818–20, 1824–30; Irish judge 1830. Da. unidentified; he m. 1834.
[8] In Baden, 70 miles south of Frankfurt and 25 NE. of Karlsruhe.
[9] Capital of Hesse, 15 miles south of Frankfurt.
[10] 35 miles south of Darmstadt.

We were delayed by our wheels, & by a carriage ahead: one can never hope to start in a vehicle newly acquired without some difficulties on the first day or two.

The Berg Strasse runs something like the Pomptine marsh road[1] under its hills—but man has done as much more here as nature there. The country is a vineyard or a garden.

By paying highly the postillions may be worked up to something like 8m. an hour, *excluding* stops, on a dead flat.

At Heidelberg (man sagt)[2] 300 English & a church. The Neckar view is only second to the Castle.

By the way, at the Ems fair last week, we saw lithographs from Paris, of the Redeemer and of the Virgin (ohne sünde geboren,[3] so addressed) purporting to be *personal likenesses*.

Archbishop Droste still appears at Frankfort, on crockery, and on pipes, amidst the many emblems which they bear, so well representing the mixed masses of men all whose tastes they seem intended to meet.

read a little Dante. German & accounts: which are perplexing enough.

Thursd. Sept. 13.

The Post at Brucksal has good beds and an active intelligent young landlord.

Detained by our misbehaving wheel until $8\frac{3}{4}$: and at almost every station for horses. 70 had been out as one postmaster told me. Consequently only 14 German miles in $11\frac{1}{2}$ hours: at about 9d. per English mile. Horses are cheaper & postilions in Baden do not expect so much.

Indian corn, Venetian blinds, and shelving verandah like roofs, remind us that we approach the South. Our road lay through a highly cultivated but not a corn country: green hills at a short distance on the left, which leaving Carlsruhe we determined at a particular point greatly to resemble the view of Lord Panmure's[4] & the Kincardineshire hills with Glenesk opening between them: at another (not far from Achern)[5] to be very like the Dunsinane &c hills seen from the road between Cupar Angus[6] and Perth.

This was holiday time and the women's dress in which blue & red predominate reminds one of the Roman States.

At Carlsruhe there were no horses: but a voiturier in a green coat proposed to bring his & take us. In half an hour he appeared in a blue frock and put to: a sign from the man of the post, he withdrew for a moment and reappeared in a postilion's livery coat and hat. He drove out of the town amidst much laughter from his brethren who were standing in a cluster at the gate.

Found the landlord at Offenburg now as when we knocked him up six years ago at midnight[7] the very perfection of activity and efficiency, full of

---

[1] See 27 Apr. 32.
[3] 'born without sin'.
[5] 32 miles SE. of Karlsruhe.
[7] Cp. 19 July 32.

[2] 'on dit'.
[4] Brechin Castle.
[6] As distinct from Fife.

information, several languages at command as completely as his servants, and a power of ready suggestion: a character common in England but rare in Germany.

Fr. Sept. 14.

$5\frac{1}{2}$ A.M. to midnight—$17\frac{1}{2}$ G[erman miles] from Offenberg to Schaffhausen:[1] say 80 miles English, and at 37.48[2] or about $9\frac{1}{3}$d. per mile.

We had today a recusant horse, a Russian carriage ahead, and waiting for horses at nearly every station: some very bad roads, viz. from Hausach[3] to Krumshiltach,[4] also contributed to delay us.

The scenery however from Offenberg to the head of the Kissing (or -en?) Thal[5] above Hornberg[6] is beautiful and increasingly so: about Hornberg (where the Poste is *very good*) quite a little Switzerland. There we emerged upon a very high and undulating country, with broad cultivated sweeps and partially wooded. Out of this 'palm'[7] rises the Danube divided by not many miles from the Rhine. The last stage down to Schaffhausen showed in the gloom of night fine outlines of a gorge into which we descended over the range which bounds the tract I have described.

At Villingen[8] a dialogue is spoken which appears to exemplify the utmost imaginable corruption in language or in pronunciation. Add to this the immobility observable almost everywhere along the line, and belated travellers are in a hopeful situation.

Sat Sept 15.

Schaffhausen. Krone. House old and tumbledown, & dirty, but beds and breakfast good. Rather too near a nolle[9] church-clock.

Off at 7, to the falls, 2 miles, bonâ fide. We were much pleased. The intermediate rocks break the line into three cascades of graduated magnitude from the Schaffhausen side: and the wrath and foam vary in the same proportion. There is a wonderful union of qualities in a waterfall: flexibility and power: continuity and change: the beautiful and the terrible: are perhaps hardly in any other case so blended.[10]

9–8.20: Schaffhausen to Constanz[11] and Rheineck.[12] $14\frac{1}{2}$ German miles— about $8\frac{3}{4}$ per mile English.

The Duchy of Baden may I think challenge comparison with any country

[1] In Switzerland, 34 miles SE. of Krummschiltach.
[2] French francs.
[3] In the Black Forest, 16 miles SE. of Offenburg.
[4] 12 miles SE. of Hausach, a solitary posthouse near the watershed between the Rhine and the Danube.
[5] Kinzig Thal.
[6] Halfway between Hausach and Krummschiltach.
[7] Cp. the Greek θέναρ, 'palm of the hand', used in Greek for an undulating expanse.
[8] 10 miles SE. of Krummschiltach.
[9] 'tolling' (dialect).
[10] Cp. *Disraeli, *Falconet*, ch. v, in Buckle, ii. 1539.
[11] 24 miles east of Schaffhausen, in Baden, on the left bank of the Rhine.
[12] Swiss town where the Rhine falls into Lake Constance.

for the variety of hats and headdresses worn by the people. In the North, and middle, the threecornered sacerdotal: in the S.W. (as I remember) the unmitigated cocked hat: in the Kissingthal the low crowned broad brim swaying downwards with its own weight—and the women with every sort of fans, flaps, and wings.

It has a great deal of very high cultivation. The corn seemed to be upon the high land.

The whole of our road today was pretty, at least. The lake of Constance seen in its breadth is a noble image of reposing might: but we wanted the sun to give a *tone* to the colouring of the picture.

We went to see the low Conciliumsaal:[1] like a floor of a warehouse in Liverpool:[2] but what was done there of good and evil! Faith broken:[3] truth immolated: a Sacrament cruelly maimed:[4] on the other hand there Papal tyranny was greatly abased.[5]

Before reaching Rudolfzell[6] we passed a young eagle sitting close by the road. He turned his back, and as we came nearer flew off, scarcely deigning us one reverted glance of scorn, he flew, not fled into the wood.[7] This was in cultivated and accessible country.

Harvest not yet over, close by the S. side of the Lake of Constance.

(*S. Sep. 16*)

On Sunday I heard two sermons & half a third. The latter was R.C. in the nice church at Thal,[8] which is occupied by both R.C.'s and Reformed[9] twice a day in succession. It appeared very good & such as might come from any of our pulpits. In the afternoon R.C. service there was magnificent music, not however all sacred enough in character, & indifferently performed. Twice as many men as women were present in the morning. It is curious that the R.C. women dress in various colours & wear the singular black headdress so difficult to describe: while the women of the two Reformed congregations which I saw were dressed invariably in black with white caps.

Saw a Reformed Baptism: the child apparently very young brought by the mother. Service seems not to speak of Baptism as conveying inherently spiritual grace.

The first of the Reformed sermons was on Deut 10. 12, 13: the fear of God in individuals, considered in its national results. The second on Rom XI.— 'Behold the goodness & severity of God.' Both were earnest and earnestly delivered: but they certainly seemed to want the distinctive character of

---

[1] 'Hall of the Council' held in 1414–18.
[2] Originally a warehouse, dating from 1388.
[3] Huss was burned, in spite of the Emperor Maximilian's safe-conduct, in 1415.
[4] Hussite doctrine that communion should be in two kinds was condemned by the Council of Constance.
[5] The council declared that a council has authority in religious matters even over a Pope.
[6] Town 14 miles east of Schaffhausen.
[7] 'Watchmen' pencilled in margin.
[8] Village 1½ miles west of Rheineck, in Switzerland.   [9] Calvinist.

Christian teaching, or material parts of it. They turned on our general duties and relations to God and spoke of us as sinners before Him but hardly brought into view the covenant.

The Sabbath appears, so far as palpable signs are concerned, to be admirably observed.

We enjoyed the valley of Thal, and the hill with its old tower above the town, commanding to the left the lake, to the right the valley of the Rhine. There is a goodlooking Inn at Thal. A sweet little recess with wood and waterfall lies on the right.—I think we see the fine hill above Feldkirch[1] from this point.

service. Vinc. Lir: [2]my proofs: conv.

Sep. 17. Monday.

Hirsch at Rheineck—fair & decent. 5 A.M.–7 P.M. $18\frac{1}{2}$ G.M. over the Adlersberg[3] to St Anthoin:[4] about same price. The ascent is very long: from Bludenz[5] or even Feldkirch to 1 G.M. beyond Stuben.[6] Feldkirch, Krone: pretty good breakfast.

Austrian Zollhaus easily passed: we were merely asked if we had anything contraband. After we were formally set free, I offered money as an acknowledgement for dispatch & civility, wh was civilly declined.

The whole of today's drive presented most interesting scenery: particularly the pass above Feldkirch, the situation of Dalaas,[7] the retrospect about $\frac{1}{4}$ hour from the top, & at it, & the downward view to the right $\frac{1}{4}$ hour after leaving it.

Crocuses grow here about $\frac{1}{2}$ hour from the top. (walking distances): & some kind of myrtle.

Very little corn in this valley: it comes up from Bregenz.[8] Much grass & hay. We met cotton from Venice coming in carts over the hill. Also Italian silk & oil from the Valteline.[9]

The Swiss watchmen are one remaining memorial of the English.[10] 'Eins, geschlagen' = past one o'clock: one might believe some of the less elderly had migrated & learnt German.

The Austrian cannoneers were practising near Feldkirck: the wall of Alpine rock returned a sound louder than the original.

In our Inn at St Anthoin were family prayers—as, they say, in all houses. The inmates of the house gather before a crucifix, & all recite together, the Lord's Prayer, the creed, & the Rosencrantz[11] which consists of the aves.—

---

[1] Town on the Ill, in Austria, 15 miles south of Rheineck.
[2] Vincenzo Linares, *Cholera in Palermo* (1838).
[3] Peak on the Arlberg pass, on the road to St. Anthoin.
[4] Austrian posthouse 40 miles east of Rheineck.
[5] Town about 26 miles SE. of Rheineck, 12 miles SE. of Feldkirch.
[6] Village 16 miles east of Bludenz (see next entry) at the foot of the Arlberg pass.
[7] Village in Klosterthal 16 miles west of St. Anton.
[8] Frontier town, Austria, on Lake Constance.
[9] Valley of the upper Adda, in Lombardy, about 50 miles in length, 12 in breadth, the key to Tyrol.
[10] 'Cannoneur
    Rog. prayers' here pencilled in margin.   [11] 'Rosary'.

The Churches here have their altars highly ornamented. On the roadsides our Saviour's is the prevalent figure: there are almost always pious inscriptions with the picture: and on the other hand one is grieved by the representations of the Father.

Sep. 18. Tues.

St Anthoin (Post, endurable) to Pradt[1]—5$\frac{1}{4}$–7$\frac{3}{4}$, 15$\frac{1}{2}$ German miles, rate about 8d per English mile.

We have been incessantly delayed in getting horses: meals too are prepared with imperturbable slowness.

But our road today was delightful: especially, from Flirsch[2] to Landeck,[3] and from Stuben to Nauders,[4] the magnificent pass of the Finster Münze. Here we had to admire the narrow cleft of entry, the bold broad rock on the left whose fore-head overhangs the road soon after, and which might I think fairly be called the round tower, and the view on leaving the Inn of three noble defiles at once. The mountain on the Inn's[5] right bank just above Nauderbach[6] is remarkable both for its steepness and its graceful hanging woods. Amidst the wild grandeur of nature, the eye traces in series the poles and emblems of the Austrian engineers who maintain a gallant strife with her.

The fort in the Nauderbach pass is well advanced: the Stuben postmaster described it to me as *schauderlich schön*.[7] The arch for the stream seemed to me to be but 12 or 13 feet by 10—a limited area one should think to provide for the eccentricities of so wild a stream.

The view of the Giesser[8](?) facing us from the E. above Landeck, of the Mont Ill[9] in coming towards Stuben, and last and greatest of the Ortlerspitz[10] after leaving Nauders, are splendid—The men and women of this country have remarkably handsome features.

Post at Landeck—fair breakfast.

Sep. 19. Wed.

Pradt, Post—Tolerable. The Inns, or many of them, on this line, are very well as bachelor's inns only.

5$\frac{1}{2}$–7$\frac{1}{4}$. Six German miles to Santa Maria,[11] & 4 Italian posts to Bolladore.[12]

---

[1] Village in Austria at the foot of the Stelvio pass, SE. of St. Anthoin; 20 miles south of Nauders.

[2] Village 7 miles east of St. Anthoin.

[3] Village 8 miles east of Flirsch, on the right bank of the Inn.

[4] Village at the Austrian end of the Finstermünz pass, 17 miles south of Landeck at the other end of the Ober-Engadin.

[5] The Inn flows through the narrow cleft of the Finstermünz.

[6] Stream flowing through the glen leading to Nauders.

[7] 'fearsomely beautiful'.

[8] The Schatzer, which towers over Landeck from the east.

[9] The Mondin, 10, 536 ft., 6 miles SW. of Stuben.

[10] 12,811 ft., the highest mountain in Austria; 25 miles south of Nauders.

[11] Second *cantoniera* (house of refuge) in the Stelvio pass, through which the Austrian overnment had lately made a road; 9 miles SW. of Pradt, just past the summit.

[12] Village on the Adda, 24 miles SSW. of Pradt.

Pradt is at the foot of the pass on the side of the Tyrol. To the pillar at the summit[1] the distance appears to be by the road about 25 miles. Some English acquaintances of mine walked up this day, making a few short cuts, under six hours.

We breakfasted at Trafoi[2]—Post; middling. On arriving, I found the doors locked: the inmates were all at Church where they go every morning for ¾ hour.—The Church is very small: founded by a person named Magazz: a picture of the day of Judgement on the walls, the Founder and his sons kneeling, in order of seniority, with their names over their heads, at the foot, on the right, his wife & daughters on the other. I have seen the same thing in Gloucester Cathedral on a tombstone.

This road presents a succession of very wild and noble prospects, in which snow and rock gradually replace streams and forests of larch and pine, and humbler vegetation. The bald cone of Madatsch:[3] the huge side of the Ortler Spitz and the glacier which measures almost its whole altitude, were very grand: and in the awful depth whose silence the torrent alone disturbs is placed a solitary Church[4] at the very foot of the mountain, served occasionally by the priest of Trafoi. There are no inhabitants near.

From Franzenshöhe[5] look up to the top: and from the top down, over twelve galleries,[6] on Franzenshöhe.

Our horses were tired and we were obliged ourselves to aid in bringing up the carriage. From Trafoi to the top, 8.25–2.20. Why do the same horses pull up twenty miles? and why are not these galleries tarred or painted? 1. for durability, 2 to keep the road dry. The peculiarity of this pass is, that it seems really to carry the traveller *among* the tops of the Alps, not merely to *avoid* them. I measured one of the largest pines and found it about 13 feet.

From Santa Maria for about 3 miles the view is not at all equal to the N.E. side; but on arriving then at the giravolte[7] by which a whole hillside appears to be occupied, the eye perceives at once all the wonderful contrivances of the road scaling the mountain, piercing the rock, escaping the avalanche;[8] and with this the ravine of the Wurmser Loch[9] into which the Adda leaps by a long succession of cascades, with an iron front of gigantic height on every side, the perfection of the savage majesty of nature, together with the most consummate manifestations of human art. I have seen nothing in any place more sublime than the Wurmser Loch: it is almost grander than the Via Mala,[10] which in some parts & points its natural features resemble. The depth, the range, the barrenness, the sternness, the

[1] 9,272 ft.; frontier of Lombardy and Tyrol.
[2] Hamlet 6 miles SW. of Pradt, just inside the Austrian frontier.
[3] Glacier issuing from the Ortlerspitz.
[4] Of the 'three holy fountains', a place of pilgrimage, where the road descends to the depth of the Madatsch glacier, which is sunk 100 ft. into the ground.
[5] First *cantoniera* SW. of Trafoi, in the Stelvio pass.
[6] Cut in the rock of the pass for the passage of the road, and to resist avalanches.
[7] 'Hairpin bends'.
[8] Completed in 1824.
[9] Gorge near Santa Maria, through which the Stelvio road goes.
[10] See 4 July 32.

27—II.

impregnable adamantine strength of the almost immeasurable walls of
rock whose masses scale the very heaven, present a scene that would repay
almost any labour, and would have aided Dante with materials for the
construction of his Inferno.

Where the valley joins another from the W. observe a stream springing
actually out of the rock.—And below Bormio,[1] notice Serra,[2] and the
scenery around it.—On the whole thus far I find the Italian side presents
as great prizes to the traveller even as the German.

The Adda floats down immense quantities of hewn wood: and I saw also
high on the N. side a great deal laid in dry water courses to be carried off
when rain falls.

This pass is traversed during 4 months, June–Sept[r]. as a carriage road:
during the remainder of the year on sledges.

read Conder;[3]—Dante, on the mountain, while waiting for the carriage
8000 feet high. (In Par. III. IV)

The driving down hill by a dark wild looking postilion with flashing eyes,
was so remarkable for rapidity and skill, as to be among the curiosities at
least, if not the wonders of the pass.

Thursd. Sep. 20.

Bolladore. Post. Beds good: bread, cheese, milk, eggs, likewise. Higher
prices on this side, as might be expected.

Bolladore to Varenna,[4] 10 posts, 6½–5¾.

The materials & workmanship of this road from Santa Maria downwards[5]
surpass, taken as a whole, anything of the kind I ever saw.

The scenery is beautiful above & about Bolladore. The valley below is on
the whole fertile & fine, but a little monotonous to persons grown so fastidi-
ous as we are. The channel built for the Adda at Tirano[6] is remarkable.
From Morbegno,[7] or on quitting it, you see the lake of Como.

Grapes in immense quantities: Indian corn often growing under the vines:
and where nothing was above the corn, sometimes cabbages below it.

Many picturesque forms & handsome faces among the people: but on the
whole they look sallow & unhealthy and are sadly afflicted with goitres.

The views of the lake are delightful from the noble road of the Austrian
government, and constantly varied. Note especially the crag which is bored
by the last series of galleries before reaching Varenna.

We have now enjoyed the magnificence of nature for four days, in almost
uninterrupted surfeit: on Como we see grandeur in its softest and most
tempered form, but it is grandeur still. We saw the view from the hill
behind Varenna at sunset. The dark masses and bold outlines of the
mountains towards Como, and also beyond Lugano,[8] with the Monte di

---

[1] Also called Worms; 10 miles SW. of Santa Maria, in Lombardy.
[2] La Serra, a narrow defile dividing the Valtelline from the territory of Bormio.
[3] Josiah *Conder, *Italy* (1831).
[4] Cp. 5 July 32.   [5] *Sc.* southwards.
[6] Town 20 miles SSW. of Bormio, in the Valtelline.
[7] In the Valtelline, 30 miles west of Tirano.
[8] On Lake Lugano, 16 miles NNW. of Como.

Maneggio[1] and its lofty peak in the foreground, were admirably relieved by the last rays of the sun above, and by the lingering remains of reflection from the water below: the boats slept on the bosom of the lake, the wealth of vineyards trees and gardens was around us, and the stillness of the scene was not broken but made palpable by the constant succession of curfews from the innumerable churches. One cannot look upon such a scene and believe how much of sin and sorrow lie within its range.

It is curious to notice how far false shame extends. The Tyrolese postilions we remarked disencumbered themselves several times of their greatcoats on entering a village: especially one of them who had a blanket to serve in that capacity which he always removed from the eyes of the mountain fashionables.

Conder seems well written.

The factories appear to increase rapidly in the Tyrol for several posts above Feldkirch.

Fr. Sep. 21.

Post at Varenna very good. Prices become higher hereabouts. Varenna to Milan 5½ Italian posts, 6½–2¾. Horses very much fagged, the dregs of the Coronation.[2]

As far as Monza[3] the road is varied and picturesque: from thence it (one may say) tunnels through lines of acacias to Milan, so completely is the view excluded.

We could not wait the requisite half an hour at Monza to see the Iron Crown.[4] The cathedral is worth seeing: there is a dim richness about its interior. The arches are pointed but in the last degree I ever saw.

Milan, Hotel de la Ville. After the necessary preparations I began my out of doors operations by inquiring for Manzoni.[5] No one about the Inn could help me—there were many Manzoni's. But mine was 'il celebre autore'. No whit the better. I went out and asked an old dignified looking priest, who was extremely kind, set out to show me the way, turned backwards and forwards half a dozen times saying 'di quà,' 'ah, meglio di quà,' 'ma, no, meglio di quà,'[6] told me I should find him *un poco stravangante*,[7] talked of the Italian language, said Metastasio[8] was very limited in his vocabulary: and that he could read Goldsmith easily, Lord Byron with difficulty, Shakespeare hardly at all—and took me within sight of the house,

---

[1] On the western shore of Lake Como.

[2] Ferdinand von Habsburg, 1793–1875, king of Hungary 1830, emperor of Austria 1835–48, often insane, was crowned king of Lombardy at Milan on 6 September 1838.

[3] Town 22 miles south of Varenna and 6 NNE. of Milan; ancient capital of the Lombard kings.

[4] The traditional crown of Lombardy, said to date from the sixth century; kept in the cathedral.

[5] Alessandro Manzoni, 1785–1873, poet, author, and patriot, for whom Verdi wrote his *Requiem*. Diarist had introduction from Rio: cp. Bowe, *Rio*, 155 ff.

[6] 'But, no, better that way'.

[7] 'a little mad'.

[8] Italian poet and librettist, 1698–1782.

where I found that the master was, unhappily for me, at his *villegiatura*.[1] Conte Casati[2] came & most kindly drove us to the Arco della Pace,[3] round a part of the Boulevards and to his club the Casino de' Nobili[4] where the Milanese gossips and politicians are satisfied with one table, and half a dozen newspapers of the size of letter-paper and foolscap.

He told us the priests at first opposed education but were beginning to concur in it. The government had long been most steady in its favour. He doubted how the amnesty would be interpreted as regards the exiles.[5] They are treated as minors and the proceeds of their properties reserved. He loves the English.

Our driver into Milan seemed very intelligent and told us that the land was cultivated by a peasant tenantry, who wrought together with their families, raising corn and then Indian corn, and paying as rent three parts out of four. Brick buildings are found warmer and are esteemed. Accordingly we saw some walls painted to assume the appearance of brick. The people eat meat. The sale of cattle is taxed, not the possession. Almost all go to school. The children of the *miserabili*,[6] gratis. The tenantry have a house found, and liberty of woodcutting. The Emperor left Milan much beloved. He has la testa un po' grossa, ma una brava persona.[7] The Empress is un po' smorta e pallida, ma una bella persona.[8] Taxes were reduced, he said one half, on the coronation. The fine granite railing by the (running) canal was paid by a legacy of Beauharnois:[9] the Austrian Gov^t. were opposed to the work, the *City* went to law with the Government, and gained the suit. This shows like more freedom than we give credit for.

Sep. 22.

Finished my letters to Mr G., H.J.G., & corrections of my proofsheets, and of the Handbook of S. Germany, for Murray.[10] Bankers, passport, post office.

Duomo before breakfast. How magnificent are the East windows: the centre has its scenes from the Revelations, & illustrative mottoes included. 'Magna Babylon' included. No one can say that this wonderful building is in effect & character *Gothic*, whatever else it may be. Most of the hangings[11] still remained in the eastern part. They are very gorgeous, and have so much gold upon the blue and crimson, that nothing but great taste and

---

[1] Country residence. See 24 Sept. 38.

[2] Gabriel Casati, 1798–1873, count and politician; mayor of Milan 1837 ff.

[3] Copied from the arch of Constantine in Rome; begun 1807 to commemorate Napoleon's victories; completed after 1815 and dedicated to the Peace of Vienna; inaugurated by Emperor Ferdinand 10 Sep. 1838.

[4] In the Palazzo Talenti.

[5] An amnesty for all political offences had been proclaimed at the recent coronation; and political refugees were invited to return.

[6] 'poor'.   [7] 'a bit thick in the head, but a good man'.

[8] 'a little languid and pale, but a beautiful woman'. (Maria) Anna (Carolina Pia), 1803–84, princess of Savoy, m. Ferdinand 1831, no c.

[9] Eugène de Beauharnais, 1781–1824, Napoleon's stepson, viceroy of Italy 1805–13.

[10] Volunteered for the edition of 1840: see Add MS 44259, ff. 6, 7.

[11] Gold embroidered hangings of silk and velvet, specially designed by the architect Sanquirico, adorned the cathedral for the coronation.

skill could save them from tawdriness. The crimson festoons of drapery on the upper part of the building are very graceful. From amidst their richness, and directly over the gorgeous baldacchino[1] and the imperial crown, projects the simple crucifix with its striking inscription below it 'Attendite ad petram, unde excisiestis.'[2] There seems to me to be great moral grandeur in this.

A part of the ornaments seem to have been merely theatrical. Seats probably fewer than in Westminster Abbey—otherwise, the view finer: no screen to bisect the edifice.

Brera. Alas for the modern exhibition;[3] extremely copious in quantity. Mensi, first in station at Florence[4] here exhibits a horror of a Marchioness.[5] Amerling, of Vienna,[6] a curious illusion of light through a crimson curtain on a reposing mother and her babe. Podesti[7] good picture of Dante & Giotto, a scene. Buttinelli a beautiful statue of Venus from the shell.[8]

Among the ancient pictures, looked chiefly at the Guercino,[9] Ab[raham] & Hagar[10] which appears to be shaded away? the St Peter and St Paul, a very fine painting, but in which the *idea*, especially of St Paul, seems inadequately represented? Sasso Ferrato's[11] Madonna & child, lovely but humanised, void of inspiration? Guercino's Ecce Homo above, marking the progress of art towards Carlo Dolce? A raccourci[12] of the dead Saviour by A. Mantegna—surely no man who felt his subject duly would have hazarded it in such an experiment? The result I thought very disagreeable. Lastly, the exquisite Nozze of Raphael:[13] there is not here any hardness of outline? but the utmost grace purity and sweetness.

Santa Maria delle Grazie[14]—to see the ruins of the celebrated Supper:[15] and the pictures in the Church,[16] including that of the Virgin. We conversed some time with the custode, a female, who showed us deposited crutches amongst other articles. These are sold monthly for the benefit of the Church: there are however pictures which record recent cures, and amongst others the alleged resuscitations of 1836 and 7, of two persons already dead, who are now living, known, whom she named & who resort habitually to the Church. One had been dead two or three hours.—First she said we must believe in, and pray to, God; then Maria Virgine. But this is not by Scripture, nor by the creed: the priest tells them so. She is the Stewardess

[1] 'canopy'.
[2] 'Look unto the rock whence ye are hewn.' Isa. li. 1.
[3] Every second year an exhibition of local art was held at the Brera gallery.
[4] Francesco Mensi, 1790–1838, Italian painter, professor at the Academy of Florence.
[5] 'Portrait of a Lady.' Cf. *Gazzetta Privilegiata di Milano*, 20 Sept. 1838.
[6] Friedrich von Amerling, Austrian painter, 1803–87.
[7] Francesco Podesti, Italian historical painter, 1800–95.
[8] A 'Venus Anadyomene' by Alessandro Puttinati, Italian sculptor, 1801–72, was in the exhibition.
[9] Giovanni Francesco Barbieri, called Guercino, painter, 1591–1666.
[10] Gen. xvi.
[11] Giovanni Battista Salvi, 1609–85, called Sassoferrato, painter.
[12] 'foreshortening'.
[13] Called by the Italians the 'Sposalizio', 'marriage of the Virgin'.
[14] Church, formerly convent of the Dominicans.
[15] 'Last Supper' of Leonardo da Vinci, mural in refectory.
[16] Frescoes.

of Divine grace; but one may be a Christian without praying to her if we pray to the Trinity. The particular picture depends for its efficacy on the lively faith with which it is regarded. We endeavoured to mitigate the Romanism of her sentiments without disturbing the devotion. Amphitheatre[1]—and home.

Sunday. Sep 23.

Found Sir G. Clark here—and the Verneys.[2]
Mr. Dalton[3] read prayers mg & aft.
Tea with the Verneys & Sermon.
Sermon at San Fedele in mg—from the corner of a large & crowded Church.[4] I could not hear it.
Vinc. Lir. finished. & Notizia de' Convertiti[5] finished. Few priests were walking out among the gay crowds in the evening.

23.[6]

At Milan I had much embarrassment as to the propriety of my leaving my family to seek a very problematical benefit for myself; and I was anxious to hear from home—a word or a syllable w^d have turned me back—but no letter came.

Monday Sep 24

Breakf. with Sir H. Verney, after packing. Saw Mr Earle & his party. He is younger than in 1832. Then went to Manzoni's country house to see him in a very fair looking carriage—with bad springs. The people here are so industrious that they have not time to speak their own beautiful language. Brusuglio[7] is no more than Brusù.

I remained an hour and a half with M. whom it was the great object of my visit here to see, and was greatly delighted with him. He appears to be a man of rather strong Transalpine[8] principles, but of fervent piety and charity. He soon went into the questions of unity and authority: and I was not loth to follow him. He said it caused him a strong and indescribable emotion to find sympathies existing between himself as a Catholic and others non-Cattolici: he hardly knew whether with more of pleasure or of pain. From asking me about my journey & return he got to Parliament, from that to the conflict of principles, the state of America, the horror of slavery there, the necessity of a living and personal authority to maintain

---

[1] Built 1806 for Napoleon by the architect Luigi Canonica, 1762–1844.
[2] Sir Harry *Verney, m. 1835 Eliza, da. of Admiral Sir George Hope; she d. 1857.
[3] Perhaps Charles Browne Dalton, 1810–93; chaplain to Lincoln's Inn 1837–46; canon of St. Paul's 1845; rector of Lambeth 1846–54, vicar of Highgate 1854–78.
[4] Built by Pellegrini (1527–96), one of the architects of Milan Cathedral.
[5] *Notizia dei protestanti convertiti alla religione cattolica dal 1794 al 1832*, Venice, 1834.
[6] This entry from Lambeth MS 1423. He also wrote this day a note on heresy, Add MS 44728, f. 151.
[7] Brussuglio, Manzoni's country estate, about 6 miles from Milan.
[8] i.e. ultramontane.

and restore unity in religion since it was from the divided state of Christendom that infidelity derived all its strength. He contended without saying that the Pope was infallible in so many words yet that his dicta were to be absolutely followed in the meantime though the promise of infallibility belonged to the Episcopate acting with and under the Pope. He argued largely for the necessity of an *absolute certainty* in all matters of faith: and for the recognition of the successor of St Peter, as the essential condition of belonging to the Church. He regarded us as being cut off from the Church by the simple fact of our having assumed the right to withdraw from the Pope's jurisdiction.—I contended for the obligatory nature of probable evidence, and that the authority of the Church was of that description: that the promise of our Lord did not extend to a security from all but from vital error: that the Church of England had not renounced Catholic communion nor anathematised the Roman Churches: that absolute certainty hardly belonged to the nature of our faculties: that we knew not since the schism of E. & W. where to find the voice of the universal Church: that we received those Councils held before it, which were Ecumenical: that though our Church did not bind her members to believe in an infallible organ of the body, yet she did not prohibit it: that we waited the time when Christendom might again be one, but I could not see what England's Church had in its power to do, or was accordingly responsible for not doing, towards that consummation for which in the meantime we must hope and pray.—He hoped that he might pray for me and for my reception of the truth: I also, in return, that the recognition of truth, and the search for its forms, might constitute a durable bond of union. I asked for permission to write to him.

He spoke warmly and highly of England, quella bella Inghilterra, tanto distinta in cotanti rispetti:[1] happy would be the day when she should be reunited: of which he saw the promise in the strong spirit of religion yet preserved in her, in her retention of the Episcopate, in the defence of the faith which she had produced, the best of any *not* from the Church (of Rome).

He spoke of alterations in their Coronation service and the reason but he wished me not to mention them as coming from him on account of their political position here.[2]

I put to him two points of fact in particular: whether the British Bishops whom Augustine *found* were of the Church—he said no; unless they believed in the successor of St Peter as the head of the Church. And whether the deposition of Bishops by the Pope under the French Concordat was lawful —He said it was though against the Canons, because by a power above the Canons. The truth is that the *Church* argument of the R.C.s, which is very strong as against popular Protestantism, is their great & real strength: and yet men who would show that this argument belongs to us & cannot be used against us, are charged with Popery.

[1] 'that beautiful England, so distinguished in so many respects.'
[2] The Iron Crown of Lombardy, which Napoleon had been the first to wear since Charles V, was placed on the head of Ferdinand I by the archbishop of Milan.

Left Milan at $2\frac{1}{4}$. $6\frac{1}{4}$ posts to Piacenza,[1] by $8\frac{3}{4}$. road flat—country most fertile—but this plain, after a little time, like the Wurmser Loch, though in the opposite sense, defies description. At sunset we had the most delicate rosy tints poured over the whole Eastern sky near the horizon. The lights were very fine, the atmosphere being moist. The bridge of boats over the Po rough bad and dear. The *doganieri*[2] of Piacenza having let us go, one began to ask for money literally choked upon it: I was determined he should speak out & pressed him: he was obliged to give it up: then the other came to the rescue and significantly put his finger into his mouth! As they had *given* us our *congè* we thought they might have something—*ma*.

Tues. Sep. 25.

San Marco at Piacenza; good. 8–$7\frac{3}{4}$. $9\frac{1}{4}$ Italian posts: spending two hours at Parma,[3] & with innumerable stops for passport, dogana;[4] &c. Asked for money five times today by doganieri. The posting is very good: and we generally changed under five minutes. The country continues rich in the extreme: we find the third crop of hay cutting, with a fourth expected: the vintage in progress: some grape wagons drawn by six oxen: the treading begun: Indian-corn-threshing on a floor in the open air (cf the threshing *floor* of Araunah the Jebusite[5]): much of the land ploughed up: the long vine festoons most beautiful.

At Piacenza, admired particularly the *men* of the bronze equestrian statues.[6] The division of the cupola of the Cathedral into so many as eight compartments has put the artist (Guercino)[7] at a disadvantage as regards his composition?

Evangelists & Sybils are mixed.

The wealth of Parma in paintings has been indeed immense.

In the Cathedral, the heads on the doorposts[8] & the families of the two artists are very beautiful. Here we find the face in Parmegiano's wife, which he so constantly reproduces.

The Ascension, in S. Giovanni,[9] is surely in too dark a position for such a picture—and the light which is admitted from pigeon hole windows below the dome is disagreeable in its effect.

I did not like the Evangelists[10] so much as (from recollection) those of Domenichino in S. Andrea[11] at Rome. Particularly those of Saint John.

---

[1] 28 miles SE. of Milan, the capital of the duchy of Piacenza, which together with the duchies of Parma and Guastalla was ruled by the archduchess Marie-Louisa.

[2] 'customs officers'.

[3] 25 miles SE. of Piacenza, capital of the duchy of Parma.

[4] 'customs'.

[5] II Samuel xxiv. 16–18.

[6] By Francesco Mocchi, on the Piazza de' Cavalli, of the two dukes Alessandro and Ranuccio Farnese. They date from 1624–6.

[7] Guercino's frescos of four prophets and four sibyls fill the eight-sided cupola.

[8] Said to be of Correggio and Parmegiano, each painted by the other.

[9] Fresco in the dome, by Correggio.

[10] Four evangelists and four fathers of the Church, in the four pendentives of the dome.

[11] San Andrea della Valle, see 14 Apr. 32.

Saw too the Stoccata[1]—Theatre[2]—(convent of St Paul shut)[3]—Academy.[4] Madonna di S. Girolamo—Madonna della Scodella,[5] by Correggio—one called Raphael & strangely termed I Cinque Santi,[6] our Lord being one—a beautiful Francesco Francia,[7] (besides one of the Dead Saviour) where every face has a tempered submission except that of the Infant Christ which is divinely radiant.—The flagellation, by Lionello Spada,[8] is powerful.

Wed. 26. Sept.

Alberto Grande at Modena,[9] good.
7–8½. Cathedral, & Palace. A large picture Gallery. Guido's San Rocco & (a) Crucifixion: both very fine: the head of the Saint in the former. In the latter, too much roundness & fulness of flesh?
9¼–12¾. 3 posts to Bologna.
Got Roman money. Went to San Petronio[10]—San Paolo[11]—Palazzo Zampieri,[12] two Francesco Francias, Madonnas, eminently beautiful. This collection is for sale. A Salvator head of Demosthenes, 30 louis asked: a Ludovico Carraci, head, at 6 louis: I would have bid for these but without advice I am afraid. Palazzo Mareschalchi[13]—all in confusion. Zambeccali[14]—pictures here as in the two former, on sale: they sound dear. Our banker describes the nobles as very needy, and all classes as depressed, and increasingly so. Delighted to refresh my memory at the Academy Gallery: especially on my two old favourites the Crucifixion & the Innocents both by Guido: the former more for[15] conception & the latter more for execution; but both for both. I like the figure embracing the cross least: it is not *divinised*.—Note here also a splendid Francia,[16] next before coming to the Innocents: & the Perugino. as also the San Pietro of Dom[enichino], the S. Cecilia, the Samson & Dead Saviour of Guido—but there are indeed too many precious pictures to be named.[17]

Th. Sep. 27.

Tre Mori at Bologna, a *branch* of San Marco, under the same master. Very comfortable.

[1] Church of the Madonna della Steccata, built round an image previously palisaded in the street.
[2] Teatro Farnese, in the Farnese palace, built 1618.
[3] A former Benedictine convent with frescoes by Correggio in the refectory.
[4] In the Farnese Palace, a school for the fine arts, with a picture gallery.
[5] Both by Correggio.
[6] Attributed to Raphael. Jesus glorified with the Virgin and St. Paul on one side, St. John the Baptist and St. Catherine on the other.
[7] Francesco Raibolini, called Il Francia, painter and goldsmith, 1460–1517.
[8] Painter, 1576–1622.   [9] 28 miles ESE. of Parma.
[10] Largest church in Bologna, 14th century.
[11] 17th century church of great magnificence.
[12] The Palazzo Sampieri had become a kind of auction mart for pictures.
[13] Famous for Correggios.
[14] Zambeccari. Here were Carraccis, Guercinos, etc.
[15] A second 'for' here deleted.   [16] Madonna and child with saints.
[17] And wrote note on Lamennais, Add MS 44728, f. 152; cp. 1 Oct. 38.

5–7¼. 9 Posts, including the passage of the Appennine,[1] to Florence, where we fixed at Schneiderffs—having failed at the Armi d'Inghilterra to which we went on account of its situation with reference to the greater objects in the city.

Between Pianoro[2] & Lojano[3] there is pretty chestnut scenery in the vale on the right: on the left a singularly mottled country, where the green and brown vegetation are mingled upon an irregular surface with frequent streaks of bare light soil. The Appennines in this part are remarkable for covering a great breadth of ground, without rising to great height. The hillocks are infinitely more numerous than the hills: large families of *cubs*[4] lie out in every direction. The view backwards as the road comes near its height *before* Lojano must be very fine in clear weather. After Filicare[5] we came upon a new region, and the line of hills to the left presented a sharpness of outline which is curiously contrasted with the luxuriantly soft light in which they lie. The descent upon Florence is steep and long: the view of the city was hidden by the dusk of evening but the eye just showed us the general outline of the picture and the mind can supply something of the rest.

Made a fair breakfast at Lojano.

In this hill country we learn that the tenants pay *half* of the produce as rent: and can subsist well on the remainder. An old priest was pointed out as *un vero Ebreo*,[6] worth 70, or 80,000£. The *factors*[7] are the class who grow rich.

At the Tuscan dogana we did as with the others; *first* having our formal dismissal: and then exercising a very limited liberality.

Here you are ordinarily assaulted on entering *every* considerable town by the Doganiere, who utters dark hints about searching: by the man of passports, who requests to be paid for detaining you. & if it be dusk by a *soidisant* porter whom you may see shutting the gate that he may open it again for your benefit.

Fr. Sep. 28.

Discussed and provisionally arranged our route to Rome. Occupied in some little matters of business & with leaving letters of introduction. Got however two hours for the Gallery[8] before three when it closes—then to dine at La Luna (our old friend of 1832), to the Cathedral, the Baptistery and the Campanile for the view which is panoramic (nearly) and very fine. The brown roofs and white walls of the houses present a mottled appearance, like, in its own kind, to that which the lower Appennines presented to us: but the frequent spots of houses among the deep green of the environs

---

[1] Consistently spelt thus, Italian fashion.
[2] Town 9 miles south of Bologna.
[3] Post station 6 miles south of Pianoro.
[4] Small hills, seeming to branch from other hills.
[5] Post and customs station on the Tuscan frontier, 5 miles south of Lojano.
[6] 'a real Jew'.
[7] Managers of estates.
[8] The Uffizi.

give great animation to the landscape, and the framework of hills around the city is singularly complete. To speak mathematically, Florence lies nearly in one of the foci of an eccentric ellipse the lines of hill forming the figure. What pleasure and advantage have we in these bird's eye views! We may judge what they are in nature, by what they are, when attained, in higher subject matter.

Certainly the return to a collection like the Gallery is more delightful than the first visit. In a matter of *art*: were it pomp the case would be otherwise. One is able to set out at once from the point which was formerly attained: and there is the pleasure of old acquaintance joined with that of the idea or the hope of progress. And yet with me these words have little meaning.—I find however the value of Rio's book[1] in my memory & notes, & wish I had the original with me. I have been applying his principles to the Frate Angelico da Fiesole,[2] to Bronzino,[3] to Lorenzo da Credi.[4] It is curious to observe how the faces in his pictures hardly ever fail whatever the number to exhibit together with considerable variety of feature an expression of real sanctity, even when the drawing of the figures is as if they had been cut out of paper with the scissors.—Bronzino appears to have painted in the pagan spirit. His descent of the Lord into Limbus[5] offends equally by the characters of many among the countenances, and by an unnecessary profusion of nudity which offends the eye, as well as taste and the subject.—A picture of the Annunciation by L. da Credi detained me long: the Angel is on one knee which one may interpret for charity's sake at least as before God, of whom and whose message his countenance as well as the uplifted forefinger show that he is full while the wings still extended announce that he has just descended. The Virgin is on her knees, overcome, nay almost horrorstruck, as if by the contrast between her unworthiness and her high destiny, the face expressing something like that sentiment of St Peter, Depart from me, for I am a sinful man, O Lord.[6]

Sat Sep. 29.

Three hours at the Pitti—but they are as drops lost in the ocean. Royal courtesy can go no further than in the free access, the wide range, the liberty of demeanour, the convenient catalogues which are here permitted and provided respectively. No one should forget to steal a moment for the magnificent *pietra dura* tables, even from the pictures.

In this gallery I suppose those great masters of the Florentine school, Fra Bartolommeo and Andrea del Sarto are to be studied to the best advantage. The former is I think much more forcible and pronounced, with equal harmony. Observe particularly his Saint Mark: and his risen Saviour yet more—except that the figures are too short.

Julius the Second[7] here is not so fresh and rich as in the Tribune?[8] But

[1] Cp. 12 Aug. 38.   [2] 1387–1455.
[3] Agnolo di Cosimo Allori, called Il Bronzino, poet and painter, 1503–63.
[4] Painter, goldsmith and sculptor, 1456–1537.
[5] Then in Florence Cathedral.   [6] Luke v. 8.
[7] Pope 1503–13. Portrait by Raphael.
[8] The other portrait by Raphael is in the Tribune of the Uffizi.

Leo X,[1] and Angiolo Doni,[2] are enough to stop every mouth. (In the Madonna del Baldacchino,[3] the mitred figure[4] has a face resembling Manzoni.—)

Guido's Cleopatra suggests that as he does not rise to angelic so neither can he fall to vicious natures. The character of Cleopatra could not be inferred from this beautiful picture by one ignorant of her history.

The Pitti is rich in Salvators. There is something in his portrait of himself indicating the bizarrerie of his genius, to whose tortuous rule he makes every subject bend. Take for instance his Peace burning the arms of Mars. Over the whole landscape he has cast an indistinct ambiguous air, almost betokening wind or tempest: peace herself looks any thing but peaceful, and one would believe rather that she was lighting the flames of Discord than burning the arms of Mars. Again what a strange conception is his poet. *Nearer* a Hogarth than the Shakespearian delineation: though I do not say, *near*.

A thunderstorm: I took refuge in the Santo Spirito convent,[5] and read the epitaphs for nearly an hour. I thought their tone on the whole quite as good as ours: a few French were for the most part indifferent. An infant son (16 mo.) of Gen. Sir Geo. Walker[6] lies buried here: I suppose allowed because he was infant.

I thought the following had much beauty.

> Qui riposa
> Nella pace del Signore
> Giuseppa Lemmi Pozzolini,
> Pia, Gentile, Misericordiosa,
> Amantissima del Marito P. Lemmi etc.
> * * * * * * * * *
>
> O Dolce Consorte!
> Quando la comun figlia
> Sara venuta all'età della ragione,
>   Io, dopo averle narrato
> Di che virtù fosti adorna,
> La condurrò a questo sepolcro
> Perchè, le lagrime spurgendovi
>   Preghi Iddio
> Di farla simile alla Madre.[7]

---

[1] Pope, 1513–21. The portrait is by Raphael.   [2] Portrait by Raphael.
[3] By Raphael.   [4] St. Augustine.
[5] Of the Austin friars. Its cloisters are filled with memorials ancient and modern.
[6] George Townshend *Walker, 1764–1842; distinguished service in Peninsular War; K.C.B. 1815; commander-in-chief of Madras 1825, general 1838.
[7] 'Here lies, in the peace of the Lord, Giuseppa Lemmi Pozzolini, godly, gentle and merciful, the affectionate wife of P. Lemmi etc.
      * * * * * * * *
O sweet wife! When our daughter has arrived at the age of reason, after having told her with what virtues thou wast adorned, I will lead her to this tomb, that here shedding tears she may pray God to make her like her mother.'

In the church most of the pictures want light. Ghirlandajos Bearing the Cross[1] is pretty visible, in the North Transept.

Evening, Marchesa Torrigiani's[2]—(Mrs Seymer's[3] introduction.) Mixed English & Italian company. Quiet & early—if compared with London.

The administration of baptisms is not improved, apparently, since 1832.[4]

I learnt in conversation that here also the peasants pay one half of the produce as rent: and are better conditioned than in Lombardy. The landlord finds the house & pays taxes.

Sunday Sep. 30.

Sermon in the Cathedral at 8¾. On the nature and glory of the Redeemer before, during, and after his Incarnation. The preacher spoke with great fluency and had evidently studied the subject with much care, for his language appeared to be not less accurate than his delivery was rapid. He concluded with a prayer, to which all the congregation knelt, of devotion and selfdedication to our Lord, and petition for this grace in order thereto. In an interval of the sermon, as usual, he more colloquially exhorted them to alms.

At five I heard another Sermon in the Santa Maria Novella: respecting the indifference of the age in religion—it dealt chiefly in generalities.

English Church at 12. Casa Ferroni. Arrangements good. We paid at the door. Here this is probably necessary. An excellent Sermon on the Lord's Supper from Mr Tennant,[5] just settled here—in whom I was happy to find an old acquaintance.

Monday Oct 1.

Finished De La Mennais singular book "Les Affaires de Rome".[6] It has some striking disclosures. The writer appears greatly bewildered: and to have lost some of the ordinary faculties while he possesses others which are extraordinary.

Also read Conder's Florence.[7] It is very strange to skip the Gallery:[8] but the book on the whole is very useful though not complete.

10¾-2¼. In the Gallery, with K. and with Tennant.

Is Corregio's Virgin in the Tribune (the small picture) adoring or only wondering? Neither the expression of the countenance nor the attitude of the hands, suit the former conception.

The face of Michael Angelo's Holy Family is wonderful: and the head of Joseph magnificent. Instead of shading away his outlines by approximating the conterminous colours or by a line of light, he heightens the hues as they

---

[1] Now in the Louvre.

[2] In the Palazzo de' Mazzi.

[3] Harriet, née Beckford, m. 1807 Henry (Ker-) Seymer, 1782–1834, naturalist; mother of H.K.-; d. 1853.

[4] See 17 Mar. 32.

[5] Ottiwell Tennant, 1780?–1863, rector of Upton, Huntingdonshire, 1821.

[6] (1836.)   [7] In his *Italy*, ii. ch. 5.

[8] *Conder does not treat the Uffizi.

approach the limiting line and strengthens the contrast. The consequence is that the outlines are as clear as those of the hardest scissor-cut figures of the old German school.

Guido's Virgin does not express the Mother of our Lord. It is more suited for a fair penitent of the 19th or 17th century. The same may be said of Carlo Dolce's rich and beautiful painting which hangs in (I think) the Sala del Baroccio.[1]

Where but in the Tribune we have six pictures by Raphael all side by side and exhibiting his three manners?[2] Of *all* the pictures in that celebrated room, give me the "Vierge au Chardonneret."

Fra Bartolommeo has something of breadth in execution? In colour and design he resembles Andrea, in the former closely? but has more grandeur of conception, and more force in execution?

Observe Leonardo's fine abbozzo[3] in the Scuola Toscana. He has sketched in outline his principle figures and then darkened the whole of the ground around them: did he then mean these figures to receive their tone from the ground? Contrast (if so) Sir T. Lawrence's Mr Wilberforce[4] where the head is finished, the figure outlined, and the Canvass, except a little round the head, naked.

I cannot appreciate the drapery of the Niobe:[5] like that of many other & specially Roman statues: its details are petty and its *ensemble* heavy: it supposes some stuff entirely without body, presents crumples rather than folds, in no degree either relieves the form or adds to its dignity, and wants that *generality* of character which is required for the ideal?

Santa Croce—bookshops—Giardino Torregiani.[6] This has considerable space & great capabilities.

Tues. Oct. 2.

Among the alabasters—at Pisani's—and marbles, at Bonelli's.[7] Revisited S. M. Novella to see the picture of the Inferno (are the popes in holes represented? I was afraid to strain in looking—)[8] and Cimabue's Madonna —rude, but there is majesty in the Infant Saviour's Countenance.

Pitti again.

Bronzino's Holy Family has much of the force of that of M[ichael] A[ngelo] in the Tribune: extreme strength & clearness without hardness of outline: rather heightening of *contrasts* there, than any *rapprochemens*.

Guido's Cleopatra, it may be observed has the same face as his Lucretia.

---

[1] Showing Galla Placidia haloed as a saint replacing an idol with a crucifix; a portrait (1675) of Felicita, second wife of the Emperor Leopold I, d. 1676.

[2] Of Perugino—Portrait of a Florentine Lady, the Vierge au Chardonneret; of Leonardo da Vinci and Fra Bartolomeo—La Fornarina, Pope Julius II; of Michael Angelo— St. John preaching; the Holy Family.

[3] 'sketch', of the adoration of the Magi.

[4] In the National Portrait Gallery, an unfinished portrait of William *Wilberforce.

[5] See 22 Mar. 32.

[6] Combined garden, dairy, and factory on the city's outskirts.

[7] Bonelli's studio was on the ground floor of Scheiderff's hotel.

[8] In the Capella Strozzi, paintings of Hell and Paradise by Bernardo and Andrea Orcagna, after Dante.

But what a contrast of characters! One is to tell which is which by the dagger and the asp respectively!

His Rebecca at the well—has much defective drawing?

The miscalled Holy Family of Sustermans[1] is most offensive: he has dared to paint Cosmo III as the Saviour and his mother as the Virgin.[2] Not to mention that the figures are so essentially modern as to offend one should think art and religion equally. One might almost turn for relief to that other misnamed Holy Family of Rubens close by: as discordant with its subject as can well be conceived. How much better has Vandyck treated this same subject in the Pitti: and how remarkable are the points of contrast between him and Rubens, arising apparently out of character, not circumstances of art.—Yet the San Francesco, which is all brown, is very fine, as Rubens here could not show his vices.

Cigoli's[3] S. Francesco is beautiful. I thought his Ecce Homo savoured too much of Carlo Dolce.

Observe in A. del Sarto's Annunciation, as compared with that of Lorenzo da Credi, the progress of *Popery*. Here the Angel has a lily, is almost on both knees, and seems to address himself wholly to the Virgin as if without sense of the Presence from which he had come. She does not kneel at all, and shows little emotion, and I thought no humility, much less revulsion.

Titian's portraits in this collection are most magnificent. Even that of Aretino is a noble painting, though, perhaps from prejudice, I could not agree with K. that the head itself is a fine one. The Magdalen seems to me most inappropriate.

Michael Angelo's Fates—one would hope not his—strongly drawn, but not equal to the subject: hardly to the three weird sisters in Macbeth or the Bride of Lammermoor.

Caravaggio's sleeping Cupid exhibits strongly his characteristic tips of light.

The figures too short in Fra Bartolommeo's Risen Saviour? The tone of colouring still lighter in the Florentine school than in the Bolognese?

Goodbye to the Pitti—with great regret. rode to Fiesole—round the town, and made calls. Also in the delightful Cascino. The Fiesole view is charming: not so the road, which is steep and not all *carriageable*. The prospect reaches away to Prato and Pistoja[4] northwards: over to Vallombrosa[5] S., and exhibits the Bolognese road.—A Franciscan convent on the top:[6] clean enough. A few are educated here for the priesthood. They learn Latin: few priests, the Frate said, know Greek. There are 16 priests in this convent. The body[7] eat twice a day: meat four times a week: have a garden: take

---

[1] Justus Sustermans, 1597–1681, Flemish painter who worked in Florence.
[2] Cosmo III, grand duke of Tuscany 1670–1723, s. of Vittoria della Rovere.
[3] Ludovico Cardi da Cigoli, 1559–1613, painter, sculptor and architect.
[4] Tuscan towns NW. of Florence.
[5] Upland meadows and valley, with the famous monastery of the Camaldules, 18½ miles SE. of Florence.
[6] Of Fiesole.
[7] 'the body' instead of 'they all'.

wine: beg through town and country: sleep seven or eight hours; rising however at midnight and for the day at four or five.

Oct. 3.[1]

Again in Florence I have had the same doubts,[2] augmented by my really finding that the eye is really very much tried in looking at pictures, and also by the strong lights of Italy, from which I had not anticipated difficulty my defect being in the lids—but still I have no letter: and it seems right to make a longer trial.

Wednesday Oct 3.

Wrote to Mr G.—Arranged about some alabasters & marbles (NB Pisani asks £6 for the Hercules & Centaur ab[out] 13. in. [high]) (Laocoon—Lotta[tori].[3]) revisited the Spirito Santo. The galleries being shut we left Florence at one. In going (7 posts) to Arezzo[5] we occupied 9h. 40m.
Arezzo—La Posta—fair accommodations, but the people of the Inn great rogues.

The country beautiful: after Ponte a Sieve,[6] the first post, the road opens on an upper valley of the Arno, highly cultivated, bounded with hills, and with fine undulations. Again after Incisa[7] there is a noble screen of Appennines to the left. The appearance of the towns is very pleasing: and they are thickly set upon this fruitful soil.
Our postilions are still much given to cracking their whips many times successively, though not so loud as in Germany, where the practice might seem to expose them to the penalty of Salmoneus.
(Qui) flammas Iovis & sonitus imitatur Olympi.[8]
They use it to warn foot passengers, or the gatekeepers of towns, or the people of the post as they approach it; or the drivers of any carriage on the road at night thus make each other aware of their approach. It is due to truth to say that they also use it to show off strength and skill—and *not* to quicken the horses: they get the *wool*[9] without the noise.

Thursday Oct 4.

6½ A.M. to 2¾ A.M. of Friday. 12 Italian posts, from Arezzo to Terni. Including the hill or mountain passes 1. of the line which bounds the

---

[1] This entry from Lambeth MS 1423.
[2] Cp. the preceding entry there, 23 Sep. 38.
[3] 'Wrestlers' of the Uffizi.
[4] 'less'.
[5] 42 miles SE. of Florence, in Tuscany.
[6] Small town and post station 7 miles east of Florence.
[7] Small town 10 miles south of Ponte a Sieve.
[8] Dum flammam Iovis et sonitus imitatur Olympi: 'While he imitates the flame of Jove and the thunder of Olympus', Aen. vi. 585. Salmoneus, Sisyphus's brother, wishing to be called a god, used to drive his chariot over a brazen bridge, to imitate the thunder, while darting burning torches on every side to imitate the lightning. He was struck by a thunderbolt.
[9] 'Much cry and little wool' says the proverb.

beautiful lake of Thrasymene[1]—(how I longed for Trench's poem—)[2] 2. of the branch Appennine between Spoleto and Terni—add the hill of Perugia,[3] which, up and down, costs an extra hour. It is very curious to observe the slow strength but resistless of these oxen. Apparently[4] they draw the carriages up the steepest hills, by a yoke which seems just to catch the backbone horizontally, (while the horses walk with loose traces) without the slightest muscular effort: but on watching their nostrils one sees that even with their immense power they feel the weight or the heat or both.

We spent two hours at Perugia—½ h. at Foligno to tea: where we found a good Inn, but people roguishly inclined, as were those of Spoleto.

Our scenery today was beautiful & varied. The road describes a considerable part of the circumference of the Lake of Thrasymene, so as to give the full enjoyment of it: and there is a beautiful backview on crossing the hill from it: on the other side a new valley opens,[5] and Perugia is after a time seen at its head, on a kind of promontory-hill, which we ascended on one side and descended on the other into the valley of the Tiber, rich and even, but with a finer line of Appenines on the left than I have before seen. The vale is bounded on the west by a lower line, and runs along the foot of the eastern mountains to Spoleto where it threads the narrow defile which extends almost to Terni. In 1832 I passed it by day:[6] on this evening with a brilliant moonlight, which is particularly advantageous in Italy because it shows the outline in which Italian views excel with great effect through the depth of shadow, which again hides what is generally weaker and deficient in variety, namely the details. A part of these hills for example are covered with wood so very low that it is not in proportion to the masses: this the moonlight suppresses.

Perugia is extremely picturesque in situation, defended by wall & fort, commanding extensive & nearly panoramic prospects, and within agreeably broken by the unevenness of the summit of the hill. We saw here in a rapid *giro*[7] the following objects.

1. The Collegio del Cambio. The sides are painted by Perugino,[8] and in a manner which gives a new idea of his great powers & very high rank as an artist. On the left of the door are, Cato of Utica—Six figures, according to the custode six philosophers, (some of them only practical) namely Numa, Pythagoras, F. Maximus, Camillus, Socrates, Trajan. (There is a vein of resemblance in these characters but it is not very easy to define in any one word—or to trace the cause of their association here unless it was in the personal sympathies & admiration of the artist)—Six figures of warriors[9]—

[1] 30 miles NW. of Terni, 9 west of Perugia; here Hannibal defeated the Romans in 217 B.C.

[2] R. C. *Trench, 'Lines written at the village of Passignano on the Lake of Thrasymene' in *The Story of Justin Martyr and other poems* (1835).

[3] 34 miles NW. of Spoleto, in the Papal States.   [4] 'without' deleted.
[5] 'of the Tiber' here deleted.   [6] Cp. 6 June 1832.
[7] 'tour'.   [8] Two sides of the hall inside.
[9] The guide's particulars were inaccurate: they were three groups of two Romans and a Greek, to represent three cardinal virtues: Lucius Lucinius, Leonidas Spartacus, and Horatius Cocles (fortitude); Publius Scipio, Pericles, and Cincinnatus (temperance); and Furius Camillus, Pittacus and Trajan (justice).

the Transfiguration (head of St. Peter most beautiful)—Adoration of the Magi—six Sibyls and as many prophets; portrait of Raphael as Daniel, and this with several more of the heads are of exquisite conception and execution: and indeed one looks here in vain for the supposed hardness and stiffness of Perugino.

The Venus, the Apollo, & two chiaroscuro horses of the cieling, are by Raphael.

Perugino has likewise here a small head of himself on the wall alone.

The adjoining Chapel is painted by Gian Nicolo Manni,[1] a pupil of P.P.: some of the heads on the cieling are much in Raphael's manner.

Passing the Palazzo Publico and a Fountain which as well as a statue of Iulius III[2] on the other side of the Duomo is by [blank],[3] we entered that edifice:

2. it is very handsome, and very light: it has a Crucifixion by Baroccio,[4] a picture of the three Saint-Protectresses,[5] (School of P.P[erugino]) and a Madonna said to be of St Luke.[6] The face is of the same type as the Cimabue's in the S. Maria Novella at Florence.

3. Close to the Duomo in the Palazzo Conestabile is a small Madonna & Infant Saviour of Raffaelle.[7] A little stiffness perceptible in some of the outlines of the Virgin's head? We were told that 2000 louis had been offered to the owner for this picture: ma. However it is highly beautiful.

4. Chiesa di S. Agostino. Here are two pictures by P. Perugino: a Baptism, and an Adoration. (While Joseph is on one knee, the Virgin is on both.)

5. On the way is the Arch of Augustus.[8] Dwarf columns are introduced in the frieze (if this term be allowable).

6. Academia.[9] We had not time for the antiquities, but found in the Gallery twelve Pinturicchio's—six small. San Girolamo on one side of the Madonna (right of door) has a noble head: & the character of the small paintings is very pleasing. (this picture is praised by Rio.)[10]

In a Glory of Perugino's the Virgin kneels on one side of our Lord, John the Baptist on the other. Corruption had not then reached its height, or at least was not fully felt in art.

A Madonna with saints by Benedetto Buonfili,[11] master of Pietro Perugino. The face of St. Jerome is to be remarked.

There are also works of Angelico da Fiesole—Innocenzo da Imola[12]—and Giovanni Spagna.[13]

[1] 1460?–1544, painter.
[2] Giovanni Maria del Monte, 1487–1555, pope Julius III 1550.
[3] The statue is by Vincenzo Danti, 1530–76, but the fountain is by Giovanni Pisano, b. ca. 1245, d. after 1314.
[4] 1535–1612, painter.
[5] SS. Flavia, Apollonia, and Caterina.
[6] Cp. 13 June 32.
[7] Called the Staffa Madonna, after the count who owned it.
[8] Probably Etruscan.
[9] Gallery of the Academy of Fine Arts.
[10] De la poésie chrétienne, 265–6.
[11] Benedetto Bonfigli, d. 1496, painter.
[12] Innocenzo Vancucci da Imola, ca. 1485– ca. 1546, painter.
[13] Giovanni di Pietro, called Lo Spagna, 1450?–1528, painter.

7. San Francesco.[1] Here we find on the western wall two Guercinos and an Agony by Guido.

On the right (south)wall—the three saint Protectresses by Sasso Ferrato: beautifully executed heads, the types of which appeared to me to be evidently taken from Guido, Raffaelle, and Titian respectively—
Another of St Francis & St Benedict—

The choir is most beautifully carved in oak after the design of Raphael, exquisite in lightness richness & variety. On the north wall a dead Saviour by Sasso Ferrato—Pietà by Buonfili—an Agony by Guercino—a St Paul (on a pillar of the nave) by Guercino, with a volume open and 'Gratiâ Dei sum quod sum, et gratia ejus quae fuit in me non fuit vacua'[2]—Angels by Perugino & Pinturicchio—Madonna by Perugino—Giuditta[3] by Sasso Ferrato—her figure is not loftily conceived—a small Madonna, purporting to be of Raffaelle, faint in colouring, with St Peter & St Paul below by a French artist, Cav. Vicare[4]—an Annunciation by Sasso Ferrato—Adoration (very fine) by Donatone d'Assisi[5]—Pietà by Perugino—& a painting by Bassano.[6]

Such are the scraps which alone I could register of the wealth of Perugia. We departed with regret.

Friday Oct 5.[7]

A.K. having spent his night, or the slender residue after our arrival,[8] in an expedition to the Falls,[9] we breakfasted & started at 9.10 for Rome where we arrived before 8. $8\frac{1}{2}$ posts. Half an hour at Narni seeing that very fine old bridge of truly Roman solidarity. The whole pass of Narni is most beautiful: not altogether an Italian beauty.

The road like those of the Papal dominions generally seems extremely ill engineered, and not well made.

The rocky dells of Civita Castellana & Nepi[10] are picturesque, and the successive basons after joining the Siena road curious. From Monte Lungo we saw the declining daylight on the dome of St Peter's, and we entered the Piazza del Popolo beneath a bright moon, in which its beauty appeared to very great advantage and not even the Dogana could destroy the enjoy-

---

[1] The following particulars all apply to the ancient church of St. Peter's, and not to any of the three churches of St. Francis in Perugia.

[2] 'By the grace of God I am what I am, and his grace which was in me was not in vain.' Adapted from I Cor. xv. 10. Vulgate: 'Gratia autem Dei sum id quod sum, et gratia ejus in me vacua non fuit.'

[3] Judith.

[4] Jean-Baptiste Cavalier Wicar or Vicare, painter, 1762–1834.

[5] Adone Doni di Assisi, painter, floruit 1580.

[6] A family of painters from Bassano, a small town NNE. of Vicenza, in the territory of Venetia, named Da Ponte. Francesco, 1475–1541; Iacopo, ca. 1510–92; Francesco the younger, 1549–92; Giovambattista 1553–1613; Leandro, 1557–1622; Girolamo 1566–1621. This painting untraced.

[7] The MS here includes, misbound, a slip of paper bearing some detailed accounts of diarist's spending in Rome some two and three months later (Add MS 44818 B, f. 37).

[8] At Terni.

[9] Cp. 6 June 32.

[10] Town 8 miles west of Civita Castellana.

ment of the sight. But entering, and still more reentering Rome, engenders a crowd of sentiments and associations to which hardly any analysis could do justice. How have here been concentrated the greatest power, the greatest blessing, the greatest mischief, that the world has known! Lodged at Serny's.[1] Walked on the Pincio.

Satur. Oct 6.

First face encountered that of an old friend the blind beggar of the Trinità del Monte.—Hunting for information about Sicily.—P.O.—S.M. del Popolo[2]—Macdonald's studio where I find busts of a number of the handsomest subjects of the day—Douglas,[3] Lady Powerscourt,[4] Lady Canning, Miss Stuart,[5] &tc.—Torlonia's—English College—St Peter's—too late to go in: ruminated on the front, which offers so much to lament. Besides that the Apostles on the top are much too crowded and almost entangled with the clock ornaments, the main design of pillars and pediment is encumbered and broken by the division into four lines of height, and nine of width, giving seven entrances, six blind windows, thirtyfive compartments in all, each with its separate set of details, none subserving the whole, all conspiring against and breaking up the general effect.—One is in some degree reconciled to windows by their having a rational position and maintaining the connection of within and without: but here they are mere holes, made as if merely to spoil the front for the sake of spoiling. Then their shapes are various and without character: arched, or flat, oblong or transverse: what has the front of St Peter's to do with those arrangements proper for an entresol? Again the small pillars surely are very injurious to the effect of the great ones: and even the cross ironwork above the gates lends its aid to impair and degrade this aspect of the building which might at so much less cost and pains have been so much more grand and effective and becoming.

It strikes me that people would do well before entering the Church for the first time to walk up and down for a little in the vestibule which would prepare the eye for the vast dimensions within.

read 'Storia del Clero Franchese'—[6]

Sunday. Oct 7.

No English Service, to our dismay, today. Prayers at home.[7] Hooker's Sermon.[8] Jewel's Apology finished.—it lowers my idea of his mental

[1] The Hotel de Londres, in the Piazza di Spagna.
[2] On the left of the Porta del Popolo, in the Piazza del Popolo.
[3] Probably Lord *Douglas, who lived chiefly on the continent.
[4] Elizabeth Frances Charlotte, 1813–84, 1st da. of Robert Jocelyn, 3rd Earl of *Roden; m. 1836 Richard Wingfield, 1815–1844, Viscount Powerscourt.
[5] Unidentified.
[6] *Storia del clero di Francia in tempo della rivoluzione. Opera dedicata alla nazione inglese dall'abate Barruel*, 3 v. (1795); from the French of Augustin Barruel by di Farfa.
[7] And wrote note on theology, Add MS 44728, f. 153.
[8] Probably of Richard *Hooker, who had been reedited in 1830. Thomas *Hooker, a Puritan divine who published many sermons (1586–1647) had no recent edition.

powers, on the whole. He clings fast to Catholic consent, while admitting the charge of separation.

Sermon, Gesù, in the forenoon. On the ministry of angels: much to be questioned, much to be learned. At four P.M. in the same Church after a short discourse from the pulpit on intemperance two priests on a platform argued, or rather acted an argument, in mezzobuffo[1] style, on anger: the one contending from the passage 'Be ye angry & sin not'[2] for the general right of anger, and the other of course confuting him, apparently with right matter, but the *manner* a thing by us perhaps hardly with fairness to be judged. The people laughed very frequently & were evidently intended to do so.

Monday Oct 8.

Gibson's Studio—the chief productions since 1832 now visible are, the wounded amazon (6 feet) and Venus with the apple, very beautiful, done, against the artist's will, for Mr Neeld.[3] He is also finishing Bp Van Mildert for Durham Cathedral.[4] But he still runs too much on Cupids and Psyches. —I should not omit that he has a splendid basso rilievo of Iocasta conjuring Eteocles and Polynices not to fight.

Miss Mackenzie's—Capitol picture gallery: where I find an Assumption older I think than Rio allows: purporting to be by Cola Matrice, Quattrocentista.[5] It is however less offensive.

Forum Some progress has been made since I was here in exhuming the bones of the skeleton of Rome, the fragments and morsels of her ancient decorations. The very order in which they are now laid tends to deepen the impression they convey of that truth, tam antiqua et tam nova,[6] of human instability, as a churchyard is more fraught with the idea of mortality than a battlefield. The most precious materials, the most elaborate workmanship, and each in such abundant quantity as if the quality were the commonest, are here seen in incessant fellowship with the rust of ages and the yet ruder traces of the hand of war.

How small too is this Forum, once the mainspring of the world. It is like the case of the little "city" of London in its commercial greatness. Upon that Via Sacra which would ill carry two carriages, not two of ours, abreast, marched successively in chains the warriors of every nation known to the geography of Rome, a science whose range was commensurate in this case alone with its Empire. Here was the broad substratum made ready for the vast edifice of the Papacy, now crumbling into dust, its

---

[1] 'half comic'.   [2] Ephes. iv. 26.

[3] Joseph Neeld, 1789–1856; inherited a goldsmith's fortune, 1827; Wiltshire magnate; M.P. Gatton 1830, Chippenham 1830–56.

[4] William *van Mildert, 1765–1836, bp. of Durham 1826; last count palatine. *Gibson's statue of him is at the north end of the chapel of nine altars in Durham Cathedral.

[5] In the chapel of the Palazzo dei Conservatori, where is lodged the Capitoline gallery. It is attributed by Rio, *De la poésie chrétienne*, 226, to Perugino; but as a rule to Cola dell'Amatrice, who however is not of the fifteenth century (a Quattrocentista) but is also of the first half of the sixteenth.

[6] 'so old yet so new'.

masses falling away, its strength revived here and there, for a time, by stimulants heterogeneous and accidental.—

Coliseum. Miss Mackenzie took me through the Borghese gardens. St Peter's: it was open, and the sweetest peace reigned, with the softened lights of evening, through its vast spaces. In this temple is combined the maximum of grandeur, with the minimum of Roman superstition. The colossal statues, the scene-like mosaics, do not suggest the idea nor one would hope promote the practice of idolatry: if there be what is offensive it is absorbed along with the other atoms in this almost infinite structure. I say it has almost a relative infinity: for its magnitude and multiplicity are such as the mind nor eye can embrace in a single view, and again I feel, we know but we do not believe it human. Here I remember almost to have experienced the first conception of unity in the Church—acquired alas! by the existing contrasts—and first to have longed for its visible attainment:[1] an object in every human sense hopeless: but not therefore the less to be desired: for the horizon of human hope is not that of Dionic power and Wisdom, of

> La Divina Potestate
> E la Summa Sapienza e 'l primo Amore.[2]

That idea has been upon the whole, I believe the ruling one of my life during the period which has since elapsed. It does not lose its force: I cannot wish that it should, when I recollect what place it held in the dying supplications of the Redeemer. But alas how much yet more sad is the frightful association which forces itself upon the mind between the gorgeous magnificence of St. Peter's, a magnificence whose value in its proper place and function I do not deny, and the fearful corruptions ingrained by long practice in that portion of the Church of which this is the master-temple.

One hears little of the exterior of the body of the Church: I suppose the front is the conductor which attracts the lightning of criticism. The side however of the building appears open to similar observations: numbers of useless blind windows, without either character in themselves, fixed relation to one another, or any to the building except what is injurious. The very dome I think loses greatly in effect upon a near approach from the mere fact of its surface being broken as if it were confectionery. And what a contrast in the *morale* of architecture between the exterior of St. Peter's—except at such a distance as merges the details—and the temple of Neptune at Paestum.[3]

Surely among the causes why the interior appears smaller than it is, one should reckon the vast bulk of the pilaster piers, which *occupy* a great deal of space and hide a great deal more: so that until after well walking about the aisles and fixing their extent in the memory we do not realise the breadth of the Church, and length alone will not do. Hence the dis-

---

[1] Cp. 31 Mar. 32.
[2] Dante, *Inferno*, iii. 55–56: 'divine power, supreme wisdom, and primal love'.
[3] Cp. 8 May 32.

appointment on entering the principal door. Might it not be worth while for someone to make the experiment of resolutely walking round the aisles before permitting himself to look at the nave at all?

8.[1]

I am up to this time without any letter—I have compunctions upon reflecting that my sister is under the escort[2] of persons not of her own family while I am here—and I find the midday sun very trying: Miss Mackenzie kindly recommends green spectacles, but directly I find that my residence here instead of assisting my eyes requires the adoption of new defences to prevent fresh mischief, I must perceive that green spectacles to me mean turning homewards. Ho pregato che piacesse a Dio di rischiararmi il sentiero del mio vero dovere, affinche Egli non mi permetta di seguire qualche mio cappriccio o volere ma solamente sia in grande sia in piccola cosa la sua somma e buona volontà.[3]

Thursday Oct 9.

Saw Sig[n] Prof. Barrone about my eyes; he recommends green glasses and proceeding with my journey: I obey. Passport business in the same quarter. I must say our offices in England are much tidier than on the continent, though we have no Corinthian capitals of Pentelic marble rolling about our dunghills. Saw the Minerva:[4] with the Statue by Michael Angelo.[5] It has a brass girdle, and a shoe or boot on the right foot of the same material. Dined at my old friend the Lepre: St Peter's afterwards. Surely one *must* look well at the details in order to appreciate the mass: for instance, at the smaller cupolas, the statuary, the aisles, and then observe that these are but pierced, like caverns in a huge rock, through the piers of the greater arches which issue into the nave. About six a man with a light walks through the Church crying as well as I could make him out 'Andeamo, signori, bisogna chiudere.'[6] The voice fills the Church and the effect is very fine.

Wrote to Farquhar—James—Lincoln—Glynne. Translated a little Dante.

Wednesd. Oct 10.

With Mr Bouleur[7] seeking for Sicilian information: then to P.O., Suscipi,[8] & other business. Also to

---

[1] This entry from Lambeth MS 1423.
[2] Instead of 'care'.
[3] 'I have prayed that it may please God to make clear to me the path of my true duty, so that He may not let me follow any caprice or will of my own, but only, in great things and in small, his supreme good will.'
[4] Church of Santa Maria sopra Minerva.
[5] Of Christ with the Cross.
[6] 'Let us go, gentlemen, we must close'.
[7] Unidentified.
[8] Untraced.

the Pantheon. How the simplicity of its front shames the details of St Peters: a centre door, and two vast niches. Some minute objects have however been added even here by later hands. This noble dome should be the more carefully observed, because we are apt to overlook it *as* a dome from the fact that it springs from the perpendicular wall at a height comparatively so small. Raphaels epitaph, or epigram, pleases me.

> Ille hic est Raphael timuit quo sospite vinci
> Rerum magna parens & moriente mori.[1]

Should it have been *quo* moriente? I like also the passage, for its truth, in the inscription: cujus spirantes prope imagines si contemplere, naturae atque artis foedus facile iuspexeris.[2]

At the *Minerva* I found a function in progress with a general Communion: & here I copied the following passage, with a very different sentiment, from a prayer to the Virgin printed & hung on the rails of one of the Chapels which has a favoured altar, with specific indulgences. "In voi, O Madre nostra, noi abbiamo collocate tutte le nostre speranze: siate voi la nostra via per andare a Gesù, il mezzo per cui riceviamo tutte le grazie necessari per conseguire la nostra eterna salute."[3]

Alas! is this practical idolatry, or not? Again "onde spirando noi col vostro dolcissimo nome sulle labbra e del vostro santissimo Figliuolo" ...[4] in spirit, like.

S Andrea della Valle[5] delights me as of old: but one must not look much at the white roof of the nave which has a bald effect. In the magnificent Evangelists of Domenichino[6] there is only the picture of the Virgin and Infant with crowns which is offensively introduced. As respects matter of *art*, I thought the angels in *chiaro scuro* placed under them had a disagreeable effect: a kind of half caryatid appearance, flattened rather than foreshortened.

Lanfranco's[7] Cupola wonderfully represents the circles of heaven rising in series, the idea of the 'di soglia in soglia' of Dante's Paradise.[8] Only one must protest against the green and very earthly wreaths upon the ribs and particularly that round the base of the lantern, which both physically and metaphysically[9] *break* up the picture.

Here too I was sorry to find on a gravestone, Magdalina Vignodinia commemorated as one

---

[1] Bembo's epitaph on Raphael concludes: 'Here is Raphael, at whose passing the great mother of the world feared she would be conquered, at whose death, feared she would die.'

[2] 'If you contemplate his almost breathing forms, you will see at once the alliance of nature with art.'

[3] 'In you, O our Mother, we have placed all our hopes: be you our way to Jesus, the means by which we receive all the graces necessary for the attainment of eternal salvation.'

[4] 'when expiring with your most sweet name on our lips and that of your most holy Son.'

[5] See 14 Apr. 32.   [6] At the four angles of the cupola.

[7] Giovanni Lanfranco, painter, 1582–1647.

[8] 'from threshold to threshold', iii. 82.

[9] 'dist[urb]' here deleted.

Clara in Deum relligione,
In Deiparam, *in* sanctos.[1]

The stone seems recent: I did not look at the death.

Bye the bye between the S. Andrea and the Farnese one turns round the corner of the rarest wonder in all Rome, a house which they are absolutely rebuilding. No eye can fail to be struck with this. I doubt whether the city can produce, almost, another case. They seem to lay as much bulk of mortar as of brick. The anomaly of the Customhouse should be rather mitigated by the fact that the new building seems to be a necessary support to the substance of the ancient skeleton whose appearance it deforms.[2]

In the afternoon, Macdonald took me to Thorwaldsen's Studio, which really holds a very high place among the sights of Rome, after the first class. The activity and fertility of his fancy is wonderful, as seen in the abundance and variety of his works. His statues and bas reliefs are as thoroughly classical in general as Flaxman's[3] drawings: and he has a noble simplicity of design: unless perhaps in the bust of Napoleon and the bas-relief of Nemesis? He seems quite equal to sacred subjects, and he has produced a magnificent colossal Statue of our Saviour, in an unstudied attitude, without any garment or decoration whatever, except one which waves in fine folds upon the figure. This according to Macdonald is his masterpiece, and he a greater sculptor than Michael Angelo, and the first of any age since that of Phidias and the Elgin marbles. Like the steam engine which makes pins and propels vessels of almost the size of towns, this artist is as much at home in his miniature reliefs, of which we saw great numbers, as in his colossal performances. It is wonderful that his genius should be able so far to reanimate a dead mythology. Göthe has tried it with a bad object in poetry, but even he has not so far succeeded.

S. Maria Maggiore. The general aspect within is light. The space is sadly cut off in chapels. Particularly those of the cupolas, which are the most highly finished parts of all, but they are like separate churches. Their arches break the main lines of the architraves in the nave very awkwardly? On the whole the impression of great size is not produced: and the flat roof is or looks low and wants relief. The exterior front labours under defects akin to those of St Peter's: with the further anomaly of the old brick tower peering over. Some of the external aspects are more house- than Church-like.

I thought the effect of the Corinthian column[4] agreeable on the whole, though the shaft does not occupy I think quite a moiety of the entire height & it would surely be much improved by the removal of the second & superfluous capital.

---

[1] 'famed for her devotion to God, to the Mother of God and to the saints'.

[2] A magnificent portico of eleven fluted Corinthian columns of marble, once the temple of Marcus Antonius, had been built up with plaster to serve as the custom house at Rome.

[3] John *Flaxman, 1755–1826, sculptor and illustrator.

[4] When Benedict XIV altered the principal front in 1741, he placed a double colonnade, the lower Ionic, the upper Corinthian.

NB. on the obelisk:[1] Xtus Dominus, quem Augustus nasciturum adoravit, & exinde se Dominum dici vetuit.[2]

Thursday Oct. 11.

$6\frac{1}{2}$–$9\frac{3}{4}$ A.M. of Friday, $20\frac{1}{4}$ posts to Naples We reached Terracina at five & had tea there. From thence we had no object in hurrying, as the gates of Capua are not unlocked till daylight.

It is curious to observe that of the crowd of Roman peasantry whom in departing early we met hastening into the city, hardly one was without upper clothing much warmer than an English peasant's, or on foot—the mule or donkey often carrying its driver together with a very respectable load.

We had a horse down this day with the postilion: but the whole occupied only about five minutes. We have had four down before: but now when our posting has (probably) ceased, it is time to remember how mercifully we have been kept from harm.

We went to the lake of Nemi; and were able to identify Wilson's beautiful picture.[3] The line of hills along the Pomptine marshes to the left is bold and varied: and hardly any part of the road is *uninteresting*: an avenue I think never wearisome: there is one of four posts in length, ending at Terracina: where we observed palm trees near the entrance to the right.

Four Neapolitan doganas infest this road! And rumours of brigands: mariuoli[4] as we heard them called. At a point between Fondi[5] and Itri,[6] our postilion dismounted, came solemnly to us, and said 'Signori, Signori, bisogna star un poc'attenti, bisogna fare une scappata qui, sempre ci sono dei mariuoli'—'Bene'[7]—he mounted, & oddly enough at the very point in the road where there were a considerable number of houses, he set his horses off at full gallop, squalling himself most vigorously, without any apparition to justify it, and seemed to us to encounter a more substantial danger in dashing us through an extremely narrow rift rather than road between two houses.

Friday Oct 12.

This day has been busily occupied in inquiries and arrangements connected with our voyage to Sicily—which we find must be tomorrow, and directed

---

[1] One of the obelisks which had flanked the entrance to the mausoleum of Augustus, and one of the four erected by Pope Sixtus V; said to have been brought from Egypt by Claudius A.D. 57; erected in 1587, opposite the choir of Santa Maria Maggiore; crowned with a star and a cross.

[2] 'Christ the Lord whom Augustus worshipped before his birth, refusing to be called Lord from that moment.' One of the inscriptions, 1587, on the pedestal (north side). The reference is to Virgil's fourth eclogue, long considered a prophecy of Christ.

[3] A water colour bought by the British Museum in 1865.

[4] 'scoundrels'.

[5] Small town 10 miles NE. of Terracina, just within the border of the kingdom of the Two Sicilies.

[6] Town 7 miles SE. of Fondi.

[7] 'Sirs, you must look out, we shall have to make a detour here, there are always scoundrels.'—'Good'.

to Palermo[1] as there is no Messina[2] boat till the 25th—our passport—we are obliged to take out a new & special one as the forms needful for the other cannot be completed—& our carriage which having carried us well thus far is now in turn becoming a weight.

At Terracina we found a fair Inn. Here [in Naples] the Gran Bretagna would not receive us for one night, even with the prospect of return. We spent to the Crocelle. The bay is much overclouded and the sea mutters inauspiciously for tomorrow. Further, having anticipated my dates by a day, I must go letterless to Sicily. Wrote to J.N.G. and H.J.C.—Finished Barruels 1st vol: it is interesting.

[On fly leaf:][3]

Diary

of a visit to Sicily & return through

Calabria.

WEG. Oct 13.......Nov. 11.38.

Private.

Saturday Oct 13.

We left Naples by the Neptune for Palermo at a few minutes past nine. The shouting and confusion amidst which we at length got on board gave place to the immediate prospect of sea-sickness: before the anchor had been ten minutes weighed I received authentic information which sent me at once to bed. However on a Messina trip there would have been more to lose: we bore away right out of the bay to the westward. I think there were more victims to seasickness than an English company of the same number would have afforded: but this was a trying voyage. In the night a genuine scirocco[4] came down upon us in the teeth of our course, and increased our lateral as much as it retarded our forward motion: all but rolling us out of bed.

Sunday Oct 14

We had been assured on all hands of arrival at 9, but to show us that these things are not in our power we had to labour on till half past two in performing the short residue of our voyage. We had not anticipated such a Sunday: nothing however is more full of practical lessons than seasickness, showing us our dependence, and the proximity of our best state of health to extreme suffering and abject prostration.

It was only however upon attempting to rise and dress that I found the

---

[1] Capital of Sicily, on the Gulf of Palermo, 214 miles SSW. of Naples.
[2] Port on the Strait of Messina, 214 miles SSE. of Naples.
[3] Entries from Add MS 44818 C until 11 Nov. 38, unless otherwise noted.
[4] Hot southerly wind blowing from Africa.

real effects of this extraordinary wind: I had read of them recently in Brydone,[1] and his description is not exaggerated. I could not have conceived such an entire relaxation of the body, such an absolute suspension of the command of one part over another, and of the will over the whole. To dress in the rudest manner was a work of almost insuperable difficulty: and to get the head into cold water was the only moment of relief: relief however was luxury.

As we entered the noble harbour, the atmosphere was extremely peculiar and what one has been taught to consider oriental: under the influence of the African visitant.[2] It had much of what is called transparency yet conveyed the idea of heaviness and of heat; while the waves were of a dark green. We could see the headlands and the general character of the scene but had not the command of the whole. As we disembarked a sailor of the steamer stood with a cutlass *drawn* to keep the faquins[3] in order. Happily the landlord of the Albion,[4] or Principe di Galles, to which we had been directed came on board and took us up to his house, neither K. nor I being fit for exertion. We found there was no English Church here: read prayers. I managed to stumble across the Piazza to a Sermon in the *Catena*[5] Church. Not above 25 present, & these women with an old man & a lad or two. It was very good: on *charity*—to be found in the Decalogue, as *hope* in the Lord's Prayer, and Faith in the Creed. He began accordingly with the first commandment, of charity or love towards God, & taught with simplicity & purity how under all the titles of creation, of preservation which is like continued creation, & of redemption by the blood of Christ from Adam's sin and our own, we were not our own but God's & bound to render to Him the whole man.

My priest's pronunciation yesterday was singular, and it appears to be that of the country. Fede he pronounced fidi: and I hear fiori again called fiuri: thus two vowels of the five are dispatched.

At[6] Naples we very much regretted that the steamboat took us away just before a Sunday, though we went in some hope of finding a Church at Palermo. The diminution of the supply of Divine ordinances is a heavy loss & drawback which in travelling one begins to experience directly upon going out of the beaten track. That is now well studded with English Churches. No doubt the loss may tend to quicken the desire and so to enhance the benefit on return but this is an advantage which God's Providence draws from the evil, & it would be unsafe to use it too freely as an element in calculations beforehand, as it is a result which may arise from every kind of sin and crime that they may excite horror in others & prove an additional safeguard.

---

[1] P. *Brydone, *A Tour of Sicily and Malta* (1817), 25.
[2] The sirocco.
[3] 'porters' (Italian *facchino*, whence French *faquin*, 'rogue').
[4] Famous English hotel on the Piazza Marina, near the Porta Felice and harbour, and the Corso Cassaro (main street).
[5] Santa Maria della Catena, in the Cassaro Morto, continuous with the Corso Cassaro.
[6] This entry, undated, is from Lambeth MS 1423.

Monday Oct 15.

We set about making our arrangements, and engaged Giuseppe Lazzara to take us round the island by Egesta,[1] Selinunti,[2] Girgenti,[3] Syracuse,[4] to Messina, with 3 mules at 9 carlines[5] a day for each—of the best quality (and they are somewhat dearer because it is harvest time) and at one piastre a day besides food and lodging for himself, if we are pleased with him. We are to pay half price for the mules on the Sundays which we rest: and to pay two days at least of return: he hoping it will be four. We got advice & assistance from Mr Goodwin[6] the English Consul & Mr Brown the Banker.

We went to S. Giuseppe[7]—where are pictures by Monrealese,[8] and marble angels in downward flight holding the holy water basins—to the Duomo where the whiteness & modernness of the interior are strongly contrasted with the antique of the outward aspect: but the church is about to be cased with marble. An old mosaic is over the side door.

The convents in the Toledo are extremely curious: they are on the third or fourth floor of the houses, and they have a sort of latticed projecting balcony apparently built out in a substantial manner. The upper room of a crowded street, with a view into it, is hardly the place for retreat from the world, & it does not give the mind fair play.

The Church architecture here does not seem quite so meretricious as in Italy. I observed this particularly in the Church at Bagaria,[9] which has a particularly neat front. The white stone of the country acquires a tawny tinge by exposure to the atmosphere, and this front had really a character. There is something singular in the sub-pilasters which emerge like shadows from under the principals. The cornice over the second order also appeared faulty.

The drive to Bagaria is about 9 miles, through the Marina[10] and the suburbs, then over an indifferent road lined with hedges of cactus, aloe, and rhododendron, to the village so named. Vines and olives, and a kind of reed used for roofs, and for training vines, and rising to the height of 20 feet, seemed to occupy this very fertile soil.

A terrace of the Palazzo Valguarnera[11] commands the two bays of

---

[1] Classical name for Segesta, 32 miles SSW. of Palermo.

[2] On the south coast, 24 miles south of Segesta.

[3] 46 miles ESE. of Selinunti.   [4] 96 miles east of Girgenti.

[5] A carline was worth about 2d.

[6] John Goodwin, British consul at Cape Verde Islands 1828, Naples 1832, Palermo 1834; living in the Palazzo Campofranco in the Piazza Valguarnera. Died 1869.

[7] In the Corso Cassaro or 'Toledo', near where it crossed the Via Nuova, the other main street.

[8] Pietro Novelli, called Monrealese, painter, 1603–47.

[9] Small town 9 miles eastward from Palermo, at the base of the isthmus separating the bay of Palermo from that of Termini; surrounded by the villas of the Palermitan nobility.

[10] A marine drive extending for about a third of a mile along the shore beneath the city walls from the mouth of the Cala, or little harbour, to the Casino di Cutò.

[11] 'Palazzo' would be more properly used for the family's town house in Palermo; this, strictly, was a 'villa', as indeed it is called a few lines below. It lay on the highest ridge of the isthmus.

Termini and Palermo. Our view was bounded to the west by the bold and varied outline of Monte Pellegrino[1] with the still more imposing promontory of Monnello,[2] and to the East by Cape Cefalù:[3] we saw the town of that name plainly at near 40 miles distance though the sky was clouded and the atmosphere anything but what would here be termed clear. The Palermo coast is more cultivated. Beyond Termini[4] the mountains seem to sweep quite down into the sea. These two ranges from the intermediate land together form a magnificent prospect, and the situation of this villa is a rare one. A rising ground above does still greater justice to the scene. The outlines here are very wild and grand, and there was something very peculiar in the mixture of transparency and softness of atmosphere with all the signs of unsettled and angry weather.

We went to the Palazzo Palagonia[5] which still forcibly exhibits the quaint fancy of a former possessor, who has in a number of strange figures applied to stone the principle of broad and grotesque caricature. He roofed some rooms with mirrors, but time has spoiled them—one of more than 40 feet each way is cased with marbles, not in the best taste. The family portraits are more indifferent than the English average, and the execution of garden statues here is extremely clumsy while the architecture is much more respectable. Further, this worthy has introduced the bust of Mahomet II[6] among those of old Greek philosophers & poets.

Palermo had a good and cheap manufacture of gloves—and is celebrated for flower seeds, and for knife handles, and agate tables. Signs of the English still remain:[7] for instance the only title which is borne on the exterior of our Inn, is "Albion Hotel". We find here an Irish Chambermaid the widow of a serjeant who has remained ever since the war. Mr & Mrs Page the former landlord & landlady are dead: one of their daughters is the wife of the present master.

It appears (Mr Brown) that the Sicilians have now lost both their own parliament and that which they had under the English.[8] At the same time a change has been made in the opposite direction: primogeniture no longer regulating the succession to landed property.[9] In consequence, the great places & fortunes are not kept up, but the land, says Mr Brown, is better

---

[1] Rocky mountain behind Palermo, rising to 1963 ft.

[2] A bay east of Monte Pellegrino, separating it from the 'promontory' of Monte Gallo, a precipice of red rock 1692 ft. high.

[3] Eastern promontory of the gulf of Termini.

[4] Town 20 miles ESE. of Palermo.

[5] Villa of the Prince of Palagonia, whose father had peopled it with sculpted monsters; the family were cousins of the royal line of Naples.

[6] 1785–1839; sultan of Turkey 1808; suppressed janissaries 1826.

[7] From the alliance of Great Britain with the royal house of Naples, which took refuge in Sicily during the Napoleonic wars under protection of a British garrison.

[8] Before the Napoleonic wars the kingdom of Sicily, though subject to Naples, preserved its independent constitution; abrogated by Ferdinand IV, 1751–1825, when he took refuge in the island in 1798. Lord William *Bentinck, 1774–1839, the British minister to him, made him accept a constitution on the English model in 1812; abolished in 1816. A rebellion in favour of one was suppressed in 1820.

[9] The Code Napoleon, which does not recognise primogeniture, was the law of the two Sicilies from 1816.

cultivated. There are however other means (witness England) of securing the cultivation, and I should regret both these changes.

The same informant gives alarming account of the prevalence of brigandage, since the introduction some 18 months ago by the King of gendarmerie instead of the old native brigand police, which rested on a singular device: the captain of the district being responsible for the amount of every robbery committed between sunrise and sunset. All these are now thrown out of employ, having declined to join the gendarmes. But it is quite impossible to know what degree of reliance should be placed on these rumours: in wild countries Fame grows much faster from earth to heaven, and her giant frame is less easily dissolved, than in ours.

We are to take with us sugar, butter, tea, and salt. 2 rot[oli]. sugar 1 rot. butter $\frac{3}{4}$ lb ($=\frac{1}{2}$ rot?) tea Rotolo is over $1\frac{1}{2}$ lb English.[1] (Lopcz brothers, workers in agate. Chess table $2\frac{2}{3}$ palmi verd antique & border, 20 p[iastr]i. Dessert knife handles 6 p[iastr]i p. doz—but no set ready. Piazza Marina.) The guide or servant provides plates & pots, knives forks & spoons. The general division of our route according to our friend Giuseppe Lazzara, is thus. One day Westward to Alcamo.[2] Three days southward to Girgenti. Sunday & a day for the antiquities there. Four days to Syracuse, Eastward. A day to visit, and Sunday. On to Messina, six days including one full and hard one for Etna.[3] To arrive in Messina, please God, on Saturday the 3rd of November; with or without our *poco di roba*[4] for the rumours of brigands are still like wasps buzzing about our ears. A Dutch traveller is just come and has seen nothing, but talks mysteriously.

Here we see public scriveners in the streets: can even our Lazzara write? Time must answer. The shops have no windows, being entirely open: they close at night with doors. The number of balconies is immense. Here the Toledo does not seem to want light, so generous is the sun: though the houses appear to be five or six stories and the street is not, we thought, more than 25 feet wide. It is bisected by the other main line,[5] and on these the town is formed, bulging out towards the sea. The piazza at the intersection, the Quattro Cantoni, is too small, but highly ornamented with the three orders[6] in upward series like the Coliseum, but not pure.

Tuesday Oct 16.

We went after breakfast to

1 The Santa Catarina. The whole interior is most elaborately wrought with marble.

2. The San Simone:[7] abounds in mosaics with which nearly the whole upper

---

[1] A rotolo was about $1\frac{3}{4}$ lbs.

[2] Town 20 miles WSW. of Palermo.

[3] 40 miles SW. of Messina, the highest active volcano in Europe.

[4] 'few things'.

[5] The Via Nova.

[6] The Quattro Cantoni or 'four corners' is an octagon 112 yards round, rising to a height of 100 ft.; each of four facades has three orders, Roman Doric, Ionic, and Composite.

[7] Popular name for the Martorana, one of the earliest Norman churches of Sicily.

walls are covered. The same class however is yet more strikingly exhibited in[1]

3. The Chiesa Palatina,[2] within the Palace itself; one exterior wall is mosaic, and the whole upper part of the interior is covered with figures of our Saviour and of Saints and scenes from Scripture or quasi Scripture history.[3] Here for instance is the baptism of St Paul and his escape down the wall. But in the one case the font, in the other the basket, from which the head emerges, are so extremely small that they could only contain a very small segment even of the shoulders. The cords of the basket too hang out of the perpendicular in a manner which shows the great rudeness of art. An attendant holds a candle by the baptism. But the aim seems to have been *bonâ fide* religious instruction, and it is extremely interesting. The ground is gold. The types of the countenances Greek. In the San Simone is one of our Saviour crowning '*POΓEPIOΣ PHX*'[4]—they being the only figures. The names of the personages are generally affixed. The arches slightly pointed. The *effect* is very pleasing and rich. The roof partly of coffettoni[5] and partly pendent

We next went to

4. The Universita and saw the gallery of pictures with a (Pseudo?) Perugino of the Assumption and an Ecce Homo professing to be of Correggio, which has surely more of Carlo Dolce. A Vandyck more probable?[6]

Here among a small parcel of antiquities from Pompeii, we saw (burnt) bread, coffee,[7] and other provisions.

Below are the marbles. Quaint and rude bassirilievi from a temple of Selinunti. A biga, with two horses drawing and one on each side which have riders. Four more: Perseus and Medusa among them. A Jupiter from Tindaro, standing—fine: and a fine *torso* of a man from the same. Some singular petrifications of bones, including elephant, hippopotamus, & others, found in a cave near Palermo. We found a set of teeth & a jawbone. The rilievi were from the metopes.

By way of fighting off the residue of that relaxation which we both feel from the scirocco, we walked up the Monte Pellegrino: said to be near 2000 feet elevation, and sheer from the sea with a broken outline and grand effect. The path begins at two miles from Palermo: and is paved for three miles to the Church of Santa Rosolia.[8] A mile of scrambling then leads to the top where there is a telegraph, and a noble view to the sea, over

[1] Margin entry: NB. exterior of the Duomo spoiled by burnished cupolas which put the granity hue of the stone out of countenance.

[2] In the Palazzo Reale, which dominates the city from the upper end of the Corso Cassaro.

[3] The raising of Tabitha by St. Peter; the meeting of St. Peter and St. Paul on the way to Rome; St. Peter and St. Paul disputing with Simon Magus; Simon Magus falling to the earth.

[4] 'King Roger' de Hauteville, 1093–1154, crowned king of Sicily 1130.

[5] 'coffers' in the ceiling, a word he compounded from Italian *coffino* or *coffiro*, a box or coffer, and *cassettoni* (from *cassa*, 'box'), the true word for a coffered ceiling.

[6] Family of Rubens and Vandyck, reputedly by Vandyck.

[7] Unknown as a beverage in Europe till *ca.* 1450. A building in Pompeii was at this time erroneously termed a 'coffee shop'.

[8] Patron saint of Palermo: her chapel is on the mountain.

Palermo and Bagaria to Cefalù; and to Mondello and the little wild bay of Sferracavallo[1] on the west. Ustica[2] is seen on a clear day. We got the first view of a steamer from Trapani[3] which brings or announces the king. This was immediately announced to the palace below.

The Church is interesting. Originally it has been a retired grotto, the roof of stalactites, from which the water is now drained by art. A front has been built across, then comes an opening unprotected from the weather, & *the* Church itself is still the grotto, in which two altars have been raised, and the marble statue of S. Rosolia with a wand and Bible said to be of solid gold, reposes under the principal one. The face and hand only are visible and seem good: but the hand is (in bad taste?) covered with rings and the clothing rich & heavy. Above is a figure looking from a small hole in the roof of the cavern,[4] in which the legend says she lived. On our way down an old man of 81 gave us some grapes. He has been on the mountain for 41 years: remembers and much likes the English: he gave us pieces of stalactite, which he said were formed of Santa Rosolia's tears; and would heal any cut or wound forthwith. This, told with great simplicity from such aged lips, was really touching and beautiful, and he knew that such a power must be of God.

Cactus grows wild on this mountain: and rich soft mould accumulates and yields vegetation in the crannies of rocks sharp literally as a knife and jagged as a saw, and everywhere pierced with small cavities.

The descent yields delightful varieties of the view of Palermo. A new prison is in course of erection by the roadside:[5] three radii belonging to a common centre, therefore I suppose on one of the improved principles.

After dinner we went to the Marina Parade, and the Giardino Publico[6]— which are delightful. In the latter, we found palms, the pepper tree which languishes like the willow, has the graceful leaf and branch of the acacia, with its own beautiful red-brown berries & a delightful fragrance: and a plant with very oriental leaves, some measuring 3 feet by 2½. Here are monuments in a grove to some of the great men of Sicily: Archimedes, Epicharmus[7] as the inventor of *palliata fabula*, and Daphnis as inventor of pastorals.[8]

Today we see Palermo in something like its natural state and we can well conceive that with an English Church it would be a delightful place of residence. It has not yet been despoiled of its own character by crowds of strangers.

We have found our Inn comfortable and reasonable, with good cooking:

---

[1] West of the Capo di Gallo.

[2] Volcanic island 40 miles NNW. of Palermo.

[3] Town on the west coast 40 miles west of Palermo.

[4] A waxen dishevelled head of the saint, looking down from the hole in the rock where her bones were found.

[5] Cp. F. Volpicelli, *Delle Prigioni* (1835), 243.

[6] La Flora, at the SE. end of the Marina, immediately outside the city.

[7] 540–450 B.C., poet and Pythagorean philosopher who on migrating to Sicily introduced comedy at Syracuse. That in which some characters wore the *pallium* or cloak was called *palliata fabula*. 'Ma' ('but') added here in margin.

[8] Sicilian shepherd, the mythological inventor of pastoral music.

and now I suppose we must bid fare-well for a little to most of what is physically agreeable. Hotel d'Albione—Piazza Marina. by L.C. de Martino.

Wednesday Oct. 17.

We started at $6\frac{1}{2}$, and at five P.M. were in the Locanda della Piazza at Alcamo. The distances are given thus:

by the guide.		In the Royal Map. (60 m. to a degree.)
5	to Monreale[1]	$3\frac{1}{2}$ (add a mile of town.)
13	to Partinico[2]	$10\frac{1}{2}$
15	to Alcamo	$10\frac{1}{2}$

The first thirteen miles are one continuous ascent through a valley the first half of which exhibits the most velvetlike and richest green I ever saw. but there are no palms which Mrs Starke[3] has inaccurately reported as a feature in the scenery of the vicinity of Palermo. The city the sea the mountains and the cultivated hollow of the vale yield beautiful and everchanging retrospects, though Monte Pellegrino, the grandest arm of the bay is hidden by the shoulder of the mountain which the road (dated I think 1765) ascends.

At Monreale we saw the Duomo or Chiesa Matrice,[4] with its bold and abundant mosaics casing the whole upper walls; the arches are relatively smaller and more decidedly pointed than in the Palermo Churches: the Church is lighter and larger: the principal doors of bronze, and a part of the exterior work resembles our Norman doors, but it is combined with other ornaments. Monrealese's picture on the stair of the adjoining convent is of St Dominic feeding persons, I believe miraculously.[5] The principal & some other heads are good.—In this convent Mr Stewart,[6] a converted Scotchman, lived, and built at his own expence a small addition to the main fabric: he left it we learn some years ago.

From Monreale to the top the character of the cultivation changes, the green becomes lighter and more broken, the sharp ragged tops of the hills draw near. I should think the pass must rise by 2000 feet. Wheat is grown near the top, from soil which lies almost in handfuls among the rocks, but of the finest quality. Accordingly we find the bread of the country, as at Partinico, remarkably fine in grain, sweet and sound, with a light tinge of brown: but it is imperfectly baked.

The descent to Partinico is through a wilder glen, less picturesque in itself, but presenting a magnificent prospect of the gulph of Castellamare,[7] and a full view in particular of its western arm terminated by the Cape of Santo Vito.[8] Nothing can be finer than its outlines; and today they were

---

[1] Town west of Palermo.
[2] Town west of Monreale.
[3] Mariana *Starke, *Travels*, 95.
[4] In Sicily a *duomo* (cathedral) is called a *chiesa matrice* (mother church).
[5] Monrealese's masterpiece depicts St. Benedict distributing bread, as symbolising his rule. [6] Unidentified.
[7] To the northward. [8] 33 miles west of Palermo.

softened to us by that extreme transparency of the distances which surprises the Englishman in Italy yet might I think surprise the Italian here
which lends grace to the most abrupt and jagged lines, without in the
slightest degree impairing the distinctness of the objects: and which only
our total want of an appropriate term, probably, obliges us to denominate
haze.—Alcamo is seen in the distance from this descent, at a moderate
elevation in the opposite corner of this rich and beautiful vale.

Our cortège is this: in front, Giuseppe on the baggage horse, Giorgio:
behind him, we come on our mules: the muleteer is sometimes on foot,
sometimes on the tail of one or other of the three animals. He exhorts us
to goad them: and Giuseppe has a little instrument, appearing like a fifth
finger, with which he does wonders in a quiet way. Seriously, they tell us,
that though our mules are now a little tired, in a day or two they will
become quite fresh: as they will get rest at night: whereas it appears that
they have been at vintage labour in which for 20 days and nights together
they do not get into the stable. This they only left last night at the Ave
Maria, to come nine miles down to Palermo. An Englishman would I think
scarcely work his beast so hard, as our muleteer, who is said to be very
respectable.

We lunched on bread and grapes, and had tea from our own resources
with the aid of milk at Alcamo: while in one of the filthiest rooms I ever
saw the fleas (and what not) too enjoyed themselves upon the newcomers.
The road thus far is carriageable and most of it is very fair. The people
are of a Bengalish hue: and one sees a child with nothing but a light shirt—
evidently not from poverty. We saw several vultures, very large: and the
Sicilian sportsmen, or cockneys of Palermo, were thick in the valley above
the city. They are content it appears with shooting rabbits, turdi[1]
(thrushes?), and stornelli[2] (starlings). Some travellers however even on this
road were carrying guns not for sport but for security.

The vintage is in full activity. We meet the grapes going home, in casks
on mules: there being I fancy few or no cross roads for wheels. We meet also
new wine (musto) in great skins, as of old. Vines bear fully in the sixth year
and live to near a hundred. Monks with their mules carry home to their
convents their casks full of grapes which they solicit from the proprietors of
vineyards and habitually receive. There it is manufactured for their own
use. The poor too are found with their little baskets of the same generous
fruit which the owners give them at this time. Excellent bunches every here
and there lie neglected in the dust of the road. As for blackberries they all
rot upon the branches, and some peasants grinned with contempt at me,
or with suprise at least, when I was plucking from a blackberry bush.
Virgil's declaration is no longer true, vaccinia nigra leguntur.[3] Ecl. 2.18.
Olive, aloe, cactus, wheat, orange, abound more or less along the road—the
wheat is grown under the olive trees and cropped in June. But the people
pay so heavily that they want the means or the energy, notwithstanding

[1] cp. 14 Oct. 38.
[2] 'sparrows'.
[3] 'the black whortle-berries are picked'.

the excellence of the soil and climate to crop more than once in the year. A mule fetches twice as much as a horse of the same size and age: or even in a greater proportion: and their prices mount up to 80 and 100 ounces[1]— forty and fifty pounds. The people are persuaded that the king procured the cholera[2] to come among them and that it was not sent by God: for whenever they began to murder persons of the upper class, the cholera ceased: and they believe that he did this to check the revolutionary spirit, or to thin the people, by means of certain fumigations! that his soldiers wore plates of brass on the arms and stomach which defended them from it! So says, and so believes, Giuseppe!

(The mountain and Church of St. Calojero: above Alcamo are very fine:[3] as is the old Norman castle above Monreale.[4])

Further: they think the priests had nothing to do with it because many of them died: & they believe that the Cardinal Archbishop[5] received the cholera in a pinch of snuff (burlesque of Nessus[6]) from one of the king's generals for refusing to be concerned in this regal manoeuvre. Justice he says is thoroughly venal: the Palermitans hanno coraggio:[7] and murders take place in the city every day. (*due parole: e par' il coltello*.)[8]

Locanda della Piazza: horribly dirty: our bags afforded us insufficient protection, though nothing I think got in for some time.

At Alcamo I saw the Host carried in procession with drums beating at the head—apparently for some invalid.

(Europa at Alcamo to be particularly avoided).

Thursday Oct 19 [sc. 18]

Alcamo to Segesta	9 miles	
Segesta to Salemi[9]	12	6 A.M.–5.20 P.M.
Salemi to Castelvetrano[10]	14	

The morning here (as K. said) truly rosy fingered, tinted the hills of Castellammare & S. Vito, as setting out from Alcamo we were directed by Giuseppe to observe the temple of Segesta, which we reached in $2\frac{1}{4}$ hours. It stands in a conspicuous position, on a panoramic hill, whose sides are everywhere steep, in some places craggy and precipitous: in perfect loneliness, and in an excellence (with some help from the late king Ferdinand) of preservation which only brings home the more forcibly that image of desolation which it presents: a fit symbol of the exhausted and deserted super-

---

[1] Of silver, Sicilian coin.

[2] Outbreak in 1837 in large towns in Sicily.

[3] Also called Monte Bonifato, with the remains of a castle on it; and the church of the Madonna dell'Autu.

[4] Castello di S. Benedetto, with the ruins of a church within the castle-yard.

[5] Cajetan, Maria Trigona e Parisi, bp. of Caltagirone 1818, abp. of Palermo 1832, cardinal 1834, d. 1837.

[6] The shirt of Nessus caused the death of Hercules.

[7] 'are brave'.

[8] 'Two words, and there is the knife'—added in margin.

[9] Town south of Segesta.

[10] Town south of Salemi.

stitions which it represents, but which still retain in so many works of genius, a beauty like this. Around it are wide ranges of undulating uplands, capable but unproductive through default of cultivation, like that human nature whose longings towards heaven were absorbed and frustrated in fictitious semblances of religion. From every point it is well seen: but best in retrospect from the wild field path by which we left the spot.

The pillars are 36. The ends present 6: the sides 14. The intercolumniations are equal to the bases. I think the length (inward) is 58 yards: the width 20. From the perpendicular side of the steps, there are projecting knobs. Drops from the cornice and the metopes. It does not appear as if the whole structure was originally clear above the ground: for a part of the excavation made to show it, which forms a kind of trench round it, is of slaty stone too regularly laid to have gathered there fortuitously. The temple is termed of Diana.

The town was on the southern side of the next hill. It is in shapeless ruins. They show a stone as the mouth of a well. The wild fig tree forces itself through the stones; illustrating Holy Scripture: [large blank] and the poet Juvenal: [blank].[1]

A theatre looks North. The diameter of the cavea[2] is (by steps) 16 yards. There are 18 rows of step seats: and one at the top of stone chairs with backs. The walls are of large stones without mortar: small ones fill the interstices. There are remains of an old pediment or frieze about the stage: and of the figure of a Satyr on each side, in relief; (on the proscenium?) Aen. 1. 427:

hic alta theatris
Fundamenta locant alii, immanesque columnas
Rupibus excidunt, *scenis decora alta futuris*.[3]

Our road today except four carriageable miles between the wretched village of Vita,[4] and the town or *paese*[5] of Salemi, was rude field path or less. We passed over extensive ranges of grassland, which repose the fifth year after bearing wheat for four. On some of these, with vast space & apparently the capability to sustain thousands, we did not meet a living soul in our long and slow passage from one extremity to the other, and could scarcely perceive one solitary hut. On others they were ploughing, with a plough ruder than in the days of Virgil: no *aures*,[6] no *dentalia*, the *temo*[7] not of eight feet projection. Two oxen (some by the bye of the horns

---

[1] Probably Job viii. 17, 'His roots are wrapped about the heap, and seeth the place of stones', and *Satire* x. 144–5, 'discutienda valent sterilis mala robora fici', 'stones which the evil strength of the wild fig suffices to split'.   [2] Where the spectators sat.

[3] 'Here some lay the deep foundations of theatres, cutting out great columns from the rocks, the decorations of a future stage'.   [4] 11 miles SW. of Alcamo.

[5] 'district'.   [6] 'mould-boards' affixed to the share-beam ('dentale').

[7] 'pole'. The passage is *Geo.* i. 169. . . .

Continuo in silvis magna vi flexa domatur
In burim et curvi formam accipit ulmus aratri,
Huic a stirpe pedes temo protentus in octo,
Binae aures, duplici aptantur dentalia dorso.

'The elm is bent with great force while yet in the woods to the form of the beam, and takes on a curve, and low on this stem, prolonged to eight feet, the pole, the two mould-boards and the share-beam with double ridge are fitted.'

can hardly be under 3 feet and they are strong in proportion,) or two horses
or mules yoked, & drawing like oxen not by regular collars but by the
strength of the backbone & upper shoulder brought to bear on the transverse bar, worked a machine apparently consisting of three pieces of wood
one of which was pointed with iron: and they plough, we are told, first
longitudinally and then transversely before sowing. Never surely were the
resources of nature so miserably met on the part of man.—In one place we
saw fifteen of these yokes of oxen ploughing together.—The sheep have
lambs twice in the year. Mille meae siculis errant in montibus agnae. Ecl.
2.21.[1]—The vines are dwarf like those in Germany.—

The succession of sea views is very fine. We did not lose the Castellamare
gulph until some time after leaving Segesta, at which point we turned out
of our westward route to the south. In a short time we opened M. St
Juliano[2]—and the sea to the W. of Trapani, with the striking islands of
Favignana and [Leranzo].[3] Soon after losing these we obtained with the
town of Salemi a wide view of southern sea: and lastly a couple of miles, or
thereabouts, from Castelvetrano, we enjoyed the prospect of its rich
valley, deeper than any we have seen, and the long line of its coast which
reaches down to Sciacca.[4] Read 3d Aen. with pleasure.[5]
Locanda della Panthiera: an inn of tolerable cleanliness: i.e. the beds were
not full of fleas, though on the other hand not entirely tenantless.

Friday Oct 19.

From 6¾ A.M.–4¼ P.M.,
Castel Vetrano to the ruins of Selinunti 9 m.
Selinunti to Sciacca . . . . . .   18 m.
Our first stage lay over the plain, through lanes abounding in the cork tree
and then over a common rank with wild bushes but almost destitute of
vegetation. In passing over some recently ploughed land we had the opportunity of seeing how ineffectively these light ploughs perform their work:
the soil was only disturbed to a depth of three or four inches, and between
the furrows were ridges of unbroken clod. It appears that there is a third
ploughing immediately after the seed is sown, & then the field is levelled.[6]
The first view of the masses of Selinuntine ruins is extremely fine. Fragments of a few pillars, and confused heaps of single stones, alone remain to
show what man has done and undone: for he has been the destroyer. I
measured the base of a pillar and found it 13 feet square in a single stone:
a fragment of architrave measured 21 feet 4 in. by 7 f. 4 in. and 4f. 10 in.
The (partially) restored column, 32 feet in circumference near the base. It
has been pieced but the rest appear to have been of this great bulk. Holes

---

[1] 'A thousand lambs of mine stray in the Sicilian mountains.'
[2] The ancient Mount Eryx.
[3] Two of the Aegadian islands, from 8 to 15 miles west and SW. of Trapani; scene of
Roman naval victory against Carthage, 241 B.C.
[4] Port 21 miles SW. of Castelvetrano.
[5] In this book of the Aeneid Aeneas lands at Drepanum (Trapani), at the foot of
mount Eryx, and here his father Anchises dies.
[6] '3 ploughings' in margin.

are drilled in some of these stones, by which probably the means of moving them were applied. In the smaller temples the columns are fluted: the greater dimensions being better able to dispense with ornaments in detail? The three which lie on this hill present considerable remains: we were content to view the smaller fragments of three others over an intervening hollow at a little distance.

This situation is not to be compared with that of Segesta: yet it is fine: the ruins almost form the eminence on which they stand, and which is just sufficient to give them some command of the plain which nearly reaches to the horizon, just limited by hills, round one half of its circumference, and of the sea which spreads its broad bosom to the other. The path by which we departed afforded us a good backward view. They abound, according to Giuseppe, with porcupines and vipers. We have only yet seen two snakes on our way, both dead: one was from four to five feet.

Arriving at about nine, in order to combine antiquity with novelty we bathed after seeing the ruins and found the fresh cold sea (for such it was) agreeable & restorative. Neither of us have yet become accustomed to the mules:[1] their motion continually works the rider backwards and forwards, so as to require considerable effort to sit firm and upright: barring the consideration of the sun, which from twelve to four was excessively hot today, I doubt whether walking to a fair pedestrian would be more fatiguing.

The cork tree in hue resembles the olive but is a shade darker: and the leaf less oblong. The bark is stripped off them to a considerable height. Selinus is no longer 'palmosa' (Aen. 3)[2] and Mrs Starke[3] has been misinformed, so far as our eyes can enable us to judge, in vaunting the palms of Sciacca—which we do not see. We passed some rice fields on our way to it.

The first view of Selinunti, and the view of Sciacca (at some 3 miles distance) and the coast stretching away to Capo Bianco, are fine. Some portion of our road lay along the shore: most of it was extremely solitary, and Giuseppe wore the mysterious look which betokens that the district is of ill repute for brigands. A large party at Selinunti came to view the ruins, each man with his musket: a party whom we met last night quitting C. Vetrano was similarly armed: and so was even the vanguard of the King's suite which we have tonight seen in Sciacca.

Sciacca is a town of 22000 persons: Castel Vetrano I think of 12 or 15,000: the people in fact live not in the country but in the towns almost exclusively, on account, one supposes, of security. One is astounded to find such populations with so little accommodation for strangers, and so low a style of general provision: but this in some measure accounts for it.

As to Virgil's plough I should observe that his description may not specifically apply to Sicily, but since this island and Africa were the joint granaries of Rome one may infer that the ploughs equalled those of which the poet wrote.

---

[1] 'mules 45' in pencil in margin. Numerous marginal notes headlining the contents of travel text, henceforward omitted.

[2] *Aen.* iii. 705. [3] *Travels*, 404.

We found the King was expected in Sciacca tonight, and as the town could not bear two such arrivals, and he had the advantage of us by sending notice, we could find no bedchamber and were glad after an airing to take up our quarters in one of the rooms of a cafè, where we got however mattrasses and pillows: our own night-bags serve as sheets. Giuseppe provided us a good maccaroni, and our tea was forthwith satisfactorily consummated.

The King and Queen arrived about 7½, too late to go to the Duomo (here called Chiesa Matrice,) to return thanks. We saw him come. The people shouted tolerably for him, and warmly for the Queen.[1] He took no notice of them on alighting, but soon appeared in a balcony, looked at them coolly through his glass while men, women (in their black mantles, the general costume here,) soldiers, mules, were struggling below in the broad torchlight: retreated—again came forward as if he had forgotten himself and made two slight bows. The Queen seemed well-looking. She was carried in a sort of carriage litter, borne by two mules with long poles, and an additional one in front to draw. The throng was dense: but an Englishman always has an advantage in a foreign crowd: particularly if he have been educated at Eton.

Saturday Oct 20.

We fared pretty well on our last night's mattrasses: everyone in Sicily should be particularly watchful of the fleas which spring upon the feet and ancles from the floors and may inadvertently be carried into bed. We find it quite necessary to look well through our bags before using them. And it is after all a question worth considering whether (on account of sleep) a person who suffers much from vermin should come to Sicily at all.

We saw yesterday a primitive millwheel: the interior skeleton was made of wooden spars crossing each other at right angles: the circumference of straw ropes wound round the former: and earthenware jars were tied by the neck to these ropes to catch the water. I was sorry to see in Sciacca, on the Casa Communale,[2] a notice to the effect that 'Monsignor Agostino, Vescovo di Girgenti, concede 40 giorni d'indulgenza a chi recitera 3 Ave Maria.'[3] I thought the use of this mischief had been confined to the Pope. Today we made

5¾–12¼.   24 miles to Monte Allegro.[4]

1¾– 7¼   18 miles to Girgenti: an hour of darkness. For some time through a deep shingle, we trailed slowly along the shore.

βῆ δ'ἀκέων παρὰ θῖνα κτλ[5]

Our first prospect was that of the bay under Girgenti itself: at sunset: night, (threatening rain) upon the East, while the red sun overspread the

---

[1] Maria Theresa, archduchess of Austria, m. Ferdinand II (as his second wife) 1837.
[2] Town hall.
[3] 'Augustine, Lord Bishop of Girgenti, grants 40 days' indulgence to anyone who recites 3 Ave Marias.'
[4] Village 17 miles SE. of Sciacca.
[5] *Iliad*, i. 34; 'took his silent way along the shore etc.'

entire west. Monte Allegro is a sad misnomer—the village is infamous for malaria—the ancient one, now deserted, on an almost conical hill, offers an almost unique spectacle: I remember a deserted town near Foligno—nothing can be more deathlike than such a combination of objects which speak to the eye and mind of life, and yet do not actually offer it: like the old illustration that a *grate* may make a person feel cold.

From this village there is more traffic on the path, which at Molo,[1] four miles from Girgenti actually becomes a carriageable road, though with extremely steep and difficult ascents and descents. It was too late for us to get the first view of the ruins.

At Monte Allegro we found, for aid towards our luncheon, the *carrubba*, a description, says K., of bean, oblong & sweet: figs dried and strung: and pomegranates. Here also we found cotton, and saw the plant in flower: it is sown in June, gathered at this time: about a foot high, yielding globular green pods, which open well packed with wool. The leaf is very like ivy, but wanting the gloss: and the field might be mistaken at a little distance for one of year-old vines.

We likewise saw the peasants cutting rice about 8 miles from Sciacca. From 120 to 150 were at work. It was carried in armfuls or some such quantity to a floor where oxen tread it and it is afterwards winnowed. The appearance is something like barley, the straw not so long; it is bearded: and one stalk carries five or six or eight ears. The ground is flooded before the sowing and remains so while the plant ripens.

Ecce iterum Crispinus[2]—once more of the plough. It seems to be composed of at the most five pieces. The bent 'aratrum'[3]—the projected temo[4]—the iron point, or vomer[5]—the pin which holds the *temo* to the aratrum—and a kind of nut to secure the pin. The weather has been dry, and they cannot now, in most places, use it until rain comes. The land is full of crevices, often large enough for a mule's or horse's foot, which remain open until winter. Looking anxiously, we could only detect two palms on our road and those very small.

Nothing can be more palpable than the whole anatomy of a Sicilian village to the hastiest passer through it. Every door is open, every inhabitant without, or at it, or in sight through it. A shop or two of wares indicated by flags projecting: no name (at Siculiana)[6] or writing of any kind on any house: some wine-stores: some mills at work: always bread & some little fruit exposed: a solitary school of six boys, a master, and a rod, while there were six hundred in the street: women spinning and knitting, a few here and there weaving: children in every degree of approximation to nakedness: and a large proportion of the population unemployed: such are the features presented at this time & in this district. I never saw a country with so little of what is *written*, in any form, exposed publicly to view.—

[1] The port of Girgenti.
[2] 'Here again Crispinus', a then well-known tag (from Juvenal iv. 1) for something that keeps cropping up.   [3] Here is a small diagram of the aratrum, 'plough'.
[4] Pole by which the plough is dragged.
[5] Ploughshare.   [6] Town 3 miles SE. of Monte Allegro.

On our road we found marks of the King's passage yesterday: for example, rice straw laid over some of the muddy stream-ditches to enable animals to get over without losing their footing.

Girgenti crowns a steep hill overlooking the ancient ruins and the sea, which always harmonises so admirably with grandeur, and particularly with grandeur that belonged to other times, for what more belongs to all time, and less to the present instant? Thus the sea assists the mind to make the necessary transition, and prepares it to comprehend and feel suitably to the occasion.

Sunday Oct 21.

Prayers.[1] At four I went to a Sermon—the Sicilian dialect, rapid chattering enunciation, and noisy children prevented my following the preacher accurately: his matter however seemed good, his manner lively, with a slight tinge of buffo. He appeared to be preaching against making light of venial sins. This was in the Redentore.[2] On my way down I went into another small Church on the left where indeed I could hear well enough, and was grieved to hear the preacher descanting on the great goodness of God in his regard to the world in that he determined to save not only the just and righteous, but even the most wicked—through the Virgin Mary! pointing to her image over the altar—and again, so as not to leave room for reference to our Lord, to save them he said *per la carità di lei*.[3]

The Sunday here is noisy and altogether out of keeping with home practice. The street under our window has been full of labouring *men* all day—the women remain at their own doors, or are found in the Churches.—All these men wear white nightcaps: the prevailing dress is the velveteen jacket & breeches, with white cotton stockings, sometimes boots, sometimes large buckles, complete the equipment. The women chiefly wear the black mantle and carry it over the head. There was a kind of little fair, apparently, of horses mules and asses yesterday.

Monday Oct 22.

Certainly we have seen better horses here than elsewhere in Sicily: but I do not know if Agrigentum has recovered the fame which it enjoyed before the time of Virgil.

Magnanimûm quondam generator equorum.[4]

We left at 9. The *Albergo del Leone* is in the Sicilian sense, clean: that is to say the bedding is not so dirty as to be full of fleas. At the same time there are of course plenty about the floors, and the beds have a fair share of bugs. We went to the Temples—miles 2½—and

1–5¼, to Palma[5] . . . . . 12.

---

[1] And wrote notes on morals, Add MS 44728, ff. 154–7.
[2] Church of the Redeemer.
[3] 'through her charity'.
[4] 'once breeder of great-hearted horses'. *Aen*. iii. 704.
[5] Palma di Montichiaro, 14 miles SE. of Girgenti.

However these are very long, and indeed are marked on the map as 14½ miles of 60 = 1 degree. = 17 Eng[lish] miles.

The road down from the town gives a fine view of the temples, as does that to Palma, until it crosses the hill termed S. Francesca di Pabla about 3 miles from Palma: but the colour of the stone, though rich and mellow in itself, is too near that of the surrounding ground, now like that of the grass of Hyde Park after a summer's drought: and there is nothing to equal the retrospect upon the Temple of Segesta, with the crags of its own hill immediately below it and the mountains of Castellamare in the distance.

The wall of the ancient Agrigentum runs along a ridge, generally in a line with the temples: it appears to have been literally hewn out of the rock which is soft: oblong, semicircular, and oval recesses, of clumsy execution are cut in it, where we learn that urns have been found: its direction is from East to West: and though on a level much below that of the modern level = the old citadel, it is lofty and conspicuous enough to justify Virgil's description

Arduus inde Acragas ostentat maxima longe
Moenia.[1]

The Temples beginning from the East stand thus.

1. Juno Lucina. At the Eastern extremity are remains not only of an exterior court, but of steps fronting those of the temple—as if for spectators of processions?—The interior length is overstated in Mrs Starke:[2] from pillar to pillar is 117 feet, and the breadth 46f. 8in. The circumference of a column at the base 14f. Only a small piece of frieze remains, towards the land: the architrave of that side is entire: and it is observable that the capitals of the columns are much more worn on the seaward or south than on the landward side. I add a rude ground plan:[3]

2. The Temple of Concord—on a knoll less elevated than the former, yet a striking situation, and very perfect. The Eastern pediment is nearly complete: a little broken at the northern extremity. It is also deformed by King Ferdinand's inscription informing us that his magnificence restored the temple: would that his modesty had also been consulted—would no place do for this cobbler except the very forehead of so august a structure?

There are six side archways carried through the walls of the cella to the N. & as many to the S: and windows also drilled through its pediments—in the middle ages.

The walls of the Cella are proportionably raised above the line formed by the outer colonnades so that these with the corresponding points of the pediments would form the supports for a slanting roof over the whole. There are apertures wrought in the stones apparently for both the greater and the minor members of such a roof.

The ground plan of this cella is not quite the same with the last. Its ex-

[1] 'Here steep Agrigentum's massive walls can be seen from afar': *Aen.* iii. 703.
[2] 378.
[3] Here there is a diagram of the steps and temple described, with the words: 'steps surrounding the temple on all sides' (see facsimile overleaf).

tremities each[1] present two pillars and two pilasters. There is a step upward at the principal door A, and also one at the barrier B, and the floor
between them is raised. At A is a communication by a small stair with the
roof. The wall was raised over both ends of the cella, over A, and over B,
to correspond with the form of the pediments and meet the roof. Three of
these four parts remain. Whether there were doors here or not, we find
that there were in some temples, or cellae: for Virgil writes (Aen 1. 448)

> Aerea cui gradibus surgebant limina, nexaeque[2]
> Aere trabes: foribus cardo stridebat aenis.[3]

But he may have anachronised here: as in the description of the Sicilian
coast which was colonised by no Greeks at the time when Aeneas could
have sailed by it.
There are a kind of old stone walls hollowed like an egg with a little-endian
aperture—for water? (of which the modern Girgenti has none—it is all
carried up, & sold)—or for grain? We came to
3. The Temple of Hercules. In total ruins. Larger than the former—in spite
of Mrs S.[4] we found the dimensions by measurement to be,
length of the Cella ab. 160 feet—
interior do of the temple—200—
length of its platform—   220.
Circumference of column, in which the Grecian architects seem to have so
beautifully applied the principles of proportion—about 18–19 feet.
Here again the ground plan of the Cella is different from either of the
foregoing.

> $\alpha\beta$, $\gamma\delta$,   being solid structures to the roof—
> $\epsilon\zeta$, $\eta\theta$,   being raised walls

with separate divisions as marked on the plan.
4. The temple of Jupiter Olympius—likewise a total wreck, but for its
space and scale, appearing among the ruins of Greek temples what St
Peter's is among modern Churches: with the statue of the giant conspicuous
in the midst upon an almost cleared area.
The deep horse shoe grooves are here visible in almost every stone, and
the large ones have two. They may have been meant to receive ropes for
hoisting? while again the simple quadrangular incisions drilled into the
great stones of some other temples, would appear designed to receive metal
clippers one at each extremity—as, if the comparison be allowable, one
sees hogsheads of sugar raised in Liverpool at this day.
At the N.W. corner is a stone like the corner of a semicolumn, and at the

---

[1] Here there is a diagram of the cella (enclosed interior), with points marked A and B
to which the text refers (see opposite).
[2] Here, as often, the diarist indicated a terminal 'que' by a q with a stroke through its
tail.
[3] 'Steps went up to a bronze threshold and the lintels were bound with bronze; the
hinge of the bronze doors groaned'.
[4] *Information for Travellers*, 379.

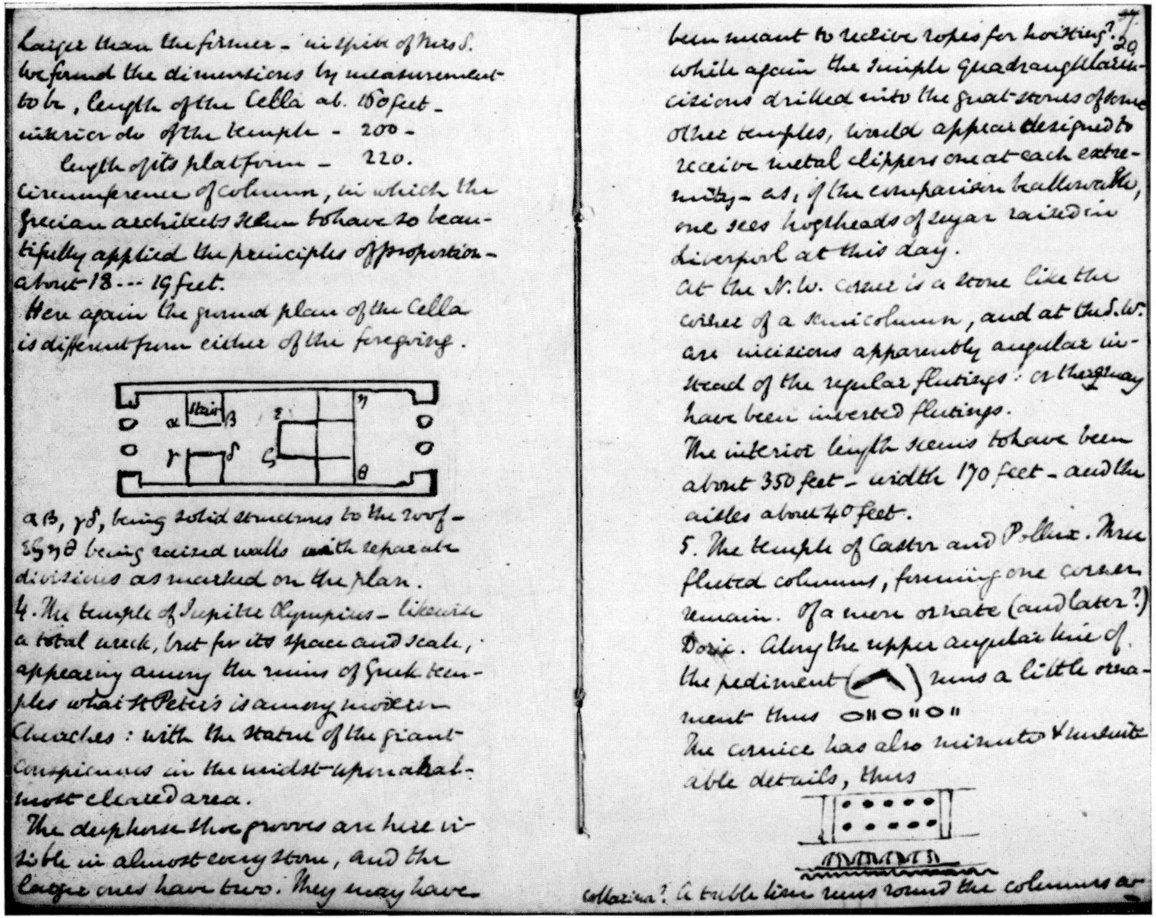

larger than the former - within of these.
...found the dimensions by measurement
to be, length of the cella ab. 80 feet.
interior ab. of the temple - 200 -
220.
length of the platform -
...correspence of column, in which the
Grecian architects then behave so beautifully applied the principles of proportion -
about 18 --- 19 feet.
Here again the ground plan of the cella
is different from either of the foregoing.

a (b, y), being extra entrances to the roof -
...being sacred walls with separate
divisions as marked on the plan.
4. The temple of Jupiter Olympius - likewise
a vast ruin, but far its finest and scale,
appearing among the ruins of Greek tem-
...what porticos is among modern
Churches: with the extent of the finest
comprised in the widest-spread that.
...enclosed area.
The diopheus thing prove are here in
...is the in almost every form, and the
...larger over have two. They may have

been meant to receive ropes for hoisting?
while again the temple quadrangulated
...cisued divided into the front-stones of the
...these couples, would appear the pro-
...receive metal clamps on each extre-
...mity - as, if the comparison (calling,
...one see hogheads of sugar carried in
...Liverpool at this day.
At the N.W. angle is a stone ... the
...edges of a monticulum, and at the later
...are numerous apparently regular instead of the regular flutings - as there they
have been indeed flutings.
The interior length seems to have been
about 350 feet - width 170 feet - and the
aisles about 40 feet.
5. The temple of Castor and Pollux. Here
placed channel, forming one corner
remain. It a more ornate (and later?)
Doric. Along the upper angular line of
the pediment (∧) was a little ornament thus ०॥०॥०॥
The cornice has also mi... to ...
...ate details, thus

...(illegible) a little line runs round the columns as

Temples at Agrigentum, 22 October 1838.
Facsimile of diary in Add MS 44818C.

Temples at Agrigentum, 22 October 1838.
Facsimile of diary in Add MS 44818C.

SW are incisions apparently angular instead of the regular flutings: or they may have been inverted flutings.

The interior length seems to have been about 350 feet—width 170 feet—and the aisles about 40 feet.

5. The Temple of Castor and Pollux. Three fluted columns, forming one corner, remain. Of a more ornate (and later?) Doric. Along the upper angular line of the pediment[1] runs a little ornament thus[2] The cornice has also minute & unsuitable details, thus.[3] collarina?[4] A treble line runs round the columns about 6 in. from the top—and another at the junction with the capitals.

We did not go to the sixth ruin, which has two columns remaining, at the extreme West.[5] All these great structures, on the same ridge, visible far and wide from hill and valley, from land and sea, must have formed a range of surpassing magnificence. By simplicity and purity of design, how much did ancient architecture produce from materials apparently scanty! We saw the tomb[6]—apparently of a vicious architecture—and retired saturated to our lunch. Four hours & a quarter brought us to Palma. Here in a Church I find

> Gesù, Giuseppe, e Maria
>> Vedono il cuor e l'anima mia:
> Gesù, Giuseppe, e Maria
>> Assistete mi nell' ultima agonia:
> Gesù, Giuseppe, e Maria
>> Spir In pace con voi l'anima mia.[7]

This is a local association of Joseph with the Virgin—found I think in some particular spots besides. It is more pleasing to record the singular inscription one sees on some of the houses and shops of Palermo: Viva la Divina Providenza! resembling that on almost every house at Aricia[8] 'Viva il sangue di Gesù Cristo'—which I suppose one should translate Blessed be the blood of Jesus Christ.

Tuesday Oct 23.

Palma. Albergo del Sole. The most uncouth looking rough plastered room, and the cleanest beds we have had: the reverse of the Sicilian rule, ornament (even to the carts) & filth. I had here my first—probably my last—

---

[1] Here there is in the text a bracketed diagram of the angle of the pediment.
[2] Here there follows a row of three small circles with two vertical strokes to the right of each circle.
[3] Diagram in text.   [4] Collar (collarino) round the capital of a column.
[5] 'View NB' pencilled against sideline in margin.
[6] Tombs said to be of the tyrants of Syracuse, either that of Phalaris, d. 552 B.C., in the city, or that of Theron, d. 472 B.C., outside it; both really Roman constructions showing near-eastern influence.
[7] 'Jesus, Joseph and Mary, look at my heart and my soul:
Jesus, Joseph and Mary, help me in my last agony:
Jesus, Joseph and Mary, May my soul expire in peace with you.'
'Vedono' misread for 'vedo', 'I give you'.
[8] Cp. 26 Apr. 32.

night the rest of which was not broken by vermin: at least I shall not expect another until Syracuse.

A singular sign attracted my eye last night. Over a tailor's door was an eagle, with a piece of tape in his mouth, and the great scissors in his claw ready to cut it! A tailor and an eagle: an eagle and a tape: what can be the associating link, the common idea, which shall explain this device of Lorenzo Amico, Sartore,[1] in Palma?

The following are some prices of principal articles in Sicily.

bread roll	. . .	4 g.[2] (would cost $\frac{3}{4}$d in Engl.)
milk, cartuccio[3] (12 oz.)	. . .	6 g.
wine, cartuccio	. . .	4, 5, 6 g.
eggs	. . .	1, 1$\frac{1}{2}$, 2 g. each
meat	. . .	12 gr. rotolo, up to 20 gr.
cheese	. . .	24 gr. rotolo
maccaroni	. . .	9 gr. rotolo
caffè	. . .	3 g. a cup, small.
grapes	. . .	2 g. 4 g, to 6 g rotolo.
potatoes	. . .	2 g rotolo.
sugar	. . .	3 g. rotolo.
butter	. . .	12 carlini, rotolo—in other seasons 4, 6, 8. Only to be had in Palermo good.

(7 Sic. oz. = 1 lb English)
(rotolo = 12 Oz. Sic.)

Traveller's prices, without doubt.

These are from our informant general, Giuseppe.

Palma . . . . . Alicata 14 m[4]   . . . . . 6$\frac{1}{2}$ . . 10 A.M.
Alicata . . . . . Villa Butera[5] 7 m . . . . . 10 a.m. . . 12 (Falconetta)
Villa B . . . . . Terra Nuova 12 m . . . . . 2$\frac{3}{4}$ PM . . 6$\frac{1}{4}$

Our first stage lay through a better cultivated country than we have lately seen. At Licata we descended upon the shore, and again at Prince Butera's Villa. The country from Licata is bald and brown, and now burnt up, there having been no considerable rain for six months! *totally* without trees, which have been tried at the Villa, and refuse to grow under the double influence of the sea air and the scorching sun: perhaps also the sulphurous soil or bottom?

We saw a family of stunted palms on our first stage. On our last, we learned the name of a common plant here, the piccolo palmieso:[6] its leaves are like a lady's fan: it is tenacious of the soil and when cut up revives, so that we see the oxen ploughing round and round these plants, which are suffered to remain in the midst of the cornfields. We had also the turpen-

[1] 'Tailor'.
[2] About $\frac{3}{4}$d.
[3] quartuccio: rather more than 1$\frac{1}{2}$ pints.
[4] They were travelling ESE. along the southern coast.
[5] Farm of the Prince of Butera Radalí, also called Torre Falconara.
[6] Piccolo palmizio: 'little palm', *chamaerops humilis*, palmetto, only species of palm family native to Europe, growing in Sicily, Sardinia, and region of Naples.

tine plant, among others, and the wild galls, our gall used for ink: a light greenish yellow ball, of tough skin, full of seeds & juice, about the size of a bigaroon cherry,[1] is the fruit. The bushes grow on the sand near the sea shore. Along this coast the answer given us is, that no rise and fall of the tide are observed.

At Alicata a wide range of coast is opened, reaching I think to the Capo Scalambri[2] which is only a few miles N. of the very southernmost point of Sicily. From Castel Vetrano our general direction has been South East. Tomorrow it turns to the N.E., leaving the coast, and makes a bow to Siragusa[3] which lies about due E. from Terra Nova. At Prince Butera's Villa, which immediately overhangs the sea, we were entertained by his Factor,[4] a Swiss, and an agricultural economist from Hanover whom he has brought here to improve his Estate. We dined with them, and they rode part of the way to Terra Nova, but the Factor armed himself for the expedition with his gun. He told us of recent robberies in this neighbourhood—in one case a peasant returning from the sale of his little produce was murdered by the brigands of the country. The pass which he pointed out as peculiarly infested by them, on our way, was under the very nose, so to speak, of a customhouse station. La dogana, he said, non se ne cura.[5]

This factor described to us some of the methods of holding land of which one is as follows. The landlord advances to the peasant 1. the seed, 2. provision for his beasts, at a certain rate. The peasant tills and gathers. The landlord withdraws from the gross produce the value of the seed and the amount of advances: the residue is equally divided between owner and cultivator.

The labourers live in the towns: come out into the country by Monday at midday: and remain until Saturday evening. Their subsistence is upon a bottle of wine and two rotoli of bread a day: they sleep in the open air or where they can. Almost all of them have donkeys.[6]

Both our informants spoke ill of the King, as avaricious & indifferent about his people—of the priests, as unchaste, habitually & notoriously—of the judiciary, as grossly venal—and lastly of the peasantry, as false in language and not to be trusted. Old customs of hospitality prevail in Sicily. A man calls at any house and asks for shelter & food for his horse—it is given as a matter of course.

The peasants salute us on the way with 'Addio'—'Vi son servo'—'Vi saluto'[7]—and among themselves according to Michaele, one mode is this: 'Viva Maria'—answered by 'Viva Gesù'.

On the Prince's Estate here are kept 30 ploughs and 150 oxen. We saw all the ploughs at work, upon the third ploughing, near the house. In other places we see ten, twelve, fifteen yoke. Some sheep, the *gentili*, only lamb

[1] The large white-and-red heart-cherry.
[2] 29 miles SSE. of Alicante.
[3] Syracuse.
[4] Named Palmi.
[5] 'The customs people don't bother'
[6] 'Tenures and condition of the people' in margin.
[7] 'God be with you'—'I am your servant'—'I salute you'.

once a year.—Sometimes the landlord *ploughs* and the occupying tenant reaps. This property pays £500 a year on an assessment of the different kinds of grain when sown at so much for a certain measure of land. Coal has been discovered at Riesi,[1] by Craig or Greig an Englishman. There are immense quantities of sulphur: but the King has granted a monopoly to a certain French company, & has laid a tax on all the rest.[2] It is smelted like a metal. The raw cotton is exported—and the tablecloths & towels we see & use are imported, from England![3] All foreigners pass by the general name of *Inglesi*. So they are or were called *Franks* among the Turks.—The people always expect them to pay much more for what they use. The schools are exceedingly few and bad: and *not* a tenth of the population, say our friends, read and write. But a certain number of the poor hill shepherds do both, keeping up these arts from generation to generation by mutual instruction. The returns from speculations in land improvement are large: and the transfer of it is at present free.

With respect to the divisions of temples, which Girgenti exhibited, the following lines of the first Aeneid are worth observing. (1.505)

> Tum foribus divae, mediâ testudine templi
> S[a]epta armis, solioque altè subnixa, resedit.[4]

as showing
1. That the line at or near the centre indicated the sanctuary.
2. for what secular purposes these edifices were made available.

Wednesday. Oct 24.

The 'English Hotel', Terra Nova, is dirty in appearance, but we had new mattrasses, and boards fresh from the carpenters: so we slept comfortably without vermin.

6½–11. 14 miles—to a stream for lunch.
1–4. 10 miles—Calata Girone.[5]

On leaving Terra Nova, we got our first view of Aetna: he peeped rather than towered over the intermediate hills, quietly smoking his pipe, as we could just discern, in the distance. Agriculture somewhat improves as we go along. Horses are yoked to the plough by saddles on the back, joined by a wooden yoke, but supported by a broad leather over the breast. The cotton plant is ploughed up like stubble. We saw white plastered kennels on the lower hills: these are for the dogs who in the winter defend the sheep hereabouts from the wolves.

We are both very weary of mule-riding. The motion is most anomalous, & most disagreeable. For each *pair* of feet moved by the mule, the body of the rider receives a distinct backward and forward impulse: the strain on

---

[1] 12 miles north of Torre Falconara (Villa Butera).
[2] See 7 Nov. 38.
[3] 'NB English' in the margin.
[4] 'Then within the goddess's doors, beneath the temple's central vault, she took her seat on a lofty throne, fenced round with weapons.'
[5] Town 17 miles NE. of Terra Nova.

the stirrups is great: & the whole body is so incessantly shaken that even the back and shoulder blades partake in the resulting aches. The mules have taken the conceit out of me, and thoroughly fatigue and unman my limbs. Uneasy as the motion is, the most singular circumstance is, that it greatly tends to produce slumber.

The shops in towns are open till eight or so in the evening, and again open with lamps at two or three hours before daybreak. One is assisted to conceive how as at Pompeii the ancients dispensed in some cases with windows, by seeing that at Licata, Terra Nova &c. there are many houses, as well as shops, which are but of one story, and have no opening but an arched door in front: so that there are whole streets without windows in them.

Another salutation exchanged by the people here is simply 'Gesù Maria'— repeated by the person to whom it is addressed.

Calata Girone is a town of 20,000 inhabitants, situated I should think at an elevation of 1500 feet, and commanding views of Mount Aetna, of the Catania valley[1] to the sea, of the Val di Noto towards Syracuse[2] (S.E.) to the sea, and of the hills with the sea in the direction of Terra Nova, S.W.: with this peculiarity, that each of the four above named prospects has an entirely different character: the first is the single unbroken outline of the Sicilian giant: the second that of a brown treeless and open valley: the third that of a rich well wooded agricultural district: the fourth that of a sea of hills.

A Belvedere has been erected on the East of the town for the enjoyment of these prospects, but the situation does not appear to be very favourable for the purpose. The town itself appears active and well conditioned in external matters: there is a great deal of handsome stonework about the exterior architecture of the Churches and houses, as may indeed be observed more or less in the other towns of Sicily. This is the best we have seen, after Palermo: and it has actually a few private carriages, drawn by *horses or fine mules.*

We went to see the repository of earthenware figures in terracotta: the artist's name is Buongiovanni, and the performances are full of talent: always excepting some absurd gilt Silenuses. The great attraction seems to be, the faithful and lively representation of national costume and character. Single figures are two *pezzi*[3] each. We found one very pretty *scene* ready to go to Palermo, the death of Polyxena. I happened to have Virgil in my pocket & pointed out the lines "O felix una ante alias"[4] &c as a motto for this piece, which the old gentleman appeared glad to have. The price was 30 oncie = 90 ducats.[5]

Locanda del Leone.[6] A filthy house: but we got clean beds and slept well contrary to all expectation.

[1] The plain of Catania, 14 miles by 8, is 14 miles NE. of Calatagirone.
[2] Named after the R. Noto; stretching 24 miles NW., and 40 miles SE., from Calatagirone to the sea.
[3] Shillings?
[4] 'O happier far than other women': *Aen.* iii. 321.
[5] Say 15 guineas.   [6] Lion Inn.

30—II.

Thursday Oct 25.

Calata Girone	...	Palagonia[1] 18 m.
		6¼ A.M. ... 11¼ A.M.
Palagonia	...	Lentini.[2] 18 m. (short)
		12½. P.M. ... 5 P.M.

Our road today commanded a fine prospect of Aetna; at the time, especially, when nothing but the Piano di Catania lay between the mountain and ourselves. Two miles or more before reaching Palagonia, we came among the lava hillocks, and one road was much bestrewed in parts with stones at some time I suppose showered from the mountain. It is curious to see how not only soil, but layers apparently of softer stone, have been formed above the lava. From Palagonia we cross the higher grounds which separate the Piano di Catania from the Vale of Scordia[3] and that of the Lago di Biviera[4] by Lentini, for the fishing of which the Prince Butera is said to receive some £1000 or £1200 a year. Until today we have had roasting suns ever since leaving Palermo: but at length we have clouds and rain.

Michele our muleteer is a character of great simplicity. Giuseppe denounces him as a creature that cannot reason, un uomo che non ragiona; but he is well worth observing in his own way. From Catania he means to carry white silk nightcaps as a present for his brother, and he is also going to buy a gown for his sister or mother—wife he has none. He produced his grano[5] of his own accord for an old beggar. He was too modest to mount behind K. on his mule the other day when the Prince Butera's factor was riding abreast & in conversation with him. K. sometimes hears him muttering 'Signore, vi ringrazio',[6] sc. for the ease & relief which he receives by mounting. He guides us tomorrow to Syracuse,[7] and it has been most amusing to see the attitude and expression with which conscious of the increased dignity of his charge he received Giuseppe's instruction for his conduct. He jabbers at an inconceivable rate: at first I used to say to him, Michele, avete la bontà di parlare sei volte più adagio, altrimente non capisco una parola, e bisognera ridirle sei volte.[8] this lost its effect, so I changed it to, Michele, vi prego, parlate un poco più presto, questo e troppo adagio[9]—all persons here seem to have a keen sense of the ridiculous[10] or of any inkling of it, and this really wrought upon him & made him for a little more intelligible.—Yesterday one of his mules was unwell. I asked this morning if he was quite well: yes, ringrazia Iddio.[11] Upon questioning him further it appeared that he had prayed to God to make the mule well, for

[1] Small town ENE. of Calatagirone.
[2] Town east of Palagonia.
[3] Town 5 miles east of Palagonia.
[4] Lake a mile west of Lentini.
[5] About a halfpenny.
[6] 'Sir, I thank you'.
[7] 32 miles SE. of Palagonia.
[8] 'Michael, have the goodness to speak six times more slowly, otherwise I don't understand a word, and you will have to say it six times again.'
[9] 'Michael, please talk a little faster, this is too slow.'
[10] 'of' deleted here.   [11] 'thank God'.

which we endeavoured to commend him. He added that he had prayed to certain saints on the subject, thinking himself unworthy to approach the Most High. A very amiable humility in the individual: but it suggests one of the scandals of the Church in these countries, which though so fond of representing the Redeemer in pictures, and especially as an Infant, yet seems to lose so much of the force of the doctrine of the Incarnation by the *interposition* of third parties, and most inadequately to teach the sympathies of the Head with the members of the body.

Some grain is already above ground, for next year. We saw sowing in progress. The seed is scattered after two ploughings. A third immediately follows, and a person goes about with a sort of mattock (?) to break the clods—but the soil is a fine soft mould. The single ploughs which we often see are I suppose where the tenant holds as in page 42.[1]—The sets of six, ten, fifteen & yoke, are probably where the landlord ploughs & sows, according to another method described to us, where in fact he only lets the land after the crop is in the ground, and the peasant gets it in and pays a certain rent per salma.[2] By the bye K. learnt from Palmi the factor, that an average working mule costs 30 oncie (£15), horse £8, ox £5, sheep 15 carlini (5/1) lamb 3 carlini. That Prince B. had four English ploughs but they were so deep that they caught the roots of the weed called the little palm, & could not be worked. Also that there is much chastity until after marriage; which takes place very early. That much may be got from the people by kind treatment. That the coal discovered by Craig (or Greig) was supposed to be of good quality. That the silk manufacture at Catania is the only one worth mentioning in the island.

Everything English is highly esteemed here. I am sorry to see, much more than elsewhere, numbers of priests and of monks, both lounging about the towns, and sitting in the cafes. The curiosity of the people is extraordinary. Not only do they stare at one extremely—which we reciprocate upon them and their interiors—but they coolly ask you who you are, whence you come, what you are doing, whither you are going. This evening several came up with us into our Inn. A lad of 12 years old or more said 'Donde siete voi altri?' 'Da una lontanissima parte della terra',[3] I told him. By and bye, when we were at tea, a well dressed man opened the door & thrust in his head: K asked him if he wanted anything: 'Niente,' he answered, 'sono venuto per curiosità.'[4] This quality seems to pervade alike all ranks and classes.

We met this morning a party of Calabrians, about six, with their conical hats, and digging implements: they came over to make drains for the fields. Sicily sadly wants water. It is saved in troughs every here and there along the roads. The streams are few, and now, low. They have dug for themselves extremely deep beds, for the most part, through the soft soil of the island, with precipitous banks of twenty, thirty, forty feet. Today

[1] *Sc.* ii. 455 above, 23 Oct. 38.
[2] A local unit of measure, equalling about 4½ acres.
[3] 'Where do you people come from?' 'From a very long way away.'
[4] 'Nothing, I came out of curiosity.'

by the bye some of the muddy feeders of the Lago di Biviero caused us some delay, for the first time from such an obstacle: but it is one which ought not to be forgotten in the calculations of a Sicilian journey.

Friday. Oct 26.

The Gran Bretagna[1]—alas for the disgrace of such an association—belonging to the Barone Girolamo[2]—alas for the peerage! is more fully stocked with fleas than any inn I have yet met with: under a semblance of cleanliness. I did not sleep a single wink during the night: I could not even remain in bed & was driven fairly forth: and on producing a light at 3 A.M. I slew five and twenty of these little animals with my own hands, and rowed the people of the house to the very top of my bent.

To save our baggage horse a long journey we left him with Giuseppe to cross from this place to Catania (2 [blank][3] miles) and take Michele with us to Syracuse. He has given us another good trait today. He gave money to a beggar who did not thank him for it. & on K's making some inquiry about it, he said the gratitude of the receiver was not to be our object in doing a kindness.

5¼ A.M.–11¼ A.M. Lentini to the junction with the Strada Rotabile[4] near the Paese Novello. 15 miles.

11¼–1¼ the new road to within a mile of Syracuse. 9 miles.

The road of the first portion is for the most part incredibly bad: and both distances are certainly underrated. The latter miles are I take it of $50 = 1°$.

From Lentini we crossed the hill behind it, & worked down very slowly upon the sea, with a rich volcanic basin afterwards prolonged in a ravine, on our right, well watered and having the sides, perhaps to a depth of 50 or 60 feet, covered with (apparently) vines and other luxuriant creepers. Wild olive, walnut, olive, carrubba, fig, trees abounded by the roadside: and scattered copiously and negligently over the landscape they gave it a very English aspect. The sun was more or less tempered by clouds. Etna has realised in snow what came yesterday to the low countries as rain: and his smoke in the enfeebled sunlight has a remarkable tint of pure silver. Even the clay paths, well beaten and (so to say) polished by the ironshod beasts of burden, shine like that metal when the sun of Sicily is in the zenith of his splendour. We left the road, to economise time, some time before reaching the gates, and finding first a charlatan guide whom we summarily dismissed much against his will, then a bonâ fide one, we set about visiting the antiquities which we had to see and which cluster together on the north side of the city. I had already had much pleasure in comparing an old Oxford card, bearing a rude delineation of the ground about Syracuse, with the fine view which was presented to us after crossing the *scala Graeca*:[5] and in the Albergo del Sole my room looks out, at the distance of

[1] At Lentini.
[2] Barone Gaetano di Girolamo, keeper of the lake and owner of the inn.
[3] 17 miles.   [4] Carriage road.
[5] Where the post road from Catania enters the plateau of ancient Syracuse, at the remains of an ancient gate, with ruins of the time of Dionysius (tyrant, 406–367 B.C.).

fifty yards, upon the old port upon whose quiet waters, scarcely spotted with here and there a solitary bark, I seem to see the proud and gilded galleys of Athens struggling to enslave the hardy ancients of this city, the long banks of oars, the decks crowded with armed men, the deadly grapple and the chequered incidents of those great and gallant seafights which the pen of Thucydides much to our labour but more to our delight has immortalised.[1]

The quarter of Achradina,[2] and indeed I believe the whole ancient site,[3] is remarkable for the ruins it does not contain, namely those of the private houses which seem to have vanished utterly away while the rugged (volcanic?) rock which preceded and supported now also survives and mocks them. In Achradina we see nothing except tombs:[4] open vaults, sarcophagi, small cavities in the rock for urns (or infants), and the square recesses in which tablets have been placed. Thus the chief signs which remain of what was once a most proud & powerful race, are those immediately associated with our mortality. And yet in these rock sepulchres themselves, in the hardihood of labour they required, in the comparative permanence of the home they gave or would have given to frail ashes which an evening breeze might irrevocably scatter, in these as well as the more material signs, of the variety extent and costliness of some of these cemeteries, we read the masculine and energetic character which belonged to states having with the solid foundation of a Doric origin, the appliances of active life in peace as well as in war, a great commercial as well as a powerful military position. But it is time for the details, such as they are. Mrs Starke's account[5] I should observe appears very imperfect, and requires the correcting and enlarging hand of some future Guide for Travellers.
We saw
1. The Amphitheatre:[6] set down by Mrs S. at 134 feet by 83.[7] I *stepped* it & think I do not much exaggerate in saying that it must be nearly 222 feet by 123 along the diameters. Here are the holes for receiving poles to support the awning, the passage for draining off the water,[8] and for casting out dead bodies from the arena: and here are some stones of the balustrade, according to our custode *passamano*,[9] having upon them the names of individuals to whom particular places belonged: one for example is marked 'Locus Statilii'.[10]

---

[1] Books vi and vii, on the Sicilian expedition and the siege of Syracuse by the Athenians.

[2] Founded, fifth century B.C., from Ortygia, the original island city.

[3] Comprising the four cities of Ortygia, Acradina, Tyche and Neapolis. The modern city has been reduced to Ortygia alone.

[4] Two Strade Sepolcrali had been discovered by 1838 (others have been discovered since); one on the borders of Acradina and Neapolis, and one near the shore. These tombs were always outside the walls of a Greek city; they serve today to mark the limits of the ancient cities of Syracuse.

[5] *Information for Travellers*, 383 ff.

[6] The principal monument of Roman Syracuse, probably dating from Augustus.

[7] Ibid. 387.

[8] With which arena was flooded for *naumachiae*, mimic sea fights.

[9] 'Lace trimming' in Italian, but 'balustrade' in Sicilian.

[10] 'Statilius's place'.

2. The Ear of Dionysius.[1] Mrs S.[2] gives the height at the entrance as 58 feet: the custode gives the height at 6×14 feet—of which it has more the appearance. It is easy upon entering this cavern to appreciate its adaptation for acoustic purposes. The more curious may be hauled up, by ropes, in an arm chair, to the orifice at which Dionysius was in the habit of eavesdropping: but there is no less operose[3] mode of access.

3. The Stone quarry,[4] now ropewalk, close at hand: very striking in its bold masses and light & shade: it is hazardous for art to compete with Nature in caverns, but this has perhaps been fortuitous: at all events the result is striking & curious.

4. An ancient staircase[5] in the solid rock now bodily overthrown, supposed to have communicated with the ear.

5. The theatre.[6] Surely the estimate of 40,000 is exaggerated unless the present remains give a very inadequate idea of the size.[7] One is almost surprised that the ancients gave such beautiful views to the seats of their theatres, as here and at Egesta—it seems like introducing a rival attraction. From this place the eye rested on the pride of Syracuse, her harbour, with the city and plain,[8] the plain bounded by the Western hills, and the city with its outlines resting on the sea.

6. Bagno di Venere.[9] Scooped in the rock—lighted by a square aperture. Four recesses: besides smaller chambers: one of these is called a chamber of tombs.—there are oblong apertures dug into the floor. The statue of Venus now in the Museum was found just over this in ploughing.[10]

7. A Private Cemetery: remains of painting in fresco: two figures on the cove of the roof: peacock (pavo) & [butterfly] (papiello) with ornaments. What peacocks indeed we are & how Death strips us.

8. The Catacombs,[11] the repositories of the dead, and the refuge of Christians during persecution—very extensive, with great variety of niches, compartments, and chambers: some remains of painting in them. some of these chambers large and lighted from the roof.

9. The subterranean Church, (of S. Marziano, the first Bp of Syracuse,)[12] purporting to have been used for its sacred purpose (according to our fratecustode) for 1800 years—& as he explained afterwards, from the time of the Apostles. Here are three crosses purporting to be very old: they have no

[1] A narrow tapering opening in the rock, winding inwards for some 200 ft.; said to have been constructed by Dionysius to hear what his prisoners in the quarry said.

[2] *Information for Travellers*, 386.

[3] 'laborious'.

[4] Latomia del Paradiso, 'Quarry of Paradise'.

[5] In the cliff above the Greek theatre, over the Ear of Dionysius.

[6] Greek theatre. The largest in Sicily; completed by 406 B.C. at the boundaries of Acradina and Neapolis, with a view over Ortygia and the port.

[7] In fact it held over 25,000.

[8] The marshes west of the port.

[9] 'Venus's bath' in Acradina.

[10] Found by excavation in 1803. There are a number of cells or troughs for the accommodation of bathers.

[11] In Acradina; said to extend for 8 miles.

[12] Beneath the church of San Giovanni, the catacombs' entrance, built where St. Paul is said to have preached and said mass during his 3 days' sojourn at Syracuse (Acts xxviii. 12). St. Martian is said to have been made a bishop by St. Peter.

figure of our Lord on them. the four Evangelists with the four creatures of the Revelations: and other frescoes[1]—respecting which one must claim some liberty of opinion.

10. Under the Church of S. Niccola is an old Piscina,[2] with pilasters reputed to be Greek. Their architrave seems to exhibit something of the principle of the arch—thus—[rough sketch] (too wide & stumpy)

11. Quarry of the Count di [blank][3] very pretty & picturesque with a good view from above, rivalling its more extensive and celebrated neighbour, the – – – –

12. Quarry of the Capuchin Convent,[4] which might be made to exhibit an extraordinary degree of beauty. It is very extensive bold and varied, & produces richly.[5] Here an Ear was commenced: & hence much of Syracuse was built.

Syracuse is now, apparently, little more than a fishing town. It had 18,000 people. Cholera swept away 3000. The populace had murdered 17. Twenty-seven were shot in consequence. The belief here, according to our waiter, ascribes it to human device—probably to the king. The little commerce of the place has declined: and the very good Inn which it contains is missing its owner. The harbour is good and the steamers remain here for a day: but this is all.

Saturday Oct 27.

6–12¾. 24 (long) miles to Fondaco d'Agnone.[6] 1½–6. 18 miles to Catania, crossing the Symethus[7] in a ferryboat.

We started under a threatening sky & with a wild wind, which soon fulfilled their menaces. Poor Michele was in great alarm; oime, sarò bagnato.[8] I asked him, 'Michele, quale ti spiace più, la pioggia, ovvero le pulci?' 'O, Signore, la pioggia vieppiù: le pulci sono niente.'[9] He can read and is in this respect ahead of Giuseppe who is of a more generally cultivated understanding.

I longed for the description of Thucydides to compare with the ground, but even from imperfect recollection one sees enough to appreciate the nature of the ground and the object of the fortifications of Epipolae[10] and Labdalum.[11] A kind of platform defended by crags runs westward[12] from Achradina: on the S. and N. it is thus naturally defended, and the fort and

---

[1] On piers and walls of the church.
[2] A subterranean reservoir, above the Amphitheatre.
[3] Latomia del Marchese Casale, west of the quarry next described.
[4] North of the Little Port, in Acradina.
[5] Flowering trees; no longer stone.
[6] Agnoni, on the east coast; 'Fondaco' is the inn there.
[7] Classical name (Symaethus) of the Giarretta or Simeto, crossed near its mouth on the coast.   [8] 'Poor me, I'll get soaked.'
[9] 'Michael, which do you most dislike, rain, or fleas?' 'O sir, rain much more: fleas are nothing.'
[10] 'Above the city.' A fifth ancient city of Syracuse, on rocky ground lying just over the city. During the siege, 415 B.C., the Athenians ran a double line of wall across it and down to the great harbour, which they occupied with their fleet.
[11] One of the forts built 414 B.C. by the Athenians in Epipolae.
[12] Instead of 'eastward'.

walls would stop hostile access from the W. The Scala Greca is cut by the line of the crags at about 3½ miles from the present city, which gives an idea of the vast extent of the ancient one: certainly most wonderful, when the limited extent of its territorial possessions is considered.

About 15 English miles from Syracuse the roads to Lentini and Catania diverge. The latter has an uninviting aspect: it surprises an English traveller when his guide or muleteer points to a lane about five feet wide, between tangled hedges, apparently blocked up with stones from the size of those used for paving to that of a good *outlier*, and says, Ecco la strada di Catania:[1] the road which leads from old Syracuse, to a city containing 80,000 people! We had as a travelling companion what would in England be called a carrier, but here *mutato nomine*,[2] in proportion to Southern grandiloquence, a courier, who with his brother go twice a week between these cities, on a mule, or if need be with more and this is the stated amount of land communication which connects them.

Some miles before reaching the Fondaco d'Agnone,[3] the road attains a noble prospect of the gulph of Catania with the beautiful city, gleaming as it did for us in the sun which had at length prevailed over a dismal morning, the proud mountain above it,[4] the Sicilian coast stretching away with very bold outlines towards Messina, and in the north-eastern distance that of Italy presenting to us a very extensive range. which reaches to the extreme S. of the peninsula, Cape Spartivento. Etna is great in appearance, and exhibits an enormous mass: yet he does not seem what he is, of Alpine height, owing I suppose partly to the absence of snow, of which the recent rain has left but a very little—previously none was visible—and partly, it is probable mainly, because its line descends so gradually towards the sea and likewise landward.

From Fondaco the path leaves on the left a *wood*: the first we have seen in Sicily after travelling 270 miles. It wanders through brakes and sand-hills, occasionally touching the shore, until nearer Catania it enters a lane and then joins a *strada rotabile* of lava, after exhibiting the face of that fearful bed which fronts the sea and still appals the passerby if he reflect upon its origin. The appearance of lava is for the most part extremely savage and corresponds with its history. In the suburb of Catania it is used for building walls and houses. We saw this day abundance of vineyards, aloe and cactus hedges, in the *sand*—absolutely—and close to the sea: and I made acquaintance with the wild rosemary, all whose leaves are prickles, but upon being bruised extremely fragrant.

Sunday Oct. 28.

After breakfast I went to the great Church of St Niccolo,[5] which has a

---

[1] 'Here is the Catania road'.   [2] 'by an altered name'.
[3] Margin entry: il golfo che receve da Euro maggior briga Dante Par. 8.68. 'The gulf tormented most by Eurus,' the east wind; *Paradiso*, viii. 68–9.   [4] Etna.
[5] Church of the convent of St. Benedict, founded on the slopes of Etna, in 1359 at St. Nicola d'Arena near Nicolosi, halfway between Catania and the summit; which name was transferred to the monastery in Catania founded 1578.

noble and beautiful organ.[1] It gave me great delight and I remained until
its majestic voice was hushed. A few of the last bars were accompanied
with the beating of a very powerful drum or kettledrums,—stop in the
instrument,[2] which reverberating through the 'longdrawn aisles'[3] & nave
produced a very singular effect.

Afterwards we had our prayers. At $3\frac{1}{2}$ I heard a Sermon in a neighbouring
Church on the forgiveness of injuries. The subject was I should think one
here especially needful, & the preacher a Dominican handles it well. He
argued it 1. from the necessity of forgiveness of injuries for the peace of
society—to our own temporal comfort—and to our eternal salvation.
2. From the express command of God our Saviour—as our Master and
Judge—and lastly as our Friend, as the Friend who took flesh and died for
us, and who requires us to give this small token of our love, to which we
should be bound even if it had not those intrinsic recommendations which
he had shown it to possess, and which it were monstrous to refuse to that
Redeemer, who desires us to regard and forgive our enemies as *in Him*.
Two other preachers were so very Sicilian that I could ill understand the
bits of their sermons which I heard. One was comparing the pains of soul &
body, & used a singular argument. The pains of the body touched its
surface but did not pervade the whole: whereas the soul had no such
defence as solidity affords to our material part. The third, in the Cathedral,
seemed to be preaching mere Romanism. The congregations are not very
large. I saw a Baptism: hurried and unimpressive as at Florence. No females
were present.

Giuseppe told me today that 52000 died of cholera in Palermo: (perhaps
this is exaggerated;) one fourth of the population. He lost his mother—a
daughter was attacked but recovered. He had made up his mind before to
be content to lose his daughter—it was so uncertain whether on growing
up they would do well—but he had most dearly loved his mother, the only
parent he had known, & this he could hardly bear. He also had, he said,
religious difficulties, & sometimes became in spite of himself "cattivo",[4]
unbelieving? when temporal want pressed him, and he saw wicked men in
great prosperity. I promised to seek solutions for these, such as are afforded
by the 37th and 73d Psalm, and the 12th chapter of the Epistle to the
Hebrews, & we are, D.V., to speak again on the subject.

In S. Niccolo I observed particularly what may often be remarked, people
sitting indifferently through the mass, in any situation, as if mere bodily
presence within the walls of the Church were enough to satisfy their duty.

(*Oct. 28*)[5]

At Catania my thoughts were much occupied by the responsibility attending the publication of my book: I mean the responsibility before God, not

---

[1] Then said to be the finest in Europe, with 72 stops, 5 sets of keys, and 2,916 pipes.
[2] These four words interlineated.
[3] Cp. *Gray's Elegy*, 39.   [4] 'bad'.
[5] Next three paragraphs from Lambeth MS 1424, where they follow the entry for 3 Nov,
38,

any consequences which might accrue to my own temporal interests, real or supposed. I had reflected much upon it before resolving, but I had never felt the reason *con* so strongly, although I do not say that they now appeared of equal strength with those *pro* But they are most weighty as impressing the necessity of deliberation. I, the worm of a moment, am bringing into permanent form the impressions of my mind, impressions which have grown or changed with the lapse of time, and which may again change or decay with its contined lapse: these I attempt to endow with the power of a perpetual voice, and that not the voice of private solicitation, addressed to one or few, and capable of being corrected in the next day or hour's conversation, but a voice attempting at least—and if the attempt fail this does not excuse me—to speak simultaneously to many, and perpetually to each of these many. So that as the sculptor ponders before he transfer his clay into marble, and deprives himself of the power of removing any further its imperfections upon discovery—so should the man who has reduced his thoughts to palpable form, to heed well all the parts and mouldings of that form, before he allow it to become a petrifaction.

But O Lord God! in whom I have wished this work to be done, I pray that it may rest in thine hand, and that both in the truth and the error of the book Thou mayest be glorified: that the minds of men may be attracted by the Truth which shall be found therein, and may espouse it: and may be aroused by its errors to seek more earnestly elsewhere for the counteracting Truths, that so Thy praise and honour may issue from them both, through Jesus Christ our Redeemer.

Having conversed with G. Lazzara on religion, and found that he had temptations from perceiving the temporal prosperity of wicked men, and from his own struggles and reverses in the world, I translated for him as well as I could into Italian passages from the 37th. and 73rd. Psalms, bearing on his subject, and from Hebrews 12th. and St Peter i. 1.—and read them to him with the earnest instance that he would abide constantly in prayer.[1]

Monday Oct 29.

Even here as we learnt from a respectable looking *cacciatore*[2] on our ride of Saturday, many among the people ascribe the Cholera to the King!

As I came into Catania a welldressed man stared at me, and turned round as he walked on to stare: I wished to see whether a reciprocal gaze would, as in England, *remind* him that there is golden mean in these matters: so I returned his compliment; without any effect: he continued after passing me to walk forwards, all the while looking backwards, and at length called out, quite civilly, from perhaps 30 yards off, 'Sei Siragusano?'—'Cosa?' 'E Siragusano vossigneria?'[3]

We hardly were able to do justice to the curiosities of this fine town, which

[1] Cp. Magnus, 37.
[2] 'man out shooting'.
[3] 'Are you a Syracusan?'—'What?' 'Are you a Syracusan, sir?'

has been rebuilt since the eruption of 1669 with a splendour sufficient to place it, I think, above Palermo in outward appearance. The streets are wide and regular, the exteriors of the houses highly ornamented, the Churches and façades numerous: we hear the population differently stated as of 45, of 60, and of 80,000 before the Cholera. We looked through the Duomo, which has paintings by Corradino[1] and others: I should think that the paintings which we have seen in Sicily generally might be easily comprehended in one description: they are of an extremely light tone in colouring, and generally represent those Italian schools which were so characterised, in an inferior form.

We visited the ancient Theatre, built with brick, lava, and mortar. According to our Cicerone the width of the Scena was 300f. Three corridors of different floors remain, or parts of them. Modern buildings and the volcanic ravages have combined to perplex the view of this fine edifice, but by taking one up and down, and by pointing out the extreme points[2] of the old building, which can I suppose be ascertained from the curve of the existing seats and passages, they contrive to convey through it a good idea of the relative positions of the ancient and the modern cities, and of the immense scale of ruin which has accompanied the eruptions of the lava. At the base is a fountain of water, which has only appeared since a recent eruption, that of 1832: and which is always higher in summer than in winter, on account, as they say, of the melting of the snows on Etna.—Near the theatre remains the front of the Odeon,[3] travestied by the modern houses which have been appended to it.

We went to the San Niccolo and again heard the magnificent organ. On the Sunday very few of the priests of the convent had been at this mass, and today I think there were more besides the officiator. We went through the convent, which is magnificent beyond any I ever saw, & must be immensely wealthy.[4] The King was lodged here during his recent visit of three days to Catania. We could only see the Museum through a grating in the door—it is of considerable extent & neatly arranged. The covers were laid for dinner: each priest, we understood, has four dishes, each lay brother and novice three: at supper they have two: in the morning they breakfast in their rooms, which appear large and airy. The garden of the Convent is very large and apparently tended with great care, abounding in beautiful flowers and marble fountains and balustrades. There are 45 priests: 15 piccoli—pupils: and 24 lay brothers. The building is of immense extent, and the lava lies around it arrested in its most menacing attitude before it had proceeded to destroy.

The Biscari Museum[5] was shut. We were quite overrun in the morning with sellers of amber which is found here & wrought, not apparently in first-rate manners into ornaments.

[1] Annibale Corradini, fl. 1590–1628, painted frescoes of the early martyrs of Catania on the outer wall of the Cathedral apse.   [2] 'Extreme points' instead of 'range'.
[3] West of the theatre, similar to it in construction and arrangement, but much smaller: used for training choruses and for musical and poetical contests.
[4] Said to be the largest monastic institution in Europe.
[5] Of antiquities of Sicily.

Having thus dispatched our immediate objects in Catania, or determined to forego them, we left our excellent Inn, the Corona, in the Corso,
near the Duomo, at $1\frac{1}{2}$ for the Etna expedition.

(1) $1\frac{1}{2}$–5. Catania to Nicolosi.[1] 12 miles. (Called by our Guide 10)
I subjoin here at once our times & distances to and from Etna for the sake
of clearness.

(2) Nicolosi to the commencement of the Bosco[2] ... $\left.\begin{array}{l}\end{array}\right\}$ 10.20 P.M.–
                                                 .. 11.45.

(3) To the end of the Bosco 11.45 .... 1.15 (A.M. of Tuesday.)

(4) To the woodman's grotto[3] .. 1.15 ...... 1.55.
Here the mules were baited by moonlight: (this road was preferred as rather
better than that by the Casa della Neve.)[4]

(5) To the Casa degli Inglesi[5] 2.30 ...... 4.45.
(Wine etc. & fire.)[6]

(6) To the brink of the great crater[7] .... $\left.\begin{array}{l}\end{array}\right\}$ 5.45 ..... 7.5.

(7) To the summit of the mountain,
   & spent about the crater, $\left.\begin{array}{l}\end{array}\right\}$ ..... 8.5.

(8) Descending to the Casa degli I., 8.5 ...... 9.5
   (Refreshments)

(9) Casa degli Inglesi to the
   Bosco ...... $\left.\begin{array}{l}\end{array}\right\}$ 9.30 ..... 11.20.

(10) To the end of the Bosco   11.20 ..... 12.15

(11) To Nicolosi[8] ....   12.15 ..... 1.20

(12) To Giarra[9] ....   2.50 ..... 7.20 P.M.
                              of Tuesday Oct. 30.

Our guide made the distances:

Catania to Nicolosi	10 m.
Nicolosi to Bosco	3 m.
Bosco to Woodm. grot.	4 m
Woodm. grot to C. degli Inglesi ...	4 m.
C. degli Inglesi to the Crater—	$1\frac{1}{2}$ m by way we took, but
	by the direct road 1 m.

Total $22\frac{1}{2}$.

[1] Small town NW. of Catania.
[2] Wooded region 6–8 miles wide, succeeding to cultivated region at Nicolosi. See next
day's entry. All dots on this page are diarist's.
[3] The Casa del Bosco.
[4] 'Snow house' 7 miles from Nicolosi, in the Bosco, hut without a door and with
leaking roof.
[5] 'Englishmen's house', a later shelter erected by English officers in 1811, beyond the
Bosco; three rooms, a small kitchen and stable for mules.
[6] Clauses 2–5 are joined by a pencilled bracket, with 5 h written in the margin.
[7] Pencilled in the margin is 1.20
                         10 h nearly
[8] Clauses 8–11 are bracketed together in pencil with $5\frac{1}{4}$ written in the margin beside it.
[9] Town 10 miles NE. of Nicolosi.

It is a good sign of a guide—and not the only good sign we had of our friend Giuseppe Bonanni, a young, handsome, active, obliging, and enthusiastic person—to underrate the distances on which his functions are charged; and they are more commonly as follows.

Catania to Nicolosi ...	12
Nicolosi to C.N.[1] 7 and thence to C.I.[2] 8, together }	15
To the top	2
Total	29

I think the latter scale comes nearer the truth than the former: at least in English miles. The height of the mountain is very variously estimated from 10,000 feet upwards: one calculation reaching 15,000.

As respects our *time* upon the distance, the pace of the mules upwards is very slow, the road often rough and always very heavy, and the animals stop incessantly: from the Casa to the top and down again, we were delayed by K's being very considerably indisposed: it required great courage in his state to proceed at all: the cause was to be lamented rather than the effect for the real difficulty was to tear one's self away. It appears that most persons are attacked with sickness in their ascent. It came upon me before reaching the Casa degli Inglesi, and in consequence I did not drink wine there, in which I think I was right. Eating a little bread & a few grapes, I became perfectly reestablished.

As respects the temperature, it was 33° at the woodman's grotto, and 33° at the Casa degli Inglesi: but a slight wind, and the slow pace of the mules, give much greater effect to the cold than would be supposed. From the Casa we were on the more especially volcanic part of the mountain, and in its present active state, its influence on the outward air must be considerable. Day was breaking as we started, and we found the air on the top temperate and agreeable. The extra covering with which we started was deposited on the way. There was frost in many places on the surface of the ground: but it appears that while the snow lies 20 palmi deep below, the cone of the mountain is clear from it in winter.

The[3] ascent is nearly uniform from Catania, though a part between Nicolosi and the wood is called plain. The country bears a volcanic aspect at every step, for lava meets the eye in a thousand forms, in roads, walls, houses: in the fields where they are detaching from it the fine mould which gathers about it: in the multitude of hills which have sprung at different times from almost every pore of Aetna, and which at different parts of the road would suggest that you are not on the ascent of a particular mountain but travelling through a range of hills: and in the broad black lines which

[1] Casa della Neve.
[2] Casa degli Inglesi.
[3] Most of the rest of this entry and of the next, and the distance table just given, in *Murray's *Sicily* (1864 ed.), 442–7.

streak the sides of the giant himself, clearly distinguishable in a bright sun from the loose ash with which it is surrounded on the higher ground.

At Nicolosi we found clean beds, and undressed. I could not sleep during the hours allotted namely from our dinner to 9½—but I listened with great interest to the distant booming of the mountain: the dignity of my reflections was somewhat disconcerted by my afterwards learning that a part of the noise was the stamping of the mules in their stable or Fondaco: but they were saved from utter discomfiture by the fact that the volcano and the mules had been copartners in producing sounds which really appeared, such are the delusions of our at least of my poor senses, to proceed from one source. At this Inn as at those of Sicily generally, on our giro, except at Palermo, Syracuse, Catania, Messina, the traveller must trust to his servant or himself, I apprehend, for his provisions: borrowing the fire, and crockery and linen where they are to be had.

From Nicolosi the road passes to the Bosco through a tract which although it belongs to the cultivated *Region,* is as dismal as anything he subsequently encounters. The Region of the wood is losing some of its interest day by day, as it is cut down alike by authorised and by illicit destroyers—of the latter we met some leading down their laden mules at one in the morning under the broad moonlight. However for the present this tract is very picturesque, like an English park, with its old oaks and abundant fern. There are also ilexes, beeches (fagi),[1] broom of a very delicate form, as a small tree six or eight feet high, (& called ginestre) and pines. Oak and fern however on this side are the staples. The ground is infinitely varied, and in this respect it would be difficult to match it. Here we found flocks browsing: they are much exposed to sheep stealers who do not touch travellers, calculating with justice that men do not carry much money to the summit of Etna. We now began to feel the cold, K. particularly: and a fire lighted at the grotto where the guardian of the wood should be, was very acceptable to us while the mules fed.

Tuesday Oct. 31 [sc. 30].

By and from this time we had a peculiar and very enjoyable view beneath us. Light fleecy clouds lay upon the sea below us—which I would compare to those of Guido's Aurora in the Rospigliosi palace at Rome[2]—the effect was precisely similar. The line of the horizon was lost in the close approximation of the hue of the clouds to that of the ocean. The line of coast, and the objects formed by its undulations, lay beneath us almost as if at arm's length. I have seen this remarked before of the view from Etna, that it seems to bring the objects below very near to the spectator: and the reason given, that as he[3] stands in a rarer and they lie in a denser medium the case is analogous to that of a pencil partly held in water of which the lower part according to a well known law of optics[4] seems to be bent towards the eye.

[1] Virgil made the plural *fagus* (*Culex*, 139).
[2] Cp. 2 June 32.
[3] Instead of 'the'.
[4] 'is bent' here deleted.

In the present instance I suppose it might be added that the effect was heightened by the circumstance that the atmosphere was much more loaded with vapours below than where we stood.

We now felt a small but very sharp wind which continued for the whole night. The mountain is rarely without more or less of it.

We passed on to the Casa degli Inglesi, occasionally walking for the sake of warmth, through the Region of Snow, so called because in winter ordinarily covered with it. We saw however (the weather having been very fine) but one patch of old winter snow, and the surface of that was covered with dark ash. It lay in a recess fronting Eastward. Our ascent was now very steep. The latter part of the stage lay over what is called the Piano del Lago:[1] and indeed it has the requisites of a plain, except a *level*: it might more accurately be called a plane,[2] because its surface though not horizontal is equable: and it lies between the Monte del Formento[3] on the left, and the Montagnola[4] and Torre del Filosofo[5] (nearest the cone) on the right, a dead waste of ash and sand, without a speck of vegetation and hardly diversified by[6] single pieces of lava here and there.

The Casa degli Inglesi has chairs, a sort of gridiron for a charcoal fire, sticks for the upward walk, and a low stand or two to serve the office of a table. Fire and closed doors soon render it under the circumstances a comfortable home. Our active lighthearted guide had no spirits, but he drank some wine of which I was afraid. We started for the crater at ¼ to six. As we ascended the top had at first been covered with thick clouds. The guide however predicted that it would be clear: and the cone gradually disrobed to our view, the showers of fiery stones becoming more and more clear until we saw them shooting over the sides of the crater and rendering it to all appearance wholly inaccessible. Bonanni doubted much of the practicability of ascending. At the Casa however he said there was a circuitous road round the cone by which on the West (the present active Crater being on the East side of the great Crater) we might make our way up.

I should have mentioned that the moon seen from the mountain had a very peculiar golden hue: and also that her form appeared to be as if upon her greatest horizontal diameter, the lower segment were a semicircle and the upper one a semi ellipse very eccentric: thus:[7] (I have no idea whether this appearance of the form could be connected with our position.)

K. notwithstanding his weakness was courageously determined to persevere, and we set out at a quarter past six. The Casa looks Eastward and we passed behind it over a rude bed of lava, bearing to the left on the South

---

[1] 'Plain of the lake', a slope of loose ashes. A lake of melted snow existed here till it was filled with lava in 1607. Here was built the Casa degli Inglesi.

[2] 'Piano' is both 'plane' and 'plain' in Italian.

[3] Two miles from the summit.

[4] Long ridge on the east edge of the crater.

[5] A ruin, made of lava fragments; Roman, but traditionally connected with Empedocles, fifth century B.C., who is supposed to have meditated here.

[6] 'a' here deleted.

[7] There follows a pencilled diagram of the moon as described.

side of the cone, making way gradually over its lower region upon the ash which really afforded a very good path: and I began rather prematurely to compare this with the wretched footing afforded by the ashes on the cone of Vesuvius. On the steeper and more regular part however we found considerable difficulty from the frozen state of this ash: there were no pieces of lava, or very few, to tread on, and my nailed shoes absolutely refused to catch the hard surface: seriously it was not easy to avoid tumbling fairly down the wall-like side along which we were clambering. It was a luxury, to me, to get into masses of black ash, in which although the foot sunk deep and slid far yet it was sure to stop somewhere—however, we made our way to the West side of the cone, and just before we reached the lip of the crater, the guide exultingly pointed out what he declared to be ordinarily the greatest sight of the mountain, namely the shadow of the cone of Etna, drawn with the utmost delicacy by the newly risen sun, but of gigantic extent: its point at this moment rested on the mountains of Palermo, probably a hundred miles off: and the entire figure was visible, the atmosphere over the mountains having become and continuing perfectly and beautifully transparent, although in the hundreds of valleys which were beneath us, from the East to the West of Sicily and from the mountains of Messina down to Cape Passaro, there were still abundant vapours waiting for a higher sun to disperse them: but we enjoyed in its perfection this view of the earliest and finest work of the greater light of heaven in the[1] passage of his light over this portion of the earth's surface. During the hour we spent on the summit, the figure of the shadow was speedily contracting: and taught us how rapid is the real rise of the sun in the heaven, although its effect is diminished to the eye by a kind of foreshortening. Stepping up to the edge of the crater, I heard the guide who was just behind me cry 'Diavolo!'[2] and as he did not seem given to these expressions I was surprised—he proceeded to explain the reason. The whole space before us said to be about a mile in circumference was when he last ascended a few days ago, one fathomless pit from which issued immense masses of smoke, it was now absolutely filled up to within a few feet[3] of the brim all round. The rocky wall frowned upon it from above, in some places begrimed from top to bottom with sulphur, or formed of it. Opposite[4] to us, as we attained the Western side & turned to enjoy the spectacle, rose on the left the highest summit of the mountain, an old peak clothed with sulphur towards the crater and reeking with its smoke upon its shelving or outward side: on the left the small cone of the[5] crater from which issue the present showers, while full between them blazed the sun now clear both of the ocean and a deep bank of cloud, with a broad stream of tempered light. The immense pit presented to us a surface in some parts as if of grey heaps of ruin, in the centre were a mass of what appeared like slate rocks: all the rest was the hard rugged impenetrable lava, in its wild forms like the sea arrested at a moment of fury by sudden petrification. On looking at these masses we saw

[1] Instead of 'his'.
[3] 'feet' written over 'inches'.
[5] 'present' here deleted.

[2] 'Devil!'
[4] Instead of 'before'.

the red heat in the clefts: and on a further inspection the guide cried out, Ecco, cammina, cammina, ecco come cammina! com'è bello![1] A great mass of lava with black exterior was detaching itself by degrees from one behind, or rather was yielding to the forward pressure: it opened like an orange and we saw the red hot fibres stretch in a broader and still broader vein until the mass had found a support in the new ground it occupied in front: as we came back on our way down this had grown black. At present, we put a stick to it—it took fire immediately—we threw pieces of stone and lava upon it; they made hardly the slightest impression upon it, so hard is it while in the fluid state—but began immediately to acquire heat—we found within a few yards, as few as *ten*, bits of ice formed on the outside of the stones of the brink by Frost, which here disputes every inch of ground with his fierce rival Fire[2]—these we threw on the lava; they hissed for a moment, and were extinct. 'A terra!'[3] exclaimed our guide as the mass came to earth. The state of the crater made his enthusiasm red hot. We were indeed extremely fortunate, and actually the first spectators of this great volcanic action: one would suppose that it portends an eruption, as the lava still everywhere proceeds and the crater is nearly filled: but at all events it is what if we were men of science would make a figure in our Journals.

To ascend the highest peak our choice lay between a precipice and a corner of the crater: we went over the lava in a very warm atmosphere, sometimes on passing a rift, too hot, for a moment or two, to breathe. We got upon the back of the peak and worked up through the sulphur clouds which here alone were seriously disagreeable. We here gazed upon the Eastern view, embracing the Messina mountains and the fine kindred outlines of the Calabrian coast, so described by Virgil: Aen. 3.414.

> Haec loca, vi quondam & vastò convulsa ruinò
> (Tantum aevi longinqua valet mutare vetustas,)
> Dissiluisse ferunt, quum protenus utraque tellus
> Una foret: venit medio vi pontus, & undis
> Hesperium Sicule latus abscidit, arvaque & urbes
> Litore diductas angusto interluit aestu.[4]

From thence it reached all along the Southern coast to Cape Passaro:

> Vivo praeterrehor ostia saxo[5]   Aen. 3.688
> Pantagiae, Megarosque sinus, Thapsumque jacentem:

(Thapsus, to the eye, is certainly one of the lowest-looking pieces of land that can be conceived: the epithet is admirable.)
And further:

> Et inde   Aen. 3.697.
> Exsupero praepingue solum stagnantis Helori.

---

[1] 'Look, there it goes, there it goes, look how it goes! How lovely!'
[2] 'and' here deleted.   [3] 'Down!'
[4] 'Once these lands were torn apart in a great catastrophe—how much change is made by distant time!—and were split, though once a single whole: the sea thrust in between them, the gulf parted Italy from Sicily, and the narrow tide washed between the fields and towns scattered along the shore.'
[5] 'I am carried beyond the mouth cut out of rock of the Pantagyas and the bay of Megara and low-lying Thapsus.'

31—II.

Hinc altas cautes projectaque saxa Pachyni
   Radimus.[1]
But our chief object from this point was the crater of the opposite side,
into which having now reached a position higher than any part of it we
had a considerable insight. We enjoyed keenly our full clear sight of the
volcanic action: and even at the moment I could not help being struck with
the remarkable accuracy of Virgil's account. The great features of this
action are, the sharp and loud clap, which perceptibly shook from time to
time the ground of the mountain under our feet: the sheet of flame, which
leapt up with a sudden[2] momentary blast, and then disappeared in smoke:
then the shower of red hot stones and lava: at this time, as we found on our
way down, lava masses of 150 or 200 lbs weight were being thrown to a
distance of probably a mile and a half: smaller ones we found even more
remote: these showers were most copious, and often came in the most rapid
succession. Even while we were ascending the exterior of the cone we saw
them alighting on its slope, and sometimes bounding down with immense
rapidity within perhaps some thirty or forty yards of our ricketty footing
on the mountain side. They disperse like the sparks of a rocket: they lay,
beneath the moon, over the mountain thicker than ever the stars in
heaven: the larger ones ascend as it were with deliberation and descend
first with speed and then with fury. Now, they passed even over our heads:
and we could pick up some newly fallen and almost intolerably hot. Lastly
there was the black-grey column which seemed smoke and was really ash,
and which was shot, from time to time, out of the very bowels of the crater
far above its edge in regular unbroken form. It was on account of these that
in ascending the guide said, do not look towards the sky or your eyes will
be filled with sand.
Now how faithfully has Virgil combined these particulars—doubtless not
without exaggeration, in his fine description: First the thunder clap, or
crack:

   horrificis juxta *tonat* Ætna ruinis:[3]   Aen. 3.571 & seqq.
Secondly the vibration of the ground to the report:
   Et, fessum quoties mutet latus, intremere omnem
   Murmure Trinacriam:[4]
Thirdly the sheet of flame:
   Attollitque globos flammarum & sidera lambit.[5]
Fourthly the smoke:
     et caelum subtexere fumo.[6]
Fifthly the fire shower:
     scopulos avulsaque viscera montis[7]

---

[1] 'Then I pass by the rich bed of the stagnant Helorus. Next we graze the high and
jagged rocks of cape Passaro.'   [2] 'blast' here deleted.
[3] 'Near by Etna *thunders* with fearful destruction'.
[4] 'And whenever he turns over all Sicily shakes'.
[5] 'and he hurls up balls of fire to singe the stars.'
[6] 'and veils the sky in smoke.'
[7] 'He belches out rocks and entrails torn from the mountain; groaning thrusts molten
stone rolled into balls into the upper air, and boils up from his lowest depths.'

Erigit eructans, liquefactaque saxa sub auras
Cum gemitu glomerat, fundoque exaestuat imo.
Sixthly: the column of ash:
atram prorumpit ad aethera nubem
Turbine fumantem piceo & candente favillâ.[1]

And this is within the limits of twelve lines. Modern poetry has its own merits: but the conveyance of information is not, generally speaking, one of them. What would Virgil have thought of authors publishing poems with *explanatory* notes (to illustrate is a different matter)—as if they were so many books of conundrums. Indeed, this vice is of very late years?

But our position was not quite secure, as the winged lava every now and then hissed and whistled past our ears: and we sorrowfully turned away from a scene which with the combination of features it exhibited on this happy morning may well be termed one of the wonders of the world, and of itself amply repays the pains of our journey to Sicily, and obliterates from recollection the vermin and the mules.

Indeed such a spectacle has higher uses. Standing in such a presence of the aweful functions and powers of Nature, the material form of Providence, a man feels that he is in respect of his physical existence, a plaything in her hands, a feather upon the wind; the paw of the lion is on him, and he feels his strength to be not little, but imperceptible, but none. And he should then desire to live more in that part of himself, which is more subtle than the flame, and which shall be, if he yield it to God's purifying dispensation's, likewise made more pure. Furthermore, one cannot but think, that these terrible orifices of the subterranean fire, are meant for this purpose, with whatever others it may be combined, to give a palpable assurance to our faith in the declarations of Scripture concerning the final conflagration of the heavens and the earth that now are. We look upon beds of lava which we know to be the graves of cities, and upon the ever fresh and fertile caverns of the mountain: we see the match and the combustibles, and nothing is hidden from us but the Hand, and the Time, which are to bring them together.

We went down, gratified and yet really burdened with the scene: K. too was weak and unwell. At the Casa we rejoined our mules and sinecure guide. Giuseppe was sleepy having been at work seven miles off at Nicolosi all yesterday: he rubbed his eyes and our own with fresh snow: which was a very agreeable application. Descending we took the road of the Casa della Neve: which is ¼ hour shorter. The Casa itself is in miserable condition. I ought to have mentioned that on our way from the *peak* we visited the piece of lava which we had seen in progress: the torture in which it writhed was over and the whole surface black: the new propulsion from behind as yet imperceptible.

We saw little on the way down but what the moon had previously shown us. We saw however a brace & a half of partridges at the top of the Bosco, probably 6000 feet above the level of the sea. The cone was no longer

---

[1] 'He hurls a dark cloud into the sky smoking with whirling pitch and glowing sparks.'

spangled with the falling showers as last night: the breadth of daylight shamed even their burning hue.

As the distance downwards to Nicolosi occupied nearly four hours, I take it at 15 (English) miles or thereabouts.

After a dinner excellently prepared by Giuseppe, we made a nominally 15, really eighteen mile stage to Giarra in a slant direction towards and round the base of Etna. The country was finely cultivated: I never saw such masses of vineyard. At Giarra, we were agreeably disappointed in flea-less beds at the Locanda di San Gaetano: where the landlord is, to say the least, a screw.

Wednesday: Oct 31.

Giarra .. Giardini 15 m. 9½ A.M.–12¾.

Giardini[1] .. La Zapaola[2] 15 m. 2½ P.M. .. 6.

Just before entering Giarra we got upon the strada maestra[3] from Messina to Catania: and before reaching Giardini we passed the fork to Palermo. The road is pretty good. The country about Giarra is very rich: it seems as if the finest of all soils were produced from the most agonizing throes of nature, as the hardiest characters are often reared amidst the severest circumstances. ὅσπερ ἐν τοῖς ἀναγκαιοτάτοις παιδεύεται, κτλ (Thuc. 1.)[4] Giarra is a flourishing commercial town. Indeed the aspect of this side of Sicily is infinitely more active and the country is cultivated as well as most parts of Italy. 'Michele quanti anni avete'? 'Trenta, Signore.' 'Siete pero certo? perche mi pare che ne avete più?' (Kinnaird added, sixty.) 'Io non so; cosi dice la madre.'[5] and his mother is 45. It is unusual for men here it appears to marry between 20 & 30, but women almost all before 20: 15 & 16 are very common ages, and at Girgenti some marry as early as at twelve.

The name Gentini, or something like it, is given in Sicily to the merino sheep, of which we see a good number.

Before reaching Giardini the road crosses the river Cantara, which marks the base of Etna on the North.

We found the road up to Taormina about 2½ miles of steep ascent, that is, to the theatre. The elevation must be of from 1000 to 1200 feet, and the position is very fine. It has a particularly intelligent custode. The dimensions according to him are 345 palmi at the longest diameter, & 245 at right angles to it. It bears the names according to circumstances, of Il Teatro, which was its function under the Greeks: of Amphitheatre to[6] which purpose it was transferred by the Romans: and of Il Palazzo, as it

---

[1] On the coast, 12 miles NNE. of Giarre.

[2] Zia Paola (from the name of the woman who kept the inn) or Marina of Palma, a small village, 14 miles NE. of Giardini.

[3] 'main road'.

[4] 'whosoever (ὅστις, Thuc.) is educated by circumstances of dire necessity, etc.'—Thucydides, I, 84.

[5] 'Michael how old are you?' 'Thirty, Sir.', 'But are you sure? for you seem older to me.' 'I don't know; that's what my mother says.'

[6] 'into' replaced by 'to'.

seems that under the Saracens it was inhabited. It has been scooped in the rock. NB. That the theatres of Segesta, of Syracuse, & of Taormina, all command very fine *views*: tho' the ancients from their works appear rather indifferent to the picturesque (Except Virgil Aen. 1 [161?].) On the other hand why a fine view *there*—unless for the intervals & while waiting for the spectacle to commence? The gradini[1] have disappeared: it may be argued that therefore they were not of stone. Some traces of stairs remain. The great merits of this ruin as it is appear to be, first its illustration of history by the traces still remaining of its own transmutations: and secondly that the physical relations of the fragments are such as to convey a good idea of the character which the whole would present. The 345 feet are exclusive of the outer corridor round the summit. The large bricks in the wall of the outer corridor, dividing it from the Inner one, are considered to show that the workmanship was Greek. They are not much deeper than those used in England, but longer, and probably broader, and of unequal lengths. In this upper corridor, said the custode, it has been thought that the nobility sat; the people below. How singular to find the relations of the stalls and the gallery so inverted as in this theory they appear to be.

The view is grand. To the North the mountains of Messina and of Calabria: including Pellaro,[2] Melito,[3] and the most southern points of Italy: to the South a range of Capes, Schiso[4] (the ancient Naxos),[5] Riposta,[6] Secca,[7] and that before Aci Reale,[8] each outlying the previous one in the most pleasing lines that can meet the eye.

A steep path brought us by another two mile walk to the road where the mules were waiting for us at 2m. from Giardini. We mounted about 3, arrived at 6 at La Zapaola, a village Inn nineteen miles from Messina: and were again favourably treated with beds free from fleas: it is to be understood that the floors in almost every such case have abundance, and the prudent traveller is always careful to guard against carrying them on his feet and legs into bed with him.

Thursday Nov. 1.

After breakfast we made our last mount on mule-back: it is fair to add that the fatigue resulting from this kind of riding has much diminished, though it is still very disagreeable.

5 A.M.–9¾. 19 miles. La Zapaola to the Gran Bretagna, Messina, well situated and a promising house.

The road runs first on a made line between the mountains and the sea,

[1] Tiered seats in the theatre.
[2] Town on Calabrian mainland, 24 miles NE. of Taormina.
[3] Melito di Porto Salvo, 27 miles ENE. of Taormina; on the extreme south coast of the mainland.
[4] Southern promontory of bay in which Giardini is situated.
[5] Ancient city destroyed by Dionysius the Elder, *ca.* 398 B.C.
[6] Shipping port a mile below Giarre.
[7] 5 miles south of Riposto.
[8] 18 miles SW. of Taormina. The cape is Point Tocco.

with some cuts that would really do credit to engineers who have had more practice than those of Sicily where the principle of 'fingers were made before forks' is still so generally applied to these assistances of locomotion. A cultivated strip then appears which slowly widens until the town is reached: and the mountains are very close upon Messina. This ground is cultivated, to all appearance, highly, with oranges, mulberries, vines, figs, olives; cactus, aloe, and abundant varieties of vegetables. It is wonderful to see how from a very little soil laid on the top of a wall and planted with cactus leaves, thick and high hedges of this massive plant arise, exhibiting a bulk of vegetation very much greater than that of the earth which is its only apparent feeder.

By such inquiries as we can make, we find that our muleteer's family are proprietors of some 30[1] acres, at least, of fine land within 9 miles of Palermo: and such land does not sell for more than 50£ the salma—about six acres or upwards as far as we can understand.[2] Other land not of so good quality is proportionately lower. And a salma planted with vines may be had for £100.

At half past seven we passed a barber shaving his victim in the open air before some houses: apparently with perfect 'ease and comfort' to his skin—I thought this worth recording, as a sign of the climate, considering the time of day, & the day of the year.

All the way along we enjoyed the Calabrian coast, and the sun rose magnificently over a low line of promontory. I must not expect to see such another morning, as we are now going to crouch under the mountains of Italy. The gradation of tints was perfect, from those of light rose colour which long preceded him, to breadth of his golden blaze when he had fairly surmounted the vapours which hung about his rising: and these steps so distinctly marked, brought to mind the beautiful verse of Scripture 'The path of the just is like the shining light (i.e. the dawning sun?) which shineth more and more unto the perfect day.'[3]

A part of the long line of the buildings of Messina is caught at ten miles distance. Reggio[4] lies lower and is seen from Taormina. This being All Saints' day, and tomorrow that of the Anime del Purgatorio,[5] we find numerous persons, apparently laymen, traversing the streets with black earthenware pans bearing a death's head and cross-bones, to beg alms: and, the confectioners' shops abundantly stocked with[6] similar insignia, as sculls, bones &c., in sugar!

Beggars abound hereabouts, of the description too termed sturdy. A traveller was robbed an hour after sunset some days back: but the men who committed the crime have both been taken. The gun is not carried for security on this side the island.

We had to make up our accounts & settle with Joseph and Michael. We

---

[1] '30' has been substituted for '40, 50, or 60'.
[2] See 25 Oct. 38.   [3] Prov. iv. 14.
[4] Port 7 miles SE. of Messina, on the extreme west coast of the mainland.
[5] 'Souls of Purgatory'.
[6] 'the' here deleted.

part with both very reluctantly: the former in particular is an able and admirable servant, and I feel tonight as if I had lost my crutches. The traveller who visits Palermo and makes the giro, cannot do better than engage Giuseppe Lazzara as his Guide. He has been in better circumstances as an innkeeper: was reduced by a very long illness: and bears his reverses with ingenuous goodhumour, I hope with a higher sentiment.

Last night from our window at La Zapaola, we had a last look at Etna: and one too most interesting. There was a broad red streak perceptible, gushing some way from the N.W. of the great crater—one of the lower parts of its circumference—which looked precisely as if the lava which we saw in progress towards the brim had now overtopped it and was making way towards the plain. For the present therefore I am quite at liberty to view this as an eruption.

At Messina[1] we find ourselves almost nonplused. No steamer, probably, for twenty days: the King having drawn them for the most part to the Palermo line: vetturini at Reggio are uncertain & long: a courier goes on Saturday but travels through Sunday: we could not reach Palermo till Wednesday & should then be quite uncertain of a boat: a Neapolitan brig offers, with the promise to sail weather permitting tomorrow evening, and we have thus still a hope, though a slender one, to reach Naples by Sunday. We have agreed with the Captain to pay him 20 ducats, find our food, & pay 2 pezzi for mattrasses. Vedremo.[2] Beggars must not be choosers.

It is curious to observe how the apparent outline of Etna changes with the point of view. Before reaching Giarra it seems as wild and broken, as from the South it had seened even: and again the line becomes gently graduated from a more distant northward position.

I should say that the ascent of Etna is not very fatiguing to the limbs: but it requires to be speedily paid off with sleep. For example, I had no sleep on Monday night, or rather between Sunday night and Tuesday night: while we were for twentysix hours of that interval engaged in actual riding or walking.

One[3] finds the precepts of Virgil in some respects observed in Sicilian agriculture, contrary to modern, at least to our Northern practice. For example: Virgil promises an abundant harvest, among others, to the man,

> qui proscisso quae suscitat acquore terga
> Rursus in obliquum verso perrumpit aratro.[4]

The land gets here, after the first ploughing, a ploughing at right angles, and another obliquely. Again: Virgil says

> Quid dicam, *jacto qui semine* cominus arva
> Insequitur, cumulosque ruit male pinguis arenae.[5]   Geo. 1. 104.

[1] 'Rio' pencilled in margin.
[2] 'We shall see'.
[3] This para. in *Murray's *Sicily* (1864 ed.), xvi.
[4] 'Who, having broken up his land by a first ploughing, turns his plough round and breaks it up again crossways.'
[5] 'Then we have him who on sowing his field immediately works it unceasingly, breaking up the infertile sandy clods,'

So we have seen immediately after the operation of sowing, along with the third ploughing, a labourer with a mattock breaking down the clods.

Further, in some instances Virgil's advice if followed would improve the aspect of Sicilian culture.

Deinde satis fluvium inducit, rivosque sonantes.[1]   ibid. 106.

Were the water saved, and used. Again:

Sic quoque, mutatis requiescunt fetibus arva.[2]   ibid. 82.

This principle is but very inadequately acted upon, by four successive years of wheat crop and then one of grass.

Again, as respects the sheep, Virgil commends Italy for this among other features:

Bis gravidæ pecudes—[3]   G.2.150

So it is here at the present day, (sup. [blank][4]) except with the Merinos, which have other advantages.

Sicily has also now the cotton plant: which we have seen, on this side of the island, of three feet and thereabouts in height, much larger than on the south. In Virgil's time this was considered Oriental.

G.2.120.   Quid nemora Æthiopum, molli canentia lanâ
          Velleraque ut foliis depectant tenuia Seres?[5]

How are we to reconcile the superiority of the grapes from the rich volcanic soil on this side of the island, with Virgil's doctrine

G.2.227   Rara sit, an supra morem si densa, requiras,
          Altera frumentis quoniam favet, altera Baccho:
          Densa magis Cereri, rarissima quaeque Lyaeo:[6]

Is it by the circumstance that in the lava soil lightness and richness are peculiarly combined?

On the other hand, he commends the Eastern aspect which is so largely afforded by the maritime base of Etna.

G 2.298   Neve tibi ad solem vergant vineta cadentem.[7]

The reed is still used here but rarely to support the vines: in Italy, there are divers methods. G 2.358.

After the vintage, which ends about Oct. 20, we see the vines in many places pruned, the leaves cropped, and the soil heaped around the root of the trunk for the winter: still according to the poet's principle.

Quaecunque premes virgulta per agros   G 2.346.
Sparge fimo pingui & multâ memor occule terrâ.

---

[1] 'And then brings in water enough in bubbling brooks.' 'sonantes' appears to be the Gladstonian emendation for 'sequentes', a dubious reading.

[2] 'So lands are rested by a change of crops.'

[3] 'Cattle pregnant twice' in the year.

[4] Cp. ii. 455 above.

[5] 'Why tell of the Ethiopian groves hoary with their soft wool, and how the Chinese pluck the slender fleeces from the leaves.'

[6] 'If you wish to find out if your soil be light or more than usually heavy, since the one is good for crops and the other for vines: the heavy soil for Ceres, and very light soil for Bacchus.' *Gladstone uses the old reading 'requiras' instead of 'requires',

[7] 'Nor let your vineyards look to the setting sun,'

Inter enim labentur aquæ, tenuisque subibit
Halitus, atque animos tollent sata![1]

As to the appearance of the people of Sicily, we have thought them very handsome on the East—and on the South side, there appears a considerable number of countenances with a negro cast of feature.[2] Their curiosity is peculiar and intensive, but it cannot be called rude. Their general manner is courteous, kindly, & respectful. I have never, I am sorry to say, observed so many lounging priests about the towns, and particularly haunting the caffès, as in this island.

It[3] is rather sad to leave one's mule after a service of near four hundred miles, without being able to like him. But the acquaintance which it gives with this race is to us one of the characteristic features of Sicilian travelling. They seem to have no sense of fatigue, of kindness, or of emulation: a light or a heavy load, a long or a short distance, a good or a bad road, provided only the pace be not rapid, are all alike without the slightest effect upon the physical composure of the mule. The wiry beast works in his own way and in no other, resenting punishment but hardly otherwise affected by it,[4] and still less accessible by any other means of influence. Michael calls his mules 'Porco'![5] when they stumble. But they really seem like[6] Frankensteins of the animal creation. Sympathy however they have: and with a faint yet wild and unnatural neighing they will sometimes recognise relationship.[7] It seems to be doubtful whether horses can be depended upon for so long a journey: but if persons do not wish to make more than 20 or 25 miles a day on the average, then I should think it quite worth their while to have horses, of course with the owner's guarantee, for the purpose of riding, while the mules may carry the heavier load of baggage.

There is little privation in the way of food, if the servant be up to his business. It is more difficult, yet not impossible, to find sleep.

Our distances have been nearly as follows: (besides 35 miles, off the giro, for Ætna.)

Palermo to Alcamo	. . .	33 m.
A. to Castel Vetrano		35 m.
C. to Sciacca	. . .	27 m.
S.—Girgenti	. .	42.
		———
		137
		———

[1] 'Whatever bushes you plant in your fields, sprinkle them with rich manure, and be careful to cover them over with plenty of earth. The rain will soak its way down, a light steam will arise, and the crops will take heart.'

[2] 'NB Carthage?' pencilled in margin against this sentence. Parts of Sicily were occupied by the Carthaginians 409–241 B.C.

[3] Next twelve lines in *Murray's *Sicily* (1864 ed.), xlvi.

[4] 'stamping constantly' here deleted.

[5] 'Pig!'

[6] 'the' here deleted.

[7] See Guedalla, Q ii. 75–76, for a retrospective comparison by *Gladstone of his relations with his mule and *Victoria's with himself; based on Add MS 44776, ff. 67–68.

Girgenti to Palma	. . .	15.
P.—Terra Nova	. . .	33.
T.—Calata Girone	—	24.
C.—Lentini	. . .	36. (nea[1]
L.—Syracuse	. . .	24. (nearer 30)
		132

Syracuse to Catania	. . .	42.
C.—Nicolosi	. . .	12.
N.—Giarra	. . .	15. (cert[ainl]y] 18)
G.—La Zapaolo	. . .	30.
La Z.—Messina	. . .	19.
		118

Palermo to Girgenti	137
Girgenti to Syracuse	132
Syracuse to Messina	118
	387

The whole I think thus counted at 387 is near 400 English miles. The expence of our mules included four days of return, which we were led to pay rather from some idea of a pledge than from believing it to be usual: we hear that *two* only are commonly given. It amounted to 42 p. 9c. = 513c:[2] including barriers about 518c: or between 5d and 5½d per mile. I believe in many parts of Germany some persons may post for 6d.

We have had rain, only for half a day on our route. A shower as we came near Messina, afforded lights which showed with the greatest beauty the peculiar terraces of the Calabrian hills.

Friday. Nov 2.

We went to the Intendenza[3] to sign for our passport: and thence to the Tasso[4] to examine our contemplated quarters. Hence to the Chiesa delle Anime di Purgatorio,[5] where a mass was chanted not to a very funereal or even solemn music, at the same time that others were constantly proceeding at the different altars of this small octagon. After mass, a sermon on the subject of the day (which is assigned to the Anime del Purgatorio) was delivered with great energy by the Padre Cavallari a Franciscan and it appears a preacher of note. His text was 'Beati misericordes, illi etenim

---

[1] Bracket left unfinished.
[2] 42 piastres 9 carlini. The carlino is reckoned at 4d.; 12 carlini to the piastre.
[3] The office of the Intendente, or Senior Administrator of Messina.
[4] The brig to Naples.
[5] A large church in the main street, the Strada Ferdinanda.

misericordiam consequentur.'[1] I write with regret that I never heard or read a composition in which the word of God was so 'made of none effect'[2] by the traditions of men. He described the gloom in which this day was invested by the Church: but he said instead of preaching in a kindred tone, he would teach them of the great privilege set before them, in their being enabled to succour those souls of the just which though they had died in faith and merits had not yet sufficiently expiated their sins, so that although the love of God yearned towards them, it could not take effect inasmuch as His Justice on the other hand tore them away to inflict the awful pains which they were now enduring. To the faithful on earth it is given to procure their release, which they are to do by means of prayers—of alms— and of masses: through these last there comes to the afflicted souls great relief during the time while they are said—and, according, he said, to St Jerome, at the time when the Host is elevated, there is an absolute suspension of pain to those on whose behalf the sacrifice is made. He had no doubt therefore in affirming, that *the zeal[3] of those who released souls from Purgatory greatly surpassed that zeal of the Apostles which we so much commend,* and by which they preached the gospel to men. For those to whom they preached were men in their sins who might or might not profit by the grace given: but these are souls already holy, and only waiting for the consummation of their holiness: infinitely then more dear to God, and thus it is a far higher work to be concerned in their redemption. And they when liberated from torture, and received in that heaven towards which they look by Christ Himself, will retain especially and first of all their gratitude to those on earth who have been the means of their release, and will powerfully intercede for them, as he instanced by a number of examples of temporal deliverances. By these reciprocal good offices the present is bound to the past, and life to death. Both then to testify against the blasphemies of those who deny the purgatorial pains of the dead: and by their own most sacred interests, he conjured his hearers to avail themselves of the means in their hands. For his own part he would esteem the having a share in liberating a sould from purgatory his best assurance of his own eternal salvation, and he concluded with an invocation to these departed spirits to remember in their prayers the preacher Cavallari who had on that day pleaded their cause, as well as the city of Messina. Amen broke from many of the auditory as he concluded: and I saw a man kiss him enthusiastically as he walked out. Alas, here was everything to be lamented: a considerable power and labour, with a knowledge of the art of preaching, perverted to teach those perilous and ruinous fictions, the expiatory power of Purgatory, the propitiation by masses for the dead, and their reciprocal advantage for the living. And these masses are (I believe) purchaseable by tariff! I have not exaggerated the sermon, at least I hope not.[4]

We went to the Duomo which has a front of the sixteenth century, very

---

[1] 'Blessed are the merciful for they shall obtain mercy' Matt. v. 7.
[2] Mark vii. 13.
[3] 'NB!' in margin here.
[4] Also wrote on theology, Add MS 44728, f. 158.

minute: old Mosaics and pillars of Egyptian granite, of the Norman time: a high altar fineered (so to say) with work imitating the Florentine pietra dura. Its Canons have, by gift of Roger the Norman, a right of wearing a mitre. One wore it during the sermon today. The Archbishop[1] passed out of the Cathedral as we went in: to his carriage & four at the door: under a green silk & gold canopy or parasol, there being no sun nor rain: some of the young ecclesiastics knelt to kiss his hand as he passed: his appearance is pleasing. Sicily has 3 Archbishoprics.[2]

We went to see the view from S. Gregorio,[3] up and down the Straights. Northwards they are closed by the Calabrian hills: open to the South. The prospect is wide, animated yet peaceful, and diversified: half an hour over it was very agreeable.

The yard $= 3\frac{1}{2}$ palmi.
The salma $= (512)$ palmi. $= 16$ tumoli.
The miglio $= 5760$ [palmi].
The aune of France $= 4\frac{1}{2}$ palmi
The braccio $= 2\frac{5}{8}$ palmi.

The cicerone (another Giuseppe, Giuseppe Nobili) proposed to take us to the High Court of Justice, which alone tries capitally: but remembered that it was Friday, and that on this day no man is tried capitally on account of the condemnation of our Lord. Here are to be had lithographs of two annual processions on Aug. 15 and [blank],[4] the first exhibits two gigantic figures dragged about the streets, and called Cham & Rhea, it being asserted that Ham the son of Noah founded Messina & that Rhea was his wife: its old name Zancle is derived from Cioclam[5] according to this theory—which word means, a metropolis. The other represents the Assumption of the Virgin, by a gigantic machine,[6] of a pyramidal form, on which not only her figure, but that of God the Father, and clouds of angels, are represented by living children. Thucydides if I remember right, or some old author, refers the name to Zancle a sickle:[7] and the land projects precisely in this form round the port. It is wonderful to observe how while nations, and languages, and religions, and cities, have passed away in succession from the spot, either by some violent catastrophe or by the slow operations of Time, the long low slip of green earth which scarcely rises from the wave and seems more frail than any of them, has survived them all. Thus is the port:[8]

---

[1] Francisco di Paola Villadicani, 1780–1861, Archbishop 1823, Cardinal 1843.

[2] Palermo, Messina, and Monreale.

[3] On the summit of an eminence behind the cathedral.

[4] On June 3rd, commemorating the letter which the Virgin was supposed to have delivered to the citizens of Messina on that date. 15 August is the festival of her assumption.

[5] As in Giuseppe Buonfiglio e Costanzo, *Messina descritta* (1606), in Lawrence Mosheim's Latin version (see J. G. Graevius, *Thesaurus Antiquitatum et Historiarum Siciliae* (1723), ii. cols. 2–3), quoting 'Berosus in Antiquitatum Libris' (1498, forgery of Giovanni Nanni a Viterbo, attributed to 3rd century B.C. Persian historian).

[6] 'on which' is here deleted.

[7] Thucydides vi, 4.

[8] Here there is an inked circle, incomplete, the lowest arc extending out to the left.

The Borsa[1] reading room appears to be courteously opened to strangers: so at least we found it. Here chair bottoms are made from the aloe: silk twisted (?): citrons cut in half and salted to go abroad: lemons & oranges packed green for the same purpose: and lemon juice also exported in casks.

I carry a letter from a Palermo Guide to Lady Coventry's servant in Rome, which is addressed 'Al ornatissimo Signore, il Signore' &c.[2]

After[3] Etna, the temples are certainly the great charm and attraction of Sicily. I do not know that there is any one among them which taken alone exceeds in interest and beauty that of Neptune at Paestum: but they have the advantage of number and variety as well as of highly interesting positions. At Segesta, the temple is enthroned in a perfect mountain solitude: and it is like a beautiful tomb of its religion, so stately, so entire: while around but for the one solitary house of the keeper there is nothing, absolutely nothing—at least in the autumn it was thus—to disturb the apparent reign of Silence and of Death. At Selinus the huge fragments on the plain seem to make an eminence themselves, and they listen to the ever young and unwearied waves which almost wash their base, and mock their desolation by the image of perpetual life and motion they present, while the tone of their heavy fall upon the beach well accords with the solemnity of the scene. At Girgenti the ridge visible to the mariner from afar is still crowned by a long line of fabrics,[4] presenting to the eye a considerable mass and regularity of structure, and the town is near and visible, yet that town is so entirely the mere phantom of its former glory within its now shrunken limits, that instead of disturbing the effect it rather seems to add a new image and enhance it. And upon them all while the light of their southern sun descends to soften and set off their beauty to the eye, how does it also illustrate the great moral form which they exhibit, the form namely of human instability, and not only this but of that instability in connection with that one and only thing namely Religion which when it is genuine can throw off what is evil in his nature and perpetuate what is capable of good. They enshrine a most pure and salutary principle of art, that namely which connects grandeur of effect with simplicity of detail: and retaining their beauty & their dignity in their decay they represent the great man when fallen as types of that almost highest of human qualities, silent yet not sullen endurance. (N.13.)[5]

I had forgotten to mention the sulphur bloom on Etna. It gathers on the stones like a low flower or dwarf moss, very delicate and fine: being the rime produced like hoar frost by evaporation when the smoke issues from the bosom of the mountain into the cold air. So also at the mouth of little apertures you see a white rime, similarly produced when the vapour exhaled is not impregnated with sulphur.

Above I have said something of the pronunciation here. Besides the e pronounced as i, and the o as u, I have sometimes heard a as e: sometimes

---

[1] Exchange.　　　　　　　　　　[2] 'To the most distinguished gentleman, Mr.' &c.
[3] This para. in *Murray's *Sicily* (1864 ed.), xxvi.
[4] 'some of them' here deleted.
[5] I.e. late entry, made on 13 November.

nn as gn: g in the middle of a word is made away with, or if retained as a guttural is imperceptible: thus one hears lao for lago: reina for regina: in some of these variations may be traced a Spanish influence? All this is quite independent of the native Sicilian dialect properly so called: of which one can only catch a word here and there.

This does not appear to be a country where any large portion of the inhabitants are very poor: but as we proceed from cold to warm climates, sitting idle becomes in comparison with labour more advantageous: and clothing rather a burden than a comfort: and certainly I have seen no country where the art of inducing rags to hold together is carried to so high a state of perfection: higher than the same art in any other country, or, one might add, than any other art in this.

Saturday Nov. 3.

An early visit to the Tasso to ascertain whether we have any hope: last night a brilliant unclouded moon & perfect serenity, today a fine fresh morning with little or no wind: yet now as then "the weather is bad—we cannot sail." In the evening, they are to sail next morning. In the morning, next evening. Pazienza.

In size the chief cities of Sicily run thus, Palermo, Messina, Catania: but in general convenience of place & beauty of architecture the order is reversed and we must read Catania, Messina, Palermo—though all are nice towns. The artisans of the towns here have much less of that squallid appearance which one deplores in England, particularly in London: owing I suppose to these three causes: the absence of gin: the purity of the atmosphere: and their sitting to work as the trades here generally do, in the open air. On the Marina is a new bronze statue of the King's Father,[1] erected by the Commune or, as it is inscribed, the S.P.Q.M.:[2] but we are told at the King's command, which certainly destroys the charm. Thus on entering Palermo it was very pretty to see that nearly every house had before it a standard for the approaching illumination, inscribed with 'Viva il Re,' or 'Viva il Re e la Reina', or 'Viva il Re e la Real Famiglia.'[3] But this also was the Commune. Surely if the voluntary principle is applicable to anything, it is to an illumination.

We have been sadly tantalised all day: the captain actually sent desiring us to be on board at one or two in the afternoon. An English captain told us he in such weather would sail: we saw a vessel beating out: and yet our Neapolitan is not man enough to go.

We had however a delightful walk up the Palermo road, five miles from our present abode: the road scales the high hills behind the town and is apparently well constructed. The hillsides are covered for the most part with arbutus, which is luxuriantly in blossom (of drops like those of lilies, but sometimes tinged with pink) and also in fruit. The views of the town and

---

[1] Francis I, 1777–1830, regent 1812–16, 1820–5, king 1825; notorious reactionary.
[2] Corporation, or Senatus Populusque Messanensis.
[3] 'Long live the King and the royal family.'

straits are diversified as the ascent winds, and all are lovely. It may be observed of the Calabrian mountains, that while these of this side are much the reverse, their upper outline is singularly even, while below their details are bold and well broken.

We contemplated even a flit with the Courier to which we should probably have resorted at first but for the Sunday: & we visited him. But only think of the arrangements of this country. He was anxious to have us, but said we must cross the straights this evening to the opposite village of San Giovanni[1] in order to ascertain whether we could have places with him— with the prospect of returning here not until tomorrow morning in case they have been occupied already. His time to Naples is about 100 hours— the distance 360 miles: a little fat flowerpot of a man, as unlike as can be imagined to the *ideal* of a conveyer of letters in England.

Noble black grapes with hardly any skin are sold here to strangers at three gransi the rotolo: or about three farthings the pound.

We passed several customhouses on entering Messina: the functionaries of each came forward to see whether in our handful of baggage we were smuggling wine, or bread, or I do not know what, into the city, and *looked* a request for money: but they were not bold enough like honest thieves to exact it at once.

Nov. 3. 1838.[2] Messina.

One should be careful of joining a subject apparently ludicrous with one which is solemn: but at all events in the privacy of this book I may say, that while tossing through the night at Lentini in pain and fever and unable to keep my bed, I found the use of that petty annoyance in realising to me the great value of the common blessing of sleep: and our absolute dependence on God for blessings small as well as great; as well as our absolute dependence on those blessings for the free possession of either our bodily or our mental faculties. And were creation armed against us, instead of being as it is obedient and subsidiary to our will, how miserable might we be made at how small a cost of means, when these little specks can raise such a fever in our blood that the mind can neither think nor repose, and the body finds them more powerful to repel sleep than fatigue to encourage it.

Sunday Nov. 4.

Prayers: failed in finding a sermon: there appeared to be few in Messina from my inquiries. The outward observance of the Lord's Day here as in Sicily generally is I should say inferior to that in Italy, there being more noise in the streets. Today a band played at midday in the public Gardens. I was sorry to count among the listeners some seven or eight sacerdotal hats. We attempted a walk to the Telegraph and were driven back by the rain.

[1] 8 miles east of Messina, on the mainland.
[2] This entry from Lambeth MS 1424. Cp. 26 Oct. 38.

As this was Sunday, we did not actively molest our Captain on the subject of departure but he sounded another false alarm, in the morning ordering us on board at four, and afterwards countermanding on the score of the weather. These marches and countermarches are in a small way rather worrying.

Sunday Nov 4.[1]

Read through Thomas a Kempis's Fourth Book on the Eucharist. I should think this or parts of it might be usefully adapted for a Tract. Ours are in general but cold and come short of teaching the Church doctrine of *food*. Finished also St Bernard. Barruel on Saturday—these with some Georgics & 3 Books of Aeneid have been my reading in Sicily.

I have seldom read anything to me more affecting than Barruel's account of the reception of the French Clergy in England.[2] The morale of that reception is very beautiful.

Monday Nov 5.

Went out after breakfast to our brig &c: the captain promised departure tomorrow morning: I went to the Anime del Purgatorio to hear a Sermon. It is a mark of the inexactness with which time is observed here, as compared with the stricter husbandry in England, that almost every answer one gets upon a point of time here is not *alle* tre but *verso* le tre:[3] to 'how long hence', not 'un ora', but 'un ora o un' ora & mezza,' or 'un altro poco.'[4] I had at length found the preacher at work, when after two or three minutes I was summoned by a message from the captain to go on board: the day was fine and the wind so fair as to render all excuses desperate: we were on board among the first. Some two hours were lost in waiting, particularly for a Monsignore[5] who is our fellow passenger on his way back to Rome, and so much of the precious wind which is needed we are told to get well beyond Stromboli[6] where they no longer dread being driven on the coast of Calabria. We got away however at half-past twelve: and rounded the Faro[7] about three, the wind being southerly and very favourable. (And here is the place to make a good report of our Inn the Gran Brettagna; which is well situated, moderate in prices, and comfortable. In Sicily however the *bellhangers* trade is as yet either unknown or it has not at all events found its way into the hotels.)[8]

Scylla[9] is still conspicuous as when Virgil wrote: a boldly projected rock,

[1] These two paragraphs from Lambeth MS 1424.
[2] Cp. 6 Oct. 38, n. 6, French edition, ii. 193 ff., on the change from the suspicion and hatred reigning in French society to the geniality and friendliness of England.
[3] Mgr. Rossi, a judge.
[4] 'Not *at* three o'clock but *about* three o'clock.'
[5] Not 'an hour', but 'an hour or an hour and a half' or 'a little more'.
[6] Island in the Lipari group, 45 miles NNW. of Messina.
[7] Long low point at the northern entrance of the Straits, 7 miles NE. of Messina, bearing a lighthouse tower (*faro*) at its tip.
[8] Brackets in pencil.
[9] On the 'toenail' of Italy, 10 miles ENE. of Messina.

precipitous towards the sea, though low as compared with the fine coast which rises behind it, and up which the Naples road winds at some distance farther from Messina. The rock is crowned with buildings I believe fortifications: and a *paese*[1] takes its name from this monster of fable. In its front are low broken rocks nearly on the level of the water, and these I suppose are the *canes*[2] whence came that barking of the waters which was of old so formidable: while the *antrum*[3] may be in the high beetling coast above.

> semel informen vasto vidisse sub antro
> Scyllam & coeruleis canibus resonantia saxa.[4]

Unless possibly *canes* may be the waves themselves, which are now called *cavalloni*: great horses. With this compare the description in Shakespeare's Henry [blank]:[5]
With respect to Charybdis, it does not seem to be so strictly identified: some declare it to be the point of the Faro which is on a horn of land nearly opposite Scylla: some to be the next Sicilian cape to the westward: none seemed to speak of it as a whirlpool.—but there is a whirlpool near the Faro called the Garofalo,[6] to which one might perhaps without impropriety apply the name. The currents in these straights are certainly very strong and considering the timidity of ancient navigation, and its servile adhesion to the shores one cannot be surprised at the exaggerations in which the features of this passage have been enveloped. Our captain crept round the inside of the horn near the Sicilian coast. The meeting of the principal and the back streams causes a considerable ripple even when there is little or no wind, and we are told mysteriously that the changes of the currents are not describable to the uninitiated and can only be comprehended by those who have long experience of the channel.

The view of Messina from the Faro is less striking than I had expected: but the whole straits are very beautiful indeed.

We congratulated ourselves on having left them, as the current acts only for ten miles outside with a continually diminishing force and we soon saw Stromboli (his fire however was wrapt in clouds) and the Lipari islands beyond which we hoped for (at worst) the open sea a good tossing, and the port of Naples. Meantime we began to realise the second of these three anticipations: and some of our mercurial passengers were reduced to the successive levels of squeamishness & vomiting.

The wind changed to the Libeccio,[7] and sank before sunset: our progress was very slow as the Captain did not make all the way of which it would have allowed, but held his course very near the wind and along the Sicilian

---

[1] 'village'.
[2] 'dogs'.
[3] 'cavern'.
[4] *Aen.* iii. 431. 'to catch sight once of monstrous Scylla in her cave and the rocks echoing with their blue dogs.'
[5] *King Henry VI*, part III, ii. v. 5–12. 'And monboni'—unidentified—added in pencil.
[6] Between the Punta Sottile and the Punta Palazzo on the Sicilian coast, opposite the village of Faro.
[7] A south-wester.

coast, that of Calabria being the great object of his apprehension: while the Neapolitan Frigate [blank], which sailed an hour or more after us, now passed between us and the Sicilian coast, and immediately crossing our line[1] bore away to the N.W. much nearer the Calabrian coast. I went down and lay in our little cabin on my bed alongside of K's. There being rain every one soon came below and almost every one was sick before dark: K, and I too, wonderful to say, held out. But fear now came among the passengers as the vessel pitched and rolled: the women shrieked a good deal and the men jabbered like geese. The little voice of the little Monsignore was heard out of his berth in the accents of piety and good sense. 'Io mi son messo qui perche incominciava soffrire dello stomaco: e adesso sto un poco meglio: (uomo mio, capitano, vi prego mandate un bassino, o una cosa, se uno vomita non c'è niente;) vi prego, Signori miei, state cheti e tranquilli: raccomenandate vi a Dio, siamo nella mano del Signore: aveste falto premura di partire voi stessi, perche dunque gridate?'[2] We pitched on till perhaps about nine o'clock: the passengers nearly all sick, and the excessive and continual groanings and other manifestations which accompany all the operations of Italian seasickness—the occasional noises when a longer and heavier roll overset any of the articles on the deck or in the cabin—the pattering of the seamen's naked feet on the deck, and their idle clamour too—and the exhortations of the passengers to one another not to be afraid, made a strange mixture. K. was asleep, and I lay listening and dosing, in a state of general incredulity as to any danger which has no other attestation than the alarms of a Neapolitan company.

The Captain however was alarmed at the idea of the Calabrian coast, and put about, of which I got the first suspicion by finding that whereas formerly my heels had tossed higher than my head (lying across the ship) now my head tossed higher than my heels. In the meantime while the men continued their discordant and most unprofitable chattering, and the little Abate from time to time demanded Heh, che cos'è, non c'è paura, siam al Faro, siam in Messina, raccommandatevi alla Madonna,[3] the women had become quiet and continued so throughout the subsequent alarm: they shrieked at the tossing, but were silent when they heard of danger: showing the truth of the observation that it is characteristic of the female sex, to judge more by signs than by proofs.

Tuesday Nov. 6.

We had rounded the Faro again and were it appears near the Garofalo, which as I have said appears to me to have the fairest claims to represent the ancient Charybdis, when Monsignore's servant came downstairs with a

[1] 'course' pencilled above 'line'.
[2] 'I put myself here because my stomach was beginning to trouble me: now I am a little better. (Captain! my good man, please send me a basin, or something, if one vomits that's nothing;) pray, gentlemen, be quiet and calm; commend yourselves to God; we are in the hand of the Lord; you yourselves urged our setting out; so why are you screaming?'
[3] 'Now, now, what's this? no need to fear, we are at the Faro, we are in Messina, commend yourselves to Our Lady.'

message purporting to be from the Captain, to say the Litany of the Saints, intimating that we were in great peril. Monsignore immediately proceeded to recommend his own soul & those of the rest, by reciting the Pater, the Ave, the Rosario, and the Atti di Fede, di Speranza, and di Charità respectively.[1] I[2] was sincerely grieved that we could not join in the general and ostensible acknowledgement of the hand of God as the ruler of the deep: but really the matter of this devotion was for us in great part so objectionable that it appeared right rather to gather one's own thoughts for one's self. The Abate I am sure did not mean it irreverently, but he went at an immense rate: few joined in the Lord's Prayer, most came in at the Ave, all were kneeling towards his berth at the Rosario: but as he finished each in succession and gave out the title of the next, it was evident by the lingering voices how he had outstripped them. It is very singular to see this ready practical belief—for I have no doubt they all considered that they were standing on the brink of eternity—combined with very palpable superstition: and in retrospect, it is very touching, though at the time the careless volubility of the general tone intercepted and prevented that effect. I went up on deck with K. for a moment:[3] we had certainly had some violent gusts of wind: we were now close on shore, the sails furled, riding with the current, abreast of the first houses & near the lights of Messina, to all appearance perfectly secure. When we had again entered the port, it was one o'clock: parties began again to compare their accounts, no one was willing to confess having carried the message which was at length[4] agreed to have come by the Abate's domestic, the Captain disowned it, though he allowed he had said a prayer might be as well: the crestfallen passengers began to recover and some to brag, one in particular complained that he had had to support the spirits of the whole company in the midst of general lamentations—'bisogna d'un poco di coraggio nel mare', 'Io sempre fo l'allegro'[5]—(this was a *tenente*[6] of the Customs—) and the Abate rebuked the Captain for putting to sea at the instance of inexperienced youths (K. and G. videlicet)—recommended prudence for the future—was greatly taken aback on learning that the supposed Captain's message was a fabrication, or at all events a mountain from a mouse—explained that he had believed the vessel was really in the Garofalo and going down, and that in consequence he was (K.) giving absolution—and concluded as he tumbled back into bed, 'questa è una cattiva cosa, quando si fa viaggio nel mare con uomini, che sono pusillanimi.'[7] We have[8] thus witnessed a remarkable scene for the alarm was perfectly bonâ fide: and it is perhaps in some degree justified by the fact that the Frigate, which is under orders to proceed

---

[1] Acts of Faith, Hope and Charity.
[2] 'omit' pencilled in margin. Diarist inserted this note at passages unsuitable for publication in a guidebook. Cp. Add MS 44259, f. 177.
[3] See i. xxxix above and D. Fraser, *M. J. Kinnaird* (1890), 22–23.
[4] 'fathered' (?) deleted.
[5] 'You need a spot of courage at sea', 'I was always all right'.
[6] 'lieutenant'.
[7] 'This is a poor show, going to sea with men who are cowards.'
[8] 'Finis' (*sc.* 'end' of omission) faintly pencilled in the margin.

with expedition to Naples, has returned like ourselves to Messina, although some hours later having re-appeared about breakfast time this morning. We ought[1] to have our own thankfulness to God who has kept us, upon that element which seems to be his own more peculiar domain of immediate and resistless action, whether it be in danger, or from it—a commander & crew of this nation cannot, as would those of our own, be deemed a self-sufficient criterion.

We resumed our quarters at the Gran Brettagna, and upon consideration had made up our poor minds to the conclusion that after this fright, and the Abate's recommendation of prudence for the future, and the really altered state of the weather to one of squalls with heavy showers and general uncertainty, Naples by sea recedes into infinite distance, and that we must willingly resume the consideration, which we had rejected at once on arriving here last week on account of its involving a Sunday's travelling on the road, of going with the Post Office Courier. We set the Servitore di Piazza[2] G. Nobili to work, saw the Courier, and the Captain: he obstreperous as the sea from which he had fled: demanded the whole of our fare: we offered half: agreed that the English consul[3] should arbitrate: we repaired to him there and then: he heard us both, & decided at once for us: having thus recovered our passport we sent Nobili to San Giovanni, over the water! to engage our places under the Courier's direction for tomorrow evening. We have thus the prospect of much expenditure of time, and some fatigue, in a land journey of 360 miles, at 3½ miles per hour, for four days and five nights without intermission: but how thankful ought we to be when we reflect that these inconveniences, now so rare and befalling us for the first time, were a few years back the common and necessary lot of those who sought to see Etna and Girgenti. I doubt not we shall find we have no cause to regret this detention and any consequent dislocation of our plans. It[4] is most useful, even if there be no other use, to be reminded to redeem our time while it is ours, by finding that it is not ours always to redeem.

On visiting this afternoon the English Captain Maxwell of the Countess of Liverpool an old Holyhead Packetboat, we find him ridiculing the return of the brig and of the frigate but not surprised at either. There was nothing he says to prevent their persevering. He made us take wine in his little cabin: and showed us some verses by a son & some by a daughter of his: those of the latter written at 15 were very pretty. The lad had been made an infidel among some[5] Americans: & afterwards came back to the faith through a Sermon which the Father took him to hear in Dublin. The weather today is rainy and squally, and we have even had snow: but Maxwell portends fair winds & a genial sky forthwith.

I have here to record a few very homespun Sicilian hints. The traveller should have *shoes* with soles as thick as can well be worn: but if there are

[1] 'om[it]' pencilled in margin.
[2] 'Berth agent', an obsolescent meaning of 'piazza' being 'midships space available for passengers'.
[3] William Wilton Barker, d. 1856, pro-consul at Messina 1816, consul there 1826.
[4] 'om[it]' pencilled in margin.
[5] Instead of 'the'.

nails in them they should not project: as I have found the inconvenience of this in mine the fabric of D[avid] Murray of Fettercairn, though they were exceedingly admired by the Guides of Etna, as they slip very much on the flags and pavements: while great thickness is necessary to resist the sharp stones and edges of the lava.[1]

An *umbrella* is greatly required against sun & rain: but it should have a leather case or it will be rubbed to pieces.

Trowsers if light should also be such as will wear for some time without being washed.

A *white hat* and an *oilskin or cloth cap* are, together, I should think the best coverings for the head. If not a white *hat*, then a white or light coloured cap.

A *Scotch plaid* is very advisable: it is a convenient shawl for walking Etna, a good coverlet when you have not regular bed-clothes, serves to mend the seat of the saddles which is sometimes very bad, & altogether I should say is preferable here to a greatcoat. A *Macintosh with a hood* would be lighter than the Sicilian leather cloaks, and I should think quite as effectual against wet.

Our *cotton bags* have not succeeded in keeping out the vermin: but they serve as a pair of sheets in case of need: and they likewise *delay* the assault of the vermin. Linen ones would be cooler.[2]

The *leather gaiters* or leggings of the country are useful against wet.

Nothing produces so much comfort in proportion to the space it occupies, as a little *tea* for the evenings. It may be boiled with or in the water: and an egg, beaten up white & yolk together, with a little warm water, is a very respectable substitute for milk. The *bread* is everywhere of good grain, tho' from Palermo to Syracuse imperfectly baked.

The *wine* is much more generous so far as we have seen it than that of Italy Germany or France.

The *milk* is generally that of goats.

Meat is commonly to be had. *Potatoes* in the principal places: so also *sugar*. *Coffee* general, & pretty good. *Maccaroni* not very general. *Sheep's cheese* of the country is peculiar but not bad. *Fish* is to be had in many places & good.

Wednesday Nov. 7

Our Captain—no, I rejoice to say, no longer ours—has still a hankering for the other half of the fare, and seems inclined as the wind continues unfavourable to spend his time in throwing good money after bad. These unenergetic people often prove in a matter of immediate and palpable lucre tenacious enough. He threatens the innkeeper and is altogether magniloquent. He likewise holds that a new development has been given to National character & that the Neapolitans are now quite as good sailors as the English.

Our Banker[3] tells us that the King has 400,000 ducats for the sulphur

---

[1] 'om[it]' pencilled in margin.   [2] 'om[it]' pencilled in margin.
[3] Probably Mr. Cailler.

monopoly which has been given to a French company partly for the sake of employing some Carlists and taking them off his pension list[1]—the Duchesse de Berri and others of that party are likewise said to be share-holders to a great extent. The company are likely to *make* £100,000 a year, & the privileges are for 10 years.[2] The King makes a great deal of money: his army should be of 60,000 men: but he does not fill up the conscriptions in some years, and pockets the money. The government is mild in its character. After the English were here, the Sicilians got a representative constitution, which also had an aristocratic branch: the franchise was large, and the people were induced or suborned to petition for its removal.[3] Their prayer was granted.

I walked up to the Telegraph, finding the way with some difficulty: a peasant of Melazzo[4] led me by a circuit, but the wildness of the hills which reminded me of Scotland well repaid me. And the view, or rather the two views, for the high ridge towards the Faro divides them, were very fine. That to the East presented the town, the straights, and several lines of the Calabrian hills: on which snow has now fallen. A ladder-road leads up to the summit along which the lines of mules and donkeys, laden with oranges, lemons, apples, were slowly winding towards their market at Messina. The hills want wood: and their luxuriant clothing of arbutus is rapidly giving place to the culture of the vine stimulated by the commerce of the city. By the port lay the coward frigate, as well as the smaller vessels to which she has afforded so plausible an apology.

Along the coast I enjoyed the fine prospect of seven or eight lines of well broken hill overlying one another: the low promontory of Milazzo lay flat beneath my station, scarcely dividing the great gulf from Rasocolmo to Calavà.[5] From this latter point one more wide range reaches to Cefalù,[6] so that I have now seen very nearly the whole of the northern coast of Sicily. The wind blew strong from the West. The sea was green, flecked with white, and spotted in larger masses with brown from the rainy looking clouds. To the North West were the Lipari islands, of which, small & great, I could count nine. Stromboli the most northerly, reared his bold form sheer from sea to sky, a nearly regular truncated cone with broad top, and the tuft of his volcanic smoke surmounting it.

I returned by the direct road. To reach this point from Messina, do not take the Strada Nuova[7] (of Palermo) at all, but go at once into the stream

---

[1] 'partly in order' here deleted.

[2] Ferdinand II had on 10 July 1838 conferred a monopoly of the Sicilian sulphur trade on a Marseilles firm, Taix and Aicard, to run from 1 August. The effect was to double the price of sulphur. The monopoly attracted criticism in England, France and Germany; its legality was questioned, and British owners of sulphur mines claimed most-favoured-nation treatment under the Anglo-Neapolitan treaty of 26 Sep. 1816, clause 4 (*BFSP* v. 586 ff.). British warships were sent to reinforce diplomatic pressure; and on 11 July 1840 the monopoly was revoked. Cp. 19 Nov. 38.

[3] In 1815. See 15 Oct. 38.

[4] Town 25 miles WNW. of Messina.

[5] Milazzo stands on a promontory dividing the gulfs of Milazzo and Patti; each about 20 miles wide; the western promontory of the latter is Cape Calavà; the eastern promontory of the former is Cape Rasocolmo.

[6] 53 miles farther west.   [7] 'New Road'.

road, i.e. that which the people frequent when the torrents do not happen to want it: take the right hand at three successive forks, and you reach the bottom of the *scala*.[1]

It is amusing to watch the pronunciation of our various friends here. Giuseppe Lazzara took breath at every fourth syllable, besides a crotchet rest after the word perchè whereever it occurred: and the courier, to whom we are now consigned, squeezes his words like a lemon and every half-minute interrupts his own narratives with a longdrawn lugubrious "Oh".

Another visit from the Captain at 3—& the song of the dying swan!

On the road to the Telegraph one sees stones appearing to contain ore, as in other places: this apropos to Mr Cailler's information, who says the island abounds in metals. We are also told that there are manufactories of cotton here—generally under the management of persons from Switzerland. We started from our Inn soon after five: waited for 2 hours on the beach, $2\frac{1}{2}$ at Villa San Giovanni opposite—$1\frac{1}{2}$ was spent in crossing the Canale: the passage is of 8 miles. Generally they do not get over at this season without a ducking: but this evening was beautiful, and as the strong current glanced from the prow, the stars in the heaven below rivalled those in the heaven above. We had two intelligent and agreeable fellow-travellers: one, who only came sixty miles, had the appearance of no more than a small farmer & made his night's journey without luggage: yet he seemed well acquainted with the history of his own country & was very anxious that the English should reunite with the Pope, which he thought they would do if Queen Victoria wd. do it for herself, as the English had always changed their religion with their sovereign.

We traversed the fine coast to Scylla and Bagnara[2] by moonlight over a broken and unfinished road. From this tract we enjoyed our parting gaze at Etna whose red lava glowed seventy miles off, & which has, even had we seen nothing else, amply repaid the labour of our journey to Sicily. At Bagnara the regular post road commences: and it is generally both well engineered and well made—excepting where it comes on a bit of Calabrian pavement which is made of stones equal in size to those of the old Roman roads but not like them compacted into a regular structure with an even surface: here the jolting was incomparable. It appears that the sum total of our distance is under 320 miles, and I have been doubting absolutely of the possibility of spending on it the allotted 100 or (in winter) 110 hours: but with the comfort that after all it is a curiosity in its way to have travelled by the slowest mail in Christendom. This satisfaction soon promised to be realised: as the $52\frac{1}{2}$ miles from San Giovanni to Monte Leone[3] occupied us from $11\frac{3}{4}$ P.M. of Wednesday, to 2 P.M. of Thursday.

Thursday Nov. 8.

After crossing the high hills above the coast to Palma,[4] we passed first

---

[1] 'staircase', used in Italian for any stepped slope.
[2] Town 7 miles ENE. of Scilla. [3] Town $43\frac{1}{2}$ miles NNE. of Bagnara.
[4] Coast town $7\frac{1}{4}$ miles north of Bagnara.

through extensive[1] tracts of wood, with the largest and most beautiful olive trees I ever saw,[2] then through a well-cultivated and undulating country, with the Appennines on our right and the sea sometimes visible on our left, to Monte Leone. We passed the little Paese of Mileto[3] where we were shown the remains of the tomb of Count Roger on a green by the road. We crossed the River Rosarno[4] today.

Calabria is divided into three provinces:

1. Calabria Citra (from Naples)
2. Calabria Ultra 1.
   2.[5]

We were today in the first[6] of which Reggio[7] is the capital, until we reached the Rosarno which is its boundary.

At Montereale[8] we had a dinner of maccaroni, pork, & fruit, such as the Director of the Post's wife could prepare for us in the family bedroom—and our present journey only permits one such meal as this a day—biscuit, or fruit, or a cup of coffee here & there, abundantly make up the rest. A lack of Inns having clean beds even greater than that which is experienced in Sicily appears to be the greatest obstacle to undertaking the tour of Calabria in a more systematic manner. Fleas abound. Monsignore very sensitive. Said he felt two on him & 'mi sentiva avvilito.'[9] Here as in Sicily the bread wine and fruit are good. The road passes over considerable tracts of very high ground, and warmer clothing is desirable here than would probably be found sufficient for the Sicilian giro.

Friday. Nov. 9.

On Wednesday night in leaving the coast we went near the snow and last night was for the most part spent at a considerable elevation: we really felt it cold. We passed into the other province of Calabria Ultra, and got beyond its capital Catansara,[10] which the road does not touch: but from Tiriolo,[11] the nearest station, we had a view of the Adriatic as it is termed—the gulf of[12] Squillace, opposite to that of S. Eufemia.

Seventy three miles of hilly country but over a well engineered road occupied us from 3½ P.M. yesterday to 2 P.M. today when we reached Cosenza.[13] Our road has lain through a very noble tract of country, broken

[1] Margin entry: 'Bosco di Solano', 'wood of Solano', a stream falling into the sea a little SW. of Bagnara; this wood lies south of Bagnara.
[2] The Piana del Oliveto, 'plain of the olive'.
[3] 26¼ miles north of Palme.
[4] The town of Rosarno, 14½ miles NNE. of Palme, is on the R. Mesima, the provincial boundary. There is no river Rosarno.
[5] Respectively northern, southern and central Calabria.
[6] Calabria Ulteriore Prima.
[7] Port on the straits of Messina, 14½ miles south of Villa S. Giovanni.
[8] A slip of the pen for Monte Leone.
[9] 'I felt myself demeaned'.
[10] Catanzaro, 16¼ miles NE. of Monte Leone.
[11] Town 5 miles NW. of Catanazaro.
[12] 'Tarentum, I suppose, forming the hollow of the foot of Italy' here lightly deleted.
[13] Town 26 miles NNW. of Tiriolo.

everywhere into mountains or hills on a mountain scale, and covered either with oak and chestnut woods, or with the results of agricultural labour. Cosenza has 18000 persons and is the capital of Calabria Citra. Its shops show great marks of abundance & indeed there is little appearance of want in this country. The law of primogeniture is abolished here as well as in Sicily. The people wear very thick woollen clothing of the darkest colours, with the conical felt hat: all adapted to the high ground and the severe winter weather which belongs to it. One is surprised however to see dark colours so common in southern countries: as contrasted with the white frocks of our northern latitudes—or the lightish blues which belong to England as well as to Germany & France.

As an Englishman I ought to have mentioned that we have passed & had a fine view of the gulph of S. Eufemia in which is situated Maida the scene of a victory gained by the British troops under Sir John Stewart over the French.[1]

Saturday. Nov 10.

Twentyfour hours & three quarters from 4 P.M. yesterday to $4\frac{3}{4}$ P.M. today have brought us to a distance of eighty miles. It is not doing justice to the country to say that these miles are evidently longer than the English: & I suppose they are those indicated in the Sicilian map, of 60 to a degree. We have travelled through a magnificent country & over a very fine road, made by the French when they held Italy. We have now crossed the main Appennine twice: once on Thursday night, to reach Cosenza where the streams pass into the gulph of Tarentum: and once this morning between Castrovillari[2] & La Rotonda.[3] The mountains are high & have snow at present on their tops. The descent upon La Rotonda is very beautiful. It is well so called, being built on a hill which appears to form a very regular cone. There are many of these in the pass, like the family of Etna: but I understand that they are calcareous, not volcanic. We passed successively through the Campo Ateniese,[4] the Valle della Rotonda,[5] crossing the Fiume Meranio;[6] the Valle di Lauria,[7] and the Valle della Rosa:[8] after which we descended on Lago Negro,[9] so named after a wretched little pond rather

[1] On 4 July 1806, when Sir John *Stuart, 1759–1815, defeated J. L. E. Reynier, 1771–1814; using line successfully against column. Till the present century, the only battle of importance fought by British troops on Italian ground.

[2] Town 36 miles north of Cosenza.

[3] Just over the border of Calabria Citeriore, in the province of Basilicata, 14 miles NW. of Castrovillari.

[4] Campotenese, a narrow strip of tableland south of La Rotonda. Also the name of a post station.

[5] South of La Rotonda.

[6] The post road crosses the Coscile river near Morano; here again perhaps the river was given the name of the town, which is 5 miles NW. of Castrovillari.

[7] Lauria lies 16 miles NW. of Morano.

[8] Perhaps another name of the Valle della Spina (Valley of the Thorn), which is north of Lauria.

[9] Town $7\frac{1}{2}$ miles NW. of Lauria, situated in a wild and gloomy position at the extremity of a narrow glen.

than lake near[1] the top of the hill. Our pass this morning was called the Dirupata di Morano,[2] from a paese of that name under the hill.

We found the Inn at Lago Negro indifferent and of a low class, plentifully supplied with nothing except fleas. Sicilian refinement has now reached to iron bedsteads: here they are of wood. Travellers would really do well on this journey to carry a little meat: as they find on the road only what is very hard, probably if poultry killed after their arrival.

We have been today in the province of Basilicata, which we quit further on at La Sala.[3] The peasantry wear the high conical hat as in Calabria Citra: and have every appearance of being a fine hardy highland population. They gather around strangers very much as in Sicily, but their curiosity is less loquacious. We see few signs of poverty. The men wear instead of shoes, in many cases, an ill made slipper of skin with the hair outwards, clumsily attached by the contortions of a string to the leg: it must take a Calabrian peasant longer to fasten his sandals than a London fine gentleman his tight boots but probably he does not put them off so frequently. The women are oftener barefooted than the men, and their features from labour and exposure have a more rugged appearance, as marble long exposed presents a more tarnished surface than granite. They appear to work harder than the male sex: we meet them everywhere carrying very heavy loads of firewood from the hills on the head: whereas the men on the road are generally with their mules or donkeys, and in most cases riding on the top of the regular burden of the beast as supernumeraries. This recals the passage in Sophocles Oed Tyr v. 347:

ὦ πάντ' ἐκείνω τοῖς ἐν 'Αιγύπτῳ νόμοις
φύσιν κατεικασθέντε καὶ βίου τροφάς.
ἐκεῖ γὰρ οἱ μὲν ἄρσενες κατὰ στεγὰς
θακοῦσιν ἱστουργοῦντες, αἱ δε συννομοι
τἄξω βίου τροφεῖα πορσύνουσ' ἀεί.[4]

This province of Basilicata which we entered before reaching La Rotonda, separates Calabria from Apulia to the N. & from the Principato di Salerno to the N.W., lying along the hollow of the foot of Italy. We again saw the Eastern sea, (the gulph of Tarentum) in crossing the Dirupata pass this morning.—This province abounds in extensive & beautiful woods; of chestnut, oak, (quercia and cerro,)[5] beech, and I think wild birch also.

We resumed our places at seven in a fresh carriage with a coupè holding two, & four places behind. Don Marco had promised great things of it but we found the jolting quite surpassed all former experience & to be such as

---

[1] 'near' instead of 'at'.

[2] Defile leading north of Morano up to the tableland of Campotenese.

[3] La Sala, 20¼ miles NNW. of Lago Negro, is in fact 18 miles beyond the frontier between Basilicata and Calabria Citeriore. The post road crossed the frontier in the range of Monte Cucuzzo, 3 miles NW. of Lago Negro.

[4] 'That pair have become in nature and ways of life like the Egyptians. For there the men sit at home weaving, while their wives ever abroad provide the food.' *Oedipus at Colonus*, 337. Cp. 3 Sept. 36.

[5] Common and turkey oak.

must be undergone in order to be believed. We continued to traverse an interesting mountain country into the Principato di Salerno. The road is remarkable for its zigzag cuts above the Ponte di Campestrino,[1] and the bridge itself is a considerable work. A lofty and broken wall of rock accompanied our track for a great distance on the left and terminated at *Postiglione* a name invented by Don Marco, who always invented a name when he did not know the right one,[2] which overlooks Eboli and a part of the plain of Salerno, rounding itself off towards the west with a front of iron, rugged, wild, and inaccessible, like such a for[ti]fication as those giants might have built who strove to scale heaven in their rebellion. But here even the wildest scenery never strikes the eye, in broad day, so as to suggest other than gentle images, so deeply is it bathed and so wonderfully are its outlines softened, by the transparency and abundance of the light.

Stopping this morning in a rude house at La Sala for a bad cup of coffee (by the bye they give one everywhere the *finest* sugar with it) we clustered round the fire where a man knelt tending the pot, an old hostler walked up and down with vehement gesticulations and loud groans and cries complaining that he had been robbed of six ducats out of a small cupboard which held his goods —he seemed a lodger—a young half naked savage crouched opposite looking in every other direction, & liable to reasonable suspicion of being the thief—we half wakened travellers were mixed with these national figures, and the dawn was blended with the firelight—then came a little naked boy of perhaps seven years old, with his clothes in his hand, tumbled down at his mother's feet, (who sat receiving the old hostler's complaints,) & mounted on her knee to be drest warming his foot all the time over the glowing embers. This might have made a tolerable picture for Teniers or for Wilkie?

Sunday Nov. 11.

Much do I regret to record this day as passed in travelling: but it was unavoidably so consumed. Our companion, who proves to be Monsignore Rossi, a criminal judge at Rome, was very anxious to stop and hear mass, which as he said discharged their obbligo: ours I told him extended to the whole day. We reached Salerno, seventy three miles from Lago Negro, at four P.M.: in twenty one hours. We came down from *Postiglione*, al. Duchessa[3] to Eboli which has an old convent for its Inn with an old brigand for the landlord: a brigand however against the French, not against the peace, and now pensioned by the Crown. The soil is beautifully soft and rich. We passed on the left the royal preserves of Persano. Calabria is a great sporting country as we were told: but they evidently have no idea of what would in England be termed abundance of game. Twenty hares in a day I was told was out of the question—six or eight a great day, often

---

[1] Just before coming to Pertosa, 13 miles NW. of La Sala, the road crosses a fine seven-arched bridge, spanning a deep ravine.

[2] But see next note.

[3] La Duquesa, 22½ miles NNW. of La Sala, was the post station 2 miles NE. of Postiglione, which actually existed on a side road.

none. There are wild boars, foxes & wolves: &, they say, bears in the Abruzzi.[1] At Eboli[2] the road detaches itself gradually from the high ground & takes the well watered plain. We dined well at the Cafè di Parigi in Salerno.[3] *Seven* more hours, (4¾–11¾ P.M.) were required to bring me to Naples.[4] K. and Monsignore remained at La Torre dell'Annunziata[5] to see Pompeii. Anxiety for my letters induced me to go on without them.

This Sunday of travelling has given me some more idea of the practice respecting its observance. In the first place one does not find here that *domestic* character which belongs to the day in England so peculiarly, nor see that so constant and so beautiful spectacle of parents & their children in company, at home (all the doors remember are open) or abroad. In the second there is much more of actual work. Carts of all kinds were on the road in considerable number coming from as well as going to the capital: peasants on their donkeys, intending probably, according to Monsignore, to visit their lands: parties of pleasure, as with us: near Eboli by the roadside there were trenchers at work & also eight or ten yoke of oxen in a field ploughing, women & children picking olives, &c. Monsignore said they could not do it without a dispensation, & that it might have been given, as respected the ploughing & sowing, because heavy rain generally falls after St Martin's day (the 12th)[6] and the seed should be in before. It was possible that the owner of that field might have a great deal to sow & might be much pressed. Indeed the number of oxen at work looked like this: but all these carts of various kinds could hardly be in the same predicament, and I thought he despaired of accounting for them. Nor would those of our country admit the reasons for the ploughing to be sufficient. Here they are certainly more lax in the country: in Sicily e.g. Michael told me that during vintage, i.e. for three weeks, they work through the Sundays as on other days.

Monsignore, who is intelligent, acute, and agreeable, as well as apparently very sound in many principles, promises to aid me in Rome: told me their judges may be lay but must wear the ecclesiastical habit: they baptize always within three days: if it is wished, upon a payment, at home: infants must have a padrino:[7] may have a madrina[8] also: these offices continue after Cresima (confirmation), but without spiritual force & perhaps other persons then take them: cresima is at 14 for boys, 12 for girls, & thereabouts: may be administered by priests under Episcopal licence.

I ought to say a few words of the character of the scenery we have witnessed. I take our journey to have been of near 400 English miles: in Neapolitan miles, I find it is, according to a corrected calculation, about 320. Much the greater part is through the mountain scenery, in which the pic-

[1] The rugged Apennine region north of Campania and east of Latium.
[2] Town 30 miles NW. of La Sala.
[3] Port 15 miles WNW. of Eboli; battlefield of 1944.
[4] 30 miles WNW. of Salerno.
[5] Port 17 miles WNW. of Salerno.
[6] 11th.
[7] 'Godfather'.
[8] 'Godmother'.

turesque and the romantic styles respectively are more happily blended than in any other country I have seen. This journey certainly presents Italy to the eye in a new point of view: the abundance of wood, the superiority of its kinds to the olives which constitute the ordinary staple, the quantity of cultivation which everywhere penetrates the forest and scales the hill, and another peculiar feature, the thickly strewn hamlets and villages nestling in some recess or crowning some hillock but almost always in beautiful and interesting positions, and with these the very sharp and bold forms into which the hills are cast, delight the eye with a continual succession of prospects at once grand and lovely. There are too a good many castles. That at Monreale [sc. Monteleone] of the Pignatelli family,[1] is the largest we have seen & is well placed: but the country is less interesting in that quarter until the road gets fairly among the Appennines which in Calabria are as superior as can possibly be conceived to their brethren in the Papal States and in Tuscany. Nothing can be more picturesque than the site of the old castle of Lauria, on a rock sharp apparently (to the southern approach) as a sugar loaf: & the little village still appears to cluster beneath it for a protection which its ruined walls cannot even afford to its interior against the winds & storms of heaven.

The towns rarely rise to any considerable size. Indeed Bari[2] the next to Naples in the whole of *this* kingdom,[3] is only rated at 30,000 inhabitants: and the third[4] has but 18,000. Agriculture disperses the population: manufactures & commerce are on the most contracted scale. In the mountains of Basilicata[5] however we found them taking loads of staves made from the cerro (green oak) to the sea shore: they go I learned to Trieste[6] and Marseilles & are exported to make casks.

The Courier is always accompanied by at least *one* gendarme. There are 8000 or 9000 of this force: mounted well, well equipped, well paid: receiving 20 ducats a month including keep of horse & clothing, & after they have paid 80 ducats for their horse, 24 ducats a month. They are looked up to by the people & are an effective police. They have the right to ask who you are & the usual police questions: to keep order on the road, and to impress private horses if necessary for the public service. (K.)

After Monsignore had removed his portly form at La Torre dell'Annunziata from his seat by my side the springs became perfectly ungovernable & I took refuge in the Coupè with the grave Don Marco who declared that our journey was one of almost unprecedented rapidity. From Messina 102 hours. From Villa San Giovanni 96 hours. I should be most thankful for all the interest and advantage which have attended it: & have only to wish they would choose their days a little better. Twenty four hours might easily be saved off the time by retrenching the stoppages.

Soon after midnight I brought my sore bones to the Crocelle, and am bound

---

[1] The Pignatelli family were as well as marquesses of Castelnuovo dukes of Monteleone, owning the Monteleone castle. (Montereale is in the northern Abruzzi, far off the diarist's route.)

[2] Capital of Apulia, port on Adriatic, 135 miles east of Naples.

[3] I.e. the Neapolitan part of the kingdom of the Two Sicilies.   [4] Brindisi.

[5] I.e. on the road northward between Lano and La Sala.   [6] Then Austrian.

in honesty to confess that the luxury of a reasonably good bed was for once indescribable.

We have made about 1000 miles since leaving Naples: which, after Sicily and Calabria seems like my house in London.

WEG. Napoli. N. 12/38.

P.S. Errors excepted. The foregoing pages have not been read over.

Route of Calabria.

Naples.		Post.
Torre dell'Annunziata		$1\frac{1}{2}$
($\frac{1}{2}$ post (royal) to be added.)		

Nocera	. . . . . .	$1\frac{1}{2}$.	3 dh.[1]
Salerno	. . . . . .	$1\frac{1}{2}$.	
Eboli	. . . . . .	2.	3 dh. & back.
Duchessa	. . . . . .	$1\frac{1}{2}$.	
Auletta	. . . . . .	$1\frac{1}{2}$.	3 dh.
Sala	. . . . . .	$1\frac{1}{2}$.	
Casalnuovo	. . . . . .	$1\frac{1}{2}$.	3 dh.
Lago Negro	. . . . . .	$1\frac{1}{2}$.	
Lauria	. . . . . .	1.	
Castelluccio	. . . . . .	1.	
Rotonda	. . . . . .	1.	
Castrovillari	. . . . . .	2.	
Tarsia	. . . . . .	2.	
Ritorto	. . . . . .	$1\frac{1}{2}$.	
Cosenza	. . . . . .	$1\frac{1}{2}$.	
Rogliano	. . . . . .	1	
Coraci	. . . . . .	2	
Tiriolo	. . . . . .	2	
Casino Chiriaco	. . . . . .	$1\frac{1}{2}$	
Torre Masdea	. . . . . .	$1\frac{1}{4}$	
Monteleone	. . . . . .	$1\frac{1}{4}$	
Rosarno	. . . . . .	2	
Paluci	. . . . . .	$1\frac{1}{2}$	
Bagnara	. . . . . .	$\frac{3}{4}$	
Villa San Giovanni	. . . . . .	$1\frac{1}{2}$	
(Reggio ... 1)		$38\frac{3}{4}$[2]	
$39\frac{3}{4}$			

[1] Draught-horses (two were normal).

[2] This list is printed in Murray's *Handbook for Travellers in Southern Italy* (1853), 439, plus equivalents of Italian posts in Italian miles and one or two extra post-stations.

Naples, Nov. 12.[1]

Dined with the Geary's: read English news: discussed with K. his plans, to see if by hook or by crook his stay could be lengthened: wrote to Mr G: and finished my Sicilian Journal. Here I must breathe. It is impossible to digest in the mind more than a certain quantity within a certain time, of what it has received through the senses.

Nov. 13.

Made purchase of gomma d'oliva[2] from

> Gennaro Lofiego
> Strada Bisignano
> No 45 Chiaja.

K. finds himself obliged to go on Thursday as only in this way can he save Sunday which he will probably be able to spend quietly at Genoa.

We went to see Mr. Kennedy[3] at the Embassy: he spoke freely of the K. of N.; but said they had been most attentive to the Queen Dowager,[4] & had if anything rather overdone it.

We took our walk to the Camaldolite Convent, which Queen Adelaide had just visited, by means of a special permission from the Pope, necessary in order to enable her to enter. We were very kindly received, (as in 1832,)[5] by one of the brethren, of whom there are 25. He would only take money for the Church or the poor—of which we preferred the latter. A heavy haze rested on land & sea, & marred with the view: which however as I had the advantage of old recollections and could dispense in part with actual sight I enjoyed intensely. The peculiar feature is, the *command* which this site appears to have over the prospect. It lies before the eye like a map or a model. Add to this that the range is immense, the variety most abundant, the colours rich and gorgeous, the forms large and grand, the historical interest very high—and upon these data I must say I do not know its equal in its own line although the view from Etna may be preferred on different grounds.

The monastery said our conductor is 1500 feet high: each foot $1\frac{1}{2}$ palmi: (however, he hesitated;) if this be the case & the palmo = ten inches, the elevation will be about 1873 feet English.[6] I am sorry to say that this delightful spot is about seven miles from our hotel—the Crocelle. By the way of the Salita del Vomere.[7] Of all monasteries, not having ostensible active

---

[1] Entries again from Add MS 44818 B, unless otherwise noted, up to 2 Dec. 38.

[2] A scented resinous gum from trunks of old olive trees; formerly used as a vulnerary.

[3] John Kennedy, 1807–45, gs. of Archibald Kennedy, 11th earl of Cassilis; m. 1834 Amelia Briggs, only d. of Samuel Briggs; secretary of British legation at Naples 1834–44, at Washington 1845.

[4] *Adelaide spent the first fortnight of this month at Naples, being treated with the utmost distinction by the royal family. Cp. Harold Acton, *The Last Bourbons of Naples* (1961), 137.

[5] Cp. 16 May 32.   [6] In fact, 1488.

[7] 'Gradient of the Vomero' leading down from that suburb to the Chiaja. This sentence in margin.

duty attached, this is the most pleasing: but it is not easy to believe that the balanced nature of man can, at least in early life, (and the youngest Brother is but 22,) so completely turn the whole of its energies inward as to render generally advantageous the foundation of religious institutions on this particular basis. Some other functions than those of prayer and study will commonly be needed in order to absorb the active energies and prevent them from harassing and spoiling the contemplative. When I look at English colleges, and think what they are in a degree & might be much more, I look back with reverential gratitude to the eulogy of Erasmus, who I think wrote of Oxford that it surpassed all monasteries.[1]

Nov 13.[2]

Naples. A long and interesting conv. with A.K. on political position, reciprocal—his personal entrance into politics in 1834, his acquaintance with Lord Durham who he says has by nature a violent temper but is quite the reverse of a cold Man, his present difficulty arising out of his religion as applied to the general principle or idea of liberal politics—in their wrong estimate of human nature. This difficulty has not yet reached a head. He has I believe upon the whole the rare blessing of a very honest conscience & God will I Trust enable it to do its work in him.

Looked over several Tracts for K. The "Breve Esposizione della Fede Generale de'Riformati"[3] I think a most unsound and objectionable publication: and the worst of it is, that a good deal of the phraseology is picked from the Articles of the Church of England.

Wednesday November 14.

After hunting gloves & money with some other matters went to the Studio & hastily visited the best sculpture:[4] liked & admired the Bacchus (Torso) and the Psyche more than ever, but especially the latter for the exquisitely high *character* of the countenance which is much above (for example) that of the Venus de' Medici. And the form appears to be idealised at least in one remarkable particular. In the Toro I liked best the trunks & attitudes of the two sons.[5] In the Hercules[6] the smallness of the head seems very remarkable: it does not strike the eye as disproportionate. In its own kind it is very wonderful for the building of those blocks of muscle.

The Cacciatore in the corridor has a hare & a brace of partridges: a net? & a knife.[7] Thus they were snarers: which one ought to be able to illustrate.

---

[1] Not in Erasmus, but referring to Cambridge in Caius, *Historia Cantabrigensis Academiae* (1574), lib. 2, p. 127, quoted in Samuel *Knight, *Life of Erasmus* (1726).

[2] These two paragraphs from Lambeth MS 1424.

[3] Untraced.   [4] Cp. 2, 14 May 32.

[5] Zethus and Amphion, straining to hold in a wild bull, to which they are binding Dirce to avenge her treatment of their mother Antiope.

[6] Exhumed with the Toro Farnese in 1540 from the Baths of Caracalla; by Glykon; legs restored by Michael Angelo.

[7] According to G. B. Finati, *Real Museo Borbonico* (1824 ff.), vii, tav. 10, the net is the end of the cord that ties the hare to the shoulder; the 'partridges' are doves.

The dying Amazon a little further on than the Cacciatore seems a fine piece of sculpture.

San Carlos.[1] The Giuramento by Mercadante.[2] I liked the music of the second and third acts. The enthusiasm of the audience appeared much more directed towards the acting than the music. No first rate voice. The part of Furio Camillo which I saw, was the more offensive for purporting to be historical.

Nov. 14.[3]

San Carlos. Saw part of the Ballet. It was called Furio Camillo[4] and purported to be in subject very grave. I hope never to see another & can have no doubt about any ballet Establishments. Indeed it has always been that as reputed, which has to my mind formed the definite reason for avoiding the Opera in London.

Thursday Nov 15.

Papers: letters: & internal arrangements: seeing Kinnaird off—a heavy loss: comparing notes with the Glynnes: read Baggs: began Monti's Crocciata:[5] dined at Mr. Kennedy's. Gay season here Jan. & Feb.—also Dec. The people winter in town: in summer they do not go to their estates but to watering places: & they do nothing, & cultivate nothing. Così Mrs. K; who seems a nice person, as well as Mr. K.

Nov 15.[6]

Sent off by A.K. & the *bag* letters to Mr. G
            J.N.G.
            Ld Mahon
            Murray (with note to A.K.)
            Rio.[7]
            Aunt J.

Friday Nov. 16.

The great disadvantage of the distance of the Studio[8] is that one finds half a dozen impediments on the way to it. Among others I found an author in a

[1] Principal theatre of Naples, and one of the largest in Europe, adjoining the Royal Palace; devoted to Italian opera.
[2] By Saviero Mercadante, 1795–1870, Neapolitan composer; first represented at the Scala in Milan in 1837.
[3] This entry from Lambeth MS 1424.
[4] A ballet with classical subject (they changed from night to night) filling intervals in the opera. The subject had a political anti-Austrian significance, as L. Furius Camillus, d. 365 B.C., was the great defender of Rome against the Gauls.
[5] *I Lombardi alla Prima Crociata* (1826), poem in 15 cantos, by Tommaso Grossi, 1790–1853; not by his contemporary Vincenzo Monti, 1754–1828.
[6] This entry from Lambeth MS 1424.
[7] On his talk with Manzoni; in Bowe, *Rio*, 158 n.
[8] At the end of the Strada Toledo, main street of Naples, farthest from the bay where *Gladstone's hotel was.

33—II.

bookseller's shop whom I greatly pleased by telling him he was like Manzoni in countenance which was the fact: & he very goodnaturedly corrected some blunders in my Italian as we spoke. He said prohibited books were all easily to be had, & were more sought & sold than any others. That not long ago a bookseller in Rome was about to fail; he printed a book to retrieve his affairs, the copies remained unsold and the matter was made worse. He went to the Pope & said he had a petition: what was it? He had printed a book & he wished it to be prohibited:—how so? in such case he would be unable to sell it? On the contrary when once it was prohibited, it would be sure to sell: the Pope according to my informant entered into the spirit of the request, prohibited the book, & the bookseller saved his affairs!

It is interesting to see on a house beyond the Chiaja and the turning to Posilipo,[1] this inscription:

> Si loca la casa di Sannazaro.[2]

Surely the *Toro* in the Studio should be viewed either from some elevation greater than that of the floor: or at least from a considerable distance. At present the eye has no *command* whatever.

The Church of San Severino appears to be inwardly (in effect) a Greek cross outwardly an oblong—by means of the architects having thrown open the aisles at their centre to the nave.[3]

I have begun Grossi's Lombardi alla Prima Crocciata. It is curious to find the representation in the Third Canto, that when the Hermit wished to leave a certain vicinity in the East, where his repute for sagacity was immense during his residence there, and where he had rejected the prayers of the inhabitants for his continuance, a party of armed ruffians attacked him on his departure to slay him in order that

> a tutela del suo corpo santo
> Quella terra di sangue si ponesse![4]

This is surely a confession of superstition in the strictest sense.

Saturday Nov. 18 [sc. 17]

I got to the Studio earlier & spent my time with much delight in the Statue & picture galleries: after putting up at home a little copy from Correggio's Sposalizio which I bought yesterday of an artist named Scardino.[5]

Among the statues are several fine Torsi besides the great ones: which the managers of these matters have not been cruel enough to restore, like the Antinous.[6]

---

[1] Western promontory of Bay of Naples.

[2] 'Here was Sannazaro's house'. Iacopo Sannazaro, 1456–1530, Neapolitan poet buried nearby, gave his name to that part of the coast.

[3] Enlarged and modernised 1490.

[4] 'under the protection of his holy body this land should rest from blood': *I Lombardi*, Canto 3, stanza 44.

[5] Unidentified.

[6] Colossal statue of Antinous as Bacchus, much restored.

The statue of the Faun carrying Bacchus a boy struck me as extremely fine.

Observe near this a head of Bacchus which is not young. Some heads named from Venus & Cleopatra do little credit to the names

The Venere et Amore[1] gives a beautiful type of Venus, but, even for this combination, too *maternal*?

The horses of the Balbi[2] are supported by great pillars under the body, the strength of the legs in marble being insufficient. Here is a testimony to the Creator's skill and wisdom in the structure of the animal itself which carries so much and so rapidly upon limbs of so small girth & of a substance much less hard.

The countenance of Socrates is not of the elevated character of Plato's in any of the busts: in some it is positively pug and snubnosed.

Is the attitude of the Aristides that of a listener?[3] I suppose certainly not of a speaker: the singularly fine drapery locks up the right hand in a manner from which there seems to be no escape.

Atlas with his *small* globe, looks *pained*. This is against the vraisemblable?

Noble bust of Homer—of Homer such as 'through seven cities famed' he begged his bread: blind & neglected: not like a bard at the table of Branksome.[4]

255. Tre Grazie, so intitled. Six illdressed women & a girl?[5]

Flora[6] may be called in the hyper-Niobe style?

Hall of Apollo[7] is offensive: concentrates the motley harlequin figures which waxwork could imitate much better.

In the Picture Gallery: Donzelli's Crucifixion,[8] observe the clouds behind the centre cross—is this the commencing of darkness?

Andrea di Salerno[9] has good heads. From his case & others, do we not find that the brilliancy & fame of his last manner did not utterly eject the style of Perugino[10] for some time from the Roman school?

Schidoni's pictures[11] appear to [have] the strangest & most arbitrary disposition of light & shade, quite without unity or connection, which gives them a mottled appearance, & offends all laws of ideal probability: here is a figure or a part of one in strong light, fetched from no one knows where,

---

[1] Venus Victrix with Cupid, from the excavation of the amphitheatre of Capua.

[2] Cp. 2 May 32.

[3] Statue now believed to be of Aeschines, Greek orator, floruit 342 B.C.

[4] Cp. *Scott's *Lay of the Last Minstrel*, canto vi, stanza 3.

[5] Bas-relief of six women taking one another by the hand and walking towards a smaller one, the first three bearing the names Euphrosyne, Aglaie and Thalia—the three Graces; the second three, nymphs; the smaller one being Telonnesus, probably eponym of Telos, one of the Cyclades.

[6] Upwards of 12 feet in height, here compared to Niobe of the Uffizi, Florence.

[7] Or Hall of Coloured Marbles, full of statuary in coloured marble or alabaster.

[8] Pietro Donzelli, 1452–1509, and his brother Ippolito, 1456–94, both have paintings of the Crucifixion.

[9] Andrea Sabatini, called da Salerno, 1484?–1530.

[10] As distinct from the semi-pagan style of the Renaissance. Cp. A.-F. Rio, *De la Poésie Chrétienne*, 220 ff.

[11] Works executed for Rannuccio I duke of Parma, from whom they passed into the Farnese collection, cp. 19 May 32.

next to this a patch of deep scuro, & this half a dozen times over in one picture.

Arcivescovado. The Chapel with the pictures[1] was locked: but may be seen tolerably through the doors. The porphyry pillars[2] outside beat all other architectural specimens.

Sunday Nov 18.

Church morning and afternoon. Only once before since Ems. I did not anticipate so much privation.[3] Good sermons from Mr. Boileau Pollen,[4] & Mr. Lushington the Chaplain. It was lately attempted to build an English Church, near the Embassy, with the understanding, that its exterior was to resemble a house: but even thus, the priests applied to the police, & the police interfered to stop it. So that toleration is still somewhat modified here. A room larger than the present is in course of preparation. In the Strada S. Caterina,[5] heard a buffo Neapolitan Sermon afterwards. Dialect strong. People greatly amused. Some good matter intermixed. He bid them seek instruction: but not the instruction of the civilisation of the day which was demoralisation.

Dined with Mr and Mrs Kennedy.

This city is noisy & most unSundaylike today: as those in Sicily. Much worse, to the sense, than Rome & Florence. Mrs K. says, that English people frequently go to balls and to the Opera here on Sundays.

Monday Nov 19.

No letter. Ahi sventurato.[6] A long draught at the papers, a sorry substitute. Walk & conversation with Sir R. Vyvyan. Grossi, Pompeii, Journal.

Found myself on the Mergellina[7] & walked to the top of the hill by the carriage road, then by the road to the right which placed me in an old foot & horse path leading back to Naples and giving with delightful variety alternate views of Pozzuoli & the country towards Camaldoli with its little vine farms on the one hand, of Naples & the bay on the other. The smoke of Vesuvius blended beautifully with the clouds in which he was wrapped. But for a small bit of the lip of the crater visible, they could hardly have been distinguished. The smoke however is more decidedly silvery.—The vines still retain most of their leaves: the poplars are bare: the acacias begin to look foolish. But the country seems always to smile under its own sun.

---

[1] St. Januarius' heavily ornamented chapel. Cp. 5 May 32.

[2] Taken from the two temples of Neptune and Apollo on which the cathedral was built.

[3] Note on theology, Add MS 44728, f. 159.

[4] George Boileau-Pollen, 1798–1847; at Christ Church; m. 1824 Elizabeth, da. of Sir James Hall, bart.; br. of Sir John Peter *Boileau; and squire of Little Bookham, Surrey, 1821; rector 1823.

[5] Near the Villa Reale (Chiaja), continuous with the Piazza Santa Maria a Cappella on which is situated the Palazzo Calabretto, where were held the services of the Church of England.

[6] 'Alas for my bad luck'.

[7] At the modern end of the Chiaja.

Read at the Embassy certain papers on the Sulphur question.[1] The Neapolitan tone I thought contemptible. One argument not sound throughout: though the case appears excellent in equity & has I learn been approved in law.

San Carlos at 10 P.M.: found the spectacle less advanced than I had calculated. Met P. & Pª. Bisignano,[2] D. & Dª. Scondito[3] in the latter's box. The 2d and 3d Acts of Giuramento I still like: especially the scene of the tombs.—The officers of the army have certain seats by privilege in the pit: they pay however. The hired boxes appear ill furnished: to judge from that which the Glynnes had. We counted seven priests in their hats coming out—and we were of the tail of the audience.

Tuesday Nov 20.

At 10½ with the Glynnes to D. Scondito's and thence to the ladies school Isabella Borbona. No. [blank].[4] Nearly three hours in going over it. We heard excellent singing and playing. The highest class compose in French, and learn English but find it very hard on account of the exceptions. Most pronounced the French well. We found heads excellently copied: they are generally fond of drawing. Priests appear to conduct the literary instruction. The Gospel is explained on Sundays & they learn a compendium of Scripture history: the Bible is not read. They have three dishes besides fruit for dinner, apparently very good: on feasts, four: on fasts, three, but no meat they do not eat less on those days: & they have soup. They walk on the terraces three hours a day. They have Sunday & half Thursday free. They may enter at 5 & remain till 18: they generally stay 8 & 10 years: & they only go out to their families unless seriously ill, on *two* days in a year. Their parents may enter the school (once a convent) to see them: otherwise friends converse through a grating. There are 180. Most of the nobles & those who can afford it send their children to this & another similar school: those who cannot educate at home. (NB. the reverse of England.) Their appearance in general was a little depressed: not shy nor forward. Some who were kneeling in the antichapel laughed much as we went through. The rooms were clean: the bedrooms beautifully so: counterpanes of green silk wadded. They hear mass every day. They learn with the branches above named Greek, & Roman, & Neapolitan history, & some geography. Sometimes none in the Infirmary, sometimes three or four. Sorelle di

[1] Cp. 7 Nov. 38, and PRO FO 70/157.

[2] Principe and Principessa Bisignano. Pietrantonio Sansaverino succeeded to title 1814; grandee of Spain of the first class, highest in rank of Neapolitan nobility, grand master of the court and superintendent of the royal household, married Maria Antonia Serra of the ducal house of Cassano, lady in waiting to the queen.

[3] Duke and Duchess Scondito, claiming to be of the many-branched Neapolitan family of the Capeces who followed Manfred in the thirteenth century; Scondito chapel in the cathedral. Family became extinct with Duke Ottavio Capece-Scondito, 1783–6, husband of Livia Sanseverino di Bisignano.

[4] No. 2. Two girls' boarding schools ('educandate') were under the patronage of the queen mother, Maria Isabella Borbona, daughter of Charles IV of Spain, second wife of Francis I, 1789–1848, one in the ancient convent of Santa Maria dei Miracoli, one in that of Sanseverino.

Carità[1] are paid to attend it. The view from the bedrooms is very delightful: of Vesuvius particularly good. The establishment retains a part of its property. The girls bring a wardrobe and pay 8 ducats a month.

San Carlino, to see Pulcincllo: he is a figure dressed in white with a black caricature mask over the upper part of his face. I could understand the patois but very imperfectly: what I caught was generally about the level of an openair harlequin stage in England with a few finer strokes intermixed. The costume is generally that of the lower orders in the streets of Naples: including an imitation of bare feet. The part of the gentleman was very decidedly the worst acted & quite out of place. At the same time the whole tone is (in painting phrase) light & suggests rather than anything else that these people are very easily amused.

Wednesday Nov. 21.

Breakfasted below & got away (after a visit from G. Nobili) at 9¼ for Pompeii. 2½ h. going, 2¼ returning: I think near 18 English miles. 3½ h. there & lunch in the carriage. Much amused at seeing in the Largo close by the San Carlino one of the best dressed of the actors of last night in the identical hat coat & trowsers (I doubt the presence of a waistcoat) in which he performed.

After all the greatest interest attaching to Pompeii is not in the view of what is on the spot, taken in detail, but rather attaches to the new and singular set of associations with which a traveller of the 19th century finds himself walking amidst the *ipsissima vestigia* of the first: amidst all the little familiar objects, arrangements, and contrivances, which of everything that has relations to man appears to have the most *proximate*: for objects which have more soul transferred into them, more satisfying in themselves, do not so immediately suggest the void which has been made by the absence of the owner or maker. On this account they do well to reserve the public buildings to the end of the day: when the interest of novelty has worn off and requires something to replace it. One wishes in vain first that the excavations could once for all be completed: and secondly & more, that it had been possible upon making the discoveries to leave them as they were, instead of dividing the *disjecta membra* between the town and the Studio of Naples. The objects seen there are as it were dead, and become narrative instead of being dramatic.

The fabric of the walls appears not to be uniform:[2] the part in large regular blocks descends from the Cyclopean manner.[3] *Footpaths* everywhere along the streets: it is singular that this useful practice shd have been so generally abandoned! Cuttings of ruts very deep: but the general surface of the pavements no where broken.—The custode described in modern terms 'quest è

---

[1] 'Sisters of Charity'.

[2] The towers and part of the walls are of *opus incertum*: stones broken into small pieces cemented with mortar and covered with stucco.

[3] i.e. derived from the Cyclopean manner: unhewn blocks of stone, without mortar, gaps filled with smaller stones, as at Mycenae and Tiryns; but at Pompeii the stones are well hewn and fit without mortar.

la dogana', 'quest'è la posta de' cavalli', & above all, at the College of the Vestals 'quest'era un convento di monache.'[1]—The triclinia[2] all small except that called of the priests in the Dî majorum. Gent[ium].[3] Tables pr[obably?] to accommodate 4 or 6. Seat 4 or 5 feet deep. General frontage of the shops 12 . . . 18 feet. The style of interior ornament is elaborately minute: not in pure taste: especially the painting the walls all over in blocks of ill assorted colour, some of them mottled as in coarse imitation of mosaic. The paintings are middling in perspective? and very few figures reach excellence. The sculptures better in general? Great wealth probably was expended here: at present, no relics of the poor discovered? The public buildings decidedly fine: the Forum must have been very much so.[4] The Amphitheatre[5] would accommodate the whole population? arena 80 paces by 60 (acc. to Cicerone): 5 seats for persons of rank &c., 12 for soldiers (as at S. Carlos the other night) in advance, 15 or 18 for the generality, boxes for women above with corridor behind. In the temple of Isis, cracks through holes under the altar. Altars of sacrifice are large: $3\frac{1}{2}$ f by 2 f. pr.? The Alexander mosaic[6] seems certainly a noble work: particularly for *composition*, and for spirit: the large eyes produce a great effect. In shading I suppose it does not reach those of the Vatican.[7] Alexander has Medusa's head on his breast. The lion's head in the same house is very fine. The wall of the chase is curious.[8] We dubbed the Casa del Poeta, "Mr Rogers's."[9] In the size of the amphith. compared with that of the theatres, we find the character of the people: not *dianoctic*.

The amphorae decline a little from the perpendicular: & their pointed bottoms would not allow them to stand. Was this to give the sediment better opportunity of depositing? was it as *port* is now laid on its side? Even these are full of ash.—Rooms very very small: as of persons depending more on the open air. At least in Christian times & countries gross vice does not exhibit its emblems by daylight on exteriors & in principal streets of cities: as in Pompeii.

Read the 'Useful Knowledge' on Pompeii:[10] Grossi.

Dined with Ld & Lady Jersey.

(By the way, a part of the joke last night was, a little boy's speaking a Neapolitan dialect so exaggerated that the Neapolitans of the play said 'non capisco una parola.'[11])

We counted 8, 9, 10 on one horse cars coming back from Pompeii.

---

[1] 'this is the customs house', 'this is the posting-station', 'that was a monastery'.
[2] Couch for reclining at meals; hence a dining-room.
[3] The Pantheon, temple of the twelve principal Roman gods.
[4] It had a Grecian Doric colonnade on three sides, marble pavings and pedestals for equestrian statues.
[5] In the SE. angle of the city walls.
[6] Of the battle of the Issus, where Alexander beat Darius 333 B.C., removed from the House of the Faun to the Museo Borbonico.
[7] Cp. 31 Mar. 32.
[8] Mosaic in the House of the Chase.
[9] In *Rogers's house in St. James's Place each room, as here, was a work of art.
[10] *Pompeii* (anon., 1831–2. 2nd ed. 1846 under name of William Clarke).
[11] 'I don't understand a word.'

Thursday. Nov 22.

Sold our carriage to Buonaccorsi[1] of the Gran Bretagna for 70 piastres. At 10 went with him & Nobili to the police about his wine. The Captain of the Tasso wishes to detain it on pretence that it belongs to Kinnaird & me, & that we owe him ten ducats. Properly speaking I was not concerned in the matter but I went in order to show readiness. We were first with the Inspector then with the Commissary: & after much uproar, several bawling at once, judgment was given against the Captain, and he was ordered to deliver the wine. Singularly enough, he insisted on holding his umbrella over my head from the carriage to the door of the office, and also seized my hand when we came away: while I cannot but pronounce him a great rogue. On the other hand I saw some further specimens of the want of general regard for truth: N[obili] said he had come from Messina at an expence of 30 piastres for this matter! & that the English Consul himself had made the award at Messina: which I corrected.

I went to Giustiniani's shop beyond the Piazza del Mercato:[2] a sight worth seeing.

Studio at 12. Pictures—Statuary (the Venus of the Casa Aurea the only one worth looking at?)[3] and the Pompeii Frescoes. While they differ very much in execution, the conception of the figure & the attitude is generally good: the only ones very beautifully drawn seem to be the Hercules about to kill Nessus[4] and its neighbour, I think of the Graces. The figures suspended in air are generally light & buoyant. The larger ones of Telephus,[5] Ulysses & Achilles,[6] Theseus with the children[7] and [blank] have much force. Those of the writing implements very instructive.[8] Some graceful borders. The insignia of a school, actually used as such, a pupil horsed, or rather bridged between two, & flogging on the point of taking place! The games of the cupids, hide and seek &c,[9] very pretty. Here is the foundation of the families of Loves which Thorwaldsen has worked out in sculpture.[10]— Ld & Lady Jersey there: some discussion about the Torso.[11] Papers. With Mr Kennedy on sulphur, &c. Dined with the Glynnes.

Friday Nov 23.

At 9 A.M. to Albergo de' Poveri: an institution on a gigantic scale for the

---

[1] The innkeeper at Messina.

[2] In the Strada Marinella; sold imitation Etruscan vases and terra cotta.

[3] Venus Callipyge, found in the 'Golden House' of Nero; shown with a number of other Venuses

[4] Group of Hercules, Nessus and Dejanira.

[5] Telephus nursed by a hind with Hercules hearing a goddess announce that he is his son.

[6] Achilles at Skyros, having his disguise as a maiden discovered by Ulysses, who was disguised as a merchant.

[7] Theseus with children kissing his hands after the slaying of the Minotaur.

[8] Fragments of paintings (cp. *Real Museo Borbonico*, i. (1824) plate XII) reproduced writing and reading tools of the ancients.

[9] Instead of 'blind man's buff'.

[10] e.g. in his 'Vintage' or 'Apple Harvest', or in a baptismal font for Copenhagen.

[11] Cp. 14 Nov. 38.

children of the poor.[1] It is said that 7000 may be received here: there are actually 4000: from childhood to manhood: supported very cheaply: and instructed in schools under the name "Lancastrian" & in arts. We saw the processes of printing, pin-making, hardware, weaving, glass blowing. The expenditure of labour appears to be very great. Handlooms alone are used, the cloth we saw was very coarse, pins are headed with the hand and it requires half a dozen beats of a little hammer worked with the foot to fix each head. The glass too was of a very inferior kind, I should suppose. Many of the children begged of us with the usual gestures & complaint— moro di fame.[2] They wear a military uniform.[3] In the school they looked intelligent: many had bad eyes & the general appearance throughout was not healthy. The means of ventilation are most abundant, but in the dormitories the air was vile, and the whole establishment had not a very clean appearance. They assemble in two chapels, twice a day. A band of thirty, most of them grown up performed for us, very well but much too loud: their drums nearly burst ours. Some of the pupils draw very well: among all the models I only saw one sacred, la jeune communiante. The walls were hung all round. Fingal & Malvina[4] were there: & I have seen the latter used as a name.—They have meat twice a week: the bread is nearly black & I think much below what the peasantry eat. The tables had a very dirty brown napkin laid for each (no cloth,) & an instrument forming a spoon at one end & fork at the other. They receive we understood a third of their earnings for their own disposal. The sand for the glass is brought from Trapani & mixed with potash or soda? so ignorant am I. The sea forms this sand from a flint shingle.—In one part of this building we counted eight stories. There is a school for the deaf & dumb: of whom there are about 30. It was not open during our visit. 76 died of cholera on its last visitation. (In Naples altogether 50,000 off 500,000, acc. to Mr Kennedy: & in Palermo 25,000.)

Capo di Monte.[5] Bolton's[6] & Michelangeli's.[7] Dined with Mr Kennedy. Lady Dering's[8] af[te]r.

At Pompeii we saw the wall where the cross *had been,* opposite to the Pagan insignia: but with the whole stucco it had slipped away.

Saturday Nov 24.

Studio. Pictures. Beautiful Perugino (Virgin & Child) in the Roman room: & pseudo or retouched Raphael near it.[9] Also a fine Pinturicchio:[10] he

---

[1] Intended by Charles III as asylum for all the poor of the kingdom, where they might learn useful arts.

[2] 'I'm dying of hunger.'   [3] Most of the boys went into the army.

[4] A hero and heroine of the Ossianic poems of which translations by Cesarotti appeared early in Italy: *Fingal* (1762); *Temora* (1763); many successive editions.

[5] Suburb on the hill, to north, crowned by the king's favourite suburban villa.

[6] Unidentified.

[7] Unidentified.

[8] Jane, youngest da. of William, 2nd Lord Kensington, m. 1832 Sir Edward Cholmeley Dering, 8th bart.; M.P. for Wexford 1830–1, for Romney 1831–2.

[9] Copy of the Entombment in the Borghese gallery.

[10] Assumption of the Virgin.

shows like A da Salerno that Raphael's change did not at once change everything.—The Baptist in Fra B.s fine picture of the Assumption has a *short* figure, like others of the same great artist?—Parmegianino's faces show no invention.

Pompeian gems. The ladies ornaments in general show very little taste or beauty of form, & are thus curiously contrasted with the generality of the vessels designed for useful purposes.—The Cameo from Adrian's villa is indeed magnificent.

Statues. The figure of the fine Crucifix lately found is unfinished: about the head & on the arms? & below the knees: but how noble a work. M. A. Lacherinus the artist, whose name is on it, was, it seems, Buonarroti's pupil. The govt. gave 8000 ducats for it.[1] For a colossal St Ambrose which Angelini[2] is executing for them they are to give 6000. The artist in his studio said it was too little. The marble costs 1000.

Nov 24.[3]

In Pr. Butera's letter to Mr Kennedy he says that the English are deservedly liked better than any other nation by all persons in this kingdom, with a few exceptions only, from the King downwards.

Sunday Nov. 25.

Church mg. & aft. Mr Lushington & Mr. Palmer preached. Heard part of a sermon in the Chiaja Church:[4] on the permanence of early habits & against the postponement of turning to God. Dinner with the Glynnes. After morning service I had, while waiting under an archway an interesting conversation about religious matters with two men, one of whom was very earnest. He begged me to become a Catholic—I told him I hoped I was one, & explained that I was not at liberty to leave the Church in England, inasmuch as it had sound doctrine & a valid ministry. I showed him some things in the prayerbook & he was very much pleased with them. He urged their miracles. He liked the free circulation of the Scriptures: & they were also much struck with the fact that during our services we do not speak to one another! while here (the other told me) they go to Church 'per parlare, & per far l'amore.'[5] They insisted on my coming home in one of their carriages, which I did.—It is impossible to open the whole subject with these persons but when they seem really set upon the essence of religion, I suppose the right way is to dwell upon what connects us both with the Redeemer.

---

[1] By Michaelangelo Naccherinus, 1550–1622; found in 1835, in a box in the church of San Spirito; placed in the Studio, soon removed to the re-dedicated church of San Carlo all'Arena.

[2] Tito Angelini, 1806–78, Neapolitan sculptor.

[3] This paragraph from Lambeth MS. 1424. He also wrote a note on the nunc dimittis, Add MS 44728, f. 160.

[4] Of Santa Teresa, attached to Carmelite monastery.

[5] 'to talk and to make love'.

Monday Nov 26.

As regards sights a *dies non*. With Mr K[ennedy] about sulphur & other papers: walk with him up the Mergellina Scala[1] & back by the Tre Case Garden:[2] which gives very nice views of the town. Dinner also with him. Mrs K. says the Neapolitans are much scandalised by the circumstances that most of the English clergymen who come here attend the balls, (including the Chaplain) which the priests do not. Clergymen so doing are always sharply criticised by the world in general: & they are also when out of their place but secondary personages.

Tuesday Nov 27.

Finished Grossi's 'Lombardi alla Prima Crocciata.' The descriptions are beautiful in a high degree, the sentiment generally pure, & the narrative interesting.

Studio. Bronzes. How rich is this small collection! The Plato for majestic ideal beauty: the Scipio Africanus, for marked and manly character: the Mercury in repose & the Faun near it[3] for the human form: are pre-eminent: the Seneca, for approximation to actual life. Besides the Discoboli, the Fauno Dansante of Pompeii, the head of Antinous, the Fauno Ubbriaco.[4]

Dined at the Villa di Napoli, at the bottom of the Toledo: which is a good restaurant.

The Mercury called in repose is not in actual motion: but his figure rests in considerable part on points, one toe, one heel, one hand—this is not repose properly so called, in order to which a large portion of the body should have actual support. He seems ready and waiting to move.—The left arm of the Faun below the left elbow is thick: probably it was meant to withdraw from the eye. Observe the glands under the jaws in imitation of the goat: & the mulberries in the hair of the Fauno Ubbriaco.

While I was buying soap in Ridolfo's shop,[5] a monk came in and begged him to read for him the address of a letter (very clearly written) which he had to deliver: being himself, as Ridolfo said, unable to read.

Wednesday Nov 28.

A very wet morning broke up a party to Vesuvius: & I was unwillingly thrown upon the (to me) unadvisable resource of reading & writing.[6]

I have been reading a French Octavo of Lectures, of which Milton is the hero:[7] a good sign. The author does more justice to Dante than to Chateaubriand, but yet his judgments on the Paradiso are most unsatisfactory: he

[1] A stepped road, generally called Rampa di Posilipo, rising abruptly behind the Mergellina.
[2] Unidentified among many villas and gardens of the hill of Posilipo.
[3] The 'sleeping Faun'.
[4] The 'drunken Faun'.
[5] On the Largo del Vasto.
[6] Fragment on St. Paul in Add MS 44728, f. 162.
[7] R. de Véricour, *Milton et la Poésie épique* (1838).

compares it with Milton's Paradise & then naturally gives the latter the preference. He calls Adam le plus beau des hommes & Eve la plus ravissante des femmes. He interprets Genesis neologically, apparently with some regard to the tone of his audience: he says 'nous ne sommes ici d'aucune religion' & begs them to assume the prepossessions of Christianity in order to judge Milton fairly. Here is that *extrinsic* handling of religion, as if it had not already established antecedently to our option relations with & claims upon us: as if Christianity were on the stage and we in the boxes. However perhaps M. de Vericour did the best he dared.

Thursday. Nov 29.

9¾ A.M.–5¾ P.M. To Vesuvius with the Glynnes. We were about half an hour on the top: & three quarters lunching & resting at the foot of the cone & on the side. The ascent is much improved since 1832:[1] being now over the lava which hardly slips at all—then in the ash. The motion of the chaise-a-porteur must however be very disagreeable & if a lady be pretty strong I should think she might try the cord[2] with advantage.

The height is said to be 3500 feet: & the ascent from Portici[3] to the top cannot I think exceed six miles. The first part of the mountain from Portici corresponds with that below Nicolosi on Etna: and one then sees & traverses something imperfectly resembling the regione del Bosco:[4] which terminates half a mile before the foot of the cone. At the top we had clouds, & sulphur frequently all but intolerable. We crossed over the great crater of 1822,[5] & the crater of 1834,[6] to the present one[7] which is 200 feet deep, and which was roaring continuously & emitting stones but they did not reach to the lip & we could not see them. However as regards the view we had it over the bay & city very delightfully in the descent: & there is a good deal of resemblance to the view towards Syracuse from Etna, the bay of Catania corresponding tho' imperfectly with that of Naples.—The blue & green sulphurs[8] were particularly beautiful. Our party amounted to thirty-eight persons, and five quadrupeds! of which number four only were principals: 12 were bearers, a guide, a gendarme, two men with the horses, two speculating on a demand for their grapes & wine, & the rest buona-mano and bottiglia-hunters.[9]

The ascent of Vesuvius has this advantage over that of Etna that it shows the breadth of the old streams of lava better.

Angrisani[10] disappoints me & I cannot go till after Sunday: thus always I find that when I have procrastinated voluntarily for a time, other involuntary postponements are sure to happen.

[1] Cp. 15 May 32. [2] Used by guides to pull travellers up the cone.
[3] Coastal town 3½ miles ESE. of Naples. [4] Cp. 29 Oct. 38.
[5] Counted as the 46th eruption of Vesuvius.
[6] 49th eruption.
[7] 50th eruption March 1838–January 1839, changing the crater to a funnel 300 ft. deep.
[8] Vapours emitted by the mountain in preparation for real eruption January 1839.
[9] Tip-hunters.
[10] He ran a service of carriages on the Naples–Rome road via Terracina on contract to the two governments; departure time fixed only when the carriage was full.

Friday Nov 30.

The Austrian Courier, my last chance and the quickest of all conveyances to Rome (in 21 hours I believe) goes next not this Friday. His regular mission once a fortnight is a proof of the vigilance of the Emperor of Austria in watching this peninsula.

Walked up the Vomero & around St Elmo.[1] The priests I observe sometimes fold a long mantle under the right and over the left shoulder crossing the breast, like the toga.—Though Naples does not, comparatively, abound in fine churches, I think in my walk I saw 32 domes, of which 27 were in sight at once.—I know not whether it be ludicrous to mark as among the minor signs of national character that the clocks here are singularly wide of one another: I heard them for a range of 25 minutes striking the same hour. —Dined with Mr Kennedy, & visited Mrs Conyngham[2] afterwards.

Saturday Dec. 1.

Wrote to H.J.G.[3]—read Craven's Travels,[4] about Calabria &c. Studio. Objects of Bassi Tempi —Pompeii mosaics—some moral horrors & little good in art; the cat & partridge & the fish may be observed.)—Bronze utensils— & Sepulchral Vases. These two last are particularly curious & the vases most beautiful. It seems singular that the representations on them shld. rarely have any intelligible connection with death. They have been found *empty* in the tombs: & probably were used first to carry the materials for sacrifices: in some of the drawings[5] they appear as thus employed. The light figure on dark ground belongs to a better state of art, they say, than the dark figure on light ground: but they are not truly distinguished as Etruscan & Greek respectively.

San Carlino to see 'le finte Inglesi'[6] & learn something in two hours of candlelight without straining the eyes. Two *miledis* give a bill for £100 as a remuneration for two bunches of flowers: and speak no English but 'I say come here' and '*Yes*' the last constantly reiterated though it is obviously the first word of which an English person gets rid. No satire seemed to be intended: but there was much fun in the piece, of which a portion is derived from the rude elements of pushing & inarticulate sound. *Miledi* was addressed as 'distintissima, amabilissima *Miss*.'[7]—Even in this small audience I found a priest—in his habit and hat.—The company act the pieces twice each evening. Water circulates between the acts: 'Volete acqua, Signori, che è fredda.'[8] The price in the pit is 15 gr.[9]

---

[1] Fortress in Vomero hill commanding Naples from NW.; formed chiefly out of an immense rock; said to communicate with Royal Palace.

[2] Unidentified.

[3] And note on absolution, Add MS 44728, f. 163.

[4] Keppel Richard *Craven, *A Tour through the Southern Provinces of the Kingdom of Naples* (1821).

[5] e.g. in vase from Nola, representing a tomb.

[6] 'The sham Englishwomen'. Improvised commedia dell'arte; author untraced.

[7] 'most distinguished and amiable Miss.'

[8] 'Do you want water, gentlemen? it's cold.'

[9] 6d.

Sunday Dec 2.

The Holy Communion. Well attended. Two Sermons from Mr Lushington. Then went to San Ferdinando, (opposite the end of the Palace) and heard one on the Virgin Mary of the class that I can only denominate horrible. The G[lynne]s whom I accompanied were similarly impressed. The service had some relation to the Immaculate Conception of the Blessed Virgin: and the preacher set forth that the Divina Maternità was something of a highly mysterious (moral) character which he seemed covertly to assimilate to the Divina Paternità: that this wonderful Creatura triumphed over original sin and was an exception to the general laws of human nature, formed by picking, like a certain Agrigentine painter, from all quarters all the choicest elements of excellence:[1] she is regina de' Cieli,[2] and Imperatrice del Mondo:[3] her virtue and glory differ in this essential respect from those of the angels and archangels, that theirs are restrained within the bounds of what is finite, *i cancelli del finito*, while hers *tocca ai cancelli del infinito*,[4] so that there can properly be no relation or comparison between them. In her are exhibited the several distinctive virtues of apostles, doctors, martyrs, virgins: in her are represented also those which belong to the heavenly circles of cherubim and seraphim angels and archangels (Cf. Dante Par. of St Francis & St Dominic):[5] *nay more*, and most of all she is invested with the extrinsic attributes of the Blessed Trinity, namely Infinite Power, Infinite Wisdom, & Infinite Love. And tho Sacred Scripture represents that (of the appeal to *Scripture* here I am not absolutely but very nearly certain) St John in the Spirit saw our Lord on his throne calling up his Spouse to her throne by his side: this was the Virgin! and he crowned her with a crown adorned[6] with lions, bears, and leopards, beasts signifying emblematically the sinners she had saved. Her part in the salvation of the world was analogous to that of Eve in its destruction. Accordingly he said let us go with confidence to her feet, and we came away I think instinctively, before his concluding prayer to the Blessed Mary, wh might too probably be the saddest and the most awful part of this alarming sermon. The preacher appeared to be considered a man of reputation. He was a monk, I think a Franciscan but the light was imperfect.

Dined with the Glynnes and prepared for a very early departure in the morning from this Circean city.

(Dec. 6.)

Monday Dec. 3. 1838.[7]

Left Naples at 5 with Angrisani's promise that we should sleep at Terracina and arrive at Rome before nightfall on Tuesday. We travelled all night and arrived at Rome between ten and eleven P.M. on Tuesday. About 3

---

[1] Zeuxis, whose 'Helen' was painted from a combination of the graces of five virgins.
[2] 'queen of heaven'.
[3] 'empress of the world'.
[4] 'touch on the bounds of the infinite'.
[5] *Paradiso*, xxxii. 29 ff.; xi. 37 ff.
[6] Instead of 'of'.
[7] Entries from Add MS 44818 D, unless otherwise noted.

hours of this were owing to a broken brace. We dined very well at Mola[1] (Gaetano's) and also found very fair provision at Cisterna.[2] No more Angrisani for me. (On Tuesday we met I think eleven carriages going South.)

An Augustinian monk of the Gesù e Maria[3] was my companion halfway in the coupè. He came at 9 Scudi[4] instead of 12: & the police made him no charge for his passport. He asked me if the river at Capua was the Tiber: & he had lived 3 years in Rome. Perhaps it was more discreditable that I was unable to inform him that it was the Vulturnus.

From Sparanisi[5] to Terracina the whole ride is varied and interesting. Here & there one sees patches of wood like those of Calabria. There is a good deal of oak & on the whole the country looks much less bare than the campagna of Naples with its merely *adjective* poplars. A poplar is among trees like a donkey among animals, not admired or loved, & endured for its use alone.

A Benedictine fellow traveller who appeared to know Sicily well said that S. Niccolo in Catania had probably 60,000 or 70,000 scudi a year. Monte Casino *was* something like this: now 18. The convents in Sicily all *virgin*.

My companion Count Theotoky[6] (Greek) complained of Sir Howard Douglas in the Ionian islands as arbitrary & severe: he talks of raising a Parliamentary discussion. I told him he should go first to C.O. & why.

Tuesday Dec. 4.

I thought myself fortunate in seeing at Genzano[7] a very lovely Raffaelle face, between that of the Madonna della Seggiola & that of the Madonna del Gatto;[8] but rather too broad.

Arriving at Rome between ten and eleven we went to the seven principal hotels before getting a shelter for the night. At length I shared a double bedded room at the Russie[9] with Theotoky & this only was obtained with the promise to remain three nights. I thought well of the house. It is clean & I imagine a trifle lower in price than Serny's and the first houses.

Wednesday Dec. 5.

Saw Lincoln and Mr Goulburn & speculated on the probable duration of the remainder of our holidays. Upon the whole a month here seemed probable and I searched for a lodging accordingly. But very few are to be had for so short a period: the people will not let for less than three & four & at high prices. The demand is immense: many were gone that very day: one

---

[1] Mola di Gaeta, 45 miles NW. of Naples, now Formia.
[2] Small town 42 miles NW. of Formia.
[3] Church and convent of discalced Augustinian Friars on the Corso.
[4] 47s. 10d. (scudo about 5s. 5d.).
[5] Town 24 miles north of Naples.
[6] Ioannes Baptistes, Count Theotokes, 1778–1865, polemicist of Corfu, minister of justice there 1824–7; Greek senator till 1850.
[7] Town 17 miles SW. of Rome.
[8] Madonna of the Chair, of Raphael, in the Pitti at Florence; of Giulio Romano, in the Studio at Naples.
[9] In the Piazza del Popolo.

vanished while I was absent conversing with Mr. Goulburn &c. At last I took a clean looking bird's nest, *al 4to*,[1] at 62 Piazza di Spagna, attracted by the convenient situation, new furniture & bedding, moderate price (only 15 sc.) & apparent respectability of the people.

Dined with the Lincolns (Sir F. Lamb[2] was of the party) & conv. with him afterwards.

Thursday Dec. 6.

Wrote to Glynne—Mr. G.—(I had found nine letters in the Post Office).

Went with Lincoln to Wiseman—to the [English] College Chapel Library and Hall—to several Churches, including the San Luigi de' Francesi[3] which has certain frescoes (v) by Domenichino: and the S.M. della Pace[4] with Raphael's fine fresco (v) of the Sibyls writing prophetically of the Saviour's birth: his prophets above:[5] and Carlo Maratta's Presentation.[6] Also the Sant Agnese, remarkable for its form:[7] the relief Statue of the Saint in the vault below appears very heavily executed.

In the afternoon we went to the Vatican and St. Peters. Mr. Gray[8] told L. that the Laocoon ought, it is supposed, to have the right hand nearer the head as the muscular tension would then in the course of nature be greater. That arm is modern.

It is very remarkable not only how many fine Fauns exist among the remains of ancient sculpture, but that there are so few or no bad ones: in that kind of grosser nature they seem to have had more facility & uniform success.

The happy moment for St Peter's is that which precedes darkness & the closing of the doors: the light through the white windows does not at all blend with the warm and rich masses of the architecture and it requires to be tinctured in default of other means with gloom. I rather believe walking about for a certain time and fixing in the mind the size of each part is after all the best specific for acquiring in a general view from one spot afterwards the size of the whole.

Made up our joint accounts.

Dec. 6.[9]

On reading Sir Sam. Scott's letter yesterday morning I reeled rather than walked away from the Post Office. Anything that is not perfect undoubting confidence appears so ungenerous: and a line from her[10] would I think have done everything, to me at least who am not her judge: but I cannot yet

---

[1] On the fourth floor.

[2] Frederick James *Lamb, 1782–1853, diplomat; ambassador to Vienna 1831–41; cr. Lord Beauvale 1839; succ. his br.* as 3rd Viscount Melbourne 1848.

[3] Near the Pantheon.

[4] Near S. Luigi dei Francesi.

[5] By Timoteo della Vite, called da Urbino, 1469?–1523; from Raphael's drawings.

[6] Maratta's Visitation; Presentation by Baldassare Peruzzi, 1481–1536.

[7] On west side of Piazza Navona; interior in form of Greek Cross.

[8] Probably John Edward *Gray, 1800–75, zoologist.

[9] This entry from Lambeth MS 1424.   [10] His sister Helen.

feel perfectly easy under circumstances so singular: alone, unprotected, in ill health: a foreigner, a Russian foreigner, a frequenter of a watering place, self-attested—and with a difficulty about religion, probably: and Sir S.s. letter is ominously wary and guarded tho' very kind in wishes: there was a time when these & tenfold more circumstances would not have caused me a moment's apprehension and even now surely surely all must be right and in a short period I shall be reviewing with regret and shame this record of my first and most involuntary thoughts.[1]

Friday Dec. 7.

Left my letters. Moved to No 62 Piazza di Spagna. Dined with Mr Goulburn. Read Ulrico e Lida.[2]
Went with L[n.] to my old friend S. Andrea della Valle—to the Minerva: what a sad want of light! Frate Angelico's Annunciation is a most beautiful work in conception and execution: the outlines good: the heads have natural grace as well as holiness: the eyes of both the Angel and the Virgin are appropriately cast down as mindful of that greater presence wherein they stand. (Visited Monsignore Rossi. He saluted me with the double kiss.)[3] The colouring is very agreeable. The intermediate figures detract from the Scriptural fidelity of the piece and also from its effect as estimated by the eye?—Here is also, as [we] were told, a painted crucifix of Giotto, exhibiting the union of the two professions of sculptor and painter. We could not see it accurately.
Thence to the Gesù—where we saw the Pope passing: he looks wonderfully fresh for a man of seventyfour: & heard a Sermon on the Immaculate Conception. The preacher seemed to make the best use of his subject that the case would admit: as Mary was not satisfied with the triumph over original sin, but glorified God in all things & advanced in holiness (he said merits) so be not you content with mere admission into a state of grace but similarly strive to live unto the Lord.

Saturday Dec. 8.

Wrote to Murray. Journal. Giansenismo.[4] Ulrico e Lida.
Overbeck's[5] Studio: little there, but that little good. A Study of a noble picture, which he is to paint for Frankfort:[6] exhibiting the influence of religion on the arts. It seems honourably emulous of Raphael's School of Athens.—With L[n] to divers Studii:[7] closed: saw nothing but Camucinni's

[1] Helen had become engaged at Ems to a twenty-six year old Polish count, Leon Sollohub, whose parents disapproved. Cp. Magnus, 38, and 17 Dec. 38, second entry.
[2] Verse tale by T. Grossi (1837).
[3] These ten words in margin.
[4] Perhaps G. Pedrelli, *Il giansenismo di un secolo* (1835).
[5] Johann Friedrich Overbeck, 1789–1869, creator of German pre-Raphaelitism; lived at Rome from 1810.
[6] For the Städel'sches Institut in Frankfurt am Main.
[7] Of living artists.

Conception in the Cappuccini:[1] which is best seen on a dark day: his weak colouring does not bear an abundant light.

This being the feast of the Immaculate Conception, i.e. the Conception of the Virgin, is kept in Rome much more strictly than the Lord's Day. The reading room[2] was absolutely closed, under penalty according to Monaldini of 50 Scudi, and all Cafès and Restaurants also during the middle of the day. It is rather sad considering the subject of the festival is a fiction & a corruption.

Sunday Dec. 9.

Our chapel very crowded with an attentive congregation.[3] Mr. Hutchinson[4] preached in the morning: Mr Sillery,[5] an Irish clergyman, in the afternoon. The number of carriages is very large: I should think eighty or upwards, & before service begins they form a long line, for a considerable time. Walked with Verney. Read B. & A. Dunn[6]—I am sorry to say a very mischievous book. Dined with L[n] & his lady & saw very singular manifestation of character in his children.

Monday Dec. 10.

Manning arrived with A. Harrison;[7] I sat through the evening with him. Went with L[n] to some shops; to look over the Gesù where the altar of Ignatius is exceedingly fine: and to the Madonna del Popolo, which besides the pictures of soft Pinturicchio and the Carlo Maratta and the fine altar-piece & Statue of Ionas in the Chigi Chapel, contains, close together, probably the three strongest monuments in Italy.[8]

Tuesday. Dec. 11.

Cardinal Fesch's[9] Gallery, Falconieri Palace, with the Verneys. We left

[1] Santa Maria della Concezione, church of the Capuchin monastery on the Piazza Barberini, south of Villa Borghese. Picture of Conception by Lanfranco over high altar destroyed by fire was replaced by that of Gioacchino Bombelli, pupil of Camuccini.

[2] Monaldini's, in the Piazza di Spagna.

[3] Notes on theology, Add MS 44728, ff. 164–5.

[4] James Hutchinson, 1805?–73, of Irchester, Northants, and St. John's College, Oxford; chaplain at Rome 1836–49, rector of Berkhampstead 1851–71.

[5] Perhaps Anthony Sillery, b. 1788 co. Louth. M.A. Trinity College, Dublin, 1826.

[6] Perhaps *Gladstone's term for two Catholic booklets, Thomas *Baddeley's 'Sure Way to find out the True Religion' (ca 1820 etc.) and 'Conversion and Edifying Death of Andrew Dunn' (1826) (reply to notorious Protestant pamphlet 'Conversion and edifying death of A.D.' (1803 etc.)).

[7] Arthur Harrison, 1819?–40, 3rd s. of Benjamin*; then at Christ Church.

[8] S. Maria del Popolo includes several frescoes and a nativity by Pinturicchio, a conception by Maratta, a nativity of the Virgin by Sebastian del Piombo, 1485?–1547, finished by Cecchino Salviati, 1510–63, a statue of Jonah by Lorenzetto, 1490–1541, acting under Raphael's direction; and the fifteenth century tomb of cardinal Cristoforo della Rovere, and those of cardinal Basso and cardinal Ascanio Sforza, both by Andrea Sansovino, sculptor, 1460–1529.

[9] Joseph Fesch, 1763–1839; Napoleon's uncle; abp. of Lyons 1802, to which he left bulk of his collection; cardinal 1803; retired to Rome 1815, while remaining abp.

our cards on a previous day: the Secretary then names a day & hour, the latter usually I believe ten. The rooms are small & the lights bad. Only a small proportion of the Cardinal's pictures are hung: there is a story that they are 30,000. The Flemish rooms are more numerous than the Italian. They seem richest in Rembrandts: & among them is a picture called by Sir Godfrey Kneller of one of the Charles II beauties, which should rather be by Sir Peter Lely?

In the Italian rooms are many Guidos, an early Crucifixion & a small Madonna & Saviour by Raphael: the expressions of the former are very sweet:—Titian's Madonna & Saviour with the Four Doctors: the heads of the Saints are fine, & their figures, the Madonna & Saviour I thought much less elevated and true. There is a picture of Beato Angelico's representing the day of Judgment with many of the visions of Dante's Inferno introduced into it & from this & the painting at Florence in the S.M. Novella we may infer that the poem had exercised a great influence, or at least had assumed a very high rank. And indeed from other signs.—In the Innermost room, which is not large, I counted I think twentytwo pictures of Holy Family's and Presepes.[1] Some of them appear, to me! egregiously misnamed. Here is a copy of a Holy Family of Raphael's by Pierin del Vaga.[2] The original must be between the Madonna of the Gold Finch at Florence, and its *pendant*.[3]

Palazzo Farnese. The noble ceiling with the frescoes of the Caracci, Domenichino, Guido, and some say a figure of Michael Angelo's nearly opposite you on entering, a little to the right—if it deserve epithets of praise in respect of design and effect, exhibits in the choice of its subjects[4] either a state of art, or a domineering influence of the patron,[5] which is miserable and degraded.

Cav. Carta's[6] Studio—awkwardly placed enough among the stables of the Barberini Palace. He is painting Lady Verney. He has a finished oil painting of Santa Rosolia in prayer within the cavern for the liberation of Palermo from the plague. The tone of colouring is neither deep nor warm, but the countenance is very beautiful and holy. Two cherubs are introduced rather watching the saint than as *ministering* spirits sent forth to them who shall be heirs of salvation.[7] Sir H.V's in evg. Mr. Cleaver[8] expounded the 32d Psalm.—Saw Ld. Carnarvon.[9]

---

[1] 'cribs'.

[2] Pietro Bonaccorsi, called del Vaga, 1500–47; copied Michael Angelo and Raphael at Rome.

[3] The pendant to Raphael's Madonna in the Uffizi is his less naturalistic Madonna del Baldachino.

[4] Pagan, supposed to represent the triumph of love.

[5] Cardinal Odoardo Farnese, 1565–1626, 2nd s. of Alexander III, duke of Parma, and of Princess Maria of Portugal.

[6] Natale Carta, Italian portraitist and historical painter, first half of the 19th century. Had worked with Camuccini.

[7] Note on painting, Add MS 44728, ff. 166–9.

[8] Probably William Cleaver, 1786–?, of Christ Church, Oxford; precentor of St. Asaph and sinecure rector of Llanvawr, Merioneth.

[9] Henry John George *Herbert, 1800–49; 3rd earl of Carnarvon 1823; Eton and Christ Church, Oxford; tory M.P. for Wootton Bassett, 1831–2.

Wednesday. Dec. 12.

Took Manning to Wiseman's where I met Sir C. Wolseley[1] and borrowed the 'Tracts for the Times' to get an idea of the Breviary.[2] W. says with some inaccuracies it is on the whole a very good account. Spent much of the afternoon in St. Peter's, looking at the monuments & pictures, hearing the vespers, & endeavouring to catch the effect of the building. The bass voices in the Choir are certainly most magnificent. I am glad to hear that in one department it is not to be reinforced.[3] Read the singular & interesting account of Cardinal Odescalchi's[4] *demission*. It is not difficult to believe him right in concluding such was the Divine Will concerning him.
Dined at Col. Blair's. Mrs. Tollemache's.[5]

Thursday Dec. 13.

At Petrucci's[6] about books on Colleges for Hope: &c. wrote to Lincoln. My Journal in extenso becomes a great nuisance & I think not unlikely to assume an epigrammatic form.—Sad news of a new revolt in Canada.[7] Very few seem to look at that question in its whole breadth.

Afternoon in the Vatican with Manning: we fell in with Mr. Severn & were so fortunate as to go through a considerable part of the statues with him. He condemned the feet of the Mercury *alias* Antinous:[8] pointed out the mark on the head of Laocoon which Canova discovered to have been the point of contact of the right hand: the omission of any sacerdotal characteristics: the eyes not turned towards the sons nor any apparent concern for them: the left thigh & leg as on the whole the finest part of the work: the smallness of the boys' heads as less pardonable than the maturity of their forms, & this common with the ancients. He thinks the Demosthenes nearly the finest statue in the Vatican: & agrees that the helmet seems to pinch the upper part of the head of Minerva Medica too much for the character.

St Peter's afterwards: another ineffectual attempt to see the P. Venturi:[9] & dined at Mr Earle's.

Friday Dec. 14.

At ten with Sir H. Verney & chaperoned by Cardinal Rivarola's[10] Secretary

[1] Sir Charles *Wolseley, 1769–1846, 7th bart. 1817, radical reformer; convert to Rome 1837.
[2] Tract 75, devoted to the Roman Breviary.
[3] Probably refers to castrati; possibly, to decree by Cardinal Ostini, November 1838, favouring masculine voice and Gregorian chant.
[4] Carlo Odescalchi, 1786–1841, resigned the cardinalate 1838 to become a Jesuit.
[5] Unidentified.   [6] A bookseller.
[7] First rebellion of French Canada occurred 1837; second after departure of Lord Durham, November 1838. See *The Times*, 3 December 1838.
[8] The Belvedere Antinous considered by G. B. A. and E. Q. Visconti, *Il Museo Pio Clementino* (1818), to be Mercury.
[9] Giacchino Ventura, 1792–1861; theatine monk famous as an advocate, following Lamennais, of freedom as the nursery of religion.
[10] Agostino Rivarola, 1758–1842; cardinal 1817, President of the Congregation of Waters and Highways.

to the Convent of the Fratelli delle Scuole Cristiane[1] at San Salvadore: where four hundred lads, generally from 7 & 8 to 15 years of age, are educated gratuitously in reading, writing, & arithmetic (up to square & cube root) with dottrina Cristiana & singing hymns, & with *qualche squarcio*[2] of geography & history intermixed, by the priests of the order. They make no use of monitors: are divided into four classes or schools: have tasks, but corporal punishment rare—it is by a strap across the hand. Their running hand is inferior I should think to that of English boys but in the writing books one finds many indications of the Italian talent for form. They are taught to read the *Latin* of the services but it is not explained. The best specimens of penmanship are highly ornamental & embellished with actual drawings of some objects, as *birds*. They attend mass daily: & close with prayer. I thought the sentiments of the *copies* from which they wrote extremely good. Their book of Doctrine explained the creed: the passage they read stated how full Jesus and the Madonna were of divine Grace.—It is impossible not to be struck with the splendid eyes which turn upon one & show like stars in this school. According to Mr Secretary, the system of mutual instruction[3] is prohibited in Rome.—The two best boys in each school were on elevated seats in the corners, but there was no movement or change of places upon a blunder. Verney remarked he had never seen a school so quiet. The masters instead of using the voice had a small instrument with a spring which *clacked*, once when there had been a mistake, twice (I think) when another boy was to go on: and the one summoned was simply indicated by pointing.

S. Agostino:[4] a function, & I could not look at what I came to hunt for: but this Church is the most remarkable I have seen for votive offerings, particularly small hearts in relief, fixed on the walls by thousands or perhaps myriads & stamped P.G.R. meaning I suppose per grazia ricevuta.[5]
At last I hit Padre Venturi and sat an hour & a half; upon most interesting subjects all the while. He began with Canada—colonies—their separation near—the design of Providence to inoculate them with civilisation & then to launch them—the doctrine of Church & State—the evil done to Christianity always from its protectors (I accorded, having of course the Pope among others in my mind)—the function of States in respect to religion—the structure of society in England—the great Revolution effected by the Reform Bill which transferred the power from the Lords to the Commons—the instability of the popular will as a support for the Church even admitting it to be at present favourable—'l'Anglicanismo va cadere—teologicamente è caduto già, quando Ld. Brougham, ministro degli affari Ecclesiastici ha dichiarato nella camera dei Lordi che non avesse mai letto

[1] Brothers of the Christian Schools, institute founded 1679 by St. Jean Baptiste de la Salle, 1651–1719. School near San Salvatore in Lauro on left bank of Tiber opposite Castle of San Angelo, built 1793 by Pius VI; others at Trinità dei Monti and (1828) near Maria dei Monti.
[2] 'a bit'.   [3] The Lancastrian system, rejected by the order.
[4] On the Piazza San Agostino, near Via della Scrofa; famous for fresco by Raphael representing prophet Isaiah with two angels.
[5] 'for grace received'.

i 39 Articoli—perche allora apparve che il sentimento della Camera fosse lo stesso col suo!—in un paese dove si dice tutto, e si ragiona tutto, bisogna esser consequente—la logica sarà più forte del governo—200 anni fa, e il governo manteneva la chiesa—adesso ci sarà la discussione, e non più la forza—ma la Provvidenza non abbandonerà l'Inghilterra, perchè ella ha molte virtù: io spero che viene il tempo quando quel titolo di Difensore della Fede avra la sua verità.'[1] These words he used, very nearly, not continuously, & allowing for blunders. He had been terribly misled upon matters of fact by the partial information which I fancy alone reaches the readers of Rome: thought the Canadians had great grievances, & that their deputations had not been attended to![2] that O'Connell and the R.C.'s had opposed the ministerial Church Rate Bill![3] & the principle of appropriating Church property to secular uses![4] He was much surprised by what I told him respecting the detriment the ministerial party had undergone, & our increase of strength, from their attacks on the Church. He thought all the great movements in England, even the Reform Bill, had been traceable to religious causes: and contended that even the present contest in Spain was religious.—This Padre is evidently a man of great force and great earnestness, & well worth cultivating.

Palazzo Colonna. A Colonna portrait by Holbein[5]—wonderful as compared with all else of his which I have seen—shows the softening & refining influence of Italy even on a formed style?—Paul Veronese's *green* Incognito,[6] characteristic & very fine—Castiglione's robe & vase painting, of an inferior order, but very striking in its own way[7]—a Holy Family of Titian, first manner, in the magnificent saloon. What gross taste is the painting of flowers and putti (yet these are by Carlo Maratta) on mirrors! The *fondo*, so important to a picture, is thus surrendered (at best) to accident, as the mirror must reflect what may happen to be opposite.— A. Caracci's peasant, eating,[8] very powerful. The Luther & Calvin have it appears been improperly so called.[9]

[1] 'Anglicanism will fall—theologically it has already fallen, when Lord Brougham minister of ecclesiastical affairs declared in the House of Lords that he had never read the 39 articles, for then it was clear that the Chamber's feeling was the same as his own!— in a country where everything is said, and everything is discussed, one must be consistent —logic will be stronger than the government—200 years ago the government supported the Church—now there will be discussion, no longer force, but Providence will not abandon England for she has many virtues: I hope the time will come when that title of Defender of the Faith will have its true meaning.'

[2] From the Legislative Assembly of Lower Canada in 1822, 1828, and 1834, to the Colonial Office.

[3] Daniel *O'Connell and other Irish members made common cause with utilitarians and free thinkers in trying to get bill abolishing Church Rate passed, cp. *H* xxii. 397, 1019, 1022.

[4] Clause 147 (ultimately excluded) of the Irish Temporalities Bill, asserting that Church property was at the disposal of Parliament, was supported by *O'Connell and Irish members in alliance with free thinkers and utilitarians, cp. *H* xvi. 1374, 1381; xvii. 1076.

[5] Lorenzo Colonna, count of Amalfi, brother of Oddone Colonna who became Pope Martin V, 1417–31.

[6] 'A Gentleman' with green curtain behind, long green satin robe, and general silver-green effect.

[7] Giovanni Bendetto Castiglione, 1610–65; painting of arms, vases, and trophies.

[8] 'The Bean-Eater'.   [9] In the ante-room; attributed to Titian.

The Baker's Tomb[1] is indeed an antiquarian curiosity. In shape it is an irregular quadrilateral: the sides from the ground, first of massive horizontal blocks: then of pillars and pilasters, vertical, without any intercolumniations: and above a frieze bearing an inscription declaratory of the name & profession, & a cornice with all the operations of the baker's business represented upon it. In the adjoining house of the Custode[2] are the figures of a man & woman in marble reclining together, fragments of a third statue, of ornaments, of weights (one with the mark of a handle, engraved XXX & weighing they say 30 lbs—but where is the handle which must have been included?) of ornaments, a very small agate bottle in the shape of a sepulchral vase, closed & having in it a transparent fluid—the height of this vessel is I think under two inches—& a stone with an inscription as follows:

Fuit Atistia Uxor Mihei
Femina Opituma Veixsit
Quojus corporis reliquias
Quod superant sunt in
Hoc panario.[3]

Dined at Mr. Goulburn's.

Saturday Dec. 15.

Petrucci's. Calls. Visited Severn's Studio: his picture of the scene before the Pantheon[4] is very beautiful: that of Rienzi addressing the people in the Forum[5] promises to be of great interest: he says Bulwer's points are feeble compared with those of the old novelists.[6] He is about beginning the visit of the Maries to the sepulchre[7] and means to follow that by the New Jerusalem descending from Heaven:[8] and in the meantime the Chaining of the Dragon is the great object of interest: a bold effort, a new subject, fierily conceived and executed, particularly I thought as regards the figure of the woman (who is to be taken for the Virgin) and St. John: who is in a green but benignant old age.[9] This picture has caused much jealousy, as

[1] Outside the Porta Maggiore, at junction of Via Labicana and Via Praenestina; just discovered.

[2] 'Watchman'. Bas-relief and stone with epitaph were afterwards affixed to front of tomb.

[3] 'Atistia was my wife, and lived a most excellent woman: what remains of her body is in this bread-basket.'

[4] 'The Roman Ave Maria', a procession after dark (called *Ave Maria* in Rome) such as took place regularly from the various oratories, with the Pantheon (Santa Maria Rotonda) in the background. This picture was commissioned by Nicholas I, then Czarevich, and came to hang in the Imperial Gallery in St. Petersburg.

[5] The scene is on the square of the capitol, dominating the forum.

[6] E. G. E. *Bulwer-Lytton, *Rienzi, the Last of the Tribunes* (1835), i. 50 ff. *Bulwer's being the only novel, reference is perhaps to old chronicles: Bracciano, *Vita di Cola di Rienzo tribuno del popolo romano*, ostensibly from a 15th century MS (1624); Fr. Du Cerceau, S.J., *Conjuration de Nicolas Gabrini dit de Rienzi, tyran de Rome en 1347* (1733); Abbé de Sade, *Mémoires pour la vie de Petrarque*, iii (1764–7), this last the source of Miss *Mitford's tragedy *Rienzi* (1828).

[7] Cp. Matt. xxviii. 1; Mark xvi. 1. [8] Cp. Rev. xxi. 2.

[9] *Severn's picture 'The Infant of the Apocalypse caught up into heaven'; cp. Rev. xii. 5–9.

it is to go to a Chapel in San Paolo, a present from Cardinal Weld[1] to the Pope.

After a dinner at the Trattoria I went again to see the Padre Venturi meaning to stay $\frac{1}{2}$ hour, whereas I staid nearly $2\frac{1}{2}$ hours: I shall now note some of the points of his conversation: & first one of Friday which I omitted, namely that in answer to a question of mine he said he did not believe Napoleon would at the time have been overthrown nor the Pope restored without England.

I asked him respecting a book on Jansenism. He deprecated all books on that subject as unprofitable & tending to revive needless controversies. The real question he said was, which is the true Church. ['] Show me the true Church: to that I give my adhesion & I will spare you all the discussions of particular doctrines. The Russians agree precisely with us in dogma, except as to the Pope—though the Greeks differ as to the Procession of the Spirit— yet the Russians sympathize more with you than with us although they do not concur in the ThirtyNine Articles. The nearer other bodies are in particular opinions, the farther from reunion. A Russian is more difficult to convert, than an atheist: a Greek, than a Turk: *an English Churchman than an English Dissenter*.[2] For where there is nullity, at least we have not positive prejudices to contend against: & nullity is better than pride— though I condemn none in particular. Out of that nothing, God can draw something. But I have good hopes of England: from the complaints of many among you respecting the great increase of the Roman Communion: and also from a certain progression of opinion in the Universities towards us. (WEG. But upon your principle this should render less & not more hopeful?) I regard this as a favourable change within the Church itself although I do not mean that it makes the members of the Church as good subjects for us to operate upon, as the Dissenters. We have also gained much by the removal of all political disqualifications, which indicates a softening of your prejudices against us, & I am certain of the re-entrance of England into the bosom of the Church. When England reenters then will all the rest. As France is *il capo del Cattolicismo*, so England is *il capo del Protestantismo*.[3] From these two countries respectively are derived the leading influences which govern the rest. When England has reentered, both Germany and the United States will follow, and unity in religion will again prevail.'

He said the first demands of Luther were just, but while he talked of reform he meant revenge. That the objects of the English sovereigns when they pretended to be political were in fact religious, & centred in the destruction of the papal power. That the Gunpowder plot was now proved to have been got up by Cecil![4] That the priests who were put to death in the reign

---

[1] Thomas, Cardinal *Weld, 1773–1837, eldest s. of Thomas Weld of Lulworth Castle, founder of Stonyhurst, and of Mary Anne, née Smyth, who m. 2ndly 1778 Thomas Fitz-herbert, 3rdly, 1785, *George, Prince of Wales; m. 1796 (wife d. 1815); priest 1818; cardinal-priest 1830; uncle of Thomas Weld-Blundell who succeeded 1837 to estates of Blundell of Ince. The picture was finally hung in San Paolo fuori la Mura 1838.

[2] 'Churchman' and 'Dissenter' each substituted for the other.

[3] 'the head of Catholicism', 'the head of Protestantism'.

[4] An often recurring tale: cp. S. R. *Gardiner, *What Gunpowder Plot Was* (1897); and *Observer*, 5 November 1967.

of Elisabeth had their life offered them if they would join the English
Church & that the affair of the oath of allegiance was a pretext! That
Charles I was not murdered for religious but for political causes. That the
oath respecting the Roman Church was taken by our Queen in the Coronation service, was to be considered as sanctioned by the English Church, &
was a shame to a civilized nation. That the R.C.'s were perhaps even farther
from the idea of intolerance than the Protestants themselves. That he did
not defend all the Roman proceedings with regard to the events of the
Reformation: what was certain was that those events were most deplorable.
That the Council of Trent was the means of the real reformation of abuses
within the Church: and that *this was the most important & valuable part of
its labours*. He could not see the connection between the attempts of James
II and the Queen's oath: (but this I think he afterwards recognised.) He
thought the Church of England taught the doctrine of private judgement
& yet most illogically claimed the assent of men to her creeds—
which could not be consistent with the idea that each man was to *seek* a
religion in the Bible. There she was more inconsequent than the pure
Protestants.

As to the reading of the Bible he admitted it to be the general *right* of the
members of the Church to resort to it as a means of grace: he denied it to be
their general *duty*. The Government in Rome takes pains *to enable all the
people to read & write: there are not 3000 in the whole of the population who
are unable to do so:* perhaps other governments did not take equal pains:[1]
having made this provision, it left them to procure the Bible for themselves.
That which the Church *did* consider essential was that they should be instructed in religion & of this she took care thro' the priesthood. 'You
strangers do not really know them. You come here to the 'quartiera di
Ginevra',[2] the Piazza di Spagna, in which there is little either of religion or
of morals: you hear some lacquey de place scoff at the priests & you put it
in your journals. Again remember 'voi sempre mettete discorsi intorno alla
religione: i Cattolici mai mettono discorsi, perche credono con una fermezza
che non può muoversi'.'[3]

I told him I was come here with the earnest & main desire of knowing how
the Roman system works: & asked him how I should set about it—he asked
me if I had been to the Conversazioni[4] of Roman society—advised seeing
the nuns administer relief in the hospitals on Sundays & told me when I
might hear a sermon out of our Church hours.

He does not consider the Bishopric of Algiers[5] as a proof of favourable
disposition on the part of Louis Philippe: *thinks religion in France has
benefited greatly by his being reputed an infidel* & by the opposition of the
government: under Napoleon there were in the diocese of Paris at Easter
80,000 tickets of Communion: in 1830 not 20,000. He seemed to think this

[1] Cp. end of 19 Dec. 38.
[2] 'Geneva quarter', where foreigners, especially Protestants, congregated.
[3] 'You always make a lot of talk about religion: Catholics don't talk, but believe with
a firmness that cannot be moved.'
[4] Sodalities of persons living under the same rule, though not under the same roof.
[5] Established 1838, suffragan of abp. of Aix.

singular principle—how different from his own reading of the change of
1829 in England—was peculiar in some degree at least, to France.
He also explained the doctrine of 'invincible ignorance';[1] in the manner
which belongs to a powerful & naturally liberal mind.

I have thus given some points of the Padre's conversation without inter-
spersing in general what I felt called upon to say either in the way of
opinion or of fact: but how does it prove that what they most of all dread
in the Church of England is the adoption of clear definite, and positive
Church principles!
He said also: Observe & consider well, that all your argument against us
is for negatives. (This is true in about the same sense of the argument of
the Jews against the polytheists.)
Verney's in evg—& long conv. with the Prussian Chargè M. de Buch[2] on
English Ecclesiastical politics.

Sunday Dec. 16.

Church at 11 & 3. Mr Hutchinson preached mg: & Mr Hare,[3] Irish, in evg.
If I do not infer too rapidly, the Irish Sermons of today & last Sunday give
me some light as to the scarcely progressive state of the Church in Ireland.

Afterwards went to the Caravita[4] where a sermon is preached between 5
& 6. Ladies are not admitted as Ave Maria is past: & Miss Glynne who went
with Sir S. was obliged to quit. I heard a beautiful sermon: with an argument of this kind. 'L'affetto il più proprio alla natura dell'uomo, è
l'amore.'[5] But this love is fixed on worthy or unworthy objects. Composed
of body and soul, we depend much on the sense & hardly love what we do
not see. Hence man before the Advent had generally forgotten God: the
Jewish nation had fallen often into idolatry: & even the Jewish saints had
desired a fuller manifestation. 'Lord, show me thy face.'[6] To enable us
to love Him, God came in the flesh. To appeal to our deepest affections, he
came, not merely palpable to sense, but as our comparison & our brother.
Enter with me the grotto of Bethlehem—behold that infant—then much
detail on eyes hands &c.—there is your God. What do you desire in the
object of your love? Power? He is omnipotent & the nations one day shall
know it.—& so on. How then can you live in sin, when by so doing you
imbrue your hands in the blood of this your brother and crucify Him
afresh?—I hurried away before this good preacher had quite concluded.
Dined with the Glynnes—read Bible—Tract on the Catholic Services[7]—&
Hook's admirable Sermon at the Visitation.[8]

---

[1] In theology, ignorance produced by failure to realise obligation to seek out the truth,
or by failure to find it when sought.
[2] Ludwig August von Buch, envoy extraordinary and charge d'affaires in Rome.
[3] John David Hare, of Trinity College, Dublin.
[4] First of Roman 'night oratories', where devotions for men took place after sunset,
founded by Fr. Pietro Caravita, S.J., about 1711, near church of St. Ignatius on the Via
del Seminario.
[5] 'The emotion most proper to man, is love.'
[6] Ps. lxxx. B.C.P. 3, 'Shew the light of thy countenance'.
[7] Tract 75 (see 12 Dec. 38).
[8] W. F. *Hook, on Acts vii. 26, at *Longley's visitation (1838).

Monday D. 17.

Letters from young Murray saying his father was to publish me on the 8th: and of more consequence from H.J.G.

Wrote to & saw Rossi. He says it is impossible for me to be present at any trials in the Courts of Cassation & Appeal: they were open to the public three years ago but are now closed.[1] He gave me a printed case, & promised another, & the code. The Government prints the speeches of the advocates & heads of the proceedings for the judges—in case un giudice si distragga oppure s'addormenti, qualcheduni essendo molto vecchj: o che un avvocato sia molto nojoso.[2] After some time to read these documents they meet & pronounce, but not until further opportunity has been given to the advocates on either side to add. In the Court of First Instance three of the four judges must concur, for a sentence of death to be past: and in that of Appeal, four of six. The Court of Cassation regards the forms of the trial. Much time is consumed: the case I have dates the first *sentence* 22 Nov. 1837: the printed speech of the advocate in appeal appears to be dated Aug. 9. 1838—& the sentence itself only extended to three years.

Cramer's[3] concert at one. The instrumental music very good: but Guglielmi[4] & Signora E. Marzi[5] do not give a very high idea of the wealth of Rome in voices, and we are not accustomed to see ladies spit on the floor in the middle of their songs.

At four, heard the newly appointed Bishop of Algiers[6] preach in the San Luigi de' Francesi on 'Come unto me'[7] &c. It was not a reasoned discourse but a simple and affectionate exhortation to turn from the idols of the world to God who is our proper end: mingled with compliments to his audience beyond the measure of Italy and quite out of our English practice.

Met Mr Abeker[8] the Prussian Chaplain at Sir H. Verney's & liked him exceedingly. Much conversation on religion in Prussia—Liturgies old & new—religion in Rome—& the general argument of Church & State, particularly as respects England—& something on literature. He thinks in Prussia Proper, which is better than most parts, $\frac{3}{4}$ of the clergy are believers—the govt. continues sometimes to appoint neologian professors of divinity, if learned men[9]—but in every University their opponents have

---

[1] Cp. 8 Jan. 51.

[2] 'in case a judge lets his mind wander or falls asleep, some of them being very old: or a barrister is very boring.'

[3] Johann Baptist Cramer, 1771–1858; German pianist and music-teacher.

[4] Iacopo Guglielmi, b. 1782, tenor; s. of Pietro Alessandro and younger b. of Pietro Carlo Guglielmi (both composers); sang in theatres of Rome, Parma, Naples, Florence, Bologna, Paris.

[5] Unidentified.

[6] Adolphe Dupuch, bp. of Algiers 1838, res. 1846, d. 1856.

[7] Matt. xi. 28.

[8] Heinrich Abeken, 1809–72, preacher to Prussian legation in Rome 1834–8, assisted Frederick William III of Prussia in ecumenical liturgical projects; became diplomat; wrote original Ems telegram 1870.

[9] E.g. Friedrich Daniel Ernst Schleiermacher, 1768–1834; and Wilhelm Martin Leberecht De Wette, 1780–1843; philosophical interpreters of Christianity and historical critics of the Bible; both on theological faculty of Berlin.

now a stand[1] & the influence of great names is now rather come round[2]—
were the govt. a free one, the difficulties of concurrent endowment would
be developed[3]—violence has been threatened in some cases to force the
Lutherans to comply with the new Liturgy,[4] by provincial authorities, wh
the govt. disapproves—in the case when the military were introduced, law
had been broken—the new Liturgy mainly compiled by the King himself—
too Evangelical for the rationalists, and unpopular on different grounds
with those who had used the Liturgies of the Reformers[5]—not accepted
through any ecclesiastical medium whatever, the clergymen being merely
individuals: except in Westphalia where there is a Presbyterian government & where some liberties were obtained in consⁿ of the acceptance. But
even there private ministers used it before the Synod[6] had consented.
There the people choose the ministers & generally well because they are
well trained: but of the two he seemed to prefer patronage—& a mixture
to either mode unmixed. In Prussia no new sect is paid: & the Anabaptists
who have in some places an organisation,[7] are not paid: but the R.C.'s, the
United Church,[8] & the Reformed.[9] He thinks & hopes the Cologne question[10] will go deeper & will ultimately show the necessity of giving more
freedom to the Protestant Church.[11] It has been very serviceable to the
R.C.s who were thought to be in a depressed state: it has brought out much
zeal & talent among them. They gain on the whole by mixed marriages,
wh are very numerous: otherwise there is little movement of either body.
In the south of Germany some R.C. congregations have become Protestant.
Boos[12] died in the Church: he was a Bavarian: of the school of the admirable
Bp Seider (?):[13] the Pope has a strong party there but the clergy of Bavaria

[1] The universities of Prussia proper, without the recently added Saxon and Rhineland
provinces, were Berlin, Breslau, Greifswald, and Königsberg. At Berlin, for instance,
Ernst Wilhelm Hengstenberg, 1802–69, a fundamentalist, was professor of theology from
1826.

[2] Heinrich Eberhard Gottlob Paulus, 1761–1851, historian and critic, Johann Gottlieb
Fichte, 1762–1814, Friedrich Wilhelm Joseph Schelling, 1775–1854, Georg Wilhelm
Friedrich Hegel, 1770–1831, philosophers; in universities of Jena, Heidelberg, Halle, and
Schleiermacher in Berlin, created tradition of rationalising criticism, arousing reaction
towards orthodoxy after Napoleonic wars: e.g. after the publication of his *Life of Jesus*
(1835) David Friedrich Strauss, 1808–74, lost his tutorship at Tübingen, and never obtained another post.

[3] The Prussian state endowed both a protestant and a catholic theological faculty in
Bonn and Breslau, and a Catholic Academy in Münster. The state also continued to pay
pastors who did not accept the Union declared by King Frederick William III of Reformed (Calvinists) and Lutherans, in 1817, or the Liturgy published by him in 1822
and again in 1824.

[4] The king's *Agende* (liturgy) led to the founding of 'free', i.e. non-state Lutheran
churches in Germany and the U.S.A.

[5] Calvinists and Lutherans.

[6] Ruling body of church government for Calvinists, consisting of lay and ecclesiastical
deputies.

[7] Called Mennonites; in the Marienburger Werder, at the mouth of the Vistula.

[8] United Lutherans and Calvinists, so named since 1817.

[9] Calvinists.   [10] Cp. 15 Aug. 38.

[11] The territorial basis of state control of protestant churches in Prussia had been deranged by acquisition of Catholic Rhineland in 1815; the Protestant churches began to
demand freedom from state control; Catholic action at Cologne gave the example.

[12] Martin Boos, 1762–1825, priest in catholic 'awakening movement' led by Bp. Sailer.

[13] Johann Michael Sailer, 1751–1832, catholic theologian, bp. of Regensburg 1822.

in general are not ultramontane. He laments exceedingly the enslaved state of the Protestant[1] religion: & longs for Bishops who were the primitive governors. He looks for improvement within the R.C. body, rather than proselytism from it.

In Rome they have about 120 Germans—his congregation sometimes reaches 50 or 60, but ordinarily from 12 to 20.—The beggars at the Roman church doors pay the Church for the right of sitting there during the quarant'ore when the Sacrament is exposed! and the bande[2] with white hoods & eye holes[3] *farm* the rights of collecting alms at particular seasons & for specific purposes! This he knows from a well informed Italian. He said an eminent Roman divine had said to Mr Bunsen what Venturi said to me about the return of England to the Church & the rest of Protestantism following it. He knows Venturi's character to be high.

The present ecclesiastical servitude of Prussia has come he thinks from the theory which allows to the state a *veto* upon *all* the acts of the Church. He recognises the distinction between the Church as an endowed Corporation—which case might be met by a very *general* and extrinsic control on the part of the State—and the Church as a body calling continually for fresh endowments from the State, which seems in argument to imply an universal controul or veto.

Dec. 17.[4]

From dearest Helen herself I learn by letter the truth of this startling intelligence:[5] and learning it from herself, I became at once confident that her chosen one is worthy. She speaks of the sacrifices to be made with the strength of a great character but with the pathos of a deeply feeling heart. Poor dear soul—does she know them yet? But I cannot judge for her. At least I cannot but see it is in no selfish spirit but in one of profound affection that she acts: and I have to pray that God may receive his glory and she her peace in this and in all the passages of a life so dear and valuable. I am ashamed of what is written above:[6] nothing so base as want of confidence.

Tuesday Dec. 18

Ch. conv. with Manning. Paper. Quarterly on Milman's Gibbon. Rienzi's life: of a simplicity like O.T. scripture, as here: "in questo tempo paura e tremore assalio li tiranni: la buona gente, come liberata da servitude, si rallegrava".[7]

Visited a German artist's Studio who has been in Sicily. It is singular that

---

[1] Instead of 'church'.

[2] 'gang'.

[3] Confraternity of White Penitents; probably the Archconfraternity of the Papal Standard, as it had many privileges.

[4] This paragraph from Lambeth MS 1424.

[5] Fragment in Magnus, 38.

[6] Lambeth MS entry for 6 Dec. 38.

[7] Re ed. *La Vita di Cola di Rienzo Tribuno del Popol Romano scritta da incerto autore nel secolo decimo quarto* (1828), 67: 'In that time did fear and trembling seize the tyrants; good people, as though freed from servitude, rejoiced.'

one does not see landscape views of places so beautifully situated as Palermo, Messina, & Catania with its gulf & Etna.

Walk with M. Abeken to S.M. Maggiore, where he showed me Platina's[1] curious monument. P was a good man of the 16th Century, biographer of the Popes, thought to sympathise too much with the Reformers:[2] there are three bits of inscription, two in good Latin, one in bad Greek. θαρσον αδελφε· καλως θνησκων παλιν φυετας.[3] The Latin which precedes is curious: & this or nearly. 'Quisquis es, si pius, Platinam & suos ne vexes: angustè jacent, et soli volunt esse.'[4]

Observe the old part of the exterior of this Church. It is supposed to be the work of Pope Liberius.[5] Benedict's inscription on the portico is a practical falsehood.[6]

S. Antonio has a marble gate of the 12th century, with the round arch.[7] The pointed arch was then used by the Normans, but not in Rome. This gate is beautiful. We went to a cypress ring in the garden of the Villa Negroni, along what Bunsen has determined to be the *agger* of Servius: it is the highest spot on this side of Rome, and commands delightfully the city, the campagna, and the hills.[8] In a mere garden road Bunsen recog-

[1] Bartolomeo Sacchi, called Platina, 1421–81, humanist; imprisoned, 1464–71, by pope Paul II; favoured from 1471 by pope Sixtus IV, director of Vatican Library 1475.

[2] *Liber de vita Christe ac omnium pontificum* (1474).

[3] 'Be of good cheer, brother; dying nobly you live again.' Correct Greek: θαρσει αδελφι· καλως θανων παλινφυη.

[4] 'Whoever you be, if you have any piety vex not Platina nor his kin: here they lie in narrow room, and would be alone': preceded by 'Xysti IV anno VIII Stephano qui vixit An. XXVII Men. VIII D. XII Platyna Fratri Benemerenti Posuit Sibique Ac Posteris', 'In the eighth year of Xystus IV Platyna set up this stone to his deserving brother Stephen who lived 27 years, eight months, 12 days, to himself and his posterity.'

[5] Pope 352–66.

[6]

'Benedicto XIV. Pont. Max.
Quod Liberianae Basilicae Lacunari Restauraverit
  De Integro Pavimentum Refecerit
Columnis ad veram Formam Redactis et expolitis
Nova Capitula Imposuerit Novas Bases Subiecerit
  Plasticum Opus omne inauraverit
Picturis Deterso Situ Venustatem Restituerit
  Absidem exornaverit
Chorum Novis Subsellis Instruxerit
Sacram Denique Aedem Antea Inconditam
Ad Elegentiam Partiumque Consensum Revocaverit
  Capitulum et Canonici Beneficentissimo Principi
    Anno Jubliei MDCCL. PP.'

'To Benedict XIV, Pope, most beneficent pastor of pastors because he repaired the ceiling of the Liberian Basilica, entirely renewed its pavement, restored their true form to the columns, polished them, gave them new capitals and new bases, gilded all the mouldings, cleaned the pictures and restored their beauty, adorned the apse, furnished the choir with new stalls; in short gave back to the sacred temple, before rude and uncouth, elegance and harmony of parts, the chapter and canons [record their gratitude] Year of the Jubilee, 1750.' Several other popes had adorned the church; Benedict XIV gave it a façade in front of the portico, and the restoration detailed in the inscription.

[7] Romanesque portal of San Antonio Abate, on Piazza Santa Maria Maggiore; built 1260.

[8] A bank some 50 ft. broad and 30 ft. high runs across the wide grounds of the Villa Negroni; rising to the highest spot in old Rome, marked by a circle of cedars and cypresses. Cp. Platner, J. Bunsen, Gerhard and Rostell, *Beschreibung der Stadt Rom* (1830), 641 ff. and iii (1838) pt. 2, 349 ff. Servius Tullius, king of Rome 578–535 B.C., built a wall enclosing the Palatine, Quirinal, Viminal, and Esquiline.

nises one of the Roman viæ.[1]—The burning under Henry IV & others have been, says Abeken, the great causes of the reduction of the city to ruins:[2] but in part also the law which made the destruction of a man's house one of the legal punishments of a criminal & which Rienzi[3] repealed.

San Luigi. The Bp[4] good & pious but rather wanted a definite subject which he promised tomorrow—the *unity* of religion. One observes in his style how low a ground French preaching is obliged to take, not of principle, but in estimating the predispositions of the audience: a continual *apology for truth*.

Wednesday, Dec. 19.

Rienzi. Quarterly on Lister.[5] Scottish Canons.[6] writing letters home. Evening in part with Manning.

Went with him to S.M. Maggiore: which under all its incrustations is very interesting. I was also at Severn's studio again to take Ld Carnarvon & Glynne to see his picture. Then S. Luigi where we had the promised sermon on religion as one, but the Bishop feared either his subject or his audience or both: he declined any examination of other claims, but recited in a summary form the history of Christianity including the reestablishment of the Popedom after the shock of the French Revolution, relying on these as evidences sufficient for his purpose.

Severn astounded at Venturi's report on Roman popular Education: quite contrary to his experience. He speaks of great ferocity inherent in the national character: lately he saw two women carried to prison of whom one brandished in triumph a large handful of hair as she passed along.

Thursday Dec. 20.

At ten, went with the G's to the S.M. sopra Minerva[7]—one of few Roman churches with Gothic arches in the nave—to Sant' Andrea—which I am never weary of admiring—and to the Chiesa Nuova[8] which contains a good deal though not of the first interest. In the Church three Rubenses (Tribune), two Baroccios in chapels, and a mosaic from Guido: in adjoining apartments a Guercino and a Guido the first of S. Fil. Neri praying, the second a Madonna & Infant Saviour: with the relics of Saint Philip Neri,

[1] The road running east from the site of the Porta Viminalis in the wall of Servius to the closed gate of the Praetorian camp. Cp. ibid. i. 642.

[2] Henry IV, 1050–1106, Emperor, destroyed the Leonine (now Vatican) city in 1084 before retreating north; the rest of the city was fired and sacked immediately after by Robert Guiscard.

[3] Eleven laws were promulgated by Rienzo in the Capitol, of which the third was: 'that no house of Rome be thrown down for any reason, but be given to the Commune'. *Vita di Cola di Rienzo*, 46.

[4] Of Algiers.

[5] On *Clarendon.

[6] 'The Code of Canons of the Episcopal Church in Scotland drawn up and enacted by an Ecclesiastical Synod holden for that purpose in Edinburgh . . . in the year . . . 1838.'

[7] Near the Pantheon, the only Gothic church in Rome.

[8] Santa Maria in Vallicella, built by St. Philip Neri, 1515–95.

his shoes, his clothes, his drawers or case, his bed & bedding which they say does not waste or fail. In the Sacristy is a cieling painted by Pietro da Cortona[1] which exhibits a most curious ocular deception. As one moves across the doorway, the cross in the picture appears to move with or rather to the eye: and its elevation is reversed according as it is viewed from the one end or the other.—Engl. College.

Vatican. Scarcely reached the pictures when the hour of closing was announced. The time allowed for viewing them is according to one of the Swiss guards from one to half past two! twice a week during the season, and once during the rest of the year. And entrance by the direct door is not allowed: a walk through the galleries of I should think near a mile is required in consequence.

Found in the long Statue gallery a new object of admiration in the head of a Niobis (daughter of Niobe).

San Luigi again. The Bishop preached on Tu es Petrus:[2] & had some good points on the necessity of a Divine source for the Sacramental grace & on holding to the Apostles: on the Roman claim he did not much particularise.

Dined at Mr Wyvill's.[3]

Friday Dec 21.

The shortest day once more. This like Advent Sunday, & my birthday (happening to fall on Dec. 29) seem intended to revive more frequently the thought of the flight of the years.—The difference at evening between this and England is very observable.

Calls: discussion of our plans for return with the Glynnes & Mr Goulburn. Called on Mr Abeken & walked with him & Stirling[4] to the vineyards on the Aventine which give fine views of the surrounding ground and ruins: the masses of the Cesars' palace,[5] and the breadth of the Coliseum. Back by the Arch of Constantine, with its discordant sculptures, the Church of St. Cosmo & Damian, with its mosaic of 6th Cent.[6]—(the vespers for the people are a litany invoking a string of saints, & they close with an Elevation—A. said, would the words were other than they are, it would be more pleasing to me than a thousand sermons—) & the Forum of Augustus, once temple of Mars Ultor,[7] where the wall of the cella remains behind three fine pillars, & terminates against the gigantic wall with which he surrounded his Forum.

---

[1] Pietro Berrettini, called da Cortona, 1596–1669.

[2] Matt. xvi. 18: the text inscribed round the inside of the dome of St. Peter's.

[3] Probably Marmaduke Wyvill, 1791–1872, of Constable, Burton, Yorkshire, liberal M.P. for Richmond, Yorkshire, 1847–65 and 1866–8.

[4] See A. K. Tuell, John *Sterling, a Representative Victorian (1941), 53, for *Sterling's account of this meeting.

[5] Tremendous ruins on Palatine hill of the Palace of the Caesars, constantly enlarged from Augustus to Nero.

[6] In the Forum, with mosaic of the Saviour and his Apostles over the Tribune.

[7] Part of the wall of the forum of Augustus was the temple of Mars Ultor, which he built to commemorate his revenge on Caesar's murderers.

Dined with the Glynnes. Mrs. Caldwell.[1] Abeken is indeed a man worth knowing alike in a religious & an intellectual & a social sense.

Saturday Dec. 22.

At ten, to St John Lateran. An ordination was in progress. The laying on of hands is not attended with an address to each individual, and I am told is repeated three times: but when the scarf ([blank])[2] is placed over the shoulders there is an address 'accipe jugum Domini'[3] &c. & when the priestly garb is laid then 'accipe vestem sacerdotalem'[4] &c. The hands are also touched, we were told with oil & then bound with a napkin.

One of the newly ordained deacons had his face covered with his hands for some time. When he removed them the eyes remained closed, as if to secure the undivided enjoyment of the vision within, light seemed to rest upon his countenance, his arms and hands lay extended as if in perfect unconsciousness, and his whole appearance beautifully betokened a happy and a holy spirit.

This solemn rite like that of Baptism loses in impressiveness from the arbitrary additions of Rome: yet is their case better than that of the mutilated Eucharist.[5]

The Pietà of Bernini below the Corsini Chapel[6] has this great advantage over the similar work of Michael Angelo in St Peter's, that by resting the head only instead of the entire figure on the knee of the Virgin, the artist has avoided all the three objectionable alternatives, of too much enlarging the Virgin's figure, of too much contracting that of the Saviour, or presenting a disproportion between the supporting and the supported.

This Church has five aisles and the Basilican form. It is the Cathedral of Rome. The Baptistery is much disfigured: when old and new are mingled in this city there never seems any care to make them harmonise, or any subordination of the new to the old—and as in the architecture of their still remaining primitive Churches, so it is, but too precisely, in their religion.

Visited San Stefano:[7] very interesting. Here are found the portico of four pillars before the outer wall: the court with a portico within that wall: the Church oblong with the oval tribuna projected from the further end: to which is added an (I suppose) innovation on the old form of the Basilica in two minor recesses to the right and left: the Bishop's chair in the centre of the tribune: those of the priests right and left: before the altar an oblong

---

[1] Probably wife of H. B. Caldwell.

[2] *Stola*, 'stole'.

[3] 'Receive the yoke of the Lord.'

[4] 'receive the priestly garment.'

[5] In one kind.

[6] First chapel opening from the left aisle as one enters the basilica: in its crypt is Pieta (1727) of Antonio Montauti, sculptor and architect, d. *ca.* 1740; perhaps from the design of Bernini.

[7] 'Clemento' pencilled above. The church of San Clemente, between the Lateran and the Coliseum, is a fourth-century church of basilican form said to be on the site of St. Paul's helper's house. (Phil. iv. 3.)

35—II.

inclosure (for the inferior clergy) and a pulpit on one side, a reading with a praying desk on the other. This oblong is of the 9th century, I believe. Over the altar rise four pillars, on them an architrave supporting a square of small low pillars quite out of proportion with the first, & from them a canopy. Here also are wellknown frescoes of Masaccio.[1] This outline is from memory & must be very inaccurate.[2] Built *before* the 5th Cent. 417. The restorations are sadly out of keeping.

Hence to San Pietro in Vincoli. The nave is very broad: hence the effect of size is realised in a remarkable degree. The date is 442 (Vasi).[3] The Liberation of St Peter by Domenichino appeared to me (considering the artist) singularly thin & weak in colouring and the effect which belongs to it. The Moses is astonishing: that it is not pleasurable, is not necessarily a reproach: but in this case I think the dissatisfaction arises from the conception being lower than the idea, or to come out of Coleridge, from the inferiority of the conception of the statue to the representation of the character. The smallness of the arches which join the tall fluted columns also diminishes from the effect of this striking Church. Here we have the Basilican form, and the seat of the Bishop in the bisecting point of the outer line of the tribune: of white marble, but made before the wisdom of men had been directed to the science & art of making easy chairs.

Spent the evening with Sterling & his friend Dr Calvert.[4] On Germanism— Oxfordism—Cathedrals. Practical conscience & practical energy, according to his experience, are the distinctions of Englishmen. Insularity produced commerce: commerce, political freedom: political freedom, the development of personal energies.—He leans to the creed of intellectual aristocracy.

Sunday Dec. 23.

Mr Cleaver, morning: "transparently good", as Manning said. Mr Hutchinson aft.—Caravita. A good sermon on purity: but the argument was rather far fetched: it was supported only by the case of the Virgin Mary, & our Saviour's never having been called impure. He spoke of Henry VIII and Luther, and somewhat strongly said that the former "si fece capo di una *setta diabolica*"[5]—because the Vicar of Christ would not allow him to put away his lawful wife! Read Pusey. Tea with the G.s. Heard there an excellent sermon of Melvill's.[6] So many sermons heard seem to require an apology: my eyes are the reason.

Monday. Christmas Eve.

Slight facts are sometimes very characteristic: and I note accordingly that

---

[1] Tommaso di ser Giovanni di Mone, called Masaccio, 1401–28 or 29, painter.

[2] Here appears a pencil plan of the church.

[3] Giuseppe Agostino Vasi, eighteenth-century engraver who produced illustrated guides to Rome.

[4] John Mitchinson Calvert, 1803?–42, of Crosthwaite, Cumberland; at Oriel; M.D. 1831; like *Sterling, consumptive, and his companion since their meeting in Madeira in the previous winter.

[5] 'made himself the head of a diabolical sect'.

[6] Two of *Melvill's sermons were in print (1833–8).

in the late frost I saw from the Vatican a number of workmen levelling a piece of ground immediately under the windows, who (even those wheeling barrow-loads of soil) were working in their cloaks.

Found the Vatican[1] closed to the public until Jan. 3. Went to the inscriptions:[2] how much might be made of them! & to the Loggia[3] which seems to be going very rapidly to decay. It remarkably displays the wealth of Scripture in subjects for art. An old & a young peasant were looking at these paintings apparently with much delight. The hand of Giulio Romano[4] & his style seem to have predominated in the work.

I went into St Peter's where Mr Macaulay,[5] whose acquaintance I might be said to possess *de jure*, came & conversed for some time. Vespers were performed here in great state before the Pope: it is sad that in these great services there is little of the appearance of devotion. Hardly any books of the vespers: may one hope that the cardinals & canons know the Psalms by heart.

Dr Wiseman this evening kindly gave me a lesson in the Missal, as I am anxious to understand & follow the service.

At nine went with Lady Brabazon & the G.s to the Sistine Chapel where the first Christmas mass is performed before the Pope: in other Churches it is not until midnight, & there is a great concourse of people. The Chapel was dark & lowering above: the attendance within the bar not very large & again few or no books though matins were sung before mass. All was over about a quarter past eleven. There is a strange & fearful interest about these things. I dare not conjecture whether the present system will or will not live long. but I can at least believe that nothing less than a wisdom most Divine can separate & discharge the evil & the good which are so subtly combined in it. Tea afterwards at Lady Brabazon's, & home late. Wrote to Kinnaird. Wrote to Lincoln.

Tuesday Christmas Day.

Our congregation in the morning suffered by 150 or 200, partly from the weather, rainy & out of harmony with the day: partly from the high mass at St. Peter's before the Pope which begins at nine A.M.—Mr Hutchinson preached: we had no afternoon service. Dined with the Ellisons.[6] This day even the cafès were shut in the morning at breakfast time & I went a begging to Manning.

Wednesday Dec. 26. St Stephen's day.

The Sistine had a mass and Latin service in the morning, to which I did not go. M. has been regretting much that these days are not observed in

---

[1] Vatican Museum.   [2] In Capitoline Museum.
[3] In the Vatican. Cp. 4 Apr. 32.
[4] Giulio di Pietro de Gianuzzi Pippi called Romano, painter, architect and engineer, 1499–1546. Painted here History of Adam and Eve; of Noah; Joseph; Moses, and the New Testament subjects.
[5] See G. O. *Trevelyan, *Macaulay, ii. 41.
[6] Cuthbert Ellison, m. 1804 Isabella Grace Ibbetson.

our Chapel: particularly with so many of our Clergy in Rome—supposed not fewer than 25 or 30.

Wrote to J.N.G. & Col. Verner.[1] Tea at Lady Verney's—afterwards at Lady Brabazon's.—Today I had a search with Mr Goulburn for the steamers, which do not promise to lie very conveniently. We visited Gibson's and Wyatt's studio. What hours artists must lose under these inflictions, and in these very short days too. It seems impossible to conceive or wish for anything more chaste than Wyatt's execution: Gibson's male figures were liked better, I thought with reason, than his females. Both labour under the defect of poverty of subjects, at least they are deficient in interest, because without a soul.

In conversing about the gold which he has placed on the heads of the Psyche group, and on the wings of the Zephyrs,[2] G[ibson] seemed to admit that the ancients did not use ornaments upon their statues excepting in the case of gods and goddesses: and that in these cases it might have been because the artist was not free to follow altogether his ideal form, but had also to produce an object such as should attract the veneration of the mass of the people: & thus approximate a little to the too often gaudy & tawdry images of the R.C. Churches of the present day.

Thursday Dec. 27. St John's day.

At ten, with the G[lynne]s to St John Lateran, where I heard part of the chanting of a mass by the Pope's choir to great advantage: standing immediately behind them I could better appreciate their power and precision. The music was likewise beautiful: between the common operatic, and the extreme severity of the Sistine style. A sermon was preached: all I could catch from a weak & distant voice seemed good: but it was little.

In the Ara Celi Church[3] I saw the Presepe, with a plate of alms chiefly copper before it & ten or fifteen peasants kneeling. At the door, within the porch, were persons selling very ungainly coloured prints of the infant Saviour.

The Presepe is thus formed: on the ground of one of the side recesses of the Church, a kind of basket (apparently) filled with hay, on this a napkin, and the wooden image of a baby decked in silver tinsel with a crown: the Virgin kneeling beside, dressed in silver & colours, but without a crown. An image of a lamb with the feet tied, & several baskets of actual oranges and apples, representing I suppose the gifts, and eight or ten figures who are to be taken for the magi and others present. Above, are a receding series of scenes with the country view for a background and in front a sort of grotto roof, while choirs of angels and painful to add the aged figures which dares to mean the Father himself, look downwards on the scene.

Evening with Manning: on Church matters & that large circle which lies around them.

Church St John L. I also visited the Santa Croce: Pinturicchio's frescoes

[1] Thomas Verner, 1774–1853, courtier; lieut-col. Antrim Militia.
[2] Psyche carried by Zephyrs, exhibited Royal Academy 1827.
[3] On the Capitol.

have been in part retouched: some beautiful heads. The Church is of the Basilican form & has a sort of elliptical porch with double columns. There are fine ancient columns along each side of the nave.)

(Ventura as I recollect intimated by holding up his fingers (instead of the word money in the posture of a table[?]) that the Anglican Church would easily be reconciled to the Roman, but for pecuniary considerations: a thought unworthy enough of such a man.

He said St Basil compared the Scripture to an apothecary's shop, containing drugs for every kind of disease, but requiring a distributor: 'e quella comparazione è *bellissima*!'[1] This shows his notion of reading the Scripture pretty clearly.

Friday Dec 28.

Papers & reading in mg.[2] Walked with Mr Ellison to S Maria e S. Francesca[3] in the forum: an ancient mosaic pavement:[4] and in the cross two old pictures[5] one of which in particular from the softness & character in general of the heads looked like Pinturicchio. S. Giovanni e Paolo:[6] a convent of 50 Passionists,[7] in the Celian,[8] commanding good views of the surrounding hills and ruins as well as of the city & towards the mountains.

This is a missionary order founded under Clement XIV[9] by way of substitute for the Jesuits. The founder a S. Paolo received the habits, as the conducting brother told us, from the arch-angel Gabriel—or Michael. He thought the Russians did not believe in the Holy Ghost. To this convent young men of family, priests, & even bishops, are sent to do penance: instead of going as formerly to S. Angelo, which is a prison. A converted Pole is now here, under voluntary mortification & offering prayer for the conversion of his mother.—This brother thought that the Russians did not believe in the existence of the Holy Ghost.

In the Church was a presepe without an infant figure—thus he told us, they represent symbolically the flight of our Lord into Egypt—but the figures of Mary & Joseph were left behind!

Went to Hofgartens in the Macelli,[10] whose bronzes ought to be seen for the beauty of their execution, though the prices render them very inaccessible. A Laocoon, the principle figure perhaps 14 inches in length,

---

[1] 'and that is a very fine comparison!' Cp. Migne, *PL*, ciii. 685.
[2] Note on church history, Add MS 44728, f. 171.
[3] Santa Maria Nova, or Santa Francesca Romana.
[4] Ninth century.
[5] Over the high altar ancient image of the Madonna said to be brought by the crusader Angleo Frangipani from Troy to Rome *ca.* 1100. On the door of the sacristy Madonna with four saints by Ibi Sinibaldo *ca.* 1475–*ca.* 1550, pupil of Perugino.
[6] Fifth century church near the Coliseum.
[7] Congregation of discalced clerks of the most Holy Cross and Passion of Our Lord Jesus Christ, founded by Paul Francis Danei (St. Paul of the Cross) 1694–1775.
[8] On SE. side of Rome.
[9] Lorenzo Ganganelli, 1705–74, pope 1769–74; confirmed rule and approved institute of the Passionists, 1769; presented this church to them.
[10] 72 Via due Macelli.

170 scudi. An arch of Constantine, perhaps 24 in. high, 700 scudi. A shepherd from that in the Capitol, of the size of the original, 420 scudi (I think). Dying gladiator for 12 in. figure, 35 sc. G. Bologna's[1] Mercury a little smaller 30 sc. But these are real & very interesting representations. Dined at Mr Earle's.

Saturday. Dec 29.

English College at 10: mass before the Cardinals, with the Pope's choir. Dr Wiseman kindly placed Manning, Harrison, & me, behind the Cardinals' bench, and one of his students, Mr Grant,[2] by us, to assist us in following the service of the Mass, with the parts of which I am beginning to acquire a little acquaintance. There were seven cardinals, I think, present: two came in the midst of the service and caused a great stir, and from their speaking, their in hardly any instance using books, their appearing in some cases to be reciting something other than the service I suppose the breviary, and their general manner, I am confirmed in the idea that the mass implies & carries less of active mental participation than the English Liturgy: in conformity with the simple observation of two Neapolitans which I have named in the journal of a former day.[3] With Manning by the Ponte Rotto to Abeken's & a conv. on Animal Magnetism & the Sister Emmerich:[4] he believes that these wounds might be produced by a power in the mind: I cannot help thinking it is more simple & more rational to refer to supernatural agency.

Went with Capt. Goulburn[5] to the Church of the Capuchins; which has a showy & soft painting over the altar by Camuccini of the Conception: this should surely have been a prohibited subject.—Pietro da Cortona: Ananias restoring the sight of St Paul.[6]

Guido—St Michael slaying the devil: the figure of the archangel is a compound, if one must speak rashly, of a dancer and a cavalier, and wants the dignity and depth suited to such a conception: it is not high enough for a St. George, me jud. Domenichino—St. Francis in extasy supported by an angel, a cold painting—and St. Francis in extasy, without the angel, a much damaged but most beautiful fresco, expressing to the life the earnest heavenward longings of a holy soul.—

Hence to Bienaimé's Studio:[7] where I chiefly observed the (reclining) Bacchante—the Diana—the Telemachus—and the Innocence. In all we seem to have graceful chaste and firm execution, with liveliness of imagination: the first figure could hardly be called chaste in conception? The sculptor was executing a figure of Andromeda chained to the rock, the price of

[1] Giovanni Bologna, sculptor, 1524–1608.
[2] Thomas *Grant, 1816 70, pro-rector of English College 1844; first bp. of Southwark 1851.
[3] Cp. 25 Nov. 38.
[4] Anna Catarina Emmerich, 1774–1824, Augustinian nun; stigmatic and ecstatic.
[5] Edward Goulburn, 1816–87, 2nd s. of Henry*, captain, later colonel, Grenadier Guards.
[6] Acts ix. 17.
[7] Luigi Bienaimé, 1795–1878; Italian sculptor, pupil of Thorwaldsen.

which (less than life) is to be 350 louis. Conv. with Manning. Tea with the G.s.—Dublin Rev. on Ap[ostolica]l succession.[1] Finished skimming Bunsen's Forum,[2] which I have by no means duly excavated.

My twentyninth birthday: how solemnly this clock strikes.

Sunday. Dec. 30.

Chapel mg & aft. Mr Hutchinson, & Mr Ottley.[3] Though we have no music & few of the externals of a Church, we have two compensations: the first, in general and stirring responses: the second, we are really all together like brethren, not like sheep of different owners in different pens.

Caravita at 5½. A familiar table Sermon[4]—on the difference between fearing relapse into sin, & the desire to avoid such: & on culpable ignorance. The former was illustrated by a game at cards, in which the player hopes earnestly to win, yet may fear to lose: but he does all he can to prevent losing, by attention to the game, for I conclude said the preacher that at cards you do not go to sleep, *alla predica forse*.[5]

He divided culpable ignorance, scholastically I suppose, into

1. temeraria.[6]   where natural sense ought to supply the requisite knowledge.
2. concomitante[7]—where intrinsic sources of information are open & are not applied to.
3. consequente.   a. diretta—called supina—
                  b. indiretta—called affettata.[8]
                  where there is a suspicion that we may be doing wrong, & that suspicion is not examined.

These he illustrated by stories of a countryman who not wishing to keep the vigils and feasts never attended his parish church in order that he might not hear them announced: and of a boy who would not learn the letter A, because that would lead to the whole alphabet, & so to writing & mathematics.

Tea with the G.s—a sermon of Melvills.

Monday Dec. 31.

At 10¼ to S. Silvestro in Capite:[9] a Messa Cantata with a band: nearly the entire interior of the Church was covered with hangings. One Cardinal attended. The bowing of the knee so constantly repeated before him as before the altar, might offend, one should think, even those to whom the latter practice does not appear faulty.

Barberini palace: where we met Sterling. The Cenci portrait[10] does not give

---

[1] v. 285 (October 1838).   [2] C. C. J. Bunsen, *Le Forum Romanum expliqué* (1835).
[3] Lawrence Ottley, 1808–61, at Trinity, Cambridge; vicar of Acton, Suffolk 1837–50; rector of Ripon 1850.
[4] One with an orderly arrangement of particulars.
[5] 'perhaps at the sermon'.
[6] 'rash'.   [7] 'concomitant'.
[8] 'consequent', 'direct', 'gross', 'indirect', 'affected'.
[9] On the Piazza di San Silvestro, east of the Corso.   [10] Cp. 4 June 32.

the idea of a character capable of very stern resolution under any circumstances. In intellect it is not deficient: & the sweetness is exquisite. If genuine it must have been painted early in Guido's life?

Albert Durer's 'Christ with the doctors': wonderful force in heads, hands, and books. Several appear to be plying at once the Youth in whom all wisdom was hidden.

Raphael's Fornarina:[1] how brilliant in execution: how unworthy in conception, of a mind in which pure visions must have dwelt so often & so long.—If there be positive indelicacy in this picture, is it not increased by the hand holding the garment on the breast?

Titian's slave—surely a lady: the flesh not in his highest character for excellence—

Domenichino's Vision of God to Adam & Eve: the figure, which means the Almighty, very bold and grand: taken according to S[terling] from M. Angelo on the vault of the Sistine.

Francesco Francia,[2] a holy family: retouched? Gian Bellini, a fine Virgin and Child.

Church of the Gesù at 2¾ to hear the Te Deum on the close of the year:[3] it was chanted alternately by choir and people. Some of the other music was very fine: but high voices are tolerated here from which the melody has utterly departed, & which would not be borne even in England.

For an hour or more the three organs played alternately pieces of music most thoroughly operatic, & often consisting of prelude & air.

At the elevation of the host a man from behind touched G. and myself rather sharply, pointed to what was doing, & said, perchè non s'inginocchiano?[4] we remained as we were without taking any notice—sitting, as (for my part at least) I had heard standing was more disagreeable to them as more conspicuous—he then said loudly so as to be heard around him— 'questi non sono Cristiani—non sono Cristiani questi; sono Inglesi'.[5]— Noone else appeared to take any notice.—I regret much to give offence, especially in such a place, by omission or commission: & had I deemed such a thing likely would have kept away: it is the first time I have heard of it here.[6]

Evening at Mr Goulburn's. I find the Times of 19th has an article on my book.[7] Dublin Review—Ventura—Missal. Bp. Andrewes.[8]

---

[1] 'Baker-girl'.
[2] Francesco di Marco Raibolini, 1450–1517, goldsmith, historical painter, engraver.
[3] He was with the Glynnes: Cp. Battiscombe, 25.
[4] 'Why don't you kneel?'
[5] 'These people are not Christians—these people are not Christians; they are English.'
[6] Notes on the Church, Add MS 44728, ff. 172–3.
[7] Long, strongly favourable leader.
[8] Probably *Tracts for the Times* 88, 'The Greek Devotions of Bishop *Andrews, translated and arranged' by *Newman. Lancelot *Andrewes, 1555–1626; bp. of Chichester, of Ely and of Winchester, preacher and high-churchman.

Tuesday Jan 1. 1839.

After visiting Manning on a matter of interest, went to S. Andrea della Valle—Messa Cantata, and a sermon by the Padre Lojacomo.[1]

As respects the first I seem now to comprehend sufficiently the Mass, as the principal, ordinary, & obligatory R.C. service for the people in general, to compare it in respect of worship with that of the Anglican Church: whose members ought to realise far more of the high privilege of Christian prayer. In the 'et cum spiritu tuo',[2] the Roman congregations appear to bid a kind of farewell to the priest: they do not so much as attempt, if one can judge from signs, to accompany of the priest through the prayers which he recites inaudibly: I should almost say it is impossible really to *pray* those prayers in the time he takes, considering what prayer really is—at all events one sees that parts of the service itself in their very language do not suppose or admit the active participation of the hearers: but as he offers a sacrifice, and offers it especially for the '*circumstantes*'[3] (see Canon of the Mass) they are thus supposed to receive a benefit by presence, independent of any real fulfilment of the high duty which brings them together.

If further evidence be wanting as to the idea of the Mass, do we not find it in the appointment of the choir to chant *other words* wholly different, while the priest is reciting the greater part of the service? of course they are not intended to occupy the people, and if they do so then manifestly they cannot be praying with the priest.

The sermon was on 'Dominus diligit misericordiam & judicium: misericordia Domini plena est terra'[4]—a very Christian exposition of the love of God illustrated by that of David for Absalom who w^d not have his son slain even when in rebellion:[5] & by the parable of the lost piece of silver[6] and others, with the exhortation to act in conformity with the drawings of this Divine Love—& an enumeration of the (ordinary) blessings of the past year, including the suspension of those lightnings from heaven wh might well consume us for our sins.

Spada Palace.[7] Of the bassi rilievi, eight in all, two seemed exceedingly fine, the Pasiphae & Minotaur, & another of warriors & a child strangled by a serpent, for which the custode would give me no better name than Archimore.[8] Could this be Alcmæon[9]—I am sadly at fault.

---

[1] Unidentified.

[2] 'and with thy spirit', response to the priests's 'the Lord be with you'.

[3] Those here present ('standing round').

[4] 'He loveth righteousness, and judgment; the earth is full of the goodness of the Lord'. Ps. xxxii. 5 (Vulgate), xxxiii. 5 (B.C.P.).

[5] II Sam. xviii. 5.

[6] Luke xi. 8.

[7] In the Piazza di Capo di Ferro on the left bank of the Tiber, near the Farnese Palace.

[8] Adrastus and Hypsipyle finding Lycurgus's son Archemorus, who had been entrusted to Hypsipyle, being strangled by a snake.

[9] Son of the hero-prophet Amphiaraus and Eriphyle.

There is a fine sitting statue of Aristotle: nothing ideal.

A curious deception from an avenue of pillars arranged like the perspective of a regular colonnade, i.e. in decreasing height. The effect of length is given.[1]

The statue supposed of Pompey has a severe masculine grandeur, with power & energy of character expressed: the drapery hangs unmeaningly & if real it would fall: also viewed from the left it makes the shoulder thick and heavy: and the short sword or dagger is on a belt which fixes it above the robe (or rather within it) & almost under the armpit.

The most striking pictures seem to be a fresco of Julius III, said of the school of Raphael[2]—St. Francis, Caravaggio—Seneca, Salvator Rosa—S. Girolamo, Albert Durer, to the life—Beatrice Cenci,[3] for its contrast with the Barberini—in character it resembles more the stepmother as there given[4]—Some, of high pretensions, looked as if repainted. Here are also Cardinal Pole[5]—a raccourci of the dead Redeemer by A. Caracci: surely this ought not to be made the subject of a mere experiment of the skill of a draughtsman: and Dido on the funeral pile by Guercino, who has in a very small degree followed the directions he might have drawn from Aen. iv. 504–21, & from the same 651–705.

Palazzo Rospigliosi. Guido's splendid fresco of the Aurora continues to be in good preservation. Boothby[6] tells me, that frescoes require to be painted on plaister while it is wet: then a considerable body of colour is imbibed and retained. Observe here, that the garments are all blown backward, while the torch, and the hair of the child who carries it, stream forward: may this be because the latter is the peculiar representative of the Sun & his course? The attitudes are graceful, the heads varied and *Raffaelesque*, the colouring warm & pure, that of the sea deep: seven Hours are visible, & there does not appear to be room left on the other side of the car for more than two others.

The twelve Apostles by Rubens appear among his higher works in point of taste and conception. Domenichino's Adam & Eve, with the crowd of birds & beasts around them, is a fanciful rather than a beautiful picture &, in a higher style, resembles one of Breughel's at the Barberini, in which flowerpainting is grossly obtruded upon landscape.

Calls. Macdonald's Studio. He is well advanced with Miss Ellison[7] who he says is very difficult. Lord Newry[8] is modelling a young Alexander there,

[1] By Francesco Borromini, 1599–1667, sculptor and architect, noted for baroque fancies.

[2] Portrait of Giammaria Ciocchi del Monte, 1487–1555, pope 1550; generally attributed to the sixteenth-century school of Il Gaetano.

[3] By Guercino.

[4] Portrait of Lucrezia Cenci, stepmother of Beatrice Cenci, by Pulzone Scipione, il Gaetani, d. 1550, in the Barberini.

[5] Reginald *Pole, 1500–58, cardinal 1536, abp. of Canterbury 1556.

[6] (Sir) Brooke William Robert Boothby, 1809–65; Christ Church and All Souls; 10th bart. 1846; rector of Elmsley, Kent 1846–52, of Welwyn 1852; writer on French literature.

[7] Sarah Caroline, da. of Cuthbert Ellison; m. 1841 (see 15 Jan. 39 n.), d. 1890.

[8] Francis Jack Needham, 1815–51, Etonian; styled Viscount Newry 1832, when his f. became 2nd earl of Kilmore; cons. M.P. Newry from 1841.

Catherine Glynne at Rome, 1838.
Bust by L. MacDonald.

his first attempt: many worse busts may be seen than this even in its present early stage. Gibson is to do another Mr Huskisson, for the townhall at Liverpool.

Mrs. Hunter Blair's[1] in evg. Dub & Ed. Rev—Journal.

Wednesday. Jan 2.

Forenoon, with the Verney's to Mr Lear's,[2] who draws beautifully: & to Mr. Colman's,[3] who imitates Mr Severn's manner, or at least has the same warm colouring: but does not yet equal him. He has a very beautiful picture of Paestum.

Afternoon, with Lord & Lady Brabazon & the G's to the baths of Caracalla[4] amidst whose vast marbles we wandered for an hour: and thence to San Paolo.[5] It is very interesting to see a grand Church in a state of progression, considering that we are in the 19th century. The cipollino columns in part remain, repaired: but such as could not thus be used, have been cut up into squares & the tribune cased with them.[6] The roof is carved in pine & gilded. At present they seem to leave the nave & to aim chiefly at restoring the tribune & transept: however the pillars of the nave are up: the intercolumniations are narrow: & there will I think be an awkward contrast between the arches over them, and the wide arch which spans the whole nave at its junction with the transept.[7]

A curious sarcophagus, of the age of Constantine, has been discovered under the altar, within the last few months:[8] a body in it. it is not finished: & the workmanship of course degenerate. One of the reliefs (of which there are two courses, & two figures, one male & the other female, busts, in the centre) seemed to be the adoration of the Magi.

The cloister[9] is curious: of very small arches, with double pillars, twisted & in every fanciful form, some of them laced with mosaic: like that we saw at Monreale.[10] (& St John Lateran[11]—(Sir S.G.)—The mosaic over the tribune has been restored: it is of the fourth century—has no Virgin—Our Lord has two Apostles on each side of him.[12] There is also a St Paul of the same

---

[1] Cp. 2 Apr. 32.

[2] Edward *Lear, 1812–88, poet and painter, lived in Rome from 1837.

[3] Charles Coleman, d. 1874, at Rome, resident there from 1835; painter and etcher.

[4] On the Via di S. Sebastiano, on the eastern slopes of the Aventine, at the southern limit of Rome.

[5] fuori le Mura, which was being repaired after the 1823 fire.

[6] A whitish marble veined with green; two cipollino columns survived the fire with the colonnade of the portico (1725). The tribune was cased with fragments of the 40 columns of the side-naves, which largely survived the fire, of proconnesian (grey-streaked) marble.

[7] Arch (440) of Galla Placidia, 386–450, half-sister of Emperor Honorius, 384–423, mother of Emperor Valentinian III, 419–455.

[8] April 1838; removed first to the cloisters, 1854 to Lateran Museum (No. 104).

[9] Of the Benedictines, to whom basilica entrusted since 1424.

[10] Cp. 17 Oct. 38.

[11] In the cloisters here also the columns have mosaic ornamentation.

[12] On the right Paul and Luke; on the left Peter and Andrew. The mosaics are however of the 13th century. Those on the arch of Galla Placidia are of the 5th century.

date[1] over a small door leading from the sacristy: & in the sacristy or chapel, are three Peruginos, two of which at least seemed worthy of the name. Home by Temple of Vesta.[2]

It is very interesting to see Claude's window in the Tempietto,[3] the house at the confluence of the Vie Sistina and Gregoriana: the middle one in the 2d piano,[4] looking along the Pincio & outwards: here then grew the inspiration of his golden glow and his magic transparency.—Nearly opposite in the Sistina (No [9]) is the house of G (?) Poussin.[5]

Evg—

Thursday. Jan 3.

Before noon to Severn's and Elsesir's[6] (Via Sistina) with the Ellisons & Glynnes. Has much been painted within the last 200 years which is of a higher order than Severn's Saint John?[7] The head seems thoroughly original, yet without anything strange, familiar when seen like ideas of a poet which awaken answering ideas having all the force of novelty yet so just and ($\pi\omega\varsigma$)[8] general, that we are unwilling to believe we were previously destitute of them.

Afternoon, to the Vatican, chiefly among the pictures. Our Lord upon the rainbow (Correggio) had a head of the type of that in the Transfiguration? but inferior.

Crivelli's dead Saviour shows the least agreeable form of the old sincere painting: much that is earnest, strong, and human, but nothing divine.

A. Mantegna's dead Saviour has a very fine head, the highest of the two elderly: but is it not a fault that the body, being nearly vertical, is neither rigid nor collapsed?

In Perugino's noble picture of the Madonna & Four Saints, why has San Luigi the *mitre*?[9] Has it any connection with his regal dignity?

In Guercino's Magdalen is not the idea of the picture rather broken up by the double action, as it were, of cherubs in the sky above, and angels with the penitent below?

Hence to the Pincio: a golden evening: the lights of this country at this season & hour are peculiar: for they are alike abundant, transparent, and brilliant: yet do not convey the idea of warmth: a contrast to our English associations.

---

[1] Reference perhaps to very ancient wooden statue of St. Paul, at the end of the first left nave.

[2] On the left bank of the Tiber, west of Palace of the Caesars.

[3] Name usually given to the classical pavilion of Bramante in the cloisters of San Pietro in Montorio on the right bank of the Tiber; but also to the three-storey house with classical portico forming junction of Via Sistina and Via Gregoriana; Claude's residence here now doubted. [4] 'storey'.

[5] Traditionally that of Nicolas Poussin, though Gaspard Dughet, 1615–75, his brother-in-law, also a landscape painter, and who adopted his name, had two houses on the Pincio.

[6] Friedrich-August Elsasser, 1810–45, German landscape and architecture painter; lived in Rome from 1832.

[7] In the 'Infant of the Apocalypse', cp. 15 Dec. 38 [8] 'as it were'.

[9] St. Louis of Sicily, 1274–97, bp. of Toulouse, not St. Louis king of France.

At 10½ PM to the Forum & Coliseum by the Hospital of Protestants[1] & under Mr Abeken's guidance.[2] From the roof of the Hospital we had two views, perfectly distinct in character: that towards the moon gave us the Albanian hills, Coliseum, Palatine, Lateran, and many more, in black masses with the outline thoroughly relieved: looking *from* the moon, we had the still Tiber and Rome in all its details with a fidelity and minuteness such as in our northern climate day alone can afford. Hard by the Forum beauties at every step: and the loveliness with magnificence of the interior of the Coliseum itself was such as left nothing to be desired. Not only should every one see these ruins by moonlight but I think perhaps see them first by moonlight: as thus only he can be prevented from doing them injustice. The perfect stillness, (the distant bells) (here & there) the actual beauty & variety of form in the ruin with its extreme richness, the (sufficient) distinctness of colour, the immense range, the entire contrast between its dead repose and its former office of inclosing almost countless thousands, the analogy between this mixture of grandeur and of ruin and the state of that nature by whose pomp and pride the mighty structure was erected and the simple cross asserting its triumphs in the midst of material so much more durable than its own—all this & much more pressed upon us: we mounted and descended, traversed, wound round, (oh for a girare)[3] gazed and said little.[4] Of particulars I must just remark that the higher side in mass affords an exquisite contrast to the lower which is more visibly & strongly broken in surface & pierced in a thousand places by moonlight.

Certainly the Coliseum should be included in Scott's category of Melrose.

> He that would see fair Melrose aright
> Must visit it by the pale moonlight.[5]

Friday Jan 4.

Morning, to the Sciarra[6] which in four rooms presents very high attractions; the whole number having any claim on visitors. The first has two fine pictures of the old school, one over a door & the other vis-a-vis: the second gives a good opportunity of picking out Claude and Both:[7] there are some by C's pupils: and by Breughel. In the third are two fine Garofalos:[8] a

[1] The 'Casa Tarpeia', built on the Tarpeian rock next to building of the Istituto di Corrispondenza Archeologica (see 8 Jan. 39), both Bunsen's foundations, near the Prussian embassy in the Palazzo Caffarelli on the Capitoline Hill.

[2] Cp. H. Abeken, *Ein schlichtes Leben in bewegter Zeit* (1898), 91.

[3] 'tour round'.

[4] But he said something to Catherine Glynne: cp. 18 Jan; 6 Feb. (first entry) 39; and Battiscombe, 26.

[5] *Lay of the Last Minstrel*, Canto II:
> If thou wouldst view fair Melrose aright
> Go visit it by the pale moonlight.

[6] Collection of prince Sciarra Colonna after division of family paintings at end of lawsuit with his brother prince Barberini, end of 18th century.

[7] Jan Both, 1618–52, Dutch painter and etcher, landscape painter influenced by Claude, lived much in Rome.

[8] Tisio Girofalo, painter, 1481–1559.

Paradise of German strength but disputed origin, with a ladder which deceives the sight as you move from side to side:[1] and the noble Moses by Guido in his first manner,[2] in which he seems as much to surpass the masters of the Bolognese school[3] in force as in his later works he fell below them. The last room contains, the Vanity and Modesty:[4] in which the real image of beauty is in the *force* of Modesty, though her figure is dowdy and rather diverts the eye from examining the face: Vanity has very fine features but the eyes are askance and the mouth strongly compressed and elongated. Why does she hold the modest jessamine? The colouring is wonderfully fresh rich and warm: nothing but warm colouring I think has a place in the picture. Here are Raphael's violinist,[5] Caravaggio's gamesters which has force & a mind though only ψυχικὸν,[6] Poussin's Erasmus,[7] figure very fine, Titian's Lady: Guido's Magdalene, called sublime—ma: Perugino's unpretending & highly beautiful St Sebastian: a curious picture in compartments by Giotto:[8] & a Death of the Virgin by Albert Durer, of extraordinary force and finish.

Afternoon—Villa Mattei terrace[9] on the Celian for the view: and to the Pope's old convent,[10] where are two frescoes by Guido one by Domenichino, a chapel in historical fresco by Marc Antonio d'Urbino,[11] & two fine statues by Nicolo [blank] scholar of Michael Angelo & really recalling him, one of the Virgin, the other of St Gregory.[12]—S. Carlo in Catinari:[13] scarcely long enough for the height? Domenichino has painted the four rests of the dome. *pendentifs*.

Dined at Col. Lindsay's[14] & evg there.

Saturday Jan 5.

Bookshops. Doria[15] at 12. This very fine gallery has but bad light for the

[1] Allegedly by Gaudenzio Ferrari, painter and sculptor, 1484?–1546.

[2] Half-length figure with the tables of the Law, early picture still in the manner of Caravaggio.

[3] Issuing from the teaching of Lodovico, 1554–1619, Agostino, 1557–1602, and Annibale, 1560–1609, Carracci: Albani, 1578–1680, Domenichino, 1581–1641, Guercino, 1591–1666.

[4] Two women half length, said to be by Leonardo da Vinci; perhaps by one of his school.

[5] Dated 1518, two years before his death: a young man, perhaps the then famous violinist Iacopo Sansecondo, cp. B. Castiglione *Cortegiano*, bk. ii, ch. 45.

[6] 'psychological'.

[7] Sketch of martyrdom of St. Erasmus, 3rd century martyr of the time of Diocletian; picture in the Vatican.

[8] Six small paintings of the Passion on one canvas.

[9] Built 1582, SE. of palace of the Caesars.

[10] San Gregorio, Camaldolese monastery near by, where Gregory XVI was abbot 1807, general 1823 of the order.

[11] On the wall of the chapel of St. Barbara, by Antonio Viviano da Urbino, 1560–1620, showing St. Gregory instructing St. Augustine of Canterbury to convert the Anglo-Saxons.

[12] Niccolo Cordieri, painter, engraver and sculptor, 1567–1612. St. Silvia, mother of St. Gregory, in her chapel; St. Gregory, in chapel of St. Andrew.

[13] NW. of the Capitol, near the left bank of the Tiber; form a Greek cross, built 1612.

[14] James Lindsay of Balcarres, had m. 1823 Anne, eldest da. of Sir Coutts Trotter; she d. after 1890.

[15] Palazzo Doria-Panfili, east of Pantheon.

most part. For my own preference I incline to Garofalo's Visitation, rich & classical yet quite accordant with the subject, and S. del Piombo's noble portrait of Andrew Doria.[1] The Claudes, and Caracci[2] landscapes are very delightful and Salvator's Cain & Abel, two S. Girolamos of Spagnoletto, and Rubens's second wife, are, it appeared to me, fine specimens of the respective artists. Raphael's two-portrait[3] is of course conspicuous. (Guercino's) ceilings in the S. Agnese! a beautiful picture. Beschreibung der Stadt Rom. I. 518.[4] Platner I see praises the Garofalo as well conceived besides having his usual merit of strength and beauty of colouring. The room of landscapes presents to the eye a mass rather dark & monotonous, but it repays examination.

Evening, to S. Maria del Popolo: how very rich is this Church! I am glad to find S. del Piombo is the original & part author of the large painting L^n & I had admired:[5] the Ionas always gains, the Pinturicchio's[6] are very sweet in expression, & the Carlo Maratta of the Conception[7] seems executed in his best manner: the head of the Virgin is Raffaellesque? Wrote to J.N.G. dined at H. Sandbach's[8] read Platner.

At S. Lorenzo in Lucina[9] I could hardly see well the Crucifixion by Guido: but I like that awful solitude exceedingly.—An image of our Lord as a child standing, alone, in a sort of petticoat, was preparing, I suppose, for the Epiphany: of course it does not correspond with the real subject of the Festival.—This as well as New Year's day is a period of presents among the Italians.

Sunday Jan 6, Epiphany.

Church mg & aft. Mr Grimshaw[10] & Mr Hutchinson. The Communion was administered to (I should think) 150 or more.

Before Church went to the Propaganda[11] where masses are performed on

[1] Genoese admiral, 1468–1560; directed maritime strength of Italy against Turkey and the Barbary pirates. Half length life-size portrait.

[2] Annibale Caracci. Six pictures of equal semicircular form, landscapes with Christian subjects: flight into Egypt; Visitation; Assumption; Laying in the tomb; Birth of Christ; adoration of the Magi; two small landscapes with St. Francis dying and two angels, St. Francis praying before a Crucifix; landscape with St. Mary Magdalene.

[3] Two half length portraits on the same canvas of men in black dress and cap, said to be (after contemporary likenesses?) of the jurists Bartolo 1314–57, and Baldo 1319 or 1327–1400.

[4] Both phrases margin entries. E. Z. Platner, C. Bunsen and others, Beschreibung der Stadt Rom, 3v. (1830–37).

[5] Opinion of Platner's (cp. Beschreibung, III, part 3, 221, note 2). Two oil paintings of the moments of creation up to the expulsion from Paradise, in the drum of the cupola between the windows, and an altar oil painting of the Nativity of the Virgin in the Chigi chapel, finished 1554 by Francesco Salviati, historical painter, 1510–63, had in recent guides to Rome been attributed to Raphael's design.

[6] Frescoes in the ceiling of the choir.   [7] In the Cibò chapel.

[8] Henry Robertson Sandbach, 1807–95, of Hafodunos, Denbighshire, 2nd s. of S.; m. 1832 Margaret Roscoe, g.d. of William *Roscoe of Liverpool.

[9] S. of Via di Fontanella, near the Corso.

[10] Thomas Shuttleworth *Grimshaw, 1778–1850, vicar of Biddenham, Bedfordshire 1808–50.

[11] College for native missionaries of different countries in the Piazza di Spagna, founded by Gregory XV 1622.

this day according to the several rituals. A Greek priest was officiating. He recited audibly.

Also to S. Silvestro where the profession of a nun was to take place: but I had to come away before the service. The Church was full, & our congregation seemed to suffer, perhaps to the extent of 150. I am told the person was under 18, and perfectly unmoved: the sermon good but severe, & compared a retracting novice to Judas Iscariot.

In the evening to Caravita: a very good sermon on the manifestation of Christ—to be spiritual as well as physical—and followed out faithfully into the resemblance of Him in all Christian virtues. Over and over again, did the preacher say, place all your hopes in Jesus Christ, place you hopes in Jesus Christ alone. And it seemed strangely discordant when he ended with 'Preghiamo adunque La Madonna'[1] &c—but afterwards he offered kneeling at the altar a beautiful and deeply penitential prayer to the Saviour. Tea with the G's.[2]

Monday Jan 7.

Sat some time with Dr. Wiseman, who kindly gave me a good deal of information. Thence to Abeken's & the Capitol:[3] where I was among the statues only. Nothing there—it might almost be said, or elsewhere—seems at all to touch the Dying Gladiator, as a model of manly form, and for its wonderful expression of pain and shame in a countenance still testifying valour while yet further clouded with the mists of coming death.[4] Yet the Antinous[5]—the Capitoline Venus (as I remember)—the rosso Faun,[6] that of Praxiteles, the bust of Alexander, the Apollo, the gilt bronze of Hercules, are each in their own way very interesting.

Hence to S. Silvestro. A priest was reading to the people from a book on the Epiphany: from his slow enunciation of two or three words at once, the long pause, & the eyes never withdrawn, I suspect he did not very easily read himself. Padre Ventura followed with a long and good sermon on 'Et vidimus stellam ejus'[7]—not a word of Popery, I think, from first to last. The *idea* was, that in the Magi we were called—& the exhortation to obey the call. He ended with prayer to the Redeemer. The Church was in course of illumination through most of his sermon. Not less than two hundred wax lights I think constituted the whole array. A Litany to the Virgin followed: chanted in somewhat theatrical style.

---

[1] 'Let us now pray to our Lady'.
[2] Notes on theology, Add MS 44728, ff. 205–7.
[3] Today the square of palaces occupying the summit of the Capitoline hill under the name of Piazza di Campidoglio. Built by Paul III from the designs of Michael Angelo. Here is the museum of the Capitol, on the east side of the piazza.
[4] Said to be statue by Kresilas, 5th century B.C., contemporary of Phidias, or a copy, 'a wounded man dying', discovered 1770.
[5] Found in Hadrian's villa, of the youth of Bithynia represented here as hero.
[6] Found in Hadrian's villa, in 'rosso antico', deep red marble with white markings and fine black veins.
[7] 'And we have seen his star', Matt. ii. 2.

Wiseman tells me parochial priests are examined before institution & that a priest *as such* is not entitled to preach.

Tuesday Jan 8.

With Mr Goulburn on the unpalatable subject of our journey. Thence, hunting for books: in Rome: what a labour! for example: for the Statutes of the Sapienza,[1] Petrucci (bookseller) referred me to the Propaganda: the Propaganda to the Stamperia Camerale:[2] and the Stamperia to the printing office: the printing office back to an upper floor of the Stamperia: where I went at one, & it was closed for dinner: again at five, & it was shut for the night.

The Church of Madonna di Loreto contains a Perugino over the high altar, not unworthy, apparently, of that great artist. The Virgin sits above: S. Sebastian & another S. on either side: below, the angels are flying charged with the Casa, and a sort of Campanile attached to it, which the Sacristan asserts is at Loreto with the Casa. I don't recollect this tower.

At $1\frac{1}{2}$ to Mr Hughes's[3] sermon in S. Silvestro. It was on 'et vidimus stellam ejus' and 'they whose names were not found written in the book of life'[4] &c. He laid the substance of religion in similitude—to the Redeemer: and preached with a very forcible and sometimes violent manner. He complained bitterly of the misconduct and profanations of English strangers in their churches: without specifying. He seemed to show a strong grasp of few ideas, a considerable tendency to coarseness, & remarkable dramatic powers in describing the condemnation of different classes at the last day for want of conformity to Christ. There were some things about merit which offended: but the whole was certainly rivetting. He is about to be made Bishop & is to repair to Gibraltar as Vicar Apostolic. The music was beautiful, yet with one most unmusical voice.

Went to the Annual meeting of the Archaeological Society. Sig. Campani[5] exhibited vases and ornaments from tombs near Corneto.[6] A golden head of the Indian Bacchus[7] had a gold chain attached to it[8] of exactly the S. American work of the present day[9]—and two golden ornaments like

[1] University of Rome, east of Piazza Navona, founded 1310 by Clement V; under control of Italian state since 1872, as 'Royal University of Roman Studies'.

[2] Palazzo Cornaro, in the Via della Stamperia east of Quirinal Gardens, 'printing works of the Papal Chancellery', to which were assigned printing and sale of state documents, government decrees, and reports on cases in the Roman courts.

[3] Mgr. Henry Hughes, of the Reformed Friars Minor; made bp. of Heliopolis in partibus infidelium and Vicar Apostolic of Gibraltar 15 March 1839; succeeded by John B. Scandella bp. of Antinoe, 1857.

[4] Rev. viii. 13.

[5] Giampetro Campana, marquis of Cavelli, b. 1808, whose palace was a museum of precious Etruscan and Roman jewellery, vases, glass, enamels, etc.; later disposed of to museums of Europe.

[6] At Tarquinia, Etruscan city.

[7] The bearded Bacchus, appearing in triumphal procession in India, dating from the campaign of Alexander.

[8] Attaching the head as a locket to the neck.

[9] Indian goldsmith's work in Mexico, Peru, etc. Cp. M. Romero de Terreros y Vincent, *Las Artes Industriales en la Nueva España* (1923), 33 ff.

buttons but having no loop were of a workmanship more minute & fine I think than I ever saw. And these are Etruscan. Ah, vixere fortes &c.[1]—
Dr. Ferlini[2] exhibited the Egyptian remains he has found in a pyramid near Meroe[3]—which it appears he has destroyed—of the height of 30 metres. Symbols of gods—Trinity in several forms: parents & a child: or three coequal heads: were among them.[4] And a most beautiful bronze vessel for incense.
Ara Celi. A good picture behind the high altar of the Holy Family, in Raphael's school & manner.[6] We were too late to enjoy Pinturicchio's frescoes.
Dined at the G's.

Wednesday Jan 9.

At 11 to the S.M. degli Angeli, S. Bernardo, & Convent.[7] The cloister is designed by M. Angelo & remarkable for simplicity. The old & modern buildings are strangely mixed up. The best view of the baths[8] I have seen is from the eminence near the agger of Servius.—The monk (a Spaniard, come within a year, but he said voluntarily) showed us an angel executed he said by Buonarroti, which seemed not to want fine points, yet hardly to be enough marked by the hand of that great man.
S. Bernardo[9] is circular, once a hall in the Baths. The coffettoni of the roof are of equal number in each of the concentric circles, (which are numerous) & each consequently in succession varies in size.
S.M. degli Angeli[10] is more grand than churchlike. Finest from the entrance. It seems to be a serious defect that the shorter arm of the cross is higher: (& I think broader.) The effect on entering, is very remarkable. Observe Algiati's epitaph:

Pietate vixit
Memoriâ vivit
Gloriâ vivet.[11]

[1] Horace, Odes, iv. 9, 25;

vixere fortes ante Agamemnona
multi; sed omnes illacrimabiles
urgentur ignotique longa
nocte, carent quia vate sacro.

'Many strong men lived before Agamemnon; but all unknown and without a tear are sunk in long night, because they lacked an inspired poet.' Quoted by Campana in his lecture, cp. *Antiche opere in Plastica discoperte, raccolte e dichiarate da Gio. Pietro Campana . . . Marchese di Cavelli . . .* (1852), i. 10. For objects described, see ibid. catalogue, Class 3, Ori, Argenti.
[2] Giuseppe Ferlini, Bolognese doctor of medicine, took service with Turks in Albania, Greeks in Roumania, General Sir Richard *Church and Egyptian government as army doctor; amateur archaeologist; first to publish (1825) description of cave in Parnassos mountains NW. of Athens.   [3] In Western Libya.
[4] See 'Cenno sugli Scavi operati nella Nubia e Catalogo degli oggetti ritrovati dal Dott. Giuseppe Ferlini Bolognese' (1837), nos. 33, 37, 41.   [5] Ibid. no. 105 or 106.
[6] Copy of Raphael picture, the Virgin with child, St. Elizabeth and St. John the Baptist.   [7] Cistercian.
[8] Of Diocletian.   [9] Cp. 30 May 32.
[10] Also in the baths of Diocletian.
[11] 'He lived in piety, he lives in memory, he will live in glory'; on Cardinal Francesco Alciati, 1542–80, jurist.

And the statue of Bruno[1]—Muzianos picture,[2] Pomarancio's (Sapphira),[3] C. Maratta's Baptism,[4] Domenichino's S. Sebastian,[5] very effective—& free from mannerism?

Borghese Gallery.[6] Requires more time than any other (Palace) in Rome: comprising a greater number, if not of capi d'opera, yet of pictures worth looking at. I am sorry the pictures of Venus, Cupids &c are put into a separate room: for this attaches to them more or less of a character which otherwise they need not have.[7] The collection is very rich in Garofalos, & generally in the Florentine & Venetian schools. The "Graces" of Titian have little or no grace, but the flesh is splendidly coloured. Here may be appreciated

'Il vero natural di Tiziano.'

The Sacred & Profane Love[8] is very finely executed: & above the former in conception, though below its own subject.

Garofalo's Conversion of St Paul is rather confused: his Holy Family in the last room very beautiful.

I was sorry to see a renowned copyist Anna (nata) Muschi[9] at work on Dolce's Virgin & child: when close by it were one by Francia, and a smaller one by Perugino, both very beautiful, the latter exquisite.

Lorenzo da Credi reappears here, to very great advantage, in a Holy Family. The Virgin kneels to worship.

There is a beautiful St. Francis by Cigolo

The Danæ of Correggio is purer than one would have anticipated: particularly the putti, who I suppose are cupids.

Parmeggiano[10] is in this gallery too: an ugly likeness[11] of Correggio: retaining & exaggerating his faults, up to gross mannerism? Not however so in all cases.

Raphael's picture of the dead Saviour carried is extremely beautiful. Is it

[1] St. Bruno, ca. 1030–1101, founder of the Carthusian order, whose monastery adjoins the church. Statue by Jean-Antoine Houdon, 1741–1828, sculptor and caster in bronze.

[2] Giovanni Girolamo Muziano, 1528–92, historical painter and decorator; of St. Jerome, St. Francis and other saints, on the wall closing the great chapel at the eastern end of the church.

[3] Cristofor Roncalli, called il cavalier dalle Pomerancie, 1552–1626; cp. Acts v. 1–10.

[4] Fresco 22 ft. high, originally in St. Peter's; in the transept.

[5] On opposite wall of the transept; like Pomerancie's, originally in St. Peter's, and replaced there by a copy in mosaic.

[6] Ground floor of Palazzo Borghese, west of the Corso.

[7] Room 6: Leda with the swan, allegedly by Leonardo da Vinci; Venus and Cupid life-size by Lucas Cranach; Venus and Adonis by Lucas Cambiaso, 1527–80 or 85, copy allegedly by Giulio Romano of Raphael's Fornarina; Venus and Cupid nearly life-size by Domenico (Mecherino) Beccafumi, ca. 1486–1551; half-length figure, said to be Venus, allegedly by Giulio Romano; Venus and Cupid with a Satyr, allegedly by Paul Veronese; Venus crowned by Cupid; Andromeda chained to the rock, by Giuseppe Cesare, called cavaliere d'Arpino, 1570–1640 or 42.

[8] Of Titian.

[9] Probably sister of Patrizio Muschi of Siena, translator of *Thomson's Seasons, 1826, for which she designed a frontispiece.

[10] Entombment of Christ.

[11] Sc. imitation.

between the 2d & the 3d manner? i.e. the Madonna del Granduca & the John the Baptist? Observe in the countenance of the bearer at the head the mixed expression of great bodily effort with mental anguish.—I did not know why the legs from the knee do not bend downwards more: like the left hand from the wrist: which shows that the body is not stark. Dr. Wiseman informed me, that according to the expression, 'equitare in croce',[1] there was some support on the cross, of old, for the feet, & also to sit on.

Hence to Mr Lewis's:[2] he draws beautifully in rich water colours.

At 3.50, S. Silvestro. Padre Ventura preached a good and able sermon, still on the subject of the Epiphany. He gave us an interpretation of the two spies,[3] from the Fathers: according to which the first, with his face away from the grapes, was the Jew: the hinder or later one who beheld them, the Christian: the fruit Christ: the pole the wood of the cradle and of the cross. So Adam & Eve hid, he said before, not nel bosco but nel legno:[4] the tree in which they hid, a type of the cross. His sermons conclude with prayer, direct to its proper Object.

Dined with Miss McKenzie. Mrs Severn[5] remarked how the veneration of images tends to secure works of art as such, from disrespect or injury by the people. She mentioned that reverence had been paid to Sir T. Lawrence's Geo. IV in the Vatican:[6] & that cases were known of the people taking off their hats to an Indian Bacchus[7] by the roadside. I have heard the same generally of their conduct in the Vatican when open to all classes.

Mr Sebright[8] asked a young Italian (son of the Count [blank]) how he wd like to be English. 'Non mi piacerebbe,' said the boy (of 12 years old,) 'dopo la morte di andare in casa del diavolo'. 'Ma come e perchè? 'Non sono tutti gli Inglesi e gli Scozzesi protestanti?' 'Si.' 'Gli compatisco assai.'[9] P. Ventura I remember spoke of the body of the English and of the Russian people as being probably included, under the doctrine of invincible ignorance, in the true Church. Torlonia's. 1½ hour arriving. 1 hour there. (Just heard (the Roman) Grisi[10] who seems to sing very well indeed.) 2 hours getting away: this however was not the host's fault. Great numbers of ecclesiastics: & a good many at cards.

---

[1] 'To ride on the Cross'.
[2] John F. *Lewis was in Italy 1838–40.
[3] Joshua, ii. 1; vi. 22, 23.
[4] 'not in the wood but in the tree.'
[5] Elizabeth Montgomerie, natural da. of Lord Montgomerie, m. Joseph *Severn 1828, d. 1862.
[6] In the Pinacotheca, copy made by Sir Thomas *Lawrence of his portrait, 1821, of *George IV in coronation robes, sent by king to Pius VII.
[7] Cp. 8 Jan. 39.
[8] Thomas Gage Saunders Sebright, 1802–64, s. of Sir John Saunders *Sebright, 7th bart.; succ. 1846.
[9] 'I shouldn't like to go after death to the house of the devil.' 'But how and why?' 'Aren't all the English and Scotch protestants?' 'Yes.' 'I am very sorry for them.'
[10] All the famous Grisi were Milanese; this singer untraced.

Thursday Jan 10.

9–10. Sat to [blank][1] at Chev. Kestner's[2]—who also tried his hand upon a sketch. Then with the G's to the Quattro Coronati.[3] Four martyred brothers. There are curious paintings in a chapel on the right before entering the Church, which represent different actions in the life of Constantine. The custode declared them to be of the 4th century,[4] & *also* to be by Giovanni da San Giovanni:[5] probably neither true. But they must be very ancient. There are two quadrangles before reaching the Church. Its form is basilican: the apsis remarkable for width. Along the nave are five arches below, and six in an upper line: the third and fourth divided by a pier instead of a pillar: and below the aisles also terminating in the same way: so that there are but four pillars in each line. The altar is in the centre of the tribune: & the bishop's chair in the ancient place: but modern?[6]

S. Prassede.[7] Originally built in 160. Here is the column of the flagellation, in an old chapel with mosaics:[8] a remarkable double flight of rosso steps to the tribune: six white marble columns in strange taste between the rails & the tribune:[9] the body of the Church is large & fine, and the mosaics of the tribune well executed & interesting. They are of the time of Pope Paschal, 822,[10] and accordingly our Saviour's stature & dignity is pre-eminent, & not put in (as it were) competition with the Virgin. Three figures are on each side of him:[11] & a representation meant apparently for the ripples of water. Overhead, a hand & similar streaks. Below is written, Jordanes.[12] The nice oval [?] of the Pope also appears. On a kind of frieze are thirteen lambs for our Lord & the apostles. On the right & left are the 24 elders, & above them the four evangelists & the symbolic "beasts". Also there is the Holy City, with precious stones in the wall.—The portico is old.

[1] One of several German artists then in Rome called Müller, who was painting the diarist at Bunsen's request.

[2] Georg August Christian Kestner, 1777–1853, art connoisseur, secretary to Hanoverian legation in Rome 1817–24, 1824–49 chargé d'affaires and minister resident in Rome for protection of English and Hanoverian interests.

[3] Church of the 'Four Crowned' Martyrs, the brothers Severianus, Carpophorus, Severus and Victorinus, Roman officials scourged to death by order of Diocletian; ca. 4th century, NW. of St. John Lateran.

[4] Chapel of St. Silvester 1140; pope 314–335, associated with conversion and donation of Constantine. Paintings of 7th and 8th centuries.

[5] Painter and genre painter 1592–1636. His paintings are in the choir.

[6] Church destroyed by Robert Guiscard 1099, rebuilt by Paschal II 1111, tribune (apse with bishop's throne) rebuilt 1624 by Cardinal Gian. Garzia Millini.

[7] Near Santa Maria Maggiore, SSW. of Baths of Diocletian. In the margin is a pencil ground-plan, with: (recesses apptly of unequal depth).

[8] Half of column in oriental jasper at which Christ supposedly scourged brought here 1223 by Cardinal Giovanni Colonna.

[9] Set up by St. Charles Borromeo, 1538–84, cardinal-priest of supposedly St. Prassede 1564; though seemingly antique, with capitals adorned with ivy and acanthus leaves wreathing in places the grooved shafts, Gothic style.

[10] Who rebuilt the church.

[11] On the left (right hand of the Saviour), St. Peter, St. Prassede, and Paschal I; on the right, St. Paul, St. Pudentiana, sister of St. Prassede, and St. Zeno.

[12] The Jordan.

S. Andrea a Monte Cavallo.[1] A beautiful small oval Church of the Jesuits with an (high) altarpiece by Borgognone,[2] and another picture by Carlo Maratta.[3] The coffettoni of the roof contract as at S. Bernardo.[4]

It is very sad to examine the prayers printed in the Churches to assist devotion. Here are words very nearly taken from one I saw today, to the B.V. 'Fatemi sapere *la dolcezza del vostro cuore*, e la vostra *forza* presso quello di Gesù.'[5] Certain of forza & dolcezza. So that He who was in all things tempted like as we are requires to be overcome by the *force* of the Virgin's feelings in our favour! And so in another place she is intreated to be our great Advocate with her son. And the idea evidently lurks of her maternal authority having to do with this subject.

My book arrived.[6] Wrote to Mr G.

Vatican at 2: among the Statues: the pictures were locked for the Czarowitch.[7] Six hours in the week, during the season, are allowed by the Pope to the public for gratuitous access to the statuary: and between three and four for the pictures: out of these hours forsooth must be appointed the visit of the Czarowitch! Certainly the Pope may do as he pleases: but we hear much of the illiberality of England with regard to public collections: we are at least as much before the Vatican as behind Florence. We went to the Sistine: what stores untold are here! This is the temple of Michael Angelo's memory, where his genius reposes in unrivalled grandeur. Especially among all the Jeremiah overpowers me: as the prophet is himself represented all but overpowered, by the solemn weight of his message and the depth of that vision which is opened before his mental eye: yet not overpowered, but rather gathered and concentrated in the meditation of one determined to perform to the uttermost the commission entrusted to him of God, and seeming to dilate into grander dimensions for his gigantic task. Ezekiel again appears to recoil from the announcement of woe: & to remonstrate with the angel pleading for a mitigation of the tidings or almost release from the task. Isiah, the prophet of evangelical joy, might one should think have shone with the gladness of that heavenly host which sang the coming of the Messiah: though in a tempered exaltation: but of this the painter has seen fit to stop short.

The Last Judgement struck me this day for its variety of postures: and the skilful suspension of the picture without a base.

S. Silvestro. Padre Ventura preached as usual & as usual well. He complained of the coolness of the R.C.'s in rendering the signs of devotion in Church: as did Hughes yesterday of their timidity before strangers. So

---

[1] Opposite Quirinal gardens, west of Baths of Diocletian. From designs of Bernini for the Jesuit novitiate, at command of Alexander VII, 1655–67.

[2] i.e. picture at the high altar by Guglielmo Courtois, called il Borgognone, 1628–79, brother of the more celebrated Jacques Curtois, also called il Borgognone, who painted the crucifixion of St. Andrew.

[3] St. Stanislaus.

[4] Cp. 30 May 32.

[5] 'Make me to know *the tenderness of your heart*, and its *force* and power over the heart of Jesus.'

[6] *The State in its relations with the Church.*

[7] The future Alexander II.

the sermon on Sunday at the Caravita reprobated the standing & leaning instead of kneeling to the Host.—He showed that the Jews deceived Herod by not quoting the entire prophecy from Micah.[1]

The wax lights are near 300: the Litany of the Virgin is sung and the Host elevated after sermon. One is constantly surprised here by the mixture of the most beautiful with the most inappropriate music, and of the finest voices with others utterly discordant or worthless.

Mr Earle died this day before eleven a.m.

Tea with G.s.—& capping verses.

Friday Jan 11.

9–11 a.m. Second sitting to Müller and the Chevalier. Calls and buying books &c. at Petrucci's. Wrote to Hope.

Heard M. de Forbin,[2] the Bp of Nancy, excluded from his diocese by the government of France, at 2 P.M. in S. Silvestro. He was long and less interesting than the others: but generally earnest and untainted. He came from the Deluge downward through all the types & the whole life of the Redeemer. He strongly exhibited the fact that our Lord was truly a martyr to the doctrine of His own divinity.

In affn. to the cloisters of St. John Lateran[3]—which are curiously constructed of small arches with mosaic in the frieze & the columns: & here an old modernised, Bishop's Chair of the Roman Cathedral is kept.[4]—Mr Bunsen supposes the obelisk[5] here to be the oldest monument in Rome & the sculpture[6] is considered fine.

Hence to the Villa Massimi:[7] where are the frescoes of Overbeck, Koch, & other Germans: from Tasso, Ariosto, & Dante.[8] I liked those of the two former best, as most equal to their subject: the latter I thought fell much below Flaxman's conception of the poet, and the Inferno in particular was unsatisfactory.

Dined at Ld Carnarvon's.

Saturday Jan 12.

9–10. Third sitting. While I was at the Chevalier's, the soldiers who attended the archaeological meeting came to be paid: & it appears there is a tariff for all so employed, as at the great parties, & at our English Church.

[1] Matt. ii. 3–5, Micah v.

[2] Charles-Auguste-Marie-Joseph Forbin-Janson, 1785–1844, bp. of Nancy and Toul 1824; forced by popular rising 1830 to quit his diocese; missionary in Canada.

[3] Cp. 2 Jan. 39.

[4] Of the 13th century, with Gothic canopy added later.

[5] Brought by Constantine from Heliopolis to Alexandria, erected by Constantius 357 in the Circus Maximus (between the Palace of the Caesars and the Aventine), erected by Pope Sixtus V 1588, in the middle of the square of St. John Lateran.

[6] The hieroglyphics with which the obelisk is covered are of finest workmanship.

[7] Opposite the Palace of the Lateran.

[8] In the ground floor of the summer pavilion, scenes from Dante's Hell and Purgatory, by Johann Karl Koch, 1806–1900, Paradise, by Philip Veith, 1793–1877, from Ariosto's *Orlando Furioso* by Julius Veit Hans Schnorr von Carolsfeld, 1794–1872, and from the *Gerusalemme Liberata* by Overbeck and Josef von Führich, 1800–76; commissioned 1821–28 by the owner Marquis Carlo Massimo.

At 10¼, a party to Trastevere:[1] on the way

S. Carlo in Catinari.[2] The cardinal virtues want characteristics suitable to a Church: & their emblems are not all easily discerned.[3] A fine head of S. Carlo in the apartment behind the high altar, by Guido: & the death of S. Anna good, by A. Sacchi.[4]

Fontana delle Tartarughe is[5] is very gracefully designed and appropriate. A Madonna projects almost over the gate of the Ghetto:[6] for the special benefit of the Jews?

S. Cecilia.[7] Statue of the body of the Saint, by Carlo Maderno,[8] with the face turned towards the ground. Would it not be more collapsed? An ancient fresco is on the wall to the right.[9]

S. Chrysogono.[10] Massive ancient granite columns, with architraves, support the wall dividing the nave & aisles. In S. Cecilia there are ancient mosaics having the name of Pascal, of the 9th century & have nearly all the same emblems as those of S. Prassede.[11] The same remark may be made about the Virgin. Two columns of porphyry support the great arch of the nave: & I should remark here as at St Paul's.

S. Maria in Trastevere:[12] Mosaics of 12th C. on the façade: Virgin in centre of saints.[13] So in the Tribune: of the same: & here the Virgin is elevated above the rest, & nearly of the same magnitude with out Saviour. Below are the scenes of *her* life.[14] A singular scene of a delivery.—On the left, in the nave, two old mosaics: nothing sacred in the subjects or origin?[15] The roof has a picture by Domenichino, of the assumption.

Palazzo Corsini.[16] The most celebrated pictures are perhaps Guercino's Ecce Homo, Titian's Woman Taken in Adultery,[17] & Salvator's Prometheus, of horrible strength. Nec coram populo pueris Medea trucidet &c.[18] I liked best, Fra Bartolomeo's Holy Family, and a small Madonna & Child of A. del Sarto's, numbered 15. These Ecce Homo's dissatisfy me: I think such a face as that of the Crucifix at Naples comes home much more, and is

---

[1] Extending on the right bank of the Tiber from Vatican City to the quay of Ripa Grande.

[2] Near the left bank, south of the Pantheon, 17th century.

[3] On the pendentives of the cupola, by Domenichino.

[4] Andrea Sacchi, historical painter and portraitist, 1599–1661.

[5] Mid-renaissance.

[6] On the left bank, near San Carlo a' Catinari.

[7] In Trastevere, near the quay of Ripa Grande.

[8] Stefano Maderno, *ca.* 1576–1636, sculptor.

[9] Also representing St. Cecilia; 10th century.

[10] NW. of St. Cecilia's, in the Trastevere; 1123, built on 4th-century church.

[11] i.e. of Christ.

[12] West of San Crisogono.

[13] Five wise and five foolish virgins.

[14] By Pietro Cavallini, *ca.* 1250–*ca.* 1330.

[15] Pagan mosaics of 1st century: a bay with boats and dolphins; ducks and other water birds.

[16] Gallery in the Trastevere; once residence of Queen Christina of Sweden.

[17] Not in catalogues of Titian's works; perhaps reproduction of fresco in St. Antony's at Padua; showing a man, about to stab his wife for suspected adultery, saved by the saint.

[18] 'Ne pueros coram populo Medea trucidet', 'let not Medea kill her children in public'; Horace, *Ars Poetica*, 185.

sublime in agony which these are not: they go out of nature & yet do not reach their subject: one of Guido's hangs above: one by Carlo Dolce opposite is most painful to contemplate. The same painter has stolen his S. Apollonia, with the tooth, from his own beautiful Magdalen.[1]

There are some fine heads in the room of portraits.—By the way I see resemblance between the faces given to Calvin and to C. Borromeo![2]

Farnesina.[3] A restored cieling, representing the fable of Amore e Psiche, after Raphael's designs, restored by C. Maratta: part of one figure had much of Raphael's hand. In the next room his genuine fresco of Galatea's flight: and a powerful head by Buonarroti.[4] Landscapes by Poussin—sadly faded.

Villa Pamfili Doria.[5] The view of St. Peter's was pretty good:[6] of the city & the hills delicious. No one to open the door of the villa itself—the gardens are Italian but varied & of some extent.

Dined with the Ellisons.

Another sermon from P. Ventura: on the marriage in Cana of Galilee. In general, very good: his exposition corresponded very much with that of Nicole:[7] he said however (and N. says something rather like it) that while Christ is the fountain of grace it is not ordinarily distributed except through the Virgin Mary: inferred from her having here made the representation.[8]

He explained the 5th verse[9] rather awkwardly I thought, as stating the distinction of the divine and human natures of Christ: but he was good and forcible on marriage.[10] Where Christ is not invited to marriages, the devil is present, said he. Some have too much depressed marriage, as the Manicheans: some have exalted it above virginity as Jovinian:[11] this passage puts it in its right place, as honourable: yet less honourable, because Simon son of Alpheus[12] whose marriage it was, was called from it to a state of celibacy in the Apostolate. The want of wine signified the exhausted state of truth in the then Church of God. The superiority of celibacy was

[1] Also in this gallery. St. Apollonia, 3rd-century martyr whose teeth were knocked out, is usually shown holding a tooth with pincers.

[2] As in portraits of Calvin by J. Vienot and of St. Charles Borromeo by Ambrogio Figino, *ca.* 1550–1597.

[3] Opposite the Palazzo Corsini on the right bank of the Tiber.

[4] Said to have been sketched in charcoal by Michelangelo in one of the lunettes; later painted by Sebastiano del Piombo.

[5] Extensive grounds outside Rome to west, laid out by Alessandro Algardi, 1602 64, sculptor.

[6] From the extremity of the grounds there is a more complete view of the flank of St. Peter's than from any other quarter.

[7] *Essais de Morale*, ix. 320 ff. (1782).

[8] Ibid. 328 f.

[9] 'And his mother saith unto the servants, whatsoever he saith unto you, do it' (John ii. 5).

[10] Margin entry: What have I to do with thee, i.e. in the thing [?] of my mission—fatal to R.C. doctrine.

[11] Fourth-century advocate of anti-asceticism. Cp. St. Jerome, *Adversus Iovinianum* (393) in Migne, *PL* xxiii. 211; doctrine condemned 390.

[12] Father of Levi in Matt. ii. 14; of James the Less, in Matt. x. 3, Mark iii. 18, Luke vi. 15, Acts i. 13; not of Simon. Hence *Gladstone's marginal comment: 'So the P[adre]'. That Simon the Canaanite was the bridegroom at the marriage in Cana was traditional but legendary.

also inferred from the fact that Anna the prophetess was a widow.[1] The change signified that from letter to spirit—law to gospel—& also prefigured transubstantiation! (But here the accidents went away with the substance: the argument seems the other way.)

Dined with the Ellisons.

Sunday Jan 13.

Church mg & aft. Mr Hutchinson twice. Between our services heard part of the Bp of Nancy: who was excellent on the two principles in man & nature of the Christian warfare which he was proceeding to apply in exhibiting the sweetness [?] of all sacrifices made for religion. This he illustrated by the respect paid to the newly appointed Bp of Algiers on his way south.

If the English have behaved with levity in the Churches here they do but alas! follow the example set them by even priests in this respect.

At the Caravita I heard another very good sermon on Ecce Agnus Dei:[2] the preacher showed that by sin we crucify the son afresh, and most earnestly besought his audience to avoid it at least for the next week & until Sunday evening when he might meet them again. There were a few spots of Romanism. Again he addressed a beautiful prayer for pardon to our Lord at the altar: but after having unlocked and opened the *ciborio*.[3]

The other day Ventura announced in the middle of his sermon that una persona di nota had lost a pin in Church, of value because it had touched the relics at Loretto: & promised a reward for its recovery. Today the priest gave notice that certain scudi had been found in the church, which would be restored to their owner: adding 'si raccommanda un' abbondante elemosina.'[4]—The French Bishop motions with his hand & desires the hearer to walk forward to a more commodious part of the Church: & all this without any indecency or *jar*—such is the difference of their manner in freedom as well as force.

Tea with the G.s.

Monday Jan 14.

9–10½. Last sitting to Muller. Papers. Shopping. Went to Mr Richmonds:[5] found only copies & studies but was very much pleased with the talent and sort of mind they exhibit.

Capitol. The Dying Gladiator seems to me to unite the expression of Strength as impersonated in determinate masculine form, with that of Beauty in the modifications of that form, to an astonishing degree, so as *of the two together* to yield a greater aggregate than any other ancient or modern statue. The Apollo in the same room is I see flabby and Sybaritish: he has the form without the formation of the male.

[1] Luke ii. 36–37.
[2] 'Behold the Lamb of God'; John i. 29, 36.
[3] The receptacle for the host.
[4] 'abundant alms are recommended'.
[5] George *Richmond, 1809–96, portrait painter; s. of Thomas*; lived in Rome 1837–9.

Ara Celi to see again the frescoes of Pinturicchio[1] so much esteemed: and the ambones.[2]

Tabulario.[3] Amid the massive remains of the ancient Record Office, the Pope's workmen are employed in opening out the old arches towards the Forum: & in enlarging the prisons. We heard the prisoners singing in strong chorus as we went by. We also visited the bronzes of the Capitol: where the wolf[4] is curious, & the *rosso* bust said to be of Theseus:[5] the Brutus[6] powerful, but in the character of the elder more than the younger & not much of either? & the shepherd[7] beautiful.

One of the rooms is painted with frescoes which claim to be by Perugino.[8]

The Chapel has four Evangelists by Caravaggio and a painting by Pinturicchio. In the Protomoteca disappointed by Canova's monument,[9] & Fra Angelico's bust: pleased with Giotto's, Scb. del Piombo's, and Fra Bartolommeo's: the head much resembles the Bp of London's, the features are larger & therefore finer.

S.M. in Cosmedine[10] (by Janus Quadrifrons &c.) has eight arches in each of the divisions of its nave from the aisles: themselves divided at the fourth by piers. Several large pillars are inserted into the walls: two by a side altar two by the chief entrance: these & the smaller ones are all ancient.[11] A step rises about midway along the nave: at the end a further rise leads to the tribune. On the intermediate space is on one side the pulpit[12] with a stair towards the door & a stair towards the altar: about $\frac{1}{2}$ foot higher than the reading desk,[13] and on the right[14] as one enters: opposite is the reading desk, with a place for the book, turned towards the tribune.[15] Behind the high altar is the Bishop's Chair, with two lions fronts sculptured on its arms: not of the oldest form.[16] This part of the Church is further elevated.

---

[1] Illustrating the life of St. Bernardino of Siena.

[2] Raised reading desks, used in early Christian churches; left and right for Epistle and Gospel.

[3] Record office of ancient Rome, SE. end of Capitol, of which portico was discovered January 1839 while prisons underneath the 14th-century Palace of the Senator were being enlarged.

[4] Capitoline wolf, early Etruscan, perhaps 296 B.C.; suckled by Romulus and Remus, modern.

[5] So given by Carlo Fea, *Nuova Descrizione* (1819), but now held to be Appius Claudius Caecus.

[6] Bronze head, said to be of L. Junius Brutus, first Roman consul, who expelled Tarquin, 509 B.C.

[7] Naked life-size boy, Etruscan style, extracting thorn from his foot; cp. Fea, *Nuova Descrizione*, 228.

[8] Incidents from the Punic war; now rather considered to be by Sodoma.

[9] By Placido Fabris, 1802–59, historical painter and portraitist, at cost of Leo XII.

[10] Third-century church on the way from Capitol and Forum to the left bank of the Tiber.

[11] Remains of 6th century B.C. temple of Ceres, turned into grain-market 4th century A.D., the church built from its ruins.

[12] The Gospel ambo; the old ambos had steps both on east and west sides.

[13] Epistle ambo.

[14] It was the rule that the reader of the Gospel should face north.

[15] Pencil sketches in margin.

[16] i.e. the simple 'cathedra', a chair with rounded back and no arms.

Dined with Mr Hamilton.[1] Mr Severn's & music in the evening.

The Pope's govt. has a revenue of 9–10 mill. scudi, & a debt of 60, almost wholly contracted since the death of Pius VII.[2] The government lands are now almost entirely sold, & pecuniary embarrassment increases.

Tuesday Jan 15.

I meant to have gone at 10 to the Umiltà[3] where a nun professed: but Wiseman called & sat two hours. He said many things interesting & material.

That P. Ventura had proposed to abrogate all the existing sentences against England by way of a step towards peace. That our refusing the common intercourse of nations was urged in objection: i.e. our having no mission at Rome

That the Pope had *told* him (W.) that he would be very much gratified by the reestablishment of diplomatic relations with England.[4]

That the Pope was excessively anxious not to do anything that might bring the Romanists of England under the controul or influence of the state & on this account opposed some measures which everyone else through necessary.

That they contemplated building a Chapel in Southwark of 220 feet by 90 and 80 high: one larger than this in the West End: & in Manchester one with a front 3 feet wider than York Minster, for which the contract had been taken at £20,000.[5] I understood that a considerable part of the funds for these purposes was to be drawn from Mr. Blundell's bequest:[6] and he told me that in order to get immediate possession of the money they had compromised the suit on the personal property, agreeing to pay the Tempests & Stonor's near £50,000: which would leave about £78,000 for their religious purposes.

That the Dublin Review had little countenance in Ireland, and there was a total want of sympathy between the Irish & English R.C.s except as regarded their communion in faith: that O'Connell had come down upon the conductors of the Review with great violence in consequence of their

---

[1] William Richard *Hamilton, 1777–1859, diplomat and antiquarian; uncle of W.K.*

[2] Debt at death of Pius VII, 1823, 1½ million scudi. He established a sinking fund, which disappeared during the reign of Leo XII, 1823–9. Cp. L. Galeotti, *Della Sovranità e del Governo temporale dei Papi* (1846), 127 ff. and N. Nada, *Metternich e le Riforme nello Stato Pontificio. La missione Sebregondi a Roma* (1832–6), on the Austrian attempt to improve finances and administration, in *Biblioteca di Storia Italiana recente*, n.s., iii (1957).

[3] Santa Maria della Umiltà, in the street of the same name, west of the Quirinal; convent built 1603, first of Dominican nuns, then of the Order of the Visitation.

[4] Cp. Add MS 44791, f. 32.

[5] Intended as pro-cathedrals, in anticipation of the restoration of the hierarchy (1850), which was already being mooted. St. George's, Southwark, built 1840–48 from the designs of Pugin; St. John the Evangelist, Salford, built 1844–8; that of London long not built, St. Mary's Moorfields, built 1826, continuing to serve as procathedral till 1869.

[6] Henry *Blundell's three children, John *Gladstone's friend C. R. Blundell and his sisters, Catherine who m. 1795 Thomas Stonor of Stonor (d. 1831) and Elizabeth, d. 1845, who m. 1787 Stephen Tempest of Broughton, fell out over division of their father's estate, of which C. R. Blundell left the bulk to Thomas Weld(-Blundell), 1808–87, of Lulworth. Cp. *DNB* v. 266–7.

not going his lengths, and that probably the Irish connection would be at once broken off & the Review become more exclusively religious.

That he himself was very unpopular in Ireland & that one of the Irish R.C. Bishops had been the author of a letter which lately appeared in the Freeman's Journal, violently attacking him.[1]

That the Irish influence on the English R.C. body was diminishing & likely to diminish: & a great anxiety for peace prevailed.

That they lamented that writers in the Tracts for the Times should have in some places cast imputations on the motives of the priesthood in general: he thought out of deference to Protestant clamour.[2]

That he condemned the principles of govt. without religion & of a secular national education: thought Wyse[3] was not supported by the R.C.s in general.

That they were about to double their number of Episcopal districts in England: & to form chapters which should have the right of election. (HEM[4] says he is to be Bp in the London District—from himself—)

That his recent Discourse[5] on the Oxford principles was from very scanty materials & had some inaccuracies. (I pushed to have it offered me, but he avoided it.) The Pope had made him print it, a great interest having been felt in the Propaganda when it was delivered.

That he thought the R.C. religion from the rapid progress it had already made might secure a national influence in the U.S. & become the national religion.

That Newman would stand in a very awkward position if the Bps in general or any number of them were to assail the general doctrines he had advocated. (Of this I said there was no likelihood.)

That he understood 700 clergymen in England held those sentiments.

That establishing some truths they might lead men on into the whole truth: but that also undoubtedly presenting men with a system much more complete than any other they had known they might stop the inquiries of many who from ultra Protestantism would otherwise have come into the RC Church & keep them in ours.

He asked to see my book: & I requested him to acquaint me with any fault of uncharitableness which he might detect in it.

He considered that there were exaggerated accounts gone abroad in England of the number of conversions to Romanism: however they had some active and influential converts.[6]

---

[1] *MacHale, on 14 November 1838, under the name of Camillus; attacking *Wiseman's *Twelve Lectures on the Connection of Science with Religion* (1836).

[2] Probably *Newman's Tract 71, 'Against Romanism' (1835), particularly 25–26.

[3] (Sir) Thomas *Wyse, 1791–1862; lib. M.P. co. Tipperary 1830–2, Waterford 1835–47; secretary to Board of Control 1846–7; British minister in Athens 1849; K.C.B. 1857. *Stanley and *Russell adopted *Wyse's plan for an Irish national board of education; *Wyse introduced bills in 1830 and 1835, which were dropped.

[4] *Manning.

[5] Read to the Accademia di religione cattolica in Rome on 16th June 1837; cp. *Annali delle Scienze Religiose*, Rome, v. 161 (1837), particularly 166 ff.: principles of the Oxford movement quoted from *Tracts for the Times*.

[6] Next two paragraphs on last page of volume.

He thought their greatest need now was of a central College in London[1] which he hoped that they would be able to build and to place in connection with the newly formed University.

He did not much desire the continuance of the Maynooth vote:[2] but would prefer that their Bishops should have each their Diocesan independent seminary in its stead: the[3] priests were at present ill educated and studied radical newspapers and magazines instead of theology.

At one with Abeken and the G's to [blank][4] studio. No. 9 P. di Spanga. He had Pompeii by a bright sun, the inner edges of the columns actually lighted: just so I saw it in 1832, golden stone in perfectly transparent air on an afternoon of May.[5] The bay of Naples by moonlight, fine chiaroscuro: & the Coliseum by moonlight which can hardly make anything but a good picture.

4 Fontane.[6] Kochs.[7] This artist died on Saturday. He has left abundant evidence of a very powerful poetic fancy: but he has not the dramatical power equally with the symbolical.

A portfolio of drawings from Dante are very splendid. I rejoice to find that an artist of genius has so given himself to the king of poets: it is a noble servitude indeed. Here is the scene of Aristotle and Homer, among others, about wh I had lately conversation with Macdonald. In the drawings one does not find the deficiencies which struck me in the frescoes generally of the Dante room.[8] Still they are below Flaxman in conception.

We saw Balaam with the angel & his ass refusing—Diana & Actaeon— The good Samaritan—Homer addressing his island audience & many more.[9] Macdonald likewise spoke to me about this last. Koch has I think erred in not giving prominence enough to the female hearers. Is it not in the hymn

χαίρετε δ'ὑμεῖς πᾶσαι

and

ὑμεῖς δ'εὖ μάλα πᾶσαι ἀποκρίνασθε κτλ.[10]

Hence to the
Villa Ludovisi,[11] which Prince Piombino[12] keeps very jealously closed with rare exceptions. The top afforded a delicious view. In an upper chamber was the *Fama* of Guercino. Unfortunately the descriptions of Homer and Vir-

---

[1] Eventually established by *Manning in 1874; closed 1878.
[2] Maynooth College, west of Dublin, founded 1795 to train Roman Catholic priests, currently got an annual grant of £9,250 of public money.
[3] Instead of 'they'.
[4] 'Ketel's?' pencilled faintly in blank. Jean Ketel, 19th-century genre painter.
[5] See 7 May 32.   [6] Strada Quattro Fontane, where Koch had lived.
[7] Joseph Anton Koch, 1768–1839.
[8] Weaknesses in anatomy, and inexperience in fresco.
[9] Pictures in Koch's studio at his death.
[10] 'Hail, all ye women', hymn to Delian Apollo, 166, addressed to the women of Delos and 'do you all, ladies, answer fair etc.' (Homer: ὑποκρίνασθε) ibid. 171 (to those inquiring who he is in whose song they delight).
[11] On the Pincio, near the northern Porta Pinciana.
[12] Luigi Boncompagni-Ludovisi, 1767–1841, prince of Piombino, duke of Soria.

gil[1] cannot I suppose be reduced to palpable form. Fame flies above with a trumpet, carrying all her canvass: below is a martial figure, a globe, Orpheus, representing the different kinds of reputation.

The red mantle is touched with peculiarly vivid colouring.

Below in one room are two landscape frescoes by Domenichino & two by Guercino: the colouring has not stood. In another, the celebrated Aurora.[2] She is the

Tithoni croceum linquens Aurora cubile.[3]

He is behind under a saffron mantle.

She on her car, with two steeds powerful and full of spirit: pieballed. Cherubs scatter lilies and flowers, & crown Aurora with a wreath. In front are two sets of Hours, three in each, & stars in the hands of several of them. Below at one end is the figure of night, asleep, with a head something like this painter's Sybil: the owl & bat, appropriate symbols: the figure of Day as a boy near, awakening. At the other end, the figure of the Morning Star personified. This fresco is not so well preserved as Guido's:[4] & has less composition and effect: more force, and more fancy.

Among the statues we looked chiefly at the majestic Roman & more than majestic Greek Juno:[5] (Abeken said he could not live with it in his room:) the Poetus and Arria[6]—he stabs himself above the collar bone and supports with the left hand her dying figure: this group is of the workmanship they say of the Dying Gladiator, & whether Greek or Roman is uncertain: The *man* is very fine indeed & yet does not bear view from *all* points like the Gladiator, & the form is less refined?

The opposite figures of two warriors, sitting, one with the hands holding round the left knee & sustaining the leg in air: the back becomes very round in this attitude: the other has the body thrown forward towards the knees by balance alone: an arm here has been most abominably restored: the head of the first has more beauty & the form is more finished: but both are indeed great in the view it appears of judges.

At seven we met at the Vatican: Sir W. James,[7] Mrs & Miss Ellison, Mr Knight,[8] the Glynnes, the Brabazons, Mr Macdonald & myself for our torch-light expedition among the statues.[9] We stood chiefly before

The Modesty, a Roman matron? opposite the Medica, Silenus, Demosthenes, the Venus Anadyomene, Nile, Minerva, and the Dacians.

The headless Niobid—sitting Tiberius. young Augustus—

---

[1] *Iliad*, ii. 93 f., *Odyssey*, xxiv. 413 f., *Aeneid*, iv. 173–190.
[2] Fresco on the ceiling of the hall on the ground floor.
[3] 'Aurora leaving the saffron bed of Tithonus', Virgil, *Georgics*, i. 447.
[4] In the Palazzo Rospigliosi.   [5] Colossal heads.
[6] When her husband Paetus was accused of conspiracy against the emperor Claudius, 41–54, Arria accompanied him to Rome for trial, and on the way stabbed herself, saying 'Paetus, it does not hurt'; whereupon he also stabbed himself.
[7] Sir Walter Charles James, 1816–93, *Castelreagh's nephew; 2nd bart. 1829, m. Miss. Ellison 1841, tory M.P. Hull 1837–47, cr. lord Northbourne 1884.
[8] Perhaps John Prescott *Knight, 1803–81, painter.
[9] The statues of the Vatican Museum might be seen by torchlight by application to the major-domo through a consul or diplomatic agent. Wax torches, of 4 lb. each, supplied by the party.

Torso—Meleager—Perseus, boxers—Apollo—Laocoon—Mercury. This last is a robust tho active figure and does not correspond with the name: nor has it now any of the *insignia*, but it is said to have had the caduceus. The Perseus says M. wants more strength of character, and a firm attitude —as it stands, it might be easily pushed over. Also the lower parts of the figure are too short. The Creugas is the finest of the boxers but both are grand, so M. also said—

In the Galleria di Statue, the Ariadne—demi figure of Love, of early & severe Greek workmanship—Amazon—Jupiter sitting—the rosso Faun— Some of the colossal figures in the Sala Rotonda—

Apollo Sauroctonus, Phocion, and the discoboli, in the Biga hall.

I had thought they would make more use of the lights[1] in projecting the masses from behind: this however was done with the Apollo & some others, including the Laocoon on its being called for.

(NB. In Titian's Profane & Sacred Love, the latter is unclothed the former clothed: & the naked is clearly the more sacred of the two.)

Tea at Mrs Ellison's.

Wednesday Jan 16.

Preparations for departure thicken. At twelve however we went to the Museo Gregoriano[2] which is very rich in Etruscan antiquities with some few others. Some of the walls are painted with copies from the tombs and there is one exact imitation of a tomb with the vases in it as found, in niches, & on the dust.

There is a fine bronze statue of a warrior below the size of life: hard but of considerable merit? Abundance of utensils, & splendidly rich ornaments chiefly sacerdotal. The gold frontlets[3] are particularly beautiful. The vases I imagine cannot equal the Naples collection.

In afternoon calls, Lewis's studio with A. Harrison—to finish my visit— & Sign. Vallati[4] No 5 Via Margutta to see his Magdalen of Correggio—the most beautiful work of the artist, I think, which I have seen. Strange as it may appear the family have at present a sentence [?] against him and it was delivered by two supplemental judges only—he has now appealed to the Reta.[5]

Divided the evening between Sterling's and Mrs Lindsay's. At the first Abeken gave some light on German philosophy. At the second, Macdonald examined some heads, mine included—

Thursday Jan 17.

Quirinal[6] with the G.s—Here are St Peter & St Paul by Fra Bartolommeo, & worthy of him: a seapiece of Bassano's, rare for the subject & more

[1] *Sc.* torches.
[2] Of the Vatican; founded 1836 by Gregory XVI, containing antiquities excavated principally 1818–36.
[3] For the heads of priests.   [4] Roman animal painter.
[5] Court of Appeal in secular causes, for the Papal States.
[6] Palace of the popes; residence of kings of Italy, 1870–1946.

interesting than are his in general. A singular Indian picture from Dyce Sombre's nuwb,[1] in which the likenesses are said to be very strong and I can believe it from his: we had an opportunity of judging from meeting him in the Vatican. The Pope's chapel has frescoes & an altarpiece by Guido:[2] & an organ in it which is not used in functions.—It seems a strange custom that the benches in the outer halls have the title of the reigning Pope painted all along them, thrice for instance on each seat for three: on each accession the new name is substituted.

Vatican: went over the pictures which suggested some ideas that I cannot now record.[3] Compare however the two Incoronazioni,[4] side by side, one in Raphael's early manner, the other from one of his latest designs, & executed by the Fattore[5] & G. Romano apparently unfinished below.

S. Onofrio.[6] Frescoes by Domenichino representing the Madonna with angels,[7] & passages of St. Jerome:[8] in the Church, Pinturicchio, Baldassare Peruzzi,[9] & a picture by A. Caracci wh did not interest.

S. Pietro in Montorio.[10] Flagellation by S. del Piombo.[11] Here is shown a place as the spot of St. Peter's crucifixion.[12] Dined with the Brabazons.

Friday Jan 18.

On this day I saw the baker's tomb again:[13] went to S. Agostino[14] which had hitherto escaped me. The votive offerings which must amount to many thousands have all according to the sacristan been deposited within 15 years.—The picture by Guercino[15] in the transept at S. Augustine's altar is a fine specimen of the artist.—Raphael's Isaiah does not satisfy after one has seen the Prophets of Michael Angelo as it falls far far beneath them in soul and character.

[1] David Ochterlony *Dyce-Sombre, 1808–51, born Sirdhana, not far from Delhi, convert to Roman Catholicism, the religion of the Begum of Sombre, his great-grandmother; came to England in 1838; whig M.P. Sudbury 1841, unseated 1842, declared mad 1843. The picture, in the Pope's antechamber, is of the consecration of the church at Sirdhana in 1822.

[2] By Guido Reni, of the life of the Virgin; and altarpiece of annunciation, others by Francesco Albani, painter, 1578–1660.

[3] Later entries from now (if not earlier) till 6 Feb. 39, completed on 2 March.

[4] Crownings of the Virgin.

[5] Giovanni Francesco Penni, 1488–1528, called Il Fattore ('the executor'), historical painter.

[6] Cp. 24 Apr. 32.

[7] In the lunette of the portico over the entrance to the church: attribution considered erroneous.

[8] Sc. from the life of St. Jerome, the church having been built 1439 with adjoining monastery of Hermits of St. Jerome by the Hieronymite Nicholas di Forca Palena.

[9] 1481–1536, painter, architect and engraver.

[10] Near Santa Maria in Trastevere, right bank of Tiber; founded by Constantine.

[11] From designs of Michel Angelo.

[12] In an adjacent courtyard, over which Donato Bramante da Urbino, 1444–1514, painter and architect, erected a Tempietto.

[13] Cp. 14 Dec. 38.

[14] At the southern extremity of the Via della Ripetta, which runs SW. from the Porta del Popolo.

[15] Of St. Augustine.

37—II.

Enjoyed a last look at S. Andrea[1] & left a note for P. Ventura. J.N.G's natale.[2]

Tea with the G.s.[3]—Packed: & after midnight

Saturday Jan 19

bade a reluctant adieu to this mysterious City: whither he should repair who wishes to renew for a time the *dream* of life.

9½ hours to Civita Vecchia.[4] Coast low and bare. Town rather good. The Inn, Europa, fed us well: but also eat a considerable portion, at least of me. We are four in company: Glynne, James, Mildmay,[5] & myself.

There is here a shop of antiquities: partly Etruscan & partly Roman. The labourers gather them & every *Sunday* morning come to negotiate for their sale with the bottegajo.[6] He is allowed to keep his shop open during the whole Sunday, as otherwise he would miss some steam-boat customers. One sees already in the shops here the results of easy intercourse with France & access to her manufactures.—Very few vessels in the harbour: from one they were unloading English fish to send to Rome.

Sunday Jan 20.

The *Tancrède*, royal war steamer, or as she is called *Paquebot de l'Etat*, was detained at Messina by foul weather: we were thus debarred of our Sunday at Leghorn:[7] sailing at midday, instead of at two yesterday: & arriving at Leghorn at 3 A.M. of Monday.

At C.V. I read Manning's Tract on modern pulpit Eloquence, written by some priest:[8] grievously complaining of the internally relaxed condition of the R.C. Church. Such is their tone, whenever one gets at them from within.

Monday Jan 21.

Landed at Leghorn to breakfast at Thompson's,[9] such an operation being out of the question on board—where however I hear the food is excellent: & all are obliged to pay. Went to Micali's.

Tuesday Jan 22.

At 12 sailed: & arrived at Marseilles[10] on Tuesday evening at 10½ against a strong headwind most of the way. There is much beautiful & bold coast to

[1] Della Valle, served by the Theatine monks, of whom Padre Ventura was one.
[2] birthday.
[3] Cp. 6 Feb. 39, pp. ii. 576–7: his proposal to Catherine Glynne. Letters in Magnus, 38–39.
[4] Port 40 miles WNW. of Rome.
[5] Paulet Henry St. John Mildmay, 1814–58, of Hazlegrove, Taunton, Somerset; Christ Church, Oxford; afterwards in army.
[6] 'Shopkeeper', called Pucci; whose gallery of antiquities were all for sale.
[7] 120 miles NW. of Civita Vecchia.
[8] Sc. 'tract given me by Manning'; perhaps the 40-page tract by G. Muttirolo 'Un Desiderio sulla predicazione', which may have appeared early in January.
[9] Hotel on the quay.   [10] About 250 miles west of Leghorn.

be seen on the passage: but I could not get sight of a great deal of it being on or in bed.

Wednesday Jan 23.

Landed in the morning & went through a pretty strict search at the Custom-house. We placed ourselves at the Hotel Beauveau[1] in the street of that name: which we found good and reasonable: better that is than inns in the commercial towns of England generally. The main event of my day was getting rid of my sickness. We are unfortunately detained an extra day through a mistake in writing for the places which caused them to be taken for the 24th instead of the 23rd.—Wrote to Rome.

Thursday Jan 24.

The day was fine & we walked about the town a good deal, and made divers provisions for our journey. The town is finely situated on the slope around its port, and flanked as it were by the Castle[2] and the Lazaretto:[3] it does not appear to have fine public buildings but it has handsome streets, the S. Ferréon[4] containing shops as showy as I have ever seen: there the old cooped and steep passages, for they are no more, have their interest & rather remind one of the old town of Edinburgh: while the business and shipping of the port, both very great in themselves, are so concentrated as to render the quays a scene of great liveliness and striking commercial activity. Everywhere there is an appearance of employment and material wellbeing: one does not see a large number either of Churches or book-seller's shops. A stall-keeper told me he sold more of Walter Scott than *any other novelist*.

I saw in the Canabière[5] at a shop appearing to serve the purpose of our house-agencies and servant's register offices, a formidable column of advertisements under the head '*à marier*'. There were eleven separate notices, all from females, ten of them widows, ages varying from 24 to 45 and 50, no other particular mentioned except the fortunes, which in one case (of a quinquagenarian advertiser) rose to no less than 400,000 francs. What a strange picture of humanity is this! Let us observe however that none of the parties were in the early stage of marriageable life, so this strange method is not absolutely preferred.

Friday Jan 25   Saturday Jan 26.   Sunday Jan. 27.

At midnight we started by the Malle Poste[6]—and our journey occupied 76 hours.

[1] Near the port.
[2] The Chateau d'If, on one of the group of islands a little west of the port.
[3] Immense public hospital covering 50 acres, to the north side of the port.
[4] Rue Saint Ferréol near the east side of the harbour.
[5] Rue de la Cannebière, striking east from the harbour to join the Cours and Rue de Rome, the street traversing the town from the north.
[6] Mail coach; limited to two or three passengers with not more than 55 lbs baggage. Faster than posting.

The cold was severe: and defence is rendered more difficult the more the duration of the trial is protracted.

The distance is called 530 miles. We had a good deal of indifferent road, & some snow: in summer the journey should be done in 70 hours, according to the courier. The carriage is of clumsy construction though a great improvement when compared with the house & mountain like Diligences on seeing which when not actually in progress one might be tempted to doubt or to deny the moveableness, of *all* things earthly.

We stopped at Avignon[1] and [Valence][2] on Friday: St. Etienne[3] and Moulins[4] on Saturday: and Briere[5] (?) only on Sunday: at most of these for an hour. There was a good deal of snow, particularly on La Republique[6] where—as might be anticipated from the name—we were in great danger of an overturn. We found a few cases of churches building. On the Sunday we saw apparently as much traffic on the road as on other days: and in the towns people standing & idling as in Girgenti[7] with this addition, that the shops in general were open: which disappointed me. There was very great cold particularly before and about dawn. Three of the nights I spent in the cabriolet:[8] the feet require very great defence—nothing appears equal to skins for this purpose. At the Inns or eating houses where we stopped we were well fed, but sometimes rather dear.—James & Mildmay we found performed the journey posting in four days and four nights. On arriving at Paris at 4½ in the morning of Monday we were obliged to have our portmanteaus opened by the city custom-house officers: barbarous enough, all things considered, although the tops were lifted up, and no more. With this delay & the slow walking of a porter overweighted with a column of luggage, Glynne & I (here parting from our fellow traveller Verner)[9] were frozen[10] by the time we reached Meurice's. I not only went to bed, but was awakened at 9, with feet stone-cold.

Monday Jan 28.

The general shop and street architecture of Paris it must be confessed very much excels that of London, besides the superiority of the city in respect of magnificent combinations as along the Rue Rivoli and the river.

Glynne and I went to see the Arch[11] & the Madeleine. Of the former I doubt whether it is equal to that at Milan.[12] Some of the sculptures on the

[1] 50 miles NW. of Marseilles.
[2] 65 miles north of Avignon.
[3] 45 miles NW. of Valence.
[4] 90 miles NW. of St. Etienne.
[5] Briare, 80 miles NNW. of Moulins.
[6] The coach.
[7] Instead of 'Sicily'.
[8] The name given on the continent to the framework fitted high behind the low-hung mail-coach, English 'dickey', for the conductor.
[9] Probably James Edward Verner, 1804–65, s. of Thomas Verner, nephew of 1st bart., at Eton with *Glynne, major London Irish Volunteers, lt.-col. in Bengal army.
[10] 'fro cold' here deleted.
[11] De Triomphe, crowning the Champs Elysées on the right bank of the Seine.
[12] Cp. 21 Sept. 38.

exterior, I mean the principal ones, are very heavy and disagreeable. And it is not a little wonderful to see in the list of military actions inscribed in the almost endless list, such names as (I think) Talavera, Salamanca, Ciudad Rodrigo, Almeida.[1] Surely they had victories enough without recording as such disaster & defeat. This arch has a very grand position, the crown of a hill which is also the finest entrance into Paris. Its scale is very grand.

As to the Madeleine[2] it is beautiful enough to make one ashamed of English works in the Ecclesiastical kind, at least in the exterior. Inside, I like neither the combination of colour, nor the complex artificial arrangement of the sides, nor the stunted dimensions of the columns of the smaller order, nor the unmeaning line of them which runs round the Tribune.[3] Outside, I could not admire the crowded & constrained pediment,[4] & heartily wished some of the ornaments about the frieze[5] away, & (of course) Corinthian for composite columns,[6] & wondered at the fatuity of the blind windows:[7] but after all, this is a magnificent peripteral temple, and at least as much above most of the modern Church architecture as it is below the purest Greek of Pæstum (the best I have seen). Outside abt 264 f. by 90?

Meurice's table d'hote presented a profusion of dishes in weary succession, and a large company of somewhat questionable order, much more American than English: & perhaps the Americans would not thank me for saying so. The general arrangements of the hotel are very good, and of a kind to save the traveller trouble in every possible way: all the prices fixed

Tuesday Jan 29.

Attempted the Louvre but in vain—it was closed until I think the beginning of March. Busy on the book stalls: & went by the quays to Notre Dame. Glynne says there is much to praise in the architecture of this Church: but its general effect is not happy: and the double aisles with massive pillars here as in St John Lateran take away very much from the magnitude of the edifice. The painted windows are striking.

It is interesting & strange to read on the walls of this Church the Monition (I am uncertain of the right appellation) of the Archbishop of Paris for the approaching season of Lent: very stringent as respects all separatists from the Church, but also high-strung as respects discipline internally; treating for example of the use of meat in Lent just as if it had been written

---

[1] Battles of Talavera and Salamanca, 1809 and 1812, were *Wellington's victories; he took Almeida and Ciudad Rodrigo in 1811 and 1812, both taken by the French in 1810.
[2] Founded 1763, converted by Napoleon into Temple of Glory 1808, dedicated 1816 to the Magdalene, completed 1843.
[3] Corinthian columns round the church, smaller Ionic columns in the Tribune.
[4] High-relief by Philippe Joseph Henri Lemaire, 1798–1880, of the Saviour at the day of Judgment with the Magdalene in supplication at his feet, with virtues and vices.
[5] Running round the exterior of the church, angels, with garlands of fruit and flowers.
[6] The columns are Corinthian.
[7] Light is transmitted through the centres of the three domes.

two hundred years ago. But now those only listen and obey who choose: and if we are to judge from appearances in Paris, few indeed they are.

Dined early at a restaurant, and left Paris at four by the Aigle[1] for Boulogne.[2] (Ln. Feb. 39.)

I was surprised to find a licentious song of which the burden was "Vive le Dimanche"—the reason assigned being, that with it came ease and dissipation. But all those who thus subject the Sabbath to their will, become themselves the slaves in turn of their necessities: this is the sure if not immediate result.

Our Aigle was a (scarcely) moving house: there was snow on the ground and the whimsical vehicle had a predilection for going down the hills sideways. We took 31 hours instead of 21 or 22—five English horses brought us in the last stage gallantly. At Abbeville[3] (Ecu de Brabant) we had an excellent *dejeuner*.

It was very sad to find two Parisians who with an Englishman were my companions in the *rotonde*, gross in their conversation both agt. decency and agt. religion: rank and blasphemous infidelity, and hardly civility upon these subjects though abundance on every other. There was a good deal of insight into the details of Parisian manners: and a picture of the Sunday balls, as the regular occasions of intrigue the most unblushing & systematic, which exceeded what anyone could have supposed. At five last Monday morning as we were walking home we met persons coming out from them.

These men extolled Paris as a perfect Paradise: & one said he had at one time settled elsewhere, but at the expence of nearly all his substance he returned.[4]

Wednesday Jan 30.

Boulogne detained us only an hour. It looked clean & rather English— though the people were all at home. The crowds of commissioners & porters beat however either England or any other country I have seen. The rate of charge denotes the neediness of the class that resides here. In my Inn (the Ship) I met a man who said something. I asked if he was going to England 'Indeed I am not' he replied with a sigh as long (perhaps) as the bills that banish him.

The Steamer was small & crowded & as it blew fresh & was very cold the prospect for the night was not of the best. Mr Church[5] kindly gave me what they called his berth—about four feet long. I was just able by packing up my legs to stretch on my back: & so escaped while nearly all were sick. We left soon after 12: three or four hours, & we were out of the rough water. At 2 P.M. we reached London Bridge.

[1] Diligence.
[2] 130 miles NNW. of Paris.
[3] 85 miles NNW. of Paris.
[4] Extracts in Magnus, 40.
[5] Unidentified.

Thursday Jan 31.

I found great civility at the Custom House, but defective arrangements &
two hours delay. Between four & five I surprised my Father in his sitting-
room younger thank God (except as to an obstruction which we hope is
temporary of his vision), than I have almost ever seen him.

(Ln. Mch 2. 39.)

London Feb. 6. 1839.[1]

In my accustomed review at the end of the past year I found that I had passed through more real depression in the earlier half of it, than ever before, and that this depression was attended with a partial diminution of sin in some of its branches: but such is the subtlety of that evil principle that one cannot tell what advances it may have made in other quarters while we are congratulating ourselves upon a partial repression of some one of its forms, because those advances are frequently veiled and imperceptible long after they have begun to be operative.

I had also another cause for useful humiliation in a circumstance connected with my journey: namely that the admission of one,[2] who has I am certain a single eye & an enlightened conscience, to the familiar intercourse of companionship in travel, had shown him the delusiveness of that gloss which I sometimes seem to wear upon my outward character, and had led him to say, and to leave unretracted, more severe sentences than have been passed upon me for a very long time if ever: as for example to express suspicions of my deliberate insincerity.

A retrospect would hardly suffice me to trace the growth & grounds of the conviction which issued in my letter of the 17th.[3] sent on the morning of the 18th to the Europa, and followed by a conversation in a walk, about noon on that day. Here again—yes, even a third time—it would appear that in incorrigible stupidity, I have been precipitate. And yet not perhaps to the extent that no suspicion of my leaning was entertained previously to the declaration then made: so at least I inferred from our discourse.

The truth is I believe my affections are more worthless than ever. Poured forth more than once & more than once repudiated they have become stale and unprofitable: and I am strangely divided between the pain of solitude in the heart and the shame of soliciting a love which I sometimes fear it is impossible for me to repay. I am so deadened and exhausted by what has taken place: my still dreams of romance have been so near my real life and their dissipation has brought so much devastation, at least the pain of devastation, upon it: that I am to one who freshly and genuinely loves, what a sacked and blackened country, seared[4] with recent conflagration, is to the green[5] shady and well watered vales which have never known the tread of the spoiler. And yet I suffered more & more from being *inwardly* alone, & I more & more felt my childish dependence: childish, not childlike, because it is gracefully appropriate to the nature of a child, whereas I fear that in my circumstances a nature truly noble would probably come to the conclusion that it had nothing left to give which would be worthy of any woman herself such as to be worthy of its

[1] Lambeth MS 1424 resumed.   [2] *Kinnaird.
[3] His proposal to Catherine Glynne.
[4] 'seared' over an illegible word; 'over and' then deleted.
[5] 'well' here deleted.

attachment.—I offer myself therefore with many conflicting feelings: but this time must I suppose be the last, were it only for shame's sake.

In her C.G. I saw what I desired, as I think distinctly developed: the admiration of sacrifice made for great objects—and a gentle not unwomanly contempt for the luxurious pleasures of the world. She said to me in a Church when we observed upon the profusion of labour bestowed in its embellishment, and the contrast between our parsimony in the house of God and our secular luxuries "do you think we can be justified in indulging ourselves in all those luxuries?" I loved her for this question:[1] oh how we want that which shall surrender, that rather which shall escape from, some at least of the burden [of] outward life, that our souls may be free to look at God and our Redeemer and to have the putting His will simply into act for their hourly & continual as well as their daily discipline. And now that she has I think kindly and generously desired, or hinted, a suspension, how sweet a thing it is to reflect, that her heart and will are entirely in the hands of God, to do as it seemeth Him fit: she is removed from all advantitious circumstances: in the clear recesses of her own mind where Divine light alone I trust shall penetrate, she will be led to a decision in which second motives will have no part.[2] May He in this and in all things be with her.— Since returning to town as well as before, I have been anxiously receiving and even seeking testimonies respecting my book. Thank God they are on the whole more favourable than I had any right to expect. Church authorities and the clergy generally so far as I can learn approve: many of them warmly: the Bp of London writes it;[3] & the Abp. of Canterbury I am told says it. My political leaders have as yet said nothing. Stephen & the doctrinaires differ in part yet sympathise. The Germans on the whole approve: including, they say, the Crown Prince of Prussia,[4] who means to have it translated: but I fancy they do not agree as to the limits of the term Catholic Church. From both Universities, I have favourable accounts. From Scotland they are mixed: those which are most definite tend to show there is considerable soreness, at which God knows I am not surprised, but I have not sought nor desired it & I trust none of it is ascribable to the manner of what has been done.

On Thursday Jan 31 I returned to C[arlton] G[ardens] & found my dear Father delightfully well—Tom in Sandwich—John in Ireland—the rest in Liverpool. We dined with the Tylers & in the evening strove to make a commencement in opening my letters and parcels.

Friday Feb. 1.

Pursued the labours of yesterday, but not yet with much effect. Dined at

---

[1] Version of question and comment in Battiscombe, 26.
[2] See 27 May, 8 June 39.   [3] Add MS 44356, ff. 149–51.
[4] Friedrich Wilhelm (IV) von Hohenzollern, 1795–1861; prince royal of Prussia 1797; fought in France 1814; friend of Bunsen's; king 1840; supported Jerusalem bishopric; espoused, then opposed, revolution of 1848; paralysed 1857.

Uncle D.s.—Much family conversation with Mr G.—& went through the Parlt lists for him to circulate his pamphlets,[1] which I read last night. Wrote to R. Caparn—H. Thompson—J.G. & Co.

Sat. Feb. 2.

Calls. Home arrangements. Wrote to Manning. Lincoln—Kessner[2]—Huddlestone—Bromley—Ramsay—J.N.G.—Jas Moncreiff—Weldon[3]—Hayward[4]—A. Gordon[5]—Beecham—W. Ward. (Nk)[6]—Burnet[7]—Simons[8]—H. Taylor—and some others. arranged corrections of my book for 3d Edition.[9]

S. 3.

St James's mg & aft. read the Bp of London's Charge[10]—poor Mr Armstrong's Three Discourses[11]—& part of Wilberforce's Essay.[12]

M. 4.

The conversations connected with my book take up no inconsiderable time: but they enable me to turn the subject over a hundred times in my mind, which in single thought would be wearisome. Acland here in evg, on Edn & my book. Wrote to Jacobson—Girdlestone—Bp of London—Murray.

T. 5.

Read Jachin[13]—Carlyle.[14]
wrote to T.G.—Mr G.—J.G. & Co
House 4½–6, and 8¼–12. Voted in 426:86 agt radical amendment to the Address.[15]
Conv. with Bonham & others on Sandwich—& wrote a draft for B. to send. meant to prevent the door from closing utterly.[16]

[1] John *Gladstone, 'The Repeal of the Corn Laws . . . Considered' (1839): he favoured them.
[2] G. A. C. Kestner.
[3] Thomas Weldon, Newark accountant.
[4] Abraham *Hayward, 1801–84, essayist; in his *Correspondence*, i. 67 (1886).
[5] Abercromby Lockhart Gordon, educationist, minister at Aberdeen.
[6] William Ward, Newark bricklayer or labourer.
[7] Unidentified.
[8] Possibly Nicholas Simons, 1810?–86, vicar of Bramfield, Suffolk, 1846.
[9] Imminent.
[10] C. J. *Blomfield, 'A Charge Delivered to the Clergy of the Diocese of London' (1838).
[11] G. Armstrong, *Abuse of Power in the State: the Cause and Support of Corrupt Doctrine in the Church . . . in Three Discourses . . . with an Address, Explanatory of the Author's Secession from the United Church of England and Ireland* (1838).
[12] H. W. *Wilberforce, *Essay on the Parochial System* (1838).
[13] W. Roberts and W. Nicholson, *The Call Upon The Church Considered in Two Essays* (1838), pt. 2: 'Jachin. The Right Hand Pillar of the Church'.
[14] T. *Carlyle, *Critical and Miscellaneous Essays: Collected and Republished*, 4v. (1839).
[15] Amdt, proposing further parliamentary reform, by *Duncombe, *H* xlv. 125.
[16] There was a vacancy at Sandwich; but Thomas Gladstone did not get offered the candidacy.

W. 6.

[Saw] Taylor, Hope, Harrison, Ph. Pusey, Gaskell, successively, on my book.
Wrote to H.J.G.—J.N.G.—H. Thompson, & Scotts—Ashley—Sir F. Palgrave.
House $3\frac{1}{2}$–$6\frac{1}{4}$.[1] Began Ld Brougham on Anc. Eloquence.[2]

Th. 7.

Saw Rio—Mr Bunsen[3]—Dear J.s. marriage: adsit Deus.[4] Wrote to T.G.—
Dr Hook—Mr Perkins (Leeds)[5]—Mr Bishop (Nottingham)—Mr G.
Started the project of sending young G. Christie[6] to Oxford that he may become a clergyman. Glynne, Doyle, Rio, Gaskell, Hope, Harrison, to dinner.[7]

Fr. 8.

Since return I have begun to read a little & thank God I think my eyes are really on the whole better. I have begun Carlyle—Merle d'Aubigne[8]—Coleridge's Letters.[9]
& read Wilberforce on Eln Committees[10]—Chandler's Address[11]—Hook's appx[12]—Mr G. on Corn Laws, & some more already noticed.
Wrote to Mr Sheppard.—Mr Hughes—Mr Macrom[13]—T.G.—J.N.G.—H.J.G.
Dined at Dss of Beaufort's.
House $4\frac{1}{2}$–$6\frac{1}{2}$.[14]

Sat 9.

Wrote to R.G.—Mr Legh (Nk)[15]—Mr Selwyn—read Carlyle—began Horner (Holland Report)[16]—see pp. xxxiv–ix.

[1] Misc. business: *H* xlv. 129.
[2] H. *Brougham, *Speeches of . . . *Brougham upon Questions Relating to Public Rights, Duties and Interests; with . . . a Critical Dissertation upon the Eloquence of the Ancients*, 4 v. (1838).
[3] Cp. F. Bunsen, *Bunsen*, i. 501 (1868).
[4] 'may God be with it'. J. N. Gladstone's marriage to Elizabeth Bateson.
[5] Possibly Charles Perkins, Leeds solicitor.
[6] Charles Henry, s. of Albany Henry, Christie; b. 1820?; at Queen's College, Oxford 1840–44; for a time curate of Lewknor, Oxfordshire.
[7] See A. F. Rio, *Epilogue à l'art chrétien* (1870), ii. 354–5.
[8] Presumably more of his *Histoire de la Réformation*.
[9] S. T. *Coleridge, ed. T. Allsop, *Letters, Conversations and Recollections*, 2 v. (1836).
[10] W. Wilberforce the younger, 'The Law and Practice of Election Committees in a Letter to the Electors of Hull' (1839).
[11] G. Chandler, 'An Inaugural Address, Delivered at the First Meeting of the Chichester Literary and Philosophical Society' (1831).
[12] W. F. *Hook, 'A Call to Union on the Principles of the English Reformation . . . with an appendix containing extracts from the Reformers' (1838).
[13] Unidentified.
[14] Misc. business: *H* xlv. 197.
[15] J. W. Lee?
[16] V. Cousin, tr. L. *Horner, *On the State of Education in Holland, as Regards Schools for the Working Classes and for the Poor* (1838).

Rio here 2½ hours[1]—2 hours with Mrs Austin[2] on Edn. book buying for self & Carlton. dined at Peel's. Not a word from him S[tanley] or G[raham] yet even to acknowledge the receipt of my poor book: but no change in manner, certainly none in P's or G.s.[3]

10. Sunday.

St James's mg & aft. Walk.
Read Merle d'Aubignè—Strype's Parker—Hook's Appx—Xtn Knowl. Report S. Scripture[4]

11. M.

Wrote to Caparn (bis) Japp,[5] Rn G., Dss Beaufort, Dealtry, Hussey.
　　N.S. Commee of Inqy 1½–5: House 6¼.[6] dined in B. Square.
read Scott on the Ballot[7]—& Acland's letters on Edn.[8]

12 T.

Wrote to Taunton—H.J.G.—Backhouse—read Exeter Edn Report[9]—Lord Durham's Amn Report[10]—Horner.
Calls: which however I am not making on my general acquaintance, in order as far as possible to avoid invitations, without noise.
House 4¾–12,[11] home to tea in the midst. Found Mr G.—Saw Mr Gildea[12] on Irish Edn—Carlton Libr. C.

13. Ash Wednesday.

Wrote to Caparn—H. Thompson—W.K. Hamilton—Mr Sherwood.[13]
read Bp of Oxford's Charge[14]—& Edinbro 1638 Meeting's proceedings.[15]
Fast until dinner—wh was at C. Mackenzie's—Church at 11—Mr Ward preached.

---

[1] See Bowe, *Rio*, 159–61.
[2] Sarah *Austin, 1793–1867, translator; née Taylor; m. 1820 John *Austin the jurist.
[3] Version of last sentence in Morley, i. 177. *Graham told Teignmouth 'he could not understand it': Teignmouth, *Reminiscences*, ii. 226 (1878). *Peel called it 'trash': T. W. *Reid, *Houghton*, i. 316n.
[4] In the *Record*.
[5] Possibly Richard Jebb, 1806–84; barrister at Lincoln's Inn 1832; vicar general of Isle of Man 1861.
[6] Wheat: *H* xlv. 228.
[7] Untraced.
[8] 'National Education. The Present State of the Question Elucidated' (1839).
[9] Exeter Diocesan Board of Education, *Report* (1839).
[10] *PP* 1839, xvii. 5: 'Report on the Affairs of British North America', signed by *Durham on 31 January, but mainly written by *Buller, foundation of Canadian independence.
[11] Education, Scottish courts, &c: *H* xlv. 273.
[12] George Robert Gildea, 1803?–87; at Trinity, Dublin; ordained 1826; provost of Tuam 1872.
[13] Unidentified.
[14] R. *Bagot, 'A Charge Delivered to the Clergy of the Diocese of Oxford' (1838).
[15] Signature of the Scottish National Covenant.

14. Th.

Wrote to G.S. Smythe (Camb)[1]—Spedding—G. Heathcote[2]—Mr Maxfield (Rev.)[3]
read Horner's Transln of Cousin.
Caparn here on Nk business. 12–1 calls & shopping—1–4½ school Commees —discussing the Catechism question—House to 6—& again 8½–12. Voted in 177:63 for retaining Eln Commee jurisdiction.[4]

15 Fr.

Wrote to Girdlestone—Rodber[5]—A.M. Campbell—G. Sinclair—Sec. Treasury[6]—T.G.
read Horner's Cousin's Holland—& Maurice.
Carlton Libr. Comm. at 3—Caparn on Nk business.
House 5–6¾[7]—dined at Ld Vernon's.[8] Lady Parke's afr.
At a conference with the Bp of London, Ld Sandon & I found him favourable to the important change we hope to see in N.S. rules respecting the use of the Catechism. He is to manage it tomorrow in the Standing Committee.

16. Sat.

Wrote to Caparn—Mrs Austin[9]—Vicar of Newark—T. Godfrey—H.J.G.—R.G.
I find I have besides family & parlty concerns & those of study, *ten* Committees on hand: Milbank, S.P.G., Church building, Metropolis Church, Commercial School, N.S. Inquiry & Correspondence, U. Canada Clergy, Addl Curates Fund, Carlton Library, O. & C. Club. These things distract & dissipate my poor mind.
Milbank Commee—dined at Pusey's to meet Bunsen. Talked through Newark matters with Caparn—finished Horner's Cousin.[10]

17. Sunday.

Commn at 8. St Jams's mg & aft.—Hearing M. Bunsen from mg to aft. Church in explanation of his views.[11] Mr Ward & Bp preached.
Sir R. Bateson & Sir S. Glynne dined.
read Quarterly on Abp of Cologne—A. Gordon (Abn)'s sermon[12]—Girdlestone's Word & Ministers[13]—Eusebius.[14]

[1] George A. F. P. S. *Smythe, 1818–57; Eton and St. John's, Cambridge; tory M.P. Canterbury 1841–52; leader of 'Young England' 1844; foreign under-secretary 1845–6; fought fellow-member 1852 (last duel in England); 7th viscount Strangford 1855.
[2] Perhaps George Heathcote, 1811–95; at Eton; wrangler, 1833; canon of Ely, 1868.
[3] John Maxfield, vicar of Norwell near Newark 1853.
[4] *Mahon's proposal that M.P.s should no longer adjudicate on contested elections was lost: *H* xlv. 432. [5] Unidentified.
[6] E. J. *Stanley. [7] D. W. *Harvey again: ibid. 446.
[8] George John Venables-*Vernon, 1803–66, Dante scholar; whip M.P. co. Derby 1831–5; 5th Lord Vernon 1835; edited *Inferno*, 3v. (1858–65).
[9] Cp. Janet A. Ross, *Three Generations of Englishwomen* (1888), 127–30.
[10] Version of extracts in Morley, i. 219—dated 1 February.
[11] Cp. F. Bunsen, *Bunsen*, i. 503.
[12] A. L. Gordon, minister at Aberdeen, on education (1839).
[13] C. *Girdlestone, 'God's Word and Ministers', a sermon (1838).
[14] 4th century ecclesiastical historian.

18. M.

Wrote to Bunsen (with 3 copies)[1]—W.R. Farquhar—T.G.—
Read a Dignitary's Letter to Bp of Exeter[2]—Fraser's Mag in answer to Hook[3]—Sydney Smith on Ballot[4]—& Emerson's oration at Dartmouth[5]—Wilberforce's Educn Sermon.[6] House 4–6$\frac{1}{4}$.[7] Calls. J.N.G. & his bride arrived in evg: I went to meet them at the railway: a strange unearthly scene. She seems a sweet person.

19. T.

Wrote to Vicar of Nk—Mrs Austin—Hope—Campbell (Eye)—Girdlestone.[8]
{Anne's death to us.}
read Terrot's Letter[9]—& Quarty of Decr on Canada.
House 5–11$\frac{1}{2}$. home to dinner. Divided in 361:172 agt. Hearing Corn Law Evidence at the Bar.[10]
Saw Rio—Doyle—Drs Chandler & Spry on Cathl plan

20 W.

Wrote to Baxter—G.S. Smythe—Caparn—read Faussit's Sermon[11]—Newman's letter.[12] long conv. with Acland & others on our Catechism question wh is going ill.
dined at Lady de Salis's.

21. Th.

Wrote to Macarthur—T.F. Elliot[13]—Mr Campbell—W. Selwyn—Lincoln.
read acct of Stockport Sunday School.[14]
calls. House 4–6$\frac{1}{2}$.[15] Glynne dined here.

22. Fr.

Wrote to Codling[16] (with Testl)—Bunsen

[1] Of his book: F. Bunsen, *Bunsen*, i. 504.
[2] A Dignitary of the Church, 'Ecclesiastical Commission' (1839).
[3] *Fraser's Magazine*, xix. (1 January 1839) on W. F. *Hook.
[4] S. *Smith, 'Ballot' (1839).
[5] R. W. Emerson, 'An Oration delivered before the Literary Societies of Dartmouth College' (1838).
[6] S. *Wilberforce, 'The Power of God's Word Needful for National Education' (1838).
[7] He spoke a few words and voted for continuing to restrict theatres in Lent: *H* xlv. 580.
[8] And note on public speaking, Add MS 44728, f. 215.
[9] [C. H. *Terrot] 'Reasons for avoiding controversy' (1839).
[10] Charles *Villiers' motion beaten: *H* xlv. 691.
[11] G. Faussett, 'The Revival of Popery' (1838).
[12] J. H. *Newman, 'A Letter to the Rev. Godfrey Faussett, . . . on Certain Points of Faith and Practice' (1838).
[13] (Sir) Thomas Frederick Elliott, 1808–80; agent-general of emigration 1837–40; assistant under-secretary, colonial office, 1847–68; K.C.M.G. 1869.
[14] Untraced.
[15] Taxes on coaches: *H* xlv. 720.
[16] Unidentified.

read Case of Minor Canons[1]—Dealtry's Charge[2]—Draft of Fifth Report & old papers & books on Cathl question. House $4\frac{1}{2}$–$8\frac{3}{4}$. Voted in 125:93 on Affirmation Bill, a mischievous measure.[3]
Lady Stanhope's in evg. music.

23 Sat.

Wrote to Lewin[4]—T.G.—Backhouse[5]—Giffard—Manning—Abeken—Kennedy—A. Williams.
Read Sir J. Graham's Address & Speech[6]—Pusey on Cathedrals &c. for Monday: it is a great subject which I do not know how to master.
calls. dined at Mrs Vansittart's.

24. S.

St James mg & aft.
Worked the subject of Cathedrals. read also Erskine[7] & Rutherford.[8]

25. M.

Wrote to T.G.
Still at work on Cathls: & full for speaking, when it appeared better to wait for a Resolution or Instruction & let 2d reading pass: as less liable to be misunderstood.
Inglis, Estcourt, & Ashley, wished me to move it: I asked Graham's frank opinion & he told me he thought it might give cause for offence, wh my speaking could not. This was my feeling too: & I decided accordingly.
The idea of the Instruction is, against *alienation*.
School meeting 2–$8\frac{1}{4}$.
House $4\frac{3}{4}$–$8\frac{3}{4}$.[9]
Read Merle d'Aubigné—Head[10] (began) aloud to Mr G.—Sydney Smith's 3d to Singleton, offensive[11]—and Selwyn's "Vox Ecclesiae".[12]

26. T.

Wrote to Hamilton—W. Selwyn—Rev A. Cooper[13]—Scott. read Head—& Ld Brougham on Queen C.[14] Rio 3 hours, on our usual range of subjects.[15]

---

[1] Untraced.
[2] W. *Dealtry, 'Obligation of the National Church (1838).
[3] Bill lost: *H* xlv. 838.
[4] Perhaps George Ross Lewin, 1810–85, of co. Clare, naval chaplain.
[5] Who was quarrelling with *Urquhart: cp. Add MS 44356, ff. 199–201.
[6] On inauguration as lord rector at Glasgow University (1839).
[7] H. *Moncreiff Wellwood, *Account of the Life and Writings of T. *Erskine* (1818).
[8] C. Thomson, *The Letters and Life of . . . Samuel *Rutherford*, 2 v. (1836).
[9] Ecclesiastical Duties and Revenues bill, 2°: *H* xlv. 848.
[10] F. B. *Head, *A Narrative* (1839); a vindication of his government of Upper Canada.
[11] S. *Smith, 'Third Letter to Archdeacon Singleton' (1839).
[12] Possibly draft of *The Voice of the Church*, 2v. of divines' writings published in monthly parts (1840), ed. anon.
[13] Allen Cooper, 1793–1851; priest at St. Mark's, North Audley Street, from 1828.
[14] For Queen *Caroline, in the house of lords, 3 and 4 October 1820; *NSH* iii. 112, 179.
[15] See Bowe, *Rio*, 160 and Add MS 44728, f. 127.

Acland on Cathls.[1] I own that *pain* has in part hindered my speaking: but my mind is resolved.

Read Authors' Association:[2] I fear there is here a fundamental error; the power of books may be tested but who shall decide on the ἦθος?[3]

Dss of Beaufort's in evg.

Yesterday O'Connell said to me in H. of C. 'I read your book; & I claim the half of you.'[4] This eveng Mr Cumming (Presbn)[5] 'I dont think your book is a Pusey book or I wd blame it as strongly as any man.'

27. W.

Wrote to T. Godfrey—Mr G.—R.G.

read Head—& began "Janet"[6] at Lady Henniker's request.

House 4½–7½.[7] Mahon to tea. Mr Hallam's in evg.—Church in mg.

28. Th.

Wrote to T.G.—Caparn—Miss Seymer—Mr Cumming—Mr C. Marryat.[8]

read Head—Janet—Turner's Engld.[9]

A morning spent amg my papers, struggling for something like order.

House 3½–7.[10] Dined at Egerton's.

Fr. Mch. One.

Bunsen & Glynne to breakf—& conv. to past midday.[11] Wrote to Mr G.—Mr Bishop—Mr Burgess—H.J.G.—House 5–8¼ and 10–1¼. Voted agt postponing 2d reading of Munl Bill—agt most of the party who were in the House[12]—[blank]—Read Janet, Head—

2 Sat.

Wrote to Caparn—Arrangement of letters—Rio to breakf—& conv. Finished Journal.

read Janet (finished) & Head (finished). Edn Commee moved a commn on Terms of Union: no seconder: it remains on record.[13]—Dined at the Speaker's. Calls.

---

[1] Presumably MS.

[2] Untraced.

[3] 'moral character'.

[4] See Morley, i. 178.

[5] John *Cumming, 1807–81, controversialist; presbyterian minister in Covent Garden 1832–79.

[6] J. R. Waddington, *Janet; or Glances at Human Nature*, 3v. (1839).

[7] He voted for *Talfourd's copyright bill, 2°: H xlv. 943.

[8] Probably Charles *Marriott, 1811–58, tractarian divine.

[9] S. *Turner, *The History of England from the Earliest Period to the Death of *Elizabeth*, 12 v. (1799–1839).

[10] Procedure: H xlv. 965.

[11] Notes in Add MS 44819, ff. 43–44.

[12] Irish railways and municipalities: ibid. 1051, 1141.

[13] Untraced.

Sunday Mch 3.

St James's mg & aft. Mr Ward & Bp.—Holy Communion.
Pusey here on Cathls. & M. Bunsen on the Church, from aft. service two hours.
read Hooker B.VII—S. Clement[1]—Vogan's Sermon[2]—Tyler's Two Sermons.[3]

M. 4.

Wrote to Abp York—Farquhar—Tyler—Sir H. Ellis[4]—R.G.—Lady F. Cole.
read Ed. Rev (Stephen) on Luther: heavy: Carlyle: Palmer, Steane[5] on the Church. Cobbett's Refn.[6] Comte Montalembert called here with Rio. Our conversation was chiefly of fact: but he is a very interesting person.[7]
H. of Lords 5–7.[8] Mrs Ede's in Evg.

T. 5.

Wrote to Rev. H. Mackenzie[9]—Morley—J.N.G. arranging Journals & MS books.
Rio brought me the news that while Montalembert was conversing here yesterday, his mother[10] died! while in France she was R.C.
read D'Aubigné—French Concordat & Articles Organiques.[11]
convv. with Acland, Inglis, Goulburn, Pusey, on Cathls.[12] Sketched a motion with A. House 5–7 and 10–12.[13]

W. 6.

Wrote to Caparn—T.G.—R.G.—Mr Philips (Leicr)[14] read Cerati (Celibat)[15]—D'Aubigné.

---

[1] W. *Jacobson, S. Clementis Romani, S. Ignatii, S. Polycarpi, Patrum Apostolorum, Quae Supersunt (1838); until 7 July 39 mention of these Fathers refers to *Jacobson's edition.

[2] T. S. L. Vogan, 'The Doctrine of the Apostolical Succession Developed and Proved' (1838).

[3] Cp. Add MS 44356, f. 207.

[4] Sir Henry *Ellis, 1777–1869, British Museum librarian 1827–56; K.H. 1833.

[5] E. Steane, 'The Reciprocal Duties of Church Members' (1835).

[6] W. *Cobbett, A History of the Protestant 'Reformation', in England and Ireland (1824–6), and The Protestant 'Reformation' Part Second (1827).

[7] See Bowe, Rio, 153. Charles Forbes René, comte de Montalembert, 1810–70, French liberal catholic author; deputy 1848–57.

[8] Irish church: H xlv. 1144.

[9] Henry Mackenzie, 1808–78; ordained 1834; vicar of St. Martin's-in-the-fields 1848–55; canon of Lincoln 1858; archdeacon 1866–78, and bishop 1870–7 of Nottingham.

[10] Elise Rosée, née Forbes, a Scottish heiress.

[11] To the concordat agreed between Bonaparte and Pius VII in 1801 the French consulate added organic articles to which the pope never agreed.

[12] See 8 Mar. 39.

[13] Navy; Canada. H xlv. 1263; 1312.

[14] Possibly William Joseph George Phillips, 1778?–1855, priest, whose s. Francis Robert Phillips, 1812?–62, was vicar of Oadby, Leicester, ca. 1840–55.

[15] L'abbé Cérati, Du Célibat (1829).

38—II.

House 5–6½.[1]
Dined at Dr Short's.[2] Lady Beresford's[3] in evg.

Th. 7.

read Cerati—Gresley's Churchman[4]—Theiner's Letter to Möhler.[5]
saw Clerk & M'Conochie on Orkney return—Rio. House 4¾–6¾ and 10–1½.[6]
Glynne, Gaskell, C. Bruce dined here. My Father likes these numbers.

Fr. 8.

read Buxton on Slave Trade[7]—Voltaire Misc.—House 9½–12. Voted
again for 2d reading Ir. Mun. Bill.[8] Meeting at Sir R. Inglis's on Cath'ls.
Our Res. adopted (of Mch 5)

Sat. 9.

Wrote to Mr Jeffs.[9] read Buxton—Catullus & Propertius—Cerati—Milbank
2½–4¼. 1½ hour with Mr G. on his Scotch (Leith) Church Constitution &
arrangements. Dined at Mrs C. Offley's.

10 Sunday.

St James m. & a. Bp N. Scotia & Mr Lonsdale. Dinner & evg alone with
Mr G.—Talked the Lpool Church Discipline over, & other matters.
Read Fenelon's Letter on reading Scripture[10]—one of MacHale's
Sermons[11]—Eusebius.[12]

11. M.

Wrote to Mr Paterson.
Wrote out copy of Mr G's paper on his Leith Church.
read Roman Statistics[13] & Buxton (finished).
House 4½–7.[14] Lady Ely's in evg.[15] U.C.C. Comm. meeting.

12 T.

wrote to M'Arthur—Willis—Buxton—R. Wilberforce. Saw Rev Mr Page[16]

[1] Highways bill, cttee.: H xlv. 1319.
[2] T. V. *Short was rector of St. George's, Bloomsbury, 1834–41.
[3] Louisa, née Beresford, d. 1851; da. of 1st Lord Decies; m. 1832 William Carr *Beresford, 1768–1854, Peninsular commander, cr. baron 1814, and Viscount Beresford 1823.
[4] W. *Gresley, Portrait of an English Churchman (1838).
[5] Probably J. A. Theiner, Merkwürdiges Umlaufschreiben (1827), reply to J. A. Möhler, Die Einheit in der Kirche (1825), which defended the papacy.
[6] Irish outrages: H xlvi. 25.
[7] T. F. *Buxton, The African Slave Trade (1839).
[8] Read 2° 300 to 39: H xlvi. 199.
[9] William Jeffs, foreign bookseller in Burlington Arcade.
[10] F. de Salignac de la Mothe Fenelon, Lettre sur la Lecture de L'Écriture Sainte (1709).
[11] Untraced.   [12] And note on Trinity, Add MS 44728, f. 220.
[13] Untraced.   [14] Lenten theatres; navy: H xlvi. 229.
[15] Anna Maria, née Dashwood, 1785–1857; 1st da. of 3rd bart.; m. 1810 John Loftus, 1770–1845, 2nd marquis of Ely 1806.
[16] James Robert Page, 1805?–86, priest and historian.

(Ir. Ed). Mr Latrobe[1] (W.I. ed.)—Rio—read Burnets Intr. to Vol 3—Celibat.
House 5–6¾ and 9½–12.[2]

13 W.

Wrote to H.J.G.—on her trying circumstances announced this morning—& to R.G.
Read Cerati's Celibat—Burnet & Appx
House 5¾–7. 10¾–1.[3] Dined at Ld Cholmondeleys.
Conv with Mr G. on H[elen].

14. Th

Wrote to Mr Waddilove—Mr Wilson. R.G.—arranging books.
Finished Cerati. It is strange that the writings of R.C. anti-celibataires are so commonly tainted—Read Burnet & Appx. Locke.
House 3¾–6½ and 10¾–12¼.[4]
Milnes Glynne &c to dinner—Mrs Vansittart's afr.

15. Fr.

Wrote to Lady Henniker.
read Ld King's Locke[5]—Carlyle.[6]
House 4½–6¾ and 9¼–2¾. Two divv. on adjournment: magnificent debater's Speech from Peel.[7]

16. Sat.

Wrote to Macarthur—H.J.G.
read Pusey to Bp of Oxford[8]—Armstrong to Abp Magee.[9] Speaker's Levee—Lady Cork's afr.

17 Sunday.

Holy Commn at 8. St James mg & aft. Bp & Mr Ward.
Bunsen here 4½–6½—Acland on Cathls.
read Pusey and Gresley[10]—

[1] Charles Joseph *Latrobe, 1801–75, traveller; governed Victoria, 1851–4, during gold rush.
[2] Corn laws: H xlvi. 333, 441, 628.
[3] Corn laws: H xlvi. 441.
[4] Corn laws: ibid. 628.
[5] P. *King, The Life of John *Locke (1830).
[6] French Revolution (1837).
[7] Corn law discussion ctd.; procedural divisions. H xlvi. 715; 749.
[8] E. B. *Pusey, 'A Letter to Richard*, Lord Bishop of Oxford, on the Tendency to Romanism imputed to Doctrines Held of Old, as Now, in the English Church' (1839).
[9] Untraced.
[10] Probably W. *Gresley, The Necessity of Zeal and Moderation in the Present Circumstances of the Church . . . in Five Sermons (1839).

18. M.

Wrote to Caparn—rewrote on 'Janet'—read Blackstone IV. 4.[1]—Pusey—
Brougham's Corn Law Speech[2]—Abp Spottiswoode.[3]
House 4–7 and 10–1¾. Voted in 342:195 agt committee on Corn Laws.[4]

19. T.

Wrote to P. Gaskell[5]—Fletcher[6]—Mr Simpson—Caparn—Oakley—
Moore[7]—S.P.C.K.
read Pusey—Palmer's Supplement[8]—Milner on Jamaica[9]—Fuller's Ch.
Hist.[10]
House 3¾–8 & 10–12.[11] H.J.G. returned—Bunsen 11–1.[12]

20 W.

Wrote to Mrs Wishlade
Church at 11.—read Locke's Life—his Essay on Study is exasperating[13]—
finished Pusey: much good & fine but oleum addit camino,[14] as a whole—
finished Milner on Jamaica—went to Lincoln's to see the electric telegraph:
by wh motion may be carried round the world in 1/12 of a second.[15]
Dined at Sir W. Wynne's.
Read Wiseman on Italian tourists.[16]

21. Th.

Wrote to Hill—& to Ld Sidmouth—Bp Ln—Sir R. Peel.—Ld Abinger, for
him.[17]
    Read Jama papers—Life of Locke—Father Paul[18]—
    Saw Mr Buchan.[19] & T.G. on G. McKenzies Bills; wrote draft of letter
accordingly: 3–4 Rose St School[20]—

22 Fr.

Read Locke—W.I. papers—went to Wimbledon & Putney heath. House
5–6½[21] and at 11 to tell of the 18 Bps—Dined at Uncle D.s.—a rubber.

---

[1] *Blackstone, *Commentaries*; on offences against God and Religion.
[2] 18 February 1839; moving for a cttee. of the whole house on the corn laws: *H* xlv. 509.
[3] J. *Spottiswoode, *History of the Church of Scotland* (1655).
[4] *H* xlvi. 859.   [5] Salford surgeon.
[6] Unidentified.   [7] Perhaps Thomas *Moore, 1779–1852, poet.
[8] To *Palmer's *Treatise on the Church*.
[9] T. H. Milner, 'The Present and Future State of Jamaica Considered' (1839).
[10] T. *Fuller, *The Church History of Britain* (1655).
[11] Irish education; trade with Mexico and Buenos Ayres: *H* xlvi. 876; 891.
[12] Note in Add MS 44819, f. 44v.
[13] 'Some Thoughts Concerning Reading and Study for a Gentleman' (1720).
[14] 'he pours oil on the flames'.
[15] Samuel Morse the codemaker had invented a practicable electric telegraph in 1838.
[16] *Dublin Review*, vi. 1 (January 1839).
[17] And theological notes, Add MS 44728, ff. 221–2.
[18] A. Bianchi-Giovini, *Biografia di Frà Paolo Sarpi*, 2 v. (1836).
[19] Possibly John Buchan, minister at Kirriemuir, Forfarshire clothmaking town.
[20] At the west end of Covent Garden.   [21] Army estimates: *H* xlvi. 1120.

23. Sat.

Wrote to Peterkin[1]—Caparn—W. Selwyn. Saw Montalembert, 1½ hour, on my book:[2] and P Gaskell.
read Bunsen's Art.[3] to Mr G. Locke (finished I)—and W.I. papers.
Milbank 2¾–5.
dined at Sir J Mordaunt's—singing.

24. Sunday.

St James mg & aft.
Saw Bunsen again & walked with him. Spoke to George on Communion—he has much dread yet not I think with an averted will—read Manning's beautiful Sermon on Rule of Faith[4]—Gresley's Churchman—& an anon but very good sermon on Fasting. (Rio m/39)[5] conv. with Mr G. on Church & Succession 1½ hour.

25. M.

Wrote to Bunsen—R.G.
read W.I. papers—King's Locke—part of Nihill[6]—saw Rio—conv. with Goulburn, & with Peel, on Jamaica—evg with the Verney's from 10.
House 5–7.[7] Commee at 2.

26 T.

Wrote to Lewin. Labouchere.[8]
read King's Locke—finished Nihill on Prison Discipline—excellent—Oakley's very able Preface[9].
saw Capt. Huntley[10]—H. Taylor.
Dined at T.G.s—whist for Mr G.

27.

wrote to Povah[11]—Corrie & Co—H. Mackenzie—Mr Thompson—J.N.G.
House 5–6¼.[12]
read Lacordaire 'Retablissement',[13] King's Locke[14]
Church at 11. Garden preached. conv. with him in aftn. Wrote.
dined at Abp of York's—family party.

[1] Alexander Peterkin, of Edinburgh; archivist of the Church of Scotland.
[2] On abp. of Cologne: see F. Bunsen, *Bunsen*, i. 491.
[3] Note in Add MS 44819, f. 45.   [4] (1838).   [5] Unintelligible.
[6] D. Nihill, 'Prison Discipline in its Relations to Society and Individuals, As Deterring from Crime, and as conducive to Personal Reformation' (1839).
[7] Supply: *H* xlvi. 1198.
[8] And note on self, Add MS 44728, f. 223.
[9] F. *Oakeley, preface to *Sermons, preached . . . in the Chapel Royal . . . Whitehall* (1839).
[10] (Sir) Henry Vere *Huntley, 1795–1864; naval capt.; cruised against slavers on W. African coast; lieutenant-governor of Gambia 1839; cr. bart. 1841.
[11] John Vigden Povah, 1803?–82, canon of St. Paul's 1833.
[12] The house had been counted out at 4.
[13] J. B. H. Lacordaire, *Mémoire pour le Rétablissement en France de l'Ordre des Frères Prêcheurs* (1839).   [14] Note in Add MS 44728, f. 225.

28. Th

Wrote to Madame Rio (at R.'s request) read Lacordaire—King's Locke—
Quarty on Oxford Theology & (in part) on Canada.
Whitehall service at 3. It ought to be most beautiful.
Mr Rogers in evg. 3½ hours with my Father & I am quite worthless to him.

29. Good Friday.

8 A.M. Holy Communion. St James mg & aft. Bp of London & Mr Ward.
read Merle d'Aubignè—Lacordaire (finished)—Manning's Appx on Rule of
Faith.[1]
Evg. with Mr G.

30. Easter Eve.

read W.I. papers—Mahon's Hist., began Vol III—Townsend's Sermon on
the Atonement: I cannot but agree in his proposition.[2]
dined at Abp of York's: on return, an involuntary game at whist.
11–1½ Mr Rogers's: met A. Tennyson, & brought him home with me.

During this Passion Week, I have had a cup of tea to breakfast, coffee
to lunch with two or three mouthfuls of oatcake to qualify it: & have
restricted my dinner a little, as I could. On Tuesday however I had wine &
biscuit at 5, expecting to speak, & knowing my voice would fail. During
Lent I have for some time been in the habit of prayer with arms extended:
& not upon any suggestion.

Slender and trifling indeed are these shadows of the "bodily exercise"
which is πρὸς ὀλίγον ὠφελιμὸς,[3] yet they follow what was yet more
trivial, and I would trust that they precede what is less so: if ever I am in
the circumstances: but I find an effect upon my eyes which should be
avoided, and I am likewise under the belief that where great & constant
excitements are applied to the mind, stronger animal support is required.
Otherwise I have a glimpse of understanding, how fasting might be
sweetened to the heart. It seems to leave a clearer temperament: and to
dispose the mind towards God: and although it may seem strange to use a
more constrained attitude in prayer, it is good for that low class of Christians to which alone I can aspire to belong, whose minds are ever wandering
from the presence of "the Lord Jesus Christ & the elect angels"[4] to some
speculation: which this remedy has a tendency to restrict.

It seems also most unequivocally true, that abstinence is much easier
than a strict temperance.

How often, how daily, & this for how many years—ever since my feet
were dipped in the turbid stream—do I ask inwardly of Him in whose lap

---

[1] H. E. *Manning, 'The Rule of Faith. An Appendix to a Sermon . . . Containing an
Examination of Certain Popular Objections' (1838).
[2] G. *Townsend, 'The Doctrine of Atonement to be Taught Without Reserve; or, the
Clergy Warned Against the Errors of . . . "Tracts for the Times, No. 80—Ad Clerum"'
(1838).
[3] 'mildly beneficial'.   [4] I Tim. v. 21.

is cast the lot of my destiny, "shall I ever be a man of study and of prayer, a man of the cell and of the lamp, of the chair, of the altar, shall I ever cast the burden from my shoulder and flee away and be at rest?" The answer is better than the affirmative which I desire: it is

> Chiniam la fronte al massimo
> Fattor.[1]

But what is my practice?

31. Easter Day.

8 A.M. Communion. St James mg & evg. Bp & Rector. wrote. Walk with Taylor.
read Rutherford—Manning—Whewell's Four Sermons.[2] Harcourt's Deluge.[3]

Monday Ap 1.

Wrote to P. Gaskell.
read letters in re H.J.G.—Merle d'Aubigné—Sam Slick[4]—(finished) Quarterly on Head.
a lesson at picquet from Mr G.—calls.

2.

Church 11 A.M. Wrote to Caparn Lewin—read Sam Slick—Merle d'Aubignè (finished I)—Eclectic on my book, not personal[5]—Mahon's Hist.
dined at Mr Egerton's—wrote

3. W.

Saw Rio; at Panorama of Rome, a faint shadow! read Slick—Locke (King, Vol. II)—Mahon's Hist—wrote for x[6]
dined at Mr G. Vernon's—music.

4 Th.

1½ hour Nat. Gall.—with Miss Trench.
read Slick—King's Locke & Appx.
Wrote for x: the name for an argument indefinite, embryo, unborn.
calls. dined in B. Square. whist.

---

[1] 'May we bow our heads before the great Creator'.
[2] W. *Whewell, 'On the Foundations of Morals' (1838).
[3] L. V. *Harcourt, *The Doctrine of the Deluge; vindicating the scriptural account from the doubts . . . cast upon it by geological speculations*, 2v. (1838).
[4] T. C. *Haliburton, *The Clockmaker; or the Sayings and Doings of Samuel Slick of Slicksville*, 2 pts. (1837, 1838).
[5] *The Eclectic Review*, new series, v. 365–85 (April 1839).
[6] See next two entries, and Add MS 44728, ff. 230–2, on ethics.

5. Fr.

read Slick—Erskine's Life (by Moncreiff)—Mahon—picquet with Mr G.
wrote a sketch of x.
Rio to breakfast.

6. Sat.

Wrote to W. Selwyn—H. Seymer.[1]
read Slick—Erskine's Life—Locke.
rode. dined at Sir S. Canning's—late.[2]

7. Sunday.

Ch mg & aft.—Communion. Lamentably few: still more lamentable however, if all carry the amount of inward disease that one at least does.
read Bp Wilson's Sermon (finished)—Manning's Appx (finished)—Gresley's
Churchman (finished)—and [blank]. In Scripture I hope now to fall in
more or less with the Lessons.

8. M.

Wrote to Abp York—Milnes—J.N.G.
D. Robertson to breakfast. Conv. & Virgil construing with him afterwards.
read Erskine's Life—Sam Slick.
House $3\frac{3}{4}$–$4\frac{1}{2}$.[3] Picquet with Mr G. rode.

9. T.

Wrote to R. Phillimore—J. Kennedy.
read Sam Slick (finished)—part of Macaulay's very kind as well as gentlemanly article in the Edinburgh[4]—and finished King's Locke & Appx—a
poor book—Sir R. Peel's on Jamaica at $1\frac{1}{2}$—House 5–10 on do. Spoke
briefly, & with reserve to keep abreast of my leaders.[5]

10 W.

Wrote to Rn G.—& to Macaulay on his Article.[6] finished the Article, &
Erskine's Life.
saw Murray on my book & on Sewell's Article:[7] Mahon on do. Spry on
Cathls. at S.P.G. Commee's meeting.
We failed in making a House for the Copyright Bill at 4—only 28 present.
The Finlays to dinner. Lady Peel's in evg.

---

[1] And on ethics, ibid. f. 233.
[2] Notes in Add MS 44819, ff. 45–46, written later in April.
[3] Misc. business: *H* xlvi. 1239.
[4] lxix. 231 (April 1839), including the historic phrase about stern unbending
Tories.
[5] Bill to suspend Jamaican constitution, 1°; diarist expressed doubts. *H* xlvi. 1243,
1276.
[6] Extracts in *Trevelyan, *Macaulay, ii. 52–53, where it is described as the only letter
*Macaulay ever kept; full texts of letter and reply in *Gleanings*, vii. 106–8.
[7] 'Oxford Theology', in the *Quarterly Review* (December 1838).

11. Th.

Wrote to Mr Simpson (& draft)—R. Caparn—& the vicar of Nk.
read Rousseau—Mahon—Stuart on N.A. Boundary.[1]
dined with the Larkinses. House & ride.

12. Fr.

Wrote to Mr G.
read S. Wilberforce's Preface &c[2]—& Mahon.
House 2–4 Nk Gas Committee: & 5–6.[3] dined at Milnes Gaskells.[4] $2\frac{1}{2}$ hours,
mg, investigating a matter disclosed yesterday[5]—Godfrey Tallents came
to breakft.

13 Sat.

Wrote to Mr G—Mr Fyvie[6]—Parkes—Apjohn[7]—Commee of Dissenters.
Finished Stuart on N.A. Boundary: read Newfoundland petition, & a
Schoolfellow (!) to Sir R. Peel.[8] rode: calls: dined at Mr G.R. Smith's,[9]
10–12 Mr Rogers's to breakf. conv. &c.—& conv. with Best.

14 Sunday.

St James. Bp, & Mr Ward.
conv. with Best. Wrote. read Jachin (finished)—Melville's Protm &
Popery[10] S. Clcm ad Cor.

15 M.

breakf. at Mahon's to meet Macaulay 10–$12\frac{1}{2}$. Afterwards much conv. on
this unhappy inquiry into Best's matters, & perusing letters much of aftn.
read Mahon, & Moncreiff's Erskine—rode. House $6\frac{1}{2}$–12.[11]

16 T.

more conv. reading & investigation. Here is a new & strange development of
human life.
read Erskinc and 'a Test for the Ballot'.[12] calls.
House at $3\frac{3}{4}$–$4\frac{3}{4}$, $5\frac{1}{2}$–6, $8\frac{3}{4}$–$10\frac{3}{4}$[13] and looking through old files of newspapers,
extract hunting.

[1] Untraced.
[2] To *Eucharistica*, an anthology he compiled (1839).
[3] Misc. business: *H* xlvi. 1321.
[4] In Albemarle Street.
[5] Cp. 15, 16, 18, 19, 20, 29 Apr. 39.
[6] Perhaps Charles Fyvie, minister at Inverness.
[7] Perhaps Michael Lloyd Apjohn, 1806–71, rector of Ballybroad, Co. Limerick, 1850.
[8] D. Jerrold, *The Schoolfellows*, a play (1835).
[9] George Robert Smith, 1793–1869, whig M.P. Midhurst 1831, Wycombe 1838–41;
nephew of 1st Lord *Carrington; m. 1818 Jane, née Maberly, who d. 1879.
[10] H. *Melvill, 'Protestantism and Popery' (1839).
[11] *Russell proposed motion approving recent policy in Ireland: *H* xlvii. 4.
[12] Untraced.
[13] Govt. of Ireland, ctd.: *H* xlvii. 94.

17. W.

read Carlyle's Hist—Erskine Appx (finished)—Mahon (finished)—Head Despatches[1]—H. of Assy in Newfoundland's Conduct.[2]
dined at Abp of Yorks[3] at 6: Concert, & House, at 9 to speak;[4] finding Shiel absent returned soon, & heard delightful music: this charms me away immeasurable distances from the excitement of politics.[5]

18 Th.

Wrote to R.G.—
More investigation about Best. It seems likely to terminate in a manner highly to his credit. Mr Simpson examined him. Poor fellow, what a tissue of the acts & sufferings of human nature does this history disclose. Independently of the *duty*, as a matter of knowledge, & of wonder, I could not regret the time. But I know one whose temptations are more & subtler: & whose impalpable offences are blacker in the sight of God than the obvious & superficial sins of such as these, in whose very hypocrisy—if the wife be[6] indeed a hypocrite, there is a comparative simplicity. read Carlyle—the Head Dispatches.
Saw Bunsen with a letter from his Crown Prince, most kind: and had a conv. with Sir R. Peel (Mema) House 4–5¼ on priv. bus. & 8–1, but unable to speak.[7]

19 Fr.

Jas Moncreiff to breakft & conv.—Best's, & other domestic matters with Mr G., occupied the morning to 12½.
Wrote Mema. read Carlyle—a book very difficult to lay down. read Pringle's W.I. pamphlet.[8] House 4–5¾ and 8–4½. Voted in 296:318, and in 299:81 on Duncombe.[9] Lost my opportunity of speaking after four night's waiting, by some misunderstanding I think or disapproval of Ld Stanley's—which is I doubt not a very useful mortification. I do not *allow* myself for a moment to feel mortified: because I simply sought to obey my superiors in this debate, which seemed the best index of my duty—and having done so, there is not the smallest right to regret losing an opportunity advantageous in a parliamentary sense because the fulfilment of duty can leave nothing to desire in retrospect: so I resist it, but the mind when wrought up & afterwards baffled, feels rather frustrate.[10]

[1] *PP* 1839 xxxiii, Sir F. B. *Head's dispatches from Toronto and *Glenelg's replies.
[2] Untraced. [3] 40 Grosvenor Square.
[4] Govt. of Ireland: *H* xlvii. 166.
[5] See Morley, i. 220–1: Morley appears to have post-dated by two days the conversation between *Peel and *Gladstone he describes.
[6] Instead of 'for the wife *seems* to know'. [7] Govt. of Ireland: *H* xlvii. 234.
[8] J. W. Pringle, 'Remarks on the State and Prospects of the West Indian Colonies' (1839).
[9] He voted for an amdt. of *Peel's, mitigating *Russell's motion; and against one of *Duncombe's favouring more reform. Earlier, he had voted in 107–70 to defeat a Newcastle railway bill. *H* xlvii. 447, 452; *Mirror*, 1892–3.
[10] See Morley, i. 220–1.

20 Sat.

wrote to Buxton.
read Carlyle.
Mr Gordon & Mr Seeley[1] 1½ hour on Church Extension—2 hours at Mr
Rickards's[2] on this very sore and mysterious business: God be thanked it
is not my part to judge anyone.
dined at Ld Harrowby's.
attempted to write out the probable speech of last night.[3]

21 S.

Communion, 8 A.M. Ch. 11.
read Manning's powerful Sermon on Natl Education[4]—Dean of Norwich's
on do[5]—S. Wilberforce's (good) book on the Eucharist—St Clement.

22 M.

Wrote to Jacobson.
Sir R. Peel's on Jama 12–1¼. N.S. (D) meeting 2¼–4. rode. House 5¼–6½ and
8–10½.[6] Mrs R. Ellice's concert. Finished "Speech".
read Carlyle & W.I. papers.

23 T.

Wrote petition to Lincoln's Inn to be dismissed. This connection was not
orig[inal]ly of my own seeking. I retire with my Father's full concurrence.
Wrote to A. Williams.
read Carlyle—Merle d'Aubigné.
party at home.
2¼–4½ meeting (priv.) on Africa at Dr Lushington's—House.[7] saw Tarbet
on Nfdd—Macpherson[8] on Jama.

24 W.

Wrote to G. Selwyn—Mahon (on book, for Quy)[9]—Corrie & Co.
read Carlyle—Canada papers—M. d'Aubigné—dined at Dr Dss of Beaufort's.
Occupied again in Best's matters.

25 Th.

Wrote to Blakesley—Rev. Mr Scott—Mr Brooks. what form of madness is
this?

[1] Robert Benton *Seeley, 1798–1886; publisher and author.
[2] Perhaps George Rickards, G. K.*'s f., Bloomsbury solicitor.
[3] Add MS 44728, ff. 235–50.
[4] H. E. *Manning, 'National Education, a sermon . . . preached on behalf of the
Chichester central schools' (1838).
[5] G. *Pellew on Heb. viii, 1, reprinted in his Sermons, ii, 252 (1848).
[6] Jamaica bill, 2° and hearing counsel: H xlvii. 459.
[7] Same, ibid. 480.   [8] Unidentified.
[9] Cp. Quarterly Review, lxiii. 151 (January 1839), on *Mahon's History of England, ii
and iii.

read Introduction to Wodrow[1]—Carlyle—Newton Smart.[2]
saw Sir R. Inglis on Church Extension.
House 4–5¾.[3] Lady F. Egertons & Mrs C. Offley's in evg.

26 Fr.

Wrote to Bunsen.
read Carlyle—finished Newton Smart.
wrote paper on African mission—House 5–6½ and 8–12.[4] King's Coll.
Council 2½–4½.

27 Sat.

Wrote to Selwyn—Mr Cursham[5]—Hatchard—read Carlyle—W. Selwyn on
Cathls[6]—& MS. reply of 'A Churchman' (referred to me by Hatchard) to
Macaulay.[6]
2½–4¼ Dr Lushington's on Africa.
dined at Colquhoun's, Putney Heath.

28. Sunday.

St James mg & aft, Dr Williamson,[7] good tone, but the ill omened words
'merit' & 'deserve' were heard. Mr Andrews[8] in aft. I grieved to hear
talk of expiation by our gifts & much more—one trusted that at least the
day for this had gone past.
2 hours 11–1 P.M. with H. on her painful & trying matters. There is a cloud
to be removed.
read S. Clement—Sam. Wilberforce (finished)—Mr Nicholson's Essay[9]—
Coleridge.

29 M.

Wrote to H. Taylor—Mr Campbell (Glasg.)—read Carlyle. began Pearce
Stevenson.[10]

[1] R. *Wodrow, *History of Sufferings of the Church of Scotland from Restoration to Revolution*, 2 v. (1721–2).
[2] N. Smart, 'The Ecclesiastical Commission Considered: and Suggestions . . . for Increasing the Efficiency of the Church Without Invading the Rights of Cathedral Establishments' (1839).
[3] Misc. business: *H* xlvii. 511.
[4] Election petitions trials bill, cttee.: ibid.
[5] Perhaps George Cursham, surgeon, of Savile Row.
[6] Untraced.
[7] Richard Williamson, 1802–65; priest 1829; D.D. 1835; headmaster Westminster School 1828–46; vicar of Pershore, Worcs., 1850–65.
[8] Gerrard Thomas Andrewes, 1795–1851; rector of All Hallows, Bread Street, 1819; chaplain to commons 1839–49; lived in Sackville Street, a few yards from St. James's, across Piccadilly.
[9] W. Nicholson, 'The Purity of the Ministry the Strength of the Church', pt. 1 of *The Call Upon the Church*, cp. 5 Feb. 38.
[10] i.e. Caroline *Norton, 'A Plain Letter to the Lord Chancellor on the Infant Custody Bill' (1839).

Mr Birkett on Distr. Prisons[1]—C.O. on African expedition[2]—Dr Newland on Irish Edn.[3]

More of poor Best, & I trust the last—How useful is a mirror!

House at 5 & 6–12½.[4]

30 T.

Wrote to Mr Lee—Sewell—Dr Hook—G. Mackenzie (writer)—Mr Roundell[5] with Introdn.

read Carlyle & (finished) Pearce Stevenson.

Saw Railway Deputn—at 12, Sir R. Peel's on Educn—determ[ine]d to take the initiative if need be—Bp of Lns afr—House $3\frac{3}{4}$–$5\frac{1}{4}$, & afr dinner[6]—& out.

Wednesday May one.

Wrote to Bonham—Mr Brooking[7]—Hatchard—

read Mence on Infant Custody[8]—Hayward's Article on do[9]—Letter to Bp of Exeter on do.[10] Carlyle—Xtn O. on my book[11]—

Monthly letters &c.

House 4–$12\frac{1}{2}$—home to tea: & missed one divn [out] of 21:20 of these were on the Copyright Bill—but the majority triumphed, I believe for the first time in such a contest.[12]

2 Th.

wrote two drafts to Mr Clarke—Caparn—Lincoln—saw S. Wilberforce & Trench—Bonham on Manchester—Mr G. on Manchester.

read Carlyle—Buxton's private volume.[13]

House 5–$6\frac{1}{4}$ and $9\frac{1}{2}$–$11\frac{1}{2}$[3]—Mrs Cunliffe's afr.

3 Fr.

read Burge's Speech—Merewether's Speech[14]—Carlyle—

getting up the Jamaica case—House $5\frac{1}{4}$–$12\frac{1}{2}$—

saw Ln on Manchester.

---

[1] Untraced.   [2] Untraced.

[3] H. Newland, 'An Examination of the Scripture Lessons, as Translated and Published by His Majesty's Commissioners of Education in Ireland' (1836).

[4] Prison bill, cttee.: *H* xlvii. 628.

[5] Unidentified.

[6] Church rates: ibid. 694.

[7] Unidentified: cp. 19 June 39.

[8] R. Mence, 'The Mutual Rights of Husband and Wife; with the draft of a Bill . . . for the Custody of Infants' (1838).

[9] Untraced.

[10] Untraced.

[11] *The Christian Observer*, xxxix. 285 (May 1839); an unfavourable review.

[12] Copyright bill, cttee.; *Talfourd persisting against Henry *Warburton, 1784?–1858, philosophical radical, wrangler 1806, M.P. Bridport 1826–41 and Kendal 1843–7. *H* xlvii. 699. The other division carried, 64–29, a Nottingham inclosure bill, 2°: ibid.

[13] T. F. *Buxton, *The Remedy* (1839); a private edition of his book on the African slave trade, published 1840.

[14] W. Burge and H. A. Merewether, at bar of H. of C., on Jamaica, 22 and 23 April 1839.

House 5¼–12½.[1] home to tea—I was to have spoken but reserve for Monday.

4 Sat.

Wrote to Mr Clark—Mr Norris.[2]
read Carlyle—Revival of Jesuitism[3]—Buxton's Suggestions (finished).
dined with the Brownriggs. Commee of Inquiry 3–4¾.

5. Sunday.

St James mg & aft & Communion. read S. Clem (finished all)—Nicholson (finished)—Maurice[4]—Nicole.[5]
the Ramsays dined.

6 M.

Carlyle—Jama case books &c—M. d'Aubignè—House at 5, and 6½–2. Spoke a dry speech to a somewhat reluctant House: I cannot work up my matter at all in such a plight: however considering what it was they behaved very well. Divided in 289:294—a loud cheer on the announcement from our people, in wh I did not join.[6]

7 T.

Wrote to Mr Clarke—Lushington—Simpson. read Vivian's conv. with Napoleon[7]—Carlyle—d'Aubignè. Eyes rather out of sorts.
Dined with T.G. singing.
House at 5: heard the announcements in Lords and Commons.[8]
    saw Gourrier[9]—Tupper—at Natl Gallery

8 Wed.

wrote Pol. Mema.[10]
read Carlyle—d'Aubigné.
prepared corrections & an Advt for my 4th Edition: & arranged with Murray.[11]
dined with the Heywoods. Anc. Music afr.

9 Th.

Wrote to Burnaby—Rd Caparn—W. Thompson jun. read M. d'Aubignè—Carlyle.

[1] Jamaica bill: *H* xlvii. 765.
[2] Henry Handley *Norris, 1771–1850, high church divine.
[3] *British Critic And Quarterly Theological Review*, xxv. 143 (January 1839).
[4] F. D. *Maurice, 'Has the Church or State the Right to Educate the Nation?' (1839).
[5] And cp. Add MS 44728, ff. 252–6.
[6] Extracts in Morley, i. 222. Jamaica bill: *H* xlvii. 921, 967. Notes in Add MS 44649, ff. 264–73.
[7] I. H. Vivian, 'Minutes of a Conversation with Napoleon Bonaparte during his Residence in Elba (first ed. *ca.* 1821; reprinted for private distribution 1839.)
[8] Ministers resigned, on account of previous night's vote: *H* xlvii. 973, 976.
[9] François Bonaventure Gourrier, French theologian.
[10] Add MS 44819, ff. 46v.–47.   [11] This ed. did not appear till 1841.

Church at 11—& Holy Communion.—If any offer be made to me I have indeed much need of guidance. Long. conv. with Acland in evg on these matters.

dined at Mr Grenville's.

10 Fr.

Wrote to Mence—Gresley[1]—Vivian[2]—C. Wood—C. Talbot. read d'Aubigné—Tupper's Poems—Carlyle—Commee at 12.

dined at Abp of York's—Lady Cork's afr, then Queens Ball where I talked with several of the old new ministers.

11 Sat.

wrote to Boler—Simpson.

dined at Mr Cotton's[3]—singing.

read Warburton's Letters[4]—d'Aub.—Carlyle.

Penitentiary Commee—rode.

Rumours of all kinds afloat: in the evening they tended towards us.—Wrote Mema.[5]

12 Sunday.

Blessed peace amidst the dim turbulence in which we are involved!

St James mg & aft. Rector & Bp.

read S. Ignatius to the Ephesians—d'Aubigné—Nicole—Oakley's three first Sermons.[6]

13 M.

Wrote to Mr Ryder—Dr Traill.

read (Tupper's) Geraldine[7]—d'Aubigné (finished Vol.2)—Carlyle.

House $4\frac{3}{4}$–$7\frac{1}{4}$: the ministerial explanations.[8] rode, papers, saw Mr Tyler & Jas Bruce.

Whist for Mr G.—

14 T.

wrote to Picasse.[9] read Carlyle—Warburton's Letters—Brougham to Lord John Russell.[10]

House $4\frac{1}{2}$–6.[11] Evg. at home—whist.

---

[1] William *Gresley, 1801–1876; divine and writer; priest of Boyne Hill 1857–76.

[2] I. H. Vivian, brother of Sir Richard Hussey *Vivian.

[3] William *Cotton, 1786–1866, banker and philanthropist; director, 1821–66, and governor, 1843–6, of bank of England; built churches in east London.

[4] W. *Warburton, *Letters from a Late Eminent Prelate to One of His Friends* (1808).

[5] Add MS 44819, f. 48.

[6] F. *Oakeley, *Whitehall Chapel Sermons* (1837).   [7] M. F. *Tupper (1838).

[8] As *Victoria and *Peel could not agree on household appointments, *Melbourne resumed office. *H* xlvii. 979; and cp. Longford, 108–15.   [9] Unidentified.

[10] H. P. *Brougham, 'Lord *Brougham's Reply to Lord John *Russell's Letter . . . on the Principles of the Reform Act' (1839).

[11] He voted in 139–91 for the Manchester and Birmingham railway bill: *Mirror* iii. 2438.

15. W.

Occupied most of the day on a Letter with respect to the late changes, which will probably never see the light;[1] it is so difficult to handle them in our sense, without touching the Queen.
read Carlyle.
house $4\frac{1}{2}$–$5\frac{3}{4}$:[2] and evg at home—picquet with Mr G.

16 Th.

wrote to H. Denison—Dr Sherriffs.
finished & corrected my 'Letter': which cannot be born—read Carlyle.
saw Doyle—& the Manchr gentlemen.
picquet with Mr G—took H. & M.E. to H. of C. wh was lighted experimentally.

17 Fr.

wrote to Kinnaird—Ponsonby—Lds Fitzwilliam,[3] Aberdeen, Haddington, Morpeth, Sir S. Canning, Verney, Nicholl. Gregson, Mr Farrer, Finch, Smith Wright—on Natl Educn meeting: & to JNG at Florence.
read Carlyle—Tupper—pamphlet on Colonial Incorporation.[4]
dined at Ld Mansfields: Abp Yorks, Mrs Brownrigg's, Apsley House & walk home.
Saw Hamilton on Church & Edn matters, Bruce & the Manchr gentn

18 Sat.

wrote to Bartlett—Sir R. Peel—S. Wilberforce.
read R. Wilberforce on Edn[5]—Carlyle—Tupper—dined at Abp of Yorks.—a little music with M.E.

19 Whitsunday.

Ch mg & evg, & Holy Communion—read Oakley (excellent)—Ignatius II & III—Hunter Gordon[6]—

20 M.

Wrote to D. of Wn—Nicholl—Mrs Sherriffs.
Church at 11. read Carlyle—'A Lady'[7]—'Registrn not Baptm'[8]—(5

---

[1] See Morley, i. 222n. The letter is in Add MS 44681, ff. 37–59.
[2] Misc. business: *H* xlvii. 1022.
[3] Charles William Wentworth-*Fitzwilliam, 1768–1857, whig M.P. Yorkshire 1807–30, Northamptonshire 1831–3; 5th earl Fitzwilliam 1833.
[4] Untraced.
[5] R. *Wilberforce, 'A Letter to the . . . Marquis of *Lansdowne, on the Establishment of a Board of National Education' (1839).
[6] H. Gordon, 'The Present State of the Controversy Between the Protestant and Roman Catholic Churches' (1837).
[7] Untraced.
[8] 'Baptism and Registration' (1837?), anonymous pamphlet.

games) picquet—Lady Murray's—Ly Antrobus's—called in B. Square[1]
(&c.)

21 T.

wrote to Hanmer—H. Wilberforce.
read Hanmer's Poems[2]—Carlyle (finished)—began Geraldine Vol 3—saw
Pinnock—Morris.
rode with H. & the G[lynne]s a little. dined in B. Square—Mrs Green's afr.

22 W.

wrote to J. Moncreiff.
saw A. Kinnaird—Mr Hulton.[3]
musie with M.E. dined with the Scotts & music. read Geraldine—Hanmer.
at the Levee.

23 Th.

Wrote to Mr Furbank[4]—Dr Kaye—J. Hope—Ld Chichester—Ld Teignmouth.[5]
read Geraldine.
Saw Sir Jas Graham on Edn & on S. Lancashire—singing. rode with H.J.G.
—O. & C.C. Commee—picquet with Mr G.—Lady Lansdowne's afr.

24 Fr.

Wrote to F. Oakley—Mr Watts Russell.
read Geraldine—Tupper's Poems (finished)—There is some vein in them?
they are unequal?—part of the Judgments in the Auchterarder Appeal.[6]
rode to Norwood with Kinnaird & saw the school: very interesting.
1–5.20—dined at Bp of London's—Mr Granville Vernon's afr.—music.

25 Sat.

wrote to Ld Chichester—Ld Teignmouth—Dr Cooke. singing.
finished Auchterarder judgments—read Geraldine—Edn Commee 2–3½—
Panorama of Rome 4–5½ with the G[lynne]s—dined at Mr Hoare's.

26. Trinity Sunday.

St James mg & aft—& Communion. On this day in particular I had occasion to feel how blessed is the Altar, on which we are appointed to lay

---

[1] 36 Berkeley Square was the Glynnes' town house.
[2] Sir J. *Hanmer, *Fra Cipolla and Other Poems* (1839).
[3] William Hulton, 1787–1864; high sheriff of Lancashire 1809; f. of W. F. See 5 June 39.
[4] Perhaps Thomas Furbank, 1792–1851; perpetual curate of Bramley, Yorks., 1839–51.
[5] Charles John Shore, 1796–1885; b. at Calcutta; went on Waterloo campaign while
up at Trinity, Cambridge; 2nd Lord Teignmouth 1834; tory M.P. Marylebone 1838–41.
[6] H. of L. endorsed the action of the Scottish judges, in accepting the appeal of Robert
Young and the earl of Kinnoull against presbytery and synod at Auchterarder, Perthshire, and the Assembly of the Church of Scotland, which led to the disruption of 1843.
H. of L. *Journals* lxxi. 239.

our body soul and spirit, our whole Hope and desire. For the moment it
was with an apparent singleness of purpose: but that as heretofore will not
last. However it waters and refreshes me, even me!
read S. Ignatius—Oakley VII–IX—Geraldine (finished). The Ramsays to
dinner.

27 M.

wrote to Caparn—Simpson—Vicar—W. Selwyn—read Auchterarder
(Ass[embl]y) proceedings: the hand of God seems to work visibly though
dimly:—King's 1st Lecture[1]—Bickersteth's City Mission Sermon: amiable
illusions?[2]
House 2½–5¾. Voted in 299:317 for Goulburn[3]—12¼–1¾ in B[er]k[eley]
Square. But what I seek is next to an impossibility.[4]
rode—dinner at home & a batch of picquet—8 games.

28 T.

Wrote to Mrs Austin.
read Irish Corporations Case, most wrongly called Epitome[5]—King's 2d
Lecture—began Mrs Austin's proof sheets.[6]
Edn meeting & House 2–5¾.[7] rode (G.s): dined at Mr Tyler's—picquet with
Mr G.—singing with M.E.

29 W.

Wrote to G. Selwyn—F. Baring—Rossellotty[8]—Rev. Mayow—Woolsey—
Hutchinson. read Mrs Austin.
an interesting meeting of 8 or 9 at Sir R.P.s at 11—on Edn & other great
subjects.
read Igiene degl'Occhi[9]—finished Corpns Case—dined at Ld Cholmondeley's—Ancient Music—Mrs Cunliffe's.
The G.s here.

30 Th.

12. Exhibn (G.s) & off to Commee (Nottm)[10] then to Bethnal Green (City)

[1] D. *King, 'Two Lectures in Reply to the Speeches of Dr. *Chalmers on Church
Extension' (1839).
[2] Preached 2 May 1839 at St. John's Chapel, Bedford Row.
[3] For the speakership: the house chose Charles *Shaw-Lefevre, 1794–1888, M.P.
Downton 1830, Hampshire 1831–57; cr. Viscount Eversley on retiring 1857; Hampshire
magnate. H xlvii. 1050.
[4] But see 8–10 June 39.
[5] Untraced.
[6] S. *Austin, On National Education (1839).
[7] Misc. business: H xlvii. 1058. He voted in 66:114 for Strood Church bill, beaten 2°:
ibid. For education meeting see A. H. D. *Acland, T. D. *Acland, 91.
[8] Unidentified: nickname?
[9] Italian pamphlet on care of eyes.
[10] Untraced.

meeting & House to 5¾ and rode—House 7½–9.[1] rode with G.s
read Oliver Twist[2]—Wardlaw[3]—Kennedy on Nat. Educn.[4]

31 Fr.

10–1 Breakfast at Mr Rogers's. G.s.
Robn & M.E. off before.
read Oliver Twist—Wardlaw.
4½–7¼ sat & rode with G.s & House to 10¾. Lady Johnstone's[5] concert with H.J.G.
saw B. Harrison—Mr Ramsay—Mr Gourrier—voted in 81:137 agt Chaplains (Prison) Clause.[6]

Saturday June One.

Wrote to Caparn (Bis)—Branstone—H.J.G.
read Oliver Twist—'True State of the Case'.[7]
dined at Abp of York's (Brougham)—Mrs Brownrigg's afr. (G.s).
Edn Commee 2¼–4. rode 6–7.
Saw Bp of Exeter—Mr Darby.[8]

Sunday 2.

St James mg & aft. & Holy Communion—read Ignatius to Smyrna—Gideon[9]—Hampden on Tradition[10]—weak.

3 M.

Wrote to Naylor[11]—Bp of Exeter—Mr Birch.
read Oliver Twist—Gideon.
Nat. Gall. (G.s) 11–1. Bk Sq. to tea 9¾–12¼—Lady Domvile's. House 5–8½.[12]
Saw Mr Hulton (S. Lanc)—Ld Colborne.

[1] Jamaica; wool trade. *H* xlvii. 1105; 1132.
[2] *Dickens.
[3] R. *Wardlaw, 'The Importance of the Voluntary Church Controversy and the Spirit in which it Ought to be Conducted' (1839).
[4] Letter in Add MS 44356, ff. 167–72.
[5] Louisa Augusta, née Harcourt, 1804–69; da. of abp. of York; m. 1825 Sir John Johnstone, 1799–1869, 2nd bart. 1807, whig M.P. Yorkshire 1830–2, Scarborough 1832–7 and from 1841.
[6] He voted against leave to appoint non-anglican prison chaplains; the numbers were 81:136. *H* xlvii. 1226.
[7] [G. P. de Sanctâ Trinitate] 'The True state of the Case Considered; or, the Oxford Tracts, the Public, Press, and the Evangelical Party' (1839).
[8] John Wareyn Darby, 1793?–1846; vicar of Wiclewood All Saints, Norfolk, 1823–32; rector of Shottesham 1832–46.
[9] *Gideon, 'The Mighty Man of Valour'* (1839); anonymous retelling of the story of Judges vi–viii.
[10] R. D. *Hampden, 'A Lecture on Tradition Read before the University, in the Divinity School, Oxford' (1839).
[11] George Naylor, *ca.* 1768–1854, vicar of Bramford, Suffolk, 1795.
[12] Canada: *H* xlvii. 1254.

4 T.

Wrote to Sir S. Glynne—Lutwidge—Oakley.
Finished Oliver Twist—read Gideon—Bp of Salisbury's Sermon[1]—Commee
12½–4 and House 6½–8½ voted in 207:81 agt £10 County householders.[2]
picquet with Mr G.

5 W.

Wrote to Mr Freshfield—Thos Wilson.
Meeting at Sir R. Peel's on Jamaica & Canada, & arrangements made.
Yesterday a S. Lancashire meeting was held: & a tacit understanding is to
remain that in case of a vacancy I am to obey them; without pecuniary
cost. Mr G. attended & did all.[3]
read Ld Durham.
3–7. ride to Highgate[4] (G.s)—dined at Lady Johnstone's—Mrs Cunliffe's
afr (G.s).

6 Th.

read Wardlaw[5]—Hoare's Charge[6]—Gideon.
rode (G.s)—Lady Cork's in evg & then Lady Wenlock's[7] (10½–1) (Gs)—
rode with H.J.G. too.
House at 2, & 8¼–9½[8]—saw O'Brien: & Brooking on Nfdd. told Mr G. my
position. Concealment became too heavy for me.[9]

7 Fr.

Wrote to D. of N—G.A. Selwyn—G. Tallents—J.G & Co—read Gideon
([blank])—most remarkable & beautiful—House 4–5.[10] Exhibn 5–7 (Gs).
breakf. at Mr Rogers's 10¼–1. (G.s)—saw Montalembert—& S. Wilberforce—
   Picquet with Mr G.—Lady S. Murrays (music)—and to Bk Sq. afterwards.

8 Sat.

Wrote to Caparn (£130).
saw Mr Dixon, late Dissg Minr,[11] on his matters—Doyle—Bruce.

---

[1] E. *Denison, 'The Church the Teacher of Her Children' (1839).
[2] Moved by *Fleetwood. *H* xlvii. 1374.
[3] There was no contest in south Lancashire in 1841; *Gladstone eventually fought the
seat in 1865.
[4] i.e. northwards out of London.
[5] R. *Wardlaw, *National Church Establishments examined* (1839).
[6] C. J. *Hoare, 'A Charge Delivered to the Clergy of the Archdeaconry of Winchester'
(1838).
[7] Caroline, née Neville, 1792–1868, Catherine Glynne's mother's sister; m. 1817 Paul
Beilby Lawley Thompson, 1784–1852, whig M.P. Wenlock 1826–32, cr. Lord Wenlock
May 1839.
[8] Election Petitions Trials bill, cttee.: *H* xlviii. 10.   [9] See Magnus, 43.
[10] He voted in 177 to 186 for the Cheltenham Improvement bill, which was lost 3°.
[11] Not further identified.

read Hints on Horsemanship[1]—Wardlaw.

dined at Sir J. Mordaunt's—Lady Shelleys[2] (near Fulham) $3\frac{1}{2}$-$6\frac{1}{2}$—I went down with the G.s—& here my Catherine gave me herself.[3] We walked apart, and with an effort she said that all doubt on my part might end. I intreated her to try & know me well: I told her what was my original destination & desire in life, in what sense & manner I remained in connection with politics[4]—all this produced no revulsion in her pure and lofty spirit. She asked for the earliest Communion, that we might go together to the altar of Christ. Blessed creature! until I escape from these distractions of business I cannot feel the boon I have received nor do her even the scanty justice that would otherwise be in my power. We agreed that I should remain silent until tomorrow: for I wished to show her the letter of September 1835,[5] and explain to her, at the least, that subject.

9 Sunday.

St James mg & aft. Mr Ward & Dr Hook. read Nicole—Oakley.

I was with Catherine between Churches, & in the afternoon. I told her what I had to say: she read the letter and rejoiced in it. It was not fear that she would view it differently, but it was the desire to fulfil an inward compact with myself, which prompted me to leave her free until she had read it: but now I freely and absolutely call her mine and I have kissed her cheek. They are all most kind: & may I have from my God a due sense of the value and the sweetness of this gift, and of the responsibility connected with it: and the power to lay it as a sacrifice before Him.—I have given her (led by her questions) these passages for canons of our living.

> Le frondi onde s'infronda tutto l'orto
> Del Ortolano Eterno, am' io cotanto
> Quanto de Lui in lor di bene è porto—[6]

then St Paul's 'Henceforth know I no man after the flesh'[7]—and Dante again

> In la sua voluntade è nostra pace:
> Ella è quel mare al qual tutto si muove.[8]

She responds at once—it seems as if in her heart there were no strongholds to cast down.[9]

10 M.

At the end of a long and checquered day—checquered with joy, business,

---

[1] G. Greenwood, *Hints on Horsemanship to a Nephew and Niece* (1839).
[2] The Glynnes' next-door-neighbour in Berkeley Square.
[3] See Morley, i. 222–3, and Magnus, 43.
[4] See 2–5, 8, 12 Aug. 30.
[5] These two phrases in Morley, i. 223. And cp. 3 Sept. 35.
[6] 'The leaves that leaf over all the Eternal Gardener's garden, I love in measure of the good that he has lavished on them.'—Dante, *Paradiso* xxxvi. 65.
[7] II Cor. v. 16; cp. i. xxx above.
[8] 'In his Will lies our peace; it is the sea towards which all moves'—*Paradiso* iii. 86.
[9] Extracts in Morley, i. 223, dated a day early.

and excitement—I sit down to write & think a little. First, how much have I said of God today, my hand coursing over the paper, & how little have I thought of Him to thank Him. My blessing is indeed very great.

I began to read in the morning but had made no way when the Bp of Vermont[1] came in. At 11¾ I went to Sir R. Peel's on Education. Thence at 12¾ to Berkeley Square. At two she and I went to the Archbishop's by his desire & he kissed Catherine twice & spoke most kindly to us both—at four I came home & saw Aunt Divie & then Mr Grenville[2]—at five I went to the House & remained till 10½ speaking ½ hour on the Jamaica Clause[3]—thence to Catherine at Lady Wenlock's, & after seeing her home I made a bow at Lady Willoughby's & came home to write again. My letters today have been to

T.G. (bis)	Mrs Wadd	H. Glynne
R.G.	Mrs Chisholm	T. Egerton
J.N.G.	Mr Rawson	A. Wood
Aunt J.	Mr Staniforth[4]	R. Phillimore
Aunt D.	Mr Ramsay	Mr Rogers[5]
Jane C.R.	W.F. Hamilton	F.H. Doyle
Mrs Larkins	W.R. Farquhar	R.M. Milnes
C. Mackenzie	Milnes Gaskell	Doyle
Miss Joy	Lady Antrobus	Canning
Mrs Jones	Lincoln	Mahon
Mrs Fellowes		

Also to Thos Wilson of Newark.

11 T.

Up rather early & wrote to Mrs Hagart—Lady Kerrison—A. Gordon—Dr Fergusson—also to Jas Hope[6]—G.A. Selwyn—H. Seymer—B. Harrison—& (on business) to Rev. Mr Murray—read Pref. to Coleridge's Table Talk. Morng Mr G. on Sologoub's letter—Mr Rogers's at 10, to breakfast with Thirlwall,[7] and talk to Lyttleton, in whom I am deeply interested, on his matters.[8] B. Square at 11½ to introduce Mr G.—Helen there 1—at 2½ H. of C. for Nk Small Debts Committee—& again 4–5.[9] then to B. Square; drove out & called on a tribe of Catherine's relations &c. including old Mr Grenville—dined in Bk: Square and two hours walk in the garden with her,

[1] John Henry Hopkins, 1792–1868; convert from agnosticism; first protestant bp. of Vermont 1832; presiding bp. of Protestant Episcopal Church 1865.
[2] Catherine Glynne's uncle Thomas *Grenville, 1755–1846, collector; Foxite M.P. Buckinghamshire 1780–4, Aldborough 1790–6, Buckingham 1796–1818; sinecurist 1800–17; left over 20,000 books to British Museum.
[3] He opposed allowing governor of Jamaica to legislate by decree: *H* xlviii. 118. Notes in Add MS 44649, f. 274.
[4] Copy in Add MS 44356, f. 287.
[5] Copy ibid. f. 286.
[6] Fragment in Magnus, 46.
[7] Connop *Thirlwall, 1797–1875, historian; fellow of Trinity, Cambridge 1818; rector of Kirby Underdale 1835–40; bp. of St. David's 1840–74.
[8] See 17 June 39.
[9] Bible in Scotland: *H* xlviii. 140.

very dear. She went at 3 with Miss Harcourt[1] to the Dss of Beaufort. Home at 11 & read &c.

12 W.

wrote to Mrs Gaskell—(Mr Dennis[2] & R.G. on business)—Bp of London— Mr Ward—F. Calvert—Sir W. Riddell—Lady F. Cole—Dr Lady Sitwell.[3] Morning, 'imaginary conversation': at one with Mr G. to Ld Braybrooke's & on to Bk. Square—My delight grows so rapidly from day to day: & yet it will not be her fault if it sinks into earthliness. But it is more than can endure. Sweet hours this day in Bkley Square: then we rode, taking Helen: and then we dined with the dear Duchess of Beaufort: & went again to No 36. We watched our *rivals*, Mary & Ld L. a good deal: O may God direct and sanctify them. Joy and kindness flow in from all quarters: what would (even) this world be, but for sin! read a little "Table Talk"—that I may not quite forget my alphabet.

13 Th.

At 11 & to 12½ to Sir R.P.s on Education & Jamaica—Catherine here from 1 to 4—I was able to tell her the F. & D. affairs throughout.[4] House 4½–5¾:[5] wrote to Sir E. Kerrison—Miss Benwell. thence to Bk Sq.— Regent's Park—Bk S.—Lady Carysfort's[6] (she is very striking)—Bk. S. again till one. How many may I conscientiously allow myself of such days?

14 Fr.

Wrote to Manning—S.F. Wood—H.H. Joy. 10½–4½: Bk Square. Long and delightful conversations, wh aid I hope in the attainment of mutual knowledge. L[yttleto]n came in; he pursues his own matters most zealously & shows many fine qualities. House 5–6¾. Petitions.[7] G[lynne]s dined in C[arlton] G[ardens]—Aunts D. & J. &c—House 11–12½[8]—in the cellar, with H. & G.s.

15 Sat.

Wrote to Branston—Butterfield.[9] Bk.S. 12¼–5: 3 hours nearly walk &c. in Kensington Gardens dove la dilettissima mi spiegò le cose che mi avea promesse con somma schietezza— io non poteva non diventare più e più invaghito di tante virtù—ecco in

---

[1] Anne, d. 1867, eldest da. of abp. of York.　　　　　　　　[2] Unidentified.
[3] I.e. Mrs. Smith Wright.
[4] Cp. Sept. 1835 and Nov. 1837.
[5] He voted in 165 to 82 against receiving a petition on Irish education from the archbishop of Tuam: *H* xlviii. 204.
[6] Elizabeth, née Grenville, 1756–1842; da. of George *Grenville and great-aunt of Catherine Glynne; m. 1787 John Joshua Proby, 1751–1828, 2nd earl of Carysfort 1789.
[7] He was among two dozen M.P.s presenting petitions against proposed education vote: *H* xlviii. 222.
[8] Education: ibid. 227.
[9] Thomas Butterfield, d. 1861; chief justice of Bermuda.

somma la lista σημερνευαρκἰλλϝαυἀνέγερτονἀνϛονἀρκουρτλευιϛμορδαυντ.[1]
rode with Mary & H.J.G.—dined with the Egertons to meet G.s—conv.
with Mr G. at night.

16 Sunday.

At 7½ to Bk S. took C. & M. to the Communion which we received together
conforme alla di lei dolcissima richiesta. Così incominciando, cos'è da
desiderare, soltanto che resti,[2] siccome in questi giorni l'ho trovato, piena
del amore di Dio e del prossimo e di sant virtu.—Quel meschino ha maritato
un altra donna nobile e ricchissima dopo aver giurato fede a essa: dice nondimeno che non è giusto supporre quel donaro per motivo del fatto infame:
o carità illustre![3]
took them back to Bk S—there again between Churches & till dinner. St
James mg & aft.—Mr G. most of evg.
read Oakley & Pusey's Preface to S. Aug.

17 M.

Wrote to Morpeth—Mrs Hagart—Lady Brabazon—T.S. Godfrey.
At 10½ to Bk Square. We talked over many subjects & made much progress. At about 3½ Lyttleton who had been there from before lunch, in a
tempest of joy tottered across the room to let us know we were his brother
and sister respectively. Mary was a good deal overcome & hid her head in
Catherine's bosom: then they fled for a little. He for a while could not in
the least control his emotions of delight—and yet he directed them towards
God.[4] He is a very noble and powerful creature. 'I never loved any other',
he said, 'I never dreamed of any other'—it was true: and this gush of
virgin affection bursting its banks was extremely moving. We adopted
address by Christian names, agreed to marry on the same day—or rather
hoped it—kissed each the other's love—
May God be with these newly betrothed. For me, I know how much of
the gloss has been brushed off my ideal: but I now know enough to be convinced that not without the faithful Providence of God have I been reserved for access to a creature so truly rare and consummate as my
Catherine.

[1] 'where my very dearest explained to me the things she had promised me, with
complete genuineness—I could not fail to become more and more attracted by such
goodness—here in fact is the list, Seymer Newark Hill Vaughan Egerton Anson Harcourt
Lewis Mordaunt'. The list is of her former suitors; cp. next n. but one.
[2] 'fissa' (fixed) deleted.
[3] 'at her very sweet request. Thus begun, thus, I hope, may she only remain; as I have
found her in these last few days, full of the love of God and of her neighbour and of holy
virtues.—That rascal, after plighting himself to her, married another high-born lady, a
very rich one: all the same, she says it is unjust to assume that money motivated the
vile deed: o perfected charity!' The 'rascal' was Colonel Francis Vernon Harcourt,
1801–80, of Buxted in Sussex; who m. 20 November 1837 Lady Catherine Julia Jenkinson, eldest da. of 3rd earl of *Liverpool; she d. 1877. Cp. Battiscombe, 19; and 30 July 39.
[4] Cp. Magnus, 34.

We rode—for peace: dined at Abp of York's—House before dinner & 11–1½: voted in 184:166 on Privilege.[1]

18 T.

Wrote to Mr Hallam—Rio—Mrs Austin—on her proofsheets, which I read. At 10½ to Bk. Square—calls with Catherine—House at 2½. and 5–6:[2] then to Ross's with C. & they came to dine with us. House (the ballot) 10½–1¾: voted in 333:216 agt it.[3]

19 W.

Wrote to C.G (bis)—Verney—Jas Alexr—Mrs Austin—Jennings. saw Messrs Brooking & Robinson[4] on Nfdd.
read Education Debate—& looked it up: but I was really not in a state to speak at night though Chas Buller had just been at my book.[5]
drove & rode with the G.s—also some time in the Square.
wrote a letter (agreed on) to Stephen, respecting allowance.
House 5½–7 (in 257:267 on Jamaica) & 9–12½.[6]
sent a snowstorm of excuses for all pending parties.

20 Th.

Wrote to Mrs Fraser—T.S. Godfrey.
read 'Taming of a Shrew'! Educn Debate. went with Helen to the drawingroom.
at 4 to Bk. Square: there till 7¾ in delight: then to H. of C. in agony: spoke at 9½ for an hour or more. There till 2½ in the morning. Voted in 275:280—very good—on Ld Stanley's motion.[7]

21. Fr.

Wrote to Selwyn—Seymer—S. Wilberforce—Mordaunt—R.G. with Macneille's statement. read Newfdd papers.
Bk. Square at 10½ (after seeing Kinnaird)—at 2, family calls with C.—House 5½–7.[8] Dined at Ld Wenlock's, a family party.

22. Sat.

Wrote to Hulton.[9]
In Berkeley Square from eleven. There is no end to our subjects, or to our interruptions. Time flies with great rapidity: & yet in retrospect one seems

---

[1] For not interfering in *Stockdale v. *Hansard. John Joseph *Stockdale, 1770–1847, publisher, claimed that *Hansard had libelled him by reprinting some observations of a parliamentary committee; *Hansard pleaded privilege. *H* xlviii. 423.
[2] Misc. business: ibid. 428.   [3] *Grote's motion lost: ibid. 504.
[4] Unidentified.   [5] Ibid. 562.
[6] Jamaica Laws bill, 3°; education. *H* xlviii. 524; 529.
[7] *Stanley's amdt., like *Gladstone's speech, sought greater clerical influence on education. Ibid. 622, 682. Notes for speech in Add MS 44649, ff. 275–7.
[8] Prisons, and police. Ibid. 701; 705.   [9] W. F. Hulton.

to have lived through months in days. At four by the Railway to Eton with the G.s & L. Went to the Society: party of cousins to dinner: on the Terrace & a delightful evening.

23 Sunday.

Datchet Church mg with Selwyn.[1] St George's in aftn. Dined with Dr Hawtrey—read S. Wilberforce[2]—walk with C. & sat much with her.

24 M.

St George's mg; then to see the boats—school—& cricket—calls on the Provost & Hawtrey—off by two o'clock train. House $5\frac{1}{4}$–$6\frac{1}{4}$ and 10–12. Voted in 273:275 on Education Vote:[3] & heard myself talked about. That of Lord Aberdeen's letter of Feb. 35 is a sore business though I am perfectly innocent.[4]

G.s &c. to dinner in C.G.

25 T.

wrote to Maj. Macarthur.

read on the Wesleyan Centenary.[5]

breakfast in Bk Sq.—Sir R. Peel's at $11\frac{3}{4}$ on Education, & on Canada.—nuptial shopping. B.S. again—Ld Devon's to dinner, & B.S. afr. But we are full of worry and all joy broken into shivers by constant interruptions. I suppose that the craving for something like continuance of repose by her side is the form which the inveterate disease of selflove has now assumed.

26 W.

Manning & Glynne to breakft. Saw Mr Robinson on Newfoundland—Sir R. Peels at $11\frac{1}{2}$ on Edn &c.—they decided there not to divide—thence to B.S. & in their little arrangements—drove with them & rode to House & shopping.

Evg, went in to Ld Stanley's to see Webster,[6] Sir W. Wynn's (G.s) & B. Square.

27 Th.

Wrote to Macdonald—Richmond—Rio[7]—read Wesleyan Centenary.

saw Ivall[8]—Macarthur (Australia)—Labouchere (at C.O.) & papers on the Coolies' case[9]—dined at Lady Carysfort's—B. Barings $\frac{1}{2}$ hour, & B. Square afr.

---

[1] G. A. *Selwyn was a curate at Windsor 1833–41. Datchet lies $1\frac{1}{2}$ miles east of Windsor. Cp. H. W. Tucker, *G. A.* *Selwyn, i. 54 (1879).

[2] S. *Wilberforce, *Sermons Preached Before the University of Oxford*, 1s. (1839).

[3] *Russell just carried supply vote to spend £30,000: *H* xlviii. 793.

[4] Untraced; presumably lobby gossip about C.O. business.

[5] *The Centenary of Methodism: being a History of the Rise and Continuance of That System* (1839).   [6] Probably Thomas *Webster, 1800–86; painter, R.A. 1846–76.

[7] Part in Bowe, *Rio* 163 n.

[8] David Ivall, Bloomsbury coachmaker. Cp. 29 June 39.   [9] Untraced.

28. Fr.

Wrote to H. Glynne.
Poor dear Helen's birthday. Oh may she reach the measure of her possible excellences.
read Wesleyan Centenary—Paradiso I.
in B.S. most of the day. dined at home. Lady Wenlocks in evg. H of C.[1]

29 Sat.

read Paradiso II.
we had been very anxious to be married by banns, but we are reluctantly compelled to give it up mainly because Stephen [Glynne] & others dislike it & it is not a matter on wh to shock people so nearly connected: partly because it *might* cause some delay.
dined in B.S.—settled the grand affair of the carriage.

30 S.

St James mg & aft.—Mr Wigram's farewells. read Wesleyan Centenary.
in B.S. between Churches & before dinner.

L[ondo]n Monday July one.

Saw Ld A. Hervey—to B.S. before 12. Wrote to H. Glynne—rode—dined in B.S. House afr,[2] & rctd to Lady Wenlock's. read Alison[3]—Dub. Rev. on Froude.[4]

2 T.

Wrote to J.N.G.
Breakf. in B.S.—routing out & struggling to arrange papers for C.—Come son felice di trovare solo un cotal difetto.[5]—Our work advances.
read Alison—Newcastle papers.
dined at Mr Grenville's—B.S. afr.

3 W.

Wrote to Ld Ashley—Labouchere—T.D. Acland—Lady Henniker—Jane Tyler—Sir W. James—W. Selwyn—G.A. Selwyn—H. Wilberforce—Rev. H. Mackenzie.
In B.S. assisting in their arrangements of books &c. They have lived with almost community of goods. Beautiful!

[1] Sugar duties, 3°: *H* xlviii. 1021.
[2] Factories bill, cttee.: *H* xlviii. 1063.
[3] A. *Alison, History of Europe During the French Revolution*, 10 v. (1833–42); vol. vii was published 1839.
[4] *Dublin Review*, vi. 416 (May 1839); on 2nd vol. of *Remains of . . . Richard H. *Froud* (1838); article by *Wiseman.
[5] 'How happy I am to find only such a weakness as this.'

Dined at home, small party—Lady Grosvenor's[1] concert afr.
H. of C.[2]

4 Th.

wrote to Mrs Fellowes—Dry—Murray—Uncle D.—Gourrier—Stretton[3]—
M.A. Fellowes.
read Wesleyan Centenary—arranging papers letters &c. most joyously the
work considered, for departure! Ivalls & B.S.
dined in B. Square.
House at $5\frac{1}{2}$ and again $10\frac{1}{2}$–$12\frac{1}{2}$.[4]
Wrote some passages on Church & State matters—an unwonted effort!

5. Fr.

Wrote to Pusey—Lutwidge—Edn Standard (with a Statement of Selwyn's
matter)[5]—Sewell.
read Centenary (finished)—St Elisabeth.[6]
at 1 to see Mr G's picture—business afr—accts—dined at Mr Ellison's,
G.s in C.G. afr.

6 Sat.

wrote to Bp Winchr—Mr Farrer—Mr W. Cotton—Dr Ferguson—Caparn—
Ramsay—Steele—R.G.—read Buxton—Quarty on Zillerthal.
B.S. at $10\frac{1}{2}$. House $12\frac{3}{4}$–$3\frac{3}{4}$.[7] dined & evg in B.S.

7. S.

St James mg & aft. Holy Communion: I had the pleasure of kneeling by
George's side.
B.S. between Churches & in evg. Conv. of half an hour with Lady Glynne[8]
whose case is very interesting. read S. Ignatius to Polycarp—Polycarp to
Philippians—J. Steele on Evidences[9]—S. Wilberforce's Sermons—Eller on
Private Judgment.[10]

---

[1] Lady Elizabeth Mary Leveson-Gower, 1797–1891, youngest da. of 1st duke of
*Sutherland, m. 1819 Richard *Grosvenor, 1795–1869, styled Viscount Belgrave 1802–31
and Earl Grosvenor 1831–45; whig M.P. Chester 1818–30 and Cheshire 1830–5, 2nd
marquess of Westminster 1845.
[2] Copyholds Enfranchisement bill, 3°: H xlviii. 1182.
[3] Unidentified.
[4] Canada; Irish municipalities. H xlviii. 1195; 1213.
[5] Untraced.
[6] Montalembert (1836).
[7] Factories bill, cttee.: H xlviii. 1415.
[8] Mary, née Neville, da. of 2nd lord Braybrooke, m. 1807 Sir Stephen Richard Glynne,
8th bart. of Hawarden, who d. 1815; she was an invalid from 1818 (see Battiscombe, 18)
and d. 1854.
[9] J. Steele, *The Philosophy of the Evidence of Christianity* (1834).
[10] I. Eller, 'A few plain words . . . on . . . Christian Unity: and on . . . Private Judgment' (1839).

8 M.

Wrote to C.G.—Eller[1]—Murray—Brooking—Caparn—Ryder—: and to
A. Kinnaird, bis, with a draft address, on the interesting matter he com-
municated in two morning visits: I was gratified but not surprised by it.[2]
Breakfast in B.S.—they went at 9.
African meeting at 2½ at Dr Lushington's. A singular but really a pleasing
mixture.
House 5–6¾.[3] Picquet with Mr G.
read Buxton's 'Remedy' (finished) & Marryat on Religion in America.[4]

9 T.

wrote to Mr G—Ld Braybrooke (both on pinmoney)—R.G.—C.G.—Mr
Armstrong—George—Brooking—saw A.K. & reconsidered draft address.
Sir R. Peel's on Canada at 11¾–1½.
saw Labouchere on Newfoundland. House 4½–5¾. Counted out—my motion
drops[5]—Picquet with Mr G.
read Wilberforce's Sermon on the Temptation.[6]

10 W.

wrote to *Mavor* (with chestnut)—C.G.—Mr G.—Neville Grenville.[7]
read Quarterly on Household.
paying bills[8] & preparing for departure.
saw Lyttelton—T. Godfrey—C. Childers—rode with Helen—dinner party.

11 Th.

Wrote to C.G. (bis)—Henry G.—Ld Braybrooke (finally yielding)—Mr
Whatham[9] (Lpool Establ. Church Society)—Robn G.—Mr Harrison—Mr
Hulton.[10] In consequence of ill accounts of Lady Charlotte N.G.[11] I post-
pone until Saturday.
House 4½–6¾ and 8½–1. Voted in 156:174 agt a very arbitrary clause wh
only a 'reform' govt cd have afforded to propose.[12]
saw D. of N. on Newark matters—kind & frank as ever.

[1] Irvin Eller, rector of Faldingworth, Lincolnshire, 1848–70. See previous note.
[2] *Kinnaird resigned his seat for Perth, in the belief that his constituents would resent
his vote for religious education (D. Fraser, *M. J. Kinnaird*, 26–27).
[3] Bank of England: *H* xlix. 3.
[4] F. *Marryatt, *A Diary in America with Remarks on Its Institutions*, 6 v. (1839), iii.
90–166.
[5] Misc. business: *H* xlix. 78.
[6] S. *Wilberforce, *Sermons Preached Before the University of Oxford*, 1 s. 137, on Matt.
iv. 1.
[7] George *Neville Grenville, 1789–1854, b. of 3rd Lord *Braybrooke, master of Magdalene, Cambridge 1810–53, rector of Hawarden 1814–34; took name of Grenville 1825 on
taking over Thomas *Grenville's estates; dean of Windsor 1846; see 25 July 39.
[8] Including £1,000 for Newark election expenses (cp. Add MS 44356, f. 316).
[9] Perhaps John Whatham, Liverpool shoemaker.
[10] Reply ibid f. 318.
[11] Charlotte, née Legge, d. 1877; da. of 3rd earl of *Dartmouth; m. G. *N. Grenville
1816.
[12] Canada Bill in cttee.: he voted to retain restriction on governor's powers to legislate.
H xlix. 214.

12 Fr.

Wrote to C.G.—Mr Dry.
Packing, paying bills &c. rode with H.J.G. Party at home.
House 4–5, various business—& 11–11½—paired agt govt on postage.[1]
finished S. Wilberforce's excellent Sermons.

13 Sat.

9–9. 200 miles to Hawarden. Dust from engine annoying to the eyes &
filthy in the carriage: I had dreaded the motion backward.[2]
Found dear Catherine well & strong tho' not stouter—a delightful evening.
The place most lovely & at its best. George Mary Henry & Stephen who
came with me, altogether a joyous circle. Even Lady G. dear soul seemed
better.
read Chalmers's Speech on Patronage.[3]

14 Sunday.

Ch mg & aft. Music very pleasing. read Nicole & Wilberforce's Parochial
System. Much & dear convn.

15 M.

Wrote to Storr[4]—Crombie—Bishop (organ)—Burnaby—Mr G.
read Wilberforce—Montalembert's Introduction to St Elisabeth.
Drive in poney chaise & much real intercourse—Virginis incertâ trepidat
formidine pectus.[5] I had opportunity for looking at the neglected side of
the question—what am I, to charge myself with the care of such a being,
and to mix her destiny in mine?

16 T.

Wrote to H.J.G.—& H. Wilberforce.
Finished H.W.s admirably powerful book—began the 'Sentimental
Journey'.[6]
drive again & much conv. music in evg.

17. W.

read Montalembert & 'Sentiml Journey'.
music in evg. Walk & visits to some poor & to the three schools—I ex-

---

[1] Penny postage: ibid. 277.
[2] By the 9.30 train from Euston to Crewe, changing in Birmingham; thence by road through Chester.
[3] T. *Chalmers, 'Remarks on the Right Exercise of Church Patronage' (1836); extracted from *Chalmers's *The Christian and Civic Economy of Large Towns*, 3v. (1821–26), i. chapters 5 and 6.
[4] Richard Storr, Newark publican.
[5] 'The maiden's breast trembles with fear of the unknown.' Cp. Ovid, *Metam.* ii. 66.
[6] *Sterne (1768).

amined the boys in Heb.XI—excellent practice, which I much wish for the opportunity of resuming: & certainly one 'doubly blessed'.

18 Th.

Wrote to Mr G—Mr Ramsay—Steele—Mrs Crauford[1]—Corrie & Co—Manning.
read Montalembert's St Elisabeth—Law agt Hoadley[2]—Kenilworth, aloud with dearest. Drive with her and M. Delicious days: few by all law human & divine. Yet not without their instruction & their profit: both I believe dwell under even the light forms of love: but on this earth instruction and profit do not usually come upon the wings of Joy so unmixed.

19 Fr.

Wrote to M'Cracken[3]—Scotts—Smith (Montrose)[4]—Jno Murray jun.
We have arranged tea for the children (400) & some little benefactions. The people also are subscribing & threaten roasting an ox: fireworks at least: £50 raised. The widows (130) & old men (about half as many) are to receive the first bedgowns & the latter waistcoats.
Saw Boydell[5] & recd from him a full account of the Colliery: wh only wants I think a village & a Church.
read Law.
billiards with C.

20 Sat.

wrote to A. Kinnaird—Doyle—Storr—RG.—read Law, Scott (ballads), Sentimental Journey (finished)—without pleasure.
read Vss to C.—drove her to Northop.[6] Music.

21 Sunday.

Church mg & aft. An extra Communion: well attended—by above 80—Henry much affected. S., G, M, C, & I present.
read St Elisabeth & Law to Hoadley.

22 M.

wrote to Mr G.—T.G.
read Law to Hoadley—& Montalembert.
The Neville's arrived.[7] Music. Rode to Northop Bazaar! my first: I hope

---

[1] Possibly w. of William Crawford, east India magnate, lib. M.P. London 1833–41.
[2] W. *Law, 'Three Letters to the Bishop of Bangor between 1717–19, in The Dispute Following the Appearance of B. *Hoadley's *Reply to the Representation of Convocation'* (1719).
[3] James and Robert McCracken, wine merchants in Old Jewry.
[4] Robert Smith, Montrose shipowner?   [5] The Glynnes' agent.
[6] Coal mining village 5 miles WNW. of Hawarden.
[7] The Braybrookes and their five sons (two of whom were killed in the Crimea) and three daughters, all b. 1820–30.

my last. Wilberforce's censure is only a little too strong for me.[1] I think they tend to disguise first principles, & that systematically. There can hardly be a greater objection, dispassionately viewed. On the other hand there is a mixture of good.

Una dolcissima passeggiata.[2]

23 Tues.

Wrote to Mr Johnson (Taxes)[3]—Walter Hamilton.—finished Montalembert's 1st vol.—& read Pole's 'Reform of England'.[4]

Miss Lyttelton[5] has the measles—& on account of apprehended disturbance 40 yeomanry are at Hagley.[6] George like a son & a man quickly decided to go to his mother[7]—which cast a shade of uncertainty over our prospects.

Many arrivals today: my Father & Helen among them.

24 W.

wrote to Corrie—Burge—Stokes[8]—W. Selwyn—Auld—A. Kinnaird—& Boydell in C's name.

Went at one to the distribution of waistcoats & bedgowns among 200 old men & widows, in the school: a most interesting sight. Helen Miss Lawley[9] & others assisted in the distribution: C. & M. sat by the door, & warmly greeted the old people as they poured their blessings & prayers before them. Read a little of Cardinal Pole.

We dined about 30. T.G. came in evg. The necessary arrangements, the settlements & pecuniary matters occupied the evening. At near 12 I walked on the terrace with 12[sc. G]—a fine night: & we ruminated & spoke together on our great felicity, until he was summoned to join the Rectory Dilly.

25 Th.

Only this night, & a little last night, have my too sound & homely slumbers been at all broken: & even this glory & poetry of life has not till this morning abated my appetite. Rose in good time, & read Ps.: breakfast about 9. Soon after 10 Sir Watkin [Williams Wynn] arrived & we set off in about 12 carriages over the grass, round the old Castle, & into & through the village. Oh what a scene! Till 12 when we started I fought almost in vain against

---

[1] Untraced.
[2] 'A most delightful journey'.
[3] Unidentified.
[4] R. *Pole, Reformatio Angliae (1556); probably the ed. tr. by H. Raikes (Chester, 1839).
[5] Caroline Lavinia, 1816–1902.
[6] *Lyttelton's seat in north Worcestershire, midway between Birmingham and Kidderminster. Cp. DLFC i. 20.
[7] Lady Sarah, née Spencer, 1787–1870, 1st da. of 2nd Earl *Spencer, m. 1813 William Henry Lyttelton, 1782–1837, 5th baron 1828; governess to *Victoria's children 1842–50.
[8] Perhaps Charles Stokes, London solicitor.
[9] Jane, only da. of 1st Lord Wenlock; m. 1846 James Archibald *Stuart-Wortley, 1805–81, M.P. Halifax 1832–7, Buteshire 1842–9.

such a gush of delight as I had not yet experienced. Such an outpouring of pure human affection on these beloved girls, combined with so solemn a mystery of religion! Every house was as a bower, the road arched & festooned, flowers & joined hands amid the green; & the deepest interest on every face: a band & procession of Societies at the head. The mass thickened as we came nearer to the Church. From the highroad all the way to the door was carpeted: the Churchyard portion strown with flowers & dear little girls with the baskets: the order perfect. George came with my Father & me after the brides. The Church was full: & as we walked up the aisle the organ & a hymn began & took away what little power of resistance I had left. At the Altar I found my beloved: we went towards the left: & were joined first: but the same opening & conclusion served. Uncle George[1] performed the service with dignity & great feeling, & *entire*—Stephen gave C. & Henry M. My beloved bore up pretty well: her soul is as high & strong as it is tender. There were many many tears. George gave way in the vestry a little: where we signed. They then changed at the Rectory & went off he for Hagley, I for Norton,[2] where I write at 5 P.M. and the beloved sleeps for a while on the sofa—We have read the two second lessons together.[3]

She has *less* cause to rejoice as well as more to weep: but with me this joy is not tempered enough, I fear, & hardly belongs to a follower of the Crucified, much less to one so false in his profession. It has been more of heaven than of earth today. Life cannot yield such another sight.

Yet it has had its warning voice. Just before setting out, we saw Lady G.: birth, beauty, riches, energy, the respect of men, all were hers: and she has not passed middle age: but she remained in uneasy depression at the Castle, & did not venture to attend while she felt being absent. How strong are the contrasts of this mortal life—whereof today has been the flower—for that mingling of sanctity, joy, & love, which sin hardly ever suffers to manifest itself on earth, & there but for a moment.

She sleeps, gently as a babe. O may I never disturb her precious peace,[4] but cherish her more dearly than myself in proportion as she is less earthly.

Wrote to Tom with congratulations on his birthday. We read the two Second Lessons: & I read Marmion to her. Walk.

26 Fr.

wrote to Stephen—& Storr.
read Bible *with* my Catherine: this daily practice will I trust last as long as our joint lives.[5] read to her Trench—Marmion—& some of my own verses.
Billiards: & drove C. & walked.
How could I express the sense of the scene of yesterday! It may seem

[1] *Neville Grenville. Facsimile certificate in Add MS 44728, f. 260.
[2] Norton Priory, 20 miles eastward, the seat of Sir Richard Brooke, 1785–1865, 7th bart. 1795, a cousin of the bride's.
[3] Version of part of this sentence in Magnus, 46.
[4] Thus far in this paragraph in Magnus, 46.
[5] Cp. 31 Aug. 39.

extravagant to dwell so much on the accompaniments: but it is because they did ennoble and sanctify the time: and did *really*, for the time, raise the heart to a high tone accordant with the spirit of the great mystery of Christian marriage.[1]

27 Sat.

Wrote to Bishop—Steele—Lady Glynne—Chester Chronicle.[2]
read the Bible, with much conv.—Marmion—Ld Lyttelton's Dialogues of the Dead[3]—Bp of London's Sp. on Education.[4] Not only every day, but nearly every hour, convince me of the brightness of my treasure, her pure, enduring brightness.[5]

28 Sunday.

Ch mg & aft. Thin. Music good: such as the South wd not supply: still it was not congregational. Walk. Read Nicole, & Wilberforce's Sixth Srm— all delightful.

29 M.

Wrote to Mary Lyttelton—& Johnson (Taxes)—T.G. These days are very full, with the study of one another in no small part;—the flower of life. read Marmion—Lalla Rookh (began).[6]
singing.

30. T.

Wrote to Stephen—Fitzmaurice—R.G.—Cursham.
read Marmion (finished)—Lalla Rookh—C's F[rancis] H[arcourt] Letters: including the noble one where she wishes Heaven may grant all happiness to them both—there is in the whole of it an astonishingly ripened spirit, & this is the crown of all.
billiards with C. rain.

31 W.

wrote to Henry Glynne—Mr G.
read Lady of the Lake (aloud)—Lalla Rookh.
Billiards with C. rain still. Long conv. on previous history.

Thursday August One.

Wrote to T.G.—Mr Macdougal—and Mrs D.R.—Mr G. read Lady of the Lake—Doyle's St Leger[7]—Lalla Rookh (finished) conv. on amusements. Walk & drive.

---

[1] Version of this phrase in Magnus, 46.
[2] Cp. Robbins, 366.   [3] G. *Lyttelton (1760).
[4] C. J. *Blomfield, 'Speech of the Lord Bishop of London on National Education, at the Public Meeting Held in Willis's Rooms' (1839).
[5] Most of this sentence in Magnus, 46.   [6] T. *Moore (1817).
[7] F. H. *Doyle, 'The Doncaster St. Leger'; published unsigned in *The New Sporting Magazine*, xv. 294 (November 1838); reprinted in *Doyle's *Miscellaneous Verses* (1840).

2 Fr.

wrote to Acland[1]—J.N.G.—Sir R. Brooke.
conv. on private judgment &c.
read Lady of the Lake—Mathilde[2]—Russell's Tour in Sicily.[3]

4 Sunday.

wrote to Montalembert in answer to his note: not well. Wrote.[4]
Conv. on Lord's Day.
read Mr Tweddell's Tracts[5]—& Atterbury's unsatisfactory Sermon on
"Charity covereth" &c.[6]

5 M.

Wrote to Sir Jas Graham—Sir R. Inglis.
read Sewell's pamphlet on the Church Discipline Bill.[7] Finished Russell's
Tour in Sicily.
Drove & walked. Called on Mr Tweddell[8] & arranged for charities.

6 T.

Wrote to M'Crackens—Tweddell—R. Carus Wilson[9]—Mary L.
read Landor's Imag. Conv.[10]
Billiards with C. Delayed in starting by nonarrival of horses & caught by
Sir R. [Brooke] who was very good natured.
We returned to Hawarden to dinner—in order to consult respecting Lady
Glynne—No less than heretofore seems to depend on C.

7 W.

Wrote to Sir J. Graham—Lady Bromley—T.S. Godfrey—Mr Grant—
Elisabeth G.—H.J.G.—read Ed. Rev. on Jamaica Bill—Montalembert's
Introdn—& Landor.
Drove with C.G.—music. Conferences on Lady G. who it is now thought
better should go to Lincoln instead of Leamington.

8 Th.

Wrote to Kitchings[11]—Wells & Lambe[12]—M'Crackens—K. Finlay—Doyle.
read Landor, who seems coarse & evil-minded—Conybeare's two first
Bampton Lectures[13]—& finished Montalembert's Introduction.

[1] Part in A. H. D. *Acland, T. D. *Acland, 109–10.
[2] Sophie Cottin's romantic novel about crusades, 6v. (1805).
[3] G. Russell, A Tour Through Sicily in the Year 1815 (1819).
[4] Add MS 44728, ff. 261–2.   [5] Untraced.
[6] F. *Atterbury, 'The Power of Charity to Cover Sin' (1708).   [7] Untraced.
[8] Robert, brother of John*, Tweddell; b. 1772; wrangler 1796; quarrelled with *Elgin
about his brother's papers 1815–6; priest at Halton, the next village to Norton.
[9] Roger Carus-Wilson, 1792–1839, of Trinity, Cambridge; vicar of Preston 1817.
[10] W. S. *Landor, Imaginary Conversations, 5 v. (1824–29).
[11] Kitching and Abutt, Conduit Street goldsmiths.
[12] Dressing-case makers of Cockspur Street.
[13] J. J. *Conybeare, Attempt to Trace the History and Ascertain the Limits of the
Secondary and Spiritual Interpretation of the Scriptures (1824).

The Lytteltons came. A beautiful meeting between the sisters.—In the evening, a servants' ball—
I did not know before the extent of sensitiveness in C's frame. From the joyful excitement of meeting her sister, her hands became cold as ice.

We went to see old Molly, severely bruised from an accident when decorating her house on the 25th. She said to me from her bed "I hope Sir you never saw any ladies & gentlemen respected as ours was"—& did not at all seem to regret.

9 Fr.

Wrote to W. Goalen—Kinnaird—G. Grant—read Landor—Conybeare—Ed. Rev. on Jamaica. walk with C.—Went to the Ferry[1] & saw the wharf steamer &c.—Music.

10 Sat.

Wrote to Bishop—Mr G.—J.N.G.—More consultns about Lady G.—who goes to Lincoln. read Landor—Conybeare—Ed. Rev. on Shelley—ride—billiards—music.

11. S.

Ch mg & aft. read H. More's Tracts—Conybeare—wrote to Mr Grant & R. Ward.

12 M.

Wrote to J.E. Tyler—J. Murray—Kinnaird—Kitching & Abutt—Wells & Lambe—Messrs Cocks[2] (signed by Cath.)—Mr Ramsay—Steele—Dr Giffard—Sir R. Inglis—read Hazlitt.
Ly Blessington's Confessions (began)[3]—went off suddenly to Lpool to secure the ferry—& arrived in 2½ hours.—Arrangements for our journey tomorrow.

13 T.

Wrote to Mr Finlay—T.G.—Mr G.—Rev. Mr [Carus] Wilson. finished Lady Blessington—read Hazlitt—shopping &c.—Off at one (the Lytteltons in company) by the Commodore for Greenock. The sea like a pond.

14 W.

Wrote to R. Ward—H. Glynne. read Hazlitt. Greenock at 8 P.M.—With great labour & some risk, got our carriages into the Dumbarton boat at 11.[4]—Posted, through rain, 22 miles to Tarbet.[5]—Fair inn, excessively crowded.

[1] Queensferry, 2 miles north of Hawarden.
[2] Cocks & Biddulph's, bankers at Charing Cross.
[3] Marguerite, Lady *Blessington, The Confessions of an Elderly Lady (1838).
[4] Dumbarton lies 7 miles east of Greenock on the opposite bank of the Clyde.
[5] Northward from Dumbarton up the western bank of Loch Lomond.

15 Th.

Wrote to Mr G.—Mrs Clark (Braemar).[1] In spite of most adverse weather
our gallant ladies & G. would set off at 1 for Inversnaid, Loch Katrine &
the Trossachs[2]—arrived at 7—two hours waiting at the Loch head.—Inn
tolerable, excessively crowded. Ran ahead to secure rooms.—We find the
boat & ferry men great rogues; as have our predecessors—The Trossachs
were pretty fresh in my recollection. Lower Lochlomond is extremely soft
& rich. But miserably clad in this atmosphere!

16 Fr.

9–12¼ Trosachs Inn to Inversnaid. The land distances hereabouts are under-
stated—By steam up the Loch—& posted 24 miles to Inverary through
the wild & grand pass of Glencroe[3]—& along the banks of the lochs. Argyle
Arms at Inverary—excellent.
read Hazlitt.
The huts at Inversnaid & Loch K. head yield very good bread, oatcake,
butter, cheese, ale! Difficulty of getting horses so great, that they ought to
be engaged before hand all along the line.

17 Sat.

The situation of Inverary is very grand and feudal. Sea as well as earth
appear to do homage to the Castle.[4] The edifice might be finer.
10 10¼—47 miles to Killin.[5] The road as far as Tynedrum[6] very hilly.
Kept for hours waiting horses. Ascent from Inverary, view of Loch Awe,
& situations of Dalmally[7] & Killin very fine. The rest wild.
Found everything ready at K. whither we sent our servants direct. Inn
(M'Tavish) very fair.

18 Sunday.

Kirk in mg—our aftn service in aftn.—A S. of S. Wilberforce in evg.
read Nicole.
Had an opportunity of seeing the adminn of the Communion in the Kirk.
The communicants are arranged along the lines of seats fronting the pulpit.
After an address & recital of passages from S. Matthew & S. Paul, which
the Minister termed 'our warrant for proceeding' the elders collected the

[1] Landlady of the Invercauld Arms.
[2] Inversnaid is 3 miles north of Tarbet, across Loch Lomond; Loch Katrine lies from
5 to 10 miles east of it, with the picturesque glen of the Trossachs at and beyond its
eastern end.
[3] Inveraray, on Loch Fyne, 40 miles WNW. of Glasgow; and 25 miles by road from
Ardlui at the head of Loch Lomond through Glen Croe, which runs NW. towards the
head of Loch Fyne.
[4] Seat of the dukes of Argyll.
[5] 34 miles ENE. of Inverary, at the head of Loch Tay.
[6] 20 miles NE. of Inverary, where Glen Lochy meets Strath Fillan.
[7] Dalmally, 12 miles NNE. of Inverary, lies 2 miles east of the NE. end of Loch Awe.

tickets from the communicants, and then drew first the platters & afterwards the cups along before them, each helping himself. The elders then replaced the vessels. The minister communicated with a second set of the people, to whome another minister came forward from the ranks to officiate. Walk with C. The spot is lovely.

19 M.

Rain does not yet leave us.
$10\frac{1}{2}$–7, 40 miles to Dunkeld[1]—seeing Taymouth[2]—magnificent in natural features, which are heightened by art & culture—& the house would be grand but for the surpassing grandeur around it—and the falls of Moness,[3] which are of perfect beauty on a small scale—the farthest, is 2 miles from the road—Lunch at Aberfeldy, good. Dunkeld is very lovely, but should be seen before Taymouth. Went over the Cathedral: half ruin, half a very neat kirk. There is something sad in the juxtaposition.
read Hazlitt.

20 T.

Grant's, Dunkeld. Good. None of our sleeping houses have been cheap. $7\frac{3}{4}$–$5\frac{1}{2}$: 57 miles to Fasque. By Blairgowrie,[4] where we breakfasted well. road then to Meigle[5] extremely bad. We had a fine afternoon & auspicious approach to Fasque. Much depends on first impressions. To beloved C. entrance into her adoptive family is much more formidable than it would be to those who had been less loved, or less influential, or less needed and leant upon in the home where she was so long as a queen.[6] We found all well & the kindest of welcomes. Music.

21 W.

Took my own to the garden stables &c. & went on the hill 12–4. Afr with her. Shot $4\frac{1}{2}$ br[ace] & 2 hares: very ill.
Music & whist with Mr G.—

22 Th.

Wrote to Mr Ramsay—Stephen—Corrie & Co—Newman.
arranging effects in dressingroom & in our (once my) turret.
music. whist. rode with Catherine in the hill woods.

23 Fr.

wrote to Caparn—Ld Chancellor—On the hill. Lytteltons came: ciceronising George.—Chess in evg.

[1] 29 miles east of Killin and 13 WNW. of Perth.
[2] Taymouth Castle, at the eastern end of Loch Tay; seat of the earls of Breadalbane.
[3] 5 miles east of the castle, south of Aberfeldy.   [4] 10 miles east of Dunkeld.
[5] 7 miles farther east, on the road to Forfar.
[6] Version of part of this sentence in Morley, i. 224.

24 Sat.

Wrote a long letter to Mr J.G. Jones on the Lpool Collegiate Institution—
& showed it to Mr G.—who approved: setting forth the necessity of founding
on Church principles. Wrote also to J.N.G.—and the Primate.
rain—billiards. walk. Chess with C.

25. S.

To Laurencekirk with C. M. & G.—Communion Sunday. The Scotch Office
is very impressive.
C. suffering from toothache Cured by laudanum.
Read Nicole—Gresley (Sermon.)[1] My Father now reads the aftn prayers.

26. M.

Wrote to Mrs Fellowes—Aunt J.—Luxmoore.
music—chess—rode with C. M. & G. up the Cairn: they were all delighted.
Began J. Edwards's Life:[2] a most feeble recommencement!

27. T.

On the hill, with Robert 12–6. Only 8 head between us.
Chess. C. & I in deadly conflict. It is too great an expenditure perhaps of
thought & interest.[3]
Read Edwards's Life.

28. W.

Wrote to Jones (Tailor)—Mrs Clark (for our Deeside party)—Mr Glover.[4]
Chess—billiards—took Glynne the Delaly[5] ride—read Edwards's Life.

29 Th.

Read Hook's powerful Sermon at Liverpool[6]—& finished Edwards's Life.
Chess—billiards—music-whist.

30. Fr.

Wrote to Mrs Clark—Mr Bennett—Chess—whist—music.
read Edwards's "Freedom of the will".
Yesterday Mr G. communicated that he means actually to transfer to us
his Demerara properties[7]—Robn to have the management—this increased

---

[1] Probably from W. *Gresley, *Sermons on Some of the Social and Political Duties of a Christian* (1839).
[2] The first vol. of S. Edwards Dwight's ed. of the *Works* of Jonathan Edwards, American congregationalist, 10v. (1830).
[3] Lenin thought the same.   [4] Unidentified.
[5] Delalie, a house a mile west of Fasque.
[6] W. F. *Hook, 'The Gospel and the Gospel Only, the Basis of Education: a Sermon Preached in St. Peter's ... Liverpool' (1839).
[7] Rest of this sentence in Morley, i. 224.

wealth so much beyond my needs with its attendant responsibility is very burdensome, however on his part the act be beautiful.

31. Sat.

Wrote to Mr Dundas.
read Ly Blessington's 'Maxims' &c—impar materiae[1]—the scale of untruths with the truisms greatly predominates. Chess—five tough games. resumed Scr[ipture] with C.—it has been intermitted, tho' our prayers have kept pretty regular.

Sunday September One.

To Laurencekirk for Church with C.G. M. & S. read Nicole. Prayers in aft.

2. M.

Off at 7¼ over the Cairn. Reached Ballater[2] 42 m. at 4½: stopped for want of horses. Geo. & I walked across from the Banchory road to Charleston[3]—up the Cairn—&c—in all I made 17 miles: 8 yesterday. We had rain—of course—& got soaked—but the beauty of the scenery more than paid us— Wrote to Farquhar.

3. T.

7¼–10, 18 m. to Braemar: the morning bright: the heather rich beyond anything, & in this moment at its very best—we were delighted & all my companions who are new to this country were in ecstasy—After breakfast at Mrs Clerk's we set off up Lochnagar—29 miles—a drosky for five to Garrawalt Bridge—Walked 25. The horse distance to the top is 14 miles. We were 7 hours absent. The Invercauld Forest is now much finer than the Mar.
The spectacle from the rocks is indeed magnificent: they beetle over the black sleeping lake in everlasting horror: no, not everlasting. They do not[4] reach round it: but form more than half a cradle: they are of very great height & extreme wildness. In 1836, I looked from their brow into mist which was almost more peaceful than the reality of the yawning chasm.[5]
C. & M. rode the bogs well but it is not easy nor agreeable. S. & G. walked. Chess—& Coleridge's Table Talk.
Yesterday G. & I. inquired the distance from Charleston as we came along & received in succession the following answers at intervals of ¼ mile more or less: 8 miles, 9, 4½. 7, 6, and so on—no two corresponding.
The Garrawalt deserves its name: its channel is generally naked rock. The views from it are glorious.

---

[1] 'unequal in subject'. Marguerite, Lady *Blessington, *Desultory Thoughts and Reflections* (1839).
[2] Cp. 6 Sept. 36.
[3] Charlestown, 10 miles east of Ballater.
[4] 'quite' here deleted.   [5] Cp. 8 Sept. 36.

4. W.

10–6. 31 miles to the top of Ben Aburd[1] & on it & back. Up thro' Invercauld forest a good path. Down by Glen Quoich, a mile longer: & forded
the Dee. The top is round but there are grand rocks & a noble view towards
the Cairngorms. We left the ladies at the top of the shank: 3 miles, probably,
from the summit. They wished to try the ascent, & were hardly dissuaded.
I walked the distance. Chess.[2] Wrote to Mr G. (bis)—Ballater & Banchory.

5 Th.

41 miles to Loch Avon[3] by the Linn of Dee. Walked. Lewis[4] rode. All went
to the Linn when rain turned them back: except Stephen who came on to
the foresters where he followed the Luibeg for Aviemore and we struck up
Glen Lui over very rough ground by Loch Etichan[5] over the shoulder of
Ben Main & to the Stone at the head of Loch Avon where I wrung my coat
thoroughly soaked—the thermomr was however 49°: & on Lochnagar top.
47°. Saw Highland women from Strathspey coming down for harvest with
heavy loads, some with babies, over these wild rough paths, through mist &
storm—O with what labour does a large portion of mankind subsist while
we 'fare sumptuously *every day*'. But they have their rest. My walk
occupied 11 hours of rather hard labour.
Yesterday we viewed the R.C. Chapel which is in excellent taste & might
be taken as a model, apparently.
Mrs Clerk's here is very comfortable, & there is here a remnant, really, of
the old idea of hospitality, now scarcely traceable & in such places least of
all—Loch Avon is on a larger scale than Lochnagar but I think the scene
is less consummate.

6 Fr.

7½–6¾. 60 miles to Fasque. Breakfast (excellent) at Monaltrie Arms, Ballater. Bait & chess at Charleston. Finished our games in the carriage. A
second pair from the Bridge of Dye.
The Dee from Ballater to the Linn shows I imagine a finer line than any
other river in Scotland & from Banchory upwards to Castleton there is a
progression in the scenery & gradual unfolding of character with enlargement of scale that are admirable. Then the red deer are no despicable sight,
nor even the ptarmigan: we saw both on Ben Aburd, in considerable numbers. The absence of the herd of tourists is that which above all renders
this a delightful trip—Chess & whist in evg.

7. Sat.

Wrote to Mr Bennett—Storr—Hogg—Wm Gladstone—& rode through the

---

[1] The Grampian summit NW. of Braemar. *Lyttleton made the journey in slippers
(Battiscombe, 39).
[2] 'Coleridge' here deleted.
[3] The loch lies 10 miles NW. of Braemar, deep in the Cairngorms.
[4] One of the maids?
[5] A mile south of the SW. end of Loch Avon.

hill wood with George—read Nicholas Nickleby No 1.[1]
Chess with G. & did duty at the whist table

8. S.

Fettn Church. Aftn prayers & sermon.
read Nicole—Finished Gresley 'on Zeal & Moderation'.[2]

9. M.

Wrote to Bishop—Ivall—Scotts—Kinnaird. The Litteltons went at 8—
carrying with them many regrets. Ruminated on plans of reading for C. &
myself which now at least ought to take form. It is high time to recommence application. Resumed Lingard—read Nickleby—Chess with C.—
whist, Drove C. & M.E.—

10. T.

Wrote on the Will—apropos to Edwards.[3]
Began S. Aug. de Symbolo.[4]—N.N. No. 3—Mathilde (resumed) with C.—
Lingard.
drove C. to Balmakewan—Chess with her.

11. W.

Wrote Notes on Edwards, & analysis.
read Mathilde—N.N. (4, 5)—Edwards.
J.N.G. came—On the hill. Chess with C.

12. Th.

Wrote to Bonham—Mr Douglas—on Edwards—read S. Aug. de Symb.
11.—Scr. with Cath—Mathilde—N.N. No 6—Edwards—Lingard.
Chess—picquet—Walked with C.

13. Fr.

Wrote on Edwards.
read Scr (I in Gr. T., she the Bible aloud, & our prayers joined)—S. Aug.—
Edwards—N.N. No 8—Mathilde—Chess—whist—in the evg. with John—

14. Sat.

Wrote on Edwards.
Scr & Gr T.—S. Aug—Edwards—N.N. No 9—Mathilde—Chess—whist—
billiards: walk, in heavy continued rain.

[1] Charles *Dickens's *Nicholas Nickleby* appeared in monthly parts in the winter of
1838–9. For a final comment, see 17 Oct. 39.
[2] W. *Gresley, *The Necessity of Zeal and Moderation in the Present Circumstances of
the Church Enforced and Illustrated in Five Sermons* (1839).
[3] Add MS 44728, ff. 279–303.
[4] *Defide et symbolo*, Migne, *PL*, xl. 180 (393). Notes in Add MS 44728, ff. 263–4.

15. *Sunday.*
Fettn mg, & home service aftn.
Read S. Aug—Nicole (finished Vol 1 of Morale, admirable but in some degre onesided.)—& Benson on Episcopacy[1] &c.
Music in Evg.

16. *M.*
Wrote to Mr Brogden.[2] Wrote on Edwards.
read Scr—S. Aug—Edwards—Mathilde—N.N. No 10—walk with Cath.— Chess—whist.

17. *T.*
Wrote on Edwards.
read Scr.—S. Aug. (I am now in the Tractatus Diversi)[3] Edwards—N.N. Nos 11, 12—Mathilde.
chess—singing. on the hill with M.G. & R. Bateson.[4]

18. *W.*
Wrote on Edwards.
read the Hastings correspondence[5]—Riland on Church Reform[6]—S. Augustine—Edwards—Mathilde (finished V.2.) Chess—singing. Drove C. & E.
C. had a good deal of sickness yesterday & today—

19. *Th.*
Wrote to G. Grant—R. Hodgson—& on Edwards—read Edwards—Riland —Mathilde—N.N. Nos 13 and 14.
walk with C. whose sickness continued—& to Mary Hay: prayer.
Chess—whist.

20. *Fr.*
Read Riland (finished) Edwards—Mathilde.
To Montrose in the carriage, to sign in presence of one of the Baillies, a power of Attorney to Stuart to manage for us in Demerara—with my brothers.
Walked home (2¾ hours)
Whist & singing.
   Quest oggi mi disse la mia carissima che cosa sentisse colla cagione del medesimo.[7]

---

[1] C. *Benson, *Discourses upon Tradition and Episcopacy* (1839).
[2] James Brogden, 1806–64; priest and author; rector of Great Henney, Essex, 1841–5; vicar of Deddington, Oxon., 1848–64.
[3] Migne, *PL* xl. 107 (397). Notes in Add MS 44728, ff. 265–6.
[4] Robert Bateson, 1816–43, s. of Sir R., cons. M.P. co. Derry 1837.
[5] 'The Victim of Scandal. Memoir of Lady Flora *Hastings (1839). Cp. Longford, 93– 127.
[6] J. Riland, 'Ecclesiae Decus et Tutamen' (1830).
[7] 'Today my darling told me what she felt, with the cause of the same' sickness: earliest signs of pregnancy.

21 Sat.

Wrote on Edwards, to J. Bruce—Mr Riland.[1]
read Nickleby No 15—S. Aug.—Edwards. Mathilde—whist—music.
Sculled the ladies on the water—

22. Sunday.

Lkirk with Cath—aftn prayers. S. Aug—Nicole (Port-royal Pieces)—
Benson (finished): very far from satisfactory, from such a man.
walked with C. music.

23. M.

Wrote on Edwards—to Mr Kennedy.
read Scr.—S. Aug (finished Tractatus Diversi)—Mathilde—Edwards—
N.N. Nos 16, 17.
Chess—whist. Walked with C. to the Garrol.

24. T.

Wrote on Edwards—& to Sir J. Forbes—& Lady Brabazon.
Read Scr—Edwards—S. Aug—(began Expositio in Joannis Ev, read
Psaltm)[2] N.N. No 18.—whist. To the bog.—C. suffers annoyance from
sickness & bears it sweetly.

25. W.

Wrote on Edwards.
S. Aug—Edwards—Scr.—Spenser (+) 1. 2.—out shooting. chess. whist.

26. Th.

Wrote on Edwards—to H. Taylor.
Scr.—S. Aug.—Edwards—Spenser—Mathilde
Drove & walked with C.—Chess—music.

27. Fr.

Wrote on Edwards.
read Scr. S. Aug.—Edwards—Mathilde.
driving for roe—chess—backgammon.

28. Sat.

Wrote on Edwards.
read Scr. S. Aug—Edwards—Mathilde.
Spenser—chess—music—walk with C.

[1] John Riland, Birmingham priest.
[2] Migne, *PL*, xxxv. 1379 (416) and xxxvi. 69 (391–415). Notes in Add MS 44728, ff. 267–78.

29. S.

To Lkirk with C. & Bateson—Prayers in aftn with a Sumner.
read S. Aug—Nicole—Woodgate's Introduction[1]—walk with C.

30. M.

Wrote on Edwards.
read Scr—S. Aug—Mathilde—Edwards (finished) Spenser Chess—walk
with C. Larkins.

£10[2] to National School Newark pd.
£10 to Prisoners Employment Society
£5   to Flintshire Dispensary

Rio. A l'île d'Aiz, par Vannes, Morbihan
Posting House—Sandiway Head Northwich.
Senhouse, Keswick Mrs A.W Aug 10–31.

---

[1] Introduction to H. P. Woodgate, *The Authoritative Teaching of the Church Shewn To Be in Conformity With Scripture, Analogy, and the Moral Constitution of Man* (1839).
[2] Next six lines on back page of volume.

[VOLUME XI]¹

Order Lance's Translation of Benezra's "Advent".²

(No. 11)

O. 1.39–S. 30.41.

Fasque October 1. 1839.

Tuesday.

wrote on Ch. & St.
read Wardlaw's Lectures (recommenced)³—Scr.—S. Aug.—Mathilde.
shooting.—chess.—some time with C.
The Ramsays & Jas Bruce came.

2. W.

read S. Aug.—Wardlaw—Mathilde—Scr.
dearest much relieved today.
rode with Bruce to the Burn. Chess.

3. Th.

read Scr—S. Aug—Wardlaw—Mathilde—J. Hope on Patronage.⁴
rode with Bruce to Drumtochtie—Chess: singing. Dinner party.—Rn &
M.E. went.

4 Fr.

Wrote to Farquhar.
read Scr.—S. Aug—Mathilde—Hope on Patronage—Wardlaw (finished)
(with Analysis)..
Bruce & the Ramsays went. Chess. Whist. Drove Cath. to Drumtochtie—
le duoli ancora⁵—

5. Sat.

read Scr.—S. Aug.—Mathilde—Hope on Patronage—Long conv. with John
on H[elen] & her matters.

¹ Lambeth MS 1425, 77 ff.
² This note on fly-leaf. E. *Irving tr. J. J. Ben-Ezra [i.e. M. Lacunza y Diaz] *The
Coming of Messiah in glory and majesty* (1812; tr. 2v. 1827).
³ Notes in Add MS 44728, ff. 304–6.
⁴ John *Hope, 'A Letter to the Lord Chancellor, on the Claims of the Church of
Scotland in Regard to its Jurisdiction and on the Proposed Changes in its Polity' (1839).
⁵ 'suffering again'.

Went to the bog with John—Chess with C.
Finished Mathilde today. The conversation of Malek Adhel is unsatisfactory: & below the general tone of the book in respect of religion: the concluding passage is beautiful.

6 Sunday.

Laurencekirk with C. E. & J. .—Aftn prayers & Sumner.
read Woodgate[1]—Hallam's First Theological Chapter[2]—S. Augustine—
Appeal to Wisdom & Piety of our Ancestors on Church Reform[3]—I suppose Riland's—I see little piety in such wisdom as this book has.

7. M.

Wrote to Mr Tyler—& on Ch. & St.—copied a letter for Mr G. read Scr.—
S. Aug.—Hallam—Hope on Patronage—whist—chess—drove Cath. to see the Goalens.

8. T.

Wrote to Crabb.
read Keble's too indulgent, but able, learned, elevated & most interesting article on my book: & wrote most of the morning on my subject. Inserted a few explanatory passages for the next Edition, a propos to his remarks.[4]
read Hope on Patronage—Scr.
chess, billiards (rain), music.

9 W.

Wrote to Mahon.
read Hope—Hallam—S. Augustine.
shooting with J.—Chess, music.

10 Th.

Wrote to Uncle D.—Mr Plater.[5]
read Hope—(finished—very lengthy, much important matter, ignorance of the English Church—)—Hallam—finished his theological chapters, in which I am sorry to find amidst such merits what is even far more grievous than his anti-Church sarcasms, such notions on original sin as in IV.
p.161[6]—read Ld J. Russell's & Ld Lansdowne's corrected speeches on Education.[7]
Drove Cath.—chess—singing.

[1] H. A. Woodgate, *The Authoritative Teaching of the Church Shewn to Be in Conformity With Scripture, Analogy, and the Moral Constitution of Man* (1839).
[2] Henry *Hallam, *Introduction to the Literature of Europe* (1837) i. 482, on religious thought from 1520 to 1550.   [3] Anonymous pamphlet by an Oxford graduate (1835).
[4] *British Critic*, xxvi. 355 (October 1839); cp. Georgina Battiscombe, *John *Keble* (1963), 212–13.
[5] Charles Eaton Plater, 1798–1854, vicar of River, Kent, 1836–47, originator of Marlborough College 1843.   [6] This sentence in Morley, i. 220.
[7] *Russell's speech on the previous 20 June, *H* xlviii. 655, and *Lansdowne's on 5 July, ibid. 1255, were both reprinted as pamphlets.

11 Fr.

Wrote to Lady Morton—Aunt J.
read Scr.—S. Aug.—began Rothe's 'Anfänge der Christlichen Kirche'.[1]
perused & corrected MS on the Church—& added to it.
rode—chess—music.

12 Sat.

read S. Aug.—Rothe—'Recent Measures for Education'[2]—Scr—further
corrected, enlarged, & analysed, MS on the Church.[3]
    Shooting with T. & J.—Chess—whist (Mr G. had returned).

13. Sunday.

Fettn—prayers & a Sumner [sermon read] in aft.—walk with C—read
Dodgson's Sermon[4]—Pott's Charge[5]—S. Aug.—Port-royal.
    did a little on my MS.

14. M.

S. Aug.—Rothe.—perused, altered, & added to Ms. 'The Church of
England'.[6]—also wrote on Ch. & St.—read 'Recent Measures'—Scr.
Chess, whist.

15 T.

Wrote to Mr P. Gaskell[7]—S. Glynne.
    read Scr—S. Aug—Rothe—'Recent Measures' (finished) a very in-
sidious production.
    beating for roe—chess—whist.

16 W.

Wrote on Ch. & St.—
    read S. Aug.—Rothe—Nickleby—
    shooting. whist. the Goalens dined.

17 Th.

Nickleby (finished). It is too long, & length will I fear sink it. The tone is
very human: he is most happy in touches of natural pathos. No Church in
the book: and the motives are not those of religion.[8] read Rothe.

[1] An essay on the early church's origins and constitution by R. Rothe (1837). Notes
in Add MS 44728, ff. 307–16.
[2] J. P. *Kay-Shuttleworth, 'Recent Measures for the Promotion of Education in
England' (1839).
[3] For fourth edition (1841). Add MS 44682 contains most of these revisions.
[4] C. Dodgson, 'Preach the Gospel' (1839).
[5] 'The rule of faith considered', a charge delivered by archdeacon J. H. *Pott (1839).
[6] Add MS 44681, ff. 416–29; became ch. vi of his Church Principles (1840).
[7] 'sonnet' here deleted.
[8] Morley, i. 320.

Working on my MS. 'Rationalism'[1]—

Beating for roe. Whist in evg. The service will now become more constant. My Father is most kind about it: but he *ought* not to want companions.

18 Fr.

Wrote to H. Glynne—Storr—Farquhar—Acland. finished my operation on MS. 'Rationalism'—drove Cath to Slateford.[2] Whist. Mr Taylor here.

read Scr.—Rothe—

19. Sat.

Wrote on Ch. & St. To Mahon.

read S. Aug.—Rothe—Scr.—Hallam's Literature (Vol II)—

took Cath. up the Garrol—she walked down. Chess.

20 S.

To Laurencekirk with C.—Prayers in aftn. read 'Recueil'[3]—wrote on Ch. & St.—

Long conv. with Mr Taylor on Private Judgment.

21.

Wrote to T.M. Gladstone—Mary Lyttelton—T.S. Godfrey. T.M.G's brother is most desirous to be a clergyman God prosper him.[4]

read S. Aug.—Rothe—Scr.—

reviewed, analysed, & added to 'Introduction' MS.

rode to Fordoun. Whist.

22.

Wrote to Mr S. Taylor (Nk)[5]—

read Scr.—S. Aug.—Rothe.—

Wrote on Ch. & St.—I am now endeavouring to reduce to some order the materials of a supplementary Chapter.

billiards (rain)—whist.

23. W.

read Scr—S. Aug—Rothe—Hallam (Vol II)

Wrote on Church—

Billiards (rain)—whist & picquet with Mr G.

---

[1] Add MS 44681, ff. 232–71; became ch. ii of *Church Principles*.

[2] The part of Edzell parish in Kincardineshire.

[3] *Receuil de plusieurs Pièces pour servir à l'histoire de Port Royal* (1740). Cp. Add MS 44682, f. 196.

[4] John Eddowes Gladstone, 1814–1901, priest 1846; vicar of St. Matthew, Wolverhampton (a crown living), 1870.

[5] John Taylor, Newark maltster?

41—ii.

24 Th.

wrote to Mrs Grant—J.R. Hope.
    read Scr—Rothe—Hallam.
    Mr G. seemed displeased at my letter to the Bp of Barbadoes: but I told
him it was seen & approved of by him.[1] I hope he will upon reflection
gladly aid the Bp.
    rain continued: almost another flood. Rode.
    Today we have an account of Lord Brougham's death. If it is true it is
very awful. And, it leaves a void in the world of mind, like the sinking of a
great ship in the deep.[2]
    Whist in evg.

25 Fr.

Wrote to Storr.
    Laboured hard & without much ostensible progress on Ch. & St. MSS.—
    I am glad to find an *if* in yesterday's journal, on the tale of Lord
Brougham's death—wh proves pure fiction—a relief.
    read Scr—S. Aug.—Hallam.
    shooting—Whist.

26. Sat.

Wrote a little on Ch. & St.—
    read Scr—S. Aug.—Rothe—Hallam.
    shooting (Luther)—whist.
    I hope dear C. who has now suffered long & much with admirable
patience & spirit from the usual sickness is at length beginning to be a
little relieved.

27. Sunday.

We went twelve to Lkirk, 8 at the Communion there.
    read Woodgate & S. Aug.—wrote.[3]

28. M.

Wrote to Smith—Wrote a little.[4]
    read Scr.—Rothe—Lingard.
    drove Cath—Whist.

[1] Letter 10 Aug. 38, asking him to inquire into educational and religious needs on
John *Gladstone's three estates in British Guiana, and offering the owner's financial help
*Coleridge's response Add MS 44356, f. 266 and 44357, f. 13, and cp. 1 Jan. 40.
    [2] See next entry, and *History of 'The Times'* (1935–52), i. 403–4.
    [3] Add MS 44728, ff. 321–2.   [4] Ibid. ff. 323–4.

29 T.

Wrote to J.N.G.
   read Scr—S. Aug.—Rothe—Lingard.
   Wrote on Ch. & St.
   Walk & free conf. with dearest C.—whist in evg.

30 W.

read Scr. S. Aug. Rothe—Lingard.
   shooting—whist.

31 Th.

read Scr.—S. Aug.—Rothe—Lingard.
   shooting (Balfour)—whist.

Novr One. Fr.

Wrote to R. Hodgson.
   read Scr.—S. Aug—Rothe—Lingard.
   walk with Cath—whist.

2. Sat.

Wrote to Lyttelton—J.E. Gladstone.
   read Scr—S. Aug.—Rothe.
   walk with Cath—whist.—

3. Sunday.

Fettn & aftn prayers.
   read S. Aug.—Rothe.

4. M.

Wrote to J.N.G. (with notes for R.B.)[1]—Mr Greene—Rev. W.M. Goalen—
Bishop—Crabb.—
   read Scr—S. Aug.—Rothe.
   walk with Cath—whist.—

5. T.

The *Toms* went. Wrote to Sir H. Dukinfield.
   read Scr—S. Aug.—Rothe.
   shooting: whist & picquet in evg—we are now so small a party—walk
with C.

[1] R. Bateson.

6. W.

wrote to Steward of Lincoln's Inn—Hatchard—Hope.[1] read Scr—S. Aug.—Rothe—
shooting, whist & picquet.

7. Th.

read Scr—S. Aug—Rothe. reperusing papers, & trying to *arrange* for the Apl Succession—but with little or no success.[2]
drove & walked with C—whist & picquet.

8 Fr.

Wrote on Sacts[3] & Succn.[4]
read Scr—S. Aug—Rothe.
I have now some reading of letters for my Father in the morning wh of course helps to reduce my time for other purposes—he is very good & kind about it.
shooting—whist & picquet.

9 Sat.

Wrote to Mrs Munro[5]—Mrs Wishlade—Col. Galloway[6]—T.S. Godfrey—Mr Gye.
read Scr—Rothe—S. Aug.
Wrote on Apl Succn.
Drove & walked with Cath—Whist, picquet.

10. Sunday.

With C. to Lkirk.—Prayers & a Sumner in aft. Heard of Sir Francis Doyle's death,[7] and wrote to F.H.D.
read S. Aug.—Scr. Comment[arie]s—Hooker.
walk with C.

11 M.

Wrote to T.G.—
read Scr—S. Aug.—Rothe—
Wrote on Apl Succession.
shooting—picquet all evg.

---

[1] *Hope-Scott, on *Keble's review of his book and on Rothe. Add MS 44214, f. 74.
[2] See 13 Nov. 39.
[3] Add MS 44681, ff. 232–343; became ch. iv of *Church Principles*.
[4] Ibid. ff. 344–412, became ch. v of the same.
[5] Probably Amelia, née Browne, m. 1817 Charles Munro of Culraine, 1794–1886, who succ. as 9th bart. 1848; d. 1849.
[6] (Sir) Archibald *Galloway, 1780?–1850; col., 58th Bengal native infantry 1836; maj.-gen. 1841; K.C.B. 1848.
[7] On 6 November 1839.

12. T.

Wrote to Hope on F.H.D.—and to Lincoln offering him my dear old mare.
read Scr—S. Aug.—Rothe—
drove C. to Arbuthnott—picquet all evg. Wrote on Apl Succn.—

13. W.

Wrote to Scotts—Blair—P. Gaskell—Lincoln's Inn. Finished on Apl Succn
—as I hope—but it is fearful to venture upon it.
read S. Aug.—Rothe—Scr.
walk & boat with C. picquet.

14. Th.

Wrote to M. Gaskell—Rose (Limerick)[1]—Walter [Hamilton].
read Scr—S. Aug.—Rothe.
Shooting: picquet & whist.—
Worked on my MSS.

15 Fr.

A long day on the additions to 'Church & State': heavy rain assisted me.
read Scr.—S. Aug.—
whist & picquet. Dear Rns birthday: God bless him.

16 Sat.

Wrote to Ld Meadowbank—Dr Locock—read S. Aug. —Scr—Rothe—
a painful occupation in hearing & reporting on H's maid—and much
conv. with my Father. Egli era distintissimamente d'avviso che consiglio
non vaglia più niente: bisognerebbe che egli reggesse le cose.[2]
Drove C.—Evg as usual.

17. Sunday.

Fettn mg. Prayers & Sumner's S. aftn.
read much of S. Augustin—Scr—Woodgate.
More of H.—Mr G postponed measures till tomorrow on account of the
Sunday.

18 M.

Wrote to Lady Morton.
read S. Aug.—Scr—Rothe[3]—
Mr G. straziato da una vera agonia scrisse una lettera e poi parlò per
un' ora con H.—tornando da lei disse che la[4] donzella P. fosse bugiarda,

[1] Richard Anderson Rose, of Ardhu, co. Limerick.
[2] 'He was distinctly of the opinion that counselling was no longer of any avail, it would be necessary for him to take things in hand.'
[3] On whom he concluded his notes, in Add MS 44728, ff. 307–16.
[4] One word deleted here.

che egli non la verrebbe altra volta per far prova dei suoi avvertimenti, che sarebbe impossibile avanzarsi mediante altro che consiglio. Io non[1] potendo dir sì, neppure ho sentito che mi fosse del dovere dire altra cosa.[2]

Evening as usual.

19. T.

Wrote to Crabb—Mrs Munro—

also to H.—una risposta alla di lei lettera: dicendo solamente che mi credessi non aver torto il Sabato passato—che volentieri parlerei delle cose che tocchino a lei, ma non sentendomi autorizzato, mi sforzarei star cheto: credendo fermamente che il di lei amore verso noi altri fosse verace e caldo; e che cosìfatte lettere non dovessero bruciarsi.[3]

finished Rothe's profound & in many points admirable book—read S. Aug.—Scr.—

out about the poacher who has killed himself.

Piquet in evg. Cath. had an attack of the heart.

20 W.

Finished St Augustine's Commentary on St John. Excepting perhaps some figurative & numerical interpretations, it is worthy throughout of the deep and luminous mind saturated with the spirit of Scripture and the Church, from which it emanated—so far as I dare to speak. read Woodgate's Bampton Lectures. Scr.—

shooting. Whist & picquet in Evg.—Dearest better much.

Alla mia lettera d'ieri non c'è risposta: benchè potesse quasi averne provocato una.[4]

21. Th.

Wrote to Brechin, Forfar, Cupar; Rn G.—Caparn—Dice la donzella che la padrona si comporti meglio.[5]

read Woodgate—Hazlitt—Scr—

The Lpool C.I. Prospectus[6] came: it seems now to be in a right form *as*

---

[1] Word much altered.

[2] 'Mr. Gladstone, racked by a real agony, wrote a letter and then talked for an hour to Helen.—Returning from her, he said that P. the maid was a liar, that he would not see her again to make proof of her warnings, that it would be impossible to make any progress except by advice. Not being able to say yes, neither did I feel it my duty to say anything else.'

[3] 'a reply to her letter: saying only that I believed I was not wrong last Saturday—that I would willingly talk about her affairs, but not feeling myself authorised, would endeavour to remain silent: firmly believing that her love for us was warm and real, and that letters like these should not be burnt.'

[4] 'There is no answer to my letter of yesterday, though one would think it would have provoked one.'

[5] 'The maid says her mistress is behaving better.'

[6] Prospectus (1839) of Liverpool Collegiate Institution, later Liverpool College: Add MS 44357, ff. 7, 45. John *Gladstone contributed £500; cp. *Newark Times*, 11 Dec. 39

respects its fundamental principle.—Wrote to Mr Whyte—Nk Times;[1] *cards.*

22 Fr.

Wrote to T.G.—Lyttelton—Mr Pendleton (Dublin)[2]—finished Woodgate: he has much valuable matter from a strong mind: especially in the latter Lectures.

finished Hazlitt. In many parts, he is exceedingly felicitous.

Drove C. and busied in preparing for departure—picquet: about which & the little else I can do for him indeed my Father has been most kind.

23. Sat.

7.20–8 P.M. to the Queensferry—there two hours improper delay: reached Dalmeny[3] at 11—tea at Kinross.

read Hallam on Shakespeare &c. to C. while kept.

24. S.

walked to Edinburgh—mg & aft. service there, a great delight. With the Ramsays between. Excellent sermons from Mr R. The new Church is pretty, might have been much prettier.—Back at 5. Dearest pretty well.—read a little of Dick.[4]

25 M.

Wrote to Cornhill[5] for quarters.

read C. Murray[6]—a walk about the place between showers: it is very sweet.—music. This is a very kind cordial family.

At 4¼, over to Dalmahoy.[7]

26. T.

Wrote to Mr G—Mr Macarthur—Mr Goalen—Dr Blair.[8]

shooting—Cath. walked a little with Lady Milton & liked her very much. In appearance she is just as two years ago. She dresses in excellent taste *plainly*, evincing thereby a higher tact. She seems to me in all respects now

---

[1] *Newark Times* unpublished, probably on controversy, ibid. 6, 13, 20 November 1839, on *Gladstone's refusal to respond, 1835, to low churchman Robert Simpson's appeal for funds to build Christ Church, Newark; closed by editor 20 November 1839.

[2] Edmund C. Pendleton, d. 1846; minister of North Strand church, Dublin; canon of Ferns 1840; m. Henrietta Benson, 1792–1875, philanthropist.

[3] The Roseberys' great house beside the Forth, 7 miles west of Edinburgh; no doubt to meet Archibald Primrose, 1809–51, styled Lord Dalmeny 1814, s. of 4th earl*; he m. 1843 *Mahons's da. Catherine Stanhope, and was f. of the 5th earl.*

[4] A. C. Dick, *Dissertation on Church Polity* (1835).

[5] 55 miles ESE. of Queensferry, in Northumberland. See 27 Nov. 39.

[6] C. A. *Murray, *Travels in North America during . . . 1834, 1835, and 1836, . . . and a Visit to Cuba and the Azore Islands*, 2 v. (1839).

[7] Lord Morton's; cp. Magnus, 47.   [8] Unidentified.

the same person that she seemed then. No one of the family ever alluded ever so indirectly to my having been here before. They were most kind to us.

Dearest C. not very well here.

There was some awkwardness in meeting Lady (F.) M. She felt it too and lingered on the handle of the door when she entered. But why should she? She has nothing to regret. I have to regret a precipitancy blamable in itself though I do not believe it at all affected the issue. In other respects, I received here a sharp instruction which I believe will chasten me for my life long with respect to all objects of my desire: combined, that is to say, with what preceded it in 1835. And I say deliberately, & I think not self-deceived, that I now see how much more wisely God judged and ordered for me: C. & I talked over these matters for two hours, and read Scr.— Wrote on Ch. MS.

27. W.

Wrote to Mr G.—Lady Wenlock.
read Cunningham's Letter to Hope[1]—& Candlish's.[2]

8–9 to Ed[inburgh]. Breakfast with the Ramsays: then to Ld Meadow-banks—Wrights'[3] (linen)—Mrs Ogilvy's—and $12\frac{1}{4}$–$6\frac{3}{4}$, 51 miles to Cornhill —a most comfortable Inn. The stages are 16, 15, 8, 12.—On Sat, we did 95.

28 Th.

$7\frac{3}{4}$ A.M.–$9\frac{1}{2}$ P.M. to Durham—75 miles (13, 13, 10, 9, 14, 15) of snow— varying from 3 & 4 to 15 & 18inches (without drift.) *Four* [horses] thrice. Cath. bore up gallantly.
Waterloo at Durham very comfortable.
Began Dunlop's answer to Hope.[4]

29. Fr.

Wrote to Mr G.—Lincoln.
$7\frac{3}{4}$–6. 72 miles to Escrick:[5] breakf. at Darlington,[6] Kings Head, excellent. Rain: luxury compared with the delays & doubts of yesterday. Most kindly received—C. is loved here nearly as a child.

30. Sat.

Wrote to J.N.G.—M. Lyttelton—Douglas (Hotel)[7] read Peter Plymley &

[1] W. *Cunningham, 'Letter to John *Hope . . . Occasioned by his Letter . . . on the Present Claims of the Church of Scotland' (1839).
[2] R. S. *Candlish, 'Remarks on the Dean of Faculty's . . . Letter to the Lord Chancellor' (1839).
[3] J. and P. Wright, linen-drapers, North Bridge.
[4] A. *Dunlop, 'An Answer to the Dean of Faculty's . . . "Letter to the Lord Chancellor"' (1839).
[5] 7 miles south of York: Wenlock's seat.
[6] 17 miles south of Durham.   [7] Unidentified.

2 Sermons of S.S.[1]—who divides Xtn doctrines into those influencing practice & those purely speculative!—Fermoy on Tone.[2]

shooting: lionised house & stables—music.

The family are alone: & this kind of visit interna molto in corto tempo.[3] They are very cordial & amiable. The moral atmosphere much clearer than in London.

Escrick. Sunday Decr One.

E. Ch. in mg: & Holy Communion. Dr Criggan[4] preached a good sermon: Low Church principles, under the inchoant modification of High: a good form. York Minster in evg: dusky grandeur, a great crowd, in a stall under the organ, could hear only the whirring vibration in the air & feel the throb of the instrument through the whole fabric of the screen.

wrote on Succn—read Br. Cr.—on Elizabethan Puritanism[5]—Abp Sharp[6]—& Chalmers's Lectures.[7]

2. M.

Early breakfast: at 8¼, 9 m. to Bishopthorpe[8]—breakf. there—and 10¾–6, 55 m. to Grove, Mr G. Vernon's[9]—The Abp looked well, but I thought a little bent. Francis Grey here: has a most pleasing manner. Rumours of early Session for Queen's marriage.

Long evg at Grove, music—G.V. gave me a very bad acct of the D. of N's affairs, which I suppose must have some basis.

3. T.

Fog a little relaxed—This place seemed pretty. 11¼–2½. 24 miles to Lincoln, flat (with one hill), by Durham Bridge over Trent. The Cathedral is a noble object nobly placed.

Lady Glynne essentially as of old. I had a sad & interesting convn with her—she, unsuspicious, mistakes my sentiments for me. She has an interest in Cath[erine] & shows it.

Well lodged at the Saracen's Head—afr 402 miles journey. Attended Minster service in aftn. Not ill done: i.e. nothing to intercept its proper delightfulness.

Read paper—Candlish—Dunlop.

[1] Sydney *Smith.

[2] P. R. Fermoy [Robert Johnson] *A Commentary on the Memoirs of T. Wolfe *Tone* (1828).

[3] 'has a deep effect on one in a short time.'

[4] Alexander Crigan, rector of Escrick 1827.

[5] *The British Critic and Quarterly Theological Review* xxvi. 152 (July 1839), on H. *Soames, *Elizabethan Religious History* (1839).

[6] Ibid. p. 101, on T. Stephen, *Life and Times of Archbishop *Sharp* (1839).

[7] Ibid. p. 228, on T. *Chalmers, *Lectures on the Establishment and Extension of National Churches* (1838).

[8] The archbishop of York's palace.

[9] Granville Harcourt-Vernon, 1792–1879, chancellor of diocese of York, m. 1814 Frances Julia Eyre, d. 1844, and lived at Grove Hall.

4. W.

Wrote to T.G.—J.G. Jones—& Journal.
    read paper—Dunlop—& chess.
    Cathl in aft with Catherine. Saw Dr Charlesworth:[1] he seems an acute man, but I think scarcely appreciates Lady G.—Arranging in my quarters.

5. Th.

Wrote to Mr G—R.G.—T.G.—Mr Rose (Limerick)—Sir Jas Graham—Lady Wenlock—Mr Simpson (Nk).
    read papers—Dunlop.
    Cathedral in aft with C.—chess—walk—began prayers in evg.

6 Fr.

Finished Dunlop—read 'Present Position of the Church'[2]—began Report of the Lethendy case.[3]
    reviewed the accounts of some years: henceforward I mean to keep, please God, a separate account of all sums given to charity and religion, in order to test & expose myself & to prevent at least falling below a certain mark.[4]
    Cathl in aftn. Yesterday we had nine (non-official) persons—today but 3 —in that glorious temple.—
    Chess—walk.

7. Sat.

Finished Lethendy case—read Brit. Mag.[5]—Voice of the Church—Speeches in Auchterarder Case, Genl Assy.[6]—
    Cathl aftn 'In Jewry'.[7] Visited the Library. Chess.

8. Sunday.

Wrote on Succession—
    Cathl at 10. St Peter's at 3. A good organ played in the vilest taste: scarcely any congregation: a sermon (Mr Naylor) of the meridian of 50 years back.—Cathl afr.

[1] E. P. Charlesworth, Lincoln physician.
[2] J. Hamilton, 'The Present Position of the Church of Scotland Explained and Vindicated' (1839).
[3] C. Gordon Robertson, *Report of the proceedings of the Court of Session in the Lethendy Case* (1839). Quoted 4th ed. *State in its Relations with the Church*, ch. vii. 19, ch. ix. 265; *Church Principles*, 482–3, for clash between Church of Scotland and Court of Session.
[4] Cp. Add MS 44804 D, ff. 30, 35; E ff. 6–70 (account books).
[5] *British Magazine and Monthly Register of Religious and Ecclesiastical Information.*
[6] 'Report of the Speeches of the Rev. Dr. *Gordon, Mr. Buchan of Kelloe, and Rev. R. S. *Candlish, in the Commission of the General Assembly, on the Auchterarder Case' (1839).
[7] Anthem on John, vii. 1.

read Non Intrusion Tracts[1]—Moncreiff's Acct of Constn of Scottish Church[2]—Willis's Address.[3]

9. M.

Wrote to Mr G.—Stretton—Caparn—Albany Christie—read Macfarlane's Remarks[4]—rather declamatory & weak.

wrote an Appx to Supplemental Chapter.[5]

Cathedral at 3¾—walk—chess.

10. T.

Wrote & arranged on Succn & on Ch. & St.—

read Mill's Principles of Toleration—irresponsibility for belief.[6]— Coleridge's Table Talk, Vol. I.

Wrote to G. Selwyn.

Cathedral at 3. "When the Son of Man"[7]—at our desire by the Dean's permission.[8]—Chess.

11. W.

Wrote to Sir J. Graham.

read Table Talk (little[9] of it, I fancy, talked at table—) Hallam's Literature—corrected, arranged, & analysed on Ch. & St.—

Cathl at 3. 'Give the Lord'[10] as yes[terda]y. D[eare]st C. in bed with cold, after fighting long.

12. Th.

Wrote to T.G.—S.R.G.—Ld Wenlock—Freshfield—Scotts—Uncle D—A. Kinnaird—Mr G.—

More of yesterday's work on Ch. & St.—

read Table Talk (finished Vol I)—(our N.T. chapters I now read daily at prayers, 2d mg lesson.

C. better.—Cathl—Chess—I make the minster 170 yards long.

---

[1] A. *Dunlop, R. S. *Candlish, C. J. Brown, T. *Guthrie, W. *Cunningham, T. *Chalmers, 'Tracts on the Intrusion of Ministers' (1839): eleven separate pamphlets, published simultaneously, against the intrusion of ministers of the Church of Scotland upon unwilling congregations.

[2] H. *Moncreiff Wellwood, 'A Brief Account of the Constitution of the Established Church of Scotland', edited and revised by J. W. *Moncreiff (1833).

[3] R. *Willis, 'An Address to those of the Roman Communion in England, Occasioned by the Late Act of Parliament for the Further Preventing the Growth of Popery' (1700).

[4] J. *Macfarlane, 'Remarks on the Tracts Lately Published, on the Intrusion of Ministers on Reclaiming Congregations' (1839).

[5] Chs. iii and iv of 4th edition State in its Relations with the Church; cp. Add MS 44681, f. 67. Appendices ibid. ff. 68–97 (rejected MSS of 4th edition).

[6] James *Mill (1837).

[7] Anthem: 'When the Son of Man shall come', Matt. xxv. 31.

[8] George Gordon, 1764–1845, priest of St. John's College, Cambridge, rector of Whittington 1812–45, vicar of Lincoln and Precentor 1827–45.

[9] 'or none' here deleted.

[10] Anthem: 'Give the Lord the honour due', Ps. xxix. 2.

13 Fr.

Wrote to D. of Newcastle.[1]
Began my (as I hope) closing Chapter on Church principles applied to the present time.
read Coleridge—Hallam.
Cathl at 3—Chess.

14 Sat.

Wrote to Caparn—Conv. with Charlesworth on Ly G. Worked upon the same papers: the matter expands under my hand.
read Coleridge. Cathl at 3.—One day our congregation (unofficial) reached 9: yesterday & today, I was alone: in wh there is something solemn.

15. Sunday.

Minster at 10. Vicar (Garvie)[2] preached very well: Aft. St Peter's (Gowts) Mr Nairne[3]—preached a beautiful Sermon—C. says Newmans.
read two of Machale's (It)[4]—& Portroyal Pieces.
wrote on Ch. Pr.—

16. M.

Wrote to A. Hart.[5]
Called on young Butler[6] & Mr Bainbridge,[7] Wesleyans—they were kind & Bu[tler] communicative.
read Coleridge.
Cathl at 3.—how I shall miss it! how dearest C. does.—
wrote on Ch. pr. in relations with Romanists.

17. T.

8–6¾ Drove over to Newark[8] to discharge my duties there. Found them in great spirits. Could only make out 28 visits. Conversed for some time with the Vicar for an Education Board: he desponds.—
All in great spirits about the coming election. The Church did not look at all less beautiful, after Lincoln.
Wrote on Ch. & St. before & after. Chess.
I found this day in returning homewards the blessing of a wife who makes home after labour a living & not merely a material thing.

---

[1] 'R. Caparn' here deleted.
[2] Richard Garvey, pluralist; vicar choral of Lincoln and headmaster of Lincoln grammar school.
[3] Charles Nairne, 1802–67, priest at St. Peter at Gowts 1837, and canon of Lincoln 1845.
[4] (Italian) Dr. *McHale's Sermons* (5 sermons), translated by Ari Torino de Luca (1832). Cp. Add MS 44681, f. 45, *Church Principles*, ch. vii.
[5] Unidentified.
[6] Perhaps Miles Butler, collector of excise, High Street, Lincoln.
[7] George Bainbridge, draper, ibid.
[8] 15 miles SW. of Lincoln.

18. W.

A longish day on Ch. pr. as affecting relations with Dissenters &c.

read Coleridge. Chess. Cathedral at 3. They sometimes make me quite happy by giving me a service book.

C. has not yet got rid of her cold, & suffers from her heart.

19 Th.

Wrote to Lincoln—T. Godfrey—Holt Yates[1]—Mr G.

Wrote on Ch. pr. as affecting internal relations.

Cathl at 3.—Farewell: what a loss. 5 today.

read Coleridge.

20 Fr.

At 9 to Newark. There 11½–2½. 11 calls, & took Cath. to both Churches, & heard the organs. Then to Clumber. Most kindly received. read Coleridge's Table Talk.

C. affected in leaving Lady G: who was moved painfully.

21. Sat.

Wrote to Mr G—R.G.—Uncle D—Acland—Lady Wenlock—Lady Glynne —Bishop—Williams (Eton).[2]

read Coleridge music—shooting with L[incol]n & Ld Edward [Clinton].

C. makes much progress in Ly Lns affections.

22. Sunday.

Service at 12¼.

read Campion's 'Rationes' & Oration on the Virgin.[3]—Rose Appx on German Protestantism.[4]

walk in aftn to Worksop.[5] Could not this noble building be saved for a College?[6]

23 M.

9–7.40. 68 miles, very hilly, to Knutsford:[7] where the Inn (George, very good) is starved by the railway.

[1] William Holt Yates, 1802–74, physician to Royal General Dispensary, London, till 1846; traveller in the East. Wrote 6 Dec. 39 from London asking for vacancy at King's College, London. Add MS 44357, f. 49.

[2] George *Williams, 1814–78, s. of Eton bookseller; priest and topographer; chaplain in Jerusalem 1841–3; dean of arts, King's College, Cambridge 1846–8.

[3] Edmund *Campion, Decem Rationes propositae in Causa Fidei et Opuscula eius selecta (1631). Cp. Church Principles, 355.

[4] H. J. *Rose, 'An Appendix to The State of the Protestant Religion in Germany; being a reply to German critiques of that Work' (1828).

[5] 20 miles NW. of Newark, in Nottinghamshire.

[6] Worksop Manor, vast Italian pile belonging to Duke of Norfolk, burned down 1761; bought by duke of *Newcastle as residence 1840.

[7] 52 miles west of Worksop, in Cheshire.

read Hallam.
wrote to Lady Bromley—D. of Newcastle.

24. T.

Wrote to T.G.—
read Bp of Chester's 'Churches Consecrated in 1839';[1] & the 'Unlawful-ness of War'.[2] The former most interesting.

9¼–1½, 32 m. to Hawarden. The Hawtreys here; & Bp of Chester on a call. Lytteltons came in evg. A happy meeting of the family. We settle in Lady G's sitting room.

Christmas Day.

Ch at 11. Communion. Church at 6½.—read Synodus Anglicana[3]—Mere-wether's Sermon[4]—Sterne.[5]—music.

26.

Wrote to J.N.G.—R.G.—Bookkeeper (JG & Co)—Mrs Martindale—Maurice—T.D. Acland.
worked on my MS.—Long conv. with Dr Hawtrey—& in a family circle, about arrangements.
Music. read Quarterly on P.O.

27.

Wrote to Mr Jones (Dispensary)
read Ed. Rev. on Education—& on Baxter, but found it (Stephen I fear) very heavy & stopped.
Shooting. chess & music in evg.

28.

Wrote to Mr G.—Ivall.
read Synodus Anglicana—Sterne, Sermons—Walker's Attempt.[6]—Gib-son's Codex[7]—Presbyterian rights asserted.[8]
Walk—chess—music.

29. Saturday.

Ch. mg & aft.—
read Moberly's two Sermm. on Ordination[9]—Hook's on 'Novelties of

---

[1] Pamphlet (1839). Cp. *Church Principles*, 384, n.   [2] Untraced.
[3] E. *Gibson (1702).
[4] F. Merewether, 'The Ministerial Succession' (1839).
[5] See 28 Dec. 39. Criticised in *Church Principles*, 457–8.
[6] John *Walker, *An Attempt towards recovering an account of the numbers and sufferings of the clergy of the Church of England, Heads of Colleges, Teachers, Scholars etc. who were sequester'd, Harrass'd, &c. in the late Times of the Grand Rebellion* (1714).
[7] E. *Gibson, *Codex Juris Ecclesiae Anglicanae* (1713).
[8] [W. F. *Hook] 'Presbyterian Rights Asserted' (1839).
[9] G. *Moberly, *Practical Sermons* (1838), 298 and 318.

Romanism'[1]—Machale's 3d—S.P.G. Report for 1839, most inttg—part of Art. in Quarty on my book.[2]

Today I complete my 30th year. The last twelvemonth has seen less done, and more received from God: a slight progress as respects relative duties: but nothing to affect myself except what tends thoroughly to abase, is suggested by the retrospect. His mercy however has vouchsafed to me that which I contemplated as a help towards heaven & I am indeed still persuaded that it is my own fault if it do not prove so. United to my Catherine, I now stand in the eye of God charged with a double responsibility; & ought the more to seek grace to meet it.

30 M.

Wrote to Mrs Martindale—Uncle D.—Ld Cholmondeley—James Hope (Worksop Manor)—

Finished Sewell's Article: valuable as respects the subject, & certainly more than kind to me.

Worked on my Appx MS.—

read Hoadley's 'Defence of Episc. Ordinns.'[3]—Bp Coleridge's Charge.[4]

31. Tuesday.

Wrote an anxious letter to Mr G. forwarding at the same time the Bps.[5]

Worked upon accounts, & arrangements, with C.G.

Shooting in aftn. party and music in evg.

read Hoadly—Bp Denison's Charge[6]—& Selwyn's Sermon.

And so flies another year into the void of the past, laden with many sins.

---

[1] W. F. *Hook, 'The Novelties of Romanism: or, Popery Refuted by Tradition' (1839).
[2] xlv. 97 (December 1839).
[3] B. *Hoadly, 'A Defence of Episcopal Ordination' (1707).
[4] W. H. *Coleridge, 'A Charge Delivered in the Cathedral Church of Barbados' (1838).
[5] Letter of *Coleridge, dated 27 Aug. 39, Add MS 44357, f. 13, in which he asked for contribution for new school, land for a chapel school, etc. on the British Guiana estates of John *Gladstone.
[6] E. *Denison, 'A Charge Delivered to the Clergy . . . of Salisbury (1839).

ADDENDA AND CORRIGENDA

(Noted while these volumes were in the press)

As the editor cannot hope to emulate the diarist's range of reading and acquaintance, he will be glad to hear, from people more expert than himself in divers fields of knowledge, of other corrigenda which can appear in a later volume.

VOLUME 1

Page	Note	Date	
2	1	29 July 25	should read: John Henry Barlow, 1795–1841, E.I.C.S.: m. 1823 the diarist's cousin Elizabeth Robertson, who d. 1831.
24	1	15 Dec. 25	add: 1823–94?; vicar of Henfield, Sussex, 1872–87.
60	6	11 July 26	add new n. after 'suspension.': Colin Robertson's partnership had failed.[1]
73	6	14 Sept. 26	add: 1797–1873.
89	1	12 Dec. 26	add: d. 1846.
95	4	23 Jan. 27	should read: see 30 Sept. 38.
105	7	11 Mar. 27	for 1845 read 1854.
108	6	27 Mar. 27	add: See J. L. Lowes, *The Road to Xanadu*, 2 ed. (1951), 16.
136	5	13 Sept. 27	add after 'Bennett': (see Add MS 44108).
137	1	17 Sept. 27	Charles Parker was Sandbach's merchanting partner.
205	8	17 Oct. 28	should end: fifth s. of 1st Lord Feversham.
205	13	18 Oct. 28	His diary while in the W.I. is now in the Liverpool Athenaeum.
208	7	27 Oct. 28	add: But see 25 July 31.
211	7	15 Nov. 28	for 1781 read 1771.
225	3	6 Feb. 29	should read: Cp. Morley, i. 53.
248	3	29 June 29	should read: Probably Isaac *Watts, eighteenth-century hymn-writer and educationist.
278	4	6 Jan. 30	should read: Jane Catherine, Colin Robertson's daughter.

[1] The editor is indebted for this information to Professor S. G. Checkland of Glasgow, who is engaged in a study of Sir John Gladstone and his family.

Page	Note	Date	
338	4	12 Jan. 31	n. should read: Frances Theodora, née Rose, 1798–1879, who m. 1817 George Sholto Douglas, 1789–1858, diplomat, 18th earl of Morton 1827.
340	5	20 Jan. 31	should be deleted.
349	4	17–19 Mar. 31	should read: 4th s. of 8th earl.
360	8	23 May 31	should be deleted.
384	4	26 Sept. 31	See Add MS 44218.
394	2	22 Nov. 31	should read: P. S. H. Payne.
398	7a	18 Dec. 31	add new n. after 'Millenarian': Unidentified.
399	3	22–24 Dec. 31	for 12 November read 7 June 1879.
459	1a	26 Mar. 32	add new n. after 'Pisani's': Alabaster shop; cp. 2 Oct. 38.
461	5	31 Mar. 32	for 1 read 2 Apr. 32.
469	6a	10 Apr. 32	insert new n. two lines from end after 'Pakenham': See 7 May 32.
482	3a	24 Apr. 32	add new n. at end: 'Eliza, née Norris, w. of T. Hunter Blair,'
564	6	31 July 32	for 11th read 10th earl.

VOLUME II

3	1a	11 Jan. 33	Add new n. after 'Wrote to Tupper': In D. Hudson, *Martin *Tupper* (1949), 17–18.
5	10	24 Jan. 33	add: Cp. Add MS 44236.
18	12	23 Mar. 33	add new n. to Mrs. Williams in last line: Frances, née Turner, m. Robert Williams 1794; d. 1841.
18	13	23 Mar. 33	add new n. to Mrs. Mundy in last line: Wife of C. G. Mundy; connexion of *Newcastle's.
19	1a	23 Mar. 33	add new n. after first name: Wife of Joseph Julian, and mother of D.W.P., Labalmondiere.
21	13	5 Apr. 33	add new n. after first name: Thomas Gayfere, priest at Bath.
27	9	6 May 33	Or perhaps William Hudleston, 1793–1855, Madras civil service, f. of his namesake.
51	1	24 July 33	add after '1824': cr. bart. 1840;
57	6	4 Sept. 33	add new n. after 'Finlays': Kirkman Finlay 1772–1842, Glasgow merchant, m. *ca.* 1795 Janet, née Struthers.

Page	Note	Date	
61	5	23 Sept. 33	Liverpool banker and tea merchant.
74	3	3 Dec. 33	should end: vicar of Kensington 1842, archdeacon of Middlesex 1843, canon of St. Paul's 1844; built St. Mary Abbott's church.
87	12	9 Feb. 34	add new n. after 'Williams': Isaac *Williams, 1802–65, theologian, at Trinity.
88	12	13 Feb. 34	should be deleted.
103	14	25 Apr. 34	for H. Sumner read bp. G. H. Sumner.
107	12	17 May 34	n. should read: Presumably a br. of J. T. H. Peter.
112	7	14 June 34	for Holbeck read Holbech.
112	7a	14 June 34	add new n. after 'Cotton': Cp. 11 May 39.
115	8	29 June 34	Cp. Lathbury, ii. 421–7.
119	1	19 July 34	n. should read: *Hayter's portrait of the diarist in the H. of C., based on the oil sketch prefaced to this vol., is in Reid, *G*, 168, and Magnus 50.
123	1	9 Aug. 34	should begin: He was staying with untraced friends, on the west
123	4	10 Aug. 34	should read: Cp. 21 July 35, n. 7.
135	4a	4 Nov. 34	add new n. after first name: T. Guthrie, surgeon, of Bervie.
142		19 Dec. 34	'Minister' should read 'Minster'.
147	7	9 Jan. 35	for '1860, judge' read: 1868, sergeant-at-law.
155	1	21 Feb. 35	add to first sentence: K.C.M.G. 1869.
156	2	27 Feb. 35	2nd and 3rd lines should be deleted.
157	2a	4 Mar. 35	add new n. at end: Richard Robert *Madden, 1798–1886, surgeon and author; just back from Jamaica.
170	3a	13 May 35	add new n. after 'Bradley's Sermon': Probably in C.* Bradley, *Practical Sermons* (1835).
174	6	4 June 35	Cp. 1 May 34.
175	3a	13 June 35	add new n. after 'Hicklin[g]': Either the journalist (cp. 1 Dec. 32) or J. Hickling, Wesleyan minister.
181	7	13 July 35	for 'n. 1' read 'n. 5'.
183	5	21 July 35	n. should read: Wife of R. P. Falkner of Newark.
183	10	22 July 35	B.A. from Magdalen Hall 1840.

Page	Note	Date	
187	5a	10 Aug. 35	add new n. after 'Mr Holford': George Peter Holford, d. 1839; penologist (cp. 29 July 35) and member of unreformed H. of C.
195	2	17 Nov. 35	should be deleted.
197	1	25 Sept. 35	add: Cp. Add MS 44236.
203	4	23 Oct. 35	add at end of bracket: and Add MS 44110.
203	7	25 Oct. 35	read *Pollok.
206	2	12 Nov. 35	should be deleted.
207	1	16 Nov. 35	n. should read: Parish clerk of Newark.
212	11	22 Dec. 35	should be deleted.
220	12	3 Feb. 36	For Lidden read *Liddon.
224	8	22 Feb. 36	should be deleted.
225	13	1 Mar. 36	add new n. after last word: Add MS 44681, ff. 29–33.
226	14	5 Mar. 36	n. should read: Dandeson Coates, 1778–1846, secretary of Church Missionary Society 1830; opposed colony in New Zealand.
227	13	9 Mar. 36	n. should read: Cp. 24 May, 4 Aug. 36.
231	6	2 Apr. 36	She d. 1856.
281	11	27 Feb. 37	Cp. 21 July 34.
289	5	9 Apr. 37	n. should read: See n. 2 on next page.
292	9a	29 Apr. 37	add new n. at end of entry: Cp. 1 July 37, n. 6.
303	3	4 July 37	add: or an Applecross connexion?
330	9a	23 Dec. 37	add new n. after 'Gladstone': Thomas Murray Gladstone, 1807–77, s. of James; Liverpool ironfounder.
352	12	4 Mar. 38	n. should read: See b. 1 on next page.
358	2	30 Mar. 38	for 'Protero' read 'Protheroe'.
359	4	2 Apr. 38	should be deleted.
361	1	7 Apr. 38	should be deleted.
362	4	11 Apr. 38	2nd sentence should be deleted.
373	5	24 May 38	should be deleted.
374	6	29 May 38	should be deleted.
380	6	23 June 38	should read: Margaret, née Gordon, m. Sir Coutts Trotter 1802; d. 1853; a cousin of *Aberdeen's.
385	16	23 July 38	add: (for whom cp. Add MSS 44238–40).
389	4	7 Aug. 38	should be deleted.
508	4a	18 Nov. 38	add new n. after 'Chaplain': Charles Lushington, 1805–ca. 1892, 3rd s. of 2nd bart.

Page	Note	Date	
546	8	1 Jan. 39	for Kilmore read Kilmorey.
567	7	15 Jan. 39	add: Cp. Add MSS 44264–5.
578	4	2 Feb. 39	add: Cp. Add MS 44207.
580	13	13 Feb. 39	should read: Probably Joseph Sherwood, parliamentary agent.
583	6	23 Feb. 39	should be deleted.
597	5	30 Apr. 39	Perhaps Henry Dawson Roundell, 1786?–1852, priest; *Selborne's uncle.
601	4a	23 May 39	add new n. after 'Dr. Kaye': John *Kaye, 1783–1853, bp. of Bristol 1820, of Lincoln 1827
606	5a	11 June 39	add new n. after 'Dr. Ferguson': (Sir) William *Ferguson, 1808–77; professor of surgery, King's College London, 1840; cr. bart. 1866.
608	1	15 June 39	Frederick Anson, 1811–85; s. of dean of Chester; fellow of All Souls; canon of Windsor 1845.
610	9	27 June 39	*PP* 1839 xxxv. 597.
614	4	14 July 39	should be deleted.
616	7	23 July 39	for 5th read 3rd
622	7	22 Aug. 39	add new n. after 'Corrie & Co.': Liverpool corn merchants, John *Gladstone's original employers.
623	4	28 Aug. 39	Frederick Robert Augustus Glover, 1800–81, priest and author.
637	1	14 Nov. 39	should read: for H. H. Rose, priest, appealing Dawson Massy, a distressed clergyman (Add MS 44357, f. 40–2).

DRAMATIS PERSONAE

An index to the whole work will appear in the concluding volume. Meanwhile it may help readers to have this list of biographical notes on the characters who have so far appeared in the diaries. Dates are usually, though not always, those of first appearance.

People with double-barrelled, or particuled, surnames appear under the last part of the name—Edwards-Moss under Moss, Smith Wright under Wright, de Grey under Grey, von Bunsen under Bunsen—except that names in M' and Mc are under Mac, Irish names in O' are under O, and D'Arcy, D'Aubigné, D'Eyncourt, D'Israeli and D'Oyley are under D.

Rulers and royal dukes are given under their regnal or Christian names. Other peers, and married women, are listed under their surnames, with cross-references from their titles and maiden names.

Titles, given in italics in this list, are ignored in its alphabetical order; which is that of surnames, followed by full forenames, of which only the initials appear. Gladstone and Gladstones are treated as one.

Halcomb, J., 10 Apr. 35
Hale, W. Hale, 4 Feb. 33
Halford, *Sir* H., *né* Vaughan, *bart.*, 19 Oct. 26
Halifax, *Viscount, see* Wood
Hall, B., 3 Jan. 37
Hall, *Sir* B., *1st Lord Llanover*, 14 May 35(?)
Hall, C. H., *dean of Christ Church*, 8 June 30n
Hall, E., *see* Boileau-Pollen
Hall, G., 23 Feb. 37
Hall, H., 27 May 37
Hall, *Sir* J., *bart.*, 18 Nov. 38n
Hall, J., *see* Gladstone
Hall, *Sir* J., *bart.*, 13 Feb. 33
Hall, P., 26 Aug. 26n
Hallam, *Mrs. née* Roberts, 5 Nov. 26
Hallam, A. H., 4 Feb. 26
Hallam, E., 16 June 37
Hallam, H., 23 Feb. 33n
Hallam, H. F., 31 July 35
Hallam, J. M., *née* Elton, 23 Feb. 33
Hallewell, J., 10 Dec. 36(?)
Halliday, *Sir* A., 23 Feb. 35
Hallifax, H. C., 4 Mar. 26
Halliwell, *see* Hallewell
Ham, 25 Apr. 31
Ham, 6 July 31
Hamilton, *dukes and duchess of, see* Douglas
Hamilton, *Mr.*, 2 Feb. 32
Hamilton, *Lord* C., 5 Mar. 35
Hamilton, E. W. T., 2 June 34
Hamilton, H., *née* Campbell, *Lady Belhaven*, 4 Jan. 37
Hamilton, J., *1st duke of Abercorn*, 15 May 30n
Hamilton, M. A., 8 July 29
Hamilton, R. M., *8th Lord Belhaven and 1st Lord Hamilton*, 4 Jan. 37
Hamilton, T., *9th earl of Haddington*, 12 Dec. 36
Hamilton, W. K., *bp. of Salisbury*, 11 Mar. 27
Hamilton, W. R., 14 Jan. 39
Hamley, E., 15 Mar. 28
Hampden, R. D., *bp. of Hereford*, 14 Nov. 31
Hanbury, A., 15 Nov. 28
Hancock, E., 29 Oct. 33(?)
Handley, Peacock and Co., 31 Oct. 25n
Handley, J., 16 Oct. 26
Handley, P., 31 Oct. 25
Handley, W., 23 July 37
Hankey, T., 2 July 35
Hanley, E., *see* Hamley

Hanmer, *Sir* J., *1st Lord Hanmer*, 9 Mar. 26
Hanmer, M. E., *see* Kenyon
Hannington, H., 4 Oct. 30
Hansard, L. G., 7 May 38
Harborough, *Earl, see* Sherard
Harcourt *family*, 28 Aug. 28n
Harcourt, A., 11 June 39
Harcourt, C. J., *née* Jenkinson, 16 June 39n
Harcourt, E. V. V., *abp. of York*, 24 June 37
Harcourt, E. L. Vernon-, *see* Norreys
Harcourt, F. V., 16 June 39
Harcourt, G. G. Vernon-, 11 May 31n
Harcourt, L. A., *see* Johnstone
Harcourt, *Sir* W. V., 24 June 37n
Hardinge, *Lady* E. J., *née* Stewart, 5 June 37
Hardinge, *Sir* H., *1st Viscount Hardinge* 18 Aug. 35
Hardwicke, *earl of, see* Yorke
Hardy, T., 2 Aug. 34
Hardy, T., 11 July 26
Hare, J. D., 16 Dec. 38
Harewood, *earl of, see* Lascelles
Hargreaves, T., 23 Dec. 28
Harrington, *earl of, see* Stanhope
Harris, G. F. R., *3rd Baron Harris of Seringapatam*, 24 Nov. 31
Harris, R., 9 Dec. 32(?)
Harris, W., 10 Feb. 29
Harrison, A., 10 Dec. 38
Harrison, B., *the younger*, 1 Feb. 29
Harrison, B., *the elder*, 4 Aug. 32
Harrison, G., 5 Aug. 26
Harrison, H., 23 Dec. 26
Harrison, M., *née* LePelly, 4 Feb. 33
Harrison, R., 12 Feb. 26
Harrison, W., 4 May 35
Harrowby, *earls of, see* Ryder
Harrowby, *Lady, see* Ryder
Hart, A., 16 Dec. 39
Hartismere, *Lord and Lady, see* Henniker-Major
Hartopp, E. B., 11 Mar. 26
Harty, W., 6 Apr. 37
Harvey, *Mrs.*, 4 Dec. 32
Harvey, G., 4 Dec. 32n(?)
Harvey, D. W., 6 Feb. 33
Harvey, R., 30 Mar. 34
Hastings, H. J., 13 Aug. 36(?)
Hasy, *Mr.* 19 June 32
Hatchard, J., 28 July 38
Hatchett, J., 3 Dec. 27
Hatherton, *Lord, see* Littleton
Hatton, G., 2 Oct. 32

44 + II.